FOURTH EDITION

The African-American Odyssey

COMBINED VOLUME

DARLENE CLARK HINE
Northwestern University

WILLIAM C. HINE
South Carolina State University

STANLEY HARROLD
South Carolina State University

PEARSON

Prentice Hall

Upper Saddle River, New Jersey 07458

Library of Congress Cataloging-in-Publication Data

Hine, Darlene Clark.
  The African-American odyssey/Darlene Clark Hine, William C. Hine, and Stanley
Harrold.—Combined volume, 4th ed.
        p. cm.
  Includes bibliographical references and index.
  ISBN-13: 978-0-13-615012-1
  ISBN-10: 0-13-615012-8
  1. African Americans.2. African Americans—History. I. Hine, William C. II. Harrold, Stanley.
III. Title.
  E185 .H533 2007
  973' .0496073—dc22   2007030305

AVP, Publisher: Charlyce Jones Owen
Editor-in-Chief, Development: Rochelle Diogenes
Development Editor: Gerald Lombardi
Senior Marketing Manager: Kate Mitchell
Director of Marketing: Brandy Dawson
Editorial Assistant: Maureen Diana
Marketing Assistant: Jennifer Lang
Operations Supervisor: Mary Ann Gloriande
Operations Specialist: Maura Zaldivar
Creative Design Director: Maria Lange/Nancy Wells
Interior and Cover Designer: Anne DeMarinis
AV Project Manager: Mirella Signoretto
Cartographer: International Mapping
Director of Media: Shannon Gattens
Senior Managing Editor: Mary Carnis
Project Manager: Denise Brown
Full-Service Production and Composition: Emily Bush/S4Carlisle Publishing Services
Permission Coordinator: Laura Rannals/S4Carlisle Publishing Services
Director, Image Resource Center: Melinda Patelli
Manager, Rights and Permissions: Zina Arabia
Manager, Visual Research: Beth Brenzel
Manager Cover Visual Research and Permission: Karen Sanatar
Image Permission Coordinator: Craig A. Jones
Photo Researcher: Rachel Lucas
Color Scanning Services: Joe Conti, Greg Harrison, Cory Skids, Rob Uibelhoer, Ron Walko
Printer/Binder: Quebecor Printing, Inc.
Cover Printer: Phoenix Color

Cover: African-American family posed for portrait seated on lawn from *Negro Life in Georgia, U.S.A.*,
photographed, compiled, and prepared by W. E. B. Du Bois, v. 4, no. 346.

Credits and acknowledgments for materials borrowed from other sources and reproduced, with
permission, in this textbook, appear on pages **C-1** to **C-4**.

Pearson Education LTD.
Pearson Education Singapore, Pte. Ltd.
Pearson Education Canada Ltd.
Pearson Education–Japan

Pearson Education Australia PTY, Limited
Pearson Education North Asia Ltd.
Pearson Educación de Mexico, S.A. de C.V.
Pearson Education Malaysia, Pte. Ltd.

10 9 8 7 6 5 4 3 2 1

ISBN-13 978-0-13-615012-1
ISBN-10 0-13-615012-8

TO
CARTER G. WOODSON & BENJAMIN QUARLES

iv

Brief Contents

Contents

PART II

SLAVERY, ABOLITION, AND THE QUEST FOR FREEDOM: THE COMING OF THE CIVIL WAR, 1793–1861 136

6

Life in the Cotton Kingdom, 1793–1861 138

7

Free Black People in Antebellum America, 1820–1861 164

12

The Meaning of Freedom: The Promise of Reconstruction, 1865–1868 296

13

The Meaning of Freedom: The Failure of Reconstruction, 1868–1877 322

16

Conciliation, Agitation, and Migration: African Americans in the Early Twentieth Century, 1895–1928 410

17

African Americans and the 1920s, 1915–1928 446

PART V

THE GREAT DEPRESSION
AND WORLD WAR II   474

18
Black Protests, The Great
Depression and the New Deal,
1929–1941   476

19
Meanings of Freedom Culture
and Society in the 1930s and
1940s, 1930–1949   508

20

The World War II Era and Seeds of a Revolution, 1936–1948 536

VISUALIZING THE PAST 564

INTERPRETING THE PAST 566

PART VI

THE BLACK REVOLUTION 568

21

The Freedom Movement, 1954–1965 570

22

The Struggle Continues, 1965–1980 604

23

Black Politics, White Backlash, 1980 to Present 638

24
African Americans at the Dawn of a New Millennium 668

MAPS, FIGURES, AND TABLES

Preface

"One ever feels his two-ness,—an American, a Negro; two souls, two thoughts, two unreconciled strivings; two warring ideals in one dark body." So wrote W. E. B. Du Bois in 1897. African-American history, Du Bois maintained, was the history of this double-consciousness. Black people have always been part of the American nation that they helped to build. But they have also been a nation unto themselves, with their own experiences, culture, and aspirations. African-American history cannot be understood except in the broader context of American history. American history cannot be understood without African-American history.

Since Du Bois's time our understanding of both African-American and American history has been complicated and enriched by a growing appreciation of the role of class and gender in shaping human societies. We are also increasingly aware of the complexity of racial experiences in American history. Even in times of great racial polarity some white people have empathized with black people and some black people have identified with white interests.

It is in light of these insights that *The African-American Odyssey* tells the story of African Americans. That story begins in Africa, where the people who were to become African Americans began their long, turbulent, and difficult journey, a journey marked by sustained suffering as well as perseverance, bravery, and achievement. It includes the rich culture—at once splendidly distinctive and tightly intertwined with a broader American culture—that African Americans have nurtured throughout their history. And it includes the many-faceted quest for freedom in which African Americans have sought to counter white oppression and racism with the egalitarian spirit of the Declaration of Independence that American society professes to embody.

Nurtured by black historian Carter G. Woodson during the early decades of the twentieth century, African-American history has blossomed as a field of study since the 1950s. Books and articles have appeared on almost every facet of black life. Yet this survey is the first comprehensive college textbook of the African-American experience. It draws on recent research to present black history in a clear and direct manner, within a broad social, cultural, and political framework. It also provides thorough coverage of African-American women as active builders of black culture.

The African-American Odyssey balances accounts of the actions of African-American leaders with investigations of the lives of the ordinary men and women in black communities. This community focus helps make this a history of a people rather than an account of a few extraordinary individuals. Yet the book does not neglect important political and religious leaders, entrepreneurs, and entertainers. And it gives extensive coverage to African-American art, literature, and music.

African-American history started in Africa, and this narrative begins with an account of life on that continent to the sixteenth century and the beginning of the forced migration of millions of Africans to the Americas. Succeeding chapters present the struggle of black people to maintain their humanity during the slave trade and as slaves in North America during the long colonial period.

The coming of the American Revolution during the 1770s initiated a pattern of black struggle for racial justice in which periods of optimism alternated with times of repression. Several chapters analyze the building of black community institutions, the antislavery movement, the efforts of black people to make the Civil War a war for emancipation, their struggle for equal rights as citizens during Reconstruction, and the strong opposition these efforts faced. There is also substantial coverage of African-American military service, from the War for Independence through American wars of the nineteenth and twentieth centuries.

During the late nineteenth century and much of the twentieth century, racial segregation and racially motivated violence that relegated African Americans to second-class citizenship provoked despair, but also inspired resistance and commitment to change. Chapters on the late nineteenth and early twentieth centuries cover the Great Migration from the cotton fields of the South to the North and West, black nationalism, and the Harlem Renaissance. Chapters on the 1930s and 1940s—the beginning of a period of revolutionary change for African Americans—tell of the economic devastation and political turmoil caused by the Great Depression, the growing influence of black culture in America, the racial tensions caused by black participation in World War II, and the dawning of the civil rights movement.

The final chapters tell the story of African Americans during the second half of the twentieth century and beginning of the twenty-first century. They portray the successes of the civil rights movement at its peak during the 1950s and 1960s and the efforts of African Americans to build on those successes during the more conservative 1970s and 1980s. Finally, there are discussions of black life at the turn of the twenty-first century and of the continuing impact of African Americans on life in the United States.

In all, *The African-American Odyssey* tells a compelling story of survival, struggle, and triumph over adversity. It will leave students with an appreciation of the central place of black people and black culture in this country and a better understanding of both African-American and American history.

New to the Fourth Edition

For the fourth edition of *The African-American Odyssey,* we have expanded or revised a number of topics, added new Profiles and Voices features, and included new information based on recent scholarship. In the early chapters there are extensive revisions to the "A Slave's Story" section and the Olaudah Equiano profile. There is a new Voices box containing Alexander Falconbridge's report on the impact of disease on slave ships during the Middle Passage, and new information on Africans in Dutch New Amsterdam. There are changes in the discussion of the founding of the Prince Hall Masons, and new coverage of the relationship between Thomas Jefferson and Sally Hemings.

In the chapters that deal with the nineteenth century, there is expanded treatment of African Americans in the Oregon Territory as well as in California at the time of the gold rush. There is a new profile of Mary Ellen Pleasant, who migrated to San Francisco. There is also new information on the role of African Americans in John Brown's raid on Harpers Ferry. There is a new Voices feature on the recollections of black nurse Susie King Taylor. There is a new discussion of the reaction to Reconstruction in the North. In addition, there is more information on the Lodge Federal Elections bill of 1890 and new coverage of the Butler Emigration bill, which was an attempt to persuade African Americans to leave the South and migrate to Africa.

For the twentieth-century chapters, there is a new profile of Dr. William Key and his wonderful horse, Jim Key. Our discussion of the Atlanta race riot of 1906 is enlarged, and we augment the examination of Julius Rosenwald and the financial assistance that led to the creation of 5,300 Rosenwald schools across the South. There is expanded coverage of black club women, and a new profile of Jane Edna Hunter and the Phillis Wheatley Association. There is more information on football player and coach Frederick Douglass "Fritz" Pollard. In addition, there is a revised and expanded dis-

cussion of A. Philip Randolph and the Brotherhood of Sleeping Car Porters, and there is new information on black novelist Nella Larsen, who wrote during the Harlem Renaissance. There is a new voices, E. D. Wixon, on being inspired by A. Philip Randolph. There are also new Profile features of political and economic advisor Robert Weaver as well as Steven Robinson and the first African-American men who served in the U.S. Marines during World War II. There is a new discussion of the GI Bill of Rights. Playwright Lorraine Hansberry is the subject of a new Profile feature. And there is a new Profile feature of U.S. Senator and presidential candidate Barack Obama. We expand our discussions of the Iraq War and the second term of President George Bush. There is new information on African Americans' access to education and housing, and there is an updated discussion of black reparations grounded in new scholarship.

Regarding events in the twenty-first century, there is a discussion of the impact of Hurricane Katrina, especially on black residents of New Orleans and on the rising number of impoverished African Americans. There is a revised and lengthier discussion of hip hop and its global significance. And there is coverage of debates among African Americans about class differences and of the recent U.S. Supreme Court decision concerning the use of race to promote diversity in schools.

Supplementary Instructional Materials

The extensive package of both traditional and electronic supplements that accompanies *The African-American Odyssey* provides instructors and students with an array of resources that combine sound scholarship, engaging content, and a variety of pedagogical tools and media to enrich the classroom experience and students' understanding of African-American history.

Instructor's Resource Manual
ISBN: 0-13-603062-9
The Instructor's Resource Manual provides summaries, outlines, learning objectives, lecture and discussion topics, and audio/visual resources for each chapter.

Test Item File
ISBN: 0-13-603068-8
Test materials include multiple-choice, essay, identification, short-answer, chronology, and map questions. To help with the assignment of supplementary material offered with the text, the Test Item File includes test questions in multiple-choice, true/false, and essay format for this material.

Prentice Hall Test Generator
ISBN: 0-13-603073-4
This commercial-quality, computerized test management program, available for Windows and Macintosh environ-

ments, allows instructors to select from testing material in the Instructor's Manual with Tests and design their own exams.

Study Guide (Volumes I and II)
Volume I: ISBN: 0-13-603046-7;
Volume II: ISBN: 0-13-603078-5
This student study aid includes a summary for each chapter, reviews key points and concepts, and provides multiple-choice, essay, and chronology questions. New to this edition of the study guide is an extensive map skills section and additional *Interpreting the Past* essays for analysis.

Primary Source Reader in African-American History (Volumes I and II)
Volume I: ISBN: 0-13-603045-9;
Volume II: ISBN: 0-13-603079-3
This collection of additional primary and secondary source material covers the social, cultural, and political aspects of African-American history. Each reading includes a short historical summary and review questions. The readings are included on the *MyHistoryLab* online study resource and on the *Exploring African-American History CD-ROM*. Many of the documents are referenced throughout the text with special call-outs to related textual material.

African American Biographies
Volume I: ISBN: 0-13-193785-5;
Volume II: ISBN: 0-13-193794-4
This collection of brief biographical sketches of the many African-American figures represented in the text serves as an indispensable companion to The *African-American Odyssey*. Students can use this as a reference to learn more about the people who have helped to shape both American and African-American history.

Prentice Hall and Penguin Bundle Program
Prentice Hall and Penguin are pleased to provide adopters of *The African-American Odyssey* with an opportunity to receive significant discounts when orders for *The African-American Odyssey* are bundled together with Penguin titles in American history. Contact your local Prentice Hall representative for details.

MEDIA RESOURCES

Exploring African-American History CD-ROM
This unique CD-ROM combines two important resources designed to enhance students' experience with *The African-American Odyssey*: *Living Words* audio excerpts, documents, map explorations, and interactive activities. A copy of the CD-ROM is included in each new copy of the textbook. For a list of the contents of the CD-ROM, see pages xxix-xxxii.

MyHistoryLab [www.myhistorylab.com]
MyHistoryLab is an easy-to-use online resource that allows instructors to assess student progress and adapt course

material to meet the specific needs of the class. This online resource enables students to diagnose their progresss by completing an online self-assessment test. Each student is provided with a customized study plan, including a variety of tools to help each fully master the material. *MyHistoryLab* offers students major resources for *The African-American Odyssey*—including quizzes organized by the main topics of each chapter, primary source documents, learning activities, and interactive maps. For instructors, *MyHistoryLab* provides images and maps from the text, additional images organized by chapter, primary source documents, video and audio clips, and PowerPoint presentations. Contact your local Prentice Hall representative for more information about this exciting new online teaching and learning resource.

Instructor's Resource CD-ROM
ISBN: 0-13-603075-0
This instructor resource contains PowerPoint™ presentations directly linked to the text; maps, figures, and graphs from *The African-American Odyssey;* lecture outlines; a gallery of over 300 images of African-American history; the full text of the Instructor's Manual; the Test Item File; and other instructional materials.

Prentice Hall's *Guide to Research Navigator™*
ISBN: 0-13-600863-1
This brief guide introduces students to tools for finding, evaluating, and using resourcese on the Internet. It includes a section on avoiding plagiarism and using sources effectively, tips for finding information related to history on the Internet and for documenting electronic sources, and an access code to the *Research Navigator™* website. Contact your local Prentice Hall representative for details about using OneSearch in your course.

Research Navigator™
This unique resource helps your students make the most of their research time. From finding the right articles and journals, to citing sources, drafting and writing effective papers, and completing research assignments, **Research Navigator™** simplifies and streamlines the entire process. Access to **Research Navigator™** is available in the *MyHistoryLab* website or with every copy of the *OneSearch* guide. For more information, contact your local Prentice Hall representative.

ACKNOWLEDGMENTS

In preparing *The African-American Odyssey* we have benefited from the work of many scholars and the help of colleagues, librarians, friends, and family.

Special thanks are due to the following scholars for their substantial contributions to the development of this textbook: Hilary Mac Austin, *Chicago, Illinois;* Brian W. Dippie, *University of Victoria*; Thomas Doughton, *Holy Cross College;* W. Marvin Dulaney, *College of Charleston*; Sherry DuPree, *Rosewood Heritage Foundation*; Peter

Banner-Haley, *Colgate University*; Robert L. Harris Jr., *Cornell University*; Wanda Hendricks, *University of South Carolina*; Rickey Hill, *Mississippi Valley State University*; William B. Hixson, *Michigan State University*; Barbara Williams Jenkins, *South Carolina State University*; Earnestine Jenkins, *University of Memphis*; Hannibal Johnson, *Tulsa, Oklahoma*; Wilma King, *University of Missouri, Columbia*; Karen Kossie-Chernyshev, *Texas Southern University*; Frank C. Martin, *South Carolina State University*; Jacqueline McLeod, *Metropolitan State University*; Freddie Parker, *North Carolina Central University*; Christopher R. Reed, *Roosevelt University*; Linda Reed, *University of Houston*; Mark Stegmaier, *Cameron University*; Robert Stewart, *Trinity School, New York*; Matthew Whitaker, *Arizona State University*; Barbara Woods, *South Carolina State University;* Andrew Workman, *Mills College*; Deborah Wright, *Avery Research Center, College of Charleston*.

We are grateful to the reviewers who devoted valuable time to reading and commenting on *The African-American Odyssey*. Their insightful suggestions greatly improved the quality of the text: Carol Anderson, *University of Missouri, Columbia*; Abel A. Bartley, *University of Akron*; Jennifer L. Baszile, *Yale University*; James M. Beeby, *West Virginia Wesleyan College*; Richard A. Buckelew, *Bethune-Cookman College*; Claude A. Clegg, *Indiana University*; Gregory Conerly, *Cleveland State University*; Delia Cook, *University of Missouri at Kansas City*; Caroline Cox, *University of the Pacific*; Mary Ellen Curtin, *Southwest Texas State University*; Henry Vance Davis, *Ramapo College of NJ*; Roy F. Finkenbine, *Wayne State University*; Abiodun Goke-Pariola, *Georgia Southern University;* Robert Gregg, *Richard Stockton College on NJ*; Keith Griffler, *University of Cincinnati*; John H. Haley, *University of North Carolina at Wilmington*; Robert V. Hanes, *Western Kentucky University*; Julia Robinson Harmon, *University of North Carolina, Charlotte*; Ebeneazer Hunter, *De Anza College*; Eric R. Jackson, *Northern Kentucky University*; Wali Rashash Kharif, *Tennessee Technological University*; Joseph Kinner, *Gallaudet University*; Eric Love, *University of Colorado-Boulder;* John F. Marszalek, *Mississippi State University*; Kenneth Mason, *Santa Monica College*; Andrew T. Miller, *Union College*; Diane Batts Morrow, *University of Georgia*; Walter Rucker, *University of Nebraska, Lincoln*; Manisha Sinha, *University of Massachusetts, Amherst*; John David Smith, *North Carolina State University at Raleigh*; Marshall Stevenson, *Ohio State University*; Betty Joe Wallace, *Austin Peay State University*; Matthew C. Whitaker, *Arizona State University*; Harry Williams, *Carleton College*; Vernon J. Williams, Jr., *Indiana University*; Andrew Workman, *Mills College*.

We wish to thank the following reviewers for their insightful comments in preparation for this fourth edition: Leslie Alexander, *The Ohio State University;* Richard A. Buckelew, *Bethune-Cookman College*; Dr. Jessie Gaston, *California State University, Sacramento*; John W. King, *Temple University*; Lester C. Lamon, *Indiana University, South Bend*; Ruddy Pearson, *American College*; Josh Sides, *California State University, Northridge*; Leslie Wilson, *Montclair State University*; Marilyn L. Yancy, *Virginia Union University*.

Many librarians provided valuable help tracking down important material. They include Aimee Berry James, Lakeshia Darby Dawson, Ruth Hodges, Doris Johnson, Minnie Johnson, Barbara Keitt the late, Andrew Penson, and Mary L. Smalls, all of Miller F. Whittaker Library, South Carolina State University; James Brooks and Jo Cottingham of the interlibrary loan department, Cooper Library, University of South Carolina; and Allan Stokes of the South Carolina Library at the University of South Carolina. Kathleen Thompson, Marshanda Smith, and Robbie Davine Clark provided important documents and other source material.

Seleta Simpson Byrd and Rosalind Hanson of South Carolina State University and Linda Werbish and Marshanda Smith of Michigan State University provided valuable administrative assistance.

Each of us also enjoyed the support of family members, particularly Barbara A. Clark, Robbie D. Clark, Emily Harrold, Judy Harrold, Carol A. Hine, Peter J. Hine, Thomas D. Hine, and Alma J. McIntosh. Finally, we gratefully acknowledge the essential help of the superb editorial and production team at Prentice Hall: Charlyce Jones Owen, Publisher, whose vision got this project started and whose unwavering support saw it through to completion; Maureen Diana, Editorial Assistant; Rochelle Diogenes, Editor in Chief of Development, and Gerald Lombardi, Development Editor, who provided valuable organizational, substantive, and stylistic insights; Maria Lange, Creative Design Director; Anne DeMarinis, who created the book's handsome design; Mary Carnis, Senior Managing Editor, and Denise Brown, Production Editor, who saw it efficiently through production; Maura Zaldivar, Manufacturing Buyer; Kate Mitchell, Senior Marketing Manager; and Pat McCarthy, Southern Editorial, who pulled together the book's supplementary material.

Darlene Clark Hine
Northwestern University

William C. Hine
South Carolina State University

Stanley Harrold
South Carolina State University

About
The African-American Odyssey

The many special features and pedagogical tools integrated within *The African-American Odyssey* are designed to make the text accessible to students. They include a variety of tools to reinforce the narrative and help students grasp key issues.

SPECIAL FEATURES: TIMELINES

PART-OPENING TIMELINES thematically organize events in African-American history and provide a reference to the many noteworthy individuals discussed in the chapters.
Brief chronologies are included throughout the chapters to provide students with a snapshot of the temporal relationship among significant events.

END-OF-CHAPTER TIMELINES establish a chronological context for events in African-American history by relating them to events in American history and in the rest of the world.

PRIMARY SOURCE DOCUMENTS AND BIOGRAPHIES

VOICES

AFRICAN AMERICANS RESPOND TO THE FUGITIVE SLAVE LAW

These two passages reflect the outrage the Fugitive Slave Law of 1850 provoked among black Americans. In the first, John Jacobs, a fugitive slave from South Carolina, urges black people to take up arms to oppose the law. In the second, from a speech he delivered a few days after the passage of the law, Martin Delany defies authorities to search his home for runaway slaves.

My colored brethren, if you have not swords, I say to you, sell your garments and buy one. . . . They said that they cannot take us back to the South; but I say, under the present law they can; and now they say unto you; let them take only dead bodies. . . . I would, my friends, advise you to show a front to our tyrants and arm yourselves . . . and I would advise the women to have their knives too.

Source: William F. Cheek, *Black Resistance before the Civil War* (Beverly Hills: Glencoe Press, 1970), 148–49.

Sir, my house is my castle; in that castle are none but my wife and my children, as free as the angels of heaven, and whose liberty is as sacred as the pillars of God. If any man approaches that house in search of a slave—I care not who he may be, whether the constable, or sheriff, magistrate or even judge of the Supreme Court—nay, let it be he who sanctioned this act to become law [President Millard Fillmore] surrounded by his cabinet as his bodyguard, with the Declaration of Independence waving above his head as his banner, and the constitution of this country upon his breast as his shield—if he crosses the threshold of my door, and I do not lay him a lifeless corpse at my feet, I hope the grave may refuse my body a resting place, and righteous Heaven my spirit a home. O, no! He cannot enter that house and we both live.

Source: Victor Ullman, *Martin R. Delany: The Beginnings of Black Nationalism* (Boston: Beacon Press, 1971), 112

How and why did these two black men justify the use of violence against those who were enforcing a law passed by Congress?

Under what circumstances is it permissible to violate the law or threaten to kill another human being?

VOICES boxes provide students with first-person perspectives on key events in African-American history. Brief introductions and study questions help students analyze these primary source documents and relate them to the text.

PROFILE boxes provide biographical sketches that highlight the contributions and personalities of both prominent individuals and ordinary people, illuminating common experiences among African Americans at various times and places.

PROFILE — IDA WELLS BARNETT

Ida Wells Barnett began life as a slave in 1862 and grew up during Reconstruction. As a young woman, she saw the worst indignities and cruelties that the Jim Crow South could inflict, but she fought back as a journalist, agitator, and reformer.

Ida Wells was one of eight children born to Jim and Lizzie Wells in Holly Springs, Mississippi. After the Civil War, she attended a school for freed people with her mother, and they learned to read and write. Her parents and one of her brothers died in the yellow fever epidemic of 1878. Sixteen-year-old Ida became mother and father to her five surviving brothers and sisters. She attended Shaw University in Holly Springs (now Rust College) and taught school in Mississippi and Tennessee.

In 1884, a railroad conductor removed Wells from a first-class car. She sued the railroad and won a $500 settlement "Dusky Damsel Gets Damages," a Memphis newspaper reported. But a higher court reversed the decision.

Wells then took up journalism and wrote a weekly column for *The Living Way*. In 1889, she bought a one-third interest in the Memphis *Free Speech and Headlight*. She wrote about racial issues and criticized black educators for the quality of black schools. In 1892 her friend Thomas Moss was lynched with two other men for the crime of running a successful grocery store. Wells expressed her rage and horror in a fiery editorial, thus beginning a lifelong crusade against lynching.

Wells blamed the white people of Memphis for her friend's murder and pointed out that more black men were lynched for challenging the myth of white superiority than for allegedly raping a white woman. She angered white people even more by writing that white women could be attracted to black men.

She blamed white clergymen and their parishioners for tolerating lynching. "[O]ur American Christians are too busy saving the souls of white Christians from burning in hell-fire to save the lives of black ones from present burning in fires kindled by white Christians."

Wells moved to Chicago and wrote a pamphlet criticizing the racism at the 1893 World's Fair: *The Reason Why the Colored American Is Not in the Columbian Exposition*. In 1895 she married Ferdinand Barnett, the owner of the Chicago *Conservator*.

After a white journalist from Missouri wrote that black women were immoral, "having no sense of virtue and altogether without character," black women including Wells Barnett founded the National Association of Colored Women in 1896.

In 1909, Wells Barnett was one of two black women who supported the founding of the National Association for the Advancement of Colored People (NAACP), although she later broke with the group because of its mostly white board of directors and what she considered its cautious stands. She also helped organize the Negro Fellowship League in 1910.

Wells Barnett became an ardent supporter of black voting rights. She believed that if enough black men and women could vote, their political power would end lynching. In 1913 she helped found the Alpha Suffrage Club, the first black women's suffrage organization in Illinois, and was a delegate to the National American Woman's Suffrage Association meeting in Washington, D.C.

Ever an agitator, she found Booker T. Washington's philosophy too timid. She was influenced by Marcus Garvey and the Universal Negro Improvement Association in the 1920s, and praised Garvey as a black leader who "made an impression on this country as no Negro before him had ever done."

She continued to write, campaign, speak out, and organize. She was directly involved in protesting the execution of black soldiers after the 1917 Houston riot. She took the lead in exposing the injustice twelve poor black farmers experienced after the Elaine riot and massacre in 1919 (see pp. 000–000). She supported A. Phillip Randolph and the formation of the Brotherhood of Sleeping Car Porters (see pp. 000–000). In 1928 she ran as a Republican for the state Senate. Only death from kidney failure in 1931 ended her efforts to secure justice for black Americans.

Barnett

SPECIAL TOPIC FEATURES

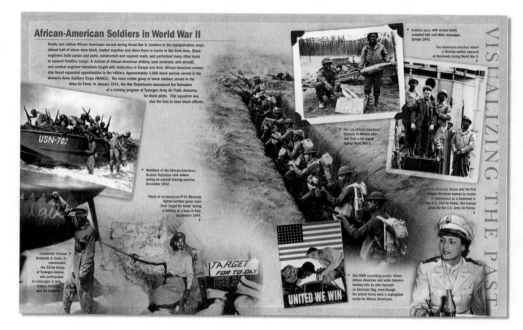

VISUALIZING THE PAST   These two-page features analyze important aspects of African-American history through photographs. A brief narrative introduction provides a careful examination of the historical implications of each topic. This feature is located at the end of each part.

INTERPRETING THE PAST   NEW to this edition, this feature includes brief primary source excerpts and visual documents on an engaging topic and provides critical thinking questions for students to explore as they analyze the connections between the historical sources. These six new spreads follow the *Visualizing the Past* features at the end of each part.

STUDY AIDS

CHAPTER OPENERS   Each chapter opens with a provocative image that gives students a visual introduction to the chapter content and **chapter opening questions** that provide an inquiry-based approach that encourages students to think about the material they are about to read.

MAPS   The text includes an abundance of maps that help students visualize the geographical context of events and grasp significant trends. **Map questions** accompany every map in the text to challenge students to review their understanding of the maps in context. Maps identified as **Map Explorations** are provided in an interactive version on the text's *Myhistorylab* website and on the *Exploring African-American History CD-ROM*. A url is provided for instant access to the map within the website. The interactive activities are designed to enhance map reading and analysis skills.

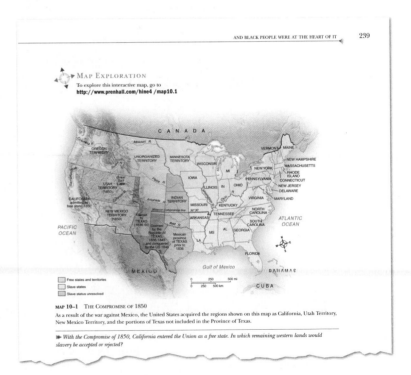

END OF CHAPTER RESOURCES

Recommended Reading and **Additional Bibliography** lists direct students to more information about the subject of each chapter. **Retracing the Odyssey** sections guide instructors and students to educational sites that explore the diverse dimensions of African-American history. **Review, Research, and Interact** is a study and research section at the end of each chapter that provides **Review Questions** to encourage students to analyze the material they have read and to explore alternative perspectives on that material; *Research Navigator*™ activities to explore topics in African-American history; relevant primary source *Documents* and *Interactive Activities* both for maps and special topics to enhance deeper understanding of the core content of the chapters. These resources are now available on the NEW online resource, *MyHistoryLab,* that accompanies the fourth edition as well as on the *Exploring African-American History CD-ROM* included in the text.

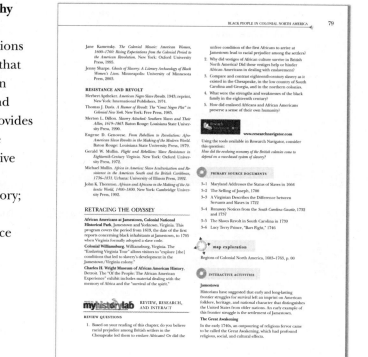

GLOSSARIES   Key Terms are first bold-faced in the chapters and included in a NEW alphabetical **Glossary of Key Terms and Concepts,** at the end of the text. A **Biographical Glossary,** also NEW to this edition, includes brief biographies of the individuals discussed throughout the text.

MyHistoryLab is an easy-to-use learning management system that allows instructors to assess student progress and adapt course material to meet the specific needs of the class. It enables students to diagnose their progress by completing an online self-assessment test.

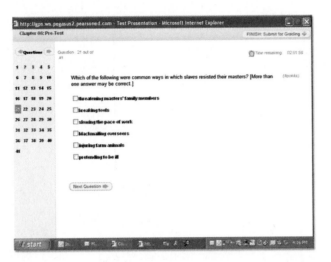

ASSESSMENT   *MyHistoryLab* allows students to test themselves and with aggregate class reports helps instructors know what content their class has mastered and where they are still struggling. Pretests and Chapter Reviews, as well as assessment within a student's study plan provide a comprehensive program for reviewing and reinforcing content.

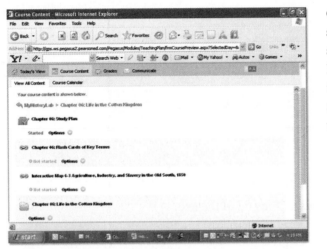

CUSTOMIZED STUDY PLAN   Generated by self-assessments, *MyHistoryLab* produces customized study plans for students and addresses different learning styles while helping students to study independently. It identifies areas of weakness and strength to focus students' attention and efforts where they are needed the most.

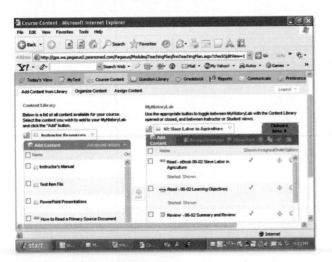

CUSTOMIZABLE LECTURE AND INTERACTIVE MATERIALS   Instructors can organize and base their course on their syllabus and on student performance. *MyHistoryLab* simplifies and enriches the teaching experience by offering text-specific materials including instructor's manuals, test banks, PowerPoint presentations, and much more.

A wealth of hands-on activities and exercises let students experience and learn firsthand. *MyHistoryLab* contains a wide variety of multimedia resources for students: an on-line eBook, documents, activities, animations, audio, and much more.

ADDITIONAL RESOURCES ON *MyHistoryLab*™   From finding the right articles and journals, to citing sources, drafting and writing effective papers, and completing research assignments, *Research Navigator*™ simplifies and streamlines the entire process.

Exploring
African-American History CDROM

LIVING WORDS AFRICAN-AMERICAN ORAL TRADITIONS

DOCUMENTS AND INTERACTIVE ACTIVITIES

PART I

BECOMING AFRICAN AMERICAN

King Mbunza

	to 1500	1500–1700

RELIGION

300s CE Axum adopts Christianity

750s Islam begins to take root in West Africa

1300s–1500s Timbukto flourishes as a center of Islamic learning

1324 Mansa Musa's pilgrimage to Mecca

c.1500 Portuguese convert Kongo kings to Christianity

CULTURE

1600s African versions of English and French—Gullah, Geechee, and Creole—begin to develop

1600s–1700s African-American folk culture appears among the slaves

POLITICS & GOVERNMENT

c.3150–30 BCE Independence of Ancient Egypt

1st century CE Fall of Kush

8th century CE Decline of Axumfite Empire in Ethiopia

c.750–1076 Empire of Ghana

1230–1468 Empire of Mali

1400s–1700s Expansion of Benin

1468–1571 Empire of Songhai

1500s Rise of Akan states

1607 Jamestown founded

1696 South Carolina Slave Code enacted

SOCIETY & ECONOMY

10th century Islamic slave trade across the Sahara and Central Africa begins

1472 First Portuguese slave traders in Benin

1481 First "slave factory" in Elmira on the Guinea coast

1502 First mention of African slaves in the Americas

1518 Spanish *Asiento* begins

c.1520 Sugar plantations begin in Brazil

1619 First African slaves arrive in Jamestown

1620s Chesapeake tobacco plantations increase the demand for slaves

1624 First black child reported born in British North America

1660s Chattel slavery emerges in the southern colonies

Phillis Wheatley

Elizabeth Freeman

James Forten

1700–1800	1800–1820	NOTEWORTHY INDIVIDUALS

c.1738 First Great Awakening: George Whitefield preaches to African Americans

1780 Lemuel Haynes becomes first ordained black Congregationalist Minister

1794 Mother Bethel Church founded in Philadelphia St. Thomas's Episcopal Church established under Absalom Jones

1740s Lucy Terry Prince publishes poetry

1760 Jupiter Hammon publishes a book of poetry

1773 Phillis Wheatley's Poems on Various Subjects

1775 Prince Hall founds first African-American Masonic Lodge

1780 First African-American mutual aid society founded in Newport Rhode Island

1787 Free African Society founded in Philadelphia

1791–1795 Benjamin Banneker's Almanac published

1793 Philadelphia's Female Benevolent Society of St. Thomas founded

1773 Massachusetts African Americans petition the legislature for freedom

1775 Black militiamen fight at Lexington and Concord

1776 Declaration of Independence

1777 Vermont prohibits slavery

1782 Virginia allows manumission

1783 Massachusetts allows male black taxpayers to vote

1787 Congress bans slavery in the Northwest Territory

1789 U.S. Constitution includes the Three-Fifths clause

1793 Congress passes First Fugitive Slave Act

1712 New York City slave rebellion

1739 Stono slave revolt in South Carolina

1776–1783 100,000 slaves flee southern plantations

1781–1783 20,000 black Loyalists depart with British troops

1793 Eli Whitney invents the cotton gin

1808 Abyssinian Baptist Church organized in New York City

1811 African Presbyterian Church established in Philadelphia under Samuel E. Cornish

1816 African Methodist Episcopal Church established

1818 Mother Bethel Church establishes the Augustine School

1807 Britain abolishes the Atlantic slave trade

1808 U.S. abolishes the Atlantic slave trade

1820 Missouri Compromise

First settlement of Liberia by African Americans

1800 Gabriel's rebellion in Charleston

1811 Deslondes's rebellion in Louisiana

King Pianky of Kush
(r. c.750 BCE)

Sudiata of Mali
(c.1235 CE)

Emperor Mansa Musa of Mali
(r. 1312–1337)

King Sunni Ali of Songhai
(r. 1464–1492)

King Askia Muhammed Toure of Songhai (r. 1492–1528)

King Nzmiga Mbembba (Affonso I) of Kongo
(r. 1506–1543)

Ayubu Sulieman Diallo of Bondu (c.1701–1773)

Jupiter Hammon
(1711–c.1806)

Crispus Attucks
(1723–1770)

Benjamin Banneker
(1731–1806)

Prince Hall
(1735–1807)

Elizabeth Freeman
(1744–1811)

Absalom Jones
(1746–1818)

Olaudah Equiano
(c.1745–1797)

James Forten
(1746–1818)

Peter Salem
(1750–1816)

Phillis Wheatley
(c.1753–1784)

Richard Allen
(1760–1831)

Paul Cuffe
(1759–1817)

Daniel Coker
(1780–1846)

Gabriel
(d. 1800)

Charles Deslondes
(d. 1811)

1

Africa

WHAT ARE THE GEOGRAPHICAL
CHARACTERISTICS OF AFRICA?

WHERE AND HOW DID HUMANS ORIGINATE?

WHY ARE ANCIENT AFRICAN
CIVILIZATIONS IMPORTANT?

WHY IS WEST AFRICA SIGNIFICANT
FOR AFRICAN-AMERICAN HISTORY?

HOW DID THE LEGACIES OF WEST AFRICAN
SOCIETY AND CULTURE INFLUENCE
THE WAY AFRICAN AMERICANS LIVED?

◀ **The craftsmen of the Kingdom of Benin** gained wide renown
for the bronze reliefs they produced. This plaque portrays a
king on horseback flanked by two attendants. British Museum,
London/Bridgeman Art Library, London/SuperStock

These [West African] nations think themselves the foremost men in the world, and nothing will persuade them to the contrary. They imagine that Africa is not only the greatest part of the world but also the happiest and most agreeable.

Father Cavazzi, 1687

◀ **A wall painting** from an Egyptian tomb shows Nubians carrying baskets and beads. Nubia had close cultural ties to ancient Egypt.

The ancestral homeland of most black Americans is West Africa. Other regions—Angola and East Africa—were caught up in the great Atlantic slave trade that carried Africans to the New World during a period stretching from the sixteenth to the nineteenth century. But West Africa was the center of the trade in human beings. Knowing the history of West Africa therefore is important for understanding the people who became the first African Americans.

That history is best understood within the larger context of the history and geography of the whole African continent. This chapter begins with a survey of the larger context. It emphasizes the aspects of the broader African experience that shaped life in West Africa before the arrival of Europeans in that region. It then explores West Africa's unique heritage and the facets of its culture that have influenced the lives of African Americans from the Diaspora—the original forced dispersal of Africans from their homeland—to the present.

A Huge and Diverse Land

Africa, the second largest continent in the world (only Asia is larger), is bounded by the Mediterranean Sea to the north, the Atlantic Ocean to the west, and the Indian Ocean and the Red Sea to the east. A narrow strip of land in its northeast corner connects it to the Arabian Peninsula and beyond that to Asia and Europe.

From north to south, Africa is divided into a succession of climatic zones (see Map 1–1). With the exception of a fertile strip along the Mediterranean coast and the agriculturally rich Nile River valley, most of the northern third of the continent consists of the Sahara Desert. For thousands of years, the Sahara limited contact between the rest of Africa—known as sub-Saharan Africa—and the Mediterranean coast, Europe, and Asia. South of the Sahara is a semidesert region known as the Sahel, and south of the Sahel is a huge grassland, or savannah, stretching from Ethiopia westward to the Atlantic Ocean. Arab adventurers named this savannah *Bilad es Sudan*, meaning "land of the black people," and the term *Sudan* designates this entire region, rather than simply the modern East African nation of Sudan. Much of the habitable part of West Africa falls within the savannah. The rest lies within the northern part of a **rain forest** that extends eastward from the Atlantic coast over most of the central part of the continent. Another region of savannah borders the rain forest to the south, followed by another desert—the Kalahari—and another coastal strip at the continent's southern extremity.

The Birthplace of Humanity

Paleoanthropologists—scientists who study the evolution and prehistory of humans—have concluded that the origins of humanity lie in the savannah regions of Africa. All people today, in other words, are very likely descendants of beings who lived in Africa millions of years ago.

Fossil and genetic evidence suggests that both humans and the forest-dwelling great apes (gorillas and chimpanzees) descended from a common apelike ancestor who lived in Africa about five to ten million years ago. The African climate was growing drier at that time, as it has continued to do into the present. Forests gave way to spreading savannahs dotted with isolated copses of trees.

The earliest known *hominids* (the term designates the biological family to which humans belong) were the *australopithecines*, who emerged about four million years ago. These creatures walked upright but other-

Map Exploration

To explore this interactive map, go to
http://www.prenhall.com/hine4/map1.1

MAP 1–1   Africa: Climatic Regions and Early Sites

Africa is a large continent with several climatic zones. It is also the home of several early civilizations.

▶ *What impact did the variety of climatic zones have on the development of civilization in Africa?*

wise retained many apelike characteristics and probably did not make stone tools. The first stone tools are
associated with the emergence—about 2.4 million
years ago—of *Homo habilis*, the earliest creature designated as within the *homo* (human) lineage. Individuals
of the *Homo habilis* species had larger brains than the
australopithecines. They butchered meat with stone
cutting and chopping tools and built shelters with
stone foundations. Like people in **hunting and gathering societies** today, they probably lived in small bands
in which women foraged for plant food and men
hunted and scavenged for meat.

Recently scientists have found *Homo habilis* fossils
in the Caucasus region of southeastern Europe. A
more advanced human, *Homo erectus*, spread even farther from Africa, reaching eastern Asia and Indonesia.
Homo erectus, who emerged in Africa about 1.6 million
years ago, is associated with the first evidence of human use of fire.

Paleoanthropologists agree that modern humans,
Homo sapiens, evolved from *Homo erectus*, but they disagree on how. According to a multiregional model,
modern humans evolved throughout Africa, Asia, and
Europe from ancestral regional populations of *Homo
erectus* and archaic *Homo sapiens*. According to the out-
of-Africa model, modern humans emerged in Africa
some 200,000 years ago and began migrating to the
rest of the world about 100,000 years ago, eventually
replacing all other existing hominid populations. Both
of these models are consistent with recent genetic evidence, and both indicate that all living peoples are
closely related. The "Eve" hypothesis, which supports
the out-of-Africa model, suggests that all modern humans are descended from a single African woman. The
multiregional model maintains that a continuous exchange of genetic material allowed archaic human
populations in Africa, Asia, and Europe to evolve simultaneously into modern humans.

Anthropologists discovered these fossilized bones of a
female australopithecus afarenisis, nicknamed "Lucy," in
1974 at Hadar, Ethiopia. Dated to 3.2 million years ago,
Lucy's bones are among the more famous in the world.
They provide strong evidence that human origins lay in
Africa.   The Cleveland Museum of Natural History

Ancient Civilizations and Old Arguments

The earliest civilization in Africa and one of the two
earliest civilizations in world history is that of ancient
Egypt (see Map 1–1), which emerged in the Nile River
valley in the fourth millennium BCE. Mesopotamian
civilization, the other of the two, emerged in the valleys
of the Tigris and Euphrates rivers in southwest Asia
with the rise of the city-states of Sumer. In both regions,
civilization appeared at the end of a long process in
which hunting and gathering gave way to agriculture.
The settled village life that resulted from this transfor-

mation permitted society to become increasingly
hierarchical and specialized. Similar processes gave
rise to civilization in the Indus valley in India around
2300 BCE, in China—with the founding of the Shang
dynasty—around 1500 BCE, and in Mexico and Andean
South America during the first millennium BCE.

The race of the ancient Egyptians and the nature
and extent of their influence on later Western civilizations have long been a source of controversy that reflects more about racial politics of recent history than
it reveals about the Egyptians themselves. It is not clear
whether they were an offshoot of their Mesopotamian

contemporaries, whether they were representatives of a group of peoples whose origins were in both Africa and southwest Asia, or whether the ancestors of both the Egyptians and Mesopotamians were black Africans. What is clear is that the ancient Egyptians exhibited a mixture of racial features and spoke a language related to the languages spoken by others in the fertile regions of North Africa and southwest Asia.

In this context the argument over the racial identity of the Egyptians is unlikely to be resolved, and they did not regard themselves in a way related to modern racial terminology. The argument began in the nineteenth century when African Americans and white liberals sought to refute claims by racist pseudoscientists that people of African descent were inherently inferior to whites. Unaware of the achievements of West African civilization, those who believed in human equality used evidence that the Egyptians were black to counter assertions that African Americans were incapable of civilization.

Recently there has been a more scholarly debate between Afrocentricists and traditionalists. Afrocentricists regard ancient Egypt as an essentially black civilization closely linked to other indigenous African civilizations to its south. They maintain that not only did the Egyptians influence later African civilizations but that they had a decisive impact on the Mediterranean Sea region, including ancient Greece and Rome. Therefore in regard to philosophy and science black Egyptians were the progenitors of Western civilization. Traditionalists respond that modern racial categories have no relevance to the world of the ancient Egyptians. The ancient Greeks, they argue, developed the empirical method of inquiry and notions of individual freedom that characterize Western civilization. What is not under debate, however, is Egypt's contribution to the spread of civilization throughout the Mediterranean region. No one doubts that in religion, commerce, and art Egypt strongly influenced the development of Greece and subsequent Western civilizations.

EGYPTIAN CIVILIZATION

Egypt was, as the Greek historian Herodotus observed 2,500 years ago, the "gift of the Nile." A gentle annual flooding regularly irrigates the banks of this great river, leaving behind deposits of fertile soil. The Nile allowed Egyptians to cultivate wheat and barley and herd goats, sheep, pigs, and cattle in an otherwise desolate region. The Nile also provided the Egyptians with a transportation and communications artery, while its desert surroundings protected them from foreign invasion. Egypt became a unified kingdom in about 3150 BCE. A succession of thirty-one dynasties ruled it prior to its incorporation into the Roman Empire during the first century BCE. Historians divide this immensely long span into several epochs. During the early dynastic period (3100–2700 BCE) and Old Kingdom (2700–2200 BCE), Egypt's kings consolidated their authority and claimed the status of gods. After a period of instability following the end of the Old Kingdom, the Middle Kingdom (2050–1650) reestablished royal authority. During the New Kingdom (1550–1100), Egypt expanded beyond the Nile valley, creating an empire over coastal regions of southwest Asia as well as Libya and Nubia in Africa. It was during the New Kingdom that Egypt's kings began using the title *pharaoh*, which means "great house." During the Post-Empire period (1100–30 BCE), Egypt fell prey to a series of outside invaders. With the invasion of Alexander the Great's Macedonian army in 331 BCE, Egypt's ancient culture began a long decline under the pressure of Greek ideas and institutions (see Map 1–2).

The way of life that took shape during the Old Kingdom, however, had resisted change for most of ancient Egypt's history. Kings presided over a strictly hierarchical society. Beneath them were classes of warriors, priests, merchants, artisans, and peasants. A class of scribes, who were masters of Egypt's complex **hieroglyphic** writing, staffed a comprehensive bureaucracy.

Egyptian society was also strictly **patrilineal** and **patriarchal**. Royal incest was customary, with each king choosing a sister to be his queen. Kings maintained numerous concubines; other men could also take additional wives if the first wife failed to produce children. Egyptian women nonetheless held a high status compared with women in much of the rest of the ancient world. They owned property independently of their husbands, oversaw household slaves, controlled the education of their children, held public office, served as priests, and operated businesses. There were several female rulers, one of whom, Hatshepsut, reigned for twenty years (1478–1458 BCE). She is depicted in carvings and monuments wearing the regalia of male rulers, including the traditional false beard.

A complex polytheistic religion shaped every facet of Egyptian life. Although there were innumerable gods, two of the more important were the sun god Re (or Ra), who represented the immortality of the Egyptian state, and Osiris, the god of the Nile, who embodied each individual's personal immortality. In Egyptian myth Osiris was murdered by his evil brother Seth and resurrected by his sister and wife Isis. This myth, originally an allegory for the seasonal rebirth of vegetation caused by the Nile's annual flooding, came to symbolize the possibility of individual immortality. Egyptians came to regard Osiris as the judge of the worthiness of souls.

Personal immortality and the immortality of the state merged in the person of the king, as expressed in Egypt's elaborate royal funerary architecture. The most dramatic examples of that architecture, the Great Pyramids at Giza near the modern city of Cairo, were built more than 4,500 years ago to protect the bodies of three prominent kings of the Old Kingdom so that their souls might successfully enter the life to come. The pyramids also dramatically symbolized the power of the Egyptian state and have endured as embodiments of the grandeur of Egyptian civilization.

KUSH, MEROË, AND AXUM

To the south of Egypt in the upper Nile River valley, in what is today the nation of Sudan, lay the ancient region known as Nubia. As early as the fourth millennium BCE, the black people who lived there interacted with the Egyptians. Recent archaeological evidence suggests that grain production and the concept of monarchy may have arisen in Nubia and subsequently spread northward to Egypt. But Egypt's population was always much larger than that of Nubia, and during the second millennium BCE, Egypt used its military power to make Nubia an Egyptian colony and control Nubian copper and gold mines. Egyptians also imported ivory, ebony, leopard pelts, and slaves from Nubia and required the sons of Nubian nobles to live in Egypt as hostages.

The hostages served as ambassadors of Egyptian culture when they returned home. As a result, Egyptian religion, art, hieroglyphics, and political structure became firmly established in Nubia. Then, with the decline of Egypt's New Kingdom at the end of the second millennium BCE, the Nubians established an independent kingdom known as Kush, which had its capital at Kerma on the upper Nile River. During the eighth century BCE, the Kushites took control of upper Egypt, and in about 750 the Kushite king Piankhy added lower Egypt to his realm. Piankhy made himself pharaoh and founded Egypt's twenty-fifth dynasty, which ruled until the Assyrians, who invaded Egypt from southwest Asia, drove the Kushites out in 663 BCE.

Kush itself remained independent for another thousand years. Its kings continued for centuries to call themselves pharaohs and had themselves buried in pyramid tombs covered with Egyptian hieroglyphics. They and the Kushite nobility practiced the Egyptian religion and spoke the Egyptian language. In 540 BCE a resurgent Egyptian army destroyed Kerma, and the Kushites moved their capital southward to Meroë. The new capital was superbly located for trade with East Africa, with regions to the west across the Sudan, and with the Mediterranean world by way of the Nile River. Trade made Meroë wealthy, and the development of a smelting technology capable of exploiting local deposits of iron transformed the city into Africa's first industrial center.

MAP 1–2   ANCIENT EGYPT AND NUBIA

▶ *What does this map indicate about the relationship between ancient Egypt and Nubia/Kush?*

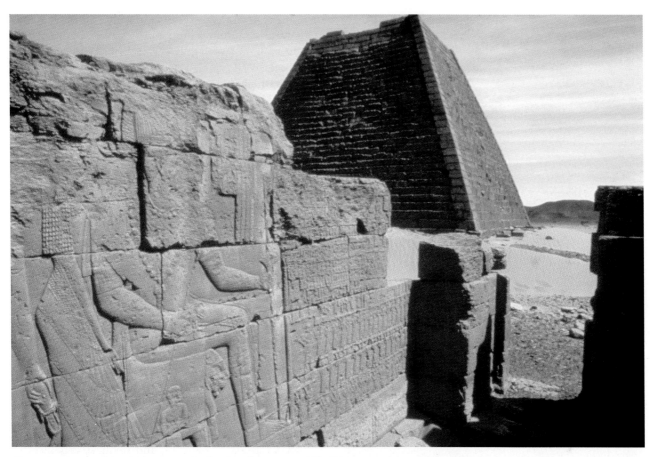

The ruined pyramids of Meroë on the banks of the upper Nile River are not as old as those at Giza in Egypt, and they differ from them stylistically. But they nonetheless attest to the cultural connections between Meroë and Egypt.

As Meroë's economic base expanded, the dependence of Kushite civilization on Egyptian culture declined. By the second century CE, the Kushites had developed their own **phonetic script** to replace hieroglyphics. An architecture derived from that of Egypt gave way to an eclectic style that included Greek, Indian, and sub-Saharan African motifs, as well as Egyptian.

Because of its commerce and wealth, Kush attracted powerful enemies, including the Roman Empire, which by 31 BCE controlled all the lands bordering the Mediterranean Sea. A Roman army invaded Kush in 23 BCE. But it was actually the decline of Rome and its Mediterranean economy that were the chief factors in Kush's destruction. As the Roman Empire grew weaker and poorer, its trade with Kush declined, and Kush, too, grew weaker. During the early fourth century CE, Kush fell to the neighboring Noba people, who in turn fell to the nearby kingdom of Axum, whose warriors destroyed Meroë.

Located in what is today Ethiopia, Axum emerged as a nation during the first century BCE as Semitic people from the Arabian Peninsula, who were influenced by Hebrew culture, settled among a local black population. By the time it absorbed Kush during the fourth century CE, Axum had become the first Christian state in sub-Saharan Africa. By the eighth century, shifting trade patterns, environmental depletion, and Islamic invaders combined to reduce Axum's power. It nevertheless retained its unique culture and its independence.

West Africa

For centuries, legend has held that the last kings of Kush retreated westward across the savannah to West Africa, bringing with them artistic motifs, the knowledge of iron making, and the concepts of divine kingship and centralized government. No archaeological evidence supports this belief. By the fifth century BCE, Garamantian **Berbers** in what is today Libya independently introduced pyramids, Egyptian gods, and

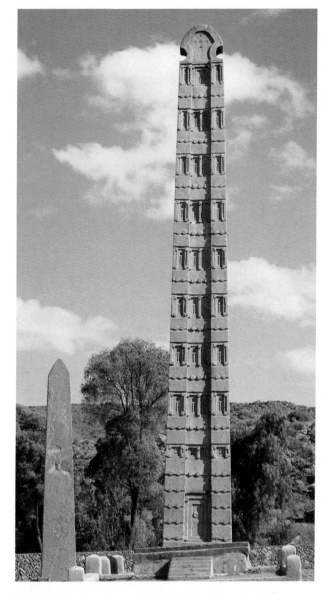

This giant stele at Axum demonstrates the spread of Egyptian architecture into what is today Ethiopia. Probably erected during the first century CE, before Axum converted to Christianity, this is the last of its kind still standing.   Copyright Werner Forman/Art Resource, NY

ancestor worship to the western Sahara region. But a distinctive West African civilization had independent roots. Iron working, for example, arose earlier in West Africa than it did at Meroë. The immediate birthright of most African Americans, then, is to be found not in the ancient civilizations of the Nile valley—although those civilizations are part of the heritage of all Africans—but thousands of miles away among the civilizations that emerged in West Africa during the first millennium BCE.

Like Africa as a whole, West Africa is physically, ethnically, and culturally diverse. Much of West Africa south of the Sahara Desert falls within the great **savannah** that spans the continent from east to west. West and south of the savannah, however, are extensive forests. They cover Senegambia (modern Senegal and Gambia), the southwestern coast of West Africa, and the lands located along the coast of the Gulf of Guinea. These two environments—savannah and forest—were home to a great variety of cultures and languages. Patterns of settlement in the region ranged from isolated homesteads and hamlets through villages and towns to cities.

West Africans began cultivating crops and tending domesticated animals between 1000 BCE and 200 CE. Those who lived on the savannah usually adopted settled village life well before those who lived in the forests. The early farmers produced grains—millet, rice, and sorghum—while tending herds of cattle and goats. By 500 BCE, beginning with the Nok people of the forest region, some West Africans were producing iron tools and weapons.

From early times, the peoples of West Africa traded among themselves and with the peoples who lived across the Sahara Desert in North Africa. This extensive trade became an essential part of the region's economy and formed the basis for the three great western Sudanese empires that successively dominated the region from before 800 CE to the beginnings of the modern era.

ANCIENT GHANA

The first known kingdom in the western Sudan was Ghana (see Map 1–3). Founded by the Soninke people in the area north of the modern republic of Ghana, the kingdom's origins are unclear. It may have arisen as early as the fourth century CE or as late as the eighth century when Arab merchants began to praise its great wealth. Its name comes from the Soninke word for king, which Arab traders mistakenly applied to the entire kingdom.

Because they possessed superior iron weapons, the Soninke were able to dominate their neighbors and forge an empire through constant warfare. Ghana's boundaries reached into the Sahara Desert to its north and modern Senegal to its south. But the empire's real power lay in commerce.

Ghana's kings were known in Europe and southwest Asia as the richest of monarchs, and the source of their wealth was trade. The key to this trade was the Asian camel, which was introduced into Africa during the first century CE. With its ability to endure long journeys on small amounts of water, the camel dramatically increased trade across the Sahara between the western Sudan and the coastal regions of North Africa.

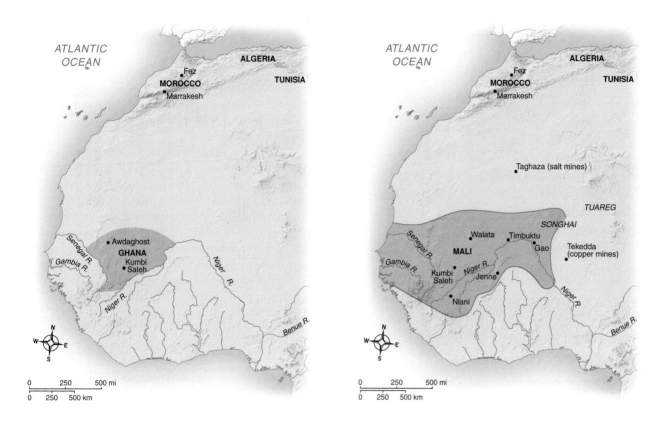

MAP 1–3   THE EMPIRES OF GHANA AND MALI

The western Sudanese empires of Ghana and Mali helped shape West African culture. Ghana existed from as early as the fourth century CE to 1076. Mali dominated the western Sudan from 1230 to 1468.

▶ *What does this map suggest concerning the historical relationship between ancient Ghana and Mali?*

Ghana traded in several commodities. From North Africa came silk, cotton, glass beads, horses, mirrors, dates, and, especially, salt—a scarce necessity in the torridly hot western Sudan. In return, Ghana exported pepper, slaves, and, especially, gold. The slaves were usually war captives, and the gold came from mines in the Wangara region to the southwest of Ghana. The Soninke did not mine the gold themselves; instead the kings of Ghana grew rich by taxing it as it passed through their lands.

Before the fifth century CE, Roman merchants and Berbers—the **indigenous** people of western North Africa—were West Africa's chief partners in the trans-Sahara trade. After the fifth century, as Roman power declined and Islam spread across North Africa, Arabs replaced the Romans. Arab merchants settled in Saleh, the Muslim part of Kumbi Saleh, Ghana's capital, which by the twelfth century had become an impressive city. There were stone houses and tombs

and as many as twenty thousand people. Visitors remarked the splendor of Kumbi Saleh's royal court. Saleh had several mosques, and some Soninke converted to Islam, although it is unclear whether the royal family joined them. Moslems dominated the royal bureaucracy and in the process introduced Arabic writing to the region.

A combination of commercial and religious rivalries finally destroyed Ghana during the twelfth century. The Almorvids, who were Islamic Berbers, had been Ghana's principal competitors for control of the trans-Sahara trade. In 992 Ghana's army captured Awdaghost, the Almorvid trade center northwest of Kumbi Saleh. Driven as much by religious fervor as by economic interest, the Almorvids retaliated decisively in 1076 by conquering Ghana. The Soninke regained their independence in 1087, but a little over a century later fell to the Sosso, a previously tributary people, who destroyed Kumbi Saleh.

LIVING WORDS

1 *Ghana: Ewe-Atsiagbekor*

DOCUMENT

Ghana and Its People in the Mid-Eleventh Century   **1-3**

AL BAKRI DESCRIBES KUMBI SALEH AND GHANA'S ROYAL COURT

Nothing remains of the documents compiled by Ghana's Islamic bureaucracy. As a result, accounts of the civilization are all based on the testimony of Arab or Berber visitors. In this passage, written in the eleventh century, Arab geographer Al Bakri describes the great wealth and power of the king of Ghana and suggests there were tensions between Islam and the indigenous religion of the Soninke.

The city of Ghana [Kumbi Saleh] consists of two towns lying in a plain. One of these towns is inhabited by Muslims. It is large and possesses twelve mosques. . . . There are imams and muezzins, and assistants as well as jurists and learned men. Around the town are wells of sweet water from which they drink and near which they grow vegetables. The town in which the king lives is six miles from the Muslim one, and bears the name Al Ghaba [the forest]. The land between the two towns is covered with houses. The houses of the inhabitants are of stone and acacia wood. The king has a palace and a number of dome-shaped dwellings, the whole surrounded by an enclosure like the defensive wall of a city. In the town where the king lives, and not far from the hall where he holds his court of justice, is a mosque where pray the Muslims who come on diplomatic missions. Around the king's town are domed buildings, woods, and copses where live the sorcerers of these people, the men in charge of the religious cult. . . .

Of the people who follow the king's religion, only he and his heir presumptive, who is the son of his sister, may wear sewn clothes. All the other people wear clothes of cotton, silk, or brocade, according to their means. All men shave their beards and women shave their heads. The king adorns himself like a woman, wearing necklaces and bracelets, and when he sits before the people he puts on a high cap decorated with gold and wrapped in a turban of fine cotton. The court of appeal [for grievances against officials] is held in a domed pavilion around which stand ten horses with gold embroidered trappings. Behind the king stand ten pages holding shields and swords decorated with gold, and on his right are the sons of the subordinate kings of his country, all wearing splendid garments and their hair mixed with gold. . . . When the people professing the same religion as the king approach him, they fall on their knees and sprinkle their heads with dust, for this is their way of showing him their respect. As for the Muslims, they greet him only by clapping their hands.

THE EMPIRE OF MALI, 1230–1468

Following the defeat of Ghana by the Almorvids, many western Sudanese peoples competed for political and economic power. This contest ended in 1235 when the Mandinka, under their legendary leader Sundiata (c. 1210–1260), defeated the Sosso at the Battle of Kirina. In the wake of this victory, Sundiata went on to forge the Empire of Mali.

Mali, which means "where the emperor resides" in Mende, the language of the Mandinka, was socially, politically, and economically similar to Ghana. It was larger than Ghana, however—stretching 1,500 miles from the Atlantic coast to the region east of the Niger River—and centered farther south, in a region of greater rainfall and more abundant crops. Sundiata also gained direct control of the gold mines of Wangara, making his empire wealthier than Ghana had been. As a result, Mali's population grew, reaching a total of eight million.

Sundiata was also an important figure in western Sudanese religion. According to legend, he wielded magical powers to defeat his enemies. This suggests that he practiced an indigenous faith. But Sundiata was also a Muslim and helped make Mali—at least superficially—a Muslim state. West Africans had been converting to Islam since Arab traders arrived in the region centuries before, although many converts continued to practice indigenous religions as well. By Sundiata's time, most merchants and bureaucrats were Muslims, and the empire's rulers gained stature among Arab states by converting to Islam.

To administer their vast empire at a time when communication was slow, Mali's rulers relied on personal and family ties with local chiefs. Commerce, bureaucracy, and scholarship also played a role in holding the empire together. Mali's most important city was Timbuktu, which had been established during the eleventh century beside the Niger River near the southern edge of the Sahara Desert. Two other cities—Walata in the northwest and Gao in the east—also functioned as economic and cultural centers.

By the thirteenth century, Timbuktu had become a major hub for trade in gold, slaves, and salt. It attracted merchants from throughout the Mediterranean world and became a center of Islamic learning. There were several mosques in the city, 150 Islamic schools, a law

What does this passage indicate about life in ancient Ghana?

According to Al Bakri, in what ways do customs in Kumbi Saleh differ from customs in Arab lands?

Source: Roland Oliver and Caroline Oliver, *Africa in the Days of Exploration* (Upper Saddle River, NJ: Prentice Hall, 1965), 9–10.

school, and many book dealers. It supported a cosmopolitan community and impressed visitors with its absence of religious and ethnic intolerance. Even though Mali enslaved war captives and traded slaves, an Arab traveler noted in 1352–1353, "the Negroes possess some admirable qualities. They are seldom unjust, and have a greater abhorrence of injustice than any other people."

The Mali Empire reached its peak during the reign of Mansa Musa (1312–1337). One of the wealthiest rulers the world has known, Musa made himself and Mali famous when in 1324 he undertook a pilgrimage across Africa to the Islamic holy city of Mecca in Arabia. With an entourage of sixty thousand, a train of one hundred elephants, and a propensity for distributing huge amounts of gold to those who greeted him along the way, Musa amazed the Islamic world. After Musa's death, however, Mali declined. The empire's leading families vied with each other for wealth and power and its subject peoples began to rebel. In 1468, one of the most powerful of its formerly subject peoples, the Songhai, captured Timbuktu, and their leader, Sunni Ali, founded a new West African empire.

Mansa Musa, who ruled the West African Empire of Mali from 1312 to 1337, is portrayed at the bottom center of this portion of the fourteenth-century Catalan Atlas. Musa's crown, scepter, throne, and the huge gold nugget he displays symbolize his power and wealth.

THE EMPIRE OF SONGHAI, 1464–1591

Like the Mandinka and Soninke before them, the Songhai were great traders and warriors. The Songhai had seceded from Mali in 1375, and under Sunni Ali, who reigned from 1464 to 1492, they built the last and largest of the western Sudanese empires (see Map 1–4). Sunni Ali required conquered peoples to pay tribute, but otherwise let them run their own affairs. Nominally a Muslim, he—like Sundiata—was reputedly a great magician who derived power from the traditional spirits.

When Sunni Ali died by drowning, Askia Muhammad Toure led a successful revolt against Ali's son to make himself king of Songhai. The new king, who reigned from 1492 to 1528, extended the empire northward into the Sahara, westward into Mali, and eastward to encompass the trading cities of Hausaland. He centralized the administration of the empire, replacing local chiefs with members of his family, substituting taxation for tribute, and establishing a bureaucracy to regulate trade.

A devout Muslim, Muhammad Toure used his power to spread the influence of Islam within the empire. During a pilgrimage to Mecca in 1497 he established diplomatic relations with Morocco and Egypt and recruited Moslem scholars to serve at the Sankore Mosque at Timbuktu. Subsequently, the mosque became a widely known center for the study of theology, law, mathematics, and medicine. Despite these efforts, by the end of Muhammad Toure's reign (the aging ruler, senile and blind, was deposed by family members) Islamic culture remained weak in West Africa outside urban areas. Peasants, who made up 95 percent of the population, spoke a variety of languages, continued to practice indigenous religions, and remained loyal to their local chiefs.

Songhai reached its peak of influence under Askia Daud between 1549 and 1582. But the political balance of power in West Africa was changing rapidly, and, lacking new leaders as resourceful as Sunni Ali or Muhammad Toure, Songhai failed to adapt. Since the 1430s, adventurers from the European country of Portugal had been establishing trading centers along the Guinea Coast, seeking gold and diverting it from the trans-Sahara trade. Their success threatened the

The Nok people of what is today Nigeria produced terracotta sculptures like this one during the first millennium BCE. They also pioneered, between 500 and 450 BCE, iron-smelting in West Africa.   Nigeria, Nok head, 900 BC–200 AD, Rafin Kura, Nok. Prehistoric West African sculpture from the Nok culture. Terracotta, 36 cms high. © Werner Forman/Art Resource, NY

MAP 1–4   WEST AND CENTRAL AFRICA, C. 1500
This map shows the Empire of Songhai (1464–1591), the Kongo kingdom (c. 1400–1700), and the major kingdoms of the West African forest region.

▶ *How did the western Sudanese empires' geographical location make them susceptible to slave trading?*

Arab rulers of North Africa, Songhai's traditional partners in the trans-Sahara trade. In 1591 the king of Morocco, hoping to regain access to West African gold, sent an army of 4,000 mostly Spanish mercenaries armed with muskets and cannons across the Sahara to attack Gao, Songhai's capital. Only 1,000 of the soldiers survived the grueling march to confront Songhai's elite cavalry at Tondibi on the approach to Gao. But the Songhai forces were armed only with bows and lances, which were no match for firearms, and the mercenaries routed them. Its army destroyed, the Songhai empire fell apart. The center of Islamic scholarship in West Africa shifted eastward from Timbuktu to Hausaland. The Moroccans soon left the region, and West Africa was with-

DOCUMENT
1-4   *Muslim Reform in Songhai*

out a government powerful enough to intervene when the Portuguese, other Europeans, and the African kingdoms of the Guinea Coast became more interested in trading for human beings than for gold.

THE WEST AFRICAN FOREST REGION

The area called the forest region of West Africa, which includes stretches of savannah, extends two thousand miles along the Atlantic coast from Senegambia in the northwest to the former kingdom of Benin (modern Cameroon) in the east. Among the early settlers of the forest region were the Nok, who around 500 BCE, in what is today southern Nigeria, created a culture noted for its iron-working technology and its terra-cotta sculptures. But significant migration into the forests

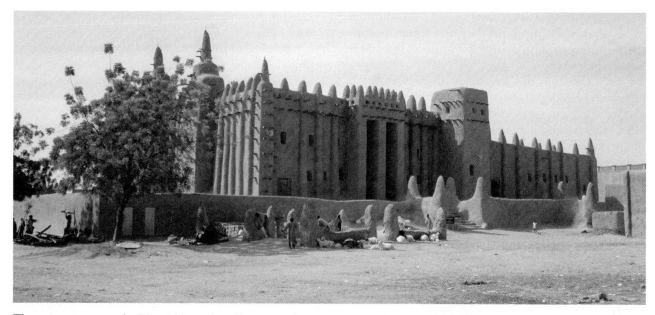

The great mosque at the West African city of Jenne was first built during the fourteenth century CE. It demonstrates the importance of Islam in the region's trading centers.   Roderick J. McIntosh, Rice University

began only after 1000 CE, as the western Sudanese climate became increasingly dry.

Because people migrated southward from the Sudan in small groups over an extended period, the process brought about considerable cultural diversification. A variety of languages, economies, political systems, and traditions came into existence. Some ancient customs survived, such as dividing types of agricultural labor by gender and living in villages composed of extended families. Nevertheless, the forest region became a patchwork of diverse ethnic groups with related, but sometimes quite different, ways of life.

Colonizing a region covered with thick vegetation was hard work. In some portions of the forest, agriculture did not supplant hunting and gathering until the fifteenth and sixteenth centuries. In more open parts of the region, however, several small kingdoms emerged centuries earlier. Benin City, for example, dates to the thirteenth century and Ife in Nigeria to the eleventh. Although none of these kingdoms ever grew as large as the empires of the western Sudan, some were powerful. The kings claimed semidivine status but their power was limited by the nobility and urban elites. Kings sought to extend their power by conquering and assimilating neighboring peoples. Secrecy and elaborate ritual marked royal courts, which were also centers of patronage for art and religion.

DOCUMENT 1-5   *Job Hortop and the British Enter the Slave Trade, 1567*

The peoples of the forest region are of particular importance for African-American history because of the role they played in the Atlantic slave trade as both slave traders and as victims of the trade. Space limitations permit only a survey of the most important of these peoples, beginning with those of Senegambia in the northwest.

The inhabitants of Senegambia shared a common history and spoke closely related languages, but they were not politically united. Parts of the region had been incorporated within the empires of Ghana and Mali and had been exposed to Islamic influences. Senegambian society was strictly hierarchical, with royalty at the top and slaves at the bottom. Most people were farmers, growing rice, millet, sorghum, plantains, beans, and bananas. They supplemented their diet with fish, oysters, rabbits, and monkeys.

To the southeast of Senegambia were the Akan states. They emerged during the sixteenth century as the gold trade provided local rulers with the wealth they needed to clear forests and initiate agricultural economies. The rulers traded gold from mines under their control for slaves, who did the difficult work of cutting trees and burning refuse. Then settlers received open fields from the rulers in return for a portion of their produce and services. When Europeans arrived, they traded guns for gold. The guns in turn allowed the Akan states to expand, and during the late seventeenth century, one of them, the Ashante, created a well-organized and densely populated kingdom, comparable in size to the modern country of Ghana.

By the eighteenth century, this kingdom not only dominated the central portion of the forest region, but also used its army extensively to capture slaves for sale to European traders.

To the east of the Akan states (in modern Benin and western Nigeria) lived the people of the Yoruba culture. They gained ascendancy in the area as early as 1000 CE by trading kola nuts and cloth to the peoples of the western Sudan. The artisans of the Yoruba city of Ife gained renown for their fine bronze, brass, and terra-cotta sculptures. Ife was also notable for the prominent role of women in conducting its profitable commerce. During the seventeenth century, the Oyo people, employing a well-trained cavalry, imposed political unity on part of the Yoruba region. They, like the

This carved wooden ceremonial offering bowl is typical of a Yoruba art form that has persisted for centuries. It reflects religious practices as well as traditional hairstyle and dress.

Ashanti, became extensively involved in the Atlantic slave trade.

Located to the west of the Oyo were the Fon people, who formed the Kingdom of Dahomey, which rivaled Oyo as a center for the slave trade. The king of Dahomey was an absolute monarch who took thousands of wives for himself from leading Fon families as a way to assure the loyalty of potential rivals.

At the eastern end of the forest region was the Kingdom of Benin, which controlled an extensive area in what is today southern Nigeria. The people of this kingdom shared a common heritage with the Yoruba, who played a role in its formation during the thirteenth century. Throughout Benin's history, a struggle for power between the Oba (king), who claimed divine status, and the kingdom's hereditary nobility marked its politics.

During the fifteenth century, after a reform of its army, Benin began to expand to the Niger River in the east, to the Gulf of Guinea to the south, and into Yoruba country to the west. The kingdom peaked during the late sixteenth century. European visitors at that time noted the size and sophistication of its capital—Benin City. There skilled artisans produced the fine bronze sculptures for which the region is still known. The city's wealthy class dined on beef, mutton, chicken, and yams. Its streets, unlike those of European cities of the time, were free of beggars.

Benin remained little influenced by Islam or Christianity, but like other coastal kingdoms, it became increasingly involved in the Atlantic slave trade. Beginning in the late fifteenth century, the Oba of Benin allowed Europeans to enter the country to trade for gold, pepper, ivory, and slaves. Initially, the Oba forbade the sale of his own subjects, but his large army—the first in the forest region to be provided with European firearms—captured others for the trade as it conquered neighboring regions. By the seventeenth century, Benin's prosperity depended on the slave trade. As the kingdom declined during the eighteenth century, it began to sell some of its own people to European slave traders.

To Benin's east was Igboland, a densely populated but politically weak region stretching along the Niger River. The Igbo people lived in one of the stateless societies common in West Africa. In these societies, families rather than central authorities governed. Village elders provided local government and life centered on family homesteads. Igboland had for many years exported field workers and skilled artisans to Benin and other kingdoms. When Europeans arrived, they expanded this trade, which brought many Igbos to the Americas (see Map 1–5).

MAP 1–5 TRANS-SAHARAN TRADE ROUTES

Ancient trade routes connected sub-Saharan West Africa to the Mediterranean coast. Among the commodities carried southward were silk, cotton, horses, and salt. Among those carried northward were gold, ivory, pepper, and slaves.

➤ *What was the significance of the trans-Sahara trade in West African history?*

Kongo and Angola

Although the forebears of most African Americans originated in West Africa, a large minority came from Central Africa. In particular they came from the region encompassing the Congo River and its tributaries and the region to the south that the Portuguese called Angola. The people of these regions had much in common with those of the Guinea Coast. They divided labor by gender, lived in villages composed of extended families, and accorded semidivine status to their kings. Like the people of West Africa, they were ensnared in the Atlantic slave trade as it grew to immense proportions after 1500.

During the fourteenth and fifteenth centuries, much of the Congo River system, with its fertile valleys and abundant fish, came under the control of the Kingdom of Kongo. The wealth of this kingdom also derived from its access to salt and iron and its extensive trade with the interior of the continent. Nzinga Knuwu, who was *Mani Kongo* (the Kongolese term for king) when Portuguese expeditions arrived in the region in the late fifteenth century, surpassed other African rulers in wel-

coming the intruders. His son Nzinga Mbemba tried to convert the kingdom to Christianity and remodel it along European lines. The resulting unrest, combined with Portuguese greed and the effects of the slave trade, undermined royal authority and ultimately led to the breakup of the kingdom and the social disruption of the entire Kongo-Angola region.

West African Society and Culture

West Africa's great ethnic and cultural diversity makes it hazardous to generalize about the social and cultural background of the first African Americans. The dearth of written records from the region south of the Sudan compounds the difficulties. But working with a variety of sources, including oral histories, traditions, and archaeological and anthropological studies, historians have pieced together a broad understanding of the way the people of West Africa lived at the beginning of the Atlantic slave trade.

FAMILIES AND VILLAGES

By the early sixteenth century, most West Africans were farmers. They usually lived in hamlets or villages composed of extended families and clans called **lineages**. Generally, one lineage occupied each village, although some large lineages peopled several villages. The members of extended families were descended from a common ancestor, and the lineages claimed descent from a mythical personage. Depending on the ethnic group involved, extended families and lineages were either patrilineal or matrilineal. In patrilineal societies, social rank and property passed in the male line from fathers to sons. In matrilineal societies, rank and property, although controlled by men, passed from generation to generation in the female line. A village chief in a matrilineal society was succeeded by his sister's son, not his own. According to the Arab chronicler Al Bakri, the succession to the throne of the empire of Ghana followed this pattern. But many West Africans lived in stateless societies with no government other than that provided by extended families and lineages.

In extended families, **nuclear families** (husband, wife, and children) or in some cases **polygynous families** (husband, wives, and children) acted as economic units. Nuclear and polygamous families existed in the context of a broader family community composed of grandparents, aunts, uncles, and cousins. Elders in the extended family had great power over the economic and social lives of its members. In contrast with ancient Egypt, strictly enforced incest taboos prohibited people from marrying within their extended family.

Villages tended to be larger on the savannah than in the forest. In both regions, people used forced earth or mud to construct small houses, which were round or rectangular in shape, depending on local tradition. The houses usually had thatched roofs, or, sometimes in the forest, they had palm roofs. In both savannah and forest, mud or mud-brick walls up to ten feet high surrounded villages. A nuclear or polygynous family unit might have several houses. In nuclear households, the husband occupied the larger house and his wife the smaller. In polygynous households, the husband had the largest house, and his wives lived in smaller ones.

Villagers' few possessions included cots, rugs, stools, and wooden storage chests. Their tools and weapons included bows, spears, iron axes, hoes, and scythes. Households used grinding stones, woven baskets, and a variety of ceramic vessels to prepare and store food. Villagers in both the savannah and forest regions produced cotton for clothing, but their food crops were quite distinct. West Africans in the savannah cultivated millet, rice, and sorghum as their dietary

PROFILE ❧ NZINGA MBEMBA (AFFONSO I) OF KONGO

Nzinga Mbemba, baptised Dom Affonso, ruled as the Mani Kongo from about 1506 to 1543 CE. His life illustrates the complex and tragic relationships between African coastal kingdoms and Europeans in search of power, cultural hegemony, and wealth.

Mbemba was a son of Nzinga Knuwu, who, as Mani Kongo, established diplomatic ties with Portugal. Portuguese vessels had reached Kongo in 1482, and in 1491 the Portuguese king sent a formal mission to Mbanza Kongo (the City of Kongo). Amid considerable ceremony, Knuwu converted to Christianity, not because of faith, but because conversion gave him access to Portuguese musketeers he needed to put down a rebellion. Mbemba served as his father's general in the ensuing successful campaign.

By 1495, internal politics and Knuwu's inability to accept Christian monogamy had led him to renounce his baptism and to banish Christians—both Portuguese and Kongolese—from Mbanza Kongo. Mbemba, who was a sincere Christian, became their champion in opposition to a traditionalist faction headed by his half-brother Mpanza. Following Knuwu's death in 1506, the two princes fought over the succession. The victory of Mbemba's forces led to his coronation as Affonso and the execution of Mpanza.

By then Mbemba had learned to speak, read, and write Portuguese. He gained at least outward respect from the Portuguese monarchy as a ruler and devout Christian missionary. Soon there were hundreds of Portuguese advisers, priests, artisans, teachers, and settlers in Mbanza Kongo and its environs. In 1516 a Portuguese priest described Mbemba as "not . . . a man but an angel sent by the Lord to this kingdom to convert it. . . . Better than we, he knows the Prophets and the Gospel of Our Lord Jesus Christ." Mbemba destroyed fetishes and shrines associated with Kongo's traditional religion, replaced them with crucifixes and images of saints, built Christian churches in Mbanza Kongo, and had some of his opponents burned.

While seeking the spiritual salvation of his nation, Mbemba hoped also to modernize it on a European model. He dressed in Portuguese clothing, sent his sons and other young men to Portugal to be educated, and began schools to educate the children of Kongo's nobility. He corresponded with Portuguese kings, and his son Dom Henrique, who became a Christian bishop, briefly represented Kongo at the Vatican, where he addressed the pope in Latin in 1513.

Mbemba put too much faith in his Portuguese patrons and too little in the traditions of his people. By 1508, Portuguese priests were trading in slaves and living with Kongolese mistresses. This disturbed Mbemba, not because he opposed slavery, but because the priests undermined his authority. He was supposed to have a monopoly over the slave trade, and increasingly his own people were subjected to that trade.

Mbemba's complaints led to a formal agreement with Portugal in 1512 called the *Regimento*, which actually worsened matters. It placed restrictions on the priests and pledged continued Portuguese military assistance. But it also recognized the right of Portuguese merchants to trade for copper, ivory, and slaves and exempted Portuguese from punishment under local law. Soon the slave trade and related corruption increased, and so did unrest among Mbemba's increasingly unhappy subjects. In 1526, Mbemba created a commission designed to ensure that only war captives could be enslaved and, when that did not work, he begged the Portuguese king that "in these kingdoms there should not be any trade in slaves or market for slaves."

In response, Portugal made alliances with Kongo's neighbors and withdrew much of its support from Mbemba, who died surrounded by scheming merchants, corruption, and dissension. In 1568—a quarter-century after his death—Kongo became a client state of Portugal, and the slave trade expanded.

Affonse I gives an audience to foreign ambassadors at his royal court. ▶

staples; kept goats and cattle for milk and cheese; and supplemented their diets with peas, okra, watermelons, and a variety of nuts. Yams, rather than grains, were the dietary staple in the forest region. Other important forest region crops included bananas and coco yams, both ultimately derived from far-off Indonesia located near southeast Asia.

Farming in West Africa was not easy. Drought was common on the savannah. In the forest, where diseases carried by the tsetse fly sickened draft animals, agricultural plots were limited in size because they had to be cleared by hand. The fields surrounding forest villages averaged just two or three acres per family.

Although there was private ownership of land in West Africa, people generally worked land communally, dividing tasks by gender. Among the Akan of the Guinea Coast, for example, men were responsible for clearing the land of trees and underbrush while women tended the fields (planting, weeding, harvesting, and carrying in the harvested produce). Women also took care of children, prepared meals, and manufactured household pottery.

WOMEN

In general, men dominated women in West Africa. As previously noted, it was common for men to take two or more wives, and, to a degree, custom held women to be the property of men. But West African women also enjoyed a relative amount of freedom that impressed Arab and European visitors. In ancient Ghana, women sometimes served as government officials. Later, in the forest region, women sometimes inherited property and owned land—or at least controlled its income. Women—including enslaved women—in the royal court of Dahomey held high government posts. Ashante noblewomen could own property, although they themselves could be considered inheritable property. The Ashante queen held her own court to administer women's affairs.

Women retained far more sexual freedom in West Africa than was the case in Europe or southwest Asia. Ibn Battuta, a Muslim Berber from North Africa who visited Mali during the fourteenth century, was shocked to discover that in this Islamic country "women show no bashfulness before men and do not veil themselves, though they are assiduous in attending prayer." Battuta was even more dumbfounded to learn that in West Africa women could have male friends and companions other than their husbands or relatives.

Sexual freedom in West Africa was, however, more apparent than real. Throughout the region **secret societies** instilled in men and women ethical standards of personal behavior. The most important secret societies were the women's *Sande* and the men's *Poro*. They initiated boys and girls into adulthood and provided sex education. They also established standards for personal conduct, especially in regard to issues of gender, by emphasizing female virtue and male honor. Other secret societies influenced politics, trade, medical practice, recreation, and social gatherings.

CLASS AND SLAVERY

Although many West Africans lived in stateless societies, most lived in hierarchically organized states headed by monarchs who claimed divine or semidivine status. These monarchs were far from absolute in the power they wielded, but they commanded armies, taxed commerce, and accumulated considerable wealth. Beneath the royalty were classes of landed nobles, warriors, peasants, and bureaucrats. Lower classes included blacksmiths, butchers, weavers, woodcarvers, tanners, and the oral historians called *griots*.

Slavery had been part of this hierarchical social structure since ancient times. Although very common throughout West Africa, slavery was less so in the forest region than on the savannah. It took a wide variety of forms and was not necessarily a permanent condition. Like people in other parts of the world, West Africans held war captives—including men, women, and children—to be without rights and suitable for enslavement. In Islamic regions, masters had obligations to their slaves similar to those of a guardian for a ward and were responsible for their slaves' religious wellbeing. In non-Islamic regions, the children of slaves acquired legal protections, such as the right not to be sold away from the land they occupied.

Slaves who served either in the royal courts of a West African kingdom or in a kingdom's armies often exercised power over free people and could acquire property. Also, the slaves of peasant farmers often had standards of living similar to those of their masters. Slaves who worked under overseers in gangs on large estates were far less fortunate. However, even for such enslaved agricultural workers, the work and privileges accorded to the second and third generations became little different from those of free people. Regardless of their generation, slaves retained a low social status, but in many respects slavery in West African societies functioned as a means of **assimilation**.

RELIGION

There were two religious traditions in fifteenth-century West Africa: Islamic and indigenous. Islam, which Arab traders introduced into West Africa, took root first in the Sudanese empires and remained more prevalent in the cosmopolitan savannah. Even there it was stronger in cities than in rural areas because it was the religion of merchants and bureaucrats. Islam fostered literacy in Arabic, the spread of Islamic learning, and the construction of mosques. Islam is resolutely monotheistic, asserting that Allah is the only God. It recognizes its founder, Muhammad, as well as Abraham, Moses, and Jesus, as prophets but regards none of them as divine.

West Africa's indigenous religions remained strongest in the forest region. They were **polytheistic** and **animistic**, recognizing a great number of divinities and spirits. Beneath an all-powerful, but remote, creator god were pantheons of lesser gods who represented the forces of nature. Other gods were associated with particular mountains, rivers, trees, and rocks. Indigenous West African religion, in other words, saw the force of God in all things.

In part because practitioners of West African indigenous religions perceived the creator god to be unapproachable, they invoked the spirits of their ancestors and turned to magicians and oracles for divine assistance. Like the Chinese, they believed the spirits of their direct and remote ancestors could influence their lives. Therefore ceremonies designed to sustain ancestral spirits and their power over the earth became central to traditional West African religions. These rituals were part of everyday life, making organized churches and professional clergy rare. Instead, family members with an inclination to do so assumed religious duties. These individuals encouraged their relatives to participate in ceremonies that involved music, dancing, and animal sacrifice in honor of deceased ancestors. Funerals were especially important because they symbolized the linkage between living and dead.

ART AND MUSIC

As was the case in other parts of the world, religious belief and practice influenced West African art. West Africans, seeking to preserve the images of their ancestors, excelled in woodcarving and sculpture in **terra-cotta**, bronze, and brass. Throughout the region, artists produced wooden masks representing in highly stylized manners ancestral spirits as well as various divinities. Wooden and terra-cotta figurines, sometimes referred to as "fetishes," were also extremely common. West Africans used them in funerals, in rituals related to ancestral spirits, in medical practice, and in coming-of-age ceremonies. In contrast to masks and fetishes, the great bronze sculptures of Benin had political functions. They were quite real-

This six-string wooden harp is a rare example of the type of instrument West African musicians and storytellers used to accompany themselves.

istic in portraying their subjects, which consisted of kings, warriors, and nobles rather than deities and spirits.

West African music also served religion. Folk musicians employed such instruments as drums, xylophones, bells, flutes, and mbanzas (predecessor to the banjo) to produce a highly rhythmic accompaniment to the dancing associated with religious rituals. A **call-and-response** style of singing also played a vital role in ritual. Vocal music, produced in a full-throated, but often raspy, style, had polyphonic textures and sophisticated rhythms.

LITERATURE: ORAL HISTORIES, POETRY, AND TALES

West African literature was part of an oral tradition that passed from generation to generation. At its most formal, it was a literature developed by specially trained poets and musicians who served kings and nobles. But West African literature was also a folk art that expressed the views of the common people.

At a king's court there could be several poet-musicians who had high status and specialized in poems

EVENTS IN AFRICA	WORLD EVENTS
• 10 million years ago •	
5–10 million years ago Separation of hominids from apes	**1.6 million years ago** *Homo erectus* beginning to spread through Eurasia
4 million years ago Emergence of *australopithecines*	
2.4 million years ago Emergence of *Homo habilis*	
1.7 million years ago Emergence of *Homo erectus*	
• 1.5 million years ago •	
100,000–200,000 years ago Appearance of modern humans	**8000 BCE** Appearance of the first agricultural settlements in southwest Asia
6000 BCE Beginning of Sahara Desert formation	
• 5000 BCE •	
5000 BCE First agricultural settlements in Egypt	**3500 BCE** Sumerian civilization in Mesopotamia
3800 BCE Predynastic period in Egypt	
c. 3150 BCE Unification of Egypt	
• 2500 BCE •	
2700–2150 BCE Egypt's Old Kingdom	**2300 BCE** Beginning of Indus valley civilization
2100–1650 BCE Egypt's Middle Kingdom	
1500 BCE	
1550–700 BCE Egypt's New Kingdom	**1600–1250 BCE** Mycenaean Greek civilization
	C. 1500 Beginning of Shang dynasty in China

glorifying rulers and their ancestors by linking fact and fiction. Drums and horns often accompanied recitations of these poems. Court poets also used their trained memories to recall historical events and precise genealogies. The self-employed poets, called **griots,** who traveled from place to place were socially inferior to court poets, but they functioned in a similar manner. Both court poets and griots were men. Women were more involved in the genre of folk literature. They joined men in the creation and performance of work songs and led in creating and singing dirges, lullabies, and satirical verses. Often these forms of literature used a call-and-response style similar to that of religious songs.

Just as significant for African-American history were the West African prose tales. Like similar stories told in other parts of Africa, these tales took two forms: those with human characters and those with animal characters who represented humans. The tales centered on human characters dealing with such subjects as creation, the origins of death, paths to worldly success, and romantic love. Such tales often involve magical objects and potions.

The animal tales aimed to entertain and to teach lessons. They focus on small creatures, often referred to as "trickster characters," which are pitted against larger beasts. Among the heroes are the hare, the spider, and the mouse. Plots center on the ability of these weak animals to outsmart larger and meaner antagonists, such as the snake, leopard, and hyena. In all instances, the animal characters have human emotions and goals. They are presented in human settings, although they retain animal characteristics.

In West Africa, these tales represented the ability of common people to counteract the power of kings and nobles. When the tales reached America, they became allegories for the struggle between enslaved African Americans and their powerful white masters.

CONCLUSION

In recent years, paleoanthropologists, archaeologists, and historians have revealed much about Africa's history and prehistory, but much remains to be learned concerning the past of this vast and diverse continent. The evolution of humans, the role of ancient Egypt in world history, and Egypt's relationship to Nubia and Kush are all topics that continue to attract wide interest.

Although all of Africa contributed to their background, the history of African Americans begins in West Africa, the region from which the ancestors of most of them were unwillingly wrested. Historians have discovered, as subsequent chapters will show, that

West Africans taken to America and their descendants in America preserved much more of their ancestral way of life than scholars once believed possible. West African family organization, work habits, language structures and some words, religious beliefs, legends and stories, pottery styles, art, and music all reached America. These African legacies, although often attenuated, influenced the way African Americans and other Americans lived in their new land and continue to shape American life.

RECOMMENDED READING

Emmanuel Kwaku Akyeampong, ed. *Themes in West Africa's History*. Athens: Ohio University Press, 2006. Provides an up-to-date interdisciplinary approach to major themes in West African history.

Robert W. July. *A History of the African People*, 5th ed. Prospect Heights, IL: Waveland, 1998. A comprehensive and current social history with good coverage of West Africa and West African women.

Roland Oliver. *The African Experience: Major Themes in African History from Earliest Times to the Present*. New York: Harper-Collins, 1991. Shorter and less encyclopedic than July's book, but innovative in organization. It also provides insightful analysis of cultural relationships.

John Reader. *Africa: A Biography of the Continent*. New York: Knopf, 1998. The most up-to-date account of early African history, emphasizing the ways the continent's physical environment shaped human life there.

Christopher Stringer and Robin McKie. *African Exodus: The Origins of Modern Humanity*. New York: Henry Holt, 1997. A very clearly written account favoring the out-of-Africa model.

John Thornton. *Africa and Africans in the Making of the Atlantic World, 1400–1689*. New York: Cambridge University Press, 1992. A thorough consideration of West African culture and its impact in the Americas.

ADDITIONAL BIBLIOGRAPHY

PREHISTORY, EGYPT, AND KUSH

William Y. Adams. *Nubia—Corridor to Africa*. Princeton, NJ: Princeton University Press, 1984.

Martin Bernal. *Black Athena: The Afroasiatic Roots of Classical Civilization*. New Brunswick, NJ: Rutgers University, 1987.

Nicholas C. Grimal. *A History of Ancient Egypt*. Oxford: Blackwell, 1993.

Donald Johanson, Lenora Johanson, and Blake Edgar. *Ancestors: In Search of Human Origins*. New York: Villard Books, 1994.

Susan Kent. *Gender in African Prehistory*. Walnut Creek, CA: Altamira, 1998.

AFRICAN-AMERICAN EVENTS | **NATIONAL EVENTS**

1000 BCE

750–670 BCE
Rule of Kushites over Egypt

540 BCE
Founding of Meroë

c. 500 BCE
Beginning of iron smelting in West Africa

50 CE
Destruction of Kush

600–336 BCE
Classical Greek civilization

500 CE

632–750 CE
Islamic conquest of North Africa

c. 750–1076 CE
Empire of Ghana; Islam begins to take root in West Africa

204 BCE–476 CE
Domination of Mediterranean by Roman Republic and Empire

500–1350 CE
European Middle Ages

c. 570 CE
Birth of Muhammad

1200 CE

1230–1468 CE
Empire of Mali

c. 1300 CE
Rise of Yoruba states

1400 CE

1434 CE
Start of Portuguese exploration and establishment of trading outposts on West African coast

c. 1450 CE
Centralization of power in Benin

1464–1591 CE
Empire of Songhai

1492 CE
Christopher Columbus and European encounter of America

1517
Reformation begins in Europe

1600 CE

c. 1650 CE
Rise of Kingdom of Dahomey and the Akan states

1610
Scientific revolution begins in Europe

Mary R. Lefkowitz and Guy MacLean Rogers, eds. *Black Athena Revisited.* Chapel Hill: University of North Carolina Press, 1996.

Donald B. Redford. *From Slave to Pharaoh: The Black Experience of Ancient Egypt.* Baltimore: Johns Hopkins Press, 2004.

Stuart Tyson Smith. *Wretched Kush: Ethnic Identities and Boundaries in Egypt's Nubian Empire.* New York: Routledge, 2003.

Derek A. Welsby. *The Kingdom of Kush: The Napatan and Merotic Empires.* Princeton, NJ: Markus Wiener, 1998.

WESTERN SUDANESE EMPIRES

Nehemiah Levtzion. *Ancient Ghana and Mali.* London: Methuen, 1973.

Nehemiah Levtzion and J. F. Hopkins, eds. *Corpus of Early Arabic Sources for West African History.* New York: Cambridge University Press, 1981.

Roland Oliver and Brian M. Fagan. *Africa in the Iron Age.* New York: Cambridge University Press, 1975.

Roland Oliver and Caroline Oliver, eds. *Africa in the Days of Exploration.* Englewood Cliffs, NJ: Prentice-Hall, 1965.

J. Spencer Trimington. *A History of Islam in West Africa.* New York: Oxford University Press, 1962.

THE FOREST REGION OF THE GUINEA COAST

I. A. Akinjogbin. *Dahomey and Its Neighbors, 1708–1818.* New York: Cambridge University Press, 1967.

Edna G. Bay. *Wives of the Leopard: Gender, Politics, and Culture in the Kingdom of Dahomey.* Charlottesville: University of Virginia Press, 1998.

Daryll Forde, ed. *African Worlds.* New York: Oxford University Press, 1954.

Robert W. July. *Precolonial Africa.* New York: Scribner's, 1975.

Robin Law. *The Oyo Empire, c. 1600–c. 1836: West African Imperialism on the Eve of the Atlantic Slave Trade.* Oxford: Clarendon, 1977.

T. C. McCaskie. *State and Society in Pre-Colonial Ashanti.* New York: Cambridge University Press, 1995.

Walter Rodney. *A History of the Upper Guinea Coast, 1545–1800.* Oxford: Clarendon, 1970.

Robert Sydney Smith. *Kingdoms of the Yoruba,* 3d ed. Madison: University of Wisconsin Press, 1988.

CULTURE

Harold Courlander, ed. *A Treasury of African Folklore.* New York: Marlowe, 1996.

Susan Denyer. *African Traditional Architecture: An Historical and Geographical Perspective.* London: Heinemann, 1978.

Ruth Finnegan. *Oral Literature in Africa.* 1970. Reprint, Nairobi: Oxford University Press, 1976.

Werner Gillon. *A Short History of African Art.* New York: Viking, 1984.

Paulin J. Hountondji. *African Philosophy: Myth and Reality.* Bloomington: University of Indiana Press, 1984.

Elizabeth Allo Isichei. *The Religious Traditions of Africa: A History.* Westport, CT: Praeger, 2004.

J. H. Kwabena Nketia. *The Music of Africa.* New York: Norton, 1974.

Oyekan Owomoyela. *Yoruba Trickster Tales.* Lincoln: University of Nebraska Press, 1977.

RETRACING THE ODYSSEY

African Americans at Jamestown, Colonial National Historical Park, Virginia. This program covers the period from 1619, the date of the first reports concerning black inhabitants at Jamestown, to 1705 when Virginia formally adopted a slave code.

National Museum of African Art, Smithsonian Institution, Washington, DC. The museum exhibits visual art from African regions south of the Sahara Desert. It includes art from ancient Benin and ancient Kerma in Nubia. There is also an exhibit of African musical instruments.

African Collection, National History Museum of Los Angeles County, Los Angeles, CA. This collection includes about five thousand objects representing African cultures.

African Gallery, University of Pennsylvania Museum of Archaeology and Anthropology, Philadelphia. The gallery includes a collection of Benin bronzes.

Chattanooga African American Museum, Chattanooga, TN. The museum includes an exhibit dealing with African culture and history.

 PRENTICE HALL **myhistorylab** *Where it's a good time to connect to the past!* REVIEW, RESEARCH, AND INTERACT

REVIEW QUESTIONS

1. What was the role of Africa in the evolution of modern humanity?

2. Discuss the controversy concerning the racial identity of the ancient Egyptians. What is the significance of this controversy for the history of African Americans?

3. Compare and contrast the western Sudanese empires with the forest civilizations of the Guinea Coast.

4. Discuss the role of religion in West Africa. What was the African religious heritage of black Americans?

5. Describe West African society on the eve of the expansion of the Atlantic slave trade. What were the society's strengths and weaknesses?

www.researchnavigator.com

Using the tools available in Research Navigator, consider these questions:

What were the key features of West African society and culture?
What place did slavery have in that society?

PRIMARY SOURCE DOCUMENTS

MAP EXPLORATION

2

Middle Passage

❖

HOW DID THE ARRIVAL
OF THE EUROPEANS AFFECT AFRICA?

HOW DID THE SLAVE TRADE IN AFRICA
DIFFER FROM THE ATLANTIC SLAVE TRADE?

WHAT WAS THE "MIDDLE PASSAGE"?

WHAT HAPPENED TO AFRICANS
AFTER THEY CROSSED THE ATLANTIC?

HOW WERE SLAVES TREATED IN THE AMERICAS?

WHY DID THE ATLANTIC SLAVE TRADE END?

ca. 1450–1809

◀◀ **After Great Britain** banned the Atlantic slave trade in 1807,
British warships enforced the ban. The people portrayed in
this early nineteenth century woodcut were rescued from a
slave ship by the H.M.S. *Undine*.

They felt the sea-wind tying them into one nation of eyes and shadows and groans, in the one pain that is inconsolable, the loss of one's shore. They had wept, not for their wives only, their fading children, but for strange, ordinary things. This one, who was a hunter wept for a sapling lance whose absent heft sang in his palm's hollow. One, a fisherman, for an ocher river encircling his calves; one a weaver, for the straw fisherpot he had meant to repair, wilting in water. They cried for the little thing after the big thing. They cried for a broken gourd.

Derek Walcott, *Omeros*

West Africans were making iron tools long before Europeans arrived in Africa.

These words of a modern black West Indian poet express the sorrow and loss the Atlantic slave trade inflicted on the enslaved Africans it tore from their homelands. This extensive enterprise, which lasted for more than three centuries, brought millions of Africans three thousand miles across the Atlantic Ocean to the Americas. It was the largest forced migration in history. By the eighteenth century, the voyage across the ocean in European ships called "slavers" had become known as the "**Middle Passage.**" British sailors coined this innocuous phrase to describe the middle leg of a triangular journey first from England to Africa, then from Africa to the Americas, and finally from the Americas back to England. Yet to-day Middle Passage denotes an unbelievable descent into an earthly hell of cruelty and suffering. It was from the Middle Passage that the first African Americans emerged.

This chapter describes the Atlantic slave trade and the Middle Passage. It explores their origins both in European colonization in the Americas and in the slave trade that had existed in Africa itself for centuries. It focuses on the experience of the enslaved people whom the trade brought to America. For those who survived, the grueling journey was a prelude to servitude on huge agricultural factories called plantations. Many who became African Americans first experienced plantation life in the West Indies—the Caribbean islands—where they were prepared for lives as slaves in the Americas through a process called "seasoning."

The European Age of Exploration and Colonization

The origins of the Atlantic slave trade and its long duration were products of Western Europe's expansion of power that began during the fifteenth century and continued into the twentieth century. For a variety of economic, technological, and demographic reasons, Portugal, Spain, the Netherlands, France, England, and other nations sought to explore, conquer, and colonize in Africa, Asia, and the Americas. Their efforts had important consequences for these areas.

Portugal took the lead during the early 1400s as ships from its ports reached Africa's western coast. Portuguese captains hoped to find Christian allies there against the Muslims of North Africa and to spread Christianity. But they were more interested in trade with African kingdoms, as were the Spanish, Dutch, English, and French who followed them.

Even more attractive than Africa to the Portuguese and their European successors as sources of trade and wealth were India, China, Japan, and the East Indies (modern Indonesia and Malaysia). In 1487 the Portuguese explorer Bartolomeu Dias discovered the Cape of Good Hope at the southern tip of Africa and thereby established that it was possible to sail around Africa to reach India and regions to its east. Ten years later Vasco da Gama initiated this route on behalf of Portuguese commerce. In between the voyages of Dias and Da Gama, a similar desire to reach these eastern regions motivated the Spanish monarchy to finance Christopher Columbus's westward voyages that began in 1492.

Columbus, who believed the earth to be much smaller than it actually is, hoped to reach Japan or India by sailing west, thereby opening a direct trade route between Spain and these eastern countries. Columbus's mistake led to his accidental landfall in the Americas. In turn, that encounter led to the European conquest, settlement, and exploitation of North and South America and the Caribbean islands, where Columbus first landed. Columbus and those who followed him quickly enslaved indigenous Americans (American Indians) as laborers in fields and mines. Almost as quickly, large numbers of indigenous peoples either died of European diseases and overwork or escaped beyond the reach of European power. Consequently, European colonizers needed additional laborers. This demand for a workforce in the Americas caused the Atlantic slave trade.

The Slave Trade in Africa

Slave labor was not peculiar to the European colonies in the Americas. Slavery and slave trading were ancient phenomena that existed in all cultures. As Chapter 1 indicates, slavery had existed in Africa for thousands of years, and slave labor was common in West Africa, although it was usually less oppressive than it became in the Americas.

When Portuguese voyagers first arrived at Senegambia, Benin, and Kongo, they found a thriving commerce in slaves. These kingdoms represented the southern extremity of an extensive trade conducted by Islamic nations that involved the capture and sale of Europeans and North African Berbers, as well as black people from south of the Sahara Desert. Although Arabs nurtured antiblack prejudice, race was not the major factor in this Islamic slave trade. Arab merchants and West African kings, for example, imported white slaves from Europe.

Insofar as it affected West Africa, the Islamic slave trade was conducted by Sudanese horsemen. The horsemen invaded the forest region to capture people who could not effectively resist—often they belonged to stateless societies. The trade dealt mainly in women and children, who as slaves were destined for lives as concubines and domestic servants in North Africa and southwest Asia. This pattern contrasted with that of the later Atlantic slave trade, which primarily sought young men for agricultural labor in the Americas. The

Although the overwhelming majority of Africans who were caught up in the Atlantic slave trade went to the Americas, a few reached Europe. This sixteenth-century drawing by German artist Albrecht Dürer depicts Katharina, a servant of a Portuguese official who lived in Antwerp. Albrecht Dürer (1471–1528). "Portrait of the Moorish Woman Katharina." Drawing. Uffizi Florence, Italy. Photograph © Foto Marburg/Art Resource, NY

West African men who constituted a minority of those subjected to the trans-Sahara slave trade were more likely to become soldiers for such North African states as Morocco and Egypt than field workers.

The demand for slaves in Muslim countries remained high from the tenth through the fifteenth centuries because many died from disease or were freed and assimilated into Arab society. The trans-Sahara slave trade therefore rivaled the extensive trade in gold across the Sahara and helped make such West African cities as Timbuktu, Walata, Jenne, and Gao wealthy. According to historian Roland Oliver, it was not until 1600 that the Atlantic slave trade reached the proportions of the trans-Sahara slave trade (see Figure 2–1).

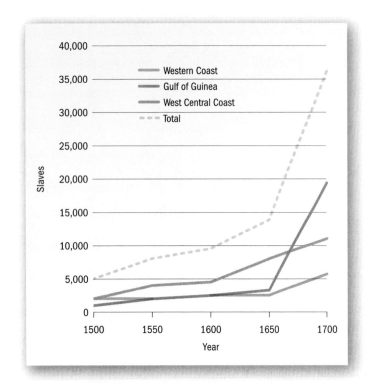

FIGURE 2–1 ESTIMATED ANNUAL EXPORTS OF SLAVES FROM WESTERN AFRICA TO THE AMERICAS, 1500–1700.

Source: John Thornton, *Africa and Africans in the Making of the Atlantic World, 1400–1680* (New York: Cambridge University Press, 1992), 118.

West African artists recorded the appearance of Europeans who came to trade in gold, ivory, and human beings. This Benin bronze relief sculpture, dating to the late sixteenth or early seventeenth century, portrays two Portuguese men.　Werner Forman, Art Resource, NY

The Origins of the Atlantic Slave Trade

When Portuguese ships first arrived off the **Guinea Coast,** their captains traded chiefly for gold, ivory, and pepper, but they also wanted slaves. As early as 1441, Antam Goncalvez of Portugal enslaved a Berber and his West African servant and took them home as gifts for a Portuguese prince. During the following decades, Portuguese raiders captured hundreds of Africans to work as domestic servants in Portugal and Spain.

But usually the Portuguese and the other European and white Americans who succeeded them did not capture and enslave people themselves. Instead they purchased slaves from African traders. This arrangement began formally in 1472 when the Portuguese merchant Ruy do Siqueira gained permission from the Oba (king) of Benin to trade for slaves, as well as gold and ivory, within the borders of the Oba's kingdom. Siqueira and other Portuguese found that a commercial infrastructure already existed in West Africa that could distribute European trade goods and procure slaves. The rulers of Benin, Dahomey, and other African kingdoms restricted the Europeans to a few points on the coast, and the kingdoms raided the interior to supply the Europeans with slaves.

Interethnic rivalries in West Africa led to the warfare that produced these slaves during the sixteenth century. Although Africans were initially reluctant to sell members of their own ethnic group to Europeans, they did not at first consider it wrong to sell members of their own race to foreigners. In fact, neither Africans nor Europeans had yet developed a concept of racial solidarity. By the eighteenth century, however, at least the victims of the trade believed that such solidarity *should* exist. Ottobah Cugoano, who had been captured and sold during that century, wrote, "I must own to the shame of my countrymen that I was first kidnapped and betrayed by [those of] my own complexion."

MAP EXPLORATION

To explore this interactive map, go to
http://www.prenhall.com/hine4/map2.1

MAP 2–1   THE ATLANTIC AND ISLAMIC SLAVE TRADES

Not until 1600 did the Atlantic slave trade reach the proportions of the Islamic slave trade. The map shows the principal sources of slaves, primary routes, and major destinations.

▶ *According to this map, which region in the Americas imported the most slaves?*

Until the early sixteenth century, Portuguese seafarers conducted the Atlantic slave trade on a tiny scale to satisfy a limited market for domestic servants on the Iberian Peninsula (Portugal and Spain). Other European countries had no demand for slaves because their workforces were already too large. But the impact of Columbus's voyages drastically changed the trade. The Spanish and the Portuguese—followed by the Dutch, English, and French—established colonies in the Caribbean, Mexico, and Central and South America. Because disease and overwork caused the number of American Indians in these regions rapidly to decline, Europeans relied on the Atlantic slave trade to replace them as a source of slave labor (see Map 2–1). As early as 1502, African slaves lived on the island of Hispaniola—modern Haiti and the Dominican Republic (see Map 2–2). During the sixteenth century, gold and silver mines in Spanish Mexico and Peru and especially

MAP 2–2 Slave Colonies of the Seventeenth and Eighteenth Centuries

This map indicates regions in North America, the West Indies, and South America that had, during the seventeenth and eighteenth centuries, significant populations of enslaved people of African descent.

▶ *What European powers controlled the regions of North America and the Caribbean islands shown in this map?*

TABLE 2–1 Estimated Slave Imports by Destination, 1451–1870

Destination	Total Slave Imports
British North America	500,000
Spanish America	2,500,000
British Caribbean	2,000,000
French Caribbean	1,600,000
Dutch Caribbean	500,000
Danish Caribbean	28,000
Brazil	4,000,000
Old World	200,000

Source: Hugh Thomas, *The Slave Trade: The Story of the Atlantic Slave Trade, 1440–1870* (New York: Simon & Schuster, 1997), 804.

sugar plantations in Portuguese Brazil produced an enormous demand for labor. The Atlantic slave trade grew to huge and tragic proportions to meet that demand (see Table 2–1).

Growth of the Atlantic Slave Trade

Because Europe provided an insatiable market for sugar, cultivation of this crop in the Americas became extremely profitable. Sugar plantations employing slave labor spread from Portuguese-ruled Brazil to the Caribbean islands (West Indies). Later the cultivation of tobacco, rice, and **indigo** in British North America added to the demand for African slaves. By 1510 Spain had joined Portugal in the enlarged Atlantic slave trade, and a new, harsher form of slavery had appeared in the Americas. Unlike slavery in Africa, Asia, and Europe, slavery in the Americas was based on race; most of the enslaved were males, and they were generally employed as agricultural laborers rather than soldiers or domestic servants. The enslaved also became **chattel**—meaning personal property—of their masters and lost their customary rights as human beings. Men and boys predominated in part because Europeans believed they were stronger laborers than women and girls. Another factor was that West Africans preferred to have women do agricultural work and therefore tended to withhold them from the Atlantic trade.

Portugal and Spain dominated the Atlantic slave trade during the sixteenth century. They shipped about 2,000 Africans per year to their American colonies, with by far the most going to Brazil. From the beginning of the trade until its nineteenth-century abolition, about 6,500,000 of the approximately 11,328,000 Africans taken to the Americas went to Brazil and Spain's colonies. Both of these monarchies granted monopolies over the trade to private companies. In Spain this monopoly became known in 1518 as the **Asiento** (meaning contract). The profits from the slave trade were so great that by 1550 the Dutch, French, and English were becoming involved. During the early seventeenth century, the Dutch drove the Portuguese from the West African coast and became the principal European slave-trading nation. For the rest of that century, most Africans came to the Americas in Dutch ships—including a group of twenty in 1619 who until recently were considered to have been the first of their race to reach British North America.

The Dutch also shifted the center of sugar production to the West Indies. England and France followed, with the former taking control of Barbados and Ja-

The Portuguese established the city of Luanda in 1575. This eighteenth-century print portrays the city when it was at its height as a center for the shipment of enslaved Africans to Brazil.   The Granger Collection

maica and the latter taking Saint Domingue (Haiti), Guadeloupe, and Martinique. With the development of tobacco as a **cash crop** in Virginia and Maryland during the 1620s and with the continued expansion of sugar production in the West Indies, the demand for African slaves grew. The result was that England and France competed with the Dutch to control the Atlantic slave trade. After a series of wars, England emerged supreme. It had driven the Dutch out of the trade by 1674. Victories over France and Spain led in 1713 to English control of the *Asiento*, which allowed English traders the exclusive right to supply slaves to all of Spain's American colonies. After 1713, English ships dominated the slave trade, carrying about 20,000 slaves per year from Africa to the Americas. At the peak of the trade during the 1790s, they transported 50,000 per year.

The profits from the Atlantic slave trade, together with those from the sugar and tobacco produced in the Americas by slave labor, were invested in England and helped fund the **Industrial Revolution** during the eighteenth century. In turn, Africa became a market for cheap English manufactured goods (see Map 2–3). Eventually, two triangular trade systems developed. In one, traders carried English goods to West Africa and exchanged the goods for slaves. Then the traders carried the slaves to the West Indies and exchanged them for sugar, which they took back to England on the third leg of the triangle. In the other triangular trade, white Americans from Britain's New England colonies carried rum to West Africa to trade for slaves. From Africa they took the slaves to the West Indies to exchange for sugar or molasses—sugar syrup—which they then took home to distill into rum.

DOCUMENT 2-1 *England Asserts Her Dominion through Legislation in 1660*

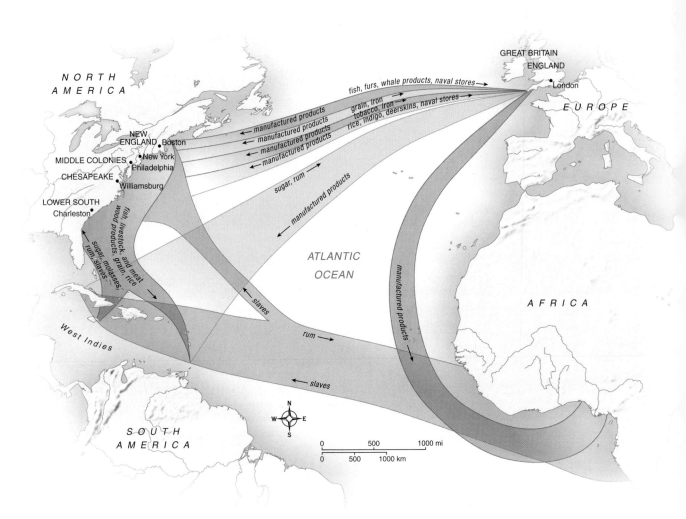

MAP 2–3 ATLANTIC TRADE AMONG THE AMERICAS, GREAT BRITAIN, AND WEST AFRICA DURING THE SEVENTEENTH AND EIGHTEENTH CENTURIES

Often referred to as a triangular trade, this map shows the complexity of early modern Atlantic commerce, of which the slave trade was a major part.

▶ *What does this map suggest about the economy of the Atlantic world between 1600 and 1800?*

The African-American Ordeal from Capture to Destination

Recent scholarship indicates that the availability of large numbers of slaves in West Africa resulted from the warfare that accompanied the formation of states in that region. Captives suitable for enslavement were a by-product of these wars. Senegambia and nearby Sierra Leone, then Oyo, Dahomey, and Benin, became, in turn, centers of the trade. Meanwhile, on the west coast of Central Africa, slaves became available as a result of the conflict between the expanding Kingdom of Kongo and its neighbors. The European traders provided the aggressors with firearms but did not instigate the wars. Instead they used the wars to enrich themselves.

Sometimes African armies enslaved the inhabitants of conquered towns and villages. At other times, raiding parties captured isolated families or kidnapped individuals. As warfare spread to the interior, captives had to march for hundreds of miles to the coast where European traders awaited them. The

In this late-eighteenth-century drawing, African slave traders conduct a group of bound captives from the interior of Africa toward European trading posts.   Culver Pictures, Inc.

raiders tied the captives together with rope or secured them with wooden yokes about their necks. It was a shocking experience, and many captives died from hunger, exhaustion, and exposure during the journey. Others killed themselves rather than submit to their fate, and the captors killed those who resisted.

Once the captives reached the coast, those destined for the Atlantic trade went to fortified structures called **factories.** Portuguese traders constructed the first factory at Elmina on the Guinea Coast in 1481—the Dutch captured it in 1637. Such factories contained the headquarters of the traders, warehouses for their trade goods and supplies, and dungeons or outdoor holding pens for the captives. In these pens, slave traders divided families and—as much as possible—ethnic groups to prevent rebellion. The traders stripped captives naked and inspected them for disease and physical defects. Those considered fit for purchase were branded like cattle with a hot iron bearing the symbol of a trading company.

In a rare account of such proceedings from a captive's point of view, Olaudah Equiano described during the 1780s how horrifying such treatment could be. The white slave traders, with their "horrible looks, red faces, and long hair," appeared to be savages who acted with a "brutal cruelty" that went beyond anything previously experienced by their victims. Many of the captives feared the Europeans were cannibals who would take them to their country for food. According to historian Gary Nash, such fears were the product of deliberate European brutalization of the captives, part of an attempt to destroy the Africans' self-respect and self-identity.

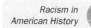
Racism in American History

THE CROSSING

After being held in a factory for weeks or months, captives faced the frightening prospect of leaving their native land for a voyage across an ocean that many of them had never before seen. Sailors rowed them out in large canoes to slave ships offshore. One English trader recalled that during the 1690s "the negroes were so wilful and loth to leave their own country, that they often leap'd out of the canoes, boat and ship, into the sea, and kept under water till they were drowned."

Once at sea, the slave ships followed the route established by Columbus during his voyages to the Americas: from the Canary Islands off West Africa to the Windward Islands in the Caribbean. Because ships taking this route enjoyed prevailing winds and westward currents, the passage normally lasted between two and three months. But the time required for the crossing varied widely. The larger ships were able to reach the Caribbean in forty days, but voyages could take as long as six months.

Both human and natural causes accounted for such delays. During the three centuries that the Atlantic slave trade endured, Western European nations often warred against each other, and slave ships became prized targets. As early as the 1580s, English "sea dogs," such as John Hawkins and Sir Francis Drake, attacked Spanish ships to steal their valuable human cargoes. Outright piracy peaked between 1650 and 1725 when demand for slaves in the West Indies greatly increased. There were also such potentially disastrous natural forces as doldrums—long windless spells at sea—and hurricanes, which could destroy ships, crews, and cargoes.

THE SLAVERS

Slave ships (called **slavers**) were usually small and narrow. A ship's size, measured in tonnage, theoretically determined how many slaves it could carry, with the formula being two slaves per ton. A large ship of 300 tons was expected to carry 600 slaves. But captains often ignored the formula. Some kept their human cargo light, calculating that smaller loads lowered mortality and made revolt less likely. But most captains were "tight packers," who squeezed human beings together in hope that large numbers would offset increased deaths. For example, the 120-ton *Henrietta Marie*, a British ship that sailed from London on its final voyage in 1699, should have been fully loaded with 240 slaves. Yet it carried 350 from West Africa when it set out for Barbados and Jamaica. Another ship designed to carry 450 slaves usually carried 600.

The cargo space in slave ships was generally only five feet high. Ships' carpenters halved this vertical space by building shelves, so slaves might be packed above and below on planks that measured only 5.5 feet long and 1.3 feet wide. Consequently, slaves had only about 20 to 25 inches of headroom. To add to the discomfort, the crews chained male slaves together in pairs to help prevent rebellion and lodged them away from women and children.

The most frequently reproduced illustration of a slaver's capacity for human cargo comes from the

Plan of the British slave ship *Brookes*, 1788. This plan, which may undercount the human cargo the *Brookes* carried, shows how tightly Africans were packed aboard slave ships.

Brookes, which sailed from Liverpool, England, during the 1780s. At 300 tons, the *Brookes* was an exceptionally large ship for its time, and the diagrams show how tightly packed the slaves were who boarded it. Although those who wished to abolish the Atlantic slave trade created the diagrams, their bias does not make the diagrams less accurate. In fact, as historian James Walvin points out in his study of the trade, the precise, unemotional renderings of the *Brookes*'s geometrically conceived design scarcely indicate the physical suffering it caused. The renderings do not show the constant shifting, crushing, and chafing among the human cargo caused by the movement of the ship at sea. Also, during storms the crew often neglected to feed the slaves, empty the tubs used for excrement, take slaves on deck for exercise, tend to the sick, or remove the dead.

Mortality rates were high because the crowded, unsanitary conditions encouraged seaboard epidemics. Between 1715 and 1775, slave deaths on French ships averaged 15 percent. The highest recorded mortality rate was 34 percent. By the nineteenth century, the death rate had declined to 5 percent. Overall, one-third of the Africans subjected to the trade perished between their capture and their embarkation on a slave ship. Another third died during the Middle Passage or during "seasoning" on a Caribbean island. It would have been slight consolation to the enslaved to learn that because of the epidemics, the rate of death among slaver crews was proportionally higher than their own.

A SLAVE'S STORY

In his book *The Interesting Narrative of the Life of Olaudah Equiano or Gustavus Vassa, the African*, published in 1789, former slave Olaudah Equiano provides a vivid account of a West African's capture, sale to traders, and voyage to America in 1755. Although recently discovered evidence suggests that Equiano *may* have been born in South Carolina rather than West Africa, scholars continue to respect the accuracy of his account. He tells the story of a young Igbo, the dominant ethnic group in what is today southern Nigeria. African slave raiders capture him when he is ten years old and force him to march along with other captives to the Niger River or one of its tributaries, where they trade him to other Africans. His new captors take him to the coast and sell him to European slave traders whose ships sail to the West Indies.

The boy's experience at the coastal slave factory convinces him he has entered a sort of hell, peopled by evil spirits. The stench caused by forcing many people to live in close confinement makes him sick to his stomach and emotionally agitated. His African and European captors try to calm him with liquor. But because he is not accustomed to alcohol, he becomes disoriented and more convinced of his impending doom. When the sailors lodge him with others below deck on the ship, he is so sick that he loses his appetite and hopes to die. Instead, because he refuses to eat, the sailors take him on deck and whip him. Later the boy witnesses the flogging of a white crewman. The man dies, and the sailors throw his body into the sea just as they disposed of dead Africans.

During the time the ship is in port awaiting a full cargo of slaves, the boy spends much time on deck. After putting to sea, however, he usually remains below deck with the other slaves where "each had scarcely room to turn himself." There, the smells of unwashed bodies and of the toilet tubs, "into which the children often fell and were almost suffocated," create a loathsome atmosphere. The darkness, the chafing of chains on human flesh, the shrieks and groans of the sick and disoriented provide "a scene of horror almost inconceivable."

When slaves are allowed to get some fresh air and exercise on deck, the crew strings up nets to prevent them from jumping overboard. Even so, two Africans, who are chained together, evade the nets and jump

into the ocean, preferring drowning to staying on board. The boy shares their desperation. As the ship goes beyond sight of land, he and the other captives believe they lose "even the least glimpse of hope of [re]gaining the shore" and returning to their country. Equiano, in his first-person narrative, insisted that "many more" would have jumped overboard "if they had not been prevented by the ship's crew."

Attempts to keep the slaves entertained and in good humor seldom succeeded. Crews sometimes forced the slaves to dance and sing, but their songs, as slave-ship surgeon Alexander Falconbridge testified, were "melancholy lamentations, of their exile from their native country." Depression among the Africans led to a catatonia that contemporary observers called melancholy or extreme nostalgia. Falconbridge noted that the slaves had "a strong attachment to their native country" and a "just sense of the value of liberty."

Although the traders, seeking to lessen the possibility of shipboard conspiracy and rebellion, separated individuals who spoke the same language, the boy described by Equiano manages to find adults who speak Igbo. They explain to him the purpose of the voyage, which he learns is to go to the white people's country to labor for them rather than to be eaten by them. He does not realize that work on a West Indian island could be a death sentence.

A CAPTAIN'S STORY

John Newton, a white captain of a slave ship, who was born in London in 1725, provides another perspective on the Middle Passage. In 1745 Newton, as an **indentured servant**, joined the crew of a slaver bound for Sierra Leone. Indentured servants lost their freedom for a specified number of years, either because they sold it or because they were being punished for debt or crime. In 1748, on the return voyage to England, Newton survived a fierce Atlantic storm and, thanking God, became an evangelical Christian. Like most people of his era, Newton saw no contradiction between his newfound faith and his participation in the enslavement and ill treatment of men, women, and children. When he became a slaver captain in 1750, he read Bible passages to his crew twice each Sunday and forbade swearing on board his vessel. But he treated his slave cargoes as harshly as any other slaver captain.

Newton was twenty-five years old when he became captain of the *Duke of Argyle*, an old 140-ton vessel that he converted into a slaver after it sailed from Liverpool on August 11, 1750. Near the Cape Verde Islands, off the coast of Senegambia, carpenters began making the

PROFILE ❧ OLAUDAH EQUIANO

For many years historians have regarded Olaudah Equiano's autobiography, *The Interesting Narrative of the Life of Olaudah Equiano or Gustavus Vassa, the African. Written by Himself* (1789), as an essential document for understanding the Atlantic slave trade. It appeared to be one of the few authentic descriptions of the trade from an African point of view. Recently, however, Equiano's African birth, if not his general accuracy, has been questioned. Vincent Carretta, author of *Equiano the African: Biograhy of a Self-Made Man* (2005), discovered two documents—a 1759 baptismal record and a 1777 ship muster roll—indicating that Equiano was born in South Carolina in about 1747 rather than—as Equiano claimed—in Nigeria in 1745. It appears that Equiano had not used an African name for himself before he published his autobiography. But, as several scholars have noted, an African in the Atlantic world during the eighteenth century had good reason to hide his true identity and claim to have been born in America. Even Carretta does not flatly assert that Equiano lied about his African birth. Carretta, in fact, validates Equiano's autobiography by treating Equiano's description of his capture, experience on the Middle Passage, and enslavement "as if it were true."

Although the controversy over Equiano's place of birth may never be resolved, it is certain that he was a young slave in Virginia when a visiting British sea captain named Michael Henry Pascal purchased him in 1754. Pascal commanded a merchant ship and employed Equiano as his personal servant. It was Pascal who gave him the name Gustavus Vassa (after the king of Sweden), which Equiano used for the rest of his life. Pascal and Equiano traveled extensively and served together in North America during the French and Indian War. As a result, both of them were with General James Wolfe at Quebec in 1759 where the British won the decisive battle of the war. Equiano also lived in England, where he received the schooling that allowed him to work as "a shipping clerk and amateur navigator on the ship of his . . . [third] master, the Quaker Robert King of Philadelphia, trading chiefly between [North] America and the West Indies."

Growing antislavery sentiment among Quakers during the eighteenth century led King to allow Equiano to purchase his freedom for forty pounds sterling in 1766. This was a considerable amount of money, amounting to more than most eighteenth-century British laborers earned in a year. Thereafter, Equiano toured the Mediterranean, sailed to the Arctic and Central America, converted to Calvinism, and became a leader in the British movement against the slave trade. In 1787 Equiano helped organize a colony for emancipated British slaves at Sierra Leone in West Africa in 1787. Just before embarking for that country, however, dissention and confusion in the enterprise cost him his position as Commissary for Stores for the Black Poor. His autobiography, which he wrote shortly thereafter, proved to be a greater contribution to the anti-slave-trade cause. The book also became a major source of income for Equiano.

In April 1792 he married an Englishwoman, Susanna Cullen, with whom he had two daughters. The couple's marriage notice recognized him "as the champion and advocate for procuring the suppression of the slave trade." When Equiano died on March 31, 1797, he was, according to Carretta, "probably the wealthiest and most famous person of African descent in the Atlantic world."

Equiano is significant for his account of the Atlantic slave trade and his service in the British struggle against that trade. His extraordinary life reveals how baseless was the assumption among Europeans and persons of European descent that black people were naturally suited for slavery.

◄ *Portrait of a Negro Man*, Olaudah Equiano, 1780s (previously attributed to Joshua Reynolds) by English School (eighteenth century).   Royal Albert Memorial Museum, Exeter, Devon, UK/Bridgeman Art Library, London/New York.

alterations required for packing many Africans below deck. Newton also put the ship's guns and ammunition in order to protect against pirates or African resistance. On October 23 the *Duke of Argyle* reached Frenchman's Bay, Sierra Leone, where Newton observed other ships from England, France, and New England anchored off-shore. Two days later, Newton purchased two men and a woman from traders at the port, but he had to sail to several other ports to accumulate a full cargo. Leaving West Africa on May 23, 1751, for the open sea, the ship reached Antigua in the West Indies on July 3 to deliver its slaves.

DOCUMENT 2-3 A Slave Ship Surgeon Writes about the Slave Trade in 1788

Poor health forced Newton to retire from the slave trade in 1754. Ten years later he gained ordination as an Anglican priest. In 1779 he became rector of St. Mary Woolnoth Church in London and served there until his death in 1807. By the late 1770s, Newton had repented his involvement in the slave trade and had become one of its leading opponents. Together with William Cowper—a renowned poet—Newton published the *Olney Hymns* in 1779. Among the selections included in this volume was "Amazing Grace," which Newton wrote as a reflection on divine forgiveness for his sins. For several reasons, Newton and other religious Britons had begun to perceive an evil in the slave trade that, despite their piety, they had failed to see earlier.

PROVISIONS FOR THE MIDDLE PASSAGE

Slave ships left Liverpool and other European ports provisioned with food supplies for their crews. These included beans, cheese, beef, flour, and grog, a mixture of rum and water. When the ships reached the Guinea Coast in West Africa, their captains purchased pepper, palm oil, lemons, limes, yams, plantains, and coconuts. Because slaves were not accustomed to European foods, the ships needed these staples of the African diet. Meat and fish were rare luxuries on board, and crews did not share them with slaves. In the voyage Equiano describes, crew members at one point caught far more fish than they could eat but threw what was left overboard, instead of giving it to the Africans who were exercising on deck. The captives "begged and prayed for some . . . but in vain." The sailors whipped those Africans who filched a few fish for themselves.

The crew usually fed the slaves twice per day in shifts. Cooks prepared vegetable pulps, porridge, and stews for the crew to distribute in buckets as the slaves assembled on deck during good weather or below deck during storms. At the beginning of the voyage, each slave received a wooden spoon for dipping into the buckets, which were shared by about ten individuals. But in the confined confusion below deck, slaves often lost their spoons. They then had to eat from the buckets with their unwashed hands, a practice that spread disease.

Although slaver captains realized it was in their interest to feed their human cargoes well, they often skimped on supplies to save money and make room for more slaves. Therefore, the food on a slave ship was often insufficient to prevent malnutrition and weakened immune systems among people already traumatized by separation from their families and homelands. As a result, many Africans died during the Middle Passage from diseases amid the horrid conditions that were normal aboard the slave ships. Others died from depression: they refused to eat, despite the crews' efforts to force food down their throats.

SANITATION, DISEASE, AND DEATH

Diseases such as malaria, yellow fever, measles, smallpox, hookworm, scurvy, and dysentery constantly threatened African cargoes and European crews during the Middle Passage. Death rates were astronomical on board the slave ships before 1750. Mortality dropped after that date because ships became faster and ships' surgeons knew more about hygiene and diet. There were also early forms of vaccinations against smallpox, which may have been the worst killer of slaves on ships. But, even after 1750, poor sanitation led to many deaths. It is important to remember that before the early twentieth century, no civilization had developed a germ theory of disease. Physicians blamed human illnesses on poisonous atmospheres and imbalances among bodily fluids.

Usually slavers provided only three or four toilet tubs below deck for enslaved Africans to use during the Middle Passage. They had to struggle among themselves to get to the tubs, and children had a particularly difficult time. Those who were too ill to reach the tubs excreted where they lay, and diseases such as dysentery, which are spread by human waste, thrived. Dysentery, known by contemporaries as the bloody flux, vied with smallpox to kill the most slaves aboard ships. Alexander Falconbridge reported that during one dysentery epidemic, "The deck, that is, the floor of [the slaves'] rooms, was so covered with blood and mucus which had proceeded from them in consequence of the flux, that it resembled a slaughter-house. It is not in the power of human imagination, to picture to itself a situation more dreadful or disgusting."

DOCUMENT 2-4 An African Captive Tells the Story of Crossing the Atlantic in a Slave Ship

THE JOURNAL OF A DUTCH SLAVER

The following account of slave trading on the West African coast is from a journal kept on the Dutch slaver
St. Jan *between March and November 1659. Although it is written from a European point of view, it clearly indicates the sort of conditions Africans faced on board such ships.*

We weighed anchor, by the order of the Hon'ble Director, Johan Valckenborch, and the Hon'ble Director, Jasper van Heussen to proceed on our voyage to Rio Reael [on the Guinea Coast] to trade for slaves for the hon'ble company.

March 8. Saturday. Arrived with our ship before Ardra, to take on board the surgeon's mate and a supply of tamarinds for refreshment for the slaves; sailed again next day on our voyage to Rio Reael.

17. Arrived at Rio Reael in front of a village called Bany, where we found the company's yacht, named the *Vrede*, which was sent out to assist us to trade for slaves.

In April. Nothing was done except to trade for slaves.

May 6. One of our seamen died. . . .

22. Again weighed anchor and ran out of Rio Reael accompanied by the yacht *Vrede*; purchased there two hundred and nineteen head of slaves, men, women, boys and girls, and set our course for the high land of Ambosius, for the purpose of procuring food there for the slaves, as nothing was to be had at Rio Reael.

June 29. Sunday. Again resolved to proceed on our voyage, as there also but little food was to be had for the slaves in consequence of the great rains which fell every day, and because many of the slaves were suffering from the bloody flux in consequence of the bad provisions we were supplied with at El Mina. . . .

July 27. Our surgeon, named Martyn de Lanoy, died of the bloody flux.

Aug. 11. Again resolved to pursue our voyage towards the island of Annebo, in order to purchase there some refreshments for the slaves. . . .

Aug. 15. Arrived at the island Annebo, where we purchased for the slaves one hundred half tierces of beans, twelve hogs, five thousand coconuts, five thousand sweet oranges, besides some other stores.

Sept. 21. The skipper called the ships officers aft, and resolved to run for the island of Tobago and to procure water there; otherwise we should have perished for want of water, as many of our water casks had leaked dry.

24. Friday. Arrived at the island of Tobago and hauled water there, also purchased some bread, as our hands had had no ration for three weeks.

Nov. 1. Lost our ship on the Reef of Rocus [north of Caracas], and all hands immediately took to the boat, as there was no prospect of saving the slaves, for we must abandon the ship in consequence of the heavy surf.

4. Arrived with the boat at the island of Curaco; the Hon'ble Governor Beck ordered two sloops to take the slaves off the wreck, one of which sloops with eighty four slaves on board, was captured by a privateer [pirate vessel].

🌲 *What dangers did the slaves and crew on board the* St. Jan *face?*

🌲 *What is the attitude of the author of the journal toward slaves?*

Source: Elizabeth Donnan, ed., *Documents Illustrative of the History of the Slave Trade to America*, 4 vols. (Washington, DC: Carnegie Institute, 1930–35), 1: 141–45.

John Newton's stark, unimpassioned records of slave deaths aboard the *Duke of Argyle* indicate even more about how the Atlantic slave trade devalued human life. Newton recorded deaths at sea only by number. He wrote in his journal, "Bury'd a man slave No. 84 . . . bury'd a woman slave, No. 47." Yet Newton probably was more conscientious than other slave-ship captains in seeking to avoid disease. During his 1750 voyage, he noted only eleven deaths. These included ten slaves—five men, one woman, three boys, and one girl—and one crewman. Compared with the usual high mortality rates, this was an achievement.

What role ships' surgeons—general practitioners in modern terminology—played in preventing or inadvertently encouraging deaths aboard slave ships is difficult to determine. Some of them were outright frauds. Even the best were limited by the primitive medical knowledge that existed between the fifteenth and nineteenth centuries. Captains rewarded the surgeons with "head money" for the number of healthy slaves who arrived in the Americas, but the surgeons could also be blamed for deaths at sea that reduced the value of the human cargo.

Many surgeons recognized that African remedies were more likely than European medications to alleviate the slaves' illnesses. The surgeons collected herbs and foods along the Guinea Coast. They also learned African nursing techniques, which they found more effective in treating on-board diseases than European procedures. What the surgeons did not understand, and regarded as superstition, was the holistic nature of African medicine. African healers maintained that body, mind, and spirit were interconnected elements of the totality of a person's well-being.

The enslaved Africans were often just as dumbfounded by the beliefs and actions of their captors. They thought they had entered a world of bad spirits when they boarded a slave ship, and they attempted to counteract the spirits with rituals from their homeland. John Newton noted that during one voyage he feared slaves had tried to poison the ship's drinking water. He was relieved to discover that they were only putting what he called "charms" in the water supply. In fact, such fetishes, representing the power of spirits, were important in West African religions. What the slaves hoped to accomplish is not clear. But Newton, as a Christian, held their beliefs in contempt. "If it please God [that] they make no worse attempts than to charm us to death, they will not harm us," he wrote.

RESISTANCE AND REVOLT AT SEA

Although Newton ridiculed African religion, he was relieved that the slaves were not planning to poison the crew or mutiny. Because many enslaved Africans refused to accept their fate, slaver captains had to be vigilant. Uprisings were common, and Newton himself put down a potentially serious one aboard the *Duke of Argyle*. Twenty men had broken their chains below deck, but were apprehended before they could assault the crew.

Most such rebellions took place while a ship prepared to set sail, the African coast was in sight, and the slaves could still hope to return home. But some revolts occurred on the open sea where it was unlikely the Africans, even if their revolt succeeded, could return to their homes or regain their freedom. Both sorts of revolt indicate that not even capture, forced march to the coast, imprisonment, branding, and sale could break the spirit of many captives. These Africans preferred to face death rather than accept bondage.

John Atkins, an English slave-ship surgeon who made many voyages between Africa and the Americas during the 1720s, noted that although the threat of revolt diminished on the high seas, it never disappeared:

> When we are slaved and out at sea, it is commonly imagined that the *Negroes*['] Ignorance of Navigation, will always be a Safeguard [against revolt]; yet, as many of them think themselves bought to eat, and more, that Death will send them into their own Country, there has not been wanting Examples of rising and killing a Ship's Company, distant from Land, though not so often as on the Coast: But once or twice is enough to shew, a Master's Care and Diligence should never be over till the Delivery of them.

Later in the eighteenth century, a historian used the prevalence of revolt to justify the harsh treatment of Africans on slave ships. Edward Long wrote that "the many acts of violence they [the slaves] have committed by murdering whole crews and destroying ships when they had it left in their power to do so, have made this rigour wholly chargeable on their own bloody and malicious disposition, which calls for the same confinement as if they were wolves or wild boars."

Failed slave mutineers could expect harsh punishment, although profit margins influenced sentences. Atkins chronicled how the captain of the *Robert*, which sailed from Bristol, England, punished the ringleaders, who were worth more, less harshly than their followers who were not as valuable. Atkins related that

PROFILE ❧ AYUBA SULIEMAN DIALLO OF BONDU

Ayuba Sulieman Diallo, known to Europeans as Job ben Solomon, was one of the many West Africans caught up in the Atlantic slave trade. But his experience was far from typical. Because he had family connections, was literate in Arabic, and used his aristocratic personality to gain favor among Europeans, Diallo was able to escape enslavement and return to his native land. His story reveals a great deal about the bonds of wealth and class in the Atlantic world during the early eighteenth century.

Diallo was born in about 1701 at the village of Marsa located in the eastern Senegambian region of Bondu. His father, the imam of the local mosque and village head, taught him Arabic and the Koran when he was a child and prepared him to become a merchant. That Samba Geladio Jegi, the future king of the nearby kingdom of Futa Toro, was a fellow student suggests the standing of Diallo's family. Diallo, following Moslem and West African custom, had two wives. He married the first of them when he was fifteen and she was eleven; he married the second when he was twenty-eight.

In February 1730, Diallo was on his way to the Gambia River to sell two slaves to an English trader when he was himself captured by Mandingo warriors and sold as well. Although the English slaver captain was willing to ransom Diallo, his ship sailed before Diallo's father was able to send the money. As a result, Diallo was shipped with other Africans to Annapolis, Maryland, and delivered to Vachell Denton, factor for William Hunt, a London merchant. Shortly thereafter, Diallo was sold to a Mr. Tolsey who operated a tobacco plantation on Maryland's eastern shore.

Although Diallo was "about five feet ten inches high . . . and naturally of a good constitution," his "religious abstinence" and the difficulties he had experienced during the Middle Passage unsuited him for fieldwork. Therefore, Tolsey assigned him to tending cattle. In June 1731, however, after a young white boy repeatedly interrupted his prayers, Diallo escaped to Dover, Delaware, where he was apprehended and jailed. There, Thomas Bluett, who, in 1734, published an account of Diallo's adventures, discovered that Diallo was literate in Arabic, pious in his religious devotions, and—according to Bluett's stereotypical notions—"no common slave." Bluett provided this information to Tolsey, who on Diallo's return allowed him a quiet place to pray and permitted him to write a letter in Arabic to his father.

The letter reached James Oglethorpe, the director of England's slave-trading Royal African Company, who arranged to purchase Diallo from Tolsey and in March 1733 transport him by ship to England. Accompanied by Bluett, Diallo learned, during the long voyage, to speak, read, and write English. In London, Bluett contacted several well-to-do gentlemen who raised sixty pounds to secure Diallo's freedom and, with the aid of the Royal African Company, return him to Senegambia. Before he departed England in July 1734, Diallo had an audience with the British monarch, met with the entire royal family, dined with members of the nobility, and received many expensive gifts.

Diallo's wives and children greeted him upon his return to his village, but otherwise much had changed during his absence. Futa Toro had conquered Bondu, Diallo's family had suffered economically as a result, the slave trade in Senegambia had intensified, and Morocco had begun to interfere militarily in the region. Grateful to his English friends, Diallo used his influence in these difficult circumstances to help the Royal African Company hold its share of the trade in slaves and gold until the company disbanded in 1752. Quite able to differentiate between his fortunes and those of others, he retained commercial ties to the British until his death in 1773.

"The Fortunate Slave," an illustration of African slavery in the early eighteenth century by Douglas Grant (1968). From "Some Memoirs of the Life of Job," by Thomas Bluett, 1734. Photo by Robert D. Rubic/Precision Chromes Inc., The New York Public Library, Research Libraries.

Captain Harding, weighing the Stoutness and Worth of the two [ringleaders], did, as in other Countries they do by Rogues of Dignity, whip and scarify them only; while three others, Abettors, but not Actors, nor of Strength for it, he sentenced to cruel Deaths; making them first eat the Heart and Liver of one of them killed. The Woman [who had helped in the revolt] he hoisted up by the Thumbs, whipp'd and slashed her with Knives, before the other Slaves, till she died.

Other slaves resisted their captors by drowning or starving themselves. Thomas Phillips, captain of the slaver *Hannibal* during the 1690s, commented, "We had about 12 negroes did wilfully drown themselves and others starved themselves to death; for 'tis their belief that when they die they return home to their own country and friends again." As we previously indicated, captains used nets to prevent deliberate drowning. To deal with starvation, they used hot coals or a metal device called a *speculum oris* to force individuals to open their mouths for feeding.

CRUELTY

The Atlantic slave trade required more capital than any other maritime commerce during the seventeenth and eighteenth centuries. The investments for the ships, the exceptionally large crews they employed, the navigational equipment, the armaments, the purchase of slaves in Africa, and the supplies of food and water to feed hundreds of passengers were phenomenal. The aim was to carry as many Africans in healthy condition to the Americas as possible in order to make the large profits that justified such expenditures. Yet, as we have indicated, conditions aboard the vessels were abysmal.

Scholars have debated how much deliberate cruelty the enslaved Africans suffered from ships' crews. The West Indian historian Eric Williams asserts that the horrors of the Middle Passage have been exaggerated. Many writers, Williams contends, are led astray by the writings of those who, during the late eighteenth and early nineteenth centuries, sought to abolish the slave trade. In Williams's view—and that of other historians as well—the difficulties of the Middle Passage were similar to those experienced by European indentured servants who suffered high mortality rates on the voyage to America.

From this perspective the primary cause of death at sea on all ships carrying passengers across the Atlantic Ocean to the Americas was epidemic disease, against which medical practitioners had few tools before the twentieth century. Contributing factors included inadequate means of preserving food from spoilage and failure to prevent fresh water from becoming contaminated during the long ocean crossing. According to Williams, overcrowding by slavers was only a secondary cause for the high mortality rates.

Such observations help place conditions aboard the slave ships in a broader perspective. Cruelty and suffering are, to some degree, historically relative in that practices acceptable in the past are now considered inhumane. Yet cruelty aboard slavers must also be placed in a cultural context. Cultures distinguish between what constitutes acceptable behavior to their own people, on the one hand, and to strangers, on the other. For Europeans, Africans were cultural strangers, and what became normal in the Atlantic slave trade was in fact exceptionally cruel in comparison to how Europeans treated each other. Slaves below deck received only one-half the space allocated on board to European soldiers, free emigrants, indentured servants, and convicts. Europeans regarded slavery itself as a condition suitable only for non-Christians. And as strangers, Africans were subject to brutalization by European crew members who often cared little about the physical and emotional damage they inflicted.

AFRICAN WOMEN ON SLAVE SHIPS

For similar reasons, African women did not enjoy the same protection against unwanted sexual attention from European men that European women received. Consequently, sailors during long voyages attempted to sate their sexual appetites with enslaved women. African women caught in the Atlantic slave trade were worth half the price of African men in Caribbean markets, and as a result, captains took fewer of them on board their vessels. Perhaps because the women were less valuable commodities, crew members felt they had license to abuse them sexually. The separate below-deck compartments for women on slave ships also made them easier targets than they otherwise might have been.

Historian Barbara Bush speculates that the horrid experience of the Middle Passage may have influenced black women's attitudes toward sexuality and procreation. This, in turn, may help explain why slave populations in the Caribbean and Latin America failed to reproduce themselves: exhaustion, terror, and disgust can depress sex drives.

DYSENTERY (OR THE BLOODY FLUX)

Alexander Falconbridge (d. 1792) served as ship's surgeon on four British slavers between 1780 and 1787. In 1788 he became an opponent of the trade and published An Account of the Slave Trade on the Coast of Africa. *Here he describes in gruesome detail conditions in slave quarters during a dysentery epidemic, which he mistakenly attributes to stale air and heat.*

Some wet and blowing weather having occasioned the portholes to be shut, and the grating to be covered, fluxes and fevers among the Negroes ensued. While they were in this situation, my profession requiring it, I frequently went down among them, till at length their apartments became so extremely hot, as to be only sufferable for a very short time. . . . It is not in the power of the human imagination, to picture to itself a situation more dreadful or disgusting. Numbers of the slaves having fainted, they were carried upon deck, where several of them died, and the rest were, with great difficulty, restored. It had nearly proved fatal to me also. The climate was too warm to admit the wearing of any clothing but a shirt, and that I had pulled off before I went down; notwithstanding which, by only continuing among them for about a quarter of an hour, I was so overcome with the heat, stench, and foul air, that I had nearly fainted; and it was not without assistance, that I could get upon deck. The consequence was, that I soon after fell sick of the same disorder, from which I did not recover for several months. . . .

The place allotted for the sick Negroes is under the half deck, where they lie on the bare planks. By this means, those who are emaciated, frequently have their skin, and even their flesh, entirely rubbed off, by the motion of the ship, from the prominent parts of the shoulders, elbows, and hips, so as to render the bones in those parts quite bare. And some of them, by constantly lying in the blood and mucus, that had flowed from those afflicted with the flux, and which . . . is generally so violent as to prevent their being kept clean, have their flesh much sooner rubbed off, than those who have only to contend with the mere friction of the ship. The excruciating pain which the poor sufferers feel from being obliged to continue in such a dreadful situation, frequently for several weeks, in case they happen to live so long, is not to be conceived or described. Few, indeed, are ever able to withstand the fatal effects of it. The utmost skill of the surgeon is here ineffectual. . . .

The surgeon, upon going between decks, in the morning, to examine the situation of the slaves, frequently finds several dead; and among the men, sometimes a dead and living Negroe

Landing and Sale in the West Indies

As slave ships neared their West Indian destinations, the crew prepared the human cargo for landing and sale. They allowed the slaves to shave, wash with fresh water, and take more vigorous exercise. Those bound for the larger Caribbean islands or for the British colonies of southern North America often received some weeks to rest in the easternmost islands of the West Indies. French slave traders typically rested their slave passengers on **Martinique**. The English preferred **Barbados**. Sale to white plantation owners followed, and then began a period of what the planters called "seasoning," a period of up to two years of acculturating slaves and breaking them in to plantation routines.

The process of landing and sale that ended the Middle Passage was often as protracted as the events that began it in Africa. After anchoring at one of the Lesser Antilles Islands—Barbados, St. Kitts, or Antigua—English slaver captains haggled with the agents of local planters over numbers and prices. They then determined whether to sell all their slaves at their first port of call, sell some of them, sail to another island, or sail to such North American ports as Charleston, Williamsport, or Baltimore. If the market looked good in the first port, the captain might still take a week or more to sell his cargo. The captain of the *James*, who landed at Barbados in 1676, just as the cultivation of cane sugar there was becoming extremely profitable, sold most of his slaves in three days. "May Thursday 25th . . . sold 163 slaves. May Friday 26th. We sold 70 slaves. May Saturday 27th. Sold 110 slaves," he recorded in his journal.

Often, captains and crew had to do more to prepare slaves for sale than allow them to clean themselves

I Just Came from the Fountain — **2** — LIVING WORDS

fastened by their irons together. When this is the case, they are brought upon the deck, and being laid on the grating, the living Negroe is disengaged, and the dead one thrown overboard. . . .

🌿 *Could slave traders have avoided the suffering described in this passage?*

🌿 *What impact would such suffering have had on those who survived it?*

Source: Alexander Falconbridge, *An Account of the Slave Trade on the Coast of Africa* (London: privately printed, 1788), in John H. Bracey Jr. and Manisha Sinha, *African American Mosaic: A Documentary History from the Slave Trade to the Twenty-first Century* (Upper Saddle River, NJ: Prentice Hall, 2004), 1: 24.

and exercise. The ravages of cruelty, confinement, and disease could not be easily remedied. According to legend, young African men and women arrived in the Americas with gray hair, and captains used dye to hide such indications of age before the slaves went to market. Slaves were also required to oil their bodies to conceal blemishes, rashes, and bruises. Ships' surgeons used hemp to plug the anuses of those suffering from dysentery in order to block the bloody discharge the disease caused.

The humiliation continued as the slaves went to market. Once again they suffered close physical inspection from potential buyers, which—according to Equiano—caused "much dread and trembling among us" and "bitter cries." Unless a single purchaser agreed to buy an entire cargo of slaves, auctions took place either on deck or in sale yards on shore. However, some captains employed "the scramble." In these barbaric spectacles, the captain established standard prices for men, women, and children, herded the Africans together in a corral, and then allowed buyers to rush pell-mell among them to grab and rope together the slaves they desired.

Falconbridge described one such "scramble" on a West Indian island. "The Negroes," he recalled, "were landed and placed together in a large yard belonging to the merchants to whom the ship was consigned. As soon as the hour agreed on arrived, the doors of the yard were suddenly thrown open and in rushed a considerable number of purchasers, with all the ferocity of brutes." As the purchasers roped together the men, women, and children they wished to purchase and quarreled among themselves, "the poor astonished Negroes were so terrified . . . that several of them . . . climbed over the walls of the courtyard and ran wild about the town, but were hunted down and retaken."

Seasoning

Seasoning followed sale. On Barbados, Jamaica, and other Caribbean islands, planters divided slaves into three categories: **Creoles** (slaves born in the Americas), old Africans (those who had lived in the Americas for some time), and new Africans (those who had just survived the Middle Passage). Creole slaves were worth three times the value of unseasoned new Africans, whom planters and Creole slaves called "salt-water Ne-

This nineteenth-century engraving suggests the humiliation Africans endured as they were subjected to physical inspections before being sold.

groes" or "Guinea-birds." Seasoning began the process of making new Africans more like Creoles.

In the West Indies, this process involved not only an apprenticeship in the work routines of the sugar plantations on the islands. It was also a means of preparing many slaves for resale to North American planters, who preferred "seasoned" slaves to "unbroken" ones who came directly from Africa. In fact, most of the Africans who ended up in the British colonies of North America before 1720 had gone first to the West Indies. By that date, the demand for slave labor in the islands had become so great that they could spare fewer slaves for resale to the North American market. Thereafter, as a result, slave imports into the tobacco-, rice-, and later cotton-growing regions of the American South came directly from Africa and had to be seasoned by their American masters. But many slaves still came to North America from the Caribbean to which they had been brought from Africa or where they had been born.

In either case, seasoning was a disciplinary process intended to modify the behavior and attitude of slaves and make them effective laborers. As part of this process, the slaves' new masters gave them new names: Christian names, generic African names, or names from classical Greece and Rome (such as Jupiter, Achilles, or Plato).

The seasoning process also involved slaves learning European languages. Masters on the Spanish islands of the Caribbean were especially thorough in

Slaves in this nineteenth-century painting are preparing a field for cultivation on the island of Antigua, a British possession in the West Indies. As had been the case in earlier centuries, the men and women work in gangs under the direction of a white overseer who carries a whip.

this regard. Consequently, although the Spanish of African slaves and their descendants retained some African words, any Spanish-speaking person could easily understand it. In the French and English Caribbean islands and in parts of North America, however, slave society produced Creole dialects that in grammar, vocabulary, and intonation had distinctive African linguistic features. These Africanized versions of French and English, including the Gullah dialect still prevalent on South Carolina's sea islands and the Creole spoken today by most Haitians, were difficult for those who spoke more standardized dialects to understand.

Seasoning varied in length from place to place. Masters or overseers broke slaves into plantation work by assigning them to one of several work gangs. The strongest men joined the first gang, or "great gang," which did the heavy fieldwork of planting and harvesting. The second gang, including women and older men, did lighter fieldwork, such as weeding. The third gang, composed of children, worked shorter hours and performed such tasks as bringing food and water to the field gangs. Other slaves became domestic servants. New Africans served apprenticeships with old Africans from their same ethnic group or with Creoles.

Some planters looked for cargoes of young people, anticipating that they might be more easily **acculturated** than older Africans. One West Indian master in 1792 recorded his hopes for a group of children: "From the late Guinea sales, I have purchased altogether twenty boys and girls, from ten to thirteen years old." He emphasized that "it is the practice, on bringing them to the estate, to distribute them in the huts of Creole blacks, under their direction and care, who are to feed them, train them to work, and teach them their new language."

Planters had to rely on old Africans and Creoles to train new recruits because white people were a minority in the Caribbean. Later, a similar demographic pattern developed in parts of the cotton-producing American South. As a result, in both regions African custom shaped the cooperative labor of slaves in gangs. But the use of old Africans and Creoles as instructors and the appropriation of African styles of labor should not suggest leniency. Although the plantation overseers, who ran day-to-day operations, could be white, of mixed race, or black, they invariably imposed strict discipline. Drivers, who directed the work gangs, were almost always black, but they carried whips and frequently punished those who worked too slowly or showed disrespect. Planters assigned recalcitrant new Africans to the strictest overseers and drivers.

Planters housed slaves undergoing seasoning with the old Africans and Creoles who were instructing them. The instructors regarded such additions to their households as economic opportunities because the new Africans provided extra labor on the small plots of land that West Indian planters often allocated to slaves. Slaves could sell surplus root vegetables, peas, and fruit from their gardens and save to purchase freedom for themselves or others. Additional workers helped produce larger surpluses to sell at local markets, thereby cutting the amount of time required to accumulate a purchase price.

New Africans also benefited from this arrangement. They learned how to build houses in their new land and to cultivate vegetables to supplement the food the planter provided. Even though many Africans brought building skills and agricultural knowledge with them to the Americas, old Africans and Creoles helped teach them how to adapt what they knew to a new climate, topography, building materials, and social organization.

The End of the Journey: Masters and Slaves in the Americas

By what criteria did planters assess the successful seasoning of new Africans? The first criterion was survival. Already weakened and traumatized by the Middle Passage, many Africans did not survive seasoning. Historian James Walvin estimates that one-third died during their first three years in the West Indies. African men died at a greater rate than African women, perhaps because they did the more arduous fieldwork.

A second criterion was that the Africans had to adapt to new foods and a new climate. The foods included salted codfish traded to the West Indies by New England merchants, Indian corn (maize), and varieties of squash not available in West Africa. The Caribbean islands like West Africa were tropical, but North America was much cooler. Even within the West Indies, an African was unlikely to find a climate exactly like the one he or she had left behind.

A third criterion was learning a new language. Planters did not require slaves to speak the local language, which could be English, French, Spanish, Danish, or Dutch, perfectly. But slaves had to speak a creole dialect well enough to obey commands. A final criterion was psychological. When new Africans ceased to be suicidal, planters assumed they had accepted their status and their separation from their homeland.

It would have suited the planters if their slaves had met all these criteria. Yet that would have required the Africans to have been thoroughly desocialized by the Middle Passage, and they were not. As traumatic as that voyage was—for all the shock of capture, separation from loved ones, and efforts to dehumanize them—most of the Africans who entered plantation society in the Americas had not been stripped of their memories or their culture. When their ties to their villages and families were broken, they created bonds with shipmates that simulated blood relationships. Such bonds became the basis of new extended families. So similar were these new synthetic families to those that had existed in West Africa that slaves considered sexual relations among shipmates and former shipmates incestuous.

As this suggests, African slaves did not lose all their culture during the Middle Passage and seasoning in the Americas. Their value system never totally repli-

After experiencing the horrors of the Middle Passage, enslaved Africans faced hard, forced labor in a new environment.

cated that of the plantation. Despite their ordeal, the Africans who survived the Atlantic slave trade and slavery in the Americas were resilient. Seasoning did modify behavior, yet the claim that it obliterated African Americans' cultural roots is incorrect. Anthropologist Melville Herskovits in 1941 raised questions about this issue that still shape debate about the African-American experience.

Herskovits asked, "What discussions of world view might not have taken place in the long hours when [Creole] teacher and [new African] pupil were together, reversing their roles when matters only dimly sensed by the American-born slave were explained [by his pupil] in terms of African conventions he had never analyzed?" How many African beliefs and methods of coping with life and the supernatural were retained and transmitted by such century. During the late 1700s, English abolitionists led by Thomas Clarkson, William Wilberforce, and Granville Sharp began a religiously oriented moral crusade against slavery and the slave trade. Because the English had dominated the Atlantic trade since 1713, Britain's growing antipathy became crucial to the trade's destruction. But it is debatable whether moral outrage alone prompted this humanitarian effort. By the late 1700s, England's industrializing economy was less dependent on the slave trade and the entire plantation system than it had been previously. To maintain its prosperity, England needed raw materials and markets for its manufactured goods. Slowly but surely its ruling classes realized it was more profitable to invest in industry and other forms of trade and to leave Africans in Africa.

So morals and economic self-interest combined when Great Britain abolished the Atlantic slave trade in 1807 and tried to enforce that abolition on other nations through a naval patrol off the coast of Africa. The U.S. Congress joined Britain in outlawing the Atlantic trade the following year. Although American, Brazilian, and Spanish slavers continued to defy these prohibitions for many years, the forced migration from Africa to the Americas dropped to a tiny percentage of what it had been at its peak. Ironically, it was the coastal kingdoms of Guinea and western Central Africa that fought most fiercely to keep the trade going because their economies had become dependent on it. This persistence gave the English, French, Belgians, and Portuguese an excuse to establish colonial empires in Africa during the nineteenth century in the name of suppressing the slave trade.

CONCLUSION

Over more than three centuries, the Atlantic slave trade brought more than eleven million Africans to the Americas. Several million died in transit. Of those who survived, most came between 1701 and 1810, when more Africans than Europeans reached the New World. Most Africans went to the sugar plantations of the Caribbean and Brazil. Only 500,000 went to the British colonies of North America, either directly or after seasoning in the West Indies. From them have come the nearly forty million African Americans alive today.

This chapter has described the great forced migration across the Atlantic that brought Africans into slavery in the Americas. We still have much to learn about the origins of the trade, its relationship to the earlier trans-Sahara trade, and its involvement with state for-

Group of Negros, as imported to be sold for Slaves.

This print, published in 1793, portrays a group of Africans who arrived during the 1720s in Suriname, in northern South America. Although the artist creates an almost festive scene, a slave trader is driving them with a stick.

private discussions? How much did African cultural elements, such as dance, song, folklore, moral values, and etiquette, offset the impulse to accept European values?

The Ending of the Atlantic Slave Trade

The cruelties associated with the Atlantic slave trade contributed to its abolition in the early nineteenth mation in West and western Central Africa. Historians continue to debate how cruel the trade was, the ability of transplanted Africans to preserve their cultural heritage, and why Britain abolished the trade in the early nineteenth century.

We are fortunate that a few Africans who experienced the Middle Passage recorded their testimony. Otherwise, we would find its horror even more difficult to comprehend. Even more important, however, is that so many survived the horrible experience of the Atlantic slave trade and carried on. Their struggle testifies to the human spirit that is at the center of the African-American experience.

RECOMMENDED READING

Barbara Bush. *Slave Women in Caribbean Society, 1650–1838.* Bloomington: University of Indiana Press, 1990. The book contains an insightful discussion of African women, their introduction to slavery in the Americas, and their experience on sugar plantations.

Basil Davidson. *The African Slave Trade: Revised and Expanded Edition.* Boston: Little, Brown, 1980. Originally published in 1961, this book has been superseded in some respects by more recent studies. But it places the trade in both African and European contexts.

Herbert S. Klein. *The Atlantic Slave Trade.* New York: Cambridge University Press, 1999. This is the most thorough and most current study of the subject.

Edward Reynolds. *Stand the Storm: A History of the Atlantic Slave Trade.* London: Allison and Busby, 1985. Reynolds concentrates on African societies and the responses of those subjected to the Atlantic slave trade.

John Thornton. *Africa and Africans in the Making of the Atlantic World, 1400–1800,* 2nd ed. New York: Cambridge University Press, 1998. Thornton emphasizes the contributions of Africans, slave and free, to the economic and cultural development of the Atlantic world during the slave-trade centuries.

ADDITIONAL BIBLIOGRAPHY

THE SLAVE TRADE IN AFRICA

Walter Hawthorne. *Planting Rice and Harvesting Slaves: Transformations along the Guinea-Bissau Coast 1400–1900.* Portsmouth, NH: Heinemann, 2003.

Bernard Lewis. *Race and Slavery in the Middle East: An Historical Enquiry.* New York: Oxford University Press, 1990.

Patrick Manning. *Slavery and African Life: Occidental, Oriental, and African Slave Trades.* New York: Cambridge University Press, 1990.

Suzanne Miers and Richard Roberts. *The End of Slavery in Africa.* Madison: University of Wisconsin Press, 1988.

Claire C. Robertson and Martin A. Klein, eds. *Slavery in Africa.* Madison: University of Wisconsin Press, 1983.

Elizabeth Savage, ed. *The Human Commodity: Perspectives on the Trans-Saharan Slave Trade.* London: Frank Cass, 1992.

John K. Thornton. *The Kingdom of Kongo: Civil War and Transition, 1641–1718.* Madison: University of Wisconsin Press, 1983.

THE ATLANTIC SLAVE TRADE

Vincent Carretta. *Equiano the African: Biography of a Self-Made Man.* Athens: University of Georgia Press, 2005.

Emma Christopher. *Slave Ship Sailors and Their Captive Cargoes 1730–1807.* New York: Cambridge University Press, 2006.

Herbert S. Klein. *The Middle Passage: Comparative Studies in the Atlantic Slave Trade.* Princeton, NJ: Princeton University Press, 1978.

Rosemarie Robotham, ed. *Spirits of the Passage: The Transatlantic Slave Trade in the Seventeenth Century.* New York: Simon & Schuster, 1997.

Lief Svalesen. *The Slave Ship Fredensborg.* Bloomington: Indiana University Press, 2000.

Hugh Thomas. *The Slave Trade: The Story of the Atlantic Slave Trade, 1440–1870.* New York: Simon & Schuster, 1997.

Vincent Bakpetu Thompson. *The Making of the African Diaspora in the Americas, 1441–1900.* New York: Longman, 1987.

John Vogt. *Portuguese Rule on the Gold Coast, 1469–1682.* Athens: University of Georgia Press, 1979.

James Walvin. *Making the Black Atlantic: Britain and the African Diaspora.* New York: Cassell, 2000.

THE WEST INDIES

Edward Brathwaite. *The Development of Creole Society in Jamaica, 1770–1820.* New York: Oxford University Press, 1971.

William Claypole and John Robottom. *Caribbean Story: Foundations.* Kingston: Longman, 1980.

Melville J. Herskovits. *The Myth of the Negro Past.* Boston: Beacon, 1941.

Clarence J. Munford. *The Black Ordeal of Slavery and Slave Trading in the French West Indies, 1625–1715.* Lewiston, NY: Mellen, 1991.

Keith Albert Sandiford. *The Cultural Politics of Sugar: Caribbean Slavery and Narratives of Colonialism.* New York: Cambridge University Press, 2000.

RETRACING THE ODYSSEY

The Henrietta Marie. This is a slave ship placed on traveling display by the Museum of Southern Florida in Miami. *The Henrietta Marie* sank in 1701 after delivering slaves to Jamaica.

SLAVE TRADE	WORLD EVENTS
900	
900–1100 Trans-Sahara trade peaks	**935** Finalization of the Koran text
	979 Sung dynasty unites China
	1236 Mongols invade Russia
	1337 French–English Hundred Years' War begins
1400	
1441 Antam Goncalvez of Portugal captures Africans	**1445** Gutenberg prints first book in Europe
1450	
1472 Ruy do Siqueira contracts with the Oba of Benin	**1453** Fall of Constantinople to the Turks
	1468 Fall of the Empire of Mali
	1492 Columbus's first voyage to the Americas
1500	
1502 African slaves are reported to be on Hispaniola	**1517** Protestant Reformation
1518 Spanish *Asiento* begins	**1519** Spanish conquest of Aztecs
1533 Sugar production begins in Brazil	
1550	
1571 Portuguese colonize Angola	**1591** Fall of the Empire of Songhai

Chattanooga African American Museum, Chattanooga, TN. The museum includes an exhibit dealing with the Atlantic slave trade.

myhistorylab   REVIEW, RESEARCH, AND INTERACT

REVIEW QUESTIONS

1. How did the Atlantic slave trade reflect the times during which it existed?

2. Think about Olaudah Equiano's experience as a young boy captured by traders and brought to a slave ship. What new and strange things did he encounter? How did he explain these things to himself? What kept him from descending into utter despair?

3. How could John Newton reconcile his Christian faith with his career as a slave-ship captain?

4. What human and natural variables could prolong the Middle Passage across the Atlantic Ocean? How could delay make the voyage more dangerous for slaves and crew?

5. How could Africans resist the dehumanizing forces of the Middle Passage and seasoning and use their African cultures to build black cultures in the New World?

www.researchnavigator.com

Using the tools available in Research Navigator, consider these questions:
Why was the history of slavery repressed for so long? Why has interest in the subject grown in the past quarter of a century?

PRIMARY SOURCE DOCUMENTS

2–1 England Asserts Her Dominion through Legislation in 1660

2–2 A Slave Tells of His Capture in Africa in 1798

2–3 A Slave Ship Surgeon Writes about the Slave Trade in 1788

2–4 An African Captive Tells the Story of Crossing the Atlantic in a Slave Ship

MAP EXPLORATION

The Atlantic and Islamic Slave Trades, p. 31

INTERACTIVE ACTIVITY

Racism in American History
Based on the writings of Olaudah Equiano and George Fitzhugh, what does the treatment of Africans suggest about the humanity of Europeans?

1600

AFRICAN-AMERICAN EVENTS	NATIONAL EVENTS
1610 Dutch drive Portuguese from Africa's west coast	**1607** Founding of Jamestown
1619 Africans reported to be in British North America	**1620** Pilgrims reach New England

1650

1662 Portuguese destroy Kongo Kingdom	**1688** England's Glorious Revolution
1674 England drives the Dutch out of the slave trade	

1700

1713 England begins its domination of the slave trade	**1728** Russian exploration of Alaska begins
c. 1745 Olaudah Equiano born	

1750

1752 British Royal African Company disbands	**1776** American Declaration of Independence
	1789 United States Constitution ratified

1800

1807 Great Britain abolishes the Atlantic slave trade	**1815** Napolean defeated at the Battle of Waterloo
1808 United States abolishes the Atlantic slave trade	

AFRICAN-AMERICAN EVENTS   NATIONAL EVENTS

3

Black People in Colonial North America

WHO WERE THE PEOPLES
OF COLONIAL NORTH AMERICA?

HOW DID BLACK SERVITUDE
DEVELOP IN THE CHESAPEAKE?

WHAT WERE THE CHARACTERISTICS
OF PLANTATION SLAVERY FROM 1700 TO 1750?

HOW DID THE EXPERIENCE OF AFRICAN AMERICANS
UNDER FRENCH AND SPANISH RULE
IN NORTH AMERICA COMPARE TO THAT
IN THE BRITISH COLONIES?

HOW DID SLAVERY AFFECT BLACK WOMEN
IN COLONIAL AMERICA?

HOW DID AFRICAN AMERICANS RESIST SLAVERY?

1526–1763

◀ **This eighteenth-century woodcut** shows enslaved black men,
women, and children engaged in the steps involved in the
curing of tobacco. Courtesy of the Library of Congress

Whereas, the plantations and estates of this Province [of South Carolina] cannot be well and sufficiently managed and brought into use, without the labor and service of negroes and other slaves; and forasmuch as the said negroes and other slaves brought unto the People of the Province for that purpose, are of barbarous, wild, savage natures, and such as renders them wholly unqualified to be governed by the laws, customs, and practices of this Province; . . . it is absolutely necessary, that such other constitutions, laws and orders, should in this Province be made and enacted, for the good regulating and ordering of them, as may restrain the disorderly rapines and inhumanity, to which they are naturally prone and induced; and may also tend to the safety and security of the people of this Province and their estates.

From the introduction to the original South Carolina Slave Code of 1696

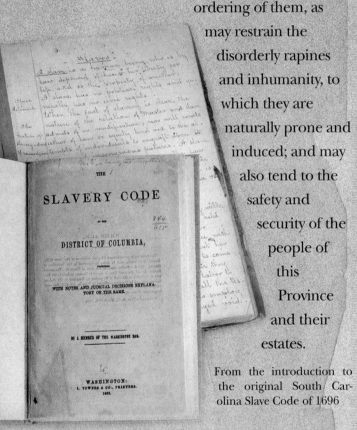

The slavery codes regulated slaves and asserted the rights of slave owners.

African Americans lived in North America for nearly three centuries before the United States gained independence from Great Britain in 1783. Most of them were held as slaves in British,

French, and Spanish colonies. Mainly for that reason the black Americans of the sixteenth, seventeenth, and early eighteenth centuries left scant written testimony about their lives. Their history, therefore, must be learned mainly through the writings of the white settlers who enslaved and oppressed them.

The passage that begins this chapter is an excellent example of what we can learn about African-American history by reading between the lines in the official publications of the colonial governments. As historian Winthrop D. Jordan points out, the founders of South Carolina in 1696 borrowed much of this section of the colony's law code from the British colony of Barbados in the Caribbean.

The code indicates that the British Carolinians believed they needed the labor of enslaved Africans for their colony to prosper. It also shows that the colonial British feared Africans and their African-American descendants. This ambivalence among white Americans concerning African Americans shaped life in colonial South Carolina and in other British colonies in North America. The same ambivalence persisted in the minds of white southerners into the twentieth century. The dichotomy of white economic dependence on black people and fear of black revolt was a central fact of American history and provided a rationale for racial oppression.

The opening passage also reveals the willingness of British and other European settlers in North America to brand Africans and their American descendants as "barbarous, wild, [and] savage." Although real cultural differences underlay such negative perceptions, white people used them to justify oppressing black people. Unlike white people, black people by the 1640s could be enslaved for life. Black people did not enjoy the same legal protection as white people and were punished more harshly.

This chapter describes the history of African-American life in colonial North America from the early sixteenth century to the end of the **French and Indian War** in 1763. It briefly covers the black experience in Spanish Florida, in New Spain's borderlands in the Southwest, and in French Louisiana, but concentrates on the British colonies that stretched along the eastern coast of the continent. During the seventeenth century, the plantation system that became a central part of black life in America for nearly two centuries took shape in the Chesapeake tobacco country and in the low country of South Carolina and Georgia. Unfree labor, which in the Chesapeake had originally involved white people as well as black people, solidified into a system of slavery based on race that also existed in the northern British colonies. African Americans responded to these conditions by intereacting with other groups, preserving parts of their African culture, seeking strength through religion, and finding ways to resist and rebel against enslavement.

The Peoples of North America

In the North American colonies during the seventeenth and eighteenth centuries, African immigrants gave birth to a new African-American people. Born in North America and forever separated from their ancestral homeland, they preserved a surprisingly large core of their African cultural heritage. Meanwhile, a new natural environment and contacts with people of American Indian and European descent helped African Americans shape a way of life within the circumstances that slavery forced on them. To understand the early history of African Americans, we must first briefly discuss the other peoples of colonial North America.

AMERICAN INDIANS

Historians and anthropologists group the original inhabitants of North America together as American Indians. (Sometimes the terms *Amerinds* and *Native Americans* are also used, with the latter term including Inuits [Eskimos].) But when the British began to colonize the coastal portion of this huge region during the early seventeenth century, the indigenous peoples who lived there had no such all-inclusive name. They spoke many different languages, lived in diverse environments, and considered themselves distinct from one another. Like other Indian peoples of the Western Hemisphere, they descended from Asians who had migrated eastward across a land bridge connecting Siberia and Alaska at least 12,000 years ago. Europeans called them Indians as a result of Christopher Columbus's mistaken assumption in 1492 that he had landed on islands near the "Indies," by which he meant near southeast Asia.

In Mexico, Central America, and Peru, American Indian peoples developed complex, densely populated civilizations with hereditary monarchies, formal religions, armies, and social classes. They built stone temples and great cities, kept official records, and studied astronomy and mathematics. Cultural developments in Mexico and the northward spread of the cultivation of maize (corn) influenced the indigenous peoples of what is today the United States. In the Southwest, the Anasazi and later Pueblo peoples developed sophisticated farming communities. Beginning around 900 CE, they produced pottery, studied astronomy, built large adobe towns, and struggled against a drying climate. Farther east in what is known as the Woodlands region, the Adena culture flourished in the Ohio River valley as early as 1000 BCE and attained the social organization required to construct large burial mounds. Between the tenth and fourteenth centuries CE, what is known as the Mississippian culture established a sophisticated civilization, marked by extensive trade routes, division of labor, and urban centers. The largest such center was Cahokia—located near modern St. Louis, Missouri—which at its peak had a population of about 30,000.

Climatic change and warfare destroyed the Mississippian culture during the fourteenth century, and only remnants of it existed when Europeans and Africans arrived in North America. By that time, a diverse variety of American Indian cultures existed in what is today the eastern portion of the United States. People resided in towns and villages, supplementing their agricultural economies with fishing and hunting. They held land communally, generally allowed women a voice in ruling councils, and—although warlike—regarded battle as an opportunity for young men to prove their bravery rather than as a means of conquest. Gravely weakened by diseases that settlers unwittingly brought from Europe, the woodlands Indians of North America's coastal regions were ineffective in resisting British settlers during the seventeenth century. Particularly in the Southeast, the British developed an extensive trade in Indian slaves.

Because American Indians were experts at living harmoniously with the natural resources of North America, they influenced the way people of African and European descent came to live there as well. Indian crops, such as corn, pumpkins, beans, and squash, became staples of the newcomers' diets. On the continent's southeastern coast, British cultivation of tobacco, another Indian crop, secured the economic survival of the Chesapeake colonies of Virginia and Maryland and led directly to the enslavement in them of Africans. The Indian canoe became a means of river transportation for black and white people,

Escaping slaves in the Carolinas during the early eighteenth century sometimes found shelter with the Tuscaroras and other Indian tribes. This map, drawn during a colonial expedition against the Tuscaroras in 1713, shows a Tuscarora fort that escaped slaves probably helped design and build.

and Indian moccasins became common footwear for everyone.

The relationships between black people and American Indians during colonial times were complex. Although Indian nations often provided refuge to escaping black slaves, Indians sometimes became slaveholders and on occasion helped crush black revolts. Some black men assisted in the Indian slave trade and sometimes helped defend European colonists against Indian attacks. Nevertheless, people of African and Indian descent frequently found themselves in similarly oppressive circumstances in Britain's American colonies. Although white officials attempted to keep them apart, social and sexual contacts between the two groups were frequent. Some interracial black-Indian settlements—and a few black-Indian-white settlements—have persisted to the present.

THE SPANISH EMPIRE

Following Christopher Columbus's voyage in 1492, the Spanish rapidly built a colonial empire in the Americas. Mining of gold and silver, as well as the production of sugar, tobacco, and leather goods, provided a firm economic foundation. But few Spanish people came to the Western Hemisphere, and Spain's colonial economy rested on the forced labor of the Indian population and,

when the Indian population declined from disease and overwork, increasingly on enslaved Africans. Overseers in the mines and fields often brutally worked Africans and Indians to death. But because the Spanish were few, some of the African and Indians who survived were able to gain freedom and become tradesmen, small landholders, and militiamen. Often they were of mixed race and identified with their former masters rather than with the oppressed people beneath them in society. African, Indian, and Spanish customs intermingled in what became a multicultural colonial society. Its center was in the West Indian islands of Cuba and Santo Domingo, Mexico, and northern South America. On its northern periphery were lands that are now part of the United States: Florida, Texas, Arizona, New Mexico, and California.

Africans came early to these borderlands. In 1526 Luis Vasquez de Ayllon brought one hundred African slaves with him from Hispaniola (modern Haiti and the Dominican Republic) in an attempt to establish a Spanish colony near what is now Georgetown, South Carolina. A decade later, slaves, who were either African or of African descent, accompanied Hernando de Soto on a Spanish expedition from Florida to the Mississippi River. In 1565 Africans helped construct the Spanish settlement of St. Augustine in Florida, which is now the oldest city in the continental United States. In 1528 a Spanish expedition that departed Cuba to search for gold in western Florida and the Gulf Coast included a slave of African descent named Esteban. Following a shipwreck, Esteban reached the coast of Texas. After a brief captivity among the local Indians, he and other survivors made their way southward to Mexico City.

THE BRITISH AND JAMESTOWN

While the powerful Spanish empire colonized warm, populous, and wealthy regions of the Americas, the relatively less powerful British acquired lands that were cooler, less populous, and deficient in easily acquired wealth. The British, like the Africans and the American Indians, were not a single nation. The British Isles—consisting principally of Britain and Ireland and located off the northwest coast of Europe—were the homeland of the English, Welsh, Scots, and Irish. The English by the seventeenth century dominated the other ethnic groups. But at that time, the Kingdom of England was, compared to Spain, a poor country notable mainly for producing wool.

England's claim to the east coast of North America rested on the voyage of John Cabot, who sailed in 1497, just five years after Columbus's first westward voyage. But, unlike the Spanish who rapidly created an empire in the Americas, the English were slow to establish themselves in the region Cabot had reached. This was partly due to the harsher North American climate, with winters much colder than in England. In addition, the English monarchy was too poor to finance colonizing expeditions and social turmoil associated with the Protestant Reformation absorbed its energies.

Attempts failed in the 1580s to colonize Newfoundland, a large island off the east coast of what is today Canada, and Roanoke Island, a small island off the coast of what is today North Carolina. It took the English naval victory over the Spanish Armada in 1588 and money raised by **joint-stock companies** to produce in 1607 at Jamestown the first permanent British colony in North America. This settlement, established by the Virginia Company of London, was located in the Chesapeake region the British called Virginia—after Queen Elizabeth I (r. 1558–1603), the so-called Virgin Queen of England. The company hoped to make a profit at Jamestown by finding gold, trading with Indians, cutting lumber, or raising crops, such as rice, sugar, or silk, that could not be produced in Britain.

None of these schemes was economically viable. There was no gold, and the climate was unsuitable for rice, sugar, and silk. Because of disease, hostility with the Indians, and especially economic failure, the settlement barely survived into the 1620s. By then, however, the experiments begun in 1612 by the English settler John Rolfe to cultivate a mild strain of tobacco that could be grown on the North American mainland began to pay off. Tobacco was in great demand in Europe, where smoking was becoming popular. Soon growing tobacco became the economic mainstay in Virginia and the neighboring colony of Maryland.

The sowing, cultivating, harvesting, and curing of tobacco required considerable labor. Yet colonists in the Chesapeake could not follow the Spanish example of enslaving Indians to produce the crop. Rampant disease had reduced the local Indian population, and those who survived eluded British conquest by retreating westward.

Unlike the West Indian sugar planters, however, the North American tobacco planters did not immediately turn to Africa for laborers. British advocates of colonizing North America had always promoted it as a solution to unemployment, poverty, and crime in England. The idea was to send England's undesirables to America, where they could provide the cheap labor tobacco planters needed. Consequently, until 1700, white labor produced most of the tobacco in the Chesapeake colonies.

AFRICANS ARRIVE IN THE CHESAPEAKE

By early 1619, there were, nevertheless, thirty-two people of African descent—fifteen men and seventeen women—living in the English colony at Jamestown. Nothing is known concerning when they arrived or from where they came. They were all "in the service of sev[er]all planters." The following August a Dutch warship, carrying seventeen African men and three African women, moored at Hampton Roads at the mouth of the James River. For many years, historians believed these were the first black people in British North America. They were part of a group of over 300 who had been taken from Angola by a Portuguese slaver that had set sail for the port of Vera Cruz in New Spain (Mexico). The Dutch warship, with the help of an English ship, had attacked the slaver, taken most of its human cargo, and brought these twenty Angolans to Jamestown. The Dutch captain traded them to local officials in return for provisions.

The Angolans became servants to the Jamestown officials and to favored planters. The colony's inhabitants, for two reasons, regarded the new arrivals and those black people who had been in Jamestown earlier to be *unfree*, but not slaves. First, unlike the Portuguese and the Spanish, the English had no law for slavery. Second, at least those Angolans, who bore such names as Pedro, Isabella, Antoney, and Angelo, were Christians, and—according to English custom and morality in 1619—Christians could not be enslaved. So, once these individuals worked off their purchase price, they regained their freedom. In 1623, Antoney and Isabella married. The next year they became parents of William, whom their master had baptized in the local **Church of England**. William may have been the first black person born in English America. He was almost certainly born free.

During the following years, people of African descent remained a small minority in the expanding Virginia colony. A 1625 census reported only twenty-three black people living in the colony, compared with a combined total of 1,275 white people and Indians. This suggests that many of the first black inhabitants had either died or moved away. By 1649 the total Virginia population of about 18,500 included only 300 black people. The English, following the Spanish example, called them "negroes." (The word "negro" means black in Spanish.) In neighboring Maryland, which was established as a haven in 1632 for persecuted English Catholics, the black population also remained small. In 1658 people of African descent accounted for only 3 percent of Maryland's population.

Black Servitude in the Chesapeake

As these statistics suggest, during the early years of the Chesapeake colonies, black people represented a small part of a labor force composed mainly of white people. From the 1620s to the 1670s, black and white people worked in the tobacco fields together, lived together, and slept together (and also did these things with American Indians). They were all unfree indentured servants.

Indentured servitude had existed in Europe for centuries. In England, parents indentured—or, in other words, apprenticed—their children to "masters," who controlled their lives and had the right to their labor for a set number of years. In return, the masters supported the children and taught them a trade or profession. Unrestrained by modern notions of human equality and democracy, masters could exercise brutal authority over those bound to them.

As the demand for labor to produce tobacco in the Chesapeake expanded, indentured servitude came to include adults who sold their freedom for two to seven years in return for the cost of their voyage to North America. Instead of training in a profession, the servants could improve their economic standing by remaining as free persons in America after completing their period of servitude.

When Africans first arrived in Virginia and Maryland, they entered into similar contracts, agreeing to work for their masters until the proceeds of their labor recouped the cost of their purchase. Indentured servitude could be harsh in the tobacco colonies because masters sought to get as much labor as they could from their servants before the indenture ended. Most indentured servants died from overwork or disease before regaining their freedom. But those who survived, black people as well as white people, could expect eventually to leave their masters and seek their fortunes as free persons.

The foremost example in early Virginia of a black man who emerged from servitude to become a tobacco planter himself is Anthony Johnson. He had arrived in the colony in 1621, and a 1625 census listed him as a servant. By 1651 he had an estate of 250 acres and was himself the master of several servants, some of

them white. Johnson was not the only person of African descent who emerged from servitude to become a free property owner during the first half of the seventeenth century. Here and there, black men seemed to enjoy a status similar to their white counterparts. During the seventeenth century, free black men living in the Chesapeake participated fully in the commercial and legal life of the colony. They owned land, farmed, lent money, sued in the courts, served as jurors and as minor officials, and at times voted.

As Johnson's story indicates, prior to the 1670s the English in the Chesapeake did not draw a strict line between white freedom and black slavery. Yet the ruling elite had from the early 1600s treated black servants differently from white servants. Over the decades, the region's British population gradually came to assume that persons of African descent were inalterably alien. This sentiment did not become universal among the white poor during the colonial period. But it was a foundation for what historian Winthrop D. Jordan calls the "unthinking decision" among the British in the Chesapeake to establish **chattel slavery**, in which slaves were legally private property on a level with livestock, as the proper condition for Africans and those of African descent.

RACE AND THE ORIGINS OF BLACK SLAVERY

Between 1640 and 1700, the British tobacco-producing colonies stretching from Delaware to northern Carolina underwent a social and demographic revolution. An economy based primarily on the labor of white indentured servants became an economy based on the labor of black slaves. In Virginia, for example, the slave population in 1671 was less than 5 percent of the colony's total non-Indian population. White indentured servants outnumbered black slaves by three to one. By 1700, however, slaves constituted at least 20 percent of Virginia's population. Probably most agricultural laborers were slaves.

Although historians debate how this extraordinary change occurred, several interrelated factors brought it about. Some of these factors are easily understood. Others are more complicated and profound because they involve basic assumptions about the American nation.

Among the economic and demographic developments that led to the mass enslavement of people of African descent in the tobacco colonies was the precedent for enslaving Africans set in the British Caribbean sugar colonies during the second quarter of the seventeenth century. Also, African slaves became cheaper as white indentured servants became more expensive. This was because poor white people found better opportunities for themselves in other regions of British North America than in the tobacco colonies. Meanwhile, as fewer English men and women agreed to indenture themselves in return for passage to those colonies, Britain gained increased control over the Atlantic slave trade.

These changing circumstances provide the context for the beginnings of black slavery as a major phenomenon in British North America. Yet race and class played the crucial role in shaping the *character* of slavery in the British mainland colonies. From the first arrival of Africans in the Chesapeake, those English who exercised authority made decisions that qualified the apparent social mobility the Africans enjoyed. The English had historically distinguished between how they treated each other and how they treated those who were physically and culturally different from them. Such discrimination had been the basis of English colonial policies toward the Irish—whom England had been trying to conquer for centuries—and the American Indians. Because the English considered Africans even more different from themselves than either the Irish or the Indians, they assumed from the beginning that Africans were generally inferior.

Therefore, although black and white servants residing in the Chesapeake during the early seventeenth century had much in common, their masters immediately made distinctions between them based on race. The few women of African descent who arrived in the Chesapeake during those years worked in the tobacco fields with the male servants, while most white women performed domestic duties. Also, unlike white servants, black servants usually did not have surnames, and early census reports listed them separately from whites. By the 1640s, black people could not bear arms, and during the same decade, local Anglican priests (although not those in England itself) maintained that persons of African descent could not become Christians. Although sexual contacts among blacks, whites, and Indians were common, colonial authorities soon discouraged them. In 1662 Virginia's **House of Burgesses** (the colony's legislature) declared that "any christian [white person]" who committed "Fornication with a negro man or woman, he or shee soe offending" would pay double the fine set for committing the same offense with a white person.

These distinctions suggest that the status of black servants had never been the same as that of white servants. But only starting in the 1640s do records indicate a predilection toward making black people slaves rather than servants. During that decade, courts in Virginia and Maryland began to reflect an assumption that it was permissible for persons of African descent to serve their master for life rather than for a set term.

DOCUMENT
3-1
Maryland Addresses the Status of Slaves in 1644

One court case, heard in 1640, involved the escape of three servants from Virginia to Maryland. One of the escapees was Dutch, another was a Scot, and the third—named John Punch—was of African descent. Following their capture and return to Virginia, a court ruled that all three should be whipped, that the Scot and Dutchman should have their terms of service extended for four years, and that Punch "being a negro . . . serve his said master or his assigns for the time of his natural life." By mid-decade, black men, women, and children often sold for higher prices than their white counterparts on the explicit provision that the black people would serve "for their Life tyme," or "for ever."

DOCUMENT
3-3
The Difference between Servants and Slaves in 1722

THE EMERGENCE OF CHATTEL SLAVERY

Legal documents and statute books reveal that, during the 1660s, other aspects of chattel slavery emerged in the Chesapeake colonies. Bills of sale began to stipulate that the children of black female servants would also be servants for life. In 1662 the House of Burgesses decreed that a child's condition—free or unfree—followed that of the mother. This ran counter to English common law, which assumed that a child's status derived from the father. The change permitted masters to exploit their black female servants sexually without having to acknowledge the children who might result from such contacts. Just as significant, by the mid-1660s statutes in the Chesapeake colonies assumed servitude to be the natural condition of black people.

DOCUMENT
3-2
The Selling of Joseph

With these laws, slavery in British North America emerged in the form that it retained until the American Civil War: a racially defined system of perpetual involuntary servitude that compelled almost all black people to work as agricultural laborers. **Slave codes** enacted between 1660 and 1710 further defined American slavery as a system that sought as much to control persons of African descent as to exploit their labor. Slaves could not testify against white people in court, own property, leave their master's estate without a pass, congregate in groups larger than three or four, enter into contracts, marry, or, of course, bear arms. Profession of Christianity no longer protected a black person from enslavement nor was conversion a cause for **manumission**. In 1669 the House of Burgesses exempted from felony charges masters who killed a slave while administering punishment.

By 1700, just as the slave system began to expand in the southern colonies, enslaved Africans and African Americans had been reduced legally to the status of domestic animals except that, unlike animals (or

PROFILE ～ ANTHONY JOHNSON

Little is known of the individual Africans and African Americans who lived in North America during the seventeenth and eighteenth centuries. A lack of contemporary accounts prevents us from truly understanding their personalities. This is also true for poorer Americans of European descent, but it is especially true of black servants or slaves. In rare instances, however, black people emerge from the bits and pieces of information preserved in court records. This is the case for Anthony Johnson and his family. Their accomplishments cast some light on African-American life in the seventeenth-century Chesapeake.

Anthony Johnson arrived at Jamestown in 1621 from England, but his original home may have been Angola. He was fortunate the following year to escape death in an Indian attack on Jamestown. He was one of four out of fifty-six inhabitants on the Bennett plantation, where he labored, to survive. He was also lucky to wed "Mary a Negro Woman," who in 1625 was the only woman residing at Bennett's.

In 1635 Johnson's master, Nathaniel Littleton, released him from further service. Johnson, like other free men of this time and place, then scrambled to acquire wealth in the form of land, livestock, and human beings. He received his own 250-acre plantation in 1651 under the "headright system" by which the colonial government encouraged population growth by awarding fifty acres of land for every new servant a settler brought to Virginia.

This meant that Johnson had become the master of five servants, some of them white. His estate was on a neck of land between two creeks that flowed into the Pungoteague River in Northampton County. A few years later, his relatives, John and Richard Johnson, also acquired land in this area. John brought eleven servants to the colony and received 550 acres, and Richard brought two and received one hundred acres.

The Johnson estates existed among white-owned properties in the same area. Like their white neighbors, the Johnsons were not part of the planting elite, but they owned their own land, farmed, and had social, economic, and legal relations with other colonists. Anthony Johnson in particular engaged in litigation that tells us much about black life in early Virginia.

In 1654, his lawsuit against his black servant John Casor and a white neighbor set a precedent in favor of black slavery, but also revealed Johnson's legal rights. Casor claimed that Johnson "had kept him his serv[an]t seven years longer than hee should or ought." Johnson, whom court records described as an "old Negro," responded that he was entitled to "ye Negro [Casor] for his life." Johnson momentarily relented when he realized that if he persisted in his suit, Casor could win damages against him. Shortly thereafter, however, Johnson brought suit against his white neighbor Robert Parker, whom Johnson charged had detained Casor "under pretense [that] the s[ai]d John Casor is a freeman." This time the court ruled in Johnson's favor. It returned Casor to him and required Parker to pay court costs.

During the 1660s, the extended Johnson family moved to Somerset, Maryland, where its members had acquired additional land. They were still prospering as planters during the early eighteenth century. Some family members moved on to New Jersey and others to Delaware, where some of them intermarried with the Nanticoke Indians. Historian John H. Russell exaggerated when he claimed in 1913 that blacks in the seventeenth century had roughly the same opportunities as free white servants. But industrious and lucky black people at that time could achieve a social and economic standing that became nearly impossible for their descendants.

Johnson

masters who abused slaves), the law held slaves to be strictly accountable for their transgressions.

BACON'S REBELLION AND AMERICAN SLAVERY

The series of events that led to the enslavement of black people in the Chesapeake tobacco colonies preceded their emergence as the great majority of laborers in those colonies. The dwindling supply of white indentured servants, the growing availability of Africans, and preexisting white racial biases affected this transformation. But the key event in bringing it about was the rebellion led by Nathaniel Bacon in 1676.

Bacon was an English aristocrat who had recently migrated to Virginia. The immediate cause of his rebellion was a disagreement between him and the colony's royal governor William Berkeley over Indian policy. Bacon's followers were mainly white indentured servants and former indentured servants who resented the control exercised by the tobacco-planting elite over the colony's resources and government. That Bacon also appealed to black slaves to join his rebellion indicates that poor white and black people still had a chance to unite against the **master class**.

Before such a class-based, biracial alliance could be realized, Bacon died of dysentery, and his rebellion collapsed. But the uprising convinced the colony's elite that continuing to rely on white agricultural laborers, who could become free and get guns, was dangerous. By switching from indentured white servants to an enslaved black labor force that would never become free or control firearms, the planters hoped to avoid class conflict among white people. Increasingly thereafter, white Americans perceived that both their freedom from class conflict and their prosperity rested on denying freedom to black Americans.

Plantation Slavery, 1700–1750

The reliance of Chesapeake planters on slavery to meet their labor needs was the result of racial prejudice, the declining availability of white indentured servants, the increasing availability of Africans, and fear of white class conflict. When, following the shift from indentured white to enslaved black labor, the demand for tobacco in Europe increased sharply, the newly dominant slave labor system expanded rapidly.

TOBACCO COLONIES

Between 1700 and 1770, some 80,000 Africans arrived in the tobacco colonies, and even more African Americans were born into slavery there (see Figure 3–1). Tobacco planting spread from Virginia and Maryland to Delaware and North Carolina and from the coastal plain to the foothills of the Appalachian Mountains. In the process, American slavery began to assume the form it kept for the next 165 years.

By 1750, 144,872 slaves lived in Virginia and Maryland, accounting for 61 percent of all the slaves in British North America. Another 40,000 slaves lived in the rice-producing regions of South Carolina and Georgia, accounting for 17 percent. Unlike the sugar colonies of the Caribbean, where white people were a tiny minority, they constituted a majority in the tobacco colonies and a large minority in the rice colonies. Also, most white southerners did not own slaves. Nevertheless the economic development of the region depended on enslaved black laborers.

The conditions under which those laborers lived varied. Most slaveholders farmed small tracts of land and owned fewer than five slaves. These masters and their slaves worked together and developed close personal relationships. Other masters owned thousands of acres of land and rarely saw most of their slaves. During the early eighteenth century, the great planters divided their slaves among several small holdings. They did this to avoid concentrating potentially rebellious Africans in one area. As the proportion of newly arrived Africans in the slave population declined later in the century, larger concentrations of slaves became more common.

Before the mid-eighteenth century, nearly all slaves—both men and women—worked in the fields. On the smaller farms, they worked with their master. On larger estates, they worked for an overseer, who was

FROM SERVITUDE TO SLAVERY

1619 Thirty-two Africans reported to be living at Jamestown; twenty more arrive

1621 Anthony Johnson arrives at Jamestown

1624 First documented birth of a black child occurs at Jamestown

1640 John Punch is sentenced to servitude for life

1651 Anthony Johnson receives estate of 250 acres

1661 House of Burgesses (the Virginia colonial legislature) recognizes that black servants would retain that status throughout their life

1662 House of Burgesses affirms that a child's status—slave or free—follows the status of her or his mother

1619–1662

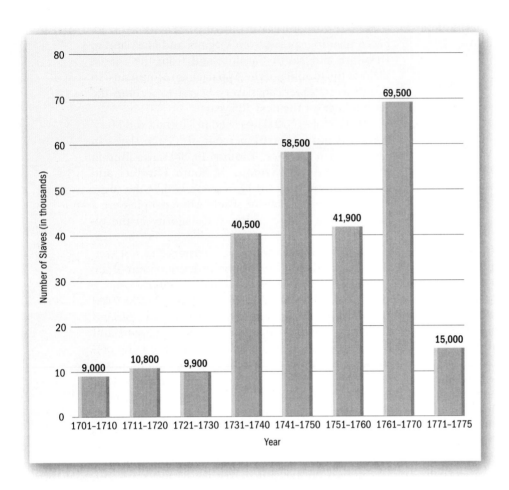

FIGURE 3–1 AFRICANS BROUGHT AS SLAVES TO BRITISH NORTH AMERICA, 1701–1775.

The rise in the number of captive Africans shipped to British North America during the early eighteenth century reflects the increasing dependence of British planters on African slave labor. The declines in slave imports during the periods 1751 to 1760 and 1771 ro 1775 resulted from disruptions to commerce associated with the French and Indian War (or Seven Years' War) and the struggle between the colonies and Great Britain that preceded the American War for Independence. Source: R. C. Simmons, *The American Colonies: From Settlement to Independence* (New York: David McKay, 1976).

tive to which both slaves and masters looked forward was the annual harvest festival. These festivals were held in both Africa and Europe and became common throughout the British colonies early in the eighteenth century.

After 1750 some black men began to hold such skilled occupations on plantations as carpenter, smith, carter, cooper, miller, sawyer, tanner, and shoemaker. By 1768 one South Carolina planter noted that "in established Plantations, the Planter has Tradesmen of all kinds in his Gang of Slaves, and 'tis a Rule with them, never to pay Money for what can be made upon their Estates, not a Lock, a Hinge, or a Nail if they can avoid it." Black women had less access to skilled occupations. When they did not work in the fields, they were domestic servants in the homes of their masters, cooking, washing, cleaning, and caring for children. These duties could be extremely taxing, because, unlike fieldwork, they did not end when the sun went down.

usually white. Like other agricultural workers, enslaved African Americans normally worked from sunup to sundown with breaks for food and rest. Even during colonial times, they usually had Sunday off.

From the beginnings of slavery in North America, masters tried to make slaves work harder and faster while slaves sought to conserve their energy, take breaks, and socialize with each other. African men regarded field labor as women's work and tried to avoid it if possible. But, especially if they had incentives, enslaved Africans could be efficient workers. One incen-

LOW-COUNTRY SLAVERY

South of the tobacco colonies, on the coastal plain or low country of Carolina and Georgia, a distinctive slave society developed (see Map 3–1). The influence of the West Indian plantation system was much stronger here than in the Chesapeake, and rice, not tobacco, became the staple crop.

The first British settlers who arrived in 1670 at Charleston (in what would later become South Carolina) were mainly immigrants from Barbados, rather than England. Many of them had been slaveholders on that island and brought slaves with them. Therefore, in the low country, black people were never indentured servants. They were chattel from the start. The region's subtropical climate discouraged white settlement and encouraged dependence on black labor the way it did in the sugar islands. During the early years of settlement, nearly one-third of the immigrants were African, most of them male. By the early eighteenth century, more Africans had arrived than white people. White Carolinians also enslaved more American Indians than other British colonists did, and during the early 1700s, Indians accounted for approximately one-quarter of

Negroes for Sale.

A Cargo of very fine stout Men and Women, in good order and fit for immediate service, just imported from the Windward Coast of Africa, in the Ship Two Brothers.—Conditions are one half Cash or Produce, the other half payable the first of January next, giving Bond and Security if required.

The Sale to be opened at 10 o'Clock each Day, in Mr. Bourdeaux's Yard, at No. 48, on the Bay.

May 19, 1784.   JOHN MITCHELL.

Thirty Seasoned Negroes

To be Sold for Credit, at Private Sale.

AMONGST which is a Carpenter, none of whom are known to be dishonest.

Also, to be sold for Cash, a regular bred young Negroe Man-Cook, born in this Country, who served several Years under an exceeding good French Cook abroad, and his Wife a middle aged Washer-Woman, (both very honest) and their two Children. Likewise, a young Man a Carpenter.

For Terms apply to the Printer.

Sales like the one announced in this 1784 broadside were common since slavery had been established in the low country ninety years earlier. South Carolina and Georgia remained dependent on imported slaves for much longer than did the Chesapeake and the North.

the colony's slave population. Carolina also became the center of an Indian slave trade. Although official colonial policy sought to keep Africans and Indians apart, black slaves sometimes helped acquire and transport Indian slaves. Carolina exported Indian slaves to the West Indies and to other mainland British colonies.

By 1740 the Carolina low country had 40,000 slaves, who constituted 90 percent of the population in the region around Charleston. In all, 94,000 Africans arrived at Charleston between 1706 and 1776, which made it North America's leading port of entry for Africans during the eighteenth century. A Swiss immigrant commented in 1737 that the region "looks more like a negro country than like a country settled by white people."

During its first three decades, Carolina supplied Barbados with beef and lumber. Because West Africans from the Gambia River region were skilled herders, white settlers sought them out as slaves. Starting around 1700, however, the low-country planters concentrated on growing rice. This crop had been grown in West Africa for thousands of years, and many of the enslaved Africans who reached Carolina had the skill required to cultivate it in America. Economies of scale, in which an industry

MAP EXPLORATION

To explore this interactive map, go to

http://www.prenhall.com/hine4/map3.1

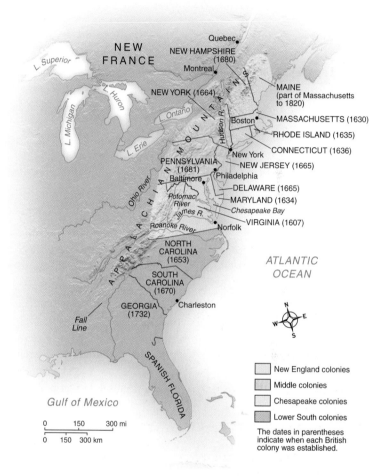

MAP 3–1   REGIONS OF COLONIAL NORTH AMERICA, 1683–1763.
The British colonies on the North American mainland were divided into four regions. They were bordered on the south by Spanish Florida and to the west by regions claimed by France.

▶▶ *How did African Americans in the British colonies benefit from the close proximity of regions controlled by France amd Spain?*

becomes more efficient as it grows larger, were more important in the production of rice than tobacco. Although tobacco could be profitably produced on small farms, rice required large acreages. Therefore, large plantations on a scale similar to those on the sugar islands of the West Indies became the rule in the low country.

In 1732 King George II of England chartered the colony of Georgia to serve as a buffer between South Carolina and Spanish Florida. James Oglethorpe, who

A DESCRIPTION OF AN EIGHTEENTH-CENTURY VIRGINIA PLANTATION

The following eyewitness account of a large Virginia plantation in Fairfax County indicates the sorts of skilled labor slaves performed by the mid-eighteenth century. George Mason, one of Virginia's leading statesmen during the Revolutionary War era, owned this plantation, which he named Gunston Hall in 1758. The account is by one of Mason's sons.

My father had among his slaves carpenters, coopers, sawyers, blacksmiths, tanners, curriers, shoemakers, spinners, weavers and knitters, and even a distiller. His woods furnished timber and plank for the carpenters and coopers, and charcoal for the blacksmith, his cattle killed for his own consumption and for sale supplied skins for tanners, curriers, and shoemakers, and his sheep gave wool and his fields produced cotton and flax for the weavers and spinners, and his orchards fruit for the distiller. His carpenters and sawyers built and kept in repair all the dwelling-houses, barns, stables, ploughs, harrows, gates, &c., on the plantations and the outhouses at the home house. His coopers made the hogsheads the tobacco was prized in and the tight casks to hold the cider and other liquors. The tanners and curriers with the proper vats &c., tanned and dressed the skins as well for upper as for lower leather to the full amount of the consumption of the estate, and shoemakers made them into shoes for the negroes. . . . The blacksmith did all the iron work required by the establishment, as making and repairing ploughs, harrows, teeth chains, bolts, &c., &c. The spinners, weavers and knitters made all the coarse cloths and stockings used by the negroes, and nearly all worn by the children of it. The distiller made every fall a good deal of apple, peach and persimmon brandy. . . . Moreover, all the beeves and hogs for consumption or sale were driven up and slaughtered there at the proper seasons, and whatever was to be preserved was salted and packed away for after distribution.

🌿 *What does this passage indicate about plantation life in mid-eighteenth-century Virginia?*

🌿 *How does the description of black people presented here compare to the passage from the South Carolina statute book that begins this chapter?*

Source: Edmond S. Morgan, *Virginians at Home: Family Life in the Eighteenth Century* (Williamsburg, VA: Colonial Williamsburg, 1952), 53–54.

received the royal charter, wanted to establish a refuge for England's poor, who were expected to become virtuous through their own labor. Consequently, in 1734 he and the colony's other trustees banned slavery in Georgia. But economic difficulties combined with land hunger among white South Carolinians soon led to the ban's repeal. During the 1750s, rice cultivation and slavery spread into Georgia's coastal plain. By 1773 Georgia had as many black people—15,000—as white people.

As on Barbados, absentee plantation owners became the rule in South Carolina and Georgia. In these colonies planters preferred to live in Charleston or Savannah where sea breezes provided relief from the heat. Meanwhile enslaved Africans on low-country plantations suffered from a high mortality rate from diseases, overwork, and poor treatment just as did their counterparts on Barbados and other sugar islands. Therefore, unlike the slave population in the Chesapeake colonies, the slave population in the low country did not grow by natural reproduction—rather than through continued arrivals from Africa—until shortly before the American Revolution.

Low-country slave society developed striking paradoxes in race relations. As the region's black population grew, white people became increasingly fearful of revolt, and by 1698 Carolina had the strictest slave code in North America. In 1721, Charleston organized a "Negro watch" to enforce a curfew on its black population, and watchmen could shoot recalcitrant Africans and African Americans on sight. Yet, as the passage that begins this chapter indicates, black people in Carolina faced the quandary of being both feared and needed by white people. Even as persons of European descent grew fearful of black revolt, the colony in 1704 authorized the arming of enslaved black men when needed for defense against Indian and Spanish raids.

Of equal significance was the appearance in Carolina and to some extent in Georgia of distinct classes among people of color. Like the low-country society itself, such classes were more similar to those in the Caribbean sugar islands than in the mainland colonies to the north. A Creole population that had absorbed European values lived in close proximity to white people in Charleston and Savannah. Members of this Creole population were frequently mixed-race relatives of their masters and enjoyed social and economic privileges denied to slaves who labored on the nearby rice plantations. Yet this urban mixed-race class was under constant white supervision.

In contrast, slaves who lived in the country retained considerable autonomy in their daily routines. The intense cultivation required to produce rice encouraged the evolution of a "task system" of labor on the low-country plantations. Rather than working in gangs as in the tobacco colonies, slaves on rice plantations had daily tasks. When they completed these tasks, they could work on plots of land assigned to them or do what they pleased without white supervision. Because black people were the great majority in the low-country plantations, they also preserved more of their African heritage than did black people who lived in the region's cities or in the more northerly British mainland colonies.

Slave Life in Early America

Little evidence survives of the everyday lives of enslaved Africans and African Americans in colonial North America. This is because they, along with American Indians and most white people of that era, were poor. They had few possessions, lived in flimsy housing, and kept no records. Yet recent studies provide a glimpse of their material culture.

Eighteenth-century housing for slaves was minimal and often temporary. In the Chesapeake, small log cabins predominated. They had dirt floors, brick fireplaces, wooden chimneys, and few, if any, windows. African styles of architecture were more common in coastal South Carolina and Georgia. In these regions, slaves built the walls of their houses with tabby—a mixture of lime, oyster shells, and sand—or, occasionally, mud. In either case, the houses had thatched roofs. Early in the eighteenth century, when single African men made up the mass of the slave population, these structures were used as dormitories. Later they housed generations of black families.

The amount of furniture and cooking utensils the cabins contained varied from place to place and according to how long the cabins were occupied. In some cabins, the only furniture consisted of wooden boxes for both storage and seating and planks for beds. But a 1697 inventory of items contained in a slave cabin in Virginia includes chairs, a bed, a large iron kettle, a brass kettle, an iron pot, a frying pan, and a "beer barrel." Enslaved black people, like contemporary Indians and white people, used hollowed-out gourds for cups and carted water in wooden buckets for drinking, cooking, and washing. As the eighteenth century progressed, slave housing on large plantations became more substantial, and slaves acquired tables, linens, chamber pots, and oil lamps. Yet primitive, poorly furnished log cabins persisted in many regions even after the abolition of slavery in 1865.

SLAVES' QUARTERS IN THE CELLAR OF THE OLD KNICKERBOCKER MANSION.

Thomas Coram, "View of Mulberry Street, (House and Street)." About 1770, Thomas Coram painted the slave quarters and the master's house at Mulberry Plantation, located near Charleston, South Carolina. The slave cabins with their high-pitched roofs were influenced by West African architecture.   Oil on paper, 10 x 17.6 cm, Gibbes Museum of Art, Carolina Art Association.

At first, slave dress was minimal during summer. Men wore breechcloths, women wore skirts, leaving their upper bodies bare, and children went naked until puberty. Later men wore shirts, trousers, and hats while working in the fields. Women wore shifts (loose, simple dresses) and covered their heads with handkerchiefs. In winter, masters provided heavier cotton and woolen clothing and cheap leather shoes. In the early years, much of the clothing, or at least the cloth used to make it, came from England. Later, as the account of George Mason's Gunston Hall plantation indicates, homespun fabric made by slaves replaced English cloth. From the seventeenth century onward, slave women brightened clothing with dyes made from bark, decorated clothing with ornaments, and created African-style headwraps, hats, and hairstyles. In this manner, African Americans retained a sense of personal style compatible with West African culture.

Food consisted of corn, yams, salt pork, and occasionally salt beef and salt fish. Slaves also caught fish and raised chickens and rabbits. When, during the eighteenth century, farmers in the Chesapeake began planting wheat, slaves baked biscuits. In the South Carolina low country, rice became an important part of African-American diets, but even there corn was the staple. During colonial times, slaves occasionally supplemented this limited diet with vegetables, such as cabbage, cauliflower, black-eyed peas, turnips, collard greens, and rutabagas, that they raised in their own gardens.

Miscegenation and Creolization

When Africans first arrived in the Chesapeake during the early seventeenth century, they interacted culturally and physically with white indentured servants and with American Indians. This mixing of peoples changed all three groups. Interracial sexual contacts—miscegenation—produced people of mixed race. Meanwhile, cultural exchanges became an essential part of the process of creolization that led African parents to produce African-American children. When, as often happened, miscegenation and creolization occurred together, the change was both physical and cultural. However, the dominant British minority in North America during the colonial period defined persons of mixed race as black. Although enslaved mulattoes—those of mixed African and European ancestry—enjoyed some advantages over slaves who had a purely African ancestry, mulattoes as a group did not receive enhanced legal status.

Miscegenation between blacks and whites and blacks and Indians was extensive throughout British North America during the seventeenth and eighteenth centuries. But it was less extensive and accepted than it was in the European sugar colonies in the Caribbean, in Latin America, or in French Canada, where many French men married Indian women. British North America was exceptional because many more white women migrated there than to Canada or the Caribbean. Therefore white men were far less likely to take black or Indian wives and concubines. Sexual relations between Africans and Indians were also more limited than they were elsewhere because the coastal Indian population had drastically declined before large numbers of Africans arrived.

Yet miscegenation between black people and the remaining Indians was extensive, and there were striking examples of black-white marriage in seventeenth-century Virginia. In 1656 in Northumberland County, a mulatto woman named Elizabeth Kay successfully sued for her freedom and immediately thereafter married her white lawyer. In Norfolk County in 1671, Francis Skiper had to pay a tax on his wife Anne because she was black. In Westmoreland County in 1691, Hester Tate, a white indentured servant, and her husband James Tate, a black slave, had four children; one was apprenticed to her master, and the other three to his.

Colonial assemblies banned such interracial marriages mainly to keep white women from bearing mulatto children. The assemblies feared that having free white mothers might allow persons of mixed race to sue and gain their freedom, thereby creating a legally recognized mixed-race class. Such a class, wealthy white people feared, would blur the distinction between the dominant and subordinate races and weaken white supremacy. The assemblies did far less to prevent white male masters from sexually exploiting their black female slaves—although they considered such exploitation immoral—because the children of such liaisons would be slaves.

The Origins of African-American Culture

Creolization and miscegenation transformed the descendants of the Africans who arrived in North America into African Americans. Historians long believed that in this process the Creoles lost their African heritage. But since Melville J. Herskovits published *The Myth of the Negro Past* in 1941, scholars have found many African legacies not only in African-American culture but in American culture in general.

The second generation of people of African descent in North America did lose their parents' native languages and their ethnic identity as Igbos, Angolas, or Senegambians. But they retained a generalized West African heritage and passed it on to their descendants. Among the major elements of that heritage were family structure and notions of kinship, religious concepts and practices, African words and modes of expression, musical style and instruments, cooking methods and foods, folk literature, and folk arts.

The preservation of the West African extended family was the basis of African-American culture. Because most Africans imported into the British colonies during the late seventeenth and early eighteenth centuries were males, most black men of that era could not have wives and children. It was not until the Atlantic slave trade declined briefly during the 1750s that sex ratios became more balanced and African-American family life began to flourish. Without that family life, black people could not have maintained as much of Africa as they did.

Even during the Middle Passage, enslaved Africans created "fictive kin relationships" for mutual support, and in dire circumstances, African Americans continued to improvise family structures. By the mid-eighteenth century, however, extended black families based on biological relationships dominated. Black people retained knowledge of their kinship ties to second and third cousins over several generations and wide stretches of territory. These extended families had roots in Africa, but were also a result of—and a reaction to—slavery. West African **incest taboos** encouraged slaves to pick mates who lived on plantations other than their own. The sale of slaves away from their immediate families also tended to extend families over wide areas. Once established, such far-flung kinship relationships helped others, who were forced to leave home, to adapt to new conditions under a new master. Kinfolk also sheltered escapees.

Extended families also influenced African-American naming practices, which reinforced family ties. Africans named male children after close relatives. This custom survived in America because boys were more likely to be separated from their parents by being sold than girls were. Having one's father's or grandfather's name preserved one's family identity. Also when, early in the eighteenth century, more African Americans began to use surnames, they clung to the name of their original master. This reflected a West African predisposition to link a family name with a certain location. Like taking a parent's name, it helped maintain family relationships despite repeated scatterings.

The result was that African Americans preserved given and family names over many generations. Black men continued to bear such African names as Cudjo, Quash, Cuffee, and Sambo, and black women such names as Quasheba and Juba. Even when masters imposed demeaning classical names, such as Caesar, Pompey, Venus, and Juno, black Americans passed them on from generation to generation.

Bible names did not become common among African Americans until the mid-eighteenth century. This was because prior to that time masters often refused to allow slaves to be converted to Christianity. As a result, African religions—both indigenous and Islamic—persisted in parts of America well into the nineteenth century. The indigenous religions in particular maintained a premodern perception of the unity of the natural and the supernatural, the secular and the sacred, and the living and the dead. Black Americans

This eighteenth-century painting of slaves on a South Carolina plantation provides graphic proof of the continuities between West African culture and the emerging culture of African Americans. The religious dance, the drum and banjo, and elements of the participants' clothing are all West African in origin.   Abby Aldrich, Rockefeller Folk Art Museum, Williamsburg, VA.

continued to perform an African circle dance known as the "ring shout" at funerals, and they decorated graves with shells and pottery in the West African manner. They looked to recently arrived Africans for religious guidance, held bodies of water to be sacred, remained in daily contact with their ancestors through **spirit possession**, and practiced **divination** and magic. When they became ill, they turned to "herb doctors" and "root workers." Even when many African Americans began to convert to Christianity during the mid-eighteenth century, West African religious thought and practice shaped their lives.

THE GREAT AWAKENING

The major turning point in African-American religion came in conjunction with the religious revival known as the Great Awakening. This extensive social movement of the mid- to late-eighteenth century grew out of growing dissatisfaction among white Americans with a deterministic and increasingly formalistic style of Protestantism that seemed to deny most people a chance for salvation. During the early 1730s in western

Massachusetts, a Congregationalist minister named Jonathan Edwards began an emotional and participatory ministry aimed at bringing more people into the church. Later that decade, George Whitefield, an Englishman who with John Wesley founded the Methodist Church, carried a similarly evangelical style of Christianity to the mainland colonies. In his sermons, Whitefield appealed to emotions, offered salvation to all who believed in Christ, and—although he did not advocate emancipation—preached to black people as well as white people.

The Great Awakening

Some people of African descent had converted to Christianity before Whitefield's arrival in North America. But two factors had prevented widespread black conversion. First, most masters feared that converted slaves would interpret their new religious status as a step toward freedom and equality. A South Carolina minister lamented in 1713 that "the Masters of Slaves are generally of Opinion that a Slave grows worse by being a Christian; and therefore instead of instructing them in the principles of Christianity . . . malign and traduce those that attempt it." Second, many slaves, as we noted previously, continued to derive spiritual satisfaction from their ancestral religions and were not attracted to Christianity.

With the Great Awakening, however, a process of general conversion began. African Americans did indeed link the spiritual equality preached by evangelical ministers with a hope for earthly equality. They tied salvation for the soul with liberation for the body. They recognized that the preaching style Whitefield and other evangelicals adopted had much in common with West African "spirit possession." As in West African religion, eighteenth-century revivalism in North America emphasized personal rebirth, singing, movement, and emotion. The practice of total body immersion during baptism in rivers, ponds, and lakes that gave the Baptist church its name paralleled West African water rites.

Because it drew African Americans into an evangelical movement that helped shape American society, the Great Awakening increased mutual black-white acculturation. Revivalists appealed to the poor of all races and emphasized spiritual equality. Evangelical Anglican, Baptist, Methodist, and Presbyterian churches welcomed black people. Members of these biracial churches addressed each other as *brother* and *sister*. Black members took communion with white members, served as church officers, and both groups were subject to the same church discipline. By the late eighteenth century, black men were being ordained as priests and ministers and—often while still enslaved—preached to white congregations. They thereby influenced white people's perception of how services should be conducted.

Black worshipers also influenced white preachers and white religion. In 1756, a white minister in Virginia noted that African Americans spent nights in his kitchen. He recorded in his diary that "sometimes, when I have awakened about two or three a-clock in the morning, a torrent of sacred harmony poured into my chamber, and carried my mind away to Heaven."

Other factors, however, favored the development of a distinct African-American church. From the start, white churches seated black people apart from white people, belying claims to spiritual equality. Black members took communion *after* white members. Masters also tried to use religion to instill in their chattels such self-serving Christian virtues as meekness, humility, and obedience. Consequently, African Americans established their own churches when they could. Dancing, shouting, clapping, and singing became especially characteristic of their religious meetings. Black spirituals probably date from the eighteenth century, and like African-American Christianity itself, they blended West African and European elements.

African Americans also retained the West African assumption that the souls of the dead returned to their homeland and rejoined their ancestors. Reflecting this family-oriented view of death, African-American funerals were often loud and joyous occasions with dancing, laughing, and drinking. Perhaps most important, the emerging black church reinforced black people's collective identity and helped them persevere in slavery.

LANGUAGE, MUSIC, AND FOLK LITERATURE

Although African Americans did not retain their ancestral languages, those languages contributed to the **pidgins** and creolized languages that became **Black English** by the nineteenth century. It was in the low country, with its large and isolated black populations, that African-English creoles lasted the longest. The Gullah and Geechee dialects of the sea islands of South Carolina and Georgia, which combine African words and some African grammatical elements with a basically English structure, are still spoken today. In other regions, where black people were less numerous, the creole languages were less enduring. Nevertheless, they contributed many words to American—particularly southern—English. Among them are *yam, banjo* (from mbanza), *tote, goober* (peanut), *buckra* (white man), *cooter* (tortoise), *gumbo* (okra), *nanse* (spider), *samba* (dance), *tabby* (a form of concrete), and *voodoo*.

Music was another essential part of West African life, and it remained so among African Americans, who preserved an antiphonal, call-and-response style of singing with an emphasis on improvisation, complex rhythms, and a strong beat. They sang while working and during religious ceremonies. Early on, masters banned drums and horns because of their potential for long-distance communication among slaves. But the African banjo survived in America, and African Americans quickly adopted the violin and guitar. At night, in their cabins or around communal fires, slaves accompanied these instruments with bones and spoons. Music may have been the most important aspect of African culture in the lives of American slaves. Eventually African-American music influenced all forms of American popular music.

West African folk literature also survived in North America. African tales, proverbs, and riddles—with accretions from American Indian and European stories—entertained, instructed, and united African Americans. Just as the black people on the sea islands of South Carolina and Georgia were most able to retain elements of African language, so did their folk literature remain closest to its African counterpart. Africans used tales of how weak animals like rabbits outsmarted stronger animals like hyenas and lions to symbolize the power of the common people over unjust rulers. African Americans used similar tales to portray the ability of slaves to outsmart and ridicule their masters.

THE AFRICAN-AMERICAN IMPACT ON COLONIAL CULTURE

African Americans also influenced the development of white culture. As early as the seventeenth century, black musicians performed English ballads for white audiences in a distinctively African-American style. Meanwhile, in the northern and Chesapeake colonies, people of African descent helped determine how all Americans celebrated. By the eighteenth century, slaves in these regions organized black election or coronation festivals that lasted for several days. Sometimes called *Pinkster* and ultimately derived from Dutch-American pre-Easter celebrations, these festivities included parades, athletics, food, music, dancing, and mock coronations of kings and governors. Although dominated by African Americans, they attracted white observers and a few white participants.

LIVING WORDS

3 *Bars Fight*

The African-American imprint on southern diction and phraseology is especially clear. Because black women often raised their master's children, generations of white children acquired African-American speech patterns and intonations. Black people also influenced white notions about portents, spirits, and folk remedies. Seventeenth- and eighteenth-century English lore about such things was not that different from West

This photograph depicts two versions of the African *mbanza*. They feature leather stretched across a gourd, a wooden neck, and strings made of animal gut. In America, such instruments became known as banjos.

African lore, and white Americans consulted black conjurers and "herb doctors." Black cooks in early America influenced both white southern and African-American eating habits. Preferences for barbecued pork, fried chicken, black-eyed peas, and collard and mustard greens owed much to West African culinary traditions.

African Americans also used West African culture and skills to shape the way work was done in the American South during and after colonial times. Africans accustomed to collective agricultural labor imposed the **"gang system"** on most American plantations. Masters learned that their slaves worked harder and longer in groups. Their work songs were also an African legacy, as was the slow, deliberate pace of their labor. By the mid-eighteenth century, masters often employed slaves as builders. As a result, African styles and decorative techniques influenced southern colonial architecture. Black

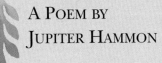

Jupiter Hammon (1711–1806?) was a favored slave living in Long Island, New York, when on Christmas day 1760 he composed "An Evening Thought. Salvation by Christ, with Penitential Cries," an excerpt of which appears here. A Calvinist preacher and America's first published black poet, Hammon was deeply influenced by the Great Awakening's emphasis on repentance and Christ's spiritual sovereignty.

Salvation comes by Jesus Christ alone,
　　The only Son of God;
Redemption now to every one,
　　That love his holy Word.
Dear Jesus we would fly to Thee,
　　And leave off every Sin,
Thy tender Mercy well agree;
　　Salvation from our King.
Salvation comes from God we know,
　　The true and only One;
It's well agreed and certain true,
　　He gave his only Son.
Lord hear our penitential Cry:
　　Salvation from above
It is the Lord that doth supply,
　　With his Redeeming Love.
Dear Jesus let the Nations cry,
　　And all the People say,
Salvation comes from Christ on high,
　　Haste on Tribunal Day.
We cry as Sinners to the Lord,
　　Salvation to obtain;
It is firmly fixt his holy Word,
　　Ye shall not cry in vain.

What elements in Hammond's poem might have appealed to African Americans of his time?

Does Hammond suggest a relationship between Christ and social justice?

Source: Dorothy Porter, ed., *Early Negro Writing, 1760–1837* (1971; reprint Baltimore: Black Classic Press, 1995).

builders introduced African-style high-peaked roofs, front porches, woodcarvings, and elaborate ironwork.

Slavery in the Northern Colonies

The British mainland colonies north of the Chesapeake had histories, cultures, demographics, and economies that differed considerably from those of the southern colonies. Organized religion played a much more important role in the foundation of most of the northern colonies than those of the South (except for Maryland). In New England, where the Pilgrims settled in 1620 and the Puritans in 1630, religious utopianism shaped colonial life. The same was true in the West Jersey portion of New Jersey, where members of the English pietist Society of Friends (Quakers) settled during the 1670s, and Pennsylvania, which William Penn founded in 1682 as a Quaker colony. Quakers, like other pietists, emphasized nonviolence and a divine spirit within all humans. These beliefs disposed some Quakers to become early opponents of slavery.

Even more important than religion in shaping life in northern British North America were a cooler climate, sufficient numbers of white laborers, lack of a staple crop, and a diversified economy. All these circumstances made black slavery in the colonial North less extensive than and different from its southern counterparts.

By the end of the colonial period during the 1770s, only 50,000 African Americans lived in the northern colonies in comparison to 400,000 in the southern colonies. In the North, black people were 4.5 percent of the total population, compared with 40 percent in the South. But, as in the South, the northern black population varied in size from place to place. By 1770 enslaved African Americans constituted 10 percent of the population of Rhode Island, New Jersey, New York, and Pennsylvania (see Figure 3–2).

New York City had a particularly large black population—20 percent of its total by 1750. This dated to 1626 when the city bore the name New Amsterdam and served as the main port of New Netherlands, a Dutch colony stretching along the Hudson River. By 1638, free and enslaved Africans constituted a large part of the city's small but cosmopolitan population. They spoke a variety of European languages and converted to a variety of Christian churches. The English conquered New Netherlands in 1664, but as late as the first decade of nineteenth century many African Americans in and about New York City still spoke Dutch.

Like all Americans during the colonial era, most northern slaves were agricultural laborers. But, in contrast to those in the South, slaves in the North typically lived in their master's house. They worked with their master, his family, and one or two other slaves on a small farm. In northern cities, which were often home-ports for slave traders, enslaved people of African descent worked as artisans, shopkeepers, messengers, domestic servants, and general laborers.

Consequently, most northern African Americans led lives that differed from their counterparts in the South. Mainly because New England had so few slaves, but also because of Puritan religious principles, slavery there was least oppressive. White people had no reason to suspect that the small and dispersed black population posed a threat of rebellion. The local slave codes were milder than in the South and, except for the ban on miscegenation, not rigidly enforced. New England slaves could legally own, transfer, and inherit property. From the early seventeenth century onward, Puritans converted to Christianity the Africans and African Americans who came among them, recognizing their spiritual equality before God.

In the middle colonies of New York, New Jersey, and Pennsylvania, where black populations were larger and hence perceived by white people to be more threatening, the slave codes were stricter and penalties harsher. But even in these colonies, the curfews imposed on Africans and African Americans and restrictions on their ability to gather together were less well enforced than they were farther south.

These conditions encouraged rapid assimilation. Because of their small numbers, frequent isolation from others of African descent, and close association with their masters, northern slaves usually had fewer opportunities to preserve an African heritage. There was an increase in African customs among black northerners between 1740 and 1770. Before that time, most northern slaves had been born or "seasoned" in the South or the West Indies. Then, during the middle decades of the eighteenth century, direct imports of African slaves into the North temporarily increased. With them came knowledge of African life. But overall, the less harsh and more peripheral nature of slavery in this region limited the retention of African perspectives, just as it allowed the slaves more freedom than most of their southern counterparts enjoyed.

Slavery in Spanish Florida and French Louisiana

Just as slavery in Britain's northern colonies differed from slavery in its southern colonies, slavery in Spanish Florida and French Louisiana—areas that later be-

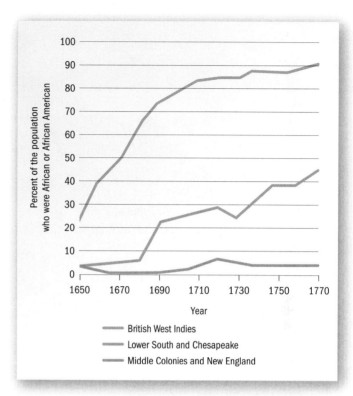

FIGURE 3–2   AFRICANS AS A PERCENTAGE OF THE TOTAL POPULATION OF THE BRITISH AMERICAN COLONIES 1650–1770.   From *Time on the Cross: The Economics of Negro Slavery* by Robert W. Fogel and Stanley L. Engerman. Copyright © 1974 by Robert W. Fogel and Stanley L. Engerman. Reprinted by permission of W. W. Norton & Company, Inc.

came parts of the United States—had distinctive characteristics. People of African descent, brought to Florida and Louisiana during the sixteenth, seventeenth, and eighteenth centuries, had different experiences from those who arrived in the British colonies. They and their descendants learned to speak Spanish or French rather than English, and they became Roman Catholics rather than Protestants. In addition, the routes to freedom were more plentiful in the Spanish and French colonies than they were in Britain's plantation colonies.

The Spanish monarchy regarded the settlement it established at St. Augustine in 1565 as primarily a military outpost, and plantation agriculture was not significant in Florida under Spanish rule. Therefore, the number of slaves in Florida remained small, and black men were needed more as soldiers than as field workers. As militiamen, they gained power that eluded slaves in most of the British colonies, and as members of the Catholic Church, they acquired social status. By

London Coffee House.

This eighteenth-century drawing of Philadelphia's London Coffee House suggests the routine nature of slave auctions in early America. The main focus is on architecture. The sale of human beings is merely incidental.   John F. Watson, "Annals of Philadelphia," being a collection of memoirs, anecdotes, and incidents of Philadelphia. The London Coffee House. The Library Company of Philadelphia.

1746 St. Augustine had a total population of 1,500, including about 400 black people. When the British took control of Florida in 1763, these local people of African descent retreated along with the city's white inhabitants to Cuba. It was with the British takeover that plantation slavery began to grow in Florida.

When the French in 1699 established their Louisiana colony in the lower Mississippi River valley, their objective, like that of the Spanish in Florida, was primarily military. In 1720 few black people (either slave or free) lived in the colony. During the following decade, Louisiana imported about six thousand slaves, most of whom were male and from Senegambia. Although they faced harsh conditions and many died, by 1731 black people outnumbered white people in the colony. Some of the Africans worked on plantations growing tobacco and indigo. But most lived in the port city of New Orleans, where many became skilled artisans, lived away from their masters, became Roman Catholics, and gained freedom. Unfortunately, New Orleans early in its history also became a place where

it was socially acceptable for white men to exploit black women sexually. This custom eventually created a sizable mixed-race population with elaborate social gradations based on the amount of white ancestry a person had and the lightness of his or her skin. Unlike the case in Florida, Louisiana's distinctive black and mixed-race population did not leave when the colony became part of the United States in 1803.

African Americans in New Spain's Northern Borderlands

What is today the southwestern portion of the United States was from the sixteenth century to 1821 the northernmost part of New Spain. Centered on Mexico, this Spanish colony reached into Texas, California, New Mexico, and Arizona. The first people of African descent who entered this huge region were members of Spanish exploratory expeditions. As we mentioned

This detail of a mural located in the Arizona capitol building shows, on its extreme right, the former slave Esteban, who wears a blue turban. During the early 1500s, shipwrecked Esteban traveled through Texas to Mexico. Later he joined Spanish expeditions that explored what are now New Mexico and Arizona.

earlier, the best known of them is Esteban, an enslaved Moor (the Spanish term for a dark-skinned Muslim) who survived a shipwreck on the Texas coast in 1529 and joined Spanish explorer Alva Núñez Cabeza de Vaca in an arduous seven-year trek from Texas to Mexico City. Esteban, a skilled interpreter, later explored regions in what are today New Mexico and Arizona. Black men also accompanied Francisco Vásquez de Coronado's 1540–1542 search across the Southwest for the mythical Seven Cities of Cibola, as well as Spanish expeditions along the upper regions of the Rio Grande in 1593 and 1598. During the seventeenth century, black soldiers participated in the Spanish conquest of Pueblo Indians. Some black or mulatto women also joined in Spanish military expeditions. The best known of them was Isabel de Olvena, who traveled with an expedition through New Mexico in 1600.

During the colonial era, however, New Spain's North American borderlands had far fewer black people than there were in the British colonies. In part this was because the total non-Indian population in the borderlands was extremely small. As late as 1792, for example, only around 3,000 colonists lived in Texas, including about 450 described as black or mulatto. There were even fewer colonists in New Mexico and California, where people of mixed African, Indian, and Spanish descent were common. Black men in the borderlands gained employment as sailors, soldiers, tradesmen, cattle herders, and day laborers. Some of them were slaves, but others had limited freedom. In contrast to the British colonies, in New Spain's border-

lands most slaves were Indians. They worked as domestics and as agricultural laborers or were marched south to Mexico where they labored in gold and silver mines.

Also in contrast to the British mainland colonies, where no formal aristocracy existed but where white insistence on racial separation gradually grew in strength, there were in New Spain's borderlands both hereditary rank and racial fluidity. In theory, throughout the Spanish empire in the Americas, "racial purity" determined social status, with Spaniards of "pure blood" at the top and Africans and Indians at the bottom. In Texas free black people and Indians suffered legal disabilities. They paid special taxes and could not own guns or travel freely. But almost all of the Spaniards who moved north from Mexico were themselves of mixed race, and people of African and Indian descent could more easily acquire status than was the case in the British colonies. In the borderlands some black men held responsible positions at Roman Catholic missions. A few acquired large land holdings called *ranchos*. In 1783 Spain's royal government began to allow black people and Indians to elevate themselves legally by paying between seven hundred and one thousand pesos, a substantial sum at the time. By this means they could acquire hereditary rank and great power over those who labored for them.

Black Women in Colonial America

The lives of black women in early North America varied according to the colony in which they lived. The differences between Britain's New England colonies and its southern colonies are particularly clear. In New England, where religion and demographics made the boundary between slavery and freedom permeable, black women distinguished themselves in a variety of ways. The thoroughly acculturated Lucy Terry Prince of Deerfield, Massachusetts, published poetry during the 1740s and gained her freedom in 1756. Other black women succeeded as bakers and weavers. But in the South, where most black women of the time lived, they had few opportunities for work beyond the tobacco and rice fields and domestic labor in the homes of their masters.

During the late seventeenth and the eighteenth centuries, approximately 90 percent of southern black women worked in the fields, as was customary for women in West Africa. White women sometimes did fieldwork as well, but masters considered black women to be tougher than white women and therefore able to do more hard physical labor. Black women also mothered their children and cooked for their families, a chore that involved

In this painting African Americans await sale to slave traders, who stand at the doorway on the left.

lugging firewood and water and tending fires as well as preparing meals. Like other women of their time, colonial black women suffered from inadequate medical attention while giving birth. But because black women worked until the moment they delivered, they were more likely than white women to experience complications in giving birth and to bear low-weight babies.

As the eighteenth century passed, more black women became house servants. Yet most jobs as maids, cooks, and body servants went to the young, the old, or the infirm. Black women also wet-nursed their master's children. None of this was easy work; those who did it were under constant white supervision and were particularly subject to the sexual exploitation that characterized chattel slavery.

European captains and crews molested and raped black women during the Middle Passage. Masters and overseers similarly used their power to force themselves on female slaves. The results were evident in the large mixed-race populations in the colonies and in the psychological damage it inflicted on African-American women and their mates. In particular, the sexual abuse of black women by white men disrupted the emerging black families in North America because black men usually could not protect their wives from it.

Although black women were more expensive than white indentured servants—because, unlike the children of white indentured servants, their children

would become their master's property—slave traders and slaveholders never valued black women as highly as they did black men. Until 1660 the British mainland colonies imported twice as many African men as women. Thereafter, the ratio dropped to three African men for every two women, and by the mid-eighteenth century, natural population growth among African Americans had corrected the sexual imbalance.

Black Resistance and Rebellion

That masters regularly used their authority to abuse black women sexually and thereby humiliate black men dramatizes the oppressiveness of a slave system based on race and physical force. Masters often rewarded black women who became their mistresses, just as masters and overseers used incentives to get more labor from field hands. But slaves who did not comply in either case faced a beating. Slavery in America was always a system that relied ultimately on physical force to deny freedom to African Americans. From its start, black men and women responded by resisting their masters as well as they could.

Such resistance ranged from sullen goldbricking (shirking assigned work) to sabotage, escape, and rebellion. Before the late eighteenth century, however, resistance and rebellion were not part of a coherent antislavery effort. Before the spread of ideas about natural human rights and universal liberty associated with the American and French revolutions, slave resistance and revolt did not aim to destroy slavery as a social system. Africans and African Americans resisted, escaped, and rebelled not as part of an effort to free all slaves. Instead, in the case of resistance, they aimed to force masters to make concessions within the framework of slavery and, in the case of escape and rebellion, to relieve themselves, their friends, and their families from intolerable disgrace and suffering.

Runaway Notices from the South Carolina Gazette, 1732 and 1737 — DOCUMENT 3-4

African men and women newly arrived in North America openly defied their masters. They frequently refused to work and often could not be persuaded by punishment to change their behavior. "You would really be surpris'd at their Perseverance," one frustrated master commented. "They often die before they can be conquered." Africans tended to escape in groups of individuals who shared a common homeland and language. When they succeeded, they usually became "outliers," living nearby and stealing from their master's estate. Less frequently, they headed west where they found a degree of safety among white frontiersmen, Indians, or interracial banditti. In 1672 Virginia's colonial government began paying bounties to anyone who killed outliers, and six decades later, the governor of South Carolina offered similar rewards. In some instances, escaped slaves, known as *maroons*—a term derived from the Spanish word *cimarron*, meaning wild—established their own settlements in inaccessible regions.

The most durable of such maroon communities in North America existed in the Spanish colony of Florida. In 1693 the Spanish king officially made this colony a refuge for slaves escaping from the British colonies, although he did not free slaves who were already there. Many such escapees joined the Seminole Indian nation and thereby gained protection during the period between 1763 and 1783 when the British ruled Florida and after 1821 when the United States took control. It was in part to destroy this refuge for former slaves that the United States fought the Seminole War from 1835 to 1842. Other maroon settlements existed in the South Carolina and Georgia backcountry and the Great Dismal Swamp of southern Virginia.

As slaves became acculturated, forms of slave resistance changed. To avoid punishment, African Americans replaced open defiance with more subtle day-to-day obstructionism. They malingered, broke tools, mistreated domestic animals, destroyed crops, poisoned their masters, and stole. Not every slave who acted this way, of course, was consciously resisting enslavement, but masters assumed that they were. In 1770, Benjamin Franklin, who owned slaves, complained to a European friend, "Perhaps you may imagine the Negroes to be mild-tempered, tractable Kind of People. Some of them indeed are so. But the Majority are of plotting Disposition, dark, sullen, malicious, revengeful and cruel in the highest Degree." Acculturation also brought different escape patterns. Increasingly, the more assimilated slaves predominated among escapees. Most of them were young men who left on their own and relied on their knowledge of American society to pass as free. Although some continued to head for maroon settlements, most sought safety among relatives, in towns, or in the North Carolina piedmont where there were few slaves.

Rebellions were far rarer in colonial North America than resistance or escape. More and larger rebellions broke out during the early eighteenth century in Jamaica and Brazil. This discrepancy resulted mainly from demographics: in the sugar-producing colonies, black people outnumbered white people by six or eight to one, but in British North America black people were a majority only in the low country. The larger the proportion of slaves in a population, the more likely they were to rebel. Also, by the mid-eighteenth century, most male slaves in the British mainland colonies were Creoles with families, who had more to lose from a failed rebellion than did the single African men who made up the bulk of the slave population farther south.

The Slaves Revolt in South Carolina in 1739   3-5   DOCUMENT

Nevertheless, there were waves of rebellion in British North America during the years from 1710 to 1722 and 1730 to 1741. Men born in Africa took the lead in these revolts, and the two most notable ones occurred in New York City in 1712 and near Charleston, South Carolina, in 1739. In New York, twenty-seven Africans, taking revenge for "hard usage," set fire to an outbuilding. When white men arrived to put out the blaze, the rebels attacked them with muskets, hatchets, and swords. They killed nine of the white men and wounded six. Shortly thereafter, local militia units captured the rebels, six of whom killed themselves. The other twenty-one were executed—some brutally. In 1741 a conspiracy to revolt in the same city led to another mass execution. Authorities put to death thirty black people and four white people, convicted of helping them.

Even more frightening for most white people was the rebellion that began at Stono Bridge within twenty miles of Charleston in September 1739. Under the leadership of a man named Jemmy or Tommy, twenty slaves, who had recently arrived from Angola, broke into a "weare-house, & then plundered it of guns & ammunition." They killed the warehousemen, left their severed heads on the building's steps, and fled toward Florida. Other slaves joined the Angolans until their numbers reached one hundred. They sacked plantations and killed approximately thirty more white people. But when they stopped to celebrate their victories and beat drums to attract other slaves, planters on horseback aided by Indians routed them, killing forty-four and dispersing the rest. Many of the rebels, including their leader, remained at large for up to three years, as did the spirit of insurrection. In 1740 Charleston authorities arrested 150 slaves and hanged ten daily to quell that spirit.

In South Carolina and other southern colonies, white people never entirely lost their fear of slave revolt. Whenever slaves rebelled or were rumored to rebel, the fear became intense. As the quotation that begins this chapter indicates, the unwillingness of many Africans and African Americans to submit to enslavement pushed white southerners into a siege mentality that became a determining factor in American history.

AFRICAN-AMERICAN EVENTS	AMERICAN EVENTS
	1450
	1492 Columbus reaches the West Indies
	1497 John Cabot's voyage to North America for England
	1500
1526 African slaves arrive at failed Spanish colony in present-day South Carolina One hundred African slaves arrive in present-day South Carolina	**1519** Spanish conquest of Aztecs
	1532 Spanish conquest of Incas
1529 Esteban shipwrecked on Texas coast	
	1550
1565 Africans help establish St. Augustine	**1565** St. Augustine established
	1587 Roanoke colony established
	1600
1619 Twenty-two Africans reported to be living in Jamestown; twenty more arrive	**1607** Jamestown established
	1612 Tobacco cultivated in Virginia by John Rolfe
1624 First documented African-American child born at Jamestown	

CONCLUSION

Studying the history of black people in early America is both painful and exhilarating. It is painful to learn of their enslavement, the emergence of racism in its modern form, and the loss of so much of the African heritage. But it is exhilarating to learn how much of that heritage Africans and African Americans preserved, how they resisted their oppressors and forged strong family bonds, and how an emerging African-American culture began to influence all aspects of American society.

The varieties of black life during the colonial period also help us understand the complexity of African-American society later in American history. Although they had much in common, black people in the Chesapeake, in the low country, in Britain's northern colonies, in Spanish Florida, in French Louisiana, and in New Spain's borderlands had different experiences, different relationships with white people and Indians, and different prospects. Those who lived in the fledgling colonial towns and cities differed from those who were agricultural laborers. The lives of those who worked on small farms were quite different from the lives of those who served on large plantations.

Finally, African-American history during the colonial era raises fundamental issues about contingency and determinism in human events. Did economic necessity, racism, and class interest make the development of chattel slavery in the Chesapeake inevitable? Or had things gone otherwise (e.g., if Bacon's Rebellion had not occurred or had turned out differently), might African Americans in that region have retained more rights and more access to freedom? What then would have been the impact on the colonies to the north and south of the Chesapeake?

RECOMMENDED READING

Ira Berlin. *Many Thousands Gone: The First Two Centuries of Slavery in North America.* Cambridge, MA: Belknap Press, 1998. Berlin presents an impressive synthesis of black life in slavery during the seventeenth and eighteenth centuries that emphasizes the ability of black people to shape their lives in conflict with the will of masters.

Winthrop D. Jordan. *White over Black: American Attitudes toward the Negro, 1550–1812.* Chapel Hill: University of North Carolina Press, 1968. This classic study provides a probing and detailed analysis of the cultural and psychological forces that led white people to enslave black people in early America.

Peter Kolchin. *American Slavery, 1619–1877.* New York: Hill and Wang, 1993. This is the best brief study of the development of slavery in America. It is particularly useful on African-American community and culture.

Philip D. Morgan. *Slave Counterpoint: Black Culture in the Eighteenth-Century Chesapeake and Lowcountry.* Chapel Hill: University of North Carolina Press, 1998. Comparative history at its best, this book illuminates the lives of black people in important parts of British North America.

Oscar Reiss. *Blacks in Colonial America.* Jefferson, NC: McFarland, 1997. Although short on synthesis and eccentric in interpretation, this book is packed with information about black life in early America.

Peter H. Wood. *Black Majority: Negroes in Colonial South Carolina from 1670 through the Stono Rebellion.* New York: Norton, 1974. This is the best account available of slavery and the origins of African-American culture in the colonial low country.

Donald R. Wright. *African Americans in the Colonial Era: From African Origins through the American Revolution,* 2d ed. Arlington Heights, IL: Harlan Davidson, 2000. Wright provides a brief but well-informed survey of black history during the colonial period.

ADDITIONAL BIBLIOGRAPHY

COLONIAL SOCIETY

Wesley Frank Craven. *The Southern Colonies in the Seventeenth Century, 1607–1689.* Baton Rouge: Louisiana State University Press, 1949.

Jack P. Greene. *Pursuits of Happiness: The Social Development of Early Modern British Colonies and the Formation of American Culture.* Chapel Hill: University of North Carolina Press, 1988.

John J. McCusker and Russell R. Menard. *The Economy of British America, 1607–1789.* Chapel Hill: University of North Carolina Press, 1985.

Gary B. Nash. *Red, White, and Black: The Peoples of Early America,* 3d ed. Englewood Cliffs, NJ: Prentice Hall, 1992.

ORIGINS OF SLAVERY AND RACISM IN THE WESTERN HEMISPHERE

Robin Blackburn. *The Making of New World Slavery: From the Baroque to the Modern 1492–1800.* New York: Verso, 1997.

David Brion Davis. *Inhuman Bondage: The Rise and Fall of Slavery in the New World.* New York: Oxford University Press, 2006.

Seymour Drescher. *From Slavery to Freedom: Comparative Studies of the Rise and Fall of Atlantic Slavery.* New York: New York University Press, 1999.

David Eltis. *The Rise of African Slavery in the Americas.* New York: Cambridge University Press, 2000.

Frank Tannenbaum. *Slave and Citizen: The Negro in the Americas.* New York: Knopf, 1946.

Betty Wood. *The Origins of American Slavery: Freedom and Bondage in the English Colonies.* New York: Hill and Wang, 1997.

1650

1640–1670
Evidence of emergence of black slavery in Virginia

1670
Carolina established

1676
Bacon's Rebellion

1693
Spanish Florida welcomes escaped slaves from the British colonies

1699
Louisiana established

1700

1712
New York City slave revolt

c. 1700
Rice cultivation begun in the Carolina low country

1739
Stono slave revolt

1732
Georgia chartered

1741
New York City revolt conspiracy

c. 1738
The Great Awakening begins

1750

1776
Declaration of Independence

1754–1763
French and Indian War

1800

AFRICAN-AMERICAN EVENTS   **NATIONAL EVENTS**

THE CHESAPEAKE

Barbara A. Faggins. *Africans and Indians: An Afrocentric Analysis of Contacts between Africans and Indians in Colonial Virginia.* New York: Routledge, 2001.

Allan Kulikoff. *Tobacco and Slaves: The Development of Southern Cultures in the Chesapeake, 1680–1800.* Chapel Hill: University of North Carolina Press, 1986.

Gloria L. Main. *Tobacco Colony: Life in Early Maryland, 1650–1720.* Princeton, NJ: Princeton University Press, 1982.

Edmund S. Morgan. *American Slavery, American Freedom: The Ordeal of Colonial Virginia.* New York: Norton, 1975.

Isaac Rhys. *The Transformation of Virginia, 1740–1790.* New York: Norton, 1982.

Mechal Sobel. *The World They Made Together: Black and White Values in Eighteenth-Century Virginia.* Princeton, NJ: Princeton University Press, 1987.

THE CAROLINA AND GEORGIA LOW COUNTRY

Judith Ann Carney. *Black Rice: The African Origins of Rice Cultivation in the Americas.* Cambridge, MA: Harvard University Press, 2001.

Alan Gallay. *The Indian Slave Trade: The Rise of the English Empire in the American South, 1670–1717.* New Haven: Yale University Press, 2002.

Daniel C. Littlefield. *Rice and Slaves: Ethnicity and the Slave Trade in Colonial South Carolina.* Baton Rouge: Louisiana State University Press, 1981.

Julia Floyd Smith. *Slavery and Rice Culture in Low Country Georgia, 1750–1860.* Knoxville: University of Tennessee Press, 1985.

Betty Wood. *Slavery in Colonial Georgia, 1730–1775.* Athens: University of Georgia Press, 1984.

THE NORTHERN COLONIES

Lorenzo J. Greene. *The Negro in Colonial New England, 1620–1776.* 1942. Reprint, New York: Atheneum, 1968.

Leslie M. Harris. *In the Shadow of Slavery: African Americans in New York City, 1626–1863.* Chicago: University of Chicago Press, 2003.

Graham R. Hodges. *Root and Branch: African Americans in New York and East Jersey, 1613–1863.* Chapel Hill: University of North Carolina Press, 1999.

Edgar J. McManus. *Black Bondage in the North.* Syracuse, NY: Syracuse University Press, 1973.

William D. Piersen. *Black Yankees: The Development of an Afro-American Subculture in Eighteenth-Century New England.* Amherst: University of Massachusetts Press, 1988.

SPANISH BORDERLANDS AND LOUISIANA

Lynn Robinson Bailey. *Indian Slave Trade and the Southwest: A Study of Slave-Taking and the Traffic in Indian Captives.* Los Angeles: Westernlore, 1966.

Gwendolyn Midlo Hall. *Africans in Colonial Louisiana: The Development of Afro-Creole Culture in the Eighteenth Century.* Baton Rouge: Louisiana State University Press, 1992.

Thomas N. Ingersoll. *Mammon and Manon in Early New Orleans: The First Slave Society in the Deep South, 1718–1819.* Knoxville: University of Tennessee Press, 1999.

John L. Kessell. *Spain in the Southwest: A Narrative History of Colonial New Mexico, Arizona, Texas, and California.* Norman: University of Oklahoma Press, 2002.

Jane Landers. *Black Society in Spanish Florida.* Urbana: University of Illinois Press, 1999.

Michael M. Swann. *Migrants in the Mexican North: Mobility, Economy, and Society in a Colonial World.* Boulder, CO: Westview, 1989.

Quintard Taylor. *In Search of the Racial Frontier: African Americans in the American West, 1528–1990.* New York: Norton, 1998.

AFRICAN-AMERICAN CULTURE

John B. Boles. *Black Southerners, 1619–1869.* Lexington: University Press of Kentucky, 1983.

Joanne Brooks. *American Lazarus: Religion and the Rise of African American and Native American Literature.* New York: Oxford University Press, 2003.

Dickson D. Bruce. *The Origins of African American Literature, 1680–1865.* Charlottesville: University Press of Virginia, 2001.

Margaret W. Creel. *A Peculiar People: Slave Religion and Community Culture among the Gullahs.* New York: New York University Press, 1988.

Sylvaine A. Diouf. *Servants of Allah: African Muslims Enslaved in the Americas.* New York: New York University Press, 1998.

Michael Gomez. *Exchanging Our Country Marks: The Transformation of African Identities in the Colonial and Antebellum South.* Chapel Hill: University of North Carolina Press, 1998.

Melville J. Herskovits. *The Myth of the Negro Past.* 1941. Reprint, Boston: Beacon, 1990.

Joseph E. Holloway, ed. *Africanisms in American Culture.* Bloomington: Indiana University Press, 1990.

Henry Mitchell. *Black Belief: Folk Beliefs of Blacks in America and West Africa.* New York: Harper & Row, 1975.

Sheila S. Walker, ed. *African Roots/American Culture: Africa and the Creation of the Americas.* Lanham: Rowman and Littlefield, 2001.

Joel Williamson. *New People: Miscegenation and Mulattoes in the United States.* New York: Free Press, 1980.

BLACK WOMEN IN COLONIAL AMERICA

Joan Rezner Gunderson, "The Double Bonds of Race and Sex: Black and White Women in a Colonial Virginia Parish," in Darlene Clark Hine, Wilma King, and Linda Reed, eds., *We Specialize in the Wholly Impossible: A Reader in Black Women's History.* Brooklyn, NY: Carlson, 1995.

Darlene Clark Hine and Kathleen Thompson. *A Shining Thread of Hope: The History of Black Women in America.* New York: Broadway, 1998, Chapter 1.

Jane Kamensky. *The Colonial Mosaic: American Women, 1600–1760: Rising Expectations from the Colonial Period to the American Revolution.* New York: Oxford University Press, 1995.

Jenny Sharpe. *Ghosts of Slavery: A Literary Archaeology of Black Women's Lives.* Minneapolis: University of Minnesota Press, 2003.

RESISTANCE AND REVOLT

Herbert Aptheker. *American Negro Slave Revolts.* 1943. Reprint, New York: International Publishers, 1974.

Thomas J. Davis. *A Rumor of Revolt: The "Great Negro Plot" in Colonial New York.* New York: Free Press, 1985.

Merton L. Dillon. *Slavery Attacked: Southern Slaves and Their Allies, 1619–1865.* Baton Rouge: Louisiana State University Press, 1990.

Eugene D. Genovese. *From Rebellion to Revolution: Afro-American Slave Revolts in the Making of the Modern World.* Baton Rouge: Louisiana State University Press, 1979.

Gerald W. Mullin. *Flight and Rebellion: Slave Resistance in Eighteenth-Century Virginia.* New York: Oxford University Press, 1972.

Michael Mullin. *Africa in America: Slave Aculturization and Resistance in the American South and the British Caribbean, 1736–1831.* Urbana: University of Illinois Press, 1992.

John K. Thornton. *African and Africans in the Making of the Atlantic World, 1400–1800.* New York: Cambridge University Press, 1992.

RETRACING THE ODYSSEY

African Americans at Jamestown, Colonial National Historical Park, Jamestown and Yorktown, Virginia. This program covers the period from 1619, the date of the first reports concerning black inhabitants at Jamestown, to 1705 when Virginia formally adopted a slave code.

Colonial Williamsburg, Williamsburg, Virginia. The "Enslaving Virginia Tour" allows visitors to "explore [the] conditions that led to slavery's development in the Jamestown/Virginia colony."

Charles H. Wright Museum of African American History, Detroit. The "Of the People: The African American Experience" exhibit includes material dealing with the memory of Africa and the "survival of the spirit."

 REVIEW, RESEARCH, AND INTERACT

REVIEW QUESTIONS

1. Based on your reading of this chapter, do you believe racial prejudice among British settlers in the Chesapeake led them to enslave Africans? Or did the unfree condition of the first Africans to arrive at Jamestown lead to racial prejudice among the settlers?

2. Why did vestiges of African culture survive in British North America? Did these vestiges help or hinder African Americans in dealing with enslavement?

3. Compare and contrast eighteenth-century slavery as it existed in the Chesapeake, in the low country of South Carolina and Georgia, and in the northern colonies.

4. What were the strengths and weaknesses of the black family in the eighteenth century?

5. How did enslaved Africans and African Americans preserve a sense of their own humanity?

 www.researchnavigator.com

Using the tools available in Research Navigator, consider this question:

How did the evolving economy of the British colonies come to depend on a race-based system of slavery?

 PRIMARY SOURCE DOCUMENTS

3–1 Maryland Addresses the Status of Slaves in 1664

3–2 The Selling of Joseph, 1700

3–3 A Virginian Describes the Difference between Servants and Slaves in 1722

3–4 Runaway Notices from the *South Carolina Gazette*, 1732 and 1737

3–5 The Slaves Revolt in South Carolina in 1739

3–6 Lucy Terry Prince, "Bars Fight," 1746

MAP EXPLORATION

Regions of Colonial North America, 1683–1763, p. 63

INTERACTIVE ACTIVITIES

Jamestown

Historians have suggested that early and long-lasting frontier struggles for survival left an imprint on American folklore, heritage, and national character that distinguishes the United States from older nations. An early example of this frontier struggle is the settlement of Jamestown.

The Great Awakening

In the early 1740s, an outpouring of religious fervor came to be called the Great Awakening, which had profound religious, social, and cultural effects.

4

Rising Expectations
African Americans and the Struggle for Independence

WHAT WAS THE CRISIS IN THE BRITISH EMPIRE?

WHAT DID THE DECLARATION OF INDEPENDENCE
MEAN TO AFRICAN AMERICANS?

HOW DID AFRICAN AMERICANS CONTRIBUTE
TO THE ENLIGHTENMENT?

WHAT ROLES DID AFRICAN AMERICANS
PLAY IN THE WAR FOR INDEPENDENCE?

HOW DID THE AMERICAN REVOLUTION WEAKEN SLAVERY?

◀◀ **African Americans fought on both sides** in the American War
for Independence. In this nineteenth-century painting, a
black Patriot aims his pistol at a British officer during the
Battle of Cowpens, fought in South Carolina in 1781. William
Ranney, "The Battle of Cowpens." Oil on Canvas. Photo by Sam Holland. Courtesy of South
Carolina State House.

To the Honorable Legislature of the State of Massachusetts Bay, January 13, 1777:

The petition of a great number of blacks detained in a state of slavery in the bowels of a free & Christian country humbly sheweth that your petitioners apprehend we have in common with all other men a natural and unalienable right to that freedom which the Great Parent of the Universe hath bestowed equally on all mankind, and which they have never forfeited by any compact or agreement whatever.

Lancaster Hill, et al.

◄ **Because of southern opposition,** the Declaration of Independence was edited to exclude criticism of the slave trade. Instead, the Declaration accused the British of inciting slaves to revolt against their masters.

As the preceding quotation indicates, African Americans of the 1770s understood the revolutionary thought of their time. When a large minority of America's white population demanded independence from Britain on the basis of a natural human right to freedom, many black Americans asserted their right to be liberated from slavery. It took a momentous change in outlook from that of earlier ages for either group to perceive freedom as a right. Just as momentous was the dawning awareness among white people of the contradiction of claiming freedom for themselves and denying it to others.

The Great Awakening had nurtured humanitarian opposition to slavery, but secular thought, rooted in the European Enlightenment, shaped a revolutionary ethos in America. According to the precepts of the Enlightenment, all humans had natural, God-given rights that could not be taken from them without their consent. In 1777 the African-American petitioners alluded to these precepts.

If the Enlightenment shaped the revolutionary discourse of the late eighteenth century, the French and Indian War, fought between 1754 and 1763, made the American struggle for independence possible. The outcome of that war, which pitted the British, Americans, and their American Indian allies against the French and their Indian allies, created a volatile situation in the thirteen British colonies. That situation, in turn, produced the American War for Independence and efforts by many enslaved African Americans to gain their freedom.

In this chapter we explore the African-American quest for liberty during the twenty years between 1763, when the French and Indian War ended, and 1783, when Britain recognized the independence of the United States. During this period, African Americans exercised an intellectual and political leadership that had far-ranging implications. A few black writers and scientists emerged, black soldiers fought in battle, black artisans proliferated, and—particularly in the North—black activists publicly argued against enslavement. Most important, many African Americans used the War for Independence to gain their freedom. Some were Patriots fighting for American independence. Others were Loyalists fighting for the British. Still others simply used the dislocations war caused to escape their masters.

The Crisis of the British Empire

The great struggle for empire between Great Britain and France created the circumstances within which an independence movement and rising black hopes for freedom developed in America. Starting in 1689 the British and French fought a series of wars in Europe, India, North America, Africa, and the Caribbean Sea. This great conflict climaxed during the French and Indian War that began in North America in 1754, spread in 1756 to Europe, where it was called the Seven Years' War, and from there spread to other parts of the world.

The war sprang from competing British and French efforts to control the Ohio River valley and its lucrative **fur trade**. In 1754 and 1755 the French and their Indian allies defeated Virginian and British troops in this region and then attacked the western frontier of the British colonies. Not until 1758 did Britain undertake a vigorous and expensive military effort that by 1763 had forced France to withdraw from North America. Britain took Canada from France and Florida from France's ally Spain. In compensation, Spain received New Orleans and the huge French province of Louisiana in central North America (see Map 4–1).

These changes had momentous consequences. Deprived of their ability to play off Britain against France and Spain, American Indian nations east of the Mississippi River had great difficulty resisting white encroachment. Although the Florida swamps remained a refuge for escaping slaves, fugitives lost their Spanish protectors. Americans no longer had to face French and Spanish threats on their frontiers. The bonds between Britain and the thirteen colonies rapidly weakened.

These last two consequences were closely linked. The colonial assemblies had not always supported the war effort against the French. American merchants had traded with the enemy. Therefore, after the war ended, British officials decided Americans should be taxed to pay their share of the costs of empire and their commerce should be more closely regulated. In England it seemed entirely reasonable that the government should proceed in this manner, but white Americans had become accustomed to governing themselves, trading with whom they pleased, and paying only local taxes. They were well aware that with the French and Spanish gone, they no longer needed British protection. Therefore, many of them resisted when the British Parliament asserted its power to tax and govern them.

During the 1760s Parliament repeatedly passed laws that many Americans considered oppressive. The Proclamation Line of 1763 aimed to placate Britain's Indian allies by forbidding American settlement west of the crest of the Appalachian Mountains. The Sugar Act of 1764 levied import duties designed, for the first time in colonial history, to raise revenue for Britain rather than simply to regulate American trade. In 1765 the Stamp Act, also passed to raise revenue, heavily taxed printed materials, such as deeds, newspapers, and playing cards.

The Stamp Act   ACTIVITY

In response, Americans at the Stamp Act Congress held in New York City in October 1765 took a first step toward united resistance. By agreeing not to import British goods, the congress forced Parliament in 1766 to repeal the Stamp Act. But the Sugar Act and Proclamation Line remained in force, and Parliament soon indicated that it remained determined to exercise greater control in America.

In 1767 it forced the New York assembly to provide quarters for British troops and enacted the Townshend Acts, named after the British finance minister, which taxed glass, lead, paint, paper, and tea imported into the colonies from Britain. Resistance to these taxes in Boston led the British government to station two regiments of troops there in 1768. The volatile situation this created led in 1770 to the Boston Massacre when a small detachment of British troops fired into an angry crowd, killing five Bostonians. Among the dead was a black sailor named Crispus Attucks, who had taken the lead in accosting the soldiers and became a martyr to the Patriot cause.

As it turned out, Parliament had repealed the Townshend duties, except the one on tea, before the massacre. This parliamentary retreat and a reaction against the bloodshed in Boston reduced tension between the colonies and Britain. A period of calm lasted until May 1773 when Parliament passed the Tea Act.

The Tea Act gave the British East India Company a monopoly over all tea sold in the American colonies. A huge but debt-ridden entity, the East India Company governed India for the British Empire. At the time, Americans drank a great deal of tea and Parliament hoped the tea monopoly would save the company from bankruptcy. But American merchants assumed the act was the first step in a plot to bankrupt them. Because it had huge tea reserves, the East India Company could sell its tea much more cheaply than colonial merchants could. Other Americans believed the Tea Act was a trick to get them to pay the tax on tea by lowering its price. They feared that once Americans paid the tax on tea, British leaders would use it as a precedent to raise additional taxes.

To prevent this from happening, in December 1773 Boston's radical Sons of Liberty dumped a shipload of tea into the harbor. Britain then sent more troops to Boston in early 1774 and punished the city economically. This action sparked resistance throughout the colonies and led eventually to American independence.

MAP EXPLORATION

To explore this interactive map, go to
http://www.prenhall.com/hine4/map4.1

French claims
Under French control
British
Disputed between Britain and France
Spanish

British
French
Spanish

1750

1763

MAP 4–1   EUROPEAN CLAIMS IN NORTH AMERICA, 1750 (LEFT) AND 1763 (RIGHT).

These maps illustrate the dramatic change in the political geography of North America that resulted from the British victory in the French and Indian War (1754–1763). It eliminated France as a North American power. France surrendered Canada and the Ohio River valley to Britain. Spain ceded Florida to Britain and, as compensation, received Louisiana from France.

▶ *What was the significance for African Americans of these political changes and, in particular, of Great Britain's acquisition of Florida?*

Patriot leaders organized the Continental Congress, which met in Philadelphia in September 1774 and demanded the repeal of all "oppressive" legislation. By November, Massachusetts Minutemen—members of an irregular militia—had begun to stockpile arms in the villages surrounding Boston.

In April 1775 Minutemen clashed with British troops at Lexington and Concord near Boston. This was the first battle in what became a war for independence. Shortly thereafter, Congress appointed George Washington commander in chief of the Continental Army. Before he took command, however, the American and British forces at Boston fought a bloody battle at Bunker Hill. After a year during which other armed clashes occurred and the British rejected a compromise, Congress in July 1776 declared the colonies to be independent states, and the war became a revolution.

PROFILE ✦ CRISPUS ATTUCKS

Crispus Attucks was a fugitive slave who escaped in 1750 at age twenty-seven from his Framingham, Massachusetts, master. Attucks's father was black, his mother Indian. His master described him as "a mulatto fellow, about 27 years old, named Crispus, 6 feet 2 inches height, short, curl'd hair, his knees nearer together than common." During his twenty years as a fugitive, Attucks worked as a sailor, with Boston as his home port.

Attucks shared the anti-British sentiment that developed after the French and Indian War. This is not surprising since the tightening restrictions Parliament placed upon American trade affected his livelihood as a seaman. In Boston British soldiers were the most obvious target of such resentment. Bostonians had insulted and thrown rocks at them for some time before Attucks joined a motley crowd that, with clubs and sticks, accosted a small detachment of troops on the chilly evening of March 5, 1770. Attucks was not the only African American in the mob. One pro-British witness described those who gathered as "saucy boys, Negroes and mulattoes, Irish Teagues and outlandish Jack Tars [sailors]."

Although eyewitness accounts differ, Attucks probably took the lead in confronting Captain Thomas Preston and the nine soldiers under his command. A black witness maintained that Attucks, "a stout man with a long cordwood stick," hit a soldier, which led the troops to fire on the mob. John Adams, who defended the soldiers in court, credited this account, and Attucks was almost certainly the first to die when the soldiers, with their backs to a wall, fired.

Samuel Adams, John's cousin, and other Patriots in Boston declared the forty-seven-year-old Attucks the first martyr to British oppression. They carried his coffin, along with those of three of the other four men who were killed, to Faneuil Hall—called the "Cradle of Liberty," because of its association with revolutionary rhetoric. There Attucks lay in state for three days with the other victims of what Americans immediately called the Boston Massacre. From this hall ten thousand mourners accompanied four hearses to Boston's Middle Burying Ground. The inscription on the monument raised to commemorate the martyrs reads:

Long as in freedom's cause the wise contend,
Dear to your country shall your fame extend;
While to the world the lettered stone shall tell
Where Caldwell, Attucks, Gray, and Maverick fell.

Bostonians celebrated the anniversary of the massacre annually until the 1840s. They revived the practice in 1858 to protest the Supreme Court's decision in *Dred Scott v. Sanford* that African Americans were not citizens of the United States. At about the same time, African Americans in Cincinnati formed the "Attucks Guards" to resist enforcement of the Fugitive Slave Law. After the Civil War, black abolitionist William C. Nell linked the service of black men in defense of the Union to Attucks's sacrifice "in defense of this nation's freedom."

Attucks has remained a symbol of African-American patriotism. In 1967, at the height of the Vietnam War, the Newark, New Jersey, board of education, at the expressed desire of the city's large black community, made March 5 an annual holiday in honor of Attucks. This was the first holiday to recognize an African American.

The death of Crispus Attucks in the ▶ Boston Massacre.

The Declaration of Independence and African Americans

The Declaration of Independence that the Continental Congress adopted on July 4, 1776, was drafted by a slaveholder in a slaveholding country. When Thomas Jefferson wrote "that all men are created equal; that they are endowed by their Creator with certain unalienable rights; that among these are life, liberty, and the pursuit of happiness," he was not supporting black claims for freedom. Men like Jefferson and John Adams, who served on the drafting committee with Jefferson, frequently distinguished between the rights of white men of British descent and a lack of rights for people of color. In 1765 Adams had written that God had "never intended the American colonists 'for Negroes . . . and therefore never intended us for slaves.'" So convinced were Jefferson and his colleagues that black people could not claim the same rights as white people that they felt no need to qualify their words proclaiming universal liberty.

The draft declaration that Jefferson, Adams, and Benjamin Franklin submitted to Congress for approval did denounce the Atlantic slave trade as a "cruel war against human nature itself, violating its most sacred rights of life and liberty in the persons of a distant [African] people." But Congress deleted this passage because delegates from the deep south objected to it. The final version of the Declaration referred to slavery only to accuse the British of arousing African Americans to revolt against their masters.

Yet, although Jefferson and the other delegates did not mean to encourage African Americans to hope the American War for Independence could become a war against slavery, that is what African Americans believed. Black people were in attendance when Patriot speakers made unqualified claims for human equality and natural rights; they read accounts of such speeches and heard white people discuss them. In response African Americans began to assert that such principles logically applied as much to them as to the white population. They forced white people to confront the contradiction between the new nation's professed ideals and its reality. Most white people did not deny that black people were human beings. White citizens therefore had to choose between accepting the literal meaning of the Declaration, which meant changing American society, or rejecting the revolutionary ideology that supported their claims for independence.

THE IMPACT OF THE ENLIGHTENMENT

At the center of that ideology was the European Enlightenment. The roots of this intellectual movement, also known as the Age of Reason, lay in Renaissance secularism and humanism dating back to the fifteenth century. But it was Isaac Newton's *Principia Mathematica*, published in England in 1687, that shaped a new way of perceiving human beings and their universe.

Newton used mathematics to portray an orderly, balanced universe that ran according to natural laws that humans could discover through reason. Newton's insights supported the rationalized means of production and commerce associated with the Industrial Revolution that began in England during the early eighteenth century. An emerging market economy required the same sort of rational use of resources that Newton discovered in the universe. But what made the Enlightenment of particular relevance to the **Age of Revolution** was John Locke's application of Newton's ideas to politics.

In his essay "Concerning Human Understanding," published in 1690, Locke maintained that human society—like the physical universe—ran according to natural laws. He contended that at the base of human laws were natural rights all people shared. Human beings, according to Locke, created governments to protect their natural individual rights to life, liberty, and private property. If a government failed to perform this basic duty and became oppressive, he insisted, the people had the right to overthrow it. Although originated nearly a century before the 1777 Massachusetts petition with which this chapter begins, Locke's ideas underlie this appeal on behalf of black liberty. Locke also maintained that the human mind at birth was a *tabula rasa* (i.e., knowledge and wisdom were not inherited but were acquired through experience). Locke saw no contradiction between these principles and human slavery, but during the eighteenth century, that contradiction became increasingly clear.

Most Americans became acquainted with Locke's ideas through pamphlets that a radical English political minority produced during the early eighteenth century. This literature portrayed the British government of the day as a conspiracy aimed at depriving British subjects of their natural rights, reducing them to slaves, and establishing tyranny. After the French and Indian War, Americans, both black and white, interpreted British policies and actions from this same perspective.

The influence of such pamphlets is clear between 1763 and 1776 when white Patriot leaders charged that the British government sought to enslave them by depriving them of their rights as Englishmen. When they made these charges, they had difficulty denying that they themselves deprived African Americans of their natural rights. George Washington, for example, declared in 1774 that "the crisis is arrived when we must assert our rights, or submit to every imposition, that can be heaped upon us, till custom and use shall make us tame and abject, as the blacks we rule over with such arbitrary sway."

AFRICAN AMERICANS IN THE REVOLUTIONARY DEBATE

During the 1760s and 1770s when powerful slaveholders such as George Washington talked of liberty, natural rights, and hatred of enslavement, African Americans listened. Most of them had been born in America, they had absorbed English culture, they were united as a people, and they knew their way in colonial society. Those who lived in or near towns and cities had access to public meetings and newspapers. They were aware of the disputes with Great Britain and the contradictions between demanding liberty for oneself and denying it to others. They understood that the ferment of the 1760s had shaken traditional assumptions about government, and many of them hoped for more changes.

The greatest source of optimism for African Americans was the expectation that white Patriot leaders would realize their revolutionary principles were incompatible with slavery. Those in England who believed white Americans must submit to British authority pointed out the contradiction. Samuel Johnson, the most famous writer in London, asked, "How is it that we hear the loudest yelps for liberty among the drivers of negroes?" But white Americans made similar comments. As early as 1763, James Otis of Massachusetts warned that "those who every day barter away other mens['] liberty, will soon care little for their own." Thomas Paine, whose pamphlet *Common Sense* rallied Americans to endorse independence in 1776, asked them to contemplate "with what consistency, or decency they complain so loudly of attempts to enslave them, while they hold so many hundred thousands in slavery; and annually enslave many thousands more."

Such principled misgivings among white people about slavery helped improve the situation for black people in the North and upper South during the war, but African Americans acting on their own behalf were key. In January 1766 slaves marched through Charleston, South Carolina, shouting "Liberty!" In the South Carolina and Georgia low country and in the Chesapeake, slaves escaped in massive numbers throughout the revolutionary era. So many slaves fled in the South that between 1770 and 1790 the percentage of black people in South Carolina's population dropped from 60.5 percent to 43.8 percent, and in Georgia from 45.2 to 36.9.

Throughout the southern colonies, rumors of slave uprisings were rife. However, it was in New England— the heartland of anti-British radicalism—that African Americans formally made their case for freedom. As early as 1701, a Massachusetts slave won his liberty in court, and there were eleven similar suits before 1750. As the revolutionary era began, such cases multiplied. In addition, although slaves during the seventeenth and early eighteenth centuries had based their **freedom suits** on contractual technicalities, during the revolutionary period, they increasingly sued on the basis of principles of universal liberty. They did not always win their cases—John Adams, a future president, was the lawyer who defeated one such case in Boston in 1768—but they set precedents.

African Americans in Massachusetts, New Hampshire, and Connecticut also petitioned their colonial or state legislatures for gradual emancipation. These petitions, worded like the one at the start of this chapter, indicate that the black men who signed them were familiar with revolutionary rhetoric. African Americans learned this rhetoric as they joined white radicals to confront British authority.

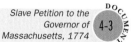
Slave Petition to the Governor of Massachusetts, 1774 — DOCUMENT 4-3

In 1765 black men demonstrated against the Stamp Act in Boston. They rioted against British troops there in 1768 and joined Crispus Attucks in 1770. Black Minutemen stood with their white comrades at Lexington and Concord. In 1773 black petitioners from Boston told a delegate to the colonial assembly, "We expect great things from men who have made such a noble stand against the designs of their *fellow-men* to enslave them. . . . The divine spirit of *freedom*, seems to fire every human breast."

The drawing portrays a black youngster joining in a Boston demonstration against the Stamp Act of 1765.

BOSTON'S SLAVES LINK THEIR FREEDOM TO AMERICAN LIBERTY

In April 1773 a committee of slaves from Boston submitted this petition to the delegate to the Massachusetts General Court from the town of Thompson. The petition, which overflows with sarcasm, demonstrates African-American familiarity with the principles of the Enlightenment and the irony of white Americans' contention that Britain aimed to enslave them. Its authors are of two minds about their society. They see both the potential for black freedom and the entrenched prejudice of white Americans. Note that the authors propose to go to Africa if they gain their freedom.

Boston, April 20th, 1773

Sir, The efforts made by the legislative of this province in their last sessions to free themselves from slavery, gave us, who are in that deplorable state, a high degree of satisfaction. We expect great things from men who have made such a noble stand against the designs of their *fellow-men* to enslave them. We cannot but wish and hope Sir, that you will have the same grand object, we mean civil and religious liberty, in view in your next session. The divine spirit of *freedom*, seems to fire every humane breast on this continent, except such as are bribed to assist in executing the execrable plan.

We are very sensible that it would be highly detrimental to our present masters, if we were allowed to demand all that of *right* belongs to us for past services; this we disclaim. Even the *Spaniards*, who have not those sublime ideas of freedom that English men have, are conscious that they have no right to all the services of their fellow-men, we mean the *Africans*, whom they have purchased with their money; therefore they allow them one day in a week to work for themselves, to enable them to earn money to purchase the residue of their time. . . . We do not pretend to dictate to you Sir, or to the Honorable Assembly, of which you are a member. We acknowledge our obligations to you for what you have already done, but as the people of this province seem to be actuated by the principles of equity and justice, we cannot but expect your house will again take our deplorable case into serious consideration, and give us that ample relief which, *as men*, we have a natural right to.

But since the wise and righteous governor of the universe, has permitted our fellow men to make us slaves, we bow in submission to him, and determine to behave in such a manner as that we can have reason to expect the divine approbation of, and assistance in, our peaceable and lawful attempts to gain our freedom.

We are willing to submit to such regulations and laws, as may be made relative to us, until we leave the province, which we determine to do as soon as we can, from our joynt labours procure money to transport ourselves to some part of the Coast of *Africa*, where we propose settlement. We are very desirous that you should have instructions relative to us, from your town, therefore we pray you to communicate this letter to them, and ask this favor for us.

In behalf of our fellow slaves in this province, and by order of their Committee.

Peter Bestes,

Sambo Freeman,

Felix Holbrook,

Chester Joie.

For the Representative of the town of Thompson.

What is the object of this petition?

What Enlightenment principles does the petition invoke?

What is the significance of the slaves' vow to go to Africa if freed?

Source: Gary B. Nash, *Race and Revolution* (Madison, WI: Madison House, 1990), 173–74.

Black Enlightenment

Besides influencing radical political discourse during the revolutionary era, the Enlightenment also shaped the careers of America's first black intellectuals. Because it emphasized human reason, the Enlightenment led to the establishment of colleges and libraries in Europe and America. These institutions usually served a tiny elite, but newspapers and pamphlets made science and literature available to the masses. The eighteenth century was also an era in which amateurs could make serious contributions to human knowledge. Some of these amateurs, such as Thomas Jefferson and Benjamin Franklin, were rich and well educated. They made discoveries in botany and electricity while pursuing political careers. What is striking is that some African Americans, whose advantages were far more limited, also became scientists and authors.

Because they had easier access to evangelical Protestantism than to secular learning, most African Americans who gained intellectual distinction during the late eighteenth century owed more to the Great Awakening than to the Enlightenment. The best known of these is Jupiter Hammon, a Long Island slave who published religious poetry in the 1760s. There were also Josiah Bishop and Lemuel Haynes, black ministers to white church congregations in Virginia and New England. But Phillis Wheatley and Benjamin Banneker, who were directly influenced by the Enlightenment, became the most famous black intellectuals of their time.

PHILLIS WHEATLEY

Wheatley came to Boston from Africa—possibly near the Gambia River—in 1761 aboard a slaver. She was seven or eight years old, small, frail, and nearly naked. John Wheatley, a wealthy merchant, purchased her as a servant for his wife. Although Phillis spoke no English when her ship docked, she was soon reading and writing in that language and studying Latin. She pored over the Bible and became a fervent Christian. She also read the fashionable poetry of British author Alexander Pope and became a poet herself by the age of thirteen.

For the rest of her short life, Wheatley wrote poems to celebrate important events. Like Pope's, Wheatley's poetry reflected the aesthetic values of the Enlightenment. She aimed to blend thought, image, sound, and rhythm to provide a perfectly balanced composition. In 1773 the Wheatleys sent her to London where her first book of poems—the first book ever by an African-American woman and the second by any American woman—was published under the title *Poems on Various Subjects, Religious and Moral*. The Wheatleys freed

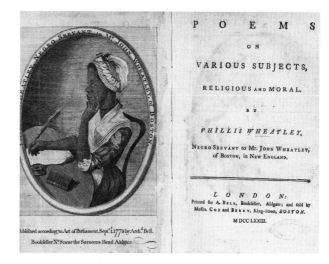

A frontispiece portrait of Phillis Wheatley precedes the title page of her first book of poetry, which was published in 1773. The portrait suggests Wheatley's small physique and studious manner.

Phillis after her return to Boston, although she continued to live in their house until both of them died. In 1778 she married John Peters, a black grocer, and was soon mired in illness and poverty. Two of her children died in infancy, and she died in December 1784 giving birth to her third child, who died with her.

Poems on Various Subjects, Religious and Moral, 1772 — DOCUMENT 4-2

Wheatley was an advocate and symbol of the adoption of white culture by black people. Before her marriage, she lived almost exclusively among white people and absorbed their values. For example, although she lamented the sorrow her capture had caused her parents, she was grateful to have been brought to America:

> 'Twas mercy brought me from my Pagan land,
> Taught my benighted soul to understand
> That there's a God, that there's a Saviour too:
> Once I redemption neither sougzht nor knew.

But Wheatley did not simply copy her masters' views. Although the Wheatleys were loyal to Britain, she became a fervent Patriot. She attended Boston's Old North Church, a hotbed of anti-British sentiment, and wrote poems supporting the Patriot cause. In early 1776, for example, she lavishly praised George Washington, "fam'd for thy valour, for thy virtues more," and received effusive thanks from the general.

Wheatley also became an advocate and symbol of John Locke's ideas concerning the influence of environment on human beings. White leaders of the Revolution and intellectuals debated whether black people

PHILLIS WHEATLEY ON LIBERTY AND NATURAL RIGHTS

Phillis Wheatley wrote the following letter to Samson Occom, an American-Indian minister, in 1774 after her return from England and as tensions between that country and its American colonies intensified. In it, she links divine order, natural rights, and an inner desire for personal liberty. She expresses optimism that Christianity and the emergence of order in Africa will lead to the end of the Atlantic slave trade. And she hopes that God will ultimately overcome the avarice of American slaveholders ("our modern Egyptians") and let them see the contradiction between their words and deeds.

February 11, 1774

Rev'd and honor'd Sir, I have this Day received your obliging kind Epistle, and am greatly satisfied with your Reasons respecting the Negroes, and think highly reasonable what you offer in Vindication of their natural Rights. Those that invade them cannot be insensible that the divine Light is chasing away the thick Darkness which broods over the Land of Africa; and the Chaos which has reign'd so long, is converting into beautiful Order, and reveals more and more clearly, the glorious Dispensation of civil and religious Liberty, which are so inseparably united, that there is little or no Enjoyment of one without the other. Otherwise, perhaps, the Israelites had been less solicitous for their Freedom from Egyptian Slavery; I don't say they would have been contented without it. By no Means, for in every human Breast, God has implanted a Principle, which we call Love of Freedom; it is impatient of Oppression, and pants for Deliverance. And by the leave of our modern Egyptians, I will assert that the same principle lives in us. God grant Deliverance in his own Way and Time, and get him honor upon all those whose Avarice impels them to countenance and help forward the Calamities of their fellow Creatures. This I desire not for their Hurt, but to convince them of the strange Absurdity of their Conduct whose Words and Actions are so diametrically opposite. How well the cry for Liberty, and the reverse Disposition for the exercise of oppressive Power over others agree, I humbly think it does not require the Penetration of a Philosopher to determine.

Phillis Wheatley

were inherently inferior in intellect to white people or whether this perceived black inferiority was the result of enslavement. Some slaveholders, such as Thomas Jefferson, who held racist assumptions about innate black inferiority, dismissed Wheatley's work as "below the dignity of criticism." But those who favored an environmental perspective considered Wheatley an example of what people of African descent could achieve if freed from oppression. She made her own views clear:

> Some view our sable race with scornful eye,
> "Their colour is a diabolic dye."
>
> Remember, *Christians*, *Negroes*, black as *Cain*,
> May be refin'd, and join th' angelic train.

BENJAMIN BANNEKER

Wheatley Poem 4 — LIVING WORDS

In the breadth of his achievement, Benjamin Banneker is even more representative of the Enlightenment than Phillis Wheatley. Like hers, his life epitomizes a flexibility concerning race that the revolutionary era briefly promised to expand.

Banneker was born free in Maryland in 1731 and died in 1806. The son of a mixed-race mother and an African father, he inherited a farm near Baltimore from his white grandmother. As a child, Banneker, whose appearance was described by a contemporary to be "decidedly Negro," attended a racially integrated school. His farm gave him a steady income and the leisure to study literature and science.

With access to the library of his white neighbor George Ellicott, Banneker "mastered Latin and Greek and had a good working knowledge of German and French." By the 1770s he had a reputation as a man "of uncommonly soft and gentlemanly manners and of pleasing colloquial powers." Like Jefferson, Franklin, and others of his time, Banneker was fascinated with mechanics and in 1770 constructed his own clock. However, he gained international fame as a mathematician and astronomer. Because of his knowledge in these dis-

🌿 *How does this letter reflect principles associated with the Enlightenment?*

🌿 *What insights does this letter provide into Wheatley's views on slavery and its abolition?*

Source: Roy Finkenbine, ed., *Sources of the African-American Past: Primary Sources in American History* (New York: Longman, 1997), 22–23.

ciplines, he became a member of the survey commission for Washington, D.C. This made him the first black civilian employee of the U.S. government. Between 1791 and 1796, he published an almanac based on his observations and mathematical calculations.

Like Wheatley, Banneker had thoroughly assimilated white culture and was keenly aware of the fundamental issues of human equality associated with the American Revolution. In 1791 he sent Thomas Jefferson, who was then U.S. secretary of state, a copy of his almanac to refute Jefferson's claim in *Notes on the State of Virginia* that black people were inherently inferior intellectually to white people. Noting Jefferson's commitment to the biblical statement that God had created "us all of one flesh," and Jefferson's words in the Declaration of Independence, Banneker called the great man to account concerning slavery.

DOCUMENT 4-6 Benjamin Banneker— Letter to Thomas Jefferson (1791)

Referring to the Declaration, Banneker wrote, "You were then impressed with proper ideas of the great valuation of liberty, and the free possession of those blessings, to which you were entitled by nature; but, Sir, how pitiable is it to reflect, that altho you were so fully convinced of the benevolence of the Father of Mankind, and of his equal and impartial distribution of these rights and privileges . . . that you should at the Same time counteract his mercies, in detaining by fraud and violence so numerous a part of my brethren, under groaning captivity and cruel oppression."

African Americans in the War for Independence

In the words of historian Benjamin Quarles, "The Negro's role in the Revolution can best be understood by realizing that his major loyalty was not to a place nor to a people, but to a principle." When it came to fighting between Patriots on one side and the British and their Loyalist American allies on the other, African Americans joined the side that offered freedom. In the South, where the British held out the promise of freedom in exchange for military service, black men eagerly fought on the British side as **Loyalists**. In the North, where white Patriots were more consistently committed to human liberty than in the South, black men just as eagerly fought on the Patriot side (see Map 4–2). In contrast, American Indians, hoping to counter white expansion westward, almost always fought on the British side.

The war began in earnest in August 1776 when the British landed a large army at Brooklyn, New York, and drove Washington's **Continental Army** across New Jersey into Pennsylvania. The military and diplomatic turning

The title page of the 1795 edition of Benjamin Banneker's *Pennsylvania, Delaware, Maryland, and Virginia Almanac.* Banneker was widely known during the late eighteenth century as a mathematician and astronomer.

point in the war came the following year at Saratoga, New York, when a poorly executed British strategy to take control of the Hudson River led British general John Burgoyne to surrender his entire army to Patriot forces. This victory led France and other European powers to enter the war against Britain. Significant fighting ended in October 1781 when Washington forced Lord Cornwallis to surrender another British army at Yorktown, Virginia.

When Washington had organized the Continental Army in July 1775, he forbade the enlistment of new black troops and the reenlistment of black men who had served at Lexington and Concord, Bunker Hill, and other early battles. Shortly thereafter, all thirteen states followed Washington's example. Several reasons account for Washington's decision and its ratification by the

MAP 4–2   MAJOR BATTLES OF THE AMERICAN WAR FOR INDEPENDENCE,
INDICATING THOSE IN WHICH BLACK TROOPS PARTICIPATED.
Black troops fought on both sides during the American War for
Independence and participated in most of the major battles.   Adapted from
The Atlas of African-American History and Politics, 1/e, by A. Smallwood and J. Elliot, © 1998, The McGraw-Hill
Companies. Reproduced with permission of The McGraw-Hill Companies.

▶ *Why is it significant that most of these battles were in the North?*

Continental Congress. Although several black men had
served during the French and Indian War, the colonies
had traditionally excluded African Americans from militia service. Like others before them, Patriot leaders
feared that if they enlisted African-American soldiers, it
would encourage slaves to leave their masters without

permission. White people—especially in the South—
also feared that armed black men would endanger the
social order. Paradoxically, white people simultaneously
believed black men were too cowardly to be effective soldiers. Although apparently contradictory, these last two
beliefs persisted into the twentieth century.

BLACK LOYALISTS

Because so many Patriot leaders resisted employing
black troops, by mid-1775 the British had taken the initiative in recruiting African Americans. From Maryland southward, during the spring of that year, rumors
circulated that the British would instigate slave revolt.
In North Carolina, for example, the white populace
believed British agents promised to reward black individuals who murdered their masters. However, no such
uprisings occurred.

Instead, many slaves escaped and sought British
protection as Loyalists. Thomas Jefferson later claimed
that thirty thousand slaves escaped in Virginia alone.
The British employed most black men who escaped to
their lines as laborers and foragers. During the siege at
Yorktown in 1781, the British used the bodies of black
laborers, who had died of smallpox, in a primitive form
of biological warfare to try to infect the Patriot army.
Even so, many black refugees fought for British or Loyalist units.

Black Loyalists were most numerous in the low
country of South Carolina and Georgia. At the end of
the war in 1783, approximately twenty thousand
African Americans left with the British forces as they
evacuated Savannah and Charleston. A few who remained became known as "the plunderers of Georgia."
They carried out guerrilla warfare there until 1786.

The most famous British appeal to African Americans to fight for the empire in return for freedom came
in Virginia. On November 7, 1775, Lord Dunmore, the
last royal governor of the Old Dominion, issued a
proclamation offering to liberate slaves who joined
"His Majesty's Troops . . . for the more speedily reducing this Colony to a proper sense of their duty to His
Majesty's crown and dignity."

Among those who responded to Dunmore's offer
was Ralph Henry, a twenty-six-year-old slave of Patrick
Henry. Perhaps Ralph Henry recalled his famous master's "Give me liberty or give me death" speech. Another who joined Dunmore's troops was James Reid,
who later became a leader of Britain's colony for former slaves in Sierra Leone on Africa's west coast. Reid's
sixteen-year-old wife came with him, and they both
served with the Royal Artillery. In 1780 at least twenty
of Thomas Jefferson's slaves joined Lord Cornwallis's
army when it invaded Virginia.

By His Excellency the Right Honorable JOHN Earl of DUNMORE, His Majesty's Lieutenant and Governor General of the Colony and Dominion of Virginia, and Vice Admiral of the fac.

A PROCLAMATION.

AS I have ever entertained Hopes, that an Accommodation might have taken Place between GREAT-BRITAIN and this Colony, without being compelled by my Duty to this most disagreeable but now absolutely necessary Step, rendered so by a Body of armed Men unlawfully assembled, firing on His Majesty's Tenders, and the formation of an Army, and that Army now on their March to attack His Majesty's Troops and destroy the well disposed Subjects of this Colony. To defeat such treasonable Purposes, and that all such Traitors, and their Abettors, may be brought to Justice, and that the Peace, and good Order of this Colony may be again restored, which the ordinary Course of the Civil Law is unable to effect; I have thought fit to issue this my Proclamation, hereby declaring, that until the aforesaid good Purposes can be obtained, I do in Virtue of the Power and Authority to ME given, by His Majesty, determine to execute Martial Law, and cause the same to be executed throughout this Colony; and to the end that Peace and good Order may the sooner be restored, I do require every Person capable of bearing Arms, to resort to His Majesty's STANDARD, or be looked upon as Traitors to His Majesty's Crown and Government, and thereby become liable to the Penalty the Law inflicts upon such Offences; such as forfeiture of Life, confiscation of Lands, &c. &c. And I do hereby further declare all indented Servants, Negroes, or others, (appertaining to Rebels,) free that are able and willing to bear Arms, they joining His Majesty's Troops as soon as may be, for the more speedily reducing this Colony to a proper Sense of their Duty, to His Majesty's Crown and Dignity. I do further order, and require, all His Majesty's Leige Subjects, to retain their Quitrents, or any other Taxes due or that may become due, in their own Custody, till such Time as Peace may be again restored to this at present most unhappy Country, or demanded of them for their former salutary Purposes, by Officers properly authorised to receive the same.

GIVEN under my Hand on board the Ship WILLIAM ... NORFOLK, the 7th Day of November, in the sixteenth Year of His Majesty's Reign.

DUNMORE.

(GOD save the KING.)

This is a broadside version of Lord Dunmore's November 7, 1775, proclamation calling on black men in Virginia to fight on the British side in the American War for Independence in return for their freedom.

Dunmore recruited black soldiers out of desperation, then became the strongest advocate—on either the British or American side—of their fighting ability. When he issued his appeal, Dunmore had only three hundred British troops and had been driven from Williamsburg, Virginia's colonial capital. Mainly because Dunmore had to seek refuge on British warships, only about eight hundred African Americans managed to reach his forces. Defeat by the Patriots at the Battle of Great Bridge in December 1775 curtailed his efforts.

But Dunmore's proclamation and the black response to it struck a tremendous psychological blow against his enemies. Of Dunmore's six hundred troops at Great Bridge, half were African Americans whose uniforms bore the motto "Liberty to Slaves." As more and more Virginia slaves escaped, masters blamed Dunmore. Throughout the war, other British and Loyalist commanders followed his example, recruiting thousands of black men who worked and sometimes fought in ex-

AFRICAN AMERICANS AND THE WAR FOR INDEPENDENCE

APRIL 18, 1775	Black Minutemen participate in Battle of Lexington and Concord.
MAY 10, 1775	The Second Continental Congress convenes in Philadelphia.
JUNE 15, 1775	Congress appoints George Washington commander in chief of the new Continental Army.
JUNE 17, 1775	Black men fight with the Patriots at Bunker Hill.
NOVEMBER 7, 1775	Lord Dunmore, the royal governor of Virginia, offers freedom to slaves who will fight for the British.
JULY 9, 1775	George Washington bans African-American enlistment in the Continental Army.
DECEMBER 30, 1775	Washington allows black reenlistments in the Continental Army.

1775

change for their freedom. In all, more African Americans became active Loyalists than Patriots during the war.

Five hundred of Dunmore's black troops died of typhus or smallpox. When he had to abandon Virginia, the remainder sailed with his fleet to New York City (which had become British headquarters in America). One of them, the notorious Colonel Tye, conducted guerrilla raids in Monmouth County, New Jersey, for several years. Until he was killed in 1780, Tye and his interracial band of about twenty-five Loyalists plundered villages, spiked cannons, and kidnapped Patriot officers. When the war ended, many black Loyalists, like those in Charleston and Savannah, joined white Loyalists in leaving the United States. Some of them went first to Acadia (now Nova Scotia) and then on to Sierra Leone, the British West African colony for former slaves that was founded in 1787. Others went to the British West Indies, where some of them faced reenslavement.

BLACK PATRIOTS

Washington's July 1775 policy to the contrary, black men fought on the Patriot side from the very beginning of the Revolutionary War to its conclusion. Prior to Washington's arrival in Massachusetts, there were black Minutemen at Lexington and Concord; and some of the same men distinguished themselves at the bloody Battle of Bunker Hill in June 1775. Among them were Peter Salem, Caesar Dickerson, Pomp Fisk, Prince Hall, Cuff Hayes, Barzillai Lew, Salem Poor, Caesar Weatherbee, and Cuff Whittemore. Lew was a veteran of the French and Indian War; Hall became a prominent black leader; and Poor, who wintered with

The black soldier in this detail from John Trumbull's contemporary oil painting *The Battle of Bunker Hill* is presumed to be Peter Salem. The battle took place in June 1775. The "Peter Salem Gun" is on display at the Bunker Hill Monument.

Washington's army at Valley Forge in 1777–1778, received a commendation for bravery at Bunker Hill.

It was Dunmore's use of African-American soldiers that prompted Washington to reconsider his ban on black enlistment. "If that man, Dunmore," he wrote in late 1775, "is not crushed before the Spring he will become the most dangerous man in America. His strength will increase like a snowball running down hill. Success will depend on which side can arm the Negro faster." After having received encouragement from black veterans, Washington, on December 30, 1775, allowed African-American reenlistment in the Continental Army. Congress, fearful of alienating slaveholders, initially would not allow him to go further. By the end of 1776, however, troop shortages forced Congress and the state governments to recruit black soldiers in earnest for the Continental Army and state militias. Even then, South Carolina and Georgia refused to permit black men to serve in regiments raised within their boundaries, although black men from these states joined other Patriot units.

The Patriot recruitment policy changed most quickly in New England. In early 1777 Massachusetts opened its militia to black men, and Rhode Island formed a black regiment. Connecticut enabled masters to free their slaves to serve as substitutes for the masters or their sons in the militia or Continental Army. New York and New Jersey adopted similar statutes.

Also in 1777, when Congress set state enlistment quotas for the Continental Army, state recruitment officers began to fill those quotas with black men so white men might serve closer to home in the militia. With considerable reluctance, the southern states of Delaware, Maryland, Virginia, and North Carolina began enlisting free black men. Of these states, only Maryland allowed slaves to serve in return for freedom, but the others sometimes allowed slaves to enlist as substitutes for their masters, and this usually led to freedom.

Black men asserted that if they were to fight in a war for liberty, their own had to be ensured. When one master informed his slave that both of them would be fighting for liberty, the slave replied "that it would be a great satisfaction to know that he was indeed going to fight for his liberty." Once an agreement to serve the Patriot cause in return for freedom had been reached, some black soldiers took new surnames. Among the newly free soldiers in a Connecticut regiment were Jeffery, Pomp, and Sharp *Liberty*, and Ned, Cuff, and Peter *Freedom*.

Except for Rhode Island's black regiment and some companies in Massachusetts, black Patriots served in integrated military units. Enrollment officers often did not specify a man's race when he enlisted, so it is difficult to know how many black men actually served in Patriot armies. The figure usually given is 5,000 black soldiers out of a total of 300,000. A few black men, such as Salem Poor, became junior officers. Others were drummers and fifers, sailors on privateers (merchant vessels armed and authorized by a government to raid enemy shipping) commissioned by the Continental Congress, and informants and spies. Like others who gathered intelligence behind enemy lines, African Americans who informed and spied risked being hanged if they were captured.

Black men fought on the Patriot side in nearly every major battle of the war (see Map 4–2). Prince Whipple and Oliver Cromwell crossed the Delaware River with Washington on Christmas night 1776 to surprise Hessian mercenaries (German troops hired to

A young French officer named Jean-Baptiste-Antoine Deverger painted this watercolor of American foot soldiers who served during the Yorktown campaign of 1781. The black solider is a light infantryman from Rhode Island's black regiment.

fight on the British side) at Trenton, New Jersey. Others fought at Monmouth, Saratoga, Savannah, Princeton, and Yorktown. In 1777 a Hessian officer reported, "No [Patriot] regiment is to be seen in which there are not Negroes in abundance, and among them are able bodied, strong and brave fellows."

There were also black women who supported the Patriot cause. As did white women, black women, such as James Reid's wife, sometimes accompanied their soldier husbands into army camps, if not into battle. A few black women also demonstrated their sympathy for the Patriots in defiance of British authority. When the British occupied Philadelphia in 1777, they put Patriot prisoners of war in the city jail. The following year, a local Patriot correspondent reported that a free black woman, "having received two hard dollars for washing, and hearing of the distress of our prisoners in the goal, went to market and bought some neck beef and two heads, with some green[s], and made a pot of as good broth as she could; but having no more money to buy bread, she got credit of a baker for six loaves of bread, all of which she carried to our unfortunate prisoners."

The Revolution and Emancipation

The willingness of African Americans to risk their lives in the Patriot cause encouraged northern legislatures to emancipate slaves within their borders. By the late 1770s, most of these legislatures were debating abolition. Petitions and lawsuits initiated by black people in

Massachusetts, Connecticut, New Hampshire, and elsewhere encouraged such consideration. But an emerging market economy, the Great Awakening, and the Enlightenment established the cultural context in which people who believed deeply in the sanctity of private property could consider such a momentous change. Economic, religious, and intellectual change had convinced many that slavery should be abolished.

Enlightenment rationalism was a powerful anti-slavery force. In the light of reason, slavery appeared to be inefficient, barbaric, and oppressive. But rationalism alone could not convince white Americans that black people should be released from slavery. White people also had to believe general emancipation was in their self-interest and their Christian duty.

In the North, where all these forces operated and the economic stake in slave labor was relatively small, emancipation made steady progress. In the Chesapeake, where some of these forces operated, emancipationist sentiment grew and many masters manumitted their slaves, but there was no serious threat to the slave system. In the low country of South Carolina and Georgia, where economic interest and white solidarity against large black populations outweighed intellectual and religious considerations, white commitment to black bondage remained absolute.

The movement among white people to abolish slavery began within the Society of Friends. This religious group, whose members were known as Quakers, had always emphasized conscience, human brotherhood, and nonviolence. Moreover, many leading Quaker families engaged in international business ventures that required educated, efficient, moral workers. This predisposed them against a system that forced workers to be uneducated, recalcitrant, and often ignorant of Christian religion. Growing numbers of Quakers concluded that slaveholding was sinful, although members of the Society of Friends had owned and traded slaves for generations.

During the 1730s Benjamin Lay, a former slaveholder who had moved from Barbados to the Quaker-dominated colony of Pennsylvania, began to exhort his fellow Friends to disassociate themselves from owning and buying slaves. By the 1740s and 1750s John Woolman, from southern New Jersey, was urging northeastern and Chesapeake Quakers to emancipate their slaves. With assistance from British Quakers, Woolman and Anthony Benezet, a Philadelphia teacher, convinced the society's 1758 annual meeting to condemn slavery and the slave trade.

An Early Abolitionist Speaks Out against Slavery in 1757 **4-1** DOCUMENT

When the conflict with Great Britain made human rights a political as well as a religious issue,

Woolman and Benezet carried their abolitionist message beyond the Society of Friends. They thereby merged their sectarian crusade with the rationalist efforts of such northern white revolutionary leaders as former slaveholder Benjamin Franklin of Philadelphia and John Jay and Alexander Hamilton—who continued to own slaves—of New York. Under Quaker leadership, antislavery societies came into existence in the North and the Chesapeake. By 1774 such societies had joined African Americans in petitioning northern legislatures and, in one instance, the Continental Congress to act against slavery or the slave trade.

> DOCUMENT 4-5
> A Free African American Petitions the Government for Emancipation of All Slaves, 1777

THE REVOLUTIONARY IMPACT

In calling for emancipation, the antislavery societies emphasized black service in the war against British rule and the religious and economic progress of northern African Americans. They also contended that emancipation would prevent black rebellions. As a result, by 1784 all the northern states except New Jersey and New York had undertaken either immediate or gradual abolition of slavery. Delaware, Maryland, and Virginia made manumission easier. Even the deep south saw efforts to mitigate the most brutal excesses that slavery encouraged among masters. Many observers believed the Revolution had profoundly changed the prospects for African Americans.

> ACTIVITY
> The American Revolution

In fact, the War for Independence dealt a heavy, although not mortal, blow to slavery (see Figure 4–1). While northern states prepared to abolish involuntary servitude, an estimated 100,000 slaves escaped from their masters in the South. In South Carolina alone, approximately 25,000 escaped—about 30 percent of the state's black population. Twenty thousand black people left with the British at the end of the war (see Map 4–3). Meanwhile, numerous escapees found their way to southern cities or to the North, where they became part of a rapidly expanding free black class.

In the Chesapeake, as well as in the North, individual slaves gained freedom either in return for service in the war or because their masters had embraced Enlightenment principles. Philip Graham of Maryland, for example, freed his slaves, commenting that holding one's "fellow men in bondage and slavery is repugnant to the gold law of God and the unalienable right of mankind as well as to every principle of the late glorious revolution which has taken place in America." The Virginia legislature ordered masters to free slaves who had fought for American independence.

Those Chesapeake slaves who did not become free also made gains during the Revolution because the war hastened the decline of tobacco raising. As planters switched to wheat and corn, they required fewer year-round, full-time workers. This encouraged them to free their excess labor force or to negotiate contracts that let slaves serve for a term of years rather than for life. Another alternative was for masters to allow slaves—primarily males—to practice skilled trades instead of doing fieldwork. Such slaves often **"hired their own time"** in return for giving their masters a large percentage of their wages.

Even those slaves who remained agricultural workers had more time to garden, hunt, and fish to supply themselves and their families with food and income. They gained more freedom to visit relatives who lived on other plantations, attend religious meetings, and interact with white people. Masters tended to refrain from the barbaric punishments used in the past, to improve slave housing, and to allow slaves more access to religion.

In South Carolina and Georgia, greater autonomy for slaves during the revolutionary era took a different form. The war increased absenteeism among masters and reduced contacts between the black and white populations. The black majorities in these regions grew larger, more isolated, and more African in culture as South Carolina and Georgia imported more slaves from Africa. The constant arrival of Africans helped the region's African-American population retain a distinctive

FIGURE 4–1   THE FREE BLACK POPULATION OF THE BRITISH NORTH AMERICAN COLONIES IN 1750, AND OF THE UNITED STATES IN 1790 AND 1800.

The impact of revolutionary ideology and a changing economy led to a great increase in the free black population during the 1780s and 1790s.

Source: *A Century of Population Growth in the United States. 1790–1900* (1909), p. 80. Data for 1750 estimated.

MAP 4–3 THE RESETTLEMENT OF BLACK
LOYALISTS AFTER THE AMERICAN WAR FOR
INDEPENDENCE

Like their white Loyalist counterparts, many
black Loyalists left with the British following the
Patriot victory. Most of those who settled in Nova
Scotia soon moved on to Great Britain or the
British free black colony of Sierra Leone. Some
black migrants to the British Caribbean were
reenslaved.   Adapted from *The Atlas of African-American History
and Politics*, 1/e, by A. Smallwood and J. Elliot, © 1998, The McGraw-Hill
Companies. Reproduced with permission of The McGraw-Hill
Companies.

▶ *What does the arrival of some black Loyalists
in Sierra Leone indicate about Great Britain's
changing attitudes toward slavery?*

culture and the Gullah dialect. The increase in master absenteeism also permitted the task system of labor to expand. As historian Peter Kolchin notes, although African Americans in the North and the Chesapeake lived in close proximity to whites and interacted with them, "in the coastal region of the lower South, most blacks lived in a world of their own, largely isolated from whites, and developed their own culture and way of life."

THE REVOLUTIONARY PROMISE

Even though the northern states were moving toward general emancipation during the revolutionary era, most newly free African Americans lived in the Chesapeake. They gained their freedom by serving in the war or escaping or because of economic and ideological change. As a result, a substantial free black population emerged in the Chesapeake after the war. Free African Americans had, of course, always lived there—Anthony Johnson is a prominent example—but before the Revolution they were few. In 1782 Virginia had only 1,800 free people within a total black population of 220,582. By 1790 the state had 12,766 free people within a total black population of 306,193. By 1810 it was 30,570 within 423,088. Free black populations also grew in Delaware and Maryland, where—unlike Virginia—the number of slaves began a long decline.

But in South Carolina and Georgia, the free black class remained tiny. Most low-country free black people were the children of white slave owners. They tended to be less independent of their former masters than their Chesapeake counterparts

and lighter complexioned because their freedom was often a result of a family relationship to their masters.

In the North and the Chesapeake, free African Americans frequently moved to cities. Boston, New York, Philadelphia, Baltimore, Richmond, and Norfolk gained substantial free black populations after the Revolution. Black women predominated in this migration because they could more easily find jobs as domestics in the cities than in rural areas. Cities also offered free black people opportunities for community development that did not exist in thinly settled farm country. Although African Americans often used their new mobility to reunite families disrupted by slavery, relocating to a city could disrupt families that had survived enslavement. It took about a generation for stable, urban, two-parent households to emerge.

Newly freed black people also faced economic difficulty, and their occupational status often declined. Frequently they emerged from slavery without the economic resources needed to become independent farmers, shopkeepers, or trades people. In the North such economic restraints sometimes forced them to remain with their former masters long after formal emancipation. To make matters worse, white artisans used legal and extralegal means to protect themselves from black competition. Therefore African Americans who had learned trades as slaves had difficulty employing their skills in freedom.

Yet, in the North and Chesapeake, most African Americans refused to work for their old masters and left the site of their enslavement. Those who had escaped had to leave; for others, leaving indicated a desire to put the stigma of servitude behind and embrace the opportunities freedom offered despite the risks. Many former masters did not understand this desire and criticized their former chattels for not staying on as hired hands. One white Virginian complained, "I cannot help thinking it is too generally the case with all those of colour to be ungrateful."

Many African Americans took new names to signify their freedom. They adopted surnames such as *Freedom, Liberty,* or *Justice* and dropped such classical given names as *Pompey* and *Caesar.* Some paid homage to their African ancestry and complexion by taking surnames such as *Africa* and *Guinea, Brown,* and *Coal.* Others, however, expressed their aspirations in a racially stratified society by replacing African given names like *Cuffee* and *Quash* with Anglicized Bible names and the surnames of famous white people.

WHEREAS the NEGROES in the counties of Briſtol and Worceſter, the 24th of March laſt, petitioned the Committees of Correſpondence for the county of Worceſter (then convened in Worceſter) to aſſiſt them in obtaining their freedom. THEREFORE,

In County Convention, June 14th, 1775.

RESOLVED, That we abhor the enſlaving of any of the human race, and particularly of the NEGROES in this country. And that whenever there ſhall be a door opened, or opportunity preſent, for any thing to be done toward the emancipating the NEGROES; we will uſe our influence and endeavour that ſuch a thing may be effected.

Atteſt. WILLIAM HENSHAW, Clerk.

The Patriot newspaper *Massachusetts Spy* published this antislavery resolution on June 21, 1775. It indicates the initiative taken by black abolitionists and the sympathetic response of white Patriots.

CONCLUSION

In the Peace of Paris signed in September 1783, Britain recognized the independence of the United States, acquiesced in American control of the territory between the Appalachian Mountains and the Mississippi River, and returned Florida to Spain (see Map 4–4). Both sides promised to return confiscated property—including slaves—to their owners, but neither side complied. As the United States gained recognition of its independence, African Americans could claim they had helped secure it. As soldiers in the Continental Army or in Patriot state militias, many black men fought and died for the revolutionary cause. Others supported the British. African Americans, like white Americans, had been divided over the War for Independence. Yet both those black men and women who chose the Patriot side and those who became Loyalists had freedom as their goal.

In this chapter, we have sought to place the African-American experience during the struggle for

MAP 4–4   NORTH AMERICA, 1783

This map shows the political geography of North America following British recognition of the independence of the United States in 1783.

▶ *Why was this division of territory important for African Americans?*

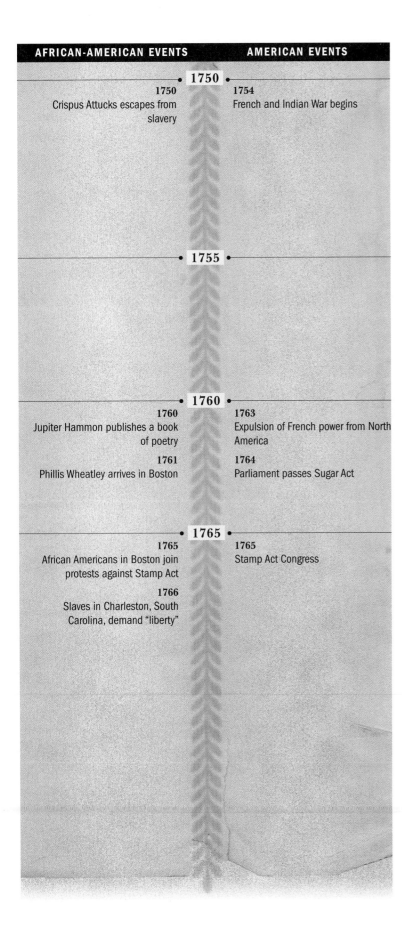

AFRICAN-AMERICAN EVENTS	AMERICAN EVENTS
1750	
1750 Crispus Attucks escapes from slavery	**1754** French and Indian War begins
1755	
1760	
1760 Jupiter Hammon publishes a book of poetry	**1763** Expulsion of French power from North America
1761 Phillis Wheatley arrives in Boston	**1764** Parliament passes Sugar Act
1765	
1765 African Americans in Boston join protests against Stamp Act	**1765** Stamp Act Congress
1766 Slaves in Charleston, South Carolina, demand "liberty"	

independence in the broad context of revolutionary ideology derived from the Enlightenment. Black men and women, such as Benjamin Banneker and Phillis Wheatley, exemplified the intellectually liberating impact of eighteenth-century rationalism and recognized its application to black freedom.

Within the context of the war and with the assistance of white opponents of slavery, African Americans combined arguments for natural rights with action to gain freedom. The American Revolution seemed about to fulfill its promise of freedom to a minority of African Americans, and they were ready to embrace the opportunities it offered. By the end of the War for Independence in 1783, slavery was dying in the North and seemed to be on the wane in the Chesapeake. The first steps toward forming free black communities were under way. Black leaders and intellectuals had begun to emerge. Although most of their brothers and sisters remained in slavery, although the slave system began to expand again during the 1790s, and although free black people achieved *at best* second-class citizenship, they had made undeniable progress. Yet African Americans were also learning how difficult freedom could be despite the new republic's embrace of revolutionary ideals.

RECOMMENDED READING

Ira Berlin and Ronald Hoffman, eds. *Slavery and Freedom in the Age of the American Revolution.* Charlottesville: University Press of Virginia, 1983. The essays in this collection focus on black life in America during the revolutionary era.

David Brion Davis. *The Problem of Slavery in the Age of Revolution, 1770–1823.* Ithaca, NY: Cornell University Press, 1975. This magisterial study discusses the influence of the Enlightenment and the Industrial Revolution on slavery and opposition to slavery in the Atlantic world.

Sylvia R. Frey. *Water from the Rock: Black Resistance in a Revolutionary Age.* Princeton, NJ: Princeton University Press, 1991. This book portrays the War for Independence in the South as a three-way struggle among Patriots, British, and African Americans. It emphasizes the role of religion and community in black resistance to slavery.

Benjamin Quarles. *The Negro in the American Revolution.* 1961. Reprint, New York: Norton, 1973. This classic study remains the most comprehensive account of black participation in the War for Independence. It also demonstrates the impact of the war on black life.

Ellen Gibson Wilson. *The Loyal Blacks.* New York: G. P. Putnam's Sons, 1976. This book discusses why many African Americans chose the British side in the War for Independence. It also focuses on the fate of those loyal blacks who departed Nova Scotia in Canada for Sierra Leone.

Arthur Zilversmit. *The First Emancipation: The Abolition of Slavery in the North*. Chicago: University of Chicago Press, 1967. Zilversmit discusses the rise of an antislavery movement in the North and the process of emancipation there during the revolutionary era.

ADDITIONAL BIBLIOGRAPHY

THE CRISIS OF THE BRITISH EMPIRE

Stephen Conway. *The British Isles and the War of American Independence*. New York: Oxford University Press, 2000.

Edward Countryman. *The American Revolution*. New York: Hill and Wang, 1975.

Douglas E. Leach. *Roots of Conflict: British Armed Forces and Colonial Americans, 1677–1763*. Chapel Hill: University of North Carolina Press, 1986.

Pauline Maier. *From Resistance to Revolution: Colonial Radicals and the Development of American Opposition to Britain, 1765–1776*. New York: Knopf, 1972.

Peter David Garner Thomas. *Revolution in America: Britain and the Colonies, 1765–1776*. Cardiff, UK: University of Wales, 1992.

THE IMPACT OF THE ENLIGHTENMENT

Bernard Bailyn. *The Ideological Origins of the American Revolution*. Cambridge, MA: Harvard University Press, 1967.

Henry Steele Commager. *The Empire of Reason: How Europe Imagined and America Realized the Enlightenment*. Garden City, NY: Anchor, 1977.

Paul Finkelman. *Slavery and the Founders: Race and Liberty in the Age of Jefferson*. London: M. E. Sharpe, 1996.

J. G. A. Pocock. *The Machiavellian Moment: Florentine Political Thought and the Atlantic Republican Tradition*. Princeton, NJ: Princeton University Press, 1975.

Frank Shuffelton, ed. *The American Enlightenment*. Rochester, NY: University of Rochester Press, 1993.

AFRICAN AMERICANS AND THE AMERICAN REVOLUTION

Lerone Bennett Jr. *Before the Mayflower: A History of Black America*, 6th ed. Chicago: Johnson, 1987, Chapter 3.

Ira Berlin. "The Revolution in Black Life," in Alfred F. Young, ed., *The American Revolution: Explorations in the History of American Radicalism*. DeKalb: Northern Illinois University Press, 1976, 349–82.

Merton L. Dillon. *Slavery Attacked: Southern Slaves and Their Allies, 1619–1865*. Baton Rouge: Louisiana State University Press, 1990, Chapter 2.

Jack P. Greene. *All Men Are Created Equal: Some Reflections on the Character of the American Revolution*. Oxford: Clarendon, 1976.

Woody Holton. *Forced Founders: Indians, Debtors, Slaves, and the Making of the American Revolution in Virginia*. Chapel Hill:

AFRICAN-AMERICAN EVENTS	NATIONAL EVENTS
1770	**1770**
Crispus Attucks is killed during Boston Massacre	Boston Massacre
1773	**1773**
Phillis Wheatley publishes a book of poetry	Boston Tea Party
Black Bostonians petition for freedom	
1775	**1775**
Black Minutemen fight at Lexington and Concord	Battles of Lexington and Concord
1776	**1776**
Lord Dunmore recruits black soldiers in Virginia	Declaration of Independence
1777	**1777**
Emancipation begins in the North	British general John Burgoyne surrenders at Saratoga
1781–1783	**1781**
20,000 black Loyalists depart with the British troops	Cornwallis surrenders at Yorktown
	1783
	Britain recognizes U.S. independence

University of North Carolina Press, 1999.

Sidney Kaplan and Emma Nogrady Kaplan. *The Black Presence in the Era of the American Revolution*. Amherst: University of Massachusetts Press, 1989.

Peter Kolchin. *American Slavery, 1619–1877*. New York: Hill and Wang, 1993, Chapter 3.

Duncan McLeod. *Slavery, Race, and the American Revolution*. New York: Cambridge University Press, 1974.

Gary B. Nash. *Forging Freedom: The Formation of Philadelphia's Black Community, 1720–1840*. Cambridge, MA: Harvard University Press, 1988.

John W. Pulis. *Moving On: Black Loyalists in the Afro-Atlantic World*. New York: Garland, 1999.

Simon Schama. *Rough Crossings: Britain, the Slaves, and the American Revolution*. New York: Ecco, 2006.

Peter H. Wood. "'The Dream Deferred': Black Freedom Struggles on the Eve of White Independence," in Gary Y. Okihiro, ed., *In Resistance: Studies in African, Caribbean, and Afro-American History*. Amherst: University of Massachusetts Press, 1986, 166–87.

ANTISLAVERY AND EMANCIPATION IN THE NORTH

Robin Blackburn. *The Overthrow of Colonial Slavery, 1776–1848*. New York: Verso, 1988, Chapter 3.

Merton L. Dillon. *The Abolitionists: The Growth of a Dissenting Minority*. New York: Norton, 1974, Chapter 1.

Dwight L. Dumond. *Antislavery: The Crusade for Freedom in America*. 1961. Reprint, New York: Norton, 1966.

Joanne Pope Melish. *Disowning Slavery: Gradual Emancipation and "Race" in New England, 1780–1860*. Ithaca, NY: Cornell University Press, 1998.

Gary B. Nash. *Freedom by Degrees: Emancipation in Pennsylvania and Its Aftermath*. New York: Oxford University Press, 1991.

———. *The Forgotten Fifth: African Americans in the Age of Revolution*. Cambridge, MA: Harvard University Press, 2006.

James Brewer Stewart. *Holy Warriors: The Abolitionists and American Slavery*. Rev. ed. New York: Hill and Wang, 1997, Chapter 1.

BIOGRAPHY

Silvio A. Bedini. *The Life of Benjamin Banneker*. New York: Scribner, 1972.

Henry Louis Gates Jr. *The Trials of Phillis Wheatley*. New York: Basic Civitas Books, 2003.

William Henry Robinson. *Phillis Wheatley and Her Writings*. New York: Garland, 1984.

RETRACING THE ODYSSEY

Colonial Williamsburg, Williamsburg, Virginia. This is the largest historical restoration site in America. It emphasizes the period on the "eve of the American Revolution." Take the "Other Half Tour," which deals with "the lives and livelihoods of eighteenth-century African Americans."

Crispus Attucks's Grave, Granary Burial Ground, Boston, Massachusetts. Attucks is buried with the other victims of the Boston Massacre.

 REVIEW, RESEARCH, AND INTERACT

REVIEW QUESTIONS

1. How did the Enlightenment affect African Americans during the revolutionary era?

2. What was the relationship between the American Revolution and black freedom?

3. What was the role of African Americans in the War for Independence? How did their choices in this conflict affect how the war was fought?

4. How did the American Revolution encourage assimilation among African Americans? How did it discourage assimilation?

5. Why did a substantial class of free African Americans emerge from the revolutionary era?

www.researchnavigator.com

Using the tools available in Research Navigator, consider these questions:
How did African Americans participate in the struggle for independence? What expectations did they have about the new nation they were helping create?

PRIMARY SOURCE DOCUMENTS

4–1   An Early Abolitionist Speaks Out against Slavery in 1757

4–2   Phillis Wheatley, *Poems on Various Subjects, Religious and Moral,* 1772

4–3   Slave Petition to the Governor of Massachusetts, 1774

4–4   An American Patriot Tries to Stir Up the Soldiers of the American Revolution, 1776

4–5   A Free African American Petitions the Government for Emancipation of All Slaves, 1777

4–6   Benjamin Banneker—Letter to Thomas Jefferson (1791)

4–7   Report on Impending Ending of Slave Trade (1792)

4–8   Mathew Carey, "A Short Account of the Malignant Fever . . ." (1793)

MAP EXPLORATION

European Claims in North America, 1750 and 1763, p. 84

INTERACTIVE ACTIVITIES

Geography of the American Revolution

Explore how the path of the American Revolution, the course of the conflict, and many of the issues confronting the United States after 1783 revolved around geography.

The Stamp Act

In 1765 Great Britain set about putting its imperial house in order. Retiring debt was a major priority, and the Stamp Act was one of several revenue measures designed to get the colonies to pay a greater share of the costs of empire.

African Americans in the New Nation

WHAT FORCES WORKED FOR BLACK FREEDOM
IN THE FIRST YEARS AFTER THE REVOLUTION?

WHY DID SLAVERY SURVIVE
IN THE NEW UNITED STATES?

WHAT WERE THE CHARACTERISTICS
OF EARLY FREE BLACK COMMUNITIES?

HOW DID THE WAR OF 1812
AFFECT AFRICAN AMERICANS?

WHAT IMPACT DID THE MISSOURI COMPROMISE
HAVE ON AFRICAN AMERICANS?

◀◀ This recent photograph portrays one of several buildings
used as slave quarters on Boone Hall Plantation, South
Carolina. Built during the mid-seventeenth century, the small
brick building housed two African-American families into the
Civil War years.

Anytime, anytime while I was a slave, if one minute's freedom had been offered to me, and I had been told I must die at the end of that minute, I would have taken it—just to stand one minute on God's earth a free woman—I would.

Elizabeth Freeman

This, my dear brethren, is by no means the greatest thing we have to be concerned about. Getting our liberty in this world is nothing to our having the liberty of the children of God. . . . What is forty, fifty, or sixty years, when compared to eternity?

Jupiter Hammon

Death or Liberty.

Proposed inscription for a flag to be used in Gabriel's planned rebellion of 1800.

◄ **Thousands of** African Americans won their own freedom by escaping to the North before the Civil War.

Except that they were all born slaves in eighteenth-century America, Elizabeth Freeman, Jupiter Hammon, and Gabriel had little in common. Freeman was an illiterate domestic servant when, in 1781, she sued for her freedom in Massachusetts. Hammon, who lived in Long Island, New York, was a poet and orthodox Calvinist preacher who enjoyed the support of his master and never sought his freedom.

Gabriel was a literate, skilled slave who in 1800 master-minded a conspiracy to overthrow slavery in Virginia.

In this chapter, we explore how African Americans as diverse as Freeman, Hammon, and Gabriel helped shape the lives of black people during America's early years as an independent republic. We also examine how between 1783 and 1820 the forces for black liberty vied with the forces of slavery and inequality. The end of the War for Independence created great expectations among African Americans. But by 1820, when the Missouri Compromise confirmed the power of slave-holders in national affairs, black people in the North and the South had long known that the struggle for freedom was far from over.

That struggle took place at the state and local as well as the regional and national levels. The forces involved in it were often impersonal. They included the emergence of a market economy based on wage labor in the North and an economy based on the production of cotton by slave labor in the South. In addition, a revolutionary ideology encouraged African Americans to seek freedom, by force if necessary.

Meanwhile, economic self-interest encouraged white northerners to limit black freedom, and fear of race war caused white southerners to strengthen the slave system.

Yet individuals and groups also shaped African-American life in the new nation. As urban, church-centered black communities arose, men and women—both slave and free—influenced culture, politics, economics, and perceptions of race. This was particularly true in the North and the Chesapeake, but also to a lesser degree in the deep South. These were years of considerable progress for African Americans, although they ended with free black people facing deteriorating conditions in the North and with slavery spreading westward across the South.

John Wesley, "Thoughts upon Slavery," 1774

DOCUMENT 5-1

Forces for Freedom

During the decades after the War for Independence ended in 1783, a strong trend in the North and the

Chesapeake favored emancipation. It had roots in economic change, evangelical Christianity, and a revolutionary ethos based on the natural rights doctrines of the Enlightenment. African Americans took advantage of these forces to escape from slavery, purchase the freedom of their families and themselves, sue for freedom in court, and petition state legislatures to grant them equal rights.

In the postrevolutionary North, slavery, although widespread, was not economically essential. Farmers could more efficiently hire hands during the labor-intensive seasons of planting and harvesting than they could maintain a year-round slave labor force. Northern slaveholders, therefore, were a tiny class with limited political power. Moreover, transatlantic immigration brought to the North plenty of white laborers, who worked cheaply and resented slave competition. As the Great Awakening initiated a new religious morality, as natural rights doctrines flourished, and as a market economy based on wage labor emerged, northern slaveholders had difficulty defending perpetual black slavery.

In Chapter 4, we saw that emancipation in the North was a direct result of the War for Independence. But the *process* of doing away with slavery unfolded in these states only after the war. Meanwhile the national Congress set an important precedent in discouraging the expansion of slavery, and antislavery societies proliferated in the North and upper South.

THE ABOLITION OF SLAVERY IN THE NORTH

1777 Vermont constitutional convention prohibits slavery within what becomes the fourteenth state

1780 Pennsylvania begins gradually abolishing slavery within its borders

1783 Massachusetts's supreme court abolishes slavery there

1784 Connecticut and Rhode Island adopt gradual abolition plans

1785 New Jersey and New York legislatures defeat gradual abolition plans

1799 The New York legislature provides for gradual abolition within its jurisdiction

1804 New Jersey becomes the last northern state to initiate gradual abolition

did the mid-Atlantic states of Pennsylvania, New York, and New Jersey (see Map 5–1). Slavery collapsed in the New England states because African Americans who lived there refused to remain in servitude and because most white New Englanders acquiesced. The struggle against slavery in the middle states was longer and harder because more white people there had a vested interest in maintaining it.

NORTHERN EMANCIPATION

In comparison to other parts of the Atlantic world, emancipation in the northern portion of the United States began early. Its first stages preceded the revolt that had by 1804 ended slavery in Haiti, the first independent black republic. It preceded by a much greater margin the initiation in 1838 of peaceful, gradual abolition of slavery in the British empire and the termination in 1848 of slavery in the French empire. Northern emancipation was exceptional in that it was not the result of force or outside intervention by an imperial power. Although free black communities were emerging throughout the Western Hemisphere, those in the North were distinctive because they included the bulk of the region's black population.

Emancipation in the North did not follow a single pattern. Instead the New England states of Massachusetts (which included Maine until Maine became a separate state in 1820), Connecticut, Rhode Island, New Hampshire, and Vermont moved more quickly than

This engraving originally appeared in Boston in 1793, with the caption, "Cuffe near him . . . grasps his hand." It suggests the progress African Americans had made in the North but also the contempt in which many white northerners held them. The object of the picture is to ridicule Massachusetts governor John Hancock for participating in a black celebration. The Library Company of Philadelphia

MAP 5–1   EMANCIPATION AND SLAVERY IN THE EARLY REPUBLIC

This map indicates the abolition policies adopted by the states of the Northeast between 1777 and 1804, the antislavery impact of the Northwest Ordinance of 1787, and the extent of slavery in the South during the early republic.

▶ *Why did the states and territories shown in this map adopt different policies toward African Americans?*

Vermont and Massachusetts (certainly) and New Hampshire (probably) abolished slavery immediately during the 1770s and 1780s. Vermont, where there had never been more than a few slaves, prohibited slavery in the constitution it adopted in 1777. Massachusetts, in its constitution of 1780, declared "that all men are born free and equal; and that every subject is entitled to liberty." Although this constitution did not specifically ban slavery, within a year Elizabeth Freeman and other slaves in Massachusetts sued under it for their freedom. Freeman, while serving as a waitress at her master's home in Sheffield, Massachusetts, overheard

"gentlemen" discussing the "free and equal" clause of the new constitution. Shortly thereafter, she contacted a prominent local white lawyer, Theodore Sedgwick Sr., who agreed to represent her in court.

Meanwhile, another Massachusetts slave, Quok Walker, left his master and began living as a free person. In response, Walker's master sought a court order to force Walker to return to slavery. This case led in 1783 to a Massachusetts Supreme Court ruling that "slavery is . . . as effectively abolished as it can be by the granting of rights and privileges wholly incompatible and repugnant to its existence." At the same time, an-

TABLE 5–1   SLAVE POPULATIONS IN THE MID-ATLANTIC STATES, 1790–1860

	1790	1800	1810	1820	1830	1840	1850	1860
New York	21,324	20,343	15,017	10,888	75	4		
New Jersey	11,432	12,343	19,851	7,557	2,243	674	236	18
Pennsylvania	3,737	1,706	795	211	403	64		

Source: Philip S. Foner, History of Black Americans, from Africa to the Emergence of the Cotton Kingdom, vol. 1 (Westport, CT: Greenwood, 1975), 374.

other judge used similar logic to grant Freeman her liberty. These decisions encouraged other Massachusetts slaves to sue for their freedom or to leave their masters because the courts had ruled unconstitutional the master's claim to his human chattel.

As a result, the first U.S. census in 1790 found no slaves in Massachusetts. Even before then, black men in the state had gained the right to vote. In 1780 Paul and John Cuffe, free black brothers who lived in the town of Dartmouth, protested with five other free black men to the state legislature that they were being taxed without representation. After several setbacks, the courts finally decided in 1783 that African-American men who paid taxes in Massachusetts could vote there. This was a notable and rare victory. Before the Civil War, only a few New England states permitted black men to vote on the same basis as white men.

New Hampshire's record on emancipation is less clear than that of Vermont and Massachusetts. In 1779 black residents petitioned the New Hampshire legislature for freedom. Evidence also indicates that court rulings based on New Hampshire's 1783 constitution, which was similar to the constitution of Massachusetts, refused to recognize human property. Nevertheless, New Hampshire still had about 150 slaves in 1792, and slavery may have simply withered away there rather than having been abolished by the courts.

In Connecticut and Rhode Island, the state legislatures, rather than individual African Americans, took the initiative against slavery. In 1784 these states adopted gradual abolition plans, which left adult slaves in bondage but proposed to free their children over a period of years. In Connecticut all children born to enslaved mothers after March 1, 1784, were to become free at age twenty-five. Rhode Island's plan was less gradual. Beginning that same March 1, it freed the children of enslaved women at birth. By 1790 only 3,763 slaves remained in New England out of a total black population there of 16,882. By 1800 only 1,339 slaves remained in the region, and by 1810 only 418 were left (108 in Rhode Island and 310 in Connecticut).

In New Jersey, New York, and Pennsylvania, the investment in slaves was much greater than in New En-

gland. After considerable debate, the Pennsylvania legislature in 1780 voted that the children of enslaved mothers would become free at age twenty-eight. Under this scheme, Pennsylvania still had 403 slaves in 1830 (see Table 5–1). But many African Americans in the state gained their freedom much earlier by lawsuits or by simply leaving their masters. Emancipation came even more slowly in New York and New Jersey. In 1785 their legislatures *defeated* proposals for gradual abolition. White revolutionary leaders, such as Alexander Hamilton and John Jay, worked for abolition in New York, and Quakers had long advocated it in New Jersey. But these states had relatively large slave populations, powerful slaveholders, and white workforces fearful of free black competition.

In 1799 the New York legislature finally agreed that male slaves born after July 4 of that year were to become free at age twenty-eight and females at age twenty-five. In 1804 New Jersey adopted a similar law that freed male slaves born after July 4 of that year when they reached age twenty-five and females when they reached age twenty-one. Under this plan, New Jersey still had eighteen slaves in 1860.

THE NORTHWEST ORDINANCE OF 1787

Nearly as significant as the actions of northern states against slavery was Congress's decision to limit slavery's expansion. During the 1780s, Congress drew its authority from a constitution known as the Articles of Confederation. The Articles created a weak central government that lacked power to tax or to regulate commerce. Despite its weaknesses, this government acquired jurisdiction over the region west of the Appalachian Mountains and east of the Mississippi River, where several states previously had conflicting land claims.

During the War for Independence, increasing numbers of white Americans had migrated across the Appalachians into this huge region. The migrants—some of whom brought slaves with them—provoked hostilities with American Indian nations. In addition, those who moved into the Old Northwest faced British

PROFILE ❧ ELIZABETH FREEMAN

Known as Mum Bett, Elizabeth Freeman showed a strength of character that impressed everyone she met. Although records are contradictory, she was probably born in 1744 in Claverack, New York. As her parents were African slaves, she was also a slave. On the death of her first master in 1758, Freeman and her sister became the property of Colonel John Ashley, a court of common pleas judge, in Sheffield, Massachusetts. She married while quite young, gave birth to her only child—a daughter—and became a widow when her husband was killed fighting on the Patriot side in the War for Independence.

Freeman, who was illiterate, may have first learned of natural rights when in 1773 a group of men met at Ashley's home to draft a protest against British policies in the American colonies. "Mankind . . . have a right to the undisturbed Enjoyment of their lives, their Liberty and Property," the document declared. She took these words to heart, and when she learned while serving as a waitress in 1780 that the state of Massachusetts had adopted a bill of rights asserting that all people were born free and equal, she was ready to apply the doctrine.

In 1781 Freeman received "a severe wound" to her arm when she attempted to protect her sister from Ashley's wife, who "in a fit of passion" was threatening her with a hot kitchen shovel. Outraged at this attack, Freeman left the Ashley home and refused to return. Instead, she engaged the legal assistance of Theodore Sedgwick Sr. in a suit for her freedom on the basis of Massachusetts's new bill of rights. The jury found in Freeman's favor and required Ashley to pay her

thirty shillings in damages. It was at this point that Mum Bett changed her name legally to Elizabeth Freeman. Shortly thereafter, the Massachusetts Supreme Court declared slavery unconstitutional throughout the state.

For the remainder of her active life, Freeman worked as a paid domestic servant in the Sedgwick household and moved with the Sedgwicks to Stockbridge in 1785. Because Theodore Sedgwick Sr.'s wife was emotionally unstable, Freeman became a surrogate mother to the Sedgwick children, who later testified to her "superior instincts," abilities as a nurse, efficiency, and bravery.

During the 1830s, Theodore Sedgwick Jr. told British writer Harriet Martineau that in 1786 some participants in Shays's Rebellion entered the Sedgwick home while Theodore Sr. was away. Acting quickly to hide the family's silver set, Freeman confronted the men with a kitchen shovel similar to the one her former mistress had used against her. While advising the men "that they 'dare not strike a woman,'" she threatened to use the shovel against any one of them who disturbed the family possessions and she managed to usher them out with only minor damage to the Sedgwicks' property.

Freeman earned enough while employed by the Sedgwicks to purchase her own home and retire. When she died she left a small estate to her daughter, grandchildren, and great grandchildren. She left another legacy with the Sedgwick children. When Theodore Jr. became an abolitionist during the 1830s he credited Freeman as the source of his conviction that black people were not inferior to white people. Earlier, Theodore's brother Charles had the following lines inscribed on Freeman's gravestone: "She never violated a trust, nor failed to perform a duty. In every situation of domestic trial, she was the most efficient helper, and the tenderest friend. Good mother fare well."

◄◄ This portrait of Elizabeth Freeman was painted in watercolor on ivory by Elizabeth Sedgwick in 1811, thirty years after Freeman initiated her famous lawsuit.

Freeman

opposition, and those who moved into the Old Southwest contested against Spanish forces for control of that area. In response to these circumstances, Congress formulated policies to protect the migrants and provide for their effective government. The new nation's leaders also disparaged the westward expansion of slavery, and Thomas Jefferson sought to deal with both issues. First, he suggested that the western region be divided into separate territories and prepared for statehood. Second, he proposed that after 1800 slavery be banned from the entire region stretching from the Appalachians to the Mississippi River and from Spanish Florida (Spain had regained Florida in 1783) to British Canada.

In 1784 Jefferson's antislavery proposal failed by a single vote to pass Congress. Three years later, Congress adopted the **Northwest Ordinance**. This legislation applied the essence of Jefferson's plan to the region north of the Ohio River—what historians call the Old Northwest. The ordinance provided for the orderly sale of land, support for public education, territorial government, and the eventual formation of new states. Unlike Jefferson's plan, the ordinance banned slavery immediately. But, because it applied only to the Northwest Territory, the ordinance left the huge region south of the Ohio River open to slavery expansion.

Even in parts of the Old Northwest, some African Americans remained unfree after 1787. The first governor of the territory forced those who had been slaves before the adoption of the ordinance to remain slaves. Then in 1803, when Ohio became a state, the remainder of the Northwest Territory legalized indentured servitude. The result was that in southern parts of what became Illinois and Indiana, a few African Americans remained in bondage well into the nineteenth century.

Yet, by preventing slaveholders from taking slaves legally into areas north of the Ohio River, the ordinance set a precedent for excluding slavery from U.S. territories. Whether Congress had the power to do this became a contentious issue after President Jefferson annexed the huge Louisiana Territory in 1803 (see p. 114). The issue continued to divide northern and southern politicians until the Civil War.

ANTISLAVERY SOCIETIES IN THE NORTH AND THE UPPER SOUTH

While African Americans participated in the destruction of slavery in the northeastern states and Congress blocked its advance into the Old Northwest, a few white people organized to spread antislavery sentiment. In 1775 Quaker abolitionist Anthony Benezet organized the first antislavery society in the world. It became the **Pennsylvania Society for Promoting the Abolition of Slavery** in 1787, and Benjamin Franklin became its president. Similar societies were founded in Delaware in 1788 and Maryland in 1789. By the end of the eighteenth century, there were abolition societies in New Jersey, Connecticut, and Virginia. Organized antislavery sentiment also arose in the new slave states of Kentucky and Tennessee. However, such societies never appeared in the deep South.

From 1794 to 1832, antislavery societies cooperated within the loose framework of the **American Convention for Promoting the Abolition of Slavery and Improving the Condition of the African Race**. Only white people participated in these Quaker-dominated organizations, although members often cooperated with black leaders. As the northern states adopted abolition plans, the societies focused their attention on Delaware, Maryland, and Virginia. They aimed at gradual, compensated emancipation. They encouraged

The title of this 1811 painting by German-American artist John Lewis Krimmel is *Pepper-Pot, a Scene in the Philadelphia Market*. Slavery still existed in Pennsylvania when Krimmel recorded this scene. It is likely, however, that the black woman who is selling pepper-pot (a type of stew) was free.   2001-196-1 Krimmel, John Lewis Pepper Pot, A Scene in the Philadelphia Market Philadelphia Museum of Art: Gift of Mr. and Mrs. Edward B. Leisenring, Jr. in honor of the 125th anniversary of the museum, 2001. Sumpter Priddy III, Inc.

masters to free their slaves, attempted to protect free black people from reenslavement, and frequently advocated sending freed black people out of the country.

Experience with emancipation in the northern states encouraged the emphasis on gradual abolition. So did the reluctance of white abolitionists to challenge the property rights of masters. Abolitionists also feared that immediate emancipation might lead masters to abandon elderly slaves and assumed that African Americans would require long training before they could be free. All of this played into the hands of slaveholders who, like Thomas Jefferson, opposed slavery in the abstract but had no intention of freeing their own slaves.

The antislavery societies of the upper South tended to be small and short lived. A Wilmington, Delaware, society established in 1788 peaked at fifty members and ceased to exist in 1800. The Maryland society organized in 1781 with 6 members grew to 250 in 1797 but disbanded in 1798. African Americans and their white friends, nevertheless, hoped that antislavery sentiment was advancing southward.

MANUMISSION AND SELF-PURCHASE

Another hopeful sign for African Americans was that after the Revolution most southern states liberalized their manumission laws. In general, masters could free individual slaves by deed or will. They no longer had to go to court or petition a state legislature to prove that an individual they desired to free had performed a "meritorious service." Virginia led the way in 1782 by repealing its long-standing ban on private manumissions. Delaware followed in 1787, as did Maryland in 1790, Kentucky in 1792, and the slaveholding territory of Missouri in 1804.

As a result, hundreds of slaveholders in the upper South began freeing slaves. Religious sentiment and natural rights principles motivated many of these masters. Even though most of them opposed general emancipation, they considered the slave system immoral. Yet noble motives were not always the most important. Masters often profited from self-purchase agreements they negotiated with their slaves. To purchase their freedom, or that of loved ones, slaves raised money over a number of years by marketing farm produce or through outside employment and paid installments to their masters. This allowed masters to enjoy income in addition to the slave's labor over the period of time the slave needed to raise the entire purchase price.

Masters also sometimes manumitted slaves who were no longer profitable investments. A master might be switching from tobacco to wheat or corn—crops that did not need a year-round workforce. Or a master might manumit older slaves whose best years as workers were behind them. Frequently, however, slaves, usually young men, presented masters with the alternative of manumitting them after a term of years or having them escape immediately.

Self-purchase often left African Americans in precarious financial condition. Sometimes they used up their savings to buy their freedom. In other instances, they went into debt to their former masters, to white lawyers who acted as their agents, or to other white people who had loaned them money to cover their purchase price. On occasion, after receiving money from a slave, masters reneged on their agreement to manumit. Many of the freedom suits that became common in the upper South during this period resulted from such unethical behavior.

THE EMERGENCE OF A FREE BLACK CLASS IN THE SOUTH

As a result of manumission, self-purchase, and freedom suits, the free black population of the upper South blossomed. Maryland and Virginia had the largest free black populations. Between 1790 and 1820, the number of free African Americans in Maryland climbed from 8,043 to 39,730 and in Virginia from 12,766 to 36,889. By 1820 the upper South (Delaware, Maryland, Virginia, District of Columbia, Kentucky, Missouri, North Carolina, and Tennessee) had a free black population of 114,070, compared with a northern free black population of 99,281. However, most of the upper South's black population remained in slavery while the North's was on the way to general emancipation. In the North, 83.9 percent of African Americans were free in 1820, compared with 10.6 percent of those in the upper South.

In the deep South (South Carolina, Georgia, Florida, Louisiana, Alabama, and Mississippi), both the percentage and the absolute numbers of free black people remained much smaller. During the eighteenth century, neither South Carolina nor Georgia restricted the right of masters to manumit their slaves, but far fewer masters in these states exercised this right after the Revolution than was the case in the Chesapeake. Manumission declined in Louisiana following its annexation to the United States. Generally, masters in the deep South freed only their illegitimate slave children, other favorites, or those unable to work. Only 20,153 free black people lived in the deep South in 1820. In North Carolina, a transitional area between the upper and deep South, the state legislature made manumission more difficult after 1777. But many masters—especially those who were Quakers—freed their slaves anyway or let them live in quasi-freedom.

The emergence of a free black class in the South, especially in the deep South, produced social strata more similar to that in Latin America than was the case in the North. As in the Caribbean, South America, and portions of Mexico, there were dominant white people, free people of color, and slaves. In southern cities, such as Charleston, Savannah, and New Orleans, some free African Americans not only identified economically and culturally with their former masters, they also acquired slaves.

Forces for Slavery

The forces for black freedom in the new republic rested on widespread African-American dissatisfaction with slavery, economic change, Christian morality, and revolutionary precepts. Most black northerners had achieved freedom by 1800, three-quarters were free by 1810, and by 1840 only 0.7 percent remained in slavery. Yet for the nation as a whole and for the mass of African Americans, the forces favoring slavery proved to be stronger. Abolition took place in the North where slavery was weak. In the South, where it was strong, slavery thrived and expanded. Virginia, for example, had 293,427 slaves in 1790, and—despite manumissions and escapes—it had 425,153 in 1820. Even more significant, although Virginia continued to have the largest population of enslaved African Americans in the country, slave populations grew more quickly in North Carolina, South Carolina, and Georgia. Meanwhile, slavery expanded westward. When Tennessee was still a territory in 1790, it had 3,417 slaves. By 1820 the state of Tennessee had 80,107 slaves.

THE U.S. CONSTITUTION

The U.S. Constitution, which went into effect in 1789, became a major force in favor of the continued enslavement of African Americans. Earlier, during the War for Independence, the Continental Congress had provided a weak central government for the United States, as each of the thirteen states retained control over its own internal affairs. The Articles of Confederation, which served as the American constitution from 1781 to 1789, formalized this system of divided sovereignty.

ACTIVITY
Ratification of the Constitution

However, by the mid-1780s, wealthy and powerful men perceived that the Confederation Congress was too weak to protect their interests. Democratic movements in the states threatened property rights. The inability of Congress to regulate commerce led to trade disputes among the states. Congress's inability to tax left it unable to maintain an army and navy. Congress could not control the western territories, and, most frightening to the wealthy, it could not help states put down popular uprisings, such as that led by Daniel Shays in western Massachusetts in 1786.

The fears Shays's Rebellion caused led directly to the Constitutional Convention in Philadelphia that in 1787 produced the Constitution under which the United States is still governed. The new constitution gave the central government power to regulate commerce, to tax, and to have its laws enforced in the states. But the convention could not create a more powerful central government without first making important concessions to southern slaveholders.

The delegates to the convention omitted the words *slave* and *slavery* from the Constitution. But they included clauses designed to maintain the enslavement of African Americans in the southern states. These clauses provided for continuing the Atlantic slave trade for twenty years, for national military aid in suppressing slave revolts, and for returning to their masters slaves who escaped to other states. The Constitution also enhanced representation for slaveholders in Congress and in the electoral college that elected the president and vice president.

Humanitarian opposition to the Atlantic slave trade had mounted during the revolutionary era. Under pressure from black activists—such as Prince Hall of Boston—and Quakers, northern state legislatures during the 1780s forbade their citizens to engage in the slave trade. Rhode Island led the way in 1787. Massachusetts, Connecticut, and Pennsylvania followed in 1788. Economic change in the upper South also prompted opposition to the trade. Virginia, for example, banned the importation of slaves from abroad nearly a decade before Rhode Island.

Yet convention delegates from South Carolina and Georgia maintained that their states had an acute labor shortage. They threatened that citizens of these states would not tolerate a central government that could stop them from importing slaves—at least not in the near future. Torn between these conflicting perspectives, the convention compromised by including a provision in the Constitution that prohibited Congress from abolishing the trade until 1808. During the twenty years prior to 1808, when Congress banned the trade, thousands of Africans were brought into the southern states. Between 1804 and 1808, for example, 40,000 entered through Charleston. Overall,

DOCUMENT
Congress Prohibits Importation of Slaves, 1807
5-4

more slaves entered the United States between 1787 and 1808 than during any other twenty-year period in American history. Such huge numbers helped fuel the westward expansion of the slave system.

Other proslavery clauses of the U.S. Constitution aimed to counteract slave rebellion and escape. The Constitution gave Congress power to put down "insurrections" and "domestic violence." It also provided that persons "held to service or labour in one State, escaping into another . . . shall be delivered up on claim of the party to whom such service or labour may be due." This clause was the basis for the **Fugitive Slave Act of 1793**, which allowed masters or their agents to pursue slaves across state lines, capture them, and take them before a magistrate. There, on presentation of satisfactory evidence, masters could regain legal custody of the person they claimed. This act did not stop slaves from escaping from Virginia and Maryland to Pennsylvania. But it did extend the power of masters into the North, force the federal and northern state governments to uphold slavery, create personal tragedies for those who were recaptured, and encourage the kidnapping of free black northerners falsely claimed as escapees.

Finally, the Constitution strengthened the political power of slaveholders through the Three-Fifths Clause. This clause was also a compromise between northern and southern delegates at the Convention. Southern delegates desired slaves to be counted toward representation in the national government but not counted for purposes of taxation. Northern delegates desired just the opposite. The **Three-Fifths Clause** provided that a slave be counted as three-fifths of a free person in determining a state's representation in the House of Representatives and in the electoral college. Slaves would be counted similarly if and when Congress instituted a per capita tax.

This gave southern slaveholders increased representation on the basis of the number of slaves they owned—slaves who, of course, had no vote or representation. The South gained enormous political advantage from it. If not for the Three-Fifths Clause, for example, northern nonslaveholder John Adams would have been reelected president in 1800 instead of losing the presidency to southern slaveholder Thomas Jefferson. For many years, this clause contributed to the domination of the U.S. government by slaveholding southerners, although the South's population steadily fell behind the North's. That Congress never instituted a per capita tax made this victory for slaveholders all the more remarkable.

Four other factors, however, were more important than constitutional provisions in fostering the continued enslavement of African Americans in the new republic: increased cultivation of cotton, the Louisiana Purchase, declining revolutionary fervor, and intensified white racism.

COTTON

The most obvious of the four developments was the increase in cotton production. By the late eighteenth century, Britain led the world in textile manufacturing. As mechanization made the spinning of cotton cloth more economical, Britain's demand for raw cotton increased dramatically. The United States led in filling that demand as a result of Eli Whitney's invention of the **cotton gin** in 1793. This simple machine provided an easy and quick way to remove the seeds from the type of cotton most commonly grown in the South.

British demand combined with the cotton gin encouraged cotton production in the United States to rise from 3,000 to 178,000 bales between 1790 and 1810. Cotton became by far the most lucrative U.S. export. Southern cotton production also encouraged the development of textile mills in New England, thereby creating a proslavery alliance between the "lords of the lash and the lords of the loom."

Cotton reinvigorated the slave-labor system, which spread rapidly across Georgia and later into Alabama, Mississippi, Louisiana, and Texas. Cotton was also cultivated in South Carolina, North Carolina, and parts of Virginia and Tennessee. To make matters worse for African Americans, the westward expansion of cotton production encouraged an internal slave trade. Masters in the old tobacco-growing regions of Maryland, Virginia, and other states began to support themselves by selling their slaves to the new cotton-growing regions (see Figure 5–1).

THE LOUISIANA PURCHASE AND AFRICAN AMERICANS IN THE LOWER MISSISSIPPI VALLEY

The Jefferson administration's purchase of Louisiana from France in 1803 accelerated the westward expansion of slavery and the **domestic slave trade**. The purchase nearly doubled the area of the United States. That slavery might extend over this vast region became an issue of great importance to African Americans. The purchase also brought under American sovereignty those black people, both free and slave, who lived in the portion of the territory that centered on the city of New Orleans. As Chapter 3 indicates, black life in this region had developed a distinctive pattern under French rule from 1699 to 1763, under Spanish rule from 1763 to 1801, and under French rule again between 1801 and 1803. Although people of African descent constituted a majority of the region's population, they were divided into two groups. First were the free people of color who referred to themselves as Creoles. They were craftsmen and shopkeepers in New Orleans and other port cities. They spoke French, belonged to the Roman Catholic Church, and aspired to equal rights with other free inhabitants. Some of them bought and sold slaves. Their numbers had increased under Spanish rule as urban slaves purchased their freedom. This route to freedom became more difficult under American sovereignty, but, as a group, Louisiana's free people of color remained optimistically integrationist in outlook.

It was, nevertheless, the second black group that grew more rapidly. It consisted of slaves, most of whom had come directly from Africa and worked on the region's plantations. Spain had encouraged white Americans to settle in the lower Mississippi Valley. The Americans, in turn, demanded more strictly enforced slave codes and the expansion of the external slave trade. At first the slaves produced tobacco and indigo, but by the 1790s sugar and cotton had emerged as the crops of the future. As demand for these crops grew, conditions for slaves in Louisiana became increasingly harsh, especially after the region became part of the United States. The slaves' rural location, their predominantly African culture, and, eventually, their Protestant religion cut them off from free people of color. In 1770 the region that later became the state of Louisiana had a slave population of 5,600. By 1810 it had 34,660, and by 1820 the slave population numbered 149,654. This tremendous growth, involving an extremely harsh form of slavery in a huge region, constituted a warning to all opponents of that institution. With the termination of the external slave trade, the notorious slave markets of New Orleans became the dreaded destination of thousands of African Americans "sold south" by their masters in the domestic slave trade.

CONSERVATISM AND RACISM

The waning of revolutionary humanitarianism and the rise of a more intense racism among white people were less tangible forces than cotton production and the Louisiana Purchase, but they were just as important in strengthening slavery. They also made life more difficult for free African Americans.

By the 1790s white Americans had begun a long retreat from the egalitarianism of the revolutionary era. In the North and the Chesapeake, most white people

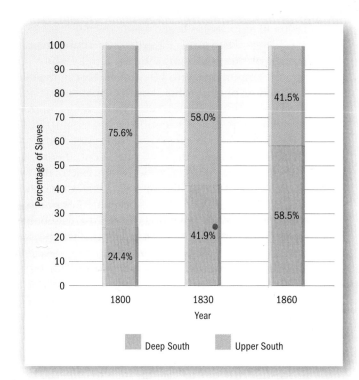

FIGURE 5–1 DISTRIBUTION OF THE SOUTHERN SLAVE POPULATION, 1800–1860.

The demand for slaves in the cotton-growing deep South produced a major shift in the distribution of the slave population.

became less willing to challenge the prerogatives of slaveholders and more willing to accept slavery as suitable for African Americans. Most Marylanders and Virginians came to think of emancipation as best left to the distant future. This outlook strengthened the slaveholders and their nonslaveholding white supporters in the deep South who had never embraced the humanitarian precepts of the Enlightenment and Great Awakening.

Increasing proslavery sentiment among white Americans stemmed, in part, from revulsion against the radicalism of the French Revolution that had begun in 1789. Reports from France of bloody class warfare, disruption of the social order, and redistribution of property led most Americans to value property rights—including rights to human property—and order above equal rights. In addition, as cotton production spread westward and the value of slaves soared, rationalist and evangelical criticism of human bondage withered. Antislavery sentiment in the upper South that had flourished among slaveholders, nonslaveholders, Deists, Methodists, and Baptists became increasingly confined to African Americans and Quakers. During the early 1800s, manumissions began a long decline.

Using race to justify slavery was an important component of this conservative trend. Unlike white people, the argument went, black people were unsuited for freedom or citizenship. The doctrines embodied in the Declaration of Independence, therefore, did not apply to them. A new scientific racism supported this outlook. As early as the 1770s, some American intellectuals challenged the Enlightenment theory that perceived racial differences were not essential or inherent but results of the different environments in which Africans and Europeans originated. Scholars instead proposed that God had created a great chain of being from lesser creatures to higher creatures. In this chain, black people constituted a separate species as close to the great apes as to white people. During the 1780s Thomas Jefferson reflected this view when he argued that "scientific observation" supported the conclusion that black people were inherently "inferior to whites in the endowments of both body and mind."

Such views became common among white northerners and white southerners. They also had practical results. During the 1790s Congress expressed its determination to exclude African Americans from the benefits of citizenship in "a white man's country." A 1790 law limited the granting of naturalized citizenship to "any alien, being a white person." Two years later, Congress limited enrollment in state militias to "each and every free, able-bodied white male citizen." These laws implied that African Americans had no place in the United States except as slaves. They suggested that the free black class was an anomaly and, in the opinion of most white people, a dangerous anomaly.

The Emergence of Free Black Communities

The competing forces of slavery and racism, on one hand, and freedom and opportunity, on the other, shaped the growth of African-American communities in the early American republic. A distinctive black culture had existed since the early colonial period. But enslavement had limited black community life. The advent of large free black populations in the North and upper South after the Revolution allowed African Americans to establish autonomous and dynamic communities. They appeared in Philadelphia, Baltimore, Newport (Rhode Island), Richmond, Norfolk (Virginia), New York, and Boston. Although smaller and less autonomous, there were also free black communities in such deep South cities as Charleston, Savannah, and New Orleans. As free black people in these cities acquired a modicum of wealth and education, they established institutions that have shaped African-American life ever since.

A combination of factors encouraged African Americans to form these distinctive institutions. First, as they emerged from slavery, they realized they would have inferior status in white-dominated organizations or not be allowed to participate in them at all. Second, black people valued the African heritage they had preserved over generations in slavery. They wanted institutions that would perpetuate their heritage.

The earliest black community institutions were mutual aid societies. Patterned on similar white organizations, these societies were like modern insurance companies and benevolent organizations. They provided for their members' medical and burial expenses and helped support widows and children. African Americans in Newport, Rhode Island, organized the first black mutual aid society in 1780. Seven years later, Richard Allen and Absalom Jones established the more famous Free African Society in Philadelphia.

Preamble of the Free African Society, 1787 — DOCUMENT 5-2

Most early free black societies admitted only men, but similar organizations for women appeared during the 1790s. In 1793 Philadelphia's Female Benevolent Society of St. Thomas took over the welfare functions of the city's Free African Society. Other black women's organizations in Philadelphia during the early republic included the Benevolent Daughters established in 1796 by Sarah Allen (the wife of the Rev. Richard Allen), the Daughters of Africa established in 1812, the American Female Bond Benevolent Society formed in 1817, and the Female Benezet begun in 1818.

These ostensibly secular societies maintained a decidedly Christian moral character. They insisted that their members meet standards of middle-class propriety and, in effect, became self-improvement as well as mutual aid societies. Members had to pledge to refrain from fornication, adultery, drunkenness, and other "disreputable behavior." By the early 1800s, such societies also organized resistance to kidnappers who sought to recapture fugitive slaves or enslave free African Americans.

Because the societies provided real benefits and reflected black middle-class aspirations, they spread to every black urban community. More than one hundred such organizations existed in Philadelphia alone by 1830. Although these societies were more common in the North than in the South, Baltimore had about thirty of them by that same year, and Charleston, South Carolina, had at least two. One of them was the Brown Fellowship, founded in 1790, which admitted only black men with light complexions. The other was open to all free black men in Charleston.

Of particular importance were the black Freemasons because, unlike other free black organizations, the Masons united black men from several northern cities. Combining rationalism with secrecy and obscure ritual, Freemasonry was a major movement among European and American men during the late eighteenth and early nineteenth centuries. Opportunities for male bonding, wearing fancy regalia, and achieving prestige in a supposedly ancient hierarchy attracted both black and white men. As historians James Oliver Horton and Lois E. Horton suggest, black people drew special satisfaction from the European-based order's claims to have originated in ancient Egypt, which black people associated with their own African heritage.

The most famous black Mason of his time was Prince Hall, the Revolutionary War veteran and abolitionist. During the 1770s he began in Boston what be-

came known as the **Prince Hall Masons**. In several respects, Hall's relationship to Masonry epitomizes the free black predicament in America.

In 1775 the local white Masonic lodge in Boston rejected Hall's application for membership because of his black ancestry. Therefore, Hall, who was a Patriot, organized African Lodge No. 1 on the basis of a limited license he secured from a British Masonic lodge associated with the British Army that then occupied Boston. The irony of this situation compounded when, after the War for Independence, American Masonry refused to grant the African Lodge a full charter. Hall again had to turn to the British Masons, who approved his application in 1787. Under this British charter, Hall in 1791 organized the African Grand Lodge of North America (later renamed the Prince Hall Grand Lodge) and became its first grand master. Even before this he had begun authorizing black lodges in other cities, including Philadelphia and Providence, Rhode Island.

THE ORIGINS OF INDEPENDENT BLACK CHURCHES

Although black churches emerged at least a decade later than black benevolent associations, the churches quickly became the core of African-American communities. Not only did these churches attend to the spiritual needs of free black people and—in some southern cities—slaves, their pastors also became the primary African-American leaders. Black church buildings housed schools, social organizations, and antislavery meetings.

This late-eighteenth-century portrait of Prince Hall (1735?–1807) dressed as a gentleman places him among Masonic symbols. A former slave, a skilled craftsman and entrepreneur, an abolitionist, and an advocate of black education, Hall is best remembered as the founder of the African Lodge of North America, popularly known as the Prince Hall Masons.

This drawing portrays Philadelphia's Bethel African Methodist Episcopal Church as it appeared in 1829. It had been built in 1793 under the direction of Richard Allen, the first bishop of the AME denomination, and had been "rebuilt" in 1803. The Library Company of Philadelphia

RICHARD ALLEN ON THE BREAK WITH ST. GEORGE'S CHURCH

It took an emotionally wrenching experience to convince Richard Allen, Absalom Jones, and other black Methodists that they must break their association with St. George's Church. Allen published the following account in 1831 as part of his autobiography, The Life Experiences and Gospel Labors of the Rt. Rev. Richard Allen. *Although many years had passed since the incident, Allen's account retains a strong emotional immediacy.*

A number of us usually attended St. George's church in Fourth street; and when the colored people began to get numerous in attending the church, they moved us from the seats we usually sat on, and placed us around the wall, and on Sabbath morning, we went to the church and the sexton stood at the door, and told us to go in the gallery. He told us to go, and we would see where to sit. We expected to take the seats over the ones we formerly occupied below, not knowing any better. We took those seats. Meeting had begun and they were nearly done singing, and just as we got to the seats, the elder said, "Let us pray." We had not been long upon our knees before I heard considerable scuffling and low talking. I raised my head up and saw one of the trustees, H M, having hold of the Rev. Absalom Jones, pulling him up off his knees, and saying, "You must get up—you must not kneel here." Mr. Jones replied, "Wait until prayer is over." Mr. H M said, "No, you must get up now, or I will call for aid and force you away." Mr. Jones said, "Wait until prayer is over, and I will get up and trouble you no more." With that he [H M] beckoned to one of the other trustees, Mr. L S to come to his assistance. He came, and went to William White to pull him up. By this time prayer was over, and we all went out of the church in a body, and they were no more plagued with us in the church. . . . We then hired a storeroom, and held worship by ourselves. Here we were pursued with threats of being disowned, and read publicly out of meeting if we did continue worship in the place we had hired; but we believed the Lord would be our friend. We got subscription papers out to raise money to build the house of the Lord.

🌿 *What appears to have sparked the confrontation Allen describes?*

🌿 *How did white church leaders respond to the withdrawal of the church's black members?*

During the late eighteenth century, as the egalitarian spirit of the Great Awakening waned among white Baptists, Methodists, and Episcopalians, separate, but not independent, black churches appeared in the South. The biracial churches spawned by the Awakening had never embraced African Americans on an equal basis with white people. Although there had initially been promising tendencies within biracial churches, as time passed white people denied black people significant influence in church governance. White parishioners also subjected African Americans to segregated seating, communion services, Sunday schools, and cemeteries. In response African Americans formed separate black congregations, usually headed by black ministers but subordinate to white church hierarchies. The first such congregations appeared during the 1770s in South Carolina and Georgia.

In contrast to these subordinate churches, a truly independent black church emerged gradually in Philadelphia between the 1780s and the early 1800s. The movement for such a church began within the city's white-controlled St. George's Methodist Church. The movement's leaders were Richard Allen and Absalom Jones, who could rely on the Free African Society they had established to help them.

These men were former slaves who had purchased their freedom: Allen in 1780 and Jones in 1783. Allen, a fervent Methodist since the 1770s, had received permis-

Raphaelle Peale, the son of famous Philadelphia portraitist Charles Wilson Peale, completed this oil portrait of the Reverend Absalom Jones (1746–1818) in 1810. Reverend Jones is shown in his ecclesiastical robes holding a Bible in his hand.

sion from St. George's white leadership to preach to black people in the evenings in what was then a simple church building. By the mid-1780s, Jones had joined Allen's congregation, and soon they and other black members of St. George's chafed under policies they considered un-Christian and insulting. But Allen's and Jones's faith that Methodist egalitarianism would prevail over racial discrimination undermined their efforts during the 1780s to create a separate black Methodist church.

DOCUMENT 5-5 *Absalom Jones, Sermon on the Abolition of the International Slave Trade, 1808*

The break finally came in 1792 when St. George's white leaders grievously insulted the church's black members. An attempt by white trustees to prevent Jones from praying in what the trustees considered the white section of the church led black members to walk out. "We all went out of the church in a body," recalled Allen, "and they were no more plagued with us in the church."

St. George's white leaders fought hard and long to control the expanding and economically valuable black congregation. Yet other white Philadelphians, led by abolitionist Benjamin Rush, applauded the concept of an independent "African church." Rush and other sympathetic white people contributed to the new church's building fund. When construction began in 1793, Rush and at least one hundred other white people joined with African Americans at a banquet to celebrate the occasion.

However, the black congregation soon split. When the majority determined that the new church would be Episcopalian rather than Methodist, Allen and a few others refused to join. The result was *two* black churches in Philadelphia. St. Thomas's Episcopal Church, with Jones as priest, opened in July 1794 as an African-American congregation within the white-led national Episcopal Church. Then Allen's Mother Bethel congregation got under way as the first truly independent black church. The white leaders of St. George's tried to control Mother Bethel until 1816. That year Mother Bethel became the birthplace of the **African Methodist Episcopal (AME) Church.** Allen became the first bishop of this organization, which quickly spread to other cities in the North and the South.

The more significant among the other AME congregations were Daniel Coker's in Baltimore, the AME Zion in New York, and those in Wilmington, Delaware; Salem, New Jersey; and Attleboro, Pennsylvania. Additional independent black churches formed at this time out of similar conflicts with white-led congregations. Among them were the African Baptist Church established in Boston in 1805 and led by Thomas Paul from 1806 to 1808, the Presbyterian Evangelical Society founded in 1811 by John Gloucester, the Abyssinian Baptist Church organized in New York City in 1808 by Paul, and the African Presbyterian Church established in Philadelphia by Samuel E. Cornish in 1822.

THE FIRST BLACK SCHOOLS

Schools for African-American children, slave and free, date to the early 1700s. In both North and South, white clergy, including Cotton Mather, ran the schools. So did Quakers, early abolition societies, and missionaries acting for the Anglican Society for the Propagation of the Gospel in Foreign Parts. But the first schools established by African Americans to instruct African-American children arose after the Revolution. The new black mutual aid societies and churches created and sustained them.

Schools for black people organized or taught by white people continued to flourish. But in other instances, black people founded their own schools because local white authorities regularly refused either to admit black children to public schools or to maintain adequate separate black schools. For example, in 1796, when Prince Hall failed to convince Boston's city council to provide a school for black students, he had the children taught in his home and that of his son Primus. By 1806 Hall's school was meeting in the basement of the new African Meeting House, which housed Thomas Paul's African Baptist Church.

Hall was not the first to take such action. As early as 1790, Charleston's Brown Fellowship operated a school for its members' children. Free black people in Baltimore supported schools during the same decade, and during the early 1800s, similar schools opened in Washington, D.C. Such schools frequently employed white teachers. Not until Philadelphia's Mother Bethel Church established the Augustine School in 1818 did a school entirely administered and taught by African Americans for black children exist.

These schools faced great difficulties. Many black families could not afford the fees, but rather than turn children away, the schools strained their meager resources by taking charity cases. Some black parents also believed education was pointless when African Americans often could not get skilled jobs. White people feared competition from skilled black workers, believed black schools attracted undesirable populations, and, particularly in the South, feared that educated free African Americans would encourage slaves to revolt.

Threats of violence against black schools and efforts to suppress them were common. The case of Christopher McPherson exemplifies these dangers.

ABSALOM JONES PETITIONS CONGRESS ON BEHALF OF FUGITIVES FACING REENSLAVEMENT

Absalom Jones wrote his petition to Congress on behalf of four black men who had been manumitted in North Carolina. Because they were in danger of being reenslaved, they had taken refuge in Philadelphia. The men, under whose names the petition appears in the Annals of Congress, *were Jupiter Nicholson, Jacob Nicholson, Joe Albert, and Thomas Pritchet. Jones provided brief accounts of their troubles. Here we include only the important general principles that Jones invoked. Southern representatives argued that accepting a petition from alleged slaves would set a dangerous precedent, and Congress refused to accept the petition.*

To the President, Senate, and House of Representatives,

The Petition and Representation of the under-named Freemen, respectfully showeth:

That, being of African descent, the late inhabitants and natives of North Carolina, to you only, under God, can we apply with any hope of effect, for redress of our grievances, having been compelled to leave the State wherein we had a right of residence, as freemen liberated under the hand and seal of humane and conscientious masters, the validity of which act of justice in restoring us to our native right of freedom, was confirmed by judgment of the Superior Court of North Carolina . . . yet, not long after this decision, a law of that State was enacted, under which men of cruel disposition, and void of just principle, received countenance and authority in violently seizing, imprisoning, and selling into slavery, such as had been so emancipated; whereby we were reduced to the necessity of separating from some of our nearest and most tender connections, and seeking refuge in such parts of the Union where more regard is paid to the public declaration in favor of liberty and the common right of man, several hundreds, under our circumstances, having, in consequence of the said law, been hunted day and night, like beasts of the forest, by armed men with dogs, and made a prey of as free and lawful plunder . . .

We beseech your impartial attention to our hard condition, not only with respect to our personal sufferings, as freemen, but as a class of that people who, distinguished by color, are therefore with a degrading partiality, considered by many, even of those in eminent stations, as unentitled to that public justice and protection which is the great object of Government. . . .

If, notwithstanding all that has been publicly avowed as essential principles respecting the extent of human right to freedom; notwithstanding we have had that right restored to us, so far as was in the power of those by whom we were held as slaves, we cannot claim the privilege of representation in your councils, yet we trust we may address you as fellow-men, who, under God, the sovereign Ruler of the Universe, are intrusted with the distribution of justice, for the terror of evil-doers, the encouragement of protection of the innocent, not doubting that you are men of liberal minds, susceptible of benevolent feelings and clear conception of rectitude to a catholic extent, who can admit that black people . . . have natural affections, social and domestic attachments and sensibilities; and that, therefore, we may hope for a share in your sympathetic attention while we represent that the unconstitutional bondage in which multitudes of our fellows in complexion are held, is to us a subject sorrowfully affecting; for we cannot conceive their condition (more especially those who have been emancipated and tasted the sweets of liberty, and again reduced to slavery by kidnappers and man-stealers) to be less afflicting or deplorable than the situation of citizens of the United States, captured and enslaved through the unrighteous policy prevalent in Algiers . . . may we not be allowed to consider this stretch of power, morally and politically, a Governmental defect, if not a direct violation of the declared fundamental principles of the Constitution; and finally, is not some remedy for an evil of such magnitude highly worthy of the deep inquiry and unfeigned zeal of the supreme Legislative body of a free and enlightened people?

🌲 *On what principles does Jones believe the U.S. government is bound to act?*

🌲 *What does Jones's petition indicate concerning the status of African Americans before the law?*

Source: *Annals of Congress*, 4 Cong., 2 sess. (January 23, 1797), 2015–18.

McPherson, a free African American, established a night school for black men at Richmond, Virginia, in 1811 and hired a white teacher. All went well until McPherson advertised the school in a local newspaper. In response, white residents forced the teacher to leave the city, and local authorities had McPherson committed to the state lunatic asylum. Nevertheless, similar schools continued to operate in the North and upper South, producing a growing class of literate African Americans.

Black Leaders and Choices

By the 1790s an educated black elite had come into existence in the North and the Chesapeake. It provided leadership for African Americans in religion, economic advancement, and racial politics. Experience had driven members of this elite to a contradictory perception of themselves and of America. On the one hand, they were acculturated, patriotic Americans who had achieved some personal well-being and security. On the other hand, they knew that American society had not lived up to its revolutionary principles. They lamented the continued enslavement of the mass of African Americans, and they had misgivings about the future.

Prominent among these leaders were members of the clergy. Two of the most important of them were Richard Allen and Absalom Jones. Besides organizing his church, Allen opened a school in Philadelphia for black children, wrote against slavery and racial prejudice, and made his home a refuge for fugitive slaves. A year before his death in 1831, Allen presided over the first national black convention.

Jones, too, was an early abolitionist. In 1797 his concern for fugitives facing reenslavement led him to become the first African American to petition Congress. His petition anticipated later abolitionists in suggesting that slavery violated the spirit of the U.S. Constitution and that Congress could abolish it.

Other influential black ministers of the late eighteenth and early nineteenth centuries were Jupiter Hammon of Long Island, Daniel Coker of Baltimore, John Chavis of Virginia, and Lemuel Haynes of New England. Hammon, who is quoted at the beginning of this chapter, became a well-known poet. Coker, who was of mixed race, conducted a school, cofounded the AME Church, and advocated black migration to Africa. Chavis also combined preaching and teaching. Born free, he served on the Patriot side in the War for Independence and entered the College of New Jersey (Princeton) in 1792. Thereafter he became a Presbyterian missionary among African Americans in Virginia, Maryland, and North Carolina and gained a wide reputation as a biblical scholar. Haynes was perhaps even better known for his intellectual accomplishments. The son of a white mother and black father, Haynes served with the Minutemen and Continental Army, spoke against slavery, and in 1780 he became the first ordained black Congregationalist minister, serving as pastor to several white congregations.

Vying with clergy for influence were African-American entrepreneurs. Prince Hall, for example, owned successful leather dressing and catering businesses in Boston, and Peter Williams, principal founder of New York's AME Zion Church, was a prosperous tobacco merchant. Another prominent black entrepreneur was James Forten of Philadelphia, described as "probably the most noteworthy free African-American entrepreneur in the early nineteenth century." Born to free parents in 1766, Forten was a Patriot during the War for Independence, learned the craft of sail making, and became the owner of his own business in 1798. For the rest of his life, he advocated equal rights and abolition.

American patriotism, religious conviction, organizational skill, intellectual inquisitiveness, and antislavery activism delineate the lives of most free black leaders in this era. Yet these leaders often were torn in their perceptions of what was best for African Americans. Hammon and Chavis were accommodationist about slavery and racial oppression. They condemned slavery and lauded human liberty, but they were not activists. They maintained that God would eventually end injustice. As late as 1836, Chavis, who lived in the South, wrote "that Slavery is a national evil no one doubts, but what is to be done? . . . All that can be done, is to make the best of a bad bargain. For I am clearly of the opinion that immediate emancipation would be to entail the greatest earthly curse upon my brethren according to the flesh."

Allen, Jones, Hall, and Forten were more optimistic than Hammon and Chavis about the ability of African Americans to mold their destiny in the United States. Although they each expressed misgivings, they believed that, despite setbacks, the egalitarian principles of the American Revolution would prevail if black people insisted on liberty. Forten never despaired that African Americans would be integrated into the larger American society on the basis of their individual talent and enterprise. Although he was often frustrated, Hall for four decades pursued a strategy based on the assumption that white authority would reward black protest and patriotism. In 1786, when Daniel Shays led his revolt of white farmers in western Massachusetts, Hall offered to raise seven hundred black volunteers to help defeat the insurgency. Allen and Jones put more emphasis on separate black institutions than did Forten or Hall. Yet they were just as willing to organize, protest, and petition to establish the rights of black people as American citizens.

PROFILE ❧ JAMES FORTEN

James Forten was one of the few black leaders of the early American republic to live well beyond that era. His long career as a determined opponent of slavery linked the time of Prince Hall and Richard Allen to that of the militant abolitionists William Lloyd Garrison and Frederick Douglass (see Chapters 8 and 9). From the 1790s until his death in 1842, Forten used his wealth and organizational talents to build a cohesive black community in Philadelphia. But he also struggled to create a broader American community based on merit rather than on racial privilege.

Forten was born in Philadelphia in 1766. Family tradition held that one of his great grandfathers was an African who had been brought to Delaware in the late 1600s. His paternal grandfather was one of the first Pennsylvania slaves to purchase his freedom.

As a child, Forten learned to read and write at a school run by Quaker abolitionist Anthony Benezet and acquired Benezet's broad humanistic philosophy. In 1781 Forten volunteered to serve as a powder boy with a cannon crew on board the American privateer *Royal Louis*. He proved himself a brave sailor in battle. He was also deeply patriotic. When taken prisoner and offered special treatment by the son of a British officer, Forten declared, "No, NO! I am here a prisoner for the liberties of my country; *I never, NEVER, shall prove a traitor to her interests.*" As a result of his defiance, Forten spent seven months on a rotting prison ship in the New York harbor.

After his release Forten walked back to Philadelphia and became an apprentice sail maker. He became foreman in 1786 and bought the business in 1798. By 1807 he employed an interracial workforce of thirty members, and by 1832 had acquired a fortune of about $100,000—a large sum at the time.

Throughout the 1780s and most of the 1790s, Forten stood aloof from Philadelphia's developing black community. He did not join the Free African Society or help establish separate black churches. Not until 1797 did he emerge as an active black leader. At that time he joined Richard Allen and Absalom Jones in establishing the African Masonic Lodge of Pennsylvania, which Prince Hall came to Philadelphia to install. Forten then joined eighty other Philadelphia African Americans to petition Congress to repeal the Fugitive Slave Law of 1793.

By 1817 Forten had become a major opponent of black migration to Africa. Although he had previously endorsed some colonization schemes, he had come to believe such efforts were racist because they assumed that black people were not suited for American citizenship. Rather than commit resources to sending African Americans to other parts of the world, he was determined to improve their standing in the United States. In 1809 he joined Allen and Jones in creating a self-improvement organization, the Society for the Suppression of Vice and Immorality. By 1830 he hoped to use the newly organized Black National Convention movement to train young black men for skilled trades.

At about the same time, Forten became an important influence on the white abolitionist leader William Lloyd Garrison. Forten welcomed Garrison to his home, introduced him to other black leaders, and helped finance his antislavery newspaper, the *Liberator*. In 1833 Forten joined Garrison, Arthur Tappan, Lewis Tappan, and other white and black abolitionists in organizing the American Antislavery Society, pledged to the peaceful immediate abolition of slavery without colonization of the former slaves and without compensation to slaveholders. Increasingly radical during his remaining years, Forten advocated an end to war, favored equal rights for women, and resisted the enforcement of the Fugitive Slave Law. He also helped establish the American Moral Reform Society. He demonstrated his commitment to women's rights in the way he raised his daughters, Sarah, Margaretta, and Harriet, who carried on his activism.

◀ James Forten, by an unknown artist.

Forten

MIGRATION

African Americans, however, had another alternative: migration from the United States to establish their own society free from white prejudices. In 1787 British philanthropists, including Olaudah Equiano, had established Freetown in Sierra Leone on the West African coast as a refuge for former slaves. As we mentioned in Chapter 4, some African Americans who had been Loyalists during the American Revolution settled there. Other black and white Americans proposed that free black people should settle western North America or in the Caribbean islands. There were great practical obstacles to mass black migration to each of these regions. Migration was extremely expensive, difficult to organize, and involved long, often fruitless, negotiations with foreign governments. But no black leader during the early national period was immune to the appeal of such proposals.

Aware of Freetown, Hall in 1787 petitioned the Massachusetts legislature to support efforts by black Bostonians to establish a colony in Africa. Although he recognized black progress in Massachusetts, Hall maintained that he and others found themselves "in many respects, in very disagreeable and disadvantageous circumstances; most of which must attend us so long as we and our children live in America." By the mid-1810s, a few influential white Americans had also decided there was no place in the United States for free African Americans. In 1816 they organized the **American Colonization Society**. Under its auspices, Coker in 1820 led the first party of eighty-six African Americans to the new colony of Liberia on the West African coast.

The major black advocate of migration to Africa during this period, however, was Paul Cuffe, the son of an Ashanti (in modern Ghana) father and Wampanoag Indian mother. He became a prosperous New England sea captain and, by the early 1800s, cooperated with British humanitarians and entrepreneurs to promote migration. He saw African-American colonization in West Africa as a way to end the Atlantic slave trade, spread Christianity, create a refuge for free black people, and make profits. Before his death in 1817, Cuffe had influenced not only Coker but also—at least temporarily—Forten, Allen, and Jones to consider colonization as a viable alternative for African Americans.

SLAVE UPRISINGS

While black northerners became increasingly aware of the limits to their freedom after the Revolution, black southerners saw the perpetuation of their enslavement. As cotton production expanded westward, as new slave states entered the Union, and as masters in such border slave states as Maryland and Virginia turned away from the revolutionary commitment to gradual emancipation, slaves faced several choices.

Some lowered their expectations and loyally served their masters. Most continued patterns of day-to-day resistance. Mounting numbers of men and women escaped. A few risked their lives to join revolutionary movements to destroy slavery violently. When just several hundred out of hundreds of thousands of slaves rallied behind Gabriel in 1800 near Richmond or Charles Deslondes in 1811 near New Orleans, they frightened white southerners and raised hopes for freedom among countless African Americans.

The egalitarian principles of the American and French revolutions influenced Gabriel and Deslondes. Unlike earlier slave rebels, they acted not to revenge personal grievances or to establish maroon communities but to destroy slavery because it denied natural human rights to its victims. The American Declaration of Independence and the legend of Haiti's Toussaint Louverture provided the intellectual foundations for their efforts. Louverture, against great odds, had led the enslaved black people of the French sugar colony of Saint Domingue—modern Haiti—to freedom and independence. This bitter and bloody struggle lasted from 1791 to 1804. Many white planters fled the island with their slaves to take refuge in Cuba, Jamaica, South Carolina, Virginia, and, somewhat later, Louisiana. The Haitian slaves carried the spirit of revolution with them to their new homes.

During the early 1790s, black unrest and rumors of pending revolt mounted in Virginia. The state militia arrested suspected plotters, who got off with whippings. In this revolutionary atmosphere, Gabriel, the human property of Thomas Prosser Sr., prepared to lead a massive slave insurrection. Gabriel was an acculturated and literate blacksmith well aware of the rationalist and revolutionary currents of his time. He was also a large and powerful man with a violent temper. In the fall of 1799 a local court convicted him of "'biting off a considerable part of [the] left Ear' of a white neighbor."

The ideology of the American Revolution shaped Gabriel's actions. He also perceived that white people were politically divided and distracted by an undeclared naval war with France. He enjoyed some secret white support and hoped that poor people generally would rally to his cause as he and his associates planned to kill those who supported slavery and take control of central Virginia.

But on August 30, 1800—the day set for the uprising—two slaves revealed the plan to white authorities

Toussaint Louverture (1744–1803) led the black rebellion in the French colony of St. Domingue on the Caribbean island of Hispaniola that led to the creation of the independent black republic of Haiti in 1804. Louverture became an inspiration for black rebels in the United States.   Stock Montage, Inc./Historical Pictures Collection

while a tremendous thunderstorm prevented Gabriel's followers from assaulting Richmond. Then Virginia governor—and future U.S. president—James Monroe quickly had suspects arrested. Gabriel, who relied on white allies to get to Norfolk, was among the last captured. In October he and twenty-six others, convicted of "conspiracy and insurrection," were hanged. By demonstrating that slaves could organize for large-scale rebellion, they left a legacy of fear among slaveholders and hope for liberation among southern African Americans.

The far less famous Louisiana Rebellion took place under similar circumstances. By the early 1800s, refugees from Haiti had settled with their slaves in what was then known as Orleans Territory. As they arrived, rumors of slave insurrection spread across the territory. The rumors became reality on January 8,

1811, when Deslondes, a Haitian native and slave driver on a plantation north of New Orleans, initiated a massive revolt in cooperation with maroons.

Although no record of Deslondes's rhetoric survives and his goals may have been less ideologically coherent than Gabriel's, he organized a force of at least 180 men and women. They marched south along the Mississippi River toward New Orleans, with leaders on horseback, and with flags and drums, but few guns. The revolutionaries plundered and burned plantations but killed only two white people and one recalcitrant slave. On January 10 a force of about 700 territorial militia, slaveholding vigilantes, and U.S. troops overwhelmed them. The "battle" was a massacre. Well-armed white men slaughtered sixty-six of the rebels and captured thirty. They tried the captives without benefit of counsel, found twenty-two (including Deslondes) guilty of rebellion, and shot them. Then they cut off the hands of the executed men and displayed them on pikes to warn other African Americans of the consequences of revolt.

THE WHITE SOUTHERN REACTION

Although Deslondes's uprising was one of the few major slave revolts in American history, Gabriel's conspiracy and events in Haiti left the more significant legacy. For generations, enslaved African Americans regarded Louverture as a black George Washington and recalled Gabriel's revolutionary message. The networks among slaves that Gabriel established continued to exist after his death. As the external slave trade carried black Virginians southwestward, they took his promise of liberation with them.

The fears that the Haitian revolution and Gabriel's conspiracy raised among white southerners deepened their reaction against the egalitarian values of the Enlightenment. Because they feared race war and believed emancipation would encourage African Americans to begin such a war, most white people in Virginia and throughout the South determined to make black bondage stronger, not weaker.

Beginning with South Carolina in December 1800, southern states outlawed assemblies of slaves, placed curfews on slaves and free black people, and made manumissions more difficult. The old colonial practice of white men on horseback patrolling slave quarters revived. Assuming that revolutionaries like Gabriel received encouragement from northern white abolitionists, white southerners became suspicious of such outsiders as Yankee peddlers, evangelicals, and foreigners. Assuming that local free African Americans were even more involved in slave uprisings, some white southerners advocated forcing them to leave. This brought about an odd alliance between white advocates of expulsion and black advocates of emigration to Africa.

The War of 1812

Many of the themes developed in this chapter—African-American patriotism, opportunities for freedom, migration sentiment, and influences pushing slaves toward revolutionary action—are reflected in the black experience during the U.S. war with Great Britain that began in 1812 and lasted until early 1815. The roots of this conflict lay in a massive military and economic struggle between Britain and France for mastery over the Atlantic world. The struggle lasted from 1793, during the French Revolution, to the defeat of Napoleon Bonaparte by a British-led coalition in 1815.

British military support for American Indian resistance in the Old Northwest, an American desire to annex Canada, and especially Britain's interference with American ships trading with Europe drew the United States into the war. Although the United States won important victories, it failed to achieve its major objective—the conquest of Canada—and the war ended in a draw. Yet many Americans regarded the war as a second struggle for independence and, as had been the case during the American Revolution, black military service and white fear of slave revolt played important roles (see Map 5–2).

When the war began, white prejudice and fear of black revolt had nearly nullified memories of the service of black Patriot soldiers during the Revolution. The Militia Act of 1792 eliminated armed black participation in all state militias except that of North Carolina. The secretary of the navy ended black service on American warships in 1798. Because of the news from Haiti and because of Gabriel's conspiracy, most white southerners joined John Randolph of Virginia in regarding African Americans as "an internal foe." When the war with Great Britain began, therefore, the southern states refused to enlist black men for fear they would use their guns to aid slave revolts. Meanwhile the lack of enthusiasm for the war among many northern-

MAP 5–2   WAR OF 1812

As during the War for Independence, African Americans fought on both sides during the War of 1812. Some joined the British army that burned Washington, D.C. Others helped the United States win control of Lake Erie in 1813 and stop the British invasion of Louisiana at the Battle of New Orleans in 1815.

▶ *What was at stake for African Americans in the War of 1812?*

ers, combined with the absence of a British threat to their part of the country, kept northern states from mobilizing black troops during 1812 and 1813.

Southern fears of slave revolt mounted during the spring of 1813 when the British invaded the Chesapeake. As they had during the Revolution, British generals offered slaves freedom in Canada or the British West Indies in return for help. In response, African

Americans joined the British army that burned Washington, D.C., in 1814 and attacked Baltimore.

The threat this British army posed to Philadelphia and New York led to the first active black involvement in the war on the American side. The New York state legislature authorized two black regiments, offered freedom to slaves who enlisted, and promised compensation to their masters. Meanwhile, African Americans in Philadelphia and New York City volunteered to help build fortifications. In Philadelphia, James Forten, Richard Allen, and Absalom Jones patriotically raised a "Black Brigade," which never saw action because the British halted when they failed to capture Baltimore.

African-American men did fight, however, at two of the war's most important battles. During the naval engagement at Put-in-Bay on Lake Erie in September 1813 that secured control of the Great Lakes for the United States, one-quarter of Commandant Oliver Hazard Perry's 400 sailors were black. Although Perry had been staunchly prejudiced against using these men, after the battle he praised their valor. At the Battle of New Orleans—fought in January 1815, about a month after a peace treaty had been negotiated (news of peace had not yet reached the area)—African Americans also fought bravely. Yet white memories of Deslondes's recent uprising almost prevented them from being allowed to fight on the American side. Many white people feared that, if mobilized, the local free black militia, which dated back to the Spanish occupation of Louisiana from 1763 to 1801, would make common cause with slaves and the British rather than take the American side. In defiance of such fears, General Andrew Jackson included the black troops in his force defending New Orleans and offered them equal pay and benefits. At least 600 free black men fought on the American side at the Battle of New Orleans, and Jackson lived up to his promise of equal treatment. It was a choice, he later informed President James Monroe, between having the free African Americans "in our ranks or . . . in the ranks of the enemy."

21 "We Have Met the Enemy and They Are Ours"

Perry's Famous Victory on Lake Erie in War of 1812, Erie, Pa.   99824

The Battle of Put-in Bay, fought on Lake Erie in September 1813, was a notable American victory during the War of 1812. This postcard suggests the prevalence of black sailors among American commandant Oliver Hazard Perry's crew.

The Missouri Compromise

After 1815, as the United States emerged from a difficult war, sectional issues between the North and South, which had been pushed into the background by constitutional compromises and the political climate, revived. The nation's first political parties—the Federalist and the Republican—had failed to confront slavery as a national issue. The northern wing of the modernizing Federalist Party had abolitionist tendencies. But during the 1790s when they controlled the national government, the Federalists did not raise the slavery issue. Then the victory of the state-rights-oriented Republican Party in the election of 1800 fatally weakened the Federalists as a national organization and brought a series of implicitly proslavery administrations to power in Washington.

It took innovations in transportation and production that began during the 1810s, as well as the rapid disappearance of slavery in the northern states, to transform the North into a region consciously at odds with the South's traditional culture and slave-labor economy. The first major expression of intensifying sectional differences over slavery and its expansion came in 1819 when the slaveholding Missouri Territory, which had been carved out of Louisiana Territory, applied for admission to the Union as a slave state. Northerners expressed deep reservations about the creation of a new slaveholding state. Many of them feared it would destroy the political balance between the sections and encourage the expansion of slavery elsewhere. The aged Thomas Jefferson called this negative northern reaction a "fire bell in the night." It awakened slaveholders to an era in which the slavery issue could no longer be excluded from national politics.

 DOCUMENT 5-6 Missouri Admitted to Statehood, Slavery at Issue, 1820

Concerned African Americans were also aware of the significance of the Missouri crisis. Black residents of Washington, D.C., crowded into the U.S. Senate gallery as that body debated the issue. Finally, Henry Clay of Kentucky, the slaveholding Speaker of the House of Representatives, directed an effort that produced in 1820 a compromise that temporarily quieted discord. This Missouri Compromise (see Map 5–3) permitted Missouri to become a slave state, maintained a sectional political balance by admitting Maine, which had been part of Massachusetts, as a free state, and banned slavery north of the 36° 30' line of latitude in the old Louisiana Territory. Yet sectional relations would never be the same, and a new era of black and white antislavery militancy soon confronted the South.

CONCLUSION

The period between the War for Independence and the Missouri Compromise was a time of transition for African Americans. On one hand, the legacy of the American Revolution brought emancipation in the North and a promise of equal opportunity with white Americans. On the other hand, by the 1790s slavery and racism had begun to grow stronger. Through a combination of antiblack prejudice among white people and African Americans' desire to preserve their own cultural traditions, black urban communities arose in the North, upper South, and, occasionally—in Charleston and Savannah, for example—in the deep South.

Spreading freedom in the North and the emergence of black communities North and South were heartening developments. There were new opportunities for education, spiritual expression, and economic growth. But the mass of African Americans remained in slavery. The forces for human bondage were growing stronger. Freedom for those who had gained it in the upper South and North was marginal and precarious.

Gabriel's conspiracy in Virginia and Deslondes's rebellion in Louisiana indicated that revolutionary principles persisted among black southerners. But these rebellions and British recruitment of slaves during the War of 1812 convinced most white southerners that black bondage had to be permanent. Therefore, African Americans looked to the future with mixed emotions. A few determined that the only hope for real freedom lay in migration from the United States.

RECOMMENDED READING

Ira Berlin. *Slaves without Masters: The Free Negro in the Antebellum South.* New York: New Press, 1974. The early chapters of this classic study indicate the special difficulties the first large generation of free black southerners faced.

Douglas R. Egerton. *Gabriel's Rebellion: The Virginia Slave Conspiracies of 1800 and 1802.* Chapel Hill: University of North Carolina Press, 1993. This most recent account of Gabriel's conspiracy emphasizes both the revolutionary context within which he acted and his legacy.

Philip S. Foner. *History of Black Americans, from Africa to the Emergence of the Cotton Kingdom.* Westport, CT: Greenwood, 1975. This is the first volume of a comprehensive three-volume history of African Americans. It is detailed and informative about black life between 1783 and 1820.

MAP EXPLORATION

To explore this interactive map, go to
http://www.prenhall.com/hine4/map5.3

MAP 5–3   THE MISSOURI COMPROMISE OF 1820
Under the Missouri Compromise, Missouri entered the Union as a slave state, Maine entered as a free
state, and Congress banned slavery in the huge unorganized portion of the old Louisiana Territory
north of the 36° 30' line of latitude.

▶▶ *Which section of the United State did the Missouri Compromise favor?*

James Oliver Horton and Lois E. Horton. *In Hope of Liberty: Culture, Community, and Protest among Northern Free Blacks, 1700–1860.* New York: Oxford University Press, 1997. This is a well-written interpretation of the northern free black community and its origins.

Sidney Kaplan and Emma Nogrady Kaplan. *The Black Presence in the Era of the American Revolution,* Rev. ed. Amherst: University of Massachusetts Press, 1989. This delightfully written book provides informative accounts of black leaders who lived during the early American republic.

Gary B. Nash. *Forging Freedom: The Formation of Philadelphia's Black Community, 1720–1840.* Cambridge, MA: Harvard University Press, 1988. This path-breaking study of a black community analyzes the origins of separate black institutions.

Donald R. Wright. *African Americans in the Early Republic, 1789–1831.* Arlington Heights, IL: Harlan Davidson, 1993. This is a brief but comprehensive account that reflects recent interpretations.

ADDITIONAL BIBLIOGRAPHY

EMANCIPATION IN THE NORTH

James D. Essig. *The Bonds of Wickedness: American Evangelicals against Slavery, 1770–1808.* Philadelphia: Temple University Press, 1982.

David N. Gellman, *Emancipating New York: The Politics of Slavery and Freedom, 1777–1827.* Baton Rouge: Louisiana State University Press, 2006.

Joanne Pope Melish. *Disowning Slavery: Gradual Emancipation and "Race" in New England, 1780–1860.* Ithaca, NY: Cornell University Press, 1998.

Gary B. Nash and Jean R. Soderlund. *Freedom by Degrees: Emancipation in Pennsylvania and Its Aftermath.* New York: Oxford University Press, 1991.

Arthur Zilversmit. *The First Emancipation: The Abolition of Slavery in the North.* Chicago: University of Chicago Press, 1967.

PROSLAVERY FORCES

Paul Finkelman. *Slavery and the Founders: Race and Liberty in the Age of Jefferson.* Armonk: M. E. Sharpe, 1996.

Duncan J. MacLeod. *Slavery, Race, and the American Revolution.* New York: Cambridge University Press, 1974.

Donald G. Nieman. *Promises to Keep: African Americans and the Constitutional Order, 1776 to the Present.* New York: Oxford University Press, 1991.

Donald L. Robinson. *Slavery in the Structure of American Politics, 1765–1820.* New York: Harcourt Brace Jovanovich, 1971.

Larry E. Tise. *Proslavery: A History of the Defense of Slavery in America, 1701–1840.* Athens: University of Georgia Press, 1987.

FREE BLACK INSTITUTIONS AND MIGRATION MOVEMENTS

Carol V. R. George. *Segregated Sabbaths: Richard Allen and the Emergence of Independent Black Churches, 1760–1840.* New York: Oxford University Press, 1973.

Eddie S. Glaude. *Exodus! Religion, Race, and Nation in Early Nineteenth-Century Black America.* Chicago: University of Chicago Press, 2000.

Sheldon H. Harris. *Paul Cuffe: Black America and the Africa Return.* New York: Simon & Schuster, 1972.

Leon Litwack. *North of Slavery: The Negro in the Free States.* Chicago: University of Chicago Press, 1961.

William A. Muraskin. *Middle-Class Blacks in a White Society: Prince Hall Freemasonry in America.* Berkeley: University of California Press, 1975.

Lamont D. Thomas. *Rise to Be a People: A Biography of Paul Cuffe.* Urbana: University of Illinois Press, 1986.

Heather Andrea Williams. *Self-Taught: African American Education in Slavery and Freedom.* Chapel Hill: University of North Carolina Press, 2005.

Julie Winch. *Philadelphia's Black Elite: Activism, Accommodation, and the Struggle for Autonomy, 1787–1848.* Philadelphia: Temple University Press, 1988.

———.*A Gentleman of Color: The Life of James Forten.* New York: Oxford University Press, 2002.

THE SOUTH

John Hope Franklin. *The Free Negro in North Carolina, 1790–1860.* 1943. Reprint, New York: Russell and Russell, 1969.

Peter Kolchin. *American Slavery, 1619–1877.* New York: Hill and Wang, 1993.

John Chester Miller. *The Wolf by the Ears: Thomas Jefferson and Slavery.* 1977. Reprint, Charlottesville: University Press of Virginia, 1991.

T. Stephen Whitman. *The Price of Freedom: Slavery and Manumission in Baltimore and Early National Maryland.* Lexington: University of Kentucky Press, 1997.

SLAVE REVOLTS, RESISTANCE, AND ESCAPES

Herbert Aptheker. *American Negro Slave Revolts.* 1943. Reprint, New York: International, 1983.

Merton L. Dillon. *Slavery Attacked: Southern Slaves and Their Allies, 1619–1865.* Baton Rouge: Louisiana State University Press, 1990.

Eugene D. Genovese. *From Rebellion to Revolution: Afro-American Slave Revolts in the Making of the Modern World.* Baton Rouge: Louisiana State University Press, 1979.

John R. McKivigan and Stanley Harrold, eds. *Antislavery Violence: Sectional, Racial, and Cultural Conflict in Antebellum America.* Knoxville: University of Tennessee Press, 1999.

AFRICAN-AMERICAN EVENTS	NATIONAL EVENTS
• 1775 •	
1775 First antislavery society formed	**1776** Declaration of Independence
1777 Vermont bans slavery	**1777** Battle of Saratoga
• 1780 •	
1780 Pennsylvania begins gradual emancipation	**1781** Articles of Confederation ratified
1781 Elizabeth Freeman begins her legal suit for freedom	**1783** Great Britain recognizes independence of the United States
1782 Virginia repeals its ban on manumission	
1783 Massachusetts bans slavery and black men gain the right to vote there	
1784 Connecticut and Rhode Island begin gradual abolition	
• 1785 •	
1785 New Jersey and New York defeat gradual emancipation	**1786** Shays's Rebellion
1787 Northwest Ordinance bans slavery in the territory north of the Ohio River	**1787** Constitutional Convention
	1789 Constitution ratified; George Washington becomes president
• 1790 •	
1793 Congress passes Fugitive Slave Law	
1794 Mother Bethel Church established in Philadelphia	
New York adopts gradual abolition plan	

Gerald W. Mullin. *Flight and Rebellion: Slave Resistance in Eighteenth-Century Virginia.* New York: Oxford University Press, 1972.

James Sidbury. *Ploughshares into Swords: Race, Rebellion, and Identity in Gabriel's Virginia, 1730–1810.* New York: Cambridge University Press, 1998. The Library Company of Philadelphia.

RETRACING THE ODYSSEY

Monticello, Charlottesville, Virginia. One hundred and thirty African Americans worked on this plantation during the late eighteenth century and early nineteenth century.

Amherst History Museum, Amherst, Massachusetts. Includes an exhibit on free black people who lived in eighteenth-century Amherst.

Afro-American Historical and Cultural Museum, Philadelphia. Includes an exhibit on the rise of black churches, 1740–1977.

 REVIEW, RESEARCH, AND INTERACT

REVIEW QUESTIONS

1. Which were stronger in the era of the early American republic, the forces in favor of black freedom or those in favor of continued enslavement?

2. How were African Americans able to achieve emancipation in the North?

3. How was the U.S. Constitution, as it was drafted in 1787, proslavery? How was it antislavery?

4. How important were separate institutions in shaping the lives of free black people during the late eighteenth and early nineteenth centuries?

5. What led Gabriel to believe he and his followers could abolish slavery in Virginia through armed uprising?

www.researchnavigator.com

Using the tools available in Research Navigator, consider this question:
How did the Missouri Compromise shape the lives of African Americans in the decades after its passage?

PRIMARY SOURCE DOCUMENTS

5–1   John Wesley, "Thoughts upon Slavery," 1774

5–2   Preamble of the Free African Society, 1787

5–3   Venture Smith Narrative, 1798

MAP EXPLORATION

The Missouri Compromise of 1820, p. 127

INTERACTIVE ACTIVITY

Ratification of the Constitution

Learn how the Federalists won the contest over ratification.

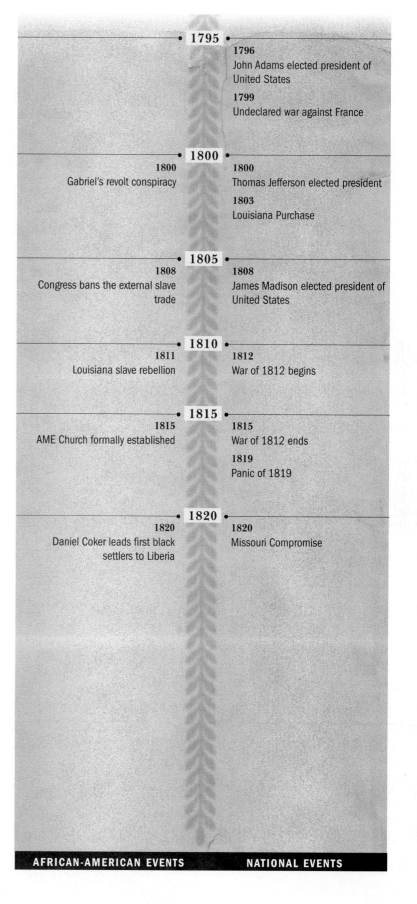

AFRICAN-AMERICAN EVENTS		NATIONAL EVENTS
	1795	**1796** John Adams elected president of United States
		1799 Undeclared war against France
1800 Gabriel's revolt conspiracy	**1800**	**1800** Thomas Jefferson elected president
		1803 Louisiana Purchase
1808 Congress bans the external slave trade	**1805**	**1808** James Madison elected president of United States
1811 Louisiana slave rebellion	**1810**	**1812** War of 1812 begins
1815 AME Church formally established	**1815**	**1815** War of 1812 ends
		1819 Panic of 1819
1820 Daniel Coker leads first black settlers to Liberia	**1820**	**1820** Missouri Compromise

THE VOYAGE TO SLAVERY

The voyage to the slavery began with captured Africans shackled together at the head, forced to march to factories where they were held in dungeons or outdoor holding pens. Many captives died from hunger, exhaustion, and exposure during the journey. Others killed themselves rather than submit to their fate, or were killed if they resisted. Families and ethnic groups were divided. Once considered fit for purchase, captives were branded like cattle with a hot iron bearing the symbol of a trading company. Those sent to the Atlantic slave trade continued the journey in the cargo space of slave ships that were only five feet high. Packed above and below ship planks that measured only five and a half feet long and one and a third feet wide, slaves had very little headroom. Male slaves were chained together in pairs. Many captains carried more slaves than a ship was built to handle, squeezing human beings together to offset increased death rates by carrying large numbers. During storms the crew often neglected to feed the slaves, empty the tubs used for excrement, take slaves on deck for exercise, tend to the sick, or remove the dead.

◀ **The manner in which slaves were stowed** on board slave ships is depicted in this set of diagrams. Slaves were crowded below deck with little or no room between them.

Fort San Sebstian in Ghana where slaves were imprisoned while awaiting transport.

Prison-type pens were used to house slaves once they arrived in America until they could be taken to market and sold. This photo shows an interior view of one such pen in Alexandria, Virginia used in the 1800s.

Tools of bondage and humiliation included iron harnesses and branding irons. At right, slave traders brand a slave with the symbol of the trading company that bought and would eventually sell her.

The first step of the voyage from Africa was called a slave coffle, a parade of slaves tied together while walking in chains after being captured by slave traders. The slaves were taken to the African coast to slave factories to be put on board ships bound for the Atlantic trade market. ▼

The arrival of slaves for sale or auction was often advertised in handbills or printed notices, beginning the experience of being viewed and treated as little more than a commodity.

Slaves were sent to ▶ **auction houses** such as this one to be sold.

Slaves endured physical torture and beatings with whips such as this one.

Shackles of the type used to restrain slaves.

TO BE SOLD & LET
BY PUBLIC AUCTION,
On MONDAY the 18th of MAY, 1829,
UNDER THE TREES.
FOR SALE,
THE THREE FOLLOWING
SLAVES,
TO BE LET,
MALE and FEMALE
SLAVES,
Also for Sale,
Fine Rice, Gram, Paddy, Books, Muslins, Needles, Pins, Ribbons &c. &c.
BLUCHER,

Charlestown, July 24th, 1769.
TO BE SOLD,
On THURSDAY the third Day
of AUGUST next,
A CARGO
OF
NINETY-FOUR
PRIME, HEALTHY
NEGROES,
CONSISTING OF
Thirty-nine MEN, Fifteen BOYS,
Twenty-four WOMEN, and
Sixteen GIRLS.
JUST ARRIVED,
In the Brigantine DEMBIA, Francis Bare, Master, from SIERRA-LEON, by
DAVID & JOHN DEAS.

AUCTION & NEGRO SALES.

THE MIDDLE PASSAGE

Most Africans were captured by other Africans in interior wars between tribes or specifically for sale as slaves. The slaves were moved to the West Coast of Africa where European and American slavers awaited to purchase a human cargo. Slavers inspected their potential cargo for health and strength. Males were preferred because the work on New World plantations would be hard. Human cargo was packed into ships' holds in the most efficient manner and carried under horrible, inhumane conditions to the New World for sale to the highest bidder. It was not unusual for Africans to prefer death to such a fate and individuals would dive overboard or even throw their children into the sea because drowning was considered a better end to that of slavery. For this reason slaves would be kept below decks in leg irons with the exception of an hour or so of exercise each day. During the exercise period slaves would be forced to jump up and down or "dance" to keep their muscles limber and the sale price for each individual at its highest level. Each day dead slaves would be cast overboard and tales abound of schools of sharks trailing slave ships for hundreds of miles.

Great excitement would surround the arrival of a slaver in the New World. Whether in South America, the Caribbean, Mexico, or British America, planters and farmers would compete enthusiastically to purchase workers for their labor. The newer territories of South Carolina and Georgia would continue the importation of slaves well into the 19th century to meet the needs of their burgeoning plantations.

What were the dehumanizing experiences faced by Africans as they were kidnapped and transported to the New World as slaves. Under what conditions were Africans taken for slavery, and what was their fate when they arrived in the New World?

The captain of a Dutch ship traded 20 Negroes for food in a deal with John Rolfe and other settlers.
▼

▶ In 1789, Olaudah Equiano provided this account of conditions on board a slave ship crossing the Atlantic Ocean.

The closeness of the place [ship's hold], and the heat of the climate, added to the number in the ship, which was so crowded that each had scarcely room to turn himself, almost suffocated us. This produced copious perspirations, so that the air soon became unfit for respiration, from a variety of loathsome smells, and brought on a sickness amongst the slaves, of which many died, thus falling victims to the improvident avarice, as I may call it, of their purchasers. This wretched situation was again aggravated by the galling of the chains, now become insupportable; and the filth of the necessary tubs, into which the children often fell, and were almost suffocated. The shrieks of the women, and the groans of the dying, rendered the whole a scene of horror almost inconceivable. Happily

▶Alexander Falconbridge served as a ship's surgeon aboard a slaver in 1788. He was so horrified by what he witnessed during that period of service that he became involved in the British abolition movement. He reported this concerning the early days of the slave trade on the coast of Africa in 1788.

When the Negroes, whom the black traders have to dispose of, are shown to the European purchasers, they first examine them relative to their age. They then minutely inspect their persons, and inquire into the state of their health; if they are afflicted with any infirmity, or are deformed; or have bad eyes or teeth; if they are lame, or weak in their joints, or distorted in the back, or of a slender make, or are narrow in the chest; in short, if they have been, or are afflicted in any manner, so as to render them incapable of much labour; if any of the foregoing defects are discovered in them, they are rejected. But if approved of, they are generally taken on board the ship the same evening. The purchaser has liberty to return on the following morning, but not afterwards, such as upon re-examination are found exceptionable.

The traders frequently beat those Negroes which are objected to by the captains and use them with great severity. It matters not whether they are refused on account of age, illness, deformity, or for any other reason. At New Calabar, in particular, the traders have frequently been known to put them to death. Instances have happened at that place that the traders, when any of their Negroes have been objected to, have dropped their canoes under the stern of the vessel, and instantly beheaded them, in sight of the captain.

◀◀ *Sugar-making in Louisiana in 1751.*

perhaps for myself I was soon reduced so low here that it was thought necessary to keep me almost always on deck; and from my extreme youth I was not put in fetters. In this situation I expected every hour to share the fate of my companions, some of whom were almost daily brought upon deck at the point of death, which I began to hope would soon put an end to my miseries . . . . One day, when we had a smooth sea and moderate wind, two of my wearied countrymen who were chained together (I was near them at the time), preferring death to such a life of misery, somehow made through the nettings and jumped into the sea: immediately another quite dejected fellow, who on account of his illness, was suffered to be out of irons, also followed their example; and I believe many more would very soon have done the same if they had not been prevented by the ship's crew who were instantly alarmed. Those of us that were the most active were in a moment put down under the deck, and there was such a noise and confusion amongst the people of the ship as I never heard before, to stop her, and get the boat out to go after the slaves. However two of the wretches were drowned, but they got the other, and afterwards flogged him unmercifully for thus attempting to prefer death to slavery.

◀ *A small boy is pulled from his grieving mother by slave traders.*

SLAVERY, ABOLITION, AND THE QUEST FOR FREEDOM

The Coming of the Civil War, 1793–1861

Anthony Burns

		1770–1820	1820–1830
RELIGION		**1775** Philadelphia Quakers organize first antislavery society in America	**1820s** Semisecret churches spread among slaves
		late 1700s –1830s Second Great Awakening	**1829** Oblate Sisters of Providence founded in Baltimore, first African-American order of Roman Catholic nuns
		1819 Episcopal Diocese of New York excludes black delegates from annual conventions	
CULTURE		**Early 1800s** Growth of folk tales among slaves	**1820s –1830s** Numerous black literary societies established in northern cities
POLITICS & GOVERNMENT		**1804–1849** Black laws in midwestern states restrict rights of African Americans	**1820** Missouri Compromise
		1807 New Jersey disfranchises black voters	**1821** New York retains property qualification for black voters
		1818 Connecticut bans new black voters	**1822** Rhode Island disfranchises black voters
SOCIETY & ECONOMY		**1784** Society for the Promotion of the Abolition of Slavery founded	**1822** Denmark Vesey's conspiracy
		1800 Gabriel's conspiracy	**1827** *Freedom's Journal* begins publication
		1812 African schools become part of Boston's public schools	
		1816 American Colonization Society founded	

Harriet Tubman

Frederick Douglas

Sojourner Truth

| 1830–1850 | 1850–1870 | |

1840s Mother Bethel Church in Philadelphia has largest black congregation in the United States

1853 Episcopal Diocese of New York readmits black delegates

1840s –1850s Paintings of Robert Duncannon

1845 *Narrative of the Life of Frederick Douglass* published

1848 Okah Tubee's fictionalized autobiography published

1852 *Uncle Tom's Cabin* published

1853 William W. Brown, first African-American novelist, publishes *Clotel*

Elizabeth Taylor Greenfield makes her singing debut in New York before a white audience

Solomon Northrup publishes *Twelve Years as a Slave*

1854 Frances Ellen Watkins Harper publishes *Poems*

1855 William C. Nell publishes *The Colored Patriots of the American Revolution*

1859 Harriet Wilson publishes first novel by an African-American woman

1832 Virginia rejects gradual emancipation

1836–1841 "Gag rule" prohibits Congress from considering petitions regarding slavery

1838 Pennsylvania disfranchises black voters

1846–1848 Mexican War

1846 Wilmot Proviso

1847 Liberia becomes an independent republic

1848 Free Soil party founded

1850 Compromise of 1850 includes stronger Fugitive Slave Act

1851 Indiana bans African Americans from residing in the state

1855–1856 "Bleeding Kansas"

1857 Dred Scott decision

1858 Arkansas reenslaves free blacks who refuse to leave the state

1859 John Brown raids Harper's Ferry

1860 Lincoln elected president

1860–1861 Eleven southern states secede and form the Confederacy

1861 Civil War begins

1831 Nat Turner's revolt

William Lloyd Garrison begins publication of *The Liberator*

1832 First black women's abolitionist organization founded

1833 American Anti-Slavery Society founded

1834 African Free Schools become part of New York's public schools

1835 Abolitionist postal campaign begins

1836 Elijah P. Lovejoy killed by antiabolitionist mob

1839 *Amistad* mutiny

1843 Henry H. Garnet's *Appeal to the Slaves*

1847 Frederick Douglass begins publication of the *North Star*

Missouri bans education of free blacks

1851 "Battle" of Christiana

1853 Rochester Convention

1854 Ashmun Institute, first black institution of higher education in the U.S., founded

1860 U.S. slave population put at 3,953,760

UNCLE TOM'S CABIN

Life in the Cotton Kingdom

WHY DID SLAVERY EXPAND
IN THE COTTON KINGDOM?

WHAT TYPES OF LABOR DID SLAVES
PERFORM IN THE SOUTH?

WHAT WAS THE DOMESTIC SLAVE TRADE?

HOW DID AFRICAN AMERICANS
ADAPT TO LIFE UNDER SLAVERY?

HOW HAVE HISTORIANS EVALUATED
SLAVERY AND SLAVES?

1793–1861

◄This 1858 woodcut portrays black men, women, and children harvesting cotton on a Georgia plantation. It indicates the large size of cotton fields and the type of labor required of slaves from childhood onward. Its rendition of black men appealed to a popular white fantasy that held African Americans to be content in slavery and physically unthreatening.   © Collection of the New York Historical Society Negative number 37628.

There may be humane masters, as there certainly are inhumane ones; there may be slaves well-clothed, well-fed, and happy, as there surely are those half-clad, half-starved, and miserable; nevertheless, the institution that tolerates such wrong and inhumanity . . . is a cruel, unjust, and barbarous one.

Solomon Northup, *Twelve Years a Slave: Narrative of Solomon Northup*

A slave buyer offers cash for men, women, and children in this 1835 advertisement.

Solomon Northup, a free black man, had been kidnapped into slavery during the 1840s. After twelve years in bondage, he finally escaped. In this passage he identifies the central cruelty of slavery. It was not that some masters failed to provide slaves with adequate food, clothing, and shelter while others did. Nor was it that some masters treated their slaves brutally while others did not. The central cruelty of slavery was that it gave masters nearly absolute power over their slaves. The sufferings of African Americans in slavery were not caused by abuses in an otherwise benevolent institution. They were caused by the institution itself.

In this chapter we describe the life of black people in the slave South from the rise of the Cotton Kingdom during the early 1800s to the eve of the Civil War in 1860. As we have indicated in previous chap-

ters, African Americans suffered brutal oppression on southern plantations. But they also developed means of coping with that oppression, resisting it, and escaping. Between 1820 and 1861, slavery in the South was at its peak as a productive system and a means of white control over black southerners. We describe the extent of that slave system, how it varied across the South, and how it operated. We investigate the slave communities that African-American men, women, and children built.

The Expansion of Slavery

Eli Whitney's invention of the cotton gin in 1793 made the cultivation of cotton profitable on the North American mainland. It was the key to the rapid and extensive expansion of slavery from the Atlantic coast to Texas. By 1811 cotton growing had spread across South Carolina, Georgia, and parts of North Carolina and Virginia. By 1821 it had crossed Alabama and reached Mississippi, Louisiana, and parts of Tennessee. It then expanded again into Arkansas, Florida, and eastern Texas (see Map 6–1). Enslaved black labor cleared forests and drained swamps to make these lands fit for cultivation.

The expansion of the cotton culture led to the removal of the American Indians—some of them slaveholders—who inhabited this vast region. During the 1830s and 1840s the U.S. Army forced the Cherokee, Chickasaw, Choctaw, Creek, and most Seminole to leave their ancestral lands for Indian Territory in what is now Oklahoma. Many Indians died during this forced migration, and the Cherokee remember it as "The Trail of Tears." Yet the Cherokees created in Oklahoma an economy dependent on black slave labor. By 1860 there were 7,000 slaves there, amounting to 14 percent of the population.

Far fewer slaves lived in the other western territories. Kansas never had more than a few dozen slaves during the 1850s and had none after 1858. In New Mexico in 1850, there were about 40 black slaves and 3,000 American Indian slaves. When Utah Territory legalized slavery in 1852, only about twenty-six enslaved black people were living there, and by 1860 Utah still had just twenty-nine black people. Although California entered the Union as a state in 1850 under a constitution that banned slavery, two years later it had more than 300 slaves, held illegally and working as prospectors or domestic servants.

PROFILE ~ SOLOMON NORTHUP

Solomon Northup's aspirations as a musician led in 1841 to his kidnapping and sale into slavery. For twelve years, he labored in the cotton and sugar regions of Louisiana, interacted with slaves and masters, and experienced firsthand what it was like to be caught up in a brutal labor system.

Northup was born free at Minerva, New York, in about 1808. His parents were prosperous farmers and he became a farmer as well, although he also worked occasionally as a violinist. He lived in Saratoga Springs with his wife and three children until March 1841 when two white men suggested that he become a musician in their circus, which was performing in Washington, D.C.

Enticed by the prospect of good wages and a chance to perform, Northup left with the two men without informing his wife or anyone else. Within two days of arriving in Washington, he was drugged, robbed of his money and free papers, chained, and sold to slave traders. After experiencing a terrible beating with a wooden paddle and a rope, Northup was shipped to New Orleans and sold to William Ford, who owned a cotton planation and sawmill in Louisiana's Red River region.

As Ford's slave, Northup worked at the mill "piling lumber and chopping logs." Northup liked Ford and regarded him to be a "model master," who treated his slaves well and read scripture to them each Sunday. But when Ford became insolvent and sold his slaves, Northup had to deal with a series of brutal masters. They employed him as a carpenter, as a field hand on cotton and sugar plantations, and finally as a slave driver.

At one point when he was cutting lumber and building cabins, Northup was surprised to have several "large and stout" black women join in the forestry work. Later he observed women engaged in other demanding physical labor. "There are lumberwomen as well as lumbermen in the forests of the South," he reported. "In fact . . . they perform their share of all the labor required by the planters. They plough, dray, drive team, clear wild lands, work on the highway and so forth."

Subsequently, Northup spent ten years as a slave of Edwin Epps, a cotton planter, who when drunk enjoyed forcing his slaves to dance. Northup noted that Epps's slaves received a meager diet of corn and bacon. They slept in crude, crowded cabins on planks of wood. During harvest season "it was rarely that a day passed by without one or more whippings" as slaves failed to pick their quota. During a three-year period, Epps hired Northup out to "sugar plantations during the season of cane-cutting and sugar making" for $1.00 per day.

Northup had become Epps's slave driver by 1852 when he was finally able to set in motion the events that led to his rescue. Deeply disturbed by being forced to whip other slaves, he conspired with a Canadian carpenter to smuggle a letter to two white businessmen in Saratoga Springs. The letter led the governor of New York to send Henry B. Northup—a member of the family that had once owned Solomon Northup's father—to Louisiana to present evidence that Solomon Northup was a free man. By January 1853 he had been reunited with his family in New York. In July of that year he published *Twelve Years a Slave*, which sold over 30,000 copies and earned him enough money to purchase a home for his family in Glens Falls, New York, where he died in 1863.

Northup

MAP 6–1   Cotton Production in the South, 1820–1860

Cotton production expanded westward between 1820 and 1860 into Alabama, Mississippi, Louisiana, Texas, Arkansas, and western Tennessee.

Source: Sam Bowers Hilliard, *Atlas of Antebellum Southern Agriculture* (Louisiana State University Press, 1984) pp. 67–71.

▶▶ *Why did cotton production spread westward?*

SLAVE POPULATION GROWTH

In the huge region stretching from the Atlantic coast to Texas, however, a tremendous increase in the number of African Americans in bondage accompanied territorial expansion. Although slave populations in Latin American countries failed to reproduce themselves and declined drastically prior to general emancipation, the slave population of the United States grew almost sixfold between 1790 and 1860, from 697,897 to 3,953,760 (see Table 6–1). Agricultural laborers constituted 75 percent of the South's slave population. But slaves were not equally distributed across the region. In western North Carolina, eastern Ten-

nessee, western Virginia, and most of Missouri there were never many slaves. The slave population grew fastest in the newer cotton-producing states, such as Alabama and Mississippi (see Map 6–2).

Virginia had the largest slave population throughout the period. But between 1820 and 1860, that population increased by only 15 percent, from 425,153 to 490,865. During the same forty years, the slave population of Louisiana increased by 209 percent, from 149,654 to 462,198, and that of Mississippi by 1,231 percent, from 32,814 to 436,631. By 1860 Mississippi had joined South Carolina as the only states that had more slaves than free inhabitants.

OWNERSHIP OF SLAVES IN THE OLD SOUTH

Slaveholders were as unevenly distributed as the slaves and, unlike slaves, were declining in number. In 1830, 1,314,272 white southerners (36 percent), out of a total white southern population of 3,650,758, owned slaves. In 1860 only 383,673 white southerners (4.7 percent), out of a total white southern population of 8,097,463, owned slaves. Even counting the immediate families of slaveholders, only 1,900,000 (or less than 25 percent of the South's white population) had a direct interest in slavery in 1860.

Almost half of the South's slaveholders owned fewer than five slaves, only 12 percent owned more than twenty slaves, and just 1 percent owned more than fifty slaves. Yet more than half the slaves belonged to masters who had twenty or more slaves. So although the typical slaveholder owned few slaves, the typical slave lived on a sizable plantation.

Since the time of Anthony Johnson in the mid-1600s, a few black people had been slaveholders, and this class continued to exist. In 1830 only 2 percent, or 3,775 free African Americans, owned slaves. Many of them became slaveholders to protect their families from sale and disruption. This was because, as the nineteenth century progressed, southern states made it more difficult for masters to manumit slaves and for slaves to purchase their freedom. The states also threatened to expel former slaves from their territory. In response to these circumstances, black men and women sometimes purchased relatives who were in danger of sale to traders and who—if legally free—might be forced by white authorities to leave a state.

Some African Americans, however, purchased slaves for financial reasons and passed those slaves on to their heirs. Most black people who became masters for financial reasons owned five or fewer slaves. But William Johnson, a wealthy free black barber of Natchez, Louisiana, owned many slaves whom he employed on a plantation he purchased. Some black women, such as Margaret Mitchell Harris of South Carolina and Betsy Somayrac of Natchitoches, Louisiana, also became slaveholders for economic reasons. Harris was a successful rice planter who inherited twenty-one slaves from her white father. She prospered by carefully managing her resources in land and slaves. By 1849, when she sold out, she had more than forty slaves and nearly 1,000 acres, which produced 240,000 pounds of rice per year.

Somayrac's case shows that economic considerations could override emotional ties between black women and their bond people. In her will, which a parish judge recorded in January 1845, Somayrac wrote that she intended to pass her human property

on to her children. She required that "my negro woman named Jane" labor to pay off family debts. She stipulated that one of her sons must own any children that Jane might produce. She even provided that a "negro boy named Solomon," who was her godson, not be manumitted until he had reached the relatively old age of thirty-five.

TABLE 6–1 U.S. Slave Population, 1820 and 1860

	1820	1860
United States	1,538,125	3,953,760
North	19,108	64
South	1,519,017	3,953,696
Upper South	965,514	1,530,229
Delaware	4,509	1,798
Kentucky	127,732	225,483
Maryland	107,397	87,189
Missouri	10,222	114,931
North Carolina	205,017	331,059
Tennessee	80,107	275,719
Virginia	425,153	490,865
Washington, D.C.	6,377	3,185
Lower South	553,503	2,423,467
Alabama	41,879	435,080
Arkansas	1,617	111,115
Florida	*	61,745
Georgia	149,654	462,198
Louisiana	69,064	331,726
Mississippi	32,814	436,631
South Carolina	258,475	402,406
Texas	*	182,566

*Florida and Texas were not states in 1820.

Source: Ira Berlin, Slaves without Masters: The Free Negro in the Antebellum South (New York: New Press, 1974), 396–97.

Slave Labor in Agriculture

About 55 percent of the slaves in the South cultivated cotton; 10 percent grew tobacco; and 10 percent produced sugar, rice, or hemp. About 15 percent were domestic servants, and the remaining 10 percent worked in trades and industries.

TOBACCO

Tobacco remained important in Virginia, Maryland, Kentucky, and parts of North Carolina and Missouri during the 1800s (see Map 6–3). A difficult crop to

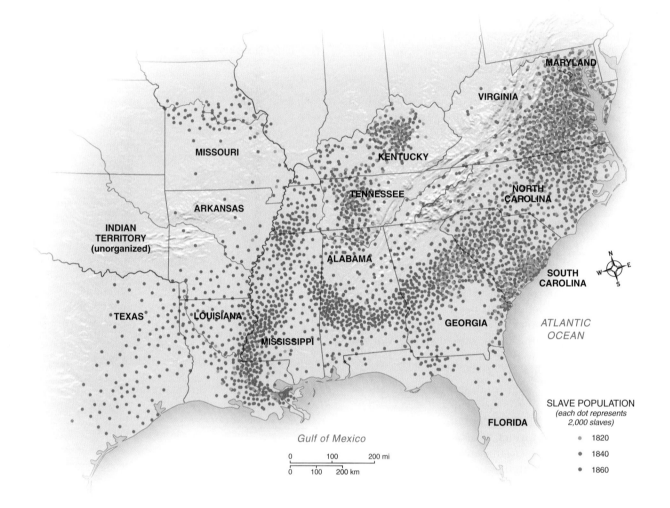

MAP 6–2 SLAVE POPULATION, 1820–1860

Slavery spread southwestward from the upper South and the eastern seaboard following the spread of cotton cultivation.

Source: Sam Bowers Hilliard, *Atlas of Antebellum Southern Agriculture* (Louisiana State University Press, 1984), pp. 29–34.

▶ *What does this map suggest concerning black life in the South?*

produce, tobacco required a long growing season and careful cultivation. In the spring slaves had to transfer seedlings from sterilized seed beds to well-worked and manured soil. Then they had to hoe weeds, pick off insects, and prune lower leaves so the topmost leaves grew to their full extent. Slaves also built scaffolds used to cure the tobacco leaves and made the barrels in which the tobacco was shipped to market.

Robert Ellett, a former slave, recalled that when he was just eight years old he worked in Virginia "a-worming tobacco." He "examined tobacco leaves, pull[ed] off the worms, if there were any, and killed them." He claimed that if an overseer discovered that slaves had overlooked worms on the tobacco plants, the slaves were whipped or forced to eat the worms. Nancy Williams, another Virginia slave, recalled that sometimes as a punishment slaves had to inhale burning tobacco until they became nauseated.

RICE

Unlike the cultivation of tobacco, which spread westward and southward from Maryland and Virginia, rice production remained confined to the low country of

South Carolina and Georgia. As they had since colonial times, slaves in these coastal regions worked according to task systems that allowed them considerable autonomy. Because rice fields needed to be flooded for the seeds to germinate, slaves maintained elaborate systems of dikes and ditches. Influenced by West African methods, they sowed, weeded, and harvested the rice crop.

Rice cultivation was labor intensive, and rice plantations needed large labor forces to grow and harvest the crop and maintain the fields. By 1860 twenty rice plantations had 300 to 500 slaves, and eight others had between 500 and 1,000. The only American plantation employing more than 1,000 slaves was in the rice-producing region. These vast plantations represented sizable capital investments, and masters or overseers carefully monitored slave productivity. Although slaves enjoyed considerable leeway in how they performed their assigned duties, those who missed a day's work risked forfeiting their weekly allowance "of either bacon, sugar, molasses, or tobacco."

SUGAR

Another important crop that grew in a restricted region was sugar, which slaves cultivated on plantations along the Mississippi River in southern Louisiana. Commercial production of sugarcane did not begin in Louisiana until the 1790s. It required a consistently warm climate, a long growing season, and at least sixty inches of rain per year.

Raising sugarcane and refining sugar also required constant labor. Together with the great profitability of the sugar crop, these demands encouraged masters to work their slaves hard. Slave life on sugar plantations was extremely harsh, and African Americans across the South feared being sent to labor on them. Historian Paul W. Gates details the work of slaves on sugar plantations:

> Fresh land was constantly being cleared, and the wood was used for fuel in the sugarhouses or was sold to steamboats. Levees had to be raised; ditching and draining was never completed. Planting, numerous hoeings, cutting, loading and unloading the cane, putting it through the mill, feeding the boilers, moving the huge hogsheads of sugar and molasses and drawing them to the boat landing, setting aside the seed cane, hauling the bagasse to the fields—all this took much labor.

Slaves did this work in hot and humid conditions, adding to the toll it took on their strength and health. Because cane could not be allowed to stand too long in the fields, harvest time was hectic. As one former slave

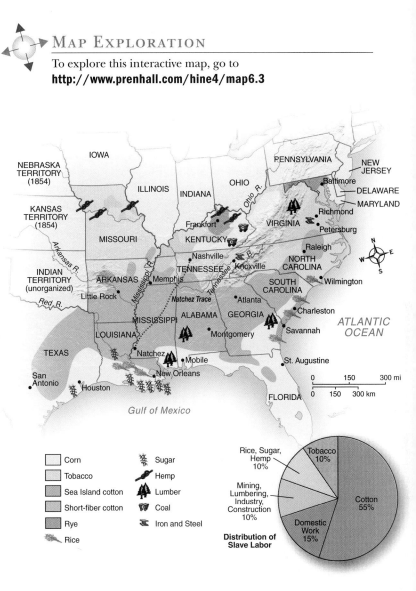

MAP EXPLORATION

To explore this interactive map, go to
http://www.prenhall.com/hine4/map6.3

MAP 6–3 AGRICULTURE, INDUSTRY, AND SLAVERY IN THE OLD SOUTH, 1850

The experience of the African American in slavery varied according to their occupation and the region of the South in which they lived.

▶▶ *To what degree did climate affect the type of crop slaves produced?*

recalled, "On cane plantations in sugar time, there is no distinction as to the days of the week. They [the slaves] worked on the Sabbath as if it were Monday or Thursday."

COTTON

Although tobacco, rice, and sugar were economically significant, cotton was by far the South's and the country's most important staple crop. By 1860 cotton exports amounted to more than 50 percent annually of the dollar value of all U.S. exports (see Figure 6–1). This was almost ten times the value of its nearest export competitors—wheat and wheat flour.

Cotton as a crop did not require cultivation as intensive as that needed for tobacco, rice, or sugar. But the cotton culture was so extensive that cotton planters as a group employed the most slave labor. By 1860 out of the 2,500,000 slaves employed in agriculture in the United States, 1,815,000 produced cotton. Cotton drove the South's economy and its westward expansion. Even in rice-producing South Carolina and sugar-producing Louisiana, cotton was dominant, and cotton plantations employed the bulk of the slave populations.

LIVING WORDS
5 *Pick a Bale of Cotton*

Although long-staple cotton continued to be grown on the sea islands of South Carolina and Georgia, most American cotton was the more hardy short-staple variety that flourished over much of the South. Demand for cotton fiber in the textile mills of Britain and New En-

gland stimulated the westward spread of cotton cultivation. This demand increased by at least 5 percent per year between 1830 and 1860. In response—and with the essential aid of Whitney's cotton gin—American production of cotton rose from 10,000 bales in 1793 to 500,000 annually during the 1820s to 4,491,000 bales in 1860. The new states of Alabama, Louisiana, and Mississippi led this mounting production.

Picturesque scenes of ripening cotton fields are part of the romantic image of the Old South that popular novels, songs, and motion pictures have perpetuated for so long. Even a former slave could recall that "few sights are more pleasant to the eye than a wide cotton field when it is in full bloom. It presents an appearance of purity, like an immaculate expanse of light, new-fallen snow." Yet such scenes mask the backbreaking labor enslaved African Americans performed and the anxiety and fear they experienced.

Potential profits drew white farmers to the rich Black Belt lands of Mississippi and Alabama during the early nineteenth century. Rapid population growth allowed Mississippi to gain statehood in 1817 and Alabama in 1819. White men with few slaves led the way into this southwestern cotton belt, and its frontier social structure allowed them to become plantation owners. Although their success was not certain and many of them failed, those who succeeded created large agricultural units because profits were directly related to the amount of cotton harvested. As a result, Mississippi and Alabama—the leading producers of cotton—had by 1860 the greatest concentration of plantations with one hundred or more slaves. Twenty-four of Mississippi's slaveholders each owned between 308 and 899 slaves.

As these large agricultural units drew in labor, the price of slaves increased. During the 1830s, a prime male field hand sold for $1,250 (about 21,000 current dollars) in the New Orleans slave market. Prices dipped during the hard times of the early 1840s. But by the 1850s, such slaves cost $1,800 (about 33,000 current dollars). Young women usually sold for up to $500 less than young men. Prices for elderly slaves dropped off sharply unless they were highly skilled.

The enslaved men and women who worked in the cotton fields rose before dawn when the master or overseer sounded the plantation bell or horn. They ate breakfast and then assembled in work gangs of twenty or twenty-five under the control of black slave drivers. They plowed and planted in the spring. They weeded with heavy hoes in the summer and harvested in the late fall. During harvest season, adult slaves picked about 200 pounds of cotton per day. Regardless of the season, the work was hard, and white overseers whipped those who seemed to be lagging. Slaves usually got a two-hour break at midday in the summer and

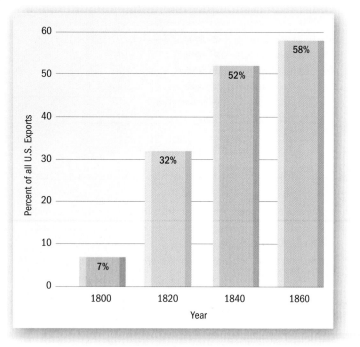

FIGURE 6–1 COTTON EXPORTS AS A PERCENTAGE OF ALL U.S. EXPORTS, 1800–1860

Cotton rapidly emerged as the country's most important export crop after 1800 and key to its prosperity. Because slave labor produced the cotton, increasing exports strengthened the slave system itself.

an hour to an hour and a half in the winter. Then they returned to the fields until sunset, when they went back to their cabins for dinner and an early bedtime enforced by the master or overseer.

Frederick Law Olmsted, a northern traveler, described a large gang of Mississippi slaves he saw in 1854 marching home early because of rain:

> First came, led by an old driver carrying a whip, forty of the largest and strongest women I ever saw together; they were all in a single uniform dress of a bluish check stuff, the skirts reaching little below the knee; their legs and feet were bare; they carried themselves loftily, each having a hoe over the shoulder, and walking with a free, powerful swing. Behind them came the [plow hands and their mules], thirty strong, mostly men, but a few of them women. . . . A lean and vigilant white overseer, on a brisk pony, brought up the rear. The men wore small blue Scotch bonnets; many of the women handkerchiefs, turban fashion. . . . They were evidently a picked lot. I thought every one could pass for a "prime" cotton hand.

OTHER CROPS

Besides cotton, sugar, tobacco, and rice, slaves in the Old South produced other crops, including hemp, corn, wheat, oats, rye, white potatoes, and sweet potatoes. They also raised cattle, hogs, sheep, and horses. The hogs, and corn and other grains, were mainly for consumption on the plantations. But all the hemp, and much of the livestock and wheat, were raised for the market. In fact, wheat replaced tobacco as the main cash crop in much of Maryland and Virginia. The transition to wheat encouraged many planters to substitute free labor for slave labor, but slaves grew wheat in the South until the Civil War.

Kentucky was the center of the hemp industry. Before the Civil War, planters used hemp, which is closely related to marijuana, to make rope and bagging for cotton bales. This tied Kentucky economically to the Deep South. But, because hemp required much less labor than rice, sugar, or cotton, Kentucky developed a distinctive slave system. Three slaves could tend fifty acres of hemp, so slave labor forces were much smaller than elsewhere. Robert Wickliffe, the largest Kentucky slaveholder during the 1840s, owned 200 slaves—a large number, but far fewer than his counterparts in the Cotton Belt.

In this engraving, which dates to about 1860, slaves harvest cotton under white supervision on a southern plantation. Note the division of labor with women picking and men packing and carrying.   The Granger Collection, New York

Enslaved black women often had the responsibility of raising their masters' young children. The women's duties sometimes forced them to neglect the needs of their own children.   From the Collection of the Louisiana State Museum

House Servants and Skilled Slaves

About 75 percent of the slave workforce in the nineteenth century consisted of field hands. But because masters wanted to make their plantations as self-sufficient as possible, they employed some slaves as house servants and skilled craftsmen. Slaves who did not have to do field labor were an elite. Those who performed domestic duties, drove carriages, or learned a craft considered themselves privileged. However, they were also suspended between two different worlds.

House slaves worked as cooks, maids, butlers, nurses, and gardeners. Their work was less physically demanding than fieldwork, and they often received better food and clothing. Nevertheless, nineteenth-century kitchen work could be grueling, and maids and butlers were on call at all hours. House servants' jobs were also more stressful than field hands' jobs because the servants were under closer white supervision.

In addition, house servants were by necessity cut off from the slave community centered in the slave quarters. Yet, as Olmsted pointed out during the 1850s, house servants rarely sought to become field hands. Conversely, field hands had little desire to be exposed to the constant surveillance house servants had to tolerate. As Olmsted put it,

Slaves brought up to housework dread to be employed at field-labor; and those accustomed to the comparatively unconstrained life of the Negro-settlement detest the close control and careful movements required of the house-servants. It is a punishment of a lazy field hand to employ him in menial duties at the house . . . and it is equally a punishment to a neglectful house-servant, to banish him to the field-gangs.

Skilled slaves tended to be even more of a slave elite than house servants. As had been true earlier, black men had a decided advantage over black women—apart from those who were seamstresses—in becoming skilled. Slave carpenters, blacksmiths, and millwrights built and maintained plantation houses, slave quarters, and machinery. Because they might need to travel to get tools or spare parts, such skilled slaves gained a more cosmopolitan outlook than field hands or house servants. They got a taste of freedom, which from the masters' point of view was dangerous.

As plantation slavery declined in the Chesapeake, skilled slaves were able to leave their master's estate to "hire their time." Either they or their masters negotiated labor contracts with employers who needed their expertise. In effect, these slaves worked for money. Although masters often kept all or most of what they earned, some of these skilled slaves merely paid their master a set rate and lived as independent contractors.

By the early nineteenth century many slaves in Delaware, Maryland, and Virginia were cultivating wheat rather than tobacco. This 1831 lithograph portrays a demonstration of Cyrus McCormick's automatic reaper. It indicates the adaptability of slave labor to new technology.

Urban and Industrial Slavery

Most skilled slaves who hired their time lived in the South's towns and cities, where they interacted with free black communities. Many of them resided in Baltimore and New Orleans, which were major ports and the Old South's largest cities. But there were others in such smaller southern urban centers as Richmond and Norfolk, Virginia; Atlanta and Augusta, Georgia; Washington, D.C.; Charleston, South Carolina; Louisville, Kentucky; and Memphis, Tennessee.

Slave populations in southern cities were often large, although they tended to decline between 1800 and 1860. In 1840 slaves were a majority of Charleston's population of 29,000. They nearly equaled white residents in Memphis and Augusta, which had total populations of 14,700 and 6,000, respectively. Slaves were almost one-quarter of New Orleans's population of 145,000 (see Map 6–4).

As the young Frederick Douglass found when his master sent him from rural Maryland to Baltimore during the late 1830s, life in a city could be much more complicated for a slave than life on a plantation. When urban slaves were not working for their masters, they could earn money for themselves, and as a result, masters had a harder time controlling their lives. Those who contracted to provide their masters with a certain amount of money per year could live on their own, buying their own food and clothing. "You couldn't pay me," observed one slave woman, "to live at home if I could help myself."

DOCUMENT 6-6 *Excerpt from Narrative of the Life of Frederick Douglass, 1845*

Urban slaves served as domestics, washwomen, waiters, artisans, stevedores, drayers, hack drivers, and general laborers. (Douglass was an apprentice caulker in a shipyard.) In general, they did the urban work that foreign immigrants undertook in northern cities. If urban slaves purchased their freedom, they usually continued in the same line of work they had done as slaves. Particularly in border cities like Baltimore, Louisville, and Washington, urban slaves increasingly relied on their free black neighbors—and sympathetic white people—to escape north. Urban masters often let slaves purchase their freedom over a term of years to keep them from leaving. In Baltimore, during the early nineteenth century, this sort of "**term slavery**" was gradually replacing slavery for life.

Industrial slavery overlapped with urban slavery, but southern industries that employed slaves were often in rural areas. By 1860 about 5 percent of southern slaves—approximately 200,000 people—worked in industry. Enslaved men, women, and children worked in textile mills in South Carolina and Georgia, sometimes beside white people. In Richmond and Petersburg, Virginia, during the 1850s, about 6,000 slaves, most of whom were male, worked in factories producing chewing tobacco. Richmond's famous Tredegar Iron Works also employed a large slave workforce. So did earlier southern ironworks in Virginia, Maryland, northern Tennessee, and southern Kentucky.

The bulk of the 16,000 people who worked in the South's lumber industry in 1860 were slaves. Under the supervision of black drivers, they felled trees, operated sawmills, and delivered lumber. Slaves also did most of the work in the naval stores industry of North Carolina and Georgia, manufacturing tar, turpentine, and related products. In western Virginia, they labored in the

MAP 6–4 POPULATION PERCENTAGES IN THE SOUTHERN STATES, 1850

The percentages of slaves, free African Americans, and white people varied from state to state. In the upper South white populations were substantially larger than black populations. In the Deep South, however, the races were more in balance.

▶ *In which two states were there black majorities in 1850, and why?*

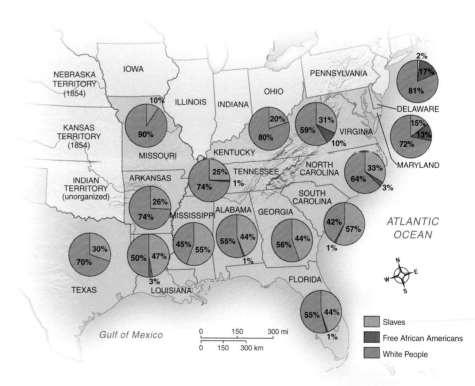

Frederick Douglass on the Readiness of Masters to Use the Whip

This passage from the Narrative of the Life of Frederick Douglass, An American Slave, *published in 1845, suggests the volatile relationship between slaves and masters that could quickly result in violence. As Douglass makes clear, masters and overseers used the whip not just to force slaves to work but also to enforce a distinction between what was proper and even laudable for white men and what was forbidden behavior for slaves.*

It would astonish one, unaccustomed to a slaveholding life, to see with what wonderful ease a slaveholder can find things of which to make occasion to whip a slave. A mere look, word, or motion—a mistake, accident, or want of power—are all matters for which a slave may be whipped at any time. Does a slave look dissatisfied? It is said, he has the devil in him, and it must be whipped out. Does he speak loudly when spoken to by his masters? Then he is getting high-minded, and should be taken down a button-hole lower. Does he forget to pull off his hat at the approach of a white person? Then he is wanting in reverence, and should be whipped for it. Does he ever venture to vindicate his conduct, when censured for it? Then he is guilty of impudence—one of the greatest crimes of which a slave can be guilty. Does he ever venture to suggest a different mode of doing things from that pointed out by his master? He is indeed presumptuous, and getting above himself; and nothing less than a flogging will do for him. Does he, while plowing, break a plough—or, while hoeing, break a hoe? It is owing to his carelessness, and for it a slave must always be whipped.

🌿 *What does Douglass imply are some of the motives that led masters and overseers to whip slaves?*

🌿 *Given the behavior by masters that Douglass describes, how were slaves likely to act around white people?*

Source: Roy Finkenbine, ed., *Sources of the African-American Past* (New York: Longman, 1997), 43–44.

salt works of the Great Kanawha River Valley, producing the salt used to preserve meat—especially the southern mainstay salt pork. During the 1820s the Maryland Chemical Works in Baltimore, which manufactured industrial chemicals, pigments, and medicines, included many slaves among its workers. Most southern industrialists hired slaves from their masters rather than buying them themselves, and the work slaves performed for them was often dangerous, as well as physically tiring. But, as historian John B. Boles points out, slaves came to prefer industrial jobs to plantation labor. Like urban slaves, industrial slaves had more opportunities to advance themselves, enjoyed more autonomy, and often received cash incentives. Industrial labor, like urban labor, was a path to freedom for some.

Punishment

Those who used slave labor, whether on plantations, small farms, in urban areas, or industry, frequently offered incentives to induce slaves to perform well. Yet slave labor by definition is forced labor based on the threat of physical punishment. Masters denied that this brutal aspect detracted from what they claimed was the essentially benign and paternalistic character of the South's "peculiar institution." After all, Christian masters found support in the Bible for using corporal punishment to chastise servants.

White southerners also believed that African Americans would not work unless threatened with beatings. Olmsted reported that in Mississippi he had observed a young girl subjected to "the severest corporal punishment" he had ever seen. The white overseer, who had administered the flogging with a rawhide whip "across her naked loins and thighs," told Olmsted that the girl had been shirking her duties. He claimed that "if I hadn't [punished her so hard] she would have done the same thing again to-morrow, and half the people on the plantation would have followed her example. Oh, you've no idea how lazy these niggers are. . . . They'd never do any work at all if they were not afraid of being whipped."

Fear of the lash drove slaves to work and to cooperate among themselves for mutual protection. Black parents and other older relatives taught slave children how to avoid punishment and still resist masters and overseers. They worked slowly—but not too slowly—and feigned illness to maintain their strength. They broke tools and injured mules, oxen, and horses to tacitly protest their condition. This pattern of covert resistance and physical punishment caused anxiety for both masters and slaves. Resistance (described in more detail in

Chapter 3) often forced masters to reduce work hours and improve conditions. Yet few slaves escaped being whipped at least once during their lives in bondage.

The Domestic Slave Trade

The expansion of the Cotton Kingdom south and west combined with the decline of slavery in the Chesapeake to stimulate the domestic slave trade. As masters in Delaware, Maryland, Virginia, North Carolina, and Kentucky trimmed excess slaves from their workforces—or switched entirely from slave to wage labor—they sold men, women, and children to slave traders. The traders in turn shipped these unfortunate people to the slave markets of New Orleans and other cities for resale. Masters also sold slaves as punishment, and fear of being "sold down river" led many slaves in the Chesapeake to escape. A vicious circle resulted: masters sold slaves south to prevent their escape and slaves escaped to avoid being sold south.

DOCUMENT
6-7 *A Slave Tells of His Sale at Auction, 1848*

Some slave songs record the anxiety of those facing separation from loved ones as a result of the domestic trade. One song laments the sale of a man away from his wife and family:

William Rino sold Henry Silvers;
Hilo! Hilo!
Sold him to de Gorgy [Georgia] trader;
Hilo! Hilo!
His wife she cried, and children bawled
Hilo! Hilo!
Sold him to de Gorgy trader;
Hilo! Hilo!

. . .

See wives and husbands sold apart,
Their children's screams will break my heart;—
There's a better day coming,
Will you go along with me?
There's a better day a coming,
Go sound the jubilee!

The number of people traded was huge and, considering that many of them were ripped away from their families, tragic. Starting in the 1820s, about 150,000 slaves per decade moved toward the southwest either with their masters or traders. Between 1820 and 1860, an estimated 50 percent of the slaves of the upper South moved involuntarily into the Southwest.

Traders operated compounds called slave prisons or slave pens in Baltimore, Maryland; Washington,

In this 1863 photograph a former Louisiana slave displays the scars that resulted from repeated whippings. Although this degree of scarring is exceptional, few slaves were able to avoid being whipped at least once in their lives. National Archives and Records Administration

D.C.; Alexandria and Richmond, Virginia; Charleston, South Carolina; and in smaller cities as well. Most of the victims of the trade moved on foot in groups called **coffles**, chained or roped together. From the 1810s onward, northern and European visitors to Washington noted the coffles passing before the U.S. Capitol. There was also a considerable coastal trade in slaves from Chesapeake ports to New Orleans and, by the 1840s, some slave traders were carrying their human cargoes in railroad cars.

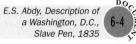
E.S. Abdy, Description of a Washington, D.C., Slave Pen, 1835 DOCUMENT 6-4

The domestic slave trade demonstrated the falseness of slaveholders' claims that slavery was a benign institution. Driven by economic necessity, profit, or a desire to frustrate escape plans, masters in the upper South irrevocably separated husbands and wives, mothers and children, brothers and sisters. Traders sometimes tore babies from their mothers' arms. The journey from the Chesapeake to Mississippi, Alabama, or Louisiana could be long and hard, and some slaves died along the way. A few managed to keep in touch with those they had left behind through letters and travelers. But most could not, and after the abolition of slavery in 1865, many African Americans used their new freedom to travel across the South looking for relatives from whom they had been separated long before.

SLAVE FAMILIES

The families that enslaved African Americans sought to preserve had been developing in America since the seventeenth century. However, such families had no legal standing. Most enslaved men and women could choose their own mates, although masters sometimes arranged such things. Masters encouraged pairings

PROFILE ⟡ WILLIAM ELLISON

The life of William Ellison, who was born a slave in the Fairfield district of South Carolina in 1790 and named *April* by his master, exemplifies several of the themes of this chapter. He was a skilled slave, used that skill to accumulate enough savings to purchase his freedom, and subsequently became a slaveholder himself. His story came to light in 1935 when three white children, playing in the crawlspace under his former home, discovered his personal papers.

The son of a slave mother and an unknown white father, Ellison received special treatment from his owner, who apprenticed him at age twelve to a broadly skilled white craftsman named William McCreight. Together with several white apprentices, Ellison learned carpentry, blacksmithing, and how to repair cotton gins. He also learned how to conduct a business. He did so well that in 1816, when he was twenty-six, he purchased himself and became a free man.

Once free, Ellison petitioned a court to change his name from his slave name *April* to *William*, in honor of his mentor—or perhaps his father. With freedom, skills, and a new name, Ellison opened a gin-making and gin-repair shop in Statesburg, South Carolina. Like the Natchez, Mississippi, barber William Johnson, Ellison achieved a respectable reputation among his white clients and neighbors as a churchgoing businessman. On the surface at least, his ties to his slave past diminished as he prospered. Because his income depended on white slaveholders, he did nothing to antagonize them.

As a result, Ellison became one of the wealthiest owners of real and personal property in the South. He owned hundreds of acres of farmland and woodland worth at least $8,250 (about 148,000 current dollars). As early as 1820, he owned two slaves. In 1830 he owned four and in 1840, twenty-six. By 1860 he owned sixty-three and was worth in personal property alone $53,000 (about 954,000 current dollars).

Ellison assigned tasks to his slaves according to their gender and age. The field hands—mostly women and children—produced eighty bales of cotton each in 1850. They also raised thousands of bushels of corn, sweet potatoes, and other vegetables each year. The gin shop workers—men and adolescent boys—worked as blacksmiths, carpenters, and mechanics.

When South Carolina seceded from the Union in December 1860 and the Civil War began a few months later, Ellison and his family were caught between two contradictory forces. During the war, South Carolina's state government considered free African Americans potential traitors and curtailed their liberty. Meanwhile, the Union moved relentlessly toward immediate, uncompensated emancipation. Ellison, who died on December 5, 1861, did not live to see the emancipation of his slaves in 1865. But his children did. They also saw the destruction of his business when its newly emancipated workers refused to continue to work for the Ellisons as free men and women.

◄ William Ellison's house near Columbia, South Carolina.

among female and male slaves because they assumed correctly that husbands and fathers would be less rebellious than single men. Masters also knew that they would benefit if their human chattel reproduced. As Thomas Jefferson put it, "I consider a [slave] woman who brings [gives birth to] a child every two years as more profitable than the best man on the farm. What she produces is an addition to the capital, while his labors disappear in mere consumption."

Families were also the core of the African-American community in slavery. Even though no legal sanctions supported slave marriages and the domestic slave trade could sunder them, many such marriages endured. Before they wed, some couples engaged in courting rituals while others rejected "such foolishness." Similarly, slave weddings ranged from simply "taking up" to religious ceremonies replete with food and frolics.

"Jumping the broom" was often part of these ceremonies, although this custom was not African but European. During the 1930s former slave Tempie Herndon recalled her wedding ceremony conducted by "de nigger preacher dat preached at de plantation church." In particular, she remembered that after the religious ceremony, "Marse George got to have his little fun" by having the newlyweds jump backward over a broomstick. "You got to do dat to see which one gwine be boss of your household," she commented. "If both of dem jump over without touchin' it, dey won't gwine be no bossin', dey just gwine be congenial." In fact, more equality existed between husbands and wives in slave marriages than in those of the masters. Southern white concepts of patriarchy required male dominance. But because black men lacked power, their wives were more like partners than servants.

Slave couples usually lived together in cabins on their master's property. They had little privacy because nineteenth-century slave cabins were rude, small, one-room dwellings that two families might have to share. But couples who shared cabins were generally better off than husbands and wives who were the property of different masters and lived on different plantations. In these cases, children lived with their mother, and their father visited when he could in the evenings. Work patterns that changed with the seasons or with the mood of a master could interfere with such visits. So could the requirement that slaves have passes to leave home.

CHILDREN

Despite these difficulties, slave parents were able to instruct their children in family history, religion, and the skills required to survive in slavery. They sang to their children and told them stories full of folk wisdom. In particular, they impressed on them the importance of

This woodcut of a black father being sold away from his family appeared in *The Child's Anti-Slavery Book* in 1860. Family ruptures, like the one shown, were among the more common and tragic aspects to slavery, especially in the upper South, where masters claimed slavery was "mild." Courtesy of the Library of Congress

extended family relationships. The ability to rely on grandparents, aunts and uncles, cousins, and honorary relatives was a hedge against the family disruption that the domestic slave trade might inflict. In this manner, too, the extended black family provided slaves with the independent resources they needed to avoid complete physical, intellectual, cultural, and moral subjugation to their masters.

During an age when infant mortality rates were much higher than they are today, those for black southerners were even higher than they were for white people. There were several reasons for this. Enslaved black women usually had to do field labor up to the time they delivered a child, and their diets lacked necessary nutrients. Consequently, they tended to have babies whose weights at birth were less than normal. In addition, enslaved infants were more likely to be subject to such postpartum maladies as rickets, tetany, tetanus, high fevers, intestinal worms, and influenza than were other children. More than 50 percent of slave children died before the age of five.

Slaveholders contributed to high infant mortality rates probably more from ignorance than malevolence. It was, after all, in the master's economic self-interest to have slave mothers produce healthy children. Masters often allowed mothers a month to recuperate after giving birth and several months thereafter off from fieldwork to nurse their babies. Although this reduced the mother's productivity, the loss might be made up by the children's labor when they entered the plantation

A SLAVEHOLDER DESCRIBES A NEW PURCHASE

In this letter to her mother, a white Louisiana woman, Tryphena Blanche Holder Fox, describes her husband's purchase of a slave woman and her children. Several things are apparent in the letter— that investing in slaves was expensive, that the white woman's only concern for the slave woman and her children was their economic value, that it was up to the white woman to supervise the new slaves, and that the slave woman showed her displeasure with her situation.

Hygiene [Jesuit Bend, Louisiana]
Sunday, Dec. 27th 1857

Dear Mother,

We are obliged to save every dollar he can "rake & scrape" to pay for a negro woman. . . . She has two likely children . . . and is soon to have another, and he only pays fourteen hundred for the three. She is considered an excellent bargain . . . he would not sell her and the children for less than $2,000. She came & worked two days, so we could see what she was capable of. . . . She was sold by a Frenchman. . . . He has a family of ten & she had all the work to do besides getting her own wood & water from the river. She was not used to do this, and gave them a great deal of trouble. . . . How much trouble she will give me, I don't know, but I think I can get along with her, passable well any how. Of course it increased my cares, for having invested so much in one purchase, it will be to my interest to see that the children are well taken care of & clothed and fed. All of them give more or less trouble. . . .

🌲 *What does Tryphena reveal about the management of slaves?*

🌲 *What does she indicate about the ability of slaves to force concessions from their masters?*

Source: Tryphena Blanche Holder Fox to Anna Rose Holder, December 27, 1857, Mississippi Department of Archives and History, Jackson, Mississippi.

workforce. Unfortunately, many infants needed more than a few months of breast-feeding to survive.

The care of slave children varied with the size of a slaveholder's estate, the region it was in, and the mother's work. House servants could carry their babies with them while they did their work. On small farms, slave women strapped their babies to their backs or left them at the edge of fields, so they could nurse them periodically, although the latter practice risked exposing an infant to ants, flies, or mosquitoes. On larger plantations, mothers could leave a child with an elderly or infirm adult. This encouraged a sense of community and a shared responsibility among the slaves for all black children on a plantation.

As children grew older, they spent much time in unsupervised play, often with white children. Boys played marbles and ball games; girls skipped rope and tended to their dolls. A game of hiding and whipping, similar to the more recent cops and robbers, was a childish commentary on a violent system.

Slave childhood was short. Early on, parents and others taught children about the realities of plantation life. By witnessing whippings—sometimes of their parents—and through admonitions from their elders, slave children learned they had to be extremely careful about what they said to white people. Deceit and guile became survival skills. Slave childhood was also short because children as young as six had to do so-called light chores. Such work became physically more taxing as a child grew older, until, between the ages of eight and twelve, the child began doing adult field-work. That slave children were subject to sale away from their families, particularly in the upper South, also accelerated their progress to adulthood.

SEXUAL EXPLOITATION

As with forced separations, masters' sexual exploitation of black women disrupted enslaved families. Abuse of black women began during the Middle Passage and continued after the abolition of slavery in the United States in 1865. Long-term relationships between masters and enslaved women were common in the nineteenth-century South. Such continuing relationships rested not on overt coercion but on masters' implicit power and authority. The relationship between Thomas Jefferson and his slave Sally Hemings is the most infamous of these. DNA and circumstantial evidence indicate that Jefferson and Hemings had a long sexual relationship that produced four children who survived to adulthood. It began in 1787 when Hemings served as caretaker to one of Jefferson's daughters at his household in Paris, where he was U.S. ambassador to France. At that time Jefferson was forty-four and Hemings was about fourteen. She was pregnant when she returned to Virginia in 1789, although the child probably died in infancy. There is evidence that Hemings and her children enjoyed special privileges on Jefferson's Monticello plantation. But, by modern standards, their relationship began with statutory rape, and Hemings's unfree status and that of her children limited her ability to resist sexual advances. Two of Hemings children, a man named Beverly and a woman named Harriet, were "allowed" to escape in 1821 or 1822. Thereafter they lived as white people in Washington, D.C. Two others, Madison and Eston, gained freedom as young men under Jefferson's will. Jefferson never freed Sally Hemings. Instead his daughter permitted her to leave Monticello shortly after his death in 1826. She lived with Madison and Eston in Charlotte, Virginia, until her death in 1835.

Even more common than relationships like that of Jefferson and Hemings were instances in which masters, overseers, and their sons forced slave women to have sex against their will. This routine conduct caused great distress. Former slave Harriet Jacobs wrote in her autobiography, "I cannot tell how much I suffered in the presence of these wrongs, nor how I am still pained by the retrospect." One of the more notorius antebellum (pre–Civil War) cases of forced sexual exploitation occurred in Missouri during the 1850s. It involved sixty-year-old Robert Newsom and Celia, a fourteen-year-old girl he had purchased in 1850. Newsom repeatedly raped Celia until she killed him in 1855. Celia's attorneys put up a spirited defense at her trial. They argued that an 1845 Missouri law that made it a crime to "take any woman unlawfully against her will and by force, menace or duress, compel her to be defiled" gave Celia a right to defend her virtue. But the white male jury convicted her of murder anyway, and she was executed.

White southerners justified sexual abuse of black women in several ways. They maintained that black women were naturally promiscuous and seduced white men. Some proslavery apologists argued that the sexual exploitation of black women by white men reduced prostitution and promoted purity among white women. These apologists ignored the devastating emotional impact of sexual exploitation on black women. They failed to note that the rape of black women by white men emphasized in the most degrading manner the inability of black men to protect their wives and daughters.

DIET

The slaves' diet hardly raised the moral issues associated with the sexual exploitation of black women by white men. The typical plantation's weekly ration of one peck of cornmeal and three to four pounds of salt pork or bacon was enough to maintain an adult's body

Freed African Americans sit outside old slave headquarters at Fort George Island in Florida.   "Remains of Slave Quarters, Fort George Island, Florida," ca. 1865, Stereograph.
© Collection of The New-York Historical Society, Negative no. 48163

weight and, therefore, appeared to be adequate. But even when black men and women added vegetables and poultry that they raised or fish and small game that they caught, this diet was (according to modern medical science) deficient in calcium, vitamin C, riboflavin, protein, and iron. Because these vitamins and nutrients are essential to the health of people who perform hard labor in a hot climate, slaves frequently suffered from chronic illnesses. They often complained about being hungry and about the poor quality of their food. As one song went,

> We raise de wheat,
> Dey gib us de corn;
> We bake de bread,
> Dey gib us de crust;
> We sif' de meal,
> Dey gib us de huss;
> We peel de meat,
> Dey gib us de skin

Yet masters and white southerners generally consumed the same sort of food that slaves ate and, in

Throughout its existence, slavery in America encouraged white men to exploit black women for sexual purposes and to abuse black men and women physically. *Virginian Luxuries,* painted c. 1810, aimed to expose and ridicule these practices.

comparison to people in other parts of the Atlantic world, enslaved African Americans were not undernourished. Although adult slaves were on average an inch shorter than white northerners, they were three inches taller than new arrivals from Africa, two inches taller than slaves who lived in the West Indies, and one inch taller than British Royal Marines.

African-American cooks, primarily women, developed a distinctive cuisine based on African culinary traditions. They seasoned foods with salt, onions, pepper, and other spices and herbs. They fried meat and fish, served sauce over rice, and flavored vegetables with bits of smoked meat. The availability in the South of such African foods as okra, yams, benne seeds, and peanuts strengthened their culinary ties to that continent. Cooking also gave black women the ability to control part of their lives and to demonstrate their creativity.

CLOTHING

Enslaved men and women had less control over what they and their children wore than how they cooked. Although skilled slaves often produced the shoes and

clothing plantation workers wore, slaves in general rarely had the time or skill to make their own clothes. They went barefoot during the warm months and wore cheap shoes, usually made by local cobblers, in the winter. Slaveholding women, with the help of trained female house servants, sewed the clothes slaves wore.

This clothing was usually made of homespun cotton or wool. Some slaves also received hand-me-downs from masters and overseers. Although the distribution of clothing varied widely over time and space, and according to the generosity of masters, slaves usually received clothing allotments twice a year. At the fall distribution, slave men received two outfits for the cold weather along with a jacket and a wool cap. At the spring distribution, they received two cotton outfits. Slave drivers wore garments of finer cloth and greatcoats during the winter. Butlers and carriage drivers wore liveries appropriate to their public duties. Slave women received at each distribution two simply cut dresses of calico or homespun. In the winter they wore capes or cloaks and covered their heads with kerchiefs or bonnets.

Because masters gave priority to clothing adult workers, small children often went naked during the warm months. Depending on their ages and the season, children received garments called *shirts* if worn by boys and *shifts* if worn by girls. "I ain' neber had no pants 'till de year befo' de [Civil] war. All de li'l boys wo' shu't-tail shu'ts, jes' a slip to de knees," recalled former Louisiana slave Jacob Branch. This androgynous garb lasted until children reached "about twelve or fourteen," when they began doing the work of adults.

Although they received standard-issue clothing, black women particularly sought to individualize what they wore. They changed the colors of clothes with dyes they extracted from roots, berries, walnut shells, oak leaves, and indigo. They wove threads of different color into their clothes to make "checkedy" and other patterns. Former slave Morris Sheppard remembered that with his mother "everything was stripedy."

To further adorn themselves, young women wore hoops under their skirts fashioned from grapevines, stiffly starched petticoats, intricately arranged turbans, and colorful kerchiefs. On special occasions they braided or twisted their hair, used rouge made from berries, eye shadow made from soot, and perfume derived from honeysuckle. Urban slaves, of course, had access to commercial products, and even plantation slaves often bought clothes, shoes, ribbons, and kerchiefs at local stores or from peddlers.

HEALTH

Low birth weight, diet, and clothing all affected the health of slaves. Before the 1830s various diseases were endemic among bond people, and death could come quickly. Much of this ill health resulted from overwork in the South's hot, humid summers, exposure to cold during the winter, and poor hygiene. Slave quarters, for example, rarely had privies, drinking water could become contaminated, and food was prepared under less than healthy conditions. Dysentery, typhus, food poisoning, diarrhea, hepatitis, typhoid fever, salmonella, and intestinal worms were common and sometimes fatal maladies.

The South's warm climate encouraged mosquito-borne diseases, the growth of bacteria, and the spread of viruses. Interaction between people of African and European descent increased the types of illnesses. Smallpox, measles, and gonorrhea were European diseases; malaria, hookworm, and yellow fever came from Africa. The sickle-cell blood trait protected people of African descent from malaria but could cause sickle-cell anemia, a painful, debilitating, and fatal disease.

African Americans were also more susceptible to other afflictions than were persons of European descent. They suffered from lactose intolerance, which greatly limited the amount of calcium they could absorb from dairy products, and from a limited ability to acquire enough vitamin D from the sunlight in temperate regions. Because many slaves lost calcium through perspiration while working, these characteristics led to a high incidence of debilitating diseases. These included, according to historian Donald R. Wright, "blindness or inflamed and watery eyes; lameness or crooked limbs; loose, missing or rotten teeth; and skin sores. Also, they made African Americans much more apt than whites to suffer from a number of often fatal diseases—tetanus, intestinal worms, diphtheria, whooping cough, pica (or dirt eating), pneumonia, tuberculosis, and dysentery."

However, black southerners constituted the only New World slave population that grew by natural reproduction. Although the death rate among slaves was higher than among white southerners, it was similar to that of Europeans. Slave health also improved after 1830 when their rising economic value persuaded masters to improve slave quarters, provide warmer winter clothing, reduce overwork, and hire physicians to care for bond people. During the 1840s and 1850s, slaves were more likely than white southerners to be cared for by a physician.

Enslaved African Americans also used traditional remedies—derived from Africa and passed down by generations of women—to treat the sick. Wild cherry bark and herbs like pennyroyal or horehound went into teas to treat colds. Slaves used jimsonweed tea to counter rheumatism and chestnut leaf tea to relieve asthma. One former slave recalled that her grandmother dispensed syrup to treat colic and teas to cure fevers and stomachaches. Nineteenth-century medical knowledge was so limited that some of these folk remedies were more effective than those prescribed by white physicians. This was especially true of kaolin, a white clay also used in ceramics, which black women used to treat dysentery.

The Socialization of Slaves

African Americans had to acquire the skills needed to protect themselves and their loved ones from a brutal slave system. Folk tales often derived from Africa, but on occasion from American Indians, helped pass such skills from generation to generation. Parents, other relatives, and elderly slaves generally told such tales to teach survival, mental agility, and self-confidence.

The heroes of the tales are animal tricksters with human personalities. Most famous is Brer Rabbit, who in his weakness and cleverness represents African Americans in slavery. Although the tales portray Brer Rabbit as far from perfect, he uses his wits to overcome threats from strong and vicious antagonists, principally Brer Fox, who represents slaveholders. By hearing these stories and rooting for Brer Rabbit, slave children learned how to conduct themselves in a difficult environment.

They learned to watch what they said to white people, not to talk back, to withhold information about other African Americans, to dissemble. In particular, they refrained from making antislavery statements and camouflaged their awareness of how masters exploited them. As Henry Bibb, who escaped from slavery, put it, "The only weapon of self defense that I could use successfully was that of deception." Another former slave, Charshee Charlotte Lawrence-McIntyre, summed up the slave strategy in rhyme: "Got one mind for the boss to see; got another for what I know is me."

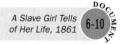

A Slave Girl Tells of Her Life, 1861   6-10   DOCUMENT

Masters tended to miss the subtlety of the divided consciousness of their bond people. When slaves refused to do simple tasks correctly, masters saw it as black stupidity rather than resistance. Sometimes outsiders, such as white northern missionary Charles C. Jones, understood more clearly what was going on. In 1842 Jones observed,

Persons live and die in the midst of Negroes and know comparatively little of their real character. The Negroes form a distinct class in the community, and keep themselves very much to themselves. They are one thing before the whites and another before their own color. Deception towards the former is characteristic of them, whether bond or free. . . . It is habit—long established custom, which descends from generation to generation.

Religion

Along with family and socialization, religion helped African Americans cope with slavery. Some masters denied their slaves access to Christianity, and some slaves ignored the religion. In New Orleans, Baltimore, and a few other locations there were Roman Catholic slaves, who were usually the human property of individual Roman Catholic masters. In Maryland during the 1830s the

Jesuits, an order of Roman Catholic priests and brothers, collectively owned approximately 300 slaves. But by the mid-nineteenth century, the overwhelming majority of American slaves practiced a Protestantism similar, but not identical, to that of most white southerners.

Charles C. Jones, The Religious Instruction of the Negroes in the United States, 1842 **DOCUMENT 6-5**

Biracial Baptist and Methodist congregations persisted in the South longer than they did in northern cities. The southern congregations usually had racially segregated seating, but black people and white people joined in communion and church discipline. They shared cemeteries. Many masters during the nineteenth century sponsored plantation churches for slaves, and white missionary organizations also supported such churches.

In the plantation churches, white ministers told their black congregations that Christian slaves must obey their earthly masters as they did God. This was not what slaves wanted to hear. Cornelius Garner, a former slave,

British artist John Antrobus completed this painting in about 1860. It is named *Plantation Burial* and suggests the importance of religion among enslaved African Americans.   John Antrobus, *Plantation Burial*, oil painting. The Historical New Orleans Collection. 1960.46

recalled that "dat ole white preacher jest was telling us slaves to be good to our marsters. We ain't keer'd a bit 'bout dat stuff he was telling us 'cause we wanted to sing, pray, and serve God in our own way." At times slaves walked out on ministers who preached obedience.

Instead of services sponsored by masters, slaves preferred a semisecret black church they conducted themselves. This was a church characterized by self-called, often illiterate black preachers. It emphasized Moses and deliverance from bondage rather than consistent theology or Christian meekness. Services were emotional and involved singing, dancing, shouting, moaning, and clapping. According to historian Peter Kolchin, African "potions, concoctions, charms, and rituals [used] to ward off evil, cure sickness, harm enemies, and produce amorous behavior" were mixed in with this black Christianity. European settlers in America during the previous century had also melded Christian and non-Christian beliefs and practices. So it is not surprising that white as well as black people continued to seek the help of African-American conjurers.

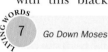

LIVING WORDS **7** Go Down Moses

The Character of Slavery and Slaves

For over a century, historians have debated the character of the Old South's slave system and the people it held in bondage. During the 1910s southern historian Ulrich B. Phillips portrayed slavery as a benign, paternalistic institution in which Christian slaveholders cared for largely content slaves. Slavery, Phillips argued—as had the slaveholders themselves—rescued members of an inferior race from African barbarism and permitted them to rise as far as they possibly could toward civilization. With different emphasis, historian Eugene D. Genovese has, since the 1960s, also placed paternalism at the heart of southern plantation slavery.

Other historians, however, deny that paternalism had much to do with a system that rested on force. Since the 1950s historians have contended that slaveholders exploited their bondpeople in a selfish quest for profits. Although some slaveholders were concerned about the welfare of their slaves, this brutal portrait of slavery is persuasive at the dawn of the twenty-first century. Many masters never met their slaves face to face. Most slaves experienced whipping at some point in their lives, and over half the slaves caught up in the domestic slave trade were separated from their families.

There is also a scholarly tradition of comparing slavery in the American South with its counterpart in Latin America. Historians note that slaves in Latin American countries influenced by Roman law and the Roman Catholic Church enjoyed more protection from abusive masters than did slaves in the United States, where English law and Protestant Christianity dominated. Routes to freedom, through self-purchase and manumission, were more available in Latin America than in the Old South. There was more interracial marriage and therefore, some historians maintain, less racism in Latin America than in the United States. But other historians have established that protections offered by law and religion to slaves in Latin America were more theoretical than practical. They argue that racism there merely took a different form than it did in the United States. Certainly the mortality rate among Latin American slaves was far greater than among slaves in the American South, which implies that the conditions under which slaves labored in Latin America were even harsher than the grim conditions slaves often faced in the American South.

The character of enslaved African Americans has also been debated. Historians such as Phillips, who were persuaded by the slaveholders' justifications of the "peculiar institution," argued that African Americans were genetically predisposed to being slaves and were therefore content in their status. In 1959 Stanley M. Elkins changed the debate by arguing that black people were not inherently inferior or submissive, but that concentration-camp-like conditions on plantations made them into childlike "Sambos" as dependent on their masters as inmates in Nazi extermination camps were on their guards.

DOCUMENT **6-9** Farm Journal Reports on the Care and Feeding of Slaves, 1836

Elkins's study stimulated the scholarship that shapes current understandings of the character of African Americans in slavery. Since the 1960s historians have argued that rather than dehumanizing them, slavery led African Americans to create institutions that allowed them some control over their lives. According to these historians, African-American resistance forced masters to accept the slaves' own work patterns and their autonomy in the slave quarters. Slaves built families, churches, and communities. Although these studies may overidealize the strength of slave communities within the brutal context of plantation slavery, they have enriched our understanding of slave life.

AFRICAN-AMERICAN EVENTS	NATIONAL EVENTS
	1810
	1812 Louisiana becomes a state
	1815
1816 William Ellison purchases his freedom	**1817** Mississippi becomes a state
1818 Suppression of Charleston's AME Church	**1819** Alabama becomes a state
1819 Frederick Douglass born in Maryland	
	1820
1822 Denmark Vesey Conspiracy, Charleston, S.C.	**1820** Missouri Compromise
	1821 Missouri becomes a state
	1824 John Quincy Adams elected president of United States
	1825
	1828 Andrew Jackson elected president
	1830
1831 Nat Turner's revolt	
1832 Virginia legislature defeats gradual abolition	
	1835
1838 Frederick Douglass apprenticed in Baltimore	**1836** Cherokee Trail of Tears
1839 *Amistad* slave revolt	

CONCLUSION

African-American life in slavery during the time of the Cotton Kingdom is a vast subject. As slavery expanded westward before 1860, it varied from region to region and according to the crops slaves cultivated. Although cotton became the South's most important product, many African-American slaves continued to produce tobacco, rice, sugar, and hemp. In the Chesapeake, slaves worked on wheat farms. Others tended livestock or worked in cities and industry. Meanwhile, enslaved African Americans continued to build the community institutions that allowed them to maintain their cultural autonomy and persevere within a brutal system.

The story of African Americans in southern slavery is one of labor, perseverance, and resistance. Black labor was responsible for the growth of a southern economy that helped produce prosperity throughout the United States. Black men and women preserved and expanded an African-American cultural heritage that included African, European, and American Indian roots. They resisted determined efforts to dehumanize them. They developed family relationships, communities, churches, and traditions that helped them preserve their character as a people.

RECOMMENDED READING

Ira Berlin. *Generations in Captivity: A History of African-American Slaves.* Cambridge, MA: Harvard University Press, 2003. Portrays slavery in the Cotton Kingdom as the product of a series of negotiations between masters and slaves over the terms of captivity.

Charles B. Dew. *Bonds of Iron: Masters and Slaves at Buffalo Forge.* New York: Norton, 1994. Dew offers an excellent account of one type of industrial slavery in the Old South.

Michael P. Johnson and James L. Roark. *Black Masters: A Free Family of Color in the Old South.* New York: Norton, 1984. This book provides a full account of William Ellison and his slaveholding black family.

Norrece T. Jones Jr. *Born a Child of Freedom, Yet a Slave: Mechanisms of Control and Strategies of Resistance in Antebellum South Carolina.* Middleton, CT: Wesleyan University Press, 1990. This book explores how masters controlled slaves and how slaves resisted.

Wilma King. *Stolen Childhood: Slave Youth in Nineteenth-Century America.* Bloomington: Indiana University Press, 1995. This is the most up-to-date account of enslaved black children. It is especially useful concerning the children's work.

Melton A. McLaurin. *Celia, a Slave.* Athens: University of Georgia Press, 1991. This is the most complete study of an enslaved woman's response to sexual exploitation.

MacLaurin establishes the social and political contexts for this famous case.

ADDITIONAL BIBLIOGRAPHY

SLAVERY AND ITS EXPANSION

Stanley M. Elkins. *Slavery: A Problem in American Institutional and Intellectual Life*, 3d ed. Chicago: University of Chicago Press, 1976.

Eugene D. Genovese. *The Political Economy of Slavery: Studies in the Economy and Society of the Slave South*. 1961. Reprint, New York: Random House, 1967.

Roger G. Kennedy. *Mr. Jefferson's Lost Cause: Land, Farmers, Slavery, and the Louisiana Purchase*. New York: Oxford University Press, 2003.

Larry Koger. *Black Slaveowners: Free Black Slave Masters in South Carolina, 1790–1860*. 1985. Reprint, Columbia: University of South Carolina Press, 1994.

Peter Kolchin. *American Slavery 1619–1877*. New York: Hill and Wang, 1993.

Donald P. McNeilly. *The Old South Frontier: Cotton Plantations and the Formation of Arkansas Society, 1819–1861*. Fayetteville: University of Arkansas Press, 2000.

John H. Moore. *The Emergence of the Cotton Kingdom in the Old Southwest*. Baton Rouge: Louisiana State University Press, 1988.

Larry Eugene Rivers. *Slavery in Florida: Territorial Days to Emancipation*. Gainsville: University Press of Florida, 2000.

Kenneth M. Stampp. *The Peculiar Institution: Slavery in the Antebellum South*. 1956. Reprint, New York: Vintage Books, 1989.

URBAN AND INDUSTRIAL SLAVERY

Ronald L. Lewis. *Coal, Iron, and Slaves: Industrial Slavery in Maryland and Virginia, 1715–1865*. Westport, CT: Greenwood, 1979.

Robert S. Starobin. *Industrial Slavery in the Old South*. New York: Oxford University Press, 1970.

Midori Takagi. *Rearing Wolves to Our Own Destruction: Slavery in Richmond, Virginia, 1782–1865*. Charlottesville: University Press of Virginia, 1999.

Richard C. Wade. *Slavery in the Cities: The South 1820–1860*. 1964. Reprint, New York: Oxford University Press, 1967.

THE DOMESTIC SLAVE TRADE

Frederic Bancroft. *Slave Trading in the Old South*. 1931. Reprint, Columbia: University of South Carolina Press, 1996.

Walter Johnson. *Soul by Soul: Life inside the Antebellum Slave Market*. Cambridge, MA: Harvard University Press, 1999.

Michael Tadman. *Speculators and Slaves: Masters, Traders, and Slaves in the Old South*. 1989. Reprint, Madison: University of Wisconsin Press, 1996.

1840

1841
Solomon Northup kidnapped

1845

1845
Betsy Somayrac's will

1845
Texas annexed as a slave state

1846
War against Mexico begins

1848
Annexation of New Mexico and California

1850

1852
Frederick Law Olmsted's first tour of southern states

1850
Compromise of 1850

1853
Solomon Northup publishes *Twelve Years a Slave*

1854
Kansas-Nebraska Act

1855

1855
Celia's trial and execution for killing her master

1856
Republican Party's first presidential election

1857
Supreme Court issues *Dred Scott* decision

1860

1860
The secession movement begins

AFRICAN-AMERICAN EVENTS   **NATIONAL EVENTS**

THE SLAVE COMMUNITY

John W. Blassingame. *The Slave Community: Plantation Life in the Antebellum South*, 2d ed. New York: Oxford University Press, 1979.

Janet Duitsman Cornelius. *Slave Missions and the Black Church in the Antebellum South*. Columbia: University of South Carolina Press, 1999.

Wilma A. Dunaway. *The African-American Family in Slavery and Emancipation*. New York: Cambridge University Press, 2003.

Eugene D. Genovese. *Roll, Jordan, Roll: The World the Slave Made*. 1974. Reprint, Vintage Books, 1976.

Herbert Gutman. *The Black Family in Slavery and Freedom*. 1976. Reprint, Vintage Books, 1977.

Charles Joyner. *Down by the Riverside: A South Carolina Community*. Urbana: University of Illinois Press, 1984.

Ann Patton Malone. *Sweet Chariot: Slave Family and Household Structure in Nineteenth-Century Louisiana*. Chapel Hill: University of North Carolina Press, 1992.

Leslie Howard Owens. *This Species of Property: Slave Life and Culture in the Old South*. 1976. Reprint, New York: Oxford University Press, 1977.

Todd L. Savitt. *Medicine and Slavery: The Diseases and Health Care of Blacks in Antebellum Virginia*. Urbana: University of Illinois Press, 1978.

Maria Jenkins Schwartz. *Born in Bondage: Growing up Enslaved in the Antebellum South*. Cambridge, MA: Harvard University Press, 2000.

ENSLAVED WOMEN

David Barry Gaspar and Darlene Clark Hine, eds. *More Than Chattel: Black Women and Slavery in the Americas*. Bloomington: University of Indiana Press, 1996.

Darlene Clark Hine, Wilma King, and Linda Reed, eds. *"We Specialize in the Wholly Impossible": A Reader in Black Women's History*. Brooklyn, NY: Carlson, 1996.

Joshua D. Rothman. *Notorious in the Neighborhood: Sex and Families across the Color Line in Virginia 1787–1861*. Chapel Hill: University of North Carolina Press, 2003.

Deborah Gray White. *Ar'n't I a Woman? Female Slaves in the Plantation South*. New York: Norton, 1985.

Jean Fagan Yellin. *Harriet Jacobs: A Life*. New York: Basic Civitas, 2003.

SLAVE CULTURE AND RELIGION

John B. Boles, ed. *Masters and Slaves in the House of the Lord: Race and Religion in the American South, 1740–1870*. Lexington: University Press of Kentucky, 1988.

Janet Duitsman Cornelius. *When I Can Read My Title Clear: Literacy, Slavery, and Religion in the Antebellum South*. Columbia: University of South Carolina Press, 1991.

———. *Slave Missions and the Black Church in the Antebellum South*. Columbia: University of South Carolina Press, 1999.

Sharla M. Fett. *Working Cures: Healing, Health, and Power on Southern Slave Plantations*. Chapel Hill: University of North Carolina Press, 2002.

Lawrence W. Levine. *Black Culture and Black Consciousness: Afro-American Folk Thought from Slavery to Freedom*. New York: Oxford University Press, 1977.

Albert J. Raboteau. *Slave Religion: The "Invisible Institution" in the Antebellum South*. New York: Oxford University Press, 1978.

RETRACING THE ODYSSEY

William Johnson House (not currently open to the public) **and Melrose Plantation**, Natchez, Mississippi. Johnson was one of the rare black slaveholders, and John T. McMurrin, the owner of Melrose Plantation, was a northern white man who became a slaveholder.

Hampton Plantation State Park, McClellanville, South Carolina. The plantation house dates to about 1750, and the outbuildings include slave cabins.

Magnolia Mound Plantation, Baton Rouge, Louisiana. This historic site includes a plantation house, outbuildings, an overseer's house, and a separate kitchen building.

Zephaniah Kingsley Plantation, Fort George Island, Florida. Kingsley's was an interracial family. Buildings on the plantation include the oldest standing plantation house in Florida and thirty-two slave quarters.

 REVIEW, RESEARCH, & INTERACT

REVIEW QUESTIONS

1. How did the domestic slave trade and the exploitation of black women by white males affect slave families?

2. Were black slaveholders significant in the history of slavery?

3. How did urban and industrial slavery differ from plantation slavery in the Old South?

4. What impact did housing, nutrition, and disease have on the lives of slaves between 1820 and 1860?

5. How did black Christianity differ from white Christianity in the Old South? How did black Christianity in the South differ from black Christianity in the North?

www.researchnavigator.com

Using the tools available in Research Navigator, consider these questions:
How did blacks resist the oppression of the slave system? What steps did whites take to eliminate resistance?

PRIMARY SOURCE DOCUMENTS

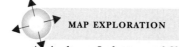

MAP EXPLORATION

Agriculture, Industry, and Slavery in the Old South, 1850, p. 145

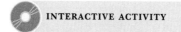

INTERACTIVE ACTIVITY

Alexis de Tocqueville

Alexis de Tocqueville's *Democracy in America* accurately discusses the rapid growth of the country and how sectional tensions might endanger the Union.

Free Black People in Antebellum America

WHAT WERE THE DEMOGRAPHICS
OF BLACK FREEDOM?

HOW DID THE POLICIES OF THE JACKSONIAN
DEMOCRATS FAVOR SLAVEHOLDERS?

HOW WAS BLACK FREEDOM
LIMITED IN THE NORTH?

WHAT WERE THE CHARACTERISTICS OF
NORTHERN BLACK COMMUNITIES?

WHAT INSTITUTIONS DID
AFRICAN AMERICANS RELY ON MOST?

HOW DID FREE AFRICAN AMERICANS
LIVE IN THE SOUTH AND IN THE WEST?

◀ **This lithograph, published in 1818** by antislavery
author Jesse Torrey Jun, depicts a free black man
still in handcuffs and leg irons after an attempt to
kidnap him into slavery. He is relating details of his
experience to a sympathetic white man. The sparsely
furnished attic room reflects the living conditions of
many free African Americans of the time.   Courtesy of
the Library of Congress

O ur vices and our degradation are ever arrayed against us, but our virtues are passed by unnoticed. And what is still more lamentable, our [white] friends, to whom we concede all the principles of humanity and religion, from these very causes seem to have fallen into the current of popular feeling and are imperceptibly floating on the stream—actually living in the practice of prejudice, while they abjure it in theory, and feel it not in their hearts. *Freedom's Journal*, March 16, 1827.

◄ **Blacks who escaped** from slavery lived in fear that they might be sought by masters who often posted monetary offers for the return of runaway slaves.

Journalist Samuel Cornish wrote this passage in 1827 when he introduced himself to his readers as the coeditor of the first African-American newspaper. He knew that pervasive white prejudice limited the lives of black people. During the forty years before the Civil War, such prejudice was nearly as common in the North as in the South. The northern states had, of course, abolished slavery, and free black people there enjoyed more rights than they did in the South. But that made many white northerners more hostile toward African Americans than white southerners generally were.

While southern legislatures considered expelling free black people from their states, northern legislatures—particularly in the Old Northwest—restricted black people's ability to move into their states. White workers North and South, fearing competition for jobs, sponsored legislation that limited most free African Americans to menial employment. White people also required most black people to live in segregated areas of cities. Yet such ghettoized African-American communities cultivated a dynamic cultural legacy and built enduring institutions.

This chapter picks up the story of free black communities begun in Chapter 5. It provides a portrait of free African Americans between 1820 and the start of the Civil War. As in the revolutionary era, the antebellum period was one of hope and fear. The numbers of free African Americans steadily increased. But, as Chapter 6 indicates, the number of slaves increased much faster. Here we begin with a review of the demographic data. We then discuss black life in the North and free black life in the South.

Demographics of Freedom

In 1820 there were 233,504 free African Americans living in the United States. In comparison there were 1,538,125 slaves and 7,861,931 white people. Of the free African Americans, 99,281 lived in the North, 114,070 in the upper South, and 20,153 in the deep South. Although throughout this period more free African Americans lived in the South as a whole than in the North, few lived in the deep South (see Map 7–1). Free people of color accounted for 2.4 percent of the American population and 3 percent of the southern population. More black women than black men were free in 1820, and—particularly in urban areas—this remained true throughout the period. As the southern states made freedom suits and manumission more difficult, the northern free black population increased more rapidly than the free black populations in either the upper or deep South.

By 1860 the free African-American population had reached 488,070. Of these, 226,152 lived in the North, 224,963 in the upper South, and 36,955 in the deep South (see Figures 7–1 and 7–2). A few thousand free black people also lived in the west beyond Missouri, Arkansas, and Texas. Meanwhile slaves had increased

MAP EXPLORATION

To explore this interactive map, go to
http://www.prenhall.com/hine4/map7.1

MAP 7–1 THE SLAVE, FREE BLACK, AND WHITE POPULATION OF THE UNITED STATES IN 1830

This map does not distinguish the slave from the free black population of the free states, although the process of gradual emancipation in several northeastern states was still under way and some black northerners remained enslaved. Source: For slave states, Ira Berlin, *Slaves without Masters: The Free Negro in the Antebellum South* (New York: New Press, 1971); for free states, *Historical Statistics of the United States* (Washington: GPO, 1960). Note: Figures for free states are rounded to the nearest thousand.

▶ *Which states had the largest and the smallest free black populations in 1830?*

Free states and territories

Slave states and territories

S - 109,588	Slave, free black,
FB - 18,710	and white populations
W - 89,441	(slave states)

| B - 10,000 | Black and white |
| W - 928,000 | populations (free states) |

to just under four million, and massive immigration had tripled the white population to 26,957,471. The proportion of free African Americans had actually dropped to just 1.6 percent of the total American population and to 2.1 percent of the southern population when the Civil War in 1861 began the process of making all black people free.

In 1860, 47.3 percent of the free black population lived in cities compared with only 32.9 percent of white people. Of the urban African Americans, 62.5 percent lived in cities with populations over 100,000. As a result, free African Americans accounted for a significantly larger percentage of the population of large cities than they did of the total American population. In the upper South city of Baltimore free black people represented 12 percent of the 212,418 residents. There, as well as in Richmond, Norfolk, and other smaller cities of the upper South, free African Americans interacted with enslaved populations to create communities embracing both groups. The largest black urban population in the North was in Philadelphia, where 22,185 African Americans made up 4.2 percent of approximately 533,000

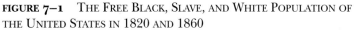

FIGURE 7–1   THE FREE BLACK, SLAVE, AND WHITE POPULATION OF THE UNITED STATES IN 1820 AND 1860

The bar graph shows the relationship among free African-American, slave, and white populations in the United States in the years 1820 and 1860. The superimposed pie charts illustrate the percentages of these groups in the population in the same years.

residents. Other important northern cities—such as New York, Boston, Providence, New Haven, New Bedford, and Cincinnati—had much smaller black populations, but they were still large enough to develop dynamic communities.

The Jacksonian Era

After the War of 1812, free African Americans—like other Americans of the time—witnessed rapid economic, social, and political change. Between 1800 and 1860, a **market revolution** transformed the North into a modern industrial society. An economy based on subsistence farming, goods produced by skilled artisans, and local markets grew into one marked by commercial farming, factory production, and national markets. The Industrial Revolution that had begun in Britain a century earlier set the stage for these changes. But transportation had to improve enormously to allow for such a revolution in America. After 1807 when Robert Fulton demonstrated the practicality of steam-powered river vessels, steamboats speeded travel on the country's inland waterways. During the 1820s a system of turnpikes and canals began to unite the North and parts of the South. Of particular importance were the National Road extending westward from Baltimore and the Erie Canal that in 1825 opened a water route from New York City to the Old Northwest. By the 1830s railroads were linking urban and agricultural regions (see Map 7–2).

As faster transportation revolutionized trade, as a factory system began to replace small shops run by artisans, and as cities expanded, northern society changed in profound ways. A large urban working class arose. Artisans and small farmers feared for their future. Entrepreneurs began to replace the traditional social elite. The North also became increasingly different from a still largely premodern South. By the 1820s northern states bristled with reform movements designed to deal with the social dislocations the market revolution had caused.

The market revolution also helped create mass political parties as communications improved and populations became more concentrated. By 1810 states had begun dropping the traditional property qualifications that had limited citizens' right to vote. One by one, they moved toward universal white manhood suffrage. This trend doomed the openly elitist Federalist Party and disrupted its foe, the Republican Party. As the market revolution picked up during the 1820s, unleashing hopes and fears among Americans, politicians recognized the need for more broadly based political parties.

A turning point came as a result of the 1824 presidential election in which four candidates ran as Republicans but none received a majority of the popular or electoral vote. War hero Andrew Jackson of Tennessee led the field, but in early 1825 Congress—exercising its duty to decide such elections—elected Secretary of State John Quincy Adams of Massachusetts. As president, Adams paradoxically represented both the old elitist style of politics and the entrepreneurial spirit of emerging northern capitalism. Adams, along with his secretary of state, Henry Clay, hoped to promote industrialization through a national program of federal government aid. But Jackson's supporter's claimed that Clay and Adams had cheated the general out of

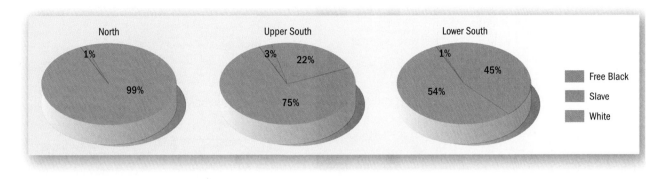

FIGURE 7–2　THE FREE BLACK, SLAVE, AND WHITE POPULATION BY REGION, 1860
These pie charts compare the free black, slave, and white populations of the North, upper South, and lower South in 1860. Note the near balance of the races in the lower South.

the presidency. Led by Martin Van Buren of New York, they organized a new Democratic Party to counter the Adams-Clay program. By appealing to slaveholders—who believed economic nationalism favored the North over the South—and to "the common man" throughout the country, the Democrats elected Jackson in 1828.

Jackson was a strong but controversial president. During the **Nullification Crisis** of 1832–1833 he acted as a nationalist in facing down the attempt of South Carolina to nullify—to block—the collection of the U.S. tariff (tax) on imports within the state. Otherwise, Jackson, who owned many slaves, promoted states' rights, economic localism, and the territorial expansion of slavery. In opposition to Jackson, Henry Clay, a Kentucky slaveholder, and others formed the Whig Party during the early 1830s.

 7-5 *Senator Sees Slavery as a "Positive Good," 1837*

A national organization that fought the Democrats for power from 1834 to 1852, the Whig Party mixed traditional and modern politics. It was a mass political party, but many of its leaders questioned the legitimacy of mass parties. It favored a nationalist approach to economic policy, which made it more successful in the North than in the South, opposed territorial expansion, worried about the growing number of immigrants, and endorsed the moral values of evangelical Protestantism. In contrast to Democratic politicians who increasingly made racist appeals to antiblack prejudices among white voters, Whigs generally adopted a more conciliatory tone regarding race. By the late 1830s, a few northern Whigs claimed their party opposed slavery and racial oppression. They were, however, exaggerating. The Whigs often nominated slaveholders for the presidency, and few Whig politicians defended the rights of African Americans.

Limited Freedom in the North

Addressing an interracial audience in Boston, white abolitionist Joseph C. Lovejoy in 1846 described the North as a land "partially free." Lovejoy was especially concerned that the Fugitive Slave Law of 1793 extended into the northern states the power of southern masters to enslave African Americans. But white northerners also limited black freedom by enacting **black laws,** by rarely allowing black men to vote, by advocating segregated housing, schools, and transportation, and by limiting African Americans' employment opportunities.

The Fugitive Slave Law endangered the freedom of northern black men, women, and children. Those who had escaped from slavery, of course, lived in fear that as long as they stayed in the United States they might be seized and returned to their erstwhile masters. But any black northerner could be kidnapped, taken to a southern state, and enslaved under the aegis of this law. Even such black leaders as Richard Allen and David Ruggles faced this threat. Ruggles, a prominent northern-born abolitionist, author, and lecturer during the 1830s and 1840s, barely escaped an attempt to haul him before a judge so he could be transported to the South. Others were less lucky, and vigilance against kidnapping became important in African-American community life in the North throughout the antebellum period.

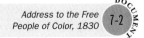 *Address to the Free People of Color, 1830* **7-2**

BLACK LAWS

As we indicated in previous chapters, the racially egalitarian impulse of the revolutionary era had by the 1790s begun to wane among white Americans. Meanwhile, the

MAP 7–2 TRANSPORTATION REVOLUTION

This map shows the principal American canals and roads built by 1830 and the principal railroad lines
built by 1850. A growing transportation network cut travel time and shipping costs, which encouraged
commerce.

▶▶ *How did the transportation revolution affect African Americans?*

dawning Romantic Age—characterized by a sentimental fascination with uniqueness—encouraged a general belief that each ethnic and racial group had its own inherent spirit that set it apart from others. As white Americans began to perceive self-reliance, intellectual curiosity, the capacity for self-government, military valor, and an energetic work ethic as inherently "Anglo-Saxon" characteristics, they began to believe other racial groups lacked these virtues. As Samuel Cornish suggested, even those white people who befriended black people considered them outsiders in a "white man's country."

Most white northerners, in fact, wanted nothing to do with African Americans. Like white southerners, they considered black people inferior in every way. They paradoxically dismissed black people as incapable of honest work and feared black competition for jobs. Contact with African Americans, they believed, had degraded white southerners and would also corrupt white northerners if they permitted it. Therefore, as historian Leon Litwack puts it, "Nearly every northern state considered, and many adopted, measures to prohibit or restrict the further immigration of Negroes" into its jurisdiction.

Such measures were more prevalent in the Old Northwest than in the Northeast. Ohio, Illinois, Indiana, Michigan, Iowa, and Wisconsin all limited or banned black immigration and discriminated against black residents. But in 1821 a bill to keep black people from entering Massachusetts failed to reach a vote in the state legislature on the grounds that it was inconsistent with "love of humanity." In Pennsylvania, which had a much larger influx of southern African Americans than Massachusetts, the legislature defeated attempts to limit their entry.

Between 1804 and 1849, Ohio's "black laws" required that African Americans entering the state produce legal evidence that they were free, register with a county clerk, and post a $500 bond "to pay for their support in case of want." State and local authorities rarely enforced these provisions, and when the Ohio Free Soil Party brought about their repeal in 1849, about 25,000 African Americans lived in the state. But these rules certainly made black people insecure. In 1829, for example, Cincinnati used them to force between 1,100 and 2,200 black residents to depart. Moreover, other provisions of Ohio's black laws were rigorously enforced, including those that prohibited black testimony against white people, black service on juries, and black enlistment in the state militia.

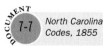

DOCUMENT 7-7 *North Carolina Codes, 1855*

In 1813 Illinois Territory threatened that African Americans who tried to settle within its borders would be repeatedly whipped until they left. In 1847,

Eliza, Nellie, and Margaret Coplan in an 1854 portrait by W. M. Prior. The Coplan family was one of the few African-American families in antebellum America affluent enough to commission such a portrait. Note the girls' fine clothing.   William Matthew Prior, American (1800–1875). "Three Sisters of the Coplan Family" 1854. Oil on canvas. 26⅞ × 36½ in. (68.3 × 92.7 cm). Request of Martha C. Karolik for the M. and M. Karolik Collection of American Paintings, 1815–1865. Courtesy, Museum of Fine Arts, Boston. Reproduced with permission. © 2001 Museum of Fine Arts, Boston. All Rights Reserved.

long after it had become a state, Illinois updated this provision, mandating that African Americans who sought to become permanent residents could be fined. Those who could not pay the fine could be sold at public auction into indentured servitude. Indiana citizens ratified a state constitution in 1851 that explicitly banned all African Americans from the state, and Michigan, Iowa, and Wisconsin followed Indiana's example. These laws testify to white prejudice and fear. They suggest how uncomfortable African Americans felt in the Old Northwest. Yet, as in Ohio, these states rarely enforced such restrictive laws. As long as they did not feel threatened, white people were usually willing to tolerate a few black people (see Table 7–1).

DISFRANCHISEMENT

The disfranchisement of black voters was, excepting most of New England, common throughout the North during the antebellum decades. The same white antipathy to African Americans that led to exclusionary legislation supported the movement to deny the right to vote to black men (no women could vote anywhere in the United States during most of the nineteenth century). Because northern antiblack sentiment was so strong in the Old Northwest, prior to the Civil War no

TABLE 7–1   BLACK POPULATION IN THE STATES
OF THE OLD NORTHWEST, 1800–1840

	1800	1810	1820	1830	1840
Ohio	337	1,899	4,723	9,574	17,345
Michigan		144	174	293	707
Illinois		781	1,374	2,384	3,929
Indiana	298	630	1,420	3,632	7,168
Iowa					188

Source: James Oliver Horton and Lois E. Horton, In Hope of Liberty: Culture, Community, and Protest among Northern Free Blacks, 1700–1860 (Oxford University Press, 1997), 104.

black men were ever allowed to vote in Ohio, Indiana, Illinois, Michigan, Wisconsin, and Iowa. But the older northern states had allowed black male suffrage, and efforts to curtail it were by-products of Jacksonian democracy.

During the eighteenth and early nineteenth centuries, the dominant elite in the northeastern states had used property qualifications to prevent poor black and poor white men from voting. Because black people were generally poorer than white people, these property qualifications gave most white men the right to vote and denied it to most black men. Under such circumstances white people saw no danger in letting a few relatively well-to-do black men exercise the franchise. It was the egalitarian movement to remove property qualifications that led to the outright disfranchisement of most black voters in the Northeast.

Both advocates and opponents of universal white male suffrage opposed allowing all black men to vote. They alleged that in certain places black men would be elected to office, morally suspect African Americans would corrupt the political process, black people would be encouraged to try to mix socially with white people, and justifiably angry white people would react violently. Therefore, the movement for universal white manhood suffrage transformed a class issue into a racial one. Although some New England states rejected disfranchisement of black voters, this was not the case in those northeastern states with the largest black populations.

New Jersey stopped allowing black men to vote in 1807 and in 1844 adopted a white-only suffrage provision in its state constitution. In 1818 Connecticut determined that, although black men who had voted before that date could continue to vote, no new black voters would be allowed. At the other extreme, Maine, New Hampshire, Vermont, and Massachusetts—none of which had a significant African-American minority—made no effort to deprive black men of the vote. In the

middle were Rhode Island, New York, and Pennsylvania, which had protracted struggles over the issue.

In 1822 Rhode Island denied that black men were eligible to vote in its elections, but in 1842 a popular uprising against the state's conservative government extended the franchise to all men, black as well as white. In New York an 1821 state constitutional convention defeated an attempt to disfranchise all black men. Instead, it raised the property qualification for black voters while eliminating it for white voters. To vote in New York, black men had to have property worth $250 (approximately 3,000 current dollars) and pay taxes, whereas white men simply had to pay taxes or serve in the state militia. This provision denied the right to vote to nearly all of the 10,000 black men who had previously voted in the state. African Americans nevertheless remained active in New York politics. As supporters of the Liberty Party in 1844, the Whig Party in 1846, and of the **Free-Soil Party** in 1848, they fought unsuccessfully to regain equal access to the polls.

A similar protracted struggle in Pennsylvania resulted in a more absolute elimination of black suffrage. From 1780 to 1837, black men who met property qualifications could vote in some of this state's counties but not in others. Then, in 1838, delegates to a convention to draft a new state constitution voted 77 to 45 to enfranchise all white men and disfranchise all black men. Although such African-American leaders as Robert Purvis, Peter Gardner, and Frederick Hinton organized to prevent the new constitution from being adopted, Pennsylvanians narrowly ratified it by a vote of 113,971 to 112,759. As late as 1855, black Pennsylvanians, arguing that without the right to vote they faced mounting repression, petitioned Congress to help them gain equal access to the polls. But their efforts failed. During the years before the Civil War, 93 percent of northern black people lived in states that either denied or severely limited black men's right to vote.

SEGREGATION

Exclusionary legislation was confined to the Old Northwest, and not all northern states disfranchised black men. But no black northerner could avoid being victimized by a pervasive determination among white people to segregate society.

Northern hotels, taverns, and resorts turned black people away unless they were the servants of white guests. African Americans were either banned from public lecture halls, art exhibits, and religious revivals or could attend only at certain times. When they were allowed in churches and theaters, they had to sit in segregated sections. Ohio excluded African Americans from state-supported poorhouses and insane asylums. In relatively enlightened Massachusetts, prominent black abolitionist and orator Frederick Douglass was "within the space of a few days . . . turned away from a menagerie on Boston Common, a lyceum [a public lecture hall] and revival meeting in New Bedford, [and] an eating house."

African Americans faced special difficulty trying to use public transportation. They could ride in stagecoaches only if there were no white passengers. As rail travel became more common during the late 1830s, companies set aside special cars for African Americans. In Massachusetts in 1841, a railroad first used the term **Jim Crow,** which derived from a blackface minstrel act, to describe these cars. Later the term came to define other forms of racial segregation as well. In cities, many omnibus and streetcar companies barred African Americans entirely, even though urban black people had little choice but to try to use these means of transportation. Steamboats accepted black passengers but refused to rent them cabins. African Americans had to remain on deck at night and during storms.

All African Americans, regardless of their wealth or social standing, endured such treatment. Frederick Douglass, who made a point of challenging segregation, refused to ride in Jim Crow train cars unless physically forced to do so. He once clung so tightly to the arms of his seat when several white men attempted to move him that the seat ripped away from its supports. In 1854, in New York City, a white streetcar conductor beat a black public school teacher named Elizabeth Jenkins who had attempted to board his vehicle. Black people, regardless of their class, also faced frequent public insult from white adults and children.

In this atmosphere, African Americans learned to distrust white people. A correspondent of Douglass's newspaper, the *North Star,* wrote in 1849 that there seemed "to be a fixed determination on the part of our oppressors in this country to destroy every vestige of self-respect, self-possession, and manly independence left in the colored people." Even when African Americans interacted with white people on an ostensibly equal basis, there were underlying tensions. James Forten's wealthy granddaughter Charlotte Forten, who attended an integrated school in Boston, wrote in her diary, "It is hard to go through life meeting contempt with contempt, hatred with hatred, fearing with too good reason, to love and trust hardly any one whose skin is white—however lovable, attractive, and congenial."

African Americans moving to northern cities were not surprised to find segregated black neighborhoods. A few wealthy black people lived in white urban neighborhoods, and a few northern cities, such as Cleveland and Detroit, had no patterns of residential segregation. But in most cases, a white belief that black neighbors led to lowered property values produced such patterns. There were "Nigger Hill" in Boston, "Little Africa" in Cincinnati, "Hayti" in Pittsburgh, and Philadelphia's "Southside." Conditions in these ghettoes were often dreadful, but they provided a refuge from constant insult and a place where black institutions could develop.

Because African Americans representing all social and economic classes lived in segregated neighborhoods, the quality of housing in them varied. But, at its worst, such housing was bleak and dangerous. One visitor called the black section of New York City's Five Points "the worst hell of America," and other black urban neighborhoods were just as bad. People lived in unheated shacks and shanties, in dirt-floored basements, or in houses without doors and windows. These conditions nurtured disease, infant mortality, alcoholism, and crime. Southern visitors to northern cities blamed the victims, insisting that the plight of many urban black northerners proved that African Americans were better off in slavery.

Black Communities in the Urban North

Northern African Americans lived in both rural and urban areas during the antebellum decades, but it was urban neighborhoods with their more concentrated black populations that nurtured black community life (see Table 7–2). African-American urban communities of the antebellum period developed from the free black communities that had emerged from slavery in the North during the late eighteenth century. The

TABLE 7–2   FREE BLACK POPULATION OF SELECTED CITIES, 1800–1850

City	1800	1850
Baltimore	2,771	25,442
Boston	1,174	1,999
Charleston	951	3,441
New Orleans	800 (estimated)	9,905
New York	3,499	13,815
Philadelphia	4,210	10,736
Washington	123	8,158

Source: Leonard P. Curry, The Free Black in Urban America, 1800–1850: The Shadow of the Dream (Chicago: University of Chicago Press, 1981), 250.

This nineteenth-century lithograph depicts a street scene in the notorious Five-Points neighborhood of New York City. Amid deteriorating buildings, black people are shown to be victims of poverty, crime, and immorality.

communities varied from city to city and from region to region, yet they had much in common and interacted with each other. Resilient families, poverty, class divisions, active church congregations, the continued development of voluntary organizations, and concern for education characterized them. Particularly in the Northeast, urban black communities attracted people of American Indian descent who often married African Americans.

THE BLACK FAMILY

As they became free, northern African Americans left their masters and established their own households. Some left more quickly than others, and in states such as New York and New Jersey, where gradual emancipation extended into the nineteenth century, the process continued into the 1820s. By then the average black family in northern cities had two parents and between two and four children. However, in both the Northeast and Old Northwest, single-parent black families, usually headed by women, became increasingly common during the antebellum period. In Cincinnati black families headed by women increased from 11 percent in 1830 to more than 22 percent in 1850. This trend may have been influenced by the difficulty black men had gaining employment. It certainly was a function of a high mortality rate among black men, which made many black women widows during their forties.

Both financial need and African-American culture encouraged black northerners to take in boarders and create extended families. By 1850 approximately one-third of black adults in such cities as Boston, Buffalo, Chicago, Detroit, and Cincinnati boarded. Economic considerations determined such arrangements, but friendship and family relationships also played a part. Sometimes entire nuclear families boarded, but most boarders were young, single, and male. As historians

James Oliver Horton and Lois E. Horton put it, "The opportunity to rely on friends and family for shelter enhanced the mobility of poor people who were often forced to move to find employment. It provided financial assistance when people were unemployed; it provided social supports for people who faced discrimination; and it saved those who had left home or run away from slavery from social isolation."

THE STRUGGLE FOR EMPLOYMENT

The rising tide of immigration from Europe hurt northern African Americans economically. Before 1820 black craftsmen had been in demand but, given the choice, white people preferred to employ other white people, and black people suffered. To make matters worse for African Americans, white workers excluded young black men from apprenticeships, refused to work with black people, and used violence to prevent employers from hiring black workers when white workers were unemployed. By the 1830s these practices had driven African Americans from the skilled trades. For the rest of the antebellum period, most northern black men performed menial day labor, although a few worked as coachmen, teamsters, waiters, barbers, carpenters, masons, and plasterers. By the 1850s black men were losing to Irish immigrants unskilled work as longshoremen, drayers, railroad workers, hod-carriers, porters, and shoe-shiners as well as positions in such skilled trades as barbering.

By 1847 in Philadelphia, 80 percent of employed black men did unskilled labor. Barbers and shoemakers predominated among those black workers with skills. Only one-half of 1 percent held factory jobs. Among employed black women, 80 percent either washed clothes or worked as domestic servants. Three-quarters of the remaining 20 percent were seamstresses. By the 1850s black women, too, were losing work to Irish immigrants. A few became prostitutes. About 5 percent of black men and women were self-employed, selling food or secondhand clothing.

Unskilled black men often could not find work. When they did work, they received low wages. To escape such conditions in Philadelphia and other port cities, they became sailors. By 1850 about 50 percent of the crewmen on American merchant and whaling vessels were black. Not only did these sailors have to leave their families for months at a time and endure brutal conditions at sea, but they also risked imprisonment if their ship anchored at southern ports.

THE NORTHERN BLACK ELITE

Despite the poor prospects of most northern African Americans, a northern black elite emerged during the

Barbering was one of the skilled trades open to black men during the antebellum years. Several wealthy African Americans began their careers as barbers.   The Granger Collection, New York

first six decades of the nineteenth century. Membership in this elite could be achieved through talent, wealth, occupation, family connections, complexion, and education. The elite led in the development of black institutions and culture, in the antislavery movement, and in the struggle for racial justice. It was also the bridge between the black community and sympathetic white people.

Although few African Americans achieved financial security during the antebellum decades, black people could become rich in many ways. Segregated neighborhoods gave rise to a black professional class of physicians, lawyers, ministers, and undertakers who served an exclusively black clientele. Black merchants could gain wealth selling to black communities. Other relatively well-off African Americans included skilled tradesmen, such as carpenters, barbers, waiters, and coachmen, who generally found employment among white people.

Although less so than among African Americans in the South, complexion influenced social standing among African Americans in the North, especially in cities like Cincinnati that were close to the South.

MARIA W. STEWART ON THE CONDITION OF BLACK WORKERS

Maria W. Stewart (1803–1879) was the first black female public speaker in the United States. She was strong willed and spoke without qualification what she believed to be the truth. At times she angered both black and white people. In the following speech, which she delivered in Boston in September 1831, Stewart criticized the treatment accorded to black workers—especially black female workers—in the North.

Tell us no more of southern slavery; for with few exceptions, although I may be very erroneous in my opinion, yet I consider our condition but little better than that. . . . After all, methinks there are no chains so galling as those that bind the soul, and exclude it from the vast field of useful and scientific knowledge. . . .

I have asked several [white] individuals of my sex, who transact business for themselves, if providing our girls were to give them the most satisfactory references, they would not be willing to grant them an equal opportunity with others? Their reply has been—for their own part, they had no objection; but as it was not the custom, were they to take them into their employ, they would be in danger of losing the public patronage.

And such is the powerful force of prejudice. Let our girls possess whatever amiable qualities of soul they may; let their characters be fair and spotless as innocence itself; let their natural taste and ingenuity be what they may; it is impossible for scarce an individual of them to rise above the condition of servants. . . .

I observed a piece . . . respecting us, asserting that we were lazy and idle. I confute them on that point. Take us generally as a people, we are neither lazy nor idle: and considering how little we have to excite or stimulate us, I am almost astonished that there are so many industrious and ambitious ones to be found. . . .

Again it was asserted that we were "a ragged set, crying for liberty." I reply to it, the whites have so long and so loudly proclaimed the theme of equal rights and privileges, that our souls have caught the flame also, ragged as we are. As far as our merit deserves, we feel a common desire to rise above the condition of servants and drudges. I have learnt, by bitter experience, that the continual hard labor deadens the energies of the soul, and benumbs the faculties of the mind; the ideas become confined, the mind barren, and, like the scorching sands of Arabia, produces nothing: or like the uncultivated soil, brings forth thorns and thistles. . . .

Most of our color have dragged out a miserable existence of servitude from the cradle to the grave. . . . Do you [women] ask, why are you wretched and miserable? I reply, look at many of the

White people often preferred to hire people of mixed race, successful black men often chose light-complexioned brides, and African Americans generally accepted white notions of human beauty.

By the 1820s the black elite had become better educated and more socially polished than its less wealthy black neighbors, yet it could never disassociate itself from them. Segregation and discriminatory legislation in the North applied to all African Americans regardless of class and complexion, and all African Americans shared a common culture and history.

Conspicuous among the black elite were entrepreneurs who, against considerable odds, gained wealth and influence in the antebellum North. As we noted in Chapter 5, James Forten was one of the first of them, and several other examples indicate the character of such people. John Remond—who as a child migrated from Curaçao, a Dutch-ruled island in the Caribbean, to Salem, Massachusetts—and his wife, Nancy Lenox Remond, became prosperous restaurateurs, caterers, and retailers. Their fortune subsidized the abolitionist careers of their son Charles Lenox Remond and daughter Sarah Parker Remond. Louis Hayden, who escaped from slavery in Kentucky in 1845, had by 1849 become a successful haberdasher and an abolitionist in Boston. Henry Boyd, like Hayden a native of Kentucky, built and operated a steam-powered furniture factory in Cincinnati during the 1840s and 1850s. Perhaps most successful were Stephen Smith and his partner William Whipper, who had extensive business interests in southeastern Pennsylvania. (See Profile box on page 180.)

Maria Stewart, "The Miseries We Tasted," 1835 **7-4** DOCUMENT

most worthy and most interesting of us doomed to spend our lives in gentlemen's kitchens. Look at our young men, smart, active, and energetic, with souls filled with ambitious fire; if they look forward, alas! What are their prospects? They can be nothing but the humblest laborers, on account of their dark complexions; hence many of them lose their ambition, and become worthless. . . .

Is Stewart correct in assuming that conditions for black northerners were little better than those for slaves?

According to Stewart, what was the impact of northern white prejudice on black workers?

Source: Maria W. Stewart, "Lecture Delivered at the Franklin Hall, Boston, September 21, 1831," as quoted in Roy Finkenbine, *Sources of the African-American Past: Primary Sources in American History* (New York: Longman, 1997), 30–32.

Black sailors were rarely allowed the command of ships, but Captain Absalom Boston was the master of the *Industry*, a whaling ship that sailed out of Nantucket in 1822.

BLACK PROFESSIONALS

The northern black elite also included physicians and lawyers. Among the physicians, some, such as James McCune Smith and John S. Rock, received medical degrees. Smith, the first African American to earn a medical degree, graduated from the University of Glasgow in Scotland in 1837 and practiced in New York City until his death in 1874. Rock, who had been a dentist in Philadelphia, graduated from the American Medical College in 1852 and practiced medicine in Boston until 1860 when he undertook the study of law. In 1865 he became the first African American to argue a case before the U.S. Supreme Court.

Either because they had been forced out of medical school or they chose not to go, other prominent black physicians practiced medicine without having earned a degree. (This was legal in the nineteenth century.) James Still of Medford, New Jersey, had meager formal education but used natural remedies to develop a successful practice among black and white people. The

multitalented Martin R. Delany, who had been born free in Charles Town, Virginia, in 1812, practiced medicine in Pittsburgh after having been expelled from Harvard Medical School at the insistence of two white classmates.

Prominent black attorneys included Macon B. Allen, who gained admission to the Maine bar in 1844, and Robert Morris, who qualified to practice law in Massachusetts in 1847. Both Allen and Morris apprenticed with white attorneys, and Morris had a particularly successful and lucrative practice. Yet white residents thwarted his attempt to purchase a mansion in a Boston suburb.

ARTISTS AND MUSICIANS

Although they rarely achieved great wealth and have not become famous, black artists and musicians were also part of the northern African-American elite. Among the best-known artists were Robert S. Duncanson, Robert Douglass, Patrick Reason, and Edmonia Lewis. Several of them supported the antislavery movement through their artistic work.

Douglass, a painter who studied in England before establishing himself in Philadelphia, and Reason, an

Educated at Oberlin College, Edmonia Lewis (1843–1911?) studied sculpture in Rome and emerged as one of the more prolific American artists of the late nineteenth century.

Elizabeth Taylor Greenfield (1817?–1876), known as the "Black Swan," was one of the more renowned vocalists of antebellum America. She made her debut in 1853 at Metropolitan Hall in New York City before an exclusively white audience.

BLACK AUTHORS

In some respects, the antebellum era was a golden age of African-American literature. Driven by suffering in slavery and limited freedom in the North, black authors portrayed an America that had not lived up to its revolutionary ideals. Black autobiography recounted life in bondage and dramatic escapes. Although the antislavery movement promoted the publication of scores of such narratives, the best known is Frederick Douglass's classic *Narrative of the Life of Frederick Douglass, an American Slave,* published in 1845.

African Americans also wrote history, novels, and poetry. In 1855 William C. Nell published *The Colored Patriots of the American Revolution,* which reminded its readers that black men had fought for freedom.

Frances Ellen Watkins Harper (1825–1911) was born free in Baltimore. During the 1850s, she published antislavery poetry and traveled across the North as an antislavery speaker.

engraver, created portraits of abolitionists during the 1830s. Reason also etched illustrations of the sufferings of slaves. Duncanson, who was born in Cincinnati and worked in Europe between 1843 and 1854, painted landscapes and portraits. Lewis, the daughter of a black man and a Chippewa woman, enrolled with abolitionist help at Oberlin College in Ohio and studied sculpture in Rome. Her works, which emphasized African-American themes, came into wide demand after the Civil War.

The reputations of black professional musicians of the antebellum period have suffered in comparison with the great tradition of black folk music epitomized by spirituals. But in Philadelphia a circle of black musicians wrote and performed a wide variety of music for orchestra, voice, and solo instruments. Similar circles existed in New Orleans, Boston, Cleveland, New York, Baltimore, and St. Louis. The best-known professional black singer of the period was Elizabeth Taylor Greenfield, who was born a slave in Mississippi and raised by Quakers in Philadelphia. Known as the "Black Swan," Taylor gained renown for her vocal range.

William Wells Brown, who had escaped from slavery in Kentucky, became the first African-American novelist. His *Clotel, or the President's Daughter*, published in 1853, used the affair between Thomas Jefferson and Sally Hemings to explore in fiction the moral ramifications of slaveholders who fathered children with their bondwomen. Another black novelist of the antebellum years was Martin R. Delany. His *Blake, or the Huts of America*, a story of emerging revolutionary consciousness among southern slaves, ran as a serial in the *Weekly Anglo-African* during 1859. Black poets included George M. Horton, a slave living in North Carolina, who in 1829 published *The Hope of Liberty*, and James W. Whitfield of Buffalo, who in 1853 lampooned the song "My Country 'tis of Thee" when he wrote the following:

> America, it is to thee
> Thou boasted land of liberty,—
> Thou land of blood, and crime, and wrong.

African-American women who published fiction during the period included Frances Ellen Watkins Harper and Harriet E. Wilson. Harper was born free in Baltimore in 1825. Associated with the antislavery cause in Pennsylvania and Maine, she published poems that depicted the sufferings of slaves. Her first collection, *Poems on Various Subjects*, appeared in 1854. Wilson published *Our Nig: Or, Sketches from the Life of a Free Black, in a Two-Story White House, North* in 1859. This was the first novel published by a black woman in the United States. In the genre of autobiographical fiction, it compared the lives of black domestic workers in the North with those of southern slaves. Wilson's book, however, received little attention during her lifetime, and until the 1980s critics believed a white author had written it.

At about the same time that Wilson wrote *Our Nig*, Hanna Crafts, who had recently escaped from slavery in North Carolina, wrote *The Bondwoman's Narrative*. Unpublished until 2002, this melodramatic autobiographical novel tells the story of a house slave and her escape.

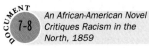

DOCUMENT 7-8 An African-American Novel Critiques Racism in the North, 1859

African-American Institutions

In the antebellum decades, the black institutions that had appeared during the revolutionary era in urban areas of the North, upper South, and—to a lesser extent—the deep South became stronger, more numerous, and more varied. This was the result of growing black populations, the exertions of the African-American elite, and the persistence of racial exclusion and segregation. Black institutions of the time included schools, mutual aid organizations, benevolent and fraternal societies, self-improvement and temperance associations, literary groups, newspapers and journals, and theaters. But, aside from families, the most important black community institution remained the church.

BLACK CHURCHES

Black church buildings were community centers. They housed schools and meeting places for a variety of organizations. Antislavery societies often met in churches, and the churches harbored fugitive slaves. All of this went hand in hand with the community leadership black ministers provided. They began schools and various voluntary associations. They spoke against slavery, racial oppression, and what they considered weaknesses among African Americans. However, black ministers never spoke with one voice. Throughout the antebellum decades, many followed Jupiter Hammon in admonishing their congregations that preparing one's soul for heaven was more important than gaining equal rights on earth.

By 1846 the independent African Methodist Episcopal (AME) Church had 296 congregations in the United States and Canada with 17,375 members. In 1848 Frederick Douglass maintained that the AME Mother Bethel Church in Philadelphia was "the largest church in this Union," with 2,000 to 3,000 worshippers each Sunday. The AME Zion Church of New York City was probably the second largest black congregation, with about two thousand members.

Most black Baptist, Presbyterian, Congregationalist, Episcopal, and Roman Catholic congregations remained affiliated with white denominations, although they were rarely represented in regional and national church councils. For example, the Episcopal Diocese of New York in 1819 excluded black ministers from its annual conventions, maintaining that African Americans "*are* socially degraded, and are not regarded as proper associates for the class of persons who attend our convention." Not until 1853 was white abolitionist William Jay able to convince New York Episcopalians to admit black representatives.

Many northern African Americans continued to attend white churches. To do so, they had to submit to the same second-class status that had driven Richard Allen and Absalom Jones to establish separate black churches in Philadelphia during the 1790s.

PROFILE ~ STEPHEN SMITH AND WILLIAM WHIPPER, PARTNERS IN BUSINESS AND REFORM

Black people living in antebellum America had great difficulty succeeding in business. In most of the states, northern and southern, African-American entrepreneurs faced limited educational opportunities, inequality before the law, disfranchisement, and pervasive antiblack prejudice. To make their fortunes, they had to compete in a marketplace dominated by whites. Yet a few African Americans, aided by skill, determination, and luck, acquired great wealth. Some who did, such as William Ellison of South Carolina (see Profile on page 152), had little sympathy for the less fortunate. But others used their affluence to better conditions for other African Americans. Black Pennsylvanians Stephen Smith and William Whipper, who linked their commercial success to reform efforts, illustrate this point.

Both Smith and Whipper were children of black mothers and white fathers. Both of their mothers were domestic servants in white households. Smith was born unfree in Dauphin County in southcentral Pennsylvania in about 1795. Whipper was born free in nearby Lancaster, Pennsylvania in about 1804. There is nothing to suggest that either of them had a formal education.

When Smith was five years old, his master apprenticed him to Thomas Boule, who owned a lumber business at Columbia in Lancaster County. During his late teens, Smith became manager of Boule's business. In 1816 he purchased his freedom, married, and began his own lumber company. Shortly thereafter, he began purchasing real estate. Not far away, Whipper grew up and struck out on his own. During the 1820s, he worked as a steam scourer in Philadelphia. There in 1834 he opened a grocery store.

◄ William Whipper, ca. 1835.
Fenimore Art Museum New York

The two men became partners in 1835. They had phenomenal success despite a mob attack that same year on their office. They operated one of the largest lumbering businesses in southeastern Pennsylvania. They expanded into selling coal. By 1842, when Smith moved to Philadelphia and left Whipper in charge of their Columbia operations, the two men had invested $9,000 (approximately 144,000 current dollars) in a bridge company and had bank deposits totaling $18,000 ($288,000). By the end of the decade, they owned—in addition to their lumber and coal business—twenty-two railroad cars and $27,000 ($432,000) worth of bank stock. They grossed $100,000 (nearly $2,000,000) per year. Smith continued to excel in real-estate acquisition, owning at one point fifty-two brick houses in Philadelphia. He was, perhaps, the richest African American in antebellum America.

When it came to reform and antislavery efforts, Whipper took the lead, but Smith was never far behind. The two men were partners in reform as well as in business. Both of them began during the 1830s as integrationists who believed, based on their own experiences, that African Americans who worked to uplift themselves would be accepted by white society. Early on, Whipper made his grocery a center for temperance and antislavery activities. He became a leader at the Black National Conventions, while Smith became an AME minister and builder of churches. They both engaged in underground railroad activities and opened their homes to people escaping from slavery. Despite their own success, however, they grew during the 1850s more pessimistic regarding peaceful reform as a means of gaining black rights in the United States. Whipper began to promote black migration to Canada. In 1858 Smith hosted a meeting at which white antislavery activist John Brown discussed his plan to incite slave revolt in the South. Clearly, Smith and Whipper as African Americans experienced the double consciousness that W. E. B. Du Bois later so eloquently identified.

Smith & Whipper

This lithograph depicts the bishops of the AME church and suggests both the church's humble origins and its remarkable growth during the antebellum years. Founder Richard Allen is portrayed at the center.

Throughout the antebellum years, northern white churches required their black members to sit in special sections during services, provided separate Sunday schools for black children, and insisted that black people take communion after white people. Even Quakers, who spearheaded white opposition to slavery in the North and South, often provided separate seating for black people at their meetings.

During the 1830s and 1840s, some black leaders criticized the existence of separate black congregations and denominations. Frederick Douglass called them "negro pews, on a higher and larger scale." Such churches, Douglass and others maintained, were part and parcel of a segregationist spirit that divided America according to complexion. Douglass also denounced what he considered the illiteracy and

anti-intellectual bias of most black ministers. Growing numbers of African Americans, nevertheless, regarded such churches as sources of spiritual integrity and legitimate alternatives to second-class status among white Christians.

SCHOOLS

Education, like religion, was racially segregated in the North between 1820 and 1860. Tax-supported compulsory public education for children in the United States began in Massachusetts in 1827 and spread throughout the Northeast and Old Northwest during the 1830s. Some public schools, such as those in Cleveland, Ohio, during the 1850s, were racially integrated. But usually, as soon as twenty or more African-American children

THE CONSTITUTION OF THE PITTSBURGH AFRICAN EDUCATION SOCIETY

Compared with black southerners, black northerners were fortunate to have access to education, and education societies were prominent among black self-improvement organizations. In January 1832 a group headed by John B. Vashon, a local black barber and philanthropist, met at Pittsburgh's African Church to establish such a society and a school. The group's motives and plans are indicated in the following extracts from its constitution.

Whereas, ignorance in all ages has been found to debase the human mind, and to subject its votaries to the lowest vices, and most abject depravity—and it must be admitted, that ignorance is the sole cause of the present degradation and bondage of the people of color in these United States—that the intellectual capacity of the black man is equal to that of the white, and that he is equally susceptible of improvement, all ancient history makes manifest; and even modern examples put beyond a single doubt.

We, therefore, the people of color, of the city and vicinity of Pittsburgh, and State of Pennsylvania, for the purpose of dispersing the moral gloom that has so long hung around us, have, under Almighty God, associated ourselves together, which association shall be known by the name of the *Pittsburgh African Education Society.* . . .

It shall be the duty of the Board of Managers . . . to purchase such books and periodicals as the Society may deem it expedient, they shall have power to raise money by subscription or otherwise, to purchase ground, and erect thereon a suitable building or buildings for the accommodation and education of youth, and a hall for the use of the Society. . . .

🌿 *Why would this group claim that black ignorance was the "sole cause" of black degradation and enslavement?*

🌿 *Why was the Pittsburgh African Education Society necessary?*

Source: Dorothy Porten, ed., *Early Negro Writing, 1760–1837* (1971; reprint, Baltimore: Black Classics, 1995), 120–22.

appeared in a school district, white parents demanded that black children attend separate schools. White people claimed that black children lacked mental capacity and lowered the quality of education. White people also feared that opening schools to black children would encourage more black people to live in the school district.

How to educate African-American children who were not allowed to attend school with white children became a persistent issue in the North. Until 1848 Ohio and the other states of the Old Northwest simply excluded black children from public schools and refused to allocate tax revenues to support separate facilities. The northeastern states were more willing to undertake such expenditures. But across the North, white people were reluctant to use tax dollars to fund education for African Americans. As a result, appropriations for black public schools lagged far behind those for public schools white children attended.

This tendency extended to cities where African-American leaders and white abolitionists had created private schools for black children. In 1812 the African School established by Prince Hall in 1798 became part of Boston's public school system. As a result, like newly created black public schools in the city, it began to suffer from inadequate funding and a limited curriculum. The African Free Schools, begun in New York City in 1787 by the New York Society for Promoting the Manumission of Slaves, had a similar fate. In 1834, when these schools became part of New York's public school system, funding and attendance declined. By the 1850s public support for the city's black schools had become negligible.

Woefully inadequate public funding resulted in poor education or none at all for most black children across the North. The few black schools were dilapidated and overcrowded. White teachers who taught in them received lower pay than those who taught in white schools, and black teachers received even less, so teaching was generally poor. Black parents, however, were often unaware that their children received an inadequate education. Even black and white abolitionists tended to expect less from black students than from white students.

Some black leaders defended segregated schools as better for black children than integrated ones. They probably feared that the real choice was between separate black schools or none at all. But, by the 1830s, most northern African Americans favored racially integrated public education, and during the 1840s Frederick Douglass became a leading advocate for such a policy. Douglass, other black leaders, and their white abolitionist allies made the most progress in Massachusetts, where by 1845 all public schools, except for those in Boston, had been integrated. After a ten-year struggle, the Massachusetts legislature finally ended segregated schools in that city too. This victory encouraged the opponents of segregated public schools across the North. By 1860 integration had advanced among the region's smaller school districts. But, except for those in Boston, urban schools remained segregated on the eve of the Civil War.

In fact, the black elite had more success gaining admission to northern colleges during the antebellum period than most African-American children had in gaining an adequate primary education. Some colleges served African Americans exclusively. Ashmum Institute in Oxford, Pennsylvania, was founded in 1854 to prepare black missionaries who would go to Africa. Ashmum, later renamed Lincoln University, was the first black institution of higher learning in the United States. Another exclusively black college was Wilberforce University, founded by the AME church in 1855 near Columbus, Ohio. Earlier some northern colleges had begun to admit a few black students. They included Bowdoin in Maine, Dartmouth in New Hampshire, Harvard and Mount Pleasant in Massachusetts, Oneida Institute in New York, and Western Reserve in Ohio. Because of its association with the antislavery movement, Oberlin College in Ohio became the most famous biracial institution of higher learning during the era. By 1860 many northern colleges, law schools, medical schools, and seminaries admitted black applicants, although not on an equal basis with white applicants.

VOLUNTARY ASSOCIATIONS

The African-American mutual aid, benevolent, self-improvement, and fraternal organizations that originated during the late eighteenth century proliferated during the antebellum decades. So did black literary and temperance associations.

Mutual aid societies became especially attractive to black women. In 1830 black women in Philadelphia had twenty-seven such organizations compared with sixteen for black men. By 1855 Philadelphia had 108 black mutual aid societies, enrolling 9,762 members, with a combined annual income of $29,600 (approximately 550,000 current dollars). Among black benevolent societies, African Dorcas Associations were especially prevalent. Originally organized in 1828 in New York City by black women, these societies distributed used clothing to the poor, especially poor schoolchildren. During the early 1830s, black women also began New York City's Association for the Benefit of Colored Orphans, which operated an orphanage that by 1851 had helped 524 children. Other black benevolent organizations in New York maintained the Colored Seaman's Home and a home for the elderly.

Meanwhile, the Prince Hall Masons created new lodges in the cities of the Northeast and the Chesapeake. Beginning during the 1840s, Black Odd Fellows lodges also became common. But more prevalent were self-improvement, library, literary, and temperance organizations. These were manifestations of the reform spirit that swept the North and much of the upper South during the antebellum decades. Closely linked to evangelical Protestantism, reformers maintained that the moral regeneration of individuals was essential to perfecting society. African Americans shared this belief and formed myriad organizations to put it into practice.

Among the more prestigious of the societies for black men were the Phoenix Literary Society established in New York City in 1833, the Philadelphia Library Company of Colored Persons begun in 1833, Pittsburgh's Theban Literary Society founded in 1831, and Boston's Adelphi Union for the Promotion of Literature and Science established in 1836. Black women had the Female Literary Society of Philadelphia begun in 1831, New York City's Ladies Literary Society founded in 1834, the Ladies Literary Society of Buffalo that emerged in the mid-1830s, and Boston's Afric-American Female Intelligence Society begun in 1832.

Black temperance societies were even more widespread than literary and benevolent organizations, although they also tended to be more short-lived. Like their white counterparts, black temperance advocates were middle-class activists who sought to stop the abuse of alcoholic beverages by those lower on the social ladder. The temperance societies organized lecture series and handed out literature that portrayed the negative physical, economic, and moral consequences of liquor. Whether such societies were effective is debatable, but they helped unite black communities.

Free African Americans in the Upper South

Life for free black people in the South during the antebellum period differed from that in the North. The free black experience in the upper South also differed from what it was in the deep South. In general, free African Americans in the North, despite the limits on their liberty, had opportunities their southern counterparts did not enjoy. Each of the southern regions, nevertheless, offered some advantages to free black residents.

The free black people of the upper South had much in common with their northern counterparts. In particular, African Americans in the Chesapeake cities of Baltimore, Washington, Richmond, and Norfolk had ties to black northerners, ranging from family and church affiliations to business connections and membership in fraternal organizations. But significant differences, which resulted from the South's agricultural economy and slavery, set free people of color in the upper South apart. Although nearly half the free black population in the North lived in cities, only one-third did so in the upper South, hampering the development of black communities there.

A more important difference was the impact of slavery on the lives of free African Americans in the upper South. Unlike black northerners, free black people in the upper South lived alongside slaves. Many had family ties to slaves and were more directly involved than black northerners in the slaves' suffering. They did so in several capacities, including efforts to prevent the sale south of relatives and friends, reimbursing masters for manumissions, and funding for freedom suits. They also earned a reputation among white southerners as inveterate harborers of escaped slaves. Southern white politicians and journalists used the close connection between free black southerners and slaves to justify limiting the freedom of the former group.

Free black people of the upper South were also more at risk of *being* enslaved than were black northerners. Except for Louisiana, with its French and Spanish heritage, all southern states assumed African Americans were slaves unless they could prove otherwise. Free black people had to carry **free papers,** which they had to renew periodically. They could be enslaved if their papers were lost or stolen, and sheriffs in the upper South routinely arrested free black people on the grounds that they might be fugitive slaves. Even when those arrested proved they were free, they were sometimes sold as slaves to pay the cost of imprisoning them. Free African Americans who got into debt in the South risked being sold into slavery to pay off their creditors.

As the antebellum period progressed, the distinction between free and enslaved African Americans narrowed in the upper South. Although a few northern states allowed black men to vote, no southern state did after 1835. In that year North Carolina followed Tennessee—the only other southern state to allow black suffrage—in revoking the right to vote among property-owning black men. Free black people of the upper South also had more difficulty traveling, owning firearms, congregating in groups, and being out after dark than did black northerners. Although residential segregation was less pronounced in southern cities than in the North, African Americans of the upper South faced a more thorough exclusion from hotels, taverns, trains and coaches, parks, theaters, and hospitals.

Free black people in the upper South also experienced various degrees of hardship in earning a living, although, during the nineteenth century, their employment expanded as slavery declined in Maryland and northern Virginia. Free persons of color in rural areas were generally tenant farmers. Some of them had to sign labor contracts that reduced them to semi-slavery. But others owned land and a few owned slaves. Free African Americans also worked in rural areas as miners, lumberjacks, and teamsters. In upper South urban areas, most free black men were unskilled day laborers, waiters, whitewashers, and stevedores; free black women worked as laundresses and domestic servants. As in the North, the most successful African Americans were barbers, butchers, tailors, caterers, merchants, and those teamsters and hack drivers who owned their own horses and vehicles. Before 1850 free black people in the upper South had less competition from European immigrants for jobs than was the case in northern cities. Therefore, although the upper South had fewer factories than the North, more free black men worked in them. This changed during the 1850s when Irish and German immigrants competed against free black people in the upper South just as they did in the North for all types of employment. As was the case in the North, immigrants often used violence to drive African Americans out of skilled trades.

These circumstances made it more difficult for free black people in the upper South to maintain community institutions. In addition, the measures white authorities adopted to prevent slave revolt greatly limited free black autonomy, and such measures became pervasive after the revolt Nat Turner led in southern Virginia in 1831. Many black churches and schools had to close or curtail their activities. The Baltimore Conference of the AME Church, which had been expanding during the 1820s, declined during the early 1830s. Some states required that black churches have white ministers, and some black ministers left for the North. Yet free black southerners persevered. During the late 1830s, new black churches organized in Louisville and Lexington, Kentucky, and in St. Louis, Missouri. Between 1836 and 1856, the Baltimore AME Conference rebounded and more than doubled its membership. By 1860 Baltimore had fifteen black churches. Louisville had nine, and Nashville, St. Louis, and Norfolk had four each. Most of these churches ministered to both enslaved and free members.

Black schools and voluntary associations also survived white efforts to suppress them, although the schools faced great challenges. Racially integrated schools and public funding for segregated black schools were out of the question in the South. Most black children received no formal education. Black churches, a few white churches, and a scattering of black and white individuals maintained what educational facilities the upper South had for black children. The schools met—often sporadically—in rooms furnished by churches or in private homes and generally lacked books, chalkboards, and student desks. Particularly noteworthy were the efforts of the Oblate Sisters of Providence, who constituted the first black Roman Catholic religious order in the United States, and John F. Cook, who for twenty years conducted a black school in Washington, D.C.

Elizabeth Clovis Lange, who was of Haitian descent, established the Oblate Sisters of Providence, an order of Roman Catholic nuns, in Baltimore in 1829 to provide a free education to the children of French-speaking black refugees from the Haitian Revolution. The sisters taught English, math, composition, and religion. Cook, who was an AME and Presbyterian minister, taught similar subjects at his Union Seminary from

EARLY BLACK LITERARY SOCIETIES	
1828	Reading Room Society (Philadelphia)
1829	New York African Clarkson Society
1830	New York Philomathean Society
1831	Female Literary Society (Philadelphia), Theban Literary Society (Pittsburgh)
1832	Afric-American Female Intelligence Society (Boston), Tyro and Literary Association (Newark, NJ)
1833	Library Company of Colored Persons (Philadelphia), Phoenix Literacy Society (New York)
1834	Minerva Literary Association (Philadelphia), Ladies Literary Society (New York), New York Garrison Literary Association Literary and Religious Institution (Hartford, CT), Washington Conventional Society (Washington, DC)

1834 until his death in 1854. Both the sisters and Cook confronted persecution and inadequate funding. Cook had to flee Washington temporarily in 1835 to avoid being killed. Nevertheless he passed his school on to his son, who kept it going through the Civil War years. Meanwhile, the Oblate Sisters had become a widely influential part of the black community. They built a chapel in Baltimore in 1836 that became the first black Catholic church in the United States.

Black voluntary associations, particularly in urban areas of the upper South, fared better than black schools. By 1838 Baltimore had at least forty such organizations, including chapters of the Prince Hall Masons, Black Odd Fellows, literary societies, and temperance groups. In Norfolk, the Masons enrolled slaves as well as freemen. As in the North, black women organized their own voluntary associations. Washington's Colored Female Roman Catholic Beneficial Society, for example, provided death benefits for its members. Black benevolent organizations in the upper South also sought to apprentice orphans to black tradesmen; sponsored fairs, picnics, and parades; and provided protection against kidnappers.

Mother Mary Elizabeth Clovis Lange, O.S.P. (c. 1784–1882), was born in Haiti. She organized the Oblate Sisters of Providence in Baltimore in 1828. This Roman Catholic order helped black refugees from Haiti and operated a school for the refugees' children.

Free African Americans in the Deep South

More than half the South's free black population lived in Maryland, Delaware, and Virginia. To the west and south of these states, the number of free people of color declined sharply. The smaller free black populations in Kentucky, Tennessee, Missouri, and North Carolina had much in common with that in the Chesapeake states. But free African Americans who lived in the deep South were different in several respects from their counterparts in other southern regions.

Neither the natural rights ideology of the revolutionary era nor changing economic circumstances led to many manumissions in the deep South. Free black people there were not only far fewer than in either the upper South or the North, they were also "largely the product of illicit sexual relations between black slave women and white men." Slaveholder fathers either manumitted their mixed-race children or let them buy their freedom. However, some free black people of the deep South traced their ancestry to free mixed-race refugees from Haiti, who sought during the 1790s to avoid that island nation's bloody revolutionary struggle by fleeing to such deep South cities as Charleston, Savannah, and New Orleans.

A three-caste system similar to that in Latin America developed in the deep South during the antebellum period. It included white people, free black people, and slaves. Most free African Americans in the region identified more closely with their former masters than with slaves. To ensure the loyalty of such free people of color, powerful white people provided them with employment, loans, protection, and such special privileges as the ability to vote and to testify against white people. Some states and municipalities formalized this relationship by requiring free African Americans to have white guardians—often their blood relatives. Some people of mixed descent crossed the racial boundary and passed as white.

The relationship between free African Americans of the deep South and their former masters was also evident in religion. An AME church existed in Charleston until 1818, when the city authorities suppressed it, fearing it would become a center of sedition. African Baptist churches existed in Savannah during the 1850s. In 1842 New Orleans's Sisters of the Holy Family became the second Roman Catholic religious order for black women in the United States. But free black people in the region were more likely than those farther north to remain in white churches largely because they identified with the white elite.

In the deep South, free African Americans—over half of whom lived in cities—were more concentrated in urban areas than were their counterparts in the North and upper South. Although deep South cities restricted their employment opportunities, free black people in Charleston, Savannah, Mobile, and New Or-

leans maintained stronger positions in the skilled trades than free black people in the upper South or the North. By 1860 in Charleston, three-quarters of the free black men worked in skilled trades. Free African Americans made up only 15 percent of Charleston's male population. Yet they constituted 25 percent of its carpenters, 40 percent of its tailors, and 75 percent of its millwrights. In New Orleans, free black men predominated as carpenters, masons, bricklayers, barbers, tailors, cigar makers, and shoemakers. In both cities, free African Americans compared favorably to white people in their ratio of skilled to unskilled workers. The close ties between free black people and the upper-class white people who did business with them explain much of this success.

Despite these ties, free black communities comparable to those in the upper South and North arose in the cities of the deep South. Although they usually lacked separate black churches as community centers, free African Americans in the region created other institutions. In Charleston the Brown Fellowship Society survived throughout the antebellum period. Charleston also had a chapter of the Prince Hall Masons, and free black men and women in the city maintained other fraternal and benevolent associations. In addition to similar sorts of organizations, the free black elite in New Orleans published literary journals and supported an opera house. During the 1850s, Savannah—where black churches did exist—had at least three black volunteer fire companies, a porters' association, and several benevolent societies.

Because black churches were rare, wealthy African Americans and fraternal organizations organized private schools for black children in the cities of the deep South. In Charleston the Brown Fellowship Society organized an academy. New Orleans had several schools, most of which were conducted in French—the first or second language for many free black people in the city. Some of the more wealthy free black families in these cities sent their children abroad for an education, and the literacy rate among free black people in both Charleston and New Orleans was markedly high for the antebellum period.

In all, free people of color in the deep South differed substantially from those in the upper South and the North. Their ties to the white slaveholding class gave them tangible advantages. However, they were not without sympathy for those who remained in slavery, and white authorities were never certain of their loyalty to the slave regime. In particular, white people feared contact between free African Americans in the port cities of the deep South and black northerners—especially black sailors. As a new round of slave unrest began in the South and a more militant northern antislavery movement got under way during the 1820s, free black people in the deep South faced difficult circumstances.

FREE AFRICAN AMERICANS IN THE FAR WEST

Free black communities in the North, upper South, and deep South each had unique features, but all of them had existed for decades by the antebellum period. In the huge region stretching from the Great Plains to the Pacific coast, which had become part of the United States by the late 1840s, free black people were rare. Black communities there were just emerging in a few isolated localities. As historian Quintard Taylor notes, the 4,000 "nominally free" African Americans who lived in California in 1860 constituted "75 percent of the free black population of the West." In the major slaveholding state of Texas, census figures indicate that a tiny free black population decreased from 397 in 1850 to 355 in 1860. The prevalence of discriminatory "black laws" in the region's states and territories partially explains the small number of free black westerners. Like similar laws in the states of the Old Northwest, these laws either banned free African Americans entirely or restricted the activities of those who were allowed to settle. Nevertheless, a few black families sought economic opportunities in the West. During the 1840s they joined white Americans in settling Oregon. The California gold rush of 1849 had by 1852 attracted about 2,000 African Americans, the great majority of whom were men, among hundreds of thousands of white Americans.

Usually black Californians lived and worked in multicultural communities that also included people of Chinese, Jamaican, Latin American, and white American descent. But in a few localities, African Americans predominated. Some black Californians were prosperous gold prospectors. Others worked as steamship stewards, cooks, barbers, laundresses, mechanics, saloonkeepers, whitewashers, porters, and domestics. By the early 1850s, there were black communities centered on churches in San Francisco, Sacramento, and Los Angeles. In 1851 Bernard Fletcher established an AME church in Sacramento, and the following year, John Jamison Moore established an AME Zion church in San Francisco. As was the case in the East, these black communities organized a variety of benevolent and self-help societies. Although most African Americans who went west were men, black women sometimes accompanied their husbands and families. The better off of them raised funds for AME churches and voluntary associations. Others

Painted in 1858 by Thomas Waterman Wood, *Market Woman* portrays a young woman carrying produce she has purchased. There is no indication of her status as either free or enslaved. The portrait provides an example of how black women dressed in antebellum America.

worked as cooks, laundresses, and prostitutes. (For more on free African Americans in California, see Chapter 10.)

CONCLUSION

During the antebellum period, free African-American communities that had emerged during the revolutionary era grew and fostered black institutions. Particularly in the urban North, life in these segregated communities foreshadowed the pattern of black life from the end of the Civil War into the twentieth century. Although the black elite could gain education, professional expertise, and wealth despite white prejudices, most northern people of color were poor. Extended families, churches, segregation, political marginality, and limited educational opportunities still influence African-American life today.

Life for free black people in the upper South and deep South was even more difficult. Presumed to be slaves if they could not prove otherwise, they confronted a greater danger of enslavement and more restrictive legislation than existed in the North. But

AFRICAN-AMERICAN EVENTS	NATIONAL EVENTS
• 1800 •	
1804 Ohio enacts black laws	1803 Louisiana Purchase
• 1805 •	
1807 New Jersey disfranchises black men	1807 Robert Fulton's steamboat is launched in New York harbor
• 1810 •	
1812 African School becomes part of Boston public school system	1812 War of 1812 begins
	1815 War of 1812 ends
• 1815 •	
1818 Connecticut bars new black voters	1819 Panic of 1819 begins
• 1820 •	
1821 New York retains property qualification for black voters	
1822 Rhode Island disfranchises black voters	
1824 Massachusetts defeats attempt to ban black migration to that state	
• 1825 •	
1827 *Freedom's Journal* begins publication	1825 John Quincy Adams becomes president of the United States
1828 African Dorcas Association is established	Erie Canal opens
1829 Cincinnati expels black residents	1827 Massachusetts pioneers compulsory public education
	1828 Andrew Jackson is elected president

energetic black communities existed in the upper South throughout the antebellum period. In the deep South, the small free black population was better off economically than were free black people in other regions, but it depended on the region's white slaveholders, who were unreliable allies as sectional controversy mounted. The antislavery movement, secession, and the Civil War would have a more profound impact on the free black communities in the South than in the North. Although it is not wise to generalize about free black people in the trans-Mississippi West, their presence on the Pacific coast in particular demonstrates their involvement in the westward expansion that characterized the United States during the antebellum years. Their West Coast communities indicate the adaptability of black institutions to new circumstances.

RECOMMENDED READING

Ira Berlin. *Slaves without Masters: The Free Negro in the Antebellum South.* New York: New Press, 1971. This classic study is still the most comprehensive treatment of free African Americans in the antebellum South.

W. Jeffrey Bolster. *Black Jacks: African American Seamen in the Age of Sail.* Cambridge, MA: Harvard University Press, 1997. *Black Jacks* explores the lives of black seamen between 1740 and 1865.

Leonard Curry. *The Free Black in Urban America, 1800–1850: The Shadow of the Dream.* Chicago: University of Chicago Press, 1981. Curry provides a comprehensive account of urban African-American life in the antebellum period.

Philip S. Foner. *History of Black America: From the Emergence of the Cotton Kingdom to the Eve of the Compromise of 1850.* Westport, CT: Greenwood Press, 1983. This second volume of Foner's three-volume series presents a wealth of information about African-American life between 1820 and 1861, especially about the northern black community.

James Oliver Horton and Lois E. Horton. *In Hope of Liberty: Culture, Community, and Protest among Northern Free Blacks, 1700–1860.* New York: Oxford University Press, 1997. The authors focus on how the northern black community responded to difficult circumstances, especially during the antebellum decades.

Leon F. Litwack. *North of Slavery: The Negro in the Free States, 1790–1860.* Chicago: University of Chicago Press, 1961. This book emphasizes how northern white people treated African Americans. It is an essential guide to the status of African Americans in the antebellum North.

Quintard Taylor. *In Search of the Racial Frontier: African Americans in the American West, 1528–1990.* New York: Norton, 1998. This is the first book-length study of black westerners.

ADDITIONAL BIBLIOGRAPHY

COMMUNITY STUDIES

Tommy L. Bogger. *Free Blacks in Norfolk, Virginia, 1790–1860: The Darker Side of Freedom.* Charlottesville: University Press of Virginia, 1997.

Letitia Woods Brown. *Free Negroes in the District of Columbia, 1790–1846.* New York: Oxford University Press, 1972.

Melvin Patrick Ely. *Israel on the Appomattox: A Southern Experiment in Black Freedom from the 1790s through the Civil War.* New York: Knopf, 2004.

Leslie M. Harris. *In the Shadow of Slavery: African Americans in New York City, 1626–1863.* Chicago: University of Chicago Press, 2003.

James Oliver Horton. *Free People of Color: Inside the African-American Community.* Washington, DC: Smithsonian Institution Press, 1993.

James Oliver Horton and Lois E. Horton. *Black Bostonians: Family Life and Community Struggle in the Antebellum North.* New York: Holmes and Meier, 1979.

Gary B. Nash. *Forging Freedom: The Formation of Philadelphia's Black Community, 1720–1840.* Cambridge, MA: Harvard University Press, 1988.

Christopher Phillips. *Freedom's Port: The African-American Community of Baltimore, 1790–1860.* Urbana: University of Illinois Press, 1997.

Bernard E. Powers Jr. *Black Charlestonians: A Social History, 1822–1885.* Fayetteville: University of Arkansas Press, 1994.

Harry Reed. *Platform for Change: The Foundations of the Northern Free Black Community, 1775–1865.* East Lansing: Michigan State University Press, 1994.

Judith Kelleher Schafer. *Becoming Free, Remaining Free: Manumission and Enslavement in New Orleans, 1846–1862.* Baton Rouge: Louisiana State University Press, 2003.

Julie Winch. *Philadelphia's Black Elite: Activism, Accommodation, and the Struggle for Autonomy, 1787–1848.* Philadelphia: Temple University Press, 1988.

STATE-LEVEL STUDIES

Barbara Jeanne Fields. *Slavery and Freedom on the Middle Ground: Maryland during the Nineteenth Century.* New Haven, CT: Yale University Press, 1985.

John Hope Franklin. *The Free Negro in North Carolina, 1790–1860.* Chapel Hill: University of North Carolina Press, 1943.

Graham Russell Hodges. *Root and Branch: African Americans in New York and East Jersey, 1613–1863.* Chapel Hill: University of North Carolina Press, 1999.

John H. Russell. *The Free Negro in Virginia, 1619–1865.* 1913. Reprint, New York: Negro Universities Press, 1969.

H. E. Sterkx. *The Free Negro in Antebellum Louisiana.* Rutherford, NJ: Fairleigh Dickinson University Press, 1972.

Timeline

1830

1831 — Maria W. Stewart criticizes treatment of black workers

1832 — Surge in European immigration begins

1834 — African Free Schools become part of New York City public school system

1832–1833 — Nullification Crisis occurs

1835

1838 — Pennsylvania disfranchises black voters

1837 — Panic of 1837 begins

Gold discovered in California

1840

1842 — Rhode Island revives black male voting

1843 — Edmonia Lewis born

1845

1845 — *Narrative of the Life of Frederick Douglass* is published

1846–1848 — War is fought against Mexico

1849 — Ohio black laws are repealed

1850

1850 — Compromise of 1850 passed

AFRICAN-AMERICAN EVENTS | **NATIONAL EVENTS**

Marina Wilkramangrake. *A World in Shadow—The Free Black in Antebellum South Carolina.* Columbia: University of South Carolina Press, 1973.

RACE RELATIONS

Francis D. Adams. *Alienable Rights: The Exclusion of African Americans in a White Man's Land, 1619–2000.* New York: Harper Collins, 2003.

Eugene H. Berwanger. *The Frontier against Slavery: Western Anti-Negro Prejudice and the Slavery Expansion Controversy.* Urbana: University of Illinois Press, 1967.

Phyllis F. Field. *The Politics of Race in New York: The Struggle for Black Suffrage in the Civil War Era.* Ithaca, NY: Cornell University Press, 1982.

Noel Ignatiev. *How the Irish Became White.* New York: Routledge, 1995.

David Roediger. *The Wages of Whiteness: Race and the Making of the American Working Class.* New York: Verso, 1991.

Joel Williamson. *New People: Miscegenation and Mulattoes in the United States.* New York: Free Press, 1980.

Carol Wilson. *Freedom at Risk: The Kidnapping of Free Blacks in America, 1780–1865.* Lexington: University Press of Kentucky, 1994.

WOMEN AND FAMILY

Virginia Meacham Gould, ed. *Chained to the Rock of Adversity: To Be Free, Black, and Female in the Old South.* Athens: University of Georgia Press, 1998.

Herbert G. Gutman. *The Black Family in Slavery and Freedom, 1750–1925.* New York: Pantheon Books, 1977.

Lynn M. Hudson. *The Making of "Mammy Pleasant": A Black Entrepreneur in Nineteenth-Century San Francisco.* Urbana: University of Illinois Press, 2003.

Jacqueline Jones. *Labor of Love, Labor of Sorrow: Black Women, Work and the Family from Slavery to the Present.* New York: Basic Books, 1985.

Wilma King. *Free Black Women during the Slave Era.* Columbia: University of Missouri Press, 2006.

Suzanne Lebsock. *The Free Women of Petersburg: Status and Culture in a Southern Town, 1784–1860.* New York: Norton, 1984.

T. O. Madden Jr., with Ann L. Miller. *We Were Always Free: The Maddens of Culpeper County, Virginia, a 200 Year Family History.* New York: Norton, 1992.

INSTITUTIONS AND THE BLACK ELITE

Vincent P. Franklin. *The Education of Black Philadelphia.* Philadelphia: University of Pennsylvania Press, 1979.

Carlton Mabee. *Black Education in New York State.* Syracuse, NY: Syracuse University Press, 1979.

Eileen Southern. *The Music of Black America,* 2d ed. New York: Norton, 1983.

Loretta J. Williams. *Black Freemasonry and Middle-Class Realities.* Columbia: University of Missouri Press, 1980.

RETRACING THE ODYSSEY

Boston African-American National Historic Site: Black Heritage Trail and Museum of Afro-American History, Boston, Massachusetts. Visitors may follow the Black Heritage Trail to historic locations located in Boston's antebellum black community on Beacon Hill. Of particular interest are the African Meeting House and the Abiel Smith School.

The Kendall Whaling Museum, Sharon, Massachusetts. Exhibits include "Heroes in the Ships: African Americans in the Whaling Industry, 1840–1900."

Chattanooga African American Museum, Chattanooga, Tennessee. A major exhibit focuses on free black businessmen in antebellum Chattanooga.

    REVIEW, RESEARCH, AND INTERACT

REVIEW QUESTIONS

1. How was black freedom in the North limited in the antebellum decades?

2. How did northern African Americans deal with these limits?

3. What was the relationship of the African-American elite to urban black communities?

4. How did African-American institutions fare between 1820 and 1861?

5. Compare black life in the North to free black life in the upper South, deep South, and California.

    www.researchnavigator.com

Using the tools available in Research Navigator, consider this question:
Compare and contrast the lives of free blacks in the North and the South. What key differences do you note?

PRIMARY SOURCE DOCUMENTS

7–1 "Reflections, Occasioned by the Late Disturbances in Charleston," 1822

7–2 Richard Allen, "Address to the Free People of Colour of These United States," 1830

7–3 Thomas R. Dew's Defense of Slavery, 1832

MAP EXPLORATION

The Slave, Free Black, and White Population of the United States in 1830, p. 167

8

Opposition to Slavery

WHY AND HOW DID ABOLITIONISM
BEGIN IN AMERICA?

HOW DID THE REVOLTS OF GABRIEL,
DENMARK VESEY, AND NAT TURNER
AFFECT AFRICAN AMERICANS?

WHAT WERE THE GOALS OF
THE AMERICAN COLONIZATION SOCIETY?

WHAT ROLE DID BLACK WOMEN PLAY
IN THE ABOLITION MOVEMENT?

WHY WAS WALKER'S *APPEAL* IMPORTANT?

◀ **This contemporary drawing** depicts the capture of Nat
Turner in October, 1831. Turner had avoided
apprehension for nearly two months following the
suppression of his revolt. The artist indicates Turner's
personal dignity. North Wind Picture Archives

Beloved brethren—here let me tell you, and believe it, that the Lord our God, as true as he sits on his throne in heaven, and as true as our Savior died to redeem the world, will give you a Hannibal [an ancient Carthaginian general], and when the Lord shall have raised him up, and given him to you for your possession, O my suffering brethren! . . . Read the history particularly of Hayti, and see how they were butchered by the whites, and do you take warning. The person whom God Shall give you, give him your support and let him go his length, and behold in him the salvation of your God. God will indeed, deliver you through him from your deplorable and wretched condition under the Christians of America.

David Walker's *Appeal*

◀ **Haitian independence** movement leader Touissant Louverture who fought successfully against the French and British provided inspiration for leaders of slave uprisings in America.

Black abolitionist David Walker wrote these words in Boston in 1829. They suggest the sense early-nineteenth-century Americans had of the nearness of God and the anguish a free black man felt about his brothers and sisters in bondage.

In his harsh language and demands for action, Walker was a precursor of the militant black and white abolitionists of the 1830s, 1840s, and 1850s. He bluntly portrayed the oppression suffered by African Americans. He urged black men to redeem themselves by defending their loved ones from abuse. If that led to violence and death, he asked, "Had you not rather be killed than be a slave to a tyrant, who takes the life of your mother, wife and dear little children?" Through his provocative language and his efforts to have his *Appeal to the Colored Citizens of the World* distributed in the South, Walker became a prophet of violent revolution against slaveholders.

Walker's *Appeal* was not just a reaction to slavery; it was also a response to a conservative brand of antislavery reform. This chapter explores the emergence, during the years between Gabriel's conspiracy in 1800 and the organization of the **American Anti-Slavery Society** in 1833, of a radical antislavery movement in the United States. We first discuss the turmoil of the period, the **Second Great Awakening,** the related social reform efforts, the two strains within the abolition movement, and the black response to African colonization. We then describe how Walker, Denmark Vesey, Nat Turner, other black leaders, and white abolitionist William Lloyd Garrison radicalized the abolition movement during the late 1820s and early 1830s. Chapter 9 traces the development of abolitionism from 1833 into the 1850s.

A Country in Turmoil

When Walker wrote his *Appeal*, the United States was in economic, political, and social turmoil. As we have shown in earlier chapters, the invention of the cotton gin in 1793 led to a vast westward expansion of cotton cultivation. Where cotton went, so did slavery. By the late 1820s, southern slaveholders and their slaves had pushed into what was then the Mexican province of Texas. Meanwhile, the states of the Old Northwest passed from frontier conditions to commercial farming. By 1825 the Erie Canal had linked this region economically to the Northeast. Later, railroads carried the Old Northwest's agricultural products to East Coast cities. An enormous amount of grain and meat also flowed down the Ohio and Mississippi rivers, encouraging the growth of such cities as Pittsburgh, Cincinnati, Louisville, St. Louis, Memphis, and New Orleans. As steamboats became common and networks of macadam turnpikes (paved with crushed stone and tar), canals, and railroads spread, travel time diminished. Americans became more mobile, families scattered, and ties to local communities weakened. For African Americans, subject to the domestic slave trade, mobility came with a high price.

The factory system, which arose in urban areas of the Northeast and spread to parts of the Old Northwest and upper South, also had a disruptive impact. Cities grew, and increased immigration from Europe meant native black and white people had to compete with foreign-born workers for employment. Farmers became more dependent on urban markets for their crops. A money economy became more pervasive, the banking industry became essential, and vast private fortunes influenced public policy. Many Americans believed forces beyond their control threatened their way of life and the nation's republican values. They distrusted change and wanted someone to blame for the uncertainties they faced. This outlook encouraged American politics to become paranoid—dominated by fear of hostile conspiracies.

They became the most ardent supporters of expanding slavery into new regions, leading their opponents to claim they were part of a "slave power" conspiracy. Most Democratic politicians also openly advocated white supremacy. Although their rhetoric demanded equal rights for all and special privileges for none, they were really concerned only with the rights of white men.

The Democratic Party's outlook toward American Indians, women, and African Americans demonstrated this. Democratic politicians led in demanding the removal of Indians to the area west of the Mississippi River, which led to the Cherokee "Trail of Tears" in 1838. Generally, Democrats also supported patriarchy, a subservient role for women in family life and the church, and their exclusion from the public sphere. And almost all Democratic leaders believed God and nature had designed African Americans to be slaves. During the 1820s and early 1830s, only a few radicals like Walker saw the hypocrisy of this outlook and contended that real democracy would embrace all men, regardless of race. Reformers did not even begin to propose equal rights for women until the late 1830s.

POLITICAL PARANOIA

The charges (discussed in Chapter 7) that John Quincy Adams and Henry Clay had cheated Andrew Jackson out of the presidency in early 1825 reflected this fear of conspiracies. What Jackson's supporters called "the corrupt bargain" and claims that Adams favored a wealthy and intellectual elite at the expense of the common white man led to the organization of the Democratic Party and the election of Jackson to the presidency in 1828. The Democrats claimed to stand for the natural rights and economic well-being of American workers and farmers against what they called the "money power," a conspiratorial alliance of bankers and businessmen.

Yet, from its start, the Democratic Party also represented the interests of the South's slaveholding elite. Democratic politicians, North and South, favored a states' rights doctrine that protected slavery from interference by the national government. They sought through legislation, judicial decisions, and diplomacy to make the right to hold human property inviolate.

The Trail of Tears, painted in 1942 by Robert Lindneux, dramatizes the westward journey of Cherokees from their homeland in Georgia to what is now Oklahoma. The Democratic Party, which championed the rights of white men, was chiefly responsible for the forced westward relocation of the Cherokees and other southeastern Indian peoples. Robert Lindneux, "The Trail of Tears" (the removal of the Cherokee Indians to the West in 1838). Oil on canvas. © The Granger Collection, New York

By the mid-1830s, those Americans who favored a more enlightened political program turned—often reluctantly—to the Whig Party, which opposed Jackson and the Democrats. The Whigs also attracted those who had supported the Anti-Masonic Party during the early 1830s. This small party epitomized political paranoia by contending that the Freemasons conspired to subvert republican government. Politicians such as Henry Clay, Daniel Webster, William H. Seward, and John Quincy Adams, who identified with the Whig Party, placed much more emphasis on Christian morality and an active national government than the Democrats did. They regarded themselves as conservatives, did not seek to end slavery in the southern states, and included many wealthy slaveholders within their ranks. But in the North, the party's moral orientation and its opposition to territorial expansion by the United States made it attractive to slavery's opponents.

The Whig Party also served as the channel through which evangelical Christianity influenced politics. In the North, Whig politicians appealed to evangelical voters. Often evangelicals themselves, some Whig politicians and journalists defended the human rights of African Americans and American Indians. They criticized the inhumanity of slaveholders and tried to limit the federal government's support for the "peculiar institution." When and where they could, black men voted for Whig candidates.

THE SECOND GREAT AWAKENING

A new era of revivalism in America motivated evangelicals to carry their Christian morality into politics. Like David Walker, they saw the hand of God everywhere. Religion, of course, had always been important in America. During the 1730s and 1740s, the religious revival known as the Great Awakening used emotional preaching and hymn singing to bring men and women to embrace Christianity and reform their lives. African Americans helped shape the Great Awakening, and American churches had first made a concerted effort to convert black people at that time. A new wave of emotional revivalism began at the end of the eighteenth century. Known as the Second Great Awakening, it lasted through the 1830s. The new evangelicalism led laymen to take control of religion from the established clergy and try to impose moral order on an increasingly turbulent American society.

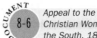

DOCUMENT 8-6 *Appeal to the Christian Women of the South, 1836*

The Second Great Awakening influenced Richard Allen and Absalom Jones's efforts to establish separate black churches in Philadelphia during the 1790s. It helped shape the character of other black churches that emerged during the 1800s and 1810s. These black churches became an essential part of the antislavery movement. However, the Second Great Awakening did not reach its peak until the 1820s. During that decade, Charles G. Finney, a white Presbyterian, and other revivalists helped democratize religion in America. At camp meetings that lasted for days, revivalists preached that all men and women—not just a few—could become faithful Christians and save their souls. Just as Jacksonian democracy revolutionized politics in America, the Second Great Awakening revolutionized the nation's spiritual life and—with greatest impact in the Northeast and Old Northwest—led many Americans, black and white, to join reform movements.

THE BENEVOLENT EMPIRE

Evangelicals emphasized "practical Christianity." Those who were saved, they maintained, would not be content with their own salvation. Instead, they would help save others. Black evangelicals, in particular, called for "a *liberating* faith" that would advance material and spiritual well-being. An emphasis on action led to what became known during the 1810s and 1820s as the **Benevolent Empire,** a network of church-related organizations designed to fight sin and save souls. The Benevolent Empire launched what is now known as antebellum or Jacksonian reform.

This social movement flourished from the 1810s through the 1850s. It consisted of voluntary associations dedicated to a host of causes: public education, self-

This 1844 lithograph by Peter S. Duval, derived from a painting by Alfred Hoffy, portrays Julianne Jane Tillman. Tillman was an AME preacher and one of the few women of her time to be employed in such a capacity.

improvement, limiting or abolishing alcohol consumption (the temperance movement), prison reform, and aid to the mentally and physically handicapped. Members of the movement also distributed Bibles and religious tracts, funded missionary activities, and discouraged prostitution. They sought to improve health through diet and medical fads, alleviate conditions for seamen, and—by the 1840s—advocated rights for women. The self-improvement, temperance, and missionary associations that free black people—and sometimes slaves—formed in conjunction with their churches in urban areas were part of this movement.

The most important of the reform societies, however, were those dedicated to the problem of African-American bondage in the United States. At first called societies for promoting the abolition of slavery, they later became known as antislavery societies. Whatever they called themselves, their members were **abolitionists,** people who favored doing away with or abolishing slavery in their respective states and throughout the country. To understand American abolitionism in the 1820s, we must return to the first abolitionist efforts that arose during the revolutionary era.

Abolitionism Begins in America

The antislavery movement in its broadest context reflected economic, intellectual, and moral changes that affected the Atlantic world during the Age of Revolution. In the United States that age forged *two* antislavery movements that continued to exist until the end of the Civil War. Although different, the two movements constantly influenced each other. The first of these movements existed in the South among slaves with the help of free African Americans and a few sympathetic white people. As we mentioned in earlier chapters, enslaved African Americans, from the seventeenth century onward, individually and in groups sought their freedom through violent and nonviolent means. Before the revolutionary era, however, these slaves only wanted to free themselves and did not seek to destroy slavery as a social system.

The second antislavery movement consisted of black and white abolitionists in the North, with outposts in the upper South. Far more white people were in this movement than in the one southern slaves conducted. In the North, white people controlled the larger antislavery organizations, although African Americans led in direct action against slavery and its influences in the North. In the upper South, African Americans could not openly establish or participate in antislavery organizations, but they cooperated covertly and informally with white abolitionists.

This second and essentially northern movement took root during the 1730s when white Quakers in New Jersey and Pennsylvania became convinced that slaveholding contradicted their belief in spiritual equality. For the rest of the eighteenth century, they advocated the abolition of slavery—at least among their fellow Quakers—in their home states and in the Chesapeake. Quakers always remained prominent in the northern antislavery movement. As members of a denomination that emphasized nonviolence, they generally expected slavery to be abolished peacefully and gradually.

The American Revolution, together with the French Revolution that began in 1789 and the Haitian struggle for independence between 1791 and 1804, revitalized both the northern and southern antislavery movements and changed their nature. The revolutionary doctrine that all men had a natural right to life, liberty, and property led other northerners besides Quakers and African Americans to endorse the antislavery cause.

Philadelphia Quakers in 1775 organized what became the first antislavery society. But when it was reorganized in 1784 as the Society for the Promotion of the Abolition of Slavery, it attracted non-Quakers. Among the first of these were Benjamin Rush and Benjamin Franklin, both of whom were influenced by natural rights doctrines. Revolutionary principles also influenced Alexander Hamilton and John Jay, who helped organize New York's first antislavery society. Prince Hall, the most prominent black abolitionist of his time, based his effort to abolish slavery in Massachusetts on universal natural rights. He contended that African Americans "have in common with all other men a natural right to our freedom."

The efforts of northern black and white abolitionists were instrumental in abolishing slavery in the North. However, the early northern antislavery movement had several limiting features. First, black and white abolitionists had similar goals but worked in separate organizations. Even white Quaker abolitionists were reluctant to mix socially with African Americans or welcome them to their meetings. Second, except in parts of New England, abolition in the North proceeded *gradually* to protect the economic interests of slaveholders. Third, white abolitionists did not advocate equal rights for black people. In most northern states, laws kept black people from enjoying full freedom after their emancipation. Fourth, early northern abolitionists did little to bring about abolition in the South, where most slaves lived.

All this indicates that neither Quaker piety nor natural rights principles created a truly egalitarian or sectionally aggressive northern abolitionism. Rather the moralistic emotionalism of the Second Great Awakening, combined with Benevolent Empire activism and the growth of northern black institutions, established a framework for a more biracial and wide-ranging antislavery movement. Even more important in providing a prod were southern slaves and their free black allies, who had their own plans for emancipation.

FROM GABRIEL TO DENMARK VESEY

Gabriel's abortive slave revolt of 1800 owed as much to revolutionary ideology as did the northern antislavery movement. The arrival of Haitian refugees in Virginia had led to slave unrest throughout the 1790s. Gabriel himself hoped to attract French revolutionary support. His conspiracy, though, was betrayed, and he and

MAP EXPLORATION

To explore this interactive map, go to
http://www.prenhall.com/hine4/map8.2

MAP 8–1   SLAVE CONSPIRACIES AND UPRISINGS, 1800–1831
Major slave conspiracies and revolts were rare between 1800 and 1860. This was in part because those that took place frightened masters and led them to adopt policies aimed at preventing recurrences.

twenty-six of his followers were executed. But the revolutionary spirit and insurrectionary network Gabriel established lived on (see Map 8–1). Virginia authorities had to suppress another slave conspiracy in 1802, and sporadic minor revolts erupted for years.

Gabriel's conspiracy had two unintended consequences. First, the Quaker-led antislavery societies of the Chesapeake declined rapidly. They had always been small and weak compared with antislavery societies in the North. They were more effective in helping free black people who were illegally held as slaves than in promoting emancipation. After Gabriel's conspiracy, these organizations either became dormant, were suppressed, or withered under pressure from public opinion. The chance all but vanished that Maryland, Virginia, and North Carolina would follow the northern example by gradually abolishing slavery.

Second, white southerners and many white northerners became convinced that, as long as black people lived among them, a race war like the one in Haiti could erupt in the United States. Slaveholders and their defenders argued that this threat did not result from the oppressiveness of slavery. On the contrary, they maintained, the slaves were naturally suited for and content in bondage. It was the growing class of free black people, they asserted, who instigated otherwise passive bondpeople to revolt.

Free African Americans were, slavery's defenders contended, a dangerous, criminal, and potentially revolutionary class that had to be regulated, subdued, and ultimately expelled from the country. No system of emancipation that would increase the number of free black people in the United States could be tolerated. Slaveholders who had never shown a willingness to free their slaves began to claim they would favor emancipation if it were not for fear of enlarging such a dangerous group. As an elderly Thomas Jefferson put it, white southerners had a wolf by the ears: once they had enslaved black people, it was impossible to free them safely. Without the restrictions slavery placed on African Americans, southern politicians and journalists argued, they would become economic competitors to white workers, a perpetual criminal class, and a revolutionary threat to white rule.

Events in and about Charleston, South Carolina, in 1822 appeared to confirm the threat. In that year black informants revealed a conspiracy for a massive slave revolt that had been organized by a free black man named Denmark Vesey. Like Gabriel before him, Vesey could read and was well aware of the revolutions that had shaken the Atlantic world. Born most likely on the Danish-ruled Caribbean island of St. Thomas, a carpenter by trade, and a former sailor who had been to Haiti, Vesey hoped for Haitian aid for an antislavery revolution in the South Carolina low country. He understood the significance of the storming of the Bastille (a fortress-prison in Paris) on July 14, 1789 that marked the start of the French Revolution and planned to start his revolution on July 14, 1822. He had read the antislavery speeches of northern members of Congress during the 1820 debates over the admission of Missouri to the Union and may have hoped for northern aid.

However, as befitted an evangelical and romantic era, religion had a more prominent role in Vesey's plot than in Gabriel's. Vesey was a Bible-quoting Methodist who conducted religious classes. Like other free black people and slaves in Charleston, he deeply resented attempts by the white authorities to suppress the city's AME church in 1818. He believed passages in the Bible about the enslavement and deliverance of the Hebrews in Egypt promised freedom for African Americans. Vesey also used aspects of African religion that had survived among low-country slaves to promote his revolutionary efforts. To reach slaves whose Christian convictions blended in with West African spiritualism, he relied on his closest collaborator, Jack Pritchard—known as Gullah Jack. A "conjure-man" born in East Africa, Pritchard distributed charms and cast spells that he claimed would make revolutionaries invincible.

Vesey and his associates planned to capture arms and ammunition and seize control of Charleston. But Gullah Jack's charms were ineffective against white vigilance and black informers. About a month before the revolt was to begin, the arrest of one of Vesey's lieutenants put local authorities on guard. Vesey moved the date of the uprising to June 16. But on June 14 a house servant revealed the conspiracy to his master, the local government called in the state militia, and arrests ensued. Over several weeks, the authorities rounded up 131 suspects. The accused received public trials, and juries convicted seventy-one of them. Thirty-five, including Vesey and Gullah Jack, were hanged. Thirty-seven were banished. Four white men—three of them foreigners—were convicted of inciting slaves to revolt. They received prison sentences and fines.

After the executions, Charleston's city government destroyed what remained of the local AME church, and white churches assumed responsibility for supervising other black congregations. Meanwhile, white South Carolinians sought to make slave patrols more efficient. The state legislature outlawed assemblages of slaves and banned teaching slaves to read. Local authorities jailed black seamen whose ships docked in Charleston until the ships were ready to leave port. Assuming that free black and white abolitionists in-spired slave unrest, white South Carolinians became increasingly suspicious of local free African Americans, as well as of white Yankees who visited their state.

THE AMERICAN COLONIZATION SOCIETY

Fear of free African Americans as a subversive class shaped the program of the most significant white anti-slavery organization of the 1810s and 1820s—but whether its aim was actually abolition is debatable. In late 1816 concerned white leaders met in Washington, D.C., to form the American Society for Colonizing Free People of Colour of the United States, usually known as the American Colonization Society (ACS). Among its founders were such prominent slaveholders as Bushrod Washington—a nephew of George Washington—and Henry Clay. In 1821 the ACS, with the support of the U.S. government, established the colony of Liberia in West Africa as a prospective home for African Americans.

The ACS had a twofold program. First, it proposed to abolish slavery gradually in the United States, perhaps giving slaveholders financial compensation for their human property. Second, it proposed to send emancipated slaves and free black people to Liberia. The founders of the ACS believed that masters would never emancipate their slaves if they thought emancipation would increase the free black population in the United States. Black and white abolitionists did not immediately perceive the moral and practical objections to this program. The ACS became an integral part of the Benevolent Empire and commanded widespread support among many who regarded themselves as friends of humanity.

Although the ACS always had its greatest strength in the upper South and enjoyed the support of slave-holders, including Francis Scott Key (who wrote the lyrics for "The Spangled Banner"), Andrew Jackson, John Tyler, and John Randolph, by the 1820s it had branches in every northern state. Such northern white abolitionists as Arthur and Lewis Tappan, Gerrit Smith, and William Lloyd Garrison initially supported colonization. They tended to emphasize the abolitionist aspects of the ACS and clung to a belief that free and soon-to-be-emancipated African Americans could choose whether to stay in the United States or go to Liberia. In either case, they hoped, black people would be free.

BLACK NATIONALISM AND COLONIZATION

Prominent black abolitionists initially shared this positive assessment of the ACS. They were part of a black nationalist tradition dating back at least to Prince Hall that—disappointed with repeated rebuffs from white people—endorsed black American migration to Africa. During the early 1800s, the most prominent advocate of this point of view was Paul Cuffe of Massachusetts. In 1811, six years before the ACS organized, Cuffe, a Quaker of African and American Indian ancestry, addressed Congress on the subject of African-American Christian colonies in Africa.

The ACS argument that appealed to Cuffe and many other African Americans was that white prejudice would never allow black people to enjoy full citizenship, equal protection under the law, and economic success in the United States. Black people born in America, went the argument for African colonization, could enjoy equal rights only in the continent of their ancestors. In the spirit of American evangelicalism, many African Americans embraced the prospect of bringing Christianity to African nations. Like white people, they considered Africa a pagan, barbaric place that could benefit from their knowledge of Christianity and republican government. Other black leaders who favored colonization objected to this view of Africa. They considered African cultures superior to those of America and Europe. They were often Africans themselves, the children of African parents, or individuals who had been influenced by Africans.

In 1815 Cuffe, who was the captain of his own ship, took thirty-four African-American settlers to the British free black colony of Sierra Leone, located just to the north of present-day Liberia. Cuffe himself would probably have later settled in Liberia if his American Indian wife had not refused to leave her native land. So, three years after Cuffe's death in 1817, AME bishop Daniel Coker led the first eighty-six African-American colonists to Liberia. Pro-ACS sentiment was especially strong among African Americans in Coker's home city of Baltimore and other Chesapeake urban areas. By 1838 approximately 2,500 colonists had made the journey and were living less than harmoniously with Liberia's 28,000 indigenous inhabitants (see Map 8–2).

In 1847 Liberia became an independent republic. But despite the efforts of such **black nationalist** advocates as Henry Highland Garnet and Alexander Crummell, only about 10,000 African-American immigrants had gone there by 1860. This amounted to just 3 percent of the increase of the black population in the United States since 1816. Well before 1860 it was clear that African colonization would never fulfill the dreams of its black or white advocates.

Other African Americans saw Haiti as a potential refuge from the oppression they suffered in the United States. Those whose ancestors had lived in the Caribbean and those who admired Haiti's revolution-

MAP 8–2   THE FOUNDING OF LIBERIA

This map shows the location of Sierra Leone and Liberia in West Africa. British abolitionists established Sierra Leone as a colony for former slaves in 1800. The American Colonization Society established Liberia for the same purpose in 1821.

▶ *Why were Sierra Leone and Liberia established in West Africa?*

Monrovia, Liberia, c. 1830. This map shows the American Colonization Society's main Liberian settlement as it existed about ten years after its founding.

ary history found it especially attractive. In 1824 about 200 men, women, and children from Philadelphia, New York City, and Baltimore went to Haiti. By the end of the 1820s, between 8,000 and 13,000 African Americans had arrived there, but African Americans found Haitian culture to be more alien than they had anticipated. They had difficulty learning French and distrusted the Roman Catholic Church to which most Haitians at least nominally belonged. By 1826 about one-third of the emigrants had returned to the United States.

BLACK OPPOSITION TO COLONIZATION

Some African Americans had always opposed overseas colonization, and, as early as 1817, such an influential black leader as James Forten wavered in his support of the ACS. Although Forten continued to endorse colonization in private, he led a meeting that year of 3,000 black Philadelphians to denounce it. By the mid-1820s, many black abolitionists in East Coast cities from Richmond to Boston had criticized colonization in general and the ACS in particular.

Among them was Samuel Cornish, who with John Russwurm began publication of *Freedom's Journal* in New York City in 1827 as the first African-American newspaper. Cornish, a young Presbyterian minister and fierce opponent of the ACS, called for independent black action against slavery. The *Journal*—reflecting the values of antebellum reform—encouraged self-improvement, education, black civil rights in the North, and sympathy among black northerners for slaves in the South. Russwurm, however, was less opposed to the ACS than was Cornish. This disagreement contributed to the suspension of the newspaper in 1829. That same year Russwurm, who was one of the first African Americans to earn a college degree, moved to Liberia.

People like Cornish regarded themselves as Americans, not Africans, and wanted to improve their condition in this country. They considered Liberia foreign and unhealthy. They had no desire to go there themselves or send other African Americans there. They feared that ACS proposals for *voluntary* colonization were misleading. They knew that nearly every southern state required the expulsion of slaves individually freed by their masters. They were aware of efforts in the Maryland and Virginia legislatures to require *all* free black people to leave or be enslaved. These efforts had little practical impact, but they made African Americans fear that colonization would be forced on them. In 1858 Arkansas actually required the reenslavement of free black people who did not leave that state. But, rather than migrate to Africa,

most of its small free black population fled to the North, Canada, Louisiana, or the Indian Territory.

By the mid-1820s most black abolitionists had concluded that the ACS was part of a proslavery effort to drive free African Americans from the United States. The ACS, they maintained in public meetings, was not an abolitionist organization at all but a proslavery scheme to force free black people to choose between reenslavement or banishment. America, they argued, was their native land. They knew nothing of Africa. Efforts to force them to go there were based on a racist assumption that they were not entitled to live in freedom in the land of their birth. "Do they think to drive us from our country and homes, after having enriched it with our blood and tears?" asked David Walker.

Black Abolitionist Women

Black women joined black men in opposing slavery. In considering their role, we should remember that the United States in the early nineteenth century had a rigid gender hierarchy. Law and custom proscribed women from engaging in all political and professional activities and in most business activities. Those women deemed by black and white Americans to be respectable—the women of wealthy families—were expected to devote themselves exclusively to domestic concerns and to remain socially aloof. Church and benevolent activities constituted their only opportunities for public action. Even in these arenas, custom relegated them to work as auxiliaries of men's organizations.

A Black Feminist Speaks Out in 1851 — DOCUMENT 8-8

This was true of the first *formal* abolitionist groups of black women. Among the leaders were Charlotte Forten, the wife of James Forten, and Maria W. Stewart, the widow of a well-to-do Boston ship outfitter. Charlotte and her daughters Sarah, Margaretta, and Harriet joined with other black and white women to found the **Philadelphia Female Anti-Slavery Society** in 1833. A year earlier, in 1832, other black women had established in Salem, Massachusetts, the first women's antislavery society. Women of the black elite also supported the education of black children, which they hoped would overcome the white prejudices that supported slavery.

Stewart's brief career as an antislavery orator provoked far more controversy than those of the Fortens or other early black abolitionist women. Influenced by Walker's *Appeal* and encouraged by William Lloyd Garrison, Stewart in 1831 and 1832 became the first American woman to address male audiences in public.

Although she directed some of her remarks to "Afric's daughters" and to "ye fairer sisters," she—as had Walker before her—pointedly called on black men actively to oppose slavery. "It is true," she told a group assembled at the African Masonic Hall in Boston in 1833, "our fathers bled and died in the revolutionary war, and others fought bravely under the command of [General Andrew] Jackson [at New Orleans in 1815], in defense of liberty. But where is the man that has distinguished himself in these modern days by acting wholly in the defense of African rights and liberty?" Such remarks from a woman cut deeply, and Stewart met such hostility from the black community that in September 1833 she retired as a public speaker. Henceforth, she labored in more conventional and respectable female ways for the antislavery cause.

Many African-American women (as well as many white women), however, did not fit the early-nineteenth-century criteria for respectability that applied to the Fortens, Stewart, and others in the African-American elite. Most black women were poor. They lacked education. They had to work outside their homes. Particularly in the upper South, these women were *practical* abolitionists.

LIVING WORDS

3 *What If I Am a Woman?*

From the revolutionary era onward, countless anonymous black women, both slave and free, living in such southern border cities as Baltimore, Louisville, and Washington, risked everything to harbor fugitive slaves. Other heroic women saved their meager earnings to purchase freedom for themselves and their loved ones. Among them was Alethia Tanner of Washington, who purchased her freedom in 1810 for $1,400 (about 16,000 current dollars). During the 1820s she went on to purchase the freedom of her sister, her sister's ten children, and her sister's five grandchildren. During the 1830s Tanner purchased the freedom of seven more slaves. Meanwhile, according to an account written in the 1860s, "Mrs. Tanner was alive to every wise scheme for the education and elevation of her race."

The Baltimore Alliance

Among the stronger black abolitionist opponents of the ACS were William Watkins, Jacob Greener, and Hezekiah Grice, associates in Baltimore of Benjamin Lundy, a white Quaker abolitionist who published an antislavery newspaper named the *Genius of Universal Emancipation*. By the mid-1820s, Watkins, a schoolteacher, had emerged, in a series of letters he published in *Freedom's Journal* and in Lundy's paper, as one of the

William Lloyd Garrison (1805–1879) sat in 1833 for this oil portrait by renowned artist Nathaniel Jocelyn. By that year Garrison was the leading American abolitionist.

more articulate opponents of colonization. Greener, a whitewasher and schoolteacher, helped Lundy publish the *Genius* and promoted its circulation. Grice, who later changed his mind and supported colonization, became the principal founder of the National Black Convention Movement, which during the 1830s, 1840s, and 1850s became a forum for black abolitionists.

In 1829 in Baltimore, Watkins, Greener, and Grice profoundly influenced a young white abolitionist and temperance advocate named William Lloyd Garrison, who later became the most influential of all the American antislavery leaders. Lundy had convinced Garrison to leave his native Massachusetts to come to Baltimore as the associate editor of the *Genius*. Garrison, a deeply religious product of the Second Great Awakening and a well-schooled journalist, had decided before he came to Baltimore that *gradual* abolition was neither practical nor moral. Gradualism was impractical, he said, because it continually put off the date of general emancipation. It was immoral because it encouraged slaveholders to go on sinfully and criminally oppressing African Americans.

Garrison, however, tolerated the ACS until he came under the influence of Watkins, Greener, and Grice. They set Garrison on a course that transformed the abolitionist movement in the United States during the early 1830s. They also initiated a bond between African Americans and Garrison that—although strained at times—shaped the rest of his antislavery career. That bond intensified in 1830 when Garrison was imprisoned in a Baltimore jail for forty-nine days on charges he had libeled a slave trader. While in jail, Garrison met imprisoned fugitive slaves and denounced—to their faces—masters who came to retrieve them.

In 1831 when he began publishing his abolitionist newspaper, *The Liberator*, in Boston, Garrison led the antislavery movement in a new, more radical direction. Although Garrison had called for the *immediate*, rather than the *gradual*, abolition of slavery before he arrived in Baltimore, he was not the first to make that demand or to oppose compensating masters who liberated their slaves. What made Garrison's brand of abolitionism revolutionary was the insight he gained from his association with African Americans in Baltimore: that immediate emancipation must be combined with a commitment to racial justice in the United States. Watkins and Greener were especially responsible for convincing Garrison that African Americans must have equal rights in America and not be sent to Africa after their emancipation. Immediate emancipation without compensation to slaveholders and without expatriation

PROFILE ～ MARIA W. STEWART

Maria W. Stewart had a brief but striking career as an abolitionist, feminist, and advocate of racial justice. She was born Maria Miller in Hartford, Connecticut, in 1803 to free parents, and she was orphaned at age five. Raised in the home of a minister, she had little formal education until she began attending "sabbath schools" when she was fifteen. In 1826 she married James W. Stewart, a successful Boston businessman nearly twice her age, in a ceremony conducted by Thomas Paul at his Boston church. When James W. Stewart died in 1829 he left her with limited means.

In 1830, caught up in the Second Great Awakening, Maria W. Stewart determined to dedicate herself to Christian benevolence. When William Lloyd Garrison began publishing the *Liberator* in 1831, she visited him at his office. Later that year, Garrison published her pamphlet *Religion and Pure Principles of Morality, the Sure Foundation on Which We Must Build*, in which she advocated abolition and black autonomy. The following year, Garrison published her second and last pamphlet, which dealt more narrowly with religion.

Meanwhile, Stewart began speaking to black organizations. In early 1832 she addressed Boston's Afric-American Female Intelligence Society. Using prophetic rhetoric, she noted that the world had entered a revolutionary age and she called on African-American women to influence their husbands and children on behalf of the cause of black freedom, equality, education, and economic advancement in America. In regard to African colonization, she said, "before I go, the bayonet shall press me through."

When in February 1833 she addressed Boston's African Masonic Lodge, Stewart overplayed her role as a prophet. She invoked the glories of ancient Africa as well as black service in the American Revolution in order to chastise black men of her time for not being more active on behalf of the liberty of their people. By claiming that black men lacked "ambition and requisite courage," she provoked her audience to respond with hoots, jeers, and a barrage of rotten tomatoes.

Daunted by this stunning rejection, Stewart determined to leave Boston for New York City. In her farewell address of September 1833, which she delivered at a schoolroom in Paul's church, she asserted that her advice had been rejected because she was a woman. Nevertheless, while acknowledging that black men must lead, she called on black women to promote themselves, their families, and their race.

During the rest of her life, Stewart sought to fulfill that role in a less flamboyant manner. In New York she joined the Female Literary Society and became for many years a public school teacher. She moved to the slaveholding city of Baltimore in 1852 to start a school for black children. During the Civil War, with the assistance of black seamstress Elizabeth Keckley, she organized a black school in Washington. Later she worked as a matron at that city's Freedmen's Hospital and organized a Sunday school for poor black children. She died at Freedmen's Hospital in December 1879.

Stewart

A BLACK WOMAN SPEAKS OUT ON THE RIGHT TO EDUCATION

Historians generally believe the antebellum women's rights movement emerged from the antislavery movement during the late 1830s. But as the following letter, published in Freedom's Journal *on August 10, 1827, indicates, some black women advocated equal rights for women much earlier:*

Messrs. Editors,

Will you allow a female to offer a few remarks upon a subject that you must allow to be all-important? I don't know that in any of your papers, you have said sufficient upon the education of females. I hope you are not to be classed with those, who think that our mathematical knowledge should be limited to "fathoming the dish-kettle," and that we have acquired enough of history, if we know that our grandfather's father lived and died. . . . The diffusion of knowledge has destroyed those degraded opinions, and men of the present age, allow, that we have minds that are capable and deserving of culture. There are difficulties . . . in the way of our advancement; but that should only stir us to greater efforts. We possess not the advantages with those of our sex, whose skins are not coloured like our own, but we can improve what little we have, and make our one talent produce two-fold. . . . Ignorant ourselves, how can we be expected to form the minds of our youth, and conduct them in the paths of knowledge? I would address myself to all mothers. . . . It is their bounden duty to store their daughters' minds with useful learning. They should be made to devote their leisure time to reading books, whence they would derive valuable information, which could never be taken from them. . . .

Matilda

🌿 *How does Matilda use sarcasm to make her point?*

🌿 *What special difficulties did black women like Matilda face in asserting their rights?*

Source: Herbert Aptheker, ed., *A Documentary History of the Negro People in the United States*, 7 vols. (1951; reprint, New York: Citadel, 1990), 1: 89.

> **DOCUMENT 8-4**
> *Abolitionist Demands Immediate End to Slavery, 1831*

David Walker's *Appeal*

Two other black abolitionists shaped Garrison's brand of abolitionism. They were David Walker and Nat Turner. This chapter begins with a quote from David Walker's *Appeal . . . to the Colored Citizens of the World*, which Walker published in 1829. As historian Clement Eaton commented in 1936, this *Appeal* was "a dangerous pamphlet in the Old South." In aggressive language, Walker furiously attacked slavery and white racism. He suggested that slaves use violence to secure their liberty. "I do declare," he wrote, "that one good black can put to death six white men." This especially frightened white southerners because Walker's *Appeal* circulated among slaves in southern ports.

> **DOCUMENT 8-3**
> *An African American Advocates Radical Action in 1829*

This drawing served as the frontispiece for Henry Highland Carnet's 1848 edition of David Walker's *Appeal . . . to the Colored Citizens of the World*. The drawing portrays a black Moses receiving divine laws guaranteeing liberty and justice.

The *Appeal* shaped the struggle over slavery in three ways. First, although Garrison was committed to peaceful means, Walker's aggressive writing style influenced the tone of Garrison and other advocates of immediate abolition. Second, Walker's desperate effort to instill hope and pride in an oppressed people inspired an increasingly militant black abolitionism. Third, Walker's pamphlet and its circulation in the South made white southerners fearful of encirclement from without and subversion from within. This fear encouraged southern leaders to make demands on the North that helped bring on the Civil War.

Nat Turner

In this last respect, Nat Turner's contribution was even more important than Walker's. Slave conspiracies had not ended with Denmark Vesey's execution in 1822. But in 1831 Turner, a privileged slave from eastern Virginia, became the first African American actually to

Well before this illustration of a man escaping from slavery appeared on the cover of *The Anti-Slavery Record* in 1837, fugitive slaves helped shape the development of the sectional controversy over slavery. Some of them became abolitionists, many aroused sympathy for the enslaved among black and white northerners, and all of them contributed to a southern white belief that the slave system required a vigilant defense.

initiate a large-scale slave uprising since Charles Deslondes had done so in Louisiana in 1811. As a result Turner inspired far greater fear among white southerners than Walker had.

During the late 1820s and early 1830s, unrest among slaves in Virginia had increased. Walker's *Appeal*, which circulated among some southern free black people by late 1829, may have contributed to this increase. Meanwhile divisions among white Virginians encouraged slaves to seek advantages for themselves. In anticipation of a state constitutional convention in 1829, white people in western Virginia, where there were few slaveholders, called for emancipation. Poorer white men demanded an end to the property qualifications that denied them the vote. As the convention approached, a "spirit of dissatisfaction and insubordination" became manifest among slaves. Some armed themselves and escaped northward. As proslavery white Virginians grew fearful, they demanded further restrictions on the ability of local free black people and northern abolitionists to influence slaves.

Yet no evidence indicates that Nat Turner or any of his associates had read Walker's *Appeal*, had contact with northern abolitionists, or were aware of divisions among white Virginians. Although Turner knew about the successful slave revolt in Haiti, he was more of a religious visionary than a political revolutionary. Born in 1800 he learned to read as a child, and as a young man, he spent much of his time studying and memorizing the Bible. He became a lay preacher and a leader among local slaves. By the late 1820s, he had begun to have visions that convinced him God intended him to lead his people to freedom through violence.

DOCUMENT

The Confessions of Nat Turner, 1831   **8-5**

After considerable planning, Turner began his uprising on the evening of August 21, 1831. His band, which numbered between sixty and seventy, killed fifty-seven white men, women, and children—the largest number of white Americans ever killed by slave rebels—before militia put down the revolt the following morning. In November, Turner and seventeen others were found guilty of insurrection and treason and were hanged. Meanwhile, panicked white people in nearby parts of Virginia and North Carolina killed more than one hundred African Americans whom they—almost always wrongly—suspected of being in league with the rebels.

Turner, like Walker and Garrison, shaped a new era in American abolitionism. The bloodshed in Virginia inspired general revulsion. White southerners—and some northerners—accused Garrison and other abolitionists of inspiring the revolt. In response,

WILLIAM WATKINS OPPOSES COLONIZATION

In response to a white clergyman who argued that migration to Africa would help alleviate the plight of African Americans, William Watkins stressed black unity, education, and self-improvement in this country.

[The Reverend Mr. Hewitt says] "Let us unite into select societies for the purpose of digesting a plan for raising funds to be appropriated to this grand object" [African colonization]. This we cannot do; we intend to let the burden of this work rest upon the shoulders of those who wish us out of the country. We will, however, compromise the matter with our friend. We are willing and anxious to "unite into select societies for the purpose of digesting a plan": for the improvement of our people in science, morals, domestic economy, &c. We are willing and anxious to form union societies . . . that shall discountenance and destroy, as far as possible, those unhappy schisms which have too long divided us, though we are brethren. We are willing to unite . . . in the formation of temperance societies . . . that will enable us to exhibit to the world an amount of moral power that would give new impetus to our friends and "strike alarm" into the breasts of our enemies, if not wholly disarm them of the weapons they are hurling against us.

🌿 *According to Watkins, how will black self-improvement societies help counter colonization?*

🌿 *What difficulties does Watkins believe African Americans must overcome to make themselves stronger in the United States?*

Source: "A Colored American [Watkins] to Editors," n.d., in *Genius of Universal Emancipation*, December 18, 1829.

Despite their knowledge of slave resistance and revolt, white abolitionists in particular tended to portray slaves as peacefully begging for deliverance. The drawing of the man in chains illustrated Quaker poet John Greenleaf Whittier's "Our Countrymen in Chains," published in 1833. By 1835, as abolitionists became more receptive to feminist perspectives, similar images of chained women began to appear.

northern abolitionists of both races asserted their commitment to a peaceful struggle against slavery. Yet both black and white abolitionists respected Turner. Black abolitionists accorded him the same heroic stature they gave Toussaint Louverture and Gabriel. Garrison and other white abolitionists compared Turner to George Washington and other leaders of national liberation movements. This tension between lip service to peaceful means and admiration for violence against slavery characterized the antislavery movement for the next thirty years.

CONCLUSION

This chapter has focused on the two principal antislavery movements in the United States before the 1830s. One movement existed in the South among slaves. The other centered in the North and the Chesapeake among free African American and white abolitionists. Both movements had roots in the age of revolution and gained vitality from evangelical Christianity. The Second Great Awakening and the reforming spirit of the Benevolent Empire shaped the northern antislavery effort. The black church, the Bible, and elements of African religion helped inspire slave revolutionaries.

Gabriel, Denmark Vesey, and Nat Turner had to rely on violence to fight slavery; northern abolitionists used newspapers, books, petitions, and speeches to spread their views. But the two movements had similarities and influenced each other. David Walker's life in Charleston at the time of Denmark Vesey's conspiracy influenced his beliefs. In turn, his *Appeal* may have influenced the enslaved. Turner's revolt helped determine the course of northern abolitionism after 1831. During the subsequent decades, the efforts of slaves to resist their masters, to rebel, and to escape influenced radical black and white abolitionists in the North.

PROFILE ～ DAVID WALKER

David Walker was born free in Wilmington, North Carolina, in 1796 or 1797. Although he learned to read and write, we know nothing of his early life. He may have attended a biracial Methodist church in Wilmington. As a young man, he traveled widely and, according to his *Appeal*, spent time in Charleston, South Carolina, where he attended a religious camp meeting in 1821. This has led historians to conjecture that Walker knew something about Denmark Vesey's conspiracy or, if he was still in Charleston in 1822, that he may even have participated in it.

By 1825 Walker was in Boston dealing in secondhand clothes. He had his own shop, lived in the city's black neighborhood, was married, and had a daughter and a son. At a time when many occupations were closed to African Americans, Walker was doing relatively well. He associated with well-established local black people, including Thomas Paul, an abolitionist minister, and William C. Nell, a foe of Boston's segregated public schools. During the late 1820s, Walker was a circulation agent in Boston for John Russwurm and Samuel Cornish's *Freedom's Journal*.

Walker, who also wrote for the *Journal*, was as conscious of the legal disabilities African Americans faced in Boston as he was of the oppressiveness of slavery. In December 1828 he addressed the Massachusetts General Colored Association on the topic of black cooperation with white abolitionists to improve the conditions of free black people and to liberate the slaves.

Not long after this, Walker became more radical. He wrote his *Appeal* and in September 1829 implemented a clandestine method to circulate it among slaves. He had black and white sailors, to whom he sold used clothes in Boston, take copies of the pamphlet to southern ports and distribute them to African Americans.

When white southerners discovered that slaves had copies of the pamphlet, southern officials demanded that the mayor of Boston stop Walker from publishing. When the mayor refused, rumors circulated that a group of white southerners had offered a reward for Walker, dead or alive. It was not surprising, therefore, that when Walker's daughter and then Walker himself died during the summer of 1830, many assumed they had been poisoned. The most recent biography of Walker, however, indicates that they died of tuberculosis.

WALKER'S

APPEAL,

IN FOUR ARTICLES,

TOGETHER WITH

A PREAMBLE

TO THE

COLORED CITIZENS OF THE WORLD,

BUT IN PARTICULAR AND VERY EXPRESSLY TO THOSE OF THE

UNITED STATES OF AMERICA.

Written in Boston, in the State of Massachusetts, Sept. 28th, 1829.

Boston:

PRINTED FOR

Walker

AFRICAN-AMERICAN EVENTS	NATIONAL AND WORLD EVENTS
1790	
	1791 Haitian Revolution begins
1795	
1796 or 1797 David Walker born	1796 John Adams elected U.S. president
	1798 Undeclared Franco-American war
1800	
1800 Gabriel's conspiracy is exposed	1800 Thomas Jefferson elected U.S. president
1803 Maria W. Stewart born	1803–1806 Lewis and Clark Expedition
1805	
1805 William Lloyd Garrison born	1807 Britain bans Atlantic slave trade
	1808 United States bans Atlantic slave trade
1810	
1811 Louisiana Slave Revolt	1812 War of 1812 begins

The antislavery movement that existed in the North and portions of the upper South was always biracial. During the 1810s and for much of the 1820s, many black abolitionists embraced a form of nationalism that encouraged them to cooperate with the conservative white people who led the ACS. As the racist and proslavery nature of that organization became clear, northern black and white abolitionists called for immediate, uncompensated general emancipation that would not force former slaves to leave the United States.

Slavery, the explicit legal disabilities imposed on free African Americans, and the widespread religious revivalism of the early nineteenth century created conditions very different from those that exist today. But some similarities between then and now are striking. As it was in the 1810s and 1820s, the United States today is in turmoil. Technological innovation and corporate restructuring have created a volatile job market, which has helped to increase interracial tension. As they did in the early nineteenth century, African-American leaders today advocate various strategies to improve black life.

Samuel Cornish, William Watkins, and others who opposed the ACS sought through peaceful means to abolish slavery and gain recognition of African Americans as American citizens. David Walker advocated a more forceful strategy to achieve the same ends. Cornish, Watkins, and Walker all cooperated with white abolitionists. Others took a position closer to black nationalism by linking the abolition of slavery to an independent black destiny in Africa.

As is true today, African Americans of the early nineteenth century, who sought to deal with the problems of their time, faced difficult choices. The strategies they followed each had virtues, weaknesses, and dangers.

RECOMMENDED READING

Merton L. Dillon. *Slavery Attacked: Southern Slaves and Their Allies, 1619–1865.* Baton Rouge: Louisiana State University Press, 1990. Integrates slave resistance and revolt with the northern abolitionist movement.

Eugene D. Genovese. *From Rebellion to Revolution: Afro-American Slave Revolts in the Making of the Modern World.* Baton Rouge: Louisiana State University Press, 1979. Places the major American slave revolts and conspiracies in an Atlantic context.

Peter P. Hinks. *To Awaken My Afflicted Brethren: David Walker and the Problem of Antebellum Slave Resistance.* University Park: Pennsylvania State University Press, 1997. The most recent biography of Walker, which places him within the black abolitionist movement and attempts to clarify what little we know about his life.

Benjamin Quarles. *Black Abolitionists.* New York: Oxford University Press, 1969. A classic study that emphasizes cooperation between black and white abolitionists.

Harry Reed. *Platform for Change: The Foundations of the Northern Free Black Community, 1775–1865.* East Lansing: Michigan State University Press, 1994. An excellent study of the relationship between free black culture in the North and antislavery action.

P. J. Staudenraus. *The American Colonization Movement, 1816–1865.* New York: Columbia University Press, 1961. Although published in the 1960s, the most recent account of the American Colonization Society.

Shirley J. Yee. *Black Women Abolitionists: A Study in Activism, 1828–1860.* Knoxville: University of Tennessee Press, 1992. Concentrates on the period after 1833, but it is the best place to start reading about black abolitionist women.

ADDITIONAL BIBLIOGRAPHY

THE RELATIONSHIP AMONG EVANGELICALISM, REFORM, AND ABOLITIONISM

Robert H. Abzug. *Cosmos Crumbling: American Reform and the Religious Imagination.* New York: Oxford University Press, 1994.

Gilbert H. Barnes. *The Antislavery Impulse, 1830–1844.* 1933. Reprint, Gloucester, MA: Peter Smith, 1973.

Douglas M. Strong. *Perfectionist Politics: Abolitionism and the Religious Tensions of American Democracy.* Syracuse, NY: Syracuse University Press, 1999.

Ronald G. Walters. *American Reformers, 1815–1860.* Baltimore: Johns Hopkins University Press, 1978.

AMERICAN ABOLITIONISM BEFORE 1831

David Brion Davis. *The Problem of Slavery in the Age of Revolution.* Ithaca, NY: Cornell University Press, 1975.

———. *The Problem of Slavery in Western Culture.* Ithaca, NY: Cornell University Press, 1966.

———. *Slavery and Human Progress.* Ithaca, NY: Cornell University Press, 1987.

Merton L. Dillon. *The Abolitionists: The Growth of a Dissenting Minority.* New York: Norton, 1974.

———. *Benjamin Lundy and the Struggle for Negro Freedom.* Urbana: University of Illinois Press, 1966.

Richard S. Newman. *The Transformation of American Abolitionism: Fighting Slavery in the Early Republic.* Chapel Hill: University of North Carolina Press, 2002.

SLAVE REVOLTS AND CONSPIRACIES

Herbert Aptheker. *American Negro Slave Revolts.* 1943; new ed., New York: International Publishers, 1974.

1815

AFRICAN-AMERICAN EVENTS	NATIONAL EVENTS
1815 Paul Cuffe leads African Americans to Sierra Leone	**1815** War of 1812 ends
1816 American Colonization Society is formed	**1816** James Madison elected U.S. president

1820

1822 Denmark Vesey's conspiracy is exposed	**1820** Missouri Compromise passed
1824 Benjamin Lundy comes to Baltimore	**1824** John Quincy Adams is elected U.S. president

1825

1827 *Freedom's Journal* begins publication	**1828** Andrew Jackson is elected U.S. president
1829 William Lloyd Garrison comes to Baltimore; David Walker's *Appeal*	

1830

1831 Nat Turner's Revolt is suppressed	**1830** Indian Removal Act passed by Congress
	1832 Great increase in migration to United States begins

1835

THE RADICAL TURN IN THE ABOLITION MOVEMENT

JULY 1829	William Lloyd Garrison joins Benjamin Lundy in Baltimore as associate editor of the *Genius of Universal Emancipation*.
SEPTEMBER 1829	David Walker's *Appeal* is published in Boston and then circulated in the South.
NOVEMBER 1829	William Watkins's anticolonization letters first appear in the *Genius*.
JUNE 1830	Garrison is sentenced to jail in Baltimore for libeling a slave trader.
AUGUST 1830	Walker dies of tuberculosis in Boston.
JANUARY 1831	Garrison begins publication of *The Liberator* in Boston.
AUGUST 1831	Nat Turner's revolt occurs.

1829–1831

Douglas R. Egerton. *Gabriel's Rebellion: The Virginia Slave Conspiracies of 1800 & 1802.* Chapel Hill: University of North Carolina Press, 1993.

———. *He Shall Go Out Free: The Lives of Denmark Vesey.* Madison, WI: Madison House, 1999.

David P. Feggus, ed. *The Impact of the Haitian Revolution on the Atlantic World.* Columbia: University of South Carolina Press, 2001.

Alfred N. Hunt. *Haiti's Influence on Antebellum America: Slumbering Volcano in the Caribbean.* Baton Rouge: Louisiana State University Press, 1988.

John Lofton. *Denmark Vesey's Revolt: The Slave Plot That Lit a Fuse to Fort Sumter.* Kent, OH: Kent State University Press, 1983.

Stephen B. Oates. *The Fires of the Jubilee: Nat Turner's Fierce Rebellion.* New York: Harper & Row, 1975.

BLACK ABOLITIONISM AND BLACK NATIONALISM

Rodney Carlisle. *The Roots of Black Nationalism.* Port Washington, NY: Kennikat, 1975.

Eddie S. Glaude. *Exodus!: Religion, Race, and Nation in Early Nineteenth-Century Black America.* Chicago: University of Chicago Press, 2000.

Leroy Graham. *Baltimore: Nineteenth-Century Black Capital.* Washington, DC: University Press of America, 1982.

Vincent Harding. *There Is a River: The Black Struggle for Freedom in America.* New York: Harcourt, Brace, Jovanovich, 1981.

Floyd J. Miller. *The Search for Black Nationality: Black Colonization and Emigration, 1787–1863.* Urbana: University of Illinois Press, 1975.

Marilyn Richardson. *Maria W. Stewart: America's First Black Woman Political Writer.* Bloomington: Indiana University Press, 1987.

Sterling Stuckey. *Slave Culture: Nationalist Theory and the Foundations of Black America.* New York: Oxford University Press, 1987.

Lamont D. Thomas. *Rise to Be a People: A Biography of Paul Cuffe.* Urbana: University of Illinois Press, 1986.

Julie Winch. *Philadelphia's Black Elite: Activism, Accommodation, and Struggle for Autonomy, 1787–1840.* Philadelphia: Temple University Press, 1988.

RETRACING THE ODYSSEY

National Afro-American Museum and Cultural Center, Wilberforce, Ohio. Exhibits on African-American history include the antislavery struggle.

Oberlin College, Oberlin, Ohio. Oberlin, one of the first racially integrated and coeducational institutions of higher learning in the United States, was an antislavery and underground railroad center. The college maintains a collection of antislavery publications.

The Amistad Research Center, Tulane University, New Orleans. This institution maintains the archives of the American Missionary Association, the largest American antislavery organization of the 1840s and 1850s.

PRENTICE HALL **myhistorylab** — REVIEW, RESEARCH, AND INTERACT
Where it's a good time to connect to the past!

REVIEW QUESTIONS

1. What did the program of the ACS mean for African Americans? How did they respond to this program?

2. Analyze the role abolitionism played (1) by Christianity and (2) by the revolutionary tradition in the Atlantic world. Which was more important in shaping the views of black and white abolitionists?

3. Evaluate the interaction of black and white abolitionists during the early nineteenth century. How did their motives for becoming abolitionists differ?

4. How did Gabriel, Denmark Vesey, and Nat Turner influence the northern abolitionist movement?

5. What risks did Maria W. Stewart take when she called publicly for antislavery action?

www.researchnavigator.com

Using the tools available in Research Navigator, consider these questions:

What forces and events fueled the antislavery movement? What role did antislavery advocates see free blacks playing in America after slavery was abolished?

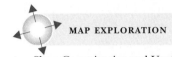

PRIMARY SOURCE DOCUMENTS

MAP EXPLORATION

Let Your Motto Be Resistance

HOW DID THE RACISM AND VIOLENCE
OF THE 1830s AND 1840s AFFECT
THE ANTISLAVERY MOVEMENT?

WHAT ROLES DID BLACK INSTITUTIONS
AND MORAL SUASION PLAY IN
THE ANTISLAVERY MOVEMENT?

HOW DID ABOLITIONISM BECOME
MORE AGGRESSIVE DURING
THE 1840s AND 1850s?

HOW DID THE VIEWS OF
FREDERICK DOUGLASS DIFFER FROM
THOSE OF HENRY HIGHLAND GARNET?

1833–1850

 In this 1867 oil painting by Theo Kaufman, a group of
women and children prepare to ford a river as they escape
from slavery. Most escapees were young men, but people of
both sexes and all age groups undertook to reach freedom in
the North or Canada. The Metropolitan Museum of Art. Gift of Erving and Joyce
Wolf, 1982/95 (1982. 443.3); Copyright © 1982 The Metropolitan Museum of Art

It is in your power to torment the God-cursed slaveholders, that they would be glad to let you go free. . . . But you are a patient people. You act as though you were made for the special use of these devils. You act as though your daughters were born to pamper the lusts of your masters and overseers. And worse than all, you tamely submit, while your lords tear your wives from your embraces, and defile them before your eyes. In the name of God we ask, are you men? . . . Heaven, as with a voice of thunder, calls on you to arise from the dust. Let your motto be RESISTANCE! RESISTANCE! RESISTANCE! No oppressed people have ever secured their Liberty without resistance.

Henry Highland Garnet, "Address to the Slaves of the United States of America"

▼ **Entitled "A Bold Stroke for Freedom,"** This illustration from William Stills, *The Underground Railroad*, depicts fugitive slaves aiming guns at slave catchers in an attempt to preserve their freedom.

When black abolitionist Henry Highland Garnet spoke these words at the National Convention of Colored Citizens, held in Buffalo, New York, on August 16, 1843, he caused a tremendous stir among those assembled. Garnet had escaped with his family from slavery in Maryland in 1824 when he was a boy. He had received an excellent education while growing up in New York and became a powerful speaker. But some of the delegates pointed out that he was far away from the slaves he claimed to address. Others believed he had called for a potentially disastrous slave revolt, and, by a narrow margin, the convention refused to endorse his speech.

Yet, in the speech, Garnet also rhetorically advised slaves, "We do not advise you to attempt a revolution with the sword, because it would be INEXPEDIENT. Your numbers are too small, and moreover the rising spirit of the age, and the spirit of the gospel, are opposed to war and bloodshed." Rather than a bloody revolt like Nat Turner's, Garnet advocated a general strike among slaves. This, he contended, would put the onus of initiating violence on the masters. Nevertheless Garnet's speech reflected a growing militancy among black and white abolitionists that shaped the antislavery movement during the two decades before the Civil War.

In this chapter we investigate the causes of that militancy and explore the role of African Americans in the antislavery movement from the establishment of the American Anti-Slavery Society in 1833 to the **Compromise of 1850.** Largely in response to changes in American culture, unrest among slaves, and sectional conflict between North and South, the biracial northern antislavery movement during this period became splintered and diverse, but also more powerful.

A Rising Tide of Racism and Violence

The growing militancy among abolitionists occurred within a context of increasing racism and violence in the United States, lasting from the 1830s through the Civil War. Garnet spoke correctly about the spirit of the gospel, but not about the spirit of his times. By the 1840s white Americans had embraced an exuberant nationalism called **Manifest Destiny** that defined political and economic progress in racial terms and legitimized war to expand the boundaries of the United States.

During this same period, American ethnologists—scientists who studied racial diversity—rejected the eighteenth-century idea that the physical and mental characteristics of the world's peoples are the product of environment. Instead, they argued that what they perceived to be racial differences are intrinsic and permanent. White people—particularly white Americans—they maintained, were a superior race culturally, physically, economically, politically, and intellectually.

This theory provided white Americans with an apparently scientific justification for the continued enslavement of African Americans and extermination of American Indians, because they deemed these groups to be inferior. Prejudice against European immigrants to the United States also increased. By the late 1840s, a movement known as *nativism* pitted native-born Protestants against foreign-born Roman Catholics, whom the natives saw as competitors for jobs and as culturally subversive.

A wave of racially motivated violence, committed by the federal and state governments as well as white vigilantes, accompanied these broad intellectual and cultural developments. Starting in the 1790s, the U.S. Army waged a systematic campaign to remove American Indians from the states and relocate them west of the Mississippi. This campaign culminated in 1838 in the Trail of Tears, when the army forced 16,000 Cherokees from Georgia to what is now Oklahoma. Many Cherokees died along the way. During the same decade, antiblack riots became common in urban America. From 1829 until the Civil War, white mobs led by "gentlemen of property and standing" attacked abolitionist newspaper presses and wreaked havoc in African-American neighborhoods.

ANTIBLACK AND ANTIABOLITIONIST RIOTS

Antiblack urban riots predated the start of immediate abolitionism during the late 1820s. But such riots became more common as abolitionism gained strength during the 1830s and 1840s (see Figure 9–1 and Map 9–1). Although few northern cities escaped racist mob attacks on African Americans and their property, riots in Cincinnati, Providence, New York City, and Philadelphia were infamous.

In 1829 a three-day riot instigated by local politicians led many black people in Cincinnati to flee to Canada. In 1836 and 1841 mob attacks on the *Philanthropist*, Cincinnati's white-run abolitionist newspaper, expanded into attacks on African-American homes and businesses. During each riot, black residents defended their property with guns. In 1831 white sailors led a mob in Providence that literally tore that city's black neighborhood to pieces. With spectators cheering them on, rioters first pulled down the chim-

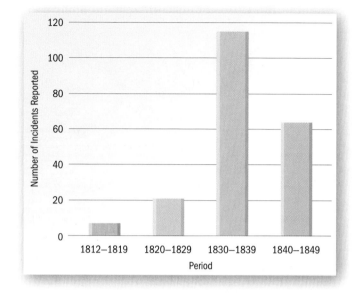

FIGURE 9–1   MOB VIOLENCE IN THE UNITED STATES, 1812–1849

This graph illustrates the rise of mob violence in the North in reaction to abolitionist activity. Attacks on abolitionists peaked during the 1830s and then declined as antislavery sentiment spread in the North.

neys of black residences and then "with a fire hook and plenty of axes and iron bars" tore down the buildings and dragged the occupants into the streets. The Rhode Island militia finally had to stop the mayhem.

In New York City in 1834, a mob destroyed twelve houses owned by black residents, a black church, a black school, and the home of white abolitionist Lewis Tappan. But no city had worse race riots than Philadelphia—the City of Brotherly Love. In 1820, 1829, 1834, 1835, 1838, 1842, and 1849, antiblack riots broke out there. In 1838 a white mob in Philadelphia burned Pennsylvania Hall, which abolitionists had just built and dedicated to free discussion. But the ugliest riot came in 1842 when Irish immigrants led a mob that assaulted members of a black temperance society, who were commemorating the abolition of slavery in the British colony of Jamaica. When African Americans defended themselves with muskets, the mob looted and burned Philadelphia's principal black neighborhood. Among those who successfully defended their homes was Robert Purvis, the abolitionist son-in-law of James Forten.

Angelina Grimké

TEXAS AND THE WAR AGAINST MEXICO

Not only northern cities experienced violence. Under President James K. Polk, the United States adopted a belligerent foreign policy, culminating in a war against the Republic of Mexico, which lasted from 1846 to

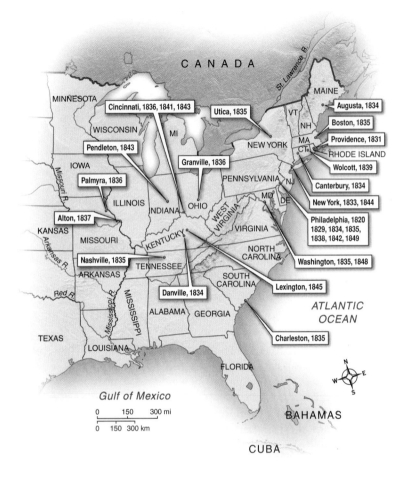

MAP 9–1 ANTIABOLITIONIST AND ANTIBLACK RIOTS DURING THE ANTEBELLUM PERIOD

African Americans faced violent conditions in both the North and South during the antebellum years. Fear among whites of growing free black communities and white antipathy toward spreading abolitionism sparked numerous antiblack and antiabolitionist riots.

▶ *Why did most of these riots occur in the Northeast?*

1848. Mexico had gained its independence from Spain in 1822 and in 1829 had abolished slavery within its borders. Meanwhile slaveholding Americans had begun settling in Texas, which was then part of Mexico, as was the gigantic region then known as California and New Mexico (and now comprising the states of California, Arizona, New Mexico, Utah, and part of Colorado). In 1836 Texas won independence from Mexico, and—as an independent slaveholding republic—applied for annexation to the United States as a slave state. Democratic and Whig Party leaders, who realized that adding a large new slave state to the

Union would divide the country along North–South sectional lines, rebuffed the application. But the desire for new territory encouraged by Manifest Destiny and an expanding slave-labor economy could not be denied. In 1844 Polk, the Democratic presidential candidate, called for the annexation of Texas and Oregon, a huge territory in the Pacific Northwest that the United States and Great Britain had been jointly administering. When Polk defeated the Whig candidate Henry Clay, who favored delaying annexation, Congress in early 1845 annexed Texas by joint resolution. This vastly expanded the area within the United States open to slavery.

In early 1846 Polk backed away from a confrontation with Great Britain over Oregon. A few months later, he provoked the war against Mexico that by 1848 forced that country to recognize American sovereignty over Texas and to cede New Mexico and California (see Map 10–1 on page 239). Immediately, the question of whether slavery would expand into these southwestern territories became a burning issue. Many white northerners assumed that slaveholders, by creating slave states out of the new territories, would dominate the federal government and enact policies detrimental to white workers and farmers.

As these sentiments spread across the North, slaveholders became fearful they would be excluded from the western lands they had helped wrest from Mexico. The resulting Compromise of 1850 (see Chapter 10) attempted to satisfy both sections. But it subjected African Americans to additional violence because part of the Compromise met slaveholders' demands for a stronger fugitive slave law. This law made it easier for masters to recapture bondpeople who had escaped to the North. It also led to an increase in attempts to kidnap free black northerners into slavery.

The Response of the Antislavery Movement

This rising tide of race-related violence caused difficulties for an antislavery movement that experienced internal racial strife and officially limited itself to peaceful means against slavery. African Americans found their most loyal white allies within the antislavery movement. But interracial understanding did not come easily. White abolitionists assumed they should set policy for their black collaborators, who became more resentful of this presumption as the 1840s progressed. Meanwhile abolitionist commitment to nonviolence weakened. It had arisen as a principled rejection of the violence that pervaded America and as a shrewd response to proslavery charges that abolitionists caused unrest among slaves. But nonviolence seemed to limit abolitionist options in an increasingly violent environment. Whether to seek greater autonomy for black abolitionists and whether to endorse violent means became contentious issues within the antislavery movement during the 1840s.

THE AMERICAN ANTI-SLAVERY SOCIETY

Well before the era of Manifest Destiny, the American Anti-Slavery Society (AASS)—the most significant abolitionist organization—emerged from a major turning point in the abolitionist cause. This was William Lloyd Garrison's decision in 1831 to create a movement dedicated to immediate, uncompensated emancipation and to equal rights for African Americans in the United States. To reach these goals, abolitionists led by Garrison organized the AASS in December 1833 at Philadelphia's Adelphi Hall. Well aware of the fears raised by Nat Turner's revolt, those assembled declared, "The society will never, in any way, countenance the oppressed in vindicating their rights by resorting to physical force."

 DOCUMENT 9-1 *American Antislavery Society Declares Its Sentiments*

No white American worked harder than Garrison to bridge racial differences. He spoke to black groups, stayed in the homes of African Americans when he traveled, and welcomed them to his home. Black abolitionists responded with affection and loyalty. They provided financial support for his newspaper, *The Liberator*, worked as subscription agents, paid for his speaking tour in England in 1833, and served as his bodyguards. But Garrison, like most other white abolitionists, remained stiff and condescending in conversation with his black colleagues, and the black experience in the AASS reflected this.

On one hand, it is remarkable that the AASS allowed black men to participate in its meetings without formal restrictions. At the time, no other American organization did so. On the other hand, that black participation was paltry. Three African Americans—James McCrummell, Robert Purvis, and James G. Barbadoes—helped found the AASS, and McCrummell presided at its first meeting. But, among sixty white people attending that meeting, these three were the only African Americans. Although three white women participated in the meeting, no black women did so. Throughout the history of the AASS, black people rarely held positions of authority.

As state and local auxiliaries of the AASS organized across the North during the early 1830s, these patterns affecting black men and women generally repeated themselves. Black men participated but did not lead, although a few held prominent offices. Among them were Barbadoes and Joshua Easton, who in 1834 joined the board of directors of the Massachusetts Anti-Slavery Society. Also, in 1837 seven black men, including James Forten, helped organize the Pennsylvania Anti-Slavery Society. Meanwhile black and white women—with some exceptions—could observe but not participate in the proceedings of these organizations. It took a three-year struggle between 1837 and 1840 over "the woman question" before an AASS annual meeting elected a woman to a leadership position, and that victory helped split the organization.

BLACK AND WOMEN'S ANTISLAVERY SOCIETIES

In these circumstances, black male, black female, and white female abolitionists formed their own auxiliaries to the AASS. Often African Americans belonged to all-black *and* to integrated, predominantly white organizations. Black men's auxiliaries to the AASS formed across the North during the mid-1830s. As we saw in Chapter 8, the earliest black women's abolitionist organization organized in Salem, Massachusetts, in 1832, a year before the AASS came into being.

The black organizations arose because of racial discord in the predominantly white organizations and because of a black desire for racial solidarity. But historian Benjamin Quarles makes an essential point when he writes that during the 1830s "the founders of Negro societies did not envision their efforts as distinctive or self-contained; rather they viewed their role as that of a true auxiliary—supportive, supplemental, and subsidiary." Despite their differences, black and white abolitionists were still members of a single movement.

Although racially integrated women's antislavery societies did not entirely overcome the racism of their time, they elevated more African Americans to prominent positions than did men's societies. Black abolitionist Susan Paul became a member of the board of the Boston Female Anti-Slavery Society when it organized in 1833. Later that year, Margaretta Forten became recording secretary of the Female Anti-Slavery Society of Philadelphia, founded by white Quaker abolitionist Lucretia Mott. In May 1837 black Quaker Sarah M. Douglass of Philadelphia and Sarah Forten—Margaretta's sister—served as delegates to the First Anti-Slavery Convention of American Women in New York City. At the second convention, Susan Paul became a vice president, and Douglass became treasurer.

The main task of all the women's antislavery societies was fund-raising. They held bake sales, organized antislavery fairs and bazaars, and sold antislavery memorabilia. The proceeds went to the AASS or to antislavery newspapers. But the separate women's societies also inspired the birth of feminism by creating an awareness that women had rights and interests that a male-dominated society had to recognize. By writing essays and poems on political subjects and making public speeches, black and white abolitionist women challenged a culture that relegated *respectable* women to domestic duties. During the 1850s famous African-American speaker Sojourner Truth emphasized that all black women through their physical labor and the pain they suffered in slavery had earned equal standing with men and their more favored white sisters.

Garnet's "Call to Rebellion" **9-4** DOCUMENT

PROFILE ~ HENRY HIGHLAND GARNET

Henry Highland Garnet rivaled Frederick Douglass as a black leader during the antebellum decades. While Douglass emphasized assimilation, Garnet emerged as an advocate of black nationalism. The two men had much in common, however, and by the time of the Civil War were almost indistinguishable in their views.

In 1824, when Garnet was nine, his family struck out from a Maryland plantation for freedom in the North. His father led the family to New York City, where Garnet enrolled in the Free African School. Influenced by his father's pride in African heritage, by vigilance against slave catchers, and by a youthful lameness that led to the amputation of one of his legs in 1840, Garnet brought a profound determination to all that he undertook. In 1835 Garnet was among twelve black students admitted to Noyes Academy at Canaan, New Hampshire. When shortly thereafter local farmers reacted by tearing down the school buildings, Garnet defended his black classmates with a shotgun. The following year he enrolled at Oneida Theological Institute located near Utica, New York. There, guided by white abolitionist Beriah Green, Garnet prepared for the Presbyterian ministry. In 1842 he became pastor of the black Presbyterian church in Troy, New York.

By that time, he had been an active abolitionist for several years. He worked closely with Gerrit Smith's radical New York wing of the Liberty Party. He also became a strong advocate of independent antislavery action among African Americans. Referring to white abolitionists, he said, "They are our allies—*Ours* is the battle." But it was within the context of the New York Liberty Party's determination to challenge slavery on its own ground that Garnet delivered his famous "Address to the Slaves" at the 1843 National Convention of Colored Citizens. By demanding what amounted to a general strike by slaves and acknowledging that violence could result, Garnet highlighted his differences with Frederick Douglass and other African Americans who remained dedicated to nonviolence.

It was Garnet's conviction that African Americans ultimately must free themselves that led him to promote migration to Africa. He always maintained that the ACS was proslavery and racist, but by 1848 he had come to believe that African colonization could become a powerful adjunct to the struggle for emancipation in the United States. Garnet's years abroad during the early 1850s strengthened him in this outlook. He served as a delegate to the World Peace Conference in Frankfurt, Germany, in 1850, spent 1851 in Great Britain, and lived in Jamaica from 1853 to 1856 as a Presbyterian missionary. Garnet returned to the United States in 1856 and in 1858 organized the African Civilization Society designed to build a strong, independent Africa through black emigration from America and the cultivation of cotton. But Garnet's views remained very much in the minority among African-American leaders, and the Civil War effectively ended his nationalist efforts.

During the war, Garnet was an early advocate of enlisting black troops in the Union armies. In 1863 he became pastor of the 15th Street Presbyterian Church in Washington, D.C., and in 1865 became the first African American to deliver a sermon in Congress. Like Douglass a staunch Republican during the postwar years, Garnet in January 1882 became the U.S. ambassador to Liberia and died there a month later.

Garnet

Wealthy black abolitionist Robert Purvis is at the very center of this undated photograph of the Philadelphia Anti-Slavery Society. The famous Quaker abolitionist Lucretia Mott and her husband James Mott are seated to Purvis's left. As significant as Purvis's central location in the photograph, is that he is the *only* African American pictured.

Black men and women also formed auxiliaries during the early 1830s to the Quaker-initiated Free Produce Association, which tried to put economic pressure on slaveholders by boycotting agricultural products produced by slaves. James Cornish led the Colored Free Produce Society of Pennsylvania, which marketed meat, vegetables, cotton, and sugar produced by free labor. With a similar aim, Judith James and Laetitia Rowley organized the Colored Female Free Produce Society of Pennsylvania. Other black affiliates to the Free Produce Association existed in New York and Ohio, and black abolitionist William Whipper operated a free produce store in Philadelphia in 1834. During the 1850s Frances Ellen Watkins Harper, one of the few prominent black female speakers of the time, always included the free produce movement in her abolitionist lectures and wrote newspaper articles on its behalf.

THE BLACK CONVENTION MOVEMENT

The dozens of local, state, and national black conventions held in the North between 1830 and 1864 were further removed from the AASS. They were a black manifestation of the antebellum American reform impulse, and their agenda transcended the antislavery cause. They, nevertheless, provided a forum for the more prominent black abolitionist men, such as Garnet, Frederick Douglass, and, later, Martin R. Delany. They also provided a setting in which abolitionism could grow and change its tactics to meet the demands of a sectionally polarized and violent time.

Hezekiah Grice, a young black man who had worked with Benjamin Lundy and William Lloyd Garrison in Baltimore during the 1820s, organized the first Black National Convention. It met on September 24, 1830, at the Bethel Church in Philadelphia with the venerable churchman Richard Allen presiding. The national convention became an annual event for the next five years, with all but one held in Philadelphia. Meanwhile, many state and local black conventions met across the North. By current standards, these conventions were small and informal—particularly those at the local level—and had no strict guidelines for choosing delegates. These characteristics, however, did not prevent the conventions from becoming effective forums for black concerns. They invariably called for the abolition of slavery and for improving the conditions of northern African Americans. Among other reforms, the conventions called for integrated public schools and the right of black men to vote, serve on juries, and testify against white people in court.

The conventions also stressed black self-help through temperance, sexual morality, education, and thrift. These causes remained important parts of the conventions' agenda throughout the antebellum years. But by the mid-1830s the national movement faltered as black abolitionists placed their hopes in the AASS.

LIVING WORDS

The Rebirth of Sojourner Truth 9

Black Community Institutions

Although the persistence of slavery and oppression helped shape the agenda of the Black Convention Movement, a maturing African-American community undergirded the movement. Free black people in the

PROFILE ❖ SOJOURNER TRUTH

Sojourner Truth does not fit easily into the history of the antislavery movement. She did not identify with a particular group of abolitionists. Instead, as her biographer Nell Irvin Painter points out, Truth served the cause by transforming herself into a symbol of the strength of all black women.

Originally named Isabella, Truth was born a slave—probably in 1797—in a Dutch-speaking area north of New York City. She had several masters, one of whom beat her brutally. Always a hard worker, she grew into a tall, muscular woman. Her voice was deep and throughout her career, enemies charged that she was really a man—despite the five children she gave birth to after her marriage in 1815.

In 1827 Truth escaped to an antislavery family who purchased her freedom. Two years later, she became a powerful revivalist preacher in New York City. Later she joined a communal religious cult, became an ardent millenarian—predicting that Judgment Day was rapidly approaching— and in 1843 took the

name Sojourner Truth. A few years later, while working at a commune in Northampton, Massachusetts, she met abolitionists Frederick Douglass and David Ruggles. This meeting led to her career as a champion of abolition and women's rights.

She lectured across the North and as far west as Kansas during the late 1840s and the 1850s. She was blunt, but eloquent, and used common sense to argue that African Americans and women deserved the same rights as white men. They did so, she insisted, because they could work as hard as white men. Truth almost always addressed white audiences and made a strong impression on them. During the Civil War, she volunteered to work among black Union troops, and President Lincoln invited her to the White House in 1864. She continued to advocate black and women's rights until her death in 1883.

Ironically, as Painter and others note, Truth probably never used the phrase "Ar'n't I a Woman?" for which she is most widely remembered. A white female journalist first attributed it to Truth years after the 1851 women's rights meeting in Akron, Ohio, at which Truth was supposed to have said it. Contemporary accounts indicate that she did not. Truth did, however, tell those assembled in Akron, "I have as much muscle as any man, and I can do as much work as any man. I have plowed and reaped and husked and chopped and mowed, and can any man do more than that?"

United States grew from 59,000 in 1790 to 319,000 in 1830. Gradual emancipation in the northern states, acts of individual manumission in the upper South, and escapes accounted for this fivefold increase. The growing free black population concentrated in such large cities as New York, Philadelphia, Baltimore, Boston, and Cincinnati. These cities had enough African Americans to provide the resources to support the churches, schools, benevolent organizations, and printing presses that created a self-conscious community. Between 1790 and 1830, this community provided the foundations for the black antislavery institutions of the decades that followed.

BLACK CHURCHES IN THE ANTISLAVERY CAUSE

Black churches were especially significant for the antislavery movement. With a few major exceptions, the leading black abolitionists were ministers. Among them were Garnet, Jehiel C. Beman, Samuel E. Cornish, Theodore S. Wright, Charles B. Ray, James W. C. Pennington, Nathaniel Paul, Alexander Crummell, Daniel A. Payne, and Samuel Ringgold Ward. Some of these men led congregations affiliated with separate African-American churches, such as the African Baptist Church or the African Methodist Episcopal (AME) Church. Others preached to black congregations affiliated with predominantly white churches. A few black ministers, such as Amos N. Freeman of Brooklyn, New York, served white antislavery congregations. These clergy used their pulpits to attack slavery, racial discrimination, proslavery white churches, and the American Colonization Society (ACS). Having covered most of these topics in a sermon to a white congregation in 1839, Daniel Payne, who had grown up free in South Carolina, declared, "Awake! AWAKE! to the battle, and hurl the hottest thunders of divine truth at the head of this cruel monster, until he shall fall to rise no more; and the groans of the enslaved are converted into the songs of the free!" Black churches also provided forums for abolitionist speakers, such as Frederick Douglass and Garrison, and meeting places for predominantly white antislavery organizations, which frequently could not meet in white churches.

BLACK NEWSPAPERS

Less influential than black churches in the antislavery movement, black newspapers still played an important role, particularly by the 1840s. Abolitionist newspapers, whether owned by black or white people, almost always faced financial difficulties. Few survived for more than a few years because *reform*, as opposed to *commercial*, newspapers were a luxury that many subscribers, black and white, could not afford. Black newspapers faced added difficulties finding readers because most African Americans were poor, and many were illiterate. Moreover, white abolitionist newspapers, such as the *Liberator*, served a black clientele. They published speeches by black abolitionists and reported black convention proceedings. Some black abolitionists argued, therefore, that a separate black press was unnecessary. An additional, self-imposed, burden was that publishers eager to get their message out almost never required subscribers to pay in advance, thereby compounding their papers' financial instability.

Nevertheless several influential black abolitionist newspapers existed between the late 1820s and the Civil War. The first black newspaper, *Freedom's Journal*, owned and edited by Samuel Cornish and John B. Russwurm, lasted only from 1827 to 1829. It showed, nevertheless, that African Americans could produce interesting and competent journalism and attract black and white subscribers. The *Journal* also established a framework for black journalism during the antebellum period by emphasizing antislavery, racial justice, and Christian and democratic values.

The most ubiquitous black journalist of the period was Philip A. Bell. Bell was either publisher or copublisher of the *New York Weekly Advocate* in 1837, the *Colored American* from 1837 to 1842, and two San Francisco newspapers, the *Pacific Appeal* and the *Elevator*, during the 1860s. But black clergyman Charles B. Ray of New York City was the real spirit behind the *Colored American*. Well aware of the need for financial success, Ray declared in 1838, "If among the few hundred thousand free colored people in the country—to say nothing of the white population from whom it ought to receive a strong support—a living patronage for the paper cannot be obtained, it will be greatly to their reproach."

Among other prominent, if short-lived, black newspapers of the 1840s and 1850s were Garnet's *United States Clarion*, published in his home city of Troy, New York; Stephen Myers's *Northern Star and Freeman's Advocate*, which was published in Albany, New York, and had many white, as well as black, subscribers; Samuel Ringgold Ward's *True American*, of Cortland, New York, which in 1850 became the *Impartial Citizen*; Martin Delany's *Mystery*, published in Pittsburgh during the 1840s; and Thomas Van Rensselaer's *Ram's Horn*, which appeared in New York City during the 1850s.

However, Frederick Douglass's *North Star* and its successor *Frederick Douglass' Paper* were the most influential black antislavery newspapers of the late 1840s and the 1850s. Heavily subsidized by Gerrit Smith, a wealthy

Frederick Douglass wrote this passage during the mid-1850s. It is from My Bondage and My Freedom, *the second of his three autobiographies. It relates with humor, not only the racial barriers that black and white abolitionists had to break, but the primitive conditions they took for granted.*

In the summer of 1843, I was traveling and lecturing in company with William A. White, Esq., through the state of Indiana. Antislavery friends were not very abundant in Indiana . . . and beds were not more plentiful than friends. . . . At the close of one of our meetings, we were invited home with a kindly-disposed old farmer, who, in the generous enthusiasm of the moment, seemed to have forgotten that he had but one spare bed, and that his guests were an ill-matched pair. . . . White is remarkably fine looking, and very evidently a born gentleman; the idea of putting us in the same bed was hardly to be tolerated; and yet there we were, and but the one bed for us, and that, by the way, was in the same room occupied by the other members of the family. . . . After witnessing the confusion as long as I liked, I relieved the kindly-disposed family by playfully saying, "Friend White, having got entirely rid of my prejudice against color, I think, as proof of it, I must allow you to sleep with me to-night." White kept up the joke, by seeming to esteem himself the favored party, and thus the difficulty was removed.

🌲 *What does this passage reveal about American life during the 1840s?*

🌲 *What does Douglass reveal about his own character?*

Source: Michael Meyer, ed., *Frederick Douglass: The Narrative and Selected Writings* (New York: Modern Library, 1984), 170–71.

white abolitionist, and attracting more white than black subscribers, Douglass's weeklies gained the support of many black abolitionist organizations. Douglass's papers were extremely well edited and attractively printed. They also employed able assistant editors, including Martin R. Delany during the late 1840s, and insightful correspondents, such as William J. Wilson of Brooklyn and James McCune Smith of New York City.

Moral Suasion

During the 1830s the AASS adopted a reform strategy based on **moral suasion**—what we would call moral *persuasion* today. This was an appeal to Americans to support abolition and racial justice on the basis of their Christian consciences and concern for their immortal souls. Slaveholding, the AASS argued, was a sin and a crime that deprived African Americans of the freedom of conscience they needed to save their souls. Slaveholding, according to the AASS, also led white masters to eternal damnation through indolence, sexual exploitation of black women, and unrestrained brutality. In addition, abolitionists argued, slavery was an inefficient labor system that enriched a few masters while impoverishing black and white southerners and hurting the entire economy of the United States.

Abolitionists, however, did not restrict themselves to criticizing white southerners. They noted that northern industries thrived by manufacturing cloth from cotton produced by slave labor. They pointed out that the U.S. government protected the interests of slaveholders in the District of Columbia, in the territories, in the interstate slave trade, and through the Fugitive Slave Act of 1793. Northerners who profited from slave labor and supported the national government with their votes and taxes, therefore, bore their share of guilt for slavery and faced divine punishment.

The AASS sought to use these arguments to convince masters to free their slaves and to persuade northerners and nonslaveholding white southerners to put moral pressure on slaveholders. To reach a southern audience, the AASS in 1835 launched the Great Postal Campaign, designed to send antislavery literature to southern post offices and individual slaveholders. At about the same time, the AASS organized a massive petitioning campaign aimed to introduce the slavery issue into Congress. Antislavery women led in circulating and signing the petitions. In 1836 over thirty thousand of the petitions reached Washington.

In the North, AASS agents gave public lectures against slavery and distributed antislavery literature. Often a pair of agents—one black and one white—traveled together on speaking tours. Ideally, the black agent would be a former slave, so he could attack the brutality and immorality of slavery from personal experience. During the early 1840s, the AASS paired fugitive slave Frederick Douglass with William A. White, a young white Harvard graduate, in a tour through Ohio and Indiana. In 1843 the Eastern New York Anti-Slavery Society paired white Baptist preacher Abel Brown with "the noble colored man," Lewis Washington. At first, all the agents were men. Later, the abolitionist organizations also employed women as agents.

The reaction to these efforts in the North and the South was not what the leaders of the AASS anticipated. As the story in the nearby *Voices* box relates, by speaking of racial justice and exemplifying interracial cooperation, the abolitionists tread new ground. In doing so, they created awkward situations that are—in retrospect—humorous. But their audiences often reacted violently. Southern postmasters burned antislavery literature when it arrived at their offices, and southern states censored the mail. Vigilantes drove off white southerners who openly advocated abolition. Black abolitionists, of course, did not attempt openly to denounce slavery while in the South.

In Congress, southern representatives and their northern allies passed the Gag Rule in 1836. It required that no petition related to slavery could be introduced in the House of Representatives. In response, the AASS sent 415,000 petitions in 1838, and Congressman John Quincy Adams (a former president) launched his long struggle against the Gag. Technically not an abolitionist, but a defender of the First Amendment right to petition Congress, Adams succeeded in having the Gag Rule repealed in 1844.

Meanwhile, in the North, mobs attacked abolitionist agents, disrupted their meetings, destroyed their newspaper presses, and burned black neighborhoods. In 1837 a proslavery mob killed Elijah P. Lovejoy, a white abolitionist newspaper editor, when he tried to defend his printing press in Alton, Illinois. On another occasion, as Douglass, White, and an older white abolitionist named George Bradburn conducted an antislavery meeting in the small town of Pendleton, Indiana, an enraged mob attempted to kill Douglass. Some of the rioters shouted, "Kill the nigger, kill the damn nigger." Douglass suffered a broken hand. A rock hit White in the head. Finally the two men escaped on foot. Years later, Douglass told White, "I shall never forget how like very brothers we were ready to dare, do, and even die for each other. . . . How I looked running you can best describe but how you looked bleeding I shall always remember."

The American and Foreign Anti-Slavery Society and the Liberty Party

In 1840 the AASS splintered. Most of its members left to establish the **American and Foreign Anti-Slavery Society** (AFASS) and the **Liberty Party,** the first antislavery political party. On the surface, the AASS broke apart over long-standing disagreements about the role of women in abolitionism and William Lloyd Garrison's broadening radicalism. By denouncing most organized religion, by becoming a feminist, and by embracing a form of Christian anarchy that precluded formal involvement in politics, Garrison seemed to many to be losing sight of the AASS's main concern. But the failure of moral suasion to make progress against slavery—particularly in the South—and the question of how abolitionists should respond to increasing signs of slave unrest also helped fracture the AASS.

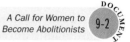

A Call for Women to Become Abolitionists 9-2

Garrison and a minority of abolitionists, who agreed with his radical critique of American society and were centered in New England, retained control of what became known as the "Old Organization." By 1842 they had de-emphasized moral suasion and had begun calling for disunion—the separation of the North from the South—as the only means of ending northern support for slavery. The U.S. Constitution, Garrison declared, was a thoroughly proslavery document that had to be destroyed before African Americans could gain their freedom.

Those who withdrew from the AASS took a more traditional stand on the role of women, believed the country's churches could be converted to abolitionism, and asserted that the Constitution could be used in behalf of abolitionism. Under the leadership of Lewis Tappan, a wealthy white New York City abolitionist, some of them formed the church-oriented AFASS. Others created the Liberty Party and nominated James G. Birney, a slaveholder-turned-abolitionist, as their candidate in the 1840 presidential election. Birney received only 7,069 votes out of a total cast of 2,411,187, and William Henry Harrison, the Whig candidate, became president. But the Liberty Party constituted the beginning of an increasingly powerful political crusade against slavery.

Black abolitionists joined in the disruption of the Old Organization. Only in New England did most black abolitionists remain loyal to the AASS. Among them were Frederick Douglass, William Wells Brown, Robert Purvis, Charles L. Remond, Susan Paul, and Sarah Douglass. As might be expected, most black clerical abolitionists joined the AFASS. Eight, including Jehiel C. Beman and his son Amos G. Beman, Christopher Rush, Samuel E. Cornish, Theodore S. Wright, Stephen H. Gloucester, Andrew Harris, and Garnet helped create the new organization. After 1840 African Americans were always more prominent as leaders in the AFASS than the AASS.

The Liberty Party also attracted black support, although few black men could vote. Particularly appealing to black abolitionists was the platform of the radical New York wing of the party led by Gerrit Smith. Philip A. Bell, Charles B. Ray, Samuel E. Cornish, Jermain Wesley Loguen, and Garnet endorsed the New

York Liberty Party and influenced its program. Of all the antislavery organizations, it advocated the most aggressive action against slavery in the South and became most directly involved in helping slaves escape.

A More Aggressive Abolitionism

The New York Liberty Party maintained that the U.S. Constitution, interpreted in the light of the Bible and natural law, outlawed slavery throughout the country—not only in the District of Columbia and in the territories, which were governed by the federal government, but in the states as well. This, the party's leaders asserted, meant Congress could abolish slavery in the southern states. More practically it meant that for slaves to escape and for others to help them escape were perfectly legal actions. They maintained that neither northern state militia nor the U.S. Army should help suppress slave revolts.

This body of thought, which dated to the late 1830s, supported growing northern abolitionist empathy with the slaves as they struggled for freedom against their masters. While the AASS disintegrated, escapes and minor rebellions proliferated in the border slave states of Maryland, Virginia, Kentucky, and Missouri as enslaved black people reacted to worsening conditions. Throughout this region the domestic slave trade threatened to tear black families apart, as the trade sent African Americans into the newly opened cotton-producing areas of the Southwest. In response, the radical wing of the Liberty Party cited the Constitution in support of slave resistance to this brutal traffic. It also encouraged black and white northerners to go south to help slaves escape.

THE *AMISTAD* AND THE *CREOLE*

Two maritime slave revolts encouraged rising militancy among northern abolitionists. The first of these revolts, however, did not involve enslaved Americans. In June 1839 fifty-four African captives aboard the Spanish schooner **Amistad,** meaning "friendship," successfully rebelled under the leadership of Joseph Cinque and attempted to sail to Africa. When a U.S. warship captured the *Amistad* off the coast of Long Island, New York, the Africans attracted the support of Lewis Tappan and other abolitionists. As a result of the abolitionists' efforts and arguments presented by Congressman Adams, the U.S. Supreme Court ruled in November 1841 that Cinque and the others were free.

Later that same month, Madison Washington led a revolt aboard the brig **Creole,** which was transporting 135 American slaves from Richmond, Virginia, to the

An increase in slave escapes helped inspire the more aggressive abolitionist tactics of the 1840s and 1850s. In this 1845 cover illustration for sheet music composed by white antislavery minstrel Jesse Hutchinson Jr., Frederick Douglass is shown in an idealized rendition of his escape from slavery in Maryland.

slave markets of New Orleans. Washington had earlier escaped to Canada from slavery in Virginia. When he returned to rescue his wife, he was captured, reenslaved, and shipped aboard the *Creole.* Once at sea, Washington and about a dozen other black men seized control of the vessel and sailed it to the Bahamas (a British colony). There local black fishermen surrounded the *Creole* with their boats to protect it, and most of the people on board immediately gained their freedom under British law. A few days later, so did Washington and the other rebels. Although Washington soon vanished, the *Creole* revolt made him a hero among abolitionists and a symbol of black bravery.

Cinque and Washington inspired others to risk their lives and freedom to help African Americans escape bondage. The New York Liberty Party reinforced this commitment by declaring that what they had done was divinely ordained and strictly legal.

THE UNDERGROUND RAILROAD

The famous **underground railroad** must be placed within the context of increasing southern white violence against black families, slave resistance, and aggressive northern abolitionism. Because the underground railroad had to be secret, few details of how it operated are known. We do not even know the origin of the term *underground railroad*. Slaves had always escaped from their masters, and free black people and some white people had always assisted them. But the organized escape of slaves from the Chesapeake, Kentucky, and Missouri along predetermined routes to Canada became much more common after the mid-1830s. A united national underground railroad with a president or unified command never existed. Instead there were different organizations separated in time and space from one another (see Map 9–2). Even during the 1840s and 1850s, most of the slaves who escaped did so on their own. Sometimes they had to fight pursuing masters.

The best documented underground railroad organizations centered in Washington, D.C., and Ripley, Ohio. In Washington Charles T. Torrey, a white Liberty Party abolitionist from Albany, New York, and Thomas Smallwood, a free black resident of Washington, began in 1842 to help slaves escape along a predetermined northward route. Between March and November of that year, they sent at least 150 enslaved men, women, and children to Philadelphia. From there, a local black vigilance committee provided the fugitives with transportation to Albany, New York, where a local, predominantly white, vigilance group smuggled them to Canada. In southern Ohio some residents, black and white, had since the 1810s helped fugitive slaves as they headed north from the slaveholding state of Kentucky. The best known of these early underground railroad operatives was John Rankin, a white Presbyterian minister who lit a lantern each night at his Ripley, Ohio, home, which sat on a hill above the north shore of the Ohio River, to serve as a beacon for escaping slaves. From the late 1840s into the Civil War years, former slave John P. Parker made the Ripley-based underground railroad more aggressive. With Rankin's support, Parker, who had purchased his freedom in 1845, repeatedly went into Kentucky to lead others to freedom.

The escapees, however, were by no means passive "passengers" in the underground railroad network. They raised money to pay for their transportation northward, recruited and helped other escapees, and

Mutiny, **painted by Hale Woodruff** in 1939, provides a dramatic and stylized portrayal of the successful uprising of African slaves on board the Spanish schooner *Amistad* in 1839. Savery Library Archives, Talladega College, Talledega, Alabama.

sometimes became underground railroad agents themselves. During the mid-1850s, Arrah Weems of Rockville, Maryland, whose freedom black and white abolitionists had recently purchased and whose daughter Ann Maria had been rescued by underground railroad agents, became an agent. She brought an enslaved infant from Washington through Philadelphia to Rochester, New York, where she met Frederick Douglass.

This was not an easy journey, and the underground railroad was always a risky business. In 1843 Smallwood had to flee to Canada as Washington police closed in on his home. In 1846 Torrey died of tuberculosis in a Maryland prison while serving a six-year sentence for helping slaves escape. Parker recalled "real warfare" in southern Ohio between underground railroad operators and slaveholders from Kentucky. "I never thought of going uptown without a pistol in my pocket, a knife in my belt, and a blackjack handy," he later recalled.

During the early 1850s, Harriet Tubman, a fugitive slave, became the most active worker on the eastern branch of the underground railroad. She was born in 1820 on a Maryland plantation, and for years her master abused her. She did not escape, however, until in 1849 he threatened to sell her and her family south. After her escape, Tubman returned about thirteen times to Maryland to help others flee. She had the help of Thomas Garrett, a white Quaker abolitionist who lived in Wilmington, Delaware, and William Still, the black leader of the Philadelphia Vigilance Association. Still, who as a child had been a fugitive slave, coordinated the work of many black and white underground agents between Washington and Canada during the 1850s.

MAP EXPLORATION

To explore this interactive map, go to
www.prenhall.com/hine4/map9.2

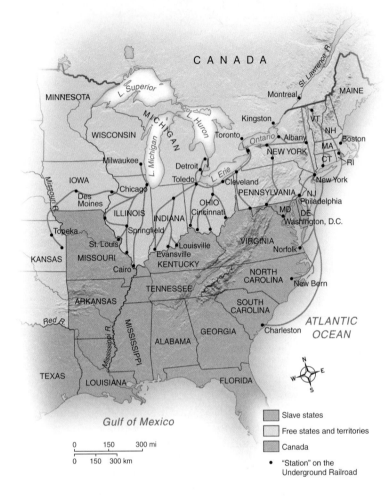

MAP 9–2   THE UNDERGROUND RAILROAD
This maps illustrates *approximate* routes traveled by escaping slaves through the North to Canada. Although some slaves escaped from the deep South, most who utilized the underground railroad network came from the border slave states.

▶ *By what means did escaping slaves travel the routes shown on this map?*

CANADA WEST

The ultimate destination for many African Americans on the underground railroad was Canada West—present-day Ontario—between Buffalo and Detroit on the northern shore of Lake Erie. Black Americans began to settle in Canada West as early as the 1820s and, because slavery was illegal in the

British empire after 1833, fugitive slaves were safe there. The stronger fugitive slave law that Congress passed as part of the Compromise of 1850 (see Chapter 10) made Canada an even more important refuge for African Americans. Between 1850 and 1860, the number of black people in Canada West rose from approximately 8,000 to at least 20,000.

There were several communal black settlements in Canada West, including the Refugee Home Society, the Buxton Community at Elgin, and the Dawn Settlement. But most black immigrants lived and worked in Toronto and Chatham. Most of them worked as craftsmen and laborers, although a few became entrepreneurs or professionals.

The chief advocate of black migration to Canada West—and the only advocate of migration who also supported racial integration—was Mary Ann Shadd Cary. Between 1854 and 1858 she edited the *Provincial Freeman*, an abolitionist paper published in Toronto, and lectured in northern cities promoting emigration to Canada. Yet, although African Americans enjoyed security in Canada, by the 1850s they also faced the same sort of segregation and discrimination that existed in the northern United States.

Black Militancy

During the 1840s growing numbers of black abolitionists advocated forceful action against slavery. This resolve accompanied a trend to create separate black antislavery organizations. The black convention movement revived during the 1840s, and there were well-attended meetings in Buffalo in 1843 (where Garnet presented his "Address to the Slaves"), in Troy, New York, in 1844, and in Cleveland in 1848. Meanwhile more newspapers owned and edited by black abolitionists appeared.

The rise in black militancy had several causes. The breakup of the AASS weakened abolitionist loyalty to the national antislavery organizations. All abolitionists, black and white, explored new types of antislavery action. Many black abolitionists became convinced that most white abolitionists enjoyed debate and theory more than action against slavery.

Influenced by the examples of Cinque, Madison Washington, and other rebellious slaves, many black abolitionists during the 1840s and 1850s wanted to do more to encourage slaves to resist and escape. This militancy inspired Garnet's "Address to the Slaves." A willingness to act rather than just talk helped make the Liberty Party—especially its radical New York wing—attractive to African Americans. However, black abolitionists, like white abolitionists, approached violence and slave rebel-

Harriet Tubman, standing at the left, is shown in this undated photograph with a group of people she helped escape from slavery. Because she worked in secret during the 1850s, she was known only to others engaged in the underground railroad, the people she helped, and a few other abolitionists.

lion with caution. As late as 1857, Garnet and Frederick Douglass described slave revolt as "inexpedient."

The black abolitionist desire to go beyond rhetoric found its best outlet in the local vigilance organizations. The most famous of these is William Still's Philadelphia Vigilance Association, which operated during the late 1840s and 1850s. Such associations appeared during the mid-1830s and often had white as well as black members. As the 1840s progressed, African Americans formed more of them and led those that already existed. In this they were reacting to a facet of the growing violence in the United States—the use of force by "slave catchers" in northern cities to recapture fugitive slaves.

Black militancy also included a willingness to charge publicly that white abolitionists did not live up to their words in favor of racial justice. Economic slights rankled African Americans the most. At the annual meeting of the AFASS in 1852, a black delegate demanded to know why Lewis Tappan did not employ a black clerk in his business. In 1855 Samuel Ringgold Ward denounced

Garrison and his associates for failing to have an African American "as clerk in an anti-slavery office, or editor, or lecturer to the same extent . . . as white men of the same calibre." These charges reflected factional struggles between the AASS and the AFASS. But they also represented real grievances among black abolitionists and real inconsistencies among their white counterparts.

Frederick Douglass

The career of Frederick Douglass illustrates the impact of the failure of white abolitionists to live up to their egalitarian ideals. Douglass was born a slave in Maryland in 1818. Intelligent, ambitious, and charming, he resisted brutalization, learned to read, and acquired a trade before escaping to New England in 1838. By 1841 he had, with Garrison's encouragement, become an antislavery lecturer, which led to the travels with William White discussed earlier.

MARTIN R. DELANY DESCRIBES HIS VISION OF A BLACK NATION

This excerpt comes from the appendix of Martin R. Delany's The Condition, Elevation, Emigration and Destiny of the Colored People of the United States, Politically Considered, *which he published in 1852. It embodies Delany's black nationalist vision.*

Every people should be the originators of their own designs, the projectors of their own schemes, and creators of the events that lead to their destiny—the consummation of their desires.

Situated as we are in the United States, many, and almost insurmountable obstacles present themselves. We are four-and-a-half millions in numbers, free and bond; six hundred thousand free, and three-and-a-half millions bond.

We have native hearts and virtues, just as other nations; which in their pristine purity are noble, potent, and worthy of example. We are a nation within a nation. . . .

But we have been, by our oppressors, despoiled of our purity, and corrupted in our native characteristics, so that we have inherited their vices, and but few of their virtues, leaving us in character, really a broken people.

Being distinguished by complexion, we are still singled out— although having merged in the habits and customs of our oppressors—as a distinct nation of people. . . . The claims of no people, according to established policy and usage, are respected by any nation, until they are presented in a national capacity.

To accomplish so great and desirable an end, there should be held, a great representative gathering of the colored people of the United States; not what is termed a National Convention, representing en masse, such as have been, for the last few years, held at various times and places; but a true representation of the intelligence and wisdom of the colored freemen. . . . A Confidential Council. . . .

By this Council to be appointed, a Board of Commissioners . . . to go on an expedition to the EASTERN COAST OF AFRICA, to make researches for a suitable location on that section of the coast, for the settlement of colored adventurers from the United States, and elsewhere.

The whole continent is rich in minerals, and the most precious metals, as but a superficial notice of the topographical and geological reports from that country, plainly show. . . . The land is ours—there it lies with inexhaustible resources; let us go and possess it. In Eastern Africa must rise up a nation, to whom all the world must pay commercial tribute.

This c. 1844 oil portrait of Frederick Douglass is attributed to E. Hammond. Douglass escaped from slavery in 1838. By the mid-1840s, he had emerged as one of the more powerful speakers of his time. He began publishing his influential newspaper, the *North Star,* in 1847.

But as time passed, Douglass, who had remained loyal to Garrison during the 1840s when most other black abolitionists had left the AASS, suspected his white colleagues wanted him to continue in the role of a fugitive slave when, in fact, he was becoming one of the premier American orators of his time. "People won't believe you ever was a slave, Frederick, if you keep on this way," a white colleague advised him.

Finally, Douglass decided he had to free himself from the AASS. In 1847 he asserted his independence by leaving Massachusetts for Rochester, New York, where he began publishing the *North Star*. This decision angered Garrison and his associates but permitted Douglass to chart his own course as a black leader. Although Douglass continued to work closely with white

🌲 *What elements of black nationalism appear in this document?*

🌲 *How does Delany perceive Africa?*

Source: Herbert Aptheker, ed., *A Documentary History of the Negro People in the United States*, 5th ed. (New York: Citadel, 1968), I: 327–28.

abolitionists, especially Gerrit Smith, he could now do it on his own terms and be more active in the black convention movement, which he considered essential to gaining general emancipation and racial justice. In 1851 he completed his break with the AASS by endorsing the constitutional arguments and tactics of the New York Liberty Party as better designed to achieve emancipation than Garrison's disunionism.

Revival of Black Nationalism

Douglass always believed that black people were part of a larger American nation and that their best prospects for political and economic success lay in the United States. He was, despite his differences with some white abolitionists, an ardent integrationist. He opposed separate black churches and predicted that African Americans would eventually disappear into a greater American identity. Most black abolitionists did not go that far, but they believed racial oppression in all its forms could be defeated in the United States.

During the 1840s and 1850s, however, an influential minority of black leaders disagreed with this point of view. Prominent among them were Garnet and Douglass's sometime colleague on the *North Star,* Martin R. Delany. Although they differed between themselves over important details, Delany and Garnet joined in favoring African-American migration and nationalism as the best means to realize black aspirations.

Since the postrevolutionary days of Prince Hall and Paul Cuffe, some black leaders had believed African Americans could thrive only as a separate nation. They suggested sites in Africa, Latin America, and the American West as possible places to pursue this goal. But it took the rising tide of racism and violence emphasized in this chapter to induce a respectable minority of black abolitionists to once again consider migration. Almost all of them staunchly opposed the African migration scheme of the ACS, which they continued to characterize as proslavery and racist. Nevertheless, Garnet conceded in 1849 that he would "rather see a man free in Liberia [the ACS colony], than a slave in the United States."

Douglass and most black abolitionists rejected this outlook, insisting the aim must be freedom in the United States. Nevertheless, emigration plans developed by Garnet and Delany during the 1850s became a significant part of African-American reform culture. Delany, a physician and novelist, was born free in western Virginia in 1812. He grew up in Pennsylvania and by the late 1840s championed black self-reliance. To further this cause, he promoted mass black migration to Latin Amer-

THE ANTISLAVERY STRUGGLE INTENSIFIES	
JUNE 1839	Joseph Cinque leads a successful revolt of enslaved Africans aboard the Spanish schooner *Amistad*
APRIL 1840	The Liberty Party nominates James G. Birney for U.S. president
NOVEMBER 1841	Madison Washington leads a successful revolt of American slaves aboard the *Creole*
MARCH 1842	Charles T. Torrey and Thomas Smallwood organize an underground railroad network to help slaves escape from Washington, D.C., and its vicinity
AUGUST 1843	Henry Highland Garnet in Buffalo, New York, delivers his "Address to the Slaves"
DECEMBER 1843	Smallwood flees to Canada to avoid arrest
JUNE 1844	Torrey is arrested in Baltimore on multiple charges of having helped slaves escape
MAY 1846	Torrey dies in the Maryland penitentiary

1839–1846

ica or Africa. "We must MAKE an ISSUE, CREATE an EVENT, and ESTABLISH a NATIONAL POSITION for OURSELVES," he declared in 1852.

If There Is No Struggle, There Is No Freedom **10** LIVING WORDS

In contrast, Garnet welcomed white assistance for his plan to foster Christianity and economic development in Africa by encouraging *some*—not all—African Americans to migrate there under the patronage of his African Civilization Society. In 1858 he wrote, "Let those who wished to stay, stay here—and those who had enterprise and wished to go, go and found a nation, if possible, of which the colored Americans could be proud."

Little came of these nationalist visions, largely because of the successes of the antislavery movement. Black and white abolitionists, although not perfect allies, awoke many in the North to the brutalities of slavery. They helped convince most white northerners that the slave-labor system and slaveholder control of the national government threatened their economic and political interests. At the same time, abolitionist aid to escaping slaves and their defense of fugitive slaves from recapture pushed southern leaders to adopt policies that led to secession and the Civil War. The northern victory in the war, general emancipation, and constitutional protection for black rights made most African Americans—for a time—optimistic about their future in the United States.

AFRICAN-AMERICAN EVENTS	NATIONAL EVENTS
1830	
1831 Publication of *Liberator* begun by William Lloyd Garrison	**1832** Andrew Jackson reelected president
1833 Formation of AASS	**1833** End of Nullification Controversy
1835	
1835 Abolitionist postal campaign	**1836** Martin Van Buren elected president; Texas independence
1839 *Amistad* mutiny	
1840	
1840 Breakup of AASS	**1840** William H. Harrison elected president
1841 *Creole* revolt	**1844** James K. Polk elected president
1843 Henry Highland Garnet's "Address to the Slaves"	

CONCLUSION

In this chapter, we have focused on the radical movement for the immediate abolition of slavery. The movement flourished in the United States from 1831, when William Lloyd Garrison began publishing the *Liberator*, through the Civil War. Garrison hoped slavery could be abolished peacefully. But during the 1840s abolitionists adjusted their antislavery tactics to deal with increasing racism and antiblack violence, both of which were related to the existence of slavery. Many black abolitionists and their white colleagues concluded that the tactic of moral suasion, typical of abolitionism during the 1830s, could not by itself achieve their goals or prevent violence against free and enslaved black people. Slave resistance also inspired a more confrontational brand of abolitionism. Most black abolitionists came to believe they needed a combination of moral suasion, political involvement, and direct action to end slavery and improve the lives of African Americans in the United States. By the late 1840s, a minority of black abolitionists contended they had to establish an independent nation beyond the borders of the United States to promote African-American rights, interests, and identity.

Although much has changed since the abolitionist era, these two perspectives remain characteristic of the African-American community today. Most African Americans prefer integration with a larger American nation. But black nationalism still has a powerful appeal. Individuals often embrace parts of both views, just as Frederick Douglass embraced some black nationalism and Henry Highland Garnet some integrationism. Similarly, reformers still debate whether peaceful persuasion is more effective than confrontation.

RECOMMENDED READING

Stanley Harrold. *The Abolitionists and the South, 1831–1861.* Lexington: University Press of Kentucky, 1995. Emphasizes the formative impact of slave resistance on northern abolitionism and the aggressiveness of that movement toward the South.

Jane H. Pease and William H. Pease. *They Who Would Be Free: Blacks' Search for Freedom, 1830–1861.* New York: Athenaeum, 1974. Deals with cooperation and conflict between black and white abolitionists. The book emphasizes conflict.

Benjamin Quarles. *Black Abolitionists.* New York: Oxford University Press, 1969. A classic study that emphasizes cooperation between black and white abolitionists.

Harry Reed. *Platforms for Change: The Foundations of the Northern Free Black Community, 1776–1865*. East Lansing: Michigan State University Press, 1994. Places black abolitionism and black nationalism within the context of community development.

Shirley J. Yee. *Black Women Abolitionists: A Study of Activism*. Knoxville: University of Tennessee Press, 1992. Discusses the activities of black women abolitionists in both white and black organizations.

R. J. Young. *Antebellum Black Activists: Race, Gender, Self*. New York: Garland, 1996. A sophisticated study of the motivation of black abolitionists.

ADDITIONAL BIBLIOGRAPHY

GENERAL STUDIES OF THE ANTISLAVERY MOVEMENT

Herbert Aptheker. *Abolitionism: A Revolutionary Movement*. Boston: Twayne, 1989.

Lawrence J. Friedman. *Gregarious Saints: Self and Community in American Abolitionism, 1830–1870*. New York: Cambridge University Press, 1982.

Stanley Harrold. *American Abolitionists*. Harlow, England: Longman, 2001.

—————. *The Rise of Aggressive Abolitionism: Addresses to the Slaves*. Lexington: University Press of Kentucky, 2004.

James Brewer Stewart. *Holy Warriors: The Abolitionists and American Slavery*, 2d ed. New York: Hill and Wang, 1997.

THE BLACK COMMUNITY

John Brown Childs. *The Political Black Minister: A Study in Afro-American Politics and Religion*. Boston: G. K. Hall, 1980.

Leonard P. Curry. *The Free Black in Urban America, 1800–1850: The Shadow of a Dream*. Chicago: University of Chicago Press, 1981.

Martin E. Dann. *The Black Press, 1827–1890*. New York: Capricorn, 1971.

James Oliver Horton and Lois E. Horton. *In Hope of Liberty: Culture, Community, and Protest among Northern Free Blacks, 1700–1860*. New York: Oxford University Press, 1997.

Patrick Rael. *Black Identity and Black Protest in the Antebellum North*. Chapel Hill: University of North Carolina Press, 2002.

David E. Swift. *Black Prophets of Justice: Activist Clergy before the Civil War*. Baton Rouge: Louisiana State University Press, 1989.

BLACK ABOLITIONISTS

Howard Holman Bell. *A Survey of the Negro Convention Movement, 1830–1861*. New York: Arno, 1969.

—————, ed. *Minutes of the Proceedings of the National Negro Conventions, 1830–1864*. New York: Arno, 1969.

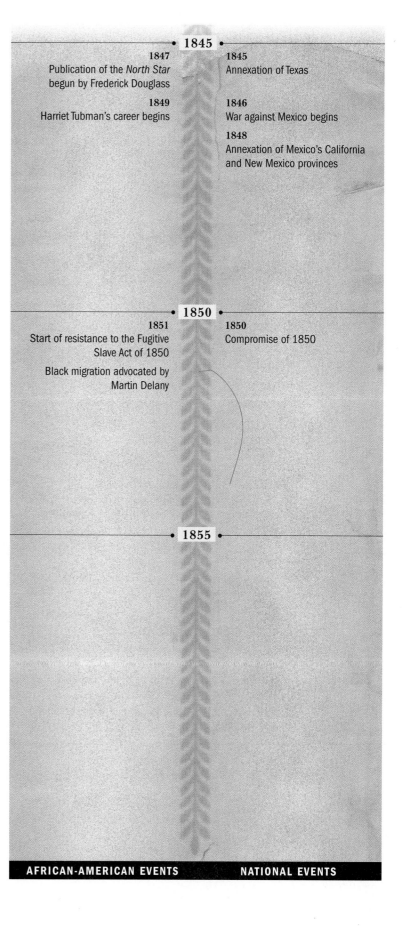

1845

1847
Publication of the *North Star* begun by Frederick Douglass

1849
Harriet Tubman's career begins

1845
Annexation of Texas

1846
War against Mexico begins

1848
Annexation of Mexico's California and New Mexico provinces

1850

1851
Start of resistance to the Fugitive Slave Act of 1850

Black migration advocated by Martin Delany

1850
Compromise of 1850

1855

AFRICAN-AMERICAN EVENTS   **NATIONAL EVENTS**

R. J. M. Blackett. *Building an Antislavery Wall: Blacks in the Atlantic Abolitionist Movement, 1830–1860.* Baton Rouge: Louisiana State University Press, 1983.

WOMEN

Blanch Glassman-Hersh. *Slavery of Sex: Feminist-Abolitionists in Nineteenth-Century America.* Urbana: University of Illinois Press, 1978.

Darlene Clark Hine, ed. *Black Women in American History: From Colonial Times through the Nineteenth Century.* 4 vols. New York: Carlson, 1990.

Julie Roy Jeffrey. *The Great Silent Army of Abolitionism: Ordinary Women in the Antislavery Movement.* Chapel Hill: University of North Carolina Press, 1998.

Gayle Tate. *Unknown Tongues: Black Women's Political Activism in the Antebellum Era 1830–1860.* East Lansing: Michigan State University Press, 2003.

Jean Fagan Yellin. *Women and Sisters: Antislavery Feminists in American Culture.* New Haven, CT: Yale University Press, 1990.

BIOGRAPHY

Catherine Clinton. *Harriet Tubman: The Road to Freedom.* New York: Little, Brown, 2003.

William S. McFeely. *Frederick Douglass.* New York: Simon & Schuster, 1991.

Nell Irvin Painter. *Sojourner Truth: A Life, A Symbol.* New York: Norton, 1996.

Joel Schor. *Henry Highland Garnet: A Voice of Black Radicalism in the Nineteenth Century.* Westport, CT: Greenwood, 1977.

James Brewer Stewart. *William Lloyd Garrison and the Challenge of Emancipation.* Arlington Heights, IL: Harlan Davidson, 1992.

Victor Ullman. *Martin R. Delany: The Beginnings of Black Nationalism.* Boston: Beacon, 1971.

UNDERGROUND RAILROAD

Keith P. Griffler. *Front Line of Freedom: African Americans and the Forging of the Underground Railroad in the Ohio Valley.* Lexington: University Press of Kentucky, 2004.

Stanley Harrold. *Subversives: Antislavery Community in Washington, D.C., 1828–1865.* Baton Rouge: Louisiana State University Press, 2003.

Wilbur H. Siebert. *The Underground Railroad from Slavery to Freedom.* 1898. Reprint, New York: Arno, 1968.

William Still. *The Underground Railroad.* 1871. Reprint, Chicago: Johnson Publishing, 1970.

BLACK NATIONALISM

Rodney Carlisle. *The Roots of Black Nationalism.* Port Washington, NY: Kennikat, 1975.

Floyd J. Miller. *The Search for Black Nationality: Black Emigration and Colonization, 1787–1863.* Urbana: University of Illinois Press, 1975.

RETRACING THE ODYSSEY

Frederick Douglass National Historic Site, Washington, D.C. This is Douglass's Cedar Hill home, which he purchased in 1878. It contains materials related to his career as an abolitionist and advocate of black rights.

"Free at Last: A History of the Abolition of Slavery in America." A "National Touring Exhibition" sponsored by the Lincoln Home National Historic Site, Springfield, Illinois, that shows how "abolition became a national issue, how the slavery issue drew politicians and moral reformers together, [and] how the efforts of escaped slaves contributed a human face to the horrors of slavery."

National Underground Railroad Freedom Center, Cincinnati. Exhibits, programs, and events dealing with "slavery and freedom," with emphasis on the Underground Railroad.

National Underground Railroad Museum, Maysville, Kentucky. Houses artifacts associated with and provides information on the Underground Railroad.

myhistorylab REVIEW, RESEARCH, AND INTERACT

REVIEW QUESTIONS

1. What was the historical significance of Henry Highland Garnet's "Address to the Slaves"? How did Garnet's attitude toward slavery differ from that of William Lloyd Garrison?

2. Evaluate Frederick Douglass's career as an abolitionist. How was he consistent? How was he inconsistent?

3. Discuss the contribution of black women to the antislavery movement. How did participation in this movement alter their lives?

4. Compare and contrast the integrationist views of Frederick Douglass with the nationalist views of Martin Delany and Henry Highland Garnet.

5. Why did black abolitionists leave the AASS in 1840?

www.researchnavigator.com

Using the tools available in Research Navigator, consider this question:
Compare and contrast the attitudes of black and white antislavery activists. What tensions existed within the antislavery movement?

PRIMARY SOURCE DOCUMENTS

 MAP EXPLORATION

 INTERACTIVE ACTIVITY

Angelina Grimké
On May 17, 1838, an antiabolition mob in Philadelphia
attacked and destroyed Pennsylvania Hall. The speaker who
provoked their fury was a young woman named Angelina
Grimké.

10

And Black People Were at the Heart of It

WHY WAS THE EXPANSION
OF SLAVERY SUCH A DIVISIVE ISSUE?

WHAT DID "FREE LABOR" MEAN
TO NINETEENTH-CENTURY AMERICANS?

HOW DID AFRICAN AMERICANS
REACT TO THE PASSAGE OF
THE FUGITIVE SLAVE LAW OF 1850?

WHY WAS THE U.S. SUPREME COURT DECISION
IN THE *DRED SCOTT* CASE SO CONTROVERSIAL?

WHAT WAS THE IMPACT OF JOHN BROWN'S
RAID ON HARPERS FERRY?

HOW DID AFRICAN AMERICANS AND WHITE
SOUTHERNERS REACT TO THE ELECTION
OF ABRAHAM LINCOLN IN 1860?

◄ **In January 1856,** Margaret Garner, her husband Robert, and
their four children escaped from Kentucky to Ohio across
the frozen Ohio River. They were pursed to the home of a
black man by slave owners as well as deputy marshals. The
Garners fiercely resisted. Robert Garner shot and wounded
one of the deputies. But when it became clear that they were
about to be apprehended, Margaret killed her daughter
rather than have the child returned to slavery.

1846–1861

The Fugitive Slave Bill, (exhibited in its hideous deformity at our previous meeting,) has already in hot haste commenced its bloody crusade o'er the land, and the liability of ourselves and our families becoming its victims at the caprice of Southern men-stealers, imperatively demands an expression, whether we will tamely submit to chains and slavery, or whether we will, at all and every hazard, Live and Die freemen.

Robert C. Nell, "Declaration of Sentiments of the Colored Citizens of Boston on the Fugitive Slave Bill!!!" 1850

◄ **An abolitionist poster** from Massachusetts condemns the fugitive Slave Law and the politicians who voted for it.

By the end of the 1840s in the United States, no issue was as controversial as slavery. Slavery, or more accurately its expansion, deeply divided the American people and led to the bloodiest war in American history. Try as they might from 1845 to 1860, political leaders could not solve, evade, or escape slavery and agree on whether to allow it to expand into the nation's western territories.

Caught in this monumental dispute were the South's nearly four million enslaved men, women, and children. Their future, as well as the fate of the country, was at stake. More than 620,000 Americans—northern and southern, black and white—would die before a divided nation would be reunified and slavery would be abolished.

Whether slavery should be permitted in the western territories was not a new issue. As early as 1787, Congress had prohibited slavery in the Northwest Territory, the area north of the Ohio River that became the states of Ohio, Indiana, Illinois, Michigan, and Wisconsin. Then in 1819 a major political controversy erupted when Missouri applied for admission to the Union as a slave state. The Missouri Compromise—which admitted Maine as a free state, Missouri as a slave state, and outlawed slavery north of the 36° 30' line of latitude (see Chapter 5)—settled that controversy, but only postponed for twenty-five years further conflict over the expansion of slavery.

The country's desire to acquire western lands intensified in the 1830s and 1840s. Most white Americans and many free black Americans assumed that the American people should occupy the entire North American continent from the Atlantic to the Pacific. It was their future, their Manifest Destiny (see Chapter 9). In 1846–1847 U.S. troops fought an eighteen-month conflict that resulted in the acquisition of more than half of Mexico and was a major step toward the fulfillment of Manifest Destiny.

The Lure of the West

Even before the war with Mexico, hundreds of Americans made the long journey west, drawn by the opportunity to settle the fertile valleys of California and the Oregon Territory, which included what is today the states of Oregon and Washington. African Americans shared these hopes and dreams. In 1844 a black Missouri farmer with the improbable name of George Washington Bush caught "Oregon fever" and set out with his wife, six children, and four other families on the 1,800-mile trek by wagon train to Oregon. Bush settled north of the Columbia River in what later became the Washington Territory because Oregon's territorial constitution forbade black settlement. Although the law was rarely enforced, black residents were legally subject to whipping every six months until they departed. The statute remained a part of Oregon state law until the 1920s.

FREE LABOR VERSUS SLAVE LABOR

Westward expansion revived the issue of slavery's future in the territories. Should slavery be legal in western lands, or should it be outlawed? Most white Americans held thoroughly ingrained racist beliefs that people of African descent were not and could never be their intellectual, political, or social equals. Yet those same white Americans disagreed vehemently on where those unfree African Americans should be permitted to labor and reside.

Most northern white people adamantly opposed allowing southern slaveholders to take their slaves into the former Mexican territories and detested the prospect of slavery spreading westward and limiting their opportunities to settle and farm those lands. Except for the increasing number of militant abolitionists, white Northerners detested both slavery as a labor system and the black people who were enslaved.

By the mid-nineteenth century, northern black and white people embraced the system of **free labor**—that is, free men and women who worked for compensation to earn a living and improve their lives. If southern slave owners managed to gain a foothold for their unfree labor on the western plains, in the Rocky Mountains, or on the Pacific coast, then the future for free white laborers would be severely restricted, if not destroyed.

11 Remembering Slavery

THE WILMOT PROVISO

In 1846, during the Mexican War, a Democratic congressman from Pennsylvania, David Wilmot, introduced a measure in Congress, the so-called Wilmot Proviso, to prohibit slavery in any lands acquired from Mexico. Wilmot later explained that he wanted neither slavery nor black people to taint territory that should be reserved exclusively for whites: "The negro race already occupy enough of this fair continent. . . . I would preserve for free white labor a fair country . . . where the sons of toil, of my own race and own color, can live without the disgrace which association with negro slavery brings upon free labor."

The Wilmot Proviso failed to become law, but white Southerners, who saw it as a blatant attempt to prevent them from moving west and enjoying the prosperity and way of life that an expanding slave-labor system would create, were enraged. They considered any attempt to limit the growth of slavery to be the first step toward eliminating it. And the possibility that slavery might be abolished, as remote as that may have seemed in the 1840s, was too awful for them to contemplate.

White Southerners had convinced themselves that black people were a childlike and irresponsible race wholly incapable of surviving as a free people if they were emancipated and compelled to compete with white Americans. Most white people believed the black race would decline and disappear if it were freed. Virginia lawyer George Fitzhugh wrote in 1854, "the negro race is inferior to the white race, and living in their midst, they would be far outstripped or outwitted in the chase of free competition. Gradual, but certain, extermination would be their fate." Thus southern white people considered slavery "a positive good"—in the words of Senator John C. Calhoun of South Carolina—that benefited both races and resulted in a society vastly superior to that of the North.

To prevent slavery's expansion, the Free-Soil Party was formed in 1848. It was composed mainly of white people who vigorously opposed slavery's expansion and the supposed desecration that the presence of black men and women might bring to the new western lands. But some black and white abolitionists also supported the Free-Soilers as a way to oppose slavery. They reasoned that even though many Free-Soil supporters were hostile to black people, the party still represented a serious challenge to slavery and its expansion. Frederick Douglass felt comfortable enough with the Free-Soil Party to attend its convention in 1848. The Free-Soil candidate for president that year was the former Democratic president Martin Van Buren. He came in a distant third behind the Whig victor and hero of the Mexican War, Zachary Taylor, who won, and the Democrat Lewis Cass. Nevertheless, ten Free-Soil congressmen were elected, and the party provided a growing forum to oppose slavery's advance.

CALIFORNIA AND THE COMPROMISE OF 1850

The discovery of gold in California in 1848 sent thousands of Americans hurrying west in 1849. The **Forty-Niners,** as these migrants were called, were almost exclusively male, and most were white Americans. But the desire to get rich had universal appeal, and the gold rush attracted Europeans, Asians (mostly Chinese), and African Americans. By 1850 nearly 900 black men (and fewer than 100 black women) were living in California, including people of African descent from Mexico, Peru, Chile, and Jamaica.

A black sailor known only as Hector deserted a naval vessel, *The Southampton,* in Monterrey, California, in 1848 and headed for the gold fields. He returned with $4,000, a large sum at the time. Another African American, Dick, brought $100,000 in gold, a veritable

Although white miners resented their presence, black men too sought riches in California in the great gold rush of 1849.

fortune, out of Tuolumne County, only to lose it all gambling in San Francisco.

As California's population soared to more than 100,000, its new residents applied for admission to the Union as a free state. White Southerners were aghast at the prospect of California prohibiting slavery, and they refused to consider its admission unless slavery was lawful there. Most Northerners would not accept this.

Into the dispute stepped Whig senator Henry Clay, who had assisted with the Missouri Compromise thirty years earlier. In 1850 the aging Clay put together an elaborate piece of legislation, **the Compromise of 1850,** designed not only to settle the controversy over California, but also to resolve the issue of slavery's expansion once and for all. Clay attempted to satisfy both sides. To placate Northerners, he proposed admitting California as a free state and eliminating the slave trade (but not slavery) in the District of Columbia. To satisfy white Southerners, he offered a stronger fugitive slave law to make it easier for slave owners to apprehend runaway slaves and return them to slavery. New Mexico and Utah would also be organized as territories with no mention of slavery (see Map 10–1).

DOCUMENT 10-1 *The Compromise of 1850*

Clay's measures were hammered into a single bill and produced one of the most remarkable debates in the history of the Senate, but it did not pass. Southern opponents like Senator John C. Calhoun of South Carolina could not tolerate the admission of California without slavery. Northern opponents like Senator William Seward of New York could not tolerate a tougher fugitive slave law. President Zachary Taylor shocked his fellow Southerners and insisted that California should be admitted as a free state, and that Clay's compromise was unnecessary. Taylor promised to veto the compromise if Congress passed it.

Clay's effort had failed—or so it seemed. But in the summer of 1850, Taylor died unexpectedly and was succeeded by Millard Fillmore, who was willing to accept the compromise. Senator Stephen Douglas, an ambitious Democrat from Illinois, guided Clay's compromise through Congress by breaking it into separate bills. California entered the Union as a free state, and a stronger fugitive slave law entered the federal legal code.

FUGITIVE SLAVE LAWS

Those who may have hoped the compromise would resolve the dispute over slavery forever were mistaken. The **Fugitive Slave Law of 1850** created bitter resentment among black and white abolitionists and made slavery a more emotional and personal issue for many white people who had previously considered slavery a remote southern institution.

DOCUMENT *Fugitive Slave Act* 9-5

Had runaway slaves not been an increasingly frustrating problem for slave owners—particularly those in the upper South states of Maryland, Virginia, and Kentucky—the federal fugitive slave law would not have needed to be strengthened in 1850. The U.S. Constitution and the fugitive slave law passed in 1793 would seem to have provided ample authority for slave owners to recover runaway slaves.

The Constitution in Article IV, Section 2, stipulates that "any person held to service or labor in one State" who ran away to another state "shall be delivered up on claim of the party to whom such service or labor may be due." The fugitive slave law of 1793 permitted slave owners to recover slaves who escaped to other states. The escaped slave had no rights—no right to a trial, no right to testify, and no guarantee of **habeas corpus** (the legal requirement that a person be brought before a court and not imprisoned illegally).

But by the 1830s and 1840s, as hundreds if not thousands of slaves escaped to freedom by way of the underground railroad, white Southerners increasingly found the 1793 law too weak to overcome the resistance

MAP EXPLORATION

To explore this interactive map, go to
http://www.prenhall.com/hine4/map10.1

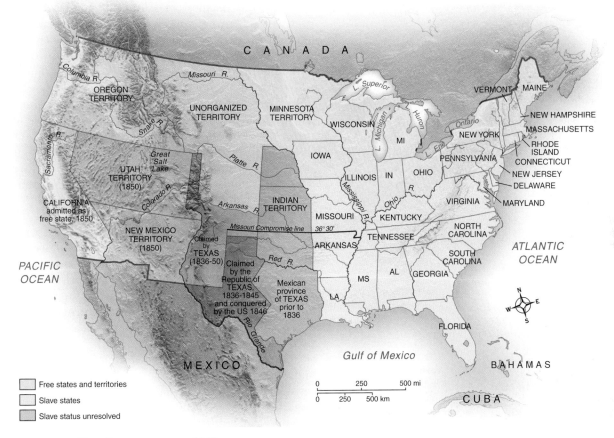

MAP 10–1   THE COMPROMISE OF 1850

As a result of the war against Mexico, the United States acquired the regions shown on this map as California, Utah Territory, New Mexico Territory, and the portions of Texas not included in the Province of Texas.

▶ *With the Compromise of 1850, California entered the Union as a free state. In which remaining western lands would slavery be accepted or rejected?*

of northern communities to the return of escapees. For example, in January 1847 four Kentuckians and a local law officer attempted to capture Adam Crosswhite, his wife, and four children after the family had escaped from slavery in Kentucky and settled on a farm near Marshall, Michigan. When the would-be abductors arrived, an old black man mounted a horse and galloped through town ringing a bell warning that the Crosswhites were in danger. Having been aroused by this "Black Paul Revere," about one hundred people helped rescue the family and put them on a railroad train to Canada. The local citizens who had aided the Cross-

whites were later sued successfully by the slave owner and fined an amount equal to the estimated value of the Crosswhites had the family been sold as slaves.

Several northern states had enacted personal liberty laws that made it illegal for state law enforcement officials to help capture runaways. (Michigan passed such a law in 1855 after the Crosswhites escaped to Canada.) Not only did many Northerners refuse to cooperate in returning fugitives to slavery under the 1793 law, but they also encouraged and assisted the escaped slaves. The local black vigilance committees that were created in many northern communities and discussed

AFRICAN AMERICANS RESPOND TO THE FUGITIVE SLAVE LAW

These two passages reflect the outrage the Fugitive Slave Law of 1850 provoked among black Americans. In the first, John Jacobs, a fugitive slave from South Carolina, urges black people to take up arms to oppose the law. In the second, from a speech he delivered a few days after the passage of the law, Martin Delany defies authorities to search his home for runaway slaves.

My colored brethren, if you have not swords, I say to you, sell your garments and buy one. . . . They said that they cannot take us back to the South; but I say, under the present law they can; and now they say unto you; let them take only dead bodies. . . . I would, my friends, advise you to show a front to our tyrants and arm yourselves . . . and I would advise the women to have their knives too.

Source: William F. Cheek, *Black Resistance before the Civil War* (Beverly Hills: Glencoe Press, 1970), 148–49.

Sir, my house is my castle; in that castle are none but my wife and my children, as free as the angels of heaven, and whose liberty is as sacred as the pillars of God. If any man approaches that house in search of a slave—I care not who he may be, whether the constable, or sheriff, magistrate or even judge of the Supreme Court—nay, let it be he who sanctioned this act to become law [President Millard Fillmore] surrounded by his cabinet as his bodyguard, with the Declaration of Independence waving above his head as his banner, and the constitution of this country upon his breast as his shield—if he crosses the threshold of my door, and I do not lay him a lifeless corpse at my feet, I hope the grave may refuse my body a resting place, and righteous Heaven my spirit a home. O, no! He cannot enter that house and we both live.

Source: Victor Ullman, *Martin R. Delany: The Beginnings of Black Nationalism* (Boston: Beacon Press, 1971), 112.

🌿 *How and why did these two black men justify the use of violence against those who were enforcing a law passed by Congress?*

🌿 *Under what circumstances is it permissible to violate the law or threaten to kill another human being?*

in Chapter 9—among them the League of Freedom in Boston and the Liberty Association in Chicago—were especially effective in these efforts. These actions infuriated white Southerners and prompted their demand for a stricter fugitive slave law.

The Fugitive Slave Law of 1850 was one of the toughest and harshest measures the U.S. Congress ever passed. Anyone apprehended under the law was almost certain to be sent back to slavery. The law required U.S. marshals, their deputies, and even ordinary citizens to help seize suspected runaways. Those who refused to help apprehend fugitives or who helped the runaway could be fined or imprisoned. The law made it nearly impossible for black people to prove they were free. Slave owners and their agents only had to provide legal documentation from their home state or the testimony of white witnesses before a federal commissioner that the captive was a runaway slave. The federal commissioners were paid $10 for captives returned to bondage but only $5 for those declared free. Supporters of the law claimed the extra paperwork involved in returning a fugitive to slavery necessitated the $10 fee. Opponents of the law saw the $10 as a bribe to encourage federal authorities to return men and women to bondage. During the time the law was in effect, 332 captives were returned to the South and slavery, and only 11 were released as free people.

The new fugitive slave law outraged many black and white Northerners. An angry Frederick Douglass insisted in October 1850 that "the only way to make the Fugitive Slave Law a dead letter is to make a half dozen or more dead kidnappers." White abolitionist Wendell Phillips exhorted his listeners to disobey the law. "We must trample this law under our feet."

Northern State Defies Fugitive Slave Act **10-3** DOCUMENT

Fugitive Slaves

The fugitive slave law did more than anger black and white Northerners. It exposed them to cruel and heart-wrenching scenes as southern slave owners and slave catchers took advantage of the new law and—with the vigorous assistance of federal authorities—relentlessly pursued runaway slaves. Many white people and virtually all black people felt genuine revulsion over this crackdown on those who had fled from slavery to freedom.

In September 1850 in New York City, federal authorities captured a black porter and returned him to slavery in Baltimore, even though he insisted that because his mother was a free woman he had not been a slave. (In each of the slave states, the law stipulated the status of the mother determined a child's legal status—free or slave.) In Poughkeepsie, New York, slave catchers captured a well-to-do black tailor and returned him to slavery in South Carolina. In Indiana, a black man was apprehended while his wife and children looked on, and he was sent to Kentucky where his owner claimed he had escaped nineteen years earlier.

Not all fugitives were forced back into bondage. A Maryland slave owner attempted to recover a black woman in Philadelphia who, he asserted, had escaped twenty-two years earlier. Since then, she had had six children, and the slave owner insisted they were also his property. In this instance, the federal commissioner ruled the woman and her children were free.

Even California was not immune to the furor over fugitive slaves. Although slavery was prohibited in the new state, several hundred black people were held illegally there as slaves in the 1850s. Nevertheless there were some slaves who ran away to the west rather than the north. Black abolitionist Mary Ellen Pleasant hid fugitive Archy Lee in San Francisco in 1858; other members of the black community provided security for runaways from as far east as Maryland.

WILLIAM AND ELLEN CRAFT

Black and white abolitionists had organized vigilance committees to resist the fugitive slave law and to prevent—by force if necessary—the return of fugitives to slavery. In October 1850 slave catchers arrived in Boston fully prepared to return William and Ellen Craft to slavery in Georgia. In 1848 the Crafts had devised an ingenious escape. Ellen's fair complexion enabled her to disguise herself as a sickly young white man who, accompanied by "his" slave, was traveling north for medical treatment. They journeyed to Boston by railroad and ship and thus escaped from slavery—or so they thought.

Slave catchers vowed to return the Crafts to servitude no matter how long it took: "If [we] have to stay here to all eternity, and if there are not enough men in Massachusetts to take them, [we] will bring some from the South." While white abolitionists protected Ellen and black abolitionists hid William, the vigilance com-

Effects of the Fugitive-Slave-Law.

Leaflets like this reflect the outrage many Northerners felt in response to the capture and reenslavement of African Americans that resulted from the passage of a tougher Fugitive Slave Law as part of the Compromise of 1850.

mittee plastered posters around Boston describing the slave catchers, calling them "man-stealers," and threatening their safety. Within days (which must have seemed slightly less than eternity), the Southerners left without the Crafts. Soon thereafter, the Crafts sailed to security in England.

SHADRACH

Black and white abolitionists were fully prepared to use force against the U.S. government and the slave owners and their agents. Sometimes the abolitionists succeeded; sometimes they did not. In early 1851, a few months after the Crafts left Boston, federal marshals apprehended a black waiter there who had escaped from slavery and given himself the name Shadrach. But a well-organized band of black men led by Lewis Hayden invaded the courthouse and escaped with Shadrach. They spirited him to safety in Canada on the underground railroad. (Shadrach later became the owner of a restaurant in Montreal.) Federal authorities brought charges against four black men and four white men who were then indicted by a grand jury for helping Shadrach, but local juries refused to convict them.

PROFILE ❧ MARY ELLEN PLEASANT

Mary Ellen Pleasant was a fascinating and influential woman of many accomplishments. But much about her life is shrouded in mystery and uncertainty. She may have been born in Georgia or Louisiana. She claimed she was born in Philadelphia in 1814 to a free woman of color. Her father may have been Asian, Native American, or even a white planter.

She did live for a time on Nantucket Island off the Massachusetts coast and then in Boston. She was an educated woman. While in New England she became acquainted with black and white abolitionists. She married John W. Smith, who was said to have been a Cuban planter. They had a daughter, Elizabeth. Her husband died in 1844. During the gold rush in 1849, she moved to California where she married John Pleasant and quickly became a prominent figure in San Francisco's African-American community. San Francisco had about 500 black residents in the mid-1850s. They included boot and saddle makers, barbers, clothing merchants, saloonkeepers, and a newspaper publisher.

The entrepreneurial spirit struck Mary Ellen Pleasant, and she was soon operating three laundries and a boarding house. She also invested in mining stock. She remained committed to abolition and assisted fugitive slaves who fled to the far West. She may have attended the 1855 Colored Convention in San Francisco, and she almost certainly met Mifflin Gibbs, who ran the first black newspaper on the Pacific Coast, *The Mirror of the Times*. (See Chapter 13 for a profile on the Gibbs brothers.)

By the late 1850s, Pleasant was in Chatham, Canada West (Ontario), where she collaborated with Martin Delany, Mary Ann Shadd Cary, and other black abolitionists. They had formed the Chatham Vigilance Committee that aided fugitive slaves escaping from the United States. She met John Brown in Chatham and reportedly donated $30,000 to his efforts to organize a slave rebellion.

Pleasant returned to California by the mid-1860s where she presided over her daughter's elegant wedding at San Francisco's A.M.E. Zion Church. Ever the entrepreneur, Pleasant operated a fashionable restaurant and a well-appointed boarding house that many people insisted was a brothel patronized by prominent white men.

Through her contacts with powerful politicians and businessmen, she accumulated information—some might call it gossip—about influential white families and the men who governed them. She used her connections to help black Californians find employment. She also worked as a housekeeper for two well-to-do white families, the Woodworths and then the Bells. Believed by some to be a voodoo queen, she was said to have developed peculiar powers over people, especially men.

Pleasant fought racial discrimination and supported legislation to permit black people to testify in California courts. She was loved and respected as well as hated and resented. She twice sued a San Francisco streetcar company that did not allow her to ride in its vehicles. She won $500 in her second suit, but the verdict was overturned on appeal.

She became renowned as "Mammy Pleasant," but she detested the nickname and did not hesitate to tell people so. At age eighty-seven she curtly informed a journalist, "Listen: I don't like to be called Mammy by everybody. Put that down. I'm not Mammy to everybody in California. I got a letter from a minister in Sacramento. It was addressed to Mammy Pleasant. I wrote back to him on his own paper that my name was Mrs. Mary E. Pleasant. . . . If he didn't have better sense he should have had better manners."

Mrs. Mary E. Pleasant died in 1904. She had accumulated considerable wealth. Her estate included diamond jewelry, 114 acres in Sonoma County, and a lot on Octavia Street in San Francisco. But in death she remained a puzzling and curious figure to many people. There was no mystery, however, to one of her final requests. She asked that her gravestone simply be inscribed: "She was a friend of John Brown."

Pleasant

THE BATTLE AT CHRISTIANA

In September 1851 a battle erupted in the little town of Christiana, in southern Pennsylvania, when a Maryland slave owner, Edward Gorsuch, arrived to recover two runaway slaves. Accompanied by several family members and three deputy U.S. marshals, they confronted a hostile and well-armed crowd of at least twenty-five black men and several white men. Black leader William Parker bluntly told Gorsuch to give up any plans to take the runaway slaves. Gorsuch refused, and a battle ensued. Gorsuch was killed, one of his sons was wounded, and several black and white men were hurt. The runaway slaves escaped to Canada.

Again the federal government made a determined effort to prosecute those who violated the fugitive slave law. President Fillmore sent U.S. Marines to Pennsylvania, and they helped round up the alleged perpetrators of the violence. Thirty-six black men and five white men were arrested and indicted for treason by a federal grand jury. But the government's case was weak, and after the first trial ended in acquittal, the remaining cases were dropped.

ANTHONY BURNS

Of all the fugitive slave cases, none elicited more support or sorrow than that of Anthony Burns. In 1854 Burns escaped from slavery in Virginia by stowing away on a ship to Boston. After gaining work in a clothing store, he unwisely sent a letter to his brother who was still a slave. The letter was confiscated, and Burns's former owner set out to capture him. Burns was arrested by a deputy marshal who, recalling Shadrach's escape, placed him under guard in chains in the

---

PROFILE ❦ THOMAS SIMS, A FUGITIVE SLAVE

By stowing away on a ship in Savannah, Georgia, in 1851, a seventeen-year-old slave named Thomas Sims escaped to Boston, where he worked as a waiter. His owner tracked him down there and had him arrested and confined in chains on the third floor of the federal courthouse in Boston. Black leader Lewis Hayden tried to free Sims, but failed. Hayden had difficulty attracting support, because many of the men whom he would ordinarily have depended on had fled when authorities began to search for those who had freed Shadrach a few weeks earlier.

One plan involved piling mattresses under Sims's window and having him jump about thirty feet to freedom. It was abandoned when bars were installed in the window. Neither Sims's lawyers' attempts to win a writ of habeas corpus nor public protests succeeded in gaining his freedom.

On April 11, 1851, a federal commissioner ordered Sims returned to slavery. He was marched from the courthouse, "protected" by three hundred armed men, and taken to a ship in the harbor. A desperate plan to free him by twenty armed men aboard another vessel failed because Sims's ship sailed for Savannah before the other ship could get under way.

Later that summer, Sims was sent to Charleston, and then to New Orleans where he was auctioned off to a brick mason from Vicksburg, Mississippi. Sims spent the next twelve years enslaved as a mason in Mississippi. In 1863, during the Civil War, when Union forces laid siege to Vicksburg, Sims again fled to freedom. He went back to Boston where he saw the return in 1865 of the all-black 54th Massachusetts Regiment from combat in South Carolina, Georgia, and Florida.

By 1877, Sims was in Washington, D.C. He obtained a job as a messenger in the Department of Justice through the intervention of U.S. Attorney General Charles Devens—the federal marshal who had arrested him in Boston in 1851.

Posters went up in many northern communities after the passage of the Fugitive Slave Law as slave catchers pursued runways. This poster appeared after Thomas Sims was sent back to slavers from Boston in 1851.

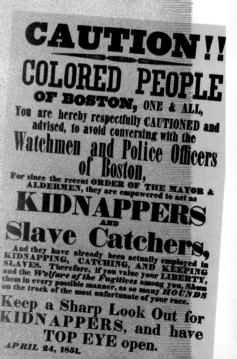

CAUTION!! COLORED PEOPLE OF BOSTON, ONE & ALL, You are hereby respectfully CAUTIONED and advised, to avoid conversing with the Watchmen and Police Officers of Boston, For since the recent ORDER OF THE MAYOR & ALDERMEN, they are empowered to act as KIDNAPPERS AND Slave Catchers, And they have already been actually employed in KIDNAPPING, CATCHING, AND KEEPING SLAVES. Therefore, if you value your LIBERTY, and the Welfare of the Fugitives among you, Shun them in every possible manner, as so many HOUNDS on the track of the most unfortunate of your race. Keep a Sharp Look Out for KIDNAPPERS, and have a TOP EYE open. APRIL 24, 1851.

federal courthouse. Efforts by black and white abolitionists to break into the courthouse with axes, guns,

Anthony Burns and a battering ram failed, although a deputy U.S. marshal was killed during the assault.

President Franklin Pierce, a northern Democrat who had been elected with southern support in 1852, sent U.S. troops to Boston, including Marines, cavalry, and artillery, to uphold the law and return Burns to Virginia. Black minister Leonard A. Grimes and the vigilance committee tried to purchase Burns's freedom, but the U.S. attorney refused. In June 1854, with church bells tolling and buildings draped in black, thousands of Bostonians watched silently—many in tears—as Anthony Burns was marched through the streets to a ship in the harbor that would take him to Virginia.

People who had shown no particular interest in nor sympathy for fugitives or slaves were moved by the spectacle of a lone black man, escorted by hundreds of armed troops, trudging from freedom to slavery. One staunchly conservative white man remarked, "When it was all over, and I was left alone in my office, I put my face in my hands and I wept. I could do nothing less." William

The **"trial" and subsequent return** of Anthony Burns to slavery in 1854 resulted in the publication of a popular pamphlet in Boston. Documents like this generated increased support—and funds—for the abolitionist cause.

Lloyd Garrison burned a copy of the Constitution on the Fourth of July as thousands looked on with approval.

Yet the government was unrelenting. A federal grand jury indicted seven black men and white men for riot and inciting a riot in their attempt to free Burns. One indictment was set aside on a technicality, and the other charges were then dropped because no Boston jury would convict the accused. Several months later, black Bostonians led by the Reverend Grimes purchased Burns for $1,300. He settled in St. Catherine's, Ontario, in Canada where he died in 1862.

Letter from Anthony Burns 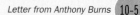 **10-5**

MARGARET GARNER

If the Burns case was the most moving, then Margaret Garner's was one of the most tragic examples of the lengths to which slaves might go to gain freedom for themselves and their children. In the winter of 1856, Margaret Garner and seven other slaves escaped from Kentucky across the Ohio River to freedom in Cincinnati. But their owner, Archibald Grimes, pursued them. Grimes, accompanied by a U.S. deputy marshal and several other people, attempted to arrest the eight fugitives at a small house where they had hidden. Refusing to surrender, the slaves fought back, but they were finally overpowered and subdued.

Before the fugitives were captured, Garner slit the throat of her daughter with a butcher knife rather than see the child returned to slavery. Before she could kill her two sons, she was disarmed. Ohio authorities charged her with murder, but by that time she had been returned to Kentucky and then sent with her surviving three children to Arkansas to be sold. On the trip down the river, her youngest child and twenty-four other people drowned in a shipwreck, thereby cruelly fulfilling her wish that the child not grow up to be a slave. Margaret Garner was later sold at a slave market in New Orleans. (Her story was the basis of Toni Morrison's novel *Beloved*, which won the 1988 Pulitzer Prize for fiction and was transformed into a film by Oprah Winfrey in 1998.)

The Rochester Convention, 1853

In 1853, while northern communities grappled with the consequences of the fugitive slave law, African-American leaders gathered for a national convention in Rochester, New York. The **Rochester Convention** warned that black Americans were not prepared to submit quietly to a government more concerned about the interests of slave owners than people seeking to free themselves from bondage. The delegates looked past the grim conditions of the times to call for greater unity among black people and to find ways to improve their economic prospects. They asserted their claims to the rights of citizenship and equal protection before the law, and they worried that the wave of European immigrants entering the country would deprive poor black Northerners of the menial and unskilled jobs on which they depended. Frederick Douglass spoke of the need for a school to provide training in skilled trades and manual arts. There was even talk of establishing a Negro museum and library.

Nativism and the Know-Nothings

Not only did many white Americans look with disfavor and often outright disgust at African Americans, they were also distressed by and opposed to the increasing numbers of white immigrants coming to the United States. Hundreds of thousands of Europeans—mostly Germans and Irish—arrived in the 1840s and 1850s. In one year—1854—430,000 people arrived on American shores.

The stark reality of mass starvation that accompanied the potato famine of the 1840s in Ireland drove thousands of Irish people to the United States, where they often encountered intense hostility. Native-born, Protestant, white Americans despised the Catholic Irish, whom they considered crude, ignorant, and all too likely to drink to excess. Irish immigrants also competed with Americans for low-paying unskilled jobs. Ugly anti-Catholic propaganda raised fears that the influence of the Vatican and the papacy would weaken American institutions. Some even charged there was a Roman Catholic conspiracy to take over the United States. Mobs viciously attacked Catholic churches and convents.

These anti-immigrant, anti-Catholic, anti-alcohol sentiments helped foster in 1854 the rise of a nativist third political party, the American Party—better known as the **"Know-Nothing Party."** (Its members were supposed to reply "I know nothing" if someone asked if they belonged to the party.) For a brief time, the Know-Nothings attracted considerable support. Feeding on resentment and prejudice, the party grew to one million strong. Most Know-Nothings were in New England, and they even for a short time took political control of Massachusetts, where many of the Irish had settled. But the party was also strong in Kentucky, Texas, and elsewhere.

Although Know-Nothings were in agreement about opposing immigrants and Catholics, they disagreed among themselves over slavery and its expansion. As a result this third party soon split into northern and southern factions and collapsed.

UNCLE TOM'S CABIN

No one contributed more to the growing opposition to slavery among white Northerners than Harriet Beecher Stowe. Raised in a deeply religious environment—her father, brothers, and husband were ministers—Stowe developed a hatred of slavery that she converted into a melodramatic, but moving, novel about slaves and their lives.

Uncle Tom's Cabin, or *Life among the Lowly,* was first published in installments in the antislavery newspaper *The National Era.* When it appeared as a book in 1852, it sold an astonishing 300,000 copies in a year. In the novel, Stowe depicted slavery's cruelty, inhumanity, and destructive impact on families through characters and a plot that appealed to the sentimentality of nineteenth-century readers. There was Little Eliza, with a babe in arms, barely escaping across the icy Ohio River from a slave owner in hot pursuit. There was Uncle Tom, the noble and devout Christian. Financial necessity forces Tom's decent master to sell the kindly slave to Simon Legree, a vicious brute and a Northerner who has embraced slavery. Legree takes perverse delight in beating Tom until the gentle old man dies.

Uncle Tom's Cabin moved Northerners to tears and made slavery more personal to readers who had previously considered it only a distant system of labor that exploited black people. In stage versions of the book that were later produced for decades across the North, Uncle Tom was transformed from a dignified man into a pitiful and fawning figure eager to please white people—hence the derogatory term *Uncle Tom.*

"Border ruffians" were armed men from Missouri who crossed the border to support pro-slavery forces in the Kansas territory. They sought the legalization of slavery in Kansas. They—as well as the opponents of slavery—were willing to resort to violence to achieve their aims.

Uncle Tom's Cabin infuriated white Southerners. They condemned it as a grossly false depiction of slavery and their way of life. They pointed out correctly that Stowe had little firsthand knowledge of slavery and had never even visited the deep South. But she had lived in Cincinnati for eighteen years and witnessed with anguish the desperate attempts of slaves to escape across the Ohio River. In response to her southern critics, Stowe wrote *A Key to Uncle Tom's Cabin,* citing the sources for her novel. Many of those sources were southern newspapers.

The Kansas-Nebraska Act

In the wake of the Compromise of 1850, the disagreement over slavery's expansion intensified and became violent. In 1854 Stephen Douglas introduced a bill in Congress to organize the Kansas and Nebraska Territories that soon provoked white settlers in Kansas to kill each other over slavery. Douglas's primary concern was to secure the Kansas and Nebraska region for the construction of a transcontinental railroad. Until 1853 it had been part of the Indian Territory the federal government had promised would not be open to white settlement. To win the support of southern Democrats, who wanted slavery in at least one of the two new territories, Douglas included a provision in the bill permitting residents of the Kansas Territory to decide for themselves whether to allow slavery (see Map 10–2).

This proposal—known as **"popular sovereignty"**—angered many Northerners because it created the possibility that slavery might expand to areas where it had been prohibited. The Missouri Compromise banned slavery north of the 36° 30' N latitude. Douglas's **Kansas-Nebraska Act** would repeal that limitation and allow settlers in Kansas, which was north of that line, to vote on slavery there. Thus, if enough proslavery people moved to Kansas and voted for slavery, slaves and their slave owners would be legally permitted to dwell on land that had been closed to them for more than thirty years.

Douglas managed to muster enough Democratic votes in Congress to pass the bill, but its enactment destroyed an already divided Whig Party and drove a wedge between the North and South. The Whig Party disintegrated. Northern Whigs joined supporters of the Free-Soil Party to form the Republican Party, which was organized expressly to oppose the expansion of slavery. Southern Whigs drifted, often without much enthusiasm, to the Democrats or Know-Nothings.

Violence soon erupted in Kansas between proslavery and antislavery forces. **"Border ruffians"** from Missouri invaded Kansas to attack antislavery settlers and to vote illegally in Kansas elections. The New England Emigrant Aid Society dispatched people to the territory and the Reverend Henry Ward Beecher encouraged them to pack "Beecher's Bibles," which were firearms and not the Word of the Lord. By 1856 Kansas had 8,500 settlers, including 245 slaves, and two rival territorial governments. Civil war had erupted— prompting the press to label the territory "Bleeding Kansas."

More than 200 people died in the escalating violence. Some 500 "Border Ruffians" attacked the antislavery town of Lawrence, damaging businesses and killing one person. Abolitionist John Brown and four of his sons sought revenge by hacking five proslavery men (none of whom actually owned slaves) to death in Pottowattamie. A proslavery firing squad executed nine Free-Soilers. John Brown reappeared in Missouri, killed a slave owner, and freed eleven slaves. Then he fled, to plan an even larger and more dramatic attack on slavery.

Harriet Beecher Stowe was a prolific writer. She wrote travel accounts, children's books, and ten adult novels. Easily her best known work was *Uncle Tom's Cabin.* It was first published in serial form in the antislavery weekly newspaper *The National Era* when Stowe was forty years old.

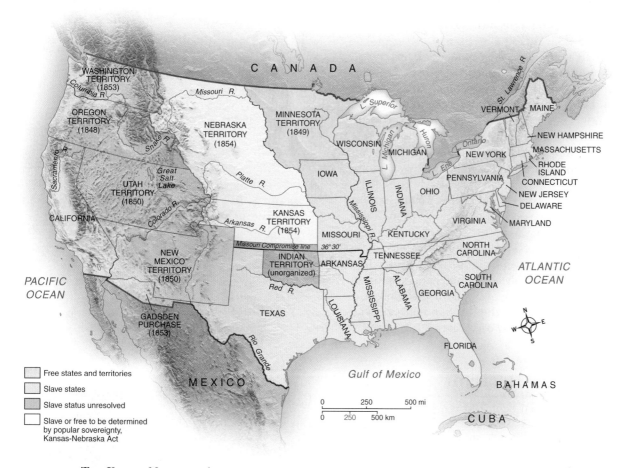

MAP 10–2   THE KANSAS-NEBRASKA ACT

This measure guided through Congress by Democratic senator Steven A. Douglas opened up the Great Plains to settlement and to railroad development. It also deeply divided the nation by repealing the 1820 Missouri Compromise Line of 36° 30' and permitting—through popular sovereignty—the people in Kansas to determine slavery's fate in that territory. Eastern Kansas became a bloody battleground between proslavery and antislavery forces.

▶ *Where exactly could slavery conceivably exist where it had previously been prohibited?*

Preston Brooks Attacks Charles Sumner

In 1856 the violence in Kansas spread to Congress. In May of that year, Massachusetts senator Charles Sumner delivered a tirade in the Senate denouncing the proslavery settlers in Kansas and the Southerners who supported them. Speaking of "The Crime against Kansas," Sumner accused South Carolina senator Andrew P. Butler of keeping slavery as his lover. Butler "has chosen a mistress to whom he has made his vows, and who . . . though polluted in the sight of the world, is chaste in his sight—I mean the harlot slavery." But-

ler was not present for the speech, but his distant cousin, South Carolina congressman Preston Brooks, was in the chamber, and Brooks did not appreciate Sumner's verbal assault on a member of his family.

Two days later, Brooks exacted his revenge. Waiting until the Senate adjourned, Brooks strode to the desk where Sumner was seated and attacked him with a rattan cane. The blows rained down until the cane shattered and Sumner tumbled to the floor, bloody and semiconscious. Brooks proudly recalled, "I gave him about thirty first rate stripes." Sumner suffered lingering physical and emotional effects from the beating and did not return to the Senate for almost four years.

Brooks resigned from the House of Representatives, paid a $300 fine, and went home to South Carolina a hero. He was easily reelected to his seat.

In the 1856 presidential election, the Democrats—although divided over the debacle in Kansas—nominated James Buchanan of Pennsylvania, another northern Democrat who was acceptable to the South. The Republicans supported a handsome military officer, John C. Fremont. Their slogan was "Free Soil, Free Speech, Free Men, and Fremont." But the Republicans were exclusively a northern party, and with the demise of the Whigs the South had become largely a one-party region. Almost no white southerners would support the Republicans, a party whose very existence was based on its opposition to slavery's expansion. Buchanan won the presidency with nearly solid southern support and enough northern votes to carry him to victory, but the Republicans gained enough support and confidence to give them hope for the 1860 election. Before then, however, the U.S. Supreme Court intervened in the controversy over slavery.

The *Dred Scott* Decision

Like most slaves, Dred Scott did not know his exact age. But when the U.S. Supreme Court accepted his case in 1856, Scott was in his fifties and had been entangled in the judicial system for more than a decade. Scott was born in Virginia, but by the 1830s he belonged to John Emerson, an army doctor in Missouri. Emerson took Scott to military posts in Illinois and Fort Snelling in what is now Minnesota. While at Fort Snelling, Scott married Harriet, a slave woman, and they had a daughter, Eliza, before Emerson returned with the three of them to St. Louis. (Another daughter, Lizzie, was born later.) In 1846, after Emerson's death, and with the support of white friends, Scott and his wife filed separate suits for their freedom. By agreement, her suit was set aside pending the outcome of her husband's litigation. Scott and his lawyers contended that because Scott had been taken to territory where slavery was illegal, he had become a free man.

Scott lost his first suit, won his second, but lost again on appeal to the Missouri Supreme Court. Scott's lawyers then appealed to the U.S. Circuit Court where they lost again. The final appeal in **Dred Scott v. Sanford** was to the U.S. Supreme Court. Although seventy-nine-year-old chief justice Roger Taney of Maryland had freed his own slaves, he was an unabashed advocate of the southern way of life. Moreover, Taney, a majority of the other justices, and

10-7 A Slave Sues for Freedom

The *Dred Scott* **case** was front page news on *Frank Leslie's Illustrated Newspaper* in 1857. Harriet and Dred with their two daughters are depicted sympathetically as members of the middle class rather than as abused and mistreated slaves.

President Buchanan were convinced that the prestige of the Court would enable it to render a decision about slavery that might be controversial but would still be accepted as the law of the land.

QUESTIONS FOR THE COURT

Taney framed two questions for the Court to decide in the Scott case: Could Scott, a black man, sue in a federal court? And was Scott free because he had been taken to a state and a territory where slavery was prohibited? In response to the first question, the Court, led by Taney, ruled that Scott—and every other black American—could not sue in a federal court because black people were not citizens. Speaking for the majority (two of the nine justices dissented), Taney emphatically stated that black people had no rights: "They had for more than a century before been regarded as beings of an inferior order; and altogether unfit to associate with the white race, either in social or political relations; and so far inferior that they had no rights which the white man was bound to respect; and that the negro might justly and lawfully be reduced to slavery for his benefit."

Taney was wrong. Although not treated as equals, free black people in many states had enjoyed rights associated with citizenship since the ratification of the Constitution in 1788. Black men had entered into contracts, held title to property, sued in the courts, and voted at one time in five of the original thirteen states.

A majority of the Court also answered no to the second question. Scott was not a free man, although he had lived in places where slavery was illegal. Scott, Taney maintained, again speaking for the Court, was slave property—and the slave owner's property rights took precedence. To the astonishment of those who opposed slavery's expansion, the Court also ruled that Congress could not pass measures—including the Missouri Compromise or the Kansas-Nebraska Act—that might prevent slave owners from taking their property into any territory. To do so, Taney implied, would violate the Fifth Amendment of the Constitution, which protected people from the loss of their life, liberty, or property without due process of law.

Following the decision, a new owner freed Dred and Harriet Scott. They settled in St. Louis, where he worked as a porter at Barnum's Hotel until he died of tuberculosis in 1858.

REACTION TO THE *DRED SCOTT* DECISION

The Court had spoken. Would the nation listen? White Southerners were delighted with Taney's decision. Republicans were horrified. But instead of earning the acceptance—let alone the approval—of most Americans, the case further inflamed the controversy over slavery. But if white Americans were divided in their reaction to the *Dred Scott* decision, black Americans were discouraged, disgusted, and defiant. Taney's decision delivered another setback to a people—already held in forced labor—who believed their toil, sweat, and contributions over the previous two-and-a-half centuries to what had become the United States gave them a legitimate role in American society. Now the Supreme Court said they had no rights. They knew better.

At meetings and rallies across the North, black people condemned the decision. Black writer, abolitionist, and women's rights advocate Frances Ellen Watkins Harper heaped scorn on the U.S. government

as "the arch traitor to liberty, as shown by the Fugitive Slave Law and the Dred Scott decision."

Young black leader H. Ford Douglas (no relation to Frederick Douglass) vented his rage at an American government and a constitution that could produce such a decision. He declared,

> To persist in supporting a government which holds and exercises the power . . . to trample a class under foot as an inferior and degraded race is on the part of the colored man at once the height of folly and the depth of pusillanimity. . . . The only duty the colored man owes to a constitution under which he is declared to be an inferior and degraded being . . . is to denounce and repudiate it, and to do what he can by all proper means to bring it into contempt.

Only Frederick Douglass could find a glimmer of hope. He believed—and events were to prove him right—that the decision was so wrong that it would help destroy slavery.

> The Supreme Court . . . [was] not the only power in the world. We, the abolitionists and the colored people, should meet this decision, unlooked for and monstrous as it appears, in a cheerful spirit. The very attempts to blot out forever the hopes of an enslaved people may be one necessary link in the chain of events preparatory to the complete overthrow of the whole slave system.

WHITE NORTHERNERS AND BLACK AMERICANS

Unquestionably, many white Northerners were genuinely concerned by the struggles of fugitive slaves, moved by *Uncle Tom's Cabin*, and disturbed by the *Dred Scott* decision. Yet as sensitive and sympathetic as some of them were to the plight of black people, most white Americans—including Northerners—remained decidedly indifferent to, fearful of, or bitterly hostile to people of color. By the 1850s, 200,000 black people lived in the northern states, and many white people there were not pleased with their presence. Many white Northerners, especially those living in southern Ohio, Indiana, and Illinois, supported the fugitive slave law and were eager to help return runaway slaves to bondage.

The same white Northerners who opposed the expansion of slavery to California or to Kansas also opposed the migration of free black people to northern states and communities. In 1851 Indiana and Iowa outlawed the emigration to their territory of black people, slave or free. Illinois did likewise in 1853. White male voters in Michigan in 1850 voted overwhelmingly—32,000 to 12,000—against permitting black men to vote. Only Ohio was an exception. In 1849 it repealed legislation excluding black people from the state.

These restrictive measures were not new. Most northern states had begun to restrict or deny the rights of black Americans in the early 1800s (see Chapter 6). Although only loosely enforced, the laws reflected the prevailing racial sentiments among many white Northerners, as did the widespread antiblack rioting of the 1830s and 1840s. During the debate over excluding black people from Indiana, a state senator explained that the Bible revealed God had condemned black people to inferiority. "The same power that has given him a black skin, with less weight or volume of brain, has given us a white skin, with greater volume of brain and intellect; and that we can never live together upon an equality is as certain as that no two antagonistic principles can exist together at the same time."

Foreign observers were struck by the depth of racism in the North. Alexis de Tocqueville, a French aristocrat, toured America in 1831 and wrote a perceptive analysis of American society. He considered Northerners more antagonistic toward black people than Southerners. "The prejudice of race appears to be stronger in the states that have abolished slavery than in those where it still exists; and nowhere is it so intolerant as in those states where servitude has never been known."

The Lincoln-Douglas Debates

In 1858 Senator Stephen Douglas of Illinois, a Democrat, ran for reelection to the Senate against Republican Abraham Lincoln. The main issues in the campaign were slavery and race, which the two candidates addressed in a series of debates around the state. In carefully reasoned speeches and responses, these experienced and articulate lawyers focused almost exclusively on slavery's expansion and its future in the Union. At Freeport, Illinois, Lincoln, a former Whig congressman, attempted to trap Douglas, the incumbent, by asking him if slavery could expand now that the *Dred Scott* decision had ruled slaves were property whom their owners could take into any federal territory. In reply, Douglas, who wanted to be president and had no desire to offend either northern or southern voters, cleverly defended "popular sovereignty" and the *Dred Scott* decision. He insisted that slave owners could indeed take their slaves where they pleased. But, he contended, if the people of a territory failed to enact slave codes to protect and control slave property, slave owners were not likely to settle there with their slaves.

Abraham Lincoln and Black People

But the **Lincoln-Douglas debates** did not always turn on the fine points of constitutional law or the fate of slavery in the territories. Thanks mainly to Douglas, who accused Lincoln and the Republicans of promoting the interests of black people over those of white people, the debates sometimes degenerated into crude and savage exchanges about which candidate favored white people more and black people less. Douglas proudly advocated white supremacy. "The signers of the Declaration [of Independence] had no reference to the Negro . . . or any other inferior or degraded race when they spoke of the equality of men." He later charged that Lincoln and the Republicans wanted black and white equality. "If you, Black Republicans, think the negro ought to be on social equality with your wives and daughters, . . . you have a perfect right to do so. . . . Those of you who believe the negro is your equal . . . of course will vote for Mr. Lincoln."

Lincoln did not believe in racial equality, and he made that plain. In exasperation, he explained that merely because he opposed slavery did not mean he believed in equality. "I do not understand that because I do not want a negro woman for a slave I must necessarily have her for a wife." He bluntly added,

I am not, nor ever have been in favor of bringing about in any way the social and political equality of the white and black races—that I am not nor ever have been in favor of making voters or jurors of negroes, nor of qualifying them to hold office, nor to intermarry with white people; and I will say in addition to this that there is a physical difference between the races which I believe will forever forbid the two races living together on terms of social and political equality.

But without repudiating these views, Lincoln later tried to transcend this blatant racism. "Let us discard all this quibbling about this man and the other man—this race and that race and the other race being inferior." Instead, he added, let us "unite as one people throughout this land, until we shall once more stand up declaring that all men are created equal." Lincoln stated unequivocally that race had nothing to do with whether a man had the right to be paid for his labor. He pointed out that the black man, "in the right to eat the bread, without leave of anybody else, which his own hand earns, he is my equal and the equal of Judge Douglas, and the equal of every living man."

PROFILE ~ MARTIN DELANY

*"I thank God for making me a man, but Delany thanks
Him for making him a black man."*
—*Frederick Douglass on Martin Delany*

Martin Delany (1812–1885) was one of the first individuals to insist persistently that people of African descent in the United States should control their own destiny. In speeches, articles, and books, he evoked pride in his African heritage and stressed the need for black people to rely on themselves, and not on the white majority.

Delany was a medical doctor, a journalist, an explorer, an anthropologist, a military officer, and a political leader. He was born free in Charlestown, Virginia (now West Virginia), but the family moved to Chambersburg, Pennsylvania, in 1822. In 1831 Martin went west to Pittsburgh where he spent most of the next twenty-five years. His education was strongly influenced by Lewis Woodson, a young African Methodist Episcopal minister. He also studied medicine as an apprentice under two white physicians.

Delany was active in the Pittsburgh Anti-Slavery Society and helped slaves escape on the underground railroad. In 1843, he married Catherine Richards, the daughter of a well-to-do black butcher, and by 1860, they had had seven children, each named for a well-known black figure: Toussaint L'Ouverture, Alexander Dumas, Saint Cyprian, Faustin Soulouque, Charles L. Redmond, and their only daughter, Ethiopia Halle.

In 1843, Delany began publishing *The Mystery,* a four-page weekly newspaper devoted to abolition. It did not thrive, and in 1847 he joined Frederick Douglass briefly as the coeditor of *The North Star* (see Chapter 9). In 1850 Delany was admitted to the Harvard Medical School with two other black students for formal training, but they were forced to leave after one term because of the protests of white students.

In 1852, he wrote and published *The Condition, Elevation, Emigration and Destiny of the Colored People of the United States*—the first major statement of black nationalism. Delany observed, "We are a nation within a nation." He recommended that people of African descent abandon the United States and migrate to Central America, South America, or Hawaii. Delany was the key figure in organizing the National Emigration Convention in Cleveland in 1854.

He and his family left the United States for Canada and lived in Canada West (currently the Province of Ontario), where he organized a meeting of black people and John Brown in 1858. He also managed to find time to write a novel, *Blake,* the fictional account of a West Indian slave who promotes revolution in the United States and leads a black rebellion in Cuba. In 1859–1860, Delany visited Liberia and explored what is today Nigeria.

Once the United States began to enlist black troops in the Civil War, Delany helped recruit black men. His son Toussaint joined the famed 54th Massachusetts Regiment. Delany himself became one of the few black men to be commissioned an officer. Major Delany went to Charleston, South Carolina, where he helped recruit two regiments of former slaves. After the war, he remained in South Carolina, where he entered politics. But he quickly grew disillusioned with the Republicans—both black and white—who dominated southern governments during Reconstruction. He did run for lieutenant governor on a reform party ticket, but he was not elected. In 1876, he astounded many black people when he supported white Democrats who favored the restoration of white political control over South Carolina. When Democrats won the election, the new governor, Wade Hampton, rewarded Delany by naming him to a minor political office. In 1878, a group of black South Carolinians and Georgians proposed migrating to Liberia. Delany supported them and became their treasurer, but he did not join them. The venture soon failed.

After he failed to win an appointment to a federal position in Washington, D.C., Delany went to Xenia, Ohio, and Wilberforce University, where his family had lived since the late 1860s. He died there in 1885.

Martin R. Delany played a key role in the emergence of black nationalism in the ▶ nineteenth century. He was an abolitionist, medical doctor and journalist. As a major he was the highest ranking black military officer commissioned during the Civil War.

Lincoln may have won the debate in the minds of many, but Douglas won the Senate election. Lincoln, however, made a name for himself that would work to his political advantage in the near future, and Douglas, despite his best efforts, had thoroughly offended many Southerners by suggesting that slave owners would not risk taking their human property to a territory that lacked a slave code. Douglas also antagonized white Southerners when he opposed the proslavery Kansas Lecompton constitution that he and many others believed had been fraudulently adopted. In two years, these disagreements over slavery would contribute to a decisive split in the Democratic Party.

John Brown and the Raid on Harpers Ferry

While Lincoln and Douglas were debating, John Brown was plotting. Following his attack on Pottowattamie in Kansas, Brown began to plan the violent overthrow of slavery in the South itself. In May 1858, accompanied by eleven white followers, he met thirty-four black people led by Martin Delany at Chatham in Canada West (now the province of Ontario) and appealed for their support. Brown was determined to invade the South and end slavery. He hoped to attract legions of slaves as he and his "army" moved down the Appalachian Mountains into the heart of the plantation system.

PLANNING THE RAID

Only one man at the Chatham gathering agreed to join the raid. Brown returned to the United States and garnered financial support from prosperous white abolitionists. Contributing money rather than risking their lives seemed more realistic to these men, who preferred to keep their identities confidential and thus came to be known as the Secret Six: Gerrit Smith, Thomas Wentworth Higginson, Samuel Gridley Howe, George L. Stearns, Theodore Parker, and Franklin Sanborn.

Brown also asked Frederick Douglass and Harriet Tubman to join him. They declined. By the summer of 1859, at a farm in rural Maryland, Brown had assembled an "army" consisting of seventeen white men (including three of his adult sons) and five black men. The black men who enlisted were Osborne Anderson, one of the Chatham participants; Sheridan Leary, an escaped slave who had become a saddle and harness maker in Oberlin, Ohio; Leary's nephew John A. Copeland, an Oberlin College student; and two escaped slaves, Shields Green and Dangerfield Newby.

Newby was determined to rescue his pregnant wife, Harriet, and their six children who were about to be sold from nearby Warrenton, Virginia, down the river to Louisiana. Harriet sent her husband a plaintive letter begging for him. "Oh Dear Dangerfield, com this fall . . . without fail . . . I want to see you so much that is one bright hope I have before me."

THE RAID

Brown's invasion began on Sunday night October 16, 1859, with a raid on Harpers Ferry, Virginia, and the federal arsenal there. Brown hoped to secure weapons and then advance south, but the operation went awry from the start. The dedication and devotion of Brown and his men were not matched by their strategy or his leadership. The first person Brown's band killed was ironically a free black man, Heyward Shepard, who was a baggage handler at the train station. The alarm then went out, and opposition gathered.

Even though they had lost the initiative, Brown and his men neither advanced nor retreated, but instead they remained in Harpers Ferry while Virginia and Maryland militia converged on them. Fighting began, and two townspeople, the mayor, and eight of Brown's men, including Sheridan Leary, Dangerfield Newby, and two of Brown's sons, were killed. Newby died carrying his wife's letter. But Brown managed to seize several hostages, among them Lewis W. Washington, the great grandnephew of George Washington.

By Tuesday morning, Brown, with his hostages and what remained of his "army," was holed up in an engine house. A detachment of U.S. Marines under the command of Robert E. Lee arrived, surrounded the building, and demanded Brown's surrender. He refused. The Marines broke in. Brown was wounded and captured.

There were about 150 adult slaves living in the vicinity of Harpers Ferry. Most of them were aware of the raid, and many of them joined the insurrection. Osborne Anderson provided pikes to slaves. Some of them were able to acquire firearms. Several of the slaves managed to flee to freedom in the North. Perhaps a dozen black men—in addition to those who accompanied Brown—died during and after the raid.

There was no massive slave uprising. Shields Green and John A. Copeland fled but were caught. Osborne Anderson eluded capture and later fought in the Civil War. Virginia quickly tried Brown, Green, and Copeland for treason. They were found guilty and sentenced to hang. But the violence did not end. In the days and weeks that followed, the barn of every juror who convicted Brown was burned. Many horses and cattle died. They were apparently poisoned.

THE REACTION

John Brown's raid had not proceeded as planned. But Brown and his men succeeded brilliantly in intensifying the deeply felt emotions of those who supported and those who opposed slavery. At first regarded as crazed zealots and insane fanatics, they showed they were willing—even eager—to die for the antislavery cause. The dignity and assurance that Brown, Green, and Copeland displayed as they awaited the gallows impressed many black and white Northerners.

Black teacher and abolitionist Frances Ellen Watkins Harper wrote to John Brown's wife two weeks before Brown was executed to express compassion and admiration for both husband and wife:

> Belonging to the race your dear husband reached forth his hand to assist, I need not tell you that my sympathies are with you. I thank you for the brave words you have spoken. A republic that produces such a wife and mother may hope for better days. Our heart may grow more hopeful for humanity when it sees the sublime sacrifice it is about to receive from his hands. Not in vain had your dear husband periled all, if the martyrdom of one hero is worth more than the life of a million cowards.

JOHN BROWN AT HARPER'S FERRY.

John Brown was captured in the Engine House at Harpers Ferry on October 18, 1859. He was quickly tried for treason and convicted. On December 2, 1859, he was hanged. His raid helped catapult the nation toward civil war.

James A. Copeland wrote home to his family that he was proud to die:

> I am not terrified by the gallows, which I see staring me in the face, and upon which I am soon to stand and suffer death for doing what George Washington was made a hero for doing. . . . Could I die in a manner and for a cause which would induce true and honest men more to honor me, and the angels more ready to receive me to their happy home of everlasting joy above? . . . I imagine that I hear you, and all of you, mother, father, sisters and brothers, say—"No, there is not a cause for which we, with less sorrow, could see you die."

Brown also eloquently and calmly announced his willingness to die as so many had died before him. "Now, if it is deemed necessary that I should forfeit my life for the furtherance of the ends of justice, and mingle my blood further with the blood of my children and with the blood of millions in this slave country whose rights are disregarded by wicked, cruel, and unjust enactments, I say, let it be done."

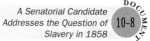

A Senatorial Candidate Addresses the Question of Slavery in 1858   DOCUMENT 10-8

For many Northerners, the day Brown was executed, December 2, 1859, was a day of mourning. Church bells tolled, and people bowed their heads in prayer. One unnamed black man later solemnly declared, "The memory of John Brown shall be indelibly written upon the tablets of our hearts, and when tyrants cease to oppress the enslaved, we will teach our children to revive his name, and transmit it to the latest posterity, as being the greatest man in the 19th century."

An Abolitionist Is Given the Death Sentence   DOCUMENT 10-9

White Southerners felt differently. They were terrified and traumatized by the raid, and outraged that Northerners made Brown a hero and a martyr. A wave of

TABLE 10–1	DEEPENING CRISIS OVER SLAVERY
1846	The Wilmot Proviso
1850	The Compromise of 1850
1854	The Kansas-Nebraska Act
1855–1856	Bleeding Kansas
1857	The *Dred Scott* Decision
1859	John Brown's Raid
1860	The Election of Lincoln as President
1860	South Carolina Secedes from the Union
1861	Formation of the Confederacy, Fort Sumter, Beginning of the Civil War

hysteria and paranoia swept the South as incredulous white people wondered how Northerners could admire a man who sought to kill slave owners and free their slaves.

Brown's raid and the reaction to it further divided a nation already badly split over slavery. Although neither he nor anyone else realized it at the time, Brown and his "army" had propelled the South toward secession from the Union—and thereby moved the nation closer to his goal of destroying slavery.

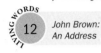
LIVING WORDS
12
John Brown: An Address

The Election of Abraham Lincoln

With the country fracturing over slavery, four candidates ran for president in the election of 1860. The Democrats split into a northern faction, which nominated Stephen Douglas, and a southern faction, which nominated John C. Breckenridge of Kentucky. The Constitutional Union Party, a new party formed by former Whigs, nominated John Bell of Tennessee. The breakup of the Democratic Party assured victory for the Republican candidate, Abraham Lincoln (see Map 10–3).

Lincoln's name was not even on the ballot in most southern states, because his candidacy was based on the Republican Party's adamant opposition to the expansion of slavery into any western territory. Although Lincoln took pains to reassure white Southerners that slavery would continue in states where it already existed, they were not in the least persuaded. A South Carolina newspaper was convinced Lincoln would abolish slavery. "[Lincoln] has openly proclaimed a war of extermination against the leading institutions of the Southern States. He says that there can be no peace so long as slavery has a foot hold in America."

A Georgia newspaper preferred a bloody civil war to a Lincoln presidency. "Let the consequences be what they may—whether the Potomac is crimsoned in human gore, and Pennsylvania Avenue is paved ten fathoms deep with mangled bodies . . . the South will never submit to such humiliation and degradation as the inauguration of Abraham Lincoln."

BLACK PEOPLE RESPOND TO LINCOLN'S ELECTION

Although they were less opposed to Lincoln than white Southerners, black Northerners and white abolitionists were not eager to see Abraham Lincoln become president. Dismayed by his contradictions and racism—he opposed slavery, but he tolerated it; he was

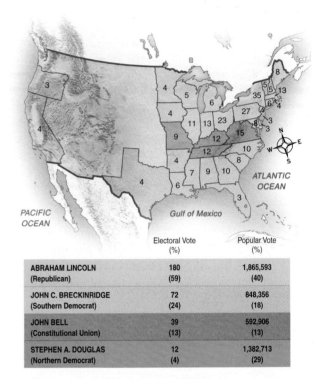

	Electoral Vote (%)	Popular Vote (%)
ABRAHAM LINCOLN (Republican)	180 (59)	1,865,593 (40)
JOHN C. BRECKINRIDGE (Southern Democrat)	72 (24)	848,356 (18)
JOHN BELL (Constitutional Union)	39 (13)	592,906 (13)
STEPHEN A. DOUGLAS (Northern Democrat)	12 (4)	1,382,713 (29)

MAP 10–3   THE ELECTION OF 1860

The results reflect the sectional schism over slavery. Lincoln carried the election although he won only in northern states. His name did not even appear on the ballot in most southern states.

▶ *How was Lincoln able to win without getting any electoral votes from the South?*

against slavery's expansion, but he condemned black Americans as inferiors—many black people refused to support him or did so reluctantly. The New York *Anglo-African* opposed both Republicans and Democrats in the 1860 election, telling its readers to depend on each other. "We have no hope from either [of the] political parties. We must rely on ourselves, the righteousness of our cause, and the advance of just sentiments among the great masses of the . . . people."

Abolitionists such as William Lloyd Garrison and Wendell Phillips believed Lincoln was too willing to tolerate slaveholding interests. But Frederick Douglass wrote, "Lincoln's election will indicate growth in the right direction" and his presidency "must and will be hailed as an anti-slavery triumph."

After Lincoln's election, black leaders almost welcomed the secession of southern states. H. Ford Douglas urged the southern states to leave the Union.

South Carolina slaves assembling an artillery piece prior to the Confederate Army's attack on Fort Sumter in Charleston in April 1861.

"Stand not upon the order of your going, but go at once. . . . There is no union of ideas and interests in this country, and there can be no union between freedom and slavery." Frederick Douglass was convinced that there were men prepared to follow in the footsteps of John Brown's "army" to destroy slavery. "I am for dissolution of the Union—decidedly for a dissolution of the Union! . . . In case of such a dissolution, I believe that men could be found . . . who would venture into those states and raise the standard of liberty there."

Disunion

When South Carolina seceded on December 20, 1860, it began a procession of southern states out of the Union. By February 1861 seven states—South Car-olina, Mississippi, Alabama, Florida, Louisiana, Georgia, and Texas—had seceded and formed the Confederate States of America in Montgomery, Alabama. Before there could be the kind of undertaking against slavery that Douglass had proposed, Abraham Lincoln tried to persuade the seceding states to reconsider. In his inaugural address of March 4, 1861, Lincoln attempted to calm the fears of white Southerners but informed them he would not tolerate their withdrawal from the Union. Lincoln repeated his assurance that he would not tamper with slavery in the states where it was already legal. "I have no purpose, directly or indirectly, to interfere with the institution of slavery in the States where it exists. I believe I have no lawful right to do so, and I have no inclination to do so."

Lincoln added that the "only" dispute between the North and South was over the expansion of slavery. He emphatically warned, however, that he would enforce

AFRICAN-AMERICAN EVENTS | NATIONAL EVENTS

1820

1820
Missouri Compromise

1825

1829
David Walker publishes his *Appeal to the Colored Citizens of the World*

1830

1831
William Lloyd Garrison begins publication of *Liberator*

1833
American Anti-Slavery Society founded

1835

1840

1845

1847
Crosswhite family eludes capture in Michigan

1846–1847
Mexican War

1848
William and Ellen Craft escape from slavery in Georgia

1846
Wilmot Proviso

1847
Mormons begin settlement of Utah

1848
Formation of the Free-Soil Party

Election of Zachary Taylor

Women's rights convention at Seneca Falls, New York

the Constitution and not permit secession. "Plainly, the central idea of secession is the essence of anarchy." He pleaded with white Southerners to contemplate their actions patiently and thoughtfully, actions that might provoke a civil conflict. "In your hands, my dissatisfied fellow-countrymen, and not in mine, is the monumental issue of civil war."

Southern whites did not heed him. Slavery was too essential to give up merely to preserve the Union. Arthur P. Hayne of South Carolina had succinctly summed up its importance in an 1860 letter to President James Buchanan. "Slavery with us is no abstraction—but a great and vital fact. Without it our every comfort would be taken from us. Our wives, our children, made unhappy—education, the light of knowledge—all lost and our people ruined forever. Nothing short of separation from the Union can save us."

Barely a month after Lincoln's inauguration, Confederate leaders demanded that U.S. Army major Robert Anderson surrender Fort Sumter, located in the harbor of Charleston, South Carolina. Anderson refused, and on April 12, 1861, Confederate artillery fired on the fort. In the aftermath, four additional states—Virginia, North Carolina, Tennessee, and Arkansas—joined the Confederacy. The Civil War had begun.

CONCLUSION

Virtually every event and episode of major or minor consequence in the United States between 1846 and 1861 involved black people and the expansion of slavery. From the Wilmot Proviso and the Compromise of 1850 to the *Dred Scott* decision and John Brown's raid, white Americans were increasingly perplexed about how the nation could remain half slave and half free. They were unable to resolve the problem of slavery's expansion.

Without the presence of black people in America, neither secession nor civil war would have occurred. Yet the Civil War began because white Americans had developed contradictory visions of the future. White Southerners contemplated a future that inextricably linked their security and prosperity to slavery. The South, they believed, could neither advance nor endure without slavery.

Northern white people believed their future rested on the opportunities for white men and their families to flourish as independent, self-sufficient farmers, shopkeepers, and skilled artisans. For their future to prevail, they insisted the new lands in the American West should exclude the slave system that white Southerners considered so vital. Neither northern nor southern white people—except for some abolitionists—ever believed people of color should fully participate as free people in American society or in the future of the American nation.

RECOMMENDED READING

Eric Foner. *Free Soil, Free Labor and Free Men: The Ideology of the Republican Party before the Civil War.* New York: Oxford University Press, 1970. An excellent overview of attitudes on free soil, slavery, and race.

Vincent Harding. *There Is a River: The Black Struggle for Freedom in America.* New York: Harcourt, Brace, Jovanovich, 1981. A tribute to and a masterful narrative about the black people who challenged the white majority in nineteenth-century America.

Leon Litwack. *North of Slavery: The Negro in the Free States, 1790–1860.* Chicago: University of Chicago Press, 1961. A story of black Northerners and the discrimination they encountered.

James McPherson. *Battle Cry of Freedom: The Civil War Era.* New York: Oxford University Press, 1988. A superb account of the crisis leading up to the Civil War and of the war itself.

David Potter. *The Impending Crisis, 1848–1861.* New York: Harper & Row, 1976. Another fine account of the events leading up to the Civil War.

ADDITIONAL BIBLIOGRAPHY

CALIFORNIA AND THE COMPROMISE OF 1850

Eugene H. Berwanger. *The Frontier against Slavery: Western Anti-Negro Prejudice and the Slave Extension Controversy.* Urbana: University of Illinois Press, 1967.

Holman Hamilton. *Prologue to Conflict: The Crisis and Compromise of 1850.* Lexington: University of Kentucky Press, 1964.

Lynn M. Hudson. *The Making of "Mammy Pleasant," a Black Entrepreneur in Nineteenth-Century San Francisco.* Urbana: University of Illinois Press, 2003.

Rudolph M. Lapp. *Blacks in Gold Rush California.* New Haven, CT: Yale University Press, 1977.

THE FUGITIVE SLAVE LAW AND ITS VICTIMS

Stanley W. Campbell. *The Slave Catchers: Enforcement of the Fugitive Slave Law, 1850–1860.* Chapel Hill: University of North Carolina Press, 1968.

Gary Collison. *Shadrach Minkins.* Cambridge, MA: Harvard University Press, 1998.

Albert J. von Frank. *The Trials of Anthony Burns.* Cambridge, MA: Harvard University Press, 1998.

AFRICAN-AMERICAN EVENTS	NATIONAL EVENTS
1850	**1850**
Fugitive Slave Act	Compromise of 1850 and the Fugitive Slave Act
1850–1860	**1852**
Fugitive slaves captured	Publication of *Uncle Tom's Cabin*
1851	Election of Franklin Pierce
Shadrach eludes capture in Boston;	**1854**
Thomas Sims returned to slavery; "Battle" at Christiana	Kansas-Nebraska Act
1853	
Black convention at Rochester, New York	
1854	
Anthony Burns returned to slavery in Boston	
1856	**1855–1856**
Margaret Garner kills her daughter in unsuccessful escape	"Bleeding" Kansas
1857	**1856**
The *Dred Scott* decision	Congressman Preston Brooks assaults Senator Charles Sumner
1859	**1858**
John Brown's raid on Harpers Ferry	The Lincoln-Douglas debates
1861	**1860**
Free black men in Charleston offer their support to South Carolina	Abraham Lincoln elected president
	South Carolina secedes from the Union
	1861
	Six more southern states secede and form the Confederacy; Civil War begins after firing on Fort Sumter in April; four more southern states join the Confederacy

Jonathan Katz. *Resistance at Christiana: The Fugitive Slave Rebellion at Christiana, Pennsylvania, September 11, 1851: A Documentary Account.* New York: Crowell, 1974.

Thomas P. Slaughter. *Bloody Dawn: The Christiana Riot and Violence in the Antebellum North.* New York: Oxford University Press, 1991.

THE 1850S

Walter Ehrlich. *They Have No Rights: Dred Scott's Struggle for Freedom.* Westport, CT: Greenwood Press, 1979.

Don E. Fehrenbacher. *The Dred Scott Case: Its Significance in American Law and Politics.* New York: Oxford University Press, 1978.

Michael F. Holt. *The Fate of Their Country: Politicians, Slavery Extension, and the Coming of the Civil War.* New York: Hill and Wang, 2005.

Robert W. Johannsen. *Stephen A. Douglas.* New York: Oxford University Press, 1973.

Kenneth M. Stampp. *America in 1857: A Nation on the Brink.* New York: Oxford University Press, 1990.

Eric Walther. *The Shattering of the Union: America in the 1850s.* Wilmington: Scholarly Resources, 2004.

JOHN BROWN AND THE RAID ON HARPERS FERRY

Louis A. DeCaro, Jr. *"Fire from the Midst of You": A Religious Life of John Brown.* New York: New York University Press, 2002.

Paul Finkelman. *And His Soul Goes Marching On: Responses to John Brown and the Harpers Ferry Raid.* Charlottesville: University of Virginia Press, 1995.

Truman Nelson. *The Old Man John Brown at Harpers Ferry.* New York: Holt, Rinehart, & Winston, 1973.

Stephen Oates. *To Purge This Land with Blood: A Biography of John Brown.* New York: Harper & Row, 1970.

Benjamin Quarles. *Blacks on John Brown.* Urbana: University of Illinois Press, 1972.

SECESSION

William L. Barney. *The Road to Secession.* New York: Praeger, 1972.

Steven A. Channing. *Crisis of Fear: Secession in South Carolina.* New York: Simon & Schuster, 1970.

Kenneth M. Stampp. *And the War Came: The North and the Secession Crisis, 1860–1861.* Baton Rouge: Louisiana State University Press, 1950.

ABRAHAM LINCOLN

Gabor Boritt, ed. *The Lincoln Enigma.* New York: Oxford University Press, 2001.

David Herbert Donald. *Lincoln.* New York: Simon & Schuster, 1995.

Stephen B. Oates. *With Malice toward None: A Life of Abraham Lincoln.* New York: Harper & Row, 1977.

Benjamin Thomas. *Abraham Lincoln: A Biography.* New York: Alfred A. Knopf, 1952.

NOVELS

Martin R. Delany. *Blake or the Huts of America.* Boston: Beacon Press, 1970.

Harriet Beecher Stowe. *Uncle Tom's Cabin, or Life among the Lowly.* New York: Modern Library, 1985.

RETRACING THE ODYSSEY

Black Heritage Trail, Boston, Massachusetts. This is a 1.6-mile walking tour of fourteen sites. It begins at the Africa Meeting House (built in 1806) and includes the four-story home of black leader Lewis Hayden and his wife Harriet as well as Augustus Saint-Gaudens's powerful 1897 *Memorial to Robert Gould Shaw and the 54th Massachusetts Regiment.*

The Old St. Louis Court House, St. Louis, Missouri. This restored structure was the scene of two of Dred Scott's trials. It contains some of the legal papers and newspaper articles involving the case.

The First Baptist Church, Chatham, Ontario, Canada. On May 28, 1858, John Brown met with members of Chatham's black community—many of whom had fled to Canada to escape the fugitive slave law. Brown appealed for support to begin an armed uprising of slaves in the South. Fire destroyed the original structure in 1907, and the current church was built in 1908.

Harpers Ferry National Park, West Virginia. Picturesquely situated in the Blue Ridge Mountains at the confluence of the Shenandoah and Potomac Rivers, this is where John Brown and his "army" in October 1859 attempted to secure weapons to begin a slave rebellion.

PRENTICE HALL myhistorylab *Where it's a good time to connect to the past!*   REVIEW, RESEARCH, AND INTERACT

REVIEW QUESTIONS

1. How and why did southern and northern white people differ over slavery? On what did white people of both regions agree and disagree about race and slavery?

2. If you were a northern African American in the 1850s, how would you have responded to the policies of the U.S. government?

3. If you were a white Southerner in the 1850s, would you have been encouraged or discouraged by U.S. government policies?

4. Why did seven southern states secede from the Union within three months after Abraham Lincoln was elected president in 1860?

5. If you were a black person—either a slave or free—would you have welcomed the secession of the southern states? How might secession affect the future of your people?

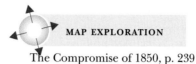 **www.researchnavigator.com**

Using the tools available in Research Navigator, consider these questions:
Why did the conflict over slavery intensify in the 1840s and 1850s? What efforts were made to resolve the conflict?

 PRIMARY SOURCE DOCUMENTS

10–1 The Compromise of 1850

10–2 The Lincoln-Douglas Debate, 1858

10–3 Northern State Defies Fugitive Slave Act, 1855

10–4 New England Writer Portrays Slavery in 1852

10–5 Letter from Anthony Burns to the Baptist Church, 1855

10–6 Vilet Lester Letter to Miss Patsey Patterson, August 19th 1857

10–7 A Slave Sues for Freedom in 1857

10–8 A Senatorial Candidate Addresses the Question of Slavery in 1858

10–9 An Abolitionist Is Given the Death Sentence in 1859

MAP EXPLORATION

The Compromise of 1850, p. 239

INTERACTIVE ACTIVITY

Anthony Burns

Anthony Burns came to embody the evils of slavery and the way in which the Fugitive Slave Law forced Northerners to support the South's "peculiar institution."

Speaking Out Against Slavery

Abolitionist literature was a mainstay of the movement to end slavery. The anti-slavery press created a wide variety of newspapers, periodicals, publications for children, reports, broadsides, sermons, and other types of printed material to bring their stand against slavery to the public. In addition, many anti-slavery organizations regularly held public meetings with speeches by prominent leaders of the movement to bring the abolitionist message to people, using music and songs to arouse the crowds. Whites, African Americans, and women were all deeply involved in these determined efforts to abolish slavery.

The title page of *The Penitential Tyrant; or, Slave Trader Reformed* by Thomas Branagan, former slave trader and owner of slaves. Branagan joined the abolitionist movement. His books were a powerful indictment of the institution of slavery.

REPORT

OF THE

HOLDEN SLAVE CASE,

TRIED AT THE

JANUARY TERM OF THE COURT OF COMMON PLEAS, FOR THE COUNTY OF WORCESTER, A. D. 1839.

Published by the
Board of Directors of the Holden Anti-Slavery Society.

WORCESTER:
PRINTED BY COLTON & HOWLAND.
1839.

THE
PENITENTIAL TYRANT;
OR,
Slave Trader Reformed:
A
PATHETIC POEM,
IN FOUR CANTOS.

BY THOMAS BRANAGAN.

THE SECOND EDITION, ENLARGED.

"AM I NOT A MAN, AND A BROTHER?"

New-York:
PRINTED AND SOLD BY SAMUEL WOOD,
No. 362, PEARL-STREET.
1807.

This illustration shows Wendell Phillips (1811–1884) speaking at a meeting to protest the trial of fugitive slave Thomas Sims in Boston. Sims was eventually returned to slavery in Savannah.

Anti-slavery activities included publishing reports on legal cases involving slaves or former slaves.

Leaflet appealing to fellow citizens to attend a meeting to hear their platform against slavery, published in Lexington, 1850.

THOMPSON, THE ABOLITIONIST.

That infamous foreign scoundrel THOMPSON, will hold forth *this afternoon*, at the Liberator Office, No. 48, Washington Street. The present is a fair opportunity for the friends of the Union to *snake Thompson out!* It will be a contest between the Abolitionists and the friends of the Union. A purse of $100 has been raised by a number of patriotic citizens to reward the individual who shall first lay violent hands on Thompson, so that he may be brought to the tar kettle before dark. Friends of the Union, be vigilant!

Boston, Wednesday, 12 o'clock.

◄ This anti-abolitionist ad announces an offer of $100 for the capture of an abolitionist.

In an effort to stir ► anti-abolitionist fervor, this broadside announces an upcoming abolitionist lecture at a local New York church.

OUTRAGE.

Fellow Citizens,

AN
ABOLITIONIST,

of the most revolting character is among you, exciting the feelings of the North against the South. A seditious Lecture is to be delivered

THIS EVENING,

at 7 o'clock, at the Presbyterian Church in Cannon-street. You are requested to attend and unite in putting down and silencing by peaceable means this tool of evil and fanaticism. Let the rights of the States guaranteed by the Constitution be protected.

Feb. 27, 1837. The Union forever!

[May 1850]

TO THE PEOPLE, Who wish to do Right!

There are thousands of persons in Kentucky who conscientiously believe, that

Slavery is injurious to the prosperity of our beloved State:—
Inconsistent with the fundamental principles of free government:—
Contrary to the natural rights of mankind:—
Adverse to a pure state of morals:—
A great hindrance to the establishment of Free Schools:—
That it depresses the energies of the laboring white man:—
And in many other ways, is

A CURSE TO THE COUNTRY.

Many of the persons who so believe, have formed themselves into a party,

OPPOSED TO THE PERPETUATION OF SLAVERY IN KENTUCKY,

Composed of such men as Henry Clay and Dr. R. J. Breckinridge, of Fayette; Judge Nicholas, Wm. L. Breckinridge and Hon. Wm. P. Thomasson, of Louisville; C. M. Clay, of Madison; Judge Monroe, of Franklin; Dr. J. C. Young, of Boyle; J. McClung, of Mason; Judge Ballinger, of Mercer; J. R. Thornton, of Bourbon, and thousands of other persons of both parties; hard-working, honest, industrious, virtuous Mechanics, Manufacturers, Laborers, Farmers and Slaveholders of the Commonwealth, who for *Talent, Education, Virtue, Uprightness of Character and Intelligence*, cant be beat in any State in the Union!

These men object to the Perpetuation of Slavery by the Constitution of the State, and so *ought* every other GOOD REPUBLICAN who loves the prosperity of his home. The *way* and the *time* to do this, belongs to the CONVENTION TO CHANGE THE CONSTITUTION, which will assemble in Frankfort in October.

This party has adopted and published a PLATFORM OF THEIR PRINCIPLES, so that every body may see that their *design is a good one*, and the *manner* in which they wish to do it, is a Peaceable, Quiet and Lawful one. For which purpose, they are going to run candidates in the various counties in the State, favorable to the two following objects, and no matter how their *enemies may misrepresent them*, we believe that a majority of the people of this State, are in favor of the principles laid down in the Plat-

THEIR PLATFORM.

1st. "The absolute prohibition of the importation of any more slaves into Kentucky."

2d. "The complete power in the People of Kentucky to enforce and perfect in or under the new Constitution, a system of gradual prospective Emancipation of Slaves."

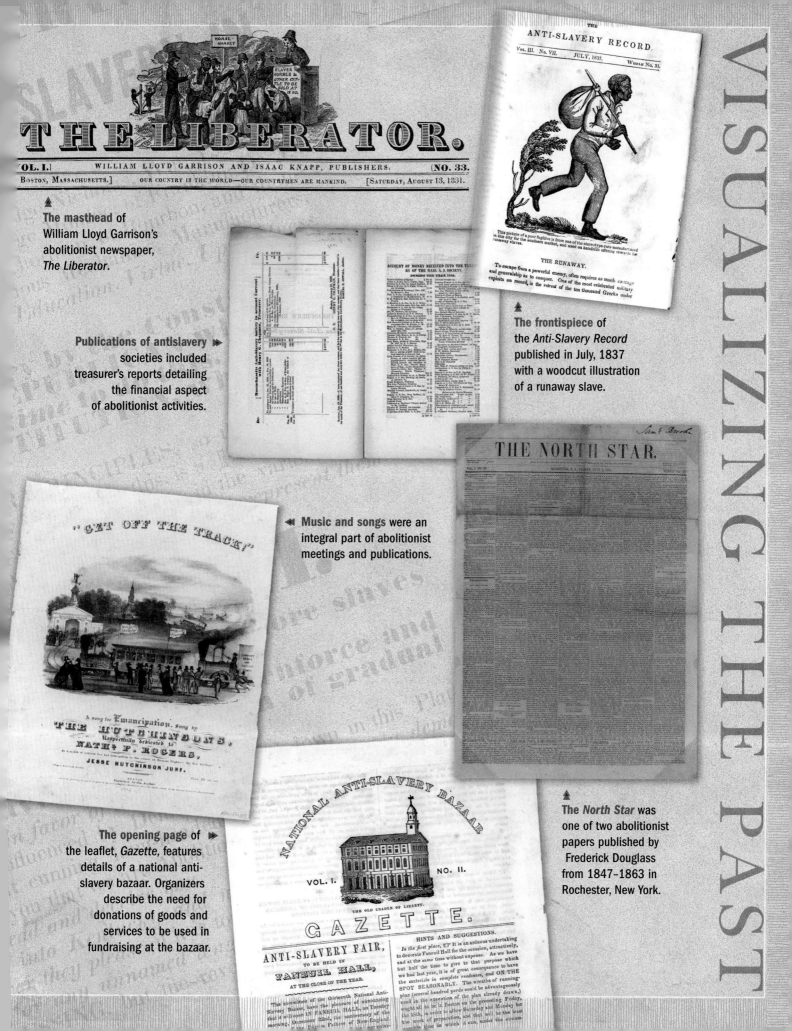

VISUALIZING THE PAST

THE LIBERATOR.

VOL. I.]   WILLIAM LLOYD GARRISON AND ISAAC KNAPP, PUBLISHERS.   [NO. 33.

BOSTON, MASSACHUSETTS.]   OUR COUNTRY IS THE WORLD—OUR COUNTRYMEN ARE MANKIND.   [SATURDAY, AUGUST 13, 1831.

▲ **The masthead** of William Lloyd Garrison's abolitionist newspaper, *The Liberator*.

Publications of antislavery ▶ societies included treasurer's reports detailing the financial aspect of abolitionist activities.

THE ANTI-SLAVERY RECORD.

Vol. III.   No. VII.   JULY, 1837.   WHOLE No. 31.

THE RUNAWAY.

▲ **The frontispiece** of the *Anti-Slavery Record* published in July, 1837 with a woodcut illustration of a runaway slave.

"GET OFF THE TRACK!"

A song for Emancipation. Sung by THE HUTCHINSONS, Respectfully dedicated to NATH. P. ROGERS,

JESSE HUTCHINSON JUNR.

◀ **Music and songs** were an integral part of abolitionist meetings and publications.

THE NORTH STAR.

▲ **The *North Star*** was one of two abolitionist papers published by Frederick Douglass from 1847–1863 in Rochester, New York.

The opening page of ▶ the leaflet, *Gazette*, features details of a national anti-slavery bazaar. Organizers describe the need for donations of goods and services to be used in fundraising at the bazaar.

NATIONAL ANTI-SLAVERY BAZAAR

VOL. I.   NO. II.

THE OLD CRADLE OF LIBERTY.

GAZETTE.

ANTI-SLAVERY FAIR, TO BE HELD IN FANEUIL HALL, AT THE CLOSE OF THE YEAR.

HINTS AND SUGGESTIONS.

SLAVE REBELLIONS

In many areas slaves outnumbered their white masters. Plantation owners and white authorities in southern slave colonies were frightened of the potential for slave rebellions and set very strict laws to restrict the movement of slaves. The Maryland General Assembly was particularly concerned in these laws about preventing the development of a class of freedmen from which slave rebellions might be spawned because of their freedom of movement. Almost one hundred years later the North Carolina state legislature would be enact stricter and much more specific slave codes.

Given the population advantage of slaves in plantation regions and the multiples of examples of slave rebellions which were known to slaves, why were slave rebellions not more frequent and more successful in southern states?

▶ SOURCE: Stono Bridge Revolt, South Carolina, 1739

They increased every minute by new Negroes coming to them, so that they were above Sixty, some say a hundred, on which they halted in a field, and set to dancing, Singing and beating Drums, to draw more Negroes to them, thinking they were now victorious over the whole Province, having marched ten miles & burnt all before them without Opposition, but the Militia being raised, the Planters with great briskness pursued them and when they came up, dismounting; charged them on foot. The Negroes were soon routed, though they behaved boldly several being killed on the Spot, many ran back to their Plantations thinking they had not been missed, but they were there taken and [sic] Shot, Such as were taken in the field also, were after being examined, shot on the Spot, And this is to be said to the honour of the Carolina Planters, that notwithstanding the Provocation they had received from so many Murders, they did not torture one Negroe, but only put them to an easy death. All that proved to be forced & were not concerned in the Murders & Burnings were pardoned, And this sudden Courage in the field, & the Humanity afterwards hath had so good an Effect that there hath been no farther Attempt, and the very Spirit of Revolt seems over. About 30 escaped from the fight, of which ten marched about 30 miles Southward, and being overtaken by the Planters on horseback, fought stoutly for some time and were all killed on the Spot. The rest are yet untaken. In the whole action about 40 Negroes and 20 whites were killed.

▶ SOURCE: Maryland Slave Code, 1664

Be it Enacted by the Right Honourable the Lord Proprietary, by the advice and Consent of the upper and lower house of this present General Assembly, That all Negroes or other slaves already within the Province And all Negroes and other slaves to be hereafter imported into the Province shall serve Durante Vita. [for the duration of their lives]

And all Children born of any Negro or other slave shall be Slaves as their fathers were for the term of their lives. . . .

Be it further Enacted by the Authority advice and Consent aforesaid, That whatsoever freeborn woman shall inter marry with any slave from and after the Last day of this present Assembly shall Serve the master of such slave during the life of her husband, And that all the Issue of such freeborn women so married shall be Slaves as their fathers were. And Be it further Enacted that all the Issues of English or other freeborn women that have already married Negroes shall serve the Masters of their Parents till they be Thirty years of age and no longer.

▶ SOURCE: Denmark Vesey Rebellion, 1822

Previous to the proposal of any plan for preventing the recurrence of similar danger, it may be useful to advert to the causes which produced the late conspiracy. The following may be assigned as some of the most obvious: —1st, The example of St. Domingo, and (probably) the encouragement received from thence.—2dly, The indiscreet zeal in favor of universal liberty, expressed by many of our fellow-citizens in the States north and east of Maryland; aided by the Black population of those States.—3dly, The idleness, dissipation, and improper indulgencies permitted among all classes of the Negroes in Charleston, and particularly among the domestics: and, as the most dangerous of those indulgencies, their being taught to read and write: the first bringing the powerful operation of the Press to act on their uninformed and easily deluded minds; and the latter furnishing them with an instrument to carry into execution the mischievous suggestions of the former.—4th, The facility of obtaining money afforded by the nature of their occupations to those employed as mechanics, draymen, fishermen, butchers, porters, hucksters, &c.—5th, The disparity of numbers between the white and black inhabitants of the City. No effort of ours can remove some of these causes, but over others we may exercise control.

▶ SOURCE: from *The Confessions of Nat Turner,* 1831

There were two whom they thought they left dead on the field at Mr. Parker's, but who were only stunned by the blows of their guns, as they did not take time to re-load when they charged on them. The escape of a little girl who went to school at Mr. Wailer's, and where the children were collecting for that purpose, excited general sympathy. As their teacher had not arrived, they were at play in the yard, and seeing the negroes approach, she ran up on a dirt chimney, (such as are common to log houses,) and remained there unnoticed during the massacre of the eleven that were killed at this place. She remained on her hiding place till just before the arrival of a party, who were in pursuit of the murderers, when she came down and fled to a swamp, where, a mere child as she was, with the horrors of the late scene before her, she lay concealed until the next day, when seeing a party go up to the house, she came up, and on being asked how she escaped, replied with the utmost simplicity, `The Lord helped her." She was taken up behind a gentleman of the party, and returned to the arms of her weeping mother. Miss Whitehead concealed herself between the bed and the mat that supported it, while they murdered her sister in the same room, without discovering her. She was afterwards carried off, and concealed for protection by a slave of the family, who gave evidence against several of them on their trial. Mrs. Nathaniel Francis, while concealed in a closet heard their blows, and the shrieks of the victims of these ruthless savages; they then entered the closet where she was concealed, and went out without discovering her. While in this hiding place, she heard two of her women in a quarrel about the division of her clothes. Mr. John T. Baron, discovering them approaching his house, told his wife to make her escape, and scorning to fly, fell fighting on his own threshold. After firing his rifle, he discharged his gun at them, and then broke it over the villain who first approached him, but he was overpowered, and slain. His bravery, however, saved from the hands of these monsters, his lovely and amiable wife, who will long lament a husband so deserving of her love. As directed by him, she attempted to escape through the garden, when she was caught and held by one of her servant girls, but another coming to her rescue, she fled to the woods, and concealed herself. Few indeed, were those who escaped their work of death. But fortunate for society, the hand of retributive justice has overtaken them; and not one that was known to be concerned has escaped.

◀ *The slave mutiny on board the* Amistad *as depicted in an 1839 newspaper report.*

▶ SOURCE: North Carolina Codes, 1855

If any slave shall be guilty of producing any forged free pass. . . shall on conviction. . . be sentenced to receive. . . lashes on his bare back, not exceeding thirty-nine. . .

No slave shall go armed with gun, sword, club or other weapon, or shall keep any such weapon, or shall hunt or range with a gun in the woods, upon any pretence whatsoever. . .

No slave shall go from off the plantation or seat of land where such slave shall be appointed to live without a certificate of leave, in writing, for so doing from his or her master or overseer.

If any slave shall teach or attempt to teach, any other slave to read or write. . . and on conviction. . . , shall be sentenced to receive thirty-nine lashes on his or her bare back.

It shall not be lawful under any pretence for any slave, or free person of colour to preach or exhort in public or in any manner to officiate as a preacher or teacher in any prayer meeting, . . .

If any number of slaves shall at any time hereafter, consult, advise or conspire to rebel or make insurrection, or shall plot or conspire the murder of any person... the slave or slaves convicted thereof... shall suffer death. . .

If any slave be found in a state of rebellion or insurrection, or shall agree to join any conspiracy or insurrection. . . shall suffer death. . .

If any free person shall join in any conspiracy, rebellion or insurrection of the slaves. . . . shall suffer death without benefit of clergy. . . .

Any emancipation, granted to any slave or slaves, as herein directed, shall be upon the express condition that he, she or they will leave the State within ninety days from the granting thereof, and never will return within the State afterwards.

It shall not be lawful for any free negro, or mulatto to migrate into this State. . .

PART III

THE CIVIL WAR, EMANCIPATION, AND BLACK RECONSTRUCTION

The Second American Revolution

Robert Brown Elliott

	1860–1865	1865–1870
RELIGION	**1865–1870s** Former slaves organize their own religious congregations across the South	**1866–1870s** Numerous black ministers elected to political office and leadership positions in the South
CULTURE		**1865–1870s** More than forty black colleges founded in the South **1867** Howard University established **1868** Elizabeth Keckley publishes *Behind the Scenes, Or Thirty Years as a Slave and Four Years in the White House* **1869** More than 100,000 students attend Freedmen's Bureau schools in the South
POLITICS & GOVERNMENT	**1861** Union Army rejects black volunteers First Confiscation Act frees slaves who had been used by the Confederate Army **1862** Militia Act authorizes recruitment of black troops for the Union Army First black troops fight for Union at Island Mountain, MO **1863** Emancipation Proclamation issued Black troops assault Battery Wagner in Charleston Harbor **1864** Fort Pillow Massacre **1865** Confederate Congress votes to enlist 300,000 black troops U.S. Congress creates the Freedmen's Bureau Thirteenth Amendment abolishes slavery Congress passes a Civil Rights Act Southern states rejoin the Union and enact black codes	**1865–1866** Black political conventions held across the South **1867** Reconstruction Acts passed by Congress **1867–1868** Black people participate in southern states' constitutional conventions **1868** Fourteenth Amendment gives black people the rights of citizenship
SOCIETY & ECONOMY	**1862** Port Royal Experiment begins in South Carolina **1863** New York City Draft Riots attack African Americans **1864** Black National Convention meets in Syracuse, NY **1865** Freedmen's Savings Bank and Trust Company established	**1866** Klu Klux Klan organized New Orleans Massacre White mob lynches twenty-four black men near Pline Bluff, AR **1869** Isaac Myers organizes the Colored National Labor Union

Charlotte Forten

Blanche K. Bruce

Elizabeth Keckley

| 1870–1880 | 1880–1900 | NOTEWORTHY INDIVIDUALS |

1870s Colored Methodist Episcopal Church established

1870s Black people organize St. Mark's, the first African-American Episcopal congregation in Charleston, SC

1902 Susie K. Taylor publishes her memoir of nursing black troops in the Union Army

1872 Charlotte Ray becomes the first African-American woman lawyer

Alcorn A&M College, the first black state university, founded in Mississippi

1870 Fifteenth Amendment prohibits disfranchisement because of race

Hiram R. Revels, first African-American U.S. senator elected; Joseph Rainey, First African-American congressman, elected

1870–1871 Enforcement Acts against Klan terrorism passed by Congress

1877 Reconstruction ends

1883 U.S. Supreme Court strikes down the Civil Rights Act of 1875

1872 Colefax Massacre in Louisiana

1874 Freedmen's Savings Bank closes

1876 Hamburg Massacre in South Carolina

Aaron A. Bradley
(1815–1881)

Elizabeth Keckley
(1818–1907)

Hiram R. Revels
(1822–1901)

Mifflin W. Gibbs
(1823–1915)

Richard H. Cain
(1825–1887)

Jonathan C. Gibbs
(c. 1827–1874)

Isaac Myers
(1835–1901)

William Whipper
(1835–1907)

James T. Rapier
(1837–1883)

Francis L. Cardozo
(1837–1903)

Charlotte Forten
(1837–1914)

P.B.S. Pinchback
(1837–1921)

Robert Smalls
(1839–1915)

Jonathan J. Wright
(1840–1895)

William H. Carney
(1840–c. 1901)

Blanche K. Bruce
(1841–1898)

Robert Brown Elliott
(1842–1884)

Frances Rollin
(1844–1901)

Susie K. Taylor
(1848–1912)

Charlotte Ray
(1850–1911)

Katherine Rollin
(1851–1876)

11

Liberation
African Americans and
the Civil War

WHEN THE CIVIL WAR BEGAN, WHAT WAS
ABRAHAM LINCOLN'S PRIMARY OBJECTIVE?

HOW DID AFRICAN AMERICANS RESPOND
AS THE CIVIL WAR BEGAN IN 1861?

HOW DID LINCOLN'S POLICIES ON SLAVERY
CHANGE AS THE CIVIL WAR CONTINUED?

WHY DID LINCOLN ISSUE THE
EMANCIPATION PROCLAMATION?

HOW DID BLACK AND WHITE PEOPLE REACT
TO THE EMANCIPATION PROCLAMATION?

HOW DID AFRICAN AMERICANS AFFECT
THE OUTCOME OF THE CIVIL WAR?

◄ **Company E** of the Fourth United States Colored Infantry at
Fort Lincoln in the District of Columbia in 1865.

1861–1865

If the muse were mine to tempt it
And my feeble voice were strong,
If my tongue were trained to measures,
I would sing a stirring song.
I would sing a song heroic
Of those noble sons of Ham,
Of the gallant colored soldiers
Who fought for Uncle Sam! . . .
Ah, they rallied to the standard
To uphold it by their might;
None were stronger in the labors,
None were braver in the fight.
From the blazing breach of Wagner
To the plains of Olustee,
They were foremost in the fight
Of the battles of the free. . . .
And their deeds shall find a record
In the registry of Fame;
For their blood has cleansed completely
Every blot of Slavery's shame.
So all honor and all glory
To those noble sons of Ham—
The gallant colored soldiers
Who fought for Uncle Sam!

From "The Colored Soldiers," 1895, by Paul Laurence Dunbar, whose father, Joshua, served with the all-black 55th Massachusetts Regiment.

◄ **185,000 black men** fought for the Union during the Civil War.

Slavery caused the Civil War. Yet when the war began in 1861, neither the Union nor the Confederacy entered the conflict with any intention or desire to change the status of black Americans. It was supposed to be a white man's war. White Southerners would wage war to make the Confederacy a separate and independent nation free to promote slavery. White Northerners took up arms to maintain the Union but not to free a single slave. African Americans who wanted to enlist in 1861 were emphatically rejected. The Union might be disrupted, but slavery was not going to be disturbed.

Both North and South expected a quick victory. No one anticipated that forty-eight months of brutal war would rip the nation apart. When the Civil War ended in April 1865, almost 620,000 Americans were dead—including nearly 40,000 black men. The Union was preserved, and four million people had been freed. Nothing in American history compares with it.

Lincoln's Aims

When the war began, as it was fought, and when it ended, President Abraham Lincoln's unwavering objective was to preserve the Union. Any policies that helped or hindered black people were subordinate to that goal. Following the attack on Fort Sumter in April 1861 and Lincoln's call for state militias to help suppress the rebellion, four more slave states—North Carolina, Virginia, Tennessee, and Arkansas—seceded from the Union and joined the Confederacy. For most of 1861, Lincoln was determined to do nothing that would drive the four remaining slave states—Delaware, Maryland, Kentucky, and Missouri—into the Confederacy. Lincoln feared that if he did or said anything that could be interpreted as interfering with slavery, those four border states would leave the Union too.

Meanwhile, Lincoln issued a call for 75,000 men to enlist in the military for ninety days of service to the national government. Thousands of black and white men, far more than 75,000, responded to the call. White men were accepted; black men were rejected. Spurned by federal and state authorities, black men remained determined to aid the cause.

Black Men Volunteer and Are Rejected

Black people recognized long before most white Northerners that the fate of the Union was inextricably tied to the issue of slavery and the future of slavery was tied to the outcome of the war. "Talk as we may," insisted the *Anglo-African*, a black New York newspaper,

> we are concerned in this fight and our fate hangs upon its issues. The South must be subjugated, or we shall be enslaved. In aiding the Federal government in whatever way we can, we are aiding to secure our own liberty; for this war can end only in the subjugation of the North or the South.

Black men in New York formed their own military companies and began to drill. In Boston, they drew up a resolution modeled on the Declaration of Independence and appealed for permission to go to war:

> Our feelings urge us to say to our countrymen that we are ready to stand by and defend our Government as equals of its white defenders; to do so with "our lives, our fortunes, and our sacred honor," for the sake of freedom, and as good citizens; and we ask you to modify your laws, that we may enlist—that full scope may be given to patriotic feelings burning in the colored man's breast.

Black men in Philadelphia volunteered to infiltrate the South to incite slave revolts but were turned down. In Washington, Jacob Dodson, a black employee of the U.S. Senate, wrote a letter to Secretary of War Simon Cameron shortly after the fall of Fort Sumter volunteering the services of local black men. "I desire to inform you that I know of some 300 reliable colored free citizens of this city who desire to enter the service for the defense of the city." Cameron curtly replied, "This Department has no intention at the present to call into the service of the government any colored soldiers."

Union Policies toward Confederate Slaves

Slaves started to liberate themselves as soon as the war began, but Union political and military leaders had no coherent policy for dealing with them. To the deep disappointment of black Northerners and white abolitionists, Union military commanders showed more

These African-American troops served as teamsters for the Union Army in Virginia. Most Northern white people—including political leaders—believed that black men lacked the courage and fortitude for combat. They expected black men would do little more as soldiers than haul freight, erect fortifications, serve guard duty, and prepare food.

concern for the interests of Confederate slave owners than for the people in bondage. In May 1861 General George B. McClellan reassured Virginia slave owners: "Not only will we abstain from all interferences with your slaves, but we will, with an iron hand, crush any attempt at insurrection on their part."

General Henry Halleck ordered slaves who escaped in the Ohio Valley returned to their owners, and General Winfield Scott, the army's chief of staff, asked that Confederate slave owners be permitted to recover slaves who crossed the Potomac River to what they believed was the freedom of Union lines. In Tennessee in early 1862, General Ulysses S. Grant returned runaway slaves to their owners if the owners supported the Union cause, but Grant put black people to work on fortifications if their owners favored secession.

"CONTRABAND"

Not all Union commanders were as callous as these generals. A month after the war began, three bondmen working on Confederate fortifications in Virginia escaped to the Union's Fortress Monroe on the coast. Their owner, a Confederate colonel, appeared at the fortress the next day under a flag of truce and demanded the return of his slaves under the 1850 Fugitive Slave Act. The incredulous Union commander, General Benjamin Butler, informed him that because

Virginia had seceded from the Union, the fugitive slave law was no longer in force. Butler did not free the three slaves, but he did not reenslave them either. He declared them "**contraband**"—enemy property—and put them to work for the Union. Soon, over a thousand slaves fled to Fortress Monroe. The white authorities may have thought of them as contraband, but it is not likely that is how they viewed themselves. Crossing Union lines, it is doubtful any slaves declared, "We are contraband." Rather, they were more apt to proclaim enthusiastically, "We are free!"

On August 6, 1861, Congress clarified the status of runaway slaves when it passed the First Confiscation Act. Any property that belonged to Confederates used in the war effort could be seized by federal forces. Any slaves used by their masters to benefit the Confederacy—and only those slaves—would be freed. Almost immediately, Union general John C. Fremont (the 1856 Republican presidential candidate) exceeded the strict limits of the act by freeing all the slaves belonging to Confederates in Missouri. President Lincoln quickly countermanded the order and told Fremont that only slaves actively used to aid the Confederate war effort were to be freed. Lincoln worried that Fremont would drive Missouri or Kentucky into the Confederacy.

Black leaders were—to put it mildly—displeased with Lincoln and with federal policies that both prohibited the enlistment of black troops and ignored the plight of the enslaved. To fight a war against the South without fighting against slavery, the institution on which the South was so thoroughly dependent, seemed absurd. Frederick Douglass stated the argument cogently: "To fight against slaveholders, without fighting against slavery, is but a half-hearted business, and paralyzes the hands engaged in it. . . . Fire must be met with water. . . . War for the destruction of liberty must be met with war for the destruction of slavery."

Others were less charitable. Joseph R. Hawley, a white Connecticut Republican, thought Lincoln was foolish to worry about whether the border states might leave the Union. "Permit me to say damn the border states. . . . A thousand Lincolns cannot stop the people from fighting slavery." In the New York *Anglo-African,* a letter writer who identified himself as "Ivanhoe" urged northern black men to decline any request to serve in Union military forces until the slaves were freed and black Northerners received treatment equal to that of white people. "And suppose we were invited [to enlist]," he asked, "what duty would we then owe to ourselves and our posterity? . . . Our enslaved brethren must be made freedmen. . . . We of the North must have all of the rights which white men enjoy; until then we are in no condition to fight under the flag [which] gives us no protection."

Lincoln did not budge. Union military forces occupied an enclave on South Carolina's southern coast and the Sea Islands in late 1861, and on May 9, 1862, General David Hunter ordered slavery abolished in South Carolina, Georgia, and Florida. Lincoln quickly revoked Hunter's order and reprimanded him. Nevertheless, thousands of slaves along the South Carolina and Georgia coast threw off their shackles and welcomed Union troops as plantation owners fled to the interior.

LINCOLN'S INITIAL POSITION

For more than a year, Lincoln remained reluctant to strike decisively against slavery. He believed the long-term solution to slavery and the race problem in the United States was the compensated emancipation of slaves followed by their colonization outside the country. That is, slave owners would be paid for their slaves; the slaves would be freed but forced to settle in the Caribbean, Latin America, or West Africa.

As a Whig congressman in 1849, Lincoln voted for a bill that would have emancipated slaves and compensated their owners in the District of Columbia if it had passed. In 1861 he tried—but failed—to persuade the Delaware legislature to support compensated emancipation. Then in April 1862, at Lincoln's urging, Republicans in Congress (against almost unanimous Democratic opposition) voted to provide funds to "any state which may adopt gradual abolishment of slavery." Lincoln wanted to eliminate slavery from the border states with the approval of slave owners there and thus diminish the likelihood that those states would join the Confederacy.

But leaders in the border states rejected the proposal. Lincoln brought it up again in July. This time he warned congressmen and senators from the border states that if their states opposed compensated emancipation they might have to accept uncompensated emancipation. They ignored his advice and denounced compensated emancipation as a "radical change in our social system" and an intrusion by the federal government into a state issue.

To many white Americans, Lincoln's support for compensated emancipation and colonization was a misguided attempt to link the war to the issue of slavery. But to black Americans, abolitionists, and an increasing number of Republicans, Lincoln's refusal to abolish slavery immediately was tragic. Antislavery advocates regarded Lincoln's willingness to purchase the freedom of slaves as an admission that he considered those human beings to be property. They deplored his seeming inability to realize the Union would not win the war unless slaves were liberated.

LINCOLN MOVES TOWARD EMANCIPATION

However, by the summer of 1862, after the border states rejected compensated emancipation, Lincoln concluded that victory and the future of the Union were tied directly to the issue of slavery. Slavery became the instrument Lincoln would use to hasten the end of the war and restore the Union. He told Secretary of the Navy Gideon Welles: "We must free the slaves or be ourselves subdued. The slaves were undeniably an element of strength to those who had their service, and we must decide whether that element should be with us or against us." Emancipation, Lincoln stressed, would "strike at the heart of the rebellion."

In cabinet meetings on July 21 and 22, 1862, Lincoln discussed abolishing slavery. Except for Postmaster General Montgomery Blair, the cabinet supported emancipation. Blair feared that eliminating slavery would cost the Republicans control of

A Ride for Liberty—The Fugitive Slaves, 1862. On March 23, 1862, artist Eastman Johnson was with General George B. McClellan's Army of the Potomac near Manassas, Virginia. Just before dawn, Johnson witnessed a family of three fleeing slavery, and he was prompted to paint the episode.   Oil on board, The Brooklyn Museum, Gift of Miss Gwendolyn O.L. Conkling

Congress in the fall elections. Secretary of State William H. Seward supported abolition but advised Lincoln not to issue a proclamation until the Union Army won a major victory. Otherwise emancipation might look like the desperate gesture of the leader of a losing cause. Lincoln accepted Seward's advice and postponed emancipation.

LINCOLN DELAYS EMANCIPATION

Nevertheless, word circulated that Lincoln intended to abolish slavery. But weeks passed, and slavery did not end. Frustrated abolitionists and Republicans attacked Lincoln. Frederick Douglass was exasperated with a president who had shown inexcusable deference to white Southerners who had rebelled against the Union:

> Abraham Lincoln is no more fit for the place he holds than was [previous president] James Buchanan. . . . The country is destined to become sick of both [General George B.] McClellan and Lincoln, and the sooner the better. The one plays lawyer for the benefit of the rebels, and the other handles the army for the benefit of traitors. We should not be surprised if both should be hurled from their places before the rebellion is ended.

In his *Prayer of Twenty Millions*, Horace Greeley, editor of the New York *Tribune*, expressed his disappointment that the president had not moved promptly against slavery, the issue that had led the southern states to leave the Union and go to war: "We ask you to consider that Slavery [is the] inciting cause and sustaining base of treason. . . . We think timid counsels in such a crisis [are] calculated to prove perilous, probably disastrous." Greeley insisted that Lincoln should have long ago warned white Southerners that their support of secession would endanger slavery.

On August 22, 1862, Lincoln replied to Greeley and offered a masterful explanation of his priorities. Placing the preservation of the Union before freedom for the enslaved, Lincoln declared, "My paramount object in this struggle is to save the Union, and is not either to save or destroy slavery. If I could save the Union without freeing any slave I would do it; and if I could save it by freeing all the slaves, I would do it; and if I could do it by freeing some and leaving others alone, I would also do that." Lincoln concluded, "I have here stated my purpose according to my view of *official* duty, and I intend no modification of my oft-expressed *personal* wish that all men, everywhere, could be free."

During the Civil War, Abraham Lincoln met with a free black family on the lawn of the Executive Mansion. A white woman and Union soldier and observers.   © Bettmann/Corbis

BLACK PEOPLE REJECT COLONIZATION

Lincoln's policy on emancipation had shifted dramatically, but he remained committed to colonization. On August 14, 1862, Lincoln invited black leaders to the White House and appealed for their support for colonization. After condemning slavery as "the greatest wrong inflicted on any people," he explained that white racism made it unwise for black people to remain in the United States. "Your race suffer very greatly, many of them, by living among us, while ours suffer from your presence. There is an unwillingness on the part of our people, harsh as it may be, for you free colored people to remain among us. . . . I do not mean to discuss this, but to propose it as a fact with which we have to deal. I cannot alter it if I would." Lincoln asked the black leaders to begin enlisting volunteers for a colonization project in Central America.

Most black people were unimpressed by Lincoln's words and unmoved by his advice. A black leader from Philadelphia condemned the president. "This is our country as much as it is yours, and we will not leave it." Frederick Douglass accused Lincoln of hypocrisy and claimed that support for colonization would lead white

men "to commit all kinds of violence and outrage upon the colored people."

Lincoln would not retreat from his support for colonization. Attempts were already under way to put compensated emancipation and colonization into effect. In April 1862 Congress enacted a bill to pay District of Columbia slave owners up to $300 for each slave they freed and to provide $100,000 to support the voluntary colonization of the freed people in Haiti or Liberia. In 1863 the government tried to settle 453 black American colonists at Ile à Vache, an island near Haiti. The settlers suffered terribly from disease and starvation. This sorry attempt at government-sponsored colonization ended in 1864 when the U.S. Navy returned 368 survivors to the United States.

The Preliminary Emancipation Proclamation

Finally on September 22, 1862—more than two months after Lincoln first seriously considered freedom for the enslaved—the president issued the Preliminary Emancipation Proclamation. It came five days after General George B. McClellan's Army of the Potomac turned back an invasion of Maryland at Antietam by General Robert E. Lee's Army of Northern Virginia. This bloody but less-than-conclusive victory allowed Lincoln to justify emancipation. But this first proclamation freed no people that September—or during the rest of 1862. Instead, it stipulated that anyone in bondage in states or parts of states still in rebellion on January 1, 1863, would be "thenceforward, and forever free." Lincoln's announcement gave the Confederate states one hundred days to return to the Union. If any or all of those states did rejoin the Union, the slaves there would remain in bondage. The Union would be preserved, and slavery would be maintained.

What were Lincoln's intentions? It might seem that he expected the Confederate leaders to give his offer serious consideration and perhaps return to the Union and thus he was willing to free the slaves only as a last resort. But Lincoln knew there was virtually no chance that white Southerners would return to the Union just because he had threatened to free their slaves. Most Confederates expected to win the war, thereby confirming secession and safeguarding slavery. White Southerners ridiculed the preliminary proclamation.

NORTHERN REACTION TO EMANCIPATION

In the Union, the Preliminary Emancipation Proclamation was greeted with little enthusiasm. Most black people and abolitionists, of course, were gratified that Lincoln, after weeks of procrastination, had finally issued the proclamation. Frederick Douglass was ecstatic. "We shout for joy that we live to record this righteous decree." In *The Liberator*, William Lloyd Garrison wrote that it was "an act of immense historical consequence." But they also worried that—however remote the possibility might be—some slave states would return to the Union by January 1, denying freedom to those enslaved.

Many white Northerners resented emancipation. One New York soldier, more concerned with defeating the South than freeing the slaves, bluntly reflected these views: "We must first conquer & then it's time enough to talk about the *dam'd niggers.*" A northern newspaper editor vilified Lincoln as a "half-witted usurper" and the Proclamation as "monstrous, impudent, and heinous . . . insulting to God as to man, for it declares those 'equal' whom God created unequal."

Even before the announcement of emancipation, antiblack riots flared in the North. In Cincinnati in the summer of 1862, Irish dock workers invaded black neighborhoods after black men had replaced the striking wharf hands along the city's river front. In Brooklyn, New York, Irish Americans set fire to a tobacco factory that employed black women and children.

POLITICAL OPPOSITION TO EMANCIPATION

Northern Democrats almost unanimously opposed emancipation. They accused Lincoln and the Republicans of "fanaticism" and regretted that emancipation would liberate "two or three million semi savages" who would "overrun the North" and compete with white working people. The Democratic-controlled lower houses of the legislatures in Indiana and Illinois condemned the Proclamation as "wicked, inhuman, and unholy." Republicans recognized the intense hostility among many white Northerners to black people. Senator Lyman Trumball of Illinois conceded that "there is a very great aversion in the West—I know it to be so in my state—against having free negroes come among us. Our people want nothing to do with the negro."

And as some Republicans had predicted and feared, the Democrats capitalized on dissatisfaction with the war's progress and with Republican support for emancipation to make significant gains in the fall elections. Democratic governors were elected in New York and New Jersey, and Democrats won thirty-four more seats in the U.S. House of Representatives, although the Republicans retained a majority. Overjoyed Democrats proclaimed, "Abolition Slaughtered." Republicans took solace that their losses were not greater.

The Emancipation Proclamation

On January 1, 1863, Abraham Lincoln issued the **Emancipation Proclamation.** It was not the first step toward freedom. Since 1861 several thousand slaves had already freed themselves, but it was the first significant effort by Union authorities to assure freedom to nearly four million people of African descent who, with their ancestors, had been enslaved for 250 years in North America. The Civil War was now a war to make people free.

Black communities and many white people across the North celebrated. Church bells pealed. Poems were written, and prayers of thanksgiving were offered. Many considered it the most momentous day in American history since July 4, 1776. Frederick Douglass had difficulty describing the emotions of people in Boston when word reached the city late on the night of December 31 that Lincoln would issue the Proclamation the next day. "The effect of this announcement was startling beyond description, and the scene was wild and grand. Joy and gladness exhausted all forms of expression, from shouts of praise to sobs and tears. . . . A Negro preacher, a man of wonderful vocal power, expressed the heartfelt emotion of the hour, when he led all voices in the anthem, 'Sound the loud timbrel o'er Egypt's dark sea, Jehovah hath triumphed, his people were free.'" Well into the twentieth century, New Year's Day was commemorated as Emancipation Day, a holiday zealously observed by black Americans in churches and with parades and celebrations.

LIMITS OF THE PROCLAMATION

Despite this excitement, the language of the Emancipation Proclamation was uninspired and unmoving. It lacked the eloquence of the Declaration of Independence or the address Lincoln would deliver after the Union victory at Gettysburg in July 1863. Lincoln dryly wrote that "as a fit and necessary measure for

THE STEPS TO EMANCIPATION

APRIL 1861	Fort Sumter is attacked; Civil War begins
MAY 1861	General Butler refuses to return escaped "contrabands" to slavery
AUGUST 1861	General Fremont orders emancipation of slaves in Missouri; Lincoln countermands him
AUGUST 1861	First Confiscation Act frees captured slaves used by Confederate Army
APRIL 1862	Congress provides funds for compensated emancipation; border states spurn the proposal
MAY 1862	General Hunter's order abolishing slavery in South Carolina, Georgia, and Florida is revoked by Lincoln
SUMMER 1862	Lincoln concludes that Union victory requires emancipation
SEPTEMBER 22, 1862	Lincoln issues Preliminary Emancipation Proclamation after Battle of Antietam
JANUARY 1, 1863	Emancipation Proclamation takes effect

1861–1863

The Emancipation Proclamation was essentially a military directive and not a ringing declaration of liberation. Nevertheless its uninspiring words would free more than three million people from bondage by 1865. Decorative copies such as this circulated for many decades after the Civil War.

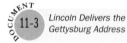

11-3 Lincoln Delivers the Gettysburg Address

suppressing said rebellion . . . I do order and declare that all persons held as slaves within said designated States, and parts of States, are, and henceforth shall be free."

Moreover, by limiting emancipation to those states and areas still in rebellion, Lincoln did not include enslaved people in the four border states still in the Union or in areas of Confederate states that Union forces had already occupied. This included forty-eight counties in western Virginia that would soon become the state of West Virginia, parts of Tennessee, and thirteen parishes (counties) in Louisiana, including New Orleans (see Map 11–1). Thus hundreds of thousands of people would remain in bondage despite the proclamation. The immediate practical effect of the Proclamation was negligible in the areas it was intended to affect. After all, slave owners in the Confederacy did not recognize Lincoln's authority, and they certainly did not free their slaves on January 1 or anytime soon thereafter. Yet the Emancipation Proclamation remains one of the most important documents in American history. It made the Civil War a war to free people, as well as to preserve the Union, and it gave moral authority to the Union cause. And as many black people had freed themselves before the Proclamation, now many more would liberate themselves after.

EFFECTS OF THE PROCLAMATION ON THE SOUTH

The Emancipation Proclamation destroyed any chance that Great Britain or France would offer diplomatic recognition to the Confederate government. Diplomatic recognition would have meant accepting the Confederacy as a legitimate state equal in international law to the Union, and it would almost surely have led to financial and military assistance for the South. British leaders, who had considered recognizing the Confederacy, now declined to support a "nation" that relied on slavery while its opponent moved to abolish it. In this sense, the Proclamation weakened the Confederacy's ability to prosecute the war.

Even more important, it undermined slavery in the South and contributed directly to the Confederacy's defeat. While the Proclamation may not have freed any of those in bondage on January 1, 1863, word of freedom spread rapidly across the South. Black people—aware a Union victory in the war meant freedom—were far less likely to labor for their owners or for the Confederacy. More slaves ran away, especially as Union troops ap-

MAP EXPLORATION

To explore this interactive map, go to
http://www.prenhall.com/hine4/map11.1

MAP 11–1 EFFECTS OF THE EMANCIPATION PROCLAMATION

When Abraham Lincoln issued the Emancipation Proclamation on January 1, 1863, it applied only to slaves in those portions of the Confederacy not under Union authority. No southern slave owners freed their slaves at Lincoln's command. But many black people already had freed themselves as well as family and friends in the aftermath of Lincoln's order. The Emancipation Proclamation was of extreme importance. It helped the Union win the war. It meant that at long last the U.S. government had joined the abolitionist movement.

▶ *Where, according to the map, did slaves reside who were to be freed under the terms of the Proclamation?*

proached. Slave resistance became more likely, although Lincoln cautioned against insurrection in the Proclamation: "And I hereby enjoin upon the people so declared to be free to abstain from all violence, unless in necessary self-defence." The institution of slavery cracked, crumbled, and collapsed after January 1, 1863.

Without emancipation, the United States would not have survived as a unified nation. Abraham Lincoln, after first failing to make the connection between eliminating slavery and preserving the Union, came to understand it fully and also grasped what freedom meant to both black and white people. In his annual message to Congress in December 1862, one month before the Proclamation, Lincoln described the importance of emancipation with a passion and feelings that were absent in the Proclamation itself. "We know how to save the Union. The world knows we do know how to save it. We—even we here—hold the power, and bear the responsibility. In giving freedom to the slave, we assure freedom to the free—honorable alike in what we give, and what we preserve."

Black Men Fight for the Union

The Emancipation Proclamation not only marked the beginning of the end of slavery, but it also authorized the enlistment of black troops in the Union Army. Just

as white leaders in the North came to realize the preservation of the Union necessitated the abolition of slavery, they also began to understand that black men were needed for the military effort if the Union was to triumph in the Civil War.

By early 1863 the war had not gone well for the all-white Union Army. Although they had won significant battlefield victories in Kentucky and Tennessee and had captured New Orleans, the war in the east was a much different matter (see Map 11–2). The Union's Army of the Potomac faced a smaller but highly effective Confederate Army—the Army of Northern Virginia—led by the remarkable General Robert E. Lee. Confederate troops forced a Union retreat from Richmond during the 1862 Peninsular campaign. Union forces lost at the first and second battles of Bull Run. Their only victory over Lee at Antietam provided Lincoln with the opportunity to issue the Preliminary Emancipation Proclamation. But that was followed by a crushing Union loss at Fredericksburg.

Much like the decision to free the slaves, the decision to employ black troops proceeded neither smoothly nor logically. The commitment to the Civil War as a white man's war was deeply entrenched, and the initial attempts to raise black troops were strongly opposed by many white Northerners. As with emancipation, Lincoln moved slowly from outright opposition to cautious acceptance to enthusiastic support for enlisting black men in the Union Army.

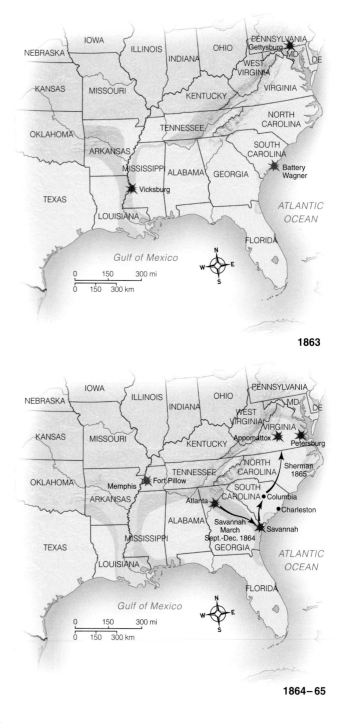

MAP 11–2   The Course of the Civil War

Although the outcome of the Civil War remained in doubt until the autumn of 1864, Union armies, as well as a Union naval blockade, applied increasing pressure on the eleven Confederate states beginning in 1862. Black people freed themselves as Union forces carved out an enclave on the South Carolina coast, captured New Orleans, and pushed through Kentucky and Tennessee into Mississippi and Arkansas. Following the successful Union siege of Vicksburg in 1863, the Confederacy was divided along the Mississippi River. In 1864 General Ulysses S. Grant's Army of the Potomac drove General Robert E. Lee's Army of Northern Virginia into entrenchments around Richmond and Petersburg. General William Tecumseh Sherman marched from Atlanta to Savannah and then into the Carolinas. Several thousand more black people liberated themselves. The war ended in April 1865 with Lee's surrender to Grant at Appomattox Court House and Joseph E. Johnston's capitulation to Sherman near Durham, North Carolina.

▶ *Based on an examination of these maps, what appears to have been the strategy of Union military forces to defeat the Confederacy?*

Although black men had fought well in the War for Independence and the War of 1812, they were legally prohibited from joining the regular U.S. Army, and the Militia Act of 1792 also barred them from the state militias. In 1861 a few black men were able to join Union units and go off to war. H. Ford Douglas, a black leader of the 1850s who had a fair complexion, enlisted in the all-white 95th Illinois Infantry, a volunteer regiment.

THE FIRST SOUTH CAROLINA VOLUNTEERS

Some Union officers recruited black men long before emancipation was proclaimed and before most white Northerners were prepared to accept, much less welcome, black troops. In May 1862 General David Hunter began recruiting former slaves along the South Carolina coast and the Sea Islands, an area Union forces had captured in late 1861. But some black men did not want to enlist, and Hunter used white troops to force black men to "volunteer" for military service. He managed to organize a five-hundred-man regiment—the **First South Carolina Volunteers.**

The former slaves were outfitted in bright red pants, with blue coats and broad-brimmed hats.

Through the summer of 1862, Hunter trained and drilled the regiment while awaiting official authorization and funds to pay them. When Congress balked, Hunter reluctantly disbanded all but one company of the regiment that August. The troops were dispersed, unpaid and disappointed. The surviving company was sent to St. Simon's Island off the Georgia coast to protect a community of former slaves.

PROFILE — ELIZABETH KECKLEY

Born a slave in 1818, Elizabeth Keckley became a skilled dressmaker for First Lady Mary Todd Lincoln. After President Lincoln's assassination in 1865, Keckley wrote one of the first personal accounts of life inside the Lincoln White House, Elizabeth Keckley had experienced the exploitation and degradation common to thousands of slave women. She was born in Dinwiddie Court House, Virginia, and spent her childhood as a slave of the Burwell family. She saw slaves beaten and slave sales divide families. She watched as a young boy was sold away from his mother so his owner could buy pigs.

Dining adolescence, she was loaned to a North Carolina slave owner and beaten and eventually raped. She reluctantly described what happened: I was regarded as fair-looking for one of my race, and for four years a white man—I spare the world his name—had base designs upon me. I do not care to dwell upon this subject for it is one that is fraught with pain. Suffice it to say that he persecuted me for four years, and I—I became a mother. The child of which he was the father was the only child I ever brought into the world.

She was later returned to one of the Burwell daughters, who took Elizabeth and her son George to St. Louis, She already knew how to sew, and she became an increasingly skilled dressmaker. She also married a slave, James Keckley, but they soon separated. As a proficient seamstress, Keckley was able to purchase herself and her son for $1,200. She learned to read and write. In 1860 she moved to Washington and attracted a prosperous clientele that included the wives of prominent politicians, such as Varma Davis; the wife of Mississippi senator Jefferson Davis, soon to be president of the Confederacy.

Shortly after the Lincolns arrived in Washington Keckley began making dresses for the First Lady and became Mrs. Lincoln's confidante and traveling companion. Keckley helped convert Mrs. Lincoln, whose family owned slaves in Kentucky, to strong antislavery views. Both women lost sons. Elizabeth Keckley's son George, was killed early in the Civil War in Missouri fighting for the Union. Eleven-year-old Willie Lincoln died of a fever in 1862 in the White House. With Mrs. Lincoln's assistance, Elizabeth Keckley founded the Contraband Relief Association to provide aid to former slaves in Washington.

In 1868 she published *Behind the Scenes: Or Thirty Years a Slave and Four Years in the White House.* Although it was a favorable account of life in the Lincoln White House, the book upset the Lincoln family. Keckley denied she had violated Mrs. Lincoln's privacy. "If I have betrayed confidence in anything I have published it has been to place Mrs. Lincoln in better light before the world. My own character as well as the character of Mrs. Lincoln, is at stake, since I have been intimately associated with the lady in the most eventful periods of her life."

Elizabeth Keckley spent the rest of her life living off the pension from her son's service as a Union soldier. She died in Washington in 1907 at the Home for Destitute Women and Children, which she had helped found years earlier.

Keckley

Although Congress failed to support Hunter, it did pass the Second Confiscation Act and the Militia Act of 1862, which authorized President Lincoln to enlist black men. In Louisiana that fall, two regiments of free black men, the Native Guards, were accepted for federal service, and General Benjamin Butler organized them into the Corps d'Afrique. General Rufus Saxton gained the approval of Secretary of War Edwin Stanton to revive Hunter's dispersed regiment and to recall the company that had been sent to St. Simon's Island.

As commander, Saxton appointed Thomas Wentworth Higginson. Higginson was an ardent white abolitionist, one of the Secret Six who had provided financial support for John Brown's raid on Harpers Ferry. Higginson was determined not merely to end slavery but to prove that black people were equal to white people, a proposition most white people regarded as preposterous. Disposing of the unit's gaudy red trousers, Higginson set out to mold this regiment of mostly former slaves into an effective fighting force. On Emancipation Day, January 1, 1863, near Beaufort, South Carolina, the First South Carolina Volunteer Regiment was inducted into the U.S. Army.

Poised with their rifles, these African-American soldiers were members of the Twenty-first U.S. Colored Infantry at the battle of Dutch Gap in Virginia in August, 1864.   Corbis/Bettmann

THE SECOND SOUTH CAROLINA VOLUNTEERS

A month later, the Second South Carolina Volunteers began enrolling ex-slaves, many from Georgia and Florida. James Montgomery, another former financial supporter of John Brown, commanded them. Montgomery was determined that the regiment would wipe out all vestiges of slavery, especially the homes, plantations, and personal possessions of families who owned slaves. But like Hunter, Montgomery found that many former slaves were reluctant to volunteer for military service, so he also used force to recruit them. He concluded that black men responded to the call to arms much the way white men did, except black men were less likely to desert once they joined the army:

> Finding it somewhat difficult to induce Negroes to enlist, we resolved to the draft. The negroes reindicate their claim to humanity by shirking the draft in every possible way; acting exactly like white men under similar circumstances. . . . The only difference that I notice is, the negro, after being drafted does not desert; but once dressed in the uniform with arms in his hands he feels himself a man; and acts like one.

THE 54TH MASSACHUSETTS REGIMENT

While ex-slaves joined the Union ranks in South Carolina, free black men in the North enlisted in what would become the most famous black unit, **the 54th Massachusetts Regiment.** In January 1863 governor of Massachusetts John A. Andrew received permission from Secretary of War Stanton to raise a black regiment, but because few black men lived in Massachusetts, Andrew asked prominent black men across the North for help. The Black Committee—as it became known—included Frederick Douglass, Martin Delany, Charles Remond, and Henry Highland Garnet.

These black leaders were convinced that by serving in the military, black men would prove they deserved to be treated as equals and had earned the right to be citizens. Frederick Douglass put it succinctly: "Once let the black man get upon his person the brass letters, U.S.; let him get an eagle on his button, and a musket on his shoulder and bullets in his pocket, and there is no power on earth which can deny that he has earned the right to citizenship." Two of Douglass's sons, Charles and Lewis, joined the 54th.

Lincoln, who had opposed emancipation and resisted enlisting black troops, became an enthusiastic supporter of black men in the Union Army. Writing to Andrew Johnson, who was the Union military governor of Tennessee, Lincoln perhaps overoptimistically predicted that "The bare sight of fifty thousand armed, and drilled black soldiers on the banks of the Mississippi, would end the rebellion at once. And who doubts that we can present that sight, if we but take hold in earnest."

Governor Andrew selected twenty-five-year-old Robert Gould Shaw to command the 54th Massachusetts Regiment. Shaw was a Harvard graduate from a prominent Massachusetts family, and he had already been wounded at the battle at Antietam. Although not an active abolitionist, he opposed slavery and was determined to prove that black men would fight well. The men the Black Committee recruited came from most of the northern states. Their average age was around twenty-five and virtually all of them were literate. They were farmers, seamen, butchers, blacksmiths, and teamsters. Only one of them had grown up in a slave state. As the ranks of the 54th filled, the 55th Massachusetts Regiment and the all-black 5th Massachusetts Cavalry Regiment were also formed.

After training from March to May 1863, on May 28, 1863, the 54th paraded through Boston to the wharf to board a ship for the trip to South Carolina and the war. Thousands of people turned out to see the black men in blue uniforms. As they passed the home of William Lloyd Garrison, he stood erect with a bust of John Brown. As they passed the customhouse where Crispus Attucks and four others had been killed in the Boston Massacre in 1770, the regiment sang "John Brown's Body." The departure of the 54th from the city was perhaps the most emotional event Boston had witnessed since Anthony Burns had been returned to slavery in 1854.

BLACK SOLDIERS CONFRONT DISCRIMINATION

But the enthusiastic departure could not disguise the discrimination and hostility that black troops faced during the war. Many white Northerners were willing to accept neither the presence of black troops nor the idea that black men could endure combat. Many white people tolerated black troops only because they preferred that a black man die rather than a white man. A crude bit of verse in an Irish dialect that reflected this racism circulated during the war:

Sambo's Right to be Kilt

Some tell us 'tis a burnin' shame
　To Make the naygers fight;

And that the thrade of bein' kilt
　Belongs but to the white;

But as for me, upon my sowl!
　So liberal are we here,

I'll let Sambo be murthered instead of myself,
　On every day of the Year.

In the same vein, a white Union soldier wrote that a "Negro can fall from a rebel shot as well as me or my friends, and better them than us."

That black troops would serve in separate, all-black units was accepted as a matter of course. No one seriously proposed to integrate black men into previously all-white regiments. In 1863 the War Department created the Bureau of Colored Troops, and the Union Army remained segregated throughout the war. The only exception was the officers of the black regiments.

Almost all black troops had white officers. Yet many white officers, convinced their military record would be tainted by such service, refused to command black troops. Others believed black men simply could not be trained for combat. Even those white officers who were willing to command black troops sometimes regarded their men as "niggers" suited only for work or fatigue duty. When the 110th U.S. Colored Infantry joined General William Tecumseh Sherman's army on its march through Georgia and South Carolina in 1864 and 1865, Sherman kept the black men out of combat. Some were armed with picks and axes; others served as hospital guards and teamsters.

Black soldiers were paid less than white soldiers. Based on the assumption that black troops would be used almost exclusively for construction, transportation, cooking, and burial details, and not for fighting, the War Department authorized a lower pay scale for them. A white private earned $13 per month; a black private earned $10 per month. This demoralized black soldiers, particularly after they had shown they were more than capable of fighting.

The 54th Massachusetts Regiment refused to accept their pay until they received equal pay. To take no compensation was an enormous sacrifice for men who had wives, children, and families to support. For some, it was more than a monetary loss. Sergeant William Walker insisted—despite orders—that the men in his company take no pay until they received equal pay. He was charged with mutiny, convicted, and shot. In Texas, a soldier in a black artillery unit from Rhode Island threatened a white officer in the dispute over pay. The white lieutenant shot and killed the black man, and the regiment's commander declined to charge the officer.

The pay issue festered in Congress for nearly two years. Finally, near the end of the war, Congress enacted a compromise, but many black soldiers remained dissatisfied. The law equalized pay between

This young man is Jackson. In the first photo he is shown as a slave who worked as a servant in the Confederate Army. In the second photo he has been freed and has joined the U.S. Colored Troops as a drummer.

black and white troops, but made it retroactive only to January 1, 1864—except for black men who had never been slaves. But the thousands of black men who had been slaves and had joined the military before January 1, 1864, would not be entitled to equal pay for the entire period of their service. The War Department compounded the problem with bureaucratic delays.

BLACK MEN IN COMBAT

Once black men put on the Union uniform, they took part in almost every battle that was fought during the rest of the Civil War. Black troops not only faced an enemy dedicated to the belief that the proper place of black people was in slavery, but they also confronted doubts about their fighting abilities among white Northerners. Yet by war's end, black units had suffered disproportionately more casualties than white units.

In October 1862 the first black unit went into combat in Missouri. James H. Lane, a white Free-Soiler, recruited five hundred black men in Kansas. Most were runaway slaves from Missouri and Arkansas. After some hasty training, they advanced against a Confed-

erate position at Island Mountain. The black troops held off an attack until reinforcements arrived, and the Confederates were repulsed. Soon thereafter, the black unit became the First Kansas Colored Infantry.

On July 17, 1863, at Honey Springs in Indian territory (now Oklahoma), the Kansas soldiers attacked a Confederate force composed of white Texans and Cherokee Indians. After an intense twenty-minute battle, the black troops broke through the southern line and won a victory, capturing the colors of a Texas regiment.

In January 1863 Thomas Wentworth Higginson led the First South Carolina Volunteers on raids on the Georgia and Florida coasts. At one point, they were surrounded at night by Confederate cavalry but managed to fight their way out and escape.

On June 3, 1863, the 54th Massachusetts Regiment arrived in South Carolina and joined the raids in Georgia. Other raids in the Carolina low country devastated rice plantations and liberated hundreds of slaves.

THE ASSAULT ON BATTERY WAGNER

Since 1861 and the Confederate capture of Fort Sumter in Charleston harbor that began the Civil War, Union leaders had been determined to retake the fort and occupy nearby Charleston—the heart of secession. In 1863 Union commanders began a combined land and sea offensive to seize the fort. But **Battery Wagner,** a heavily fortified installation on the northern tip of Morris Island, guarded the entrance to the harbor.

Frustrated in their initial efforts to enter the harbor, Major General Quincy A. Gilmore and Rear Admiral John Dahlgren decided on a full-scale assault on Wagner. After an unsuccessful attack by white troops, Colonel Shaw volunteered to lead the 54th in a second attack on the battery.

To improve the Union's chances, artillery fired more than nine thousand shells on Wagner on July 18, 1863. Everyone but the fort's Confederate defenders was convinced that no one could survive the bombardment. In fact, only 8 of the 1,620 defenders had been killed.

At sunset, 650 men of the first brigade of the 54th prepared to lead more than 5,000 Union troops in storming the battery. The regiment was tired and hungry but eager for the assault. Colonel Shaw offered brief words of encouragement to his troops: "Now I want you to prove yourselves men."

At 7:45 P.M., the 54th charged and was met by heavy rifle and artillery fire. Within minutes, the sand was littered with injured and dying men. Sergeant Major Lewis Douglass (the son of Frederick Douglass) was among those who took part. The 54th reached the walls only to be thrown back in hand-to-hand combat. Shaw was killed.

Sergeant Major William H. Carney, although wounded four times, saved the regiment's flags. Thirty-seven years later, in May 1900, he was awarded the Congressional Medal of Honor for his gallantry that night.

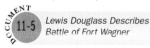

DOCUMENT 11-5 *Lewis Douglass Describes Battle of Fort Wagner*

Although white troops fought to support the 54th, the attack could not be sustained, and the battle was over by 1 A.M. But within days, the courage of the 54th was known across the North, putting to rest—for a time—the myth that black men lacked the nerve to fight.

The day after the attack, Shaw and twenty of his men were buried in a trench outside Wagner. Several wounded men had drowned when the tide came in. Altogether 246 black and white men were killed, 890 were wounded, and 391 were taken prisoner. Forty-two percent of the men of the 54th were killed or injured, and 80 men were taken prisoner.

On the evening of July 18, 1863, more than six hundred black men led by their white commander, Colonel Robert Gould Shaw, attacked the heavily fortified Battery Wagner on Morris Island near the southern approach to Charleston harbor. They made a frontal assault through withering fire and managed to breach the battery before Confederate forces threw them back. Shaw was killed and the 54th suffered heavy losses. It was a defining moment of the Civil War, demonstrating to skeptical white people the valor and determination of black troops.

Union forces never took Wagner. The Confederates abandoned Charleston as the war was ending in February 1865. Black Union troops—the 21st U.S. Colored Infantry and the 55th Massachusetts Regiment—occupied the city. Years later Charles Crowley recalled the scene. "Never, while memory holds power to retain anything, shall I forget the thrilling strain of music of the Union, as sung by our sable soldiers when marching up Meeting Street with the battle stained banners flapping in the breeze."

OLUSTEE

On February 20, 1864, the 54th fought again and was joined by two black regiments—the First North Carolina and the Eighth U.S. of Pennsylvania—and six white regiments at the battle at Olustee in northern Florida. After almost five hours of bloody combat, Confederate forces prevailed and forced a Union retreat. The 54th had marched 110 miles in 100 hours prior to entering the engagement.

LEWIS DOUGLASS DESCRIBES THE FIGHTING AT BATTERY WAGNER

After the failed assault on Battery Wagner, Lewis Douglass wrote this letter home to his wife Amelia.

Lewis Douglass
JULY 20 [1863]

My Dear Amelia:

I have been in two fights, and am unhurt. I am about to go in another I believe tonight. Our men fought well on both occasions. The last one was desperate. We charged that terrible battery on . . . Fort Wagner and were repulsed. . . . I escaped unhurt from amidst that perfect hail of shot and shell. It was terrible. . . . This regiment has established its reputation as a fighting regiment. Not a man flinched, though it was a trying time. Men fell all around me. . . . Our men would close up again, but it was no use. . . . How I got out of that fight alive I cannot tell, but I am here. My dear girl, I hope again to see you. I must bid you farewell should I be killed. Remember if I die, I die in a good cause. I wish we had a hundred thousand colored troops. We would put an end to this war.

Your own loving

Lewis

🌿 *How graphic is this description of combat?*

🌿 *Does Douglass explain what motivated him as well as his fellow troops?*

🌿 *Does this account of combat differ in any way from the way a white soldier might describe it?*

Source: Carter G. Woodson, ed., *The Mind of the Negro as Reflected in Letters Written during the Crisis 1800–1860* (1926). Washington: The Association for the Study of Negro Life and History

THE CRATER

But as impressive as black troops often were in battle, northern commanders sometimes hesitated to commit black men to combat. In 1864, after Union troops laid siege to Petersburg, Virginia, white soldiers of the 48th Pennsylvania, who had been coal miners before the war, offered to dig a tunnel and set off an explosion under Confederate lines. General Ambrose Burnside agreed to the plan and assigned black troops to be prepared to lead the attack after the blast.

Four tons of powder were placed in the tunnel, but only hours before the blast was set to go off, Burnside's superior, General George Meade, replaced the black troops with inadequately trained white soldiers commanded by an alcoholic. Meade either lacked confidence in the black unit or was worried he would be blamed for using black men as shields for white soldiers if the attack failed.

On July 30, 1864, at 4:45 A.M., what was perhaps the largest man-made explosion in history up to that time buried a Confederate regiment and an artillery battery and created a crater 170 feet long, 60 feet wide, and 30 feet deep. But the white Union troops rushed down into the crater instead of fanning out around it in pursuit of the stunned enemy. While the Union soldiers marveled at the destruction, the Confederates launched a counterattack that threw back the Union troops, including the black troops that were finally brought forward. Some of the black men were murdered after they surrendered. More than four thousand Union troops, many of them black, were killed or wounded.

The Confederate Reaction to Black Soldiers

On June 7, 1863, Confederate forces attempting to relieve the Union siege of Vicksburg attacked a Union garrison defended by black troops at Milliken's Bend on the Mississippi River. Although armed with outdated muskets and not fully trained, the defenders fought off the Confederate attack. Assistant Secretary of War Charles A. Dana claimed that their valor would change the attitudes of white people toward the use of black troops. "The bravery of the blacks completely revolutionized the sentiment of the army with regard to the employment of negro troops. I heard prominent officers who formerly in private sneered at the idea of negroes fighting express themselves after that as heartily in favor of it."

The southern soldiers who lost at Milliken's Bend, however, felt differently. Enraged by having to fight black troops, they executed several black men captured during the engagement and sold others into slavery.

THE ABUSE AND MURDER OF BLACK TROOPS

Confederate leaders and troops refused to recognize black men as legitimate soldiers. Captured black soldiers were persistently abused and even murdered, rather than treated as prisoners of war. Confederate

Secretary of War James A. Seddon ordered that captured black soldiers be executed. "We ought never to be inconvenienced with such prisoners . . . summary execution must therefore be inflicted on those taken."

Protests erupted across the North after Confederate authorities decided to treat eighty men of the 54th Massachusetts Regiment who had been captured in the attack on Battery Wagner not as prisoners of war, but as rebellious slaves. Frederick Douglass refused to recruit any more black men and held Abraham Lincoln personally responsible for tolerating the mistreatment of black prisoners. "How many 54ths must be cut to pieces, its mutilated prisoners killed, and its living sold into slavery, to be tortured to death by inches, before Mr. Lincoln shall say, 'Hold, enough!'"

Lincoln issued General Order 11, threatening to execute southern troops or confine them to hard labor. "For every soldier of the United States killed in violation of the laws of war a rebel soldier shall be executed, and for every one enslaved by the enemy or sold into slavery a rebel soldier shall be placed at hard labor on the public works, and continued at such labor until the other shall be released and receive the treatment due to a prisoner of war."

Lincoln's order did not prevent the Confederates from sending the men of the 54th to trial by the state of South Carolina. The state regarded the black soldiers as either rebellious slaves or free black men inciting rebellion. Four black soldiers went on trial in Charleston police court, but the court declared it lacked jurisdiction. The black prisoners were eventually sent to prisoner of war camps.

THE FORT PILLOW MASSACRE

The Civil War's worst atrocity against black troops occurred at **Fort Pillow** in Tennessee on April 12, 1864. Confederates under the command of Nathan Bedford

In April 1864 fifteen hundred Confederate forces under General Nathan Bedford Forrest attacked and captured Fort Pillow, a Union installation on the Mississippi River forty miles north of Memphis, Tennessee, that was defended by 550 black and white troops. After the Union forces surrendered, Confederate troops executed some of the black soldiers. Forrest and his men denied the atrocity, but there is little doubt it occurred.

Forrest slaughtered 300 black troops and their white commander, William F. Bradford, after many of them had surrendered. (After the Civil War, Forrest gained notoriety as a founder of the Ku Klux Klan. Before the war he had been a slave trader.) The Fort Pillow Massacre became the subject of an intense debate in Lincoln's cabinet. But rather than retaliate indiscriminately—as required by General Order 11— the cabinet decided only to punish those responsible for the killings, if and when they were apprehended, but no one was punished during or after the war. Instead, black troops exacted revenge themselves. In fighting around Petersburg, Virginia, later that year, black soldiers shouting, "Remember Fort Pillow!" reportedly murdered several Confederate prisoners.

Captain Charles Francis Adams Jr. reported, "The darkies fought ferociously. . . . If they murdered prisoners, as I hear they did . . . they can hardly be blamed." There were many other instances of racial atrocities committed by Confederate troops during the remainder of the war.

Fort Pillow Massacre

On their own, Union commanders in the field also retaliated for the Confederate treatment of captured black troops. When captured black men were virtually enslaved and forced to work at Richmond and Charleston on Confederate fortifications that were under Union attack, Union officers put Confederate prisoners to work on Union installations that were under fire. Aware they were not likely to be treated as well as white soldiers if they were captured, black men often fought desperately.

Black Men in the Union Navy

Black men had a tradition of serving at sea and had been in the U.S. Navy almost continuously since its creation in the 1790s. In the early nineteenth century, there were so many black sailors that some white people tried to ban black men from the navy. Nor did black sailors serve in segregated units. Naval crews were integrated.

Nonetheless, black sailors encountered rampant discrimination and exploitation during the Civil War. They were paid less than white sailors. They were assigned the hardest and filthiest tasks, such as loading coal and tending the boilers, on the navy's new steam-powered vessels. Many were stewards who waited on white officers. White officers and sailors often treated black sailors with contempt. On the USS *Constellation* in 1863, the three white crew members regularly referred to the thirty-three black sailors as "God-damned nigger," "black dog," and "black bitches" and kicked and swore at them.

But some white men respected and admired the black sailors. One observed, "We never were betrayed when we trusted one of them, they were always our friends and were ready, if necessary, to lay down their lives for us." (He did not say whether white men were willing to lay down their lives for black men.) About 30,000 of the 120,000 men who served in the Union Navy were black sailors.

Liberators, Spies, and Guides

Besides serving as soldiers and sailors, black men and women aided themselves and the Union cause as lib-

Robert Smalls was born a slave in Beaufort, South Carolina, in 1839. In May 1862 while still a slave and working as a pilot in Charleston on a 150-foot Confederate vessel, *The Planter*, Smalls devised an audacious plan to seize the ship. With the ship's white officers enjoying a night on the town, Smalls sailed *The Planter* with family and friends aboard to the Union Navy outside the harbor. Smalls' exploits created a sensation in the North. He went on to become a successful Republican politician in South Carolina in the decades following the Civil War.

erators, spies, guides, and messengers. At about 3 A.M. on May 13, 1862, Robert Smalls, a twenty-three-year-old slave, fired the boiler on *The Planter*, a Confederate supply ship moored in Charleston harbor. With the aid of seven black crewmen, Smalls sailed *The Planter* past Confederate fortifications, including Fort Sumter, to the Union fleet outside the harbor and to freedom. Smalls liberated himself and fifteen other slaves, including the families of several crewmen and his own wife, daughter, and son.

Smalls managed the daring escape because he knew the South Carolina coast and was familiar with Confederate navigation signals and regulations. He became an overnight hero in the North, a slave who wanted freedom and had possessed the leadership, knowledge, and tenacity to liberate sixteen people.

In 1863 Harriet Tubman organized a spy ring in the South Carolina low country, and in cooperation with the all-black Second South Carolina Volunteer Regiment, she helped organize an expedition that destroyed plantations and freed nearly eight hundred slaves, many of whom joined the Union Army.

In Richmond in 1864, slaves helped more than one hundred escaped Union prisoners of war. Other slaves drew sketches and maps of Confederate fortifications and warned Union forces about troop movements. A black couple near Fredericksburg, Virginia, cleverly transmitted military intelligence to Union general Joseph Hooker. The woman washed laundry for a Confederate officer and hung shirts and blankets in patterns that conveyed information to her husband, who was a cook and groom for Union troops and relayed the information to Union officers.

Mary Elizabeth Bowser was a former slave who worked as a servant at the Confederate White House in Richmond. She overheard conversations by President Jefferson Davis and his subordinates, and—because she was literate—she covertly examined Confederate correspondence. She relayed the information to Union agents until the Confederates became suspicious. Bowser and slave Jim Pemberton managed to flee after unsuccessfully trying to burn down the mansion to distract their pursuers.

In Virginia's Shenandoah Valley, slave John Henry Woodson was a guide for Union general Philip H. Sheridan's cavalry in 1864 and 1865. Woodson was the father of Carter G. Woodson, who would become the "father" of black history in the twentieth century.

Violent Opposition to Black People

No matter how well black men fought, no matter how much individual black women contributed, and no matter how many people—black and white—died "to make men free," many white Northerners, both civilian and military, remained bitter and often violently hostile to black people. They used intimidation, threats, and terror to injure and kill people of color.

THE NEW YORK CITY DRAFT RIOT

Irish Catholic Americans, themselves held in contempt by prosperous white Protestants, indulged in an orgy of violence in New York City in July 1863. The New York draft riot arose from racial, religious, and class antagonisms. Poor, unskilled Irish workers and other white Northerners were convinced by leading Democrats, including New York governor Horatio

Seymour, that the war had become a crusade to benefit black people.

The violence began when federal officials prepared to select the first men to be drafted by the Union for military service. An enraged mob made up mostly of Irish men attacked the draft offices and any unfortunate black people who were in the vicinity. Many of the Irish men were angry because black men had replaced striking Irish stevedores on the

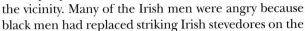

Testimony from Victims of Draft Riots   11-4   DOCUMENT

PROFILE ⬥ HARRIET TUBMAN

Long before her death in 1913, Harriet Tubman had achieved legendary status. Although she never led a slave revolt like Nat Turner or Joseph Cinque, she was personally responsible for freeing more slaves than any other individual in American history.

Thomas Wentworth Higginson, an abolitionist and commander of the First South Carolina Volunteers, called her "the greatest heroine of the age." He added, "Her tales of adventure are beyond anything in fiction and her ingenuity and generalship are extraordinary. I have known her for some time—the slaves call her Moses."

Harriet Tubman was born in 1821 or 1822 on Maryland's eastern shore, one of eleven slave children of Harriet Greene and Benjamin Ross. When a teenager, she was struck in the head by a rock or chunk of metal hurled by an overseer at a fleeing slave. The incident left her plagued by seizures and with an ugly scar that she sometimes covered with a turban.

In 1849 she married John Tubman, a free black man. Fearing that she would be sold following the death of her owner, she escaped to Pennsylvania, but her husband refused to go with her. He had married another woman, and he died shortly after the Civil War.

Tubman—like Sojourner Truth—never learned to read or write. She had, however, a deep reservoir of religious faith that sustained her and helped inspire her return to slave states again and again to free people held in bondage. She made at least fifteen trips south in ten years as a conductor on the Underground Railroad. Working with the support of William Still and the General Vigilance Committee in Philadelphia and Quaker abolitionist Thomas Garrett in Wilmington, Delaware, she led between 70 and 80 people to freedom on 14 trips to Maryland's Eastern Shore between 1849 and 1860. Among them were her sister, her sister's two children, and her parents. Tubman also assisted as many as 200 other people escape slavery. She never lost a passenger.

Aware that she had a hefty reward on her head Tubman devised detailed plans and elaborate disguises to elude capture. She feigned insanity, she pretended to be feeble, she forged passes, and she acquired real railroad tickets. She also packed a gun, as much to goad any of her charges whose courage might waver as to protect herself.

In 1862, during the Civil War, Tubman journeyed to the South Carolina low country where Union military forces had established a base. She worked as a nurse, cook, scout, and liberator. She made her way up the Combahee River and helped more than seven hundred slaves to freedom. She was on Morris Island in 1863 when the 54th Massachusetts Regiment attacked Battery Wagner.

After the war, she married Nelson Davis, a Union veteran who died in 1888. She and several of her supporters spent years in a determined effort to gain her federal pension. They finally succeeded in securing an award of $20 a month that was based on her husband's military service rather than her contributions to the Union cause.

Tubman was active in the women's rights movement of the late nineteenth century. She attended several women's rights conventions and she was friends with Susan B. Anthony. She also worked to help elderly ex-slaves who faced insecurity and uncertainty after emancipation. She bought a home in Auburn, New York, and eventually died there.

Many Americans talk about freedom, but not many have done as much to make it a reality for as many people as did Harriet Tubman.

Tubman

city's wharves the month before and because rich white Northerners could purchase an exemption from the draft.

The riot went on for four days. The
poorly trained city police could not control
it. Black people were beaten and lynched.
The Colored Orphan Asylum was burned
to the ground, although the children had
already fled. The mob attacked businesses
that employed black people. Protestant
churches were burned. Rioters set fire to
Horace Greeley's New York *Tribune*. The
houses of Republicans and abolitionists
were attacked and destroyed. The violence
and destruction did not end until the U.S.
Army arrived. Soldiers who had been fighting Confederates at Gettysburg two weeks
earlier found themselves firing on New
York rioters.

UNION TROOPS AND SLAVES

White Union troops who brutalized southern freedmen sometimes exceeded the
savagery of northern civilians. In November 1861 men
from the 47th New York Regiment raped an eight-year-
old black girl. Later, in Virginia, a Connecticut soldier
told what men in his regiment did to a pair of black
women. They took "two niger wenches . . . turned them
on their heads, & put tobacco, chips, sticks, lighted cig-
ars & sand into their behinds." On Sherman's march
through Georgia in 1864, a drunk Irish soldier from an
Ohio regiment shot into a crowd of black children,
badly wounding one youngster. He was tried and convicted but released on a technicality and returned to
the army.

However, not all white troops behaved despicably.
Others sympathized with slaves. Some Union soldiers
wanted to fight for the liberation of black people. One
Wisconsin private wrote, "I have no heart in this war if
the slaves cannot be free." Many were visibly moved by
the desire of slaves for freedom. A Union officer noted
that those who believed slaves were satisfied with slavery were wrong. "It is claimed the negroes are so well
contented with their slavery; if it ever was so, that day
has ceased." Several Union soldiers wept when they
witnessed a daughter reunited with her mother ten
years after they had been separated in a slave sale.

Refugees

Throughout the war, black people took advantage of
the hostilities to free themselves. It was not easy. Con-

During the draft riot in New York City in July 1863, black people were
attacked, beaten, and killed. A mob lynched this black man near Clarkson
street. *Illustrated London News*, August 8, 1863

federate authorities did not hesitate to reenslave or
even execute black people who sought freedom. Six
black people were hanged near Georgetown, South
Carolina, in 1862 when they were captured as they attempted to reach Union forces.

As Union armies plunged deep into the Confederacy in 1863 and 1864, thousands of black people liberated themselves and became refugees. When General
William Tecumseh Sherman's army of 60,000 troops
laid waste to Georgia in 1864, an estimated 10,000 former slaves followed his troops to Savannah, although
they lacked adequate food, clothing, and housing.
Sherman did not like black people, and his troops
tried with little success to discourage the refugees. As
one elderly black couple prepared to leave a plantation, Union soldiers as well as their master urged them
to remain. They declined in no uncertain terms. "We
must go, freedom is as sweet to us as it is to you."

Black People
and the Confederacy

The Confederacy was based on the defense of slavery,
and it benefited from the usually coerced, but sometimes willing, labor of black people. Slaves toiled in

southern fields and factories during the Civil War. The greater the burden of work the slaves took on, the more white men there were who could become soldiers. When the war began, southern whites believed their disadvantage in manpower—the twenty-two northern states had 22,339,989 people and the eleven Confederate states had 9,103,332 (5,449,462 white people, 3,521,110 slaves, and 132,760 free black people)—would be partly offset by the slaves whose presence would free a disproportionately large number of white Southerners to go to war. While slaves would tend cotton, corn, and cattle, white southern men would fight.

THE IMPRESSMENT OF BLACK PEOPLE

As the war went on, the demand for more troops and laborers in the Confederacy increased. Slave owners were first asked and then compelled to contribute their slave laborers to the war effort. In July 1861 the Confederate Congress required the registration and enrollment of free black people for military labor. In the summer of 1862 the Virginia legislature authorized the **impressment** of 10,000 slaves between the ages of eighteen and forty-five for up to sixty days. The owners would receive $16 per month per slave.

But many slave owners who enjoyed the benefits of forced labor did not themselves want to be forced to turn their slaves over to state authorities. In October 1862 President Davis asked Virginia to draft 4,500 black people to build fortifications around Richmond, so that "whites could fight more and dig less."

The most important factory in the South was the Tredegar Iron Works in Richmond. During the war, more than twelve hundred slaves and free black men worked there in every capacity—from unskilled laborers to engineers—manufacturing artillery, locomotives, nails, and much more. Other black men across the South loaded and unloaded ships, worked for railroads, and labored in salt works.

In South Carolina in 1863, Confederate officials appealed to slave owners to provide 2,500 slaves to help fortify Charleston. The owners offered fewer than 1,000. During the Union bombardment of Fort Sumter, 500 slaves were employed in the difficult, dirty, and dangerous work of building and rebuilding the fort. Slaves were even forced into combat. Two Virginia slaves who were compelled to load and fire Confederate cannons near Yorktown were shot and killed.

Although many slave owners resisted the impressment of their bondmen, many white Southerners who did not own slaves were infuriated when the Confederate conscription law in 1862 exempted men who owned twenty or more slaves from military service. This "twenty nigger law" (later reduced to fifteen) meant that poor white men were drafted while wealthier planters remained home, presumably to supervise and discipline their slaves. One Mississippi soldier deserted the Confederate Army, claiming he "did not propose to fight for the rich men while they were home having a good time." Although the law was widely criticized, planters—always a small percentage of the white southern population—dominated the Confederate government and would not permit the repeal of the exemption.

CONFEDERATES ENSLAVE FREE BLACK PEOPLE

After Lincoln's Emancipation Proclamation, Confederate president Jefferson Davis issued a counterproclamation in February 1863 declaring that free people would be enslaved, "all free negroes within the limits of the Southern Confederacy shall be placed on the slave status, and be deemed to be chattels . . . forever." This directive was not widely enforced. Davis, however, went on to order Confederate armies that invaded Union states to capture free black people in the North and enslave them. "All negroes who shall be taken in any of the States in which slavery does not now exist, in the progress of our arms, shall be adjudged, immediately after their capture, to occupy slave status."

This was done. Several hundred northern black people were taken south after Confederate forces invaded Pennsylvania in 1863 and fought at Gettysburg. Robert E. Lee's Army of Northern Virginia at Greensburg, Pennsylvania, captured at least fifty black people. A southern victory in the Civil War could conceivably have led to the enslavement of more than 300,000 free black residents of the Confederate States.

BLACK CONFEDERATES

Most of the labor black people did for the Confederacy was involuntary, but there were a few free black men and women who offered their services to the southern cause. In Lynchburg, Virginia, in the spring of 1861, seventy free black people volunteered "to act in whatever capacity may be assigned them." In Memphis in the fall, several hundred black residents cheered for Jefferson Davis and sang patriotic songs. These demonstrations of black support were made early in the conflict when the outcome was still much in doubt and long before the war became a crusade against slavery.

The status of many free black Southerners remained precarious. In Virginia in 1861, impressment laws, like those applying to slaves, compelled free black men to work on Confederate defenses around Richmond and Petersburg. Months before the war, South Carolina considered forcing its free black population to choose between enslavement and exile. The legislature rejected the proposal, but it terrified the state's free black people. Many people of color there had been free for generations. Fair in complexion, they had education, skills, homes, and businesses. Some even owned slaves. When the war came, many were willing to demonstrate their devotion to the South in a desperate attempt to gain white acceptance before they lost their freedom and property.

In early 1861, before the formation of the Confederacy, but after the secession of South Carolina, eighty-two free black men in Charleston petitioned Governor Francis W. Pickens "to be assigned any service where we can be useful." To distinguish themselves from slaves and to show their solidarity with white Southerners, they proclaimed, "We are by birth citizens of South Carolina, in our veins is the blood of the white race in some half, in others much more, our attachments are with you, our hopes of safety and protection is in South Carolina, our allegiance is due alone to her, in her defence we are willing to offer up our lives and all that is dear to us." Pickens rejected the petition, but white South Carolinians were pleased at this show of loyalty.

White southern leaders generally ignored offers of free black support unless it was for menial labor. But in Charleston, when the city was under siege between 1863 and 1865, black and white residents were grateful that volunteer fire brigades composed of free black men turned out repeatedly to fight fires caused by Union artillery.

PERSONAL SERVANTS

Other black men contributed in different ways to the Confederate military effort. Black musicians in Virginia played for Confederate regiments and received the same pay as white musicians. Well-to-do white men often took their slaves—personal servants—with them when they went off to war. The servants cooked, cleaned uniforms, cared for weapons, maintained horses, and even provided entertainment. Some were loyal and devoted. They cared for owners who were wounded or fell sick. They accompanied the bodies of dead masters home.

Being the personal servant for a soldier was hard and sometimes dangerous work. Those close to combat could be killed or injured. One father warned his son not to take Sam, a valuable slave, into battle. "I hear you are likely to have a big battle soon, and I write to tell you not to let Sam go into the fight with you. Keep him in the rear, for that nigger is worth a thou-

sand dollars." The father evidently placed a higher value on the slave than on his son.

BLACK MEN FIGHTING FOR THE SOUTH

Approximately 144,000 black men from the southern states fought with the Union Army. Most had been slaves. Although it was technically not legal until almost the end of the war, a much, much smaller number of black men did fight for the Confederacy. White New York troops claimed to have encountered about seven hundred armed black men in late 1861 near Newport News, Virginia. In 1862 a black Confederate sharpshooter positioned himself in a chimney and shot several Union soldiers before he was finally killed. Fifty black men served as pickets for the Confederates along the Rappahannock River in Virginia in 1863.

John Wilson Buckner, a free black man with a light complexion, enlisted in the First South Carolina Artillery. As a member of the well-regarded free black Ellison family of Stateburg, South Carolina, Buckner was considered an "honorary white man." He fought for the Confederacy in the defense of Charleston at Battery Wagner in July 1863 and was wounded just before the 54th Massachusetts Regiment assaulted the fort.

Some black civilians supported the war effort and stood to profit if the South won. Buckner's uncles grew corn, sweet potatoes, peas, sorghum, and beans on the Ellison family plantation to feed Confederate troops. By hiring out horses, mules, and slaves they owned, the Ellisons had earned nearly $1,000 by 1863. By 1865 they had paid almost $5,000 in taxes to the Confederacy, nearly one-fifth of their total income. They also patriotically invested almost $7,000 in Confederate bonds and notes. Like prosperous white families, the Ellisons lost most of this investment with the defeat of the Confederacy. At war's end, the bonds were as worthless as Confederate cash, and the eighty slaves the Ellisons owned—worth approximately $100,000—were free people (see Chapter 6).

Other black Southerners also suffered economically from the Confederate defeat. Richard Mack, a South Carolina slave, went off to war as a personal servant. After his master died, he became an orderly for another Confederate officer. He worked hard and accumulated a large sum in Confederate currency. He later joked, "If we had won, I would be rich."

In Virginia, free black people and slaves also contributed to the Confederate cause. Pompey Scott of Amelia County gave $20 to the war effort. William, a slave who had amassed $150, invested in Confederate State Loan Bonds. Lewis, a Mecklenburg County slave,

Black troops were among the first Union military forces to "liberate" the devastated city of Charleston, South Carolina, in the waning weeks of the Civil War. On February 21, 1865, the 55th Massachusetts Regiment occupied Charleston. Black residents—many of them former slaves—eagerly welcomed the soldiers. Defeated and discouraged white residents remained secluded indoors.   *Harper's Weekly*, March 18, 1865

was not permitted to join a Confederate cavalry unit as a bugler, so he donated his bugle and $20 to the Confederacy.

White Southerners effusively praised the few black people who actively supported the South. Several states awarded pensions to black men who served in the war and survived. Henry Clay Lightfoot was a slave in Culpeper, Virginia, who went to war as a body servant of Captain William Holcomb. After the war, he bought a house, raised a family, and was elected to the Culpeper town council. He collected a pension from Virginia, and when he died in 1931, the United Daughters of the Confederacy draped his coffin in a Confederate flag.

BLACK OPPOSITION TO THE CONFEDERACY

Although many white Southerners and some Northerners believed most slaves would support their mas-

ters, in fact most did not. When a slave named Tom was asked if slaves would fight for their masters, he replied, "I know they say dese tings, but dey lies. Our masters may talk now all dey choose; but one ting's sartin,—dey don't dare to try us. Jess put de guns in our hans, and you'll soon see dat we not only knows how to shoot, but who, to shoot. My master wouldn't be wuff much ef I was a soldier."

THE CONFEDERATE DEBATE
ON BLACK TROOPS

By late 1863 and 1864, prospects for the Confederacy had become grim. The Union naval blockade of southern ports had become increasingly effective, and the likelihood of British aid had all but vanished. Confederate armies suffered crushing defeats at Vicksburg and Gettysburg in 1863 and absorbed terrible losses in Tennessee, Georgia, and Virginia in 1864.

As defeat loomed, some white Southerners began to discuss the possibility of arming black men. Several southern newspapers advocated it. In September 1863 the Montgomery (Alabama) *Weekly Mail* admitted it would have been preposterous to contemplate the need for black troops earlier in the war, but it had now become necessary to save the white South:

> We are forced by the necessity of our condition—by the insolence and barbarity of the enemy, by his revengeful and demoniacal spirit—to take a step which is revolting to every sentiment of pride, and to every principle that governed our institutions before the war. But the war has made great changes, and we must meet those changes, for the sake of preserving our very existence. It is a matter of necessity, therefore, that we should use every means within our reach to defeat the enemy. One of these, and the only one which will checkmate him, is the employment of negroes in the military service of the Confederacy.

In early 1864 Confederate general Patrick Cleburne recommended enlisting slaves and promising them their freedom if they remained loyal to the Confederacy. Cleburne argued that this policy would gain recognition and aid from Great Britain and would disrupt Union military efforts to recruit black Southerners. Yet most white Southerners considered arming slaves and free black men an appalling prospect. Jefferson Davis ordered military officers, including Cleburne, to cease discussing the issue.

Most white Southerners were convinced that to arm slaves and put black men in gray uniforms defied the assumptions on which southern society was based. Black people were inferior, and their proper status was to be slaves. The Richmond *Whig* declared in 1864 that "servitude is a divinely appointed condition for the highest good of the slave." It was absurd to contemplate black people as soldiers and as free people. Georgia politician Howell Cobb explained that slaves could not be armed. "If slaves will make good soldiers our whole theory of slavery is wrong."

The Civil War for white Southerners was a war to prevent the abolition of slavery. Now white southern voices were proposing abolition to preserve the southern nation. North Carolina senator Robert M. T. Hunter opposed any attempt to enlist slaves and free them. "If we are right in passing this measure we were wrong in denying to the old government the right to interfere with the institution of slavery and to emancipate slaves. Besides, if we offer slaves their freedom . . . we confess that we were insincere, were hypocritical, in asserting that slavery was the best state for the negroes themselves."

Nevertheless, as the military situation deteriorated, the South moved toward employing black troops. In November 1864 Virginia governor William Smith enthusiastically supported the idea. "There is not a man that would not cheerfully put the negro in the Army rather than become a slave himself. . . . Standing before God and my country, I do not hesitate to say that I would arm such portion of our able-bodied slaves population as may be necessary." In February 1865 Jefferson Davis and the Confederate cabinet conceded, "We are reduced to choosing whether the negroes shall fight for us or against us."

The opinion of General Robert E. Lee was critical to determining whether the Confederacy would decide to arm black men. No Southerner was more revered and respected. Lee had freed nearly two hundred slaves in keeping with the instructions of his father-in-law George Washington Parke Custis's will in 1862. That will provided that the slaves be emancipated within five years of Custis's death in 1857.

With his army struggling to survive a desperate winter around Petersburg and Richmond, Lee announced in February 1865 that he favored both enrolling and emancipating black troops. "My own opinion is that we should employ them without delay." He believed their service as slaves would make them capable soldiers. "They possess the physical qualities in an eminent degree. Long habits of obedience and subordination, coupled with moral influence which in our country the white man possesses over the black, furnish an excellent foundation for that discipline which is the best guarantee of military efficiency."

Less than a month later in March 1865, although many white Southerners still opposed it, the Confederate Congress voted to enlist 300,000 black men between the ages of eighteen and forty-five. They would receive the same pay, equipment, and supplies as white soldiers. But those who were slaves would not be freed unless their owner consented and the state where they served agreed to their emancipation.

It was a desperate measure by a nearly defeated government and did not affect the outcome of the conflict. Before the war ended in April, authorities in Virginia managed to recruit some black men and send a few into combat. By the end of March, one company of thirty-five black men—twelve free black men and twenty-three slaves—was organized. On April 4, 1865, Union troops attacked Confederate supply wagons that the black troops were guarding in Amelia County. Less than a week later, Lee surrendered to Grant at Appomattox Court House, and the Civil War ended.

AFRICAN-AMERICAN EVENTS	NATIONAL EVENTS
• 1860 •	
	November 1860 Abraham Lincoln wins the presidential election
	December 1860 South Carolina secedes from the Union
• 1861 •	
April–May 1861 Black men volunteer for military service and are rejected	**February 1861** The Confederate States of America is formed
August 1861 First Confiscation Act	**March 1861** Lincoln inaugurated
	April 1861 The firing on Fort Sumter begins the Civil War
	November 1861 Union military forces capture the Sea Islands and coastal areas of South Carolina and Georgia
• 1862 •	
May 1862 Robert Smalls escapes with *The Planter* and sixteen slaves	**September 1862** Battle of Antietam is fought
May–August 1862 The First South Carolina Volunteers, an all-black regiment, forms	
September 1862 Lincoln announces the Preliminary Emancipation Proclamation	
October 1862 Black troops see combat for the first time in Missouri	
• 1863 •	
January 1, 1863 Lincoln issues the Emancipation Proclamation	**March 1863** The U.S. government enacts a Conscription Act
January–March 1863 Troops recruited for the 54th and the 55th Massachusetts Regiments	**July 1863** Battles of Vicksburg and Gettysburg
June 1863 Battle of Milliken's Bend	
July 1863 Assault on Battery Wagner; New York City draft riots; Battle at Honey Springs	

CONCLUSION

The Civil War ended with the decisive defeat of the Confederacy. The Union was preserved. The long ordeal of slavery for millions of people of African descent was over. Slavery—having thrived in America for nearly 250 years—was finally abolished by an amendment to the U.S. Constitution. Congress passed the Thirteenth Amendment on January 31, 1865. It was ratified by twenty-seven states and declared in effect on December 18, 1865.

Were it not for the presence and labors of more than four million black people, there would have been no Civil War. Had it not been for the presence and contributions of more than 185,000 black soldiers and sailors, the Union would not have won. Almost forty thousand of those black men died in combat and of disease during the war. Twenty-one black men were awarded the Congressional Medal of Honor for heroism during the conflict.

No one better represents the dramatic shift in attitudes and policies toward African Americans during the Civil War than Abraham Lincoln. When the war began, Lincoln insisted it was a white man's conflict to suppress an insurrection of rebellious white Southerners. Black people, Lincoln remained convinced, would be better off outside the United States. But the war went on, and thousands of white men died. Lincoln issued the Emancipation Proclamation and welcomed the enlistment of black troops. The president came to appreciate the achievements and devotion of black troops and condemned the mean-spiritedness of white Northerners who opposed the war. Lincoln wrote in 1863, "And then there will be some black men who can remember that, with silent tongue, and clenched teeth, and steady eye, and well-poised bayonet, they have helped mankind on to this great consummation; while, I fear, there will be some white ones, unable to forget that, with malignant heart, and deceitful speech, they have strove to hinder it."

RECOMMENDED READING

Lerone Bennett. *Forced into Glory: Abraham Lincoln's White Dream.* Chicago: Johnson, 2000. Bennett is highly critical of Lincoln's attitudes and actions in this thought-provoking account.

Dudley Taylor Cornish. *The Sable Arm: Negro Troops in the Union Army, 1861–1865.* New York: Norton, 1956. The best single study of black men in the military during the war.

John Hope Franklin. *The Emancipation Proclamation.* Garden City, NY: Doubleday, 1963. A work written to commemorate the centennial of the Proclamation.

Michael P. Johnson and James L. Roark. *Black Masters: A Free Family of Color in the Old South.* New York: Norton, 1984. A splendid depiction of life among prosperous free black people before and during the Civil War.

Ervin Jordon. *Black Confederates and Afro Yankees in Civil War Virginia.* Charlottesville: University of Virginia Press, 1995. A rich study of life and society among African Americans in Virginia during the war.

James McPherson. *Battle Cry of Freedom: The Civil War Era.* New York: Oxford University Press, 1988. A superb one-volume account of the Civil War.

George W. Williams. *History of the Negro Troops in the War of the Rebellion.* New York: Harper & Row, 1888. An account of black soldiers in the war by America's first African-American historian.

ADDITIONAL BIBLIOGRAPHY

MILITARY

Joseph T. Glatthaar. *Forged in Battle: The Civil War Alliance of Black Soldiers and White Officers.* New York: The Free Press, 1990.

———. *The March to the Sea and Beyond: Sherman's Troops in the Savannah and Carolina Campaign.* New York: New York University Press, 1985.

Herman Hattaway and Archer Jones. *How the North Won: A Military History of the Civil War.* Urbana: University of Illinois Press, 1983.

Geoffrey Ward and Ken Burns. *The Civil War.* New York: Alfred A. Knopf, 1990.

Stephen R. Wise. *Gate of Hell: Campaign for Charleston Harbor, 1863.* Columbia: University of South Carolina Press, 1994.

AFRICAN AMERICANS AND THE WAR

Peter Burchard. *One Gallant Rush: Robert Gould Shaw and His Brave Black Regiment.* New York: St. Martin's Press, 1965.

George S. Burkhardt. *Confederate Wrath: No Quarter in the Civil War.* Carbondale: Southern Illinois University Press, 2007.

John Cimpach. *Fort Pillow: A Civil War Massacre and Public Memory.* Baton Rouge: Louisiana State University Press, 2005.

Catherine Clinton. *Harriet Tubman: The Road to Freedom.* Boston: Little, Brown, 2004.

Ella Forbes. *African American Women during the Civil War.* New York: Garland, 1998.

Kate Clifford Larson. *Bound for the Promised Land: Harriet Tubman, Portrait of an American Hero.* New York: Ballantine, 2004.

Leon Litwack. *Been in the Storm So Long: The Aftermath of Slavery.* New York: Alfred A. Knopf, 1979.

Edward A. Miller. *Gullah Statesman: Robert Smalls from Slavery to Congress, 1839–1915.* Columbia: University of South Carolina Press, 1995.

1864

AFRICAN-AMERICAN EVENTS	NATIONAL EVENTS
February 1864 Battle at Olustee	**November 1864** Lincoln is reelected
April 1864 Fort Pillow Massacre	**November–December 1864** Sherman makes his march to the sea

1865

AFRICAN-AMERICAN EVENTS	NATIONAL EVENTS
February 1865 Black troops lead the occupation of Charleston	**February 1865** Charleston falls
	March 1865 Richmond falls
March 1865 Confederate Congress approves the enlistment of black men	
	April 1865 Lee surrenders at Appomatox; Lincoln is assassinated
December 1865 Thirteenth Amendment ratified	

AFRICAN-AMERICAN EVENTS   NATIONAL EVENTS

Benjamin Quarles. *The Negro in the Civil War.* Boston: Little, Brown, 1953.

Willie Lee Rose. *Rehearsal for Reconstruction: The Port Royal Experiment.* Indianapolis: Bobbs Merrill, 1964.

Noah A. Trudeau. *Like Men of War: Black Troops in the Civil War, 1862–1865.* Boston: Little, Brown, 1998.

Gregory J. W. Urwin, ed. *Black Flag over Dixie: Racial Atrocities and Reprisals in the Civil War.* Carbondale: Southern Illinois University Press, 2004.

Bell I. Wiley. *Southern Negroes, 1861–1865.* New Haven, CT: Yale University Press, 1938.

DOCUMENTS, LETTERS, AND OTHER SOURCES

Virginia M. Adams, ed. *On the Altar of Freedom: A Black Soldier's Civil War Letters from the Front.* [Corporal James Henry Gooding]. Amherst: University of Massachusetts, 1991.

Ira Berlin et al., eds. "Freedom: A Documentary History of Emancipation, 1861–1867," Series 1, Volume I, *The Destruction of Slavery.* New York: Cambridge University Press, 1985.

———. "Freedom: A Documentary History of Emancipation, 1861–1867," Series 1, Volume III, *The Wartime Genesis of Free Labor: The Lower South.* New York: Cambridge University Press, 1990.

Robert F. Durden. *The Gray and the Black: The Confederate Debate on Emancipation.* Baton Rouge: Louisiana State University Press, 1972.

Michael P. Johnson and James L. Roark, eds. *No Chariot Letdown: Charleston's Free People of Color on the Eve of the Civil War.* Chapel Hill: University of North Carolina Press, 1984.

James McPherson. *The Negro's Civil War: How American Negroes Felt and Acted during the War for the Union.* New York: Pantheon, 1965.

Edwin S. Redkey, ed. *A Grand Army of Black Men: Letters from African American Soldiers in the Union Army, 1861–1865.* New York: Cambridge University Press, 1992.

REMINISCENCES

Thomas Wentworth Higginson. *Army Life in a Black Regiment.* Boston: Beacon Press, 1962.

Elizabeth Keckley. *Behind the Scenes: Or Thirty Years a Slave and Four Years in the White House.* New York: Oxford University Press, 1968.

Susie King Taylor. *Reminiscences of My Life in Camp.* Boston: Taylor, 1902.

RETRACING THE ODYSSEY

The Penn Center, St. Helena Island, South Carolina. Beginning in 1862, black and white teachers from the North began offering instruction to former slaves on the Carolina coast. Laura Towne and Ellen Murray helped establish Penn school amid the oak trees draped in Spanish moss. The school closed in 1948. During the 1950s and 1960s, civil rights leaders, including Dr. Martin Luther King Jr., gathered at Penn to discuss strategy. Today Penn Center provides programs on health, literacy, land ownership, and agriculture. It serves as a cultural and community center, and there is a museum among the historic buildings.

Olustee Battlefield State Historic Site, Olustee, Florida. In February 1864 the largest Civil War battle in Florida was fought at Olustee, which is almost fifty miles west of Jacksonville. About one-third of the Union troops were black men. There is a museum with exhibits and artifacts.

Fort Pillow State Park, Tennessee. This was the scene of the April 1864 battle in which Confederate forces attacked the black and white Union defenders of the fort. About 238 black men were killed, some during the battle and others after they surrendered. There is a visitor center, museum, and trail to the fortifications.

The Crater, Petersburg National Battlefield, Virginia. The longest siege in American military history occurred in and around the town of Petersburg in 1864 and 1865. Union forces attempted to break Confederate lines by setting off an enormous explosion in July 1864. Poor leadership and inept execution turned the Union advantage to disaster for the white and black troops who took part. Portions of the trenches and the crater are still visible.

Harriet Tubman Museum, Auburn, New York. In 1896 the famed liberator of slaves bought this property and made it her home. She died here in 1913. The African Methodist Episcopal Zion Church operates the house as a museum. Harriet Tubman is buried nearby at Fort Hill Cemetery.

 REVIEW, RESEARCH, AND INTERACT

REVIEW QUESTIONS

1. How did the Union's purposes in the Civil War change between 1861 and 1865? What accounts for those changes?

2. How did policies of the Confederate government toward slaves change during the Civil War? What were those changes, and when and why did they occur?

3. When the Civil War began, why did northern black men volunteer to serve in the Union army if the war had not yet become a war to end slavery?

4. To what extent did Abraham Lincoln's policies and attitudes toward black people change during the Civil War? Does Lincoln deserve credit as "the Great Emancipator"? Why or why not?

5. What was the purpose of the Emancipation Proclamation? Why was it issued? Exactly what did it accomplish?

6. What did black men and women contribute to the Union war effort? Was it in their interests to participate in the Civil War? Why or why not?

7. Why did at least some black people support the southern states and the Confederacy during the Civil War?

8. Was the result of the Civil War worth the loss of 620,000 lives?

www.researchnavigator.com

Using the tools available in Research Navigator, consider this question:
Why were African Americans who wanted to enlist rejected in 1861?

PRIMARY SOURCE DOCUMENTS

11–1 The Working Men of Manchester, England, Write to President Lincoln on the Question of Slavery in 1862

11–2 President Lincoln Responds to the Working Men of Manchester on the Subject of Slavery in 1863

11–3 President Abraham Lincoln Delivers the Gettysburg Address in 1863

11–4 "If It Were Not for My Trust in Christ I Do Not Know How I Could Have Endured It": Testimony from Victims of New York's Draft Riots, July 1863

11–5 "I Hope to Fall with My Face to the Foe": Lewis Douglass Describes the Battle of Fort Wagner, 1863

11–6 Retaliation in Camp, 1864

11–7 Elizabeth Keckley, *Thirty Years a Slave, and Four Years in the White House*, 1868

11–8 Paul Laurence Dunbar, "The Colored Soldiers," 1896

MAP EXPLORATION

Effects of the Emancipation Proclamation, p. 275.

INTERACTIVE ACTIVITIES

Fort Pillow Massacre
In this activity, you will examine the events surrounding the atrocity against black troops at Fort Pillow.

A Nation Divided: The Civil War
What role did African Americans play in gaining their own freedom, and how did their struggle affect the lives of ordinary people?

12

The Meaning of Freedom: The Promise of Reconstruction

❖

WHAT DID FREEDOM MEAN TO NEARLY
FOUR MILLION PEOPLE WHO HAD BEEN SLAVES?

HOW SUCCESSFUL WERE MOST FORMER SLAVES
IN ACQUIRING LAND OF THEIR OWN?

WHAT WAS THE FREEDMEN'S BUREAU
AND HOW EFFECTIVE WAS IT?

WHY WAS EDUCATION SO IMPORTANT
TO AFRICAN AMERICANS?

WHAT WAS THE PURPOSE
OF THE FOURTEENTH AMENDMENT?

HOW DID AFRICAN AMERICAN MEN
GAIN THE RIGHT TO VOTE?

1865–1868

◄ **In an idealized rendering,** artist J. W. Watts depicted a Union
soldier reading the Emancipation Proclamation to a group
of astonished freed people. In some cases it took weeks for
slaves to learn that the U.S. government had declared an end
to slavery. Reportedly in remote areas of Texas, slaves did not
find out about freedom until 'Juneteenth' of 1865.

Many Thousand Gone

No more auction block for me,
No more, no more,
No more auction block for me,
Many thousand gone.

No more driver's lash for me,
No more, no more,
No more driver's lash for me,
Many thousand gone.

No more peck of salt for me,
No more, no more,
No more peck of salt for me,
Many thousand gone.

No more iron chain for me,
No more, no more.
No more iron chain for me,
Many thousand gone.

An African American Emancipation Song

◀ **Many freed blacks** returned to the South looking for family who had been sold away.

What did freedom mean to a people who had endured and survived 250 years of enslavement in America? What did the future hold for nearly four million African Americans in 1865? Freedom meant many things to many people. But to most former slaves, it meant that families would stay together. Freedom meant that women would no longer be sexually exploited. Freedom meant learning to read and write. Freedom meant organizing churches. Freedom meant moving around without having to obtain permission. Freedom meant that labor would produce income for the laborer and not the master. Freedom meant working without the whip. Freedom meant land to own, cultivate, and live on. Freedom meant a trial before a jury if charged with a crime. Freedom meant voting. Freedom meant citizenship and having the same rights as white people.

Years after slavery ended, a former Texas slave, Margrett Nillin, was asked if she preferred slavery or freedom. She answered unequivocally, "Well, it's dis way, in slavery I owns nothin' and never owns nothin'. In freedom I's own de home and raise de family. All dat causes me worryment and in slavery I has no worryment, but I takes freedom."

The End of Slavery

With the collapse of slavery, many black people were quick to inform white people that whatever loyalty, devotion, and cooperation they might have shown as slaves had never been a reflection of their inner feelings and attitudes. Near Opelousas, Louisiana, a Union officer asked a young black man why he did not love his master, and the youth responded sharply. "When my master begins to lub me, den it'll be time enough for me to lub him. What I wants is to get away. I want to take me off from dis plantation, where I can be free."

In North Carolina, planter Robert P. Howell was deeply disappointed that a loyal slave named Lovet fled at the first opportunity. "He was about my age and I had always treated him more as a companion than a slave. When I left I put everything in his charge, told him that he was free, but to remain on the place and

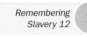

Remembering Slavery 12

LIVING WORDS

take care of things. He promised me faithfully that he would, but he was the first one to leave . . . and I did not see him for several years."

Emancipation was a traumatic experience for many former masters. A Virginia freedman remembered that "Miss Polly died right after the surrender, she was so hurt that all the negroes was going to be free." Another former slave, Robert Falls, recalled that his master assembled the slaves to inform them they were free. "I hates to do it, but I must. You all ain't my niggers no more. You is free. Just as free as I am. Here I have raised you all to work for me, and now you are going to leave me. I am an old man, and I can't get along without you. I don't know what I am going to do." In less than a year, he was dead. Falls attributed his master's death to the end of slavery. "It killed him."

DIFFERING REACTIONS OF FORMER SLAVES

Other slaves bluntly displayed their reaction to years of bondage. Aunt Delia, a cook with a North Carolina family, revealed that for a long time she had secretly gained retribution for the indignity of servitude. "How many times I spit in the biscuits and peed in the coffee just to get back at them mean white folks." In Goodman, Mississippi, a slave named Caddy learned she was free and rushed from the field to find her owner. "Caddy threw down that hoe, she marched herself up to the big house, then, she looked around and found the mistress. She went over to the mistress, she flipped up her dress and told the white woman to do something. She said it mean and ugly. This is what she said: 'Kiss my ass!'"

In contrast, some slaves, especially elderly ones, were fearful and apprehensive about freedom. On a South Carolina plantation, an older black woman refused to accept emancipation. "I ain' no free nigger! I is got a marster and mistiss! Dee right dar in de great house. Ef you don' b'lieve me, you go dar an' see."

REUNITING BLACK FAMILIES

As slavery ended, the most urgent need for many freed people was finding family members who had been sold away from them. Slavery had not destroyed the black family. Husbands, wives, and children went to great lengths to reassemble their families after the Civil War. For years and even decades after the end of slavery, advertisements appeared in black newspapers appealing for information about missing kinfolk. The following notice was published in the *Colored Tennessean* on August 5, 1865:

Saml. Dove wishes to know of the whereabouts of his mother, Areno, his sisters Maria, Neziah and Peggy, and his brother Edmond, who were owned by Geo. Dove of Rockingham County, Shenandoah Valley, Va. Sold in Richmond, after which Saml. and Edmond were taken to Nashville, Tenn., by Joe Mick; Areno was left at the Eagle Tavern, Richmond. Respectfully yours, Saml. Dove, Utica, New York.

In North Carolina a northern journalist met a middle-age black man "plodding along, staff in hand, and apparently very footsore and tired." The nearly exhausted freedman explained that he had walked almost six hundred miles looking for his wife and children who had been sold four years earlier.

There were emotional reunions as family members found each other after years of separation. Ben and Betty Dodson had been apart for twenty years when Ben found her in a refugee camp after the war. "Glory! glory! hallelujah," he shouted as he hugged his wife. "Dis is my Betty, shuah. I foun' you at las'. I's hunted and hunted till I track you up here. I's boun' to hunt till I fin' you if you's alive."

Other searches had more heart-wrenching results. Husbands and wives sometimes learned that their spouses had remarried during the separation. Believing his wife had died, the husband of Laura Spicer remarried—only to learn after the war that Laura was still alive. Sadly, he wrote to her but refused to meet with her. "I would come and see you but I know I could not bear it. I want to see you and I don't want to see you. I love you just as well as I did the last day I saw you, and it will not do for you and I to meet."

Tormented, he wrote again pledging his love. "Laura I do not think that I have change any at all since I saw you last—I thinks of you and my children every day of my life. Laura I do love you the same. My love to you never have failed. Laura, truly, I have got another wife, and I am very sorry that I am. You feels and seems to me as much like my dear loving wife, as you ever did Laura."

One freedman testified to the close ties that bound many slave families when he replied bitterly to the claim that he had had a kind master who had fed him and never used the whip. "Kind! yes, he gib men corn enough, and he gib me pork enough, and he neber gib me one lick wid de whip, but whar's my wife?—whar's my chill'en? Take away de pork, I say; take away de corn, I can work and raise dese for myself, but gib me back de wife of my bosom, and gib me back my poor chill'en as was sold away."

Land

As freed people embraced freedom and left their masters, they wanted land. Nineteenth-century Americans of virtually every background associated economic security with owning land. Families wanted to work land and prosper as self-sufficient yeomen. Former slaves believed their future as a free people was tied to the possession of land. But just as it had been impossible to abolish slavery without the intervention of the U.S. government, it would not be possible to procure land without federal assistance. At first, federal authorities seemed determined to make land available to freedmen.

SPECIAL FIELD ORDER #15

Shortly after his army arrived in Savannah—after having devastated Georgia—Union general William T. Sherman announced that freedmen would receive land. On January 16, 1865, he issued **Special Field Order #15.** This military directive set aside a 30-mile-wide tract of land along the Atlantic coast from Charleston, South Carolina, 245 miles south to Jacksonville, Florida. White owners had abandoned the land, and Sherman reserved it for black families. The head of

each family would receive "possessory title" to forty acres of land. Sherman also gave the freedmen the use of army mules, thus giving rise to the slogan, "Forty acres and a mule."

Within six months, 40,000 freed people were working 400,000 acres in the South Carolina and Georgia low country and on the Sea Islands. Former slaves generally avoided the slave crops of cotton and rice and instead planted sweet potatoes and corn. They also worked together as families and kinfolk. They avoided the gang labor associated with slavery. Most husbands and fathers preferred that their wives and daughters not work in the fields as slave women had had to do.

THE PORT ROYAL EXPERIMENT

Meanwhile, hundreds of former slaves had been cultivating land for three years. In late 1861 Union military forces carved out an enclave around Beaufort and Port Royal, South Carolina, that remained under federal authority for the rest of the war. White planters fled to the interior, leaving their slaves behind. Under the supervision of U.S. Treasury officials and northern reformers and missionaries who hurried south in 1862, ex-slaves began to work the land in what came to be

Former slaves assembled in a village near Washington, D.C. Black people welcomed emancipation, but without land, education, or employment, they faced an uncertain future.

known as the **"Port Royal Experiment."** When Treasury agents auctioned off portions of the land for nonpayment of taxes, freedmen purchased some of it. But northern businessmen bought most of the real estate and then hired black people to raise cotton.

White owners sometimes returned to their former lands only to find that black families had taken charge. A group of black farmers told one former owner, "We own this land now, put it out of your head that it will ever be yours again." And on one South Carolina Sea Island, white men were turned back by armed black men.

The Freedmen's Bureau

As the war ended in early 1865, Congress created the Bureau of Refugees, Freedmen, and Abandoned Lands—commonly called the **Freedmen's Bureau.** Created as a temporary agency to assist freedmen to make the transition to freedom, the bureau was placed under the control of the U.S. Army and General Oliver O. Howard was put in command. Howard, a devout Christian who had lost an arm in the war, was eager to aid the freedmen.

The bureau was given enormous responsibilities. It was to help freedmen obtain land, gain an education, negotiate labor contracts with white planters, settle legal and criminal disputes involving black and white people, and provide food, medical care, and transportation for black and white people left destitute by the war. However, Congress never provided sufficient funds or personnel to carry out these tasks.

The Freedmen's Bureau never had more than 900 agents spread across the South from Virginia to Texas. Mississippi, for example, had twelve agents in 1866. One agent often served a county with a population of 10,000 to 20,000 freedmen. Few of the agents were black because few military officers were black. John Mercer Langston of Virginia was an inspector of schools assigned to the bureau's main office in Washington, D.C.; Major Martin R. Delany worked with freedmen on the South Carolina Sea Islands.

The need for assistance was desperate as thousands of black and white southerners endured extreme privation in the months after the war ended. The bureau established camps for the homeless, fed the hungry, and cared for orphans and the sick as best it could. It distributed more than thirteen million rations—consisting of flour, corn meal, and sugar—by 1866. The bureau provided medical care to a half million freedmen and thousands of white people who were suffering from smallpox, yellow fever, cholera, and pneumonia. Many more remained untreated.

In July 1865 the bureau took a first step toward distributing land when General Howard issued Circular 13 ordering agents to "set aside" forty-acre plots for freedmen. But the allocation had hardly begun when the order was revoked, and it was announced that land already distributed under General Sherman's Special Field Order #15 was to be returned to its previous white owners.

The reason for this reversal in policy was that President Andrew Johnson, who had become president after Lincoln's assassination in April 1865, began to pardon hundreds and then thousands of former Confederates and restore their lands to them. General Howard was forced to tell black people that they had to relinquish the land they thought they had acquired. In a speech before some 2,000 freedmen on South Carolina's Edisto Island in October 1865, Howard pleaded with his audience to "lay aside their bitter feelings, and to become reconciled to their old

OFFICE OF THE FREEDMEN'S BUREAU, MEMPHIS, TENNESSEE.
[SEE PAGE 376.]

Freedmen's Bureau agents often found themselves in the middle of angry disputes over land and labor that erupted between black and white southerners. Too often the Bureau officers sided with the white landowners in these disagreements with former slaves. *Harper's Weekly,* July 25, 1868

A FREEDMEN'S BUREAU COMMISSIONER TELLS FREED PEOPLE WHAT FREEDOM MEANS

In June 1865 Charles Soule, the commissioner of contracts for the Freedmen's Bureau, told a gathering of freedmen in Orangeburg, South Carolina, what to expect and how to behave in the coming year:

You are now free, but you must know that the only difference you can feel yet, between slavery and freedom, is that neither you nor your children can be bought or sold. You may have a harder time this year than you have ever had before; it will be the price you pay for your freedom. You will have to work hard, and get very little to eat, and very few clothes to wear. If you get through this year alive and well, you should be thankful. . . . You cannot be paid in money, for there is no good money in the District, nothing but Confederate paper. Then, what can you be paid with? Why, with food, with clothes, with the free use of your little houses and plots. You do not own a cent's worth except yourselves.

You do not understand why some of the white people who used to own you do not have to work in the field. It is because they are rich. If every man were poor, and worked in his own field, there would be no big farms, and very little cotton or corn raised to sell; there would be no money, and nothing to buy. Some people must be rich, to pay the others, and they have the right to do no work except to look out after their property.

Remember that all of your working time belongs to the man who hires you: therefore you must not leave work without his leave not even to nurse a child, or to go and visit a wife or husband. When you wish to go off the place, get a pass as you used to, and then you will run no danger of being taken up by our soldiers.

In short, do just about as the good men among you have always done. Remember that even if you are badly off, no one can buy and sell you: remember that if you help yourselves, GOD will help you, and trust hopefully that next year and the year after will bring some new blessing to you.

🌲 *According to Soule, what is the difference between slavery and freedom?*

🌲 *Does freedom mean that freed people will have economic opportunities equal to those of white people?*

🌲 *How should freed people have responded to Soule's advice?*

Source: Ira Berlin et al., "The Terrain of Freedom: The Struggle over the Meaning of Free Labor in the U.S. South," *History Workshop* 22 (Autumn 1986): 108–30.

masters." A black man shouted a response, "Why, General Howard, why do you take away our lands? You take them from us who are true, always true to the Government! You give them to our all-time enemies. This is not right!"

A committee rejected Howard's appeal for reconciliation and forgiveness and they insisted the government provide land:

> You ask us to forgive the landowners of our island. You only lost your right arm in war and might forgive them. The man who tied me to a tree and gave me 39 lashes and who stripped and flogged my mother and my sister and who will not let me stay in his empty hut except I will do his planting and be satisfied with his price and who combines with others to keep away land from me well knowing I would not have anything to do with him if I had land of my own— that man I cannot well forgive.

Howard was moved by these appeals. He returned to Washington and attempted to persuade Congress to make land available. Congress refused, and President Johnson was determined that white people would get their lands back. It seemed so sensible to most white people. Property that had belonged to white families for generations simply could not be given to freedmen. Freedmen saw matters differently. They deserved land that they and their families had worked without compensation for generations. Freedmen believed it was the only way to make freedom meaningful and to gain independence from white people. As it turned out, most freedmen were forced off land they thought should belong to them.

SOUTHERN HOMESTEAD ACT

In early 1866 Congress attempted to provide land for freedmen with the passage of the **Southern Homestead Act.** More than three million acres of public land were set aside for black people and white southerners who had remained loyal to the Union. Much of this land, however, was unsuitable for farming and consisted of swampy wetlands or unfertile pinewoods. More than 4,000 black families—three-quarters of them in Florida—did claim some of this land, but many of them lacked the financial resources to cultivate it. Eventually southern timber companies acquired much of it, and the Southern Homestead Act largely failed.

SHARECROPPING

To make matters worse, by 1866 bureau officials tried to force freedmen to sign labor contracts with white landowners—putting black people once again under white authority. Black men who refused to sign contracts could be arrested. Theoretically, these contracts were legal agreements between two equals: landowner and laborer. But they were seldom freely concluded. Bureau agents usually sided with the landowner and pressured freedmen to accept unequal terms.

Occasionally, the landowner would pay wages to the laborer. But because most landowners lacked cash to pay wages, they agreed to provide the laborer with part of the crop. The laborer, often grudgingly, agreed to work under the supervision of the landowner. The contracts required labor for a full year; the laborer could neither quit nor strike. Landowners demanded that the laborers work the fields in gangs. Freedmen resisted this system. They sometimes insisted on making decisions involving planting, fertilizing, and harvesting as they sought to exercise independence (see Map 12–1).

Thus it took time for a new form of agricultural labor to develop. But by the 1870s, the system of **sharecropping** had emerged and dominated most of the South. There were no wages. Freedmen worked land as families—not in gangs—and not under direct white supervision. When the landowner provided seed, tools, fertilizer, and work animals (mules, horses, oxen), the black family received one-third of the crop. There were many variations on these arrangements, and frequently black families were cheated out of their fair share of the crop.

Freed women washing laundry along a creek near Circleville, Texas, ca. 1866.

The Black Church

In the years after slavery, the church became the most important institution among African Americans other than the family. Not only did it fill deep spiritual and inspirational needs, it offered enriching music, provided charity and compassion to those in need, developed community and political leaders, and was free of white supervision. Before slavery's demise, free black people and slaves often attended white churches where they were encouraged to participate in religious services conducted by white clergymen and where they were treated as second-class Christians.

Once liberated, black men and women organized their own churches with their own ministers. Most black people considered white ministers incapable of delivering a meaningful message. Nancy Williams recalled, "Ole white preachers used to talk wid dey tongues widdout sayin' nothin', but Jesus told us slaves to talk wid our hearts."

Northern white missionaries were sometimes appalled by the unlettered and ungrammatical black preachers who nevertheless communicated effectively and emotionally with their parishioners. A visiting white clergyman was genuinely impressed and humbled on hearing a black preacher who lacked education, but more than made up for it with devout faith. "He talked about Christ and his salvation as one who understood what he said. . . . Here was an unlearned man, one who could not read, telling of the love of Christ, of Christian faith and duty in a way which I have not learned."

Other black and white religious leaders anguished over what they considered moral laxity and displaced values among the freed people. They preached about honesty, thrift, temperance, and elimination of sexual promiscuity. They demanded an end to "rum-suckers, bar-room loafers, whiskey dealers and card players among the men, and to those women who dressed finely on ill gotten gain."

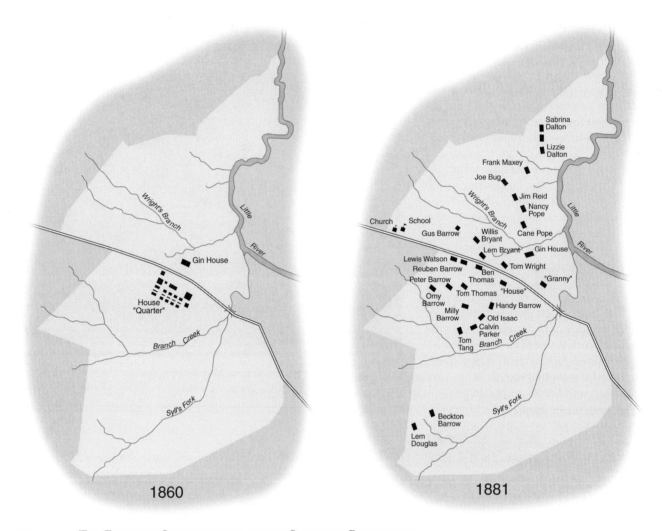

MAP 12–1 The Effect of Sharecropping on the Southern Plantation: The Barrow Plantation, Oglethorpe County, Georgia.

With the end of slavery and the advent of sharecropping, black people would no longer agree to work in fields as gangs. They preferred to have each family cultivate separate plots of land, thereby distancing themselves as much as possible from slavery and white supervision.

▶ *Although many freed people worked the same land that they had as slaves, how does this map suggest the changes experienced by black people in family life, religion, education, and their relationships with white people?*

Church members struggled, scrimped, and saved to buy land and to build churches. Most former slaves founded Baptist and Methodist churches. These denominations tended to be more autonomous and less subject to outside control. Their doctrine was usually simple and direct without complex theology. Of the Methodist churches, the African Methodist Episcopal (AME) church made giant strides in the South after the Civil War.

In Charleston, South Carolina, the AME church was resurrected after an absence of more than forty years. In 1822, during the turmoil over the Denmark Vesey plot, the AME church was forced to disband and its leader, Morris Brown, had to flee (see Chapter 8).

But by the 1870s, three AME congregations were thriving in Charleston. In Wilmington, North Carolina, the 1,600 members of the Front Street Methodist Church decided to join the AME church soon after the Civil War ended. They replaced the longtime white minister, the Reverend L. S. Burkhead, with a black man.

White Methodists initially encouraged cooperation with black Methodists and helped establish the Colored (now Christian) Methodist Episcopal church (CME). But the white Methodists lost some of their fervor after they tried but failed to persuade the black Methodists to keep political issues out of the CME church and to dwell solely on spiritual concerns.

The Presbyterian, Congregational, and Episcopal churches appealed to the more prosperous members of the black community. Their services tended to be more formal and solemn. Black people who had been free before the Civil War were usually affiliated with these congregations and remained so after the conflict. Well-to-do free black people in Charleston organized St. Mark's Protestant Episcopal Church when they separated from the white Episcopal church. But they retained their white minister Joseph Seabrook as rector. Poorer black people of darker complexion found churches like St. Mark's decidedly unappealing. Ed Barber visited, but only one time.

"When I was trampin' 'round Charleston, dere was a church dere called St. Mark, dat all de society folks of my color went to. No black nigger welcome dere, they told me. Thinkin' as how I was bright 'nough to git in, I up and goes dere one Sunday, Ah, how they did carry on, bow and scrape and ape de white folks. . . . I was uncomfortable all de time though, 'cause they were too "hifalootin" in de ways, in de singin', and all sorts of carryin' ons."

The Roman Catholic Church made modest inroads among black southerners. There were all-black parishes in St. Augustine, Savannah, Charleston, and Louisville after the Civil War. For generations prior to the conflict, large numbers of well-to-do free people of color in New Orleans had been practicing Catholics, and their descendants remained faithful to the church. On Georgia's Skidaway Island, Benedictine monks established a school for black youngsters in 1878 that survived for nearly a decade.

Religious differences among black people notwithstanding, the black churches, their parishioners, and clergymen would play a vital role in Reconstruc-

Hundreds of black churches were founded across the South following the Civil War, and they grew spectacularly in the decades that followed. This illustration shows a congregation crowded into Richmond's First African Baptist Church in 1874.

tion politics. More than one hundred black ministers were elected to political office after the Civil War.

Education

Freedom and education were inseparable. To remain illiterate after emancipation was to remain enslaved. One ex-slave master bluntly told his former slave, Charles Whiteside, "Charles, you is a free man they say, but Ah tells you now, you is still a slave and if you lives to be a hundred, you'll STILL be a slave, cause you got no education, and education is what makes a man free!"

Almost every freed black person—young or old—desperately wanted to learn. Elderly people were especially eager to read the Bible. Even before slavery ended, black people began to establish schools. In 1861 Mary Peake, a free black woman, opened a school in Hampton, Virginia. On South Carolina's Sea Islands, a black cabinetmaker began teaching openly after having covertly operated a school for years. In 1862 northern missionaries arrived on the Sea Islands to begin teaching. Laura Towne and Ellen Murray, two white women, and Charlotte Forten, a black woman, opened Penn school on St. Helena's Island as part of the Port

Charlotte Forten came from a prominent Philadelphia family of color. She joined hundreds of black and white teachers who migrated South during and after the Civil War to instruct the freed people. Some teachers remained for a few months. Others stayed for a lifetime. Charlotte Forten—shown here in an 1866 photograph—taught on the South Carolina Sea Islands from 1862 to 1864.

DOCUMENT 12-1 *Life on the Sea Islands*

Royal Experiment. They enrolled 138 children and 58 adults. By 1863 there were 1,700 students and 45 teachers at 30 schools in the South Carolina low country.

With the end of the Civil War, northern religious organizations in cooperation with the Freedmen's Bureau organized hundreds of day and night schools. Classes were held in stables, homes, former slave cabins, taverns, churches, and even—in Savannah and New Orleans—in the old slave markets. Former slaves spent hours in the fields and then trudged to a makeshift school to learn the alphabet and arithmetic. In 1865 black ministers created the Savannah Educational Association, raised $1,000, employed fifteen black teachers, and enrolled 600 students.

In 1866 the Freedmen's Bureau set aside $500,000 for education. The bureau furnished the buildings while former slaves hired, housed, and fed the teachers. By 1869 the Freedmen's Bureau was involved with 3,000 schools and 150,000 students. Even more impressive, by 1870 black people had contributed $1 million to educate their people.

BLACK TEACHERS

Although freedmen appreciated the dedication and devotion of the white teachers affiliated with the missionary societies, they usually preferred black teachers. The Reverend Richard H. Cain, an AME minister who came south from Brooklyn, New York, said that black people needed to learn to control their own futures. "We must take into our own hands the education of our race. . . . Honest, dignified whites may teach ever so well, but it has not the effect to exalt the black man's opinion of his own race, because they have always been in the habit of seeing white men in honored positions, and respected."

Black men and women responded to the call to teach. Virginia C. Green, a northern black woman, felt compelled to go to Mississippi. "Though I have never known servitude they are . . . my people. Born as far north as the lakes I have felt no freer because so many were less fortunate. . . . I look forward with impatience to the time when my people shall be strong, blest with education, purified and made prosperous by virtue and industry." Hezekiah Hunter, a black teacher from Brooklyn, New York, commented in 1865 on the need for black teachers. "I believe we best can instruct our own people, knowing our own peculiarities—needs—necessities. Further—I believe we that are competent owe it to our people to teach them our speciality." And in Malden, West Virginia, when black residents found that a recently arrived eighteen-year-old black man could read and write, they promptly hired him to teach.

In some areas of the South, the sole person available to teach was a poorly educated former slave equipped primarily with a willingness to teach his or her fellow freedmen. One such teacher explained, "I never had the chance of goen to school for I was a slave until freedom. . . . I am the only teacher because we can not doe better now." Many northern teachers, black and white, provided more than the basics of elementary education. Black life and history were occasionally read about and discussed. Abolitionist Lydia Maria Child wrote *The Freedmen's Book*, which offered short biographies of Benjamin Banneker, Frederick Douglass, and Toussaint Louverture. More often northern teachers, dismayed at the backwardness of the freedmen, struggled to modify behavior and to impart cultural values by teaching piety, thrift, cleanliness, temperance, and timeliness.

Many former slaves came to resent some of these teachers as condescending, self-righteous, and paternalistic. Sometimes the teachers, especially those who were white, became frustrated with recalcitrant students who did not readily absorb middle-class values. Others, however, derived enormous satisfaction from teaching freedmen. A Virginia teacher commented, "I think I shall stay here as long as I live and teach this people. I have no love or taste for any other work, and I am happy only here with them."

BLACK COLLEGES

Northern churches and religious societies established dozens of colleges, universities, academies, and institutes across the South in the late 1860s and the 1870s. Most of these institutions provided elementary and secondary education. Few black students were prepared for actual college or university work. The **American Missionary Association**—an abolitionist and Congregationalist organization—worked with the Freedmen's Bureau to establish Fisk in Tennessee, Hampton in Virginia, Tougaloo in Alabama, and Avery in South Carolina. The primary purpose of these schools was to educate black students to become teachers.

In Missouri, the black enlisted men and the white officers of the 62nd and 65th Colored Volunteers raised $6,000 to establish Lincoln Institute in 1866, which would become Lincoln University. The American Baptist Home Mission Society founded Virginia Union, Shaw in North Carolina, Benedict in South Carolina, and Morehouse in Georgia. Northern Methodists helped establish Claflin in South Carolina, Rust in Mississippi, and Bennett in North Carolina. The Episcopalians were responsible for St. Augustine's in North Carolina and St. Paul's in Virginia. These and many other similar institutions formed the foundation for the historically black colleges and universities.

RESPONSE OF WHITE SOUTHERNERS

White southerners considered efforts by black people to learn absurd. For generations, white Americans had looked on people of African descent as abjectly inferior. When significant efforts were made to educate former slaves, white southerners reacted with suspicion, contempt, and hostility. One white woman told a teacher, "I do assure you, you might as well try to teach your horse or mule to read, as to teach these niggers. They can't learn."

Black and white land-grant colleges stressed training in agriculture and industry. In this late-nineteenth-century photograph, Hampton Institute students learn milk production. The men are in military uniforms, which was typical for males at these colleges. Military training was a required part of the curriculum.

Most white people were well aware that black people could learn. Otherwise, the slave codes that prohibited educating slaves would have been unnecessary. After slavery's end, some white people went out of their way to prevent black people from learning. Countless schools were burned, mostly in rural areas. In Canton, Mississippi, black people collected money to open a school—only to have white residents inform them that the school would be burned and the prospective teacher lynched if it opened. The female teacher at a freedmen's school in Donaldsonville, Louisiana, was shot and killed.

Other white southerners grudgingly tolerated the desire of black people to acquire an education. One planter bitterly conceded in 1870, "Every little negro in the county is now going to school and the public pays for it. This is one hell of [a] fix but we can't help it, and the best policy is to conform as far as possible to circumstances."

Most white people adamantly refused to attend school with black people. No integrated schools were established in the immediate aftermath of emancipation. Most black people were more interested in gaining an education than in caring whether white students attended school with them. When black youngsters tried to attend a white school in Raleigh, North Carolina, the white students stopped going to it. For a brief time in Charleston, South Carolina, black and white children attended the same school, but they were taught in separate classrooms.

Violence

In the days, weeks, and months after the end of the Civil War, an orgy of brutality and violence swept across the South. White southerners—embittered by their crushing defeat and unable to adjust to the end of slave labor and the loss of millions of dollars worth of slave property—lashed out at black people. There were beatings, murders, rapes, and riots, often with little or no provocation.

Black people who demanded respect, wore better clothing, refused to step aside for white people, or asked to be addressed as "mister" or "missus" were attacked. In South Carolina, a white clergyman shot and killed a black man who protested when another black man was removed from a church service. In Texas, one black man was killed because he failed to remove his hat in the presence of a white man and another for refusing to relinquish a bottle of whiskey. A black woman was beaten for "using insolent language," and a black worker in Alabama was killed for speaking sharply to a white overseer. In Virginia, a black veteran was beaten after announcing he had been proud to serve in the Union Army.

In South Carolina, a white man asked a passing black man whom he belonged to. The black man replied that he no longer belonged to anybody. "I am free now." With that, the white man roared, "Sas me? You black devil!" He then slashed the freedman with a knife, seriously injuring him. The sheriff of DeWitt County, Texas, shot a black man who was whistling "Yankee Doodle." A Freedmen's Bureau agent in North Carolina explained the intense white hostility. "The fact is, it's the first notion with a great many of these people, if a Negro says anything or does anything that they don't like, to take a gun and put a bullet into him, or a charge of shot." In Texas another Freedmen's Bureau officer claimed that white people simply killed black people "for the love of killing."

There was also large-scale violence. In 1865 University of North Carolina students twice attacked peaceful meetings of black people. Near Pine Bluff, Arkansas, in 1866, a white mob burned a black settlement and lynched twenty-four men, women, and children. An estimated 2,000 black people were murdered around Shreveport, Louisiana. In Texas, white people killed 1,000 black people between 1865 and 1868.

In May 1866 in Memphis, white residents went on a brutal rampage after black veterans forced local police to release a black prisoner. The city was already beset with economic difficulties and racial tensions caused in part by an influx of rural refugees. White people, led by Irish policemen, invaded the black sec-

---

PROFILE ⟋ CHARLOTTE E. RAY

Charlotte E. Ray became the first African American woman to earn a law degree and the first woman admitted to the practice of law in Washington, D.C. She was born on January 13, 1850, in New York City. One of seven children, her parents were the Reverend Charles B. Ray and his second wife, Charlotte Augusta Burroughs Ray. They were firm believers in the rights of African Americans and in their potential for success.

Charlotte attended Myrtilla Miner's Institution for the Education of Colored Youth in Washington, D.C. Myrtilla Miner, a white educator from upstate New York, was determined to demonstrate that black women were as capable of high moral and mental development as white women.

Charlotte completed high school at Miner's in 1869, and she then taught at the Normal and Preparatory Department of the recently established Howard University. She also enrolled in law classes at Howard and wrote a thesis analyzing corporations.

She graduated from the law school in 1872, and a month later was admitted to the bar in Washington, D.C. She opened an office and planned to practice real estate law. As a real estate lawyer, she could avoid court appearances and the discrimination that women attorneys encountered. She often used her initials, C. E. Ray, so that her clients would not suffer because their legal counsel could be identified as a woman.

Because of the Panic of 1873 and the ensuing economic depression and the difficulties of being a black woman in a white male profession, Ray gave up the practice of law. She supported women's rights and in 1876 attended the annual meeting of the National American Woman Suffrage Association in New York City. By 1879, she had returned to New York and taught school in Brooklyn. Some time before 1886, she had married, but little is known of her husband. Charlotte Ray died of acute bronchitis on January 11, 1911.

Ray

tion of Memphis and destroyed hundreds of homes, cabins, and shacks as well as churches and schools. Forty-six black people and two white men died.

On July 30, 1866, in New Orleans, white people—angered that black men were demanding political rights—assaulted black people on the street and in a convention hall. City policemen, who were mostly Confederate veterans, shot down the black delegates as they fled in panic waving white flags in a futile attempt to surrender. Thirty-four black people and three of their white allies died. Federal troops eventually arrived and stopped the bloodshed. General Philip H. Sheridan characterized the riot as "an absolute massacre."

Little was done to stem the violence. Most Union troops had been withdrawn from the South and demobilized after the war. The Freedmen's Bureau was usually unwilling and unable to protect the black population. Black people left to defend themselves were usually in no position to retaliate. Instead, they sometimes attempted to bring the perpetrators to justice. In Orangeburg, South Carolina, armed black men brought three white men to the local jail who had been wreaking violence in the community. In Holly Springs, Mississippi, a posse of armed black men apprehended a white man who had murdered a freedwoman.

For black people, the system of justice was thoroughly unjust. Although black people could now testify against white people in a court of law, southern juries remained all white and refused to convict white people charged with harming black people. In Texas in 1865 and 1866, 500 white men were indicted for murdering black people. Not one was convicted.

The Crusade for Political and Civil Rights

In October 1864 in Syracuse, New York, 145 black leaders gathered in a national convention. Some of the century's most prominent black men and women attended, including Henry Highland Garnet, Frances E. W. Harper, William Wells Brown, Francis L. Cardozo, Richard H. Cain, Jonathan J. Wright, and Jonathan C. Gibbs. They embraced the basic tenets of the American political tradition and proclaimed that they expected to participate fully in it.

Anticipating a future free of slavery, Frederick Douglass optimistically declared "that we hereby assert our full confidence in the fundamental principles of this government . . . the great heart of this nation will ultimately concede us our just

Race Relations and Reconstruction

claims, accord us our rights, and grant us our full measure of citizenship under the broad shield of the Constitution."

Even before the **Syracuse Convention,** northern Republicans met in Union-controlled territory around Beaufort, South Carolina, and nominated the state's delegates to the 1864 Republican national convention. Among those selected were Robert Smalls and Prince Rivers, former slaves who had exemplary records with the Union Army. The probability of black participation in postwar politics seemed promising indeed.

But northern and southern white leaders who already held power would largely determine whether black Americans would gain any political power or acquire the same rights as white people. As the Civil War ended, President Lincoln was more concerned with restoring the seceded states to the Union than in opening political doors for black people. Yet Lincoln suggested that at least some black men deserved the right to vote. On April 11, 1865, he wrote, "I would myself prefer that [the vote] were now conferred on the very intelligent, and on those who serve our cause as soldiers." Three days later Lincoln was assassinated.

Presidential Reconstruction under Andrew Johnson

Vice President Andrew Johnson then became president and initially seemed inclined to impose stern policies on the white South while befriending the freedmen. He announced that "treason must be made odious, and traitors must be punished and impoverished." In 1864 he had told black people, "I will be your Moses, and lead you through the Red Sea of War and Bondage to a fairer future of Liberty and Peace." Nothing proved to be further from the truth. Andrew Johnson was no friend of black Americans.

Born poor in eastern Tennessee and never part of the southern aristocracy, Johnson strongly opposed secession and was the only senator from the seceded states to remain loyal to the Union. He had nonetheless acquired five slaves and the conviction that black people were so thoroughly inferior that white men must forever govern them. In 1867 Johnson argued that black people could not exercise political power and they had "less capacity for government than any other race of people. No independent government of any form has ever been successful in their hands. On the contrary, wherever they have been left to their own devices they have shown a constant tendency to relapse into barbarism."

A NORTHERN BLACK WOMAN ON TEACHING FREEDMEN

Blanche Virginia Harris was born in 1842 in Monroe, Michigan. She graduated from Oberlin College in 1860. She became the principal of a black school in Norfolk, Virginia, attended by 230 students. She organized night classes for adults and a sewing society to provide clothing for impoverished students. Later, she taught in Mississippi, North Carolina, and Tennessee. In the following letter she describes her experiences in Mississippi:

23 January 1866
Natchez, Miss.

I have been in this city now nearly five months. . . . The colored teachers three in number, sent out by the [American Missionary] Association to this city, have been brought down here it is true. And then left to the mercy of the colored people or themselves. The distinction between the two classes of teachers (white and colored) is so marked that it is the topic of conversation among the better class of colored people.

My school is very large, some of them pay and some do not. And from the proceeds I pay the board of my sister and myself, and also for the rent of two rooms; rent as well as board is very high so I have to work quite hard to meet my expenses. I also furnish lights, wood and coal. I do not write this as fault-finding, far from it. I shall be thankful if I can in any way help. I sometimes get discouraged. . . .

I have become very much attached to my school; the interest they manifest in their studies pleases me. I will now tell you how I employ my time. From 8 A.M. until 2 P.M. I teach the children. At 3 P.M. I have a class of adults and at night I have night school.

One afternoon we have prayer meeting, another sewing school. And another singing school. I hope my next letter may be more interesting to you.

Very Respectfully,

Blanche Harris

Why was the race of the teacher of such concern?

What did Harris find difficult about teaching and what did she find rewarding?

Source: Ellen NicKenzie Lawson, ed., *The Three Sarahs: Documents of Antebellum Black College Women* (New York: Edward Mellon Press, 1984).

Johnson quickly lost his enthusiasm for punishing traitors. Indeed, he began to placate white southerners. In May 1865 Johnson granted blanket amnesty and pardons to former Confederates willing to swear allegiance to the United States. The main exceptions were high former Confederate officials and those who owned property valued in excess of $20,000, a large sum at the time. Yet even these leaders could appeal for individual pardons. And appeal they did. By 1866 Johnson had pardoned more than 7,000 high-ranking former Confederates and wealthier southerners. Moreover, he had restored land to those white people who had lost it to freedmen.

Johnson's actions blatantly encouraged those who had supported secession, owned slaves, and opposed the Union. He permitted longtime southern leaders to regain political influence and authority only months after the end of America's bloodiest conflict. As black people and radical Republicans watched in disbelief, Johnson appointed provisional governors in the former Confederate states. Leaders in those states then called constitutional conventions, held elections, and prepared to regain their place in the Union. Johnson merely insisted that each Confederate state formally accept the **Thirteenth Amendment** (ratified in December 1865, it outlawed slavery) and repudiate Confederate war debts.

The southern constitutional conventions gave no consideration to the inclusion of black people in the political system or to guaranteeing them equal rights. As one Mississippi delegate explained, "'Tis nature's law that the superior race must rule and rule they will."

Black Codes

After the election of state and local officials, white legislators gathered in state capitals across the South to determine the status and future of the freedmen. With little debate, the legislatures drafted the so-called **black codes.** Southern politicians gave no thought to providing black people with the political and legal rights associated with citizenship.

The black codes sought to ensure the availability of a subservient agricultural labor supply controlled by white people. They imposed severe restrictions on freedmen. Freedmen had to sign annual labor contracts with white landowners. South Carolina required black people who wanted to establish a business to purchase licenses costing from $10 to $100. The codes permitted black children ages two to twenty-one to be apprenticed to white people and spelled out their duties and obligations in detail. Corporal punishment was legal.

PROFILE ❧ AARON A. BRADLEY

At a time when many white people considered even the most reserved, refined, and well-educated black man holding political office a disgrace, Aaron Bradley's presence in politics was outrageous. White southerners regarded him as a dangerous revolutionary. White Republicans, who normally would have been his allies, considered him belligerent and uncooperative. But most freedmen admired and supported him. Like him or not, he was a major figure in Georgia politics during Reconstruction.

Bradley was born a slave in about 1815 in South Carolina. His father was probably white. He belonged to Francis W. Pickens, who was South Carolina's governor when the state seceded (see Chapter 10). For a time, Bradley worked as a shoemaker in nearby Augusta, Georgia. At about age twenty, he escaped and went to Boston where he studied law and met black and white abolitionists.

In 1865, after the war, Bradley moved to Savannah where he took up the cause of the freedmen and opened a school. He worked closely with the city's black longshoremen and the low country and Sea Island rice field workers.

Bradley demanded that black families keep the land they had occupied under Sherman's Special Field Order #15. He believed that black people had to have land to prosper. He criticized the Freedmen's Bureau for attempting to force black people off the land and argued that President Johnson should be impeached for supporting Confederate landowners rather than black and white people who were loyal to the Union.

Bradley also insisted that black people deserved the rights to vote, testify in court, and have jury trials. After he urged black farmers to defend their land by force, federal authorities charged him with advocating insurrection. He was sentenced to a year's confinement but was soon paroled. Almost immediately, another fiery speech got him in trouble again and he had to leave Georgia.

He returned to Boston and renewed his pleas for land for the freedmen. He wrote the head of the Freedmen's Bureau, General Oliver O. Howard: "My great object is, to give you Back-bone, and as the Chief Justice of 4 millions of Colored people, and Refugees; You can not, and must not, be a Military Tool, in the hands of Andrew Johnson."

In 1867, Bradley returned to Savannah and attacked the system of sharecropping. He complained that freedmen were compelled to work involuntarily and asked that black men be permitted to arm themselves. He also argued that justice would be fairer if the courts included black men. Although the Freedmen's Bureau considered Bradley a troublemaker, he never backed down.

In 1867, black farmers and workers elected Bradley to the state constitutional convention, but he was soon expelled. Then he was elected to the state senate—only to be expelled again along with all the black members of the Georgia legislature.

Meanwhile, Bradley carried on a running battle with Savannah's mayor, a former Confederate colonel affiliated with the Ku Klux Klan. He threatened the "KKK and all Bad Men, . . . if you strike a blow the man or men will be followed, and the house in which he or they shall take shelter, will be burned to the ground."

In 1868, Bradley organized black workers to arm themselves to retain the lands that they believed belonged to them. For a month, black men controlled parts of Chatham County outside Savannah. Eventually, federal authorities jailed one hundred of them. Bradley again fled north.

He returned to Georgia in 1870 and reclaimed his senate seat after Congress forced the legislature to seat its black members. He supported measures to remove Savannah's mayor, reduce taxes on workers, and institute an eight-hour workday.

Democrats regained control of Georgia politics in 1872, and Bradley and the Republicans were swept from power. He ran for Congress in South Carolina in 1874 but lost. He supported black migration to Liberia and Florida, but he moved to St. Louis and died there in 1881.

Aaron Bradley was certainly not a typical Reconstruction leader. He maintained few close ties to black or white politicians. He was constantly embroiled in factional disputes. He did not cooperate with middle-class black leaders and had no ties with local churches and their clergymen—a rarity among black politicians.

He dressed in expensive and flashy clothes. He could be pompous, abrasive, and intemperate. White people universally detested him. Yet Bradley remained exceedingly popular among freedmen.

Bradley

Employers were designated "masters" and employees "servants." The black codes also restricted black people from loitering or vagrancy, using alcohol or firearms, hunting, fishing, and grazing livestock. The codes did guarantee rights that slaves had not possessed. Freedmen could marry legally, engage in contracts, purchase property, sue or be sued, and testify in court. But black people could not vote or serve on juries. The black codes conceded—just barely—freedom to black people.

Black Conventions

Alarmed by these threats to their freedom, black people met in conventions across the South in 1865 and 1866 to protest, appeal for justice, and chart their future. Men who had been free before the war dominated the conventions. Many were ministers, teachers, and artisans. Few had been slaves. Women and children also attended—as spectators, not delegates—but women often offered comments, suggestions, and criticism. These meetings were hardly militant or radical affairs. Delegates respectfully insisted that white people live up to the principles and rights embodied in the Declaration of Independence and the Constitution.

At the AME church in Raleigh, North Carolina, delegates asked for equal rights and the right to vote. At Georgia's convention they protested against white violence and appealed for leaders who would enforce the law without regard to color. "We ask not for a Black Man's Governor, nor a White Man's Governor, but for a People's Governor, who shall impartially protect the rights of all, and faithfully sustain the Union."

Delegates at the Norfolk meeting reminded white Virginians that black people were patriotic. "We are Americans. We know no other country. We love the land of our birth." But they protested that Virginia's black code caused "invidious political or legal distinctions, on account of color merely." They requested the right to vote and added that they might boycott the businesses of "those who deny to us our equal rights."

Two conventions were held in Charleston, South Carolina—one before and one after the black code was enacted. At the first, delegates stressed the "respect and affection" they felt toward white Charlestonians. They even proposed that only literate men be granted the right to vote if it were genuinely applied to both races. The second convention denounced the black code and insisted on its repeal. Delegates again asked for the right to vote and the right to testify in court. "These two things we deem necessary to our welfare and elevation." They also appealed for public schools

and for "homesteads for ourselves and our children." White authorities ignored these and other black conventions and their petitions. Instead they were confident they had effectively relegated the freedmen to a subordinate role in society.

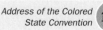

Address of the Colored State Convention 12-6

By late 1865 President Johnson's Reconstruction policies had aroused black people. One black Union veteran summed up the situation. "If you call this Freedom, what do you call Slavery?" Republicans in Congress also opposed Johnson's policies toward the freedmen and the former Confederate states.

The Radical Republicans

Radical Republicans, as more militant Republicans were called, were especially disturbed that Johnson seemed to have abandoned the ex-slaves to their former masters. They considered white southerners disloyal and unrepentant, despite their military defeat. Moreover, radical Republicans—unlike moderate Republicans and Democrats—were determined to transform the racial fabric of American society by including black people in the political and economic system.

Among the most influential radical Republicans were Charles Sumner, Benjamin Wade, and Henry Wilson in the Senate and Thaddeus Stevens, George W. Julian, and James M. Ashley in the House. Few white Americans have been as dedicated to the rights of black people as these men. They had fought for the abolition of slavery. They were reluctant to compromise. They were honest, tough, and articulate but also abrasive, difficult, self-righteous, and vain. Black people appreciated them; many white people excoriated them. One black veteran wrote Charles Sumner in 1869, "Your name shall live in our hearts forever." A white Philadelphia businessman commented on Thaddeus Stevens, "He seems to oppose any measure that will not benefit the nigger."

RADICAL PROPOSALS

Stevens, determined to provide freedmen with land, introduced a bill in Congress in late 1865 to confiscate 400 million acres from the wealthiest 10 percent of southerners and distribute it free to freedmen. The remaining land would be auctioned off in plots no larger than 500 acres. Few legislators supported the proposal. Even those who wanted fundamental change considered confiscation a gross violation of property rights.

Bearing a remarkable resemblance to a slave auction, this scene in Monticello, Florida, shows a black man auctioned off to the highest bidder shortly after the Civil War. Under the terms of most southern black codes, black people arrested and fined for vagrancy or loitering could be "sold" if they could not pay the fine. Such spectacles infuriated many northerners and led to demands for more rigid Reconstruction policies.

Instead, radical Republicans supported voting rights for black men. They were convinced that black men—to protect themselves and to secure the South for the Republican Party—had to have the right to vote.

Moderate Republicans, however, found the prospect of black voting almost as objectionable as the confiscation of land. They preferred to build the Republican Party in the South by cooperating with President Johnson and attracting loyal white southerners.

The thought of black suffrage appalled northern and southern Democrats. Most white northerners—Republicans and Democrats—favored denying black men the right to vote in their states. After the war, proposals to guarantee the right to vote to black men were defeated in New York, Ohio, Kansas, and the Nebraska Territory. In the District of Columbia, a vote to permit black suffrage lost 6,951 to 35. However, five of the six New England states as well as Iowa, Minnesota, and Wisconsin did allow black men to vote.

As much as they objected to black suffrage, most white northerners objected even more strongly to defiant white southerners. Journalist Charles A. Dana described the attitude of many northerners. "As for negro suffrage, the mass of Union men in the Northwest do not care a great deal. What scares them is the idea that the rebels are all to be let back . . . and made a power in government again, just as though there had been no rebellion."

In December 1865 Congress created the Joint Committee on Reconstruction to determine whether the southern states should be readmitted to the Union. The committee investigated southern affairs and confirmed reports of widespread mistreatment of black people and white arrogance.

THE FREEDMEN'S BUREAU BILL AND THE CIVIL RIGHTS BILL

In early 1866 Senator Lyman Trumball, a moderate Republican from Illinois, introduced two major bills. The first was to provide more financial support for the Freedmen's Bureau and extend its authority to defend the rights of black people.

The Freedmen's Bureau **DOCUMENT 12-4**

FEDERAL RECONSTRUCTION LEGISLATION

1865 Freedmen's Bureau established

1865 Thirteenth Amendment passed and ratified

1866 Freedmen's Bureau Bill and the Civil Rights Act
of 1866 passed over Johnson's veto

1866 Fourteenth Amendment passed (ratified 1868)

1867 Reconstruction Acts passed over Johnson's veto

The second proposal became the first **Civil Rights Act** in American history. It made any person born in the United States a citizen (except Indians) and entitled them to rights protected by the U.S. government. Black people would possess the same legal rights as white people. The bill was clearly intended to invalidate the black codes.

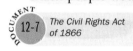

DOCUMENT 12-7 The Civil Rights Act of 1866

JOHNSON'S VETOES

Both measures passed in Congress with nearly unanimous Republican support. President Johnson vetoed them. He claimed that the bill to continue the Freedmen's Bureau would greatly expand the federal bureaucracy and permit too "vast a number of agents" to exercise arbitrary power over the white population. He insisted that the civil rights bill benefited black people at the expense of white people. "In fact, the distinction of race and color is by the bill made to operate in favor of the colored and against the white race."

DOCUMENT 12-8 President Johnson's Veto of the Civil Rights Act of 1866

The Johnson vetoes stunned Republicans. Although he had not meant to, Johnson drove moderate Republicans into the radical camp and strengthened the Republican Party. The president did not believe Republicans would oppose him to support the freedmen. He was wrong. Congress overrode both vetoes. The Republicans broke with Johnson in 1866, defied him in 1867, and impeached him in 1868 (failing to remove him from office by only one vote in the Senate).

The Fourteenth Amendment

To secure the legal rights of freedmen, Republicans passed the **Fourteenth Amendment.** This amendment fundamentally changed the Constitution by compelling states to accept their residents as citizens and to guarantee that their rights as citizens would be safeguarded.

Its first section guaranteed citizenship to every person born in the United States. This included virtually every black person. It made each person a citizen of the state in which he or she resided. It defined the specific rights of citizens and then protected those rights against the power of state governments. Citizens had the right to due process (usually a trial) before they could lose their life, liberty, or property.

> All persons born or naturalized in the United States, and subject to the jurisdiction thereof, are citizens of the United States and of the State wherein they reside. No State shall make or enforce any law which shall abridge the privileges or immunities of citizens of the United States; nor shall any State deprive any person of life, liberty, or property, without due process of law; nor deny to any person within its jurisdiction the equal protection of the laws.

Eleven years after Chief Justice Roger Taney declared in the *Dred Scott* decision that black people were "a subordinate and inferior class of beings" who had "no rights that white people were bound to respect," the Fourteenth Amendment vested them with the same rights of citizenship other Americans possessed.

The amendment also threatened to deprive states of representation in Congress if they denied black men the vote. The end of slavery had also made obsolete the Three-Fifths Clause in the Constitution, which had counted slaves as only three-fifths (or 60 percent) of a white person in calculating a state's population and determining the number of representatives each state was entitled to in the House of Representatives. Republicans feared that southern states would count black people in their populations without permitting them to vote, thereby gaining more representatives than those states had had before the Civil War. The amendment mandated that the number of representatives each state would be entitled to in Congress (including northern states) would be reduced if that state did not allow adult males to vote.

Democrats almost unanimously opposed the Fourteenth Amendment. Andrew Johnson denounced it, although he had no power to prevent its adoption. Southern states refused to ratify it except for Tennessee. Women's suffragists felt badly betrayed because the amendment limited suffrage to males. Despite this opposition, the amendment was ratified in 1868.

Radical Reconstruction

By 1867 radical Republicans in Congress had wrested control over **Reconstruction** from Johnson, and they then imposed policies that brought black men into the political system as voters and officeholders. It was a dramatic development, second in importance only to emancipation and the end of slavery.

Republicans swept the 1866 congressional elections despite the belligerent opposition of Johnson and the Democrats. With two-thirds majorities in the House and Senate, Republicans easily overrode presidential vetoes. Two years after the Civil War ended, Republicans dismantled the state governments established in the South under President Johnson's authority. They instituted a new Reconstruction policy.

Republicans passed the first of three **Reconstruction Acts** over Johnson's veto in March 1867. It divided the South into five military districts, each under the command of a general (see Map 12–2). Military personnel would protect lives and property while new civilian governments were formed. Elected delegates in each state would draft a new constitution and submit it to the voters.

UNIVERSAL MANHOOD SUFFRAGE

The Reconstruction Act stipulated that all adult males in the states of the former Confederacy were eligible to vote, except for those who had actively supported the Confederacy or were convicted felons. Once each state had formed a new government and approved the Fourteenth Amendment, it would be readmitted to the Union with representation in Congress.

The advent of radical Reconstruction was the culmination of black people's struggle to gain legal and political rights. Since the 1864 black national convention in Syracuse and the meetings and conventions in the South in 1865 and 1866, black leaders had argued that one of the consequences of the Civil War should be the inclusion of black men in the body politic. The achievement of that goal was due to their persistent and persuasive efforts, the determination of radical Republicans, and, ironically, the obstructionism of Andrew Johnson, who had played into their hands.

BLACK POLITICS

Full of energy and enthusiasm, black men and women rushed into the political arena in the spring and summer of 1867. Although women could not vote, they joined men at the meetings, rallies, parades, and picnics

MAP EXPLORATION

To explore this interactive map, go to
http://www.prenhall.com/hine4/map12.2

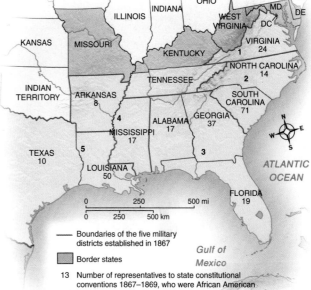

MAP 12–2   CONGRESSIONAL RECONSTRUCTION

Under the terms of the First Reconstruction Act of 1867, the former Confederate states (except Tennessee) were divided into five military districts and placed under the authority of military officers. Commanders in each of the five districts were responsible for supervising the reestablishment of civilian governments in each state.

▶ *In which states were African Americans a majority of delegates to that state's constitutional convention?*

that accompanied political organizing in the South. For many former slaves, politics became as important as the church and religious activities. Black people flocked to the Republican Party and the new Union Leagues.

The **Union Leagues** had been established in the North during the Civil War, but they expanded across the South as quasi-political organizations in the late 1860s. The Leagues were social, fraternal, and patriotic groups in which black people often, but not always, outnumbered white people. League meetings featured ceremonies, rituals, initiation rites, and oaths. They gave people an opportunity to sharpen leadership skills and gain an informal political education by discussing issues from taxes to schools.

With the adoption of radical Republican policies, most black men eagerly took part in political activities. Political meetings, conventions, speeches, barbecues, and other gatherings also attracted women and children.

SIT-INS AND STRIKES

Political progress did not induce apathy and a sense of satisfaction and contentment among black people. Gaining citizenship, legal rights, and the vote generated more expectations and demands for advancement. For example, black people insisted on equal access to public transportation. After a Republican rally in Charleston, South Carolina, in April 1867, several black men staged a "sit-in" on a nearby horse-drawn streetcar before they were arrested. In Charleston, black people were permitted to ride only on the outside running boards of the cars. They wanted to sit on the seats inside. Within a month, due to the intervention of military authorities, the streetcar company gave in. Similar protests occurred in Richmond and New Orleans.

Black workers also struck across the South in 1867. Black longshoremen in New Orleans, Mobile, Savannah, Charleston, and Richmond walked off the job. Black laborers were usually paid less than white men for the same work, and this led to labor unrest during the 1860s and 1870s. Sometimes the strikers won; sometimes they lost. In 1869 a black Baltimore longshoreman, Isaac Myers, organized the National Colored Labor Union.

The Reaction of White Southerners

White southerners grimly opposed radical Reconstruction. They were outraged that black people could claim the same legal and political rights they possessed. Such a possibility seemed preposterous to people who had an abiding belief in the absolute inferiority of black people. A statement by Benjamin F. Perry, whom Johnson had appointed provisional governor of South Carolina in 1865, captures the depth of this racist conviction. "The African," Perry declared, "has been in all ages, a savage or a slave. God created him inferior to the white man in form, color and intellect, and no legislation or culture can make him his equal. . . . His hair, his form and features will not compete with the caucasian race, and it is in vain to think

Black men vote in 1868 after the passage of the 1867 Reconstruction acts. Notice that it is not a secret ballot. It was possible to see the ballots in the voting jar.

of elevating him to the dignity of the white man. God created differences between the two races, and nothing can make him equal."

Some white people, taking solace in their belief in the innate inferiority of black people, concluded they could turn black suffrage to their advantage. White people, they assumed, should easily be able to control and manipulate black voters just as they had controlled black people during slavery. White southerners who believed this, however, were destined to be disappointed, and their disappointment would turn to fury.

CONCLUSION

Why were black southerners able to gain citizenship and access to the political system by 1868? Most white Americans did not suddenly abandon 250 years of deeply ingrained beliefs that people of African descent were their inferiors. The advances that African Americans achieved fit into a series of complex political developments after the Civil War. Black people themselves had fought and died to preserve the Union, and they had earned the grudging respect of many white people and the open admiration of others. Black leaders in meetings and petitions insisted that their rights be recognized.

White northerners—led by the radical Republicans—were convinced that President Andrew Johnson had made a serious error in supporting policies that permitted white southerners to retain pre–Civil War leaders while the black codes virtually made freedmen slaves again. Republicans were determined that white southerners realize their defeat had doomed the prewar status quo. Republicans established a Reconstruction program to disfranchise key southern leaders while providing legal rights to freedmen. The right to vote, they reasoned, would give black people the means to deal more effectively with white southerners while simultaneously strengthening the Republican Party in the South.

The result was to make the mid- to late 1860s one of the few high points in African-American history. During this period, not only was slavery abolished, but black southerners were able to organize schools and

AFRICAN-AMERICAN EVENTS	NATIONAL EVENTS
1862	
March 1862 The beginning of the Port Royal Experiment in South Carolina	**February 1862** Julia Ward Howe publishes the first version of "Battle Hymm of the Republic" in the *Atlantic Monthly*
	July 1862 Morrell Land-Grant College Act signed into law by Abraham Lincoln
1864	
October 1864 Black national convention in Syracuse, New York	**November 1864** Abraham Lincoln reelected
1865	
January 1865 General Sherman's Special Field Order #15	**April 1865** Abraham Lincoln is assassinated; Andrew Johnson succeeds to presidency
March 1865 Freedmen's Bureau established	**May 1865** Andrew Johnson begins presidential Reconstruction
September–November 1865 Black codes enacted	**June–August 1865** Southern state governments are reorganized
	December 1865 Thirteenth Amendment to the Constitution is ratified
1866	
February 1866 Southern Homestead Act	**November 1866** Republican election victories produce greater than two-thirds majorities in House and Senate
March 1866 President Johnson's vetoes of bill to extend the Freedman's Bureau and the Civil Rights bill	
April 1866 Override of Johnson's veto of the Civil Rights bill by Congress	
May 1866 Memphis riot	
July 1866 New Freedmen's Bureau bill enacted by Congress over Johnson's veto; New Orleans riot	

churches, and black people throughout the South acquired legal and political rights that would have been incomprehensible before the war. Yet black people did not stand on the brink of utopia. Most freedmen still lacked land and had no realistic hope of obtaining much, if any, of it. White violence and cruelty continued almost unabated across much of the South. Still, for millions of African Americans, the future looked more promising than it had ever before in American history.

RECOMMENDED READING

Ira Berlin and Leslie Rowland, eds. *Families and Freedom: A Documentary History of African-American Kinship in the Civil War Era.* New York: Cambridge University Press, 1997. A collection of documents that conveys the aspirations and frustrations of freedmen.

David W. Blight. *Race and Reunion: The Civil War in American Memory.* Cambridge: Harvard University Press, 2001. This outstanding study shows how white Americans "remembered" the Civil War and were able to reconcile their sectional differences by essentially forgetting the role and contributions of African Americans.

W. E. B. Du Bois. *Black Reconstruction in America: An Essay toward a History of the Part Which Black Folk Played in the Attempt to Reconstruct Democracy in America, 1860–1880.* New York: Russell & Russell, 1935. A classic account of Reconstruction challenging the traditional interpretation that it was a tragic era marked by corrupt and inept black rule of the South.

Eric Foner. *Reconstruction: America's Unfinished Revolution, 1863–1877.* New York: Harper & Row, 1988. The best and most comprehensive account of Reconstruction.

Herbert G. Gutman. *The Black Family in Slavery and Freedom, 1750–1925.* New York: Oxford University Press, 1976. An illustration of how African-American family values and kinship ties forged in slavery endured after emancipation.

Steven Hahn. *A Nation under Our Feet: Black Political Struggles in the Rural South from Slavery to the Great Migration.* Cambridge, MA: Harvard University Press, 2003. In a sophisticated analysis, Hahn explores the ways in which African Americans conceived of themselves as political people and organized from slavery through Reconstruction and disfranchisement to the growth of Marcus Garvey's Universal Negro Improvement Association in the 1920s.

Tera W. Hunter. *To 'Joy My Freedom: Southern Black Women's Lives and Labors after the Civil War.* Cambridge, MA: Harvard University Press, 1997. An examination of the interior lives of black women, their work, social welfare, and leisure.

Gerald D. Jaynes. *Branches without Roots: Genesis of the Black Working Class in the American South, 1862–1882.* New

York: Pantheon, 1986. The changes in work and labor in the aftermath of slavery.

Leon F. Litwack. *Been in the Storm Too Long: The Aftermath of Slavery*. New York: Alfred A. Knopf, 1979. A rich and detailed account of the transition to freedom largely based on recollections of former slaves.

ADDITIONAL BIBLIOGRAPHY

EDUCATION

James D. Anderson. *The Education of Blacks in the South, 1860–1935*. Chapel Hill: University of North Carolina Press, 1988.

Ronald E. Butchart. *Northern Schools, Southern Blacks, and Reconstruction: Freedmen's Education, 1862–1875*. Westport: Greenwood Press, 1981.

Edmund L. Drago. *Initiative, Paternalism, and Race Relations: Charleston's Avery Normal Institute*. Athens: University of Georgia Press, 1990.

Robert C. Morris. *Reading, 'Riting, and Reconstruction: The Education of the Freedmen in the South, 1861–1890*. Chicago: University of Chicago Press, 1981.

Joe M. Richardson. *Christian Reconstruction: The American Missionary Association and Southern Blacks, 1861–1890*. Athens: University of Georgia Press, 1986.

Brenda Stevenson, ed. *The Journals of Charlotte Forten Grimke*. New York: Oxford University Press, 1988.

Heather Andrea Williams. *Self-taught: African-American Education in Slavery and Freedom*. Chapel Hill: University of North Carolina Press, 2005.

LAND AND LABOR

Paul A. Cimbala and Randall M. Miller, eds. *The Freedmen's Bureau and Reconstruction*. New York: Fordham University Press, 1999.

Barbara J. Fields. *Slavery and Freedom on the Middle Ground: Maryland during the Nineteenth Century*. New Haven, CT: Yale University Press, 1985.

Jacqueline Jones. *Labor of Love, Labor of Sorrow: Black Women, Work and Family, from Slavery to the Present*. New York: Basic Books, 1985.

Edward Magdol. *A Right to the Land: Essays on the Freedmen's Community*. Westport, CT: Greenwood Press, 1977.

Claude F. Oubre. *Forty Acres and a Mule: The Freedmen's Bureau and Black Landownership*. Baton Rouge: Louisiana State University Press, 1978.

Dylan C. Penningroth. *The Claims of Kinfolk: African American Property and Community in the Nineteenth-Century South*. Chapel Hill: University of North Carolina Press, 2003.

Roger L. Ransom and Richard Sutch. *One Kind of Freedom: The Economic Consequences of Emancipation*. New York: Cambridge University Press, 1977.

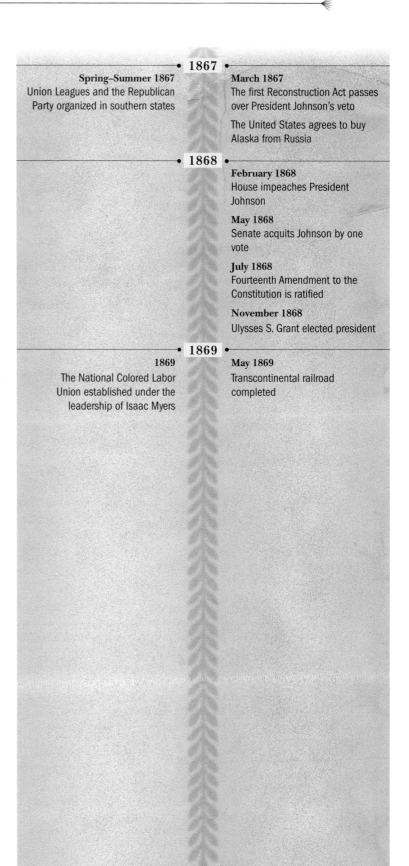

1867

Spring–Summer 1867
Union Leagues and the Republican Party organized in southern states

March 1867
The first Reconstruction Act passes over President Johnson's veto

The United States agrees to buy Alaska from Russia

1868

February 1868
House impeaches President Johnson

May 1868
Senate acquits Johnson by one vote

July 1868
Fourteenth Amendment to the Constitution is ratified

November 1868
Ulysses S. Grant elected president

1869

1869
The National Colored Labor Union established under the leadership of Isaac Myers

May 1869
Transcontinental railroad completed

AFRICAN-AMERICAN EVENTS   **NATIONAL EVENTS**

Willie Lee Rose. *Rehearsal for Reconstruction: The Port Royal Experiment.* Indianapolis: Bobbs Merrill, 1964.

Julie Saville. *The Work of Reconstruction: From Slave to Wage Labor in South Carolina, 1860–1870.* New York: Cambridge University Press, 1994.

James D. Schmidt. *Free to Work: Labor, Law, Emancipation, and Reconstruction, 1815–1880.* Athens: University of Georgia Press, 1998.

Leslie A. Schwalm. *A Hard Fight for We: Women's Transition from Slavery to Freedom in South Carolina.* Urbana: University of Illinois Press, 1997.

BLACK COMMUNITIES

John W. Blassingame. *Black New Orleans, 1860–1880.* Chicago: University of Chicago Press, 1973.

Cyprian Davis. *The History of Black Catholics in the United States.* New York: Crossroad, 1990.

Robert F. Engs. *Freedom's First Generation: Black Hampton, Virginia, 1861–1890.* Philadelphia: University of Pennsylvania Press, 1979.

William E. Montgomery. *Under Their Own Vine and Fig Tree, the African American Church in the South 1865–1900.* Baton Rouge: Louisiana State University Press, 1993.

Bernard E. Powers, Jr. *Black Charlestonians: A Social History, 1822–1885.* Fayetteville: University of Arkansas Press, 1994.

Clarence E. Walker. *A Rock in a Weary Land: The African Methodist Episcopal Church during the Civil War and Reconstruction.* Baton Rouge: Louisiana State University Press, 1982.

James M. Washington. *Frustrated Fellowship: The Black Baptist Quest for Social Power.* Macon, GA: Mercer University Press, 1986.

RETRACING THE ODYSSEY

The Avery Research Center for African-American History and Culture, Charleston, South Carolina. In 1865 the American Missionary Association opened a private school for black youngsters that served the Charleston community until 1954. The renovated structure currently contains an archive, a restored classroom, and exhibits devoted to African-American life in the Carolina low country.

Shaw University and St. Augustine's College, Raleigh, North Carolina. These are two of the many black colleges established during Reconstruction. The Baptists founded Shaw in 1865, and its impressive Estey Hall has survived almost 130 years. The Episcopal Church and the Freedmen's Bureau collaborated to found St. Augustine's in 1867.

Fisk University, Nashville, Tennessee. The American Missionary Association established Fisk in 1866.

Magnificent Jubilee Hall is the nation's oldest building dedicated to the higher education of black students. It was completed in 1876. There is an impressive collection of European and American art on the campus at the Carl Van Vechten Art Gallery.

St. Stephen African Methodist Episcopal Church, Wilmington, North Carolina. Following the Civil War, black members of the Front Street Methodist Church withdrew and founded their own church on Red Cross Street. In 1880 they began construction of the current building. For a time parishioners met in the basement while work continued on the imposing and ornate sanctuary above them.

PRENTICE HALL **myhistorylab** REVIEW, RESEARCH, AND INTERACT
Where it's a good time to connect to the past!

REVIEW QUESTIONS

1. How did freedmen define their freedom? What did freedom mean to ex-slaves? How did their priorities differ from those of African Americans who had been free before the Civil War?

2. What did the former slaves and the former slaveholders want after emancipation? Were these desires realistic? How did former slaves and former slaveholders disagree after the end of slavery?

3. Why did African Americans form separate churches, schools, and social organizations after the Civil War? What role did the black church play in the black community?

4. How effective was the Freedmen's Bureau? How successful was it in assisting ex-slaves to live in freedom?

5. Why did southern states enact black codes?

6. Why did radical Republicans object to President Andrew Johnson's Reconstruction policies? Why did Congress impose its own Reconstruction policies?

7. Why were laws passed to enable black men to vote?

8. Why did black men gain the right to vote but not possession of land?

9. Did congressional Reconstruction secure full equality for African Americans as American citizens?

Research Navigator.com
RESOURCES FOR COLLEGE RESEARCH ASSIGNMENTS

www.researchnavigator.com

Using the tools available in Research Navigator, consider this question:
Who supported radical Reconstruction? Why?

PRIMARY SOURCE DOCUMENTS

MAP EXPLORATION

INTERACTIVE ACTIVITIES

Reconstruction: The Struggle to Define the Meaning of Freedom
This activity highlights some of the complexities that faced the nation following the Civil War and the emancipation of nearly four million people who had been held as slaves.

IntegrationQuest: Race Relations and Reconstruction
Take the part of an historian, an educator, or a presidential aide to learn about the mood in America during the Reconstruction years.

13

The Meaning of Freedom: The Failure of Reconstruction 1868–1877

WHAT POLITICAL OFFICES WERE BLACK MEN ELECTED TO—AND NOT ELECTED TO—DURING RECONSTRUCTION?

WHAT ISSUES MOST CONCERNED BLACK POLITICAL LEADERS?

WHY WERE SO MANY WHITE SOUTHERNERS BITTERLY AND VIOLENTLY OPPOSED TO BLACK AND WHITE REPUBLICANS EXERCISING POLITICAL POWER?

WHAT WAS THE PURPOSE OF THE KU KLUX KLAN AND HOW EFFECTIVE WAS IT?

WHAT WAS THE PURPOSE OF THE FIFTEENTH AMENDMENT?

HOW AND WHY DID BLACK AND WHITE REPUBLICAN LEADERS LOSE CONTROL OF EVERY SOUTHERN STATE BY 1877?

◄ These are the first African Americans to serve in the U.S. Congress. Standing, left to right: Robert C. DeLarge, representative, South Carolina; Jefferson Long, representative, Georgia; Seated, left to right: U.S. Senator Hiram R. Revels, Mississippi; Benjamin S. Turner, representative, Alabama; Josiah T. Walls, representative, Florida; Joseph H. Rainey, representative, South Carolina; Robert B. Elliott, representative, South Carolina.

1868–1877

Let us with a fixed, firm, hearty, earnest, and unswerving determination move steadily on and on, fanning the flame of true liberty until the last vestige of oppression shall be destroyed, and when that eventful period shall arrive, when, in the selection of rulers, both State and Federal, we shall know no North, no East, no South, no West, no white nor colored, no Democrat nor Republican, but shall choose men because of their moral and intrinsic value, their honesty and integrity, their love of unmixed liberty, and their ability to perform well the duties to be committed to their charge.

From a speech delivered in 1872, by Jonathan J. Wright, Associate Justice of the South Carolina Supreme Court

▼ **An African-American attorney** confers with white colleagues during an historic session of the Supreme Court in the late 1800s.

In 1868, for the first time in American history, thousands of black men would elect hundreds of black and white leaders to state and local offices across the South. Would this newly acquired political influence enable freedmen to complete the transition from slavery to freedom? Would political power propel black people into the mainstream of American society? Equally important, would white southerners and northerners accept black people as fellow citizens?

Events in the decade from 1867 to 1877 generated hope that black and white Americans might learn to live together on a compatible and equitable basis. But these developments also raised the possibility that black people's new access to political power would fail to resolve the racial animosity and intolerance that persisted in American life after the Civil War.

Constitutional Conventions

Black men as a group first entered politics as delegates to constitutional conventions in the southern states in 1867 and 1868. Each of the former Confederate states, except Tennessee, which had already been restored to the Union, elected delegates to these conventions. Most southern white men were Democrats. They boycotted these elections to protest both Congress's assumption of authority over Reconstruction and the extension of voting privileges to black men. Thus the delegates to the conventions that met to frame new state constitutions to replace those drawn up in 1865 under President Johnson's authority were mostly Republicans joined by a few conservative southern Democrats. The Republicans represented three constituencies. One consisted of white northern migrants who moved to the South in the wake of the war. They were disparagingly called **carpetbaggers,** because they were said to have arrived in the South with all their possessions in a single carpetbag. A second group consisted of native white southerners, mostly small farmers in devastated upland regions of the South who hoped for economic relief from Republican governments. This group was known derogatorily as **scalawags,** or scoundrels, by other southern white people. African Americans made up the third and largest Republican constituency.

Of the 1,000 men elected as delegates to the ten state conventions, 265 were black. Black delegates were a majority only in the South Carolina and Louisiana conventions. In most states, including Alabama, Georgia, Mississippi, Virginia, North Carolina, Arkansas, and Texas, black men made up 10 percent to 20 percent of the delegates. At least 107 of the 265 had been born slaves; about 40 had served in the Union Army. Several were well-educated teachers and ministers; others were tailors, blacksmiths, barbers, and farmers. Most went on to hold other political offices in the years that followed.

These delegates produced impressive constitutions. Unlike previous state constitutions in the South, the new constitutions ensured that all adult males could vote, and except in Mississippi and Virginia, they did not disfranchise large numbers of former Confederates. They conferred broad guarantees of civil rights. In several states they provided the first statewide systems of public education. These constitutions were progressive, not radical. Black and white Republicans hoped to attract support from white southerners for the new state governments these documents created by encouraging state support for private businesses, especially railroad construction.

ELECTIONS

Elections were held in 1868 to ratify the new constitutions and elect officials. The white Democratic response varied. In some states, Democrats boycotted the elections. In others, they participated, but voted against ratification, and in still other states they supported ratification and attempted to elect as many Democrats as possible to office. Congress required only a majority of those voting—not a majority of all registered voters—to ratify the constitutions. In each state a majority of those voting eventually did vote to ratify, and in each state, black men were elected to political offices.

BLACK POLITICAL LEADERS

Over the next decade, 1,465 black men held political office in the South. Although black leaders individually and collectively enjoyed significant political leverage, white Republicans dominated politics during Reconstruction. In general, the number of black officials in a state reflected the size of that state's African-American population. Black people were a substantial majority of the population in just Mississippi and South Carolina, and most of the black officeholders came from those two states and Louisiana, where black people were a bare majority. In most states, such as Arkansas, North Carolina, Tennessee, and Texas, where black people made up between 25 percent and 40 percent of the population, far fewer black men were elected to office (see Table 13–1).

Southern black men cast ballots for the first time in 1867 in the election of delegates to state constitutional conventions. The ballots were provided by the candidates or political parties, not by state or municipal officials. Most nineteenth-century elections were not by secret ballot.

Initially, black men chose not to run for the most important political offices because they feared their election would further alienate already angry white southerners. But as white Republicans swept into office in 1868, black leaders reversed their strategy, and by 1870 black men had been elected to many key political positions. No black man was elected governor, but Lieutenant Governor P. B. S. Pinchback served one month (from December 1872 to January 1873) as governor in Louisiana after the white governor was removed from office. Blanche K. Bruce and Hiram Revels represented Mississippi in the U.S. Senate. Beginning with Joseph Rainey in 1870 in South Carolina, fourteen black men served in the U.S. House of Representatives during Reconstruction. Six men served as lieutenant governors. In Mississippi and South Carolina, a majority of the representatives in state houses were black men, and each of these states had two black speakers of the house in the 1870s. Jonathan J. Wright, quoted at the beginning of this chapter, served seven years as a state supreme court justice in South Carolina. Four black men served as state superintendents

TABLE 13–1   AFRICAN-AMERICAN POPULATION AND OFFICEHOLDING DURING RECONSTRUCTION IN THE STATES SUBJECT TO CONGRESSIONAL RECONSTRUCTION

	African-American Population in 1870	African Americans as Percentage of Total Population	Number of African-American Officeholders during Reconstruction
South Carolina	415,814	58.9	314
Mississippi	444,201	53.6	226
Louisiana	364,210	50.1	210
North Carolina	391,650	36.5	180
Alabama	475,510	47.6	167
Georgia	545,142	46.0	108
Virginia	512,841	41.8	85
Florida	91,689	48.7	58
Arkansas	122,169	25.2	46
Texas	253,475	30.9	46
Tennessee	322,331	25.6	20

Source: Eric Foner, *Freedom's Lawmakers: A Directory of Black Officeholders during Reconstruction* (New York: Oxford University Press, 1993), p. xiv; *The Statistics of the Population of the United States, Ninth Census (1873)*, p. xvii.

of education, and Francis L. Cardozo served as South Carolina's secretary of state and then treasurer. During Reconstruction, 112 black state senators and 683 black representatives were elected. There were also 41 black sheriffs, 5 black mayors, and 31 black coroners. Tallahassee, Florida, and Little Rock, Arkansas, had black police chiefs.

Many of these men—by background, experience, and education—were well qualified. Others were not. Of the 1,465 black officeholders, at least 378 had been free before the Civil War, 933 were literate, and 195 were illiterate (we lack information about the remaining 337). Sixty-four had attended college or professional school. In fact, fourteen of the leaders had been students at Oberlin College in Ohio, which began admitting both black and female students before the Civil War.

Black farmers and artisans—tailors, carpenters, and barbers—were well represented among those who held political office. There were also 237 ministers and 172 teachers. At least 129 had served in the Union Army, and 46 had worked for the Freedmen's Bureau.

Several black politicians were wealthy, and a few were former slave owners. Antoine Dubuclet, who became Louisiana's treasurer, had owned more than one hundred slaves and land valued at more than $100,000 before the Civil War. Former slave Ferdinand Havis became a member of the Arkansas House of Representatives. He owned a saloon, a whiskey business, and two thousand acres near Pine Bluff, where he became known as "the Colored Millionaire."

Hiram R. Revels represented Mississippi in the U.S. Senate from February 1870 until March 1871, completing an unexpired term. He went on to serve as Mississippi's secretary of state. He was born free in Fayetteville, North Carolina, in 1822. He attended Knox College in Illinois before the Civil War. In 1874 he abandoned the Republican Party and became a Democrat. By the 1890s he had acquired a sizable plantation near Natchez.

Although black men did not dominate any state politically, a few did dominate districts with sizable black populations. Before he was elected to the U.S. Senate, Blanche K. Bruce all but controlled Bolivar County, Mississippi, where he served as sheriff, tax collector, and superintendent of education. Former slave and Civil War hero Robert Smalls was the political "kingpin" in Beaufort, South Carolina. He served successively in the South Carolina house and senate, and in the U.S. House of Representatives. He was also a member of the South Carolina constitutional conventions in 1868 and 1895.

DOCUMENT 13-3 *Blanche K. Bruce, Speech in the Senate, 1876*

The Issues

Many, but not all, black and white Republican leaders favored increasing the authority of state governments to promote the welfare of all the state's citizens. Before the Civil War, most southern states did not provide schools, medical care, assistance for the mentally impaired, or prisons. Such concerns—if attended to at all—were left to local communities or families.

EDUCATION AND SOCIAL WELFARE

Black leaders were eager to increase literacy and promote education among black people. Republican politicians created statewide systems of public education throughout the South. It was a difficult and expensive task, and the results were only a limited success. Schools had to be built, teachers employed, and textbooks provided. To pay for it, taxes were increased in states still reeling from the war.

In some communities and in many rural areas, schools were not built. In other places, teachers were not paid. Some people—black and white—opposed compulsory education laws, preferring to let parents determine whether their children should attend school or work to help the family. Some black leaders favored a poll tax on voting if the funds it brought in were spent on the schools. Thus, although Reconstruction leaders established a strong commitment to public education, the results they achieved were uneven.

Furthermore, white parents refused to send their children to integrated schools. Although no laws required segregation, public schools during and after Reconstruction were invariably segregated. Black parents were usually more concerned that their children should have schools to attend than whether the schools were integrated. New Orleans, however, was an exception; it provided integrated schools.

Reconstruction leaders also supported higher education. In 1872 Mississippi legislators took advantage of the 1862 federal Morrill Land-Grant Act, which provided states with funds for agricultural and mechanical colleges, to found the first historically black state university: Alcorn A&M College. Although the university was named after a white Republican governor, James L. Alcorn, former U.S. senator Hiram Revels was its first president. The South Carolina legislature created a similar college and attached it to the Methodist-sponsored Claflin University.

Black leaders in the state legislature compelled the University of South Carolina, which had been all white, to admit black students and hire black faculty. Many, but not all, of the white students and faculty left. Several black politicians enrolled in the law and medical programs at the university. Richard Greener, a black Harvard graduate, served on the university's faculty and was its librarian.

Despite the costs, Reconstruction leaders also created the first state-supported institutions for the insane, the blind, and the deaf in the South. Some southern states during Reconstruction began to offer medical care and public health programs. Orphanages were established. State prisons were built. Black leaders also supported revising state criminal codes, eliminating corporal punishment for many crimes, and reducing the number of capital crimes.

CIVIL RIGHTS

Black politicians were often the victims of racial discrimination when they tried to use public transportation and accommodations such as hotels and restaurants. Rather than provide separate arrangements for black customers, white-owned businesses simply excluded black patrons. This was true in the North as well as the South. Robert Smalls, for example, the Civil War hero who had commandeered a Confederate supply ship to escape from Charleston in 1862 (see Chapter 11), was unceremoniously ejected from a Philadelphia streetcar in 1864. After protests, the company agreed to accept black riders. In Arkansas, Mifflin Gibbs (see *Profile: The Gibbs Brothers*) and W. Hines Furbish successfully sued a local saloon after they had been denied service. In South Carolina, Jonathan J. Wright won $1,200 in a lawsuit against a railroad after he had purchased a first-class ticket but had been forced to ride in the second-class coach.

Black leaders were determined to open public facilities to all people, in the process revealing deep divisions between themselves and white Republicans. In several southern states they introduced bills to prevent proprietors from excluding black people from restaurants, barrooms, hotels, concert halls, and auditoriums, as well as railroad coaches, streetcars, and steamboats. Many white Republicans and virtually every Democrat attacked such proposals as efforts to promote social equality and gain access for black people to places where they were not welcome. The white politicians blocked these laws in most states. Only South Carolina—with a black majority in the house and many black members in the senate—enacted such a law, but it was not effectively enforced. In Mississippi, the Republican governor James L. Alcorn vetoed a bill to outlaw racial discrimination by railroads. In Alabama and North Carolina, civil rights bills were defeated, and Georgia and Arkansas enacted measures that encouraged segregation.

PROFILE ~ THE GIBBS BROTHERS

Among the many black leaders who emerged during Reconstruction were the Gibbs brothers, who had political careers in two different states, Arkansas and Florida. Mifflin W. Gibbs and Jonathan C. Gibbs grew up in a well-to-do free black family in Philadelphia, where their father was a respected Methodist minister. But their paths diverged, and they spent little time together as adults.

Mifflin was born in 1823 and became a building contractor. By the 1840s, he was an active abolitionist. With the discovery of gold in California in 1849, he went west and eventually established California's first black newspaper, *The Mirror of the Times*. He led a protest in 1851 against a provision in the California constitution that denied black men the right to vote. In 1858 he left California for Canada, again because gold had been discovered. He spent more than ten years in Canada as a businessman involved in real estate and a coal company. In 1866 he was elected to the Victoria City Council in British Columbia. He returned to the United States in 1869. In 1870 he graduated from the law program at Oberlin College.

Mifflin moved to Arkansas in 1871 and was elected Little Rock Municipal Judge in 1873. Although defeated for reelection, he remained deeply involved in Republican Party politics and was a delegate to every Republican national convention from 1876 to 1904. In 1897, Republican president William McKinley appointed him U.S. consul to Madagascar, a French island colony off the East Coast of Africa, where he served until 1901. He died in 1915. A black high school in Little Rock was named in his honor.

Jonathan, born in 1827 or 1828, also joined the abolitionist movement. Rejected by eighteen colleges because of his color, he finally graduated from Dartmouth in 1852. He then went to Princeton Theological Seminary and became a Presbyterian minister in Troy, New York.

Jonathan attended the 1864 National Black Convention in Syracuse, New York, taught briefly at a freedmen's school in North Carolina, and then spent two years in Charleston, South Carolina. There he joined those black leaders who favored limiting the right to vote to literate men if that restriction were applied both to black and white people.

In 1867, Jonathan moved to Florida, where he became a key Republican leader and the state's highest-ranking black official. He was elected to the 1868 Florida constitutional convention and was appointed secretary of state by the Republican governor. Although defeated for a seat in Congress in 1868, he remained one of Florida's most visible black leaders and was repeatedly threatened by the Ku Klux Klan. In 1873, another Republican governor appointed him state superintendent of education. Jonathan Gibbs died in 1874, but his son Thomas went on to serve in the Florida House of Representatives, where he was instrumental in the establishment of Florida A&M University.

◀ **Mifflin** Gibbs was probably the only African American in the nineteenth century elected to political office in two nations. He served as a city councilman in Victoria, British Columbia, in Canada in the late 1860s, and he was elected a judge in Little Rock, Arkansas, in 1873.

Gibbs Brothers

Economic Issues

Black politicians sought to promote economic development in general and for black people in particular. For example, white landowners sometimes arbitrarily fired black agricultural laborers near the end of the growing season and then did not pay them. Some of these landowners were dishonest, but others were in debt and could not pay their workers. To prevent such situations, black politicians secured laws that required laborers to be paid before the crop was sold or at the time when it was sold. Some black leaders who had been slaves also wanted to regulate the wages of laborers, but these proposals invariably failed because most Republicans did not believe states had the right to regulate wages and prices.

Legislators also enacted measures that protected the land and property of small farmers against seizure for nonpayment of debts. Black and white farmers who lost land, tools, animals, and other property because they could not pay their debts were unlikely ever to recover financially. "Stay laws" prohibited, or "stayed," authorities from taking property. Besides affording financial protection to hard-pressed poor farmers, Republicans hoped these laws would attract political support from white yeomen and draw them away from their attachment to the Democratic Party.

LAND

Black leaders were unable to initiate programs that would provide land to landless black and white farmers. Many black and white political leaders believed the state had no right to distribute land. Again, South Carolina was the exception. Its legislature created a state land commission in 1869.

The commission could purchase and distribute land to freedmen. It also gave the freedmen loans on generous terms to pay for the land. Unfortunately, the commission was corrupt, inefficiently managed, and it had little fertile land to distribute. However, despite its many difficulties, the commission enabled more than 14,000 black families and a few white families to acquire land in South Carolina. Their descendants still possess some of this land today.

Although some black leaders were reluctant to use the states' power to distribute land, others had no qualms about raising property taxes so high that large landowners would be forced to sell some of their property to pay their taxes. Abraham Galloway of North Carolina explained, "I want to see the man who owns one or two thousand acres of land, taxed a dollar on the acre, and if they can't pay the taxes, sell their property

to the highest bidder . . . and then we negroes shall become the land holders."

Sharecropping after the Civil War   DOCUMENT 13-5

BUSINESS AND INDUSTRY

Black and white leaders had an easier time enacting legislation to support business and industry. Like most Americans after the Civil War, Republicans believed that expanding the railroad network would stimulate employment, improve transportation, and generate prosperity. State governments approved the sale of bonds supported by the authority of the state to finance railroad construction. In Georgia, Alabama, Texas, and Arkansas, the railroad network did expand. But the bonded debt of these states soared and taxes increased to pay for it. Moreover, railroad financing was often corrupt. Most of the illegal money wound up in the pockets of white businessmen and politicians. Black politicians rarely had access to truly large financial transactions.

So attractive were business profits that some black political leaders formed corporations. They invested modest sums and believed—like so many capitalists—that the rewards outweighed the risks. In Charleston, twenty-eight black leaders (and two white politicians) formed a horse-drawn streetcar line they called the Enterprise Railroad to carry freight between the city wharves and the railroad terminal. Black leaders in South Carolina also created a company to extract the phosphate used for fertilizer from riverbeds and riverbanks in the low country. Neither business lasted long. Black men found it far more difficult than white entrepreneurs to finance their corporations.

Black Politicians: An Evaluation

Southern black political leaders on the state level did create the foundation for public education, for providing state assistance for the blind, deaf, and insane, and for reforming the criminal justice system. They tried, but mostly failed, to outlaw racial discrimination in public facilities. They encouraged state support for economic revival and expansion.

But black leaders could not create programs that significantly improved the lives of their constituents. Because white Republicans almost always outnumbered them, they could not enact an agenda of their own. Moreover, black leaders often disagreed among themselves about specific issues and programs. Class and prewar status frequently divided them. Those leaders who had not been slaves and had not been raised in rural isolation were less likely to be concerned with land and agricultural labor. More prosperous black leaders showed more interest in civil rights and encouraging business. Even when they agreed about the need for public education, black leaders often disagreed about how to finance it and whether it should be compulsory.

Republican Factionalism

Disagreements among black leaders paled in comparison to the internal conflicts that divided the Republican Party during Reconstruction. Black and white Republicans often disagreed on political issues and strategy, but the lack of party cohesion and discipline was even more harmful. The Republican Party in the South constantly split into factions as groups fought with each other. Most disagreements were over who should run for and hold political office.

During Reconstruction, hundreds of would-be Republican leaders—black and white—sought public offices. If they lost the Republican nomination in county or state conventions, they often bolted and formed a competing slate of candidates. Then Republicans ran against each other and against the Democrats in the general election. It was not a recipe for political success.

These bitter and angry contests were based less on race and issues than on the desperate desire to gain an office that would pay even a modest salary. Most black and white Republicans were not financially well off; public office assured them a modicum of economic security.

Ironically, these factional disputes led to a high turnover in political leadership and the loss of that very economic security. It was difficult for black leaders (and white leaders too) to be renominated and reelected to more than one or two terms. Few officeholders served three or four consecutive terms in the same office during Reconstruction. This made for inexperienced leadership and added to Republican woes.

Opposition

Even if black and Republican leaders had been less prone to internecine conflict and more effective in adopting a political platform, they might still have failed to sustain themselves for long. Most white southerners led by conservative Democrats remained absolutely opposed to letting black men vote or hold office. As a white Floridian put it, "The damned Republican Party has put niggers to rule us and we will not suffer it." Of course, because black people voted did not mean they ruled during Reconstruction, but

many white people failed to grasp that. Instead, for most white southerners, the only acceptable political system was one that excluded black men and the Republican Party.

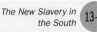
The New Slavery in the South   13-4   DOCUMENT

As far as most white people were concerned, the end of slavery and the enfranchisement of black men did not make black people their equals. They did not accept the Fourteenth Amendment. They attacked Republican governments and their leaders unrelentingly. White southerners blamed the Republicans for an epidemic of waste and corruption in state government. But most of all, they considered it preposterous and outrageous that former slaves could vote and hold political office.

James S. Pike spoke for many white people when he ridiculed black leaders in the South Carolina House of Representatives in 1873:

> The body is almost literally a Black Parliament. . . . The Speaker is black, the Clerk is black, the doorkeepers are black, the little pages are black, the chairman of the Ways and Means is black, and the chaplain is coal-black. At some of the desks sit colored men whose types it would be hard to find outside of Congo; whose costume, visages, attitudes, and expression only befit the forecastle of a buccaneer. It must be remembered, also, that these men, with not more than a half a dozen exceptions, have been themselves slaves, and that their ancestors were slaves for generations.

Pike's observations circulated widely in both the North and the South.

White southerners were determined to rid themselves of Republicans and the disgrace of having to live with black men who possessed political rights. White southerners would "redeem" their states by restoring white Democrats to power. This did not simply mean defeating black and white Republicans in elections; it meant removing them from any role in politics. White southerners believed any means—fair or foul—were justified in exorcising this evil.

The Ku Klux Klan

If the presence of black men in politics was illegitimate—in the eyes of white southerners—then it was acceptable to use violence to remove them. This thinking gave rise to militant terrorist organizations, such as the **Ku Klux Klan,** the Knights of the White Camellia, the White Brotherhood, and the Whitecaps. Threats, intimidation, beatings, rapes, and murder, such groups believed, would restore conservative white Democratic rule and force black people back into subordination.

PROFILE ~ THE ROLLIN SISTERS

Few women, black or white, were as influential in Reconstruction politics as the Rollin sisters of South Carolina. Although they could not vote or hold political office, the five sisters, and especially Frances and Katherine, were closely associated with the black and white Republican leadership in South Carolina. With their education, knowledge, and charm, these black women affected political decisions and policies.

The sisters were born and raised in the elite antebellum free black community in Charleston. Their father, William Rollin, a prosperous lumber dealer, traced his ancestors back to French Catholic families in Haiti. He insisted that his daughters obtain a first-rate education. Frances, who was born in 1844, was sent to Philadelphia to take the "ladies course" at the Quaker's Institute for Colored Youth. At least two of the other sisters attended school in Boston. After the war, Frances joined other members of Charleston's prominent people of color and taught at schools sponsored by the American Missionary Association. She also found time to write the biography of the black abolitionist leader Martin Delany. This was the first major nonfiction work published in America by a black woman, but she felt compelled to identify the author as a male, Frank A. Rollin.

In 1867 and 1868, as black men were entering the political arena, the Rollin sisters also gravitated to politics. Against her father's wishes, Frances married one of Reconstruction South Carolina's most controversial figures, William Whipper, a black attorney from Philadelphia who settled in Beaufort, South Carolina, after the war. (Whipper was the nephew of the antebellum black Pennsylvania businessman, also named William Whipper, profiled on p. 180.) He was elected to the state constitutional convention and then the South Carolina House of Representatives. Whipper was a tough, able, shrewd, and not altogether honest politician. He enjoyed an expensive lifestyle. Most white people detested him.

While the legislature was in session, the Whippers and the Rollin sisters took up residence in Columbia, the state capital. There, the sisters were extraordinarily popular. They were well educated, intelligent, refined, and sophisticated. One observer described them as "ravishingly beautiful." Katherine Rollin was frequently seen with white State Senator George W. McIntyre.

The Rollin sisters were enthusiastic proponents of women's rights and women's suffrage. They enlisted the wives of prominent black and white Republican politicians in their cause. Charlotte and Katherine organized a women's rights convention in Columbia in 1870 and formed the South Carolina Branch of the American Women's Suffrage Association.

Charlotte Rollin pleaded for the right to vote.

We ask suffrage not as a favor, not as a privilege, but as a right based on the grounds that we are human beings and as such entitled to human rights. While we concede that woman's ennobling influence should be confined chiefly to the home and society, we claim that public opinion has had a tendency to limit a woman's sphere to too small a circle and until woman has the right of representation this will last, and other rights will be held by insecure tenure.

Their black and white male allies tried to amend South Carolina's constitution to enable women to vote. After a bitter debate, the legislature rejected women's suffrage.

After the Democrats regained political power in 1877, the Rollin sisters left for the North. Charlotte and Louise settled with their mother in Brooklyn, New York. William and Frances Whipper and their five children moved to Washington, D.C., in 1882, where he practiced law and she was a clerk in the General Land Office. Three of their children survived to adulthood. Their sole son, Leigh Whipper, was a prominent stage and screen actor in the 1940s and 1950s. Sometime in the 1890s, Frances joined her husband in Beaufort. She died there in 1901.

Frances Rollin Whipper was author, teacher, political activist, wife, and mother. With ▶ her sisters, she was deeply involved in Reconstruction politics in South Carolina.

Rollin Sisters

The Ku Klux Klan was founded in Pulaski, Tennessee, in 1866. It was originally a social club for Confederate veterans who adopted secret oaths and rituals—similar to the Union Leagues, but with far more deadly results. One of the key figures in the Klan's rapid growth was former Confederate general Nathan Bedford Forrest, who became its grand wizard. The Klan drew its members from all classes of white society, not merely from among the poor. Businessmen, lawyers, physicians, and politicians were active in the Klan as well as farmers and planters.

The Klan and other terrorist organizations functioned mainly where black people were a large minority and where their votes could affect the outcome of elections. Klansmen virtually took over areas of western Alabama, northern Georgia, and Florida's panhandle. The Klan controlled the up country of South Carolina and the area around Mecklenburg County, North Carolina. However, in the Carolina and Georgia low country where there were huge black majorities, the Klan rarely, if ever, appeared.

DOCUMENT 13-2 Organization and Principles of the Ku Klux Klan, 1868

Although the Klan and similar societies were neither well organized nor unified, they did reduce support for the Republican Party and helped eliminate its leaders. Often wearing hoods and masks to hide their faces, white terrorists embarked on a campaign of violence rarely matched and never exceeded in American history.

Mobs of marauding terrorists beat and killed hundreds of black people—and many white people. Black churches and schools were burned. Republican leaders were routinely threatened and often killed. The black chairman of the Republican Party in South Carolina, Benjamin F. Randolph, was murdered as he stepped off a train in 1868. Black legislator Lee Nance and white legislator Solomon G. W. Dill were murdered in 1868 in South Carolina. In 1870 black lawmaker Richard Burke was killed in Sumter County, Alabama, because he was considered too influential among "people of his color."

As his wife looked on, Jack Dupree—a local Republican leader—had his throat cut and was eviscerated in Monroe County, Mississippi. In 1870 North Carolina senator John W. Stephens, a white Republican, was murdered. After Alabama freedman George Moore voted for the Republicans in 1869, Klansmen beat him, raped a girl who was visiting his wife, and attacked a neighbor. An Irish-American teacher and four black men were lynched in Cross Plains, Alabama, in 1870. Notorious Texas outlaw John Wesley Hardin openly acknowledged he had killed several black Texas state policemen.

White men attacked a Republican campaign rally in Eutaw, Alabama, in 1870 and killed four black men and wounded fifty-four other people. After three black leaders were arrested in 1871 in Meridian, Mississippi,

for delivering what many white people considered inflammatory speeches, shooting broke out in the courtroom. The Republican judge and two of the defendants were killed, and in a wave of violence, thirty black people were murdered, including every black leader in the small community. In the same year, a mob of five hundred men broke into the jail in Union County, South Carolina, and lynched eight black prisoners who had been accused of killing a Confederate veteran.

Nowhere was the Klan more active and violent than in York County, South Carolina. Almost the entire adult white male population joined in threatening, attacking, and murdering the black population. Hundreds were beaten and at least eleven killed. Terrified families fled from their homes into the woods. Appeals for help were sent to Governor Robert K. Scott (see *Voices: An Appeal for Help against the Klan*).

But Scott did not send aid. He had already sent the South Carolina militia into areas of Klan activity, and even more violence had resulted. The militia was made up mostly of black men, and white terrorists retaliated by killing militia officers. Scott could not send white men to York County because most of them sympathized with the Klan. Thus Republican governors like Scott responded ineffectually. Republican-controlled legislatures passed anti-Klan measures that made it illegal to appear in public in disguises and masks, and they strengthened laws against assault, murder, and conspiracy. But enforcement was weak.

A few Republican leaders did deal harshly and effectively with terrorism. Governors in Tennessee, Texas, and Arkansas declared martial law and sent in hundreds of well-armed white and black men to quell the violence. Hundreds of Klansmen were arrested, many fled, and three were executed in Arkansas. But when Governor William W. Holden of North Carolina sent the state militia after the Klan, he succeeded only in provoking an angry reaction. Subsequent Klan violence in ten counties helped Democrats carry the 1870 legislative elections, and the North Carolina legislature then removed Holden from office.

Outnumbered and outgunned, black people in most areas did not retaliate against the Klan, and the Klan was rarely active where black people were in a majority and prepared to defend themselves. In the cause of white supremacy, the Klan usually attacked those who could not defend themselves.

The West

During the 1830s the U.S. government forced the Five Civilized Tribes—the Cherokee, Chickasaw, Choctaw, Creek, and Seminole—from their southern home-

Head Quarters "Klu Klux"
Blood! Blood!! Blood!!!
First Quarter Bloody Moon
April 27 1868
To
H. C. Warmoth
        Villain. Beware! Your doom
is sealed—Death now awaits you. The
Midnight Owl Screames.

        Revenge! Revenge!! Revenge!!!
Klu Klux Klan
By Order of Grand Giant
Bloody Knights
Klu Klux Klan
Prepare Death now awaits you.

The flowing white robes and cone-shaped headdresses associated with the Ku Klux Klan today are mostly a twentieth-century phenomenon. The Klansmen of the Reconstruction era, like these two men in Alabama in 1868, were well armed, disguised, and prepared to intimidate black and white Republicans. The note is a Klan death threat directed at Louisiana's first Republican governor, Henry C. Warmoth.

lands to Indian Territory in what is now Oklahoma. By 1860 Native Americans held 7,367 African Americans in slavery. Many of the Indians fought for the Confederacy during the Civil War. Following the war, the former slaves encountered nearly as much violence and hostility from Native Americans as they did from southern white people. Indians were reluctant to share their land with freedmen, and they vigorously opposed policies that favored black voting rights.

Gradually and despite considerable Indian prejudice, some African Americans managed to acquire tribal land. Also, the Creeks and the Seminoles permitted former slaves to take part in tribal government. Black men served in both houses of the Creek legislature—the House of Warriors and the House of Kings. An African American, Jesse Franklin, served as a justice on the Creek tribal court in 1876. In contrast, the Chickasaw and Choctaw were absolutely opposed to making concessions to freed people, and thus the U.S. government ordered federal troops onto Chickasaw and Choctaw lands to protect the former slaves.

FEDERAL RECONSTRUCTION LEGISLATION

1869	Fifteenth Amendment passed (ratified 1870)
1870	Enforcement Act passed
1871	Ku Klux Klan Act passed
1875	Civil Rights Act of 1875 passed

1869–1875

Elsewhere on the western frontier, black people struggled for legal and political rights and periodically participated in territorial governments. In 1867 two hundred black men voted—although white men protested—in the Montana territorial election. In the Colorado Territory, William Jefferson Hardin, a barber, campaigned with other black men for the right to vote, and they persuaded 137 African Americans (91 percent of Colorado's black population) to sign a petition in 1865 to the territorial governor appealing for an end to

An Appeal for Help against the Klan

H. K. Roberts, a black lieutenant in the South Carolina state militia, described Klan terror in York County in late 1870 to Governor Robert K. Scott. Roberts desperately appealed for aid to protect Republicans and defend the black community.

ANTIOCH P.O.
YORK COUNTY S.C.

Dec. the 6th 1870. To Your Excelency R. K. Scott

Sir I will tell you that on last friday night the 2nd day of this [month] 8 miles from here thier was one of the worst outrages Commited that is on record in the state from 50 to 75 armed men went to the house of Thomas Blacks a colored man fired shots into the house and cald for him he clibed up in the loft of the house they fired up their and he came down jumped out at a window ran about 30 steps was shot down then they shot him after he fell they then draged him about 10 steps and cut his throat from ear to ear their was about 30 bullet holes in his body some 50 to one hundred shots in the house. . . . [They] abused his wife and enquired for one or two more colored men some of the colored people are leaving and a great many lying out in the woods and they reports comes to me evry day that they Ku Kluxs intend to kill us all out and I heard yesterday that they had 30 stands of arms. . . . I wish you would give me 20 or 25 men or let me enroll that many and I will stop it or catch some of them or send some U S Soldiers on for I tell you their must be something don and that quick to for I do believe that they intend to beat and kill out the Radical party in the upper Counties of the state where the vote is close if we was to have the ellection now the Radicals would turn [out] to vote their ticket I leave the matter with you I hope you will wright back to me by return mail and let me heare what you think you can do for us up here I cant tell whether I can hold my own or not I know some men that stay with us at night for safety but if they come as strong as they were the other night they may kill me and all of my men I remain yours truly as ever

H.K. Roberts, Lieut.
Commanding Post
of State Guards Kings Mountain

a white-only voting provision. In 1867 black men in Colorado finally did gain the right to vote. Hardin later moved to Cheyenne and was elected in 1879 to the Wyoming territorial legislature.

The Fifteenth Amendment

The federal government under Republican domination tried to protect black voting rights and defend Republican state governments in the South. In 1869 Congress passed the **Fifteenth Amendment,** which was ratified in 1870. It stipulated that a person could not be deprived of the right to vote because of race: "The right of citizens of the United States to vote shall not be denied or abridged by the United States or by any State on account of race, color, or previous condition of servitude." Black people, abolitionists, and reformers hailed the amendment as the culmination of the crusade to end slavery and give black people the same rights as white people.

Northern black men were the amendment's immediate beneficiaries because before its adoption, black men could vote in only eight northern states. Yet to the disappointment of many, the amendment said nothing about women voting and did not outlaw poll taxes, literacy tests, and property qualifications that could disfranchise citizens.

The Enforcement Acts

In direct response to the terrorism in the South, Congress passed the **Enforcement Acts** in 1870 and 1871, and the federal government expanded its authority over the states. The 1870 act outlawed disguises and masks and protected the civil rights of citizens. The 1871 act—known as the Ku Klux Klan Act—made it a federal offense to interfere with an individual's right to vote, hold office, serve on a jury, or enjoy equal protection of the law. Those accused of violating the act would be tried in federal court. For extreme violence, the act authorized the president to send in federal troops and suspend the writ of **habeas corpus.** (Habeas corpus is the right to be brought before a judge and not be arrested and jailed without cause.)

What prompted Roberts to write this letter?

Would Roberts have had any reason to exaggerate the violence in York County?

According to Roberts, what motivated white men to attack?

Source: H. K. Roberts to Governor Robert K. Scott, South Carolina Department of Archives and History.

Black congressmen, who had long advocated federal action against the Klan, endorsed the Enforcement Acts. Representative Joseph Rainey of South Carolina wanted to suspend the Constitution to protect citizens. "I desire that so broad and liberal a construction be placed on its provisions, as will insure protection to the humblest citizen. Tell me nothing of a constitution which fails to shelter beneath its rightful power the people of a country."

Armed with this new legislation, the Justice Department and Attorney General Amos T. Ackerman moved vigorously against the Klan. Hundreds of Klansmen were arrested—seven hundred in Mississippi alone. Faced with a full-scale rebellion in late 1871 in South Carolina's up country, President Ulysses S. Grant declared martial law in nine counties, suspended the writ of habeas corpus, and sent in the U.S. Army. Mass arrests and trials followed, but federal authorities permitted many Klansmen to confess and thereby escape prosecution. The government lacked the human and financial resources to bring hundreds of men to court for lengthy trials. Some white men were tried, mostly before black juries, and were imprisoned or fined. Comparatively few Klansmen, however, were punished severely, especially considering the enormity of their crimes.

The North and Reconstruction

Although the federal government did reduce Klan violence for a time, white southerners remained convinced that white supremacy must be restored and Republican governments overturned. Klan violence did not overthrow any state governments, but it gravely undermined freedmen's confidence in the ability of these governments to protect them. Meanwhile, radical Republicans in Congress grew frustrated that the South and especially black people continued to demand so much of their time and attention year after year. There was less and less sentiment in the North to continue support for the freedmen and involvement in southern affairs.

Many Republicans in the North lost interest in issues and principles and became more concerned with elections and economic issues. By the mid-1870s there was more discussion in Congress of patronage, veterans' pensions, railroads, taxes, tariffs, the economy, and monetary policy than about civil rights or the future of the South.

This optimistic 1870 illustration exemplifies the hopes and aspirations generated during Reconstruction as black people gained access to the political system. Invoking the legacy of Abraham Lincoln and John Brown, it suggests that African Americans would soon assume their rightful and equitable role in American society.

The American political system was awash in corruption by the 1870s, which detracted from concerns over the South. Although President Ulysses S. Grant was a man of integrity and honesty, many men in his administration were not. They were implicated in an assortment of scandals involving the construction of the transcontinental railroad, federal taxes on whiskey, and fraud within the Bureau of Indian Affairs. Nor was the dishonesty limited to Republicans. William Marcy "Boss" Tweed and the Democratic political machine that dominated New York City were riddled with corruption as well.

Many Republicans began to question the necessity for more moral, military, and political support for African Americans. They were convinced that African Americans had demanded too much for too long from the national government. Former slaves had become citizens and had the right to vote and hold political office. Therefore, they did not need additional help or legislation from the federal government. Equality for black people would come from their labor as free men, which would produce wealth and acceptance by white people. Any legislation Congress might enact, many northern white people believed, could not create equality.

BLACK LEADERS SUPPORT THE PASSAGE OF A CIVIL RIGHTS ACT

Black congressmen Robert Brown Elliott of South Carolina and James T. Rapier of Alabama both spoke passionately in favor of the Sumner civil rights bill in 1874. Both men had been free before the war. Both were lawyers, and although they each accumulated considerable wealth, both died in poverty in the 1880s.

[James T. Rapier]

I must confess it is somewhat embarrassing for a colored man to urge the passage of this bill, because if he exhibit an earnestness in the matter and expresses a desire for its immediate passage, straightaway he is charged with a desire for social equality, as explained by the demagogue and understood by the ignorant white man. But then it is just as embarrassing for him not to do so, for, if he remains silent while the struggle is being carried on around, and for him, he is liable to be charged with a want of interest in a matter that concerns him more than anyone else, which is enough to make his friends desert his cause. So in steering away from Scylla I may run upon Charybdis. But the anomalous, and I may add the supremely ridiculous, position of the Negro at this time, in this country, compel me to say something. Here his condition is without comparison, parallel alone to itself. Just that the law recognizes my right upon this floor as a law-maker, but that there is no law to secure to me any accommodations whatever while traveling here to discharge my duties as a Representative of a large and wealthy constituency. Here I am the peer of the proudest, but on a steamboat or car I am not equal to the most degraded. Is not this most anomalous and ridiculous?

[Robert Brown Elliott]

The results of the war, as seen in Reconstruction, have settled forever the political status of my race. The passage of this bill will determine the civil status, not only of the Negro but of any other class of citizens who may feel themselves discriminated against. It will form the capstone of that temple of liberty begun on this continent under discouraging circumstances, carried on in spite of the sneers of monarchists and the cavils of pretended friends of freedom, until at last it stands in all its beautiful symmetry and proportions, a building the grandest which the world has ever seen, realizing the most sanguine expectations and the highest hopes of those who in the name of equal, impartial and universal liberty, laid the foundation stone.

The Chicago Tribune, a Republican newspaper, had wearied of black agitation by 1874. "Is it not time for the colored race to stop playing baby? The whites of America have done nobly in outgrowing old prejudices against them. They cannot hurry this process by law. Let them obtain social equality as every other man, woman, and child in the world obtain it,—by showing themselves in their lives the social equals of those with whom they wish to consort. If they do this, year by year the prejudices will die away."

Other northern white people, swayed by white southerners' views of black people, began to doubt the wisdom of universal manhood suffrage. Many white people who had nominally supported black suffrage began to believe the exaggerated complaints about corruption among black leaders and the unrelenting claims that freedmen were incapable of self-government. Some white northerners began to conclude that Reconstruction had been a mistake.

Economic conditions contributed to changing attitudes. A financial crisis—the Panic of 1873—sent the economy into a slump for several years. Businesses and financial institutions failed, unemployment soared, and prices fell sharply. In 1874 the Democrats recaptured a majority in the House of Representatives for the first time since 1860 and also took political control of several northern states.

The Freedmen's Bank

One of the casualties of the financial crisis was the **Freedmen's Savings Bank,** which failed in 1874. Founded in 1865 when hope flourished, the Freedmen's Savings and Trust Company had been chartered by Congress but was not connected to the Freedmen's Bureau. However, the bank's advertising featured pictures of Abraham Lincoln, and many black people assumed it was a federal agency. Freedmen, black veterans, black churches, fraternal organizations, and benevolent societies opened thousands of accounts in the bank. Most of the deposits totaled under $50, and some amounted to only a few cents.

🌲 *If black men had the right to vote and serve in Congress, why was a civil rights law needed?*

🌲 *Who would benefit most from the passage of this bill?*

🌲 *What distinction do the two congressmen draw between social discrimination and political rights?*

Sources: *Congressional Record*, vol. II, part 1, 43d Congress, 1st session, pp. 565–67; Peggy Lamson, *The Glorious Failure* (New York: Norton, 1973), p. 181.

Although the bank had many black employees, its board of directors consisted of white men. They unwisely invested the bank's funds in risky ventures, including Washington, D.C., real estate. With the Panic of 1873, the bank lost large sums in unsecured railroad loans. To restore confidence, its directors asked Frederick Douglass to serve as president and persuaded him to invest $10,000 of his own money to help shore up the bank. Douglass lost his money, and African Americans from across the South lost more than $1 million when the bank closed in June 1874. Eventually about half the depositors received three-fifths of the value of their accounts, but many African Americans believed the U.S. government owed them a debt. Well into the twentieth century, they wrote to Congress and the president in unsuccessful efforts to retrieve their hard-earned money.

The Civil Rights Act of 1875

Before Reconstruction finally expired, Congress made one final—some said futile—gesture to protect black people from racial discrimination when it passed the **Civil Rights Act of 1875.** Strongly championed by Senator Charles Sumner of Massachusetts, it was originally intended to open public accommodations including schools, churches, cemeteries, hotels, and transportation to all people regardless of race. It passed in the Republican-controlled Senate in 1874. But House Democrats held up passage. It was not enacted until 1875 and then largely as a solemn gesture to Sumner, who had died in 1874. In its final form, the bans on discrimination in churches, cemeteries, and schools were deleted.

The act stipulated "That all persons . . . shall be entitled to the full and equal enjoyment of the accommodations, advantages, facilities, and privileges of inns, public conveyances on land or water, theaters, and other places of public amusement." After its passage, no attempt was made to enforce these provisions, and in 1883 the U.S. Supreme Court declared it unconstitutional. Justice Joseph Bradley wrote that the Fourteenth Amendment protected black people from discrimination by states but not by private businesses. Black newspapers likened the decision to the *Dred Scott* case a quarter century earlier.

The End of Reconstruction

Reconstruction ended as it began—in violence and controversy. Democrats demanded "**redemption**"—a word with biblical and spiritual overtones. They wanted southern states restored to conservative, white political control. By 1875 those Democrats had regained authority in all

On January 6, 1874, Robert Brown Elliott delivered a ringing speech in the U.S. House of Representatives in support of the Sumner civil rights bill. Elliott was responding in part to words uttered the day before by Virginia congressman John T. Harris, who claimed that "there is not a gentleman on this floor who can honestly say he really believes that the colored man is created his equal." P.S. Duval and Son, Come and join us brothers; Civil War; Philadelphia, PA; ca. 1863. Chicago Historical Society ICHi-22051.

the former Confederate states except Mississippi, Florida, Louisiana, and South Carolina (see Map 13–1). Democrats had redeemed Tennessee in 1870 and Georgia in 1871. Democrats had learned two valuable lessons. First, few black men could be persuaded to vote for the Democratic Party—no matter how much white leaders wanted to believe former slaves were easy to manipulate. Second, intimidation and violence would win elections in areas where the number of black and white voters was nearly equal. The federal government had stymied Klan violence in 1871, but by the mid-1870s, the government had become reluctant to send troops to the South to protect black citizens.

Did Reconstruction Work for the Freed People? ACTIVITY

VIOLENT REDEMPTION

In Alabama in 1874, black and white Republican leaders were murdered, and white mobs destroyed crops and homes. On Election Day in Eufaula, white men killed seven and injured nearly seventy unarmed black voters. Black voters were also driven from the polls in Mobile. Democrats won the election and "redeemed" Alabama.

White violence accompanied every election in Louisiana from 1868 to 1876. After Republicans and Democrats each claimed victory in the 1872 elections,

MAP EXPLORATION

To explore this interactive map, go to
http://www.prenhall.com/hine4/map13.1

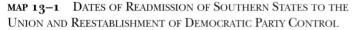

MAP 13–1   DATES OF READMISSION OF SOUTHERN STATES TO THE UNION AND REESTABLISHMENT OF DEMOCRATIC PARTY CONTROL

Once conservative white Democrats regained political control of a state government from black and white Republicans, they considered that state "redeemed." The first states the Democrats "redeemed" were Georgia, Virginia, and North Carolina. Louisiana, Florida, and South Carolina were the last. (Tennessee was not included in the Reconstruction process under the terms of the 1867 Reconstruction Act.)

▶ *In which states did black and white Republicans hold political control for the shortest and longest periods of time?*

black people seized the small town of Colfax along the Red River to protect themselves against a Democratic takeover. They held out for three weeks, and then on Easter Sunday in 1873, a well-armed white mob attacked the black defenders, killing 105 in the worst single day of bloodshed during Reconstruction. In 1874 the White League almost redeemed Louisiana in an astonishing wave of violence. Black people were murdered, courts were attacked, and white people refused to pay taxes to the Republican state government. Six white and two black Republicans were murdered at Coushatta. In September, President Grant finally sent federal troops to New Orleans after 3,500 White Leaguers attacked and

nearly wiped out the black militia and the Metropolitan Police. But the stage had been set for the 1876 campaign.

THE SHOTGUN POLICY

In 1875 white Mississippians, no longer fearful the national government would intervene in force, declared open warfare on the black majority. The masks and hoods of the Klan were discarded. One newspaper publicly proclaimed that Democrats would carry the election, "peaceably if we can, forcibly if we must." Another paper carried a bold banner: "Mississippi is a white man's country, and by the eternal God we'll rule it."

White Mississippi unleashed a campaign of violence known as the **"shotgun policy"** that was extreme even for Reconstruction. Many Republicans fled and others were murdered. In late 1874 an estimated three hundred black people were hunted down outside Vicksburg after black men armed with inferior weapons had lost a "battle" with white men. In 1875 thirty teachers, church leaders, and Republican officials were killed in Clinton. The white sheriff of Yazoo County, who had married a black woman and supported the education of black children, had to flee the state.

Mississippi governor Adelbert Ames appealed for federal help, but President Grant refused: "The whole public are tired out with these annual autumnal outbreaks in the South . . . [and] are ready now to condemn any interference on the part of the Government." No federal help arrived. The terrorism intensified, and many black voters went into hiding on Election Day, afraid for their lives and the lives of their families. Democrats redeemed Mississippi and prided themselves that they—a superior race representing the most civilized of all people—were back in control.

In Florida in 1876, white Republicans noted that support for black people in the South was fading. They nominated an all-white Republican slate and even refused to renominate black congressman Josiah Walls.

THE HAMBURG MASSACRE

South Carolina Democrats were divided between moderate and extreme factions, but they united to nominate former Confederate general Wade Hampton for governor after the **Hamburg Massacre.** The prelude to this event occurred on July 4, 1876—the nation's centennial—when two white men in a buggy confronted the black militia that was drilling on a town street in Hamburg, a small, mostly black town. Hot words were exchanged, and days later, Democrats demanded the militia be disarmed. White rifle club members from around the state arrived in Hamburg and attacked the armory, where forty black members of the militia defended themselves. The rifle companies brought up a cannon and reinforcements from nearby Georgia. After the militia ran low on ammunition, white men captured the armory. One white man was killed, twenty-nine black men were taken prisoner, and the other eleven fled. Five of the black men identified as leaders were shot down in cold blood. The rifle companies invaded and wrecked Hamburg. Seven white men were indicted for murder. All were acquitted.

The Hamburg Massacre incited South Carolina Democrats to imitate Mississippi's "shotgun policy." It also forced a reluctant President Grant to send federal troops to South Carolina. In the 1876 election campaign, hundreds of white men in red flannel shirts turned out on mules and horses to support Wade Hampton in his contest against incumbent Republican governor Daniel Chamberlain and his black and white allies. When Chamberlain and fellow Republicans tried to speak in Edgefield, they were ridiculed, threatened, and shouted down by six hundred Red Shirts, many of them armed.

Democrats attacked, beat, and killed black people to prevent them from voting. Democratic leaders instructed their followers to treat black voters with contempt. "In speeches to negroes you must remember that argument has no effect on them. They can only be influenced by their fears, superstition, and cupidity. . . . Treat them so as to show them you are a superior race and that their natural position is that of subordination to the white man."

As the election approached, black people in the up country of South Carolina knew it would be exceedingly dangerous if they tried to vote. But in the low country, black people went on the offensive and attacked Democrats. In Charleston, a white man was killed in a racial melee. At a campaign rally at Cainhoy, a few miles outside Charleston, armed black men killed five white men.

A few black men supported Wade Hampton and the Red Shirts. Hampton had a paternalistic view of black people and, although he considered them inferior to white people, promised to respect their rights. Martin Delany believed Hampton and the Democrats were more trustworthy than unreliable Republicans; Delany campaigned for Hampton and was later rewarded with a minor political post. A few genuinely conservative black men during Reconstruction also supported the Democrats and curried their favor and patronage. Most black people despised them. When one black man gave his support to the Democrats, his wife threw him and his clothes out, declaring she would prefer to "beg her bread" than live with a "Democratic nigger."

THE "COMPROMISE" OF 1877

Threats, violence, and bloodshed accompanied the elections of 1876, but the results were confusing and

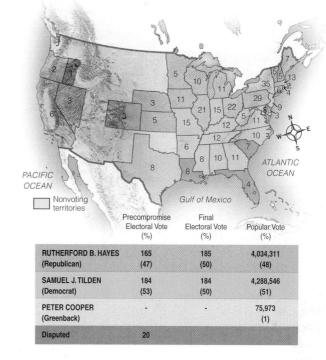

	Precompromise Electoral Vote (%)	Final Electoral Vote (%)	Popular Vote (%)
RUTHERFORD B. HAYES (Republican)	165 (47)	185 (50)	4,034,311 (48)
SAMUEL J. TILDEN (Democrat)	184 (53)	184 (50)	4,288,546 (51)
PETER COOPER (Greenback)	-	-	75,973 (1)
Disputed	20		

MAP 13–2   THE ELECTION OF 1876

Although Democrat Samuel Tilden appeared to have won the election of 1876, Rutherford B. Hayes and the Republicans were able to claim victory after a prolonged political and constitutional controversy involving the disputed electoral college votes from Louisiana, Florida, and South Carolina (and one from Oregon). In an informal settlement in 1877, Democrats agreed to accept electoral votes for Hayes from those states, and Republicans agreed to permit those states to be "redeemed" by the Democrats. The result was to leave the entire South under the political control of conservative white Democrats. For the first time since 1867, black and white Republicans no longer effectively controlled any former Confederate state.

▶ *What factors explain the loss of political power by southern Republicans?*

contradictory. Samuel Tilden, the Democratic presidential candidate, won the popular vote by more than 250,000, and he had a large lead over Republican Rutherford B. Hayes in the electoral vote. Hayes had won 167, but Tilden had 185, and the 20 remaining electoral college votes were in dispute. Both Democrats and Republicans claimed to have won in Florida, Louisiana, and South Carolina, the last three southern states that had not been redeemed. (There was also one contested vote from Oregon.) Whoever took the twenty electoral votes of the three contested states (and Oregon) would be the next president (see Map 13–2).

AFRICAN-AMERICAN EVENTS	NATIONAL EVENTS
1865	**1865**
The Freedmen's Savings Bank and Trust Company is established	Freedmen's Bureau established
	1866
	President Johnson vetoes Freedmen's Bureau Bill and civil rights bill; Congress overrides both vetoes
	Ku Klux Klan is founded in Pulaski, Tennessee
1867	**1867**
1867–1868	**1867**
Ten southern states hold constitutional conventions	Congress takes over Reconstruction and provides for universal manhood suffrage
1867	**1868**
Howard University established in Washinton, D.C.	Fourteenth Amendment to the Constitution is ratified
1868	Ulysses S. Grant elected president
Black political leaders elected to state and local offices across the South	
1869	**1869**
1870	**1869**
Hiram R. Revels is elected to the U.S. Senate and Joseph H. Rainey is elected to the U.S. House of Representatives	Knights of Labor founded in Philadelphia
Congress passes the Enforcement Act	**1870**
	Fifteenth Amendment to the Constitution is ratified
	John D. Rockefeller incorporates Standard Oil Co. in Cleveland

There was a prolonged controversy, and the constitutional crisis over the outcome of the 1876 election was not resolved until shortly before Inauguration Day in March 1877. Although not a formal compromise, an informal understanding known as the **Compromise of 1877** ended the dispute. Democrats accepted a Hayes victory, but Hayes let southern Democrats know he would not support Republican governments in Florida, Louisiana, and South Carolina. Hayes withdrew the last federal troops from the South, and the Republican administration in those states collapsed. Democrats immediately took control.

Redemption was now complete. Each of the former Confederate states was under the authority of white Democrats. Henry Adams, a black leader from Louisiana, explained what had happened. "The whole South—every state in the South had got into the hands of the very men that held us as slaves."

CONCLUSION

The glorious hopes that emancipation and the Union victory in the Civil War had aroused among African Americans in 1865 appeared forlorn by 1877. To be sure, black people were no longer slave laborers or property. They lived in tightly knit families that white people no longer controlled. They had established hundreds of schools, churches, and benevolent societies. The Constitution now endowed them with freedom, citizenship, and the right to vote. Some black people had even acquired land.

But no one can characterize Reconstruction as a success. The epidemic of terror and violence made it one of the bloodiest eras in American history. Thousands of black people had been beaten, raped, and murdered since 1865, simply because they had acted as free people. Too many white people were determined that black people could not and would not have the same rights that white people enjoyed. White southerners would not tolerate either the presence of black men in politics or white Republicans who accepted black political involvement. Gradually most white northerners and even radical Republicans grew weary of intervening in southern affairs and became convinced again that black men and women were their inferiors and were not prepared to participate in government. Reconstruction, they concluded, had been a mistake.

Furthermore, black and white Republicans hurt themselves by indulging in fraud and corruption and by engaging in angry and divisive factionalism. But even if Republicans had been honest and united, white southern Democrats would never have accepted black people as worthy to participate in the political system.

Southern Democrats would accept black people in politics only if Democrats could control black voters. But black voters understood this, rejected control by former slave owners, and were loyal to the Republican Party—as flawed as it was.

But as grim a turn as life may have taken for black people by 1877, it would get even worse in the decades that followed.

RECOMMENDED READING

Eric Foner. *Freedom's Lawmakers: A Directory of Black Office-holders during Reconstruction.* New York: Oxford University Press, 1993. Biographical sketches of every known southern black leader during the era.

John Hope Franklin. *Reconstruction after the Civil War.* Chicago: University of Chicago Press, 1961. An excellent summary and interpretation of the postwar years.

William Gillette. *Retreat from Reconstruction, 1869–1879.* Baton Rouge: Louisiana State University Press, 1979. An analysis of how and why the North lost interest in the South.

Thomas Holt. *Black over White: Negro Political Leadership in South Carolina.* Urbana: University of Illinois Press, 1979. A masterful and sophisticated study of black leaders in the state with the most black politicians.

Michael L. Perman. *Emancipation and Reconstruction, 1862–1879.* Arlington Heights, IL: Harlan Davidson, 1987. Another excellent survey of the period.

Howard N. Rabinowitz, ed. *Southern Black Leaders of the Reconstruction Era.* Urbana: University of Illinois Press, 1982. A series of biographical essays on black politicians.

Frank A. Rollin. *Life and Public Services of Martin R. Delany.* Boston: Lee and Shepard, 1883. This is the first biography of a black leader by an African American. The author was Frances A. Rollin, but she used a male pseudonym.

ADDITIONAL BIBLIOGRAPHY

RECONSTRUCTION IN SPECIFIC STATES AND TERRITORIES

M. Thomas Bailey. *Reconstruction in Indian Territory: A Story of Avarice, Discrimination, and Opportunism.* Port Washington, NY: Kennikat Press, 1972.

Jane Dailey. *Before Jim Crow: The Politics of Race in Post Emancipation Virginia.* Chapel Hill: University of North Carolina Press, 2000.

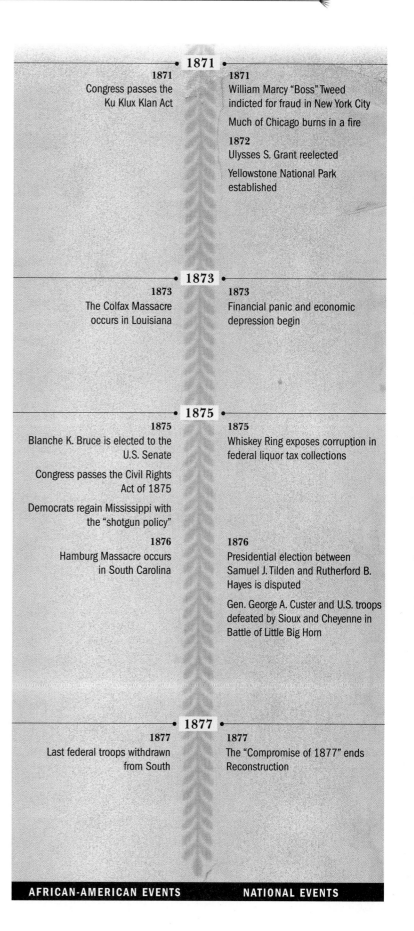

1871

1871
Congress passes the Ku Klux Klan Act

1871
William Marcy "Boss" Tweed indicted for fraud in New York City

Much of Chicago burns in a fire

1872
Ulysses S. Grant reelected

Yellowstone National Park established

1873

1873
The Colfax Massacre occurs in Louisiana

1873
Financial panic and economic depression begin

1875

1875
Blanche K. Bruce is elected to the U.S. Senate

Congress passes the Civil Rights Act of 1875

Democrats regain Mississippi with the "shotgun policy"

1875
Whiskey Ring exposes corruption in federal liquor tax collections

1876
Hamburg Massacre occurs in South Carolina

1876
Presidential election between Samuel J. Tilden and Rutherford B. Hayes is disputed

Gen. George A. Custer and U.S. troops defeated by Sioux and Cheyenne in Battle of Little Big Horn

1877

1877
Last federal troops withdrawn from South

1877
The "Compromise of 1877" ends Reconstruction

AFRICAN-AMERICAN EVENTS   **NATIONAL EVENTS**

Edmund L. Drago. *Black Politicians and Reconstruction in Georgia.* Athens: University of Georgia Press, 1982.

———. *Hurrah for Hampton: Black Red Shirts in South Carolina during Reconstruction.* Fayetteville: University of Arkansas Press, 1998.

Luther P. Jackson. *Negro Officeholders in Virginia, 1865–1895.* Norfolk, VA: Guide Quality Press, 1945.

Peter Kolchin. *First Freedom: The Responses of Alabama's Blacks to Emancipation and Reconstruction.* Westport, CT: Greenwood, 1972.

Merline Pitre. *Through Many Dangers, Toils, and Snares: The Black Leadership of Texas, 1868–1900.* Austin, TX: Eakin Press, 1985.

Joe M. Richardson. *The Negro in the Reconstruction of Florida, 1865–1877.* Tallahassee: Florida State University Press, 1965.

Buford Stacher. *Blacks in Mississippi Politics, 1865–1900.* Washington, DC: University Press of America, 1978.

Ted Tunnell. *Crucible of Reconstruction: War, Radicalism and Race in Louisiana, 1862–1877.* Baton Rouge: Louisiana State University Press, 1984.

Charles Vincent. *Black Legislators in Louisiana during Reconstruction.* Baton Rouge: Louisiana State University Press, 1976.

Joel Williamson. *After Slavery: The Negro in South Carolina: 1861–1877.* Chapel Hill: University of North Carolina Press, 1965.

NATIONAL POLITICS: ANDREW JOHNSON AND THE RADICAL REPUBLICANS

Michael Les Benedict. *A Compromise of Principle: Congressional Republicans and Reconstruction.* New York: Norton, 1974.

Dan T. Carter. *When the War Was Over: The Failure of Self-Reconstruction in the South, 1865–1867.* Baton Rouge: Louisina State University Press, 1983.

Michael W. Fitzgerald. *The Union League Movement in the Deep South.* Baton Rouge: Louisiana State University Press, 1989.

Eric L. McKitrick. *Andrew Johnson and Reconstruction, 1865–1867.* Chicago: University of Chicago Press, 1960.

James M. McPherson. *The Struggle for Equality: Abolitionists and the Negro in the Civil War and Reconstruction.* Princeton, NJ: Princeton University Press, 1964.

Hans L. Trefousse. *The Radical Republicans: Lincoln's Vanguard for Racial Justice.* Baton Rouge: Louisiana State University Press, 1969.

ECONOMIC ISSUES: LAND, LABOR, AND THE FREEDMEN'S BANK

Elizabeth Bethel. *Promiseland: A Century of Life in a Negro Community.* Philadelphia: Temple University Press, 1981.

Carol R. Bleser. *The Promised Land: The History of the South Carolina Land Commission, 1869–1890.* Columbia: University of South Carolina Press, 1969.

Sharon Ann Holt. *Making Freedom Pay: North Carolina Freed People Working for Themselves, 1865–1900.* Athens: University of Georgia Press, 2000.

Lynda J. Morgan. *Emancipation in Virginia's Tobacco Belt.* Athens: University of Georgia Press, 1992.

Donald G. Nieman. *To Set the Law in Motion: The Freedmen's Bureau and Legal Rights for Blacks, 1865–1869.* Millwood, NY: KTO, 1979.

Carl R. Osthaus. *Freedmen, Philanthropy and Fraud: A History of the Freedman's Savings Bank.* Urbana: University of Illinois Press, 1976.

Heather Cox Richardson. *The Death of Reconstruction: Race, Labor, and Politics in the Post–Civil War North, 1865–1901.* Cambridge: Harvard University Press, 2001.

VIOLENCE AND THE KU KLUX KLAN

George C. Rable. *But There Was No Peace: The Role of Violence in the Politics of Reconstruction.* Athens: University of Georgia Press, 1984.

Allen W. Trelease. *White Terror: The Ku Klux Klan Conspiracy and Southern Reconstruction.* New York: Harper & Row, 1973.

Lou Falkner Williams. *The Great South Carolina Ku Klux Klan Trials, 1871–1872.* Athens: University of Georgia Press, 1996.

AUTOBIOGRAPHY AND BIOGRAPHY

Mifflin Wistar Gibbs. *Shadow & Light: An Autobiography.* Lincoln: University of Nebraska Press, 1995.

Peter D. Klingman. *Josiah Walls.* Gainesville: University Presses of Florida, 1976.

Peggy Lamson. *The Glorious Failure: Black Congressman Robert Brown Elliott and Reconstruction in South Carolina.* New York: Norton, 1973.

Edward A. Miller. *Gullah Statesman: Robert Smalls: From Slavery to Congress, 1839–1915.* Columbia: University of South Carolina Press, 1995.

Loren Schweninger. *James T. Rapier and Reconstruction.* Chicago: University of Chicago Press, 1978.

Okon E. Uya. *From Slavery to Public Service: Robert Smalls, 1839–1915.* New York: Oxford University Press, 1971.

RETRACING THE ODYSSEY

Howard University, Washington, D.C. The Freedmen's Bureau founded this national university in 1867. Also located on the campus is the Moorland-Spingarn Research Center, one of the country's richest archives in African-American history.

Wilberforce University and the National Afro-American Museum and Cultural Center, Wilberforce, Ohio. Wilberforce University opened in 1856 and was named after English abolitionist William Wilberforce. The AME church took over the school in 1863. It contains exhibits, an art gallery, and theater, and has a picnic area.

Union Bank Building, Tallahassee, Florida. For a time during Reconstruction, a branch of the Freedmen's Savings and Trust Company was located here. The building, constructed in 1840, originally served as a planters' bank. It is currently part of the Museum of Florida History and includes its African-American History teacher in-service program.

The Robert Smalls Home, Beaufort, South Carolina. The Civil War hero and black political leader bought this house in 1863. He had lived on the premises as a slave, and it remained in his hands until his death in 1915.

 REVIEW, RESEARCH, AND INTERACT

REVIEW QUESTIONS

1. What issues most concerned black political leaders during Reconstruction?

2. What did black political leaders accomplish and fail to accomplish during Reconstruction? What contributed to their successes and failures?

3. Were black political leaders unqualified to hold office so soon after the end of slavery?

4. To what extent did African Americans dominate southern politics during Reconstruction? Should we refer to this era as "Black Reconstruction"?

5. Why was it so difficult for the Republican Party to maintain control of southern state governments during Reconstruction?

6. What was "redemption"? What happened when redemption occurred? What factors contributed to redemption?

7. How did Reconstruction end?

8. How effective was Reconstruction in assisting black people to make the transition from slavery to freedom? How effective was it in restoring the southern states to the Union?

Research Navigator.com RESOURCES FOR COLLEGE RESEARCH ASSIGNMENTS **www.researchnavigator.com**

Using the tools available in the Research Navigator, consider this question:
Why did so many whites in the North lose interest in the situation of blacks in the South?

PRIMARY SOURCE DOCUMENTS

13–1 Diary of Joseph Addison Waddell, 1865

13–2 Organization and Principles of the Ku Klux Klan, 1868

13–3 Blanche K. Bruce, Speech in the Senate, 1876

13–4 The New Slavery in the South—An Autobiography

13–5 "When We Worked on Shares, We Couldn't Make Nothing": Henry Blake Talks about Sharecropping after the Civil War

MAP EXPLORATION

Dates of Readmission of the Southern States to the Union and Reestablishment of Democratic Party Control, p. 338, **http://www.prenhall.com/hine4/map13.1**

INTERACTIVE ACTIVITY

Did Reconstruction Work for the Freed People?
How did newly freed slaves attempt to build lives for themselves? What were the principal obstacles they faced?

Higher Education for African Americans Begins

Three black colleges were founded before the Civil War. In Pennsylvania, Cheney University opened in 1837, followed by the establishment of Lincoln University in 1854. In 1856, Wilberforce University was founded in Ohio. After the Civil War, northern black and white missionary groups fanned out across the South and—frequently with the assistance of Freedmen's Bureau officials—founded colleges, institutes, and normal schools in the former slave states in the late 1860s and the 1870s. Most of these institutions provided elementary and secondary education. Few black students were prepared for actual college or university work. Even so, black colleges soon offered academic and trade courses and professional and military training. A comprehensive list of current black colleges and universities is included on page A-12.

▶ The faculty of Tuskegee Institute poses for a portrait with Mr. and Mrs. Booker T. Washington and Andrew Carnegie, the industralist (all seated in the front row.)

▲ Students perform experiments in the biological laboratory at Agricultural and Mechanical College in Greensboro, North Carolina, which began in 1892 as a land-grant college.

◀ The choir of Fisk University, Nashville, Tennessee, poses in front of the school's organ. Founded in 1866 as a liberal arts college and affiliated with the United Church of Christ, Fisk was also the home of the famed Jubilee singers, who performed in fund-raising concerts in the United States and Europe in the 1870s.

A class learns the craft ▶ of woodworking at Clafin University, Orangeburg, South Carolina, circa 1899. The university was founded in 1869 and affiliated with the United Methodist Church.

This 1850s lithograph offers a view of the buildings that comprised Wilberforce University in Xenia, Ohio, founded as a black college in 1856 by the Methodist Episcopal Church and named after the abolitionist, William Wilberforce.

These classes in dressmaking and capillary physics at Hampton Institute, (now University) in Virginia illustrate the range of studies available. Hampton was founded as a private university in 1868.

"Tuskegee Normal and Industrial Institute."

The Howard University law graduating class of 1900 poses on the campus in formal attire.

Students gathered on the campus of Berea College, in Berea, Kentucky, which was founded after the Civil War. Established by the Reverend John G. Fee in 1865, the college provided educational opportunities to black and white students, both men and women.

Howard University in Washington, D.C. provided education for African Americans in many professions, including dentistry. Howard first opened its doors in 1867 as a public university.

VISUALIZING THE PAST

REALITIES OF FREEDOM

The Freedmen's Bureau established in 1865 by Congress provided freedmen with clothing, temporary shelter, food, and series of freedmen's schools across the South. Southern response was to fall into the use of terror to deter blacks from becoming economically independent using the agencies of groups like the Ku Klux Klan. Sharecropping was an insidious economic arrangement that also placed both whites and blacks in a form of economic slavery to large land holders in the South of the post-Civil War era.

Share cropping, tenant farming, and peonage were new forms of slavery adopted in the South following the Civil War.

Following emancipation, what economic and social opportunities existed for African Americans in the United States? How did these various opportunities available to freedmen improve their life and that of their families after the official end to slavery?

▶ An Act to Establish a Bureau for the Relief of Freedmen and Refugees, 1865

Be it enacted, That there is hereby established in the War Department, to continue during the present war of rebellion, and for one year thereafter, a bureau of refugees, freedmen, and abandoned lands, to which shall be committed, as hereinafter provided, the supervision and management of all abandoned lands, and the control of all subjects relating to refugees and freedmen from rebel states, or from any district of country within the territory embraced in the operations of the army, under such rules and regulations as may be prescribed by the head of the bureau and approved by the President. The said bureau shall be under the management and control of a commissioner to be appointed by the President, by and with the advice and consent of the Senate. . .

▶ Excerpts from a Share Cropper Contract, 1882

To every one applying to rent land upon shares, the following conditions must be read, and agreed to.

To every 30 or 35 acres, I agree to furnish the team, plow, and farming implements, except cotton planters, and I do not agree to furnish a cart to every cropper. The croppers are to have half of the cotton, corn and fodder (and peas and pumpkins and potatoes if any are planted. . .

Croppers are to have no part or interest in the cotton seed raised from the crop planted and worked by them. No vine crops of any description, that is, no watermelons, muskmelons, . . . squashes or anything of that kind, except peas and pump-

kins, and potatoes, are to be planted in the cotton or corn. All must work under my direction. All plantation work to be done by the croppers. . . .

For every mule or horse furnished by me there must be 1000 good sized rails . . . hauled, and the fence repaired as far as they will go, the fence to be torn down and put up from the bottom if I so direct. All croppers to haul rails and work on fence whenever I may order. Rails to be split when I may say.

Each cropper to clean out every ditch in his crop, and where a ditch runs between two croppers, the cleaning out of that ditch is to be divided equally between them.... The cleaning out of all ditches

must be done by the first of October. The rails must be split and the fence repaired before corn is planted.

Each cropper must keep in good repair all bridges in his crop or over ditches that he has to clean out and when a bridge needs repairing that is outside of all their crops, then any one that I call on must repair it. . . .

No cropper to work off the plantation when there is any work to be done on the land he has rented, or when his work is needed by me or other croppers. Trees to be cut down on Orchard, House field & Evanson fences, leaving such as I may designate. . . .

The New Slavery in the South

The Senator had bought an additional thousand acres of land, and to his already large cotton plantation he added two great big saw-mills and went into the lumber business. Within two years the Senator had in all nearly 200 negroes working on his plantation—about his half of them free laborers, so-called, and about half of them convicts. The only difference between the free laborers and the others was that the free laborers could come and go as they pleased . . . The troubles of the free laborers began at the close of the ten-year period. To a man, they all wanted to quit when the time was up . . . . And just when we thought that our bondage was at an end we found that it had really just begun. Two or three years before, or about a year and a half after the Senator had started his camp, he had established a large store, which was called the commissary. All of us free laborers were compelled to buy our supplies— food, clothing, etc.—from that store. . . . In this store we were charged all sorts of high prices for goods, because every year we would come out in debt to our employer. If not that, we seldom had more than $5 or $10 coming to us—and that for a whole year's work. Well, at the close of the tenth year, when we kicked and meant to leave the Senator, he said to some of us with a smile (and I never will forget that smile—I can see it now) . . .

Word was sent out for all of us to meet him at the commissary at 2 o'clock. There he told us that, after we had signed what he called a written acknowledgment of our debts, we might go and look for new places. The storekeeper took us one by one and read to us statements of our accounts. According to the books there was no man of us who owed the Senator less than $100; some of us were put down for as much as $200. I owed $165, according to the bookkeeper. These debts were not accumulated during one year, but ran back for three and four years, so we were told . . . we fellows didn't care anything about the amounts—we were after getting away; and we had been told that we might go, if we stepped up, we did, and made our marks. That same night we were rounded up by a constable and ten or twelve white men, who aided him, and we were locked up, every one of us, in one of the Senator's stockades. The next morning it was explained to us by the two guards appointed to watch us that, in the papers we had signed the day before, we had not only made acknowledgment of our indebtedness, but that we had also agreed to work for the Senator until the debts were paid off by hard labor. And from that day forward we were treated just like convicts. Really we had made ourselves lifetime slaves, or peons, as the law called us. But, call it slavery, peonage, or what not, the truth is we lived in a hell on earth what time we spent in the Senator's peon camp. . . .

"When We Worked on Shares, We Couldn't Make Nothing"

After freedom, we worked on shares a while. Then we rented. When we worked on shares, we couldn't make nothing, just overalls and something to eat. Half went to the other man and you would destroy your half if you weren't careful. A man that didn't know how to count would always lose. He might lose anyhow. They didn't give no itemized statement. No, you just had to take their word. They never give you no details. They just say you owe so much. No matter how good account you kept, you had to go by their account and now, Brother, I'm tellin' you the truth about this. It's been that way for a long time. You had to take the white man's work on note, and everything. Anything you wanted, you could git if you were a good hand. You could git anything you wanted as long as you worked. If you didn't make no money, that's all right; they would advance you more. But you better not leave him, you better not try to leave and get caught. They'd keep you in debt. They were sharp. Christmas come, you could take up twenty dollar, in somethin' to eat and much as you wanted in whiskey. You could buy a gallon of whiskey. Anything that kept you a slave because he was always right and you were always wrong it there was difference. If there was an argument, he would get mad and there would be a shooting take place.

Slave croppers and their families were evicted from the plantation they were working after being convicted of engaging in a conspiracy to retain their homes. This picture was taken just after the evictions before the families were moved into a tent colony.

PART IV

SEARCHING FOR SAFE SPACES

WC Handy

	1860–1900	1900–1910

RELIGION

1880s -1890s Holiness Movement and Pentecostal churches spread among African Americans

1886 Augustus Tolten ordained first African-American Roman Catholic priest in Rome

1890 Baptist churches count 1,300,000 southern black members, making them the largest African-American denomination

CULTURE

1887 Black players banned from major league baseball

1890s -1920s Emergence of jazz and the Blues among southern blacks

1899 Scott Jopin writes the "Maple Leaf Rag"

1900 James W. Johnson writes "Lift Every Voice and Sing"

1901 Booker T. Washington publishes *Up From Slavery*

1903 W.E.B. DuBois publishes *The Souls of Black Folk*

1905 *The Defender* begins publication in Chicago

1908 Jack Johnson wins heavyweight championship in boxing

POLITICS & GOVERNMENT

1869–1889 Four black regiments stationed on the Western frontier

1881 First Jim Crow law segregates trains in Tennessee

1882 South Carolina disenfranchises black voters

1892 Populist Party attracts many black voters

1896 *Plessy v. Ferguson* upholds "separate but equal" doctrine of racial segregation

1898 First black officers command black troops in the Spanish-American War

1899–1901 George H. White serves as the South's last black congressman until 1972

SOCIETY & ECONOMY

1867 Independent Order of St. Luke founded

1868 Hampton Institute founded

1870 Howard University Law School founded

1881 Tuskegee Institute founded

1886 Washington County, Texas, race riot

1887 National Colored Farmers' Alliance formed

1892 155 African Americans lynched in the U.S.

1895 Booker T. Washington addresses the Cotton States Exposition in Atlanta

1896 National Association of Colored Women founded

1903 St. Luke Penny Savings Bank established in Richmond

1904 Boule (Sigma Phi Beta) formed

1905 Niagara Movement begins

1906 Brownsville Affair

Atlanta Riot

1908 Springfield Riot

National Association of Colored Graduate Nurses founded

1909 NAACP established

Nora Neale Hurston

Countee Cullen

Jack Johnson

1910–1920

1920–1940

1920 Baseball's Negro League organized

1922 Claude McKay publishes *Harlem Shadows*

1924 Jessica R. Faucet publishes *There is Confusion*

1925 Countee Cullen publishes *Color*
Alain Locke publishes *The New Negro*

1926 Carter Woodson organizes Negro History Week
Langston Hughes publishes *The Weary Blues*

1927 James W. Johnson publishes *God's Trombones*

1928 Duke Ellington debuts at the Cotton Club
Claude McKay publishes Home to Harlem

1929 Fats Waller's "Ain't Misbehavin" opens on Broadway

1930 James W. Johnson publishes *Black Manhattan*

1933 James W. Johnson publishes his autobiography
Along the Way

1937 Zora Neale Hurston publishes *Their Eyes
Were Watching God*

1920 Nineteenth Amendment grants female suffrage
with support from black women

1927 *Nixon v. Herndon* strikes down the white
primary laws

1914 President Woodrow Wilson defends
racial segregation

1917–1918 Over 1,000 black men serve as officers
in World War I

1910 Urban League founded
Negro Fellowship League founded

1914 Universal Negro Improvement Association founded

1915 Reemergence of the Ku Klux Klan

1917 East St. Louis riot
Houston riot

1919 Chicago riot
Elaine, Arkansas riot
Pan-African Congress meets in Paris
Marcus Garvey founds the Black Star Line

1925 National Bar Association founded
A. Philip Randolph founds the Brotherhood
of Sleeping Car Porters

Lewis Latimer (1848–1928)

George H. White
(1852–1918)

Booker T. Washington
(1856–1915)

Johnson C. Whittaker
(1858–1931)

Ida Wells Barnett
(1862–1931)

Mary Church Terrell
(1863–1954)

C. J. Walker (1867–1919)

Scott Joplin (1868–1917)

W.E.B. Dubois (1868–1963)

William J. Seymour
(1870–1922)

James W. Johnson
(1871–1938)

W.C. Handy (1873–1958)

Carter Woodson
(1875–1950)

Jack Johnson (1878–1946)

Gertrude "Ma" Rainey
(1886–1939)

Marcus Garvey (1887–1940)

A. Philip Randolph
(1889–1979)

Jelly Roll Morton
(1890–1941)

Claude McKay (1890–1948)

Bessie Smith
(1894–1937)

Jean Toomer (1894–1962)

Florence Mills (1895–1927)

Paul Robeson (1898–1976)

Duke Ellington
(1899–1974)

Zora Neale Hurston
(1901–1960)

Langston Hughes
(1902–1967)

Countee Cullen
(c. 1903–1946)

Fats Waller (1904–1943)

14

White Supremacy Triumphant: African Americans in the South in the Late Nineteenth Century

HOW DID MANY BLACK POLITICAL LEADERS
MANAGE TO REMAIN IN OFFICE AFTER
RECONSTRUCTION ENDED IN 1877?

WHAT METHODS WERE USED
TO DISFRANCHISE BLACK VOTERS?

HOW, WHERE, AND WHY DID SEGREGATION
OF THE RACES BEGIN?

WHAT DOES *JIM CROW* MEAN?

WHY DID AFRICAN AMERICANS
BEGIN TO LEAVE THE SOUTH?

◀ **The Moses Speese family** acquired a homestead near
Westerville in Custer County, Nebraska. This 1888
photograph shows the extended family assembled in front of
their sod house. They have installed a windmill to provide
power to pump water from a well. They also possess two
teams of horses. Solomon D. Butcher Collection Nebraska State Historical Society

The supremacy of the white race of the South must be maintained forever, and the domination of the negro race resisted at all points and at all hazards—because the white race is the superior race. This is the declaration of no new truth. It has abided forever in the marrow of our bones, and shall run forever with the blood that feeds Anglo-Saxon hearts.

Henry Grady, editor of the Atlanta *Constitution*, 1887

I remember a crowd of white men who rode up on horseback with rifles on their shoulders. I was with my father when they rode up, and I remember starting to cry. They cursed my father, drew their guns and made him salute, made him take off his hat and bow down to them several times. Then they rode away. I was not yet five years old, but I have never forgotten them.

Benjamin E. Mays on his childhood in Epworth, South Carolina, in 1898

After the Civil War southern whites used terror and mob violence to repress African-American demands for political rights and social equality.

Black people struggled against a rising tide of white supremacy in the late nineteenth century. White southerners—and most white northerners, for that matter—had long been convinced that as a race they were superior to black people intellectually

and culturally. They were certain that black people—because of their inferiority—could play only a subservient role in society. During slavery, white southerners had taken that subservience for granted. With the Civil War and with slavery's end, black people allied themselves with radical Republicans during Reconstruction, and they effectively challenged white supremacy as they became citizens and participated in the political system. The federal government established and enforced—although unevenly—the rights of all citizens to enjoy equal protection of the law and due process of law. But the commitment of the Republicans and the federal government wavered, waned, and then largely collapsed by the mid-1870s.

As memories of the Civil War dimmed and antagonism between white northerners and southerners faded, many northern white people who had expressed at least some sympathy for former slaves and hostility toward southern rebels immediately after the war became less concerned with the South. They were increasingly preoccupied with the frontier West or with opportunities presented by the Industrial Revolution that was so dramatically transforming American society.

Congress, the president, and especially the Supreme Court abandoned the commitment to protect civil and legal rights of African Americans. Political and judicial leaders embraced a laissez-faire approach to social and economic issues. The government would keep its hands off the rapidly expanding railroad, steel, and petroleum industries. Neither would government intervene to safeguard the rights of black citizens. The Supreme Court interpreted the Fourteenth Amendment to protect corporations from government regulation, but it failed to protect the basic rights of black people.

As a result, the conservative white Democrats who had regained political power in the South were no more than mildly fearful that the U.S. government or Republicans would intrude as white authority expanded over virtually every aspect of the lives of southern African Americans in the last quarter of the nineteenth century. Between 1875 and 1900, black people in the South were gradually excluded from politics. They were segregated in public life and denied equal, even basic, rights. They were forced to behave in a demeaning and deferential manner to white people. Most of them were limited to doing menial agricultural and domestic jobs that left them poor and dependent on white landowners and merchants. They were often raped, lynched, and beaten. The southern system of justice was systematically unjust.

Unwilling and unable to tolerate such conditions, some African Americans left the South for Africa or the American West. However, most black people remained in the South, where many acquired a semblance of education, some managed to purchase land, and a few even prospered.

Politics

In the late nineteenth century, black people remained important in southern politics. Black men served in Congress, state legislatures, and local governments. They received federal patronage appointments to post offices and custom houses. But as southern Democrats steadily disfranchised black voters in the 1880s and 1890s, the number of black politicians declined until the political system was virtually all white by 1900 (see Figure 14–1).

When Reconstruction ended in 1877 and the last Republican state governments collapsed, black men who held major state offices were forced out. In South Carolina, Lieutenant Governor Richard H. Gleaves resigned in 1877, but not without a protest. "I desire to place on record, in the most public and unqualified manner, my sense of the great wrong which thus forces me practically to abandon rights conferred on me, as I fully believe by a majority of my fellow citizens of this State."

15 *A Republican Textbook for Colored Voters*

For a time, some conservative white Democrats accepted limited black participation in politics as long as no black leader had power over white people and black participation did not challenge white domination. South Carolina's governor Wade Hampton even assured black people that he respected their rights and would appoint qualified black men to minor political offices. Hampton condescendingly told black people in 1878, "We propose to protect you and give you all your rights; but while we do this you cannot expect that we should discriminate in your favor, and say because you are a colored man, you have the right to rule the State.

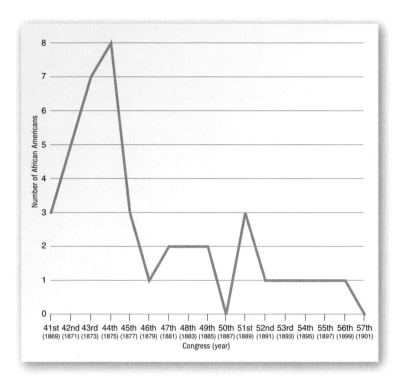

FIGURE 14–1 AFRICAN-AMERICAN REPRESENTATION IN CONGRESS, 1867–1900

Black men served in the U.S. Congress from Joseph Rainey's election in 1870 until George H. White's term concluded in 1901. All were Republicans.

We say to you that we intend to take the best men we can find to represent the State, and you must qualify yourselves to do so before you can expect to be chosen."

Paternalistic Democrats like Hampton did appoint black men to lower-level positions. Hampton, for example, appointed Richard Gleaves and Martin Delany trial justices. In turn, some black men supported the Democrats. A few black Democrats were elected to state legislatures in the 1880s. Some had been Democrats throughout Reconstruction; others had abandoned the Republican Party.

Most black voters, however, remained loyal Republicans even though the party had become a hollow shell of what it had been during Reconstruction. Its few white supporters usually shunned black Republicans. The party rarely fielded candidates for statewide elections, limiting itself to local races in regions where Republicans remained strong.

BLACK CONGRESSMEN

Democrats skillfully created oddly shaped congressional districts to confine much of the black population of a state to one district, such as Mississippi's third district, South Carolina's seventh, Virginia's fourth, and North Carolina's second. A black Republican usually represented these districts while the rest of the state elected white Democrats to Congress. This diluted black voting strength, and it reduced the number of white people represented by a black congressman. Thus Henry Cheatham of North Carolina, John Mercer Langston of Virginia, Thomas E. Miller of South Carolina, and George H. White of North Carolina were elected to the House of Representatives long after Reconstruction had ended (see Table 14–1).

But like their predecessors during Reconstruction, these black men wielded only limited power in Washington. They could not persuade their white colleagues to enact significant legislation to benefit their black constituents. They did, however, get Republican presidents to appoint black men and women to federal positions in their districts—including post offices and custom houses—and they spoke out about the plight of African Americans. North Carolina's George H. White, for example, rebuked white leaders for their readiness to label black people as inferior while denying them the means to prove otherwise. "It is easy . . . to taunt us with our inferiority, at the same time not mentioning the causes of this inferiority. It is rather hard to be accused of shiftlessness and idleness when the accuser . . . closes the avenues for labor and industrial pursuits to us. It is hardly fair to accuse us of ignorance when it was made a crime under the former order of things to learn enough about letters to even read the Word of God."

DEMOCRATS AND FARMER DISCONTENT

Black involvement in politics survived Reconstruction, but it did not survive the nineteenth century. Divisions within the Democratic Party and the rise of a new political party—the Populists—accompanied successful efforts to remove black people entirely from southern politics.

Militant Democrats stridently opposed the more moderate and paternalistic conservatives who took charge after Reconstruction. In the eyes of the militants, these redeemers seemed too willing to tolerate

TABLE 14–1 BLACK MEMBERS OF THE U.S. CONGRESS, 1870–1901

Dates	Name	State	Occupation	Prewar Status
1. 1870–1879	Joseph H. Rainey	South Carolina	Barber	Slave, then free
2. 1870–1873	Jefferson Long	Georgia	Tailor, storekeeper	Slave
3. 1870–1873	Hiram Revels*	Mississippi	Barber, minister, teacher, college president	Free
4. 1871–1877	Josiah T. Walls	Florida	Editor, planter, teacher, lawyer	Slave
5. 1871–1873	Benjamin Turner	Alabama	Businessman, farmer, merchant	Slave
6. 1871–1873	Robert C. DeLarge	South Carolina	Tailor	Free
7. 1871–1875	Robert B. Elliott	South Carolina	Lawyer	Free
8. 1873–1879	Richard H. Cain	South Carolina	AME minister	Free
9. 1873–1875	Alonzo J. Ransier	South Carolina	Shipping clerk, editor	Free
10. 1873–1875	James T. Rapier	Alabama	Planter, editor, lawyer, teacher	Free
11. 1873–1877, 1882–1883	John R. Lynch	Mississippi	Planter, lawyer, photographer	Slave
12. 1875–1881	Blanche K. Bruce*	Mississippi	Planter, teacher, editor	Slave
13. 1875–1877	Jeremiah Haralson	Alabama	Minister	Slave
14. 1875–1877	John A. Hyman	North Carolina	Storekeeper, farmer	Slave
15. 1875–1877	Charles E. Nash	Louisiana	Mason, cigar maker	Free
16. 1875–1887	Robert Smalls	South Carolina	Ship pilot, editor	Slave
17. 1883–1887	James E. O'Hara	North Carolina	Lawyer	Free
18. 1889–1893	Henry P. Cheatham	North Carolina	Lawyer, teacher	Slave
19. 1889–1891	Thomas E. Miller	South Carolina	Lawyer, college president	Free
20. 1889–1891	John M. Langston	Virginia	Lawyer	Free
21. 1893–1897	George W. Murray	South Carolina	Teacher, farmer	Slave
22. 1897–1901	George H. White	North Carolina	Lawyer	Slave

*Revels and Bruce served in the Senate, and the twenty remaining black legislators served in the House of Representatives.

even limited black participation in politics while showing little interest in the needs of white yeoman farmers. Dissatisfied independents, "readjusters," and other disaffected white people resented the domination of the Democratic Party by former planters, wealthy businessmen, and lawyers who often favored limited government and reduced state support for schools, asylums, orphanages, and prisons while encouraging industry and railroads. Nor did the redeemer and paternalistic Democrats always agree among themselves. Some did favor agricultural education, the establishment of boards of health, and even separate colleges for black students. This lack of redeemer unity permitted insurgent Democrats and even Republicans sometimes to exploit economic and racial issues to undermine Democratic solidarity.

Many farmers felt betrayed as the Industrial Revolution transformed American society. They fed and clothed America, but large corporations, banks, and railroads increasingly dominated economic life. Wealth was concentrated in the hands of big industrialists and financiers. Farmers were no longer self-sufficient, admired for their hard work and self-reliance. They now depended on banks for loans, were exploited when they bought and sold goods, and found themselves at the mercy of railroads when they shipped their agricultural commodities. As businessmen got richer, farmers got poorer.

Small independent (yeoman) farmers in the South suffered from a sharp decline in the price of cotton between 1865 and 1890. Overwhelmed by debt, many lost their land and were forced into tenant farming and sharecropping. By 1890 most farmers, both black and white—between 58 percent and 62 percent in each state in the deep South—worked land they did not own.

In response to their economic woes and political weakness, farmers organized. In the 1870s they formed the Patrons of Husbandry, or Grange. Initially a social and fraternal organization, the Grange promoted the formation of cooperatives and involvement in politics. Grangers especially favored government regulation of the rates railroads charged to transport crops. By the early 1880s, many hard-pressed small farmers turned to farmers' alliances. The first of these was the Southern Farmers' Alliance, which formed in Texas. Alliances soon spread throughout the South and northward into the states of the Great Plains and westward to the Pacific coast. These organizations further encouraged farmers to buy and sell products cooperatively and to unite politically. They favored railroad regulation, currency inflation (to increase crop prices and ease debt burdens), and support for agricultural education. By 1888 many of them joined in the National Farmers' Alliance.

THE COLORED FARMERS' ALLIANCE

Although the alliances were radical on economic issues, they were conservative on racial issues and did not challenge the racial status quo. The Southern Alliance did not include black farmers, who instead formed their own **Colored Farmers' Alliance.** It spread from Texas across the South in 1888 and 1889 and claimed over one million members. Even if it did not have that many supporters, the Colored Farmers' Alliance was one of the largest black organizations in American history. When the white alliances met in St. Louis in 1889, so did the black alliance—in a separate convention. The alliances maintained strict racial distinctions but promised to cooperate to resolve their economic woes.

However, black and white alliance members did not always see their economic difficulties from the same perspective. Some of the white farmers owned the land that the black farmers lived on and worked. Black men saw their alliance as a way of getting a political education. In 1891 sixteen black men organized a branch of the Colored Farmers' Alliance in St. Landry Parish in Louisiana. Their purpose was to help their race and their families and to acquire enough information to vote effectively. "This organization is for the purpose of trying to elevate our race, to make us better citizens, better husbands, better fathers and sons, to educate ourselves so that we may be able to vote more intelligently on questions that are of vital importance to our people."

But white people were less certain that they wanted black men to vote at all—intelligently or otherwise. Many white alliance members harbored serious doubts about the right of black men to vote, and they opposed electing black men to office. Paradoxically, they also encouraged black men to vote as long as the black voters supported candidates the alliances backed. By the late 1880s, alliance-backed candidates in the South were elected to state legislatures, to Congress, and to four governorships.

THE POPULIST PARTY

By 1892 many alliance farmers threw their political support to a new political party—the People's Party, generally known as the **Populist Party**—that mounted a serious challenge to the Democrats and Republicans. Convinced that neither of the traditional parties cared about the plight of American farmers and industrial workers, the Populists hoped to wrestle political control of the nation's economy from bankers and industrialists and their allies in the Republican and Democratic parties and to let the "people" shape the country's economic destiny. The Populists favored no less than the federal government takeover of railroads, telegraph, and telephone companies. The new party wanted the government to operate a loan and marketing program known as a subtreasury system to benefit farmers. The Populists ran candidates for local and state offices and for Congress. In 1892 they nominated James B. Weaver of Iowa for president. The Populists urged southern white men to abandon the Democratic Party and southern black men to reject the Republican Party and to unite politically to support the Populists.

The foremost proponent of black and white political unity was Thomas Watson of Georgia. He and other Populist leaders believed economic and political cooperation could transcend racial differences. During the 1892 campaign, Watson explained that black and white farmers faced the same economic exploitation, but that they failed to cooperate with each other because of race. "The white tenant," he said,

> lives adjoining the colored tenant. Their homes are almost equally destitute of comforts. Their living is confined to bare necessities. They are equally burdened with heavy taxes. They pay the same high rent for gullied and impoverished land. . . .
>
> Now the Peoples' Party says to these two men, You are kept apart that you may be separately fleeced of your earnings. You are made to hate each other because upon that hatred is rested the keystone of the arch of financial despotism which enslaves you both. You are deceived and blinded that you may not see how this race antagonism perpetuates a monetary system which beggars both.

Despite such remarks, Watson was not calling for improved race relations. He opposed economic exploitation that was disguised by race, but when Democrats accused him of promoting racial reconciliation, he denied it and bluntly supported segregation to a black audience:

> They say I am an advocate of social equality between the whites and the blacks. THAT IS AN ABSOLUTE FALSEHOOD, and the man who utter[s] it knows it, I have done no such thing, and you colored men know it as well as the men who formulated the slander. It is best for your race and my race that we dwell apart in our private affairs. It is best for you to go to your churches, and I will go to mine; it is best that you send your children to the colored school, and I'll send my children to mine; you invite your colored friends to your home, and I'll invite my friends to mine.

Years after the failure of the Populists, Watson became a racial demagogue who warmly and thoroughly

supported white supremacy. But in 1892 Watson and the Populists desperately wanted black and white voters to support Populist candidates. The Populists lost the national election that year and again in 1896, although they did win several congressional and governor's races. Southern Democrats, furious and outraged at the Populist appeal for black votes, resorted again to fraud, violence, and terror to prevail. When a biracial coalition of black and white Populists succeeded in taking political control of Grimes County in east Texas, Democrats massacred first the black and then the white leaders in 1900.

Nor is it a coincidence that in the elections of 1892, when the Democrats carried every southern state, there was an explosion of violence. Democrats were determined to destroy the Populist challenge. That year 235 people were lynched in the United States, more than in any other year in U.S. history.

The Populist challenge heightened the fears of southern Democrats that black voters could tip the balance of elections if the white vote split. But many black people were suspicious of the Populist appeals and remained loyal to the Republican Party. The Republican Party in the South, however, was a much weaker organization than it had been during Reconstruction because many of its supporters could no longer vote. Years before the alliances and the Populists emerged, southern Democrats had begun to eliminate the black vote.

Disfranchisement

As early as the late 1870s, southern Democrats had found ways to undermine black political power. Violence and intimidation, so effective during Reconstruction, continued in the 1880s and 1890s. Frightened, discouraged, or apathetic, many black men stopped voting. Black sharecroppers and renters could sometimes be intimidated or bribed by their white landlords not to vote, or to vote for candidates the landlord favored.

There was also simple injustice. In 1890 black congressman Thomas E. Miller ran for reelection and won—or so he thought. But he was charged with using illegal ballots and declared the loser. He appealed to the South Carolina Supreme Court, which ruled that although his ballots were printed on the required white paper, it was "white paper of a distinctly yellow tinge." He did not return to Congress.

EVADING THE FIFTEENTH AMENDMENT

More militant and determined Democrats in the South were not content to rely on an assortment of unreliable methods to curtail the black vote. Some "legal" means had to be found to prevent black men from voting. However, the Fifteenth Amendment to the Constitution was a serious obstacle to this goal. It explicitly stated that the right to vote could not be denied on "account of race, color, or previous condition of servitude."

White leaders worried that if they imposed what were then legally acceptable barriers to voting—literacy tests, poll taxes, and property qualifications—they would disfranchise many white as well as black voters. But resourceful Democrats committed to white supremacy found ways around this problem. In 1882, for example, South Carolina passed the Eight Box Law, a primitive literacy test that required voters to deposit separate ballots for separate election races in the proper ballot box. Illiterate voters could not identify the boxes unless white election officials assisted them.

MISSISSIPPI

Mississippi made the most concerted and successful effort to eliminate black voters without openly violating the Fifteenth Amendment. Black men had continued to vote in Mississippi despite hostility and intimidation. In 1889 black leaders from forty Mississippi counties protested the "violent and criminal suppression of the black vote." In response white men called a constitutional convention to do away with the black vote.

With a single black delegate and 134 white delegates, the convention adopted complex voting requirements that—without mentioning race— disfranchised black voters. Voting required proof of residency and payment of all taxes, including a two-dollar poll tax. A person who had been convicted of arson, bigamy, or petty theft—crimes the delegates associated with black people—could not vote. People convicted of so-called white crimes—murder, rape, and grand larceny—could vote.

Above all, the new Mississippi Constitution required voters to be literate, but with a notable exception. Illiterate men could still qualify to vote by demonstrating that they understood the Constitution if the document was read to them. It was taken for granted that white voting registrars would accept almost all white applicants and fail most black applicants seeking to register under this provision.

SOUTH CAROLINA

Black voting had been declining in South Carolina since the end of Reconstruction. In the 1876 election, 91,870 black men voted; in the 1888 election, only 13,740 did. Unhappy that even so few voters might decide an election, U.S. senator Benjamin R. Tillman

A rural black man "freely" exercises his right to vote. Notice the bottle of whiskey next to the ballot box.   Library of Congress

won approval for a constitutional convention in 1895. The convention followed Mississippi's lead and created an "understanding clause," but not without a vigorous protest from black leaders.

Six black men and 154 white men were elected to the South Carolina convention. Two of the black men—Robert Smalls and William Whipper (see Chapter 13)—had been delegates to the 1868 constitutional convention. The six black men protested black disfranchisement. Thomas E. Miller explained that it was not just a matter of black power, but that the basic rights of citizens were at stake. "The Negroes do not want to dominate. They do not and would not have social equality, but they do want to cast a ballot for the men who make their laws and administer the laws. I stand here pleading for justice to a people whose rights are about to be taken away with one fell swoop."

It was all for naught. Black voters were disfranchised in South Carolina. White delegates did not even pretend that elections should be fair. William Henderson of Berkeley County admitted

> We don't propose to have fair elections. We will get left at that every time. . . . I tell you, gentlemen, if we have fair elections in Berkeley we can't carry it. There's no use to talk about it. The black man is learning to read faster than the white man. And if he comes up and can read you have got to let him vote. Now are you going to throw it out. . . . We are perfectly disgusted with hearing so much about fair elections. Talk all around, but make it fair and you'll see what'll happen.

The Spread of Disfranchisement

	State	Strategies
1889	Florida	Poll tax
	Tennessee	Poll tax
1890	Mississippi	Poll tax, literacy test, understanding clause
1891	Arkansas	Poll tax
1893, 1901	Alabama	Poll tax, literacy test, grandfather clause
1894, 1895	South Carolina	Poll tax, literacy test, understanding clause
1894, 1902	Virginia	Poll tax, literacy test, understanding clause
1897, 1898	Louisiana	Poll tax, literacy test, grandfather clause
1899, 1900	North Carolina	Poll tax, literacy test, grandfather clause
1902	Texas	Poll tax
1908	Georgia	Poll tax, literacy test, understanding clause, grandfather clause

1889–1908

Source: Goldfield et al., *The American Journey* (Upper Saddle River, NJ: Prentice Hall, 2004), p. 550.

THE GRANDFATHER CLAUSE

In 1898 Louisiana added a new twist to **disfranchisement.** Its **grandfather clause** stipulated that only men who had been eligible to vote before 1867—or whose father or grandfather had been eligible before that year—would be qualified to vote. Because virtually no black men had been eligible to vote before 1867—most had just emerged from slavery—the law immediately disfranchised almost all black voters. In Louisiana in 1896, 130,000 black men voted; in 1904, 1,342 voted.

Except for Kentucky and West Virginia, each southern state had enacted elaborate restrictions on voting by the 1890s. As a result, few black men continued to vote, and no black men were elected to office.

The "Force Bill"

Republicans in Congress in the meantime had made a futile and final attempt to protect black voting rights. In 1890 Massachusetts representative Henry Cabot Lodge introduced a bill to require federal supervision of elections in congressional districts where fraud and intimidation were alleged. White southerners were enraged at the prospect of federal interference in elections, and they labeled the legislation the "Force bill" because they believed—incorrectly—that it would force black rule over white people.

This **Federal Elections Bill** easily passed in the House of Representatives, but it failed in the Senate after a thirty-three-day Democratic filibuster. That ended the last significant attempt to protect black voting rights in the South until the passage of the Voting Rights Act in 1965.

Segregation

When black attorney T. McCants Stewart visited Columbia, South Carolina, in 1885, he told readers of the New York *Age* that he had been pleasantly received and had encountered little discrimination. "I can ride in first class cars on the railroads and in the streets. I can go into saloons and get refreshments even as in New York. I can stop in and drink a glass of soda and be more politely waited upon than in some parts of New England." Stewart's visit occurred before most segregation laws requiring separation of the races in public places had been enacted. In fact, the word *segregation* was almost never used before the twentieth century.

Not that black and white people mingled freely in the 1880s and the 1890s. They did not. Since Reconstruction, schools, hospitals, asylums, and cemeteries had been segregated. Many restaurants and hotels did not admit black people, and many black people did not venture where they felt unwelcome or where they were likely to meet hostility. But what came to be known as "Jim Crow" had not yet become legally embedded in the southern way of life.

The Black Laws **16** LIVING WORDS

JIM CROW

The term *Jim Crow* originated with a minstrel show routine called "Jump Jim Crow" that a white performer, Thomas "Daddy" Rice, created in the 1830s and 1840s. Rice blackened his face with charcoal and ridiculed black people. How Rice's character came to be synonymous with segregation and discrimination is not clear. What is clear is that by the end of the nineteenth century, Jim Crow and segregation were rapidly expanding in the South, greatly restricting the lives of African Americans.

In the decades following slavery's demise, segregation evolved gradually as an arrangement to enforce white control and domination. Many white southerners resented the presence of black people in public facilities, places of entertainment, and business establishments. If black people were—as white southerners believed—a subordinate race, then their proximity in shops, parks, and on passenger trains suggested an unacceptable equality in public life.

Moreover, many black people acquiesced in some facets of racial separation. During Reconstruction, people of color formed their own churches and social organizations. Black people were invariably more comfortable around people of their own race than they were among white people. Furthermore, black southerners often accepted separate seating in theaters, concert halls, and other facilities that previously had been closed to them. Segregation represented an improvement over exclusion.

SEGREGATION ON THE RAILROADS

Many white people particularly objected to the presence of black people in the first-class coaches of trains. Before segregation laws, white passengers and railroad conductors sometimes forced black people who had purchased first-class tickets into second-class coaches. In 1889 black Baptists from Savannah bought first-class tickets to travel to a convention in Indianapolis. News was telegraphed ahead, and they were confronted by a white mob at a railroad stop in Georgia where they were threatened and beaten. A white man shoved a pistol into the breast of a black woman who had screamed in fear. He demanded, "You G-d d-d heffer, if you don't hush your mouth and get out of here, I will blow your G-d d-d brains out."

In another instance, a young black woman, Mary Church (later Mary Church Terrell), was traveling alone in a first-class coach when the conductor attempted to move her to the second-class car. She managed to remain but only after informing the conductor that she would send a telegram to her father telling him "you are forcing me to ride all night in a Jim Crow car. He will sue the railroad for compelling his daughter who has a first-class ticket to ride in a second-class car."

The first segregation laws involved passenger trains. Despite the spirited opposition of black politicians, the Tennessee legislature mandated segregation on railroad coaches in 1881. Florida passed a similar law in 1887. The railroads opposed these laws, but not because they wanted to protect the civil rights of black people. Rather, they were concerned about the expense of maintaining separate cars or sections within cars for black and white people. Whether they could pay for a first-class ticket or not, most black passengers found themselves confined to grimy second-class cars

To enforce segregation on a railroad coach, a rather shabbily attired conductor evicts a well-dressed black man from a first-class coach so that he will not pose a danger to a white woman and her child.   Corbis/Bettmann

crowded with smoking and tobacco-chewing black and white men. Hitched at the head of the train just behind the smoke-belching locomotive, these cars were filthy with soot and cinders.

PLESSY V. FERGUSON

In 1891 the Louisiana legislature required segregated trains within the state, despite opposition from a black organization, the American Citizens' Equal Rights Association of Louisiana, the state's eighteen black legislators, and the railroads.

In a test case, black people challenged the Louisiana law and hoped to demonstrate its absurdity by enlisting the support of a black man who was almost indistinguishable from a white person. In 1892 Homer A. Plessy bought a first-class ticket and attempted to ride on the coach designated for white people. Plessy, who was only one-eighth black, was arrested for violating the new segregation law.

The case—*Plessy v. Ferguson*—wound its way through the judicial system. Plessy's lawyers argued that segregation deprived their client of equal protection of the law guaranteed by the Fourteenth Amendment. But

MAJORITY AND DISSENTING OPINIONS ON *PLESSY V. FERGUSON*

The Supreme Court's 8-to-1 decision in Plessy v. Ferguson *sanctioned legal segregation and opened the way for a host of segregation laws throughout the South. The majority opinion ruled that segregation was constitutional so long as both races were provided equal facilities. In practice, of course, the facilities for African Americans were invariably inferior to those for white people.*

From Justice Henry Brown of Michigan's majority opinion:

The object of the [Fourteenth] amendment was undoubtedly to enforce the absolute equality of the two races before the law, but in the nature of things it could not have been intended to abolish distinctions based upon color, or to enforce social, as distinguished from political, equality, or a commingling of the two races upon terms unsatisfactory to either.

We consider the underlying fallacy of the plaintiff's argument to consist in the assumption that the enforced separation of the two races stamps the colored race with a badge of inferiority. If this be so, it is not by the reason of anything found in the act, but solely because the colored race chooses to put that construction upon it. . . . If the two races are to meet on terms of social equality, it must be the result of natural affinities, a mutual appreciation of each other's merits and a voluntary consent of individuals. . . . Legislation is powerless to eradicate racial instincts or to abolish distinctions based upon physical differences. . . . If one race be inferior to the other socially, the Constitution of the United States cannot put them upon the same plane.

From Justice John Marshall Harlan of Kentucky, the lone dissent:

In my opinion, the judgement this day rendered will, in time, prove to be quite as pernicious as the decision made by this tribunal in the Dred Scott Case. . . . But it seems that we have yet, in some of the states, a dominant race, a superior class of citizens, which assumes to regulate the enjoyment of civil rights, common to all citizens, upon the basis of race. The present decision, it may well be apprehended, will not only stimulate aggressions, more or less brutal and irritating, upon the admitted rights of colored citizens, but it will encourage the belief that it is possible, by means of state enactments, to defeat the beneficent purposes which the people of the United States had in view when they adopted the recent amendments of the Constitution, by one which

in 1896 the U.S. Supreme Court in an 8-to-1 decision upheld Louisiana's segregation statute. Speaking for the majority, Justice Henry Brown ruled that the law, merely because it required separation of the races, did not deny Plessy his rights, nor did it imply he was inferior. The lone dissenter from this "separate but equal" doctrine, Justice John Marshall Harlan, whose father had owned slaves, likened the majority opinion to the *Dred Scott* decision thirty-nine years earlier. Thus with the complicity of the Supreme Court, the Fourteenth Amendment was emasculated. It no longer afforded black Americans equal treatment under the law. After the *Plessy* decision, southern states and cities passed hundreds of laws that created an American apartheid—an elaborate system of racial separation.

From Plessy v. Ferguson **14-7** DOCUMENT

STREETCAR SEGREGATION

In the late nineteenth century, before the automobile, the electric streetcar was the primary form of public transportation in American cities and towns. Beginning with Georgia in 1891, states and cities across the South segregated these vehicles. In some communi-

the blacks of this country were made citizens of the United States and of the states in which they respectively reside and whose privileges and immunities, as citizens, the states are forbidden to abridge. . . . What can more certainly arouse race hate, what more certainly create and perpetuate a feeling of distrust between these races, than state enactments which in fact proceed on the ground that the colored citizens are so inferior and degraded that they cannot be allowed to sit in public coaches occupied by white citizens? . . . But in view of the Constitution, in the eyes of the law, there is in this country no superior, dominant, ruling class of citizens. There is no caste here. Our Constitution is color-blind, and neither knows nor tolerates classes among citizens. In respect of civil rights, all citizens are equal before the law.

🌿 *What does Justice Brown mean when he distinguishes between political and social equality? How does his position compare to that of Congressmen Rapier and Elliott when they argued for civil rights in 1874?* *(see p. 336)*

🌿 *With what arguments does Justice Harlan counter the majority opinion?*

Source: 163 U.S. 537 United States Reports: *Cases Adjudged in the Supreme Court* (New York: Banks and Brothers, 1896).

ties, the streetcar companies had to operate separate cars for black and white passengers; in other towns they designated separate sections within individual cars. The companies often resisted segregation, citing the expense of duplicating equipment and hiring more employees.

But black people were even more bitterly opposed to Jim Crow streetcars. During Reconstruction, they had fended off streetcar discrimination with boycotts and sit-ins. Thirty years later, they tried the same techniques. There were streetcar boycotts in at least twenty-five southern cities between 1891 and 1910. Black people refused to ride segregated cars in Atlanta, Augusta, Jacksonville, Montgomery, Mobile, Little Rock, and Columbia. They walked or took horse-drawn hacks. Initially, the boycotts succeeded in Atlanta and Augusta, where segregation was briefly abandoned. The boycotts seriously hurt the streetcar companies.

Black people also attempted to form alternative transportation companies in Portsmouth and Norfolk, Virginia, and in Chattanooga and Nashville, Tennessee. In 1905 the black community in Nashville organized a black-owned bus company and committed $25,000 to it. They purchased five buses, but they could not raise enough capital to keep the company going, and it failed after a few months.

SEGREGATION PROLIFERATES

Jim Crow proceeded inexorably. "White" and "colored" signs appeared in railroad stations, theaters, auditoriums, and restrooms and over drinking fountains. Southern white people were willing to go to any length to keep black and white people apart. Courtrooms maintained separate Bibles for black and white witnesses "to swear to tell the truth." By 1915 Oklahoma mandated white and colored public telephone booths. New Orleans attempted to segregate customers of black and white prostitutes, but only achieved mixed results.

Although *Plessy v. Ferguson* required "separate but equal" facilities for black and white people, when facilities were made available to black people, they were inferior to those afforded white people. Often, no facilities at all were provided for people of color. They were simply excluded. Few hotels, restaurants, libraries, bowling alleys, public parks, amusement parks, swimming pools, golf courses, or tennis courts would admit black people. The only exceptions would be black people who accompanied or assisted white people. For example, a black woman caring for a white child could visit a "white-only" public park with the child, but she dare not visit it with her own child.

Racial Etiquette

Since slavery, white people had insisted that black people act in an obedient and subservient manner. Such behavior made white dominance clear. After emancipation, white southerners sought to maintain that dominance through a complex pattern of racial etiquette that determined how black and white people dealt with each other in their day-to-day affairs.

Black and white people did not shake hands. Black people did not look directly into the eyes of

The Pullman Company manufactured and operated passenger, sleeping, and dining cars for the nation's railroads. The company employed black men to serve and wait on passengers who were usually white people. Black porters and attendants were expected to be properly deferential as they dealt with passengers.   © Collection of the New York Historical Society white people. They were supposed to stare at the ground when addressing white men and women. Black men removed their hats in the presence of white people. White men did not remove their hats in a black home or in the presence of a black woman. Black people went to the back door, not the front door, of a white house. A black man or boy was never to look at a white woman. A black man in Mississippi observed, "You couldn't smile at a white woman. If you did you'd be hung from a limb." It was a serious offense if a black male touched a white woman, even inadvertently.

White customers were always served first in a store, even if a black customer had been the first to arrive. Black women could not try on clothing in white businesses. White people did not use titles of respect—mister, missus, miss—when addressing black adults. They used first names, or "boy" or "girl," or sometimes even "nigger." Older black people were sometimes called "auntie" or "uncle." But black people were expected to use mister, missus, and miss when addressing white people, including adolescents. "Boss" or "cap'n" might do for a white man.

Violence

In the late nineteenth century, the South was a violent place. Political and mob violence, so prevalent during Reconstruction, continued unabated into the 1880s and 1890s as Democrats often used armed force to drive the dwindling number of black and white Republicans out of politics.

WASHINGTON COUNTY, TEXAS

In 1886 in Washington County in eastern Texas, Democrats were determined to keep the political control that they had won in 1884 only through fraud. Masked Democrats tried to seize ballot boxes in a Republican precinct. But armed black men resisted and, with a shotgun blast, killed one of the white men. Eight black men were arrested. A mob of white men in disguise broke into the jail, kidnapped three of the black men, and lynched them. Three white Republicans fled for their lives, but convinced federal authorities to investigate. The U.S. attorney twice tried to secure convictions for election fraud. The first trial ended in a hung jury, the second in acquittal. The white Democratic sheriff did not investigate the lynching. But the black man charged with firing the shotgun was sentenced to twenty-five years in prison.

THE PHOENIX RIOT

In the tiny South Carolina community of Phoenix in 1898, a white Republican candidate for Congress urged black men to fill out an affidavit if they were not permitted to vote. This produced a confrontation with Democrats. Words were exchanged, shots were fired, and the Republican candidate was wounded. White men then went on a rampage through rural Greenwood County. Black men were killed—how many is unknown. Others, including Benjamin Mays's father, as related in one of the quotes that opens this chapter—had to humiliate themselves by bowing down and saluting white men.

Alex Manly and the 1898 Wilmington "Race Riot" **14-5** DOCUMENT

THE WILMINGTON RIOT

While white men roamed Greenwood County in search of black victims, an even bloodier riot erupted in Wilmington, North Carolina. Black and white men shared power as Republicans and Populists in Wilmington's city government, and white Democrats bitterly resented it. With the encouragement of the *Wilmington News and Observer*, the Democrats were determined to drive the legitimately elected political leaders from power and would not hesitate to use vio-

Black men fought unsuccessfully to defend themselves in the Wilmington, North Carolina, riot in November 1898.   North Carolina Department of Cultural Resources

lence to do so. Alfred Moore Wadell, a former Confederate and U.S. congressman, vowed in a speech to "choke the Cape Fear [River] with carcasses."

In the midst of this tense situation, Alex Manly, the young editor of a local black newspaper, the *Daily Record*, wrote an editorial condemning white men for the sexual exploitation of black women. Manly also suggested that black men had sexual liaisons with rural white women, which infuriated the white community. "Poor white men are careless in the matter of protecting their women, especially on the farms. . . . Tell your men that it is no worse for a black man to be intimate with a white woman than for a white man to be intimate with a colored woman. . . . Don't think ever that your women will remain pure while you are debauching ours."

A white mob that included some of Wilmington's business and professional leaders destroyed the newspaper office. Black and white officials resigned in a vain attempt to prevent further violence. But at least a dozen black men—and perhaps many more—were murdered. Some 1,500 black residents of Wilmington fled. White people then bought up black homes and property at bargain rates. Alfred Moore Wadell was installed as Wilmington's new mayor. Black congressman George H. White, who represented Wilmington and North Carolina's second district, served the remainder of his term and then moved north. He ruefully remarked, "I can no longer live in North Carolina and be a man." White was the last black man to serve in Congress from the South until the election of Andrew Young in Atlanta in 1972.

THE NEW ORLEANS RIOT

Robert Charles was a thirty-four-year-old literate laborer who had migrated to New Orleans from rural Mississippi. Infuriated by lynching, he was tantalized by the prospect of emigration to Liberia promoted by AME Bishop Henry M. Turner. On July 23, 1900, Charles and a friend were harassed by white New Orleans police officers. One of the officers attempted to beat Charles with a nightstick. Failing to subdue the large black man, the officer then drew a gun. Charles pulled out his own gun, and each man wounded the other. Charles fled and for a time evaded authorities. He was tracked down to a rooming house where he had secluded himself with a Winchester rifle with which he proceeded to shoot his tormentors. Eventually, a white mob that numbered as many as twenty thousand gathered. In the meantime, Charles—an expert marksmen—methodically shot twenty-seven white people, killing seven, including four policemen. Finally, burned out of the dwelling, Charles was shot and

his corpse stomped beyond recognition by enraged white people. Four days of rioting ensued in which at least a dozen black people were killed and many more injured.

LYNCHING

Lynching had become common in the South by the 1890s. Between 1889 and 1932, 3,745 people were lynched in the United States (see Figure 14–2). An average of two to three people were lynched every week for thirty years. Most lynchings happened in the South, and black men were usually the victims. Sometimes white people were lynched. In 1891 in New Orleans eleven Italians were lynched for alleged involvement with the Mafia and for the murder of the city's police chief. For black southerners, violence was an ever-present possibility. Rarely did a sheriff or police officer protect a potential victim, and even if one did, that protection was often not enough.

The people who carried out the lynchings were never apprehended, tried, or convicted. Prominent community members frequently encouraged and even participated in lynch mobs. White political leaders, journalists, and clergymen rarely denounced lynching in public. The Atlanta *Constitution* dismissed lynching

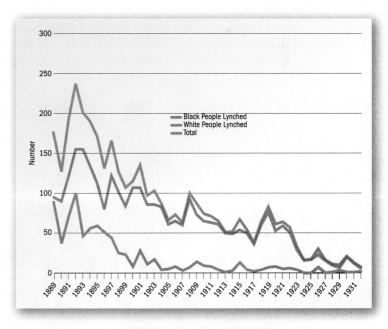

FIGURE 14–2   LYNCHING IN THE UNITED STATES: 1889–1932

Depending on the source, statistics on lynching vary. It was difficult to assemble information on lynching, particularly in the nineteenth century. Not every lynching was recorded.   Source: *The Negro Year Book*, 1931–32, p. 293.

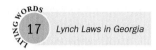

17 *Lynch Laws in Georgia*

as relatively inconsequential. "There are places and occasions when the natural fury of men cannot be restrained by all the laws in Christendom."

There was no such thing as a civilized lynching. Lynchings were barbaric, savage, and hideous. Such mob brutality was another manifestation of white supremacy. Black people were murdered, beaten, burned, and mutilated for trivial reasons—or for no reason. Most white southerners justified lynching as a response to the raping of white women by black men. But many lynchings involved no alleged rape, and even when they did, the victims often had no connection to the alleged offense.

After a white family was murdered in Statesboro, Georgia, in 1904, Paul Reed and Will Cato were convicted of murder and then seized by a mob that invaded the courtroom. They were burned alive in front of a large crowd. Then the violence spread. Albert Roger and his son were lynched "for being Negroes." A black man named McBride attempted to protect his wife who had had a baby three days earlier. He "was beaten, killed, and shot to death."

Mobs often attacked black people who had achieved economic success. In Memphis, Thomas Moss with two friends opened the People's Grocery Company in a black neighborhood. The store flourished, but it competed with a white-owned grocery. "[T]hey were succeeding too well," one of Moss's friends observed. After the white grocer had had the three black men indicted for conspiracy, black people organized a protest and violence followed. The three black men were jailed. A white mob attacked the jail,

Lynchings were common and public events in the South at the turn of the century. Often hundreds of people took part in and witnessed these gruesome spectacles.

lynched them, and then looted their store. Ida B. Wells, a newspaper editor and a friend of Moss, was heartbroken. "A finer, cleaner man than he never walked the streets of Memphis." She considered his lynching an "excuse to get rid of Negroes who were acquiring wealth and property and thus keep the race terrorized and keep the nigger down." Responding to the incident in her paper, Wells began a lifelong crusade against lynching. (See *Profile: Ida Wells Barnett.*)

Although less often than men, black women were also lynched. In 1914 in Wagoner County, Oklahoma, seventeen-year-old Marie Scott was lynched because her brother had killed a white man who had raped her. In Valdosta, Georgia, in 1918 after Mary Turner's husband was lynched, she publicly vowed to bring those responsible to justice. Although she was eight months pregnant, a mob considered her determination a threat. They seized her, tied her ankles together, and hanged her upside down from a tree. A member of the mob slit her abdomen, and her nearly full-term child fell to the ground. The mob stomped the infant to death. They then set her clothes on fire and shot her.

Ida B. Wells, a Red Record **14-3**

RAPE

Although white people often justified lynching as a response to the presumed threat black men posed to the virtue of white women, white men routinely harassed and abused black women. There are no statistics on such abuse, but it surely was more common than lynching. Like lynching, rape inflicted pain and suffering, and it demonstrated the power of white men over black men and women.

Black men tried to keep their wives and daughters away from white men. They refused to permit black women to work as maids and domestics in homes where white men were present. One black man commented in 1912, "I believe nearly all white men take, and expect to take, undue liberties with their colored female servants, not only the fathers, but in many cases the sons also." A black man could not easily protect a black woman. He might be killed trying to do it, as an Alabama clergyman pointed out. "[W]hite men on the highways and in their stores and on the trains will insult our women and we are powerless to resent it as it would only be an invitation for our lives to be taken."

Many white people believed black women "invited" white males to take advantage of them. Black women were considered inferior, immoral, and lascivious. White people reasoned it was impossible to defend the virtue of black women because they had none. Governor Coleman Blease of South Carolina pardoned black and white men found guilty of raping black women. "I

PROFILE ⤙ IDA WELLS BARNETT

Ida Wells Barnett began life as a slave in 1862 and grew up during Reconstruction. As a young woman, she saw the worst indignities and cruelties that the Jim Crow South could inflict, but she fought back as a journalist, agitator, and reformer.

Ida Wells was one of eight children born to Jim and Lizzie Wells in Holly Springs, Mississippi. After the Civil War, she attended a school for freed people with her mother, and they learned to read and write. Her parents and one of her brothers died in the yellow fever epidemic of 1878. Sixteen-year-old Ida became mother and father to her five surviving brothers and sisters. She attended Shaw University in Holly Springs (now Rust College) and taught school in Mississippi and Tennessee.

In 1884, a railroad conductor removed Wells from a first-class car. She sued the railroad and won a $500 settlement. "Dusky Damsel Gets Damages," a Memphis newspaper reported. But a higher court reversed the decision.

Wells then took up journalism and wrote a weekly column for *The Living Way.* In 1889, she bought a one-third interest in the Memphis *Free Speech and Headlight.* She wrote about racial issues and criticized black educators for the quality of black schools. In 1892 her friend Thomas Moss was lynched with two other men for the crime of running a successful grocery store. Wells expressed her rage and horror in a fiery editorial, thus beginning a lifelong crusade against lynching.

Wells blamed the white people of Memphis for her friend's murder and pointed out that more black men were lynched for challenging the myth of white superiority than for allegedly raping a white woman. She angered white people even more by writing that white women could be attracted to black men.

She blamed white clergymen and their parishioners for tolerating lynching. "[O]ur American Christians are too busy saving the souls of white Christians from burning in hell-fire to save the lives of black ones from present burning in fires kindled by white Christians."

Wells moved to Chicago and wrote a pamphlet criticizing the racism at the 1893 World's Fair: *The Reason Why the Colored American Is Not in the Columbian Exposition.* In 1895 she married Ferdinand Barnett, the owner of the Chicago *Conservator.*

After a white journalist from Missouri wrote that black women were immoral, "having no sense of virtue and altogether without character," black women including Wells Barnett founded the National Association of Colored Women in 1896.

In 1909, Wells Barnett was one of two black women who supported the founding of the National Association for the Advancement of Colored People (NAACP), although she later broke with the group because of its mostly white board of directors and what she considered its cautious stands. She also helped organize the Negro Fellowship League in 1910.

Wells Barnett became an ardent supporter of black voting rights. She believed that if enough black men and women could vote, their political power would end lynching. In 1913 she helped found the Alpha Suffrage Club, the first black women's suffrage organization in Illinois, and was a delegate to the National American Woman's Suffrage Association meeting in Washington, D.C.

Ever an agitator, she found Booker T. Washington's philosophy too timid. She was influenced by Marcus Garvey and the Universal Negro Improvement Association in the 1920s, and praised Garvey as a black leader who "made an impression on this country as no Negro before him had ever done."

She continued to write, campaign, speak out, and organize. She was directly involved in protesting the execution of black soldiers after the 1917 Houston riot. She took the lead in exposing the injustice twelve poor black farmers experienced after the Elaine riot and massacre in 1919 (see p. 434). She supported A. Phillip Randolph and the formation of the Brotherhood of Sleeping Car Porters (see p. 458). In 1928 she ran as a Republican for the state Senate. Only death from kidney failure in 1931 ended her efforts to secure justice for black Americans.

Barnett

am of the opinion," he said in 1913, "as I have always been, and have very serious doubts as to whether the crime of rape can be committed upon a negro."

Migration

In 1900 AME minister Henry M. Turner despaired for black people in America. "Every man that has the sense of an animal must see that there is no future in this country for the Negro. [W]e are taken out and burned, shot, hanged, unjointed and murdered in every way. Our civil rights are taken from us by force, our political rights are a farce."

It is therefore not surprising that thousands of African Americans fled poverty, powerlessness, and brutality in the South. What is perhaps surprising is that more did not leave. In the 1910s, 90 percent of black Americans still lived in the southern states. And of those who left the South, most did not head north along the old underground railroad. The Great Migration to the northern industrial states did not begin until about 1915. Emigrants of the 1870s, 1880s, and 1890s were more likely to strike out for Africa or move west to Kansas, Oklahoma, and Arkansas, or move from farms to southern towns or cities.

THE LIBERIAN EXODUS

When white Democrats redeemed Mississippi in 1875 with the "shotgun policy," a group of black people from Winona, Mississippi, wrote to Governor Adelbert Ames "to inquire about the possibility of moving to Africa. [W]e the colored people of Montgomery County are in a bad fix for we have no rights in the county and we want to know of you if there is any way for us to get out of the county and go to some place where we can get homes . . . so will you please let us know if we can go to Africa?"

They did not go to Africa, but some black Georgians and South Carolinians did. In 1877 black leaders in South Carolina, including AME minister and congressman Richard H. Cain, probate judge Harrison N. Bouey, and Martin Delany, urged black people to migrate to Liberia. Many black communities and churches caught "Liberia Fever" while black people in upper South Carolina still felt the trauma of the political terror that had ended Reconstruction.

A white journalist described the situation in Chester County: "At some places in this county the desire to shake off the dust of their feet against this Democratic State is so great, that they are talking of selling out their crops and their personal effects, save what they would need in their new home." They were

Milking a goat in Liberia.   Library of Congress

given promising although sometimes inaccurate information about Liberia: one potato in Liberia, they were told, could feed an entire family.

Several black men organized the Liberian Exodus Joint Stock Steamship Company. They raised $6,000 and hired a ship, the *Azor,* for the trip to Africa. The ship left Charleston in April 1878 with 206 migrants aboard and 175 left behind because there was not enough room for them. With inadequate food and fresh water and no competent medical care, twenty-three migrants died at sea. The ship arrived in Liberia on June 3.

Once settled in Liberia, several of the migrants prospered. Sam Hill established a seven-hundred-acre coffee plantation, and C. L. Parsons became the chief justice of the Liberian Supreme Court. But others did less well, and some returned to the United States. The Liberian Exodus Company experienced financial difficulties and could not pay for further voyages.

In a paradoxical twist in 1890, South Carolina Democrat Matthew C. Butler introduced an emigration bill in the U.S. Senate to appropriate $5 million per year to transport African Americans who volunteered to migrate to Africa. Butler was a former Confederate general who had helped redeem South Carolina. Most African Americans—including Frederick Douglass and Robert Smalls—opposed the legislation, but some, including AME minister Henry McNeil Turner, supported it. Butler's bill never passed. (See the *Profile* feature on Turner in Chapter 15.)

THE EXODUSTERS

In May 1879 black delegates from fourteen states met in a convention in Nashville presided over by Congressman John R. Lynch of Mississippi. The convention resolved to support migration. The delegates declared that "the colored people should emigrate to those States and Territories where they can enjoy all the rights which are guaranteed by the laws and Constitution of the United States." They also asked Congress—in vain—to appropriate $500,000 for this venture.

Nevertheless, black people headed west. Between 1865 and 1880, 40,000 black people known as **"Exodusters"** moved to Kansas. Several hundred were persuaded to migrate by Benjamin "Pap" Singleton, a charismatic ex-slave and cabinetmaker from Tennessee. Six black men were instrumental in founding the Kansas town of Nicodemus in 1877. Named after an African prince who bought his freedom, Nicodemus thrived for a few years in the 1880s with a hotel, two newspapers, a general store, a drugstore, a school, and three churches. Several of the businesses were white owned. Edwin P. McCabe, a black native of Troy, New York, settled for a time in Nicodemus, and in 1882 Kansas voters elected him state auditor.

By 1890, however, Nicodemus went into a decline from which it never recovered. Three separate railroads were built across Kansas, but each avoided Nicodemus, spelling economic ruin for the community. Edwin McCabe moved to Oklahoma and helped found the black town of Langston. Eventually more black people settled in Oklahoma than in Kansas. By 1900 African Americans possessed 1.5 million acres in Oklahoma worth $11 million. In 1889 Congress had enacted legislation eliminating Indian Territory in Oklahoma, dispossessing the Five Civilized Tribes of their land and dismantling tribal government. More than two dozen black towns, including Boley and Liberty, were founded in Oklahoma. There were nearly fifty black towns in the West by the early twentieth century, including Allensworth, California; Blackdom, New Mexico; and Dearfield, Colorado. Other black migrants settled in rural and isolated portions of Nebraska, the Dakotas, and Colorado, as well as elsewhere on the Great Plains and in the Rocky Mountains (see Map 14–1).

Many black and white people who moved west after the Civil War took advantage of the 1862 Homestead Act that provided 160 acres of federal land free to those who would settle on it and farm it for at least five years. (Alternatively, a settler could buy the land for $1.25 per acre and possess it after six months' residency.) Life on the frontier was often a bleak, dreary, and lonely exis-

With their meager belongings, these African Americans await the arrival of a steamboat in about 1878 to transport them to Kansas or perhaps another western location.

tence where trees were few and rain infrequent. People lived in sod houses and relied on cow (or buffalo) chips for heat and cooking fuel as they struggled to endure.

Railroads encouraged migration by offering reduced fares. Some western farmers and agents were eager to sell land, but some of it was of little value. Some of the white residents of Mississippi and South Carolina, which had large black majorities in their population, were glad to see the black people go. Others were alarmed at the loss of cheap black labor.

Some black leaders opposed migration and urged black people to stay put. In 1879 Frederick Douglass insisted that more opportunities existed for black people in the South than elsewhere. "Not only is the South the best locality for the Negro on the ground of his political powers and possibilities, but it is best for him as a field of labor. He is there, as he is nowhere else, an absolute necessity." Robert Smalls urged black people to come to his home county of Beaufort, South Carolina, "where I hardly think it probable that any prisoner will ever be taken from jail by a mob and lynched."

MIGRATION WITHIN THE SOUTH

Many black people left the poverty and isolation of farms and moved to nearby villages and towns in the South. Others went to larger southern cities including Atlanta, Richmond, and Nashville, where they settled in growing black neighborhoods. Urban areas offered

MAP 14–1   AFRICAN-AMERICAN POPULATION OF WESTERN TERRITORIES AND STATES, 1880–1900

Although most African Americans remained in the South following the Civil War, thousands of black people moved west and settled on farms and ranches. Others migrated to small towns that were populated mostly by former slaves.

more economic opportunities than rural areas. Although black people were usually confined to menial labor—from painting and shining shoes to domestic service—city work paid cash on a fairly regular basis, whereas rural residents received no money until their crops were sold. Towns and cities also afforded more entertainment and religious and educational activities. Black youngsters in towns spent more time in school than rural children, who had to help work the farms.

Black women had a better chance than black men of finding regular work in a town, although it was usually as a domestic or cleaning woman. This economic situation adversely affected the black family. Before the

increase in migration, husband and wife headed 90 percent of black families. But with migration, many black men remained in rural areas where they could get farm work while women went to urban communities. Often these women became single heads of households.

Black Farm Families

Most black people did not leave the South or move to towns. They remained poverty-stricken sharecroppers and renters on impoverished land white people owned. They were poorly educated. They lacked political power. They were always in debt. Many rural black families remained precariously close to involuntary servitude in the decades after Reconstruction.

Many black and white people were little better off than medieval serfs. They lived in drafty, leaky cabins without electricity or running water. Outdoor toilets created health and hygiene problems. Medical care was often unavailable. Diets were dreary and unbalanced—mostly pork and cornbread—and deficient in vitamins and protein.

SHARECROPPERS

Most black farm families (and many white families as well) were sharecroppers. Sharecropping had emerged during Reconstruction as landowners allowed the use of their land for a share of the crop. The landlord also usually provided housing, horses or mules, tools, seed, and fertilizer, as well as food and clothing. Depending on the agreement or contract, the landowner received from one-half to three-quarters of the crop.

Sharecropping lent itself to cheating and exploitation. By law, verbal agreements were considered contracts. In any case, many sharecroppers were illiterate and could not have read written contracts. The landowner informed the sharecropper of the value of the product raised—typically cotton—as well as the value of the goods provided to the sharecropping family. Black farmers who disputed white landowners put themselves in peril. Although many sharecroppers were aware the proprietor's calculations were wrong, they could do nothing about it. Also, cotton brokers and gin owners routinely paid black farmers less than white farmers per pound for cotton. A forlorn ditty circulating among black people in the South in the late nineteenth century captured this inequity:

> A naught's a naught, and a figger's a figger—
> All fer de white man—none fer de nigger!

Black men were forced to accept the white man's word. One Mississippi sharecropper explained, "I have been living in this Delta thirty years, and I know that I have been robbed every year; but there is no use jumping out of the frying pan into the fire. If we ask any questions we are cussed, and if we raise up we are shot, and that ends it."

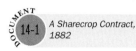 **14-1** *A Sharecrop Contract, 1882*

RENTERS

When they could, black farmers preferred renting to sharecropping. As tenants, they paid a flat charge to rent a given number of acres. Payment would be made in either cash—perhaps $5 per acre—or, more typically, in a specified amount of the crop—two bales of cotton per twenty acres. Tenants usually owned their own animals and tools. As Bessie Jones explained, "You see, a sharecropper don't ever have nothing. Before you know it, the man done took it all. But the renter always have something, and then he go to work when he want to go to work. He ain't got to go to work on the man's time. If he didn't make it, he didn't get it."

CROP LIENS

In addition to the landowner, many sharecroppers and renters were also indebted to a local merchant for food, clothing, tools, and farm supplies. The merchant advanced the merchandise but took out a **lien** on the crop. If the sharecropper or renter failed to repay the merchant, the merchant was legally entitled to all or part of the crop once the landowner had received his payment. Merchants tended to charge high prices and high interest rates. They usually insisted that farmers plant cotton before they would agree to a lien. Cotton could be sold quickly for cash.

PEONAGE

Many farmers fell deeply into debt to landowners and merchants. They were cheated. Bad weather destroyed crops. Crop prices declined. Farmers who were in debt could not leave the land until the debt was paid. If they tried to depart, the sheriff pursued them. This was called **peonage,** and it amounted to enslavement, holding thousands of black people across the South in a state of perpetual bondage. Peonage violated federal law, but the law was rarely enforced. When landowners and merchants were prosecuted for keeping black people in peonage, white juries acquitted them.

BLACK LANDOWNERS

Considering the incredible obstacles against them, black farm families acquired land at an astonishing rate after the Civil War. Many white people refused to sell land to black buyers, preferring to keep them dependent. Black people also found it difficult to save enough money to purchase land even when they could find a willing seller. Still, they steadily managed to accumulate land.

Some black families had kept land that had been distributed in the Carolina and Georgia low country under the Port Royal Experiment and Sherman's Special Field Order #15 (see Chapter 11). In 1880 black people on South Carolina's Sea Islands held ten thousand acres of land worth $300,000.

By 1900 more than 100,000 black families owned their own land in the eight states of the deep South (see Figure 14–3). Black land ownership increased

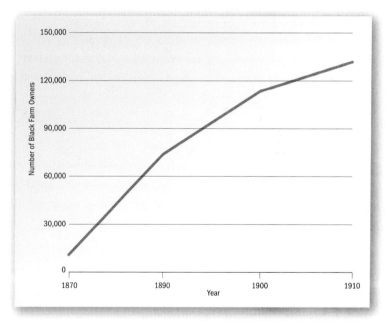

FIGURE 14–3 BLACK FARM OWNERS IN ALABAMA, ARKANSAS, FLORIDA, GEORGIA, LOUISIANA, MISSISSIPPI, SOUTH CAROLINA, AND TEXAS: 1870–1910

It was very difficult for black families to acquire land. Many former slaves had barely enough money to survive, and saving money to buy land was almost impossible. Moreover, many white people would not sell land to black people. Thus it is remarkable that so many black families purchased land in the decades after emancipation. Source: Loren Schweninger, *Black Property Owners in the South, 1790–1915*, p. 164.

CASH AND DEBT FOR THE BLACK COTTON FARMER

Benjamin E. Mays was born in 1895 in Epworth, South Carolina. He was the youngest and eighth child of parents who had been slaves and whose lives revolved around agriculture. Mays went on to South Carolina State College, to Bates College in Maine, and to the University of Chicago. He became the president of Morehouse College in Atlanta where he served as a mentor to Martin Luther King Jr. Mays delivered the eulogy at King's funeral in 1968.

As I recall, Father usually rented forty acres of land for a two-mule farm, or sixty acres if we had three mules. The rent was two bales of cotton weighing 500 pounds each, for every twenty acres rented. So the owner of the land got his two, four, or six bales of cotton out of the first cotton picked and ginned.

To make sixteen bales of cotton on a two-mule farm was considered excellent farming. After four bales were used to pay rent, we would have twelve bales left. The price of cotton fluctuated. If we received ten cents a pound, we would have somewhere between five and six hundred dollars, depending on whether the bales of cotton weighed an average of 450, 475, or 500 pounds. When all of us children were at home we, with our father and mother, were ten. We lived in a four-room house, with no indoor plumbing—no toilet facilities, no running water.

We were never able to clear enough from the crop to carry us from one September to the next. We could usually go on our own from September through February; but every March a lien had to be placed on the crop so that we could get money to buy food and other necessities from March through August, when we would get some relief by selling cotton. Strange as it may seem, neither we nor our neighbors ever raised enough hogs to have meat year round, enough corn and wheat to insure having our daily bread, or cows in sufficient numbers to have enough milk. The curse was cotton. It was difficult to make farmers see that more corn, grain, hogs, and cows meant less cash but more profit in the end. Cotton sold instantly, and that was cash money. Negro farmers wanted to feel the cash—at least for that brief moment as it passed through their hands into the white man's hands!

🌿 *What might have led to greater independence for people like the Mays family?*

🌿 *Why were southern black and white families so large?*

Source: Benjamin E. Mays, *Born to Rebel: An Autobiography* (New York: Charles Scribner, 1971), pp. 5–6.

more than 500 percent between 1870 and 1900. Most black people possessed small farms of about twenty acres. In many cases these small plots of land were subsequently subdivided among sons and grandsons, making it more difficult for their families to prosper. But some black farmers owned impressive estates. Prince Johnson had 360 acres of excellent Mississippi Delta land. Freedman Leon Winter was the richest black man in Tennessee, with real estate worth $70,000 in 1889. Florida farmer J. D. McDuffy had an 800-acre farm near Ocala and raised cantaloupes, watermelons, cabbages, and tomatoes. Texas freedman Daniel Webster Wallace had a 10,000-acre cattle ranch. Few black people inherited large estates. Most of these landowners had been born into slavery. In the decades after emancipation, they managed to accumulate land—usually just a few acres at a time.

WHITE RESENTMENT OF BLACK SUCCESS

Many white southerners found it difficult to tolerate black economic success. They resented black progress and lashed out at those who had achieved it. When one rural black man built an attractive new house, local white people told him not to paint it—lest it look better than theirs. He accepted the advice and left the dwelling bare.

When automobiles arrived in the early twentieth century, Henry Watson, a well-to-do black farmer in Georgia, drove a new car to town. Enraged white people surrounded the car, forced Watson and his daughter out at gunpoint, and burned the vehicle. Watson was told, "From now on, you niggers walk into town, or use that ole mule if you want to stay in this city."

In 1916 Anthony Crawford, the owner of 427 acres of prime cotton land in Abbeville, South Carolina, secretary of the Chapel AME Church, a married man with sixteen children, was arrested and then released after he quarreled with a local white merchant over the price of cotton seed. But a mob, infuriated that Crawford spoke so bluntly to a white man, went after him. "When a nigger gets impudent we stretch him out and paddle him a bit," exclaimed one white man. But Crawford resisted and crushed the skull of a white attacker. The mob then stabbed and beat Crawford before the sheriff rescued him and put him in jail. Several hours later, a second mob broke into the jail and beat him to death. His body was left hanging at the fairgrounds. After his first beating, Crawford had told a friend, "I thought I was a good citizen." The coroner's jury ruled that his death had occurred at the hands of persons unknown.

PROFILE ~ JOHNSON C. WHITTAKER

Shortly after 6 A.M. on April 6, 1880, West Point's lone black cadet, Johnson C. Whittaker, was found lying unconscious on the floor of his room in the barracks. He was splattered with blood. His hands were tied together, and his feet were tied to the bed. In the months that followed, Whittaker's case attracted nationwide attention.

Whittaker was born a slave in 1858 on Mulberry Plantation near Camden, South Carolina, the son of a house slave and a free man. In 1876 white Republican congressman Solomon L. Hoge nominated Whittaker to West Point.

During his first year at the Academy, Whittaker roomed with the only other black cadet, Henry O. Flipper. But Flipper graduated in 1877—the first black man to graduate from the Academy—and Whittaker spent the next four years completely ostracized as the only remaining black cadet. White cadets refused to associate or room with him. Quiet and studious, he established a creditable academic record, but when he failed an exam in 1878, he was required to repeat a year.

When he was found bloody and bound, Whittaker claimed he had been assaulted by three masked men after receiving a warning note the day before. A Court of Inquiry, however, declared that he had mutilated himself. Whittaker then insisted on a court martial to prove his innocence. In February 1881, that court martial convened in New York City.

Whittaker was charged with conduct unbecoming an officer and with lying. After four months of testimony, the court found him guilty. The court determined that Whittaker was "shamming"—making it all up to avoid failing an exam. Major Asa Bird Gardiner told the court: "Negroes are noted for their ability to sham and feign." Gardiner maintained that Whittaker was unfit. "By his own story the accused has shown himself a coward without one redeeming quality. . . . his mental attitude [was] inferior to the average Anglo-Saxon."

The court ordered Whittaker dishonorably discharged, fined one dollar, and sentenced to a year's hard labor. But the controversy did not end. In March 1882, President Chester Arthur overturned the verdict. But on the same day, the secretary of war, Robert Lincoln (Abraham's son), ordered Whittaker discharged from West Point.

Whittaker spent most of the rest of his life working with young black people at South Carolina State College and at Douglass High School in Oklahoma City. He died in South Carolina in 1931 at age 72. Whittaker had two sons. Both were commissioned officers and served in all-black units in World War I.

Whittaker summed up the meaning of his experience at West Point in a speech after the court martial found him guilty.

West Point has tried to take from me honor and good name, but West Point has failed. I have honor and manhood still left me. I have an education which none can take from me. That education has come to me at fearful cost. The government may not wish me to use it in her service, but I shall use it for the good of my fellow men and for the good of those around me. . . . Poverty and sneers can never crush manhood. With God as my guide, duty will be my watchword, I can, I must, I will win a place in life!

In July 1995, President Bill Clinton posthumously awarded Johnson C. Whittaker his commission in the United States Army.

Johnson C. Whittaker was the sole black cadet at West Point in 1880. Ostracized and ▶ shunned by white cadets, he was court-martialed and convicted of conduct unbecoming an officer. Although the conviction was overturned by President Chester Arthur, Whittaker was dismissed from the Military Academy in 1882. Courtesy Cecil Whittaker McFadden

Black and white men serve on a jury together during Reconstruction but they segregate themselves.

African Americans and Southern Courts

The southern criminal justice systems yielded nothing but injustice to black people who ran afoul of it. Southern lawmakers worried incessantly about what they considered the growing black crime problem, and they worked diligently to control the black population. They enacted laws and ordinances to regulate the behavior of black people. Vagrancy laws made it easy to arrest any idle black man or one who was passing through a community. Contract evasion laws ensnared black people who attempted to escape peonage and perpetual servitude.

SEGREGATED JUSTICE

The legal system also became increasingly white after Reconstruction. Black police officers were gradually eliminated, and white policemen acquired a deserved reputation for brutality. Fewer and fewer black men served on juries, which were all white by 1900. (No women served on southern juries.) When black men were accidentally called for jury duty, they were rejected. In Alabama, a black man called for a local grand jury insisted on serving until he was beaten and forced to step down. Judges were white men. Most attorneys were white. The few black lawyers faced daunting hurdles. Some black defendants believed—correctly—that they would be found guilty and sentenced to a longer term if they retained a black attorney rather than a white one. Court personnel treated black plaintiffs, defendants, and witnesses with contempt, referring to them as "niggers," "boy," and "gal." Black people were rarely "mister" or "missus" in court proceedings.

A black defendant could not get justice. Black men and women were more often charged with crimes than white people. They were almost always convicted, regardless of the strength of the evidence or the credibility of witnesses. In one of the few instances when a black man was found not guilty of killing a white man, the defendant's attorney advised him to leave town because local white people were unlikely to accept the verdict. He fled, but returned twenty years later and was castrated by two white men.

Race was always the priority with jurors. Even when black people were the victims of crime, they were punished. In 1897 in Hinds County, Mississippi, a white man beat a black woman with an axe handle. She took him to court only to have the justice of the peace rule that he knew of "no law to punish a white man for beating a negro woman."

Juries rarely found white people guilty of crimes against black people. In a Georgia case in 1911, the evidence against several white people for holding black families in peonage was so overwhelming that the judge virtually ordered the jury to return a guilty verdict. Nonetheless, after five minutes of deliberation, the jury found the defendants not guilty. Many black and white people were astonished in 1898 in Shreveport, Louisiana, when a jury actually found a white man guilty of murdering a black man. He was sentenced to five years in prison.

Black people could receive leniency from the judicial system, but it was not justice. They were much less likely to be charged with a crime against another black person, such as raping a black woman, than against a white person. Black people often were not charged with crimes such as adultery and bigamy because white people considered such offenses typical of black behavior.

Black defendants who had some personal or economic connection to a prominent white person were less likely to be treated or punished the same way as black people who had no such relationship. In Vicksburg, Mississippi, a black woman watched as the black man who had murdered her husband was acquitted because a white man intervened. Those black people known as "a white man's nigger" had a decided advantage in court.

Black people received longer sentences and larger fines than white people. In Georgia, black convicts served much longer sentences than white convicts for the same offense—five times as long for larceny, for example. An eighty-year-old black preacher went to prison "for what a white man was fined five dollars." In New Orleans, a black man was sentenced to ninety days in jail for petty theft. According to a local black newspaper, it was "three days for stealing and eighty-seven days for being colored."

THE CONVICT LEASE SYSTEM

Conditions in southern prisons were indescribably wretched. Black prisoners—many incarcerated for vagrancy, theft, disorderly conduct, and other misdemeanors—spent months and years in oppressive conditions and were subjected to the unrelenting abuse of white authorities. But conditions could and did get worse.

Southern politicians devised the **convict lease system** in the late nineteenth century. Businesses and planters leased convicts from the state to build railroads, clear swamps, cut timber, tend cotton, and work mines. The company or planter had to feed, clothe, and house the prisoners. Of course, the convicts were not paid. The state and local community was not only freed of the burden of maintaining prisons and jails but also received revenue. For example, South Carolina was paid three dollars per month per prisoner. Some states and counties found this so remunerative that law enforcement officials were encouraged to charge even more black men with assorted crimes so they could contribute to this lucrative enterprise.

Leased convicts endured appalling treatment and conditions. They were shackled and beaten. They were overworked and underfed; they slept on vermin-infested straw mattresses and received little or no medical care. They sustained terrible injuries on the job and at the hands of guards; diseases proliferated in the camps. Hundreds died, meaning they had, in effect, been sentenced to death for their petty crimes.

Businessmen and planters found such cheap labor almost irresistible, and black prisoners found it "nine kinds of hell." It was worse than slavery because these black lives had no value to either the government or the businesses involved in this sordid system. As one employer explained in 1883, "But these convicts; we don't own em. One dies, get another." The inhumanity of convict leasing became such a scandal that states outlawed it by the early twentieth century. Convicts were returned to state-operated penitentiaries.

CONCLUSION

With the end of the Civil War and slavery in 1865, more than four million Americans of African descent had looked with hope and anticipation to the future. Four decades later, there were more than nine million African Americans, and more than eight million of them lived in the South. The crushing burden of white supremacy increasingly limited their hopes and aspirations. The U.S. government abandoned black people to white southerners and their state and local governments. The federal government that had assured their rights as citizens during Reconstruction ignored the legal, political, and economic situation that entrapped most black southerners.

AFRICAN-AMERICAN EVENTS	NATIONAL EVENTS
	• 1875 •
	1877 Reconstruction ends
	• 1880 •
1880 Cadet Johnson C. Whittaker is assaulted at West Point	**1880** James Garfield elected President
1881 Tennessee enacts the first law segregating passenger trains	**1880s** Southern Farmers' Alliance forms, beginning Farmers' Alliance movement
Tuskegee Institute founded	**1881** President James Garfield assassinated Clara Barton establishes the Red Cross
	• 1885 •
1886 Riot occurs in Washington County, Texas	**1886** Haymarket affair in Chicago kills seven police officers and four strikers
1887 National Colored Farmers' Alliance is formed	**1887** Congress creates the Interstate Commerce Commission Dawes Act permits individual Indian families to own reservation land
1889–1908 Southern states disfranchise black voters Florida segregates passenger trains	**1889** *Wall Street Journal* established

Although the Thirteenth Amendment abolished slavery, thousands of black people were hopelessly trapped in peonage; thousands of others labored as sharecroppers and renters, indebted to white landowners and merchants. Yet more than 100,000 black families managed to acquire farms of their own by 1900. Many black farmers had also organized and participated in the Colored Farmers' Alliance and the Populist Party, although it brought few tangible benefits.

The Fourteenth Amendment had guaranteed the rights of citizenship that included due process of law. No state could deprive a person of life, liberty, or property without a court proceeding. The amendment also ensured each citizen equal protection of the law. But the Supreme Court had ruled that racial segregation in public places did not infringe on the right to equal protection of the law. And as for the right to life, hundreds of black people had lost their lives at the hands of lynch mobs by the early 1900s.

The Fifteenth Amendment stipulated that race could not be used to deprive a man of the right to vote. Nevertheless, southern states circumvented the amendment with poll taxes, literacy tests, and the grandfather clause. Thus, by 1900, after black men had held political offices across the South for the previous thirty years, no black person served in any elected political position in any southern state.

White people clearly regarded black Americans as an inferior race not entitled to those rights that the Constitution so emphatically set forth. What could black people do about the intolerance, discrimination, violence, and powerlessness they had to endure? What strategies, ideas, and leadership could they use to overcome the burdens they were forced to bear? What realistic chances did they have of overcoming white supremacy? How could black people organize to gain fundamental rights that were guaranteed to them?

RECOMMENDED READING

Edward L. Ayers. *The Promise of the New South: Life after Reconstruction.* New York: Oxford University Press, 1992. An excellent overview of how people lived in the late-nineteenth-century South.

Leon Litwack. *Trouble in Mind: Black Southerners in the Age of Jim Crow.* New York: Alfred A. Knopf, 1998. In moving words and testimony, black people describe what life was like in a white supremacist society.

Rayford Logan. *The Negro in American Life and Thought: The Nadir, 1877–1901.* New York: Dial Press, 1954. Explorations of the contours and oppressiveness of racism.

Benjamin E. Mays. *Born to Rebel: An Autobiography*. New York: Charles Scribner, 1971. Eloquent and graphic recollection of what it was like to grow up black in the rural South at the turn of the century.

C. Vann Woodward. *The Strange Career of Jim Crow*. New York: Oxford University Press, 1955. The evolution of legal segregation in the South.

ADDITIONAL BIBLIOGRAPHY

STATE AND LOCAL STUDIES

Eric Anderson. *Race and Politics in North Carolina, 1872–1901: The Black Second*. Baton Rouge: Louisiana State University Press, 1981.

David Cecelski and Timothy B. Tyson, eds. *Democracy Betrayed: The Wilmington Race Riot and Its Legacy*. Chapel Hill: University of North Carolina Press, 1998.

Helen G. Edmonds. *The Negro and Fusion Politics in North Carolina, 1894–1901*. Chapel Hill: University of North Carolina Press, 1951.

William Ivy Hair. *Carnival of Fury: Robert Charles and the New Orleans Riot of 1900*. Baton Rouge: Louisiana State University Press, 1976.

Neil R. McMillen. *Dark Journey: Black Mississippians in the Age of Jim Crow*. Urbana: University of Illinois Press, 1989.

David M. Oshinsky. *"Worse Than Slavery": Parchman Farm and the Ordeal of Jim Crow Justice*. New York: The Free Press, 1999.

H. Leon Prather. *We Have Taken a City: Wilmington Racial Massacre and Coup of 1898*. Rutherford: Fairleigh Dickinson University Press, 1984.

George B. Tindall. *South Carolina Negroes, 1877–1900*. Columbia: University of South Carolina Press, 1952.

Vernon Wharton. *The Negro in Mississippi, 1865–1890*. Chapel Hill: University of North Carolina Press, 1947.

BIOGRAPHIES AND AUTOBIOGRAPHIES

Albert S. Broussard. *African-American Odyssey: The Stewarts, 1853–1963*. Lawrence: University Press of Kansas, 1998.

Alfreda Duster, ed. *Crusade for Justice: The Autobiography of Ida B. Wells*. Chicago: University of Chicago Press, 1972.

Henry O. Flipper. *The Colored Cadet at West Point*. New York: Arno Press, 1969.

John F. Marszalek Jr. *Court Martial: The Army vs. Johnson Whittaker*. New York: Scribner, 1972.

John F. Marszalek Jr. *A Black Congressman in the Age of Jim Crow: South Carolina's George Washington Murray*. Gainesville: University Press of Florida, 2006.

Linda McMurry. *To Keep the Waters Troubled: The Life of Ida B. Wells*. New York: Oxford University Press, 1998.

Patricia A. Schechter. *Ida B. Wells-Barnett and American Reform, 1882–1930*. Chapel Hill: University of North Carolina Press, 2001.

1890

1891
Georgia segregates streetcars

1892
235 people are lynched in the United States, 155 of them African American, the most in American history

1890
11 Italians lynched in New Orleans

James A. Naismith invents basketball in Springfield, Massachusetts

1892
The Populist Party challenges the Democrats and Republicans in national elections

Homestead strike at the Carnegie steel plant near Pittsburgh

Grover Cleveland elected to a second term as president

1893
Panic of 1893 begins a serious economic depression

1895

1896
In *Plessy v. Ferguson*, the U.S. Supreme Court upholds legal segregation

1898
The Phoenix riot occurs in South Carolina

The Wilmington riot occurs in North Carolina

1899–1901
Term of George H. White of North Carolina ends—the South's last black congressman until 1972

1896
Republican William McKinley is elected president; Populist Party holds last national campaign

1898
Eugene V. Debs helps found what will become the Socialist Party

United States annexes Hawaii

1899
William McKinley reelected president

1900

1900
New Orleans riot

AFRICAN-AMERICAN EVENTS   **NATIONAL EVENTS**

POLITICS AND SEGREGATION

Grace Hale. *Making Whiteness: The Culture of Segregation in the South, 1890–1940*. New York: Pantheon Books, 1998.

J. Morgan Kousser. *The Shaping of Southern Politics: Suffrage Restriction and the Establishment of the One-Party South, 1880–1910*. New Haven, CT: Yale University Press, 1974.

Michael Perman. *Struggle for Mastery: Disfranchisement in the South, 1888–1908*. Chapel Hill: University of North Carolina Press, 2001.

Thomas Adams Upchurch. *Legislating Racism: The Billion Dollar Congress and the Birth of Jim Crow*. Lexington: University of Kentucky Press, 2004.

LYNCHING

James Allen, Hinton Als, John Lewis, and Leon F. Litwack. *Without Sanctuary: Lynching Photography in America*. Santa Fe, NM: Twin Palms Books, 2000.

W. Fitzhugh Brundage. *Lynching in the New South: Georgia and Virginia, 1880–1930*. Urbana: University of Illinois Press, 1993.

W. Fitzhugh Brundage, ed. *Under Sentence of Death: Lynching in the South*. Chapel Hill: University of North Carolina Press, 1997.

Sandra Gunning. *Race, Rape, and Lynching: The Red Record of American Literature, 1890–1912*. New York: Oxford University Press, 1996.

National Association for the Advancement of Colored People. *Thirty Years of Lynching in the United States, 1889–1918*. New York: NAACP, 1919.

Diane Sommerville. *Rape & Race in the Nineteenth Century South*. Chapel Hill: University of North Carolina Press, 2004.

Stewart E. Tolnay and E. M. Beck. *A Festival of Violence: An Analysis of Southern Lynchings, 1882–1930*. Urbana: University of Illinois Press, 1995.

THE WEST

Robert G. Athearn. *In Search of Canaan: Black Migration to Kansas, 1879–80*. Lawrence: Regents Press of Kansas, 1978.

Jacob U. Gordon. *Narratives of African Americans in Kansas, 1870–1992*. Lewiston, NY: Edward Mellon Press, 1993.

Nell Irvin Painter. *Exodusters: Black Migration to Kansas after Reconstruction*. New York: Alfred A. Knopf, 1977.

Quintard Taylor. *In Search of the Racial Frontier: African Americans in the American West, 1528–1990*. New York: Norton, 1998.

MIGRATION, MOBILITY, AND LAND OWNERSHIP

William Cohen. *At Freedom's Edge: Black Mobility and the Southern White Quest for Racial Control, 1861–1915*. Baton Rouge: Louisiana State University Press, 1991.

Pete Daniel. *The Shadow of Slavery: Peonage in the South, 1901–1969*. Urbana: University of Illinois Press, 1972.

Edward Royce. *The Origins of Southern Sharecropping*. Philadelphia: Temple University Press, 1993.

Loren Schweninger. *Black Property Owners in the South, 1790–1915*. Urbana: University of Illinois Press, 1990.

RETRACING THE ODYSSEY

Great Plains Black Museum, Omaha, Nebraska. Contains information and artifacts on black homesteaders and on the role that black women played in migration and settlement on the Plains.

Nicodemus National Historic Site, Nicodemus, Kansas. W. R. Hill was a black real estate agent who founded Nicodemus in 1877. By 1887 over 250 people lived in the town. The absence of a railroad led to a prolonged decline of what had been a small thriving community. Most of the town's original structures have not survived.

Langston, Oklahoma, and Langston University. Langston was one of the many all-black towns established after the Civil War. In 1897 the town set aside forty acres to create a black land-grant university. The town and university are named for John Mercer Langston, a prominent nineteenth-century black leader and congressman from Virginia.

Historic District, Boley, Oklahoma. Boley was an all-black town incorporated in 1905. Many of the town's residents left when the economy collapsed during the Great Depression. Some of the historic black businesses and buildings still stand.

Black American West Museum and Heritage Center, Denver, Colorado. Founded by Paul Stewart, this museum is dedicated to the black pioneers of the frontier West including cowboys, soldiers, barbers, and homesteaders. It has artifacts, photographs, recordings, and other memorabilia of nineteenth- and early-twentieth-century African Americans. It is located in the former home of Dr. Justina Ford, a pioneer and black woman physician who delivered seven thousand babies of virtually every ethnic background.

 REVIEW, RESEARCH, AND INTERACT

REVIEW QUESTIONS

1. How were black people prevented from voting despite the provisions of the Fifteenth Amendment?

2. What legal and ethical arguments did white Americans use to justify segregation?

3. Why did the South experience an epidemic of violence and lynching in the late nineteenth century?

4. Why didn't more black people migrate from the South in this period?

www.researchnavigator.com

Using the tools available in Research Navigator, consider this question:

What forces fueled violence against blacks in the South?

PRIMARY SOURCE DOCUMENTS

DATA EXPLORATION

15

Black Southerners Challenge White Supremacy

1867-1917

WHAT KINDS OF EDUCATIONAL OPPORTUNITIES WERE
AVAILABLE TO AFRICAN AMERICANS
BY THE LATE NINETEENTH CENTURY?

WHY WERE RELIGIOUS BELIEFS AND ACTIVITIES
SO IMPORTANT TO SO MANY AFRICAN AMERICANS?

WHY DID BLACK MEN IN THE U.S. ARMY ENGAGE
IN COMBAT AGAINST NATIVE AMERICANS,
THE SPANISH, AND FILIPINOS?

WHAT KINDS OF BUSINESSES DID BLACK MEN
AND WOMEN OWN AND OPERATE?

WHAT OPPORTUNITIES EXISTED FOR
AFRICAN-AMERICAN MEN AND WOMEN
IN THE LEGAL AND MEDICAL PROFESSIONS?

WHO WERE SOME OF THE PROMINENT
AFRICAN AMERICANS IN MUSIC AND SPORTS
BY THE EARLY TWENTIETH CENTURY?

◄ **Several hundred black African-American cowboys**
participated in the development of the western cattle empire
in the decades after the Civil War. This photo depicts a group
of those cowboys near Bonham, Texas, in 1909.   The Erwin E.
Smith Collection of the Library of Congress on deposit at the Amon Carter Museum.
Fort Worth, Texas

The Anglo-Saxon said to the negro, in most haughty tones: "in this great 'battle for bread,' you must supply the brute force while I will supply the brain." . . . He will contribute the public funds to educate the negro and then exert every possible influence to keep the negro from earning a livelihood by means of that education.

They pay our teachers poorer salaries than they do their own; they give us fewer and inferior school buildings and they make us crawl in the dust before the very eyes of our children in order to secure the slightest concessions. . . .

In school, they are taught to bow down and worship at the shrine of men who died for the sake of liberty, and day by day they grow to disrespect us, their parents[,] who have made no blow for freedom. But it will not always be thus!

Black novelist Sutton E. Griggs in *Imperium in Imperio,* 1899

Young African-American children being taught washing and ironing at a primary school in Hampton, Virginia, in the 1890s.▼

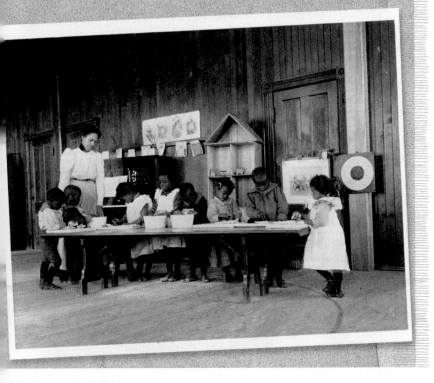

Industrialization and the rise of large, powerful corporations transformed the American economy in the late nineteenth century. As millions of European immigrants crowded into the cities of the North and Midwest to find jobs in the nation's new factories, agriculture production increased and prices declined, impoverishing many rural southerners. Most black people—nearly eight million—remained in the southern states, where they struggled to confront the malignant effects of white supremacy. Living in a society that largely sought to disregard their rights and to exclude them from its institutions and culture, black Americans increasingly relied on their own resources and depended on their own communities to adjust to the forces of white supremacy and to forge a path into the future.

Some African Americans turned to education to elevate themselves and their people, but they disagreed about the most appropriate approach. Some African-American men sought to advance themselves and prove their worth to American society through military service. By the late nineteenth century, however, black Americans mostly relied on each other and the people and institutions in their own communities to sustain themselves. As they had during Reconstruction, they continued to organize and support churches, schools, and colleges. They established businesses and sometimes formed labor unions and went on strike. They founded their own hospitals. They expressed themselves in music by creating ragtime, jazz, and blues. At times they were allowed to participate with white people in organized sports such as professional boxing, baseball, and college football. More often, they formed their own athletic teams. African Americans refused to allow white supremacy to prevent them from creating a meaningful place for themselves in American society.

Social Darwinism

Pseudoscientific evidence and academic scholarship bolstered the conviction of many Americans that white people, especially those of English and Germanic descent—Anglo-Saxons—were culturally and racially superior to nonwhites and even other Europeans. Sociologists Herbert Spencer and William Graham Sumner drew on Charles Darwin's theory of evolution and concluded that life in modern industrial societies mirrored life in the animal kingdom. This theory, called social Darwinism, held that through a process of natural selection, the strong would thrive, prosper, and reproduce while the weak would falter, fail, and die. Life was a struggle; only the fittest survived.

Social Darwinism applied to both individuals and "races." It conveniently justified great disparities in wealth, suggesting that such men as John D. Rockefeller and Andrew Carnegie were rich because they were "fit," whereas many European immigrants and most African Americans were poor and unlikely to succeed because they were "unfit." The same logic explained the strength and prosperity of the United States, Great Britain, and Germany compared to countries such as Spain and Italy and conveniently explained why African, Asian, and Latin American societies seemed so backward and primitive. In absorbing this ideology of class and race, many Americans and Europeans came to believe they had a responsibility—a duty—to introduce the political, economic, and religious benefits and values of Western cultures to the "less advanced" and usually darker peoples of the globe. This presumed responsibility was summed up in the words of the English poet Rudyard Kipling as "the white man's burden."

Social Darwinism increasingly influenced the way most Protestant white Americans perceived their society, leading them to believe people could be ranked from superior to inferior based on their race, nationality, and ethnicity. Black people were invariably ranked at the bottom of this hierarchy, and the eastern and southern European immigrants who were flooding the country only slightly above them. Black people were capable, so the reasoning went, of no more than a subordinate role in a complex and advanced society as it rushed into the twentieth century. And if their position was biologically ordained, why should society devote substantial resources to their education?

Education and Schools

A black youngster who wanted an education in the late nineteenth century faced formidable obstacles. Most black people were poor farmers who had few opportunities for an education and even fewer prospects for a

career in business or one of the professions. It is remarkable—and a testimony to black perseverance—that so many black people did manage to acquire some education and to free themselves from illiteracy (see Figure 15–1).

Gaining even a rudimentary education was not easy. Rural schools for black children rarely operated for more than thirty weeks a year. Because of the demands of fieldwork, most black youngsters could not attend school on a regular basis. Brothers and sisters sometimes alternated work and school with each other on a daily basis. Benjamin Mays was nineteen years old before he went to school for more than four months a year—and even then 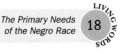 he had to defy his father's demand that he leave school in February to work on the farm.

Schools were often dilapidated shacks. They lacked plumbing, electricity, books, and teaching materials. Some schools were in churches and homes.

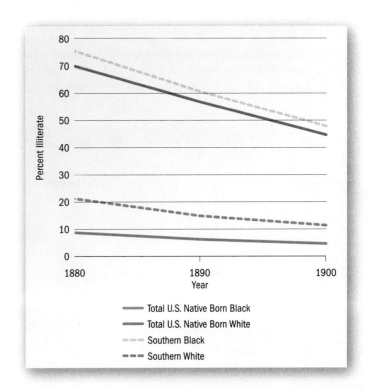

FIGURE 15–1   BLACK AND WHITE ILLITERACY IN THE UNITED STATES AND THE SOUTHERN STATES, 1880–1900

Although more than half of adult black southerners were still illiterate in 1900, black people had made substantial progress in education during the last two decades of the nineteenth century. This progress is especially remarkable considering the difficulties black youngsters and adults faced in acquiring even an elementary education.

Teachers were poorly paid and often poorly prepared. Septima Clark remembered her first teaching experience on Johns Island on the South Carolina coast in the early twentieth century:

> Here I was, a high-school graduate, eighteen years old, principal in a two-teacher school with 132 pupils ranging from beginners to eighth graders, with no teaching experience, a schoolhouse constructed of boards running up and down, with no slats on the cracks, and a fireplace at one end of the room that cooked the pupils immediately in front of it but allowed those in the rear to shiver and freeze on their uncomfortable, hard, back-breaking benches.

SEGREGATED SCHOOLS

Although southern states could not afford to support even one first-rate public school system, each of them operated separate schools for black and white children (see Table 15–1). The South had almost no public black high schools. In 1915 in twenty-three southern cities with populations of more than 20,000, including Tampa, New Orleans, Charleston, and Charlotte, there was not one black public high school. But these twenty-three cities had thirty-six high schools for white youngsters. In 1897 over the vehe-

TABLE 15–1 SOUTH CAROLINA'S BLACK AND WHITE PUBLIC SCHOOLS, 1908–1909

Black Schools		White Schools
2,354	Public Schools	2,712
894	Men Teachers	933
1,802	Women Teachers	3,247
181,095	Total Pupils	153,807
123,481	Average Attendance	107,368
77	Pupils per School	55
63	Pupils per Teacher	35
14.7	Average Number of Weeks of School	25.2
$118.17	Average Yearly Salary for Men Teachers	$479.79
$91.45	Average Yearly Salary for Women Teachers	$249.13
$308,153.16	Total Expenditures	$1,590,732.51

Source: Department of Education Annual Report, South Carolina, 1908–09, pp. 935, 961.

School for most southern black students and teachers was a part-time activity. Because of the demands of agriculture, few rural students, black or white, attended school more than six months a year. Very few teachers were graduates of four-year college programs. The situation was better in urban communities and upper South schools, where the school year lasted longer and education was better financed. But all public schools were segregated in the South.

ment protests of the black community, white school officials in Augusta, Georgia, closed Ware High School, the black secondary school, and transformed it into a black primary school. The U.S. Supreme Court in 1899 in *Cumming v. Richmond County [Georgia] Board of Education* unanimously refused to accept the contention of black parents that the elimination of the black high school violated the "separate but equal" doctrine announced in the *Plessy v. Ferguson* case three years earlier. Augusta was left with two white high schools—one for males and one for females, and none for black people.

Young black people who sought more than a primary education often had to travel to a black college or university that offered a high school program. For example, in 1911, at the age of sixteen, Benjamin Mays boarded a train and traveled one hundred miles to South Carolina State College and enrolled in the seventh grade. He graduated from high school there in 1916 at the age of twenty-two and then graduated from Maine's Bates College four years later.

In many communities, black people, with the assistance of churches and northern philanthropists, operated private academies and high schools, such as Fort Valley High and Industrial School in Georgia and Mather Academy in Camden, South Carolina, to fill the void created by the lack of public schools. Typically students were charged a modest tuition, and those who attended came from the more prosperous families of the black community. In 1890 the number of black youngsters between the ages of fifteen and nineteen attending black public or private high schools in the South was 3,106. By 1910 that number had risen to 26,553.

THE HAMPTON MODEL

Some black people and many white people regarded education for black youngsters as a pointless exercise. Benjamin Mays's father put little value in education: "My greatest opposition to going away to school was my father. When I knew that I had learned everything that I could in the one-room Brickhouse School and realized how little that was, my father felt that this was sufficient—that it was all I needed. . . .He was convinced that education went to one's head and made him a fool and dishonest." In 1911 South Carolina's governor Coleman Blease was even more blunt: "Instead of making an educated negro, you are ruining a good plow hand and making a half-trained fool."

Many of those who did value schooling were convinced the most appropriate education for a black child was industrial or domestic training. Black youngsters, these people maintained, should learn skills they could teach others and use to make themselves productive members of the community.

Hampton Normal and Agricultural Institute was founded in 1868 in Virginia and was dominated for decades by Samuel Chapman Armstrong, a white missionary with strong paternalistic inclinations. Hampton trained legions of African Americans and Native Americans to teach skills and to embrace the importance of hard work, diligence, and Christian morality. Armstrong stressed learning trades, such as shoemaking, carpentry, tailoring, and sewing. Hampton placed little emphasis on critical or independent thinking. Students were taught to conform to middle-class values. Armstrong cautioned against black involvement in politics, and he acquiesced in Jim Crow racial practices. The chapel walls at Hampton featured pictures of Robert E. Lee and Andrew Johnson.

WASHINGTON AND THE TUSKEGEE MODEL

Armstrong's prize student and Hampton's foremost graduate was Booker T. Washington, who became the nation's leading apostle of industrial training and one of the preeminent leaders and most remarkable men—black or white—in American history. Washington was born a slave in western Virginia in 1856. His father was a white man whose identity is unknown. He was raised by his mother, Jane, in an unimpressive, but tidy, cabin of split logs on a small farm. As a child, he was employed at a salt works and in coal mines. He was also a houseboy for a prominent white family. He attended a local school where he learned to read and write.

Intensely ambitious, Washington set off for Hampton Institute in 1872. While there, he was much affected by Armstrong and his curriculum and method of instruction. He worked his way through school and taught for two years at Hampton after graduating. In 1881 he accepted an invitation to found a black college in Alabama—Tuskegee Institute. The result was an institution, which he forged almost single-handedly, that reflected his experience at Hampton and the influence of Armstrong.

From the day he arrived at Tuskegee until his death in 1915, Washington worked tirelessly to persuade black and white people that the surest way for black people to advance was by learning skills and demonstrating a willingness to do manual labor. In a famous speech at the Cotton States Exposition in Atlanta in 1895 (whose impact is discussed in Chapter 16), Washington told his segregated audience, "No race can prosper till it learns that there is as much dignity in tilling a field as in writing a poem. It is at the bottom of life we must begin, and not at the top."

Booker T. Washington was the most influential black leader in America by 1900. White business and political leaders were reassured by his message that black people themselves were responsible for their economic progress and that people of color should avoid a direct challenge to white supremacy. Although W. E. B. Du Bois appreciated Washington's commitment to the advancement of black people, he believed more emphasis should be placed on developing an educated elite who would take the lead in solving the race problem. Washington was a southerner who looked for practical solutions to the problems of everyday life; Du Bois was a northerner who stressed the need for intellectual advancement.

Washington believed that if black people acquired skills and became prosperous small farmers, artisans, and shopkeepers, they would in time earn the respect and acceptance of white Americans and eventually eradicate the race problem—all without unseemly protest and agitation.

The Atlanta Exposition Address **15-1** DOCUMENT

Washington's message earned accolades from white political leaders and philanthropists, who were more inclined to support the promotion of trades and

THOMAS E. MILLER AND THE MISSION OF THE BLACK LAND-GRANT COLLEGE

In 1896 the South Carolina General Assembly established the Colored Normal, Industrial, Agricultural and Mechanical College of South Carolina. It derived funds from the Morrill Acts of 1862 and 1890 and from the state itself. Its first president was former black congressman and lawyer Thomas E. Miller. In an address to the Bamberg County Colored Fair in 1897, Miller embraced the Hampton and Tuskegee models as he described the mission of his institution:

The work of our college is along the industrial line. We are making educated and worthy school teachers, educated and reliable mechanics, educated, reliable and frugal farmers. We teach your sons and daughters how to care for and milk the cows, how to make gilt-edged butter, how to make cheese, what kind of fertilizer each crop needs, the natural strength and productive qualities of the various soils, and last to make a compost heap and how to take care of it. We teach them how to make a wagon, plow and hoe, how to shoe a horse and nurse him when sick. We teach your children how to keep books and typewrite, we teach your girls how to make a dress or undergarment, how to cook, wash and iron. We teach your boys how to make and run an engine, how to make and control electricity, we teach them mechanical and artistic drawing, house and sign painting.

Given the racial climate of the 1890s, why was or wasn't agricultural and mechanical training the most suitable education for most black youngsters?

If a young black person did learn the skills mentioned by Miller, was he or she educated for an inferior place in society?

Source: I. A. Newby, *Black Carolinians, A History of Blacks in South Carolina from 1895 to 1968* (Columbia: University of South Carolina Press, 1973), p. 263.

skills among black people than an academic and liberal education. Steel magnate Andrew Carnegie, impressed by Washington, financed the construction of twenty-nine buildings on the campuses of black schools and colleges. White railroad executive William H. Baldwin provided millions of dollars for black industrial education, and the John F. Slater Fund poured large sums of money into vocational education. Julius Rosenwald, the longtime head of retail giant Sears and Roebuck, consulted closely with Washington, and contributed liberally to black education across the South. Disciples of Washington and graduates of Tuskegee fanned out across the South as industrial and agricultural educational training for black youngsters proliferated.

The Morrill Act, which Congress passed in 1862, entitled each state to the proceeds from the sale of federal land (most of it in the West) for establishing land-grant colleges to provide agricultural and mechanical training. However, southern states did not admit black students to their A&M (Agricultural and Mechanical) schools. A second Morrill Act, however, passed in 1890 and permitted states to establish and fund separate black land-grant colleges. The 1890 act accelerated the development of practical education through the appropriation of federal money to such institutions as Alcorn A&M in Mississippi, Florida A&M, Southern University in Louisiana, Langston in Oklahoma, and Tuskegee Institute. By 1915 there were sixteen black land-grant colleges.

Most of the institutions were not actually colleges. Few of their students graduated with bachelor's degrees, and many of them were enrolled in primary and secondary programs. Virtually all the students at the black land-grant schools had to take courses in trades, agriculture, and domestic sciences. Most of the schools required students to do manual labor for which they were paid small sums. Students built and maintained the campuses, and they raised the food served in the school cafeteria. Many of the students were in the "normal" curriculum, which prepared them to teach at a time when most states did not require a college degree for a teaching certificate. Students enrolled in "normal" schools or programs earned a licentiate of instruction that certified them to teach.

Annual Report of the Tuskegee Normal and Industrial Institute

19

LIVING WORDS

CRITICS OF THE TUSKEGEE MODEL

Not everyone shared Washington's stress on industrial and agricultural training for young black men and women to the near exclusion of the liberal arts, including literature, history, philosophy, and languages. Washington's program, some critics charged, seemed to be designed to train black people for a subordinate role in American society. Black people, they worried, would continue to labor much as they had in slavery, and not far removed from it.

W. E. B. Du Bois, a Fisk- and Harvard-trained scholar, and AME Bishop Henry M. Turner believed education went beyond mere training and the acquisition of skills. It involved intellectual growth and development. It would confront racial problems. It would create wise men. According to Du Bois, "The function of the Negro college, then, is clear, it must maintain standards of popular education, it must seek the social regeneration of the Negro, and it must help in the solution of problems of race contact and cooperation. And finally, beyond all this, it must develop men."

Many of the private black colleges resisted the emphasis on agricultural and mechanical training. American Missionary Association schools such as Fisk, Talladega, and Tougaloo; AME schools such as Allen, Paul Quinn, and Morris Brown; and Methodist institutions such as Claflin, Bennett, and Rust still promoted the liberal arts and taught Latin, Greek, mathematics, and natural sciences. Henry L. Morehouse of the American Baptist Home Missionary Society explained the purpose of education was to develop strong minds. He believed gifted intellectuals—a "talented tenth" as he characterized them in 1896—could lead people forward. Du Bois likewise stressed the need for the best educated 10 percent of the black population to promote progress and to advance the race.

DOCUMENT 15-5 *The Talented Tenth, 1903*

In fairness to Washington, he did not deny the importance of a liberal arts education, but he also believed industry was the foundation to progress:

> On such a foundation as this will grow habits of thrift, a love of work, economy, ownership of property, bank accounts. Out of it in the future will grow practical education, professional education, and positions of public responsibility. Out of it will grow moral and religious strength. Out of it will grow wealth from which alone can come leisure and the opportunity for the enjoyment of literature and the fine arts.

Ultimately, however, Washington was wrong to believe education for black people that focused on economic progress would earn the respect of most white Americans. As Du Bois explained, most white people preferred ignorant and unsuccessful black people to educated and prosperous ones:

> If my own city of Atlanta had offered it to-day the choice between 500 Negro college graduates—forceful, busy, ambitious men of property and self-respect—and 500 black cringing vagrants and criminals, the popular vote in favor of the criminals would be simply overwhelming. Why? Because they want Negro crime? No, not that they fear Negro crime less, but that they fear Negro ambition and success more. They can deal with crime by chain gang and lynch law, or at least they think they can, but the South can conceive neither machinery nor place for the educated, self-reliant, self-assertive black man.

As Chapter 16 discusses, the disagreement among black leaders over the most suitable form of education would expand by the early twentieth century into a larger controversy. What began as a disagreement over the value of practical education would become a passionate debate among Washington, Du Bois, and others over the most effective strategy—accommodation or confrontation—for overcoming Jim Crow and white supremacy.

Church and Religion

In a world in which white people otherwise so thoroughly dominated the lives and limited the possibilities of black people, the church had long been the most important institution—after the family—that African Americans controlled for themselves. After the Civil War, black people organized their own churches and religious denominations, which grew and thrived as sources of spiritual comfort and centers of social activity. Black clergymen were often the most influential members of the black community.

In 1890 the South had more black Baptists than all other denominations combined. Baptist congregations were more independent and under less supervision by church hierarchy than other denominations. Bishops, for example, in the African Methodist Episcopal Zion church and the African Methodist Episcopal (AME) church exercised considerable authority over congregations, as did Methodist and Presbyterian leaders. Many black people (and many southern white people as well) preferred the autonomy of the Baptist churches (Figure 15–2).

But whatever the denomination, the church was integral to the lives of most black people. It fulfilled spiritual needs through sermons and music. It gave black people the opportunity, free from white interference, to plan, organize, and lead. It was especially a sanctuary for black women, who immersed themselves in church activities. Although church members usually had little money to spare, they helped the sick, the bereaved, and people displaced by fires and natural disasters. Black congregations also helped thousands of youngsters attend school and college.

The church service itself was the most important aspect of religious life for most black congregations. Parishioners were expected to participate in the service and not merely listen quietly to the minister's sermon. Black people had long considered white church services too sedate. One black school principal believed black people gave added meaning to Christianity: Whereas "the white man gives it system, logic and abstraction, the Negro is necessary to impart feeling,

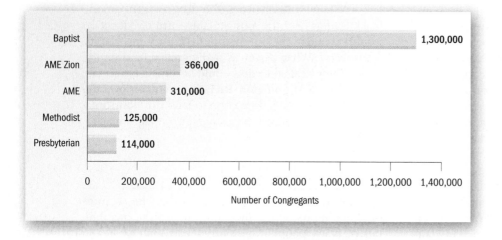

FIGURE 15–2 CHURCH AFFILIATION AMONG SOUTHERN BLACK PEOPLE: 1890

The vast majority of black southerners belonged to Baptist, Methodist, and Presbyterian congregations in the late nineteenth century, although there were about 15,000 black Episcopalians and perhaps 200,000 Roman Catholics. Source: Edward L. Ayers, *The Promise of the New South*, pp. 160–61.

sanctioned emotions, heart throes and ecstasy." In most black churches, members punctuated the minister's call with many an "Amen." They testified, shouted, laughed and cried, and sometimes fainted. Choirs provided joyful music and solemn songs.

Most congregations did not want scholarly sermons or theologically sound addresses. When Frederick Jones, a well-dressed new black minister in North Carolina, offered a deliberate message brimming with rationality, he was met with silence and rebuked by a senior member of the congregation. "Dese fellers comes out heah wid dere starched shirts, and dey' beaver hats, and dere kid gloves, but dey don't know nuffin b[o]ut 'ligion.' The next time Jones preached, he had changed his clothes and delivered a passionate sermon.

Many black ministers had little or no education. Benjamin E. Mays's father told him the clergy did not need an education. "God called men to preach; and when He called them, He would tell them what to say!" Poorly prepared and unqualified clergymen who relied on ungrammatical and rhetorical appeals disturbed some black leaders. In 1890 Booker T. Washington claimed that "three-fourths of the Baptist ministers and two-thirds of the Methodists are unfit, either mentally or morally, or both, to preach the Gospel to any one or to attempt to lead any one." W. E. B. Du Bois wanted black churches free of "the noisy and unclean leaders of the thoughtless mob" and the clergy replaced by thoughtful "apostles of service and sacri-

fice." But a black Alabama farmer observed that solemn and erudite preachers would not survive: "You let a man preach de true Gospel and he won't git many nickels in his pocket; but if he hollers and jumps he gits all the nickels he can hold and chickens besides."

Although infrequently, black women sometimes led congregations. Nannie Helen Burroughs established Women's Day in Baptist churches. Women delivered sermons and guided the parishioners. But Burroughs complained that Women's Day quickly became more an occasion to raise money than to raise women.

THE CHURCH AS SOLACE AND ESCAPE

For many black people, the emotional involvement and enthusiastic participation in church services was an escape from their dreary and oppressive daily lives. Growing up in rural Greenwood County, South Carolina, Benjamin E. Mays admitted that his Baptist preacher, James F. Marshall, who barely had a fifth-grade education, "emphasized the joys of heaven and the damnation of hell" and that the "trials and tribulations of the world would all be over when one got to heaven." But Mays understood the need for such messages to assuage the impact of white supremacy. "Beaten down at every turn by the white man, as they were, Negroes could perhaps not have survived without this kind of religion."

Black clergymen like Marshall refused to challenge white supremacy. Even veiled comments might invite retaliation or even lynching. When a visiting minister began to criticize white people to Marshall's congregation, Marshall immediately stopped him. Despite the reluctance of many black clergymen to advocate improvement in race relations, many white people still viewed black religious gatherings as a threat. Black churches were burned and black ministers assaulted and killed with tragic regularity in the late-nineteenth-century South.

Black clergymen, like their white counterparts, often stressed middle-class values to their congregations while suggesting that many black people found themselves in shameful situations because of their sinful ways. They urged them to improve their behavior. The black clergyman at Mount Ever Rest Colored Church in rural Mississippi warned his congregation to quit their "cussin; lyin; stealin; crap shootin; whisky drinkin; and backbiting one another to de white folks." Black people who had acquired sinful reputations sometimes received funeral sermons that consigned them to eternal damnation in a fiery hell. As Benjamin Mays recalled, "The church was usually full at funerals, especially if the deceased had been well known; and when a man of bad reputation died the church was jammed."

There were black religious leaders who publicly and vigorously opposed white supremacy and insisted that black people stand up for their rights. AME Bishop Henry M. Turner persistently spoke out on racial matters. In 1883 after the U.S. Supreme Court declared the 1875 Civil Rights Act unconstitutional, Turner called the Constitution "a dirty rag, a cheat, a libel and ought to be spit upon by every Negro in the land."

THE HOLINESS MOVEMENT
AND THE PENTECOSTAL CHURCH

Not all black people belonged to mainline denominations. The Holiness movement and the emergence of Pentecostal churches affected Methodist and Baptist congregations. Partly in reaction to the elite domination and stiff authority of white Methodism, the Holiness movement gained a foothold among white people and then spilled over among black southerners. Holiness churches ordained women such as Neely Terry to lead them. Holiness clergy preached that sanctification allowed a Christian to receive a "second blessing" and to feel the "perfect love of Christ." Believers thus achieved an emotional reaffirmation and a new state of grace.

The Church of God in Christ (COGIC) became the leading black Holiness church. After a series of successful revivals in Mississippi and Memphis, two black former Baptists—Charles Harrison Mason and C. P. Jones—founded COGIC in 1907. However, Mason was expelled after reporting that "a flame touched [his] tongue," and his "language changed." He had spoken in tongues. Mason then organized the Pentecostal General Assembly of the Church of God in Christ, and he assigned several black men to serve as bishops in Mississippi, Arkansas, Texas, Missouri, and California. In 1911 Mason appointed Lizzee Woods Roberson to lead the Woman's Department, a post she held until 1945. She transformed that department into a financial powerhouse for COGIC.

In the meantime, Charles Fox Parham, a dynamic white minister, had founded the Pentecostal church in the early twentieth century in the Houston-Galveston area of Texas. William J. Seymour, who was born a slave in Louisiana, played a key role in the development of the church. After hearing black people speak in tongues in Houston, he went to Los Angeles, where he and others also began to speak in tongues. There he founded the

Nannie Helen Burroughs and other black women came together at the Banner State Woman's National Baptist Convention in the early twentieth century. In addition to her involvement with the Baptist woman's movement, Burroughs was devoted to industrial education as well as voting rights for black men and women. She was also active with the National Association of Colored Women, serving as the chair of its anti-lynching committee.   Courtesy of the Library of Congress

highly evangelistic church that became the Pentecostal church. It attracted enormous interest and grew rapidly.

Charles Harrison Mason joined the Pentecostal movement, and under his leadership the Reorganized Church of God in Christ became the leading Pentecostal denomination. It soon spread across the South among black and white people. Although there were tensions between black and white believers, the Pentecostal church was the only movement of any significance that crossed the racial divide in early-twentieth-century America.

ROMAN CATHOLICS AND EPISCOPALIANS

Most African Americans belonged to one of the Baptist or Methodist churches. Booker T. Washington reportedly observed that "If a black man is anything but a Baptist or Methodist, someone has been tampering with his religion." Nevertheless, black people also belonged to other churches and denominations—or occasionally belonged to no organized religious group.

About 200,000 African Americans were Roman Catholics in 1890. They were rarely fully accepted by the church or white Catholics. In the South they were segregated in separate churches with separate parish schools.

PROFILE 〜 HENRY MCNEAL TURNER

Henry McNeal Turner began as a supporter of racial harmony and a U.S. patriot. As he aged, however, he became steadily more disenchanted with the way white Americans contradicted their professed dedication to the principles of fairness and justice by their treatment of black Americans.

Turner was born to free black parents in Newberry, South Carolina, in 1834. After his father's death, he worked in cotton fields and learned to be a blacksmith and a carriage maker. He also learned to read and write while working for a white lawyer. Drawn to religion, he was licensed to preach by the Methodist Episcopal church, a white denomination. In 1859 he moved to Baltimore and was ordained in the AME church. He then became pastor of Union Bethel Church, the largest black congregation in Washington, D.C. During the Civil War, he served as a chaplain with the First Regiment of U.S. Colored Troops.

After the war, he briefly worked for the Freedmen's Bureau in Georgia. In an Emancipation Day address in Savannah in 1866 he praised the American flag and predicted that white people would soon accept black people.

Turner became active in Republican politics and was elected to the 1867–1868 Georgia constitutional convention, where he was the only black delegate to favor a literacy requirement for voting. He also supported a measure to help white planters who had not paid their taxes to keep their land. He conceded that "no man in Georgia has been more conservative than I. Anything to please white folks has been my motto."

In 1868 Turner was elected to the Georgia House of Representatives. When white legislators voted to remove the thirty-two black representatives, he objected: "I shall neither fawn nor cringe before any party, nor stoop to beg for my rights. . . . I am here to demand my rights, and to hurl thunderbolts at the men who dare to cross the threshold of my manhood." The black lawmakers were reinstated.

In 1880 he was elected one of the twelve bishops in the AME church and became president of Morris Brown College in Atlanta, where he served until 1900. He also became an advocate of emigration to Africa and supported the Liberian Exodus of 1877. Turner supported women's suffrage and ordained a woman as a deacon in the AME church in 1888, but the AME Council of Bishops withdrew the appointment.

Turner had little tolerance for those who considered Christianity a white man's religion. He asserted that "God is a Negro" and attacked those who "believe God is a white-skinned, blue-eyed, projecting-nosed, compressed-lipped, and finely-robed white gentleman."

He helped establish and edited a monthly AME newspaper, the *Voice of Missions.* In its pages he took a progressively black nationalist stance and criticized white supremacy and lynching. Growing older and angrier, he told black readers of the *Voice of Missions* to get guns and attack white predators. "Let every Negro in this country who has a spark of manhood in him supply his house with one, two, or three guns. . . and when your domicile is invaded. . . turn loose your missiles of death and blow the fiendish wretches into a thousand giblets."

He denounced black soldiers who fought to suppress the Philippine Insurrection. "I boil over with disgust when I remember that colored men from this country. . . are there fighting to subjugate a people of their own color. . . . I can scarcely keep from saying that I hope the Filipinos will wipe such soldiers from the face of the earth. . . . To go down there and shoot innocent men and take the country away from them, is too much for me to think about."

Embittered and tired, Turner lost faith in the intentions of white people and no longer praised the flag. "I used to love what I thought was the grand old flag, and sing with ecstasy about the Stars and Stripes, but to the Negro in this country the American flag is a dirty and contemptible rag. . . . Without multiplying words, I wish to say that hell is an improvement on the United States where the Negro is concerned."

Bishop Henry McNeal Turner died of a heart attack in 1915. He was married four times, outliving three wives and all but two of his children.

Courtesy of the Library of Congress

The most prominent black Catholics in nineteenth-century America came from the Healy family. Eliza Clark was a slave who had nine children by Michael Healy, an Irish-Catholic plantation owner in Georgia. Unlike many white men, Healy genuinely cared for Eliza and their children, although by law he could not marry a black woman. The children were educated in northern schools. James A. Healy graduated from the Jesuit-run Holy Cross College in Massachusetts and was ordained a priest at Notre Dame Cathedral in Paris in 1854. He later became a bishop in Portland, Maine.

Patrick Healy also attended Holy Cross and became the first black Jesuit priest in the United States. He served eight years as president of Georgetown University in Washington. Eliza Healy took vows as a nun and was the headmistress of a Catholic school in Vermont. Most white people were unaware of the racial ancestry of the Healys, and members of the family did not openly acknowledge being African American even when other black Catholics asked for their support. Bishop James Healy, for example, refused on three occasions to speak to the Congress of Colored Catholics, an association of black Catholics that met at least four times in northern cities between 1889 and 1893. Its members were mainly concerned with the discrimination they faced in the Roman Catholic Church and with the educational opportunities that were available—or more often that were not available—to black Catholic children in church schools.

Augustus Tolton was another African-American priest, and there was no question about his color. Because no American seminary would accept him, he was educated and ordained in 1886 in Rome. For a time, he presided over a parish in Quincy, Illinois, made up mainly of Irish and German Catholics. Unlike Bishop Healy, Tolten did speak to the Congress of Colored Catholics in Philadelphia in 1892.

Mother Mathilda Beasley came from a prominent free black family in Savannah. Her efforts to establish a community of Franciscan sisters in rural Georgia ultimately failed. In New Orleans, where there were sizable numbers of black Catholics of French and Spanish descent, the Sisters of Blessed Sacrament established a black high school in 1915 that became Xavier University in 1925.

Fairly or unfairly, most African Americans identified black Episcopalians with wealth and privilege. Many of those Episcopalians traced their heritage to free black families before the Civil War. By 1903 approximately 15,000 members of black Episcopal parishes worshipped in Richmond, Raleigh, Charleston, and other urban communities in the North and South.

Although he rarely mentioned it, James A. Healey's mother was black and a slave. He graduated from Holy Cross College, was ordained a Roman Catholic Priest in Paris in 1854, and became the Bishop of Portland, Maine, in 1875.   © College at the Holy Cross and Special Collections

Red versus Black: The Buffalo Soldiers

After the Civil War, the U.S. Army was reduced to fewer than 30,000 troops. Congressional Democrats tried to eliminate black soldiers and their regiments from this small force, but radical Republicans, led by Massachusetts senator Henry Wilson, prevailed to keep the military open to black men. The Army Reorganization Act of 1869 maintained four all-black regiments: the 9th and 10th Cavalry Regiments and the 24th and 25th Infantry Regiments. These four regiments spent most of the next three decades on the western frontier. Nearly 12,500 black men served during the late nineteenth century in these segregated units commanded—as black troops had been during the Civil War—by white officers. Unlike in the Civil War, however, many of these white officers were southerners, and all too frequently, they held black men in low regard.

Military service in the West was wretched for white troops and invariably worse for black soldiers. Too often officers considered black troops lazy, undisciplined, and cowardly. Black regiments were assigned mainly to the New Mexico and Arizona territories and to west Texas because the army thought black people tolerated heat better than white people did. The ancestors of the slaves were "from the tropics," claimed army quartermaster general Montgomery C. Meigs, and "not from the Northern or Southern extremities of Africa but from the Torrid Zone almost entirely." Most black soldiers were thus compelled to endure the hot, dry, and dusty Southwest desert. Still some black troops were sent to Kansas, Colorado, and the Dakotas, where they confronted instead howling blizzards, subzero temperatures, and frostbite (see Map 15–1).

DISCRIMINATION IN THE ARMY

Black troops faced more than adverse weather. The army routinely provided them inferior food and inadequate housing. Whereas white soldiers received dried apples and peaches, canned tomatoes, onions, and potatoes, black troops were given foul beef, bad bread, and canned peas unfit for human consumption. In 1867 white troops at Fort Leavenworth in Kansas lived in barracks while black troops were forced to sleep in tents on wet ground. Black regiments were allotted used weapons and equipment. The army sent its worst horses—often old and lame—to the black cavalry.

What the Government Is Doing for Our Colored Boys **20** LIVING WORDS

Long stretches of boredom, tedious duty, and loneliness marked army life for black and white men in the West. Weeks and months might pass without combat. Commanders constantly had to deal with desertion and alcoholism. Black soldiers were much less likely to desert or turn to drink than were white troops. For example, in 1877 eighteen men deserted from the all-black 10th Regiment, and 184 white soldiers deserted from the all-white 4th Regiment. Black troops realized that although army life could be harsh and dangerous, it compared favorably to the civilian world, which held few genuine opportunities for them. Army food was poor, but the private's pay of $13 per month was regular. Moreover, black troops developed immense pride in themselves as professional soldiers.

The Plains Indians who fiercely resisted U.S. forces were so impressed with the performance of their black adversaries that they called them "**buffalo soldiers.**" Indians associated the hair of black men with the shaggy coat of the buffalo, a sacred animal. Black troops considered it a term of respect and began to use it themselves. The 10th Cavalry displayed a buffalo in their unit emblem.

The Negro as Soldier **21** LIVING WORDS

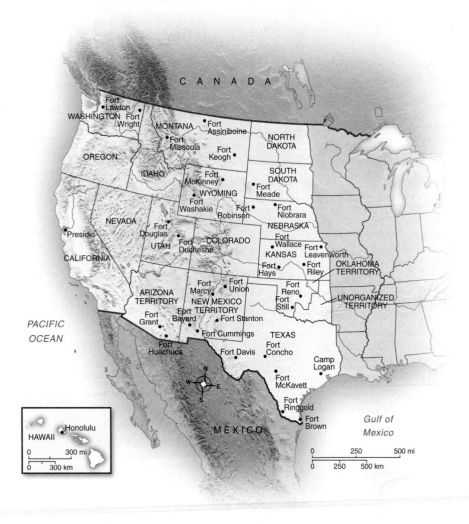

MAP 15–1   MILITARY POSTS WHERE BLACK TROOPS SERVED, 1866–1917

Black troops in the 9th and 10th Calvary and the 24th and 25th Infantry were assigned almost exclusively to western military posts from the end of the Civil War until the early twentieth century.

THE BUFFALO SOLDIERS IN COMBAT

It was ironic that white military authorities would employ black men to subdue red people. Most black soldiers, however, had no qualms about fighting Indians, protecting white settlers and railroad construction gangs, or apprehending bandits and cattle rustlers. From the late 1860s to the early 1890s, the four black regiments repeatedly engaged hostile Indians. In September 1867, seven hundred Cheyenne attacked fifty U.S. Army scouts along a dry riverbed in eastern Colorado. The scouts held out for over a week until the 10th Cavalry rescued them. For more than twelve months in 1879 and 1880, the 9th and 10th Cavalry fought the Apaches under Chief Victorio in New Mexico and Texas in a campaign of raid and counterraid. The Apaches slipped across the Mexican border and then returned to southwest Texas. In clashes at Rattlesnake Springs and near Fresno Spring, the 10th killed more than thirty Apaches before Victorio fled again to Mexico, where he was killed by the Mexican Army. But the 9th and 10th Cavalry deserve most of the credit for Victorio's defeat, with their dogged pursuit of the Apaches for months over hundreds of miles of rugged terrain.

In 1879, however, 10th Cavalry troops protected Kiowa women and children from Texas Rangers. In other instances black troops protected Chickasaw and Cherokee farmers from an attack by Kiowa and Comanche bands.

In late 1890 military units including the 9th Cavalry were sent to the Pine Ridge Reservation in South Dakota where Sioux Indians were holding an intense religious ceremony known as the Ghost Dance. Confined to reservations, some Indians—out of desperation and yearning for the past—believed their fervent participation in the Ghost Dance would bring both their ancestors and the almost extinct buffalo back to the Great Plains. Then white people would vanish, and Indian life would be restored to what it had been decades earlier. But white authorities considered the Ghost Dance a dangerous act of defiance.

On December 29, the 7th Cavalry attempted to disarm a band of Sioux at Wounded Knee on the Pine Ridge Reservation. Shooting erupted, and 146 Indian men, women, and children, and 26 soldiers were killed. The 9th Cavalry, 108 miles away in the Badlands, rode the next day through a blizzard and arrived tired and freezing to come to the aid of elements of the 7th Cavalry. The 9th spent the remainder of the bitter winter guarding the surviving Sioux. A black private, W. H. Prather, observed, "The Ninth, the Ninth were the first to come, will be the last to leave, we poor devils, and the Sioux are left to freeze."

CIVILIAN HOSTILITY TO BLACK SOLDIERS

Despite the gallant performance of the buffalo soldiers, civilians frequently treated them with hostility.

Several black men who were in the 10th Cavalry enjoy some time to themselves near St. Mary's, Montana, in 1894. Within four years they would be in combat against Spanish troops in Cuba during the Spanish American War.   Montana Historical Society, Helena

In southern Texas in 1875, Mexicans ambushed five black soldiers, killed two of them, and mutilated their bodies. The next day the infuriated white commander of the 9th Cavalry, Colonel Edward Hatch, rode out with sixty soldiers and apprehended the Mexicans. A local grand jury indicted nine of them for murder, but the only one tried was acquitted, and the other eight were released without a trial. Hatch, another white officer, and three buffalo soldiers were then indicted for breaking into and burglarizing the shack where the Mexicans had sought refuge. The charges were eventually dropped, but the five men had to hire their own lawyers.

In 1877 fifty-four black troops from the 9th Cavalry intervened successfully in a tense political and ethnic dispute between white and Mexican residents of El Paso, Texas. The 9th also found itself dispatched to police the so-called Johnson County War in Wyoming between big and small ranchers in 1890. The black troops deployment was arranged by one of the state's U.S. senators, who favored the big ranchers, and the presence of black soldiers angered small ranchers, as it was intended to do. Racial violence and bloodshed soon erupted between residents of the town of Suggs, who had run two black soldiers out of town, and several of the soldiers who had disobeyed orders. The troops were withdrawn after the town was shot up and one soldier killed.

A west Texas newspaper, the *Bellville Countryman*, summarized the attitudes of many white westerners when it complained that "the idea of a gallant and high-minded people being ordered and pushed around by an inferior, ignorant race is shocking to the senses. "

Brownsville

One of the worst examples of hostility to black troops, the so-called **Brownsville affair**, also occurred in Texas. In 1906 the 1st Battalion of the 25th Infantry was transferred from Fort Niobrara, Nebraska, to Fort Brown in Brownsville, Texas, along the Rio Grande. The black soldiers immediately encountered discrimination from both white people and Mexicans in this border community. More than four out of five of Brownsville's residents were Hispanic. Black people were not permitted in public parks, and white businesses refused to serve them. Several times civilians provoked and attacked individual black soldiers.

Shortly after midnight on August 14, shooting erupted in Brownsville. About 150 shots were fired. One man died, and a Hispanic policeman and the editor of a Spanish-language newspaper were injured. Black troops were blamed for the violence when clips and cartridges from the army's Springfield rifles were found in the street. Two military investigations concluded that black soldiers did the shooting. The army could not identify the specific soldiers responsible because no one would confess or name the alleged perpetrators.

With no hearing or trial, President Theodore Roosevelt dismissed three companies of black men—167 soldiers—from the army. They were barred from rejoining the military and from government employment and were denied veterans' pensions or benefits. The black community, which had supported Roosevelt, reacted angrily. Booker T. Washington, a Roosevelt supporter, privately wrote, "There is no law, human or divine, which justifies the punishment of an innocent man." Washington added, "I have the strongest faith in the President's honesty of intention, high mindedness of purpose, sincere unselfishness and courage, but I regret for all these reasons all the more that this thing has occurred."

Republican senator James B. Foraker of Ohio later led a Senate investigation that upheld Roosevelt's dismissals. But Foraker, a strong opponent of Roosevelt, questioned the guilt of the black men. The clips and cartridges that served as evidence were apparently planted. After Roosevelt left office in 1909, the War Department reinstated fourteen of the soldiers. In 1972 the Justice Department determined that an injustice had occurred. The black soldiers were posthumously awarded honorable discharges. The only survivor of the Brownsville affair—Dorsie Willis—received $25,000 from Congress and the right to treatment at veterans' facilities.

African Americans in the Navy

Naval service was even more unappealing than life in the army. In the late nineteenth century, as the navy made the transition from timber and sail to steam and steel, approximately one sailor in ten was a black man. Although the navy's ships were technically integrated, in that black and white sailors served on them together, white sailors were hostile to black sailors. They would not eat or bunk with them or take orders from them. Increasingly, and to enforce a de facto shipboard segregation, black sailors were restricted to stoking boilers in the bowels of naval vessels and to cooking and serving food to white sailors.

Although several black men enrolled as midshipmen at the Naval Academy in the 1870s, they faced social ostracism and none of them graduated. Not until 1949 did a black man graduate from the academy.

The Black Cowboys

Black men before, during, and after the Civil War were familiar with horses and mules. As slaves, they tended and cared for animals. Some black men served with the 9th and 10th U.S. Cavalry Regiments and gained experience with horses. By the 1870s and 1880s, black men joined several hundred Mexicans, Native Americans, and white men on the long cattle drives from Texas to Kansas, Nebraska, and Missouri. There were probably no more than a few hundred black cowboys in the late nineteenth and early twentieth centuries.

Tending cattle was monotonous, difficult, and dirty work. Yet it required considerable skill as a rider to manage hundreds of head of ornery and stinking animals. Cowboys had to tolerate weather that ranged from incredibly hot to bitter cold. They had to be willing to consume unappetizing food for weeks at a time. There was no bed to sleep in each night, and their closest companion most days and nights was the horse they rode.

Black cowhands sometimes endured discrimination and abuse. They had to tame the toughest horses, work the longest hours, and face hostility in saloons, hotels, brothels, and shops in towns like Dodge City, Abilene, or Cheyenne. Still, many black cowboys earned the respect of white ranchers and cattle barons. Bose Ikard had been born a slave in Mississippi and went to work for Texas cattleman Charles Goodnight after the Civil War. Goodnight praised Ikard: "He was my detective, banker, and everything else in Colorado, New Mexico, and the other wild country I was in. . . . We went through some terrible trials during those four years on the trail. . . . [Ikard] was the most skilled and trustworthy man I had."

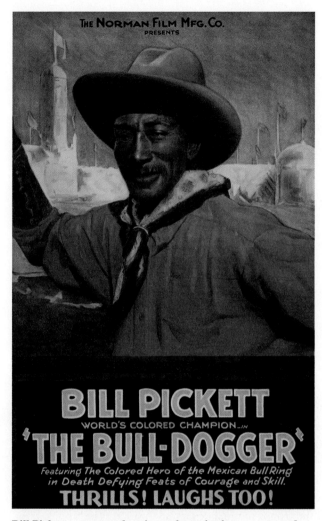

THE NORMAN FILM MFG. CO.
PRESENTS

BILL PICKETT
WORLD'S COLORED CHAMPION...IN
'THE BULL-DOGGER'
Featuring The Colored Hero of the Mexican Bull Ring
in Death Defying Feats of Courage and Skill.
THRILLS! LAUGHS TOO!

Bill Pickett was an authentic cowboy who became one of the first black movie stars. "The Bull-Dogger" was a 1922 black-and-white silent film aimed at attracting black audiences. (No copies of the film are known to have survived.) Pickett's skill as a bull-dogger was legendary. He would ride alongside a steer, jump off his horse, and grab the animal by the horns. He then wrestled it to the ground by sharply biting the animal's upper lip or nose. Pickett was the hit of the 1904 Cheyenne Frontier Days rodeo in Wyoming. Museum of the American West Collection, Autry National Center

The Spanish-American War

With the western frontier subdued by 1890, many Americans concluded that the United States should expand overseas. European nations had already carved out extensive colonies in Africa and Asia. Many, but by no means all, Americans favored the extension of U.S. political, economic, and military authority to Latin America and the Pacific. In 1893 the U.S. Navy and American businessmen toppled the monarchy in Hawaii, and the United States annexed that chain of islands in 1898.

The same year, the United States went to war to liberate Cuba from Spanish control. As in the Civil War, black men enlisted, fought, and died. Twenty-two black sailors were among the 266 men who died when the battleship USS *Maine* blew up in Havana harbor, the event that helped trigger the war. Many black Americans were convinced, as they had been in previous wars, that the willingness of black people to support the war against Spain would impress white Americans sufficiently to reduce or even eliminate white hostility. E. E. Cooper, editor of the Washington *Colored American*, declared that the war would bring black people and white people together in "an era of good feeling the country over and cement the races into a more compact brotherhood through perfect unity of purpose and patriotic affinity." The war, he asserted, would help white Americans "unloose themselves from the bondage of race prejudice."

Many black and white Americans, however, questioned the American cause. Some black people saw the war as an effort to extend American influence and racial practices, including Jim Crow, beyond U.S. borders. The Reverend George W. Prioleau, chaplain of the 9th Cavalry, wondered why black Americans supported what he considered a hypocritical war:

> Talk about fighting and freeing poor Cuba and of Spain's brutality. . . . Is America any better than Spain? Has she not subjects in her very midst who are murdered daily without a trial of judge or jury? Has she not subjects in her own borders whose children are half-fed and half-clothed, because their father's skin is black. . . . Yet the Negro is loyal to his country's flag.

Whether or not they harbored doubts, black men by the thousands served in the Spanish-American War and in the Philippine Insurrection that followed it. Shortly before war was declared, the army ordered its four black regiments of regular troops transferred from their western posts to Florida to prepare for combat in Cuba. President William McKinley also appealed for volunteers. The War Department designated four of the black volunteer units "immune regiments" because it believed that black men would tolerate the heat and humidity of Cuba better than white troops and that black people were immune or at least less susceptible to yellow fever, which was endemic to Cuba. (Yellow fever was carried by mosquitoes, but this was unknown in 1898. Most people believed the disease was caused by the tropical Caribbean climate.)

Black Men in Battle in Cuba

On October 1, 1898, a letter appeared in the Illinois Record, *a black newspaper, from one of the men in the 10th Cavalry. The author was probably John E. Lewis, and he wrote the letter from Montauk Point on the eastern tip of Long Island in New York, where black and white troops were sent after the war. Lewis described the enthusiastic reaction of the Rough Riders to the 9th and 10th Cavalry, but he complained that the contributions of the black soldiers were too often overlooked and ignored.*

The Rough Riders were mustered out on the 12th and 13th [of September], and when Colonel Roosevelt bade the regiment good-bye he paid a glowing tribute to the 9th and 10th Cavalry, especially in saving them from ambush.

Mr. Editor, if your readers could have heard the Rough Riders yell when the 10th Cav. was mentioned as the 'Smoked Yankees' and that they were of a good breed, they would have been doubly proud of the members of their race who rendered such signal service on the battle field. . . .

When a troop of the 10th made their famous charge of 3,000 yards under the command of Capt. [William J.] Beck, the non-commissioned officers, all colored, distinguished themselves in a manner that will redound to the glory of the race. Among those who distinguished themselves are Carter Smith, acting 1st Sergeant, Sgts. Geo. Taylor, James F. Cole, James H. Williams, Smith Johnson and Corpl. Joseph G. Mitchell who was wounded at San Juan.

All are soldiers whose names should go down in history. They never faltered in the thickest of the battle; they encouraged on in a rain of shot and shell and showed by their actions that they were the leaders. They did not hesitate to take the lead, and when that charge was made it was "save your cartridges, don't waste a shot."

The half will never be told of their deeds upon the battlefield. All deserve praise from the private up, but the praise has been given those who should have been in the lead instead of laying in the rear under cover. And yet they say that the black is not fit to lead.

If our war reports would only give credit where credit is due there would be no need writing these poorly composed lines that your readers might know of the deeds and hardships their dear ones have passed through.

You will read that colored troops, or companies did so and so, but the white papers never mention a name and the world only knows one who has done an act of bravery as a Negro soldier, nameless and friendless. It was never mentioned how, at that famous charge of the 10th Cav. And the rescue of the Rough Riders at San

State militia (national guard) units were also called into federal service, and several states, including Alabama, Ohio, Massachusetts, Illinois, Kansas, Virginia, Indiana, and North Carolina, sent all-black militias, as well as white units. But Georgia's governor refused to permit that state's black militia to serve, and New York would not permit black men to enlist in its militia. The states typically followed the federal example and kept black men confined to all-black units commanded by white officers, but there were exceptions.

BLACK OFFICERS

The buffalo soldiers of the 9th and 10th Cavalry and the 24th and 25th Infantry remained under the leadership of white officers. But the men of several volunteer units insisted they be led by black officers: "No officers, no fight." So for the first time in American military history, black men commanded all-black units: the 8th Illinois, the 23rd Kansas, and the 3rd North

Juan Hill, the yell was started by a single trooper of C Troop, 10th Cav. and was carried down the line.

Brave 1st Sgt. Adam Huston at the head of his troop commanded "forward" which seemed into almost certain death. In him the troop found an able leader; Lieut. [E. D.] Anderson who was in command and fell to the rear and when the command "Forward March," was given, the brave Major [Theodore J.] Wint only smiled, for he admired bravery and did not change the command although he knew that the troops was in a desperate position. The troops were carried safely through. . . .

Will it ever be known how Sgt. Thomas Griffith of Troop C cut the wire fence along the line so that the 10th Cav. and Rough Riders could go through?

Never once did these brave men give thought to danger. . . .

The Spaniard would have sent our army home in disgrace had it not been for the daring and almost reckless charge of the Negro regiments. God was with them in that charge and no man who has ever seen the place will say that it was possible to make the charge without being slaughtered. . . .

[Unsigned]

What is the source of the bitterness revealed in this letter?

What motivated black men to risk their lives in combat in the Spanish-American War?

Do any portions of this account seem strained, exaggerated, or unreliable? Why or why not?

Source: Willard B. Gatewood Jr., *Smoked Yankees and the Struggle for Empire: Letters from Negro Soldiers, 1898–1902* (Urbana: University of Illinois Press, 1971), pp. 76–78.

Carolina. Mindful that many people doubted the ability of black men to lead, the colonel of the 8th Illinois cautioned his men, "If we fail, the whole race will have to shoulder the burden." The War Department also permitted black men to serve as lieutenants with other black volunteer units, but all higher-ranking officers were white men. Charles Young, a black graduate of West Point who was serving as a military science instructor at Wilberforce University in Ohio, was given command of Ohio's 9th Battalion, and he served with distinction and was promoted from captain to colonel.

As black and white troops assembled in Georgia and Florida before departing for Cuba, black men soon realized a U.S. uniform did not lessen white racial prejudice. White civilians in Georgia killed four black men of the 3rd North Carolina. All-white juries acquitted those who were charged with the murders. After the white proprietor of a drug store in Lakeland, Florida, refused to serve a black soldier at the soda fountain, a mob of black troops gathered. The proprietor was pistol whipped, and another white man was killed by a stray bullet before the troops were disarmed. In Tampa, where the troops were embarking for Cuba, a bloody all-night riot broke out after drunken white soldiers from Ohio decided to shoot at a black child for target practice. Twenty-seven black soldiers and three white soldiers were seriously injured. Is it surprising that when the men of the all-black 3rd Alabama adopted an injured crow as the unit mascot, they named it Jim?

Most of the black units never saw combat. White military authorities considered black men unreliable and inadequately trained for combat. Black volunteer units stayed behind in Florida when white units embarked for Cuba. However, the four regiments of regular black troops, the buffalo soldiers, did go to Cuba, where they performed well despite the doubts and persistent criticism of some white men. The Spanish troops were impressed enough to give the black men the nickname "smoked yankees."

A SPLENDID LITTLE WAR

In the summer of 1898, U.S. troops arrived in Cuba. Black men of the 10th Cavalry fought alongside Cuban rebels, many of whom were themselves black. Four black American privates earned the Congressional Medal of Honor for their part in an engagement in southwestern Cuba. Black and white troops were best remembered for their role in the assault on San Juan and Kettle Hills overlooking the key Cuban port of Santiago in eastern Cuba. Santiago was the main Spanish naval base in Cuba and its capture would break Spain's hold over the island.

In this assault, black soldiers from the 24th Infantry and the 9th and the 10th Cavalry Regiments fought alongside white troops including Theodore Roosevelt's volunteer unit, the Rough Riders. In the fiercest fighting of the war and amid considerable confusion, black and white men were thrown together as they encountered withering Spanish fire. Although for a time the outcome was in doubt, they took the high ground overlooking Santiago harbor. White soldiers praised the performance of the black troops. One commented, "I am not a negro lover. My father fought with Mosby's Rangers [in the Confederate Army] and I was born in the South, but the negroes saved that fight." In his campaign for vice president in 1900, Theodore Roosevelt stated that black men saved his life during the battle. Later, however, Roosevelt reversed himself and accused several black men of cowardice.

AFTER THE WAR

As hostilities concluded, men of the 24th Infantry agreed to work in yellow fever hospitals after white regiments refused the duty. About half the black soldiers—some 471 men—contracted yellow fever. Other black troops arrived in Cuba after the war to serve garrison duty. The 8th Illinois and the 23rd Kansas built roads, bridges, schools, and hospitals. The black men were especially pleased at the lack of discrimination and absence of Jim Crow in Cuba. Some black soldiers discussed the possibility of organizing emigration to Cuba, but nothing came of it. Still other black troops from the 6th Massachusetts joined in the invasion of Puerto Rico as the United States took that island from Spain.

The Philippine Insurrection

With the resounding victory in the Spanish-American War, many Americans decided their nation had an obligation to uplift those less fortunate peoples who had been part of the Spanish Empire. Thus, President William McKinley and American diplomats insisted the United States acquire Guam, Puerto Rico, and the Philippines from Spain in the Treaty of Paris that ended the war in December 1898. The Filipinos, like the Cubans, had long opposed Spanish rule and fully expected the American government to support their independence. Instead, they were infuriated to learn that the United States intended to annex the Philippines. The Filipinos, under Emilio Aguinaldo, switched from fighting the Spanish to fighting the occupying U.S. forces.

WOULD BLACK MEN FIGHT BROWN MEN?

Many black and white Americans denounced the U.S. effort to take the Philippines. They were unconvinced the Filipinos would benefit from American benevolence. Some wondered if by oppressing the Filipinos, African-American soldiers in that distant land were helping to lessen racial oppression in the United States. AME Bishop Henry Turner termed U.S. intervention in the Philippines an "unholy war of conquest," and Booker T. Washington believed the Filipinos "should be given an opportunity to govern themselves." In a grim, but humorous, attempt to taunt those who proclaimed the superiority of white civilization, a group of black men formed the "Black Man's Burden Association."

Opposition to U.S. involvement in the Philippines notwithstanding, black men in the military served throughout the campaign in the Pacific islands. The black troops included the regular 25th Infantry and 24th Infantry, the 9th Cavalry, and the 48th and 49th Volunteer Regiments. Through propaganda, the Filipino rebels attempted to convince black troops to abandon the cause. Posters reminded "The Colored American Soldier" of injustice and lynching in the United States. White troops did not help by calling Filipinos "niggers." Although many black soldiers had reservations about the fighting, they remained loyal. By the time the conflict ended with an American victory in 1902, only five black men had deserted. David Fagen of the 24th Infantry joined Filipino forces and became an officer, fighting American troops for two years before he was killed. Two black men from the 9th Cavalry were executed for desertion; fifteen white soldiers who deserted had their death sentences commuted.

Although black men had served with distinction as professional soldiers for forty years after the Civil War—on the frontier, in Cuba, and in the Philippines—the army little valued their achievements and sacrifice, as the Brownsville affair showed. White military and political leaders persistently relied on passions and prejudices over evidence of achievement. Time and again, these circumstances dashed the hopes of those black civilians and soldiers who believed the performance of black troops would challenge white supremacy and demonstrate that black citizens had earned the same rights and opportunities as other Americans.

Black Businesspeople and Entrepreneurs

Well-educated black men and women stood no chance of gaining employment with any major business or industrial corporation at the turn of the century. White males not only monopolized management and supervisory positions, but also occupied nearly every job that did not involve manual labor. In 1899 black novelist Sutton E. Griggs described the frustrations that an educated black man encountered:

> He possessed a first class college education, but that was all. He knew no trade nor was he equipped to enter any of the professions. . . .He would have made an excellent drummer, [salesman] clerk, cashier, government official (county, city, state, or national), telegraph operator, conductor, or anything of such a nature. But the color of his skin shut the doors so tight that he could not even peep in. . . .It is true that such positions as street laborer, hod carrier, cart driver, factory hand, railroad hand were open to him; but such menial tasks were uncongenial to a man of his education and polish.

Although white supremacy and the proliferation of Jim Crow severely restricted opportunities for educated black people, those same limitations enabled enterprising black men and women to open and operate businesses that served black clientele. By the early twentieth century, black Americans not only had their own churches and schools, but they had also established banks, newspapers, insurance companies, retail businesses, barbershops, beauty salons, and funeral parlors. Virtually every black community had its own small businesses, markets, street vendors, and other entrepreneurs.

Some black men and women established thriving and substantial businesses. In Atlanta, Union Army veteran Alexander Hamilton was a successful building contractor. He supervised construction of the Good Samaritan Building, oversaw the erection of buildings on the Morris Brown College campus, and built many of the impressive houses on Peachtree Street. Hamilton employed both black and white workmen on his projects.

Alonzo Herndon was a former slave who also achieved financial success in Atlanta. He operated a fashionable barbershop on Peachtree Street that served well-to-do white men. The shop had crystal chandeliers and polished brass spittoons. Herndon expanded and opened two other shops, eventually employing seventy-five men. He also founded the Atlanta Life Insurance Company, the largest black stock company in the world.

In Montgomery, Alabama, H. A. Loveless, a former slave, became a butcher and then diversified his business operations by opening an undertaking establishment and operating a hack and dray company. By 1900 Loveless also ran a coal and wood yard and sold real estate.

In Richmond, Virginia, Maggie Lena Walker—the secretary-treasurer of the Independent Order of St. Luke, a mutual benefit society, and a founder of the St. Luke's Penny Savings Bank—became the wealthiest black woman in America. Also in Richmond, former slave John Dabney owned an exclusive catering business that served wealthy white Virginians. He catered two state dinners for President Grover Cleveland. He used his earnings to purchase several houses and to invest in real estate.

Madam C. J. Walker may have been the most successful black entrepreneur of them all. Born Sarah Breedlove in 1867 on a Louisiana cotton plantation, she married at age fourteen and was a widowed single parent by age twenty. She spent the next two decades struggling to make ends meet. In 1905 with $1.50, she developed a formula to nourish and enrich the hair of black women. She insisted it was not a process to straighten hair.

She sold the product door to door in Denver but could not keep up with the demand. The business rapidly expanded and became a thriving enterprise that employed hundreds of black women. She established the company's headquarters in Indianapolis. In the meantime, she married Charles Joseph Walker and took his name and the title Madam. As she accumulated wealth, she shared it generously with Bethune Cookman College, Tuskegee Institute, and the NAACP. She was a major contributor to the NAACP's antilynching campaign. When she died of a stroke at age fifty-one in 1919, she was reportedly a millionaire.

Despite such successes, most black people who went into business had difficulty surviving, and many failed. Too often they depended on black customers who were themselves poor. White-owned banks were unlikely to provide credit to aspiring black businesspeople. And even the wealthiest black entrepreneurs did not come close to possessing the wealth the richest white Americans accumulated.

African Americans and Labor

Thousands of black southerners worked in factories, mills, and mines. Although most textile mills refused to hire black people except for janitorial duties, many black laborers toiled in tobacco and cigarmaking facilities, flour mills, coal mines, sawmills, turpentine camps, and on railroads. Black women worked for white families as cooks, maids, and laundresses. Black workers usually were paid less than white men employed in the same capacity. Conversely, white working people frequently complained they were not hired because employers retained black workers who worked for less pay. In 1904 in Georgia white railroad firemen went on strike in an unsuccessful attempt to compel railroad operators to dismiss black firemen. There was persistent antagonism between black and white laborers.

UNIONS

When white workers formed labor unions in the late nineteenth century, they usually excluded black workers. The Knights of Labor, however, founded in 1869, was open to all workers (except whiskey salesmen, lawyers, and bankers), and by the mid-1880s counted 50,000 women and 70,000 black workers among its nearly 750,000 members. But by the 1890s, after unsuccessful strikes and a deadly riot in Chicago, the Knights had lost influence to a new organization, the American Federation of Labor (AFL). Founded in 1886, the AFL was ostensibly open to all skilled workers, but most of its local craft unions barred women and black tradesmen. In contrast, the United Mine Workers (UMW), formed in 1890, encouraged black coal miners to join the union

In less than two decades in the early twentieth century, Sarah Breedlove rose from abject poverty to become extraordinarily wealthy as Madam C. J. Walker.

PROFILE ～ MAGGIE LENA WALKER

By the early twentieth century, Maggie Lena Walker was a successful businesswoman, community leader, and one of the wealthiest black women in America. She was also an ardent advocate for her race and her gender. She was born Maggie Mitchell in Richmond, Virginia, on July 15, 1867, to Elizabeth Draper, a laundress. Her mother married William Mitchell in 1870. Young Maggie was much influenced by the determination, fortitude, and hard work of her mother. Throughout her childhood, she helped her mother wash, iron, and carry laundry.

Maggie Mitchell graduated from a normal school in 1883 and taught primary school. She was active in the First African Baptist Church and remained a committed member for life. In 1886 she married Armstead Walker. Her views on marriage were progressive. Explaining the responsibilities that she shared with her husband, she wrote, "Since marriage is an equal partnership, I believe that the woman and the man are equal in power and should by consultation and agreement, mutually decide as to the conduct of the home and the government of the children."

The Independent Order of St. Luke was one of many black mutual aid societies that flourished in the nineteenth century. Black people contributed small sums of money and, in the event of sickness or death, the society paid benefits to members or their survivors. But the Order was also a fraternal and social organization that stressed racial pride as well as compassion, generosity, and charity.

Maggie Lena Walker became active in the order at the age of fourteen in 1881. She was elected Grand Matron and became the Right Worthy Grand Secretary in 1899. When she assumed her duties, the Order had $31.61 in funds and 1,080 members. She proved to be a dynamic leader and an inspirational speaker. She traveled extensively and spoke regularly to members. She stressed racial concerns and attacked discrimination and lynching. She appealed to audiences to patronize black enterprises. By the early twentieth century under Walker's guidance, the order operated in twenty-two states. Its membership had increased, and its financial standing had improved. In 1924 the Independent Order of St. Luke had funds totaling $3,480,540.

The Order ran a newspaper, the *St. Luke Herald*, and a bank with Maggie Lena Walker as president. She was the first black woman to serve as the chief executive of a bank in the United States. The bank subsequently merged with two other banks and became the Consolidated Bank and Trust Company, with Walker as president. She was especially pleased that the bank enabled black customers to purchase homes. By 1920, 645 black families had acquired their houses with the financial assistance of the bank.

Walker was deeply concerned with the plight of black women, and she made certain that the Order employed black women in significant positions. In 1909 she paid homage to women of color:

And the great all absorbing interest, this thing which has driven sleep from my eyes and fatigue from my body, is the love I bear women, our Negro women, hemmed, circumscribed, with every imaginable obstacle in our way, blocked and held down by the fears and prejudices of the whites, ridiculed and sneered at by the intelligent blacks.

Maggie Lena Walker became a wealthy woman and lived in a twenty-two-room house. She was deeply involved in community affairs and organizations. She supported Virginia Union University, which later awarded her an honorary degree, and the Industrial School for Colored Girls. She worked with the Piedmont Tuberculosis Sanitarium for Negroes. She served on Richmond's Council for Colored Women and with the Virginia Federation of Colored Women's Clubs, and she was among the prominent women who helped organize the Council of Women of the Darker Races. She joined the National Association of Colored Women in 1912 and was active in the NAACP. She was also a committed Republican and ran unsuccessfully for state superintendent of public instruction. She died on December 15, 1934.

National Park Service, Maggie L. Walker, National Historic Site

Walker

rather than serve as strikebreakers. By 1900 approximately 20,000 of the 91,000 members of the UMW were black men. The Industrial Workers of the World (IWW), a revolutionary labor organization founded in 1905, brought black and white laborers together in, among other places, the Brotherhood of Timber Workers in the Piney Woods of east Texas.

In 1869 a Baltimore ship caulker, Isaac Myers, organized the National Colored Labor Union, which lasted for seven years. It discouraged strikes and encouraged its members to work hard and be thrifty. It lost whatever effectiveness it had when it was largely taken over by Republican leaders during Reconstruction.

STRIKES

During the late nineteenth and early twentieth centuries, although some strikes by unions won concessions from business owners, most failed because owners could rely on strikebreakers and the police or national guard to intervene and bring the strikes to an often violent end. For a time, black shipyard workers in southern ports did achieve some success. Black stevedores who loaded and unloaded ships endured oppressive conditions and long hours for low pay. They periodically went on strike in Charleston, Savannah, and New Orleans. The Longshoremen's Protective Union in Charleston won several strikes in the 1870s. In Nashville in 1871 black dockyard workers went on strike, demanding twenty cents an hour. Steamboat owners broke the strike by hiring state convicts for fifteen cents an hour.

Black and white laborers who toiled in the Louisiana sugarcane fields earned an average of $13 a week in the 1880s. They were paid in scrip—not cash—that was redeemable only in stores the planters owned where prices were exorbitant. Workers lived in 12' × 15' cabins that they rented from the planters. In some ways, it was worse than slave labor.

Although the state militia had broken previous strikes, nine thousand black and one thousand white workers responded to a call for a new strike in 1887 by organizers from the Knights of Labor. They quit the sugar fields in four parishes (as Louisiana counties are called) to demand more pay. The strike was peaceful, but planters convinced the governor to send in the militia. The troops fired into a crowd at Pattersonville and killed four people. The next day local officials killed several strikers who had been taken prisoner. In the town of Thibodaux, "prominent citizens" organized and armed themselves and had martial law declared. More than thirty-five unarmed black people, including women and children, were killed in their homes and churches. Two black strike leaders were lynched. The strike was broken.

Black washerwomen went on strike in Atlanta in 1881. The women, who washed laundry by hand for white families, refused to do any more until they were guaranteed $1 per twelve pounds of laundry. The strike was well organized through black churches, and it spread to cooks and domestics. A strike committee used persuasion and intimidation to ensure support. Some three thousand black people joined the strike. White families went two weeks without clean clothes. However, Atlanta's white community broke the strike. Police arrested strike leaders for disorderly conduct. Several black women were fined from $5 to $20. The city council threatened to require each member of the Washer Women's Association of Atlanta to purchase a city business license for $25. Although the strike gradually ended without having achieved its goal, it did demonstrate that poor black women could organize effectively.

Although most southern black people worked long hours in cotton fields, thousands toiled in factories, mills, and mines. Here black women stem tobacco in a Virginia factory under the supervision of a white man.

Black Professionals

Like business and labor, the medical and legal professions were strictly segregated. Most black physicians, nurses, and lawyers attended all-black professional schools in the late nineteenth century. Black people in need of medical care were either excluded from white hospitals or confined to all-black wards. Black physicians were denied staff privileges at white hospitals. Thus black people in many communities formed their own hospitals. Most were small facilities with fifty or fewer beds.

MEDICINE

In 1891 Dr. Daniel Hale Williams established Provident Hospital and Training Institute in Chicago, the first black hospital operated solely by African Americans. In 1894 the Freedmen's Hospital was organized in Washington, D.C., and it later affiliated with Howard University. Frederick Douglass Memorial Hospital and Training School was founded in Philadelphia in 1895. Dr. Alonzo McClennan in cooperation with several other black physicians established the Hospital and Training School for Nurses in Charleston, South Carolina, in 1897.

In 1900 Williams, explaining why black medical institutions were necessary, wrote,

> In view of this cruel ostracism, affecting so vitally the race, our duty seems plain. Institute Hospitals and Training Schools. Let us no longer sit idly and inanely deploring existing conditions. Let us not waste time trying to effect changes or modifications in the institutions unfriendly to us, but rather let us seek to promote the doctrine of helping and stimulating our race.

By 1890 there were 909 black (most of whom were male) physicians practicing in the United States. They served a black population of 7.5 million people. Barred from membership in the American Medical Association, black doctors organized the National Medical Association in Atlanta in 1895. Most black doctors had been educated at seven black medical schools that included Leonard Medical School at Shaw University in Raleigh, North Carolina; Flint-Goodridge Medical College in New Orleans; Meharry Medical School in Nashville; and the Howard University School of Medicine in Washington, D.C.

In 1910, in a report issued by the Carnegie Foundation for the Advancement of Teaching, Abraham Flexner recommended improving medical education in the United States by eliminating weaker medical schools. He suggested raising admission standards and expanding laboratory and clinical training in the stronger schools. As a result of the implementation of these recommendations, 60 of 155 white medical schools closed, and among black medical schools, only Howard and Meharry survived. By 1920 there were

3,885 black physicians. Many had completed medical school before the Flexner report was compiled.

The number of black women physicians was actually declining. In 1890 there were ninety black women practicing medicine, and by 1920 there were sixty-five. The number of medical schools had decreased, and most black and white men considered medicine an inappropriate profession for women. But black women also had to contend with the opposition of white women. Isabella Vandervall was a 1915 graduate of New York Medical College and Hospital who was accepted for an internship at the Hospital for Women and Children in Syracuse. When she appeared in person, however, the hospital's female administrator rejected Vandervall, ". . . we can't have you here! You are colored!"

Nursing was another matter. By 1920 there were 36 black nurse training schools and 2,150 white nursing schools. White nurses resented the competition from black nurses for positions as private duty nurses. And the black physicians who ran nurse training schools exploited their students by hiring them out, as part of their training, for private duty work but requiring them to relinquish their pay to the schools. Moreover, many people—black and white—regarded black nurses more as domestics than as trained professionals. Unlike white nurses, for example, black nurses were usually addressed by their first names. To confront such obstacles, fifty-two black nurses met in New York City in 1908 and formed the National Association of Colored Graduate Nurses (NACGN). By 1920 the NACGN had five hundred members.

Black physicians and nurses struggled to provide medical care to people who were often desperately ill and sought treatment only as a last resort. Disease and sickness flourished among people who were ill nourished, poorly clad, and inadequately housed. Tuberculosis, pneumonia, pellagra, hookworm, and syphilis afflicted many poor black people—as they also did poor white people. Bessie Hawes, a 1918 graduate of Tuskegee Institute's Nurse Training program, described the kind of situation she faced in rural Alabama:

> A colored family of ten were in bed and dying for the want of attention. No one would come near. I was glad of the opportunity. As I entered the little country cabin, I found the mother in bed. Three children were buried the week before. The father and the remainder of the family were running a temperature of 102–104. Some had influenza, others had pneumonia. No relatives or friends would come near. I saw at a glance I had work to do. I rolled up my sleeves and killed chickens and began to cook. . . . I milked the cow, gave medicine, and did everything I

More than five million people visited the 1904 St. Louis World's Fair. Perhaps the most popular attraction was a horse, Beautiful Jim Key, and his African-American owner, Dr. William Key.

On the Fair's opening day, President Theodore Roosevelt's feisty twenty-year old daughter Alice, accompanied by Congressman Nicholas Longworth, went to see the horse that had already captured the hearts and minds of hundreds of thousands of Americans over the previous seven years. Using his mouth, Beautiful Jim Key plucked the correct letters from a specially constructed metal frame that contained the alphabet and arranged them on a display rack to spell "Alice Roosevelt." Then, prompted by a member of the audience, the horse spelled "Longworth" and added it to Alice Roosevelt's name. It was prophetic. Two years later the Republican congressman married the president's daughter, and she became Alice Roosevelt Longworth.

William Key was born a slave in Winchester, Tennessee, in 1833, the son of a slave woman who had Cherokee ancestry and an unidentified white man. From childhood, Key demonstrated a fondness for animals and an ability to work with and care for them. Permitted by his owners to learn to read and write, he became a self-taught veterinarian whom local black and white people called "Dr. Key."

He also learned the art of diplomacy. During the Civil War he simultaneously helped slaves escape while protecting his owner's two sons who went off to fight for the Confederate Army. For these latter efforts, he was arrested by Union officials, held prisoner for six weeks, and threatened with hanging.

Following the war and emancipation, Key acquired enough wealth as a veterinarian to purchase land near Shelbyville, Tennessee. A shrewd businessman and gambler, he sold patent medicine—Keystone Liniment—and regularly won at poker. Dr. Key also purchased an Arabian horse that had been relegated to circus performances in Mississippi. He bred the neglected and weary mare, and she produced a sickly, scrawny colt, whom he named Jim Key, in 1889. Through years of kind and patient training, Key transformed this unimpressive horse into a splendid, powerful, and talented animal.

The veterinarian possessed an uncanny capacity to communicate with Beautiful Jim Key, sometimes through indecipherable Cherokee and African words. The horse could add, subtract, multiply, and divide numbers that totaled less than thirty. In one show he was asked to multiply four times five, then add five, and subtract three. He promptly plucked the card with twenty-two from the rack, causing one journalist to wonder, "What will he learn next, square roots?" The brainy horse learned the alphabet and how to read basic names and words. Asked by audience members, he spelled such words as "physics," "constitution," and "Pennsylvania." He could make change by selecting the correct coins out of a specially built National Cash Register.

In 1897 a white entrepreneur and showman from Cincinnati, Albert Rogers, persuaded Dr. Key to collaborate with him, and Rogers managed and promoted the black veterinarian and his horse for the next decade. Key and Rogers stressed the kind and gentle treatment of animals before virtually every audience. (Key never used a whip.) Beautiful Jim Key was eventually inducted into honorary membership in the American Humane Association, its only nonhuman member.

But it was Beautiful Jim Key's intelligence and knowledge that attracted the crowds. In 1897 President William McKinley visited the Nashville World's Fair and sat in amazement in the Negro Building as Beautiful Jim Key selected the names of cabinet members from a rack as they were read to him.

With the emergence of Jim Crow, Dr. Key and his horse performed before segregated audiences across the South. On some occasions, William Key would hold special shows "open to all." But in those instances, the audience was invariably all black.

There were those who doubted the intelligence of Beautiful Jim Key. Some thought the doctor had devised some secret means of communicating answers to the horse. In 1901 Beautiful Jim Key was scrutinized by a group of Harvard professors. After witnessing two performances, the scholars declared that there was no trickery involved. Dr. Key had simply educated an intelligent animal.

The man and his horse finally retired to the Key estate near Shelbyville. William Key died at age seventy-six in 1909. His magnificent horse survived him to die at age twenty-three in 1912.

could to help conditions. I worked day and night trying to save them for seven days. I had no place to sleep. In the meantime the oldest daughter had a miscarriage and I delivered her without the aid of any physicians. . . .I only wished that I could have reached them earlier and been able to have done something for the poor mother.

THE LAW

Unlike black physicians and nurses, who were excluded from white hospitals, black lawyers were permitted to practice in what was essentially a white male court system. But white judges and attorneys did not welcome them. Rather than create additional problems for themselves, black defendants and plaintiffs often retained white lawyers in the hope that white legal counsel might improve their chances of receiving justice. As a result, many black attorneys had a hard time making a living from the practice of law.

The American Bar Association (ABA) would not admit black attorneys to membership. Attorney William H. Lewis, a graduate of Amherst College and the Harvard Law School who was appointed an assistant U.S. attorney general by President William Howard Taft in 1911, was expelled by the ABA in 1912 when its leaders discovered he was black. The leaders defended his expulsion by claiming the association was mainly a social organization. In 1925 black lawyers—led by Howard Law School graduate George H. Woodson—organized the National Bar Association.

In 1910 the United States had about eight hundred black lawyers. Some, like Lewis, had attended white law schools, such as Harvard or the University of South Carolina, during Reconstruction in the 1870s. Others attended black law schools such as Howard or Allen University's law school in South Carolina. Still other black men (and white men) learned the law by reading and working in the law offices of practicing attorneys.

Very few black women were lawyers. Charlotte Ray was the first (see p. 308). In 1900 there were ten black women practicing law. There were over 700 black men and 112,000 white men engaged in the legal profession. Lutie A. Lytle, who graduated from Central Tennessee Law School in 1879, later returned to that black institution and became the first black woman to be a law professor in the United States.

Music

In the half century after the Civil War, music created and performed by black people evolved into the uniquely American art forms of ragtime, jazz, and blues. The roots of these extraordinary musical innovations are obscure and uncertain. Some late-nineteenth-century music can be traced to African musical forms and rhythms. One source is slave work songs; another is the spirituals of the slavery era.

Traveling groups of black men, some of them ex-slaves, put on minstrel shows that featured "coon songs" after the Civil War. Many black Americans resented these popular shows as caricatures and exaggerations of black behavior. At least six hundred "coon songs" that attracted a predominantly white audience were published by 1900 including "All Coons Look Alike to Me," "Mammy's Little Pickaninny," and "My Coal Black Lady."

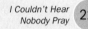 *I Couldn't Hear Nobody Pray* 22 LIVING WORDS

Most black people did not perform in or enjoy the demeaning minstrel shows. They had other forms of musical entertainment. "The Civil Rights Juba," published in 1874, was a precursor to ragtime. In 1871 the Fisk University Jubilee Singers began the first of many fund-raising concert tours that entertained black and white audiences in the United States and Europe for years thereafter with slave songs and spirituals. Other black colleges and universities also sent choirs and singers on similar trips.

RAGTIME

Ragtime, which emerged in the 1890s, was composed music, written down for performance on the piano. Ragtime pieces were not accompanied by lyrics and not meant to be sung. The creative genius of the form, Scott Joplin, was born in Texarkana, Texas, in 1868. He learned to play on a piano his mother bought from her earnings as a maid, and he may have had some training in classical music. Joplin subsequently learned to transfer complex banjo syncopations to the piano as he fused European harmonies and African rhythms. He traveled to Chicago in 1893 and played at the Columbian Exposition. He soon began to write ragtime sheet music that sold well. In 1899 he composed his best-known tune, the "Maple Leaf Rag," named after a social club (brothel) in Sedalia, Missouri. It sold an astonishing one million copies.

Maple Leaf Rag 28 LIVING WORDS

JAZZ

Jazz gradually replaced ragtime in popularity in the early twentieth century. Unlike ragtime, jazz was mostly improvised, not composed, and it was not confined to the piano. Jazz incorporated African and European musical elements drawn from such diverse sources as plantation bands, minstrel shows, riverboat

Scott Joplin (1868–1917) was one of America's most prolific composers, and his name is indelibly linked with ragtime. Although ragtime's popularity faded by the 1920s, Joplin's reputation and compositions were resurrected in 1974 when the Hollywood film, *The Sting* relied on Joplin's 1902 rag, "The Entertainer," for its soundtrack. In 1976 Scott Joplin was posthumously awarded the Pulitzer Prize for music.

ensembles, and Irish and Scottish folk tunes. The first jazz bands emerged in and around New Orleans where they played at parades, funerals, clubs, and outdoor concerts. Instead of the banjos, pipes, fifes, and violins of earlier black musical groups, these bands relied more on brass, reeds, and drums.

Ferdinand J. La Menthe, regarded as the first prominent jazz musician, was born in 1890 and grew up in a French-speaking family in New Orleans. Young La Menthe played several musical instruments before settling on the piano. He was also a superb composer and arranger. Later he changed his name to Morton and came to be known as Jelly Roll Morton. He played in the "red light" district of New Orleans known as Storeyville, where he was also a pool shark and gambler. He moved to Los Angeles in 1917 and to Chicago in 1922, where he subsequently led and recorded with "Morton's Red Hot Peppers." He died in 1941.

THE BLUES

In rural, isolated areas of the South, poor black people composed and sang songs about their lives and experiences. W. C. Handy, the father of the blues, later recalled, "Southern Negroes sang about everything. Trains, steamboats, steam whistles, sledge hammers, fast women, mean bosses, stubborn mules." They accompanied themselves on anything from a guitar to a harmonica to a washboard. They played in juke joints (rural nightclubs), at picnics, lumber camps, and urban nightclubs.

Handy, who was born in Florence, Alabama, in 1873, took up music despite the opposition of his devoutly Christian parents. He learned to play the guitar, although his mother and father regarded it as the "devil's plaything." He later led his own nine-man band. In the Mississippi Delta in 1903, Handy encountered "primitive," or "boogie," music unlike anything he had heard before. Handy was not initially impressed by the mostly unskilled and itinerant musicians whose lives swirled around cheap whiskey, gambling, prostitution, and violence. "Then I saw the beauty of primitive music. They had the stuff people wanted. It touched the spot. Their music wanted polishing, but it contained the essence. People would pay money for it." Handy went on to compose many tunes including "Memphis Blues" and "St. Louis Blues."

Handy was not the only musician to "discover" the blues. Gertrude Pridget sang in southern minstrel shows. In 1902 she heard a young black woman in a small Missouri town sing forlornly about a lover who had left her. Pridget took the song and included it in her shows. In 1904 she married William "Pa" Rainey and became "Ma" Rainey. Rainey proceeded to create other "blues" songs based on ballads, hymns, and the experiences of black people. As "Mother of the Blues," she recorded extensively and continuously in the 1920s and 1930s.

By 1920 two forms of American music were well along in their evolution—jazz and the blues. Both drew on African and American musical elements as well as on European styles. But most of all, jazz and the blues represented the experiences of African Americans and the creativity of the exceptional musicians who developed and performed the music.

Sports

While talented black men and women were making dramatic musical innovations, black athletes found that white athletes and sports entrepreneurs were increasingly opposed to the presence of black men in the boxing ring and on the playing field. In boxing, black men regularly fought white men through the end of the nineteenth century. But many white people, especially southerners, were offended by the practice. In 1892 George Dixon, a black boxer, won the world featherweight title, and some white men cheered his victory, distressing a Chicago journalist. "It was not pleasant," he complained, "to see white men applaud a negro for knocking another white man out. It was not pleasant to see them crowding around 'Mr.' Dixon to congratulate him on his victory, to seek an introduction with 'the distinguished colored gentleman' while he puffed his cigar and lay back like a prince receiving his subjects." Despite such opinions, there was never any official prohibition of interracial bouts.

JACK JOHNSON

The success of another black boxer, heavyweight Jack Johnson, angered many white Americans. Johnson was born in Galveston, Texas, in 1878 and became a professional boxer in 1897. Between 1902 and 1907 he won fifty-seven bouts against black and white fighters. In 1908 he badly beat the white heavyweight champion, Tommy Burns, in Australia. Many white boxing fans were unwilling to accept Johnson as the champion and looked desperately for "a great white hope" who could defeat him. Jim Jeffries, a former champion, came out of retirement to take on Johnson. In a brutal fight under a scorching sun in Reno, Nevada, in 1910, Johnson knocked Jeffries out in the fifteenth round.

Johnson's personal life, as well as his prowess in the ring, provoked white animosity. Having divorced his black wife, he married a white woman in 1911. Several months later, overwhelmed by social ostracism, she committed suicide. After Johnson married a second white woman, he was convicted of violating the Mann Act, which made it illegal to transport a woman across state lines for immoral purposes. In Johnson's case the "immorality" was his marriage to white women. Sentenced to a year in prison and fined $1,000, Johnson fled to Canada and then to France to avoid punishment. He lost his title to Jesse Willard in 1915 in Havana in the twenty-sixth round in a fight many people believe that Johnson threw. He returned to the United States in 1920 and served ten months in Leavenworth Prison.

BASEBALL

Baseball was a relatively new sport that became popular after the Civil War. As professional baseball developed in the 1870s and 1880s, both black and white men competed to earn money playing the game. It was not easy. They were the nation's first professional athletes, but professional baseball was unstable. Teams were formed and dissolved with depressing regularity. Players moved from team to team. Some thirty black men played professional baseball in the quarter century after the Civil War.

White players led by Adrian Constantine "Cap" Anson of the Chicago White Stockings tried to get baseball club owners to stop signing black men to contracts. Anson, who was from Iowa, bitterly resented having to play against black men. In 1887 International League officials rescinded a rule that had permitted them to sign black baseball players. One black player, Weldy Wilberforce Walker, protested the exclusion in a letter to *Sporting Life*. He insisted black men be judged by their skills, not by their color. "There should be some broader cause—such as lack of ability, behavior, and intelligence—for barring a player, rather than his color. It is for these reasons and because I think ability and intelligence should be recognized first and last—at all times and by everyone—I ask the question again, 'Why was the law permitting colored men to sign repealed, etc.?' " There was no intelligent answer to Walker's question. But Jim Crow was

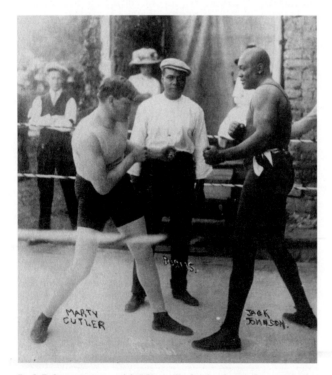

Jack Johnson spars with Marty Cutler in the early twentieth century. Johnson was a superb fighter whose ability to defeat white boxers rankled many white men. But Johnson's involvement with white women infuriated them even more and led to his imprisonment.

now on the baseball diamond. Moses Fleetwood Walker—Weldy's brother—was the last black man to play major league baseball in the nineteenth century as a catcher with Toledo of the American Association. No black men would be allowed to play with white men in major league baseball until Jackie Robinson joined the Brooklyn Dodgers in 1947.

In reaction to their exclusion, black men formed their own teams. By 1900 there were five black professional teams including the Norfolk Red Stockings, the Chicago Unions, and the Cuban X Giants of New York. The Negro Leagues would be an integral (but not integrated) part of sports for the next half century.

BASKETBALL AND OTHER SPORTS

James Naismith invented basketball in 1891 in Springfield, Massachusetts. Black youngsters were playing organized basketball by 1906 in YMCAs and later YWCAs in New York City, Philadelphia, and Washington, D.C. By 1910–1911 Howard University and Hampton Institute had basketball teams. In horse racing, black jockeys regularly won major races. Willie Simms won the Kentucky Derby in 1894, 1895, 1896, and 1898. Bicycling and bicycle racing were enormously popular by the 1890s, and in 1900 a black rider, Marshall W. "Major" Taylor, won the U.S. sprint championship.

COLLEGE ATHLETICS

Generally, white colleges and universities in the North that admitted black students would not let them participate in intercollegiate sports. (Southern colleges and universities did not admit black students.) There were, however, exceptions. In 1889 W. T. S. Jackson and William Henry Lewis played football for Amherst College. Lewis was the captain of the team in 1890. As a law school student, Lewis played for Harvard and was named to the Walter Camp All-American team in 1892. (Lewis became a distinguished attorney who was forced out of the American Bar Association because of his color. See the section "The Law" in this chapter.) White institutions with black players often encountered the racism so rampant during the era. In 1907 the University of Alabama baseball team canceled a game with the University of Vermont after learning the Vermont squad had two black infielders. Moreover, black players were frequently subjected to abuse from opposing teams and their fans.

Intercollegiate athletics emerged at black colleges and universities in the late nineteenth century. White schools occasionally played black institutions. The Yale Law School baseball team, for example, played Howard in 1898. But black college teams were far more likely to play each other. The first football game between two black colleges took place on December 27, 1892, when Biddle University (today Johnson C. Smith University) defeated Livingston College in Salisbury, North Carolina.

Eventually black athletic conferences were formed. The Central Intercollegiate Athletic Association (CIAA) was organized in 1912 with Hampton, Howard, Virginia Union, and Shaw College in Raleigh, North Carolina, among its early members. The Southeastern Conference was established in 1913 and consisted of Morehouse, Fisk, Florida A&M, and Tuskegee, among others. In Texas in 1920, five black colleges founded the Southwestern Athletic Conference: Prairie View A&M, Bishop College, Paul Quinn College, Wiley College, and Sam Houston College.

CONCLUSION

White supremacy was debilitating, discouraging, and dangerous, but black Americans were sometimes able to turn Jim Crow to their advantage. To lessen the effects of white racism and to improve the economic status of black people, educators like Samuel Chapman Armstrong and Booker T. Washington recommended agricultural and mechanical training for most black Americans. But critics such as W. E. B. Du Bois stressed the need to cultivate the minds as well as the hands of black people to develop leaders.

Black men served with distinction in all-black military units in the Indian wars, the Spanish-American War, and the Philippine Insurrection. But no matter how loyal or how committed black men in uniform were, the white majority never fully trusted nor displayed confidence in them. African Americans could only react with dismay and outrage when President Theodore Roosevelt dismissed 167 black soldiers in 1906 in the Brownsville affair.

As they tried to shape their own destinies in the late nineteenth century, black Americans organized a variety of institutions. Mostly barred from white schools, churches, hospitals, labor unions, and places of entertainment, they developed businesses and facilities to serve their communities. Black businesses, organizations, and institutions functioned in an environment mostly free from white control and interference. Black people relied on their own experiences and imaginations to create new forms of music. They participated in sports with white athletes

AFRICAN-AMERICAN EVENTS	NATIONAL EVENTS
1860	
	1862 Morrill Land-Grant Act is passed to support agricultural and mechanical education
1865	
1867 Independent Order of St. Luke is founded in Baltimore	**1867** U.S. purchases Alaska from Russia
1868 Hampton Institute is founded	**1869** Cincinnati "Red Stockings" is organized as the first professional baseball team
	Rutgers and Princeton play the first college football game
1869–1898 Four regiments of black soldiers serve on the western frontier	
1870	
1870 Howard University Law School is established	**1873** Panic of 1873 is followed by major depression
1875	
1880	
1881 Tuskegee Institute is founded	**1881** Clara Barton establishes the Red Cross
1885	
1887 Black players are barred from major league baseball	
1890	
1891 Dr. Daniel Hale Williams founds Provident Hospital in Chicago	**1890** Second Morrill Act is passed
1892 First black college football game: Biddle vs. Livingstone	**1891** John D. Rockefeller funds the establishment of the University of Chicago
	1892 Grover Cleveland elected to a second term as president

but more often played separately from them as segregation and white hostility spread.

Although black people recognized their churches, hospitals, schools, and businesses were often inadequately financed and usually less imposing than those of white people, they also knew that at a black school or church, in a black store, or in the care of a black physician or nurse, they would not be abused, mistreated, or ridiculed because of their color.

RECOMMENDED READING

James D. Anderson. *The Education of Blacks in the South, 1860–1931.* Chapel Hill: University of North Carolina Press, 1988. Anderson is highly critical of the education and philosophy promoted and provided by Hampton Institute and Tuskegee Institute.

Edward L. Ayers. *The Promise of the New South: Life after Reconstruction.* New York: Oxford University Press, 1992. This wide-ranging study encompasses almost every aspect of life in the late-nineteenth-century South, including religion, education, sports, and music.

Sutton E. Griggs. *Imperium in Imperio.* New York: Arno Press reprint, 1899. This novel describes the formation of a separate black nation in Texas at the end of the nineteenth century.

Leon Litwack. *Trouble in Mind: Black Southerners in the Age of Jim Crow.* New York: Alfred A. Knopf, 1998. The author lets the words of black people of the time, including lawyers, physicians, and musicians, explain what life was like in an age of intense white supremacy.

Leon Litwack and August Meier, eds. *Black Leaders in the Nineteenth Century.* Urbana: University of Illinois Press, 1988. This volume contains eighteen brief but valuable biographical essays.

Benjamin E. Mays. *Born to Rebel.* New York: Scribner, 1971. Mays's autobiography includes penetrating insights into religion and education among rural black southerners.

Howard N. Rabinowitz. *Race Relations in the Urban South, 1865–1890.* New York: Oxford University Press, 1978. The author examines black life in Atlanta, Montgomery, Nashville, Raleigh, and Richmond.

Mim Eichler Rivas. *Beautiful Jim Key: The Lost History of a Horse and a Man Who Changed the World.* New York: William Morrow, 2005. Here is a fascinating and warm account of how a former slave trained an exceptional horse, and the two of them then became hugely successful entertainers by the early twentieth century.

Quintard Taylor. *In Search of the Racial Frontier.* New York: W. W. Norton, 1998. This is a fine survey and analysis of the role of African Americans in the West from the sixteenth century to 1990.

ADDITIONAL BIBLIOGRAPHY

EDUCATION

Eric Anderson and Alfred A. Moss Jr. *Dangerous Donations: Northern Philanthropy and Southern Black Education, 1902–1930.* Columbia: University of Missouri Press, 1999.

Peter M. Ascoli. *Julius Rosenwald: The Man Who Built Sears, Roebuck and Advanced the Cause of Black Education in the American South.* Bloomington: Indiana University Press, 2006.

James D. Anderson and V. P. Franklin, eds. *New Perspectives on Black Education.* Boston: G. K. Hall, 1978.

Henry A. Bullock. *A History of Negro Education in the South from 1619 to the Present.* Cambridge, MA: Harvard University Press, 1967.

Mary S. Hoffschwelle. *The Rosenwald Schools in the American South.* Gainesville: University Press of Florida, 2006.

RELIGION

Stephen W. Angell. *Bishop Henry McNeal Turner and African American Religion in the South.* Knoxville: University of Tennessee Press, 1992.

Cyprian Davis. *The History of Black Catholics in the United States.* New York: Crossroad, 1990.

Harold T. Lewis. *Yet with a Steady Beat: The African American Struggle for Recognition in the Episcopal Church.* Valley Forge, PA: Trinity Press International, 1996.

Iain MacRobert. *The Black Roots and White Racism of Early Pentecostalism in the USA.* Basingstoke, England: Macmillan, 1988.

James M. O'Toole. *Passing for White: Race, Religion, and the Healy Family, 1820–1920.* Amherst: University of Massachusetts Press, 2002.

Edwin S. Redkey, ed. *The Writings and Speeches of Henry McNeal Turner.* New York: Arno Press, 1971.

Clarence E. Walker. *A Rock in a Weary Land: The African Methodist Episcopal Church during the Civil War and Reconstruction.* Baton Rouge: Louisiana State University Press, 1982.

THE MILITARY AND THE WEST

John M. Carroll, ed. *The Black Military Experience in the American West.* New York: Liveright, 1973.

Willard B. Gatewood, ed. *Smoked Yankees and the Struggle for Empire: Letters from Negro Soldiers, 1898–1902.* Urbana: University of Illinois Press, 1971.

William Loren Katz. *The Black West.* New York: Touchstone Books, 1996.

William H. Leckie. *The Buffalo Soldiers: A Narrative of the Negro Cavalry in the West.* Norman: University of Oklahoma Press, 1967.

Paul W. Stewart and Wallace Yvonne Ponce. *Black Cowboys.* Broomfield, CO: Phillips, 1986.

John D. Weaver. *The Brownsville Raid.* New York: Norton, 1971.

Timeline

1895

AFRICAN-AMERICAN EVENTS

1895
Booker T. Washington addresses the Cotton States Exposition in Atlanta

1899
Scott Joplin composes the "Maple Leaf Rag"

NATIONAL EVENTS

1895
Sears Roebuck and Company form a retail mail order business

1899
Cumming v. Richmond County [Georgia] Board of Education eliminates Augusta's black high school

1900

1903
St. Luke Penny Savings Bank is established in Richmond with Maggie Lena Walker as president

1901
President William McKinley assassinated; Vice President Theodore Roosevelt becomes president

1903
Henry Ford organizes the Ford Motor Co.

Wilbur and Orville Wright launch the first powered aircraft at Kitty Hawk, North Carolina

1905

1908
National Association of Colored Graduate Nurses is founded in New York City; Jack Johnson wins the heavyweight championship in boxing

1908
William Howard Taft elected president

1910

1915

LABOR

Tera W. Hunter. *To 'Joy My Freedom: Southern Black Women's Lives and Labors after the Civil War.* Cambridge, MA: Harvard University Press, 1997.

Gerald D. Jaynes. *Branches without Roots: Genesis of the Black Working Class in the American South, 1862–1882.* New York: Oxford University Press, 1986.

THE PROFESSIONS

V. N. Gamble. *The Black Community Hospital: Contemporary Dilemmas in Historical Perspective.* New York: Garland, 1989.

Darlene Clark Hine. *Speak Truth to Power: Black Professional Class in United States History.* Brooklyn, NY: Carlson, 1996.

Gertrude Woodruff Marlowe. *A Right Worthy Grand Mission: Maggie Lena Walker and the Quest for Black Economic Empowerment.* Washington, DC: Howard University Press, 2003.

J. Clay Smith Jr. *Emancipation: The Making of the Black Lawyer, 1844–1944.* Philadelphia: University of Pennsylvania Press, 1993.

J. Clay Smith Jr., ed. *Rebels in Law: Voices in History of Black Women Lawyers.* Ann Arbor: University of Michigan Press, 1998.

Susan L. Smith. *Sick and Tired of Being Sick and Tired: Black Women's Health Activism in America, 1890–1950.* Philadelphia: University of Pennsylvania Press, 1995.

Thomas J. Ward Jr. *Black Physicians in the Jim Crow South.* Fayetteville: University of Arkansas Press, 2003.

MUSIC

W. C. Handy. *Father of the Blues: An Autobiography.* New York: Macmillan, 1941.

John Edward Hasse, ed. *Ragtime, Its History, Composers, and Music.* London: Macmillan, 1985.

William Howland Kenney. *Jazz on the River.* Chicago: University of Chicago Press, 2005.

Alan Lomax. *Mr. Jelly Roll: The Fortunes of Jelly Roll Morton, New Orleans Creole and "Inventor of Jazz."* New York: Grove Press, 1950.

Gunther Schuller. *Early Jazz: Its Roots and Musical Development.* New York: Oxford University Press, 1968.

SPORTS

Ocania Chalk. *Black College Sport.* New York: Dodd, Mead, 1976.

Neil Lanctot. *Negro League Baseball: The Rise and Ruin of a Black Institution.* Philadelphia: University of Pennsylvania Press, 2004.

Robert W. Peterson. *Only the Ball Was White: Negro Baseball: A History of Legendary Black Players and All-Black Professional Teams before Black Men Played in the Major Leagues.* New York: Prentice-Hall, 1970.

Andrew Ritchie. *Major Taylor: The Extraordinary Career of a Championship Bicycle Racer.* San Francisco: Bicycle Books, 1988.

Randy Roberts. *Papa Jack: Jack Johnson and the Era of White Hopes.* New York: Free Press, 1983.

RETRACING THE ODYSSEY

Hampton University, Hampton, Virginia. Founded by Samuel Chapman Armstrong with the assistance of the American Missionary Association, Hampton Normal and Agricultural Institute opened in 1868 to train former slaves (and later Native Americans) in agricultural and mechanical skills. Virginia Hall (1874), Memorial Church (1886), the Hampton Museum, and the giant Emancipation Oak are all located on this picturesque campus overlooking Chesapeake Bay and Hampton Roads.

Tuskegee Institute National Historic Site, Tuskegee, Alabama. What is now Tuskegee University opened in 1881 and remained under the leadership of Booker T. Washington until his death in 1915. His home—The Oaks—was built by students and is now a museum. His grave and memorial are also on the campus, as is the George Washington Carver Museum.

Alonzo F. Herndon Home, Atlanta, Georgia. Herndon was the founder of the Atlanta Life Insurance Company and one of the wealthiest black men in America by the early 1900s. His fifteen-room mansion with immense white pillars was finished in 1910 and is open to the public. It is furnished with antiques, Roman and Venetian glass, as well as ornate artwork.

Maggie L. Walker National Historic Site, Richmond, Virginia. Built in 1883, this twenty-two-room Victorian mansion was home to the Walker family from 1904 to 1934 and is now open for tours. There is a visitor center that contains exhibits on the life of Maggie Lena Walker and the Jackson Ward community.

Madame C. J. Walker Center, Indianapolis, Indiana. In 1910 C. J. Walker (Sarah Breedlove) moved her thriving hair care and beauty products business from Denver to Indianapolis. The four-story triangular building was completed in 1919 shortly after Walker's death. It housed manufacturing facilities and was home to a beauty college that trained Walker's agents to care for the hair of African-American women and to sell Walker's products. It is currently a community center and theater.

Dunbar Hospital, Detroit, Michigan. This red brick structure was built in 1892 and served as a hospital for Detroit's black community from 1918 to 1928. It is currently operated by the Detroit Medical Society, and it has exhibits, medical devices, photographs, and papers documenting the medical care available to black Detroit.

REVIEW, RESEARCH, AND INTERACT

REVIEW QUESTIONS

1. How and why did the agricultural and mechanical training offered by Hampton Institute and Tuskegee Institute gain so much support among both black and white people? Why did black colleges and universities emphasize learning trades and acquiring skills?

2. How compatible was the educational philosophy of the late nineteenth century with the racial ideology of that era?

3. Of what value was an education for a black person in the 1890s or early 1900s? To what use could a black person put an education? What exactly was the benefit of an education?

4. What purpose did the black church serve? What were the strengths and weaknesses of the black church? What roles did black clergymen play in late-nineteenth-century America?

5. How could a black man in the U.S. Army justify participating in wars against Native Americans, the Spanish, and the Filipinos? What motivated black soldiers to serve? How well did they serve?

6. Did black people derive any benefits from the growth and expansion of segregation and Jim Crow?

7. Why did ragtime, jazz, and the blues emerge and become popular?

8. How did segregation affect the development of amateur and professional athletics in the United States?

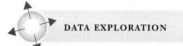 **www.researchnavigator.com**

Using the tools available in Research Navigator, consider this question:
What place did religion have in late-nineteenth-century African-American life?

PRIMARY SOURCE DOCUMENTS

15–1 Booker T. Washington, The Atlanta Exposition Address

15–5 W. E. B. Du Bois, The Talented Tenth, 1903

DATA EXPLORATION

Black and White Illiteracy in the United States and the Southern States, 1880–1900, p. 381.

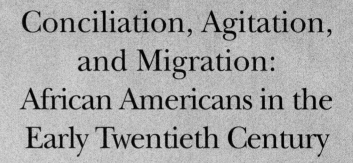

16

Conciliation, Agitation, and Migration:
African Americans in the Early Twentieth Century

1895–1928

ON WHAT ISSUES DID BOOKER T. WASHINGTON
AND W. E. B. DU BOIS AGREE AND DISAGREE
IN THEIR EFFORTS TO PROMOTE
THE ADVANCEMENT OF AFRICAN AMERICANS?

WHAT WERE THE PURPOSES
AND AIMS OF THE NAACP?

HOW DID BLACK WOMEN FOSTER
PROGRESS AMONG AFRICAN AMERICANS?

HOW DID AFRICAN AMERICANS CONTRIBUTE TO
U.S. PARTICIPATION IN WORLD WAR I?

WHY WAS THERE SO MUCH RACIAL VIOLENCE
IN THE EARLY TWENTIETH CENTURY?

WHY DID SO MANY AFRICAN AMERICANS LEAVE
THE SOUTH IN THE 1910s AND 1920s?

◀◀ **Although Tuskegee Institute** stressed agricultural and
vocational subjects, students did enroll in math, science, and
English courses. Here students in a U.S. history class are
involved in a discussion of Virginia's founding in the early
seventeenth century. Notice that the male and female
students are segregated and that the classroom features the
portraits of three U.S. presidents and several American
flags. Courtesy of the Library of Congress

The wisest among my race understand that the agitation of questions of social equality is the extremest folly, and that progress in the enjoyment of all privileges that will come to us must be the result of severe and constant struggle rather than of artificial forcing. No race that has anything to contribute to the markets of the world is long in any degree ostracized. It is important and right all privileges of the law be ours, but it is vastly more important that we be prepared for the exercises of these privileges.

Booker T. Washington, Atlanta Cotton States and International Exposition, September 18, 1895

Mr. Washington distinctly asks that black people give up, at least for the present three things,—
First, political power,
Second, insistence on civil rights,
Third, higher education of Negro youth,—
and concentrate all their energies on industrial education, the accumulation of wealth, and the conciliation of the South.

W. E. B. Du Bois, *The Souls of Black Folk*, 1903

◄ **The first issue** of *The Crisis* monthly magazine edited by W.E.B. Du Bois, was published in November 1910.

As the twentieth century dawned, black and white Americans had profoundly different views on the future of black people in America. Most white people believed black Americans were an inferior race capable of little more than manual labor and entitled to only the most basic legal rights. Black Americans rejected that assertion and worked for a more equitable place in society. Black scholar W. E. B. Du Bois announced in 1903 that race would be the century's most critical issue. "The problem of the twentieth century is the problem of the color line—the relation of the darker to the lighter races of men in Asia and Africa, in America and the islands of the sea."

Black people refused to accept the inferiority to which they had been consigned. They devised strategies and organized institutions to enable them to prosper in a hostile society. However, African Americans and their leaders disagreed about how to secure the constitutional rights and the material comforts that so many white Americans took for granted. Some, following W. E. B. Du Bois, a founder of the Niagara Movement and the National Association for the Advancement of Colored People (NAACP), favored a frontal assault on discrimination, disfranchisement, and Jim Crow in the quest for racial progress. Others, following Booker T. Washington of the Tuskegee Institute, cautioned against the vigorous pursuit of civil rights and political power and insisted that agricultural and industrial training would generate prosperity and self-sufficiency among people of color.

The emergence of the club movement among black women and other self-help organizations (see Chapter 15) enabled more prosperous black people to aid those suffering acutely from poverty and prejudice. The black elite, often reviled for ostentatious social displays, came to be designated the **Talented Tenth,** and many of them took seriously their responsibilities to aid their brethren.

When the United States entered World War I in 1917, black men responded patriotically, as they had in previous conflicts. They joined a Jim Crow military that was fighting to make the world safe for democracy. But black people in America were not safe, and democracy did not prevail. Riots and racial violence erupted before, during, and after the war.

In the meantime, one of the most important episodes in American history—a vast and prolonged migration of hundreds of thousands of rural black southerners to northern cities—began in earnest after 1910. Drawn mainly by economic opportunities, black people moved to New York, Philadelphia, Cleveland, Chicago, and other urban centers.

Race and the Progressive Movement

By the first decade of the twentieth century, many Americans were concerned and even alarmed about the rapid economic and social changes that confronted the United States, including industrialization, the rise of powerful corporations, the explosive growth of cities, and the influx of millions of immigrants. Their apprehensions spawned a disparate collection of efforts at reform known as the progressive movement. In general, progressives believed America needed a new social awareness to deal with the new social and economic problems. But most of the middle- and upper-class white people who formed the core of the movement showed little interest in white racism and its impact. Indeed, many were racists themselves. They were primarily concerned with the concentration of wealth in monopolies such as Standard Oil, with pervasive political corruption in state and local governments, and with the plight of working-class immigrants in American cities. They cared deeply about the debilitating effects of alcohol, tainted food, and prostitution, but little about the grim impact of white supremacy. When Upton Sinclair wrote his muckraking novel *The Jungle* to expose the exploitation of European immigrants in Chicago meatpacking houses, he depicted black people as brute laborers and strikebreakers.

The reforms of the progressive movement nonetheless offered at least a glimmer of hope that racial advancement was possible. If efforts were made to improve America, was it not possible that there be some advances achieved in policies and conditions affecting black Americans? But how much militancy or forbearance was necessary to achieve significant racial progress? Did it even make sense for black people to demand a meaningful role in a nation that despised them? Perhaps it

was wiser to turn inward and rely on each other rather than plead for white recognition and respect.

Booker T. Washington's Approach

Booker T. Washington's commitment to agricultural and industrial education served as the basis for his approach to "the problem of the color line." By the beginning of the twentieth century, Washington was convinced that black men and women who had mastered skills acquired at institutions like Tuskegee and Hampton would be recognized, if not welcomed, as productive contributors to the southern economy. Washington believed economic acceptance would lead in due course to political and social acceptance.

The Tuskegee leader eloquently outlined his philosophy in the speech he delivered at the opening ceremonies of the Cotton States Exposition in Atlanta in 1895 (see Chapter 15). Black people, he told his segregated audience, would find genuine opportunities in the South. "[W]hen it comes to business, pure and simple, it is in the South that the Negro is given a man's chance in the commercial world." Washington added that black people should not expect too much but should welcome menial labor as a first step in the struggle for progress. Ever optimistic, he looked for opportunities while deprecating those who complained. "Nor should we permit our grievances to overshadow our opportunities." He told white listeners that the lives of black and white southerners were historically linked, and that black people were far more loyal and steadfast than newly arrived immigrants. "[I]n our humble way, we shall stand by you with a devotion that no foreigner can approach, ready to lay down our lives, if need be, in defence of yours, interlacing our industrial, commercial, civil, and religious life with yours in a way that shall make the interests of both races one."

Address at the Atlanta Exposition LIVING WORDS 24

Then, in a striking metaphor, Washington reassured white people that cooperation between the races in the interest of prosperity did not endanger segregation. "In all things that are purely social we can be as separate as the fingers, yet one as the hand in all things essential to mutual progress." Finally, Washington implied that black people need not protest because they were denied rights white men possessed. Instead, he urged his black listeners to struggle steadily rather than make defiant demands. "The wisest among my race understand that the agitation of questions of social equality is the extremest folly, and that progress in the enjoyment of all the privileges that will come to us must be the result of severe and constant struggle rather than of artificial forcing." Washington was convinced that as African Americans became productive and made economic progress, white people would concede them their rights.

The speech was warmly received by both white and black listeners and by those who read it when it was widely reprinted. T. Thomas Fortune, the black editor of the New York *Age*, told Washington that he had replaced Frederick Douglass (who died in 1895) as a leader. "It looks as if you are our Douglass, the best equipped of the lot of us to be the single figure ahead of the procession."

But not everyone was complimentary. The black editor of the *Washington Bee*, W. Calvin Chase, complained, "He said something that was death to the Afro-American and elevating to white people." Bishop Henry M. Turner of the AME church added that Washington "will have to live a long time to undo the harm he has done our race."

White people regarded Washington's speech as moderate, sensible, and altogether praiseworthy. Almost overnight he was designated the spokesman for African Americans. Washington accepted the recognition and took full advantage of it.

WASHINGTON'S INFLUENCE

Booker T. Washington was a complex man. Many people found him unassertive, dignified, and patient. Yet he was ambitious, aggressive, and opportunistic as well as shrewd, calculating, and devious. He had an uncanny ability to determine what he might say to other people that would elicit a positive response from them. He became extraordinarily powerful. In the words of his assistant, Emmett J. Scott, Washington was "the Wizard of Tuskegee."

After the Atlanta speech, Washington's influence soared. He received extensive and mostly positive coverage in black newspapers. Some of that popularity stemmed from admiration for his leadership and agreement with his ideas. But Washington also cultivated and flattered editors, paid for advertisements for Tuskegee, and subsidized struggling journalists.

He was especially effective in dealing with prominent white businessmen and philanthropists. William H. Baldwin, vice president of the Southern Railroad, was so impressed with Washington's management of Tuskegee that Baldwin agreed to serve as the chairman of Tuskegee's board. Washington developed support among the nation's industrial elite including steel magnate Andrew Carnegie and Julius Rosenwald, the head of Sears, Roebuck, and Company. They trusted

Booker T. Washington had access to and influence among the most powerful political and business leaders in the United States. Here he shares the podium with President Theodore Roosevelt. Washington persuaded Republican leaders like Roosevelt to appoint black men to an assortment of federal offices and convinced businessmen to contribute sizable sums to black colleges and universities. Nevertheless, some African Americans criticized the Tuskegee leader for not speaking out more candidly in opposition to white supremacy and Jim Crow.

Washington's judgment and invariably consulted him before contributing to black colleges and universities. Washington assured them of the wisdom of investing in the training of black men and women in agricultural and mechanical skills. These students, he repeatedly reminded donors, would be self-sufficient and productive members of southern society.

For example, Rosenwald traveled to Tuskegee, consulted with Washington, and agreed over time to contribute several million dollars to construct public schools for black youngsters across the fifteen southern states. Between 1913 and 1932, over 5,300 schools ranging in size from one to six classrooms were built. Julius Rosenwald insisted that local communities provide a substantial portion of the funds. Of the 28 million dollars spent on constructing these Rosenwald schools, black communities contributed 19 percent, Rosenwald donated 16.5 percent, white people provided 4.5 percent, while state and local governments were responsible for 60 percent. Some white communities, however, absolutely refused to have these schools built even after local black people and Rosenwald agreed to share the financial responsibility for the schools. Black children in those communities received little, if any, education.

THE TUSKEGEE MACHINE

Washington advised black people to avoid politics, but he ignored his own advice. Although he never ran for office or was appointed to a political position, Washington was a political figure to be reckoned with. His connections to white businesspeople and politicians gave him enormous influence. Critics and admirers alike referred to him as "the Wizard of Tuskegee." With his influence, his connections, and his organizational skills, Washington operated what came to be known as "**The Tuskegee Machine.**" In 1896 he supported winning Republican presidential candidate William McKinley over the Democratic and Populist William Jennings Bryan. Washington got along superbly with McKinley's successor, Theodore Roosevelt. Although Roosevelt subscribed to social Darwinism (see Chapter 15) and regarded black Americans as inferiors, he liked and respected Washington.

In 1901 Roosevelt invited Washington to dinner at the White House, where Roosevelt's wife, daughter, three sons, and a Colorado businessman joined them. Black people applauded, but the white South, alarmed by such a flagrant breach of racial etiquette (black people did not dine with white people), recoiled in disgust. Mississippi senator James K. Vardaman was so angry that he claimed the White House was "so saturated with the odor of the nigger than the rats have taken refuge in the stable." Roosevelt was unmoved, and a few days later the two men dined again together at Yale University. Still, Roosevelt never invited Washington for another meal at the Executive Mansion.

Washington and Roosevelt regularly consulted each other on political appointments. In the most notable case, Washington urged Roosevelt to appoint William D. Crum, a black medical doctor, as the collector of customs for the port of Charleston, South Carolina. White southerners, led by Senator Benjamin R. Tillman, a South Carolina Democrat, opposed Crum's appointment and delayed final confirmation by the Senate for nearly three years. With Washington's assent, Roosevelt appointed black attorney and former all-American football player William Lewis to be U.S. district attorney in Boston. Several years later, President William Howard Taft appointed Lewis assistant attorney general of the United States. (For more details on Lewis, see Chapter 15.)

Most of Washington's political activities were not public. He secretly helped finance an unsuccessful court case against the Louisiana grandfather clause. (The statute disfranchised those voters—black men—whose grandfathers had not possessed the right to vote; see Chapter 14.) Washington provided funds to carry two cases challenging Alabama's grandfather clause to the U.S. Supreme Court, which ultimately rejected both on a technicality. He tried to persuade railroad executives to improve the conditions on segregated coaches and in station waiting rooms. He worked covertly with white attorneys to free a black farm laborer imprisoned under Alabama's peonage law. In many of these secret activities, Washington used code names in correspondence to hide his involvement. In the Louisiana case he was identified only as X.Y.Z.

Washington was a conservative leader who did not directly or publicly challenge white supremacy. He was willing to accept literacy and property qualifications for voting if they were equitably enforced regardless of race. He also opposed women's suffrage. He attacked lynching only occasionally. But he did write an annual letter to white newspapers filled with data on lynchings that had been compiled at Tuskegee. Washington let the grim statistics speak for themselves rather than denounce the injustice himself.

Washington founded the National Negro Business League in 1900 and served as its president until he died in 1915. The league brought together merchants, retailers, bankers, funeral directors, and other owners and operators of small enterprises. It helped promote black businesses in the black community and brought businessmen together to exchange information. Moreover, the league's annual meetings allowed Washington to develop support for the Tuskegee Machine from black businessmen who were community leaders from across the nation. Similarly, he worked closely with leaders in black fraternal orders such as the Odd Fellows and Pythians.

OPPOSITION TO WASHINGTON

Years before Washington rose to prominence, there were black leaders who favored a direct challenge to racial oppression. In 1889 delegates representing twenty-three states met to form the Afro-American League in Chicago. The league's main purpose was to press for civil and political rights guaranteed by the U.S. Constitution. "The objects of the League are to encourage State and local leagues in their efforts to break down color bars, and in obtaining for the Afro-American an equal chance with others in the avocations of life . . . in securing the full privileges of

W. E. B. Du Bois
on Being Black
in America

W. E. B. Du Bois's The Souls of Black Folk *(1903) contained perhaps the most eloquent statement ever written on being black in white America. The difficulties of their circumstances, Du Bois believed, create a double consciousness among Americans of African descent.*

After the Egyptian and Indian, the Greek and Roman, the Teuton and Mongolian, the Negro is a sort of seventh son, born with a veil, and gifted with second-sight in this American world,—a world which yields him no true self-consciousness, but only lets him see himself through the revelation of the other world. It is a peculiar sensation, this double-consciousness, this sense of always looking at one's self through the eyes of others, of measuring one's soul by the tape of a world that looks on in an amused contempt and pity. One ever feels his two-ness,—an American, a Negro; two souls, two thoughts, two unreconciled strivings; two warring ideals in one dark body, whose dogged strength alone keeps it from being torn asunder.

The history of the American Negro is the history of this strife,—this longing to attain self-conscious manhood, to merge his double self into a better and truer self. In this merging he wishes neither of the older selves to be lost. He would not Africanize America, for America has too much to teach the world and Africa. He would not bleach his Negro soul in a flood of white Americanism, for he knows that Negro blood has a message for the world. He simply wishes to make it possible for a man to be both a Negro and an American, without being cursed and spit upon by his fellows, without having the doors of Opportunity closed roughly in his face.

🌲 *Why, in the judgment of W. E. B. Du Bois, is it impossible for a black person to be simply an American?*

🌲 *Would Du Bois agree, based on his concept of double consciousness, that African Americans have a separate identity and separate culture from other Americans?*

Source: Du Bois, *The Souls of Black Folk* (New York: Library of America, 1903), pp. 8–9.

citizenship." But the league did not flourish, and it was eventually displaced by the Niagara Movement.

Opposition to Washington's conciliatory stance on racial matters steadily intensified. William Monroe Trotter became the most vociferous critic of Booker T. Washington and the Tuskegee Machine. Trotter was the Harvard-educated editor of the Boston *Guardian*, and he savagely attacked Washington as "the Great Traitor," "the Benedict Arnold of the Negro Race," and "Pope Washington." At a 1903 meeting of the National Negro Business League in Boston, Trotter stood on a chair and interrupted a speech by Washington, defiantly asking, "Are the rope and the torch all the race is to get under your leadership?" Washington ignored him, and the police arrested the editor for disorderly conduct. He spent thirty days in jail for what newspapers labeled "the Boston Riot."

W. E. B. Du Bois

William Edward Burghardt Du Bois, who was twelve years younger than Booker T. Washington, would eventually eclipse the influence and authority of the Wizard of Tuskegee. Du Bois emerged as the most significant black leader in America during the first half of the twentieth century. Whereas Washington's life had been shaped by slavery, poverty, and the industrial work ethic fostered at Hampton Institute, Du Bois was born and raised in the largely white New England town of Great Barrington, Massachusetts. It was a small community where he encountered little overt racism and developed a passion for knowledge.

Du Bois possessed, as he put it, "a flood of Negro blood, a strain of French, a bit of Dutch, but, thank God! no Anglo-Saxon." He graduated from Great Barrington High School at a time when few white and still fewer black youngsters attended more than primary school. He went south to Fisk University in Nashville and graduated at age twenty. He was the first black man to earn a Ph.D. (in history) at Harvard in 1895, and he pursued additional graduate study in Germany.

Du Bois was perhaps the greatest scholar-activist in American history. He was an intellectual, at ease with words and ideas. He wrote sixteen nonfiction books, five novels, and two autobiographies. He was a fearless activist determined to confront disfranchisement, Jim Crow, and lynching. Whereas Washington solicited the goodwill of powerful white leaders and was comfortable with a gradual approach to the eradication of white supremacy, Du Bois was impatient with white people who accepted or ignored white domination. Moreover, he had little tolerance for black people who were unwilling to demand their civil and political rights.

This early-twentieth-century illustration depicts a dapper young W. E. B. Du Bois (1868–1963). He was a key figure in opposing Booker T. Washington's Tuskegee Machine. Du Bois helped found the NAACP and edited its publication, *The Crisis*, for two decades.

Du Bois was well aware that he and Washington came from dissimilar backgrounds:

> I was born free. Washington was born a slave. He felt the lash of an overseer across his back. I was born in Massachusetts, he on a slave plantation in the South. My great-grandfather fought with the Colonial Army in New England in the American Revolution. I had a happy childhood and acceptance in the community. Washington's childhood was hard. I had many more advantages: Fisk University, Harvard, graduate years in Europe. Washington had little formal schooling.

THE SOULS OF BLACK FOLK

Du Bois was not always critical of Washington. Following Washington's speech at the Cotton States Exposition in 1895, Du Bois, then a young Harvard Ph.D. teaching at Ohio's Wilberforce University, wrote to praise him. "Let me heartily congratulate you upon your phenomenal success at Atlanta—it was a word fitly spoken." But in 1903, the same year as Trotter's arrest in the "Boston Riot," Du Bois, by then an Atlanta University professor, published *The Souls of Black Folk.* One of the major literary works of the twentieth century, it contained the first formal attack on Washington and his leadership.

In a provocative essay, "Of Booker T. Washington and Others," Du Bois conceded it was painful to challenge Washington, a man so highly praised and admired. "One hesitates, therefore, to criticise a life which, beginning with so little, has done so much. And yet the time is come when one may speak in all sincerity and utter courtesy of the mistakes and shortcomings of Mr. Washington's career, as well as the triumphs." Du Bois attacked Washington for failing to stand up for political and civil rights and higher education for black Americans. Du Bois found even more infuriating Washington's willingness to compromise with the white South and Washington's apparent agreement with white southerners that black people were not their equals. "Mr. Washington represents in Negro thought the old attitude of adjustment and submission . . . and Mr. Washington's programme practically accepts the alleged inferiority of the Negro races."

In concluding, Du Bois stressed that he agreed with Washington on some issues but disagreed even more about significant ones, and that on these issues it was vital to oppose Washington:

> So far as Mr. Washington preaches Thrift, Patience, and Industrial Training for the masses, we must hold up his hands and strive with him....But so far as Mr. Washington apologizes for injustice, North or South, does not rightly value the privilege and duty of voting, belittles the emasculating effects of caste distinctions, and opposes higher training and ambition of our brighter minds,—so far as he, the South, or the Nation, does this,—we must unceasingly and firmly oppose them.

Washington worried the opposition of Trotter, Du Bois, and others would jeopardize the flow of funds from white philanthropists to black colleges and universities. In an effort to reconcile with his opponents, he organized a meeting with them, funded by white philanthropists, at Carnegie Hall in New York City in 1904. But Du Bois and other opponents of Washington came to the gathering determined to adopt a radical agenda. When Washington loyalists monopolized the proceedings, Du Bois quit in disgust.

THE TALENTED TENTH

Du Bois, joined by a small cadre of black intellectuals, then set out to organize an aggressive effort to secure the rights of black citizens. He was convinced that the advancement of black people was the responsibility of the black elite, those he called the Talented Tenth, meaning the upper 10 percent of black Americans. Education, he believed, was the key:

> Work alone will not do it unless inspired by the right ideals and guided by intelligence. Education must not simply teach work—it must teach Life. The Talented Tenth of the Negro race must be made leaders of thought and missionaries of culture among people. No others can do this work, and Negro colleges must train men for it. The Negro race, like all other races, is going to be saved by its exceptional men.

THE NIAGARA MOVEMENT

In 1905 Du Bois carried the anti-Washington crusade a step further and invited a select group to meet at Niagara Falls, in Canada. The twenty-nine delegates to this meeting insisted that black people no longer quietly accept the loss of the right to vote. "We believe that [Negro] American citizens should protest emphatically and continually against the curtailment of their political rights." They also demanded an end to segregation, declaring, "All American citizens have the right to equal treatment in places of public entertainment." They appealed for better schools, health care, and housing; protested the discrimination endured by black soldiers; and criticized the racial prejudice of most churches as "wrong, unchristian and disgraceful to the twentieth century civilization." Perhaps most important, the Niagara gathering insisted that white people did not know what was best for black people. "We repudiate the monstrous doctrine that the oppressor should be the sole authority as to the rights of the oppressed."

The Niagara Movement that emerged from this meeting attracted four hundred members and remained active for several years. Du Bois composed annual addresses to the nation designed to arouse black and white support. But the Niagara Movement was no match for the powerful, efficient, and well-financed Tuskegee Machine. Washington used every means at his disposal to undermine the movement. Black newspaper editors like the *Washington Bee's* W. Calvin Chase, who had earlier attacked Washington's Atlanta Compromise address, were paid to attack Du Bois and to praise Washington. Washington dispatched spies to Niagara meetings to report on the organization's activities.

Washington sent a telegram requesting that black lawyer Clifford Plummer infiltrate the first Niagara

DOCUMENT
16-2 *The Niagara Movement, Declaration of Principles, 1905*

meeting: "See Plummer at once. Give him fifty dollars. Tell him to go to Buffalo tonight or tomorrow morning ostensibly to attend Elks convention but to report fully what goes on at meeting. . . . Get into meeting, if possible but be sure [to get] name of all who attend and what they do." Washington let it be known that black federal employees might lose their positions if they joined in the Niagara Movement.

There were also internal problems among Niagara members. Du Bois was an inexperienced leader, and difficulties developed between Du Bois and Trotter. In 1908 the Niagara Movement virtually collapsed. Most black and white Americans were not prepared to support an organization that seemed so uncompromising in its demands.

The NAACP

As the Niagara Movement expired, the National Association for the Advancement of Colored People (NAACP) came to life. There was no direct link between the demise of the Niagara Movement and the rise of the NAACP. But the relatively small numbers of people—black and white—who felt comfortable with the Niagara Movement's assertive stance on race were inclined to support the NAACP. In its early years the NAACP was a militant organization dedicated to racial justice. White leaders dominated it and white contributors largely financed it.

A few white progressives were deeply concerned about the rampant racial prejudice manifested so graphically in lynchings, Jim Crow, black disfranchisement, and a vicious riot in 1908 in Springfield, Illinois—Abraham Lincoln's hometown. After a gathering of leaders in January 1909 in New York City, Oswald Garrison Villard issued a call on February 12—Lincoln's birthday—to "all believers in democracy to join a national conference to discuss present evils, the voicing of protests, and the renewal of the struggle for civil and political liberty."

Villard was the president and editor of the New York *Evening Post* and the grandson of abolitionist William Lloyd Garrison. Prominent progressives endorsed the call, including social workers Lillian Wald and Jane Addams, literary scholar Joel E. Spingarn, and respected attorneys Clarence Darrow and Moorfield Storey.

W. E. B. Du Bois, Ida Wells Barnett, and Mary Church Terrell were the black leaders most involved in the formation of the NAACP.

USING THE SYSTEM

The NAACP was determined that black citizens should fully enjoy the civil and political rights the Constitution guaranteed to all citizens. It relied on the judicial

The founders of the Niagara Movement posed in front of a photograph of the falls when they met at Niagara Falls, Ontario, Canada, in 1905. W. E. B. Du Bois is second from the right in the middle row. Photographs and Prints Division, Schomburg Center for Research in Black Culture. The New York Public Library, Astor, Lenox, and Tilden Foundations

THE EMERGENCE OF NATIONAL AFRICAN-AMERICAN ORGANIZATIONS

1889	Afro-American League organized in Chicago
1892	Colored Women's League of Washington formed
1893	New Era Club founded in Boston
1895	National Federation of Afro-American Women organized in Boston
1896	National Association of Colored Women (NACW) formed in Washington
1897	American Negro Academy founded in Washington
1897	First Phillis Wheatley home established in Detroit
1900	National Negro Business League established in Boston
1905	Niagara Movement organized in Niagara Falls, Ontario, Canada
1909	National Association for the Advancement of Colored People (NAACP) founded in New York City
1910	National League on Urban Conditions among Negroes (Urban League) formed in New York City

1889–1910

and legislative systems in what would be a persistent and decades-long effort to secure those rights. The NAACP won its first major legal victory in 1915 when the Supreme Court overturned Oklahoma's grandfather clause in *Guinn v. United States*. But poll taxes and literacy tests continued to disfranchise black citizens.

In 1917, in a case brought by the Louisville NAACP branch and argued before the Supreme Court by Moorfield Storey, the court struck down a local law that enforced residential segregation by prohibiting black people and white people from selling real estate to people of the other race. The NAACP also tried in 1918 to secure a federal law prohibiting lynching. With the assistance of Congressman Leonidas Dyer, a white St. Louis Republican, the antilynching measure—the Dyer bill—passed in the House of Representatives in 1922 over vigorous Democratic opposition. But the Senate blocked it, and it never became law.

DU BOIS AND *THE CRISIS*

W. E. B. Du Bois was easily the most prominent black figure associated with the NAACP during its first quarter century. He became director of publicity and research and edited the NAACP publication, *The Crisis*, while largely leaving leadership and administrative tasks to others.

With *The Crisis*, Du Bois the scholar became Du Bois the propagandist. In the pages of *The Crisis*, he denounced white racism and atrocities and demanded that black people stand up for their rights. "Agitate, then, brother; protest, reveal the truth and refuse to be silenced. . . . A moment's let up, a moment's acquiescence, means a chance for the wolves of prejudice to get at our necks." He would not provoke violence, but he would not tolerate mistreatment either. "I am resolved to be quiet and law abiding, but to refuse to cringe in body or in soul, to resent deliberate insult, and to assert my just rights in the face of wanton aggression." These were not the even-tempered, cautious words of Booker T. Washington to which so many Americans had grown accustomed. *The Crisis* became required reading in many black homes. By 1913 it had 30,000 subscribers, when the membership of the NAACP was only 3,000.

Crisis Magazine 25
LIVING WORDS

WASHINGTON VERSUS THE NAACP

In 1909, with the founding of the NAACP, Oswald Garrison Villard tried to reassure Washington the ary Church Terrell lived from the year of the Emancipation Proclamation (1863) to the year that the U.S. Supreme Court declared segregated schools unconstitutional (1954). During those nine decades, she exemplified the African-American leaders whom W. E. B. Du Bois called the Talented Tenth. The daughter of slaves, she acquired a superb education and became prominent in Washington's black elite. She was ever conscious of her social status, education, and fair complexion. She was also absolutely dedicated to the elimination of Jim Crow and the cause of African-American women.

Mary Church was born in Civil War Memphis and raised during Reconstruction. She led a sheltered life and went on to Oberlin College where she studied classics, became proficient in languages, and earned an M.A. In 1891 she married Robert H. Terrell, a Harvard graduate who had earned a law degree at Howard. He was an auditor in the U.S. Treasury Department and later became a District of Columbia municipal judge.

Mary Church Terrell immersed herself in literary, social, and political activities. She spearheaded the creation of the Colored Women's League and became the first president of the National Association of Colored Women (NACW) in 1896. Terrell believed that well-to-do black women had a responsibility to assist struggling and poorer women of color.

Terrell was an inspirational speaker. She spoke in 1904 at the International Congress of Women in Berlin—in German, French, and English. Mamie Garvin Fields recalled a speech Terrell delivered in Charleston, South Carolina, in 1916:

Oh, my, when I saw her walk onto that podium in her pink evening dress and long white gloves, with her beautifully done hair, she was the Modern Woman. . . . Regal, intelligent, powerful,

reaching out from time to time with that long glove, she looked and sounded like the Modern Woman that she talked about.

Terrell was active in the NAACP, which was not easy in light of her close relationship with Booker T. Washington and his wife, Margaret Murray Washington. She could not afford to alienate Washington because he possessed enough influence to prevent her husband's reappointment as judge. Terrell managed to convince Washington that she supported him, but in fact, she was devoted to the NAACP and its program. She served on its board, and spoke forcefully on civil rights. She risked the wrath of President Theodore Roosevelt after she criticized his dismissal of three companies of black soldiers following the Brownsville incident (see Chapter 15). She presented President William Howard Taft with NAACP petitions against lynching. She wrote articles attacking chain gangs, peonage, disfranchisement, and lynching. She worked with progressive organizations, such as the Women's International League for Peace and Freedom, and supported women's suffrage and the Nineteenth Amendment.

The Terrells were active in Washington's black elite—the Four Hundred. They attended balls, concerts, and parties, traveled extensively, and belonged to Washington's most exclusive black congregation, the Lincoln Temple Congregational Church, and she was active in Delta Sigma Theta sorority.

Mary Church Terrell consistently opposed racial discrimination and protested to Oberlin College officials when her daughters encountered more prejudice as students than she had. A lifelong Republican, she opposed Democratic President Franklin Roosevelt's inaction on civil rights in the 1930s. At the age of eighty-seven she demonstrated against Thompson's Restaurant, an all-white establishment in Washington, D.C. Her death in 1954 ended her campaign against Jim Crow and for women's rights.

Mary Church Terrell summed up her legacy in her 1940 autobiography, *A Colored Woman in a White World.* "This is the story of a colored woman living in a white world. It cannot possibly be like a story written by a white woman. A white woman has only one handicap to overcome—that of sex. I have two—both sex and race. I belong to the only group in this country which has two such huge obstacles to surmount. Colored men have only one—that of race."

Terrell

organization posed no threat and to gain his support for the new association. "It is not to be a Washington movement, or a Du Bois movement. The idea is that there shall grow out of it, first, an annual conference . . . for the discussion by men of both races of the conditions of the colored people, politically, socially, industrially and educationally."

Many black leaders and members of the NAACP, however, despised Washington and his ideology, and Washington returned the sentiment. With the assistance of his followers, he worked to subvert the new organization. Washington looked on Du Bois as little more than the puppet of white people, who dominated the leadership of the NAACP, and the Tuskegee leader declined to debate Du Bois. One of Washington's aides commented that "it would be entirely out of place for Dr. Washington to enter into any discussion with a man occupying the place that Dr. Du Bois does, for the reason that Dr. Washington is at the head of a large institution . . . . Dr. Du Bois, on the other hand, is a mere hired man, as it were, in an institution completely controlled by white people."

Charles Anderson, a Tuskegee loyalist in New York City, wrote to Washington in 1909 that the NAACP was meeting secretly and he would attempt to disrupt its efforts. "I will find out as much about them as possible and let you know the facts. I am doing all I can to discredit this affair." Washington relied again on allies who were editors of black newspapers to criticize the NAACP.

He also wrote Clark Howell, the white editor of the Atlanta *Constitution*, to attack Du Bois. "I think that it is too bad that an institution like Atlanta University has permitted Dr. Du Bois to go on from year to year stirring up racial strife in the South." Washington later told an alumnus of Tuskegee that the main aim of the NAACP was to destroy Washington and Tuskegee. "As a matter of straight fact, this organization is for the purpose of tearing down our work wherever possible and I think none of our friends should give it comfort."

Washington became so obsessed with the NAACP that he was not above manipulating white supremacists to damage those connected with the association. When he learned that a group of black and white progressives associated with the NAACP were going to gather at the Café Boulevard in New York City in 1911, he allowed Charles Anderson to alert the hostile white press, which gleefully described the multiracial dinner in the most inflammatory terms. "Fashionable White Women Sit at Board with Negroes, Japs and Chinamen to Promote 'Cause' of Miscegenation" proclaimed one headline. The New York *Press* added, "White women, evidently of the cultured and wealthier classes, fashionably attired in low-cut gowns, leaned over the tables to chat confidentially with negro men of the true African type."

Ultimately, Washington's efforts to ruin the NAACP and to reduce the influence of its supporters failed. By the time of his death in 1915, the NAACP had grown steadily to over six thousand members and fifty local branches. Its aggressive campaign for civil and political rights replaced Washington's strategy of progress through conciliation and accommodation.

The Urban League

In 1910 the National League on Urban Conditions among Negroes was founded in New York City. The goal of this social welfare organization, soon known simply as the Urban League, was to alleviate conditions black people encountered as they moved into large cities in ever-increasing numbers in the early twentieth century. Like the NAACP, black and white progressives created the Urban League. It worked to improve housing, medical care, and recreational facilities among black residents who lived in segregated neighborhoods in New York, Philadelphia, Atlanta, Nashville, Norfolk, and other cities. The league also assisted youngsters who ran afoul of the law, and it helped establish the Big Brother and Big Sister movements.

Black Women and the Club Movement

Years before the Urban League and the NAACP were founded, black women began creating clubs and organizations. The local groups that began forming in the 1870s and 1880s, such as the Bethel Literary and Historical Association in Washington, D.C., were mainly concerned with cultural, religious, and social matters. But many of the mostly middle-class women active in these clubs eventually became less interested in tea and gossip and more involved with community problems. In 1893 black women in Boston founded the New Era Club. They published a monthly magazine, *Woman's Era*, that featured articles on fashion, health, and family life.

In 1895 a New Era Club member, Josephine St. Pierre Ruffin, enraged by white journalist James W. Jack's vilification of black women as "prostitutes, thieves, and liars" who were "altogether without character," issued a call to "Let Us Confer Together" that drew 104 black women to a meeting in Boston. The result was the formation of the National Federation of Afro-American Women, which soon included thirty-six clubs in twelve states. In the meantime, the Colored Women's League of Washington, D.C., which had been founded in 1892, published an appeal in *Woman's Era* for black women to organize a national association at the 1895 meeting of the National Council of Women. At that gathering, representatives from several local black women's clubs organized the National Colored Woman's League.

THE NACW: "LIFTING AS WE CLIMB"

The two groups—The National Federation of Afro-American Women and the National Colored Woman's League—merged in 1896 to form the National Association of Colored Women (NACW), with Mary Church Terrell elected the first president. The NACW adopted the self-help motto "Lifting as We Climb," and in the reforming spirit of the progressive age, they stressed moral, mental, and material advancement. By 1914 there were 50,000 members of the NACW in 1,000 clubs nationwide.

Middle- and upper-class black club women were sometimes more concerned with the morality and behavior of black men and women than with civil rights and white supremacy. They opposed premarital sex and warned against the evils of alcohol.

There were occasionally unpleasant disagreements and conflicts among the club women. Margaret Murray Washington—Booker T. Washington's wife—served as NACW president from 1912 to 1916, and the organization's *National Notes* was published at Tuskegee until 1922. Not everyone was fond of this arrangement. Ida Wells Barnett was particularly incensed and claimed that the Tuskegee Machine censored the publication. Meanwhile Mary Church Terrell found Barnett abrasive and contentious. Terrell managed to exclude the Chicago leader from the initial NACW meeting in 1896. There were also regional rivalries and ideological disputes as well as sensitivity over the light complexion of leaders like Terrell.

More important than these internal struggles were the efforts of black women to confront the problems black people encountered in urban areas as rural southerners migrated by the thousands in the second and third decades of the twentieth century. The NACW clubs worked to eradicate poverty, end racial discrimination, and promote education, including the formation of kindergartens and day nurseries. Members cared for older people, especially former slaves. They aided orphans; assisted working mothers by providing nurseries, health care, and information on child rearing; and established homes for delinquent and abandoned girls.

PHILLIS WHEATLEY CLUBS

Black women also formed Phillis Wheatley clubs and homes across the nation (named in honor of the eighteenth-century African-American poet). The resi-

dences offered living accommodations for single, black working women in many cities where they were refused admittance to YWCA facilities. Some Phillis Wheatley clubs also provided nurseries and classes in domestic skills. In Cleveland, nurse Jane Edna Hunter organized a residence for single, black working women who could not find comfortable and affordable housing. In 1911, she formed the Working Girls' Home Association for cleaning women, laundresses, and private duty nurses. With association members contributing five cents a week, Hunter opened a twenty-three-room residence in 1913 that expanded to a seventy-two-room building in 1917.

ANNA JULIA COOPER AND BLACK FEMINISM

"Only the BLACK WOMAN can say 'when and where I enter, in the quiet, undisputed dignity of my womanhood, without violence and without suing or special patronage, then and there the whole Negro race enters with me.'" So wrote Anna Julia Cooper in the late nineteenth century. Not only was Cooper convinced that black women would play a decisive role in shaping the destiny of their people, she labored to dispel the stereotype that black women lacked refinement, grace, and morality.

Cooper was born a slave in Raleigh, North Carolina, in 1858 and graduated from St. Augustine's School. She then earned a bachelor's degree from Oberlin College in 1884. Speaking and writing with increasing confidence and authority, she published *A Voice from the South by a Black Woman of the South* in 1892. In this collection of essays she stressed the pivotal role that black women would play in the future, and she chastised white women for their lack of support. In 1900 she addressed the Pan African Conference in London.

Cooper was principal of Washington's famed M Street Colored High School (later Paul Laurence Dunbar High School) from 1901 to 1906. She was forced out in 1906 amid allegations that supporters of the powerful Tuskegee Machine resented Cooper's emphasis on academic preparation over vocational training. She went on to teach for four years at Missouri's Lincoln University before returning to M Street High as a teacher. Fluent in French, she earned a Ph.D. at the Sorbonne in Paris.

She was active with the NACW, the NAACP, and YWCA. Married in 1877, her husband died only two years later. Cooper found time following his death to take in and raise five children. She died in 1964 at age 105.

WOMEN'S SUFFRAGE

Historically, many black women had supported women's suffrage. Before the Civil War, many abolitionists, including Mary Ann Shadd Cary, Sojourner

PROFILE ~ JANE EDNA HUNTER AND THE PHILLIS WHEATLEY ASSOCIATION

In the early twentieth century, no one was more committed to improving the lives of young black women than Jane Edna Hunter. Trained as a nurse, she migrated to Cleveland, where she founded the Phillis Wheatley Association.

Born Jane Harris in 1882 in Pendleton, South Carolina, she had a fair complexion because her father was the son of a slave woman and a white overseer. For a time she believed that her light color made her superior to darker friends and family members, especially her mother.

Her beloved father died when she was ten. She had little schooling as a child, but she was able to enroll at Ferguson Williams College in Abbeville, South Carolina, at age fourteen. Later her mother prodded her to marry Edward Hunter, a man forty years her senior. The marriage lasted all of fifteen months. Jane Edna Hunter never remarried.

She came to reject her color consciousness and embraced her heritage as a black woman "—I was to be overwhelmed by the realization that I was, above and beyond all, my Mother's child—a Negro; that I was proud of the blood of my ancestors; that my life henceforth was to be a solemn dedication to the people of my Mother's race!"

She received training as a nurse in Charleston at the Canon Street Hospital and Training School for Nurses and then at the Dixie Hospital and Training School at Hampton Institute. In 1905 she moved to Cleveland, Ohio. She immediately encountered difficulties as a young black woman in a big city. In search of a place to stay, she unintentionally knocked on the door of a brothel.

No white hospital would hire her as a nurse, and she worked as a cleaning woman while she lived in a series of unsavory boarding houses. "In the average rooming house of that period . . . the Negro girl had to pay a dollar and a quarter a week for a small, low-roofed, poorly furnished room. She was charged extra for the use of the laundry and gas. If she wished to invite a caller, she was frequently required to clean the whole house in payment for the privilege. The use of the bath tub, when there was one, was discouraged."

The Young Women's Christian Association in Cleveland did not extend its benevolence to black women, and they were not permitted to live at YWCA residential facilities. Jane Edna Hunter took it upon herself to persuade the white women who ran the YWCA to support the establishment of a separate housing facility for black women. But some black people—"a small group of club women, who blessed with prosperity, had risen from the servant class and now regarded themselves as the arbiters and guardians of colored society"—opposed her efforts to create a residence for black women.

Nevertheless, the Phillis Wheatley Home opened in 1911. It was named in honor of the former slave who had become a prominent eighteenth-century poet in colonial America. The first facility had twenty-three rooms. Hunter worked with white leaders to expand the size and services of what became the Phillis Wheatley Association. In doing so, she was subjected to more criticism by black leaders that she was too conciliatory and too willing to follow the lead of white people simply to gain access to their funds.

Ambitious and determined, she earned a law degree and passed the bar in 1926. She presided over the construction of an eleven-story residence for black women that was completed in 1927. It featured a beauty school, dining facilities, a nursery school, and the Booker T. Washington Playground. The Phillis Wheatley Association also operated a summer camp for children and served as an employment agency for black women. Critics complained because many of the jobs were as domestics for well-to-do white families and accused Hunter of providing dead-end positions that kept black people in a subordinate status.

Hunter also shrewdly invested in Cleveland real estate, and was active for decades in the National Association of Colored Women (NACW), even though it included many of the same women who had opposed her efforts. She served as a trustee of Ohio's Central State University. In 1937 she was awarded the NAACP's Spingarn Medal. She retired in 1946. When she died in 1971 she left most of her estate of nearly $500,000 to the Phillis Wheatley Foundation.

Truth, and Frederick Douglass, had also backed women's suffrage. Cary and Truth tried unsuccessfully to vote after the war. Black women, such as Caroline Remond Putnam of Massachusetts, Lottie Rollin of South Carolina, and Frances Ellen Watkins Harper of Pennsylvania, attended conventions of the mostly white American Woman's Suffrage Association in the 1870s.

Black women were also involved in the long struggle for women's suffrage on the state level. Ida Wells Barnett was a leader in the Illinois suffrage effort. By 1900 Wyoming, Utah, Colorado, and Idaho permitted women to vote, and by 1918 women in seventeen northern and western states had gained the vote. But as more women won voting rights, women's suffrage became more controversial. The proposed Nineteenth Amendment to the U.S. Constitution drove a wedge between black and white advocates of women's political rights. Many opponents of women's suffrage, especially white southerners, warned that granting women the right to vote would increase the number of black voters. Some white women advocated strict literacy and educational requirements for voting in an effort to limit the number of black voters, both women and men.

The Struggle for Women's Suffrage

As it turned out, only two southern states—Kentucky and Tennessee—ratified the Nineteenth Amendment before its adoption in 1920. Black suffragists understood that the right to vote meant political power, and political power could be exercised to acquire civil rights, improve education, and gain respect. White southerners also grasped the importance of voting rights. Thus despite the Nineteenth Amendment, large numbers of black people in the south—both men and women—remained unable to vote.

The Black Elite

Many of the black leaders described by W. E. B. Du Bois as the Talented Tenth formed protest organizations, joined reform efforts, and organized self-help groups. The leaders were middle- and upper-class black people who were better educated than most Americans—black or white.

THE AMERICAN NEGRO ACADEMY

In 1897, Episcopal priest Alexander Crummel met with sixteen other black men in Washington, D.C., to form the American Negro Academy. This scholarly organization was made up of "men of African descent" who assembled periodically to discuss and publish works on history, literature, religion, and science. Among those who attended the initial gathering were W. E. B. Du Bois, Paul Laurence Dunbar, Kelly Miller, and Francis Grimke.

Crummel was an elderly but dynamic and distinguished leader who did not hesitate to express his deeply felt convictions on race, religion, and Africa. He had been born in 1818 in New York and spent several years in Liberia in the 1850s and 1860s as an Episcopal missionary. Crummel died in 1898, but the Academy survived as a vibrant intellectual and elitist society.

Carter G. Woodson, Alain Locke, Arthur Schomburg, and James Weldon Johnson subsequently joined its ranks before it eventually disbanded in 1928. It afforded black intellectuals an opportunity to ponder what it meant to be black in America and to develop their racial consciousness, thus nurturing ideas and concepts that would mature during the Harlem Renaissance.

Most members of the Academy supported women's rights and women's suffrage. Consequently it was exceedingly ironic that black women were not invited to become members of the Academy, although several black women, including Anna Julia Cooper, Ida Wells Barnett, and Mary Church Terrell, were easily the intellectual equals of the male participants.

THE UPPER CLASS

By the early twentieth century, there were several hundred wealthy African Americans. These black aristocrats were as sophisticated, refined, and conscious of

James Van der Zee was a prominent black photographer in Harlem whose photos frequently depicted the community's well-to-do residents. This is a wedding party in 1926.

their status as any group in American society. They distanced themselves from less affluent black and white people and lived in expensive houses. Many of them possessed fair complexions. They were medical doctors, lawyers, and businessmen. Although they possessed vastly more wealth than most Americans, their wealth paled in comparison to the huge fortunes of the richest American families, such as the Rockefellers, Carnegies, and Vanderbilts.

The black elite formed exclusive organizations that jealously limited membership to the small black upper class. In the 1860s the Ugly Fishing Club was transformed into an organization made up of New York City's wealthiest black men. It soon came to be known simply as the Ugly Club, and its membership spread to Newport, Rhode Island, Baltimore, and Philadelphia. In 1904 two wealthy Philadelphia physicians, a dentist, and a pharmacist formed Sigma Pi Beta, better known as Boulé. It was restricted to male college graduates, and it aimed to provide "inspiration, relaxation, intellectual stimulation, and brotherhood." Boulé expanded to seven chapters in cities that included Chicago and Memphis, but its membership totaled a mere 177.

Organizations like the Diamondback Club and the Cosmos Club in Washington, the Loendi Club in Pittsburgh, and the Bachelor-Benedict Club in New York sponsored luxurious banquets, dances, and debutante balls. Several of these groups owned ornate clubhouses. These elite societies and cliques typically competed to demonstrate social exclusivity and preeminence.

FRATERNITIES AND SORORITIES

Among the black elite were also the African Americans who established the Greek letter black fraternities and

---

PROFILE ◆ LEWIS LATIMER, BLACK INVENTOR

Lewis H. Latimer (1848–1928) was a draftsman, inventor, and pioneer in the electrical industry. During his lifetime, Latimer was awarded eight patents for his inventions. He was born in Chelsea, Massachusetts, in 1848. His parents had fled from slavery and settled in Boston where abolitionists including William Lloyd Garrison and Frederick Douglass raised funds to purchase their freedom.

After a year in the Union Navy during the Civil War, Latimer worked as an office boy for the patent solicitor firm of Crosby and Gould. There he taught himself drafting. As a draftsman, Latimer worked closely with inventors and began to tinker with ideas for inventions. In 1874, he received his first patent for improving the toilet on passenger railroad cars. He developed a flushing mechanism that prevented the upflow of sewage and cinders. He also executed drawings for Alexander Graham Bell's patent application for the telephone. Latimer later worked on electric lights, and in 1882 he received a patent for producing carbon filaments that made electric lighting more practical.

Latimer became superintendent of the incandescent lamp department of the United States Electric Lighting Company and supervised the installation of lights for buildings in the United States and Canada. In 1883, Thomas A. Edison hired Latimer as an engineer, chief draftsman, and expert witness in patent infringement cases. In 1890, Latimer published a book entitled *Incandescent Lighting: A Practical Description of the Edison System*. He served as chief draftsman for the General Electric/Westinghouse Board of Patent Control when it was established in 1896.

Men who had worked with Thomas A. Edison joined together in 1918 as the Edison Pioneers to preserve memories of their early days working together and to honor Edison's genius and achievements. Latimer was a founding member and the only African-American Edison Pioneer. He died in Flushing, New York, on December 11, 1928.

Lewis H. Latimer published *Incandescent Lighting: A Practical Description of the Edison System*—one of the first books on electric lighting—in 1896.

Schomburg Center for Research in Black Culture/Art Resource

sororities. In 1906 seven students at Cornell University formed Alpha Phi Alpha, the first college fraternity for black men. Within a few years, it had chapters at the University of Michigan, Yale, Columbia, and Ohio State. The first black sorority, Alpha Kappa Alpha, was founded in 1908 at Howard University.

Several other Greek letter organizations were subsequently launched at Howard: Omega Psi Phi fraternity in 1911, Delta Sigma Theta sorority in 1913, Phi Beta Sigma in 1914, and Zeta Phi Beta sorority in 1920. In addition, in 1911 Kappa Alpha Psi fraternity was founded at Indiana University, and Sigma Gamma Rho sorority was formed in Indianapolis in 1922.

Besides providing college students with an opportunity to enjoy each other's company, the black fraternities and sororities stressed scholarship, social graces, and community involvement. Alpha Phi Alpha created the "Go to High School, Go to College" campaign in 1919. Kappa Alpha Psi adopted the "Guide Right" program to assist black youngsters in 1922. In 1923 Alpha Kappa Alpha opened a mobile health clinic in Mississippi. For seven years from 1935 to 1941 during the depths of the Great Depression, Alpha Kappa Alpha sponsored free health clinics in Mississippi under the guidance of Dr. Dorothy Ferebee of the Howard University Medical School. It was the first time many black people there had received professional medical attention.

Presidential Politics

Since Reconstruction, black voters had loyally supported the Republican Party and its presidential candidates. "The Party of Lincoln" welcomed that support and periodically rewarded black men with federal jobs. Republican presidents Theodore Roosevelt (1901–1909) and William Howard Taft (1909–1913) continued that policy.

FRUSTRATED BY THE REPUBLICANS

But other presidential actions more than offset whatever goodwill these appointments generated. Roosevelt discharged three companies of black soldiers after the Brownsville incident in 1906, and Taft tolerated restrictions on black voters in the South and encouraged the development of a "lily white" Republican Party, removing black people from federal jobs in the region.

In 1912 the Republican Party split in a bitter feud between President Taft and Theodore Roosevelt, and a third political party—the Progressive Party—emerged. The Progressives nominated Roosevelt to run against Taft and the Democratic candidate, Woodrow Wilson. But as the delegates at the Progressive convention in Chicago sang the "Battle Hymn of the Republic," south-

ern black men who had come to the gathering stood outside the hall, denied admission by white Progressives.

WOODROW WILSON

It was not a complete shock that militant black leaders like William Monroe Trotter and W. E. B. Du Bois urged black voters to support Woodrow Wilson, the Democrat, in the 1912 presidential election. Wilson was the reform governor of New Jersey, and he had been president of Princeton University. Trotter and Du Bois were impressed with Wilson's academic background and his promise to pursue a progressive policy toward black Americans. Du Bois wrote,

> Wilson is a cultivated scholar and he has brains. We have, therefore, a conviction that Mr. Wilson will treat black men and their interests with foresighted fairness. He will not advance the cause of an oligarchy in the South, he will not seek further means of 'jim crow' insult, he will not dismiss black men wholesale from office, and he will remember that the Negro has a right to be heard and considered.

But as president, Wilson proved to be no friend of black people. Born in Virginia and raised in South Carolina, Wilson had thoroughly absorbed white southern racial views. Federal agencies and buildings were fully segregated early during Wilson's tenure. In 1914 Trotter and a black delegation met with Wilson to protest segregation in the treasury department and the post office. Wilson defended separation of the races as a means to avoid friction. Trotter vehemently disagreed, and Wilson became visibly irritated. The president warned that he would no longer meet with the group if Trotter remained their spokesman.

Black Men and the Military in World War I

In 1915–1916 Wilson faced more than problems with dissatisfied black people. United States–Mexican relations had steadily deteriorated after a revolution and civil war in Mexico. War in Europe threatened to draw the United States into conflict with Germany.

THE PUNITIVE EXPEDITION TO MEXICO

In 1914 war almost broke out between the United States and Mexico when U.S. marines landed at Vera Cruz after an attack on American sailors. Then, in March 1916, Francisco "Pancho" Villa, one of the participants in Mexico's civil war, led a force of Mexican

PROFILE ~ GEORGE WASHINGTON CARVER AND ERNEST EVERETT JUST

George Washington Carver and Ernest Everett Just each rose from humble beginnings in the nineteenth century to become highly regarded biologists. Carver was born in 1864 or 1865 to slave parents in Diamond Grove, Missouri. Eager to learn, he spent much of his youth engaged in menial labor around Missouri, Iowa, and Kansas as he acquired an uneven education. He spent a year at Simpson College and then enrolled at Iowa State University in 1891 at age twenty-five as its sole black student. He compiled a superb academic record, participated in an array of student activities, and took charge of the campus greenhouse. He became fascinated with botany and focused on mycology (the study of fungi) and cross-fertilization.

Just was born in Charleston, South Carolina, in 1883 and grew up on nearby James Island, where his mother toiled in phosphate mines following the death of his father. He attended local schools and earned a teacher training certificate in 1899 from what is now South Carolina State University. Just went on to Kimball Union Academy in New Hampshire, and he graduated with honors from Dartmouth College in 1907 with a major in biology and minors in Greek and history.

Just was hired by Howard University in Washington, D.C., and spent the rest of his teaching career there. In 1911 he helped establish Omega Psi Phi, which emerged as a major black fraternity. Although hired to teach English and rhetoric, he soon changed to zoology and biology, the subjects in which he had developed an abiding interest. He spent several summers at the Marine Biology Laboratory at Woods Hole, Massachusetts, and earned a Ph.D. in zoology from the University of Chicago in 1916.

While Just felt more at home engaged in research in a laboratory, Carver felt more comfortable experimenting with crops in a field. At the invitation of Booker T. Washington, Carver left a promising career at Iowa State in 1896 to take charge of the agriculture program at Tuskegee Institute. Having studied with two men at Iowa State—James Wilson and Henry C. Wallace—who became U.S. secretaries of agriculture, Carver established political ties to Washington, D.C., that greatly benefitted Tuskegee. He became the director of the nation's only black agricultural experiment station.

Carver was a superb teacher in and out of the classroom, but he was a less-than-efficient administrator who sometimes clashed with Booker T. Washington. Carver committed himself to working with impoverished black farmers, seeking to make them more productive and less dependent on cotton. He sponsored outreach programs and farmers' institutes. He discovered hundreds of uses for the protein-rich peanut. And he experimented extensively with sweet potatoes.

Carver became a folk hero by the 1930s with his gregarious personality and self-effacing demeanor. He never married and lived in a student dormitory at Tuskegee. He wore a tattered coat with a fresh flower in the lapel. Though he never earned more than $1,200 a year, he gave more than $60,000 to Tuskegee before he died in 1943.

Just, confronted with the lack of opportunities available to a dedicated black scientist at white universities, pursued his research in the fertilization of marine animals at Woods Hole. But even there some scientists shunned him and others patronized him. Nevertheless, by 1928 he had published thirty-five articles, mostly on fertilization. Awarded a sizable grant from the Julius Rosenwald Foundation, he spent much of the 1930s engaged in research in Italy, Germany, and France. In 1939 he published *Biology of the Cell Surface*.

Just married Ethel Highwarden, a Howard faculty member, in 1912. They had three children, but later divorced. In 1939 he married Maid Hedwig Schnetzler, a German scientist. Just died of cancer in 1941.

Both George Washington Carver and Ernest Everett Just were awarded the NAACP's Spingarn Medal—Just in 1915 and Carver in 1923.

rebels across the border into New Mexico in an effort to provoke war between Mexico and the United States. Fifteen Americans were killed, including seven U.S. soldiers. In response, Wilson dispatched a "punitive expedition" that eventually numbered 15,000 U.S. troops under the command of General John J. "Black Jack" Pershing. Pershing acquired the nickname "Black Jack" after commanding black troops in Cuba during the Spanish-American War.

U.S. forces, including the black 10th Cavalry (see Chapter 15), spent ten months in Mexico in a futile effort to capture Villa. White officers commanded the 10th Cavalry, as had been the case with black troops since the Civil War. But Lieutenant Colonel Charles Young, an 1889 black graduate of the U.S. Military Academy at West Point, helped lead the regiment.

Young led the black troops against a contingent of Villa's rebels who had ambushed an element of the 13th Cavalry, a white unit, at Santa Cruz de Villegas.

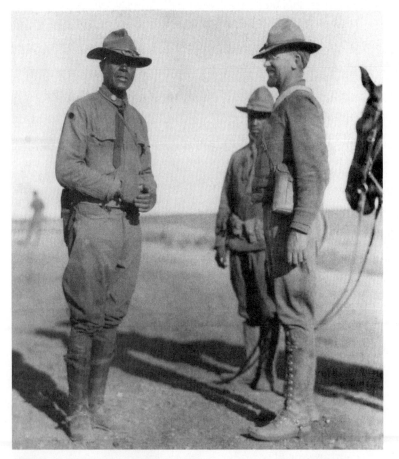

Lieutenant Colonel Charles D. Young, an 1889 graduate of the U.S. Military Academy at West Point who served in Cuba, the Phillippines, Haiti, and Mexico, was not permitted to command troops during World War I. He returned to military service at the end of the war and was sent to Liberia to help train that country's army. He died while on furlough in Nigeria in 1922.

Major Frank Tompkins of the 13th was so relieved to be rescued that he reportedly exclaimed to Young, "By God, Young, I could kiss every black face out there." Young supposedly replied, "If you want to, you may start with me." U.S. troops were withdrawn from Mexico in 1917 as the probability increased that the United States would enter World War I against Germany.

WORLD WAR I

When World War I erupted in Europe in August 1914, Woodrow Wilson and most Americans had no intention and no desire to participate. Wilson promptly issued a proclamation of neutrality. Running for reelection in 1916 on the appealing slogan "He Kept Us Out of War," Wilson narrowly defeated Republican Charles Evans Hughes. Repeated German submarine attacks on civilian vessels and the loss of American lives infuriated Wilson and many Americans as a gross violation of U.S. neutral rights. On April 6, 1917, Congress declared war on Germany. Most African Americans supported the war effort. As in previous conflicts, black people sought to demonstrate their loyalty and devotion to the country through military service. "If this is our country," declared W. E. B. Du Bois, "then this is our war. We must fight it with every ounce of blood and treasure."

Some white leaders were less enthusiastic about the participation of black men. One southern governor wondered about the wisdom of having the military train and arm thousands of black men at southern camps and posts. General Pershing argued for the use of black troops, but insisted on white leadership. "Under capable white officers and with sufficient training, Negro soldiers have always acquitted themselves creditably."

BLACK TROOPS AND OFFICERS

There were about 10,000 black regulars in the U.S. Army in 1917: the 9th and 10th Cavalry regiments and the 24th and 25th Infantry regiments. There were more than 5,000 black men in the navy, but virtually all of them were waiters, kitchen attendants, and stokers for the ships' boilers. The Marine Corps did not admit black men. During World War I, the newly formed Selective Service system drafted more than 370,000 black men—13 percent of all draftees—although none of the local draft boards had black members. Several all-black state National Guard units were also incorporated into federal service.

Although the military remained rigidly segregated, there was political pressure from black newspapers and the NAACP to commission black officers to lead black troops. The War Department created an officer training school at Fort Des Moines, Iowa. Nearly 1,250 black may say or others may think; it matters not what constitutions may contain or statutes provide, wherever the negro is in sufficient numbers to imperil the white man's civilization or question the white man's supremacy the white man is going to find some way around the difficulty. And that is just as true in the North as it is in the South. You need not deceive yourselves about that. The feeling against the negro in Illinois when he gets in the white man's way is quite as strong, more bitter, less regardful of the negro's feelings and conditions than it is in Mississippi.

The racial violence that had permeated southern life in the late nineteenth century expanded into northern communities as many white Americans responded with hostility to the arrival of black migrants from the South. Black people defended themselves, and casualties among both races escalated (see Map 16–1).

ATLANTA, 1906

In 1906—eleven years after Booker T. Washington delivered his Cotton States Exposition address there—white mobs attacked black residents in Atlanta. Several factors aggravated white racial apprehensions in the city. In 1902 four black and four white people had been killed in a riot there. Many rural black people, attracted by economic opportunities, had moved to Atlanta. But white residents considered the newcomers more lawless and immoral than the longtime black residents. The Atlanta newspapers—*The Constitution*, *The Journal*, and *The Georgian*—ran inflammatory accounts about black crime and black men who brutalized white women. Many of these stories were false or exaggerated. Two white Democrats—Hoke Smith and Clark Howell—were engaged in a divisive campaign for a U.S. Senate seat in 1906, and both candidates stirred up racial animosity.

MAP 16–1 MAJOR RACE RIOTS, 1900–1923

In the years between 1900 and 1923, race conflicts and riots occurred in dozens of American communities as black people migrated in increasing numbers to urban areas. The violence reached a peak in the immediate aftermath of World War I during the Red Summer of 1919. White Americans—in the North and South—were determined to keep black people confined to a subordinate role as menial laborers and restricted to well-defined all-black neighborhoods. African Americans who had made significant economic and military contributions to the war effort and who had congregated in large numbers in American cities insisted on participating on a more equitable basis in American society.

▶ *Were the causes of each of these riots similar, or were the reasons for the upsurge in racial violence unique to each situation?*

There were also determined and ultimately successful efforts under way to disfranchise black voters in Georgia.

On a warm Saturday night, September 22, 1906, a white man jumped on a box on Decatur Street, one of Atlanta's main thoroughfares, and waved an Atlanta newspaper emblazoned with the headline THIRD AS-SAULT. He hollered, "Are white men going to stand for this?" The crowd roared, "No! Save our women!" "Kill the niggers." A five-day orgy of violence followed.

The mayor, police, and fire departments vainly tried to stop the mob. Thousands of white people roamed the streets in search of black victims. Black people were indiscriminately tortured, beaten, and killed. White men pulled black passengers off streetcars. They destroyed black businesses. As white men armed themselves, the police disarmed black men. Black men and women who surrendered to marauding white mobs in hopes of mercy were not spared. Black men who fought back only further infuriated the crazed white crowd. Twenty-five black people and one white person died, and hundreds were injured in the riot.

Du Bois hurried home to Atlanta from a trip to Alabama to defend his wife and child. He waited on his porch with a shotgun for a mob that never came. He later explained, "I would without hesitation have sprayed their guts over the grass." In New York, black editor T. Thomas Fortune called for a violent black response: "It makes my blood boil. I would like to be there with a good force of armed men to make Rome howl." Fortune demanded retribution. "I cannot believe that the policy of non-resistance in a situation like that of Atlanta can result in anything but contempt and massacre of the race."

Booker T. Washington looked for a silver lining in the awful affair by noting that "while there is disorder in one community there is peace and harmony in thousands of others." He said that black resistance would merely result in more black fatalities. Washington went to Atlanta and appealed for racial reconciliation.

A Committee of Safety of ten black and ten white leaders was formed. Charles T. Hopkins, an influential white Atlantan, warned in strong paternalist terms, "If we let this dependent race be butchered before our eyes, we cannot face God in the judgement day." But little real racial cooperation resulted. Black minister Henry Hugh Proctor worked with white leaders and often seemed to agree with them that Atlanta's main problem was black crime, not white racism.

No members of the white mob were brought to justice. Black Georgia voters were disfranchised. Atlanta's streetcars were segregated. The city had no public high school for black youngsters. The Carnegie Library did not admit black people, and the Atlanta police force had no black officers.

SPRINGFIELD, 1908

Two years later in August 1908, white citizens of Springfield, Illinois, attacked black residents in an episode that led to the creation of the NAACP in 1909. George Richardson, a black man, was falsely accused of raping a white woman. The sheriff managed to save Richardson by getting him out of town. But an angry mob tore into Springfield's small black population. Six black people were shot and killed, two were lynched, dozens were injured, and damage in the thousands of dollars was inflicted on black homes and businesses. About two thousand black people were driven out of the community.

There was even more violence in the second decade of the twentieth century as major racial conflicts occurred between 1917 and 1921 in East St. Louis, Illinois; Houston, Texas; Chicago; Elaine, Arkansas; and Tulsa, Oklahoma. Smaller violent confrontations occurred at Washington, D.C.; Charleston, South Carolina; Knoxville, Tennesse; Omaha, Nebraska; and Waco and Longview, Texas. Although different incidents sparked each riot, the underlying causes tended to be similar. White residents were concerned that recently arrived black migrants would compete for jobs and housing.

EAST ST. LOUIS, 1917

East St. Louis, Illinois, was a gritty industrial town of nearly sixty thousand across the Mississippi River from St. Louis, Missouri. About 10 percent of the inhabitants were black. The town's schools, public facilities, and neighborhoods were segregated. Racial tensions increased in February 1917 after 470 black workers were hired to replace white members of the American Federation of Labor who had gone on strike against the Aluminum Ore Company. On July 1 several white people drove through a black neighborhood firing guns. Shortly after, two white plainclothes police officers drove into the same neighborhood and were shot and killed by residents who may have believed the drive-by shooters had returned.

Angry white mobs then sought revenge. Black people were mutilated and killed, and their bodies were thrown into the river. Black homes, many of them little more than cabins and shacks, were burned. Hundreds of black people were left homeless. The police joined the rioters. Thirty-five black people and eight white people died in the violence.

The NAACP sent W. E. B. Du Bois and Martha Gruening to East St. Louis. They compiled a twenty-four-page report, "Massacre at East St. Louis," that documented instance after instance of brutality. "Negroes were 'flushed' from the burning houses, and ran for their lives, screaming and begging for mercy. A Negro crawled into a shed and fired on the white men.

Guardsmen started after him, but when they saw he was armed, turned to the mob and said: 'He's armed boys. You can have him. A white man's life is worth the lives of a thousand Negroes.'"

To protest the riot, the NAACP organized a silent demonstration in New York City, and thousands of well-dressed black people marched to muffled drums down Fifth Avenue.

HOUSTON, 1917

A month after the East St. Louis riot, black soldiers in Houston attacked police officers and civilians. The Third Battalion of the 24th Infantry recently had been transferred from Wyoming and California to Camp Logan near Houston, where the black troops came face to face with Jim Crow. Streetcars and public facilities were segregated. Local white and Hispanic people regularly called the black troops "niggers."

On August 23 a black soldier tried to prevent a police officer, Lee Sparks, from beating a black woman. Sparks clubbed the soldier and hauled him off to jail. Corporal Charles W. Baltimore later attempted to de-

termine what had happened, and he was also beaten and incarcerated. Both soldiers were later released. But a rumor circulated that Baltimore had been slain. Led by Sergeant Vida Henry, black men sought revenge.

About one hundred armed black soldiers mounted a two-hour assault on the police station. Fifteen white residents—including five policemen—one Mexican American, four black soldiers, and two black civilians were killed. The army arrested 118 black soldiers, 63 of whom were charged with mutiny. Three separate court-martials were held over the next several months. The NAACP retained the son of Texas legend Sam Houston to help defend them. Eight black men, however, agreed to testify against the defendants. Thirteen black troops were hanged (including Corporal Baltimore) after the first court-martial. Later seven more were executed, seven others were acquitted, and the remainder were sentenced to prison terms ranging from two years to life.

While the Houston violence prompted some political and military leaders to call for the abolition of the black regiments, W. E. B. Du Bois eulogized the first thirteen black soldiers to be executed: "Thirteen young men, strong men, soldiers who have fought for

On July 28, 1917, the NAACP organized a silent march in New York City to protest the East St. Louis, Illinois, race riot in which thirty-five black people died as well as to denounce the ongoing epidemic of lynchings. The marchers were accompanied by the beat of muffled drums.

a country which never was wholly theirs; men born to suffer ridicule, injustice and, at last, death itself." In the meantime, Lee Sparks remained on the Houston police force and killed two black people later that year.

CHICAGO, 1919

Between 1916 and 1919, the black population of Chicago doubled as migrants from the South moved north in search of jobs, political rights, and humane treatment. Many encountered a violent reception. A severe housing shortage strained the boundaries between crowded, segregated black neighborhoods and white residential areas. In the months after World War I ended in November 1918, racial tensions increased as black men were hired to replace striking white workers in several industries in Chicago.

The Chicago riot began on Sunday, July 27, 1919—one day after black troops were welcomed home with a parade down the city's Michigan Avenue. Eugene Williams, a young black man, was swimming in Lake Michigan and inadvertently crossed the invisible boundary that separated the black and white beaches and bathing areas. He was stoned by white people and drowned. Instead of arresting the alleged perpetrators, the police arrested a black man who complained about police inaction.

Williams's death set off a week of violence that left twenty-three black people and fifteen white people dead. More than five hundred were injured, and nearly one thousand were left homeless after fire raged through a Lithuanian neighborhood. Not only did police fail to stem the violence, they often joined roaming white mobs as they attacked black pedestrians and streetcar passengers. Black men formed a barrier along State Street to stop the advance of white gangs from the stockyard district. Three regiments of the Illinois National Guard were sent into the streets, but the violence ended only on Saturday, August 1, as heavy rains kept people indoors.

During the riot, the Chicago *Defender*, the city's black newspaper, reported many violent incidents. "In the early [Tuesday] morning a thirteen-year-old lad standing on his porch at 51st and Wabash Avenue was shot to death by a white man who, in an attempt to get away, encountered a mob and his existence became history. A mounted policeman, unknown, fatally wounded a small boy in the block of Dearborn Street and was shot to death by some unknown rioter."

ELAINE, 1919

In the fall of 1919, black sharecroppers in and around Elaine, Arkansas, attempted to organize a union and withhold their cotton from the market until they re-

ceived a higher price. Deputy sheriffs tried to break up a union meeting in a black church, and one of the deputies was killed. In retaliation, white people killed dozens of black people. No white people were prosecuted, but twelve black men were convicted of the deputy's murder. They were sentenced to death, and sixty-seven other black men received prison terms of up to twenty years. Many were tortured and beaten while they were held in jail. Ida Wells Barnett and the Equal Rights League generated enormous publicity about the case. The NAACP appealed the convictions, and in 1923 the Supreme Court overturned them. The court agreed with NAACP attorney Moorfield Storey that the defendants had not received a fair trial.

TULSA, 1921

Violence erupted in Tulsa, Oklahoma, on May 31, 1921, after still another black man was accused of rape. Dick Rowland allegedly assaulted a white woman elevator operator, and rumors circulated that white men intended to lynch him. To protect Rowland, who was later found innocent, black men assembled at the courthouse jail where white men also gathered. Angry words were exchanged, and shooting erupted. Several black and white men died in the chaos that ensued.

Black men retreated to their neighborhood, known as Greenwood, to protect their families and homes. The governor dispatched the National Guard, and the sheriff removed Rowland from the jail to an unknown location. By the morning of June 1, some five hundred white men confronted about one thousand black men across a set of railroad tracks. White men in automobiles were also cruising around the black residential area. Approximately fifty armed black people defended themselves in a black church near the edge of their neighborhood as white men advanced on them. The attackers set fire to the church. As black people fled the burning building, they were shot. More fires were set. About two thousand black residents managed to escape to a convention hall. Forty square blocks and more than one thousand of Greenwood's homes, churches, schools, and businesses went up in flames. White men even utilized aircraft for reconnaissance and to drop incendiary devices on Greenwood. As many as three hundred black people and twenty white people may have perished in what was perhaps the worst episode of civilian violence in American history until September 11, 2001.

Following a three-and-a-half-year investigation, an eleven-member commission in 2001 made a series of recommendations to the Oklahoma legislature to offer a measure of restitution. The legislators declined to set aside funds for survivors, but they did appropriate $750,000 to formulate plans for a museum and memorial. They also created a Greenwood Redevelopment Authority and instituted a scholarship program.

ROSEWOOD, 1923

During the first week of January 1923, the small town of Rosewood, Florida, was destroyed and its black residents driven out or killed. Rosewood was a mostly black community—it had a few white inhabitants—located in the pinewoods of west central Florida not far from the Gulf of Mexico. On New Year's Day, Fannie Taylor, a married white woman from a nearby town, claimed she had been raped and beaten by a black man. Many white people quickly assumed Jessie Hunter was responsible. Other white people believed Mrs. Taylor wanted to divert attention from herself because she had a white lover who was not her husband.

White men sought Hunter and vengeance. Unable to locate him, they brutally beat Aaron Carrier, who may have helped Taylor's white lover escape. The mob shot and killed Samuel Carter after savagely mutilating him. Tensions dramatically escalated.

On January 4 a band of angry white men invaded Rosewood. Black people were prepared to defend themselves. Led by Sylvester Carrier and his mother Sarah, many townspeople had congregated in the Carrier home. The mob unleashed a hail of gunfire into the residence, killing Sarah Carrier. Two white men who attempted to gain entry into the home were shot and killed. Shooting continued until the mob's supply of ammunition was depleted on January 5.

The following day a mob of 250, including Ku Klux Klan members from Gainesville, invaded, burned, and destroyed Rosewood. The community's black residents fled to the nearby woods and swamps with little more than the clothes on their backs, never to return. Rosewood was no more.

The precise number of black people who died will never be known. It may have been well over one hundred. In 1994 the Florida legislature appropriated $2.1 million to survivors of Rosewood and to families who lost property in the assault. Although seven decades had elapsed, ten survivors were still alive and collected $150,000 each. But it proved impossible for many black people to verify they had been in Rosewood in 1923 or that they were kin to people who had owned property in the town. Much of the money was not disbursed.

The Great Migration

The Great Migration of African Americans from the rural South to the urban North began as a trickle of people after the Civil War and became a flood of human be-

This is the Greenwood neighborhood of Tulsa, Oklahoma, in flames during the riot in June 1921.

ings by the second decade of the twentieth century (see Table 16–1). Between 1910 and 1940, 1.75 million black people left the South. As a result, the black population outside the South doubled by 1940. Most of the initial wave of migrants was younger people born in the 1880s and 1890s, who had no recollection of slavery but anticipated a better future for themselves and their families in the North.

WHY MIGRATE?

People moved for many reasons. Often they were both pushed from their rural circumstances and pulled toward urban areas. The push resulted from disasters in southern agriculture in the 1910s. The boll weevil destroyed cotton crops across the South from Mexico to the Carolinas, and floods devastated Mississippi and Alabama in 1915. The pull resulted from labor shortages created by World War I in northern industry and manufacturing. The war all but ended European immigration to the United States, eliminating a main source of cheap labor. At the same time, European governments and the United States placed huge orders for war material with northern factories. Thousands of jobs became available in steel mills, railroads, meatpacking plants, and the automobile industry. Northern businessmen sent labor agents to recruit southern workers.

Many southern white people reacted ambivalently to the loss of black residents. They welcomed the departure of people they held in such low regard, but they also worried about the loss of tenants and sharecroppers. Southern states and municipalities required labor agents to obtain licenses to recruit workers. Angry

TABLE 16–1   BLACK POPULATION GROWTH IN SELECTED NORTHERN CITIES, 1910–1920

	1910		1920		
	Number	**Percentage***	**Number**	**Percentage***	**Percentage Increase**
New York	91,709	1.9%	152,467	2.7%	66.3%
Chicago	44,103	2.0	109,458	4.1	148.2
Philadelphia	84,459	5.5	134,229	7.4	58.9
Detroit	5,741	1.2	40,838	4.1	611.3
St. Louis	43,960	6.4	69,854	9.0	58.9
Cleveland	8,448	1.5	34,451	4.3	307.8
Pittsburgh	25,623	4.8	37,725	6.4	47.2
Cincinnati	19,739	5.4	30,079	7.5	53.2
Indianapolis	21,816	9.3	34,678	11.0	59.0
Newark	9,475	2.7	16,977	4.1	79.2
Kansas City	23,566	9.5	30,719	9.5	30.4
Columbus	12,739	7.0	22,181	9.4	74.1
Gary	383	2.3	5,299	9.6	1,283.6
Youngstown	1,936	2.4	6,662	5.0	244.1
Buffalo	1,773	.4	4,511	.9	154.4
Toledo	1,877	1.1	5,691	2.3	203.2
Akron	657	1.0	5,580	2.7	749.3

*"Percentage" refers to percentage of city's population; "Percentage Increase" refers to growth of black population.

Source: U.S. Department of Commerce.

white landowners and businessmen threatened some of these agents and forced them to leave southern towns.

Black newspapers, such as the Pittsburgh *Courier* and especially the Chicago *Defender*, encouraged black southerners to move north. Black railroad porters and dining car employees distributed thousands of copies of the *Defender* throughout the South. One unnamed black man wrote in the *Defender* that sensible men would leave the poverty, injustice, and violence of the South for the cold weather of the North. "To die from the bite of frost is far more glorious than that of the mob. I beg of you, my brothers, to leave that benighted land. You are free men."

A black resident of one of South Carolina's Sea Islands explained in 1917 that he left to earn more money. "I could work and dig all year on the Island and best I could do would be to make $100 and take a chance of making nothin'. Well, I figured I could make 'roun' thirty or thirty-five dollars every week and at that rate save possibly $100 every two months." Like many migrants, he moved more than once. He first went to Savannah, and then to Philadelphia, before finally settling in Brooklyn, New York.

Black people who departed the South escaped the most blatant forms of Jim Crow and the injustice in the judicial system. Black women fled the sexual exploitation of white and black men. Black people in the North could vote. The North offered better public schools. In the early twentieth century the South had almost no public high schools for black youngsters, and the longer school year in the urban North was not tied to the demands of planting and harvesting crops.

Some black people migrated to escape the dull, bleak, impoverished life and culture of the rural South. One young woman left South Carolina's St. Helena Island in 1919. "[I] got tired of the Island. Too lonesome. Go to bed at six o'clock. Everything dead. No dances, no moving picture show, no nothing. 'Coz every once in a while they would have a dance, but here you could go to 'em every Saturday night. That's why people move more than anything else."

The decision to migrate could take years of pondering and planning. To depart was to leave family, friends, and familiar surroundings behind for the uncertainty, confusion, and rapid pace of urban communities. Migrants often first moved to southern towns or cities and then headed for a larger city. Poet and writer Langston Hughes was born in Joplin, Missouri, in 1902 and moved to Lincoln, Illinois. "I had no sooner graduated from grammar school in Lincoln than we moved from Illinois to

Letters from the Great Migration   16-4

Cleveland. My stepfather sent for us. He was working in a steel mill during the war, and making lots of money. But it was hard work, and he never looked the same afterwards."

Some people made the decision to move impulsively. After she was fired from her nursing position at Hampton Institute in Virginia in 1905, Jane Edna Hunter decided to go to Florida, but changed her mind:

En route, I stopped at Richmond, Virginia, to visit with Mr. and Mrs. William Coleman, friends of Uncle Parris.

They were at church when I arrived; so I sat on the doorstep to await their return. After these good friends had greeted me, Mrs. Coleman said, 'Our bags are packed to go to Cleveland, Jane. We are going to take you with us.' I was swept off my feet by the cheerful determination of the Colemans. My trunk, not yet removed from the station, was rechecked to Cleveland.

Most migrants maintained a genuine fondness for their southern homes and kinfolk. They returned regularly for holidays, weddings, and funerals. Kelly Miller, who had grown up in South Carolina, spent years as a scholar and teacher at Howard University in Washington, D.C., but he still had "an attachment for the old state that time and distance cannot destroy. After all, we love to be known as a South Carolinian." Thousands of black migrants routinely sent money home to the South. Over the years, several million dollars earned in the North flowed into southern communities.

DESTINATIONS

Although many black southerners went to Florida, most migrants from the Carolinas and Virginia settled in Washington, Philadelphia, and New York (see Map 16–2). Black people who left Georgia, Alabama, and Mississippi tended to move to Pittsburgh, Cleveland, and Detroit. Migrants from Louisiana, Mississippi, and Arkansas often rode the Illinois Central Railroad to Chicago. Once they experienced a metropolis, many black people then resettled in smaller communities. Migrants to Philadelphia, for example, moved on to Harrisburg or Altoona, Pennsylvania, or to Wilmington, Delaware.

Few black southerners moved west to California, Oregon, or Washington. There were only 22,000 black residents of California in 1910. Substantial black migration west did not occur until the 1930s and 1940s. But in 1920 Mallie Robinson made the long trek west. Deserted by her husband Jerry, she set out with her five children (including one-year-old Jackie who would become a baseball legend) and eight other relatives. They boarded a train in Cairo, Georgia, traveled to Los Angeles, and settled in nearby Pasadena. Mallie's half brother, who had already moved west, assured her she would be closer to heaven in California.

However, most black migrants found their destination was neither near heaven nor the Promised Land. Black people congregated in all-black neighborhoods—Harlem in New York City, Chicago's South Side, Paradise Valley in Detroit, Cleveland's East Side, and the Hill District of Pittsburgh—that later would be called ghettoes. White property owners resisted selling or renting real estate to black people outside the confines of these neighborhoods. And many southern black migrants themselves, wary of white hostility, preferred to live among black people, often friends and family who had preceded them north.

MIGRATION FROM THE CARIBBEAN

Many descendants of Africans who had been slaves in the sugarcane fields of the West Indies joined the migration of black southerners to towns and cities in the North. Between 1900 and 1924, 102,000 West Indians came to the United States. Most came from British colonies including Jamaica, Barbados, and Trinidad and Tobago. But people also arrived from French-held Guadaloupe and Martinique; Dutch colonies of Aruba, Curacao, and Montserrat; and the Danish Virgin Islands (which the United States acquired in 1917). Some of these migrants were middle-class professionals and skilled workers, but a sizable number were black men from Barbados, Jamaica, and elsewhere who had been employed as laborers on the construction of the Panama Canal from 1904 until 1914.

Although white Americans tended to lump all people of color together, regardless of their complexion or origin, the West Indies often did not mix easily or comfortably with African Americans. Some spoke Dutch and French. Those who came from British islands were usually members of the Anglican Church and not Baptists or Methodists. Almost all of the newcomers sent money home to family members who remained in the West Indies. Moreover, many of the Caribbean arrivals were temporary residents. As many as one-third of them would return to the West Indies. In 1924 Congress imposed rigid restrictions on immigration to the United States, and migration from the Caribbean dropped drastically.

Northern Communities

Even before the Civil War, most northern cities had small free black populations. By the late nineteenth century, southern migrants began to gravitate to these urban areas and make their presence felt. Black residents

A Migrant to the North Writes Home

People who migrated to northern communities often wrote home to describe their new surroundings and experiences and to confess they missed their old homes. One unidentified black man who had moved to Philadelphia made his feelings known to a medical doctor.

Philadelphia, Pa., Oct. 7, 1919

Dear Sir:

I take this method of thanking you for yours early responding and the glorious effect of the treatment. Oh. I do feel so fine. Dr. the treatment reach me almost ready to move I am now housekeeping again I like it so much better than rooming. Well Dr. with the aid of God I am making very good I make $75 per month. I am carrying enough insurance to pay me $20 per week if I am not able to be on duty. I don't have to work hard. dont have to mister every little white boy comes along I havent heard a white man call a colored nigger you no now—since I been in the state of Pa. I can ride in the electric street and steam cars any where I get a seat. I dont care to mix with white what I mean I am not crazy about being with white folks, but if I have to pay the same fare I have learn to want the same accomidation. and if you are the first in a place here shoping you dont have to wait until the white folks get thro tradeing yet amid all this I shall ever love the good old South and I am praying that God may give every well wisher a chance to be a man regardless of his color, and if my going to the front [World War I] would bring about such conditions I am ready any day—well Dr. I dont want to worry you but read between the lines; and maybe you can see a little sense in my weak statement the kids are in school every day I have only two and I guess that all. Dr. when you find time I would be delighted to have word from the good old home state. Wife join me in sending love you and yours.

🌿 *What is the letter writer's main reason for having migrated?*

🌿 *What was more important to this man, better living standards or the sense of liberation he enjoyed in Philadelphia?*

Source: Emmett J. Scott, ed., "Letters of Negro Migrants of 1916–1918," *Journal of Negro History* 4 (July 1, 1919), in Fishel and Quarles, *The Negro American: A Documentary History*, pp. 398–99.

established churches, social organizations, businesses, and medical facilities. They gained representation in community and political affairs.

There was less overt segregation in the North. Most northern states, as well as California, had enacted laws in the late nineteenth century that prohibited racial discrimination in public transportation, hotels, restaurants, theaters, and barbershops. Most of these states also forbade segregated schools. However, passage of such laws and their enforcement were two different matters. Many white businesses and communities ignored the statutes and embraced Jim Crow, especially in areas along the Ohio River in southern Ohio, Indiana, and Illinois.

CHICAGO

As early as 1872, Chicago had a black policeman, and in 1876 John W. E. Thomas became the first black man elected to the Illinois Senate. Black physician Daniel Hale Williams established African-American-staffed Provident Hospital on Chicago's South Side in 1891. By 1900 black Chicagoans were the twelfth largest ethnic group in the city, behind such European immigrant groups as the Irish, Poles, and Germans.

Chicago's black population surged during the first three decades of the twentieth century as migrants poured into the city. Black institutions flourished. In 1912 an NAACP branch was established. By 1920 black Chicago had eighty Baptist and thirty-six Methodist churches. The Olivet Baptist Church grew from 3,500 members in 1916 to 9,000 by 1922. Because the downtown YMCA barred black men, black people raised $50,000 and Julius Rosenwald of Sears, Roebuck, and Company contributed $25,000 to build the Wabash YMCA for the black community in 1913. However, many black Chicagoans considered this a surrender to segregation and insisted that black men should be admitted to the white YMCA.

The Chicago *Defender* was the city's leading black newspaper. Its founder, Robert S. Abbott, the son of slaves, began publishing the *Defender* in 1905, and by 1920 it had a nationwide circulation of 230,000. Chicago's first black bank, Jesse Binga's State Bank, was established in 1908, and in 1919 Frank L. Gillespie organized the Liberty Insurance Company.

In 1915 black Chicago's political influence expanded when Oscar DePriest was elected second ward alderman. Two other black men were elected to the city council by 1918. DePriest was then elected to the U.S. House of Representatives as a Republican in 1928, becoming the first black congressman since North Carolina's George White left the House in 1901.

As the number of black people in Chicago swelled, racial tensions increased and exploded in the 1919 race

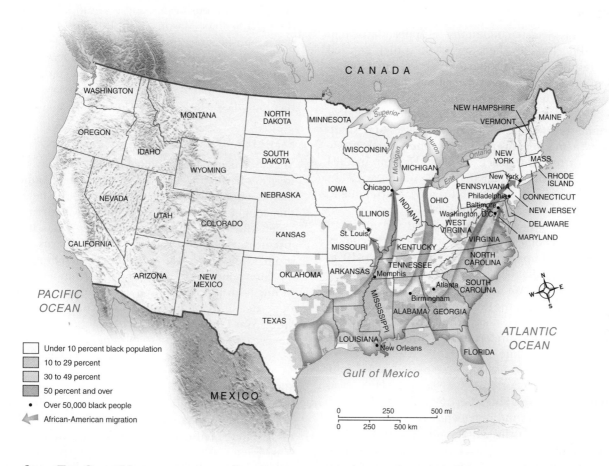

MAP 16–2 THE GREAT MIGRATION AND THE DISTRIBUTION OF THE AFRICAN-AMERICAN POPULATION IN 1920
Although several hundred thousand black southerners migrated north in the second and third decades of the twentieth century in the largest internal migration in American history, most African Americans remained in the southern states.

▶ *Why did most African Americans stay in the South if so many opportunities beckoned in the North?*

riot. Competition for jobs was a critical issue. White employers, such as the meatpacking companies, regularly replaced white strikers with black workers. Black men usually did not hesitate to take such jobs because most labor unions would not admit them. But a few weeks before the riot in 1919, the Amalgamated Meatcutters Union tried to sponsor a unity parade of black and white stockyard workers. The police prohibited it because, some observers believed, the meatpacking companies feared that black and white working men might unite.

Housing was an even more divisive issue than employment. Chicago's black population was almost entirely confined to an eight-square-mile area on the South Side east of State Street. Prosperous black people who could afford more expensive housing outside the area could not purchase it because of their race. As the black population grew, housing became more congested, and crime and vice increased.

Langston Hughes described the similar housing situation his family experienced in Cleveland:

Rents were very high for colored people in Cleveland, and the Negro district was extremely crowded, because of the great migration. It was difficult to find a place to live. We always lived, during my high school years, either in an attic or a basement, and paid quite a lot for such inconvenient quarters. White people on the east side of the city were moving out of their frame houses and renting them to Negroes at double and triple the rents they could receive from others. An eight room house with one bath would be cut up into apartments and five or six families crowded into it, each two-room kitchenette apartment renting for what the whole house had rented for before.

HARLEM

Harlem was a white community in upper Manhattan that had declined by the latter 1800s. It then enjoyed an incredible building boom that occurred in anticipation of the construction of the subway that would link upper Manhattan to downtown New York City by the early twentieth century. But real estate speculators overbuilt and were left with empty houses and apartments. Facing foreclosure, many white property owners sold or rented to black people in Harlem. In 1904 Philip A. Payton formed the Afro American Realty Company that sold homes and rented apartments to black clients before it failed in 1908.

Harlem's white residents opposed the influx of black people. Some of them formed the Harlem Property Owners' Improvement Corporation in 1910 to block black settlement. Its founder, John G. Taylor, warned in 1913, "We are approaching a crisis, it is a question of whether the white man will rule Harlem or the Negro." However, many white property owners—eager for a profit—preferred to sell to black people than to maintain white unity.

As thousands of black people moved to Harlem, many left the "Tenderloin" and "San Juan Hill" areas of Manhattan's West Side where New York's black residents had lived in the nineteenth century. The construction of Pennsylvania Station forced many to vacate the "Tenderloin." Black churches took the lead in the "On to Harlem" movement as they occupied churches formerly used by white denominations. Some of the black churches were among the largest property owners in Harlem.

St. Philip's Protestant Episcopal Church, the wealthiest black church in the United States and noted for its solemn services and elite parishioners, moved from West 25th Street in the "Tenderloin" in 1910 to Harlem. In 1911 St. Philip's purchased ten apartment houses on West 135th Street between Lenox and Seventh Avenues for $640,000. The Reverend Adam Clayton Powell Sr. and the Abyssinian Baptist Church, St. Mark's Episcopal Church, and the African Methodist Episcopal Zion Church ("Mother Zion") also moved to Harlem and acquired extensive real estate holdings there. The black churches helped make Harlem a black community.

As the black population increased in Harlem, large houses and apartments were often subdivided among working families that could not rent or buy in other areas of New York. They paid higher prices for real estate than white people did. The average Harlem family paid $9.50 a room per month; white working families paid $6.50 for similar accommodations elsewhere in New York.

By 1920, 75,000 black people lived in Harlem (see Map 16–3). Harlem became the "Negro Capital of the World." Black businesses and institutions, including the Odd Fellows, Masons, Elks, Pythians, the NAACP, the Urban League, and the YMCA and YWCA moved to Harlem. Black newspapers—the *New York News* and *Amsterdam News*—opened in Harlem to compete with the older *New York Age*. One resident observed, "If my race can make Harlem, good lord, what can't it do?"

FAMILIES

Migration placed black families under enormous strains. Relatives frequently moved north separately. Fathers or mothers would leave a spouse and children behind as they sought employment and housing. Children might be left with grandparents for extended periods. In other instances, extended family members—cousins, in-laws, brothers and sisters—crowded into limited living space.

Men generally found more opportunities for work in northern industries than women did. There was a huge demand for unskilled labor during and after World War I. In 1915 Henry Ford astounded industrial America when he began to pay employees of the Ford Motor Company in Detroit the unprecedented sum of $5 per day, and that included black men and occasionally black women. Rarely, however, would a black man be promoted beyond menial labor. Except for some opportunities in manufacturing during the war, black women were confined to domestic and janitorial work. Mary Ellen Washington recalled the experience in her family. "In the 1920s my mother and five aunts migrated to Cleveland, Ohio, from Indianapolis and, in spite of their many talents, they found every door except the kitchen door closed to them."

Black women employed as domestics lived with white families, worked long hours, and saw more of their white employer's children than they did their own. One maid explained her dreary and unhappy situation:

> I am now past forty years of age and am the mother of three children. My husband died nearly fifteen years ago. . . . For more than thirty years—or since I was ten years old—I have been a servant in one capacity or another in white families.
>
> I frequently work from fourteen to sixteen hours a day. I am compelled . . . to sleep in the house. I am allowed to go home to my own children, the oldest of whom is a girl of 18 years, only once in two weeks, every other Sunday afternoon—even then I'm not permitted to stay all night. . . . I don't know what it is to go to church; I don't know what it is to go to a lecture or entertainment of any kind; I live a treadmill life. . . . You might as well say that I'm on duty all the time—from sunrise to sunrise, every day in the week. I am the slave, body and soul, of this family.

MAP EXPLORATION

To explore this interactive map, go to
http://www.prenhall.com/hine4/map16.3

African-American Population
- 1911
- 1920
- 1930

MAP 16–3 THE EXPANSION OF BLACK HARLEM, 1911–1930

Before the American Revolution, Harlem was a small Dutch village located at the northern end of Manhattan Island. In the early twentieth century, African Americans transformed it into a thriving black metropolis. Migrants who arrived either after a short trip of just a few miles from the "Tenderloin" or "San Juan Hill" sections of midtown Manhattan or after much longer journeys from the Carolinas or Georgia took over block after block of Harlem homes and apartments.

▶ *Why did African Americans settle in Harlem and not elsewhere in New York City?* Adapted from Steven Watson, *The Harlem Renaissance* (New York: Pantheon Books, 1996).

Some vulnerable younger women were lured into prostitution in the intimidating urban environment. Black women's organizations worked to prevent newly arrived migrants from falling prey to sexual exploitation. They did not always succeed. Some women made a calculated decision to turn sex to their economic advantage. Sara Brooks caustically commented, "Some women woulda had a man to come and live in the house and had an outside boyfriend too, in order to get the house paid for and the bills. They meet a man and if he promises 'em four or five dollars to go to bed, they's grab it. That's called sellin' your own body, and I wasn't raised like that."

Despite the stresses and pressures, most black families survived intact. Most northern black families, al-though hardly well to do, were two-parent households. Women headed comparatively few families. Fathers were present in seven of ten black families in New York City in 1925. But the Great Migration transformed southern peasants into an urban proletariat.

CONCLUSION

In 1900 Booker T. Washington was the nation's most influential black leader. He soothed white people and reassured black Americans as he counseled conciliation, patience, and agricultural and mechanical training as the most effective means to bridge the racial

AFRICAN-AMERICAN EVENTS	NATIONAL EVENTS
• 1895 •	
1895 Frederick Douglass dies; Booker T. Washington delivers Cotton States Exposition address	**1896** William McKinley is elected president
1896 *Plessy v. Ferguson* is decided	**1898** Spanish-American War begins
1898 Riot erupts in Wilmington, North Carolina	**1899** Philippine insurrection begins
• 1900 •	
1900 New Orleans riot	**1900** William McKinley reelected
1903 W. E. B. Du Bois publishes *The Souls of Black Folk*	**1901** McKinley is assassinated; Theodore Roosevelt becomes president
	1903 Boston defeats Pittsburgh in the first World Series
	1904 Theodore Roosevelt is elected president
• 1905 •	
1905 Niagara Movement is founded at Niagara Falls, Ontario; the *Defender* is founded in Chicago	**1905** Thomas Dixon publishes *The Clansman;* the film *Birth of a Nation* is based on the novel
1906 Brownsville affair occurs; Atlanta riot occurs	**1906** Upton Sinclair publishes *The Jungle* The San Francisco earthquake kills nearly 700 people
1908 Springfield riot occurs	**1908** William Howard Taft is elected president
1909 NAACP is founded	**1909** Robert E. Peary and Matthew Henson, an African American, reach the North Pole with four Eskimos

divide. His 1895 speech at the Cotton States Exposition in Atlanta elicited support and praise from both white and black listeners.

The Wizard of Tuskegee, as Washington was known, had little appreciation for criticism and did not hesitate to attack his opponents, including William Monroe Trotter and W. E. B. Du Bois. He worked to subvert the Niagara Movement and the NAACP. But support for Washington and his conservative strategy gradually diminished as the NAACP openly confronted racial discrimination. Washington died in 1915. By 1920 the NAACP assumed the lead in the struggle for civil rights as it fought in the courts and legislatures.

The Talented Tenth of black Americans, distinguished by their educational and economic resources, promoted "self-help" through a variety of organizations—from women's groups to fraternities and sororities—to enhance their own status and to help less affluent black people.

As black men served in World War I and as thousands of black southerners migrated north, many white Americans became alarmed that African Americans were not as content with their subordinate and isolated status as Booker T. Washington had suggested they were. Some white Americans responded with violence in race riots as they attempted to prevent black Americans from assuming a more equitable role in American society. By 1920, despite white opposition, black Americans had demonstrated they would not accept economic subservience and the denial of their rights.

RECOMMENDED READING

W. E. B. Du Bois. *The Souls of Black Folk.* New York: Library of America, 1903. An essential collection of superb essays.

John Hope Franklin and August Meier. *Black Leaders of the Twentieth Century.* Urbana: University of Illinois Press, 1982. A series of "mini biographies" of fifteen people including Washington, Du Bois, T. Thomas Fortune, and Ida Wells Barnett.

Willard Gatewood. *Aristocrats of Color: The Black Elite, 1880–1920.* Bloomington: Indiana University Press, 1990. An examination of the lives and activities of well-to-do black people.

Lawrence Otis Graham. *One Kind of People: Inside America's Black Upper Class.* New York: HarperCollins, 1999. An informative history and analysis of black America's wealthiest families and organizations.

Louis R. Harlan. *Booker T. Washington: The Making of a Black Leader, 1856–1901.* New York: Oxford University Press, 1972; and *Booker T. Washington: The Wizard of Tuskegee, 1901–1915.* New York: Oxford University Press, 1983. The definitive two-volume biography of Washington.

David Levering Lewis. *W. E. B. Du Bois: Biography of a Race, 1868–1919.* New York: Henry Holt and Co., 1993; and *W. E. B. Du Bois: The Fight for Equality and the American Century, 1919–1963.* New York: Henry Holt and Co., 2001. A magisterial and exhaustive account of the ninety-five-year life and times of Du Bois.

Deborah Gray White. *Too Heavy a Load: Black Women in Defense of Themselves.* New York: Norton, 1999. An exploration of the contours of black women's history in the twentieth century.

ADDITIONAL BIBLIOGRAPHY

LEADERSHIP CONFLICTS AND THE EMERGENCE OF AFRICAN-AMERICAN ORGANIZATIONS

Tamara L. Brown, Gregory Parks, and Clarenda M. Phillips, eds. *African American Fraternities and Sororities: The Legacy and the Vision.* Lexington: University of Kentucky Press, 2005.

Kevin K. Gaines. *Uplifting the Race: Black Leadership, Politics, and Culture in the Twentieth Century.* Chapel Hill: University of North Carolina Press, 1996.

Charles F. Kellogg. *NAACP: A History of the National Association for the Advancement of Colored People.* Baltimore: Johns Hopkins University Press, 1967.

August Meier. *Negro Thought in America, 1880–1915.* Ann Arbor: University of Michigan Press, 1967.

Michele Mitchell. *Righteous Propagation: African Americans and the Politics of Racial Destiny after Reconstruction.* Chapel Hill: University of North Carolina Press, 2004.

Jacqueline Moore. *Booker T. Washington and W. E. B. Du Bois and the Struggle for Racial Uplift.* Wilmington, Delaware: Scholarly Resources, 2003.

Alfred A. Moss Jr. *American Negro Academy: Voice of the Talented Tenth.* Baton Rouge: Louisiana State University Press, 1981.

B. Joyce Ross. *J. E. Spingarn and the Rise of the N.A.A.C.P.* New York: Atheneum, 1972.

Lawrence C. Ross Jr. *The Divine Nine: The History of African-American Fraternities and Sororities.* New York: Kensington Books, 2000.

Elliott Rudwick. *W. E. B. Du Bois.* New York: Atheneum, 1968.

Nancy Weiss. *The National Urban League, 1910–1940.* New York: Oxford University Press, 1974.

Shamoon Zamir. *Dark Voices: W. E. B. Du Bois and American Thought, 1888–1903.* Chicago: University of Chicago Press, 1995.

AFRICAN-AMERICAN WOMEN IN THE EARLY TWENTIETH CENTURY

Elizabeth Clark-Lewis. *Living In, Living Out: African American Domestics in Washington, D.C., 1910–1940.* Washington, DC: Smithsonian Institution Press, 1994.

1910

1910
National Urban League is founded in New York City

1912
W. E. B. Du Bois endorses Woodrow Wilson for president

1910
The Mann Act prohibits the transporation of a woman across state lines for immoral purposes

1912
Woodrow Wilson is elected president

1914
World War I breaks out in Europe

1915

1915
Guinn v. United States overturns the Oklahoma grandfather clause

Booker T. Washington dies

1917
East St. Louis riot occurs; Houston riot occurs

1919
Chicago riot occurs; Elaine, Arkansas, riot occurs

1915
A German submarine sinks the British liner, *The Lusitania*

1916
United States sends punitive expedition to Mexico; Woodrow Wilson is reelected

1917
United States enters World War I

1918
World War I ends

1919
Treaty of Versailles is negotiated

1920

1920
Harlem becomes "The Negro Capital of the World"

1921
Tulsa riot occurs

1923
Rosewood destroyed

1920
Nineteenth Amendment (Women's Suffrage) is ratified; Warren Harding is elected president

1925

AFRICAN-AMERICAN EVENTS   **NATIONAL EVENTS**

Anna Julia Cooper. *A Voice from the South*. New York: Oxford University Press, 1988.

Cynthia Neverdon-Morton. *Afro-American Women of the South and the Advancement of the Race, 1895–1925*. Knoxville: University of Tennessee Press, 1998.

Jacqueline A. Rouse. *Lugina Burns Hope: A Black Southern Reformer*. Athens: University of Georgia Press, 1989.

Stephanie J. Shaw. *What a Woman Ought to Be and to Do: Black Professional Women Workers during the Jim Crow Era*. Chicago: University of Chicago Press, 1996.

Rosalyn Terborg-Penn. *African American Women in the Struggle for the Vote, 1850–1920*. Bloomington: Indiana University Press, 1998.

AFRICAN AMERICANS IN THE MILITARY IN THE WORLD WAR I ERA

Arthur E. Barbeau and Florette Henri. *Black American Troops in World War I*. Philadelphia: Temple University Press, 1974.

Edward M. Coffman. *The War to End All Wars: The American Military Experience in World War I*. Madison: University of Wisconsin Press, 1986.

Arthur W. Little. *From Harlem to the Rhine: The Story of New York's Colored Volunteers*. New York: Covici, Friede, 1936.

Bernard C. Nalty. *Strength for the Fight: A History of Black Americans in the Military*. New York: Free Press, 1986.

CITIES AND RACIAL CONFLICT

Michael D'Orso. *Rosewood*. New York: Boulevard Press, 1996.

St. Clair Drake and Horace R. Clayton. *Black Metropolis: A Study of Negro Life in a Northern City*. 2 vols. Chicago: Harcourt, Brace and Co., 1945.

Sherry Sherrod Dupree. *The Rosewood Massacre at a Glance*. Gainesville, FL: Rosewood Forum, 1998.

Scott Ellsworth. *Death in a Promised Land: The Tulsa Race Riot of 1921*. Baton Rouge: Louisiana State University Press, 1982.

David Fort Godshalk. *Veiled Visions: The 1906 Atlanta Race Riot and the Reshaping of American Race Relations*. Chapel Hill: University of North Carolina Press, 2005.

Robert V. Haynes. *A Night of Violence: The Houston Riot of 1917*. Baton Rouge: Louisiana State University Press, 1976.

Hannibal Johnson. *Black Wall Street, from Riot to Renaissance in Tulsa's Historic Greenwood District*. Austin, TX: Eakin Press, 1998.

David M. Katzman. *Before the Ghetto: Black Detroit in the Nineteenth Century*. Urbana: University of Illinois Press, 1973.

Kenneth L. Kusmer. *A Ghetto Takes Shape: Black Cleveland, 1870–1930*. Urbana: University of Illinois Press, 1976.

Gregory Mixon. *The Atlanta Riot: Race, Class, and Violence in a New South City*. Gainesville: University Press of Florida, 2005.

Kevin J. Mumford. *Interzones: Black/White Sex Districts in Chicago and New York in the Early Twentieth Century*. New York: Columbia University Press, 1997.

Gilbert Osofsky. *Harlem: The Making of a Ghetto, 1890–1930*. New York: Harper & Row, 1966.

Christopher Reed. *The Chicago NAACP and the Rise of Black Professional Leadership, 1910–1966*. Bloomington: Indiana University Press, 1997.

Elliott M. Rudwick. *Race Riot at East St. Louis, July 2, 1917*. Cleveland: World Publishing, 1966.

Roberta Senechal. *The Sociogenesis of a Race Riot: Springfield, Illinois, in 1908*. Urbana: University of Illinois Press, 1990.

Allan H. Spear. *Black Chicago: The Making of a Negro Ghetto, 1890–1920*. Chicago: University of Chicago Press, 1967.

Joe William Trotter Jr. *Black Milwaukee: The Making of an Industrial Proletariat, 1915–1945*. Urbana: University of Illinois Press, 1985.

William Tuttle. *Chicago in the Red Summer of 1919*. New York: Atheneum, 1970.

Lee E. Williams. *Anatomy of Four Race Riots: Racial Conflict in Knoxville, Elaine (Arkansas), Tulsa, and Chicago, 1919–1921*. Hattiesburg: University and College Press of Mississippi, 1972.

THE GREAT MIGRATION

Peter Gottlieb. *Making Their Own Way: Southern Blacks' Migration to Pittsburgh, 1916–1930*. Urbana: University of Illinois Press, 1987.

James Gregory. *The Southern Diaspora: How the Great Migrations of Black and White Southerners Transformed America*. Chapel Hill: University of North Carolina Press, 2005.

James R. Grossman. *Land of Hope: Chicago, Black Southerners, and the Great Migration*. Chicago: University of Chicago Press, 1989.

Florette Henri. *Black Migration, 1900–1920*. Garden City, NY: Anchor Press, 1975.

Carole Marks. *Farewell—We're Good and Gone: The Great Black Migration*. Bloomington: Indiana University Press, 1989.

Milton C. Sernett. *Bound for the Promised Land: African American Religion and the Great Migration*. Durham, NC: Duke University Press, 1997.

Joe William Trotter Jr., ed. *The Great Migration in Historical Perspective*. Bloomington: Indiana University Press, 1991.

AUTOBIOGRAPHY AND BIOGRAPHY

W. E. B. Du Bois. *Dusk of Dawn*. New York: Harcourt, Brace & Co., 1940.

———. *The Autobiography: A Soliloquy on Viewing My Life from the Last Decade of Its First Century*. New York: International Publishers, 1968.

Stephen R. Fox. *The Guardian of Boston: William Monroe Trotter*. New York: Atheneum, 1970.

Jane Edna Hunter. *A Nickel and a Prayer*. Cleveland: Elli Kani Publishing, 1940.

Adrienne Lash Jones. *Jane Edna Hunter: A Case Study of Black Leadership, 1910–1950*. Brooklyn, NY: Carlson Publishing, 1990.

Kenneth R. Manning. *Black Apollo of Science: The Life of Ernest Everett Just*. New York: Oxford University Press, 1983.

Linda O. McMurry. *George Washington Carver: Scientist and Symbol*. New York: Oxford University Press, 1981.

Arnold Rampersad. *The Art and Imagination of W. E. B. Du Bois*. Cambridge, MA: Harvard University Press, 1976.

Mary Church Terrell. *A Colored Woman in a White World*. New York: Arno Press reprint, 1940.

Emma Lou Thornbrough. *T. Thomas Fortune*. Chicago: University of Chicago Press, 1970.

Booker T. Washington. *Up from Slavery*. New York: Doubleday, 1901.

RETRACING THE ODYSSEY

The Booker T. Washington National Monument, Hardy, Virginia. Booker T. Washington lived his first nine years on this farm. A museum and restored schoolhouse depict rural life in nineteenth-century America, especially for slaves.

The George Washington Carver National Monument, Diamond, Missouri. George Washington Carver was born a slave here in 1864 or 1865 in a cabin that no longer exists. The 210-acre park has a visitor center that has exhibits on Carver's life as well as a short film about his boyhood. There are also nature trails and the Carver Science Discovery Center.

The 369th Historical Society, New York, New York. The 369th all-black regiment distinguished itself during World War I in combat alongside French units. Previously it had been the 15th Infantry Regiment of the New York National Guard. The 369th armory contains a museum that features weapons, equipment, and photos of black troops from World War I to Operation Desert Storm of 1991.

The Greenwood Cultural Center, Tulsa, Oklahoma. The Greenwood Cultural Center has a permanent exhibit of forty-five photos taken during the 1921 riot that devastated the Greenwood community. There is also a replica of one of the houses that was destroyed. The center maintains exhibits on other aspects of local black history as well, and it is home to a Jazz Hall of Fame.

The Smithsonian Institution: National Museum of American History: From Field to Factory, Washington, D.C. This major exhibit depicts the lives and experiences as well as the hopes and disappointments of the people who migrated from the rural South to the industrial North between 1915 and 1940. It includes a tenant farmer's house, a train station, and a Philadelphia row house as it examines the economic and racial factors that motivated thousands of black people to leave their homes and surroundings.

REVIEW, RESEARCH, AND INTERACT

REVIEW QUESTIONS

1. Compare and evaluate the strategies promoted by Booker T. Washington with those of W. E. B. Du Bois and the NAACP.

2. On which issues did Washington and Du Bois agree and disagree?

3. Assess Washington's contributions to the advancement of black people.

4. To what extent did middle-class and prosperous black people contribute to progress for their race? Were their efforts effective?

5. Why did most African Americans support U.S. participation in World War I? Was that support justified?

6. What factors contributed to race riots and violence in the World War I era?

7. Why did many black people leave the South in the 1920s? Why didn't this migration begin earlier or later?

8. What factors affected the decision to migrate or stay?

www.researchnavigator.com

Using the tools available in Research Navigator, consider this question:
Compare and contrast W. E. B. Du Bois's and Booker T. Washington's approach to the position of black Americans in early-twentieth-century society. What were the key differences in the two men's positions?

PRIMARY SOURCE DOCUMENTS

16–1 W. E. B. Du Bois, from *The Souls of Black Folk*, 1903

16–2 The Niagara Movement, Declaration of Principles, 1905

16–3 Platform Adopted by the National Negro Committee, 1909

16–4 Letters from the Great Migration, 1916–1917

16–5 "Our Reason for Being": A. Philip Randolph Embraces Socialism, 1919

MAP EXPLORATION

The Expansion of Black Harlem, 1911–1930, p. 441

INTERACTIVE ACTIVITIES

The Struggle for Women's Suffrage

From the time of the American Revolution through World War I, American women fought to gain the right to vote.

African Americans
and the 1920s

1915–1928

WHY WAS THE KU KLUX KLAN
SO POPULAR AND POWERFUL IN THE 1920s?

WHY DID THE UNIVERSAL NEGRO IMPROVEMENT
ASSOCIATION AND MARCUS GARVEY APPEAL
TO SO MANY AFRICAN AMERICANS?

WHAT ROLE DID A. PHILIP RANDOLPH
PLAY WITH THE BROTHERHOOD
OF SLEEPING CAR PORTERS?

WHAT SUBJECTS AND ISSUES CONCERNED
BLACK WRITERS AND POETS DURING
THE HARLEM RENAISSANCE?

WHY WAS IT SO DIFFICULT FOR
PROFESSIONAL BLACK ATHLETES
TO EARN A LIVING IN THE 1920s?

◄ **The fight to stop lynchings** was one of the NAACP's most important campaigns in the early twentieth century. In the 1920s the NAACP fought unsuccessfully to secure antilynching legislation in Congress, but persisted with demonstrations and protests like this one at the Crime Conference in Washington D.C., to keep the issue in the public arena. Courtesy of the Library of Congress

I, TOO

I, too, sing America.

I am the darker brother.
They send me to eat in the kitchen
When company comes.
But I laugh,
And eat well,
And grow strong.

To-morrow
I'll sit at the table
When company comes
Nobody'll dare
Say to me,
"Eat in the kitchen"
Then.

Besides, they'll see how beautiful I am
And be ashamed,—
I, too, am America.

—Langston Hughes, 1926

A sign of the times. Until the struggles of the modern civil rights movement, Jim Crow racism was a fact of life throughout the South. ▼

COLORED
← WAITING ROOM →

Many Americans had difficulty adjusting to life after World War I. The Allied victory brought little long-term satisfaction or security, and the U.S. Senate's rejection of the Treaty of Versailles, and therefore membership in the League of Nations, in 1920 left many Americans disillusioned. The Bolshevik Revolution in Russia in 1917 and labor agitation at home in-

creased anxiety and heightened fears of radicals. Racial and ethnic intolerance escalated as thousands of rural black southerners continued to stream into northern cities, and more than 800,000 immigrants arrived in America in 1920 and 1921.

Americans shunned Europe and its problems and closed their eyes to the imperfections of American society. Enthusiasm for progressive reforms faded as many Americans concluded that governmental efforts to mitigate poverty, control vice, improve working conditions, and regulate big business had been excessive. Middle-class Americans became preoccupied with making money and with acquiring—usually on credit and for the first time—automobiles, radios, and home appliances.

Many native white Americans, convinced that black people and immigrants—especially Jewish and Catholic immigrants—posed a threat to their Anglo-Saxon ethnic purity, ever more fervently embraced social Darwinism. Many sought reassurance in organizations that stressed religious, racial, and national pride. Millions of white Americans joined the revived Ku Klux Klan in the 1920s as it promoted white supremacy, American patriotism, and Protestant values.

Led by the NAACP, African Americans denounced injustice and pressed for inclusion in society, for the enforcement of civil rights, and for economic opportunities. Black workers—notably the members of the **Brotherhood of Sleeping Car Porters (BSCP)**—organized and demanded recognition and improved working conditions, hours, and wages. But the 1920s also saw hundreds of thousands of African Americans enthusiastically support Marcus Garvey and the **Universal Negro Improvement Association (UNIA).** Garvey celebrated black nationalism and urged his followers to forsake white America, take pride in themselves, and look to Africa. And the 1920s also saw black culture blossom and flourish as the artists, writers, musicians, and entertainers of the Harlem Renaissance celebrated black life and society.

Strikes and the Red Scare

In 1919 and 1920, Americans were bewildered and angered by labor unrest and afraid the communists (or "Reds") in the new Soviet Union would try to incite a revolution in America. There were 3,600 strikes in 1919 as workers who had deferred demands during the war for pay raises and improved working conditions walked off their jobs. More than 300,000 steel workers in Pittsburgh and Gary, Indiana, struck, including 7,000 unskilled black steel workers in Pittsburgh. In a demonstration of solidarity with striking shipyard workers, most of Seattle's working people shut the city down in a general strike. Americans were even more alarmed when police officers in Boston went on strike. Many worried that labor agitation was a prelude to revolution.

Political leaders exacerbated these feelings by warning that communists and foreign agents were plotting to overthrow the government. Woodrow Wilson's attorney general A. Mitchell Palmer grimly warned Americans of the Red menace and the threat aliens posed. He ordered 249 aliens deported and some 6,000 arrested and imprisoned in gross violation of their rights, but it was an action that many Americans warmly approved. Palmer went too far, however, when he predicted the Red revolution would begin in the United States on May 1, 1920. There was no revolution, and confidence in Palmer waned. There were, however, several terrorist bombings, including one on Wall Street in September 1920 that killed thirty-three people. Moreover, evidence indicates that some business leaders supported the Palmer raids as a means of discouraging workers from forming and joining labor unions and participating in strikes.

Prompted in part by the **Red Scare,** xenophobia (fear of foreigners) swept the nation in the 1920s. Two Sicilian immigrants, Nicola Sacco and Bartolomeo Vanzetti, who were anarchists, were charged in 1920 with a murder that had occurred during a payroll robbery near Boston. They were found guilty, and after a prolonged controversy they were executed in 1927. But their supporters believed the guilty verdict was due more to their foreign origins and radical beliefs than to conclusive proof they had committed the murder.

Varieties of Racism

The entrenched racism of American society found continued expression in more than one form in the 1920s. There was the sophisticated racism associated with supposedly scholarly studies that reflected the ideology of social Darwinism. There was also the raw bigotry that manifested itself in various aspects of popular culture and in the ideology of the increasingly popular Ku Klux Klan.

SCIENTIFIC RACISM

Many white Americans believed the United States was under siege as European immigrants and black migrants flooded American cities. Pseudoscholars gravely warned about the peril these "inferior" peoples posed. In 1916 Madison Grant published *The Passing of the Great Race*. Grant warned that America was committing "race suicide" because northern Europeans and their descendants—the Great Race—were being diluted by inferior people from eastern and southern Europe. Lothrop Stoddard's *The Rising Tide of Color* in 1920 argued that people of color would never be equal to white Americans. Stoddard stated his case unequivocally in 1927:

> Even a general knowledge of historical and scientific facts suffices to show the need for a racial basis to our national life,—as it has been, and as we intend that it shall be. We know that our America is a White America. "America," in the traditional sense of the word, was founded by White men, who evolved institutions, ideals, and cultural manifestations which were spontaneous expressions of their racial temperament and tendencies. And the overwhelming weight of both historical and scientific evidence shows that only so long as the American people remains White will its institutions, ideals, and culture continue to fit the temperament of its inhabitants,—and hence continue to endure.

These racist claims were cloaked in the trappings of legitimate scholarship, and they strengthened the cause of white supremacy in the 1920s and helped "protect" America from the "threat" of immigration. In 1921 and in 1924, Congress imposed quotas that severely restricted immigration from southern and eastern Europe, Latin America, and the Carribean, and prohibited it entirely from Asia.

THE BIRTH OF A NATION

In 1915 D. W. Griffith released *The Birth of a Nation*, a cinematic masterpiece and historical travesty based on Thomas Dixon's 1905 novel *The Clansman*. Both the book and the film purported to depict Reconstruction in South Carolina authentically. In this account, immoral and ignorant Negroes joined by shady mulattoes and greedy white Republicans ruthlessly seize control of state government until the heroic and honorable Ku

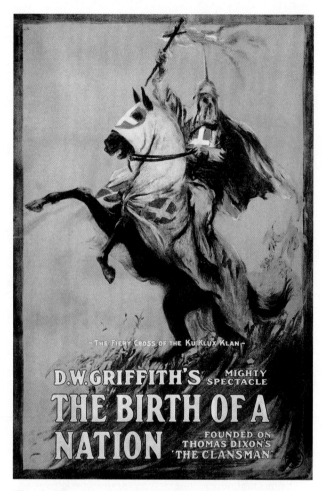

The glorification of the Ku Klux Klan in D. W. Griffith's *The Birth of a Nation,* reflected in this publicity poster, outraged African Americans. The NAACP protested when the silent film was first distributed in 1915 and again when a sound version was released in 1930. The demonstrations attracted publicity to both the film and the NAACP.

Klux Klan saves the state and rescues its white womanhood. The film was enormously popular. President Woodrow Wilson had it screened in the White House. It grossed $18 million (254 million in 2000 dollars) and helped assure a future for Metro Goldwyn Mayer (MGM), which produced it. It also distorted public perceptions about Reconstruction and black Americans.

The NAACP was enraged by *The Birth of a Nation* and fought to halt its presentation. W. E. B. Du Bois complained in *The Crisis* that in the film "the Negro [was] represented either as an ignorant fool, a vicious rapist, a venal or unscrupulous politician or a faithful but doddering idiot." The motion picture unleashed racist violence. After seeing the film in Lafayette, Indiana, an infuriated white man killed a young black man. In Houston, white theatergoers shouted, "Lynch him!"

during a scene in which a white actor in blackface pursued the film's star, Lillian Gish. In front of a St. Louis theater, white real estate agents passed out circulars calling for residential segregation.

Thanks largely to NAACP opposition, the film was banned in Pasadena, California; Wilmington, Delaware; and Boston. With an election looming in Chicago, Republican mayor "Big Bill" Thompson appointed AME bishop Archibald Carey to the board of censors, which temporarily banned the film there. When the sound version of *The Birth of a Nation* was released in 1930, the NAACP renewed its opposition. Ironically, the NAACP campaign may have provided publicity that attracted more viewers to the film. By the same token, however, the campaign also helped increase NAACP membership.

THE KU KLUX KLAN

The Ku Klux Klan (KKK), which disappeared after Reconstruction, was resurrected a few months after *The Birth of a Nation* was released. On Thanksgiving night in 1915, William J. Simmons and thirty-four other men gathered at Stone Mountain near Atlanta, and in the flickering shadows of a fiery cross, they brought the Klan back to life.

The Ku Klux Klan that rose to prominence and power in the 1920s stood for white supremacy—and more. Klansmen styled themselves as "100 percent Americans" who opposed perceived threats from immigrants as well as black Americans. The Klan claimed to represent white, Anglo-Saxon, Protestant America. With European immigrants flocking to America, William Simmons announced the United States was no melting pot. "It is a garbage can! . . . When the hordes of aliens walk to the ballot box and their votes outnumber yours, then that alien horde has got you by the throat."

The Klan found enormous support among apprehensive white middle-class Americans in the North and West. Many of these people believed the liberal, immoral, and loose lifestyles they associated with urban life, immigrants, and African Americans threatened their religious beliefs and conservative cultural values. The Klan attacked the theory of evolution, fought for the prohibition of alcoholic beverages, and claimed to uphold the "sanctity" of white womanhood. The KKK opposed Jews, Roman Catholics, and black people. Klansmen often used violent intimidation to convey their patriotic, religious, and racial convictions. They burned synagogues and Catholic churches. They beat, branded, and lynched their opponents.

By 1925 the Klan had an estimated 5 million members, and 40,000 of them marched in Washington,

D.C., that year. The Klan attracted small businessmen, shopkeepers, clerks, Protestant clergymen, farmers, and professional people. It was open only to native-born white men, but it also had a Women's Order, a Junior Order for boys, and a Tri K Klub for girls. The Klan was active in Oregon, Colorado, Illinois, and Maine, and it became a potent political force in Indiana, Oklahoma, and Texas. In those three states in particular, candidates for public office who refused to support or join the Klan stood little chance of election.

The Klan was also a highly effective moneymaking machine. Its leaders collected millions of dollars in initiation fees, membership dues, and income from selling Klan paraphernalia. But the Klan declined rapidly in the late 1920s when its leaders fought among themselves. Its claim to uphold the purity of white womanhood was damaged when one of its leaders, D. C. Stephenson, was arrested in Indiana and charged with raping a young woman who subsequently committed suicide. Stephenson was sentenced to life in prison, and the Klan never fully recovered.

PROTEST, PRIDE, AND PAN-AFRICANISM: BLACK ORGANIZATIONS IN THE 1920S

African Americans responded to racism and to larger cultural and economic developments in the 1920s in several ways. The NAACP forged ahead with its efforts to secure constitutional rights and guarantees by advocacy in the political and judicial systems. Many working-class black people who had migrated to northern cities were attracted to the racial pride promoted by Marcus Garvey and the Universal Negro Improvement Association. There were also ongoing attempts to foster racial cooperation among peoples of African descent and to exert diplomatic influence through the work of several Pan-African congresses that were held during the first three decades of the twentieth century.

THE NAACP

During its second decade, the NAACP expanded its influence and increased its membership. In 1916 James Weldon Johnson (who wrote "Lift Every Voice and Sing") joined the NAACP as field secretary. He played a pivotal role in the organization's development and in its growth from nine thousand members in 1916 to ninety thousand in 1920. Johnson traveled tirelessly, recruiting members and establishing branches. He journeyed to rural southern communities, to northern cities, and to the West Coast.

Johnson impressed both black and white people. He got along well with W. E. B. Du Bois—not always an easy task, considering Du Bois's sometimes haughty and acerbic demeanor. Johnson was an excellent diplomat who could negotiate and compromise, but he could also be blunt when necessary. He methodically reported the gruesome details of lynchings, and when some NAACP directors complained in 1921 that these graphic descriptions offended people, Johnson stood his ground. "What we need to do is to root out the thing which makes possible these horrible details. I am of the opinion that this can be done only through the fullest publicity."

In 1918 Johnson hired Walter White to assist him. White was from Atlanta and, like Johnson, a graduate of Atlanta University. White's very fair complexion permitted him to move easily among white people to investigate racial discrimination and violence. Although his domineering personality offended some NAACP officials and supporters, White devoted his life to the organization and to racial justice.

Johnson and the NAACP fought hard in Congress to secure passage of the Dyer antilynching bill in 1921 and 1922 (see Chapter 16). The legislation ultimately failed, but the NAACP succeeded in publicizing the persistence of barbaric behavior by mobs in a nation supposedly devoted to fairness and the rule of law. It was the first campaign by a civil rights organization to lobby Congress, and—like the attempt to block *The Birth of a Nation*—it won favorable publicity and goodwill for the NAACP.

Johnson blamed the Dyer bill's failure on Republican senators. He charged that the Republican Party took black support for granted because southern Democrats remained openly committed to white supremacy, and therefore black people had little choice but to vote Republican: "The Republican Party will hold the Negro and do as little for him as possible, and the Democratic Party will have none of him at all." He warned, however, that black voters in the North would abandon the Republicans:

LIVING WORDS

The Creation 28

> The Negro can serve notice that he is no longer a part of the agreement by voting in the coming elections in each State against Republicans who have betrayed him, who are in league with the Ku Klux Klan, who are found to be hypocrites and liars on the question of the Negro's essential rights, and by letting them know he has done it. I am in favor of doing the job at once.

Johnson pointed out that black voters in Harlem had elected a black Democrat to the state legislature.

The NAACP continued to rely on the judicial system to protect black Americans and enforce their civil rights. By the 1920s the Democratic Party in virtually every southern state barred black people from membership, which excluded them from voting in Democratic primary elections. The result was what was known

THE NEGRO NATIONAL ANTHEM: "LIFT EVERY VOICE AND SING"

In 1900, to celebrate Abraham Lincoln's birthday, James Weldon Johnson wrote "Lift Every Voice and Sing." His younger brother John Rosamond Johnson composed music to accompany the words. It was published in 1921 and soon thereafter—with the encouragement of the NAACP—the song was embraced as the Negro national anthem. (In 1998 the New Yorker *magazine suggested it replace the "Star-Spangled Banner" as the U.S. national anthem.)*

–1–

Lift every voice and sing, 'til earth and heaven ring, Ring with the
　harmonies of liberty
Let our rejoicing rise, high as the list'ning skies,
Let it resound loud as the rolling sea.
Sing a song full of the faith that the dark past has taught us,
Sing a song full of the hope that the present has brought us;
Facing the rising sun of our new day begun
Let us march on till victory is won.

–2–

Stony the road we trod, bitter the chast'ning rod
Felt in the days when hope unborn had died
Yet with a steady beat, have not our weary feet
Come to the place for which our fathers sighed?
We have come over a way that with tears has been watered,
We have come, treading our path thro' the blood of the slaughtered
Out from the gloomy past, 'til now we stand at last
Where the white gleam of our bright star is cast.

–3–

God of our weary years, God of our silent tears
Thou who has brought us thus far on the way
Thou who hast by Thy might, led us into the light
Keep us forever in the path, we pray.
Lest our feet stray from the places, our God, where we met Thee
Lest our hearts, drunk with the wine of the world, we forget Thee
Shadowed beneath Thy hand, may we forever stand
True to our God, true to our native land.

What does James Weldon Johnson mean in the last line: "True to our God, true to our native land"? To what native land does he refer?

Do the words of the song apply to all Americans or only to African Americans? Would the song be appropriate as the American national anthem?

as "white primaries." Because the Republican Party had almost ceased to exist in most of the South, victory in the Democratic primary elections led invariably to victory in the general election. In 1924 the NAACP, in cooperation with its branch in El Paso, filed suit over the exclusion of black voters from the Democratic primary in Texas. In 1927 the Supreme Court ruled in *Nixon v. Herndon* that the Democratic primary was unconstitutional—the first victory in what would become a twenty-year legal struggle to permit black men and women to vote in primary elections across the South.

In Detroit in 1925, black physician Ossian Sweet and his family moved into an all-white neighborhood. For several nights a mob threatened the Sweet family and other people who joined in their defense. One evening, shots were fired from the Sweet home that killed a white man. Twelve occupants of the house were charged with murder. The NAACP retained Clarence Darrow and Arthur Garfield Hayes, two of the nation's finest criminal attorneys, to defend the Sweets. The Sweets pleaded self-defense, and after two trials, they were acquitted.

"UP YOU MIGHTY RACE": MARCUS GARVEY AND THE UNIA

With several million loyal and enthusiastic followers, Marcus Garvey's Universal Negro Improvement Association (UNIA) became the largest mass movement of black people in American history. The UNIA enabled people—often dismissed by the white majority for having no genuine history or culture—to celebrate one another and their heritage and to anticipate a glorious future. Garvey was an energetic, charismatic, and flamboyant leader who wove racial pride, Christian faith, and economic cooperation into a black nationalist organization that had spread throughout the United States by the early 1920s.

Garvey was born in 1887 in the British colony of Jamaica, the eleventh child in a rural family. He quit school at age fourteen and became a printer in Kingston, the island's capital; he was promoted to foreman before he was fired in 1907 for prolabor activities during a strike. He traveled to Costa Rica, Panama, Ecuador, and Nicaragua and became increasingly disturbed over the conditions black workers endured in fields, factories, and mines. He returned to Jamaica and with a growing appreciation of the power of the written and spoken word, he set out to educate himself. He spent two years in London, where he sharpened his oratorical and debating skills discussing the plight of black people with Africans and people from the Caribbean.

He returned to Jamaica and founded the UNIA in 1914. With the slogan "One God! One Aim! One

PROFILE ❧ JAMES WELDON JOHNSON

James Weldon Johnson was a man of immense talents. At various times he was a lawyer, diplomat, journalist, teacher, and gifted writer of prose and poetry. Most important, he was an effective and dynamic civil rights leader.

Johnson was born in 1871 in Jacksonville, Florida, to parents who had not been slaves. His father was a waiter in a fashionable hotel, and his mother was a schoolteacher. He received his secondary and collegiate education at Atlanta University, where he also earned a master's degree. He read law in the office of a white Jacksonville attorney and was admitted to the Florida bar. In 1902 he moved to New York City.

With his brother John Rosamond and black entertainer Robert Cole, he became part of a successful songwriting team. They contributed two musical numbers to Theodore Roosevelt's 1904 presidential campaign: "You're All Right Teddy" and "The Old Flag Never Touched the Ground." Johnson's connection to the Republican Party and his support for Booker T. Washington helped secure diplomatic appointments for him. Johnson spent seven years as a consul in Venezuela and Nicaragua. In 1910 he married Grace Neal, the sister of a prominent New York real estate broker.

With the election in 1912 of Woodrow Wilson, a Democrat, Johnson's diplomatic career ended. He became an editorial writer for the *New York Age*. He also published anonymously *The Autobiography of an Ex-Colored Man*. In 1916 Joel Spingarn, the president of the NAACP, asked Johnson to take a leadership role with that organization, and Johnson—who had not openly supported the NAACP before Booker T. Washington's death in 1915—became its field secretary.

Johnson spent the next fourteen years with the NAACP. In 1920 he became chief executive, responsible for the association's day-to-day operations. He had organized the silent march on Fifth Avenue on July 28, 1917, to protest the East St. Louis riot (see Chapter 16). He publicized lynchings. He recruited members and established new branches. In 1920 in *The Nation*, he documented the mistreatment of Haitians by U.S. troops who had occupied that Caribbean nation. He supported black workers and A. Philip Randolph and the Brotherhood of Sleeping Car Porters. He arranged legal counsel for Ossian Sweet in Detroit in 1925 after Sweet and several of his supporters were charged with murder.

Johnson also managed to write prolifically and imaginatively. In 1920, he wrote "The Creation: A Negro Sermon." He wrote "God's Trombones: Seven Negro Sermons in Verse" in 1927 and many other works of prose and poetry. In 1930 he finished *Black Manhattan,* which traced the cultural contributions of black people in music, poetry, and theater to New York City from the seventeenth to the twentieth centuries.

Like so many civil rights leaders, Johnson could be inconsistent in his stands on racial issues. Though dedicated to the proposition that black and white people should enjoy equal access to public facilities, he supported an all-black YMCA in Harlem and the separate training of black military officers during World War I. He opposed moving NAACP headquarters from Fifth Avenue to Harlem. He supported building an all-black veteran's hospital at Tuskegee, Alabama, as long as it would be staffed by black physicians and nurses. He appreciated Marcus Garvey's emphasis on black pride, but he considered the back-to-Africa movement as an attempt to escape from America's racial problems rather than a solution to them.

In 1930 Johnson left the NAACP to become a professor of creative writing at Fisk University in Nashville. He left the NAACP a far more visible and stronger organization than he had found it in 1916. At Fisk, he worked with some of the twentieth century's leading black scholars, including Horace Mann Bond, Alrutheus A. Taylor, and E. Franklin Frazier. Historian John Hope Franklin was one of his students. Johnson's autobiography, *Along the Way*, was published in 1933. He died in an automobile accident in 1938.

Johnson

A member of Marcus Garvey's United Negro Improvement Association stands outside a UNIA club in New York City. The UNIA had a tremendous impact on black communities in the North and the South during the 1920s, providing religious leadership, business opportunities, and a sense of dignity to its many followers.

Destiny!" he stressed the need for black people to organize for their own advancement. Garvey had read Booker T. Washington's *Up from Slavery* and was much impressed with Washington's emphasis on self-help and on progress through education and the acquisition of skills. Garvey also—like Washington—could criticize black people for their lack of progress: "The bulk of our people are in darkness and are really unfit for good society." They had no right to aspire to equality because they had "done nothing to establish the right to equality."

Garvey came to the United States in 1916 just as thousands of African Americans were migrating to cities. A dynamic speaker whose message resonated among the disaffected urban working class, Garvey quickly built the UNIA into a major movement. He urged his listeners to take pride in themselves as they restored their race to its previous greatness. "We must canonize our own saints, create our own martyrs, and elevate to positions of fame and honor black men and women who have made their distinct contributions to our racial history." He reminded people that Africa had a remarkable past. "Africa was peopled with a race of cultured black men, who were masters in art, science and literature; men who were cultured and refined; men, who, it was said, were like the gods. . . . Black men, you were once great; you shall be great again." He insisted that his followers change their thinking. "We have outgrown slavery, but our minds are still enslaved

to the thinking of the Master Race. Now take these kinks out of your mind, instead of out of your hair."

With the formation of the New York division of the UNIA in Harlem in 1917, Garvey exhorted, "Up you mighty race!" as he commanded black people to take control of their destiny. Still, he blamed them for their predicament. "That the Negro race became a race of slaves was not the fault of God Almighty . . . it was the fault of the race." Their salvation would result from their own exertion and not from concessions by white people.

Garvey's message and the UNIA spread to black communities large and small. He regularly couched his rhetoric in religious terms, and he came to be known as the Black Moses, a messiah. Garvey dwelled on Christ's betrayal as he identified himself with Jesus. "If Garvey dies, Garvey lives." "Christ died to make men free, I shall die to give courage and inspiration to my race."

Garvey's followers enjoyed the pageantry, ceremonies, and titles that were a part of the UNIA. The African Legionnaires and the Black Cross Nurses, resplendent in their uniforms, assembled in New York's Liberty Hall, and they paraded through Harlem. They prayed from The Universal Negro Catechism and reflected on their connection to Africa: "O Blessed Lord Jesus, redeem Africa from the hands of those who exploit and ravish her."

Garvey and the UNIA also established businesses that employed nearly one thousand black people. The weekly newspaper, *Negro World,* promoted Garvey's ideology. In New York City, the Negro Factories Corporation operated three grocery stores, two restaurants, a printing plant, a steam laundry, and a factory that turned out uniforms, hats, and shirts for UNIA members. The association also owned buildings, vehicles, and facilities in other cities. Garvey proudly declared to white Americans that the UNIA "employs thousands of black girls and black boys. Girls who could only be washer women in your homes, we made clerks, stenographers. . . . You will see from the start we tried to dignify our race."

Although Garvey and the UNIA are most frequently associated with urban communities in the North, the UNIA also spread rapidly through the rural South in the 1920s. Black farmers and sharecroppers established UNIA chapters from Virginia to Louisiana, and the Garvey movement and the *Negro World* could be found in such remote communities as Kinston, North Carolina; Ty Ty, Georgia; and Cotton Plant, Arkansas.

Garvey may be best remembered for his proposal to return black people to Africa by way of the Black Star Line, a steamship company he founded in 1919. Garvey sold stock in the company for five dollars a share, and he hoped to establish a fleet with black officers and crew members. In 1920 the company purchased the *Yarmouth,* a dilapidated vessel that became the first

Jamaican-born Marcus Garvey arrived in the United States in 1916 and quickly rose to prominence as the head of the Universal Negro Improvement Association. Garvey appears here in a 1924 parade in Harlem attired in a uniform similar to those worn by British colonial governors in Jamaica, Trinidad, and elsewhere.

ship in the fleet. Garvey raised enough capital to buy two additional ships, the *Kanawha* and the *Booker T. Washington,* but he lacked the financial resources to maintain them or to transport anyone to Africa.

Moreover, Garvey knew it was unrealistic to expect several million black residents of the Western Hemisphere to join the back to Africa enterprise, but he genuinely believed the UNIA could liberate Africa from European colonial rule. "Wake up Ethiopia! Wake up Africa! Let us work towards the one glorious end of a free, redeemed and mighty nation." The UNIA adopted a red, green, and black flag for the proposed African republic that represented the blood, land, and race of the people of the continent.

The UNIA attempted to establish a settlement on the Cavalla River in southern Liberia. Garvey also petitioned the League of Nations to permit the UNIA to take possession of the former German colony of Tangaruyka (today's Tanzania) in East Africa. But the major colonial powers in Africa—Britain and France—and

the United States thwarted Garvey's plans, and the UNIA never gained a foothold on the continent.

The U.S. government and several black American leaders also worked diligently to undermine the UNIA and Garvey. J. Edgar Hoover and the Bureau of Investigation (the predecessor of the FBI) considered Garvey a serious threat to the racial status quo. Hoover employed black agents to infiltrate the UNIA and compile information that could be used to deport Garvey, who had never become an American citizen.

Garvey had few friends or admirers among African-American leaders because he and they differed fundamentally on strategy and goals. Garvey deplored efforts to gain legal and political rights within the American system. By appealing to the black masses, he rejected Du Bois's notion that the Talented Tenth would lead the race to liberation. He mocked the NAACP as the National Association for the Advancement of Certain People. Not long after he arrived in the United States, Garvey visited the NAACP office in New York, and he commented sourly that it was essentially a white organization. "There was no representation of the race there that any one could recognize. . . . [Y]ou had to be as near white as possible, otherwise there was no place for you as stenographer, clerk or attendant in the office of the National Association for the Advancement of 'Colored' People."

Garvey called W. E. B. Du Bois a "lazy, dependent mulatto." In return, Du Bois described Garvey as "a little, fat black man, ugly but with intelligent eyes and big head," who was "the most dangerous enemy of the Negro race in America and the world . . . either a lunatic or a traitor." A. Philip Randolph, the black labor leader, was no less critical, calling Garvey "the supreme Negro Jamaican Jackass," an "unquestioned fool and ignoramus."

Unlike African-American leaders, Garvey believed black and white people had separate destinies, and he regarded interracial cooperation as absurd. Thus Garvey considered a meeting he had with Ku Klux Klan leaders in Atlanta in 1922 consistent with his racial views. He praised the white supremacist organization. "They are better friends to my race, for telling us what they are, and what they mean, thereby giving us a chance to stir for ourselves." He added that "every white man is a Klansman . . . and there is no use lying about it."

In 1922 Garvey and three other UNIA leaders were arrested and indicted on twelve counts of fraudulent use of the U.S. mail to sell stock in the Black Star Line. Eight African-American leaders wrote to the U.S. attorney general to condemn Garvey and insist on his prosecution. Although Garvey was guilty of no more than mismanagement and incompetence, he was eventually found guilty and sent to the federal penitentiary in Atlanta in 1925. President Calvin Coolidge commuted his sentence in 1927, and he was deported.

MARCUS GARVEY APPEALS FOR A NEW AFRICAN NATION

Marcus Garvey and the UNIA offered hope to African Americans in the 1920s. In the following words, Garvey passionately calls for African Americans and West Indians to support the creation of a new African nation.

For five years the Universal Negro Improvement Association has been advocating the cause of Africa for the Africans—that is, that the Negro peoples of the world should concentrate upon the object of building up for themselves a great nation in Africa. . . .

It is only a question of a few more years when Africa will be completely colonized by Negroes, as Europe is by the white race. What we want is an independent African nationality, and if America is to help the Negro peoples of the world establish such a nationality, then we welcome the assistance.

It is hoped that when the time comes for American and West Indian Negroes to settle in Africa, they will realize their responsibilities and duty. It will not be to go to Africa for the purpose of exercising an over-lordship over the natives, . . .

It will be useless, as stated before, for bombastic Negroes to leave America and the West Indies to go to Africa, thinking that they will have privileged positions to inflict upon the race that bastard aristocracy that they have tried to maintain in this Western world at the expense of the masses. Africa shall develop an aristocracy of its own, but it shall be based upon service and loyalty to race. Let all Negroes work toward that end. . . .

The time has really come for the Asiatics to govern themselves in Asia, as the Europeans are in Europe and the Western world, so also is it wise for the Africans to govern themselves at home, and thereby bring peace and satisfaction to the entire human family.

So Negroes, I say, through the Universal Negro Improvement Association, that there is much to live for. I have a vision of the future, and I see before me a picture of redeemed Africa, with her dotted cities, with her beautiful civilization, with her millions of happy children going to and fro. Why should I lose hope, why should I give up and take a back place in this age of progress? . . .

Africa shall reflect a splendid demonstration of the worth of the Negro, of the determination of the Negro, to set himself free and to establish a government of his own.

The UNIA barely survived the loss of its inspirational leader, and it declined steadily in the late 1920s and the 1930s. The various UNIA businesses closed, and its property—including the *Yarmouth*—was sold. Garvey was never permitted to return to the United States, and he died in London in 1940. However, his legacy persisted. The Reverend Earl Little, a Baptist minister and the father of Malcolm X, belonged to the UNIA and much admired Garvey. Malcolm X recalled his father's association with Garvey: "I remember hearing that he had black followers not only in the United States but all around the world, and I remember how the meetings always closed with my father saying, several times, and the people chanting after him, 'Up, you mighty race, you can accomplish what you will!'"

PAN-AFRICANISM

As diametrically opposed as Garvey and Du Bois were on most matters, they shared an abiding interest in Africa. Garvey, Du Bois, and other black leaders believed people of African descent from around the world should come together to share their heritage, discuss their ties to the continent, and explore ways to moderate—if not eliminate—colonial rule in Africa, a concept termed **Pan-Africanism.**

By 1914 Britain, France, Germany, Portugal, Belgium, Spain, and Italy had established colonies across almost all of Africa. Only Liberia and Ethiopia (then called Abyssinia) remained independent. The Europeans assumed the "white man's burden" in their imperialist "scramble" for Africa. Christian missionaries sought to convert Africans, and European companies exploited Africa's human and natural resources. As they gained control over the continent, the European powers confirmed their conviction that they represented a superior race and culture.

The first Pan-African Congress had convened in London in 1900 and was organized principally by Henry Sylvester Williams, a lawyer from Trinidad who

🌿 *On what logical basis does Garvey rest his call for a black homeland in Africa? How realistic was this call in the 1920s for nationhood in Africa?*

🌿 *Who does Garvey believe should lead (or should not lead) the new African nation? What are the qualifications for such leadership?*

🌿 *What vision does Garvey offer for what the globe will look like in the future? Does he suggest how peoples of various colors will coexist?*

Source: David Levering Lewis, ed., *The Portable Harlem Renaissance Reader* (Viking Penguin, 1994), had resided in Canada and then London. Du Bois attended and chaired the Committee on the Address to the Nations of the World. He called for the creation of "a great central Negro state of the world." But Du Bois did not insist on the immediate withdrawal of the European powers from Africa. Instead he offered a modest recommendation that would provide "as soon as practicable the rights of responsible self-government to the black colonies of Africa and the West Indies."

The second Pan-African Congress met in Paris for three days in February 1919, near Versailles, where the peace conference ending World War I was assembled. There were fifty-eight delegates from sixteen nations. Du Bois was among the sixteen African Americans in attendance. (None of them had been to Africa.) Marcus Garvey did not attend. The delegates took seriously the Fourteen Points that U.S. president Woodrow Wilson had proposed to fashion the postwar world. They were especially interested in the fifth point, which called for the interests of colonial peoples to be given "equal weight" in the adjustment of colonial claims after the war. The congress recommended that the League of Nations assume authority over the former German colonies in East Africa. The League later established mandates over those colonies but delegated authority to administer those mandates to Britain, France, and Belgium. Two more Pan-African Congresses in the 1920s met in Brussels and London but also failed to influence the policies of the colonial powers.

Labor

The arrival of thousands of black migrants in American cities during and after World War I changed the composition of the industrial workforce and intensified pressure on labor unions to admit black members. By 1916 twelve thousand of the nearly fifty thousand workers in the Chicago stockyards were black people. In Detroit, black laborers made up nearly 14 percent of the workforce in the automobile industry. The Ford Motor Company employed 50 black people in 1916 and 2,500 by 1920.

Yet even with the Industrial Revolution and the Great Migration, more than two-thirds of black workers in 1920 were employed in agriculture and domestic service (see Figure 17–1). Less than 20 percent were

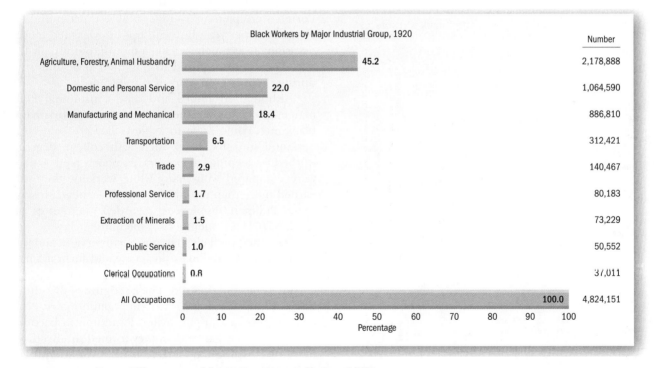

FIGURE 17–1 BLACK WORKERS BY MAJOR INDUSTRIAL GROUP, 1920

By 1920 thousands of African Americans had moved to northern cities and were employed in a variety of mostly unskilled and low-paying industrial jobs that nonetheless paid more than farm labor. Still, agriculture remained the largest single source of employment among black people, and agriculture and domestic service together employed more than two-thirds of African-American men and women. About 5 percent were employed in "white-collar" jobs. Source: Sterling D. Spero and Abram L. Harris, *The Black Worker: The Negro and the Labor Movement* (1928), 81.

engaged in manufacturing. Many black men and women remained confined to the rural South. Those who were part of industrial America disproportionately worked in the dreary, dirty, and sometimes dangerous unskilled jobs that paid the least. Still, work in the factories, mills, and mines paid more than agriculture (Figure 17–2). But even those with skills were usually not admitted to the local craft unions that made up the AFL. More than fifty trade unions within the AFL had no black members. Unions that did admit black workers included those representing cigar makers, coal miners, garment workers, and longshoremen.

By the World War I years, the NAACP and the Urban League regularly appealed to employers and unions to accept black laborers. The Urban League attempted to convince business owners that black employees would be efficient and reliable. But many employers preferred to divide black and white workers by hiring black men and women as strikebreakers, thereby enraging striking white workers. In 1918 Urban League officials met with Samuel Gompers, the longtime president of the AFL, and he agreed to bring more black people into the federation, but there were few tangible results. The Urban League did succeed in persuading the U.S. Department of Labor to establish a Division of Negro Economics to advise the secretary of labor on issues involving black workers.

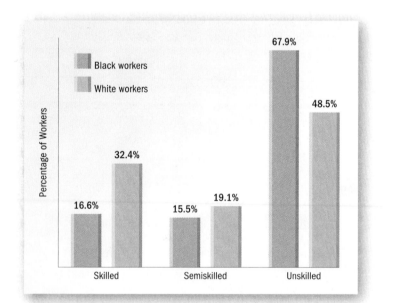

FIGURE 17-2   BLACK AND WHITE WORKERS BY SKILL LEVEL, 1920
Only one-third of black workers, compared to slightly more than one-half of white workers, found employment in skilled or semiskilled jobs in 1920.   Source: Sterling D. Spero and Abram L. Harris, *The Black Worker: The Negro and the Labor Movement* (1928), 85.

THE BROTHERHOOD OF SLEEPING CAR PORTERS

By the 1920s the Pullman Company, which owned and operated passenger railroad coaches, was the single largest employer of black people in the United States. More than twelve thousand black men worked as porters on Pullman railroad cars. After founding the Pullman Palace Car Company in 1867, George Pullman decided to employ only black men as porters—on the assumption that prosperous white people were accustomed to being waited on by black servants. Furthermore, black employees could be and were paid less than white workers.

Pullman porters toiled for upward of four hundred hours each month to maintain the coaches and serve the passengers. Porters had to prepare the cars before the train's departure and service them after the train arrived at its destination, although they were paid only for the duration of the trip. They assisted passengers, shined shoes (they had to purchase the polish themselves), and arranged sleeping compartments. Considered mere servants by most passengers, porters had little time for rest. To add to the indignity, white travelers invariably referred to these black men as "George," no matter what their actual name was. Porters were paid an average of $67.50 per month—about $810 per year. But with tips, they earned more, occasionally as much as $300 a month, but usually far less. They were required to buy their own uniforms during their first ten years of employment.

Although strenuous and time consuming, Pullman employment was the most satisfactory work many black men could hope to achieve. Barred from business and industry, black men with college degrees worked as sleeping car porters. As poorly paid as they were compared with many white workers, they still earned more than most black schoolteachers. Most of these Pullman employees regarded themselves as solid, respectable members of the middle class.

It seemed unlikely that men as subservient and unobtrusive as the Pullman porters would form a labor union to challenge one of America's most powerful corporations. But they did. The key figure in this effort was A. Philip Randolph. In 1925 a gathering of Pullman porters in Harlem invited Randolph to become their "general organizer" as they formed the Brotherhood of Sleeping Car Porters (BSCP). Randolph accepted the invitation.

A. PHILIP RANDOLPH

Randolph was a socialist with superb oratorical skills who had earned a reputation as a radical on the streets of Harlem. He was born in 1889 in Crescent City, Florida.

He attended high school at Cookman Institute (later Bethune-Cookman College) and migrated to New York City in 1911, where he attended City College and joined the Socialist Party. In 1913 he married Lucille Campbell Greene. She was a prosperous beauty shop owner who contributed financially to many of her husband's causes. With Chandler Owen, he founded *The Messenger,* a monthly socialist journal that drew the attention of federal agents because they regarded it as the only radical Negro magazine. Randolph vigorously opposed American involvement in World War I. In 1919 Department of Justice officials arrested Randolph and Owen for violating the Espionage Act and held them briefly.

Randolph was an improbable militant. He was handsome, dignified, impeccably dressed, and aloof. Save for his color, he could have been mistaken for the sort of Wall Street broker or powerful corporate attorney he detested. But blessed with a rich baritone voice, he "damned the classes and exalted the masses" and maintained an unwavering commitment to economic and racial change. He became one of the nation's foremost protest leaders and remained so for more than five decades.

Randolph faced the daunting task of recruiting support for the brotherhood, winning recognition from the Pullman Company, and gaining the union's acceptance by the AFL. There was considerable opposition, much of it from within the black community. Many porters were too frightened to join the brotherhood. Black clergymen counseled against union activities. Black newspapers, including the Chicago *Defender,* editorially opposed the BSCP.

But Randolph persevered with the assistance of Milton Webster, who became vice president of the brotherhood after Randolph assumed the presidency. With the slogan "Service not servitude," the two men recruited members, organized the brotherhood, and attempted to negotiate with the Pullman Company. Pullman executives ignored Randolph's overtures. They fired porters who joined the union, infiltrated union meetings with company agents, and organized the Employees' Representation Plan, an alternative company union that they claimed actually represented the black employees.

Although the NAACP and the Urban League strongly supported the BSCP, progress was painfully slow. In 1928 Randolph threatened to call a strike against the Pullman Company, but he called it off after AFL president William Green promised modest assistance to the as-yet unrecognized union. Green's offer simply saved face for Randolph. It is unlikely that a strike would have succeeded or that most porters would have followed Randolph's leadership and left the trains. The Great Depression of the 1930s brought layoffs and

In this painting by Betsy G. Reyneau, A. Philip Randolph hardly resembles the militant agitator, activist, and labor leader he was. He became the head of the Brotherhood of Sleeping Car Porters, and he eventually rose to power in the American Federation of Labor. He planned the first March on Washington in 1941 and was responsible for organizing the 1963 March on Washington.

mass resignations from the brotherhood. The AFL barely responded to repeated charges of discrimination by Randolph, the NAACP, and the Urban League. The BSCP nearly collapsed. Not until the passage of legislation during President Franklin D. Roosevelt's New Deal in the mid-1930s did the BSCP make substantial gains.

The Harlem Renaissance

For most of American history, most black and white Americans have shown little interest in serious literature or intellectual developments. The 1920s were no exception. People were far more fascinated by sports,

THE HARLEM RENAISSANCE

1919   Claude McKay publishes "If We Must Die"

1920   Eugene O'Neill's *The Emperor Jones* opens, featuring Charles Gilpin; Langston Hughes publishes *The Negro Speaks of Rivers*

1922   *Shuffle Along*, by Noble Sissle and Eubie Blake, opens on Broadway with Florence Mills and Josephine Baker; Claude McKay publishes *Harlem Shadows*

1923   Jean Toomer publishes *Cane;* the Cotton Club opens; *Opportunity: A Journal of Negro Life*, edited by Charles S. Johnson and supported by the National Urban League, begins publication

1924   Jessie R. Fauset publishes *There Is Confusion;* Walter White publishes *The Fire in the Flint;* Paul Robeson stars in Eugene O'Neill's drama *All God's Chillun Got Wings*

1925   Countee Cullen publishes his book of poetry, *Color;* James Weldon Johnson publishes *The Book of American Negro Spirituals; The New Negro*, edited by Alain Locke, is published

1926   Langston Hughes publishes *The Weary Blues;* George Schuyler's "The Negro Art Hokum" appears in *The Nation; The Savoy Ballroom* opens; Wallace Thurman publishes one issue of *Fire;* Florence Mills dies

1927   Langston Hughes publishes *Fine Clothes to the Jew;* James Weldon Johnson publishes *God's Trombones: Seven Negro Sermons in Verse*

1928   Claude McKay publishes *Home to Harlem;* Duke Ellington's band appears at the Cotton Club; Nella Larsen publishes *Quicksand*

1929   Jessie R. Fauset publishes *Plum Bun;* Wallace Thurman publishes *The Blacker the Berry. . . ;* Claude McKay publishes *Banjo;* Countee Cullen publishes *The Black Christ;* Nella Larsen publishes *Passing;* Fats Waller's *Ain't Misbehavin'* opens on Broadway

1930   James Weldon Johnson publishes *Black Manhattan*

1931   Jessie R. Fauset publishes *The Chinaberry Tree*

1933   Jessie R. Fauset publishes her last novel, *Comedy American Style;* James Weldon Johnson publishes his autobiography, *Along the Way*

1934   Wallace Thurman dies

1935   Zora Neale Hurston publishes *Mules and Men*

1937   Zora Neale Hurston publishes *Their Eyes Were Watching God*

1919–1937

automobiles, the radio, and popular music than they were by poetry, plays, museums, or novels. Still, the 1920s witnessed a proliferation of creative works by a remarkable group of gifted writers and artists. Among white writers, T. S. Eliot, Ezra Pound, Edith Wharton, Ernest Hemingway, Sinclair Lewis, Eugene O'Neill, Willa Cather, and F. Scott Fitzgerald produced literary works that explored a range of themes but were mostly critical of American life and society. Eliot, Pound, Wharton, Fitzgerald, and Hemingway found American culture so unappealing that they exiled themselves in Europe.

Black intellectuals congregated in Manhattan and gave rise to the creative movement known as the **Harlem Renaissance.** Alain Locke promoted *The New Negro.* Poets, novelists, and painters probed racial themes and grappled with what it meant to be black in America. There was no precise beginning to this renaissance. As early as 1920, W. E. B. Du Bois wrote in *The Crisis* that the nation was on the verge of a "renaissance of American Negro literature." In 1925 the New York *Herald Tribune* declared that America was "on the edge, if not already in the midst of, what might not improperly be called a Negro renaissance." No matter when it began, the Harlem Renaissance produced a stunning collection of artistic works, especially in creative writing, that continued into the 1930s.

The Harlem Renaissance

BEFORE HARLEM

There had certainly been serious cultural developments among African Americans before the 1920s. From 1897 to 1928, the American Negro Academy functioned as a forum for the Talented Tenth as men such as Alain Locke, Kelly Miller, and Du Bois reflected on race and color.

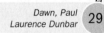
The City Negro, 1925   17-4

At the turn of the century, novelist Charles W. Chestnutt depicted a young black woman's attempt to pass for white in *The House behind the Cedars,* and he wrote about racist violence in the post-Reconstruction South in *The Marrow of Tradition.* Ohio poet Paul Laurence Dunbar wrote evocatively of black life, frequently relying on black dialect, before he died at age thirty-four in 1906. Henry Ossawa Tanner attended the Pennsylvania Academy of Fine Arts and had an illustrious career as a painter. Shortly after he produced "The Banjo Lesson" in 1893, Tanner left for Paris and spent most of the rest of his life in Europe. He died there in 1937.

Dawn, Paul Laurence Dunbar   29

Carter G. Woodson, the son of Virginia slaves, earned a Ph.D. at Harvard in history and founded the Association for the Study of Negro Life and History in 1915. He stressed the need for the scholarly examination of Negro history and established the *Journal of Negro History* and the *Negro History Bulletin.* He also founded Associated Publishers to publish books on black history. Woodson wrote several major works, including *The Negro in Our History*. In 1926 he established Negro History Week during February. Not surprisingly, Woodson became known as the "father of Negro history."

During the bloody Red Summer of 1919 when racial violence erupted in Chicago and elsewhere, Claude McKay, a Jamaican who settled—like Marcus Garvey—in New York City, wrote a powerful poem, "If We Must Die," in response to the brutal attacks by white people in Chicago on black residents:

> If we must die, let it not be like hogs
> Hunted and penned in an inglorious spot,
> While round us bark the mad and hungry dogs,
> Making their mock at our accursèd lot.
> If we must die, O let us nobly die,
> So that our precious blood may not be shed
> In vain; then even the monsters we defy
> Shall be constrained to honor us though dead!
> O kinsmen! We must meet the common foe!
> Though far outnumbered let us show us brave,
> And for their thousand blows deal one deathblow!
> What though before us lies the open grave?
> Like men we'll face the murderous, cowardly pack,
> Pressed to the wall, dying, but fighting back!

LIVING WORDS
30 *If We Must Die, Claude McKay*

McKay left the United States for the Soviet Union in 1922 and spent the next twelve years in Europe. In 1928, while in France, he wrote *Home to Harlem*, a novel that depicted life among pimps, prostitutes, loan sharks, and petty criminals. McKay was not on cordial terms with the African-American intellectuals who formed the core of the Harlem Renaissance, and he did not consider himself part of the Talented Tenth. He later commented, "I was an older man and not regarded as a member of the renaissance, but more as a forerunner."

WRITERS AND ARTISTS

Few white Americans and still fewer black Americans had access to a college education in the early twentieth century. Only slightly more than two thousand African Americans were pursuing college degrees by 1920. Yet the writers and artists who came to be associated with the Harlem Renaissance were the products of some of the nation's finest schools, and with the exception of Zora Neale Hurston, they did not come from isolated, rural southern communities. Hurston was born in Notasulga, Alabama, and raised in the all-black town of Eatonville, Florida, near Orlando. She attended Morgan State University and Howard University, and graduated from Barnard College. Alain Locke was a native of Philadelphia and Phi Beta Kappa graduate of Harvard. He was the first African American to win a Rhodes scholarship to

Oxford University, and he also earned a Ph.D. in philosophy from Harvard. Aaron Douglas was born in Kansas and was an art major at the University of Nebraska.

Langston Hughes was born in Joplin, Missouri, graduated from high school in Cleveland, and attended Columbia University before he graduated from Pennsylvania's Lincoln University. Jessie Fauset came from a prominent Philadelphia family of color. She was a graduate of Cornell University and a member of Phi Beta Kappa; she earned an M.A. from the University of Pennsylvania in romance languages. Jean Toomer was born in Washington, D.C., and he was raised largely by his grandparents in a fashionable white neighborhood. Toomer went to the University of Wisconsin and then the Massachusetts College of Agriculture. Wallace Thurman was born in Salt Lake City and attended both the University of Utah and the University of Southern California. Countee Cullen was a native of Lexington, Kentucky, and a Phi Beta Kappa graduate of New York University. Nella Larsen was the only major writer connected to the Harlem Renaissance who did not have a college degree. A native of Chicago, she graduated from the nurse training program at New York City's Lincoln Hospital.

The Renaissance gradually emerged in the early 1920s and then expanded dramatically later in the decade as more creative figures were drawn to Harlem. In 1923 Jean Toomer published *Cane*, a collection of stories and poetry about southern black life. It sold a mere five hundred copies, but it had a major impact on Jessie Fauset and Walter White. Fauset was the literary editor of *The Crisis*, and in 1924 she finished *There Is Confusion*, the first novel published during the Renaissance. Her novels explored the manners and color consciousness among well-to-do negroes. Walter White, who was James Weldon Johnson's assistant at the NAACP, published *The Fire in the Flint* in 1924, a novel that dealt with a black physician who confronted white brutality in Georgia.

In the meantime, *The Crisis*, as well as *Opportunity*, a new publication of the Urban League, published the poetry and short stories of black authors, including Langston Hughes, Countee Cullen, and Zora Neale Hurston. White publishers were also attracted to black literary efforts. In 1925 *Survey Graphic* published a special edition devoted to black life and culture called "Harlem: Mecca of the New Negro." Howard University professor Alain Locke then edited *The New Negro*, which drew much of its material from *Survey Graphic* as well as *Opportunity* and included silhouette drawings with Egyptian motifs by Aaron Douglas. In his opening essay, Locke explained Harlem's literary significance: "Harlem has the same role to play for the new Negro as Dublin has had for the New Ireland or Prague for the New Czechoslovakia."

DOCUMENT
The New Negro, 1925 **17-5**

Aaron Douglas, *Aspects of Negro Life: From Slavery through Reconstruction,* **1934,** oil on canvas, 60 × 139". Artist Aaron Douglas (1899–1979) was born in Topeka, Kansas, and was the sole black student at the University of Nebraska when he graduated in 1922. He moved to Harlem in 1925 and shortly after that visited Paris, where he met celebrated black artist Henry Ossawa Tanner. Douglas returned to Harlem and then taught art at Fisk University in Nashville from 1937 to 1966. His paintings reflected his deep interest in the African-American experience. Notice the Ku Klux Klan as well as black soldiers in this work.   Schomburg Center for Research in Black Culture, Art & Artifacts Division, The New York Public Library, Astor, Lenox and Tilden Foundation

Sharp disagreements erupted during the Harlem Renaissance over the definition and purpose of black literature. Some, such as Alain Locke, W. E. B. Du Bois, Jessie Fauset, and Benjamin Brawley, wanted black writers to promote positive images of black people in their works. They hoped inspirational literature could help resolve racial conflict in America, and they believed black writers should be included in the larger (and mostly white) American literary tradition. Claude McKay, Langston Hughes, and Zora Neale Hurston disagreed. They portrayed the streets and shadows of Harlem and the lives of poor black people in their poetry and stories. In *The Ways of White Folks,* Hughes ridiculed the notion that writers could promote racial reconciliation. One of his characters derisively declares, "Art would break down color lines, art would save the race and prevent lynchings! Bunk!"

W. E. B. Du Bois commented caustically after he read Claude McKay's bawdy *Home to Harlem,* "I feel distinctly like taking a bath." Du Bois was less than impressed with Jake, the novel's protagonist, who is intimately involved with the reality of life in Harlem that included opium, alcohol, and sex. Alain Locke dismissed McKay as a mere propagandist, and McKay in turn called Locke "a dyed-in-the-wool pussy-footing professor." Black critic George Schuyler's "The Negro Art Hokum"

in *The Nation* ridiculed black writers who contended that black people even had their own expressive culture that was separate from that of white people. "As for the literature, painting, and sculpture of Afroamericans—such as there is—it is identical in kind with the literature, painting, and sculpture of white Americans."

Langston Hughes meanwhile defended the authenticity of black art and literature but insisted the approval or disapproval of white people and black people was of little consequence:

> We younger Negro artists who create now intend to express our individual dark-skinned selves without fear or shame. If white people are pleased, we are glad. If they are not, it doesn't matter. We know we are beautiful. And ugly too. The tom-tom cries and the tom-tom laughs. If colored people are pleased we are glad. If they are not, their displeasure doesn't matter either. We build our temples for tomorrow, strong as we know how, and we stand on top of the mountain, free within ourselves.

Hughes pursued racial themes in *Fine Clothes to the Jew* (1927), which contained "Red Silk Stockings," a poem that depicted young black women who were tempted by liaisons with white men, a subject that offended some readers:

During the summer of 1927, three of the major figures associated with the Harlem Renaissance visited the Booker T. Washington Memorial on the Tuskegee Institute campus in Alabama. One can only wonder what pointed comments about the "Wizard of Tuskegee" were exchanged as (from left to right) Jessie Fauset, Langston Hughes, and Zora Neale Hurston posed to have their photograph taken.

Red Silk Stockings

Put on yo' red silk stockings,
Black gal.
Go out an' let de white boys
Look at yo' legs.
Ain't nothin' to do for you, nohow.
Round this town.—
You's too pretty.
Put on yo' red silk stockings, gal,
An' tomorrow's chile'll
Be a high yaller.
Go out an' let de white boys
Look at yo' legs.

Even more upsetting to those who wanted to safeguard the reputation of black people was Wallace Thurman, who arrived in New York in 1925. Thurman worked briefly at *The Messenger,* the socialist publication that had been absorbed by A. Philip Randolph's Brotherhood of Sleeping Car Porters. He was a voracious

reader with a brilliant mind and an eccentric personality who attracted many loyal admirers. He once wrote, "I cannot bear to associate with the ordinary run of people. I have to surround myself with individuals who for the most part are more than a trifle insane."

In 1926 Thurman published *Fire,* a journal that lasted only one issue but managed to incite enormous controversy and leave Thurman deeply in debt. *Fire* included Thurman's short story "Cordelia the Crude," about a prostitute, and a one-act play by Zora Neale Hurston, *Color Struck.* Hurston effectively replicated the speech of rural black southerners while depicting the jealousy a darker woman feels when a light-skinned rival tries to take her man. Black critic Benjamin Brawley complained that with *Fire* "vulgarity had been mistaken for art."

Thurman, who was a dark black man, antagonized still more people when *The Blacker the Berry . . .* was published in 1929. In it he described the tribulations and sorrows of Emma Lou, a young woman who did not mind being black, "but she did mind being too black." The book made it plain that many black people had absorbed a color prejudice that they did not hesitate to inflict on darker members of their own race.

Unlike Thurman, Nella Larsen wrote about black people who were indistinguishable from white people. Her novel, *Quicksand,* depicted the life of Helga Crane who, like Larsen herself, had a Danish mother and a black father. In *Passing,* Larsen dealt with a young black woman who passed for white and, indeed, married a white racist.

WHITE PEOPLE AND THE HARLEM RENAISSANCE

Like many of the writers associated with the Harlem Renaissance, Zora Neale Hurston had a pen that sliced like a scalpel. She called the white people who took an interest in Harlem "Negrotarians," and she labeled her black literary colleagues the "Niggerati." But no matter how they were described, black and white people developed pleasant but often uneasy relationships during the Renaissance.

No white man was more attracted to the cultural developments in Harlem than photographer and writer Carl Van Vechten. In 1926 he caused a furor with his novel *Nigger Heaven.* Many people were offended by the title, which referred to the balcony where black patrons had to sit in segregated theaters and auditoriums. The novel dealt with the coarser aspects of life in Harlem, which irritated Du Bois, Fauset, and Countee Cullen. But Van Vechten's purpose was in part a call for a more honest depiction of the black experience, and James Weldon Johnson, Walter White, and Langston Hughes approved of the novel.

Most black writers and artists welcomed the encouragement, support, and financial backing they received from white authors, critics, and publishers. White writers, including Eugene O'Neill, Sherwood Anderson, Sinclair Lewis, and Van Wyck Brooks, were fascinated by black people and interested in the works of black authors. Major publishers, such as Alfred A. Knopf, brought out the works of Harlem writers. Black and white literary figures sometimes gathered for cocktails, small talk, and music at Carl Van Vechten's spacious apartment on West 55th Street.

The attention and support of white people were sometimes accompanied by condescension and disdain. Too many "Negrotarians" considered Harlem and its inhabitants exotic, curious, and uncivilized. They found life in Harlem—its clubs, music, and entertainers, as well as its poetry, prose, and painting—energetic, lively, and sensual compared to white life and culture. Black culture was also—many white people believed—unsophisticated and primitive, which is what made it so fascinating. Black writers like Langston Hughes, Claude McKay, and Countee Cullen wanted to depict black life realistically—from its gangsters to its gamblers. But they and other black artists resented the notion that black culture was inherently crude and unrefined.

White patrons like Amy Spingarn, whose husband Joel was president of the NAACP board of directors, and Charlotte Osgood "Godmother" Mason supported black writers and artists. Spingarn helped finance Langston Hughes's education at Lincoln University. "Godmother" Mason was a wealthy widow who offered substantial amounts of money to black artists. She worked closely with Alain Locke, who helped identify Langston Hughes, Zora Neale Hurston, and Aaron Douglas, among others, who became her "godchildren." Mason wanted no publicity for herself, but the acceptance of her money had its costs. Mason gave Hughes $150 a month and Hurston $200 a month, as well as an automobile. She also gave Hughes expensive clothing and writing supplies. In return, Mason demanded that the black writers keep her fully informed about their activities, and she did not hesitate to tell them when they were not productive enough. She also tried to influence what they wrote. She preferred that black writers confine themselves to exotic themes. As helpful as Mason's financial assistance and personal encouragement were, she created a system of dependency, and Hughes and Hurston finally broke free from the arrangement. Hughes later fondly recalled, "I can only say that those months when I lived by and through her were the most fascinating and fantastic I have ever known."

Harlem's cultural icons sometimes congregated away from the curiosity and paternalism of white admirers. The plush twin townhouses of A'Lelia Walker at 108–110 West 136th Street also attracted Harlem's literary figures as well as entertainers. Walker was the daughter of black cosmetics millionairess Madam C. J. Walker. Although she read little herself, A'Lelia Walker enjoyed hosting musicians, writers, and artists at "The Dark Tower," as she called it. Her home was named for Countee Cullen's column, "The Dark Tower," that appeared regularly in *Opportunity*. But Harlem artists also gathered in the much less luxurious surroundings of "Niggerati Manor" on 267 West 136th Street. This was a rooming house where Thurman, Hurston, and Hughes resided in the late 1920s.

The profusion of literary works associated with the Harlem Renaissance did not so much end as fade away. Black writers remained active into the 1930s. Zora Neale Hurston wrote her two most important works then—*Mules and Men* in 1935 and *Their Eyes Were Watching God* in 1937. Claude McKay and Langston Hughes continued to write and have their work published. But the Great Depression that began in 1929 devastated book and magazine sales. Subscriptions to *The Crisis* and *Opportunity* declined, and both journals published fewer works by creative writers. Many black intellectuals left Harlem. James Weldon Johnson and Aaron Douglas went to Fisk University in Nashville.

W. E. B. Du Bois had a falling out with the NAACP and returned to Atlanta University. Alain Locke remained on the faculty at Howard University. Jessie Fauset married an insurance executive and took up housekeeping after her last novel was published in 1931. Nella Larsen was charged unjustly with plagiarism. She quit writing and resumed her career as a nurse. Wallace Thurman died an alcoholic in 1934. Countee Cullen taught French at DeWitt Clinton High School in New York City where James Baldwin was one of his students in the late 1930s.

Harlem and the Jazz Age

As powerful and important as these black literary voices were, they were less popular than the entertainers, musicians, singers, and dancers who were also part of the Harlem Renaissance. Without Harlem, the 1920s would not have been the Jazz Age. From wailing trumpets, beating drums, dancing feet, and plaintive and mournful songs, Harlem's clubs, cabarets, theaters, and ballrooms echoed with the vibrant and soulful sounds of African Americans. By comparison, white American music seemed sedate and bland.

Black and white people flocked to Harlem to enjoy themselves—and to break the law. In 1919–1920, the Eighteenth Amendment and the Volstead Act prohibited the manufacture, distribution, and sale of alcoholic beverages. But liquor flowed freely in Harlem's fancy establishments and smoky dives. Musicians and entertainers, such as Harlem's working-class residents, had migrated there from elsewhere. The blues and their sorrowful tales of troubled and broken relationships arrived from the Mississippi Delta and rural South. Jazz had its origins in New Orleans, but it drew on ragtime and spirituals as it moved up the Mississippi River to Kansas City and Chicago on its way to Harlem.

The Cotton Club was Harlem's most exclusive and fashionable nightspot. Opened in 1923 by white gangster Owney Madden to peddle illegal beer, it catered to well-to-do white people who regarded a trip to Harlem as a foreign excursion. The Cotton Club's entertainers and waiters were black, but the customers were white. Black patrons were not admitted. The club featured well-choreographed and fast-paced two-hour revues that included a chorus line of attractive young women—all brown skinned, all under twenty-one years old, and all over 5'6" tall. No dark women appeared. Music was provided by assorted ensembles. Cab Calloway might sing "She's Tall, She's Tan and She's Terrific" or "Cotton Colored Gal of Mine."

In 1928 Edward K. "Duke" Ellington and his orchestra began a twelve-year association with the Cotton Club. Although Ellington had not yet begun to compose his own music in earnest, his band already had an elegant, sophisticated, and recognizable African-American sound. Another club, Connie's Inn, also served a mostly white clientele. Thomas "Fats" Waller played a rambunctious piano at Connie's. Waller's father was the deacon at the Abyssinian Baptist Church in Harlem, and his mother was the organist. The songs and music their son wrote, including "Honeysuckle Rose" and "Ain't Misbehavin'," were hardly sacred, but they were popular. Connie's also put on stunning musical revues, perhaps the best known of which was *Hot Chocolates*. Dancers who performed at Connie's included the legendary Bill "Bojangles" Robinson and Earl "Snakehips" Tucker. A young cornetist from New Orleans, Louis Armstrong, played briefly at Connie's. Armstrong amazed listeners with his virtuoso trumpet and his gravelly singing voice.

Harlem's black residents avoided the Cotton Club and Connie's Inn. They were more likely to step into one of Harlem's less pretentious and less expensive establishments, such as the Sugar Cane. The beer and liquor were cheap. The food was plentiful. The music was good, and there were no elaborate production numbers. Even less impressive clubs and bars remained open after the legal closing hour of 3 A.M. "Arrangements" were made with the police, who looked the other way as the music and alcohol continued through the night. Musicians from "legal" clubs drifted into the after-hours joints and played until dawn.

Another popular—and sometimes necessary—form of entertainment among Harlemites was the rent party. Housing costs in Harlem were extravagant, and white people and real estate agents refused to rent or sell to black people in most other areas of New York City. To make the steep monthly rent payments, apartment dwellers would push the furniture aside and begin cooking chicken, chitterlings, rice, okra, and sweet potatoes. They would distribute a few flyers and hire a musician or two. The party was usually on a Saturday or a Thursday night. (Most domestic servants had Thursdays off.) Partygoers paid ten cents to fifty cents for admission. Food and liquor were sold. With a decent crowd, the month's rent was paid.

SONG, DANCE, AND STAGE

Black women became popular as singers and dancers in Harlem and then often appeared in Broadway shows and revues. Florence Mills entranced audiences with her diminutive singing voice in several Broadway productions including *Plantation Review, Dixie to Broadway,* and *Blackbirds* before she died of appendicitis in 1927. Adelaide Hall also appeared in *Blackbirds* and later opened her own nightclubs in London and Paris. Ethel Waters worked her way up from smoky gin joints in Harlem basements, where she sang risqué and comic songs, to Broadway shows, and then to films. Many years later she toured with Billy Graham's religious crusades and revivals.

White men wrote many of the popular Broadway productions that starred black entertainers. In 1921, however, Eubie Blake and Noble Sissle put on *Shuffle Along*, which became a major hit. Its most memorable tune was "I'm Just Wild about Harry." Sissle and Blake wrote several more shows, including *Chocolate Dandies* in 1924. It was created especially for a thin, lanky, dark, and funny young lady named Josephine Baker. But in 1925 Baker left New York and moved to Paris, where she starred in the *Revue Nègre*, which created a sensation in the French capital. She remained in France for the rest of her life.

White playwright Eugene O'Neill wrote serious drama involving black people. Charles Gilpin and then Paul Robeson appeared in performances of O'Neill's *Emperor Jones*. Robeson—who went on to an illustrious performing career—was a graduate of Rutgers University, where he was an all-American football player. He earned a law degree at Columbia University but abandoned the law for the stage. He appeared in numerous productions, including O'Neill's *All God's Chillun Got Wings*, Shakespeare's *Othello*, Gershwin's *Porgy and Bess*, and Kern and Hammerstein's *Showboat*. He often sang spirituals in his magnificent, rich voice and later recorded many of them.

LIVING WORDS

Swing Low, Sweet Chariot 31

PROFILE ~ BESSIE SMITH

No one personified the blues more than Bessie Smith. She knew the blues. She sang the blues. She lived the blues. She was the "Empress of the Blues." During the 1920s, no singer in America was more popular than she was.

Bessie Smith was born in poverty on April 15, 1894, in Chattanooga, Tennessee. She was one of seven children of a Baptist preacher, William Smith, and his wife, Laura. Bessie's parents and two brothers died while she was still a child and the surviving children were raised by an older sister, Viola.

With her brother Andrew accompanying her on the guitar, Bessie began to sing on Chattanooga street corners to earn money for the family, an apprenticeship that helped shape her career. In 1912 she toured briefly with a musical group that featured Gertrude "Ma" Rainey. In 1913 she worked in Atlanta for ten dollars a week plus tips. Her fame spread and soon she was touring the South. By the 1920s she was singing in Philadelphia and Atlantic City.

Initially her voice was considered too rough for the infant recording industry. But in 1923 Frank Walker signed her to a contract with Columbia Records. She recorded what were known in the 1920s as "race" records, produced for black audiences by white recording companies. Her first recordings included "Downhearted Blues" and "Gulf Coast Blues." Her second session brought "Tain't Nobody's Business If I Do." She sold an astonishing 780,000 records within months.

In 1925 she recorded "St. Louis Blues" and "Careless Love" with Louis Armstrong—their only recordings together. She toured major cities, including Pittsburgh, Cleveland, and Chicago, in a private railroad coach and huge crowds lined up at clubs and theaters to hear her. Though it could sound coarse, she had a striking and appealing voice that conveyed the depths of her emotions and experiences.

She knew of what she sang. When she sang "Money Blues," "Pickpocket Blues," or "Empty Bed Blues," she revealed the pathos, but also the humor, that so many black people had experienced. Smith's blues tore at the raw feelings that sociologists and academics missed when they discussed poverty, unemployment, alcoholism, or sexual relationships. Her blues were firmly grounded in African-American oral and musical traditions.

Bessie Smith was not a delicate woman. She was married twice. Her first husband, Earl Love, died shortly after they married. Her second marriage, to Jack Gee, was marked by jealousy, drinking, and physical conflict and ended in separation in 1930. She had a profusion of lovers—male and female. Her warmest and most enduring relationship was with Richard Morgan, a Chicago bootlegger.

People did not trifle with Bessie Smith. A large lady, over two hundred pounds, she ate, drank, and fought to excess. She could be mean, contentious, and violent. She physically attacked others and was herself attacked. But she also had a sweet and loyal side and could be helpful, generous, and compassionate. However, she seemed fond of some of the sleaziest, most dangerous nightclubs in America. She could not resist Detroit's Koppin Theater, a den of debauchery. She admitted wanting to go where "the funk was flying."

She continued to record even after record sales declined during the Depression. Her last recording session included "Nobody Knows When You're Down and Out." Bessie Smith died at age forty-three in 1937 in a car accident near Clarksdale, Mississippi. Perhaps Louis Armstrong summed up her musical legacy best. "She used to thrill me at all times, the way she could phrase a note with a certain something in her voice no other blues singer could get. She had music in her soul and felt everything she did."

Smith

Noble Sissle and Eubie Blake were the first two black entertainers who dressed elegantly in tuxedos, and not as minstrel players. They collaborated on writing the lyrics and composing the music for *Shuffle Along*, which opened on Broadway in 1921 and played for 504 performance. The show's hit tune was "I'm Just Wild About Harry." In 1948 Harry Truman resurrected it as his campaign song and went on to defeat Republican Thomas Dewey and win the presidency.   Maryland Historical Society. Baltimore, MD

Sports

Sports flourished in America in the 1920s. Americans worshiped their athletic heroes. Babe Ruth and Jack Dempsey were as well known as President Calvin Coolidge. Professional athletics, especially baseball and boxing, expanded dramatically. Professional football and basketball emerged later. Black men had been banned from major league baseball in 1887 (see Chapter 15). Nevertheless, in 1901 New York Giants' manager John J. McGraw signed a black man, Charlie Grant, to play second base. McGraw claimed that Grant was "Chief Tokohoma," a full-blooded Cherokee Indian. Chicago White Sox owner Charles Comiskey knew otherwise, and Grant did not play in the major leagues.

Playing among themselves, black baseball players barely made a living as they moved from team to team in an ever-fluctuating and disorganized system that saw teams come and go with monotonous regularity. No leagues functioned effectively for the black teams and players. Owners of the black teams were sometimes involved in organized crime. William A. Greenlee, for example, was the proprietor of the Pittsburgh Crawfords, and he made most of his money from the numbers racket.

Black players crisscrossed the country on trains and in automobiles as they played each other in small towns and large cities for meager amounts of money shared from gate receipts. It was an insecure and nomadic life. The black clubs kept few individual or team statistics, and their financial records were frequently in disarray.

RUBE FOSTER

Andrew "Rube" Foster was the father of black baseball in twentieth-century America. He was a crafty pitcher from Texas who combined athletic skills with mental dexterity. In 1911 he founded the Chicago American Giants, and he pitched with them regularly until 1915 and then mainly managed after that. As fine an athlete as Foster was, he was an even more talented organizer and administrator.

In 1919 in the Chicago *Defender*, he argued for the establishment of a Negro baseball league. In 1920 he was the catalyst in the formation of the eight-team **Negro National League** and became its president and secretary. It was the first stable black league, with franchises in Kansas City, St. Louis, Indianapolis, Detroit, Dayton, and two teams in Chicago. The eighth team was the Cuban Stars.

Foster and the new league took advantage of the migration of black people to northern cities. The black ball clubs usually played late in the afternoon or in the early evening so fans could attend after a day's work. (This was before night baseball.) Sunday doubleheaders in Chicago or Kansas City might draw eight thousand to ten thousand people. Players were paid regularly, and athletes on Foster's Giants earned at least $175 a month. The biggest obstacle black teams faced was the lack of their own fields or stadiums. They were forced to rent, often at exorbitant rates, from major league clubs, which frequently kept the profits from concessions.

Black baseball thrived—more or less—in the 1920s, thanks mostly to Foster's force of personality and dedication. He was a tireless worker and strict disciplinarian, but the pressure may have been too much. In 1926 he suffered a mental breakdown and died in 1930. The loss of Foster—combined with the impact of the Depression—severely disrupted the league system.

AFRICAN-AMERICAN EVENTS	NATIONAL EVENTS
1919	
1919 Pan-African Congress meets in Paris Black Star Line is founded by Marcus Garvey and the UNIA	1919 Aliens rounded up and deported by A. Mitchell Palmer Eighteenth Amendment (Prohibition) is ratified Volstead Act is passed
1920	
1920 Rube Foster organizes the Negro National League in baseball	1920 U.S. Senate rejects the Treaty of Versailles Nineteenth Amendment is ratified; women gain the right to vote Warren Harding is elected president
1921	
1921 Tulsa, Oklahoma, race riot occurs	1921 Congress establishes quotas to limit immigration
1922	
1922 Dyer antilynching bill passes in U.S. House, fails in Senate Marcus Garvey meets with KKK leaders in Atlanta KKK virtually takes over the state of Oklahoma	
1923	
	1923 President Harding dies in office Investigation of government corruption in the Teapot Dome scandal begins

Andrew "Rube" Foster was the father of black baseball. An outstanding pitcher, he reportedly taught major-league-great Christy Mathewson how to throw the screwball. He became the owner and manager of the Chicago American Giants, and he was the founder of the Negro National League. His teams won the pennant in 1920, 1921, and 1922. He was elected to the Baseball Hall of Fame in Cooperstown in 1981.

COLLEGE SPORTS

Football, baseball, basketball, and track and field were popular at the collegiate level. Amateur sports were not as rigidly segregated as professional baseball. Black men continued to play for white northern universities, although few teams had more than one black player. Paul Robeson was on the Rutgers football team in 1916 that played against Frederick Douglass "Fritz" Pollard and Brown University. Pollard was the first black man to play in the Rose Bowl, where his Brown team lost to Washington State in 1916.

Pollard went on to play professional football in the 1920s during the early years of the National Football League (NFL). He played for four NFL teams, including Milwaukee and Providence. In 1921 he became the first African-American head coach in the league when he took charge of the Akron team. Later he coached an independent all-black team, the Chicago Black Hawks. Pollard, who died in 1986, was inducted into the National Football League Hall of Fame in 2005.

Black college players on white teams encountered discrimination when the teams traveled. Spectators taunted and threatened them. The Big Ten had an unwritten agreement that basketball coaches would not accept black players. All-white college teams sometimes refused to play against schools with black players. In 1920 Virginia's Washington and Lee University canceled a football game against Washington and Jefferson College of Pennsylvania because Charles West, a black man, played in the Washington and Jefferson backfield.

Sports in black colleges and universities thrived in the 1920s. Baseball and football were the most popular spectator events. Traditional rivalries attracted large crowds. Several schools played baseball religiously each Easter Monday. In 1926 Livingstone College defeated Biddle University (now Johnson C. Smith University) before a crowd of six thousand in Charlotte, North Carolina. With the migration of black people to the North, black colleges began to play football in northern cities. Howard and Lincoln played to a scoreless tie before eighteen thousand people in Philadelphia on Thanksgiving in 1925. Hampton and Lincoln played at New York's Polo Grounds on the edge of Harlem in 1929 in a game won by Lincoln 13–7 before ten thousand spectators.

CONCLUSION

For African Americans who lived through it, the 1920s must have seemed little more than a depressing continuation of earlier decades. Little appeared to have changed. Racial violence and lynching persisted. *The Birth of a Nation* mocked black people and inflamed racial animosity. "Experts" offered "proof" that people of color were inferior and threatened America's ethnic purity. The Ku Klux Klan became a formidable organization again. Millions of white men joined the Klan, and millions of other Americans supported it.

Nevertheless, some genuinely positive developments in the 1920s gave hope for a more promising future. The NAACP became an organization to be reckoned with as it fought for antilynching legislation in Congress and for civil and political rights in the courts. Its membership exceeded 100,000 during the 1920s. Although many black and white Americans ridiculed Marcus Garvey for his flamboyant style and excessive rhetoric, he offered racial pride and self-respect as he enrolled hundreds of thousands of black people in the UNIA.

Black workers made very little progress as they sought concessions from big business and representation within the ranks of organized labor. A. Philip Randolph founded the Brotherhood of Sleeping Car Porters and began a struggle with the Pullman Company and the American Federation of Labor that would begin to pay off in the 1930s.

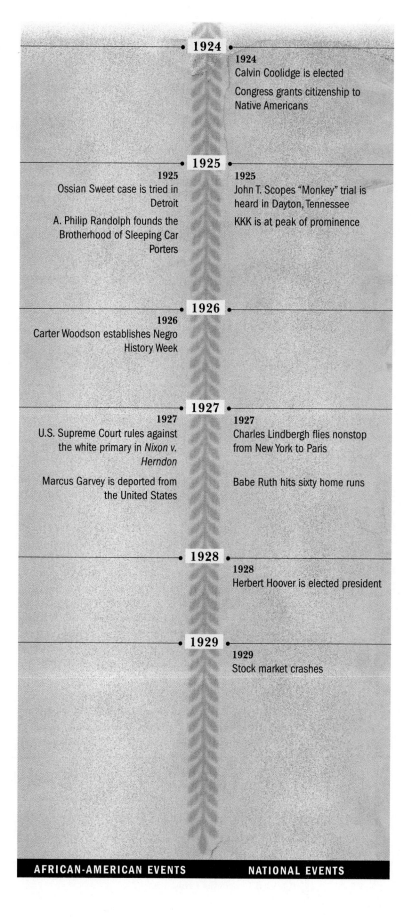

1924

1924
Calvin Coolidge is elected

Congress grants citizenship to Native Americans

1925

1925
Ossian Sweet case is tried in Detroit

A. Philip Randolph founds the Brotherhood of Sleeping Car Porters

1925
John T. Scopes "Monkey" trial is heard in Dayton, Tennessee

KKK is at peak of prominence

1926

1926
Carter Woodson establishes Negro History Week

1927

1927
U.S. Supreme Court rules against the white primary in *Nixon v. Herndon*

Marcus Garvey is deported from the United States

1927
Charles Lindbergh flies nonstop from New York to Paris

Babe Ruth hits sixty home runs

1928

1928
Herbert Hoover is elected president

1929

1929
Stock market crashes

AFRICAN-AMERICAN EVENTS   NATIONAL EVENTS

The Harlem Renaissance was a cultural awakening in literature and the arts that was unprecedented in African-American history. A torrent of words poured forth from novelists, essayists, and poets. Although they disagreed—sometimes vehemently—on the purposes of black art, the writers and artists who were a part of the Renaissance had an enduring impact. The Renaissance allowed thoughtful and creative men and women to grapple with what it meant to be black in a society in which the white majority had defined the black minority as inferior, incapable, and culturally backward. Hereafter African Americans were less likely to let other people characterize them in demeaning ways.

Black musicians, dancers, singers, entertainers, and athletes made names for themselves and contributed to popular culture in a mostly urban environment. As the nation moved into the 1930s, it remained to be seen whether the modest but real progress of the 1920s would be sustained.

RECOMMENDED READING

William H. Harris. *Keeping the Faith: A. Philip Randolph, Milton P. Webster and the Brotherhood of Sleeping Car Porters, 1925–1937.* Urbana: University of Illinois Press, 1977. This is an excellent account of the struggle of Randolph and the BSCP for recognition.

David Levering Lewis. *When Harlem Was in Vogue.* New York: Alfred A. Knopf, 1981. Lewis captures the life and vitality of Harlem in the 1920s.

David Levering Lewis, ed. *The Portable Harlem Renaissance Reader.* New York: Penguin Books, 1994. Essays, poems, and excerpts from the works of virtually every writer associated with the Renaissance are contained in this volume.

Nancy MacLean. *Behind the Mask of Chivalry: The Making of the Second Ku Klux Klan.* New York: Oxford University Press, 1994. This is the most recent study of the revived KKK.

Arnold Rampersad. *The Life of Langston Hughes, Vol. 1, 1902–1941: I, Too, Sing America.* New York: Oxford University Press, 1986. Here is a rich study of a complex and extraordinary man and writer.

Judith Stein. *The World of Marcus Garvey: Race and Class in Modern Society.* Baton Rouge: Louisiana State University Press, 1991. This is an effective examination of Garvey and the Universal Negro Improvement Association.

ADDITIONAL BIBLIOGRAPHY

THE KU KLUX KLAN

David M. Chalmers. *Hooded Americanism: A History of the Ku Klux Klan.* New York: Franklin Watts, 1965.

Kenneth T. Jackson. *The Ku Klux Klan in the City.* New York: Oxford University Press, 1967.

THE NAACP

Kevin Boyle. *Arc of Justice: A Saga of Race, Civil Rights, and Murder in the Jazz Age* [the Ossie Sweet case]. New York: Henry Holt, 2004.

Charles F. Kellogg. *NAACP: A History of the National Association for the Advancement of Colored People.* Baltimore: Johns Hopkins University Press, 1967.

Robert L. Zangrando. *The NAACP Campaign against Lynching, 1909–1950.* Philadelphia: Temple University Press, 1980.

BLACK WORKERS, A. PHILIP RANDOLPH, AND THE BROTHERHOOD OF SLEEPING CAR PORTERS

Jervis B. Anderson. *A. Philip Randolph: A Biographical Portrait.* New York: Harcourt, Brace, Jovanovich, 1973.

Beth Tompkins Bates. *Pullman Porters and the Rise of Protest Politics in Black America, 1925–1945.* Chapel Hill: University of North Carolina Press, 2001.

David E. Bernstein. *Only One Place of Redress: African Americans, Labor Regulations and the Courts from Reconstruction to the New Deal.* Durham, NC: Duke University Press, 2001.

Paula F. Pfeffer. *A. Philip Randolph: Pioneer of the Civil Rights Movement.* Baton Rouge: Louisiana State University Press, 1990.

Jack Santino. *Miles of Smiles, Years of Struggle: Stories of Black Pullman Porters.* Urbana: University of Illinois Press, 1989.

MARCUS GARVEY AND THE UNIVERSAL NEGRO IMPROVEMENT ASSOCIATION

Randall K. Burkett. *Garveyism as a Religious Movement: The Institutionalization of a Black Civil Religion.* Metuchen, NJ: Scarecrow Press, 1978.

E. David Cronon. *Black Moses: The Story of Marcus Garvey and the Universal Negro Improvement Association.* Madison: University of Wisconsin Press, 1955.

Marcus Garvey. *Philosophy and Opinions of Marcus Garvey.* New York: Atheneum, 1969.

Theodore Kornweibel, Jr. *Seeing Red: Federal Campaigns against Black Militancy, 1919–1925.* Bloomington: Indiana University Press, 1998.

THE HARLEM RENAISSANCE

Arna W. Bontemps, ed. *The Harlem Renaissance Remembered.* New York: Dodd, Mead, 1972.

Nathan Huggins. *Harlem Renaissance.* New York: Oxford University Press, 1971.

Bruce Kellner, ed. *The Harlem Renaissance: A Historical Dictionary of the Era.* Westport, CT: Greenwood Press, 1984.

Steven Watson. *The Harlem Renaissance: Hub of African American Culture, 1920–1930.* New York: Pantheon, 1995.

BIOGRAPHIES AND AUTOBIOGRAPHIES

Pamela Bordelon, ed. *Go Gator and Muddy the Water: Writings by Zora Neale Hurston from the Federal Writers Project.* New York: Norton, 1999.

Wayne F. Cooper. *Claude McKay, Rebel Sojourner in the Harlem Renaissance: A Biography.* Baton Rouge: Louisiana State University Press, 1987.

Robert C. Cottrell. *The Best Pitcher in Baseball: The Life of Rube Foster; Negro League Giant.* New York: New York University Press, 2001.

Thadious M. Davis. *Nella Larsen: Novelist of the Harlem Renaissance.* Baton Rouge: Louisiana State University Press, 1994.

Robert Hemenway. *Zora Neale Hurston: A Literary Biography.* Urbana: University of Illinois Press, 1977.

Gloria T. Hull. *Color, Sex, and Poetry: Three Women Writers of the Harlem Renaissance.* Bloomington: Indiana University Press, 1987.

George Hutchinson. *In Search of Nella Larsen: A Biography of the Color Line.* Cambridge: Harvard University Press, 2006.

James Weldon Johnson. *Along the Way.* New York: Viking Press, 1933.

Cynthia E. Kerman. *The Lives of Jean Toomer: A Hunger for Wholeness.* Baton Rouge: Louisiana State University Press, 1987.

Eugene Levy. *James Weldon Johnson: Black Leader, Black Voice.* Chicago: University of Chicago Press, 1973.

RETRACING THE ODYSSEY

The Studio Museum of Harlem, New York City. Founded in 1967, this museum displays a rich and diverse array of art and artifacts by black artists from Africa, the Caribbean, and America and thus maintains the legacy of the Harlem Renaissance.

Abyssinian Baptist Church, New York City. The best known church in Harlem and home to a huge congregation, it was led for most of the first three-quarters of the twentieth century by the Rev. Adam Clayton Powell Sr. and then his son, the Rev. Adam Clayton Powell Jr. The present structure was completed in 1923 and contains a small museum.

Paul Laurence Dunbar Home, Dayton, Ohio. Dunbar was born in 1872 in Dayton. He purchased this two-story brick house in 1903 and lived in it until his death in 1906. His mother resided in it until 1936. It is open to the public and features exhibits, artifacts, photos, and papers from Dunbar's life and era.

The Negro Leagues Baseball Museum, Kansas City, Missouri. Devoted to the history of African Americans and baseball from the 1860s to the 1950s, the museum opened in 1991 and contains films, exhibits, and interactive computer stations. Its Field of Legends features twelve life-sized bronze sculptures that honor the men who contributed the most to black baseball.

 REVIEW, RESEARCH, AND INTERACT

REVIEW QUESTIONS

1. To what extent, if any, had the intensity of white supremacy changed by the 1920s from what it had been two to three decades earlier?

2. What examples of progress could leaders like W. E. B. Du Bois, James Weldon Johnson, A. Philip Randolph, and Marcus Garvey point to in the 1920s?

3. Why did so many African-American leaders reject Marcus Garvey?

4. How did the black nationalism of the Universal Negro Improvement Association differ from the white nationalism of the Ku Klux Klan?

5. What economic opportunities existed for African Americans who had migrated to northern cities?

6. How do you explain the emergence of the literary and artistic movement known as the Harlem Renaissance?

7. How distinctive were black writers, artists, and musicians? Were their creative works essentially a part of American culture or separate from it?

8. Were there any genuine reasons for optimism among African Americans by the late 1920s?

 www.researchnavigator.com

Using the tools available in Research Navigator, consider these questions:
What factors explain the resurgence of white racism in the 1920s? How did blacks respond?

PRIMARY SOURCE DOCUMENTS

17–2 "If You Believe the Negro Has a Soul: Back to Africa" with Marcus Garvey, 1921

17–3 Elsie Johnson McDougald on "The Double Task: The Struggle of Negro Women for Sex and Race Emancipation," 1925

17–4 Charles S. Johnson, *The City Negro*, 1925

17–5 Alain Locke, from *The New Negro*, 1925

17–6 Charles McKay, "White Houses," 1925

17–7 The Harlem Renaissance: George Schuyler Argues against "Black Art," 1926

17–8 Hiram Evans, The Klan's Fight for Americanism, 1926

DATA EXPLORATION

Black Workers by Major Industrial Group, 1920, p. 457

INTERACTIVE ACTIVITY

Harlem Renaissance

The Harlem Renaissance is not simply a story of individual and group achievement. What was the significance of so many writers, painters, musicians, photographers, poets, and other artists all gathering in the same place?

GOING BACK TO AFRICA

The American Colonization Society (ACS), organized in 1817 to resettle African Americans in Africa, established the colony of Liberia in West Africa as a prospective home for African Americans in 1821. By the 1820s there were branches of the ACS in every northern state dedicated to helping blacks immigrate to Liberia. Prominent black abolitionists also endorsed migration to Africa. During the early 1800s, a prominent advocate of migration, Paul Cuffe of Massachusetts, took thirty-four African-Americans on his own ship to the black colony of Sierra Leone, located just to the north of present-day Liberia. AME church bishop Daniel Coker led the first eighty-six African-American colonists to Liberia in 1820–21. By 1838 approximately twenty-five hundred colonists had made the journey to Liberia. In 1877, black leaders in the south urged black people to migrate to Liberia, beginning a "Liberian Exodus," as many black communities and churches caught "Liberia Fever."

Joseph Jenkins Roberts (left), the first and seventh president of Liberia, emigrated from Virginia to Liberia in 1829.

Jane Roberts (right), the first lady of Liberia, who came to Liberia in 1824.

A map showing Monrovia, Liberia, ca. 1830 after the settlement of slaves in Liberia by the American Colonization Society.

The presidential mansion ▶ in Monrovia, Liberia was the home of President Roberts in 1847.

Cape Palmas, an original settlement of the Maryland Colonization Society, was established to civilize and bring Christianity to the native Africans. The mission, known as Mount Vaughan, educated many of Liberia's indigenous tribes.

John Brown Russwurm was ▶ the publisher of *Freedom's Journal,* the first African-American newspaper. After suspension of the newspaper in 1829, Russwurm moved to Liberia. He was one of the first African Americans to earn a college degree.

In this notarized letter, Henry Bonds appealed to the American Colonization Society for help in immigrating to Liberia.

▶ **These souvenir photographs** of a coffee plantation and Ashmun Street in Monrovia were produced in Liberia for distribution at the 1893 World's Columbian Exposition in Chicago, Illinois.

The Baptist Church is ▶ the oldest church in Liberia, dating back to before emancipation, when inhabitants of Monrovia were mainly escaped slaves.

The first black immigrants to Liberia traveled on the *Azor,* a ship sponsored by the Liberian Exodus Company. This collection of letters describes this maiden voyage as miserable and cramped. About twenty-three people died during the voyage.

▼

The Massachusetts Colonization Society offered membership certification to prospective emigrants.

VISUALIZING THE PAST

THE RETURN OF SUBJUGATION: "JUMPING JIM CROW"

The news of the Emancipation Proclamation, and the 13th, 14th, and 15th amendments to the U.S. Constitution appeared to herald a new age for African Americans. Those hopes were soon dashed against the political realities of the end of Reconstruction and a lack of support for African American citizenship rights by the Republican and Democratic governments of the last half of the 19th century. When white supremacists and the planter elite regained control of state governments in the South, one of their first actions was to strip blacks of their right to vote through violence and threat of violence. The threats were not hollow. Lynching, murders, whippings, and other forms of brutality were brought to bear upon African Americans to prevent them from exercising their rights of suffrage.

African Americans did not submit to this intimidation without protest. In 1865, as soon as they realized their rights were under attack, the blacks of South Carolina organized a convention to protest the Black Codes that stripped them of their rights. Some African Americans sought sanctuary by leaving the South. The rapid growth of jobs in northern cities during both the First World War and the Second World War would intensify the desire of blacks to move north.

Having gained emancipation, the right to vote, and the ability to hold public office, African Americans were returned to a status of second-class citizenship and subjugation after the end of Reconstruction. How did this happen?

▶ Thomas Dartmouth Rice as "Jim Crow"

Thomas Dartmouth Rice was a white actor in the first half of the 19th century who developed a minstrel act involving a crippled old black slave called "Jim Crow." Dressed in black face and ragged clothing, Rice would dance around the stage singing a song in black dialect with the following refrain:

Weel about and turn about and do jis so,
Eb'ry time I weel about and jump Jim Crow.

Jim Crow eventually became a stereotype for blacks and later was applied to the segregation laws that oppressed blacks and kept them in a second class existence. The image of "Jim Crow" ridiculed and lampooned Africans Americans for a full century.

▶ Blanche K. Bruce, Speech in the Senate, 1876

The conduct of the late election in Mississippi affected not merely the fortunes of partisans—as the same were necessarily involved in the defeat or success of the respective parties to the contest—but put in question and jeopardy the sacred rights of the citizen. . . .

The evidence in hand and accessible will show beyond peradventure that in many parts of the State corrupt and… threats, and violence were practiced directly upon the masses of voters in such measures and strength as to produce grave apprehensions for their personal safety and as to deter them from the exercise of their political franchises. . . .

▶ Ida B. Wells, A Red Record, 1895

Not all or nearly all of the murders done by white men, during the past thirty years in the South, have come to light, but the statistics as gathered and preserved by white men, and which have not been questioned, show that during these years more than ten thousand Negroes have been killed in cold blood, without the formality of judicial trial and legal execution.

Address of the Colored State Convention to the People of the State of South Carolina, 1865

. . . You have by your Legislative actions placed barriers in the way of our educational and mechanical improvement; you have given us little or no encouragement to pursue agricultural pursuits. . . [and] reduce us to a serfdom, intolerable to men born amid the progress of American genius and national development.

. . . We simply desire that we shall be recognized as men; that we have no obstructions placed in our way; that the same laws which govern white men shall direct colored men; that we have the right of trial by a jury of our peers, that schools be opened or established for our children; that we be permitted to acquire homesteads for ourselves and children; that we be dealt with as others, in equity and justice.

We claim the confidence and good-will of all classes of men; we ask that the same chances be extended to us that freemen should demand at the hands of their fellow-citizens. We desire the prosperity and growth of this State and the well being of all men, and shall be found ever struggling to elevate ourselves and add to the national character; and we trust the day will not be distant when you will acknowledge that by our rapid progress in moral, social, religious and intellectual development that you will cheerfully accord to us the high commendation that we are worthy, with you, to enjoy all political emoluments

Letter from the Great Migration, 1916–1917

De Ridder, La., April 29, 1917

Dear sir: there is lots of us southern mens wants transportation and we want to leave ratway as soon as you let us here from you some of us is married mens who need work we would like to bring our wife with us there is 20 head of good mens want transportation and if you need us let us no by return mail we all are redy only wants here from you there may be more all of our peoples wont to leave here and i want you to send as much as 20 tickets any way I will get you up plenty hands to do most any kind of work all you have to do is to send for them. looking to here from you.

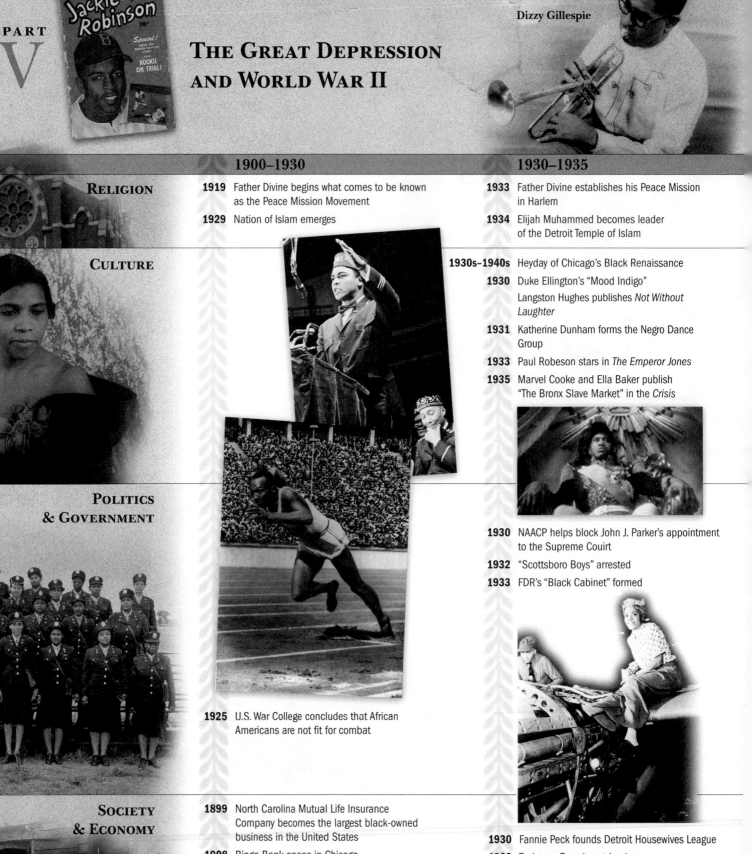

PART V

Dizzy Gillespie

THE GREAT DEPRESSION AND WORLD WAR II

	1900–1930	1930–1935
RELIGION	**1919** Father Divine begins what comes to be known as the Peace Mission Movement **1929** Nation of Islam emerges	**1933** Father Divine establishes his Peace Mission in Harlem **1934** Elijah Muhammed becomes leader of the Detroit Temple of Islam
CULTURE		**1930s–1940s** Heyday of Chicago's Black Renaissance **1930** Duke Ellington's "Mood Indigo" Langston Hughes publishes *Not Without Laughter* **1931** Katherine Dunham forms the Negro Dance Group **1933** Paul Robeson stars in *The Emperor Jones* **1935** Marvel Cooke and Ella Baker publish "The Bronx Slave Market" in the *Crisis*
POLITICS & GOVERNMENT	**1925** U.S. War College concludes that African Americans are not fit for combat	**1930** NAACP helps block John J. Parker's appointment to the Supreme Court **1932** "Scottsboro Boys" arrested **1933** FDR's "Black Cabinet" formed
SOCIETY & ECONOMY	**1899** North Carolina Mutual Life Insurance Company becomes the largest black-owned business in the United States **1908** Binga Bank opens in Chicago	**1930** Fannie Peck founds Detroit Housewives League **1932** Tuskegee Experiment begins **1935** Mary M. Bethune founds the National Council of Negro Women National Negro Congress founded NAACP sues to integrate University of Maryland School of Law

Mahalia Jackson

James Baldwin

Ralph Bunche

| 1935–1940 | 1940–1950 | NOTEWORTHY INDIVIDUALS |

1936 Jesse Owens wins four gold medals at the Berlin Olympics

1937 Joe Louis wins heavyweight championship

1939 Billie Holiday premiers "Strange Fruit"

Marian Anderson sings at the Lincoln Memorial

"Bojangles" Robinson organizes Black Actors Guild

1940s Black musicians introduce bebop

1940–1948 Oscar Micheaux's films

1940 Richard Wright publishes *Native Son*

1941 Mary Dawson founds the National Negro *Opera* Company

1942 Margaret Walker publishes *For My People*

1945 Nat King Cole becomes the first black star to have his own radio variety show

1947 Jackie Robinson becomes first black major leagues baseball player

1948 Alice Coachman becomes the first African-American woman to win an Olympic gold medal

1952 Ralph Ellison publishes *Invisible Man*

1936 African-American voters switch to the Democratic Party

1937 William Hastie named first black federal judge

1938 Oscar DePriest elected, first African-American congressman from the North

1941 U.S. Army forms Tuskegee Air Squadron

1942 Marine Corps accepts first African Americans

1943 Navy officer schools accept African Americans

1944 Adam Clayton Powell elected to Congress

Port of Chicago "mutiny"

U.S. Supreme Court declares "white primaries" unconstitutional

1945 U.S. Army desegregates its Nurse Corps

1946 President Truman creates the Committee on Civil Rights

1948 Executive Order 9981 desegregates the U.S. military

1950 State Department revokes Paul Robeson's passport

1951 House Un-American Activities Committee indicts W.E.B. DuBois

1954 *Brown v. Board of Education* declares "separate but equal" unconstitutional

1936 First National Negro Congress held

1937 Mary M. Bethune organizes conference on the Negro and Negro Youth

1940s Many African Americans move from agriculture to jobs in industry

1941 A. Philip Randolph organizes The March on Washington Movement

1942 CORE founded

1943 Detroit race riots

1944 *An American Dilemma* published

Southern Regional Council established

1946 Journey of Reconciliation begins

1950 Ralph Bunche becomes the first African-American recipient of the Nobel Peace Prize

George H. White (1852–1918)

Charles C. Spaulding (1874–1952)

Dr. Matilda A. Evans (1872–1935)

Mary McLeod Bethune (1875–1955)

"Bojangles" Robinson (1878–1949)

Father Major J. Divine (1879–1965)

Oscar Micheaux (1884–1951)

Daisey A. Lampkins (1884–1965)

Dox Thrash (1892–1965)

Elijah Muhammed (1897–1975)

Hattie McDaniel (1898–1952)

Maude E. Callen (1898-1990)

Aaron Douglas (1899–1988)

Thomas Dorsey (1899–1993)

Mabel K. Staupers (1890–1989)

Selma Burke (1900–1995)

Anna Bontemps (1902–1973)

Ella Baker (1903–1986)

Ralph Bunche (1904–1971)

William H. Hastie (1904–1976)

Richard Wright (1908–1960)

Thurgood Marshall (1908–1993)

Bayard Rustin (1910–1987)

Katherine Dunham (1910–2006)

Mahalia Jackson (1912–1972)

Jesse Owens (1913–1980)

Juanita Mitchell (1913–1992)

Joe Louis Barrow (1914–1981)

Ralph Ellison (1914–1994)

Billie Holiday (1915–1959)

Margaret Walker (1915–1998)

Dizzy Gillespie (1917–1993)

Jackie Robinson (1919–1972)

Charlie "Bird" Parker (1920–1955)

James Baldwin (1924–1987)

Constance B. Motley (1931–2006)

Imamu Amari Baraka, aka LeRoi Jones (1934–)

18

Black Protest, the Great Depression, and the New Deal

WHAT FACTORS CAUSED THE GREAT DEPRESSION
OF THE 1930s?

HOW DID BLACK PROTEST
DURING THE GREAT DEPRESSION
INFLUENCE THE NEW DEAL?

WHY DID AFRICAN AMERICANS
SHIFT THEIR POLITICAL ALLEGIANCE
TO THE DEMOCRATIC PARTY?

HOW DID THE NEW DEAL
AFFECT AFRICAN AMERICANS?

WHAT ROLE DID THE COMMUNIST PARTY
AND ORGANIZED LABOR PLAY IN RADICALIZING
BLACK AMERICANS DURING THE 1930s?

◄◄ **Photographer Margaret Bourke White** captured the
contrast between the American dream of prosperity—for
white families—and the harsh realities of life for black
Americans during the Depression. The collapse of the
economy spurred the search for radical critiques and
solutions to deal with the desperate conditions millions of
African Americans endured. Separate economic
development and the creation of parallel institutions and
organizations was one option. But was it practicable? Getty

1929–1941

The depression brought everyone down a peg or two. And the Negro had but a few pegs to fall.

Langston Hughes

The only thing that we not only can, but must do, is voluntarily and insistently to organize our economic and social power, no matter how much segregation it involves. Learn to associate with ourselves and to train ourselves in methods of democratic control within our own group. Run and support our own institutions.

W. E. B. Du Bois

▼ **The Great Depression** pushed many black Americans to the edge of despair.

For African Americans, the Great Depression was both an era of suffering made worse by the horrors and burdens of American racism and a time of profound political change, demographic shifts, and social activism that would lay the foundation for the progress of ensuing decades. At the beginning of the economic collapse, most African Americans were either trapped in the already failing southern agricultural system or eking out a bare existence at the margins of the booming urban economy. The fall of the economy pushed many black Americans to the edge of starvation, throwing them off the land and out of the small niches they had carved out in other occupations. Coming out of the southern-dominated Democratic Party, President Franklin Roosevelt's New Deal program for fighting the Depression might have simply reinforced existing racism, as in fact it did to some extent. From another perspective, the emerging political power of African-American voters in the North, the continuing development of civil rights organizations, and the growth of an antiracist agenda among radicals and labor unions created the preconditions for a profound change in American politics. Amid economic despair, peonage, lynchings, and labor conflict, black men, women, and their children saw glimmers of hope in protests against racial segregation and radical critiques of capitalist exploitation. Their protests helped shape the policies and programs of the New Deal. The 1930s were thus the dark dawn of a new era.

The Cataclysm, 1929–1933

The Great Depression was a cataclysm. National income fell from $81 billion in 1929 to $40 billion in 1932. Americans lost faith in banks, and the resulting panic deepened the despair. Overnight millions of Americans lost their life savings in bank closings and foreclosures. Individual Americans responded by buying fewer consumer goods and, in turn, businesses cut back production, investment, and payrolls. The result was a downward spiral of economic activity made worse by increasing numbers of unemployed. According to the American Federation of Labor (AFL), the number of unemployed people increased from 3,216,000 in January 1930 to 13,689,000 in March 1933 (see Figure 18–1). The standard of living of nearly everyone from farmers to small businessmen and entrepreneurs to wage laborers dropped to a fraction of what it had been before 1929.

Most people blamed the stock market crash and Republican president Herbert Hoover for the hard times, but the explanation is more complicated. Although still a hotly debated issue, the Great Depression was probably caused by a combination of factors, including rampant speculation, corporate capitalism's drive for markets and profits unchecked by federal regulation, the failure of those in the government or private sector to understand the workings of the economy, a weak international trading system, and, most important, the great inequality of wealth and income that limited the purchasing power of millions of Americans.

HARDER TIMES FOR BLACK AMERICA

The collapse of the American economy hit African Americans particularly hard. Most black people remained in the rural South mired in an increasingly exploitive agricultural system. Indeed, the Depression exacerbated the key problems besetting cash-crop production in the 1920s. Consumer demand for cotton and sugar fell with the economy, but as farmers grew more of these crops to make ends meet, the supply of these staples increased. The result was a catastrophe, with prices for cotton—still the mainstay of the southern economy—plunging from eighteen cents a pound in 1929 to six cents in 1933. Families of black sharecroppers and tenant farmers, nearly powerless in the

Dealing with Hard Times

rural South, found themselves reduced to starvation or thrown off the land.

The hard times also struck those 1.5 million African Americans who had escaped the South for northern urban communities (see Table 18–1). Even during the height of the prosperous 1920s, black Americans suffered layoffs and witnessed a steady deterioration in their living standards. After 1929 the same forces that impoverished those in the countryside swept those in urban areas further toward the economic margins as waves of refugees from the farms crowded into the cities (see Table 18–2). By 1934, when the federal government noted that 17 percent of white citizens could not support themselves, the figure for black Americans had increased to 38 percent overall. In Chicago the jobless rate for African-American men was 40 percent, in Pittsburgh 48 percent, in Harlem 50 percent, in Philadelphia 56 percent, and in Detroit 60 percent. The figures were even more dire for black workers in southern cities. In Atlanta, Georgia, 65 percent of black workers needed public assistance, and in

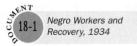
18-1 *Negro Workers and Recovery, 1934*

Norfolk, Virginia, a stunning 80 percent had to apply for welfare.

African Americans lost jobs in those parts of the economy where they had gained a tenuous foothold. Before 1929 jobs in low-status or poorly paid occupa-

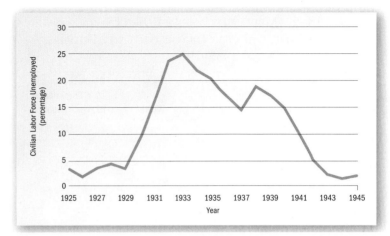

FIGURE 18–1   UNEMPLOYMENT, 1925–1945

With the collapse of the American economy, unemployment soared in the 1930s. New Deal programs alleviated some of the suffering, but full recovery did not come until the defense industries swung into action with the U.S. entry into World War II.

tions such as garbage collection, foundries, or domestic service had been regarded as "negro work" and hence were generally immune from white competition. As desperation set in, white southerners not only competed for these jobs, but they also used the old tactics of terror and intimidation to compel employers to fire black people. Unions, north and south, continued to exclude African Americans from membership and pressured manufacturers to hire white people.

TABLE 18–1   DEMOGRAPHIC SHIFTS: THE SECOND GREAT MIGRATION, 1930–1950

Year	Region	Black Population	Total Population	% Black
1930	Northeast	1,146,985	34,427,091	3.33
	Midwest	1,262,234	38,594,100	3.27
	Southeast	7,079,626	25,680,803	27.57
	South Central	2,281,951	12,176,830	18.74
	Mountain	30,225	3,701,789	0.82
	Pacific	90,122	8,622,047	1.05
1950	Northeast	2,018,182	39,477,986	5.11
	Midwest	2,227,876	44,460,762	5.01
	Southeast	7,793,379	32,659,516	23.86
	South Central	2,432,028	14,517,572	16.73
	Mountain	66,429	5,074,998	1.31
	Pacific	507,043	15,114,964	3.35

Source: U.S. Bureau of the Census Release, 1991, and Statistical Abstract, 1990. Also see Schomburg Center, The New York Public Library: African American Desk Reference (New York: John Wiley & Sons, 1999), pp. 100–101.

TABLE 18–2 MEDIAN INCOME OF BLACK FAMILIES COMPARED TO THE MEDIAN INCOME OF WHITE FAMILIES FOR SELECTED CITIES, 1935–1936

City and Type of Family	Black	White	Black Income as a Percentage of White Income
Husband–Wife Families			
New York	$980	$1,930	51%
Chicago	$726	$1,687	43%
Columbus	$831	$1,622	51%
Atlanta	$632	$1,876	34%
Columbia	$576	$1,876	31%
Mobile	$481	$1,419	34%
Other Families			
Atlanta	$332	$940	35%
Columbia	$254	$1,403	18%
Mobile	$301	$784	38%

Source: Gunnar Myrdal et al., An American Dilemma (New York: Harper and Brothers, 1944).

Black women workers, overwhelmingly concentrated in domestic service and laundry work, were affected even more than black men. There were fewer jobs because many families could no longer afford domestic help. With many impoverished women coming into the cities, those white people with the money to hire help found they could pay almost nothing and still employ these desperate women. In 1935 two black women, Marvel Cooke and Ella Baker, published an exposé of the exploitation of these women laborers in *The Crisis.* They entitled the article "The Bronx Slave Market" because the buying and selling of labor reminded them of the old slave marts in the antebellum South. Cooke and Baker described how the street corner market worked: "The Simpson avenue block exudes the stench of the slave market at its worst. Not only is human labor bartered and sold for a slave wage, but human love also is a marketable commodity." The black women gathered on particular street corners and waited as well-to-do white women selected them for a day's labor. They received "wages as low as 15 to 25 cents an hour, some working only two or three hours a day." Some black people were hired but never paid.

African Americans were no strangers to adversity, and many used the survival strategies developed through centuries of hardship to eke out an existence during the first years of the Great Depression. Survival demanded that black women pool their resources and adhere to a collective spirit that found such fertile ground in segregated northern neighborhoods. In

Chicago, for example, women and their families lived in crowded tenements in which they shared bathrooms and other facilities including hot plates, stoves, and sinks. They bartered and exchanged goods and services because money was so scarce. One woman might dress the hair of a neighbor in return for permission to borrow her dress or use her pots and pans. Another woman might trade bread and sugar or some other household staple for milk, beans, or soap. Grandmothers watched over children as their mothers went to look with rising futility for a domestic job. They helped each other as best they could.

Rural black women, like their urban sisters, had to rely on their individual and collective ingenuity to survive. As one observer of black women household heads in rural Georgia noted, "In their effort to maintain existence, these people are catching and selling fish, reselling vegetables, sewing in exchange for old clothes, letting out sleeping space, and doing odd jobs. They understand how to help each other. Stoves are used in common, wash boilers go their rounds, and garden crops are exchanged and shared." Nonetheless, the depth and duration of this downturn pressed these mutual aid strategies to the breaking point. By 1933 the clock seemed to have been turned back to 1865, when many African Americans could claim to own little more than their bodies.

BLACK BUSINESSES IN THE DEPRESSION: COLLAPSE AND SURVIVAL

Members of the black business and professional class also experienced economic losses. African Americans who had built successful businesses and professional practices in medicine and law, for example, faced the same Depression-borne problems as other businesses, but they suffered even more because the communities on which they depended were poorer. A description of two kinds of business, banking and insurance, illustrates how black enterprises stood or fell during the economic crisis.

The Binga Bank, Chicago's first black-owned-and-operated financial institution, had been founded in 1908 by its president Jesse Binga (1865–1950), a Detroit-born real estate broker who had worked as a barber and a Pullman porter. Binga had managed the bank so effectively that by 1930 its deposits had grown to more than $1.5 million. Binga once boasted he could lay claim to more footage on State Street, Chicago's principal thoroughfare, than any other man in the city. The Binga Bank was, during its early years, an important symbol of successful black capitalism and as such represented the hopes and aspirations of

A market woman in the 1930s with burdens on her head and in her arms. Black women drew upon proven strategies of self-help, hard work, and communal sharing to survive the Great Depression.

Chicago's black people. But the bank's assets were too heavily invested in mortgage loans to black churches and fraternal societies, many of which could not meet their payments after their members lost their jobs. Binga refused to seize the properties of these community institutions, but his restraint, coupled with financial improprieties, led to the bank's failure. On July 31, 1930, Illinois state bank auditors padlocked the institution and filed a federal misuse-of-funds charge against the once proud financier. Sentenced to prison in 1932, Binga was pardoned by President Franklin Delano Roosevelt a year later. However, he never rebuilt his bank or his fortune.

Some black businesses did survive the economic cataclysm, although often in a much weakened state. Among the fortunate businesses still standing when prosperity finally returned in the 1940s were the leading insurance companies, such as Atlanta Life, Supreme Life, Golden State, and the North Carolina Mutual Life Insurance Company. Atlanta Life Insurance Company, for ex-ample—founded by a former Georgia slave, Alonzo Franklin Herndon, in 1905—not only survived the Depression but recorded substantial profit. Between 1931 and 1936, the company's assets increased by more than $1 million. This was in part because insurance companies such as Atlanta Life provided an essential service for African Americans, particularly in an era before government provided social security, and could thus depend on a continued flow of premiums. And unlike Binga Bank, the officers of the Atlanta Life Insurance Company drastically reduced the percentage of their investment capital that secured mortgage loans in the black community.

The North Carolina Mutual Life Insurance Company, in Durham, weathered the Great Depression under the astute leadership of Charles Clinton Spaulding (1874–1952), a former manager of a black cooperative grocery store. In 1899 Spaulding joined with two other African Americans to transform the insurance company into the nation's largest black business. His partners were John Merrick, a former slave and leading realtor and barber (he owned six barbershops, three for whites and three for blacks), and his uncle, Dr. Aaron McDuffie Moore, Durham's only black physician. Following on the heels of the great migration to the North, Spaulding expanded the company's territory into Virginia, Maryland, and the District of Columbia. The company adhered to the thrift, hard work, and self-help philosophy so ardently expressed by Booker T. Washington. It remains today one of the three largest black-owned insurance companies in the United States.

Many of the 250 black hospitals, clinics, and nursing training schools that black physicians, such as Dr. Daniel Hale Williams, had launched since the 1890s were unable to survive the ravages of the Depression. Confronting a diminishing clientele and worsening health among black people, some black physicians began encouraging their patients to demand admission to the segregated government-operated hospitals and clinics. At the outset of the Depression, Dr. Matilda A. Evans (1872–1935) of Columbia, South Carolina, an 1897 graduate of the Woman's Medical College in Philadelphia, mobilized a diverse constituency of black parents, professionals, and religious and business leaders to persuade the state board of health to allocate money to provide free inoculations and immunization shots to black schoolchildren. Other health-care professionals volunteered to conduct free medical and dental examinations. When Evans's Columbia Clinic opened in July 1930, over seven hundred patients showed up. This short-lived clinic reflected Evans's belief that health care was a state responsibility just as important as the provision of free public education. The black South Carolina newspaper, the *Palmetto Leader*,

Dr. Matilda A. Evans (1872–1935) A remarkable black woman physician, Dr. Matilda A. Evans of Columbia, South Carolina, believed in the importance of establishing institutions and organizations that would enable black people to survive and from which they could fight to end racial segregation and discrimination. In the opening decades of the twentieth century, Dr. Evans established two hospitals and founded a nursing training school. She organized the Good Health Association of South Carolina, edited *The Negro Health Journal,* and served a term as president of the Palmetto Medical Association.

declared in October 1930 that "evidence keeps on piling on top of evidence to the effect that the Columbia Clinic is just proving to be, and will yet stand as the most important effort sponsored for our group in Columbia within the last half century." The deteriorating economic conditions of both the state of South Carolina and its people made it impossible to sustain this effort. But the Columbia Clinic movement taught black people a powerful lesson about how to mobilize to achieve change and thus raised, as Evans anticipated it would, black consciousness about the need to apply pressure on the state to gain greater access to public resources.

THE FAILURE OF RELIEF

Before Franklin Roosevelt's New Deal, private charities or, as a last resort, state and local governments were responsible for providing relief from economic hardships. Even in good times these institutions provided too little for all those in need. Moreover, African Americans had a much harder time getting aid than white people and were given less when they did get it. The Depression made it impossible for the nation's charitable organizations to meet the needs of more than a small portion of the hungry, homeless, and unemployed millions. In turn, state and local governments could not or would not provide unemployment insurance or increased welfare benefits to ease the pain and suffering of those most vulnerable to the economic disaster. Even when these governments wanted to help, the magnitude of the economic collapse so lowered tax receipts as to make it nearly impossible for relief agencies to act.

Despite the great need to alleviate the economic disaster, President Herbert Hoover hesitated to act. Steeped in the free-market orthodoxy of his time, he believed government should do little to interfere with the workings of the economy. Nevertheless, he did more to counteract a depression than any previous president had done. Hoover tried to convince businesses to retain employees and not to cut wages, believing companies would understand that by doing so they would contribute to the health of the general economy and promote their own long-term interests. The president also approved loans to banks, railroads, and insurance companies by the Reconstruction Finance Corporation, a federal agency set up to rescue large corporations. He hoped these businesses would reinvigorate production, create new jobs, and restore consumer spending. His faith was misplaced; businesses, seeking to save themselves, took the government loans and still laid off workers.

Hoover's reluctance to use the federal government to intervene in the economy extended to the provision of relief. He suggested that local governments and charities should address the needs of the unemployed, the homeless, and the starving masses. Hoover was not a callous person, but he was trapped in a rigid ideology. He watched with dismay the wandering groups of men, women, and children who began settling into what they called, with grim humor, "Hoovervilles," sordid clusters of shacks made of tin, cardboard, and burlap adjacent to railroad tracks and dumps. Still, he refused to allow the federal government to provide relief directly.

Hoover's inactivity was bad enough, but his politics were as racist as that of the Democratic Party. He wanted to create a white Republican Party in the South and cultivated white southerners by attempting to appoint judge John Parker of North Carolina, who believed in "separate but equal," to the U.S. Supreme Court and by displacing black Republican Party leaders. Hoover's policy was not new; for decades the national Republican Party had treated black voters with contempt and often declined to reward them with patronage appointments. This policy took on a different meaning during the early 1930s against the backdrop of black suffering. As NAACP director Walter White put it, Hoover

> sat stolidly in the White House, refusing bluntly to receive Negro citizens who wished to lay before him the facts of their steadily worsening plight or to consider any remedial legislation or governmental action. His attitude toward Negroes caused me to coin a phrase, which gained considerable currency, particularly in the Negro world, in which I described Hoover as "the man in the lily-White House."

Black Protest during the Great Depression

During the 1930s African-American men and women initiated their own agenda and determined to use every resource at their disposal to destroy the obstacles to racial justice and barriers to equal opportunity. The NAACP sponsored a legal campaign against educational discrimination and political disfranchisement led by Charles Houston and Thurgood Marshall, mobilized black communities, and sustained hope in struggle. Black people benefited from the New Deal, but less than white people did. The disparity between black and white lives was a spur to action. The juxtaposition of black subordination and misery alongside the new forms of federal aid so willingly distributed to white citizens convinced black Americans to intensify their own struggle for their American rights. Many em braced radical critiques of American capitalism, but few ever considered communism a viable alternative to American democracy. Black people would emerge from the Depression more determined than ever to make democracy work for them.

THE NAACP AND CIVIL RIGHTS STRUGGLES

During the 1930s the NAACP developed a new effectiveness as an advocate for African-American civil rights. The biracial organization took the lead in pressing the government to protect African-American rights and to eliminate the blatant racism in govern-

ment programs. Part of the reason for this new dynamism was the astute leadership of Walter White, a man whose physical characteristics could have easily permitted him to pass for white—he had blond hair and blue eyes—and turn away from the problems of black people. Instead he became an insistent voice of protest, personally investigating forty-two lynchings and eight race riots, and he was an ardent lobbyist for civil rights legislation and racial justice. Throughout the 1930s African Americans of all hues moved into leadership positions in the NAACP and added their names to the membership roles of its many branches.

The new dynamism of the NAACP became apparent in 1930 when Walter White took a prominent role in the successful campaign to defeat Hoover's nomination of circuit court judge John J. Parker of North Carolina to a seat on the U.S. Supreme Court. Parker had infuriated the organization because he openly embraced white supremacy, stating, for example, that the "participation of the Negro in politics is a source of evil and danger to both races." The NAACP formed a coalition with the American Federation of Labor to derail the Parker nomination. Although the NAACP could take only part of the credit, White trumpeted the victory and let it be known that African Americans would not be silent while "the Hoover administration proposed to conciliate southern white sentiment by sacrificing the Negro and his rights."

DU BOIS IGNITES A CONTROVERSY

The NAACP had critics, even within its own ranks. Many younger black people criticized its focus on civil liberties and deplored it for ignoring the economic misery of most African Americans. In 1934 W. E. B. Du Bois, editor of the NAACP's journal *The Crisis*, joined the chorus. Criticizing what he considered the group's overemphasis on integration, Du Bois advocated a program of self-determination he hoped would permit black people to develop "an economic nation within a nation." Du Bois acknowledged that this internal economy could only meet part of the needs of the African-American community. But he insisted it could be developed and expanded in many ways: "This smaller part could be so important and wield so much power that its influence upon the total economy of Negroes and the total industrial organization of the United States would be decisive for the great ends towards which the Negro moves."

The black intellectual community quickly attacked Du Bois for advocating "voluntary segregation." Sociologist E. Franklin Frazier, for example, called the idea of black businesses succeeding within a segregated economy a black upper-class fantasy and social myth. Nevertheless, Du Bois held fast to his position that the NAACP should continue to oppose legal segregation yet combine that opposition with vigorous support to improve segregated institutions as long as discrimination persisted. He was eventually forced from the editorship of *The Crisis*, but his resignation did not end the controversy. By the late 1930s the NAACP had developed, alongside its older activities, a much greater emphasis on economic policy and worked to develop stronger ties to the burgeoning labor movement.

CHALLENGING RACIAL DISCRIMINATION IN THE COURTS

A dramatic expansion of its legal campaign against racial discrimination enhanced the NAACP's effectiveness. Central to this project was the hiring of Charles Hamilton Houston, a Harvard-trained African-American lawyer and scholar, to lead it. Houston had been vice dean of Howard University Law School, which he had

transformed into a powerful institution for training black attorneys in the intricacies of civil rights law. At the NAACP, Houston laid out a plan for a legal program to challenge inequality in education and the exclusion of black people from voting in the South. Houston used lawsuits both to force state and local governments to live up to the Constitution and to inspire community organization. "This is no star performance," he said of his strategy. "My ideal of administration is to make the movement self-perpetuating. . . . Our idea should be to press upon the opposition and public that what we have is a real program, sweeping up . . . [from] popular demand."

Houston did not focus directly on eliminating segregation but rather sought to force southern states to equalize their facilities. Studies by the NAACP had revealed great disparities in per capita expenditures for white and black students, and huge differences in salaries paid to white and black teachers. In Georgia, for example, the average annual per pupil expenditure for white students was $36.29, compared with $4.59 for black students. White teachers' salaries averaged $97.88 per month, whereas black teachers received only $49.41. Houston was no supporter of segregation. He hoped to use litigation to secure judgments that would so increase the cost of separate institutions that states would be forced to abandon them.

To execute his agenda, Houston convinced Walter White to hire his former student at the Howard University Law School, Thurgood Marshall, in 1936. Marshall was born in Baltimore in 1908. His father was a dining-car waiter and club steward; his mother had been a teacher before her marriage. During the 1930s Marshall and Houston focused on bringing greater parity between black and white teachers, a project they hoped would increase NAACP membership among teachers, their students, and parents. The two men, working with a remarkable network of African-American attorneys, also attempted to end discrimination against black men and women in professional and graduate schools. Inequalities were obvious here because many southern states offered no graduate facilities of any kind to black students. Like other campaigns, this focus on graduate education was intended to establish precedents that might be used to gain equality in other areas and as an organizing tool

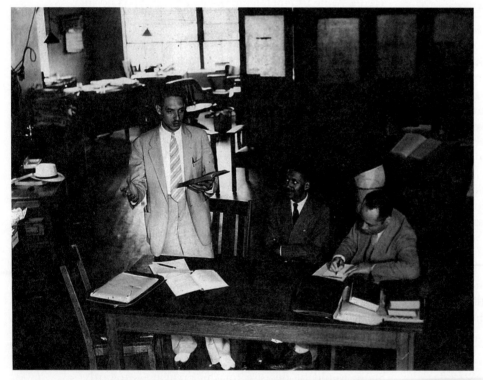

Thurgood Marshall (1908–1993). Charles Hamilton Houston (1895–1950), and Donald Gaines Murray. In 1935, attorneys Marshall and Houston handled Donald Murray's suit against the University of Maryland Law School. In 1938 Murray became the first African American to graduate from a southern state school. Thus began the relentless black attack against segregated education in America.   Courtesy Library of Congress for developing strong local NAACP branches. The first significant accomplishment in the NAACP's legal campaign against segregation in graduate and professional education was the U.S. Supreme Court's 1938 decision in *Gaines v. Canada*. The Supreme Court ordered the state of Missouri to provide black citizens an opportunity to study law in a state-supported institution. Failure to do so, the Court held, would violate the equal protection of the law clause of the Fourteenth Amendment to the U.S. Constitution. Although Lloyd Gaines, the prospective student for whom the case was brought, disappeared before the final resolution of this challenge, Missouri hastily established a law school for African Americans at the historically black Lincoln University. In the 1940s several southern states, including North Carolina, Texas, Oklahoma, and South Carolina, followed Missouri's lead and established law schools for their black citizens.

Thurgood Marshall and the NAACP were encouraged by the *Gaines* decision to persist in challenging the constitutionality of the "separate but equal" doctrine. The case of *Sipuel v. Board of Regents of the University of Oklahoma* (1947) was another such effort. In this case Ada Lois Sipuel sought admission to the law school of the University of Oklahoma at Norman. In accordance with state statutes she was refused admission but granted an out-of-state tuition award. Thurgood Marshall argued that this arrangement failed to meet the needs of the state's black citizens. The Supreme Court declared that Oklahoma was obliged under the equal protection clause of the Fourteenth Amendment to provide a legal education for Sipuel. The case established the principle that the state had to provide a separate law school for African-American students in their home states.

Heman Sweatt, a black mail carrier, tested this principle in a suit against the University of Texas Law School. In *Sweatt v. Painter* (1950), the U.S. Supreme Court again sided with the NAACP lawyers. In response to Sweatt's initial challenge, Texas had created a separate law school that had inadequate library facilities, faculty, and support staff. It was separate but hardly equal. Marshall and local Texas black lawyers argued that the legal education offered Sweatt at the black law school was so inferior it violated the equal protection clause of the Fourteenth Amendment. Marshall declared, "whether the University of Texas Law School is compared with the original or new law school for Negroes, we cannot find substantial equality in the educational opportunities offered white and Negro law students by the state. In terms of number of the faculty, variety of courses and opportunity for specialization, size of the student body, scope of the library, availability of law review and similar activities, the Uni-

versity of Texas Law School is superior." The victories registered in these early cases laid the legal foundation for the 1954 *Brown v. Topeka Board of Education* decision.

The fight against political disfranchisement also helped mobilize local and state communities and branches. Nowhere was this more apparent than in Texas. In 1923 the Texas legislature enacted the Terrell law, which expressly declared, "In no event shall a Negro be eligible to participate in a Democratic primary election . . . in . . . Texas." In the one-party South, the primary elections were more important than the general elections, which often merely rubber-stamped the choice made in the primary. Thus to be denied the right to vote in Democratic Party primary elections was to be disfranchised. The NAACP developed a case to test the constitutionality of the Terrell law and commenced a twenty-year battle through the courts. The Texas branches of the NAACP raised money and coordinated local involvement in the campaign to overthrow the Democratic white primary that disfranchised so many black Texans.

The Texas white primary fight was the most sustained and intense effort that any NAACP chapter undertook during the interwar period. It began in the 1920s and won its first victory when the Supreme Court ruled in 1927 in *Nixon v. Herndon* that the Texas Democratic primary was unconstitutional (see Chapter 17). At the national headquarters, Charles H. Houston and Thurgood Marshall orchestrated the assault. Their efforts were rewarded in subsequent decisions that further chipped away at the legal basis for the white primary. Finally, in 1944 the U.S. Supreme Court issued a ruling in *Smith v. Allwright* that ended the white primary altogether. It was the NAACP's greatest legal victory to that time. Many more would soon follow.

BLACK WOMEN AND COMMUNITY ORGANIZING

Black women made exceptional contributions to the NAACP during the 1930s through their successful fund-raising efforts and membership drives. Three agitators for racial justice were Daisy Adams Lampkin (c. 1884–1965), Juanita Mitchell (1913–1992), and Ella Baker (1903–1986). These women worked closely with White and the NAACP throughout the Depression and World War II. Lampkin, a native of Washington, D.C., in 1915 became the president of the Negro Women's Franchise League, a group dedicated to fighting for the vote. During World War I she directed Liberty Bond sales in the black community of Pennsylvania's Allegheny County and in Pittsburgh, selling some $2 million worth of government securities. In 1930 Walter White enlisted her as regional field secretary of the

The NAACP in the 1930s and 1940s depended on the formidable fund-raising talents of black women like Daisy Lampkin (shown here in a black Baptist church), Ella Baker, and Juanita Mitchell. These women played a major role in building NAACP membership.

NAACP, a post she held until she was made national field secretary in 1935. She continued raising funds for the NAACP and played leading roles within organized black womanhood.

Juanita E. Jackson was born in Hot Springs, Arkansas, and raised in Baltimore, Maryland. She earned a degree in education from the University of Pennsylvania in 1931, then returned to Baltimore, where she helped found the City-Wide Young People's Forum. This organization encouraged young people to discuss and plan attacks on such scourges as unemployment, segregation, and lynching. The success of the group, which she headed from 1931 to 1934, attracted Walter White's attention, and he subsequently offered her the leadership of the NAACP's new youth program. From 1935 to 1938 she served as NAACP national youth director. In 1938 Jackson married fellow civil rights activist Clarence Mitchell, had four sons, and directed the NAACP's voter registration campaigns. In 1950 she received a law degree from the University of Maryland. As the first black woman ad-mitted to practice law in Maryland, she embarked on a series of cases that helped destroy racial segregation on the state's public beaches and in its public schools.

Ella Baker, who became one of the most important women in the civil rights movement of the 1950s and 1960s, began her life's work during the Depression. Born in Norfolk, Virginia, Baker moved to New York City in 1927 and worked as a waitress and as an organizer involved in radical politics. She was also on the staff of two local newspapers, *The American West Indian News* and the *Negro National News*. Within two years after her arrival she had cofounded with George Schuyler the Young Negroes' Cooperative League in Harlem. The group practiced collective decision making and attempted to involve all segments of the community in the cooperatives. As she worked with the young men and women, Baker developed a strong belief in grassroots mobilization. Meanwhile, she also worked with women's and labor groups, such as the Harlem Housewives Cooperative, the Women's Day Workers and Industrial League, and the YWCA. In 1935 she served as publicity director of the Sponsoring Committee of the National Negro Congress. In 1936 she worked as a teacher with the WPA and eventually became an assistant project supervisor of the WPA. Walter White was impressed with her relentless organizing and management skills. After much persuasion Baker accepted, in 1941, White's offer to become an assistant field secretary of the NAACP. This position enabled her to travel across the country and throughout the South, making friendships that would serve her well in the coming decades. From 1943 to 1946 Baker worked as director of NAACP branches and measurably enhanced the membership of the organization. After resigning from the NAACP she joined the staff of the New York Urban League.

Other black women organized outside the NAACP. Black women in Detroit provide a potent illustration of this kind of activity. On June 10, 1930, fifty black women responded to a call issued by Fannie B. Peck, wife of Reverend William H. Peck, pastor of the two-thousand-member Bethel African Methodist Episcopal Church and the president of the Booker T. Washington Trade Association. Out of this initial meeting emerged the Detroit Housewives' League, an organization that combined economic nationalism and black women's self-determination to help black families and businesses survive the Depression. Peck had been inspired by M. A. L. Holsey, secretary of the National Negro Business League. Holsey described the directed spending campaigns that enabled housewives in Harlem to consolidate their economic power to persuade businesses to hire black women and children. Peck became convinced that such an organization would be equally as successful in Detroit. An admirer recalled that Peck effectively "focused the attention of women on the most essential, yet most unfamiliar factor in the building of homes, communities, and nations, namely, 'The Spending Power of Women.'"

The Detroit organization grew rapidly. By 1934 ten thousand black women belonged to it. According to Peck, the black woman had finally realized "that she has been traveling through a blind alley, making sacrifices to educate her children with no thought as to their obtaining employment after leaving school." The only requirement for membership was a pledge to support black businesses, buy black products, and patronize black professionals, thereby keeping money in the community. The league quickly spread to other cities. Housewives' leagues in Chicago, Baltimore, Washington, Durham (North Carolina), Harlem, and Cleveland used boycotts of merchants who refused to sell black products and employ black children as clerks or stock persons to secure an estimated 75,000 new jobs for black people.

AFRICAN AMERICANS AND THE NEW DEAL

In 1932, the third year of the Great Depression, voters elected New York governor Franklin Delano Roosevelt to the presidency with a total of nearly 23 million votes. Roosevelt's lopsided victory over Hoover, who received fewer than 16 million votes, demonstrated the country's loss of faith in the Republican Party and its economic philosophy and heralded the emergence of a new electoral coalition. The new president appealed to the Democratic Party's base of support in the white South, but to this group he added a coalition of western farmers, industrial workers, urban voters from the white ethnic groups in northern cities, and reform-minded intellectuals. For the time being, however, black Americans still clung to the Republican banner. In Chicago, for example, less than 25 percent of black voters cast their ballots for Roosevelt. But this was the last election in which the party of Lincoln could take them for granted. In his first term Roosevelt inaugurated a multitude of programs to counter the Depression—collectively known as the New Deal—that would shift the allegiance of African Americans. Initially his programs continued past patterns of discrimination against African Americans, but by 1935 the New Deal was providing more equal benefits and prompting profound social changes. The result was a new political order that ultimately undermined key portions of the edifice of American racism.

ROOSEVELT AND THE FIRST NEW DEAL, 1933–1935

During his first one hundred days in office, Franklin Roosevelt pressed through Congress a profusion of bold new economic initiatives that came to be known as the first New Deal. To combat the Depression, Roosevelt, unlike Hoover, followed no predetermined plan. Instead he favored experimentation—tempered by political expediency—over ideology as the guide to federal action. With little resistance Congress passed the president's sprawling and complex laws aimed at overhauling the nation's financial, agricultural, and industrial systems. Most hoped, vainly as it turned out, that these changes would eventually bring a return to prosperity. In the meantime Roosevelt moved forcefully to counter the immediate suffering of the unemployed with a massive emergency federal relief effort. Many of the first New Deal's programs benefited both white and black people, but the strength of white southerners in the Democratic Party and the nearly complete lack of African-American political power in the South caused much of this early program to be unfairly administered.

The Agricultural Adjustment Act (AAA), designed to protect farmers by giving them subsidies to limit production and thereby stabilize prices, illustrates the key benefits and problems African Americans experienced during the first New Deal. The theory underlying the AAA was that creating scarcity would increase agricultural prices. So farmers would be paid to grow less. The program provided for sharecroppers and tenant farmers to get part of the subsidies and allowed new rural relief agencies to dispense supplementary income to off-season wageworkers.

This program helped many African Americans, mainly because it pumped billions of dollars into an economic sector on which over 4.5 million black people relied for their livelihood. Also, the AAA was designed to remedy the problems of those farmers—disproportionately African American—who were overreliant on such cash crops as cotton. By 1929 three out of four black farmers, compared with two out of five white farmers, received at least 40 percent of their gross income from cotton. The flow of money from the AAA did, for a time, slow the exodus of black people from farming. Fewer left the farms in the first two years of the program than in the two years before it began. Indeed, from a broader perspective, the New Deal appears to have slowed the rate at which black people left the land. During the 1930s only 4.5 percent of African Americans abandoned farming, compared with 8.6 percent who did so during the 1920s.

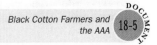

Black Cotton Farmers and the AAA 18-5

But if the AAA brought real benefits to black farmers, it was often, contrary to protections written into the law, administered unfairly and corruptly. Local control of the AAA resided in the hands of the Extension Service and County Agricultural Conservation Committees, which were supposed to represent all farmers. The county agents, however, were often the planters themselves, and the committees mirrored southern politics as a whole by excluding black people. African Americans were further disadvantaged by the system of unilateral bookkeeping and oppressive credit relations between landlords and tenants. During the first two years of the AAA, black farmers complained bitterly that white landlords simply grabbed and pocketed the millions of dollars of benefit checks they were supposed to forward to tenants. To compound the injury, some planters then evicted the sharecroppers and tenants from the land.

The experience of African Americans with the National Industrial Recovery Act (NIRA) mimicked the problems with the AAA. The NIRA was intended to promote the revival of manufacturing by allowing various industries to cooperate in establishing codes of conduct to govern prices, wage levels, and employment practices, all of which were to be overseen by a National Recovery Administration (NRA). The NRA oversaw the drafting of the codes but faced tremendous resistance from employers and unions in eliminating racial disparities in wage rates and working conditions. Even when African-American advocates did win wage increases for occupations in which black people predominated, the result was often a shift to white labor. These policies prompted some African-American newspapers and protest organizations to claim that "NRA" really stood for the "Negro Removal Agency" or "Negroes Robbed Again." To the relief of many African-American advocates and workers, the U.S. Supreme Court declared the NIRA unconstitutional in spring 1935.

The New Deal's national welfare programs included the Federal Emergency Relief Administration (FERA), the Civilian Conservation Corps (CCC), Public Works Administration (PWA), and Civil Works Administration (CWA). Although inadequate and unfairly administered on local levels, these programs were often the only thing standing between black people and starvation. FERA provided funds for local and state relief operations to restart and expand their programs. The program pulled millions of people back from the brink of starvation. Because African Americans suffered greater economic devastation, they received benefits at a higher rate than whites. In most cities north and south, 25 to 40 percent of African Americans were on relief rolls that FERA funded wholly or in part. Direct welfare, however, was deemed by many in the Roosevelt administration to be debilitating, so it emphasized hiring the unemployed for public works projects. The CWA was a temporary agency created to help people through the winter of 1933–1934. The Civilian Conservation Corps (CCC) built segregated camps to employ young men and to take them away from the poverty and hopelessness of urban areas.

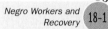

Negro Workers and Recovery 18-1 DOCUMENT

Dayton Jones of the FERA in California devised an ingenious plan that negated the CCC's regulations prohibiting segregation. In a June 26, 1935, letter, Jones shared his proposal for effective internal segregation within the camps with W. Frank Persons, the CCC's director of selections:

> It is a known fact that colored boys make efficient kitchen and dining-room aides, and in addition the vast majority of colored youths enjoy this type of work. By being assigned to work as cooks' helpers, kitchen police and in the preparation of raw vegetables for the men such as peeling and slicing potatoes, a good proportion of the colored members in most camps could be absorbed in this manner. Segregation of the colored boys in the mess halls is prevalent in a number of camps by virtue of actual necessity to prevent racial difficulties. Under my plan this segregation would automatically be accomplished because of the fact that kitchen help must necessarily eat at a time when other than the rest of the enrollees take their meals. By assigning these colored boys to this particular type of work the segregation could be accomplished with no one realizing that segregation was being effected.
> (Quoted in Olen Cole Jr., *The African-American Experience in the Civilian Conservation Corps* [Gainesville: University Press of Florida, 1999], p. 20)

Despite protests from the NAACP, the California camps, at least, instituted segregation. Effective August 9, 1935, all CCC districts in California transferred their African-American enrollees into "five colored companies." Yet despite the segregation, former enrollees conceded that their experience in the CCC helped them secure better jobs and a middle-class life after World War II. By the time the CCC was abolished in 1945, more than 200,000 African-American youth had taken part in the program.

These relief programs included substantial numbers of African Americans and helped many through the worst parts of the Depression. But the programs also tended to be less helpful to black people than they were to whites. In its early days, the CCC, for example, was a tightly segregated institution, with only about 5 percent of its slots going to black youths during its first year. Likewise, although FERA tended to be administered fairly in northern cities, in the South it reached few of those in need.

BLACK OFFICIALS IN THE NEW DEAL

The first New Deal was not completely bleak for African Americans. In addition to the benefits, however grudgingly disbursed, that they derived from New Deal relief programs, African Americans also gained new influence and allies within the Roosevelt administraton. Their experience reflected both the growing availability of highly trained African Americans for government service and the emerging consciousness among white liberals about the problems—and potential electoral power—of black people.

Black people found a staunch ally in First Lady Eleanor Roosevelt. She was revered for her relentless commitment to racial justice. She arranged meetings at the White House for some black leaders. She cajoled her husband to consider legislation on behalf of black rights. She personally defied Jim Crow laws by refusing to sit in a "white only" section while attending a meeting in the South. Moreover, she wrote newspaper columns calling for "fair play and equal opportunity for Negro citizens." Roosevelt further endeared herself to black Americans when she resigned her membership in the Daughters of the American Revolution after that organization refused to allow a young black opera singer, Marian Anderson, to perform at its Constitution Hall in Washington in 1939. (Administration officials subsequently arranged for Anderson to perform in front of the Lincoln Memorial on Easter Sunday before a crowd of 75,000. The first song she sang was "My Country, 'Tis of Thee.")

Eleanor Roosevelt was joined by other liberals to press the cause of racial justice and to seek the appointment of African Americans throughout the government. Early in 1933 President Roosevelt acceded to their request that he appoint someone in his administration to assume responsibility for ensuring that African Americans received fair treatment. He asked Harold Ickes, a former president of the Chicago chapter of the NAACP, and a white man whom most black Americans recognized as a tried and true friend, to make this happen. Ickes invited Clark Foreman, a young white Georgian who had rejected his region's racism, to handle the assignment. Foreman recognized the irony of a white man representing black people in the government and immediately began to recruit highly trained African Americans. Similar efforts to bring African Americans into government positions were made by Eleanor Roosevelt, Ickes, and other administration officials such as Daniel

Roosevelt's "black cabinet" in a 1938 photograph. Mary McLeod Bethune is in the center of the front row. The advisers included Robert Weaver, Eugene Kinckle Jones, Ambrose Caliver, and William H. Hastie, among many others.

Roper, secretary of commerce, and Harry Hopkins, FDR's relief administrator. The result was that doors to the government began opening in an unprecedented way. For the first time, the government employed professional black architects, lawyers, engineers, economists, statisticians, interviewers, office managers, social workers, and librarians. The Department of Commerce hired Eugene K. Jones, on leave from the National Urban League. The National Youth Administration brought in Mary McLeod Bethune, and the Department of Interior employed William H. Hastie and Robert Weaver. Ira De A.

Reid joined the Social Security Administration, and Lawrence W. Oxley worked for the Department of Labor, with Ambrose Caliver serving in the Office of Education.

A core of highly placed African Americans became linked in a network called the Federal Council on Negro Affairs, more loosely known as **Roosevelt's "black cabinet."** Mary McLeod Bethune was a leader of this body, which consisted primarily of "New Deal race specialists." It numbered twenty-seven men and three women working mostly in temporary emergency agencies such as the Works Progress Administration (WPA)

PROFILE ～ ROBERT C. WEAVER

Robert C. Weaver (1907–1997) was born in Washington, D.C. His parents and his teachers at the elite Dunbar High School (which boasted a host of distinguished black alumni, including Charles Houston and William Hastie) instilled in him pride in being a black American. After Dunbar, Weaver went to Harvard, where he earned his undergraduate degree in 1925 and a Ph.D. in economics in 1933, despite the open hostility of professors who doubted that black people were capable of doing serious intellectual work. Such racist thinking only hardened Weaver's resolve to succeed.

Armed with impressive credentials, but bleak job prospects, Weaver returned to Washington, where—together with his Harvard classmate John P. Davis—he founded the Negro Industrial League (NIL) and the Joint Committee on Economic Recovery (JCER) to advocate on behalf of black workers. They attracted sponsorships from twenty-four black and white organizations, including the National Baptist Convention, the AME church, the NAACP, the United Mine Workers, the Elks, the Catholic Interracial Council, and the Young Women's Christian Association. Within months Weaver was able to claim that the NIL and the JCER represented over one million black people.

This broad-based coalition demanded that the Roosevelt administration appoint black advisers or "experts" to key New Deal agencies. In 1935, Weaver succeeded a white southerner as the adviser on Negro affairs in the Department of the Interior and together with Mary McLeod Bethune became co-leader of the "black cabinet," an informal collective of African Americans who served in the Roosevelt administration's second New Deal.

Weaver remained in government service until 1944, as director of the Office of Race Relations at the United States Housing Authority; he established guidelines that ensured that black workers would be employed on all government-funded housing projects.

Under President John F. Kennedy, Weaver rejoined the government in 1961. As a key figure in the administration, he persuaded Kennedy to issue an executive order banning racial discrimination in federal housing programs. In 1966, under Kennedy's successor, Lyndon B. Johnson, Weaver became Secretary of Housing and Urban Development, the nation's first African-American cabinet secretary. He spearheaded the passage of the Housing Act of 1968, which expanded opportunities for black home ownership. Weaver died in New York City in 1997.

1. What characteristics or combination of factors contributed to Weaver's success as an administrator?

2. Why was the "black cabinet" important during the New Deal?

Weaver

and included such stalwarts as housing administrator Robert Weaver. This group met every Friday in Bethune's Washington home; a smaller and younger group met occasionally in Robert Weaver's apartment. This cadre of advisers pressured the president and the heads of federal agencies to adopt and support color-blind policies and lobbied to advance the status of black Americans.

BLACK SOCIAL SCIENTISTS AND THE NEW DEAL

Many black intellectuals, scholars, and writers believed the social sciences could be used to adjudicate race relations in the country, and during the New Deal they found greater receptiveness to their work than ever before. Nearly two hundred African Americans received Ph.D.s during the 1930s, more than four times the combined total from the first three decades of the century. Several of these young scholars reached the top ranks of the social sciences, studying the economic, political, and sociological problems of black people with a depth of experience and theoretical sophistication lacking in earlier generations of scholars. In sociology E. Franklin Frazier and Charles S. Johnson took the lead. Frazier's pioneering studies of black families, although now dated, placed him at the forefront of debates on social policy. As the editor of *Opportunity*, the journal of the Urban League, throughout the 1930s, Johnson published insightful critiques of American racial practices and policies, as well as the work of emerging black novelists, poets, and playwrights. Meanwhile Ralph Bunche became well known within the field of political science, and Abram Harris and Robert Weaver gained renown in economics.

Historians such as Carter G. Woodson, Lorenzo Greene, Benjamin Quarles, and John Hope Franklin advanced the idea that black people had been active agents in the past and not simply the passive objects of white people's actions. Through the Association for the Study of Negro Life and History as well as Negro History Week, Woodson and his coworkers Greene, Alrutheus Taylor, and Monroe Work deployed their scholarship to dismiss claims of black inferiority. Their scholarly emphasis on racial pride, achievement, and autonomy helped raise black morale.

The increasing importance of black scholars became apparent late in the 1930s when the Carnegie Corporation, a philanthropic foundation, sponsored a major study of black life. Although the study was led by Gunnar Myrdal, a Swedish social scientist, nearly half the large staff of scholars were African Americans, and several, particularly Bunche, had a major impact on the work. Published in 1944 as *An American Dilemma,*

this massive study profoundly affected public understanding of how racism undermined the progress of African Americans, and it helped set the agenda for the civil rights movement.

AFRICAN AMERICANS AND THE SECOND NEW DEAL

By late 1935, after two years marked by a slow recovery, much of the first New Deal lay in shambles. The U.S. Supreme Court had invalidated major parts of it, and a conservative backlash was emerging against the Roosevelt administration. In response Roosevelt pressed for a second burst of legislation marked by the passage of the Social Security Act (SSA), the National Labor Relations Act (NLRA), the creation of the Works Progress Administration (WPA), and other measures considerably more radical than those that had come in 1933. The NLRA, for example, helped unions get established and grow. The SSA provided the rudiments of a social welfare system as well as unemployment and

One of the most effective New Deal agencies, the Works Projects Administrations offered African Americans numerous opportunities for vocational training. Young men learned from experienced craftsmen. As this 1942 photo illustrates, the intricate lathe operations instruction prepared the trainee with skills that could be used in the defense industries. Courtesy Library of Congress

A BLACK SHARECROPPER DETAILS ABUSE IN THE ADMINISTRATION OF AGRICULTURAL RELIEF

This is one of many letters black sharecroppers sent to the NAACP in search of assistance to halt the mass evictions and abuse of New Deal relief efforts.

ALABAMA
June 21, 1934

Dear Sir:—

I am writing you these few lines ask you if it is any possible chance of you fining out just why F.E.R.A. office here in . . . refuse to gave me work when I have six in family to care for and also my wife's mother who is over 65 years old and been under the Doctor care for the past seven years of course my wife has a little job but its not with the relief work which some weeks she makes five dollars and some weeks less with four children to take care off which range in age 8–6–4–3 years old and we have $5 per month rent and also $1.74 per week Insurance which that don't enclude Food and Clothing and Fuel to burn. Now Mr. White in the past two and half months I am being going to the relief office trying to get on the relief work and it seem like it is empossible and also just before the first of April I went up to the relief office and explain my case to Mr . . . , the man that gave out the work cards and he gave me a food order for the amount of $2—two dollars and also I got some work to do. But as soon as I got paid for the 24 hours work he came to me to collect $2 for the food order that he gave me and I refuse to gave him $2 and I havent been able to get any more work to do and I have been going up to the office each day sence. But they tell me at the office that they cant gave me work because my wife is working. Of course if that maybe the case I can gave you the name and the address of at least a hundred families where there is two and three in one family who are working on the relief project and I know of at least twenty single men with no one but theirself to take care of and are working twenty-four hours every week and they got to gave their foreman one dollar each every week if they want to stay on the job.

Now Mr. White the white man who my wife work for and my wife told him that they refuse to gave me work because she was working for me and he went up to relief office to see about it But they told him that they didnt cut me out of work because my wife were working but they cut me off because I were unable to do the work. and of course I know that to be very much untrue. The

retirement insurance. This new set of laws, known as the second New Deal, survived legal challenges and changed the United States, particularly by strengthening the role of the federal government.

Roosevelt's leftward political shift helped him win the 1936 presidential election in a landslide. This election cemented a new electoral coalition that yoked the southern wing of the Democratic Party with more liberal farmers and working-class voters who were labor union members in the North and West. The Democratic Party began to win the votes of the large African-American populations in the great cities of the North. The Great Migration had effectively relocated tens of thousands of prospective black voters in northern urban centers, traditional strongholds of Democratic

trouble is I refuse to be a fool like so many of my race here and else where around here to pay for a food order that is supose to be giving to the needy free of charge but lots are paying for them and also paying for their job. Of course Mr. White I am colored and when you go up to the relief office The Colored people is treated just as if they were dogs and not human beings. I have been up in the office and I have seen with my own eyes my color kicked and beaten down a whole flight of stairs. I have seen everything done except been murder. Understand Mr. White the little job that my wife has isn't on the relief is a private and everybody that is head of any thing here in the relief office is kin to one another. Now Mr. White the lady that is head of the relief is Mrs. . . .which I saw here once since I was cut off from work and I explained my case to her and she told that she would send a investigator around to my home the next morning whose name is Miss.el;and she told me that when I gave Mr. . . .the $2 for the food order she would O.K. my work card. Mr. White if possible will you please fine out for me just what is the reason they refuse to gave me work when I have six in family and rent to pay. Insurance, Doctor bill, milk bill, buy food and clothing and with only my wife at work it is impossible Mr. White.

🌲 *What conditions led the writer to seek help from Walter White and the NAACP?*

🌲 *What were some of the reasons, both implied and noted, that prevented even more black people from protesting economic inequality?*

Source: Herbert Aptheker, ed., *A Documentary History of the Negro People in the United States, 1933–1945* (New York: Citadel Press Books, 1990), pp 58–60.

PROFILE ❧ MARY MCLEOD BETHUNE

Mary McLeod Bethune played a powerful role in Roosevelt's black cabinet, but this was only one of the many forums in which she exercised consummate leadership and diplomatic skill. Bethune's life and work are major links connecting the social reform efforts of post-Reconstruction black women to the civil rights protest activities of the generation emerging after World War II. All the various strands of black women's struggle for education, political rights, racial pride, and sexual autonomy are united in Bethune's writings, speeches, and organizational work.

Bethune, born on July 10, 1875, near Mayesville, South Carolina, graduated from Scotia Seminary in 1894 and entered Dwight Moody's Institute for Home and Foreign Missions in Chicago. After teaching in mission schools, she settled in Daytona, Florida, where she founded the Daytona Educational and Industrial Institute for Training Negro Girls. Reflecting on her work years later, Bethune recalled, "The school expanded fast. In less than two years I had two hundred fifty pupils. . . . I concentrated more and more on girls, as I felt that they especially were hampered by lack of educational opportunities." Eventually, however, she agreed to merge with Cookman Institute, an educational facility for black boys under the auspices of the Methodist Church. Thus, in 1923 the now coeducational institution was renamed Bethune-Cookman College.

During the 1920s Bethune became the leader of the National Association of Colored Women, a federation of women's clubs. As the NACW's president she attempted to turn the organization away from its previous focus on self-help and moral uplift and toward broader goals. Although she made progress, by 1935 she had become frustrated by the NACW's caution and founded the National Council of Negro Women (NCNW), an "organization of organizations." The women present at the creation of the NCNW were the who's who of black women's activism. They included educators Charlotte Hawkins Brown and Mary Church Terrell; executive director of the National Association of Colored Graduate Nurses Mabel K. Staupers; NAACP national field director Daisy Lampkin; and Addie W. Hunton, former president of the Empire State Federation of Women's Clubs and of

the International Council of Women of the Darker Race. Eventually, the NCNW included twenty national affiliates and ninety local councils located in cities, towns, and rural communities across the country. Club engagement strengthened their resolve to struggle for black rights and provided safe space for them to develop the skills and networks that proved critical in the post–World War II civil rights movement.

With the New Deal Bethune became a Democratic Party activist and a government official. She had a close personal relationship with First Lady Eleanor Roosevelt that gave her access to the president that few others enjoyed. She and Eleanor Roosevelt had persuaded the president that the National Youth Administration (NYA) needed a Negro division to assure that benefits would be distributed fairly. When the organization started, Bethune was named the NYA's Director of Negro Affairs. She was the first African-American woman to hold a high position in the government. Bethune supported the administration during the 1936 campaign by helping to convince African Americans that their best interests lay with the Democratic rather than Republican Party.

One of Bethune's many noteworthy accomplishments was the 1937 conference held by the Department of Labor on the Problems of the Negro and Negro Youth, at which Eleanor Roosevelt delivered a key speech. During the session entitled "Security of Life and Equal Protection under the Law" the conference called for a federal antilynching law, equal access to the ballot in federal elections, and elimination of segregation and discrimination on interstate carriers. This was a virtual blueprint of the agenda of the civil rights movement. No other general meeting on civil rights during the Roosevelt administration generated the interest, support, and publicity of this 1937 conference. With this Negro Youth conference, Bethune assumed the middle ground of black politics.

Bethune

Party machines, such as in Chicago. Institutionalized housing segregation combined with the often conscious choice to live in their own neighborhoods concentrated the black electorate and increased its political power. This power had already appeared in the 1928 election of Republican Oscar De Priest to the U.S. House of Representatives, the first African-American congressman from the North. In 1934, reflecting a shift in partisan allegiance, Chicago's black voters elected Democrat Arthur W. Mitchell to Congress to replace De Priest. Mitchell, a registered Republican at the outset of the Great Depression, switched to the Democratic Party and thus became the first black Democrat ever to win a seat in the House of Representatives.

Mitchell's election was only the beginning of the change in black people's political party identification. The powerful black press fanned the shifting winds and many more black urban dwellers developed an intense interest in politics. They began to connect political power with the prospect of improving their economic conditions. By the end of the decade, black urban voters garnered noteworthy influence in key states such as Illinois, Ohio, Pennsylvania, and New York. This political consciousness led to the election of black state legislators in California, Illinois, Indiana, Kansas, Kentucky, New Jersey, New York, Ohio, Pennsylvania, and West Virginia.

In another indication of change, some Democrats began supporting antilynching legislation. Congressman Mitchell gave a strong speech printed in the *Congressional Record* in 1935 supporting President Roosevelt as an antilynching advocate. "No President," he declared, "has been more outspoken against the horrible crime of lynching than has Mr. Roosevelt. In speaking of lynching some time ago he characterized it as 'collective murder' and spoke of it as a crime which blackens the record of America." Mitchell told black audiences, "Let me say again, the attitude of the administration at the White House is absolutely fair and without prejudice, insofar as the Negro citizenry is concerned."

So the 1936 election results revealed that Roosevelt had captured the allegiance of most African-Americans. Robert Vann, editor of the Pittsburgh *Courier,* had urged black people, after casting their ballots, to go home to "turn Lincoln's picture to the wall." There are many complex reasons for this revolutionary transformation in black political allegiance. The shift to the Democratic Party did not occur without anxiety. At least some black people feared that by joining the party they would open the door for even more white southern Democrats to assume national political power and thwart black advancement. But by 1936 most African-American voters were willing to take the risk.

The increased participation of African Americans in the Democratic Party sent chills down the spines of the white southern elite. The tension between black Democrats and white conservative Democrats erupted at the party's 1936 convention in Philadelphia. The seating of thirty-two black Democratic Party delegates provoked the wrath of southern politicians. The selection of a black Baptist minister to open one session with a prayer especially outraged South Carolina senator Ellison D. "Cotton Ed" Smith, who, accompanied by Mayor Burnet Maybank of Charleston, South Carolina, and one or two other delegates, marched ostentatiously off the floor, proclaiming that they refused to support "any political organization that looks upon the Negro and caters to him as a political and social equal." Smith declared he was "sick of the whole damn thing." Undaunted, the black minister simply observed that "Brother Smith needs more prayer." The next day when Congressman Mitchell of Illinois took to the floor, Ed Smith repeated his walkout. The South Carolina delegation subsequently adopted a protest resolution denouncing the appearance of black men on the convention's program. The protests of southern white politicians, however, had no effect on the political decisions of black men and women. Heeding the advice of the NAACP, they voted their personal interests.

Despite the rise of black people in the Democratic Party, southern congressmen succeeded in excluding many African Americans from key government programs. For example, they insisted on denying the benefits of the National Labor Relations Act and Social Security Act to agricultural laborers and domestic servants. These white southerners could not, however, stop the tilt toward fairer administration of programs or the revival of the push for equal rights, which had lain all but dormant since the end of the Reconstruction era.

An examination of the Works Progress Administration (WPA) illustrates the changes that the second New Deal and the increasing shift of African Americans to the Democratic Party wrought. The WPA, with Harry Hopkins (1890–1946) as its head, was created to employ the unemployed. Under Hopkins's direction, and sustained with $1.39 billion in federal funds, the WPA put thousands of men and women to work building new roads, hospitals, city halls, courthouses, and schools. Under the aegis of the WPA, American citizens built bridges, ports, and local water-supply systems. Larger-scale projects included the Lincoln Tunnel under the Hudson River connecting New York and New Jersey, the Triborough Bridge system linking Manhattan to Long Island, and the Bonneville and

Boulder Dams. (Boulder Dam was later renamed the Hoover Dam by a Republican-controlled Congress in 1946.)

The WPA was administered far more fairly than were the first New Deal programs. The national government explicitly rejected racial discrimination and worked to make sure local officials complied. Although far from perfect, by 1939 it provided assistance to one million black families on a far more equitable basis than ever before.

The same pattern prevailed in the WPA's four arts programs—the Federal Art Project, the Federal Music Project, the Federal Theater Project, and the Federal Writers Project—which employed thousands of musicians, intellectuals, writers, and artists. A fifth program, the Historical Records Survey, created in 1937, sent teams of writers, including Zora Neale Hurston, to collect folklore and study various ethnic groups. One team collected the life histories and reminiscences of some two thousand former slaves.

Between 1935 and 1943, the WPA helped artists display their talents and made their work widely available. Among the black artists hired to adorn government buildings, post offices, and public parks were Aaron Douglas, Charles Alston, Richmond Barthe, Sargent Johnson, Archibald Motley Jr., and Augusta Savage. Savage was a sculptor who worked in clay, marble, and bronze; she established arts schools in the 1930s— the Savage School of Arts and Crafts, Savage Studios, and the Uptown Art Laboratory. She became the first director of the Harlem Community Art Center in 1937. Her students included Jacob Lawrence, William Artis, Norman Lewis, and Elton Fax.

The Federal Theater Project established sixteen black theater units. Among their most notable productions was a version of *Macbeth* set in Haiti with an all-black cast. White actor John Houseman and black actress Rose McClendon directed the Harlem Federal Theater Project. This project—more than the others— proved controversial due to the fear of communist influence and the leftist political views of some African-American writers and performers.

Organized Labor and Black America

The relationship of African Americans to labor unions changed profoundly during the 1930s. Before this time most local unions affiliated with the national American Federation of Labor barred black people or restricted them to segregated locals. The railroad

unions, which called themselves "brotherhoods," excluded black workers entirely. The New Deal, especially after 1935, did much to transform the labor movement. The National Labor Relations Act and the militancy of workers provided the opportunity to organize the nation's great mass production industries. Still, leaders of the AFL dragged their feet, unwilling to incorporate into their unions the masses of unskilled workers, many of whom were African American or recent European immigrants. Frustrated by this situation, in 1935 John L. Lewis (1880–1969), head of the United Mine Workers, and his followers formed the Committee for Industrial Organization (CIO) to take on the task.

National Labor Relations Act **18-2** DOCUMENT

Unlike the AFL, the CIO was committed to interracial and multiethnic organizing and so enabled more African Americans to participate in the labor movement. Its leaders knew it was in organized labor's best interest to admit black men and women to membership. As one black union organizer said, "We colored folks can't organize without you and you white folks can't organize without us." But it took a massive change in outlook to achieve this unity. By 1940 the CIO had enlisted approximately 210,000 black members. Unions that valued and sustained interracial cooperation included the International Mine, Mill, and Smelter Workers; the Food, Tobacco, and Agricultural Workers Union; and the United Farm Equipment and Metal Workers.

A. Philip Randolph's Brotherhood of Sleeping Car Porters (BSCP) remained with the AFL, but it also benefited from New Deal legislation. In 1934 Congress had amended the Railway Labor Act in a way that helped the BSCP overcome the opposition of the Pullman Company. The law required that corporations bargain in good faith with unions if the unions could demonstrate through elections monitored by the National Mediation Board that they genuinely represented the corporations' employees. The Pullman Company resisted, but in 1937, long after an election certified the BSCP as the workers' representative, the company finally recognized the brotherhood. Then—and only then—did the AFL grant the BSCP full membership as an international union. After more than twelve years, A. Philip Randolph and thousands of black men won their struggles against a giant corporation and a powerful labor organization. These were no small victories.

Although most black people in unions were men, some unions also represented and helped improve the lives of black working women. For example, there had been a rigid hierarchy among workers in the tobacco

A. PHILIP RANDOLPH
INSPIRES A YOUNG
BLACK ACTIVIST

In 1928 young E. D. Nixon heard A. Philip Randolph speak, and it changed Nixon's life. He became president of the Montgomery branch of the Brotherhood of Sleeping Car Porters that year and remained in the post until 1964. During that period he played a leading role in mobilizing and organizing the Montgomery Bus Boycott ignited by Rosa Parks's arrest for refusing to relinquish her seat to a white male passenger. He recalls Randolph's speech in the following passage.

When I heard Randolph speak [in 1928], it was like a light. Most eloquent man I ever heard. He done more to bring me in the fight for civil rights than anybody. Before that time, I figure that a Negro would be kicked around and accept whatever the white man did. I never knew the Negro had a right to enjoy freedom like everyone else. When Randolph stood there and talked that day, it make a different man out of me. From that day on, I was determined that I was gonna fight for freedom until I was able to get some of it for myself.

Source (Quoted in Studs Turkel, *Hard Times*, pp. 119). New York; The New Press, pbk ed. 2000), 119. pub. 1970. (Orig.)

industry since the early nineteenth century, one of the few areas of the economy outside agriculture or domestic service that employed many black women. Jobs were assigned on the basis of race and gender, with black women receiving the most difficult and tedious job, that of "stemmer." In 1939 stemmer Louise "Mama" Harris instigated a series of walkouts at the I. N. Vaughn Company in Richmond. The strikes, which were supported by CIO affiliates, including the white women of the International Ladies Garment Workers Union, led to the formation of the Tobacco Workers Organizing Committee, another CIO affiliate. In 1943 black women union leaders and activists, including Theodosia Simpson and Miranda Smith, were involved in a strike against the R. J. Reynolds tobacco company to force it to the negotiating table. Smith later became southern regional director of the Food, Tobacco, Agricultural, and Allied Workers of America. It was the highest position held by a black woman in the labor movement up to that time.

The Communist Party and African Americans

Throughout the 1930s the Communist Party intensified its support of African Americans' efforts to address unemployment and job discrimination and to seek social justice. Some African Americans were attracted to the party because of its militant antiracism and its determination to be interracial. The party expelled members who exhibited racial prejudice and gave black men key leadership positions. James Ford, an African American, ran as the party's vice-presidential candidate in the election of 1932. Although few black men and women actually joined the Communist Party, some became increasingly sympathetic to left-wing ideas and prescriptions as the Depression wore on.

Many black workers were drawn to the Communist Party because it criticized the refusal of organized white labor to include them. The communists maintained that "the low standard of living of Negro workers is made use of by the capitalists to reduce the wages of the white workers." They chided "the mis-leaders of labor, the heads of the reformist and reactionary trade union organizations" for refusing to organize black workers. They insisted "this anti-Negro attitude of the reactionary labor leaders helps to split the ranks of labor, allows the employers to carry out their policy of 'divide and rule,' frustrates the efforts of the working class to emancipate itself from the yoke of capitalism, and dims the class-consciousness of the white workers as well as of the Negro workers." Indeed, much of the push for racial equality within the CIO emanated from those connected with the party.

THE INTERNATIONAL LABOR DEFENSE AND THE "SCOTTSBORO BOYS"

The *Scottsboro* case brought the Communist Party to the attention of many African Americans. The case began when nine black youths who had caught a ride on a freight train in Alabama were tried, convicted, and sentenced to death for allegedly raping two white women. Their ordeal began on the night of March 25, 1931, when they were accosted by a group of young white hobos. A fight broke out. The black youths threw the white youths off the train. The losers filed a complaint with the Scottsboro, Alabama, sheriff, charging that black hoodlums had viciously assaulted them. The sheriff ordered his deputies to round up every black person on the train. The sweep netted the nine young black men: Ozie Powell, Clarence Norris, Charlie Weems, Olen Montgomery,

PROFILE ✦ ANGELO HERNDON

In the South, the Communist Party gravitated toward those areas where black and white laborers were grossly exploited. The party's efforts in Georgia, Alabama, and Mississippi produced black organizers such as Hosea Hudson, Nate Shaw, and Angelo Herndon, who by virtue of their activism became targets of white supremacists.

In 1932, young organizer Angelo Herndon was arrested, tried, and convicted in Atlanta for inciting insurrection. One of thirteen children, Herndon was born May 6, 1913, in Ohio. Seeking better opportunities, Herndon, at age thirteen, escaped the poverty of his home region to work in the coal mines in Alabama. At eighteen he was already a seasoned miner but deeply disillusioned and angry at the exploitation of coal miners. He attended a meeting called by the Communist Party and was impressed by its commitment to equality, both racial and social. He joined the party and poured enormous energy into organizing and recruiting members from among the mine workers and the unemployed. In 1934, Angelo Herndon explained why he joined the party:

> All my life I'd been sweated and stepped on and Jim-Crowed. I lay on my belly in the mines for a few dollars a week, and saw my pay stolen and slashed, and my buddies killed. I lived in the worst section of town, and rode behind the "Colored" signs of streetcars, as though there was something disgusting about me? I heard myself called "nigger" and "darky" and I had to say "Yes, sir" to every white man. . . . I had always detested it, but I had never known that anything could be done about it. And here, all of a sudden, I had found organizations . . . that weren't scared to come out for equality for the Negro people, and for the rights of workers. The Jim-Crow system, the wage-slave system, weren't everlasting after all! It was like all of a sudden turning a corner on a dirty, old street and finding yourself facing a broad, shining highway. . . . I felt then, and I know now, that the Communist program is the only program that the Southern workers—whites and Negroes both—can possibly accept in the long run. It's the only program that does justice to the southern worker's ideas that everybody ought to have an equal chance, and that every man has rights that must be respected.

The party sent Herndon to Atlanta, Georgia, where he organized an interracial relief group and staged peaceful demonstrations against hunger. This was to prove his undoing. One week later, while picking up his mail at the post office, he was arrested on the charge that he had violated an old ordinance forbidding black and white people from mingling together. Herndon's trial and conviction made him the best-known African-American communist in the nation. The case underscored the fear that white southerners had concerning the specter of social equality across racial lines. The Communist Party assigned a young black attorney, Benjamin Davis Jr. of Atlanta, to represent Herndon. Davis challenged the constitutionality of the ordinance as well as Atlanta's jury system, which excluded African Americans from service. Davis's defense was unsuccessful and the judge sentenced Herndon to twenty years on a chain gang. The severity of the sentence and the judge's racist sentiments sparked a nationwide movement to free Herndon as black organizations, labor unions, and religious groups joined with the Communist Party to fight for Herndon's immediate release. After four years of appeals, in 1937 the United States Supreme Court, in a 5-to-4 decision, declared Georgia's slave insurrection law unconstitutional and ordered the state to let him go.

Herndon

The "Scottsboro Boys," a case of southern justice gone awry, attracted international attention and fueled competition between the NAACP and the Communist Party. In this 1937 photograph the NAACP's Juanita E. Jackson Mitchell visits with the Scottsboro Boys. Nine unemployed black young men accused of raping two white women mill workers on a Southern Railroad freight car on March 25, 1931, were sentenced to death, with one exception. Eugene Williams's life was spared because he was only thirteen. Victoria Price and Ruby Bates recanted their stories, but it made no difference. The United States Supreme Court overturned the death convictions and sentences in two landmark cases, one of which established the right of the accused to competent legal counsel.

Willie Robertson, Haywood Patterson, Eugene Williams, Andy Wright, and Roy Wright. The police also discovered two young white women: nineteen-year-old Victoria Price and seventeen-year-old Ruby Bates.

Afraid of being arrested, and perhaps ashamed of being hobos, Price and Bates falsely claimed that the nine black youths had sexually assaulted them. On the basis of that accusation, the **"Scottsboro Boys"** (ranging in ages from thirteen to twenty) were given a hasty trial. They never had a chance. Their white court-appointed attorney came to court drunk each day. Three days after the trial started, and fifteen days after their arrest, the jurors found all of them guilty. Eight received the death sentence, and the youngest, a thirteen-year-old, was sentenced to life imprisonment, even though medical examinations of Price and Bates proved that neither had been raped.

While other organizations either dawdled or refused to intervene, the Communist Party's International Labor Defense (ILD) rushed to the aid of the "boys" by appealing the conviction and death sentence to the U.S. Supreme Court. The case produced two important decisions that reaffirmed black people's right to the basic protections that all other American citizens enjoyed. In *Powell v. Alabama* (1932), the Court

ruled that the nine Scottsboro defendants had not been given adequate legal counsel and that the trial had taken place in a hostile and volatile atmosphere. Asserting that the youths' right to due process as set forth in the Fourteenth Amendment had been violated, the Court ordered a new trial. Alabama did as instructed, but the new trial resulted in another guilty verdict and sentences of death or life imprisonment. The ILD promptly appealed, and in *Norris v. Alabama* (1935) the Supreme Court decided that all Americans have the right to a trial by a jury of their peers. The systematic exclusion of African Americans from the Scottsboro juries, the Court held, denied the defendants equal protection under the law, which the Fourteenth Amendment guaranteed. Chief Justice Charles Evans Hughes pointed out that no black citizens had served on juries in the Alabama counties for decades, even though many were qualified to serve. The Court noted that the exclusion was blatant racial discrimination and called for yet another trial.

Despite these stunning defeats and increasing evidence that the "boys" had been falsely convicted, Alabama still pursued the case. Even when Ruby Bates publicly admitted the rape charge had been a hoax, white Alabamians ignored her. Finally, in 1937 Alabama dropped its charges against five of the nine men, and in the 1940s the state released those still in jail. Altogether, nine innocent black men had collectively served some three-quarters of a century in prison. Clarence Willie Norris, however, escaped and fled to Michigan, returning decades later to receive a ceremonious pardon from Governor George Wallace. When a reporter asked Norris how he felt, he declared, "I'm just glad to be free." The experience had taught him "to stand up for your rights, even if it kills you. That's all life consists of."

DEBATING COMMUNIST LEADERSHIP

Throughout the *Scottsboro* case, the NAACP tried unsuccessfully to wrest control from the Communist Party. Indeed, as the case evolved, tensions and competition between the Communist Party and the NAACP for leadership of black America flared into open hostility. At first, the NAACP had hesitated to defend accused rapists, but it moved more decisively after the Communist Party had taken the lead.

The contest between the NAACP and the communists reveals the differences between the two groups. The party organized protest marches and demonstrations and used its press to denounce more cautious middle-class organizations. In Harlem, for example, the communists staged a 1931 protest march that attracted over three thousand black men and women and ended with an address by Ada Wright, the mother of two of the defendants, who praised the ILD for its help. The NAACP countered with a carefully orchestrated campaign that questioned the sincerity and effectiveness of the communists and sought to repair its own reputation as a respectable and effective advocate for African Americans.

Black public opinion divided in its evaluation of the party. Some black men and women applauded the communists. Journalist Eugene Gordon wrote,

> Negro workers think of the countless times
> Communists have been beaten insensible for
> defending . . . Negro workers. . . .They see the ILD . . .
> supported by the Communist Party, rushing to the
> defense of the nine Negro youths at Scottsboro
> before other Negro organizations in the country
> condescended to glance superciliously in their
> direction. . . .Seeing and hearing all these things, the
> Negro worker in the United States would be a fool
> not to recognize the leadership that he has been
> waiting for since his freedom.

Historian Carter G. Woodson praised the Communist Party in the *New York Age*:

> I have talked with any number of Negroes who call
> themselves Communists, and I have never heard one
> express a desire to destroy anyone or anything but
> oppression. . . .Negroes who are charged with being
> Communists advocate the stoppage of peonage,
> equality in employment of labor. . . .If this makes a
> man "Red," the world's greatest reformers belong to
> this class, and we shall have to condemn our greatest
> statesmen, some of whom have attained the
> presidency of the United States.

But other African Americans ridiculed the party. George Schuyler, a columnist for the Pittsburgh *Courier*, used his razor-sharp wit to castigate the party and persuade black people that its claim to champion African Americans was a lie. Schuyler objected to the communists' "campaign of vilification . . . against the NAACP":

> No Ku Kluxer ever denounced the latter organization
> more vigorously and unfairly. The Communists know
> they are lying when they assert time and time again
> that the NAACP wants to see the boys convicted and
> is betraying the race. They have quite the same sort
> of grooved mentality as Ku Kluxers, Garveyites and

other race fanatics, black and white. The course they tentatively pursue is held the only true one and whoever takes exception is denounced as an enemy of humanity, even though they may have to change that course in a few months.

Although most African Americans applauded the antiracist work that the Communist Party supported and performed, there was no chance they would defect from the traditional American political system, as W. E. B. Du Bois wrote in 1931:

> American Negroes do not propose to be the shock
> troops of the Communist Revolution, driven out in
> the front to death, cruelty and humiliation in order
> to win victories for white workers. . . .Negroes know
> perfectly well that whenever they try to lead
> revolution in America, the nation will unite as one
> fist to crush them and them alone.

THE NATIONAL NEGRO CONGRESS

The infighting between the Communist Party and other groups doomed a major attempt to unite all the disparate African-American protest groups into the **National Negro Congress (NNC).** John P. Davis, a Washington-based economist, organized the NNC, modeling it on his experience as the executive secretary of the Joint Committee on National Recovery (JCNR), a coalition of black groups that pressed for fairness in the early New Deal. The NNC was to be a federation of organizations on a national scale supported by regional councils. Over 800 delegates representing 585 organizations attended its first meeting, held in Chicago in 1936. However, prominent black activists, leaders, and intellectuals were conspicuously absent, notably those associated with the NAACP. A. Philip Randolph was elected president, and Davis became the executive secretary. The group resolved not to be dominated by any one political faction and to build on the strength of all parts of the black community. Although handicapped by lack of funds, the NNC initially worked effectively at the local or community level. With branches in approximately seventy cities, the organization gained for its members increased employment opportunities, better housing, and adequate relief work. The NNC also prodded labor unions, in particular the CIO, to fight for better conditions and higher wages for black workers.

At the NNC's second meeting in Philadelphia in 1937, a skeptical Davis maintained that the Democratic Party would never allow black people to benefit justly and fairly from the New Deal. Eventually the increasing importance of communists in the NNC alienated most other groups and reduced the organization's ability to

Hoboing in Alabama

Ralph Ellison, the noted author of the great novel Invisible Man (1952), here vividly recalls his harrowing experience as a young black "hobo" in the aftermath of the arrest of the "Scottsboro Boys."

During June of 1933, I found myself traveling by freight train in an effort to reach Tuskegee Institute in time to take advantage of a scholarship granted me. Having little money and no time left in which to earn the fare for a ticket, I grabbed an armful of freight car, a form of illegal travel quite common during the Great Depression. In fact, so many young men, young women, prostitutes, gamblers, and even some quite respectable but impoverished elderly and middle-aged couples were hoboing that it was quite difficult for the railroad to control such passengers. I justify this out of sheer desperation, college being my one hope of improving my condition.

But I was young and adventurous and regarded hoboing as the next best thing to floating down the Mississippi on a raft. My head was full of readings of the Rover Boys and Huckleberry Finn. I converted hoboing into a lark until I found myself in the freight yards of Decatur, Alabama, where two white railroad detectives laying about them with the barrels of long nickel-plated .45 revolvers forced some forty or fifty of us, black and white alike, off the train and ordered us to line up along the tracks. For me, this was a most frightening moment. Not only was I guilty of stealing passage on a freight train, but I realized that I had been caught in the act in the town where, at that very moment, the Scottsboro case was being tried. The case and the incident leading to it were widely reported in the black press, and what I had read of the atmosphere of the trial led me to believe that the young men in the case had absolutely no possibility of receiving a just decision. As I saw it, the trial was a macabre circus, a kangaroo proceeding that would be soon followed by an enactment of the gory rite of lynching, that ultimate form of racial victimage.

I had no idea of what the detectives intended to do with me, but given the atmosphere of the town, I feared that it would be most unpleasant and brutal. I, too might well be a sacrificial scapegoat, simply because I was the same race as the accused young men then being prepared for death. Therefore, when a group of white boys broke and ran, I plunged into their midst, and running far closer to the ground than I had ever managed to do as a high school football running back, I kept running and moving until I came to a shed with a railroad loading dock, under which I

speak for the majority of black people. By 1940 it was greatly weakened. Randolph was voted out of office, and the once-promising NNC became little more than a front group for the Communist Party.

The Tuskegee Study

The 1930s marked the rising prominence of black scholars and intellectuals, but, paradoxically, the decade also witnessed the worst manifestation of racism in American science. This most shocking episode of virulent bigotry and racial mistreatment occurred in Macon County, Alabama. There, in 1932, U.S. Public Health Service (USPHS) officials initiated a major study of syphilis, a sexually transmitted disease that can cause paralysis, insanity, and heart failure. For the subjects of its program—entitled the Tuskegee Study of Untreated Syphilis in the Male Negro—the USPHS recruited 622 black men, all of them poor sharecroppers and the majority illiterate. Of these men, 431 had advanced cases of syphilis; the rest were free of the disease and served as controls for comparison.

The **Tuskegee Study** was called a treatment program, but it turned out to be an experiment, designed to chart the progression and development of a potentially fatal disease. To gain the trust of the men, the government doctors centered their work at Tuskegee Institute and hired a black nurse, Eunice Rivers, who convinced the men they had "bad blood" and needed special treatment. Although the drug penicillin, which could cure the disease, became available in the 1940s, the sharecroppers never received it. Instead, they were given ineffective placebos, which they were told would cure them.

scooted; and there I remained until dawn, when I grabbed the first thing that was smoking and headed south.

A few days later I reached Tuskegee, but that scrape with the law—the fear, the horror and sense of helplessness before legal injustice—was most vivid in my mind, and it has so remained.

🌿 *How does Ralph Ellison's experience as a hobo illuminate the nature of race relations in the South?*

🌿 *How did the "Scottsboro Boys" case increase Ellison's sense of vulnerability? Why were so many people engaged in "hoboing"? How did the black experience of "hoboing" differ from that of white Americans?*

Source: Ralph Ellison, "Perspective of Literature," in *Going to the Territory* (New York: Vintage Books, 1995), pp. 324–25.

Initially the Tuskegee Study was to last only six to twelve months, but it was repeatedly extended. The men received regular physical examinations, which included a painful lumbar puncture. This insertion of a needle into the spinal cord to obtain fluid for diagnosis often caused the men severe headaches, and in a few isolated cases it resulted in paralysis and even death. For almost forty years, Tuskegee Study doctors observed the men, keeping careful records of their health and performing autopsies on those who died; but they never treated them for syphilis. So little understood was the Tuskegee Study that men not only remained in the program but believed they were fortunate to have the physical examination, the hot lunches provided on examination days, and the burial allowance the government guaranteed their families. The medical community knew of the Tuskegee experiment, but the general public learned of it only in 1972 when a reporter broke the story. Black attorney Fred D. Gray of Alabama sued the U.S. government on behalf of the participants and their families, but before the case went to trial, the government made a $9 million settlement to the Tuskegee survivors and the descendants of those who had died.

Tuskegee Experiment patients (1932–1972) From 1932 to 1972, the U.S. Public Health Service (USPHS) conducted an experiment on approximately 400 black Alabama sharecroppers to trace the evolution of untreated syphilis. The men were never informed that they had the disease, nor were they given penicillin when it became available. On May 16, 1997, President Bill Clinton on behalf of the U.S. government finally apologized for this cruel and clearly racist experiment on human subjects.

CONCLUSION

Notable political changes occurred during the early 1930s: the NAACP came of age, black women found their voice, white left-wing leaders joined with black men and women in interracial alliances, organized labor bridged the race chasm, and black men and women switched from the Republican Party to the Democratic Party. The New Deal had stimulated some economic recovery and, more important, laid the basis for a strong national state and a political coalition that, beginning with World War II, would sharply challenge the nation's racial system.

RECOMMENDED READING

John Egerton. *Speak Now against the Day: The Generation before the Civil Rights Movement in the South.* New York: Alfred A. Knopf, 1994. An excellent survey of the period before the southern civil rights era, with chapters on the Depression in the South and black and white southerners' reactions to it.

Darlene Clark Hine. "The Corporeal and Ocular Veil: Dr. Matilda A. Evans (1872–1935) and the Complexity of Southern History," *Journal of Southern History,* 70, no. 1 (February 2004): 1–34. A case study of the strategies pursued by a black woman physician to provide health care for impoverished African Americans in Columbia, South Carolina, during the opening decades of the twentieth century.

James H. Jones. *Bad Blood: The Tuskegee Syphilis Experiment.* New York: Free Press, 1981. A comprehensive study of the Tuskegee experiment.

Robin D. G. Kelley. *Hammer and Hoe: Alabama Communists during the Great Depression.* Chapel Hill: University of North Carolina Press, 1990. A splendid study of the radicalizing activism of working people in the steel industry and on the farm during the 1930s. Kelley does an excellent job of showing why the communists appealed to black workers.

Mark Naison. *Communists in Harlem during the Depression.* Urbana: University of Illinois Press, 1983. A well-researched and clear-sighted study of the Communist Party in Harlem and the history of the National Negro Congress.

Susan Reverby. *Tuskegee Truths: Rethinking the Tuskegee Syphillis Study.* Chapel Hill: University of North Carolina Press, 2000. Delightful collection of essays reflecting diverse perspectives on this significant medical experiment.

Harvard Sitkoff. *A New Deal for Blacks: The Emergence of Civil Rights as a National Issue, Vol. I: Depression Decade.* New York: Oxford University Press, 1978. An important work that covers the New Deal era and presents it as a period when the groundwork for the civil rights movement was laid.

AFRICAN-AMERICAN EVENTS	NATIONAL EVENTS
• 1929 •	
	1929 October, Stock Market on Wall Street crashes
• 1930 •	
1930 Fannie Peck forms Detroit Housewives' League NAACP campaigns successfully to block John J. Parker's appointment to the Supreme Court	
• 1931 •	
1931 The "Scottsboro Boys" are arrested	
• 1932 •	
1932 In *Powell v. Alabama*, Supreme Court rules that Scottsboro defendants lacked adequate counsel The Tuskegee experiment begins	**1932** Franklin D. Roosevelt elected president
• 1933 •	
1933 The "black cabinet" is formed	**1933** Roosevelt launches the first New Deal

Patricia Sullivan. *Days of Hope: Race and Democracy in the New Deal Era*. Chapel Hill: University of North Carolina Press, 1996. An invaluable study showing how the ideas of civil rights and democracy were forged in the New Deal South.

Raymond Wolters. *Negroes and the Great Depression: The Problem of Economic Recovery*. Westport, CT: Greenwood, 1974. A solid survey of African Americans in the Depression that covers its impact on African Americans, the workings of the black cabinet, and the effects of the New Deal agencies on the lives of black Americans.

ADDITIONAL BIBLIOGRAPHY

POLITICS

Adam Fairclough. *Better Day Coming: Blacks and Equality, 1890–2000*. New York: Viking, 2001.

Kenneth W. Goings. *"The NAACP Comes of Age": The Defeat of Judge John J. Parker*. Bloomington: Indiana University Press, 1990.

Charles V. Hamilton. *Adam Clayton Powell, Jr., the Political Biography of an American Dilemma*. New York: Atheneum, 1991.

Darlene Clark Hine. *Black Victory: The Rise and Fall of the White Primary in Texas*. New edition with essays by Darlene Clark Hine, Steven F. Lawson, and Merline Pitre. Columbia: University of Missouri Press, 2003.

John B. Kirby. *Black Americans in the Roosevelt Era: Liberalism and Race*. Knoxville: University of Tennessee Press, 1980.

Christopher R. Reed. *The Chicago NAACP and the Rise of Black Professional Leadership, 1910–1966*. Bloomington: Indiana University Press, 1997.

Mark V. Tushnet. *The NAACP's Legal Strategy against Segregated Education, 1925–1950*. Chapel Hill: University of North Carolina Press, 1987.

Nancy J. Weiss. *Farewell to the Party of Lincoln: Black Politics in the Age of Lincoln*. Princeton, NJ: Princeton University Press, 1983.

LABOR

Lizabeth Cohen. *Making a New Deal: Industrial Workers in Chicago, 1919–1939*. New York: Cambridge University Press, 1990.

Olen Cole Jr., *The African-American Experience in the Civilian Conservation Corps*. Gainesville: University of Florida Press, 1999.

Dennis C. Dickerson. *Out of the Crucible: Black Steelworkers in Western Pennsylvania, 1875–1980*. Albany, NY: SUNY Press, 1986.

William H. Harris. *The Harder We Run: Black Workers since the Civil War*. New York: Oxford University Press, 1982.

August Meier and Elliott Rudwick. *Black Detroit and the Rise of the UAW*. New York: Oxford University Press, 1979.

EDUCATION

James D. Anderson. *The Education of Blacks in the South, 1860–1935*. Chapel Hill: University of North Carolina Press, 1988.

Richard Kluger. *Simple Justice: The History of Brown v. Board of Education and Black America's Struggle for Equality*. New York: Random House, 1976; new rev. ed., 2004. A new chapter assesses the fifty year impact of *Brown*.

Mark V. Tushnet. *Making Civil Rights Law: Thurgood Marshall and the Supreme Court, 1935–1961*. New York: Knopf, 1994.

Francille Rusan Wilson, *The Segregated Scholars: Black Social Scientists and the Creation of Black Labor Studies, 1890–1950*. Charlottesville, University of Virginia Press, 2006.

BLACK RADICALISM

Dan Carter. *Scottsboro: A Tragedy of the American South*. Baton Rouge: Louisiana State University Press, 1969.

Vanessa Northington Gamble. *Making a Place for Ourselves: The Black Hospital Movement, 1920–1945*. New York: Oxford University Press, 1995.

Kenneth W. Goings. *Mammy and Uncle Mose: Black Collectibles and American Stereotyping*. Bloomington: Indiana University Press, 1994.

Michael K. Honey. *Southern Labor and Black Civil Rights: Organizing Memphis Workers*. Urbana: University of Illinois Press, 1993.

Jacqueline Jones. *Labor of Love, Labor of Sorrow: Black Women, Work, and the Family from Slavery to the Present*. New York: Basic Books, 1985.

Nicholas Natanson. *The Black Image in the New Deal: The Politics of FSA Photography*. Knoxville: University of Tennessee Press, 1992.

Daryl Michael Scott. *Contempt and Pity: Social Policy and the Image of the Damaged Black Psyche, 1880–1996*. Chapel Hill: University of North Carolina Press, 1997.

Mark Solomon. *The Cry Was Unity: Communists and African Americans, 1917–1936*. Jackson: University Press of Mississippi, 1998.

Richard W. Thomas. *Life for Us Is What We Make It: Building Black Community in Detroit, 1915–1945*. Bloomington: Indiana University Press, 1992.

Thomas J. Ward Jr. *Black Physicians in the Jim Crow South*. Fayetteville: University of Arkansas Press, 2003.

ECONOMICS

Charles T. Banner-Haley. *To Do Good and to Do Well: Middle Class Blacks and the Depression, Philadelphia, 1929–1941*. New York: Garland, 1993.

Alexa Benson Henderson. *Atlanta Life Insurance Company: Guardian of Black Economic Dignity*. Tuscaloosa: University of Alabama Press, 1990.

1934
1934 Elijah Muhammad becomes leader of the Nation of Islam. W. E. B. Du Bois resigns from the NAACP

1935 Mary McLeod Bethune forms the National Council of Negro Women. *Norris v. Alabama* establishes right to trial by a jury of one's peers. Free Angelo Herndon Campaign begins. The National Negro Congress is formed

1935 The CIO is formed. Roosevelt's second New Deal—Social Security Act, National Labor Relations Act, and the Works Progress Administration

1936 African Americans shift allegiance to the Democratic Party. Mary McLeod Bethune is named director of the Division of Negro Affairs

1936 FDR is reelected in a landslide

1937 William Hastie is named first black federal judge. Bethune organizes conference on Problems of the Negro and Negro Youth

AFRICAN-AMERICAN EVENTS   NATIONAL EVENTS

Robert E. Weems Jr. *Black Business in the Black Metropolis: The Chicago Metropolitan Assurance Company, 1924–1985.* Bloomington: Indiana University Press, 1996.

BIOGRAPHY AND AUTOBIOGRAPHY

Andrew Buni. *Robert L. Vann of the Pittsburgh Courier.* Pittsburgh: University of Pittsburgh Press, 1974.

Henry Louis Gates Jr. and Evelyn Brooks Higginbotham, eds. *African American Lives.* New York: Oxford University Press, 2004.

Spencie Love. *One Blood: The Death and Resurrection of Charles R. Drew.* Chapel Hill: University of North Carolina Press, 1996.

Genna Rae McNeil. *Groundwork: Charles Hamilton Houston and the Struggle for Civil Rights.* Philadelphia: University of Pennsylvania Press, 1983.

Nell Irvin Painter. *The Narrative of Hosea Hudson: His Life as a Negro Communist in the South.* Cambridge, MA: Harvard University Press, 1979.

Paula F. Pfeffer. *A. Philip Randolph, Pioneer of the Civil Rights Movement.* Baton Rouge: Louisiana State University Press, 1990.

Barbara Ransby. *Ella Baker and the Black Freedom Movement.* Chapel Hill: University of North Carolina Press, 2003.

George S. Schuyler. *Black and Conservative: The Autobiography of George S. Schuyler.* New Rochelle, NY: Arlington House, 1966.

Gilbert Ware. *William Hastie: Grace under Pressure.* New York: Oxford University Press, 1984.

Roy Wilkins with Tom Mathews. *Standing Fast: The Autobiography of Roy Wilkins.* New York: Da Capo Press, 1994.

RETRACING THE ODYSSEY

Apollo Theatre, New York City. When other venues were closed to African Americans, many talented men and women destined to become top performers in twentieth-century America launched their careers at the Apollo Theatre. Since the 1930s, performers such as Duke Ellington, Count Basie, Charlie Parker, Bessie Smith, Billie Holiday, and Ella Fitzgerald have graced the Apollo stage. Renowned comedians such as Bill Cosby, Richard Pryor, and Redd Foxx honed their talents here, as well as numerous others.

Bethune Museum and Archives, Washington, D.C. Mary McLeod Bethune, born in 1875 in Mayesville, South Carolina, was one of the most politically engaged black women in the first half of the twentieth century. She was the president of Bethune-Cookman College in Daytona Beach, Florida, when President Franklin Delano Roosevelt appointed her Director of Negro Affairs of the National Youth Council. An ardent black clubwoman, Bethune is celebrated as the founder, in 1935, and first president of the National Council of Negro Women (NCNW). It remains a significant umbrella group for organizations of black women. The Bethune Museum and Archive Center was her home and headquarters of the NCNW from 1943 to 1966. It contains exhibits and sponsors programs that emphasize the contributions of African-American women to American society. The archive contains important manuscript collections and other research materials pertaining to the NCNW and to black women's history.

Wright Museum of African-American History, Detroit, Michigan. This is the largest African-American history museum in America. Its the Field to Factory exhibit documents the Great Migration of African Americans from the rural South to the industrial North during the twentieth century. It sponsors a variety of educational programs throughout the year.

myhistorylab REVIEW, RESEARCH, AND INTERACT

REVIEW QUESTIONS

1. Why did African Americans support the Democratic Party and abandon their long association with the Republican Party?

2. How did black radicalism influence Roosevelt's New Deal policies and programs?

3. How did black people respond to and survive the Great Depression? How did the experiences of black women during the Depression reflect their race, class, and gender status in American society?

4. How did the New Deal adversely affect black sharecroppers, tenants, and farmers? What were the political, social, and economic repercussions of the large-scale migration of African Americans out of the South during the 1930s?

5. What role did racism play in the Tuskegee experiment and the "*Scottsboro Boys*" case?

6. Why were W. E. B. Du Bois's *The Crisis* editorials about segregation so divisive and explosive? How did black activists and scholars respond to the idea of voluntary self-segregation?

www.researchnavigator.com

Using the tools available in Research Navigator, consider these questions:

What role did the federal government play in combating racism in the 1930s? What role did the courts play?

PRIMARY SOURCE DOCUMENTS

18–1 Lester B. Granger, Negro Workers and Recovery, 1934
18–2 National Labor Relations Act, 1935
18–4 Luther C. Wandall, a Negro in the CCC, 1935
18–5 E. E. Lewis, Black Cotton Farmers and the AAA, 1935

DATA EXPLORATION

Unemployment, 1925–1945, p. 481

INTERACTIVE ACTIVITY

Dealing with Hard Times

This activity looks at ways in which people coped with the Great Depression and at some of the alternatives proposed to change the political and economic system that led to it.

19

Meanings of Freedom Culture and Society in the 1930s and 1940s

HOW DID THE CHICAGO RENAISSANCE
DIFFER FROM THE HARLEM RENAISSANCE
OF THE 1920s?

HOW DID AFRICAN AMERICANS MERGE A DISTINCT
AESTHETIC WITH A DEMAND FOR SOCIAL JUSTICE?

HOW DID AFRICAN AMERICANS CREATE
AND EMPLOY POPULAR CULTURE TO COUNTERACT
NEGATIVE STEREOTYPES OF BLACK PEOPLE?

WHAT NATIONAL AND INTERNATIONAL FORCES
SHAPED THE EVOLUTION OF JAZZ?

WHO WERE SOME OF THE MAJOR
BLACK CULTURAL AMBASSADORS TO
WHITE AMERICA DURING THE 1930s AND 1940s?

◀◀ **Black Olympian Jesse Owens** powerfully challenged Adolf
Hitler's master race ideology with his outstanding
performance in track and field competition at the 1936
Olympic Games in Berlin. He won four gold medals.

1930–1949

He would not Africanize America, for America has too much to teach the world and Africa. He would not bleach his Negro soul in a flood of white Americanism, for he knows that Negro blood has a message for the world. He simply wished to make it possible for a man to be both a Negro and an American, without being cursed and spit upon by his fellows, without having the doors of opportunity closed roughly in his face. This, then, is the end of his striving: to be a co-worker in the kingdom of culture, to escape both death and isolation, to husband and use his best powers and his latent genius.

W. E. B. Du Bois, *The Souls of Black Folk: Essay and Sketches*

Pitching great Lerov Satchel Paige warms up at New York's Yankee Stadium in 1942. ▼

W. E. B. Du Bois commented often on the gifts black people had given to America. Even before he wrote the passage that opens this chapter, Du Bois had proclaimed, "We are the first fruits of this new nation. . . .We are the people whose subtle sense of song has given America its only American music, its only American fairy tales, its only touch of pathos and humor amid its money-getting plutocracy." African-American "destiny is not a servile imitation of Anglo-Saxon culture, but a stalwart originality which shall unswervingly follow Negro ideals."

A key theme in black life during the 1930s and 1940s was the many strategies African Americans devised to protest segregation, discrimination, and disfranchisement, and to resist the negative racial stereotypes and the appropriation of black culture by white entrepreneurs. At heart this was a quest to shape the representation of black people in American society and create a viable black culture for a rapidly urbanizing people. A central issue in this chapter is the extent to which black culture during the 1930s and 1940s became a source of strength—cultural power—that helped African Americans define and assert themselves within American society.

Cultural power allowed African Americans to define and create new images that replaced the distortion of the true appearance, intellect, religious practice, and family values of black people in American society. The new black cultural power had to fight the well-worn stereotypes of the dumb and lazy black man, the selfless mammy, and the promiscuous dark Venus. As we have seen throughout this book, black people were disfranchised and socially and economically marginalized. But in the arts, black people drove a small wedge into the wall of racism through which they could explode onto America's center stage. In the performing arts, talented African Americans, such as singer and actor Paul Robeson (1898–1976), who starred in the memorable role of Shakespeare's Othello on Broadway in 1930 and in the now classic film *Show Boat* in 1936, compelled the attention of white Americans. The 1930s and 1940s was ironically—also a time when most black people were suffering from the combined effects of the Depression and the entrenched Jim Crow regime—were a fertile period in the history of black expressive culture.

Paul Robeson (1898–1976) as "Othello" in 1943. A man of astonishing magnetism and creative power, Paul Robeson became, in 1943, the first black actor to play "Othello" in the United States. He was fluent in many languages, produced over 300 recordings of spiritual and folk music gathered from around the world, and appeared in eleven motion pictures. An unflinching proponent of freedom from racism and want, Robeson received the NAACP's Spingarn Medal in 1945.   Courtesy of the Library of Congress

Black Culture in a Midwestern City

During the 1930s and 1940s, black migrants flocked to St. Louis, swelling its population to make it the fifth largest city in the United States. Yet because of segregation and discrimination, the black community in St. Louis developed institutions to address its own educational and cultural needs. Attention has usually focused on St. Louis's contributions to popular culture, but there was also considerable interest in the city in classical music. Black community residents had to struggle to secure training in this genre of music and for opportunities to perform it:

> St. Louis! The town where Scott Joplin and Tom Turpin used to play ragtime. The town that W. C. Handy made famous in his great song, "The St. Louis Blues." The town where Josephine Baker started out as a $15.00 a week waitress, and end[ed] up in Paris as one of the most glamorous stars of the

international theater. St. Louis, the town that gave a laugh-hungry world the joy of E. Simms Campbell and his rib-tickling cartoons of Esquire and King Features fame. The town where the riverboats used to run from New Orleans with Louis Armstrong's horn blasting the night away.

Langston Hughes's words recall the possibilities and excitement that life in a midwestern city held for black people. St. Louis is in the heart of a region often considered remote from the nation's cultural centers. Yet it has produced outstanding jazz musicians, and Chuck Berry virtually invented rock and roll there. A closer look at black support for classical music in St. Louis during the 1930s and 1940s reveals the interior diversity of black community life—even though white St. Louisians marginalized or ignored the contributions of black artists in the city. But not all black musicians wanted to play ragtime and jazz, and many resented being relegated to these forms.

Schools, churches, labor, and media within the St. Louis black community had to create opportunities for black children to study, appreciate, and perform classical music. The two largest black newspapers, the St. Louis *Argus* and the St. Louis *American*, publicized recitals and concerts. Two all-black institutions supported classical music education: Lincoln University in Jefferson City (founded in 1866 as a school created by and for black Civil War veterans and their families) and Sumner High School (founded in 1875 as the first secondary school for black people west of the Mississippi).

By the 1940s Lincoln University had become the institution for training St. Louis musicians, and its music instructors were active in the black community's cultural affairs. Sumner High School had orchestras, bands, choirs, and glee clubs. Many of its music teachers had advanced degrees from prestigious music departments. The most influential teacher was Kenneth Billups, an arranger, composer, and founding director of the Legend Singers, a black professional chorus.

The Legend Singers appeared with the St. Louis Symphony and with the Municipal Opera Company (MUNY) in productions of *Show Boat*, where they dressed in demeaning slave costumes. Billups's response to criticism of these appearances indirectly addressed the dilemma of black artists in a racially restrictive environment:

> I've seen situations where I felt inwardly . . . I might have had to do some things; for example, let's take this Showboat thing at MUNY Opera. There is the need of a black chorus to go there, and I had the privilege of doing that with my Legend Singers, simply because one of the first requirements was to have a black chorus.

Black churches, including Antioch Baptist, Central Baptist, and Berea Presbyterian, sponsored religious programs highlighting the works of both black and white composers. Local 197 of the American Federation of Musicians and the St. Louis Music Association, which was the local branch of the National Association of Negro Musicians, promoted black performing organizations and training. These groups sponsored choirs, orchestras, and other musical organizations and devoted part of their members' dues to scholarships and summer choirs for boys and girls.

The Black Culture Industry and American Racism

Black American artists had to confront institutional racism in the culture industry. Individual black creative artists could rarely afford to produce and disseminate their work. This power often resided in the hands of record companies, publishers, and the owners of radio stations and film studios. Yet black artists in the 1930s and 1940s were shaping a new black consciousness that would erupt in the 1950s as the modern civil rights movement. Paul Robeson, a graduate of Rutgers University and Columbia University Law School, not only won acclaim as a great performing artist but he established friendships with African freedom fighters such as Kwame Nkrumah in Ghana, Jomo Kenyatta in Kenya, and Dr. Nnamdi Azikiwe of Nigeria, and he received the NAACP's most prestigious award, the Spingarn Medal, in 1945. The U.S. government, however, revoked Robeson's passport in 1950 because of his support for radical social and economic reform, and his advocacy of black internationalism.

The political content of black art provoked heated debates among black artists. Many black Americans insisted that music, the visual and performing arts, literature, and oratory serve both a functional and an aesthetic purpose. They expected black artists not only to create beauty, but also to use their art to further black freedom from white oppression across the black Diaspora and to forge significant cultural and political linkages. African-American artists and intellectuals joined with people of African descent throughout the Diaspora in support of Ethiopian resistance against Italian aggression in 1935. Still, the involvement of white people in the marketing and use of black culture for disparate reasons created tension among black artists during these decades. Although many white Americans had long appreciated black culture, some had also appropriated it for their own profit.

During the late 1930s and 1940s, corporate America recognized the money that could be made in producing and marketing black culture. But there was a problem: black artists had to be made "acceptable" if they were to be successfully marketed to affluent white consumers. These artists had to compromise, mask, and subordinate their true feelings and expressiveness if they wanted to earn income from their work. Artists who exhibited the right combination of showmanship, charm, and talent could reap some of the financial rewards their creativity generated. The paradox of the black performer—using your art to entertain your oppressor—was nowhere more apparent than in music.

The Music Culture from Swing to Bebop

Ironically, the very creativity that white Americans valued and often appropriated depended on the artists' ability to preserve some intellectual and emotional autonomy. Black artists had to juxtapose the requirements of earning a living with the need to remain true to their art. Black musicians continuously had to refine, expand, and perfect their art not only for themselves and each other but also for a white-dominated marketplace. In many respects black music is virtually synonymous with black culture, and segregation or self-imposed separation often made possible the creation of new cultural expressions. Music encapsulates and reflects the core values and underlying tensions and anxieties in black communities. In black music we witness cultural producers developing strategies of resistance against white domination.

The Great Depression wrought havoc on the vibrant black culture industry of the 1920s. Record sales in 1932 were only a sixth of those in 1927. Black musicians like Louis Armstrong had enjoyed a golden age of creativity during the 1920s. The record companies had their separate black music labels and sold thousands of records to southern migrants to the big cities. New bands sprouted up from Kansas City to Chicago; Memphis to Detroit; Washington, D.C., to New York. Los Angeles, San Francisco, and Seattle had their own black music enthusiasts and performers. The territorial (traveling) bands took the music to the outposts of black America, and the big bands under Fletcher Henderson, Duke Ellington, Count Basie, and Cab Calloway played in white urban dance halls and ballrooms that admitted black people only as staff or entertainers.

New York was where black musicians felt they had to go to prove themselves. After entertaining affluent white people or providing backup music for the Apollo

Theater in Harlem, black musicians discarded their masks of docility and deference and made a different sound in their own space and on their own time in late-night jam sessions. The small clubs, such as Monroe's Uptown House and Minton's Playhouse in Harlem a few blocks from the Apollo Theater, became the most fertile sites for innovation in melody, tempo, and dexterity. In them a new kind of jazz was born.

The big band swing style that became popular in the 1930s transformed white American culture. Swing emerged as white bands reduced the music of the more innovative black bandleaders to a broadly appealing formula based on a swinging 4/4 beat, well-blended saxophone sections, and pleasant-sounding vocals. The big swing bands of the 1930s played written-out, completely arranged music. The popularity of swing helped boost the careers of black and white bandleaders, but it also led to a creative slump that disheartened many of the younger black musicians. Tired of swing's predictability, they began improvising in the jazz clubs, sharpening their reflexes, ears, and minds.

In the 1940s at least seven musicians were among the men most responsible for making a revolution in jazz, ushering in a new sound and dimension that became known, scornfully at first, as bebop. These musicians were Charlie Parker, Dizzy Gillespie, Thelonious Monk, Bud Powell, Kenny Clarke, Max Roach, and Ray Brown. Bebop featured complex rhythms and harmonies and highlighted improvisation. Gillespie (1917–1993) said that Kansas City–born Charlie "Yardbird" and then just "Bird" Parker (1920–1955) was "the architect of the style." "Yard and I," Gillespie reminisced, "were so close, so wrapped up in one another, that he would think 'three,' and I would say 'four,' and I would say 'seven,' and he'd say 'eight.' . . . It wasn't difficult for us, really together, sometimes it sounded like one horn playing, and sometimes it was one horn, but sometimes it was both of us sounding like one horn."

Bebop met resistance from white America. The nation was about to enter World War II and was too preoccupied to switch from the big band swing ballroom dancing music to bebop. Moreover, because jazzmen played in small, intimate clubs, not big bands, they had more freedom from the expectations of white society. Bebop music was of such enduring quality, however, that it shaped the contours of American popular culture and style for two generations. Before long, bebop became the principal musical language of jazz musicians around the world.

Bebop was a way of life and had its own attendant styles whose nuances depended on class status and, perhaps, age. Gillespie helped create one side of bebop style in dress, language, and demeanor. He began to wear dark glasses on stage to reduce the glare from lights after he had cataract surgery. He grew a goatee because shaving every day irritated his bottom lip. He wore pegged pants, jackets with wide lapels, and a beret when men were still wearing hats with brims. Other bebop musicians emulated and modified this attire. For example, they wore cashmere jackets without lapels. Beboppers also created their own slang, hip Black English that mingled colorful and obscene language. They challenged convention in other ways too, engaging in a freewheeling lifestyle that often included love across the color line. There was also a downside to bebop. Some musicians became drug addicts, engaged in parasitical relationships with women, and spent their money recklessly.

Black working-class young men adopted their own style of talking and of hip dressing, reflected in their zoot suits and conked hair. Zoot suits featured high-waisted, baggy, pegged pants and long draped coats. A sixteen-year-old Malcolm Little (later to take the name Malcolm X) purchased a zoot suit when he moved to Boston and plunged into hipster culture. His first zoot suit was sky blue with a matching hat, gold watch chain, and a monogrammed belt. To savor this new identity, he recalled, "I took three of those twenty-five cent sepia-toned, while-you-wait pictures of myself, posed the way 'hipsters' wearing their zoots would 'cool it'—hat dangled, knees drawn close together, feet wide apart, both index fingers jabbed toward the floor." He then mastered the lindy hop dance style and took to the floor of the Roseland Ballroom, where he shed his life as an unskilled wageworker and became someone freer and more empowered. He recalled the Ballroom's patrons' escape from their dreary urban lives: "They'd jam pack that ballroom, the black girls in way out silk and satin dresses and shoes, their hair done in all kinds of styles, the men sharp in their zoot suits and crazy conks, and everybody grinning and greased and gassed."

Bebop was the dominant black music of the war decade, but after 1945 returning veterans preferred a slower-paced music, simple love songs, and melodies. This contributed to bebop's waning and led to more transformations. All artistic innovation extracts a high price. Bebop was no exception. Many of the most talented musicians, like Billie Holiday, discussed later in this chapter, paid that price in lives decimated by drugs, poverty, sickness, and broken relationships. Few black musicians received the respect, recognition, and financial rewards from white America that their creativity warranted. Ultimately, white Americans wanted the art, but not the artists.

PROFILE ∽ CHARLIE PARKER, 1920–1955

Charlie Parker was one of the most innovative and influential of all American musicians. With his inspired saxophone playing; his technical mastery of his instrument; his melodic, rhythmic, and harmonic innovations, he was one of the architects of modern jazz, or "bebop." His playing challenged his contemporaries, profoundly influenced subsequent generations of jazz musicians, and helped transform jazz from entertainment to one of America's most respected art forms. But Parker was also troubled by drug addiction, mental instability, and tumultuous personal relationships.

Charles Parker Jr. was born on August 29, 1920, in Kansas City, Kansas. In 1927, his family moved across the state line to Kansas City, Missouri. He had little formal musical instruction. But Kansas City had a rich, dynamic jazz scene. Pianist and composer Mary Lou Williams remembered the freewheeling atmosphere this way: "Now, at this time, which was still Prohibition . . . [m]ost of the night spots were run by politicians and hoodlums, and the town was wide open for drinking, gambling, and pretty much every form of vice. Naturally, work was plentiful for musicians though some of the employers were tough people." Young Parker became a fixture at many of the local clubs, where he also acquired a heroin habit that plagued him for the rest of his life.

In 1939, searching for a wider audience and hoping to learn from the great instrumentalists of the time, Parker left Kansas City for New York, then the jazz capital of the country. In New York, Parker began to sit in, or "jam," at Harlem nightclubs such as Monroe's and Minton's. In 1942 he was back in Kansas City playing as a member of Jay McShann's band, a popular "territory band" that traveled as far north as Lincoln, Nebraska, and as far south as New Orleans, Louisiana. During this time he acquired the nickname "Bird."

Parker left the McShann Band in 1942 to join pianist Earl Hines's band in New York. In March and April 1943, all the following musicians were in the band with Parker: "Little" Benny Harris, Bennie Green, Wardell Gray, and vocalists Billy Eckstine and Sarah Vaughan. This collection of talent reflected a musical environment that fostered innovation. New ideas spread by word of mouth from musician to musician and in late-night jam sessions. It was from the close collaboration between Parker and Dizzy Gillespie in this period that bebop emerged.

Charlie Parker joined the first bebop big band, formed by Billy Eckstine in 1944. Eckstine's friend and valet, Bob Redcross, remembers a particular night when the band was at its best.

Everybody was on. [Art] Blakey was on; John [Gillespie] was on; Bird was on; Bidd [Johnson] was on; everybody. Man, they upset this place. They had people screaming and hollering.

In the same year a recording of Parker's composition, "Red Cross," the first to be copyrighted in his name, was released on the Savoy label.

Parker and Gillespie first recorded together commercially in 1945. Gillespie formed his first bebop big band and took it on a tour of the South as part of the "Hepations 1945" package tour. Also in 1945, Parker led an expanded group at the Spotlite club that included trumpeter Miles Davis, tenor saxophonist Dexter Gordon, bassist Leonard Gaskin, and drummer Stan Levey. During a disastrous trip to California, Parker had a nervous breakdown and spent several months at Camarillo State Hospital.

In 1947, when Parker returned to New York, he formed his "classic" quintet, with trumpeter Miles Davis, drummer Max Roach, pianist Duke Jordan, and Tommy Potter on bass. The recordings produced by this quintet, four sides on the Savoy label, are the foundation on which much of Parker's reputation rests.

In 1949, in a fitting tribute to his genius by his contemporaries, a New York nightclub, "Birdland," was named for him. Charlie Parker died in New York on March 12, 1955.

Popular Culture for the Masses: Comic Strips, Radio, and Movies

The masses of African Americans participated in more accessible black popular culture outlets. Everyone needed relief from the bleakness and despair of the Depression years. Comic strips, radio programs, and movies were affordable forms of artistic creativity that allowed momentary escape. Newspapers were widely shared, passing from hand to hand, and whole families gathered around the radio for nightly programs of comedy and music. For black city dwellers, the movies offered momentary escape from poverty and want.

THE COMICS

African Americans quickly noted the difference between the fun that black people made of each other and the mockery white people made of them. These differences were reflected in tone, intent, and sympathetic versus derisive laughter. During the Depression, comic strips in newspapers and comic books featuring superheroes diverted the attention of millions of Americans. Comic strips in black newspapers entertained, but also affirmed, the values and ideals of black people. They portrayed humorous situations and elaborated tales of intrigue and action.

The Philadelphia *Independent*, a black paper, ran a serial in the 1930s called "The Jones Family." This strip, drawn by an editorial cartoonist named Branford, was a good example of the dual function of entertaining and affirming. The strip emphasized black people's desire for achievement and respectability. The plot centered around the young Jones boy's search for the "good life" of money, success, love, and a happy marriage. But at every turn he confronts a harsh environment. Unable to get a job because of the Depression, he becomes an outlaw and narrowly escapes jail. He is constantly "on the run" from oppression. His only consolations are his family and his beautiful, ever-faithful girlfriend.

"The Jones Family" illuminates the gray areas that most African Americans, regardless of their class, faced when attempting to live rational and coherent lives in the northern cities. Although they espoused and cherished middle-class values, they often had to live among poverty, crime, and racial oppression. The black comic strips sought to provide entertaining, nonjudgmental prescriptions and blueprints for middle-class life, but to more cynical and alienated black people they seemed to be promoting unattainable values and lifestyles.

"Food for Thought," editorial cartoon by Rosie Nelson, illustrated by Branford. Comic strips not only provided humor and distraction from all manner of woes that beset black people during the Great Depression, they also operated as a public space for commentary on important personal and political issues.   © International Negro Press, 1936

RADIO AND RACE

Although there were individual exceptions, during the Depression black performers in radio and film were marginalized, exploited, or excluded. Commercial radio operated to deliver an audience of white consumers to white advertisers, and it denied black people jobs as announcers, broadcast journalists, or technicians. White entertainers schooled in blackface minstrelsy portrayed black radio characters. The major labor unions involved in the entertainment side of the radio industry restricted membership to white people. Still—with its offerings of vaudeville, big bands, drama, and comedy—radio provided relief from the miseries of the Depression to all Americans, black as well as white.

The most popular comedy radio program in the early 1930s—a precursor to the soap operas and sitcoms that were to become staples of radio and television programming—was *The Amos 'n' Andy Show.* The inauguration of this program was a significant moment in radio history. The title roles were played by two white performers, Charles Correll and Freeman Gosden, who wrote and performed scripts laced with oxymorons and malapropisms. Skillful showmen, Correll and Gosden ingratiated themselves in Chicago's black community, appearing at parades and posing with black children. The Chicago *Defender* endorsed them and they received standing ovations at the Regal Theater in Chicago's black South Side. Part of the amusement they generated derived from their mispronounced words, garbled grammar, and their show's minstrel ambience. Each episode highlighted an improbable situation involving the black cab driver (Amos) and his gullible overweight friend (Andy). Other characters included the scheming con artist Kingfish, his overbearing wife Sapphire, and his domineering mother-in-law, Mama. On radio, Gosden and Correll furnished voices for the members of Amos and Andy's fraternal lodge and for a whole array of other characters. The characters and their humor reinforced unflattering racial and gender stereotypes, but the show was not mean spirited. Some of the characters conducted themselves with dignity, modeling such positive values as marital fidelity, strong families, hard work, and economic independence. An *Amos 'n' Andy* movie, *Check and Double Check*—released in 1930 when hard times made black entertainers grateful for any employment they could get—featured music by Duke Ellington's orchestra. The movie introduced Ellington to a wider audience of affluent white people and enhanced his reputation.

Black audiences recognized the minstrel stereotyping in *Amos 'n' Andy*, yet many among them still enjoyed the show. A vocal component of the ever more sophisticated and urbanized black population, however, complained that this show, and other radio programs, reinforced negative images—of black women as bossy Sapphires or Mammies and black men as childish clowns—in the nation's consciousness. Educator and activist Nannie Helen Burroughs considered the show demeaning. Robert L. Vann, editor of the Pittsburgh *Courier*, argued that it exploited African Americans for white commercial gain. Vann sponsored a petition to the Federal Communications Commission to ban the show, but his efforts were futile.

By the 1940s *The Amos 'n' Andy Show* was less popular. In the early 1950s, it had a brief life as a television series, this time with black actors. Alvin Childress, an experienced stage actor and director, became Amos, and Spencer Williams Jr., who had written, directed,

and starred in several independent all-black movies, played Andy. Tim Moore assumed the role of the Kingfish of the Mystic Knights of the Sea Lodge; Johnny Lee portrayed the shyster lawyer, Algonquin J. Calhoun.

For almost two decades, *Amos 'n' Andy* was the only depiction of black people on the nation's airwaves. Its negative stereotypes of African Americans buttressed white people's notions of their own superiority. The show never demonstrated how the characters' race affected their lives or the psychological or economic costs of racism. It taught white America that it was permissible to laugh at striving black men and women.

The best-known and most successful African American on network radio in the late 1930s was Eddie Anderson, who played Jack Benny's sidekick Rochester in NBC's *The Jack Benny Show.* Like the characters in *Amos 'n' Andy*, Anderson's character reinforced negative racial stereotypes. Anderson rationalized his role in a way that suggests discomfort with it:

> I don't see why certain characters are called stereotypes. The Negro characters being presented are not labeling the Negro race any more than "Luigi" is labeling the Italian people as a whole. The same goes for "Beulah," who is not playing the part of thousands of Negroes, but only the part of one person, "Beulah." They're not saying here is the portrait of the Negro, but here is "Beulah."

The post-Depression era witnessed the emergence of black disc jockeys on urban radio who played the blues, gospel, and jazz and who attracted listeners with their sharp banter and fast but smooth talking style. The number of black disc jockeys rose from sixteen in 1946 to over five hundred by 1955. These disc jockeys used their radio shows not only to entertain and to sell records, but also to promote the careers of black musicians. As awareness of the potential buying power of black consumers sank in, both white- and black-owned businesses eagerly moved to sponsor black-appeal radio programs.

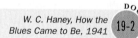
W. C. Haney, How the Blues Came to Be, 1941 DOCUMENT 19-2

RACE, REPRESENTATION, AND THE MOVIES

In the 1930s and 1940s—after the introduction of sound in motion pictures—black and white producers began to make what were known as **race films** for **African-American audiences.** Except for these race films, white film executives, since the beginning of the film industry, had cast black men and women in roles designed to comfort, reassure, and entertain white audiences. Continuing this trend, African Americans in Hollywood movies of the 1930s were usually cast in servile roles and often portrayed as buffoons. For example, the first black actor to receive major billing in American films, Stepin Fetchit (1902–1985, born Lincoln Theodore Monroe Perry), purportedly earned $2 million in ten years playing a cringingly servile, dim-witted, slow-moving character.

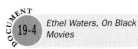
Ethel Waters, On Black Movies
19-4

Black performers appeared as servants in many other box-office successes during the Depression era. Among them were Gertrude Howard and Libby Taylor, who played servants to Mae West's characters in *I'm No Angel* (1933) and *Belle of the Nineties* (1934). In *Imitation of Life* (1934), Louise Beavers played a black servant whose light-skinned daughter, played by Fredi Washington, tries to pass for white. The black tap dancer and stage performer Bill "Bojangles" Robinson was featured in four popular films—*The Little Colonel* (1935), *The Littlest Rebel* (1935), *Just around the Corner* (1938), and *Rebecca of Sunnybrook Farm* (1938)—as a servant to white child star Shirley Temple.

The film that most firmly cemented the role of black Americans as servants in the American consciousness was *Gone with the Wind* (1939). Hattie McDaniel and Butterfly McQueen were the black "stars" in this epic adaptation of Margaret Mitchell's romanticized literary salute to the Old South. McDaniel had played servant or "Mammy" roles throughout the 1930s. The image of Mammy, the headscarf-wearing, obese, dutiful black woman who preferred nurturing white families to caring for her own children, appealed to white America. But in *Gone with the Wind*, McDaniel gave the performance of a lifetime and in 1940 became the first African American to win an Oscar. Many in the black community criticized her for playing "female Tom" roles. Defensively, McDaniel retorted she would rather play a maid and earn $700 a week than be one and earn only $7 a week. Some black actors such as McDaniel, dismayed by their relegation to demeaning roles, formed the Fair Play Committee (FPC) to lobby the white-dominated movie industry for more substantial roles, to get rid of dialect speech, and to ban the term *nigger* from the screen. But in the *Beulah* radio show, which premiered in 1947, McDaniel again played a wise but subservient maid who provides the family that employs her with advice, guidance, and direction.

Eventually, during and after World War II, Hollywood developed more sophisticated race-directed movies. Of particular significance was the positive, even romanticized, portrayal of black Americans in a movie financed by the War Department to gain support among African Americans for the U.S. role in World War II. *The Negro Soldier*, directed by Frank Capra in 1944, played to vast audiences of enthusiastic black people. But even before the *The Negro Soldier*, some motion pictures had displayed African Americans positively. Paul Robeson made two movies, *The Emperor Jones* (1933) and *Show Boat* (1936), in which he attempted to change how black men and women were represented on screen. He proclaimed in 1934, "In my music, my plays, my films I want to carry always this central idea: to be African. Multitudes of men have died for less worthy ideals; it is even more eminently worth living for." Robeson's films, however, were not box-office successes, and he left the United States to pursue his career in Europe. There his commitment to communism and leftist politics made him a target of the anticommunist hysteria that gripped the United States as the Cold War took hold in the late 1940s (see Chapter 20).

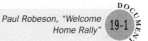
Paul Robeson, "Welcome Home Rally" **19-1**

To succeed commercially, African-American filmmakers had to disguise their dissent or create art purely for other black people. One of the most enterprising black filmmakers, Oscar Micheaux (1884–1951), made films aimed primarily at the black public, a group that

Louise Beavers (1908–1962) was a splendid actress whose talent was largely restricted to "mammy" roles. Here she appears with Claudette Colbert in a scene from the melodramatic film *Imitation of Life* (1934), which deals with the theme of black people passing for white.

Hollywood directors and producers of race movies ignored or insulted with stereotypical representations. Unlike the dominant Hollywood stereotypes, the black men and women in Micheaux's films were often educated, cultured, and prosperous. Micheaux endowed black Americans with cinematic voice and subjectivity. His films featured middle-class or identity issues such as "passing for white."

Micheaux produced more than thirty feature films between 1919 and 1948. In 1932, he released *The Exile*, the first sound motion picture to be made by, with, and for black Americans. The following year he produced *Veiled Aristocrats*, about passing for white among Chicago's black professional class. The characters in the film are considered "aristocrats" because they are descended from the white gentry of the Old South and Europe; they are "veiled" because of their color. The plot turns on the revelation that the wealthy "white" heroine is actually "colored," which enables her to marry the talented mulatto hero.

Micheaux tried to transform Hollywood without changing it, much as members of the black bourgeoisie struggled to be included in American society. His films capture the dilemma of black double consciousness. As W. E. B. Du Bois put it, black people always experienced that "peculiar sensation," that "sense of always looking at one's self through the eyes of others, of measuring one's soul by the tape of a world that looks on in amused contempt and pity." Black culture existed within and was shaped by, while simultaneously transforming, American culture. To the degree that black Americans had been assimilated, white American culture was their culture as well.

The white ethnic immigrants who created Hollywood were determined to help marginal and excluded groups like Jews and Italians assimilate into the American mainstream. Hollywood sought to create the illusion that these groups belonged to the power elite. However, these Hollywood entrepreneurs did not do the same for African Americans. Their films during the Depression represented black people as unassimilable. A small cadre of black filmmakers and actors created independent films and showed them in cinema houses exclusively for black patrons. Following the lead of pioneers like Micheaux, they created an alternative cinema in which they introduced nuanced and fully human characters.

The Black Chicago Renaissance

Black culture flourished during the 1930s and 1940s, decades otherwise noted for economic depression and global warfare. African-American musicians thrived in cities as far from Harlem as Kansas City (Missouri), Dallas, Denver, and Oklahoma City. They created a southwestern style of jazz with blues inflection. Jazz pianist Mary Lou Williams (1910–1981) worked in Kansas City during the 1930s. She recalled, "I found Kansas City to be a heavenly city—music everywhere in the Negro section of town, and fifty or more cabarets rocking on Twelfth and Eighteenth Streets." The southwestern musical style rivaled the West Coast jazz scene (that often included black and Latino musicians) that radiated from Los Angeles to Portland, Seattle, San Francisco, and Oakland, and reached as far as Honolulu and found patrons in such Asian cities as Yokohama in Japan, Shanghai and Hong Kong on the coast of China, and Manila in the Philippines.

But in many respects, Chicago was the center of black culture during the 1930s and 1940s. In contrast to some of the artists of the "Harlem Renaissance," the leading writers in Chicago harbored no illusions that art would solve the problems caused by white supremacy and black subordination. Although a western regional literary aesthetic did not emerge during these decades, a midwestern renaissance did flourish. The Chicago writers of the 1930s and 1940s emphasized the idea that black art had to combine aesthetics and function. It had to serve the cause of black freedom.

Arna Bontemps (1902–1973) was to the **Chicago Renaissance** what Alain Locke had been to the Harlem Renaissance. "The Depression," Bontemps asserted,

> put an end to the dream world of renaissance Harlem and scattered the band of poets and painters, sculptors, scholars and singers who had in six exciting years made a generation of Americans aware of unnoticed and hitherto unregarded creative talents among Negroes. . . .What they did not dream was that a second awakening, less gaudy but closer to realities, was already in prospect. . . .One way or the other, Harlem got its renaissance in the middle twenties, centering around the *Opportunity* contests and the Fifth Avenue Awards Dinners. . . .Ten years later Chicago reenacted it on WPA [Works Progress Administration] without finger bowls but with increased power.

Born in Louisiana, Bontemps migrated in 1935 from California to Chicago, where he met Richard Wright and joined the South Side Writers Group, which Wright founded in 1936. The Group included poet Margaret Walker and playwright Theodore Ward. It offered criticism and moral support to black writers. Bontemps's own writing was influenced by his association with the group. After 1935 his novels and short stories reflected a militant restlessness and revolutionary spirit. In 1936 he published *Black*

Thunder about the nineteenth-century slave conspiracy led by Gabriel and in 1939 *Drums at Dusk* about the Haitian Revolution and Toussaint L'Ouverture (1746–1803). Richard Wright's writings also celebrated resistance, but with more nuance. He published *Uncle Tom's Children* in 1938 and his masterpiece, *Native Son*, in 1940.

Among the artists who launched their careers on WPA funds were Margaret Walker and Willard Motley. Walker attracted widespread attention when her collected poems appeared as the book *For My People* in the Yale Series of Younger Poets. Willard Motley worked with a radio group while writing his powerful novel *Knock on Any Door* (1947), which depicted the transformation of an Italian-American altar boy into a criminal headed for the electric chair. The novel invited comparisons with Wright's *Native Son*.

Before the 1930s several black intellectuals misjudged the potential of Chicago to become a vibrant center of black culture. In the late 1920s, black social scientists Charles S. Johnson and E. Franklin Frazier expressed disdain for black Chicago's artistic and intellectual prospects. Frazier proclaimed that "Chicago has no intelligentsia," and in 1923 Johnson asked rhetorically,

> Who can write of lilies and sunsets in the pungent shadows of the stockyards? . . . It is no dark secret why literary societies fail, where there are no Art exhibits or libraries about, why periodicals presuming upon an I.Q. above the age of 12 are not read, why so little literature comes out of the city. No, the kingdom of the second ward [the black neighborhood] has no self-sustaining intelligentsia, and a miserably poor acquaintance with that of the world surrounding it.

Johnson did, however, admit one saving grace in Chicago's cultural wasteland: "[I]t leads these colored United States in its musical aspirations with, perhaps, the best musical school in the race, as these go."

Johnson and Frazier were too harsh. Just as Chicago's industrial economy attracted working-class black people, it also nurtured artists who drew inspiration from and reflected this stratum of moving and striving, strolling and styling black people who wanted to transgress class and geographical lines. These working-class people aspired to enjoy the middle-class life of accomplishment and consumption. A critical pulse point on Chicago's South Side came to be known as Bronzeville. It measured and reflected the reality of the lives of ordinary working-class people. As Harlem had its 125th Street, Chicago had 35th and State Street and 47th and South Park (now Martin Luther King Jr. Drive). Chicago was heir to the Harlem Renaissance. In 1930 Langston Hughes published *Not without Laughter*,

Archibald Motley (1891–1981) captures in *Barbecue* (1934) the exuberance and vitality of nightlife in Chicago's Bronzeville. Motley was a major artistic talent during Chicago's Black Renaissance of the 1930s and 1940s.   Oil on canvas, 36 1/4 × 40 1/8 in. The Howard University Gallery of Art, Washington, D.C.

the first major novel about the black experience in Chicago. Hughes moved to the city himself in 1941 and wrote often for the widely read Chicago *Defender*. The city epitomized urban industrial America. As the northern terminus of the Illinois Central Railroad and the home of the *Defender*, it had long attracted displaced agricultural workers from the southern cotton fields, and by 1930 it had a black population of 233,903. The migrants arrived eager to absorb Chicago's hard-driving blues and jazz culture.

During the 1920s a discernible class structure among African Americans emerged in Chicago, fueled in part by the new migrants. These men and women expanded the consumer base and gave rise to a cadre of educated professionals and entrepreneurs who developed an appreciation for the arts. The Black Metropolis, as social scientists St. Clair Drake and Horace R. Cayton designated Chicago's South Side, became a black city within a city. Black businesses, such as banks and insurance companies, formed the financial foundation. Entrepreneur Walter L. Lee started Your Cab Company and each day put on the streets a half-dozen chauffeur-uniformed drivers of vehicles. In the late 1940s, John Johnson would launch a publishing empire with such magazines as *Negro Digest*, *Jet*, and *Ebony*. These businesses depended less on white patronage

PROFILE ❧ LANGSTON HUGHES

Langston Hughes identified with poor and working-class black people. He used his poetry, prose, and playwriting skills to make the dignity and beauty of black people visible and known.

Hughes once referred to himself as "a literary sharecropper." Admirers called him a range of names—"Poet Laureate of the Negro People," for starters. During his career he produced fifteen volumes of poetry, two collections of short stories, one novel, two volumes of autobiography—*The Big Sea* (1940), and *I Wonder as I Wander* (1956)—and fifteen plays, along with librettos, scripts, essays, songs, translations, anthologies, children's stories, biographies and histories for the young, and two decades of weekly newspaper columns. He recorded the humor, wisdom, dialects, moods, and music of black people. One of the best examples of his social poetry was "The Negro Speaks of Rivers":

I've known rivers:
I've known rivers ancient as the world and older than the flow
of human blood in human veins.
My soul has grown deep like the rivers.
I bathed in the Euphrates when dawns were young.
I built my hut near the Congo and it lulled me to sleep.
I looked upon the Nile and raised the pyramids above it.
   I heard the singing of the Mississippi when Abe
         Lincoln went down to New Orleans, and
            I've seen its muddy
            bosom turn all golden in the sunset.
            I've known rivers:
            Ancient, dusky rivers.
            My soul has grown deep like the rivers.

Hughes was born in Joplin, Missouri, in 1902 and was raised by his maternal grandmother, Mary Langston. His father, James Hughes, emigrated to Mexico, and his mother Carrie Langston remarried. Hughes became fascinated

by black urban folk culture, which had been transplanted from the rural South by the Great Migration. He joined his mother in Cleveland in 1916, attended an integrated high school, and began to publish. Hughes had ambivalent feelings about his parents, who left him adrift, emotionally and financially. He dropped out of Columbia University in 1922, lived in Harlem, and traveled to Europe and Africa.

With the publication of *The Weary Blues* in 1926, his career took off. Hughes was enraptured by the language of the blues—its warmth, stoicism, incongruous humor, ironic laughter mixed with tears, and the "pain that was swallowed in a smile." In 1943 he introduced in his Chicago *Defender* column the character Jesse B. Semple, a racially conscious barfly philosopher—unlettered, but wise. The college-educated, somewhat uptight narrator of the series interrogates Semple about black life, from love of women and watermelon to the fortunes of rich gospel singers and the whereabouts of leaders who hide from the black people they lead. At one point Semple observed:

Not only am I half dead right now from pneumonia,
but everything else has happened to me! I've been cut,
shot, stabbed, run over, hit by a car, and tromped by a
horse. I have also been robbed, fooled, deceived, two-
timed, double-crossed, dealt seconds, and mightily near
blackmailed—but I'm still here! . . . I have been fired,
laid off, and last week given an indefinite vacation,
also Jim Crowed, segregated, barred out, insulted,
eliminated, called black, yellow, and red, locked in,
locked out, locked up, and also left holding the bag.

In 1932 Hughes visited Moscow, where he felt comfortable and appreciated. He was impressed by the absence of Jim Crow segregation and discrimination and ignored Stalin's oppression and murders. But Hughes was never a member of the Communist Party and eventually become disillusioned with the Soviet Union. Hughes remains an enduring symbol of the artist who championed black folk culture as authentic American culture.

Source: Poem from *Collected Poems* by Langston Hughes. (c) 1994 by the Estate of Langston Hughes. Used by permission of Alfred A. Knopf, a division of Random House, Inc.

Hughes

than on black support. It was in their best interest to support the arts and provide venues for performances.

 34 *"Backwater Blues" from Leadbelly's Last*

Revolutionary work in music also occurred in Chicago. It was a pioneering center both for recording and performing music. As black music became a commodity, influential black disc jockeys like Al Benson (Arthur B. Leaner was his real name) appeared on the radio in Chicago. Benson, a migrant from Mississippi, proved to be as skilled a businessman as he was a cultural impresario. By 1948 Benson was hosting shows on three different radio stations. Readers of the *Defender* voted him the "Mayor of Bronzeville." A determined entrepreneur, Benson arranged "first play rights" with record producers and distributors, catapulting Chicago into a major launch site for new releases. Diverse artists including Muddy Waters and Mahalia Jackson benefitted from airplay on Benson's programs. Historian Adam Green concludes that as a consequence of the power and machinations of black disc jockeys, "black popular music would never again face the disastrous conditions of destitution and near-erasure it faced during the depression."

Music was the primary inspiration for the creativity that characterized black cultural movements in America. Avant-garde developments in black music preceded black cultural activity in the visual arts, poetry, drama, dance, literature, film, and sports. Cultural creativity was a potent force for black liberation and occurred simultaneously in different locations in America.

Within the confines of the South Side of Chicago, black musical giants, such as trumpeter Louis Armstrong (1898–1971) and his wife, Lillian Hardin Armstrong (1898–1971), a well-known and respected jazz pianist, performed and nurtured a distinct jazz culture. "Lil" Armstrong was born in Memphis, Tennessee, and received formal music training at Fisk University, the Chicago College of Music (earning a teaching certificate in 1924), and the New York College of Music (graduated in 1929). "Lil" Hardin Armstrong led her own band and was talented at arranging, composing, and singing. She played with great performers of the day and befriended Louis Armstrong when he arrived in Chicago. They were married in 1924. Lil Armstrong eventually encouraged her husband to leave King Oliver's Creole Jazz Band and to join Fletcher Henderson in New York. The Armstrongs were divorced in 1938. She continued her recording career with Decca records under the name Lil Hardin.

Duke Ellington in his autobiography, *Music Is My Mistress*, remarked,

> Chicago always sounded like the most glamorous place in the world to me when I heard the guys in Frank

Holliday's poolroom talking about their travels. . . . They told very romantic tales about nightlife on the South Side. By the time I got there in 1930, it glittered even more . . . the Loop, the cabarets . . . city life, suburban life, luxurious neighborhoods—and the apparently broken-down neighborhoods where there were more good times than any place in the city.

At this point Ellington was recording some of his best jazz, such as *Mood Indigo* (1930) and *Ko-Ko* (1940). Ellington's stay in Chicago left a powerful impression on vocalist Joe Williams. Williams recalled,

> I used to arrange my classes so that I could get home in time to hear a program they [Ellington's band] had in Chicago called "Red Hot and Low Down." . . . The program's theme was Ellington's East St. Louis Toodle-oo. Later on, they changed the theme to "Sepia Panorama." Then they changed it again, to "Take the 'A' Train." But I used to come home early from high school so that I could hear Duke Ellington on the radio.

The seeds that blossomed into full-bodied jazz culture were planted across America at the turn of the century. The most famous musicians, however, all went to or passed through Chicago. As the Chicago Jazz Age came into its own, the beguiling tune "Pretty Baby" became the city's theme song. It was written by Tony Jackson, whom Jelly Roll Morton (the self-proclaimed "inventor of jazz") called "maybe the best entertainer the world has ever seen." The South Side, specifically along State Street between 31st and 35th, was the beating heart of the city's Jazz Age. Although Chicago did not replace New York as the major location for the aspiring jazz musician, it was the place you went to prove you had what it took to make a name for yourself.

GOSPEL IN CHICAGO: THOMAS DORSEY

The term *gospel* designates the traditional religious music of the black church. It was nurtured and flourished in Chicago's Holiness, Sanctified, Pentecostal, Baptist, and Methodist churches, in storefronts, or large edifices. Gospel music became the backbone of urban and contemporary black religion and is deeply entrenched in worship. The use of instruments—tambourines, drums, pianos, horns, guitars, and Hammond organs—characterizes gospel and distinguishes it from the earlier spiritual and black folk music. During the 1930s and 1940s, it developed its own idioms and performance techniques.

The doctrines of black "folk churches" encourage free expression, group participation, spontaneous

MARGARET WALKER ON BLACK CULTURE

In 1942 poet Margaret Walker (1915–1998) published For My People, *the most important collection of poetry written by a participant in the Black Chicago Renaissance before Gwendolyn Brooks's* A Street in Bronzeville *(1945). In a 1992 collection of her essays, Walker reflected on the meaning and significance of black culture:*

> *Black culure has two main streams: a sociological stream . . . and an artistic stream. . . .In this artistic stream black culture has five branches. These are language, religion, art, music, and literature. . . .*

Black music is perhaps the most acceptable of our black culture. The modern world is willing to accept the unique character of African rhythms and the language of the drum. White America, in general, reluctantly admits that black American music is the American music and most indigenous to our culture. In every category or classification of music, moreover, Black America has achieved monumentally. With a broad base of folk music—spirituals and gospel music, seculars (blues, work songs, prison hollers)-individuals have risen in notable achievement in classical, popular, and various forms of jazz. From Black Patti to Marian Anderson and Leontyne Price, the great black American singer has gained worldwide eminence. Roland Hayes, William Warfield, Todd Duncan, the late Ellabelle Davis, Dorothy Maynor, and Mattiwilda Dodds are notable black artists known the world over. Our blues singers like Bessie Smith, Ma Rainey, and B. B. King; folk singers like Leadbelly, and the greats like Louis Armstrong, Jimmie Lunceford, and Count Basie; great composers like Scott Joplin, Eubie Blake, Charlie Parker, and the incomparable Duke Ellington are significant contributors to the modern world and all represent the undeniable genius of the black American musician.

Individual achievement, while part of our general cultural picture, is not all. It is in language and religion that Black Americans as a group have made a significant contribution to the national fiber of American life and to the modern world. As spiritual creatures we have shown through unmerited suffering that we have a sense of humanity that can enrich the moral fiber and contribute to a new world ethos. Our black culture is aware of human needs and human values. Handicapped as we have been by a racist system of dehumanizing slavery and segregation, our American history of nearly five hundred years reveals that our cultural and spiritual gifts brought from our African past are still intact. It is not only that we

testimonies, prayers, witnessing, and music. Singers and choirs rarely perform the same songs in the same way more than once. The performer must pay attention to the quality of the sound and to the careful manipulation of timbre, range, and shading. The style of the delivery uses the whole body in synchronized movement. The mechanics of the delivery are designed to intensify the performance, giving it added textual variation and melodic improvisation. Performers expand a melody by a variety of technical devices, including repetition, shouts, slides, slurs, moans, and grunts. The supporting piano and organ frequently engage in call-and-response interplay.

Gospel singer Pearl Williams-Jones makes clear the distinction between black church music and music of the other churches: "The traditional liturgical forms of plain chant, chorales, and anthems do not fulfill the needs of traditional black folk religious worship and rituals."

are singers and dancers, poets and prophets, great athletes and perceptive politicians—but we are also a body of charismatic and numinous people yet capable of cultic fire as seen in our black churches and still creative enough in intellect to signal the leap forward into a new and humanistic age. We are the authors of the new paradigm. . . .

How then has black culture been disseminated and kept alive? Black culture has survived in the black institutions of Black America. In the black family, the Black Church, the black school, the black press, the black nation, and the black world. This is where our black culture has survived and thrived. This is where it must continue to grow. The ground of common humanity is not yet a reality in the modern world but when it comes as it must in the twenty-first century, Black Africa, and black humanity must be as always the foundation on which it stands and from which it logically proceeds. One world of international brotherhood does not negate the nationalism of black people. It only enforces and re-enforces our common humanity.

According to Walker, what external factors influenced and sustained black culture? What are some of the central themes in black culture?

What political and symbolic use have African Americans made of black culture?

Source: *On Being Female, Black, and Free:* Essays by Margaret Walker, 1932–1992, edited by Maryemma Graham, 1997. Jackson; University of Mississippi Press, 1997. Reprinted by permission of Maryemma Graham.

In Chicago, Thomas Dorsey (1899–1993)—one of Chicago's leading composers of the blues since the mid-1920s—was most responsible for developing black urban gospel. Dorsey's genius lay in his ability to synthesize elements of the blues with religious hymns to create a gospel blues. His gospel pieces, performed with a ragtime-derived, boogie-woogie piano accompaniment, radiated an urban religious spirit. In 1930 Dorsey gained widespread attention when gospel singer Willie Mae Ford Smith (1904–1994) performed his "If You See My Savior, Tell Him That You Saw Me" at the National Baptist Convention meeting in Chicago. Two years later, in 1932, Dorsey's place in musical history was assured when Theodore Frye, with Dorsey at the piano, performed in the Ebenezer Baptist Church in Chicago his now classic gospel song, "Take My Hand, Precious Lord." The song had a profound impact on gospel performers and their audiences. Dorsey's abundant works provided a foundation for shout worship in the urban Protestant churches formed by transplanted black southerners in the 1930s and succeeding decades.

One of the greatest gospel singers, Chicago-based Mahalia Jackson (1911–1972), sang and promoted Dorsey's songs all over the country on the church circuit and at religious conventions between 1939 and 1944. Jackson once said of the music, "Gospel songs are the songs of hope. When you sing them you are delivered of your burden." During the Depression and World War II, gospel became big business.

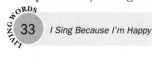
LIVING WORDS
33   *I Sing Because I'm Happy*

CHICAGO IN DANCE AND SONG: KATHERINE DUNHAM AND BILLIE HOLIDAY

The influence of the WPA in Chicago was especially reflected in dance. Dance has always been an integral part of African-American life, and the dances of black people have always been important in the American theater. The first performances by black dancers given within and taken seriously by the concert dance world occurred in the 1930s. The first "Negro Dance Recital in America" was performed in 1931 by the New Negro Art Theater Dance Company, co-founded by Edna Buy and Hemsley Winfield. In that same year, Katherine Dunham (1909–2006) founded the Negro Dance Group in Chicago, which survived thanks to WPA support. As Dunham later recalled, "Black dancers were not allowed to take classes in studios in the '30s. I started a school because there was no place for blacks to study dance. I was the first to open the way for black dancers and I was the first to form a black dance company."

One of America's premier dance artists, the internationally acclaimed Katherine Dunham (1909–2006) performed in the Bobli Gardens in Florence, Italy, in 1950. A talented choreographer, anthropologist, and writer, Dunham founded one of the first black dance companies. She was an outspoken critic of Jim Crow segregation.

Dunham was unique. Trained in anthropology, she studied African-based ritual dance in the Caribbean. In 1938 her troupe stunned an audience with the sexual vitality of its performance of one of her works. When the company, now renamed the Katherine Dunham Dance Company, performed in February 1940, audiences and critics were awed. The *New York Times* declared, "With the arrival of Katherine Dunham on the scene the development of a substantial Negro dance Art begins to look decidedly bright." The reviewer continued,

> Her performance with her group at the Windsor Theater may very well become a historic occasion, for certainly never before in all efforts of recent years to establish the Negro dance as a serious medium has there been so convincing and authoritative approach. . . . The potential greatness of the Negro dance lies in its discovery of its own roots and the crucial nursing of them into growth and flower. . . .It is because she has showed herself to have both the objective quality of the student and the natural instinct of the artist that she has done such a truly important job.

What kept audiences returning to Dunham dance performances, however, was the dancer's bold sensuality. A reviewer of *Tropical Revue*, for example, wrote that it was "likely to send thermometers soaring to the bursting point. . . .Tempestuous and torrid, raffish and revealing." The *New York Sun* marveled, "Shoulders, midsections and posteriors went round and round. Particularly when the cynosure was Miss Dunham, the vista was full of pulchritude."

Dunham explained her motivation:

> I felt a new dance form was needed for black people to be able to appear in any theater in the world and be accepted and exciting. One of the prerequisites of art is uniqueness. Rather than taking years to build a classical ballet company for blacks, I decided to create a dance with an authentic base for black people. Through my anthropological work, I studied primitive and folk dances and created the Dunham dance from them.

The success in New York led to film offers. The producers of the all-black musical extravaganza *Cabin in the Sky* hired the dance troupe and gave the feature role of Georgia Brown to Dunham. The role gave Dunham, as the *Times* dance critic wrote, the chance "to sizzle." But it also undermined her seriousness, allowing white audiences to view her as the stereotypical sultry black sexpot.

Nevertheless, the profits from the film funded the dancers' stage performances and Dunham's research. In 1943 Dunham moved to New York and opened the Katherine Dunham School of Arts and Research, which trained artists not only in dance but in theater, literature, and world cultures.

Dunham was not afraid to protest racial segregation, even though it hurt her popularity. In the early 1940s, she denounced discrimination. In 1944 in Louisville, Kentucky, after a performance, Dunham announced, "We are glad we have made you happy. We hope you have enjoyed us. This is the last time I shall play Louisville because the management refuses to let people like us sit by people like you. Maybe after the war we shall have democracy and I can return." Dunham is important for two reasons. First, she was a gifted and talented pioneer in dance whose choreography inspired future generations. Second, she underscored the responsibility that a black artist had to the black community to fight racism.

Billie Holiday (1915–1959), another great performer whose career took shape during the Depression, also used her art to challenge the oppression of black people. Holiday, popularly known as "Lady Day," began singing at age fifteen and was discovered three years later by John Hammond, a Chicago jazz producer and promoter. In 1933 Hammond arranged for Holiday's first recording session, and in 1934 she made her debut at the Apollo Theater in Harlem. An incomparable singer known for subtle and artful improvisation, she left a wealth of recordings.

Black Visual Art

Chicago artists, such as Charles White, Elizabeth Catlett, and Eldzier Cortor, and Harlem's Jacob Lawrence, celebrated both rural and urban working-class black people while implicitly criticizing the racial hierarchy of power and privilege. Their art belonged to the social realism school that flourished in the United States in the 1930s. Social realist art was intensely ideological. It strove to fuse propaganda—both left wing and right wing—to art to make it socially and politically relevant.

As the Depression worsened, black artists became even more determined to use their art to portray the crisis in capitalism. This involved depicting social and racial inequality. Chicago's Charles White wrote that "paint is the only weapon I have with which to fight what I resent. If I could write I would write about it. If I could talk I would talk about it. Since I paint, I must paint about it."

Defense Worker, a painting by Dox Thrash, reflects these concerns. Completed in 1942, just after the United States had entered World War II, it shows an isolated black worker looming over the horizon. The heroic proletarian imagery alludes to the dream of a racially integrated labor force, equal opportunity, and social reform in the wake of the New Deal and the sudden demand for labor triggered by the war.

The Harmon Foundation sponsored five juried exhibitions (1926–1931, 1933) of the work of black artists. The William E. Harmon Awards for Distinguished Achievement among Negroes celebrated black artists in the hope they would serve as role models for others. William E. Harmon, a real estate investor from Iowa, established the New York–based foundation in 1925. In the 1930s the WPA established art workshops and community art centers in black urban communities such as Chicago (Southside Community Art Center), Cleveland (Karamu House Artist Association), Detroit (Heritage House), and Harlem (Harlem Art Workshop and the Harlem Community Art Center) to teach art to neighborhood young people and provide work for artists. Sculptor Augusta Savage, as the first director of the Harlem Community Art Center, presided over more than 1,500 students enrolled in day and evening classes in drawing, painting,

PROFILE ✦ BILLIE HOLIDAY AND "STRANGE FRUIT"

"Strange Fruit," which Billie Holiday first performed in 1929, became her signature piece. It was written by a white schoolteacher who went by the name of Lewis Allan (his real name was Abel Meerpol). While the lyrics capture the brutality of lynching, it was Holiday's incomparable vocal style and delivery that gave the song its political, emotional, and cultural power and made it the antilynching anthem:

Southern trees bear a strange fruit,
Blood on the leaves and blood at the root,
Black body swinging in the Southern breeze,
Strange fruit hanging from the poplar trees.
Pastoral scene of the gallant South,
The bulging eyes and the twisted mouth,
Scent of magnolia sweet and fresh,
And the sudden smell of burning flesh!
Here is a fruit for the crows to pluck
For the rain to gather, for the wind to suck,
For the sun to rot, for a tree to drop.
Here is a strange and bitter crop.

"Every time she sang that song," recalled Barney Josephson, a New York nightclub owner, it was unforgettable. . . . I made her do it as her last number. . . . When she sang "Strange Fruit" she never moved. Her hands were down. She didn't even touch the mike. With the little light on her face. The tears never interfered with her voice, but the tears would come and just knock everybody in that house out.

Billie Holiday was born Eleanora Fagan in Philadelphia, Pennsylvania, on April 7, 1915 to teenagers Sadie Fagan and Clarence Holiday. She grew up in Baltimore, Maryland, and became perhaps the greatest jazz singer ever recorded, a unique improviser and soloist. She set the standards to which future vocalists such as Sarah Vaughan, Carmen McRae, and Lena Horne would aspire. Much attention has focused on the tragic and destructive dimensions of her private life, but it is her musical talent that compels interest and admiration. Holiday used her talent to do more than to entertain; she challenged and often disturbed her listeners, especially with her soul-shattering rendition of "Strange Fruit." While frequently factually inaccurate, Holiday's autobiography, *Lady Sings the Blues* (1956), and the equally distorted 1972 movie staring Diana Ross emphasize her struggle against sexism and racism within the music world and society. Holiday appeared in two movies. In 1935 she performed in Duke Ellington's short film *Symphony in Black*, singing "Big City Blues." In 1946 she performed three songs in a movie, *New Orleans*, opposite her musical mentor Louis Armstrong. Saxophonist Lester Young, who began recording with Holiday in 1937, gave her the nickname "Lady Day." By the late 1940s, Holiday's addiction to drugs was hurting her career. In 1947 she entered a private clinic, but was unable to stay clean. Following her discharge, the police arrested her for possession, and she served nine and one-half months at the Federal Reformatory for Women at Alderson, West Virginia. New York officials revoked her cabaret card and prohibited her from performing in night clubs in the city. Still, she gave concerts in other cities and went on international tours. A year before her death, Holiday recorded her most popular album, "Lady in Satin" (1958). She died in New York City on July 17, 1959. Thousands of friends and fans attended the funeral, a formal requiem high mass held at Saint Paul the Apostle Cathedral. She was buried in Saint Raymond's Catholic Cemetery in the Bronx.

Billie Holiday (1915–1959) was one of the greatest jazz singers of all time. ▸ Between 1935 and 1938, she released some eighty titles on the Brunswick label for marketing to the black jukebox audience. Getty Images Inc.—Hulton Archieve Photos sculpture, printmaking, and design. Among the teachers was Selma Burke (1900–1995), who sculpted the relief of Franklin D. Roosevelt that appears on the dime.

One of the initiatives of the Federal Arts Project, another New Deal agency, was to sponsor the creation of murals in public buildings, such as post offices and schools, that celebrated American ideals. Murals by black artists celebrated the heritage, contributions to society, and struggles of African Americans. Aaron Douglas, a leading painter of such public art, spoke about his work and that of his colleagues in a 1936 essay, "The Negro in American Culture":

> One of our chief concerns has been to establish and maintain recognition of our essential humanity, in other words, complete social and political equality. This has been a difficult fight as we have been the constant object of attack by all manner of propaganda from nursery rhymes to false scientific racial theories. . . .In this struggle the rest of the proletariat almost invariably has been arrayed against us. . . .But the Negro artist, unlike the white artist, has never known the big house. He is essentially a product of the masses and can never take a position above or beyond their level.

Douglas and other black artists pressed the WPA to appoint more African Americans to its local boards and to hire them for more projects. The Harlem Artists Guild and the Arts and Crafts Guild in Chicago provided forums where black artists could meet and plan strategies to foster the visual arts and support the social and political issues that affected black people's lives.

Black Literature

Black literature, like black art, has been assessed in terms of what it reveals about the social, cultural, and political landscape at a given historical moment. The most distinguishing feature of black literature may be the way that black writers have attempted to create spaces of freedom in their work, to liberate place, a trait that also marks black religious culture and folk cultural practices, such as storytelling. Black literature, like all black cultural production, is valued both for aesthetic reasons on its own and for the way it represents the struggles of black people to attain freedom. In their work black writers in the 1930s and 1940s felt obliged to address questions of identity and to define and describe urban life to the dispossessed and impoverished black migrants to the cities. They tried to delineate the dimensions of a shared American heritage by portraying the specific contributions that African Americans had made to American society. Finally, and perhaps most ambitiously, black writers explored the issue of the rights African Americans were entitled to as Americans and the demands they could and should make on the state and society.

RICHARD WRIGHT'S *NATIVE SON*

In 1940 Richard Wright (1908–1960) published *Native Son*, the first of many important novels by Depression-generation black authors. Reviewers hailed it as "the new American tragedy." Its tale of the downfall of the young Bigger Thomas could be read as a warning about how economic hardship combined with segregation and discrimination could lead young black men to lash out in violence and rage. Setting out for an interview for a job as a chauffeur, Bigger meets with his neighborhood friends who want him to help them rob a grocery store. Bigger's

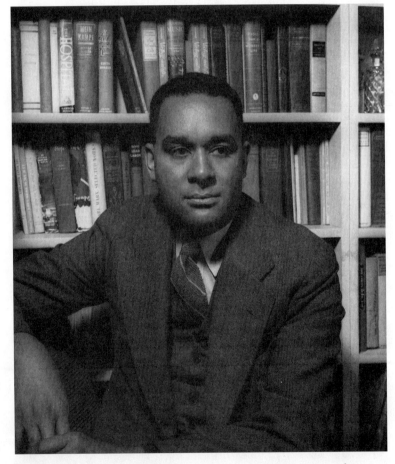

Richard Wright (1908–1960) was the first black writer to commandeer serious attention in mainstream American literature. In *Native Son* (1940) and *Black Boy* (1945), Wright provided incisive critiques of American racism. He received support from the Federal Writers Project and in his early works he poignantly portrayed the pathos of black southern migrants to the urban industrial North.   Courtesy of the Library of Congress fear of whites prevents him from going along. Instead, he picks a fight to camouflage his fear and avoid committing the crime. Bigger gets the chauffeur's job, which requires him to drive the wealthy Dalton family. On his first assignment, he is supposed to drive young Mary Dalton to a university lecture. But she talks him into picking up her boyfriend, Jan—a communist—and taking them to a restaurant in the black neighborhood. Jan and Mary are oblivious to the offensively patronizing way they treat Bigger. After dinner Bigger drives them around the city while they drink and make love in the back seat.

When Jan leaves, Bigger takes an intoxicated Mary home. Because Mary is too drunk to walk, Bigger carries her to her room and is putting her to bed when blind Mrs. Dalton comes to check on her daughter. Bigger panics. He covers Mary's head with a pillow to keep her quiet. When Mrs. Dalton leaves, Bigger discovers he has inadvertently smothered Mary. He then burns her body in the basement furnace. Not fully grasping what he has done, Bigger writes a ransom note signed with a phony name to make it seem that Mary has been kidnapped. When Mary's remains are discovered, Bigger flees. Fearing she might betray him, Bigger then murders his girlfriend, Bessie. Bigger is captured, tried, and condemned. The remainder of the novel explores the hysteria and bigotry that envelop the case, the harsh criminal justice system, the insensitivity of the Communist Party, which seeks to exploit Bigger's plight, and the poverty and social ills that plagued Chicago's African-American communities during the Depression.

At the center of the drama is Wright's exploration of how Bigger comes to terms with his murder of Mary and Bessie. In conversations with Max, his communist lawyer, he realizes his irrational fear of white people had caused him to kill the two women. Bigger realizes he was in fact a product of his experiences in the ghetto. At the end of the novel he says, "What I killed for I am."

Wright's novel poignantly and chillingly thrust the impact of urbanization and racism on black men and women into the collective consciousness of the American people. One white critic declared, "Speaking from the black wrath of retribution, Wright insisted that history can be punishment. He told us the one thing even the most liberal whites preferred not to hear: that Negroes were far from patient or forgiving, that they were scarred by fear, that they hated every moment of their suppression even when seeming most acquiescent, and that often enough they hated us the decent and cultivated white men who from complicity or neglect shared in the responsibility of their plight."

In his closing arguments, the lawyer, Max, describes the psychological conditions that led Bigger to

kill and warns of the destructive potential of suppressed black rage:

> The hate and fear which we have inspired in him, woven by our civilization into the very structure of his consciousness and into his blood and bones, into the hourly functioning of his personality, have become the justification of his existence. . . .Kill him and swell the tide of pent up lava that will some day break loose, not in a single, blundering crime, but in a wild cataract of emotion that will brook no control.

Native Son was an immediate success. It became a Book-of-the-Month Club selection and has sold millions of copies.

JAMES BALDWIN CHALLENGES WRIGHT

Wright's influence on American literature has been immense. He was the first African-American writer to enjoy an international reputation and showed that success and militancy were not mutually exclusive. A younger generation of black writers, however, especially James Baldwin (1924–1987), took issue with Wright. African Americans, they argued, need not all be portrayed as hapless victims of American racism. In a famous short essay, "Everybody's Protest Novel," in 1949, Baldwin argued that Bigger's tragedy was not that he was black, poor, and scared, but that he had accepted "a theology that denies him life, that he admits the possibility of his being sub-human and feels constrained, therefore, to battle for his humanity according to those brutal criteria bequeathed him at his birth." Baldwin concluded, "The failure of the protest novel lies in its rejection of life, the human being, the denial of his beauty, dread, power, in its insistence that it is his categorization alone which is real and which cannot be transcended." In turn, Wright accused Baldwin of trying to destroy his reputation and of betraying all African-American writers who wrote protest literature. "What do you mean, protest!" Wright demanded. "All literature is protest. You can't name a single novel that isn't protest."

Richard Wright, "Are We Solving America's Race Problem?" 1945 **DOCUMENT 19-5**

Baldwin answered Wright in a second essay in 1951 entitled, "Many Thousand Gone." "Wright's work," Baldwin declared, "is most clearly committed to the social struggle. . . .[T]hat artist is strangled who is forced to deal with human beings solely in social terms; and who has, moreover, as Wright had, the necessity thrust on him of being the representative of some thirteen million people. It is a false responsibility (since writers are not congressmen) and impossible, by its nature, of fulfillment."

The controversy ended the budding friendship between Wright and Baldwin, and Baldwin, whose work would soon include many powerful and revealing novels and insightful essays, inherited the mantle of "best-known black American male writer" (see Chapter 22).

RALPH ELLISON AND *INVISIBLE MAN*

The most intricate novel about the black experience in America written during this era was Ralph Ellison's (1914–1994) *Invisible Man*, which won the National Book Award for fiction in 1952. Partially autobiographical, it traces the life of a young black man from his early years in a southern school (a thinly disguised Tuskegee Institute) through his migration to New York City. The novel explores class tensions within American society and within the black community. It illuminates the interaction between white and black Americans with a balanced, incisive perspective.

Although he wrote many essays, *Invisible Man* was Ellison's only completed novel. He argued that the black tradition teaches one "to deflect racial provocation and to master and control pain. . . . It is a tradition which abhors as obscene any trading on one's own anguish for gain or sympathy. . . . It takes fortitude to be a man and no less to be an artist. Perhaps it takes even more if the black man would be an artist." He concluded, "It would seem to me, therefore, that the question of how the 'sociology of his existence' presses upon the Negro writer's work depends upon how much of his life the individual writer is able to transform into art."

Echoing Du Bois's now classic characterization of the "twoness" of the African-American character, Ellison observed, "[Black people] are an American people who are geared to what is and who yet are driven by a sense of what it is possible for human life to be in this society."

African Americans in Sports

It is in the arena of professional sports that black Americans have demonstrated what human life can achieve when unconstrained by racism. The experiences of black men and women in American sports are a microcosm of their lives in American society. The privileges whites enjoyed in sports in this era paralleled the disadvantages and exclusions that were a constant part of black life. In the 1930s two black athletes, Jesse Owens and Joe Louis, captured the world's attention and inspired African Americans with pride, hope, and pleasure.

JESSE OWENS AND JOE LOUIS

Jesse Owens (1913–1980) was born on an Alabama sharecropping farm but grew up in Cleveland, Ohio. A talented runner, he studied at Ohio State University and prepared for the 1936 Olympics, which were to be held in Berlin, the capital of Nazi Germany. Many African-American leaders objected to participating in the games because they believed this would help legitimate the Nazi myth of the superiority of the so-called Aryan race. Owens participated to debunk that myth and he succeeded, becoming the first Olympian ever to win four gold medals. Although Hitler left the stadium to avoid congratulating Owens, his snub meant little to African Americans who relished Owens's victory over racism.

Joe Louis Barrow (1914–1981), like Owens, was the son of Alabama sharecroppers. His family migrated to Detroit, Michigan, when he was twelve. Although his mother wanted him to be a violinist, Joe Louis—he dropped the name Barrow—had other interests. As a youth, Louis displayed impressive boxing ability and won a string of local victories. In 1935 he faced former heavyweight champion Primo Carnera. A record crowd of 62,000 attended the fight in New York. The fight had political overtones. Louis was fighting an Italian-American at a time when Benito Mussolini, the fascist dictator of Italy, was about to invade Ethiopia; this was the oldest black independent nation in Africa, whose ruler, Emperor Haile Selassie, many black Americans admired. Sports writers and police were amazed to observe everybody cheering when Louis beat Carnera in the sixth round.

Louis won the world heavyweight title against James J. Braddock in 1937 and beat the German Max Schmeling in a symbolic victory over Nazism in 1938. Louis retained the world heavyweight title until 1949.

BREAKING THE COLOR BARRIER IN BASEBALL

Although African Americans were integrated in track and in boxing, professional baseball remained strictly segregated until after World War II. Despite the hardships of the Depression, however, virtually every major black community tried to field its own baseball team. The Negro National League, which had folded in 1932, was revived in 1934, and a second league, the Negro American League, formed in 1937. Many of the players in the Negro leagues, including such legends as Josh Gibson, Satchel Paige, Leon Day, and Cool Papa Bell, would have equaled or excelled their white counterparts in the major leagues, but, except for Paige, they never had the chance.

Jackie Robinson (1919–1972) broke baseball's color barrier when he joined the Brooklyn Dodgers in 1947. He silently endured considerable hostility and threats from angry white citizens.

AFRICAN-AMERICAN MILESTONES IN SPORTS

1934	The Negro National League is revived
1936	Jesse Owens wins four gold medals at Berlin Olympics
1937	Joe Louis defeats James J. Braddock to win world heavyweight title; the Negro American League is formed
1938	Joe Louis defeats the German Max Schmeling
1947	Jackie Robinson signs with the Brooklyn Dodgers to become the first black major-league baseball player; Dodgers win the National League Pennant
1948	Alice Coachman wins a gold medal in the high jump to become the first black woman Olympic champion
	Larry Doby joins the Cleveland Indians, becoming the first black player in the American League; Brooklyn Dodgers hire their second black player, Roy Campanella
1949	Jackie Robinson wins the National League's Most Valuable Player Award

1934-1949

In 1947, however, major-league baseball, which had been a white man's game since the departure of Fleetwood Walker in 1887, became integrated again when Jackie Robinson (1919–1972) signed to play with the Brooklyn Dodgers. In 1945 Branch Rickey, the general manager of the Dodgers, decided to sign a black ball player to improve the Dodgers' chances of winning the National League pennant and the World Series. After scouting the Negro Leagues, he signed twenty-six-year-old Jackie Robinson.

Robinson was the ideal choice. He was a superb athlete and a man of fortitude and immense determination. Born in Georgia and raised in southern California, he had been an All-American running back in football at UCLA and then had played baseball for the legendary Kansas City Monarchs of the Negro leagues. Robinson was also committed to black people and racial progress. Robinson played the 1946 season for the Brooklyn Dodgers minor-league team in Montreal, where he and his wife Rachel were warmly received by the Canadians. But spring training in segregated Florida was difficult to endure.

Robinson broke the color barrier when he opened at first base for the Dodgers in April 1947. Taunted, ridiculed, and threatened by some spectators and players, he responded by playing spectacular baseball. He won the Rookie of the Year honors in 1947, and the Dodgers won the National League pennant. Robinson retired in 1957 but remained outspoken on racial issues until his death from diabetes in 1972.

In July 1947 Larry Doby became the first black player in the American League when he joined the Cleveland Indians. As other major-league teams also signed black players, the once-popular Negro Leagues withered.

Black Religious Culture

Just as black religion was the "invisible institution" that helped African Americans survive slavery, the black church was the visible institution that helped hundreds of thousands of migrants adjust to urban life while affirming an enduring set of core values consisting of freedom, justice, equality, and an African heritage. There was, of course, no single "black church." The term is a shorthand way of referring to a pluralistic collection of institutions, including most prominently seven independent, historic, and black-controlled denominations: the African Methodist Episcopal Church; the African Methodist Episcopal Zion Church; the Christian Methodist Episcopal Church; the National Baptist Convention, Incorporated; the National Baptist Convention of America, Unincorporated; the

Progressive National Baptist Convention; and the Church of God in Christ. Together, these denominations account for more than 80 percent of all black Christians.

The black church helped black workers make the transition from being southern peasants to being part of a northern urban proletariat. Yet the relationship between black religious tradition and the secular lives of black people was always changing. The blues and jazz performed in nightclubs were transformed into urban gospel music. Many of the nightclub musicians and singers received their training and held their first public performances in their churches. During the Depression, the black church helped black people survive by enabling them to pool their resources and by offering inspiration and spiritual consolation. Here we focus on alternative religious groups that became prominent during the 1930s and 1940s and addressed specific needs growing out of the Depression and the traumatic experience of relocating to alien and often hostile northern cities. Elijah Muhammad's Nation of Islam and Father Divine's Peace Mission Movement combined secular concerns with sacred beliefs. Both strengthened a sense of identity, affirmation, and community among their members.

THE NATION OF ISLAM

The Nation of Islam emerged in 1929, the year Timothy Drew died. Drew, who took the name Nobel Drew Ali, was founder of the Moorish Science Temple of America, which flourished in Chicago, Detroit, and other cities in the 1920s. After his death, a modified version of the Moorish Science Temple emerged in 1930 in Detroit. It was led by a mysterious door-to-door peddler of silks and other items that supposedly originated in Africa, known variously as Wallace D. Fard, Master Farad Muhammad, or Wali Farad. He wrote two manuals of instruction, *The Secret Ritual of the Nation of Islam* and *Teaching for the Lost-Found Nation of Islam in a Mathematical Way*. His teachings that black people were the true Muslims attracted many poor residents in Depression-era Detroit. In addition to the beliefs of Nobel Drew Ali, Fard's Nation of Islam also taught a mixture of Koranic principles, the Christian Bible, his own beliefs, and those of nationalist Marcus Garvey.

In 1934, after establishing a Temple of Islam, Fard disappeared, and one of his disciples, Elijah Poole (1897–1975), renamed Elijah Muhammad by Fard, became leader of the Detroit temple and then of a second temple in Chicago. The Nation attracted the attention of federal authorities during World War II when its members refused to serve in the military. Muhammad was arrested in May 1942 on charges of inciting his followers to resist the draft and was imprisoned in Milan, Michigan, until 1946. After his release he settled in Chicago and began to expand his movement.

The Nation of Islam taught that black people were the earth's original human inhabitants who had lived, according to Elijah Muhammad, in the Nile Valley. Approximately six thousand years ago, a magician named Yakub produced white people. These white people proved so troublesome that they were banished to Europe, where they began to spread evil. Their worst crime was their enslavement of black people. Elijah Muhammad taught that white supremacy was ending and black people would rediscover their authentic history and culture. To prepare for the coming millennium, he instructed members to adhere to a code of behavior that included abstaining from many traditionally southern black foods, especially pork. Members subscribed to a family-centered culture in which women's role was to produce and rear the next generation. The Nation also demanded part of the South for a black national state.

FATHER DIVINE AND THE PEACE MISSION MOVEMENT

Father Major Jealous Divine (c. 1877–1965) was born George Baker in Savannah. Like Elijah Muhammad, little is known about his early life. He captured attention in 1919 when he settled with twenty followers in Sayville, New York, and began what became known in the 1930s as the Peace Mission Movement. Divine secured domestic jobs for many of his followers on the surrounding estates and preached a gospel of hard work, honesty, sobriety, equality, and sexual abstinence. He provided free, or nearly free, meals and shelter for anyone who asked. In 1930 he changed his name to Father Divine. His Peace Movement espoused a racially neutral and economically empowering dogma that appealed to poor and needy black and white urbanites by offering them spiritual guidance and mental and physical healing. The movement embodied ideas from the New Thought, Holiness, Perfectionist, and Adventist religions. Hundreds of people traveled to see Father Divine on weekends, feast at his communal banquet table, and listen to his promises of heaven on earth. The feasts were symbolic of the early Christian Eucharist and became the defining practices of Divine's religion.

In 1931 the police arrested Divine and eighty followers on charges of being a "public nuisance." Three days after a judge sentenced Divine to a year in jail and a $500 fine, the judge died of a heart attack. Divine was quoted as saying, "I hated to do it." The conviction was reversed, and Divine's reputation as a master of cosmic forces soared. Some of his followers now believed he was God. Aside from the belief in the divinity of Father Divine, members of the Peace Movement were drawn to the mission's strong emphasis on ending racial prejudice and economic inequalities.

In 1933 Divine moved his headquarters to Harlem, where his Peace Mission Movement prospered, eventually purchasing key real estate and housing projects called "heavens." These acquisitions and other businesses in the Midwest enhanced Divine's ability to provide shelter, jobs, and incomes for his followers. He launched a journal entitled *New Day* in 1937 and used it to disseminate his teachings. Divine also protested social injustice and encouraged his followers to become politically engaged. Between 1936 and 1940, he lobbied strenuously for a federal antilynching law. At the time of Divine's death in 1965, the holdings of the Peace Mission were estimated to be worth $10 million. Father Divine's movement echoed the Protestant ethic: work hard; keep both your mind and body healthy; eat right; dress properly; keep good company; and avoid all manner of evil and vice.

others were excluded or relegated to demeaning, stereotypical roles. This bias and negative typecasting motivated innovative filmmakers to develop alternative films and artistic institutions that allowed a more balanced and accurate representation of black life and culture to develop. Such creative ventures seldom produced the profits that white entrepreneurs reaped from marketing black cultural productions to white consumers. The mass appeal and unparalleled success of entertainers such as Louis Armstrong and Duke Ellington should not obscure the fate of those artists who refused to entertain white America and instead sought to oppose racism and social and economic injustice. They remained poor and unnoticed by the dominant culture.

Still, black counterculture artists had a tremendous impact on America and on the spread of black internationalism. Black artists reflected a growing pride and a determination to resist complete assimilation into white culture. The comic strips, the Semple stories of Langston Hughes, the black press, and the black church preserved black people's dignity. Black culture prepared black people for the next level of struggle against the American Jim Crow regime and against all ideologies of white supremacy across the black Diaspora.

CONCLUSION

The Depression ushered in a period of intense hardship, but as this chapter indicates, it was also a period in which black Americans had an unprecedented impact on American culture. Black people excelled in sports, arts, drama, and music. The Works Progress Administration (WPA) funded a wide spectrum of artists whose cultural productions were accessible, inclusive, and populist.

The Chicago Black Renaissance reflected the impact of the WPA on the lives and fortunes of hundreds of artists. A new generation of black jazz musicians transformed black music into an art form that won worldwide admiration and emulation. Black musicians weaned Americans from swing to bebop, and gospel music became a dynamic genre that satisfied the needs of the black urban migrants to express their spiritual and communal feelings. Popular disc jockeys of black-appeal radio programs helped to make black music commercially profitable.

These positive changes were made against a backdrop of entrenched racism. Although some African Americans found satisfying jobs in film and radio, many

RECOMMENDED READING

William Barlow. *Voice Over: The Making of Black Radio.* Philadelphia: Temple University Press, 1999. A lucidly written, informative cultural history of the evolution of black radio and the personalities who made it a powerful instrument for disseminating black music, culture, language, and politics, and for constructing an African-American public sphere.

Scott DeVeaux. *BeBop: A Social and Musical History.* Berkeley: University of California Press, 1997. A perceptive study of the creative artistry and lives of the pivotal black professional musicians in the jazz world during the 1930s and 1940s and how they made bebop into a commercially successful art movement.

Manthia Diawara, ed. *Black American Cinema.* New York: Routledge, 1993. A collection of provocative essays. Three examine the work of filmmaker Oscar Micheaux. Others provide fresh interpretations of the recent independent cinema movement.

Melvin Patrick Ely. *The Adventures of Amos 'n' Andy: A Social History of an American Phenomenon.* New York: Free Press, 1991. A subtle and penetrating examination of the complexities of racial stereotyping in one of the most influential and controversial radio and television programs in the history of media race relations.

AFRICAN-AMERICAN EVENTS / NATIONAL EVENTS

AFRICAN-AMERICAN EVENTS	NATIONAL EVENTS
1932	**1932**
1932 Thomas Dorsey's "Take My Hand, Precious Lord"	1932 Franklin D. Roosevelt elected president
1933	
	1933 Approximately thirteen million Americans out of work
1934	
1935	**1935**
1935 Donald Murray and NAACP file suit to integrate University of Maryland School of Law	1935 Committee for Industrial Organization (CIO) established; WPA created
1936	
1936 Jesse Owens wins four gold medals in the Berlin Olympics	
1937	
1937 Joe Louis becomes heavyweight champion; Katherine Dunham receives Guggenheim Award to investigate dance in Haiti, Jamaica, Trinidad, and Martinique	
1938	**1938**
	1938 CIO separates from the AFL
1939	**1939**
1939 Billie Holiday sings "Strange Fruit" for the first time; Marian Anderson performs at Lincoln Memorial after DAR bars her from Constitution Hall; "Bojangles" Robinson organizes the Black Actors' Guild	1939 World War II begins in Europe
1940	
1940 Richard Wright publishes *Native Son*; Hattie McDaniel receives an Oscar for her role in *Gone with the Wind*	

Samuel A. Floyd Jr. *The Power of Black Music: Interpreting Its History from Africa to the United States.* New York: Oxford University Press, 1995. An excellent overview of the history of black music with an insightful comparison of the Harlem and Chicago flowerings.

ADDITIONAL BIBLIOGRAPHY

ART

Michael D. Harris and Moyo Okediji. *Colored Pictures: Race and Visual Representation.* Chapel Hill: University of North Carolina Press, 2003.

Sharon F. Patton. *African-American Art.* New York: Oxford University Press, 1998.

Richard J. Powell. *Black Art and Culture in the 20th Century.* New York: Thames and Judson, 1997.

William E. Taylor and Harriet G. Warkel. *A Shared Heritage: Art by Four African Americans.* Bloomington: Indiana University Press, 1996.

CHICAGO RENAISSANCE

Wallace Best. *Passionately Human, No Less Divine: Religion and Culture in Black Chicago, 1915–1932.* Princeton, NJ: Princeton University Press, 2005.

Robert Bone. "Richard Wright and the Chicago Renaissance." *Callaloo,* 9, no. 3 (1986): 446–68.

Adam Green. *Selling the Race: Culture, Community, and Black Chicago, 1940–1955.* Chicago: University of Chicago Press, 2007.

Anne Meis Knupfer. *The Chicago Black Renaissance and Women's Activism.* Urbana: University of Illinois Press, 2006.

Craig Werner. "Leon Forrest, the AACM and the Legacy of the Chicago Renaissance." *The Black Scholar,* 23, no. 3/4 (1993): 10–23.

CULTURE

St. Clair Drake and Horace R. Cayton. *Black Metropolis: A Study of Negro Life in a Northern City.* New York: Harper & Row, 1962.

Gerald Early, ed. *"Ain't But a Place": An Anthology of African American Writing about St. Louis.* St. Louis: Missouri Historical Society Press, 1998.

Geneviève Fabre and Robert O'Meally, eds. *History and Memory in African-American Culture.* New York: Oxford University Press, 1994.

Kenneth W. Goings. *Mammy and Uncle Mose: Black Collectibles and American Stereotyping.* Bloomington: Indiana University Press, 1994.

Jacqueline Goldsby. *A Spectacular Secret: Lynching in American Life and Literature.* Chicago: University of Chicago Press, 2006.

Joseph E. Harris, ed. *Global Dimensions of the African Diaspora.* Washington, DC: Howard University Press, 1993.

Robin D. G. Kelley. *Race Rebels: Culture, Politics, and the Black Working Class.* New York: Free Press, 1994.

Lawrence Levine. *Black Culture and Black Consciousness: Afro-American Folk Thought from Slavery to Freedom.* New York: Oxford University Press, 1977.

Tommy L. Lott. *The Invention of Race: Black Culture and the Politics of Representation.* Malden, MA: Blackwell, 1999.

Daryl Scott. *Contempt and Pity: Social Policy and Image of the Damaged Black Psyche, 1880–1996.* Chapel Hill: University of North Carolina Press, 1997.

Mel Watkins. *On the Real Side: Laughing, Lying, and Signifying.* New York: Simon & Schuster, 1994.

Robert E. Weems Jr. *Desegregating the Dollar: African American Consumerism in the Twentieth Century.* New York: New York University Press, 1998.

DANCE

Katherine Dunham. *A Touch of Innocence.* London: Cassell, 1959.

Terry Harnan. *African Rhythm—American Dance.* New York: Knopf, 1974.

FILMS

Donald Bogle. *Brown Sugar: Eighty Years of America's Black Female Superstars.* New York: Crown, 1980.

Thomas Cripps. *Making Movies Black: The Hollywood Message Movie from World War II to the Civil Rights Era.* New York: Oxford University Press, 1993.

Jane M. Gaines. *Fire and Desire: Mixed-Race Movies in the Silent Era.* Chicago: University of Chicago Press, 2001.

Jacqueline Najuma Stewart. *Migrating to the Movies: Cinema and Black Urban Modernity.* Berkeley: University of California Press, 2005.

LITERATURE

Ralph Ellison. "The World and the Jug." In Joseph F. Trimmer, ed., *A Casebook on Ralph Ellison's Invisible Man* (pp. 172–200). New York: T. Y. Crowell, 1972.

Michael Fabre. *The Unfinished Quest of Richard Wright.* Iowa City: University of Iowa Press, 1973.

Henry Louis Gates and Nellie Y. McKay, eds. *Norton Anthology of African American Literature.* New York: Norton, 1997.

Joyce Ann Joyce. *Richard Wright's Art of Tragedy.* New York: Warner Books, 1986.

Robert G. O'Meally. *The Craft of Ralph Ellison.* Cambridge, MA: Harvard University Press, 1980.

Arnold Rampersad. *The Life of Langston Hughes.* New York: Oxford University Press, 1986.

Margaret Walker. *Richard Wright, Daemonic Genius: A Portrait of the Man, a Critical Look at His Work.* New York: Morrow, 1988.

AFRICAN-AMERICAN EVENTS

1941
Mary Lucinda Cardwell Dawson founds the National Negro Opera Company

1942
Margaret Walker publishes *For My People*; Dox Thrash paints "Defense Worker"; Johnson Publishing launches *Negro Digest*

1945
Nat King Cole becomes first black star with his own network (NBC) radio variety show; Johnson Publishing launches *Ebony Magazine*

1947
Jackie Robinson becomes the first black major-league baseball player

1948
Alice Coachman becomes first black woman Olympic champion

NATIONAL EVENTS

1941
United States enters World War II

1945
Roosevelt dies, Truman becomes president; United States drops atomic bombs on Hiroshima and Nagasaki; World War II ends

Timeline years: 1941, 1942, 1943, 1944, 1945, 1946, 1947, 1948

MUSIC AND RADIO

William Barlow. *Looking Up at Down: The Emergence of Blues Culture*. Philadelphia: Temple University Press, 1989.

Thomas Brothers, ed. *Louis Armstrong: In His Own Words*. New York: Oxford University Press, 1999.

Jack Chalmers. *Milestones I: The Music and Times of Miles Davis to 1960*. Toronto, Canada: University of Toronto Press, 1983.

John Chilton. *The Song of the Hawk: The Life and Recordings of Coleman Hawkins*. Ann Arbor: University of Michigan Press, 1990.

Linda Dahl. *Morning Glory: A Biography of Mary Lou Williams*. New York: Pantheon Books, 2000.

Miles Davis and Quincy Troupe. *Miles: The Autobiography*. New York: Simon & Schuster, 1989.

Duke Ellington. *Music Is My Mistress*. New York: Da Capo Press, 1973.

John Birks Gillespie and Wilmot Alfred Fraser. *To Be or Not . . . to Bop: Memoirs/Dizzy Gillespie with Al Fraser*. New York: Doubleday, 1979.

Farah Jasmine Griffin. *If You Can't Be Free, Be a Mystery: In Search of Billie Holiday*. New York: Oxford University Press, 2001.

Michael Harris. *The Rise of Gospel Blues: The Music of Thomas Andrew Dorsey in the Urban Church*. New York: Oxford University Press, 1992.

Allan Keiler. *Marian Anderson: A Singer's Journey*. New York: Scribner, 2000.

Robert G. O'Meally. *Lady Day: The Many Faces of Billie Holiday*. New York: Arcade Publishers, 1991.

Thomas Owens. *Bebop: The Music and Its Players*. New York: Oxford University Press, 1955.

Barbara Dianne Savage. *Broadcasting Freedom: Radio, War, and the Politics of Race, 1938–1948*. Chapel Hill: University of North Carolina Press, 1999.

Jules Schwerin. *Got to Tell It: Mahalia Jackson, Queen of Gospel*. New York: Oxford University Press, 1992.

Alyn Shipton. *Groovin' High: The Life of Dizzy Gillespie*. New York: Oxford University Press, 1999.

Eileen Southern. *The Music of Black Americans: A History*, 2d ed. New York: Norton, 1983.

Quintard Taylor. *In Search of the Racial Frontier: African Americans in the American West, 1528–1900*. New York: Norton, 1998.

J. C. Thomas. *Chasin' the Trane: The Music and Mystique of John Coltrane*. Garden City, NY: Doubleday, 1975.

Dempsey J. Travis. *Autobiography of Black Jazz*. Chicago: Urban Research Press, 1983.

SPORTS

Arthur Ashe, with the assistance of Kip Branch, Ocania Chalk, and Francis Harris. *A Hard Road to Glory: A History of the African-American Athlete*. New York: Warner Books, 1988.

Richard Bak. *Joe Louis: The Great Black Hope*. New York: Da Capo Press, 1998.

Robert Peterson. *Only the Ball Was White: A History of Legendary Black Players and All-Black Professional Teams*. New York: McGraw-Hill, 1984.

Arnold Rampersad. *Jackie Robinson: A Biography*. New York: Alfred A. Knopf, 1997.

Jackie Robinson. *I Never Had It Made*. New York: G. P. Putnam's Son, 1972.

Jeffrey T. Sammons. *Beyond the Ring: The Role of Boxing in American Society*. Urbana: University of Illinois Press, 1988.

RELIGION

Claude Andrew Clegg III. *An Original Man: The Life and Times of Elijah Muhammad*. New York: St. Martin's Griffin, 1997.

C. Eric Lincoln and Lawrence H. Mamiya. *The Black Church in the African American Experience*. Durham, NC: Duke University Press, 1990.

Elijah Muhammad. *The True History of Elijah Muhammad: Autobiographically Authoritative*. Atlanta: Secretrius Publications, 1997.

Jill Watts. *God, Harlem USA: The Father Divine Story*. Berkeley: University of California Press, 1992.

Robert Weisbrot. *Father Divine and the Struggle for Racial Equality*. Urbana: University of Illinois Press, 1983.

RETRACING THE ODYSSEY

Harold Washington Library Center, Chicago, Illinois. Named in honor of Chicago's first African-American mayor, Harold Washington, the ten-story library, art, and computer reference center features the Harold Washington Archives and Collections (on the 9th floor), collection the Chicago Blues Archive, and the work of several African-American artists. Jacob Lawrence contributed a mural-sized mosaic entitled "Events in the Life of Harold Washington," on the north wall of the library.

DuSable Museum of African-American History, Chicago, Illinois. Artist Margaret Goss Burroughs opened the Ebony Museum in 1961 in her home in Chicago. She moved it in 1973 to its present location at Washington Park and renamed it the DuSable Museum of African-American History. The DuSable Museum honors the accomplishment of Jean Baptiste Pointe DuSable, a Haitian-born immigrant who arrived in Chicago in 1779 and was the first non-Indian to settle in the area. The museum houses an extensive collection of artifacts, art, books, and civil rights documents and sponsors a diverse array of cultural and educational programs and exhibits.

Carter G. Woodson Regional Library, Chicago, Illinois. This branch of the Chicago Public Library, named in honor of the "Father of Black History," Carter G. Woodson, contains a wealth of photographs, books, documents, and manuscript collections concerning the artists and authors, women's clubs, and social institutions that detail the Black Chicago Renaissance. The Vivian Harsah Collection of Afro-American History and Literature contains over 70,000 volumes by Langston Hughes, Richard Wright, Gwendolyn Brooks, and Arna Bontemps, among others.

PRENTICE HALL
myhistorylab
Where it's a good time to connect to the past!

REVIEW, RESEARCH, AND INTERACT

REVIEW QUESTIONS

1. How did the Great Depression affect black culture? What role did the New Deal's Works Progress Administration (WPA) play in democratizing black culture? How did black religious culture change during this era?

2. How did black artists, musicians, filmmakers, and writers negotiate the dilemma of dual consciousness as articulated by W. E. B. Du Bois? Which parts of black art did white corporate executives find easiest to appropriate and shape for white consumption?

3. How did swing-era big band music lead to bebop? What problems did the bebop musicians encounter? How did black music affect American culture?

4. How did Hollywood films portray black Americans during the 1930s and 1940s? How did these images affect white Americans' attitudes and behavior toward black Americans? How did these representations contribute to the emergence of an alternative or independent black cinema?

5. How did the cultural production of the Chicago Renaissance compare with that of the Harlem Renaissance? Why did black athletes become prominent during the 1930s and 1940s? What was their impact on American culture? How did the experiences of black sports figures reflect the status of race relations in the United States?

Research Navigator.com
RESOURCES FOR COLLEGE RESEARCH ASSIGNMENTS

www.researchnavigator.com

Using the tools available in Research Navigator, consider these questions:
What were the major themes of black literature? Who read the work of black writers?

PRIMARY SOURCE DOCUMENTS

19–1 Paul Robeson "Welcome Home Rally," June 19, 1949

19–2 W. C. Haney, How the Blues Came to Be, 1941

19–3 Marian Anderson, "Easter Sunday"

19–4 Ethel Waters, On Black Movies

19–5 Richard Wright, "Are We Solving America's Race Problem?" 1945

The World War II Era and the Seeds of a Revolution

HOW DID AFRICAN AMERICANS USE
THE WORLD WAR II CRISIS
TO PROTEST RACIAL DISCRIMINATION?

WHAT ROLE DID AFRICAN-AMERICAN
PHYSICIANS AND NURSES PLAY
IN THE STRUGGLE TO DESEGREGATE
THE U.S. MILITARY DURING WORLD WAR II?

HOW DID THE WAR EXACERBATE TENSIONS
AND COMPETITION OVER HOUSING AND JOBS
BETWEEN BLACK AND WHITE AMERICANS?

HOW DID THE ITALIAN INVASION OF ETHIOPIA
HELP TO SHAPE BLACK INTERNATIONALISM?

WHY DID RALPH BUNCHE
RECEIVE A NOBEL PEACE PRIZE?

1936–1948

◄◄ **Racial segregation** as practiced by the U.S. military reminded African Americans of their second-class status in America. The World War II crisis made impossible continued acquiescence to blatant inequalities. The black "Double V" campaign sought victory against racism on home and foreign fronts. National Archives and Records Administration

The treatment that the Negro soldier has received has been resented not only by the Negro soldier but by the Negro civilian population as well. In fact, any straight-thinking person with a sense of justice and right, without any respect to color or race, must realize the dangers inherent in the evil practices that have been permitted to exist in the Army. It is not a pleasant thought for Negroes to ponder that their tax money is being spent to help maintain an army that has little regard for the real principles of democracy.

David H. Bradford, *The Louisville Courier Journal*, September 2, 1941

◄ **Truman's order** to desegregate the armed forces in 1948 marked the victory of a long struggle by black civilians and soldiers to win full integration into the nation's military.

Between 1939 and 1954, the role of the United States in the world was transformed. The victory in World War II of the Allies—the Soviet Union, Great Britain, the United States, and dozens of other countries—over the Axis powers of Germany, Italy, and Japan marked the emergence of America as the dominant global power. This international role placed new constraints on the nation's domestic policies, particularly when, after the Axis surrender in 1945, mutual suspicions between the United States and the Soviet Union quickly developed into the Cold War. This long conflict, which lasted until 1989, led to a vast expansion in the size and power of the federal government, particularly its military, and cast a long shadow over domestic politics.

International events replaced the Great Depression as the defining force in the lives of African Americans. In preparing for and in fighting World War II, America finally emerged from the Depression and laid the basis for an era of unprecedented prosperity. Industrial and military mobilization resulted in the movement of millions of people, many of them African American, from agriculture into the cities. This population shift substantially increased black voting strength in the North and West, which, combined with a moral recoil from the savage racial policies of the Nazis, drove the issue of black equality to the forefront of national politics. Moreover, hundreds of thousands of black men and women learned new skills and ideas while serving in the armed forces and many resolved to come home and claim their rights. Events abroad and in the United States during the 1940s heightened black consciousness and led to a more aggressive militancy among local leaders and black citizens in southern states.

The Cold War also had a tremendous impact on African Americans and their struggle for freedom. The two sides of this conflict avoided direct confrontation with each other; instead, to a great degree, they enlisted the peoples of Africa, Asia, and Latin America as proxies. U.S. leaders, seeking to convince these peoples of America's virtues as a democracy, were pressed to address the segregation and racial discrimination that remained firmly imbedded in the basic fabric of American life. The U.S. Department of State sponsored worldwide tours of outstanding black jazz musicians to represent the positive dimensions of American culture. Still, the advocacy groups and black press that had come of age during the 1930s and 1940s focused attention on fighting racism and demanded the full rights and responsibilities of citizens for all people. The result was a powerful movement for civil rights that many liberal white Americans and, increasingly, key institutions in the national government supported.

These favorable developments, however, provoked strong resistance. Egged on by their politicians, white southerners used all the power at their command to defend segregation. The emerging hostilities with the Soviet Union prompted many white conservatives to charge that all those seeking to fight racial injustice were in fact agents of the communist enemy. These contrary currents—the push for a new democracy, on one hand, and the Cold War mentality, on the other— would indelibly place their stamp on the emerging civil rights movement.

On the Eve of War, 1936–1941

As the world economy wallowed in the Great Depression, the international order collapsed in Europe and Asia. Germany under the dictatorship of Adolf Hitler (1889–1945) and Italy under the dictatorship of Benito Mussolini (1883–1945) created an alliance, known as the Axis, aimed to take economic and political control of Europe. These fascist dictators advocated a political program based on extreme nationalism that brutally suppressed internal opposition and used violence to gain their will abroad. Germany was the dominant partner in the Axis. Its Nazi, or National Socialist Party, in part blamed communists and foreign powers for the nation's economic depression and loss of power. But more than by anticommunism, however, Hitler was driven by a virulent form of racism and Anglo-Saxon supremacy. Unlike racists in the United States, he focused his hatred on Jews, blaming them for all Germany's social and economic problems. But the Nazis also despised black people and considered them inferior human beings. They discriminated against Germans with African ancestors and banned jazz as "nigger" music. Through the late 1930s, the Germans and Italians embarked on a series of military campaigns that placed much of Central Europe under their power. In August 1939 Germany signed a nonaggression pact with the Soviet Union, a prelude to a September 1 attack on Poland by Germany, which the Soviets joined a few weeks later. Britain and France reacted to the invasion by declaring war on Germany, thus beginning World War II.

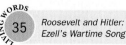

35 *Roosevelt and Hitler: Buster Ezell's Wartime Song*

As Germany and Italy pursued their plans in Europe during the 1930s, the empire of Japan sought to extend its power and territory in Asia. The Japanese considered themselves the foremost power in the Far East and wanted to drive out or supplant the European states, mainly Britain, France, and the Netherlands, and the United States, which had extensive economic interests and colonial possessions in Asia. (The United States controlled the Philippines, Hawaii, Guam, and other Pacific islands.) Japan's aggressive and expansionist policies also led to conflict with the Soviet Union in Manchuria and with the Nationalist regime in China, against which the Japanese became involved in a long and bloody struggle in the 1930s. The United States supported China and encouraged the European powers to resist Japanese demands for economic and territorial concessions in their Asian colonies. Japan's alliance with Nazi Germany and fascist Italy further aggravated United States–Japanese relations, which deteriorated rapidly after the outbreak of World War II in Europe in September 1939. These tensions led to war on December 7, 1941, when the Japanese bombed American warships at Pearl Harbor, Hawaii, and launched a massive offensive against British, Dutch, and American holdings throughout the Pacific.

Pearl Harbor **36**

President Franklin D. Roosevelt watched the events in Europe and Asia with growing concern, but he had only a limited ability to react. Despite its large economy, America was not a preeminent military power at the time. FDR had trouble convincing Congress to enlarge the army and navy because a significant segment of the American population, the isolationists, believed the United States had been hoodwinked into fighting World War I and should avoid again becoming entangled in a foreign war. During the late 1930s, the president had managed to overcome some of this opposition and had won the authority to increase the size of the nation's armed forces. By early 1940 the United States had instituted its first peacetime draft to provide men for the U.S. Army and Navy.

AFRICAN AMERICANS AND THE EMERGING WORLD CRISIS

Many African Americans responded to the emerging world crisis with growing activism. When Ethiopia was invaded by Italy in 1935, it was, along with Liberia and Haiti, one of three black-ruled nations in the world, and black communities throughout the United States organized to send it aid. In New York, black nurses under the leadership of Salaria Kee raised money to purchase medical supplies, and black physician John West volunteered to treat wounded Ethiopians at a hospital supported by black American donations. Mass meetings in support of the embattled Ethiopians were held in New York City under the auspices of the Provisional Committee for the Defense of Ethiopia and the Ethiopian World Federation. Similar rallies occurred in other large cities while reporters from black newspapers, such as J. A. Rogers of the Pittsburgh *Courier*, brought the horror of this war home to their readers. Although it was a violation of American law for its citizens to engage in active combat in Ethiopia, over seventeen thousand African Americans indicated a desire to help Emperor Haile Selassie (r. 1930–1974) resist the Italian invasion. Despite fierce resistance, the Italians won the war, in part, by using poison gas. The conflict alerted many African Americans to the dangers of fascism, reawakened interest in, and identification with, Africa, and fanned the flames of black internationalism, which was destined to become even more pronounced after World War II.

A civil war in Spain had stimulated renewed activism among leftist African Americans. In 1936 the left-leaning Spanish Republic became embroiled in a civil war against a fascist movement led by General Francisco Franco (1892–1975), whom Germany and Italy supported. About a hundred African Americans traveled to Spain in 1936–1937 to serve with the Abraham Lincoln Battalion, an integrated fighting force of three thousand American volunteers. Among the African Americans were two women: Salaria Kee, who actually nursed the wounded on the battlefield, and Chicagoan Thyra Edwards, who participated in the Medical Bureau and North American Committee to Aid Spanish Democracy. Support of the Abraham Lincoln Battalion reflected a commitment by a few African Americans to the communists' vision of internationalism. Mobilization for war, however, would soon bring most black people and their organizations into the fight against fascism abroad and for equality and justice in the United States.

A. PHILIP RANDOLPH AND THE MARCH ON WASHINGTON MOVEMENT

In 1939 and 1940, the American government, along with the governments of France and Britain, spent so much on arms that the U.S. economy was finally lifted out of the Depression. But the United States mobilized its economy for war and rebuilt its military in keeping with past practices of discrimination and exclusion. As unemployed white workers streamed into aircraft factories, shipyards, and other centers of war production, most jobless African Americans were left waiting at the gate. Most aircraft manufacturers, for example, would hire black people only in janitorial positions no matter

what their skills. Many all-white AFL unions enforced closed-shop agreements that prevented their employers from hiring black workers who were not members of the labor organization. Government-funded training programs regularly rejected black applicants, often reasoning that training them would be pointless given their poor prospects of finding skilled work. The United States Employment Service (USES) filled "whites-only" requests for defense workers. The military itself made it clear that although it would accept black men in their proportion to the population, about 11 percent at the time, it would put them in segregated units and assign them to service duties. The navy limited black servicemen to menial positions; the Marine Corps and the Army Air Corps refused to accept them altogether.

Jim Crow in the Army Camps, 1940   **DOCUMENT 20-4**

Horace Pippins's (1888–1946) *Mr. Prejudice* (1943) hammers a wedge of racism through a giant V (the sign of victory). It is a powerful expression of black Americans' ongoing struggle against racial discrimination, segregation, and violence even within a nation at war against facism and Nazism and the spread of communism.   Oil on canvas. 18 × 14 inches. Philadelphia Museum of Art, gift of Dr. and Mrs. Matthew T. Moore. Photo by Graydon Wood. 1984-108-1

WHY SHOULD WE MARCH?

What Are Our Immediate Goals?

1. To mobilize five million Negroes into one militant mass for pressure.

2. To assemble in Chicago the last week in May, 1943, for the celebration of

"WE ARE AMERICANS – TOO" WEEK

And to ponder the question of Non-Violent Civil Disobedience and Non-Cooperation, and a Mass March On Washington.

15,000 Negroes Assembled at St. Louis, Missouri
20,000 Negroes Assembled at Chicago, Illinois
23,500 Negroes Assembled at New York City
Millions of Negro Americans all Over This Great Land Claim the Right to be Free!

FREE FROM WANT!
FREE FROM FEAR!
FREE FROM JIM CROW!

"Winning Democracy for the Negro is Winning the War for Democracy!" — A. Philip Randolph

Posters like this sought both to attract black support for A. Philip Randolph's March on Washington Movement and to convince political leaders of the strength of the movement.   Courtesy of the Library of Congress

When a young African-American man wrote the Pittsburgh *Courier* and suggested a "Double V" campaign—victory over fascism abroad and over racism at home—the newspaper adopted his words as the battle cry for the entire race. Fighting this struggle in a nation at war would be difficult, but the effort led to the further development of black organizations and transformed the worldview of many African-American soldiers and civilians. Embodying the spirit of the "Double V" campaign, African-American protest groups and newspapers criticized discrimination in the defense program. Two months before the 1940 presidential election, the NAACP, the Urban League, and other groups pressed President Roosevelt to take action. The president listened to their protests, but aside from a few token gestures—appointing Howard University Law School dean William Hastie as a "civilian aide on Negro affairs" in the Department of War and promoting Benjamin O. Davis, the senior black officer in the army, to brigadier general—he responded with little of substance. As a result, during late 1940 the

NAACP and other groups staged mass protest rallies around the nation. With the election safely won, the president, anxious not to offend white southern politicians he needed to back his war program, refused even to meet with black leaders.

In January 1941 A. Philip Randolph, who was president of the Brotherhood of Sleeping Car Porters and who had been working with other groups to get Roosevelt's attention, called on black people to unify their protests and direct them at the national government. He suggested that ten thousand African Americans march on Washington under the slogan "We loyal Negro-American citizens demand the right to work and fight for our country." In the coming months Randolph helped create the March on Washington Movement (MOWM), which soon became the largest mass movement of black Americans since the activities of Marcus Garvey's Universal Negro Improvement Association of the 1920s. The MOWM's demands included a presidential order forbidding companies with government contracts from engaging in racial discrimination, eliminating race-based exclusion from defense training courses, and requiring the USES to supply workers on a nonracial basis. Randolph also wanted an order to abolish segregation in the armed forces and the president's support for a law withdrawing the benefits of the National Labor Relations Act from unions that refused to grant membership to black Americans. Departing from the leadership tactics of most other African-American protest groups of the time, Randolph prohibited white participation and encouraged the participation of the black working class.

Randolph's powerful appeal captured the support of many African Americans who had not before taken part in the activities of middle-class-dominated groups like the NAACP. Soon he alarmed the president by raising the number expected to march to 50,000. Roosevelt, fearing the protest would undermine America's democratic rhetoric and provide grist for the German propaganda mills, dispatched First Lady Eleanor Roosevelt and New York City mayor Fiorello La Guardia to dissuade Randolph from marching. Their pleas for patience fell on deaf ears, compelling Roosevelt and his top military officials to meet with Randolph and other black leaders. The president offered a set of superficial changes, but the African Americans stood firm in their demands and raised the stakes by increasing their estimate of the number of black marchers coming to Washington to 100,000. By the end of June 1941, the president capitulated and had his aides draft **Executive Order 8802**, prompting Randolph to call off the march. It was a grand moment. "To this day," NAACP leader Roy Wilkins wrote in his autobiography, "I don't know if he would have been able to turn out enough marchers to make his point stick . . . but, what a bluff it was. A tall, courtly black man with Shakespearean diction and the stare of an eagle had looked the patrician Roosevelt in the eye—and made him back down."

EXECUTIVE ORDER 8802

On the surface at least, the president's order marked a significant change in the government's stance. It stated in part:

> I do hereby affirm the policy of the United States that there shall be no discrimination in the employment of workers in the defense industry or government because of race, creed, color, or national origin.

The order instructed all agencies that trained workers to administer such programs without discrimination. To ensure full cooperation with these guidelines, Roosevelt created the Fair Employment Practices Committee (FEPC) with the power to investigate complaints of discrimination. The order said nothing about desegregation of the military, but private assurances were made that the barriers to entry in key services would be lowered.

Executive Order 8802, although it was the first major presidential action countering discrimination since Reconstruction, was no new Emancipation Proclamation. Black excitement with the order soon soured as many industries, particularly in the South, evaded its clear intent and engaged in only token hirings. What the black community learned in this instance and would witness repeatedly in the decades to come was that mere articulation of antidiscrimination principles and the establishment of commissions and committees did not lead to eradication of inequalities. Moreover, the order did not mention union discrimination. Nonetheless, the threat of the march, the issuance of the executive order, and the creation of the FEPC marked the formal acknowledgment by the federal government that it bore some responsibility for protecting black and minority rights in employment. Black activists and their allies would have to continue their fight if the order was to have any meaning. Randolph sought to lead them but would find it difficult to do so because of the opposition of key government agencies—notably the military—the political power of southern congressmen, and a belief among white people that winning the war took precedence over racial issues.

Executive Order 8802, 1941 **20-1** DOCUMENT

Race and the U.S. Armed Forces

The demands of A. Philip Randolph and other black leaders and health-care professionals to end segregation in the armed forces initially met stiffer resistance than their pleas for change in the civilian sector. Black men were expected to serve their country, but at the beginning of the war, most were assigned to segregated service battalions, relegated to noncombat positions, kept out of the more prestigious branches of the service, and faced tremendous obstacles to appointment as commissioned officers. This situation was particularly galling because military segregation was a symbol of the rampant discrimination black men and women encountered in their daily lives.

During the prewar mobilization period, 1940–1941, black physicians and leaders of their black professional organization, the National Medical Association (NMA), remembering the segregation they experienced during

PROFILE ❧ STEVEN ROBINSON AND THE MONTFORD POINT MARINES

When seventeen-year-old Steven Robinson joined the military in May 1942, he was among the first African Americans to become U.S. Marines. From its founding in 1798 until World War II, the Marine Corps accepted only white men. President Franklin Roosevelt's Executive Order 8802 ended that racial exclusion but did not outlaw segregation in the military.

With grim reluctance, the Marine Corps began to accept black men. The Commandant of the Corps, Major General Thomas Holcomb, disdained the prospect of black marines: "If it were a question of having a Marine Corps of 5,000 whites or 250,000 Negroes, I would rather have the whites." The Marine Corps would not allow black men to train with white recruits at Parris Island in South Carolina. Instead, it established a separate training facility for black men at Montford Point in North Carolina.

Robinson immediately encountered hostility as he traveled south for basic training. For the first time, he experienced segregated railroad coaches and stations. He inadvertently entered a white waiting room in Rocky Mount, North Carolina, and was curtly instructed to leave. "So I went out the door and as I went out the door, something [said], look, look back and I looked back, I looked over at the station, at the entrance to the station, and I saw a sign. It had to be three feet in width and maybe five feet in length and it says 'For White Only.'"

During basic training Robinson impressed white drill instructors and officers, and he was promoted to platoon sergeant before departing for the war in the Pacific. On the troop train to the West Coast, black marines were refused service when they tried to buy Coca-Colas in Arizona. They did see German and Italian prisoners of war enjoying the company of American women in restaurants, bars, and clubs that would not admit African Americans.

Doubting their fitness, the Marine Corps did not want black men in combat, and most of the Montford Point marines were assigned support roles in ammunition and depot companies. Nevertheless, the black marines participated in several major amphibious operations in the Pacific, including Iwo Jima.

Robinson and a contingent of black marines went ashore on Iwo Jima on February 19, 1945, and took part in some of the fiercest fighting of World War II. One of Robinson's close friends, Jimmy Wilkins, was mortally wounded. "Jimmy was on my right shoulder about two feet [away] when he got hit. And he was killed. . . . everybody liked him in the platoon. I mean, he was just a likable seventeen-year-old young teenager. And I might add, a good Marine." Wilkins was also one of the marines who had not been able to buy a Coke in Arizona.

Robinson and other marines were aware that they were fighting to defeat two enemies. "We were fighting the war against the bigotry at home and fighting the war against the bigotry overseas. And we were fighting the war to liberate people who had more liberty than we had."

Combat photographers and filmmakers generally avoided documenting the activities of the black marines, but Robinson as well as other black marines did witness the famous flag raising on Mount Suribachi. Robinson would spend 106 days on Iwo Jima. More than 6,000 marines and 21,000 Japanese troops died on the small volcanic island before the Americans gained control.

Nearly 20,000 black men trained at Montford Point during and immediately after World War II. In 1949, as a result of President Harry Truman's Executive Order 9981, the Marine Corps began to integrate, and the separate training facility at Montford Point closed. Black marines would be trained and would fight along side white marines in Korea, Vietnam, Afghanistan, and Iraq.

Taking advantage of the G.I. Bill of Rights after World War II, Steven Robinson graduated from the University of Pittsburgh, and earned a law degree. He practiced law for more than fifty years in Warren, Ohio, where he was active in state and local politics. Robinson died in 2006.

These are among the very first African-American men to serve in ▶ the U.S. Marine Corps. Beginning in 1942 they trained at a separate facility at Montford Point near Camp Lejune North Carolina.

Robinson

World War I, queried the War Department about their status. In a new war, would black physicians be integrated into the medical corps or required to practice in separate facilities set aside for sick and wounded black soldiers? In a 1940 speech, Dr. G. Hamilton Francis underscored the concerns of black doctors: "Our nation is again preparing to defend itself against aggression from without. Today, we are ready and willing to contribute all of our skill and energy and to wholeheartedly enlist our services as members of the medical profession, but we must be permitted to take our right places, as evidenced by our training, experience, and ability."

INSTITUTIONAL RACISM IN THE AMERICAN MILITARY

Much of the armed forces' racial policy derived from negative attitudes and discriminatory practices common in American society. Reflecting this ingrained racism, a 1925 study by the American War College concluded that African Americans were physically unqualified for combat duty, were by nature subservient and mentally inferior, believed themselves to be inferior to white people, were susceptible to the influence of crowd psychology, could not control themselves in the face of danger, and did not have the initiative and resourcefulness of white people.

Based on this and later studies, the War Department laid out two key policies in 1941 for the use of black soldiers. Although they would be taken into the military at the same rate as white inductees, African Americans would be segregated and would serve primarily in noncombat units. Responding with characteristic disdain for those who criticized these policies, Under Secretary of War Robert Patterson wrote the following:

> The Army is not a sociological laboratory; to be effective it must be organized and trained according to principles which will insure success. Experiments to meet the wishes and demands of the champions of every race and creed for the solution of their problems are a danger to efficiency, discipline and morale and would result in ultimate defeat. Out of these fundamental thoughts have been evolved broad principles relating to the employment of all persons in the military service.

In creating these policies, the army and navy ignored evidence of the fighting ability that African Americans had shown in previous wars, confirmed by the heroism of Dorie Miller during the attack on Pearl Harbor. Miller was the son of Texas sharecroppers who had enlisted in the navy in 1938 and, like all black sailors in the navy at the time, he had been assigned to

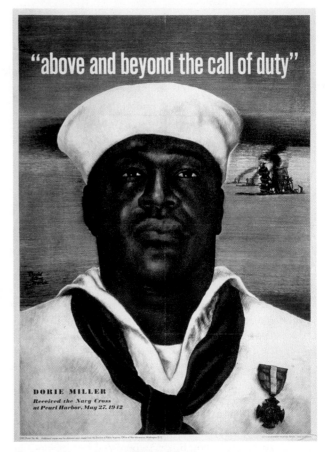

"above and beyond the call of duty"

DORIE MILLER
Received the Navy Cross
at Pearl Harbor, May 27, 1942

This World War II War Department recruitment poster recognizes the heroism of Dorie Miller (1919–1948) at Pearl Harbor. His bravery, however, did not alter the navy's policy of restricting black sailors to the kitchens and boiler rooms of navy vessels.   Courtesy of the Library of Congress

mess attendant duty. In other words, he was a cook and a waiter. When the Japanese air force attacked the naval base on December 7, 1941, the twenty-two-year-old Miller was below decks on the battleship *Arizona*. When his captain was seriously wounded, Miller braved bullets to help move him to a more protected area of the deck. He then took charge of a machine gun, shooting down at least two and perhaps six enemy aircraft before running out of ammunition. Miller had never before fired the gun. On May 27, 1942, the navy cited him for "distinguished devotion to duty, extraordinary courage and disregard for his own personal safety" and awarded him a Navy Cross. The navy then sent Miller back to mess duty without a promotion.

THE COSTS OF MILITARY DISCRIMINATION

Although the War and Navy Departments held to the fiction of "separate but equal" in their segregation program, their policies gave black Americans inferior re-sources or excluded them entirely. Sick and injured black soldiers received treatment in segregated wards in hospitals located on military bases. Black physicians were allowed only to treat black military personnel. Segregation at army camps most often meant that black soldiers were placed in the least desirable spots and denied the use of officers' clubs, base stores, and recreational areas. Four-fifths of all training camps were located in the South, where black soldiers were harassed and discriminated against off base as well as on. Even on leave, black soldiers were not offered space in the many hotels the government leased and had to make do with the limited accommodations that had been available to black people before the war. For southern African Americans, even going home in uniform could be dangerous. For example, when Rieves Bell of Starkville, Mississippi, was visiting his family in 1943, three young white men cornered him on a street and attempted to strip off his uniform. Bell fought back and injured one of them with a knife. The army could not save him from the wrath of local civilian authorities who tried and sentenced Bell to three and a half years in the notorious Parchman state penitentiary for the crime of self-defense.

Perhaps most galling was to see German prisoners of war accorded better treatment than African-American soldiers. Dempsey Travis of Chicago recalled his experiences at Camp Shenango, Pennsylvania: "I saw German prisoners free to move around the camp, unlike black soldiers who were restricted. The Germans walked right into the doggone places like any white American. We were wearin' the same uniform, but we were excluded." In 1944 black servicemen stationed at Fort Lawton in Washington State objected to living and working conditions that were inferior to those granted to Italian prisoners of war. Not only did the Italians receive lighter work assignments than the black Americans, but some Italian POWs were allowed to go to local bars that refused to admit African Americans. The tension and resentment erupted into a full-scale riot on August 14, 1944, when black soldiers stoned the barracks housing Italian prisoners. One prisoner was killed and twenty-four others injured. A court-martial convicted twenty-three black servicemen.

Due to the military's policies, most of the nearly one million African Americans who served during World War II did so in auxiliary units, notably in the transportation and engineering corps. Soldiers in the transportation corps, almost half of whom were black, loaded supplies and drove them in trucks to the front lines. Operating in the Redball or Whiteball express, the names for the trucking operations used to supply the American

forces as they drove toward Germany in 1944 and 1945, African Americans braved enemy fire and delivered the fuel, ammunition, and other goods that made the fight possible. Black engineers built camps and ports, constructed and repaved roads, and performed many other tasks to support frontline troops.

Black soldiers performed well in these tasks but were often subject to unfair military discipline. In Europe, black soldiers were executed in vastly greater numbers than whites even though African Americans made up only 10 percent of the total number of soldiers. One of the most glaring examples of unfair treatment was the navy's handling of a "mutiny" at its Port Chicago base north of San Francisco. On July 17, 1944, in the worst home-front disaster of the war, an explosion at the base killed 320 American sailors, of whom 202 were black ammunition loaders. In the following month 328 of the surviving ammunition loaders were sent to fill another ship. When 258 of them refused to do so, they were arrested. Eventually the Navy charged fifty men with mutiny, convicted them, and sentenced them to terms of imprisonment ranging from eight to fifteen years at Terminal Island in Southern California. The NAACP's Thurgood Marshall filed a brief on behalf of the fifty men arguing that they had been railroaded into prison because of their race, but to no avail.

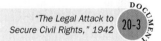
"The Legal Attack to Secure Civil Rights," 1942   DOCUMENT 20-3

SOLDIERS AND CIVILIANS PROTEST MILITARY DISCRIMINATION

In military segregation, black American leaders, including A. Philip Randolph; Walter White of the National Association for the Advancement of Colored People (NAACP); both T. Arnold Hill and Lester Granger of the National Urban League; New York Congressman Adam Clayton Powell Jr.; Robert Vann, editor of the Pittsburgh *Courier*; Arthur N. Vaughn of the National Medical Association, and Mabel K. Staupers of the National Association of Colored Graduate Nurses, among others, identified a formidable but vulnerable target. Employing a variety of strategies they mobilized the black civilian workforce, black women's groups, college students, and an interracial coalition to participate in resistance to this blatant inequality. They provoked a public dialogue with government and military officials at a pivotal moment when America's leaders most desired to present a united democratic front to the world.

Examples of black protest abound. In 1942 the NAACP's *The Crisis*, and *Opportunity*, the organ of the National Urban League, published numerous editorials denouncing the army's segregation policy. Walter White

William H. Hastie earned his LLB in 1930 and his SJD in 1935 at Harvard Law School. He taught at Howard University Law School, where he, along with Charles Hamilton Houston, trained the first generation of civil rights lawyers, the most illustrious of whom were Thurgood Marshall and Oliver Hill. In 1943, the NAACP presented Hastie with the Spingarn Medal. Appointed by President Harry Truman in 1949, Hastie became the first black American to serve as a federal judge. He sat on the Third Circuit Court of Appeals until 1971.

traveled across the country and throughout the world visiting camps and making contacts with black soldiers and their white officers. He inundated the War Department and the president with letters citing examples of improper, hostile, and humiliating treatment of black servicemen by military personnel and in the white communities in which bases were located. Frustration with continued military intransigence, however, forced William Hastie into a dramatic protest. He tendered his resignation as an adviser on Negro affairs on January 5, 1943.

BLACK WOMEN IN THE STRUGGLE TO DESEGREGATE THE MILITARY

The role of black women in the struggle to desegregate the military has often been overlooked, but their mili-

tancy contributed to the effort. A 1942 editorial in The *Crisis* suggested why:

> [T]he colored woman has been a more potent factor in shaping Negro society than the white woman has been in shaping white society because the sexual caste system has been much more fluid and ill-defined than among whites. Colored women have worked with their men and helped build and maintain every institution we have. Without their economic aid and counsel we would have made little if any progress.

The most prominent example of black women's struggle is found in the history of the National Association of Colored Graduate Nurses (NACGN). Mabel K. Staupers, its executive director, led an aggressive fight to eliminate quotas established by the U.S. Army Nurse Corps. Although many black nurses volunteered their services during World War II, they were refused admittance into the navy, and the army allowed only a few to serve. To draw attention to the unfairness of quotas, Staupers requested a meeting with Eleanor Roosevelt. In November 1944 First Lady Roosevelt and Staupers met, and Staupers described black nurses' troubled relationship with the armed forces. She informed the First Lady Roosevelt that 82 black nurses were serving 150 patients at the all-black station hospital at Fort Huachuca, Arizona, at a time when the army was complaining of a dire nursing shortage and debating the need to draft nurses. Staupers expounded on the practice of using black women to care for German prisoners of war. She asked, rhetorically, if this was to be the special role of the black nurse in the war? Staupers elaborated, "When our women hear of the great need for nurses in the Army and when they enter the service it is with the high hopes that they will be used to nurse sick and wounded soldiers who are fighting our country's enemies and not primarily to take care of these enemies."

Soldiers and sailors also resisted segregation and discrimination while in the service. Their action included well-organized attempts to desegregate officers' clubs. At Freeman Field, Indiana, for example, one hundred black officers refused to back down when their commanders threatened to arrest them for seeking to use the officers' club. In other bases African-American soldiers responded with violence to violence, intimidation, and threats. Their actions, although put down with dispatch, prompted the army brass to reevaluate their belief in the military efficiency of discrimination.

THE BEGINNING OF MILITARY DESEGREGATION

In response to the militancy of black officers, civil rights leaders, and the press, the War Department made changes and began to take on the challenge of reeducating soldiers, albeit in a limited fashion. The Advisory Committee on Negro Troop Policies was charged with coordinating the use of black troops and developing policy on social questions and personnel training. In 1943 the War Department also produced its own propaganda film—*The Negro Soldier*, directed by Frank Capra—to alleviate racial tensions. This patronizing film emphasized the contributions black soldiers had made in the nation's wars since the American Revolution and was designed to appeal to both black and white audiences.

The War Department also attempted to use propaganda to counter black protest groups and the claims of discrimination found in the black press. The key to this effort was fighter Joe Louis, whom the army believed was "almost a god" to most black Americans. "The possibilities for using him," a secret internal report stated, "are almost unlimited, such as touring the army camps as special instructor on physical training; exhibition bouts, for use in radio or in movies; in a movie appearance a flashback could be shown of Louis knocking out Max Schmeling, the champion of the Germans." The same report also mentioned other prominent black men and women who had "great value in any propaganda programs. Other athletes like Ray Robinson, also track athletes, etc.; name bands like Cab Calloway, [Jimmy] Lunceford; stage, screen and concert stars like Ethel Waters, Bill Robinson, Eddie Anderson, Paul Robeson, etc." The effect of this propaganda barrage is impossible to gauge, but it did little to counter the real incidents of prejudice and discrimination that most black people experienced in their daily lives.

Racism remained strong throughout the war, but the persistent push of protest groups and the military's need for soldiers gradually loosened its grip. After the attack on Pearl Harbor, nearly all the services had to relax their restrictions on African Americans. The navy, previously the most resistant service, began to accept black men as sailors and noncommissioned officers. By 1943 it allowed African Americans into officer training schools. The Marine Corps, exclusively white throughout its history, began taking African Americans in 1942. Black officers were trained in integrated settings in all services except the U.S. Army's Air Corps. The War Department even acted to compel recalcitrant commanding officers to recommend black servicemen for admission to the officer training schools, and soon, over two thousand a year were graduated.

African-American women nurses served at station hospitals at home and abroad. They resented the quotas and discrimination and fought to end segregation in the U.S. military. Still, black nurses such as Lt. Florie E. Grant provided expert care for prisoners-of-war, as shown in this October 7, 1942, image of her in a hospital ward in England.

Many African Americans also saw combat, although under white officers. Several African-American artillery, tank destroyer, antiaircraft, and combat engineer battalions fought with distinction in Europe and Asia. Military prejudice seemed to be borne out by the poor showing of the all-black 92nd Combat Division, but investigation revealed that its failure was the result of poor training and leadership by a white officer with no confidence in his men. After the Battle of the Bulge, a massive late-1944 German counterattack, 2,500 black volunteers fought in integrated units. The experiment would not be repeated during the war, but its success laid the groundwork for later changes. Although subject to many of the same kinds of discrimination as African-American men, African-American women also found expanded opportunities in the military. Approximately four thousand black women served in the Women's Army Auxiliary Corps (WAACs).

Mabel Staupers's efforts also bore fruit in early 1945. When the War Department claimed there was a shortage of nurses, Staupers mobilized nursing groups of all races to write letters and send telegrams protesting the discrimination against black nurses in the U.S. Army and Navy Nurse Corps. There was an immediate groundswell of public support to remove quotas. Buried beneath an avalanche of telegrams from an inflamed public, the War Department declared an end

WILLIAM H. HASTIE RESIGNS IN PROTEST

In January 1943 William H. Hastie, who had been on leave from his post as dean of the Howard University Law School, resigned as civilian aide to Secretary of War Henry L. Stimson to protest official failure to outlaw discrimination in the military. Hastie had taken the position in 1940, and throughout his tenure he had experienced frustration and hostility in attempting to secure equal treatment for black men and women in uniform. In his letter of resignation, which he published in the Chicago Defender, he explains that the U.S. Army Air Forces' reactionary policies and discriminatory practices were the immediate catalyst to his resignation:

The Army Air Forces are growing in importance and independence. In the post war period they may become the greatest single component of the armed services. Biased policies and harmful practices established in this branch of the army can all too easily infect other branches as well. The situation had become critical. Yet, the whole course of my dealings with the Army Air Forces convinced me that further expression of my views in the form of recommendations within the department would be futile. I, therefore, took the only course which can, I believe, bring results. Public opinion is still the strongest force in American life.

To the Negro soldier and those who influence his thinking, I say with all the force and sincerity at my command that the man in uniform must grit his teeth, square his shoulders and do his best as a soldier, confident that there are millions of Americans outside of the armed services, and more persons than he knows in high places within the military establishment, who will never cease fighting to remove every racial barrier and every humiliating practice which now confront him. But only by being, at all times a first class soldier can the man in uniform help in this battle which shall be fought and won.

When I took office, the Secretary of War directed that all questions of policy and important proposals relating to Negroes should be referred to my office for comment or approval before final action. In December, 1940, the Air Forces referred to me a plan for a segregated training center for Negro pursuit pilots at Tuskegee. I expressed my entire disagreement with the plan, giving my reasons in detail. My views were disregarded. Since then, the Air Command has never on its own initiative submitted any plan or project to me for comment or recommendation. What information I obtained, I had to seek out. Where I made proposals or recommendations, I volunteered them.

to quotas and exclusion. On January 10, 1945, the army opened its Nurse Corps to all applicants without regard to race, and five days later the navy followed suit. Within a few weeks, Phyllis Daley became the first black woman inducted into the navy's Nurse Corps. Over three hundred black nurses were eventually accepted into the Army Nurse Corps.

THE TUSKEGEE AIRMEN

The most visible group of black soldiers served in the U.S. Army Air Force. In January 1941 the War Department announced the formation of an all-black Pursuit Squadron and the creation of a training program at Tuskegee Army Air Field, Alabama, for black pilots.

This situation reached its climax in late December, 1942, when I learned through army press releases sent out from St. Louis and from the War Department in Washington that the Air Command was about to establish a segregated officer candidate school at Jefferson Barracks, Mo., to train Negro officers for ground duty with the Army Air Forces. Here was a proposal for a radical departure from present army practice, since the officer candidate-training program is the one large field where the army is eliminating racial segregation.

Moreover, I had actually written to the Air Command several weeks earlier in an attempt to find out what was brewing at Jefferson Barracks. The Air Command replied as late as December 17, 1942, giving not even the slightest hint of any plan for a segregated officer candidate school. It is inconceivable to me that consideration of such a project had not then advanced far enough for my office to have been consulted, even if I had not made specific inquiry. The conclusion is inescapable that the Air Command does not propose to inform, much less counsel with, this office about its plans for Negroes.

Why did African Americans fight so relentlessly to end segregation in the U.S. military? What did the military represent or symbolize to the nation?

Under what circumstances did African Americans appear to accept segregation and the establishment of separate programs such as the Tuskegee Airmen? Why, then, did African Americans object strenuously to the military's efforts to provide equal but separate facilities and educational programs?

Source: William H. Hastie, "Why I Resigned," Chicago *Defender*, February 6, 1943. Reprinted courtesy of the Chicago *Defender*.

Unlike all other units in the army, the 99th Squadron and the 332nd Group, made up of the 100th, 301st, and 302nd Squadrons, had black officers. The 99th went to North Africa in April 1943 and flew its first combat mission against the island of Pantelleria on June 2. Later the squadron participated in the air battle over Sicily, operating from its base in North Africa, and supported the invasion of Italy. The squadron regularly engaged German pilots in aerial combat. General Benjamin O. Davis Jr. commanded the 332nd Group when it was deployed to Italy in January 1944. In July the 99th was added to the 332nd and the Group participated in campaigns in Italy, France, Germany, and the Balkans.

The **Tuskegee Airmen** amassed an impressive record. They flew over 15,500 sorties and completed 1,578 missions. During the two hundred missions in which they escorted heavy bombers deep into Germany's Rhineland, not one of the "heavies" was lost to enemy fighter opposition. They destroyed 409 enemy aircraft, sank an enemy destroyer, and knocked out numerous ground installations. They were well regarded and recognized for their heroism. They accumulated 150 Distinguished Flying Crosses, a Legion of Merit, a Silver Star, 14 Bronze Stars, and 744 Air Medals. Tuskegee pilot Coleman Young (1919–1997; mayor of Detroit 1973–1993) recalled, "once our reputation got out as to our fighting ability, we started getting special requests for our group to escort their group, the bombers. They all wanted us because we were the only fighter group in the entire air force that did not lose a bomber to enemy action. Oh, we were much in demand."

THE TRANSFORMATION OF BLACK SOLDIERS

A new generation of African Americans became soldiers during World War II, and many would emerge from the experience with an enhanced sense of themselves and a commitment to the fight for black equality. They returned home with a broader perception of the world and a transformed consciousness. Unlike the black soldiers in World War I, a greater percentage of those drafted at the outset of World War II had attended high school and more were either high school or college graduates. Some black soldiers brought so-called radical ideas with them as they were drafted and sent to segregated installations. The urban and northern black servicemen and women and many of the southern rural recruits had a strong sense of their own self-worth and dignity. In their study of Chicago, sociologists St. Clair Drake and Horace Cayton noted the following:

At least half of the Negro soldiers—and Bronzeville's men fall into this class—were city people who had

William Baldwin became the first African-American recruit for general services in the U.S. Navy. This June 2, 1942, photograph of Baldwin reflects the end of the Navy's policy to assign black men to mess attendants and other menial or subservient positions. National Archives and Records Administration

lived through a Depression in America's Black Ghettoes, and who had been exposed to unions, the Communist movement, and to the moods of racial radicalism that occasionally swept American cities. Even the rural southern Negroes were different this time—for the thirty years between the First and Second World War has seen a great expansion of school facilities in the South and distribution of newspapers and radios.

Serving in the armed forces first exposed many African Americans to a world outside the segregated South and nurtured a budding internationalism among them. Haywood Stephney of Clarksdale, Mississippi, recalled that when he first encountered segregation in the military he simply thought it was supposed to be that way. He explained, "Because you grow up in this situation you don't see but one side of the coin. Having not tasted the freedom or the liberty of being and doing like other folks then you didn't know what it was like over across the street. So we accepted it." Like many others, his experiences during the war quickly removed him from "total darkness" and raised fundamental questions about the racial system of the nation.

Douglas Conner, another Mississippi veteran, captured the collective understanding of the social and political meaning of the war shared by the men in his unit, the 31st Quartermaster Battalion stationed in Okinawa: "The air people in Tuskegee, Dorie Miller, and

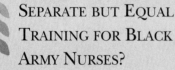

SEPARATE BUT EQUAL TRAINING FOR BLACK ARMY NURSES?

In August 1944 Mabel Staupers received this reply from Under Secretary of War Robert Patterson in response to her query about a segregated training center the army had established at Fort Huachuca, Arizona, for black nurses:

AUGUST 7, 1944
Mrs. Mabel K. Staupers R.N.,
Executive Secretary,
National Association of Colored Graduate Nurses, Inc.,
1790 Broadway,
New York 19, N.Y.

Dear Mrs. Staupers:

Thank you for your letter of July 19 with reference to the establishment of the first basic training center for Army Negro nurses at Fort Huachuca.

In establishing the first basic training center for Army Negro nurses at Fort Huachuca, the War Department desired that these nurses receive the best possible training and the most valuable experience for the type of service they would be required to render as Army nurses. It is the policy of the War Department to assign Negro nurses to those hospitals where there is a substantial number of Negro troops in relation to the personnel of the entire installation. The trainee at Fort Huachuca will therefore have the advantage of serving in a facility and under conditions parallel to those under which she will serve as an Army nurse.

You may be assured that the facilities for training afforded Negro nurses at Fort Huachuca will in no way be inferior to those of other similar establishments, and in their subsequent assignments these nurses will have full opportunity to render valuable service to the Army.

Sincerely yours,

(Signed) ROBERT P. PATTERSON

ROBERT P. PATTERSON,

Under Secretary of War

The distinguished World War II record of the "Tuskegee Airmen," pilots who trained and fought in all-black fighter squadrons, confounded the expectations of white officers who doubted that black men had the ability or nerve to pilot fighter aircraft.   Courtesy of the Library of Congress

the others gave the blacks a sense that they could succeed and compete in a world that had been saying that 'you're nothing.'" Conner insisted that "because of the world war, I think many people, especially blacks, got the idea that we're going back, but we're not going back to business as usual. Somehow we're going to change this nation so that there's more equality than there is now." The personal transformation that Conner and others experienced, combined with a number of international, national, and regional forces, laid the foundation for a modern movement for freedom of opportunity.

🌿 *How does Patterson's letter reflect the U.S. military's position that "separate but equal" did not constitute discrimination against African Americans?*

🌿 *Why did Mabel Staupers and the National Association of Colored Graduate Nurses object to the establishment of separate training facilities for black women?*

Source: War Department Files, File #2912, National Archives, Washington, DC.

Black People on the Home Front

Just as they did in the military, African Americans on the home front fought a dual war against the Axis and discrimination. Black workers and volunteers helped staff the factories and farms that produced goods for the fight while also purchasing war bonds and participating in other defense activities. The changes brought on by the war also created new points of conflict while exacerbating preexisting problems and occasionally igniting full-scale riots. Throughout the war, protest groups and the black press continued to fight employment discrimination and political exclusion.

BLACK WORKERS: FROM FARM TO FACTORY

The war accelerated the migration of African Americans from rural areas to the cities. Even though the

PROFILE ～ MABEL K. STAUPERS (1890–1989)

Mabel K. Staupers was born in Barbados, in the British West Indies, on February 27, 1890, to Thomas Clarence and Pauline (Lobo) Doyle. Mother and daughter emigrated to New York in 1903; Mabel's father joined them later. In 1917 Mabel became a naturalized citizen of the United States. In short order, Mabel married James Max Keaton, from whom she was later divorced, and received her RN diploma from Freedmen's Hospital School of Nursing in Washington, D.C. She worked as a private-duty nurse in Washington, D.C. and in New York City, where she helped to organize, and served as the superintendent of from 1920 to 1922, the Booker T. Washington Sanatorium, an inpatient clinic for African Americans with tuberculosis. This was one of the few facilities in New York City that permitted black physicians to treat their patients when they were hospitalized. Most other hospitals denied black medical professionals attending or staff privileges and positions. Staupers further honed her organizing and leadership skills when she became executive secretary of the Harlem Committee of the New York Tuberculosis and Health Association, serving from 1922 to 1934. In 1935, Staupers joined with Mary McLeod Bethune to found the National Council of Negro Women. Staupers also accepted the challenge of revitalizing the National Association of Colored Graduate Nurses (NACGN), becoming its first executive director in 1934, and served until 1949, when she was named the organization's president. Under her stewardship the NACGN, in 1951, officially dissolved, and black nurses gained membership in the American Nursing Association.

Staupers's organizing and leadership talent was put to its greatest test during World War II. With verve and perfect timing she mobilized wide-ranging support to end quotas that the U.S. military had established to limit the numbers of black nurses accepted into the Armed Forces Nurse Corps. While the army initially indicated that it would accept fifty-six black nurses to work in the hospital units at Camp Livingston in Louisiana and Fort Bragg in North Carolina, the navy refused to accept any black women nurses. The matter came to a head when, in January 1945, President Franklin D. Roosevelt announced his support of legislation to draft nurses. Staupers was appalled that the government would entertain such a notion when hundreds of black women nurses were available and eager to serve. She led the struggle to end quotas and discrimination against black women nurses in the armed forces. In 1961 Staupers published her account of this struggle in a book entitled, *No Time for Prejudice: A Story of the Integration of Negroes in Nursing in the United States* (New York: Macmillan, 1961). In recognition of her courageous and relentless struggle against racial discrimination, the NAACP awarded Staupers the Spingarn Medal in 1951. An array of honors followed. In 1967, New York Mayor John V. Lindsay gave her a citation of appreciation, which read, "To an immigrant who came to the United States and by Individual Effort through Education and Personal Achievement has become an Outstanding American Leader and Distinguished Citizen of America." She died of pneumonia at her home in Washington, D.C., in 1989.

farm economy recovered during the war, the lure of high-paying defense jobs and other urban occupations tempted many black farmers to abandon the land. By the 1940s the bitter experiences of the previous decades had made it clear there was little future in the cotton fields. Boll weevils, competition from other parts of the world, and mechanization reduced the need for black labor. Indeed, by the end of the war, only 28 percent of black men worked on farms, a decline of 13 percent since 1940. More than 300,000 black men left agricultural labor between 1940 and 1944 alone.

The wartime need for workers, backed by pressure from the government, helped break down some of the barriers to employing African Americans in industry. During the war the total number of black workers in nonfarm employment rose from 2,900,000 to 3,800,000. Nearly all industries relaxed their resistance to hiring African-American workers, and thousands moved into previously whites-only jobs. African Americans found employment in the aircraft industry, and likewise tens of thousands were employed in the nation's shipyards.

With so many of their men away at war, black women increasingly found work outside the laundry and domestic service that had previously been their lot. Nationally 600,000 black women—400,000 of them former domestic servants—shifted into industrial jobs. As one aircraft worker wryly put it, "Hitler was the one that got us out of the white folks' kitchen." Even those women who stayed in domestic work often saw their wages improve as the supply of competing workers dwindled.

The abundance of industrial jobs helped spur and direct the migration of African Americans during and after World War II. Some 1.5 million migrants, nearly 15 percent of the population, left the South, swelling the black communities in northern and western cities that had significant war industries. By 1950 the proportion of the nation's black population living in the South had fallen from 77 percent to 68 percent. The most dramatic rise in black population was in southern California. Because of its burgeoning aircraft industry and the success of civil rights groups and the federal government in limiting discrimination, Los Angeles saw its relatively small African-American community increase by more than 340,000 during the war. During the war many unions became more open to African-American workers. As black men and women took jobs in industries, many joined unions. Between 1940 and 1945, black union membership rose from 200,000 to 1.25 million. Those unions connected to the CIO, particularly the United Automobile Workers, were the most open to black membership, whereas AFL affiliates were the most likely to treat African Americans as second-class members or to con-

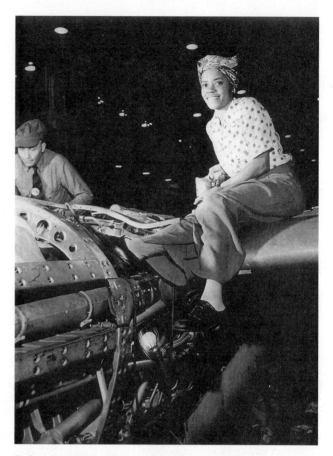

Before World War II, few white women, and still fewer black women, worked in heavy industries, but with so many men in the armed forces, women were recruited for jobs in shipyards and airplane factories, like this aircraft worker. Between 1940 and 1944, the percentage of black women in the industrial workforce increased from 6.8 percent to 18 percent.

tinue to exclude them altogether. Some white unionized workers continued to oppose hiring black workers, even going on strike to prevent it, but their resistance was often deflected by the union leadership, the government, or employers. The growth in black membership did not end racism in unions, even in the CIO, but it did provide African Americans a stronger foundation upon which to protest continuing discrimination in employment.

THE FEPC DURING THE WAR

After President Roosevelt issued the executive order banning job discrimination in defense industries with government contracts, thousands of impoverished black southerners rushed to cities in the Pacific Northwest, especially to Seattle. Wartime Seattle had offered jobs in its shipyards, in logging-truck manufacturing, and at the Boeing aircraft production plants. By the end of World War II, Boeing had employed over twelve hundred black workers, approximately 3 percent of its labor force. African Americans also accounted for 7 percent of Seattle's shipyard workers. By 1948 black families in Seattle boasted a median income of $3,314, a mere 10 percent lower than the median for the nation's white families. But the economic good fortune of black workers on the West Coast was not typical of other regions of the country.

In the middle West and on the East Coast, many African Americans criticized industry's failure to heed the call to end economic discrimination. Responding to the ineffectiveness of the Fair Employment Practices Committee during the first years of the war, in May 1943 President Roosevelt issued Executive Order 9346. The order established a new Committee on Fair Employment Practice, increased its budget, and placed its operation directly under the Executive Office of the President. Roosevelt appointed Malcolm Ross, a combative white liberal, to head the committee. Ross proved to be more effective than the committee's previous leadership. He initiated nationwide hearings of cases concerning discrimination in the shipbuilding and railroad industries. These proceedings caused embarrassment for companies and brought some compliance with the FEPC's orders. Resistance, however, was more common. In Mobile, Alabama, for example, the white employees of the Alabama Dry Dock and Shipbuilding Company opposed the FEPC's efforts to pressure the company to promote twelve of the seven thousand African Americans it employed in menial positions to racially mixed welding crews. The white workers went on a rampage, assaulting fifty African Americans. The FEPC thereupon withdrew its plan and acquiesced in the traditional Jim Crow arrangements for all work assignments. White workers retained their more lucrative positions. As a result of this kind of intransigence, the committee failed to redress most of the grievances of black workers. A concerted effort to continue the committee after the war was defeated.

ANATOMY OF A RACE RIOT: DETROIT, 1943

One of the bloodiest race riots in the nation's history took place in 1943 in Detroit, Michigan, where black and white workers were competing fiercely for jobs and housing. Relations between the two communities in the city had been smoldering for months, with open fighting in the plants and on the streets. White racism, housing segregation, and economic discrimination were part of the problem. The brutality of white police officials was an especially potent factor. Tensions were so palpable that weeks before the riot NAACP leader Walter White had warned that the city could explode in violence at any moment.

The immediate trigger for the riot was a squabble on June 20 between groups of white and black bathers at the segregated city beaches on Belle Isle in the Detroit River. Within hours, two hundred white sailors from a nearby base joined the white mob that pursued and attacked individual black men and women. A rumor that white citizens had killed a black woman and thrown her baby over the bridge spread across the city. The riot was in full swing, spreading quickly along Woodward Avenue, the city's major thoroughfare, into Paradise Valley, where some 35,000 southern black migrants had, in the spring of 1943, joined the city's already crowded black population. By Monday morning downtown Detroit was overrun with white men roaming in search of more victims. At first the mayor refused to acknowledge that the situation had gotten out of hand, but by Tuesday evening he could no longer deny the crisis.

Six thousand federal troops had to be dispatched to Detroit to restore order. When the violence ended, thirty-four people had been killed (twenty-five black and nine white people) and more than seven hundred injured. Of the twenty-five black people who died, the Detroit police killed seventeen. The police did not kill any of the white men who assaulted African Americans or committed arson. Property damage exceeded $2 million and one million man-hours were lost in war production.

In the aftermath, the city created the Mayor's Interracial Committee, the first permanent municipal body designed to promote civic harmony and fairness. Despite the efforts of labor and black leaders, many white people in Detroit, including Wayne County prosecutor William E. Dowling, blamed the black press and the NAACP for instigating the riot. Dowling and others accused the city's black citizens of pushing too hard for economic and political equality and insisted that they operated under communist influence. One of many commissioned reports concluded that black leaders provoked the riot because they had compared "victory over the axis . . . [with] a corresponding overthrow in the country of those forces which . . . prevent true racial equality." In contrast, black leaders, radical trade unionists, and members of other ethnic organizations, especially Jewish groups, blamed, "the KKK, the Christian Front, the Black Dragon Society, the National Workers League, the Knights of the White Camelia, the Southern Voters League, and similar organizations based on a policy of terror and . . . white supremacy."

THE G.I. BILL OF RIGHTS AND BLACK VETERANS

In 1944, President Roosevelt signed the Servicemen's Readjustment Act, or the G.I. Bill of Rights, a piece of legislation that would profoundly shape developments in American life and society. The act rewarded the sacrifices and accomplishments of black and white veterans in the war with college tuition allowances, stipends for books, and guaranteed loans of up to $2,000 (a substantial sum at the time) at low interest rates, with which to purchase homes or launch small businesses. Congress would eventually pay approximately $14.5 billion for the G.I. Bill's provisions.

By 1947, veterans accounted for half of the college student population. The G.I. Bill made possible the upward mobility of a generation of American men who entered professions and trades and purchased homes that would become the basis of future wealth. Between 1950 and 1960, Americans built more than 13 million new homes—11 million of them were in the suburbs, where one-quarter of the entire population relocated after the war. The G.I. Bill fueled the boom in higher education, transportation, and the construction industries that undergirded the postwar prosperity America enjoyed.

While many black veterans benefited from the G.I. Bill of rights, they never received their fair share of funds and assistance. Mississippi Congressman John E. Rankin sabotaged the transformative potential of the G.I. Bill by insisting that state and local veterans' administrators control the distribution of the benefits. The resulting racial disparities were predictable in southern states. In Mississippi, by the summer of 1947, local officials had approved over three thousand VA home loans, but only two went to African-American veterans. In northern urban areas, real estate agencies and banks practiced redlining and denied black men mortages in desirable areas. The denial of loans and the violence that often erupted when black families attempted to move into suburban areas curtailed upward and outward mobility. Roosevelt may have thought he was signing a color-blind law, but the actual execution of the law proved otherwise.

OLD AND NEW PROTEST GROUPS ON THE HOME FRONT

The NAACP grew tremendously during the war, and by its end stood poised for even greater achievements. Under the editorial direction of Roy Wilkins, the circulation of the NAACP's *The Crisis* grew from 7,000 to 45,000. During the war, *The Crisis* was one of the most important sources for information on the status of black men and women. The NAACP's membership increased from 50,000 in 1940 to 450,000 at the end of the war. Even more important, much of this growth occurred in the South, which had more than 150,000 members by 1945. Supreme Court victories and especially close monitoring of the "Double V" campaign help explain these huge increases.

With success, however, came conflict and ambivalence. Leaders split over the value of integration versus self-segregation and questioned the benefit of relying so heavily on legal cases rather than paying more attention to the concerns and needs of working-class black men and women. Wilkins acknowledged the organization's uncertainty and indecisiveness:

> The war was a great watershed for the NAACP. We had become far more powerful, and now the challenge was to keep our momentum. Everyone knew the NAACP stood against discrimination and segregation, but what was our postwar program to be? Beyond discrimination and segregation, where would we stand on veterans, housing, labor-management relations, strikes, the Fair Employment Practices Commission, organizations at state levels, education? What would we do to advance the fight for the vote in the South? . . . We had a big membership . . . but we didn't know how to use them.

In 1944 southern white liberals joined with African Americans to establish the Southern Regional Council (SRC). This interracial coalition, an important example of the local initiative of private citizens, was devoted to expanding democracy in a region better known for the political and economic oppression and exploitation of its black citizens. The SRC conducted research and focused attention on the political, social, and educational inequalities endemic to black life in the South. Although its patient, gradualist program would soon be overtaken by the events of the 1950s and 1960s, the SRC challenged the facade of southern white supremacy.

In 1942 a far more strident group called the Congress of Racial Equality (CORE) had been formed. It pursued different tactics from those of the NAACP, Urban League, and other existing civil rights groups. CORE began in Chicago when an interracial group of Christian pacifists gathered to find ways to make America live up to the ideals of equality and justice on which it based its war program. Activists James Farmer and Bayard Rustin were key in getting the group off the ground. Unlike the NAACP, CORE was a decentralized, intensely democratic organization. CORE dedicated itself to the principles of nonviolent direct action as expounded by Indian leader Mohandas Gandhi. Over the course of the war this pacifist organization expanded to other cities and challenged segregation in the North with sit-ins and other protest tactics that the civil rights movement would later adopt.

African Americans found many ways to fight discrimination. Women were central to these efforts. Throughout the 1940s, in countless communities across the South and the middle West, black women organized women's political councils and other groups to press for integration of public facilities—hospitals,

---

PROFILE ～ BAYARD RUSTIN (1910–1987)

Bayard Rustin, the preeminent strategist of nonviolent resistance, was born on March 17, 1910, in West Chester, Pennsylvania. Rustin worked behind the scenes to give shape and coherence to the modern civil rights movement. During his youth he belonged to the Young Communist League. But in the 1940s he, along with Pauli Murray and James Farmer, became a staff member of the pacifist organization Fellowship of Reconciliation (FOR) and experimented with Gandhian techniques of nonviolent resistance to racial injustice. In 1942, Rustin and Farmer were active in founding the Congress of Racial Equality (CORE). A year later, Rustin refused to be drafted, rejecting even the traditional Quaker compromise of alternative service in an army hospital. Convicted of violating the Selective Service Act, he served three years in a federal penitentiary in Ashland, Kentucky.

> While in prison, Rustin honed the philosophy that would guide his life, which he summed up this way: There are three ways in which one can deal with an injustice. (a) One can accept it without protest. (b) One can seek to avoid it. (c) One can resist the injustice nonviolently. To accept it is to perpetuate it. To avoid it is impossible. To resist by intelligent means, and with an attitude of mutual responsibility and respect, is much the better course.

> Upon release from prison, Rustin became race relations secretary for FOR and participated in countless protest organizations. He organized a Free India Committee and directed A. Philip Randolph's Committee against Discrimination in the Armed Forces. He orchestrated CORE's 1947 Journey of Reconciliation, a precursor to the Freedom Rides of 1961, in which sixteen black and white men traveled by bus through the upper South to test new federal laws prohibiting segregated services in interstate transportation. Outside Chapel Hill, North Carolina, the group was assaulted and arrested. Rustin and three of his colleagues were sentenced to thirty days on a road gang, of which he served twenty-two days. In the late 1950s Rustin served as an important adviser to Martin Luther King Jr. and was one of the key figures in nearly all phases of the civil rights movement of the 1950s and 1960s.

Rustin, who was gay, fought oppression all his life. After the ebbtide of the civil rights movement he shifted his attention to combating homophobia. He declared shortly before his death on August 24, 1987, that "the barometer of where one is on human rights questions is no longer the black community, it's the gay community. Because it is the community which is most easily mistreated."

Bayard Rustin spent his life actively engaged in civil rights causes. He ▶ struggled against discrimination during the 1940s, was special assistant to Martin Luther King, Jr. in the 1940s, acted as a behind-the-scenes architect of the March on Washington in 1963, and was executive director of the A. Philip Randolph Institute. Robert Maas captures his quiet dignity in this 1982 photograph.   Robert Maas/CORBIS

Rustin

swimming pools, theaters, and restaurants—and for the right to pursue collegiate and professional studies. Others were galvanized by the war and took advantage of the limited social and political spaces afforded them to create lasting works in the arts, literature, and popular culture. Women whose names would become virtually synonymous with the modern civil rights movement in the 1950s and 1960s helped lay its foundation in the World War II era. Ella Baker was accumulating contacts and sharpening her organizing skills as she served as the NAACP field secretary. Rosa Parks began resisting segregation laws on Montgomery, Alabama, buses in the 1940s.

Black college students also began protesting segregation in public accommodations. The spark that ignited the Howard University campus civil rights movement came in January 1943. Three sophomore women, Ruth Powell from Massachusetts and Marianne Musgrave and Juanita Morrow from Ohio, sat at a lunch counter near the campus and were refused service. They demanded to see the manager and vowed to wait until he came. Instead of the manager, two policemen arrived who instructed the waitress to serve them. When the check arrived the trio learned they had been charged 25 cents each instead of the customary 10 cents. They placed 35 cents on the counter, turned to leave, and were arrested. Ruth Power later reported that "the policemen who arrested us told us we were being taken in for investigation because he had no proof that we weren't 'subversive agents.'" In fact, no charges were lodged against the women. The purpose of their arrest had been to intimidate them, but the incident instead fanned the smoldering embers of resentment in the Howard University student body.

The Transition to Peace

After the German surrender in May 1945 and the Japanese surrender in August 1945, the United States began the transition to peace. Many of the gains of black men and women were wiped away as the armed forces demobilized and the factories began reinstituting the discriminatory hiring systems in place before the conflict. Access to fair, decent, and affordable housing remained a sore issue, as did the inequalities in educational opportunities and the continuing scourge of police brutality. Thus, as the country tried to regain its prewar footing, it was clear that segregation and discrimination would face a huge challenge in the coming years and that the African-American community was ready, willing, and able to fight in ways undreamed of in earlier eras.

The Cold War and International Politics

As the defeat of the Axis powers neared in early 1945, the United Nations began planning for the peace. Within a short time, however, the opposing interests of the Soviet Union and the United States led to a long period of intense hostility that became known as the Cold War. This conflict soon led to a division of Europe into two spheres, with the Soviets dominating part of Germany and the nations to its east and a coalition of democratic capitalist regimes allied with the United States in the west. Thereafter the overriding goal of the United States and its allies was the "containment" of communism. To this end, the North Atlantic Treaty Organization (NATO) was formed in 1949 to provide a military counterforce to Soviet power in Europe while American dollars helped rebuild Western Eu-

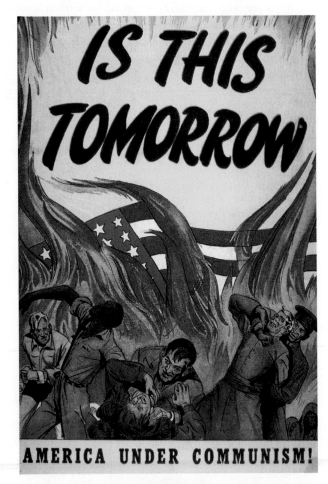

America's Cold War propaganda targeted all citizens, black and white. This anticommunism poster was one of many designed to remind Americans of threats to their freedom and to fan the flames of patriotism.

rope's war-shattered economy. The United States forged a similarly close relationship with Japan. Much of the rest of the world, however, became contested terrain during the Cold War.

As the nations of Asia and Africa gained independence from colonial domination over the ensuing decades, the United States struggled to keep them out of the Soviet orbit. It did so through foreign aid, direct military force, and, occasionally, through clandestine operations run by the Central Intelligence Agency (CIA). These military interventions were matched by a rising diplomatic and propaganda effort to convince the emerging nations of the world that the United States was a model to be emulated and an ally to be trusted.

The Cold War had an enormous influence on American society precisely when the powerful movement for African-American rights was beginning to emerge. The long conflict resulted in the rise of a permanent military establishment in the United States. Small in scope before World War II, the reorganized American military enlisted millions of men and women by the early 1950s and claimed most of the national budget. The federal government also grew in power during the war and provided a check on the control that white southerners had so long exercised over race relations in their region. American policy makers also became concerned about the nation's ability to win the allegiance of Africans and other nonwhite people who formed the population of the emerging nations. The Soviet Union possessed a powerful propaganda advantage because it could discredit American sincerity by pointing to the deplorable state of race relations within the United States. Hence, during the Cold War, external pressures reinforced efforts to change American racial policy.

AFRICAN AMERICANS IN WORLD AFFAIRS: W. E. B. DU BOIS AND RALPH BUNCHE

The Cold War gave new importance to the voices of African Americans in world affairs. Two men, W. E. B. Du Bois and Ralph Johnson Bunche (1904–1971), represent alternative strategies for responding to this opportunity. Du Bois took a highly critical approach to American policy. For half a century he had linked the fate of African Americans with that of Africans, and by 1945 was widely hailed as the "Father of Pan-Africanism". In that year he directed the Fifth Pan-African Congress, which met in Manchester, England. The Africans who had been radicalized by World War II dominated the conference and encouraged it to denounce Western imperialism. Du Bois considered the United States a protector of the colonial system and opposed its stance in the Cold War. On returning from the Manchester congress, he declared,

> We American Negroes should know . . . until Africa is free, the descendants of Africa the world over cannot escape their chains. . . . The NAACP should therefore put in the forefront of its program the freedom of Africa in work and wage, education and health, and the complete abolition of the colonial system.

In contrast to Du Bois, scholar diplomat Ralph Bunche opted to work within the American system. Bunche held a Harvard doctorate in government and international relations and had spent much of the 1930s studying the problems of African Americans. During World War II the American government found his expertise on Africa of tremendous value, and Bunche became one of the key policy makers for the region. Bunche's analysis of events and changes in Africa and the Far East after World War II led to his appointment as adviser to the U.S. delegation at the San Francisco conference that drafted the United Nations (UN) Charter. In 1948 he served as acting mediator of the UN Special Committee on Palestine, and in 1949 he negotiated an armistice between Egypt and Israel. He received the Spingarn Medal of the NAACP in 1949, and in 1950 he became the first African American to receive the Nobel Peace Prize. Although Bunche worked in concert with national policy makers, he was committed to winning independence for African nations and freedom for his own people. As he wrote,

> Today, for all thinking people, the Negro is the shining symbol of the true significance of democracy. He has demonstrated what can be achieved with democratic liberties even when grudgingly and incompletely bestowed. But the most vital significance of the Negro . . . to American society . . . is the fact that democracy which is not extended to all of the nation's citizens is a democracy that is mortally wounded.

ANTICOMMUNISM AT HOME

The rising tensions with the Soviet Union affected all aspects of domestic life in the United States. Conservatives used fears of communist subversion to attack anyone who advocated change in America. This included people who were, or had been, members of the Communist Party, union members, liberals, and people who had fought for African-American rights. The Truman administration (1945–1952) responded to fears of subversion by instituting government loyalty programs. Government employees were dismissed for the merest suspicion of disloyalty. Militant American anticommunism reached a feverish peak in the immediate postwar years and gave rise to an explosion of red-baiting hysteria that led to the rise of Wisconsin Republican senator Joseph McCarthy (1909–1957) and the House Un-American Activities Committee (HUAC). The relentless pursuit of "communist sympathizers" by McCarthy and the HUAC ruined many lives. The HUAC in particular hounded people in the media and in the entertainment industry. Even so prominent a figure as W. E. B. Du Bois was ripe for attack. On February 8, 1951, the HUAC indicted him for allegedly serving as an "agent of a foreign principal" in his work with the Peace Information Center. In November a federal judge dismissed all charges against Du Bois. The government had been unable to prove he was an agent of communism. Despite Du Bois's past contributions, fear and personal malice prevented most African-American leaders from defending him.

PAUL ROBESON

Paul Robeson was one of the most tragic victims of these anticommunist witch-hunts. This fine scholar and star collegiate athlete, Columbia Law School graduate, consummate performer, and star of stage and screen had always been an advocate for the rights of African Americans and workers. During the 1930s he worked closely with the Communist Party (although he was never a member), becoming one of the most famous defenders of the Soviet Union. Many leftists of the time became disaffected with the USSR after its 1939 pact with Hitler and after its brutal repressiveness became clear. Robeson, however, doggedly stuck to his belief in Soviet communism through the 1940s and beyond.

In the late 1940s, Robeson's pro-Soviet views and inflammatory statements aroused the ire of the U.S. government and its red hunters. A statement he made at the communist-dominated World Congress of the Defenders of Peace in Paris in 1949 provoked particular outrage. "It is unthinkable," Robeson said, "that American Negroes would go to war on behalf of those [the United States] who have oppressed us for generations against a country [the Soviet Union] which in one generation has raised our people to full human dignity of mankind." Later in 1949 crowds of rock-throwing locals twice disrupted a Robeson concert in Peekskill, New York, the first time preventing the concert from being held, the second time terrorizing performers and audience members at the concert's conclusion.

Throughout the 1940s Robeson consistently linked the struggles of black America with the struggles of black Africa, brown India, yellow Asia, the black men and women of Brazil and Haiti, and oppressed workers throughout Latin America. Robeson also refused to sign an affidavit concerning past membership in the Communist Party. In response, the U.S. State Department revoked his passport in 1950, explaining "the action was taken because the Department considers that Paul Robeson's travel abroad at this time would be contrary to the best interest of the United States." The travel ban remained in effect until ruled unconstitutional by the Supreme Court in 1958.

Robeson had combined his art and his politics to launch a sustained attack against racial discrimination, segregation, and the ideology of white supremacy and black inferiority as practiced in American society. During the Cold War the state would tolerate no such dissent by even a world-acclaimed black artist.

HENRY WALLACE AND THE 1948 PRESIDENTIAL ELECTION

Robeson's struggles illustrate how conservative attacks choked off left-wing involvement in the struggle for black equality. The attacks destroyed Robeson's brilliant singing career. The increasing importance of black votes to Democrats, however, meant that key elements of the African-American liberation struggle remained at the center of national politics. Nowhere was this more apparent than in the 1948 presidential election.

President Harry S. Truman was not expected to win this election because he faced a strong challenge from Thomas Dewey, the popular and well-financed Republican governor of New York. Truman's problems were compounded by a challenge from his former secretary of commerce Henry Wallace, who had been Roosevelt's vice president from 1941 to 1945. Wallace ran on the ticket of the communist-backed Progressive Party, which sought to take the votes of liberals, leftists, and civil rights advocates disappointed by Truman's moderation. Wallace also supported a peaceful accommodation with the Soviet Union. To undercut Wallace's challenge, Truman began to press Congress to pass liberal programs.

DOCUMENT 20-5 Henry Wallace, Radio Address, 1948

Black votes in key northern states were central to Truman's strategy for victory. African Americans in these tightly contested areas could make the difference between victory and defeat, so Truman, to retain their allegiance, sought to demonstrate his administration's support of civil rights. In January 1948 he embraced the findings of his biracial Committee on Civil Rights and called for their enactment into law. The committee's report, "To Secure These Rights," was a blueprint for changing the racial caste system in the United States. It recommended passage of federal antilynching legislation, ending discrimination at the ballot box, abolishing the poll tax, desegregating the military, and a whole range of other measures.

The reaction of white southern politicians was swift and threatening, causing Truman to pause; but as the election neared, fear of black abandonment at the polls became so great that the Democratic convention passed a strong pro–civil rights plank. Many white southerners, led by South Carolina's governor Strom Thurmond, bolted from the convention and formed their own States' Rights, or "Dixiecrat," Party. The Dixiecrats carried South Carolina, Alabama, Mississippi, and Louisiana in the election; Wallace carried no state. The failure of the bulwark of white supremacy to prevent the Democratic Party from advocating African-American rights, and Truman's ultimate victory despite the defection of hard-line racists, represented a profound turning point in American politics.

DESEGREGATING THE ARMED FORCES

The importance of the black vote, the fight for the allegiance of the emerging nations, and the emerging civil rights movement hastened the desegregation of the military. In February 1948 a communist coup in Czechoslovakia raised the possibility of war between the United States and the Soviet Union and heightened concerns among military leaders about the willingness of African Americans to serve yet again in a Jim Crow army. When President Truman reinstated the draft in March 1948, A. Philip Randolph, who, in a replay of the March on Washington scenario, had formed the League for Non-Violent Civil Disobedience against Military Segregation in 1947, warned the nation that black men and women were fed up with segregation and Jim Crow and would not take a Jim Crow draft lying down. New York congressman Adam Clayton Powell Jr. also supported this stance. He declared there weren't enough jails in America to hold the black men who would refuse to bear arms in a Jim Crow army. On June 24, 1948, the Soviet Union heightened tensions even further when it imposed a blockade on West Berlin. On July 26 Truman, anticipating war between the superpowers and hoping to shore up his support among black voters for the approaching November elections, issued **Executive Order 9981**, officially desegregating the armed forces.

Executive Order 9981, which mandated "equality of treatment and opportunity for all persons in the armed services without regard to race, color, religion,

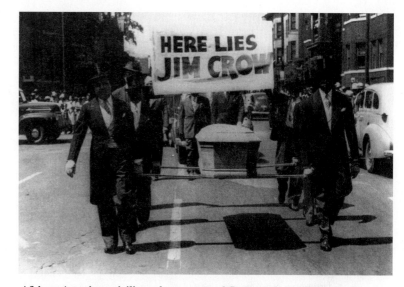

African-American civilians demonstrated firm resolve to end racial segregation at home while Americans fought to make the world safe for democracy. The NAACP Detroit branch's 1994 "Parade for Victory" featured pallbearers with caskets as they marched behind a sign that proclaimed "here lies JIM CROW." It conveyed the sentiment, if not the reality. But Jim Crow's days were numbered.

or national origin," signaled the victorious culmination of a decades-long struggle by black civilians and soldiers to win full integration into the nation's military. After Truman signed the order, Randolph and Grant Reynolds, a former minister and co-chair of the League for Nonviolent Civil Disobedience against Military Segregation, disbanded the organization and called off marches planned for Chicago and New York.

Executive Order 9981, 1948 **20-6** DOCUMENT

Not until 1950 and the outbreak of the Korean War, however, was Truman's order fully implemented. The war reflected the American Cold War policy of containment, which was intended to stop what American leaders believed to be a worldwide conspiracy orchestrated by Moscow to spread communism. In 1950 North Koreans, allied with the Soviets, attacked the American-supported government in South Korea and launched the "hot war" in the midst of the Cold War. After the North Koreans invaded South Korea, the United States under UN auspices intervened. Heavy casualties early in the war depleted many white combat units. Thus, early in 1951, the army acted on Truman's executive order and authorized the formal integration of its units in Korea. By 1954 the army had disbanded its last all-black units, and the armed forces became one of the first sectors of American society to abandon segregation.

AFRICAN-AMERICAN EVENTS	NATIONAL AND WORLD EVENTS
	• 1936 •
	1936 Abraham Lincoln Brigade goes to Spain to resist Franco
	• 1938 •
	1938 German troops overrun Austria **1939** Germany invades Poland, beginning World War II
	• 1940 •
1941 Dorie Miller, hero of Pearl Harbor, receives Navy Cross A. Philip Randolph organizes March on Washington Movement	**1940** Benito Mussolini and Hitler form Axis Germany conquers most of Western Europe Selective Training and Service Act begins Roosevelt wins reelection to third term **1941** Executive Order 8802 is issued Japan attacks Pearl Harbor; America joins World War II
	• 1942 •
1942 Congress of Racial Equality (CORE) is founded in Chicago Charity Adams (Early) becomes first black woman commissioned officer in the Women's Army Auxiliary Corps (WAACs) First black cadets graduate from flying school at Tuskegee, Alabama **1943** William H. Hastie resigns in protest from War Department Race riots in Mobile, Detroit, and Harlem The black 99th Pursuit Squadron flies its first combat mission	**1942** 100,000 Japanese Americans interred in camps **1943** Roosevelt signs G.I. Bill Servicemen's Readjustment Act provides funds for housing and education after the war

CONCLUSION

The years between 1940 and 1954 were a dynamic period of black activism and witnessed a rising international consciousness among African Americans. The quest for racial justice in the military and on the home front became an integral part of the ongoing struggle for economic, political, and social progress. President Roosevelt's Executive Order 8802 was a significant victory for A. Philip Randolph's March on Washington Movement and for black workers who were able to appeal racial discrimination in defense industries to the Fair Employment Practices Commission. The rise of fascism in Europe alarmed black and white Americans who correctly perceived ideologies based on racial tyranny and state dominance to be inimical to individual freedom and democracy. World War II also had far-reaching consequences. It profoundly transformed black servicemen and servicewomen.

Following victory in World War II, the Cold War created a climate in America that was both hospitable and hostile to the African-American freedom movement. Radicals such as Paul Robeson and W. E. B. Du Bois found no place in the movement or in American society. Moderate organizations, such as the NAACP-LDEF, pursuing their goals within the ideological and legal constraints of the nation, would meet with some success. The coming civil rights movement would, however, soon expand this narrow field of action and pave the way for a more varied, vibrant, and successful challenge to racism.

RECOMMENDED READING

John D'Emilio. *Lost Prophet: The Life and Times of Bayard Rustin.* New York: Simon & Schuster, 2003. A first-rate, well-written, thoughtful biography of a key, although often underappreciated, leader in the long struggle for social justice for all Americans.

Mary L. Dudziak. *Cold War Civil Rights: Race and the Image of American Democracy.* Princeton, NJ: Princeton University Press, 2000. An excellent study of the intricacies of Cold War diplomacy and the centrality of race issues and a splendid analysis of the Truman administration's commitment to civil rights.

Darlene Clark Hine. "Black Professional and Race Consciousness: Origins of the Civil Rights Movement, 1890–1950." *The Journal of American History,* 89, no. 4 (2003): 1279–94. A detailed discussion of the struggle of black physicians and nurses to end the racial segregation of medicine in the armed forces during World War II.

Paula F. Pfeffer. *A. Philip Randolph, Pioneer of the Civil Rights Movement.* Baton Rouge: Louisiana State University

Press, 1990. A richly insightful biography of a pioneering labor leader and activist whose March on Washington Movement in 1941 was essential to the formation of the first Fair Employment Practices Committee and the integration of the armed services.

William R. Scott. *The Sons of Sheba's Race: African-Americans and the Italo-Ethiopian War, 1935–1941.* Bloomington: Indiana University Press, 1993. A detailed and illuminating account of African-American responses to the Italian invasion of Ethiopia and the growth of black internationalism.

Laura Wexler. *Fire in a Canebrake: The Last Mass Lynching in America.* New York: Scribner's, 2003. A riveting and sobering account of the lynching by a white mob of four victims on July 25, 1946, in Walton County, Georgia, at Moore's Ford Bridge. The book is a poignant study of the pernicious power of racism in the wake of the global holocaust of World War II.

ADDITIONAL BIBLIOGRAPHY

AFRICAN AMERICANS AND THE MILITARY

Robert Allen. *Port Chicago Mutiny: The Story of the Largest Mass Mutiny in U.S. Naval History.* New York: Warner Books-Amistad Books, 1989.

Richard Dalfiume. *Desegregation of the U.S. Armed Forces: Fighting on Two Fronts 1939–1953.* Columbia: University of Missouri Press, 1969.

Charles W. Dryden. *A-Train: Memoirs of a Tuskegee Airman.* Tuscaloosa: University of Alabama Press, 1997.

Charity Adams Earley. *One Woman's Army: A Black Officer Remembers the WAC.* College Station: Texas A&M University Press, 1989.

Darlene Clark Hine. *Black Women in White: Racial Conflict and Cooperation in the Nursing Profession, 1890–1950.* Bloomington: Indiana University Press, 1989.

Ulysses Lee. *The Employment of Negro Troops.* Washington, DC: Center of Military History, 1990.

Melton A. Mclaurin. *The Marines of Montford Point: America's First Black Marines.* Chapel Hill: University of North Carolina Press, 2007.

Neil McMillen, ed. *Remaking Dixie: The Impact of World War II on the American South.* Jackson: University Press of Mississippi, 1997.

Mary Penick Motley. *The Invisible Soldier: The Experience of the Black Soldier, World War Two.* Detroit: Wayne State University Press, 1975.

Alan M. Osur. *Blacks in the Army Air Forces during World War II: The Problem of Race Relations.* Washington, DC: Office of Air Force History, 1977.

Lou Potter. *Liberators: Fighting on Two Fronts in World War II.* New York: Harcourt Brace Jovanovich, 1992.

Timeline

1944

AFRICAN-AMERICAN EVENTS

1944
Adam Clayton Powell Jr. is elected to U.S. House of Representatives, from Harlem

U.S. Supreme Court overthrows the white primary in *Smith v. Allwright*

1945
Mabel Staupers secures an end to discrimination against black nurses in the military

Du Bois, Bethune, White, and Bunche attend UN founding

Paul Robeson receives NAACP Spingarn Medal

NATIONAL EVENTS

1944
D-Day, Allied invasion of German-occupied France, begins

Roosevelt wins his fourth term

Roosevelt wins his fourth term

The Battle of the Bulge begins last major German counteroffensive

1945
United Nations founded

FDR dies; Truman becomes president

Germany surrenders

U.S. bombs Hiroshima and Nagasaki; Japan surrenders

1946

1947
The Journey of Reconciliation project begins; it is the precursor to the 1961 Freedom Rides

1946
President Truman creates the Committee on Civil Rights

1948

1948
Ada Lois Sipuel v. Board Regents is decided

Truman's Executive Order 9981 desegregates the military

1949
Whites riot against Robeson concerts in Peekskill, New York

1948
Truman wins presidential election with support of black voters

1950

1950
Sweatt v. Painter is decided
McLaurin v. Oklahoma is decided

1950–1953
Korean War is fought

1952

1952
Colonel Benjamin O. Davis Jr. is appointed commander of the 51st Fighter Interceptor Wing in Korea

1954

1954
Brown v. Board of Education declares the "separate but equal" doctrine unconstitutional

AFRICAN-AMERICAN EVENTS   **NATIONAL EVENTS**

Stanley Sandler. *Segregated Skies: All-Black Combat Squadrons of WWII.* Washington, DC: Smithsonian Institution Press, 1992.

Howard Sitkoff. "Racial Militancy and Interracial Violence in the Second World War," *Journal of American History,* 58, no. 3 (1971): 663–83.

Paul Stillwell, ed. *The Golden Thirteen: Recollections of the First Black Naval Officers.* Annapolis, MD: Naval Institute Press, 1993.

BLACK URBAN STUDIES

Albert Broussard. *Black San Francisco: The Struggle for Racial Equality in the West, 1900–1954.* Lawrence: University of Kansas Press, 1993.

Dominic Capeci. *The Harlem Riot of 1943.* Philadephia: Temple University Press, 1977.

Dominic Capeci. *Race Relations in Wartime Detroit: The Sojourner Truth Housing Controversy of 1942.* Philadelphia: Temple University Press, 1984.

Dominic Capeci and Martha Wilkerson. *Layered Violence: The Detroit Rioters of 1943.* Jackson: University Press of Mississippi, 1991.

Lawrence B. DeGraaf. "Significant Steps on an Arduous Path: The Impact of World War II on Discrimination against African Americans in the West." *Journal of the West,* 35, no. 1 (1996): 24–33.

St. Clair Drake and Horace R. Cayton. *Black Metropolis: A Study of Negro Life in a Northern City.* New York: Harcourt Brace, 1945.

August Meier and Elliott Rudwick. *Black Detroit and the Rise of the UAW.* New York: Oxford University Press, 1979.

Robert Shogan and Tom Craig. *The Detroit Race Riot: A Study in Violence.* New York: Chilton Books, 1964.

Richard W. Thomas. *Life for Us Is What We Make It: Building Black Community in Detroit, 1915–1945.* Bloomington: Indiana University Press, 1992.

BLACK AMERICANS, DOMESTIC RADICALISM, AND INTERNATIONAL AFFAIRS

Beth Tompkins Bates. *Pullman Porters and the Rise of Protest Politics on Black Americans, 1925–1945.* Chapel Hill: University of North Carolina Press, 2001.

William C. Berman. *The Politics of Civil Rights in the Truman Administration.* Columbus: Ohio State University Press, 1970.

John Morton Blum. *V Was for Victory: Politics and American Culture during World War II.* New York: Harcourt Brace Jovanovich, 1996.

Richard M. Freeland. *The Truman Doctrine and the Origins of McCarthyism.* New York: New York University Press, 1985.

Herbert Garfinkel. *When Negroes March: The March on Washington Movement in the Organizational Politics for FEPC.* New York: Atheneum, 1973.

Joseph Harris. *African American Reactions to War in Ethiopia, 1936–1941.* Baton Rouge: Louisiana State University Press, 1994.

Gerald Horne. *Black and Red: W. E. B. Du Bois and the Afro-American Response to the Cold War.* Albany: State University of New York Press, 1986.

Sudarshan Kapur. *Raising Up a Prophet: The Afro-American Encounter with Gandhi.* Boston: Orbis, 1992.

Andrew Edmund Kersten. *Race and War: The FEPC in the Midwest, 1941–46.* Urbana: University of Illinois Press, 2000.

George Lipsitz. *Rainbow at Midnight: Labor and Culture in the 1940s.* Urbana: University of Illinois Press, 1994.

August Meier and Elliott Rudwick. *CORE: A Study in the Civil Rights Movement, 1942–1968.* Urbana: University of Illinois Press, 1975.

Gail Williams O'Brien. *The Color of the Law: Race, Violence and Justice in the Post–World War II South.* Chapel Hill: University of North Carolina Press, 1999.

Brenda Gayle Plummer. *Rising Wind: Black Americans and U.S. Foreign Affairs, 1935–1960.* Chapel Hill: University of North Carolina Press, 1996.

Linda Reed. *Simple Decency and Common Sense: The Southern Conference Movement, 1938–1963.* Bloomington: Indiana University Press, 1991.

Patricia Scott Washburn. *A Question of Sedition: The Federal Government's Investigation of the Black Press during World War II.* New York: Oxford University Press, 1986.

AUTOBIOGRAPHY AND BIOGRAPHY

Andrew Buni. *Robert Vann of the Pittsburgh Courier.* Pittsburgh: University of Pittsburgh Press, 1974.

Martin Bauml Duberman. *Paul Robeson: A Biography.* New York: Ballantine Press, 1989.

Shirley Graham Du Bois. *His Day Is Marching On: A Memoir of W. E. B. Du Bois.* New York: Lippincott, 1971.

Kenneth R. Janken. *Rayford W. Logan and the Dilemma of the African-American Intellectual.* Amherst: University of Massachusetts Press, 1993.

Spencie Love. *One Blood: The Death and Resurrection of Charles Drew.* Chapel Hill: University of North Carolina Press, 1996.

Manning Marable. *W. E. B. Du Bois: Black Radical Democrat.* Boston: Twayne, 1986.

Constance Baker Motley. *Equal Justice under Law: An Autobiography.* New York: Farrar, Straus and Giroux, 1998.

Pauli Murray. *Song in a Weary Throat: An American Pilgrimage.* New York: Harper & Row, 1987.

Bayard Rustin. *Troubles I've Seen.* New York: HarperCollins, 1996.

Studs Terkel, ed. *The Good War.* New York: Pantheon, 1984.

Brian Urquhart. *Ralph Bunche: An American Life.* New York: Norton, 1993.

Gilbert Ware. *William Hastie: Grace under Pressure.* New York: Oxford University Press, 1984.

Roy Wilkins with Tom Mathews. *Standing Fast: The Autobiography of Roy Wilkins.* New York: Da Capo Press, 1994.

RETRACING THE ODYSSEY

National Museum of the Tuskegee Airmen at Historic Fort Wayne (Indiana). This museum documents the achievements of the combat aviators who served as a segregated unit of the U.S. Armed Forces in World War II. They received their training at the Army Air Corps base in Tuskegee, Alabama. During World War II these black aviators shot down enemy aircraft, bombed barges and enemy power stations, and successfully escorted other fighter pilots to their missions across Europe.

Port Chicago Naval Magazine National Memorial, Concord Naval Weapons Station, California. The memorial contains artifacts and exhibits. Much of the base is now a wildlife preserve.

 REVIEW, RESEARCH, AND INTERACT

REVIEW QUESTIONS

1. How did World War II alter the status of African Americans? What were some of the consequences of so many black servicemen fighting in Europe against fascism and Nazism?

2. How did black women participate in the campaign to desegregate the U.S. military and in the Abraham Lincoln Brigade? How did Mabel Staupers win acceptance of black women into the military nurses corps?

3. What were the consequences of the "Double V" campaign? How did African-American civilians indicate their support of black servicemen? What institutional

resources were African Americans able to marshal in their campaign for victory against racism at home?

4. How did World War II affect the status of black workers in America? What was the significance of A. Philip Randolph's March on Washington Movement, and how did President Roosevelt respond to it?

5. Why did the Cold War originate, and what is its significance for black activism? How did the World War II era promote the rising internationalization of African-American consciousness? How did the State Department attempt to downplay black dissent in America, and why?

6. Why did President Harry S. Truman decide to desegregate the U.S. military?

 www.researchnavigator.com

Using the tools available in Research Navigator, consider this question:
How did the military experience of African Americans affect their expectations when they returned home to the United States?

PRIMARY SOURCE DOCUMENTS

20–1 Executive Order 8802, 1941

20–3 Thurgood Marshall, "The Legal Attack to Secure Civil Rights," 1942

20–4 *Jim Crow in the Army Camps*, 1940, and *Jim Crow Army*, 1941

20–5 Henry Wallace, Radio Address, 1948

20–6 Executive Order 9981: Desegregation of the Armed Forces, 1948

African-American Soldiers in World War II

Nearly one million African Americans served during World War II. Soldiers in the transportation corps, almost half of whom were black, loaded supplies and drove them in trucks to the front lines. Black engineers built camps and ports, constructed and repaved roads, and performed many other tasks to support frontline troops. A number of African-American artillery, tank destroyer, anti-aircraft, and combat engineer battalions fought with distinction in Europe and Asia. African-American women also found expanded opportunities in the military. Approximately 4,000 black women served in the Women's Army Auxiliary Corps (WAACs). The most visible group of black soldiers served in the Army Air Force. In January 1941, the War Department announced the formation of a training program at Tuskegee Army Air Field, Alabama, for black pilots. This squadron was also the first to have black officers.

◄◄ **Members of the African-American Seabee Battalion** rush ashore during an assault training exercise, December 1942.

Pilots of an American P-51 Mustang fighter-bomber group learn their 'target for today' during a briefing at a base in Italy, September 1944.
▼

**Lieutenant Colonel ►
Benjamin O. Davis, Jr.** commanded the 332nd Group of Tuskegee Airmen, who participated in campaigns in Italy, France, Germany, and the Balkans.

Soldiers pose with mortar shells scrawled with anti-Hitler messages, Europe 1943.

Two American orderlies escort a German soldier captured at Normandy during World War II.

The 1st African American Division in Arizona take aim from a slit trench during World War II.

Willa Beatrice Brown was the first African American woman to receive a commission as a lieutenant in the U.S. Civil Air Patrol. She trained pilots for the U.S. Army Air Forces.

This WWII recruiting poster shows African American and white laborers working side by side beneath an American flag, even though the armed forces were a segregated reality for African Americans.

UNITED WE WIN

THE GREAT DEPRESSION AND WORLD WAR II

During the Great Depression African Americans were among the poorest of the nation's population and suffered accordingly. In the massive New Deal relief programs mounted by the Roosevelt administration, blacks were the "last hired and first fired."

Throughout WWII, African Americans soldiers fought under a cloud of military prejudice and discrimination. The war experience, though, inculcated many black soldiers with a commitment to fight discrimination.

How successful were African Americans in promoting their own equality under the presidential administration of Franklin D. Roosevelt during the Great Depression and World War II? What specific efforts were launched by African Americans to achieve that goal?

▶ Black Workers in New Deal, 1934

Negro labor in St. Louis, MO., has shown the way for colored workers throughout the country to make an aggressive attack against prejudiced and discriminatory policies on the part of certain sections of the American labor movement.

For many months in the midst of the depression, Negroes saw all municipal work in building trades turned over to white union workers who steadfastly refused to allow a Negro mechanic to work with them. . . . the Negroes' patience snapped at sight of a $2,000,000 colored hospital being erected in the middle of their own neighborhood, built with municipal and Federal funds, with no Negro carpenters, bricklayers, painters, or other skilled workers, allowed on the job.

Out of this resentment, guided and advised by the St. Louis Urban League, grew a Negro labor organization of building trades workers whose avowed aim was to protect the interests of Negro workers under the recovery program. . . .

"The National Urban League is, therefore, initiating the establishment of Workers' Councils as active aggressive units through which all Negro workers may obtain union recognition, increase their power for collective action and equal pay, and participate in the improvement of the status of all workers— white and black."

▶ A Negro in the CCC, 1935

During the two years of its previous existence I had heard many conflicting reports concerning the Civilian Conservation Corps, President Roosevelt's pet project. . . . So it was with some apprehension that I surveyed the postal card instructing me to see Miss A. at the Home Relief Bureau the following Friday. At this Bureau I signed a paper, of which I kept two copies, and the Bureau one. This paper asserted that I was "accepted for enrollment," and should report the following Monday "to U.S. Army authorities for further registration.". . .

We reached Camp Dix about 7:30 that evening. As we rolled up in front of headquarters an officer came out to the bus and told us: "You will double-time as you leave this bus, remove your hat when you hit the door, and when you are asked questions, answer 'Yes, sir,' and 'No, sir.'"

And here it was that Mr. James Crow [Jim Crow] first definitely put in his appearance. When my record was taken at Pier I, a "C" was placed on it. When the busloads were made up at Whitehall street an officer reported as follows: "35, 8 colored." But until now there had been no distinction made.

But before we left the bus the officer shouted emphatically: "Colored boys fall out in the rear." The colored from several buses were herded together, and stood in line until after the

Jim Crow in the Army, 1940

The leadership for the insulting Jim-Crow policy was given by the national Administration in legalizing the maintenance and formation of Jim-Crow regiments. On October 9 [1940], an ominous statement was issued from the White House through the President's secretary, Stephen Early:

"The policy of the War Department is not to intermingle colored and white personnel in the same regimental organization. This policy has proven satisfactory over a long period of years, and to make changes would produce situations destructive to morale and detrimental to preparations for national defense. For similar reasons the War Department does not contemplate assigning colored reserve officers other than those of the medical corps and chaplains to existing Negro combat units of the regular army. . . ."

Two questions automatically arise in the minds of young Americans: Is this tremendous draft army being created for national defense? Are the Negroes who are now being placed in Jim-Crow regiments considered a part of the nation? The simple truth is that purpose for which this armed force is being created is not for defense of the nation, but rather for profits and empire to benefit the rich. Negroes are excluded in this concept of the nation in the eyes of Wall Street. . . . How dare the President of the United States speak the name of "civilization," "democracy," "freedom," "culture," and "world order"! What can better expose this entire set-up than the reactionary attitude of the Administration toward one-tenth of America's citizenry?

Navy Recommendation Regarding Military Desegregation, 1942

The Navy of the United States is composed, except for messmen, of members of the white race. This condition has arisen because those in control have believed and experience has demonstrated that the white man is more adaptable and more efficient in the various conditions that are involved in the making of an effective man-of-war. The nation is now at war and the induction into the Navy of increasing numbers of Negroes in the wider field of activities cannot fail to increase the difficulties of preparing for war and distract the attention of the Navy from concentrating all its efforts toward winning a complete victory.

The Board strongly recommends that members of the colored race be accepted for enlistment only in the mess branch. . . .

from Franklin D. Roosevelt's Executive Order 8802, 1941

. . . I do hereby reaffirm the policy of the United States that there shall be no discrimination in the employment of workers in defense industries or government because of race, creed, color, or national origin, and I do hereby declare that it is the duty of employers and of labor organizations, in furtherance of said policy and of this order, to provide for the full and equitable participation of all workers in defense industries, without discrimination because of race, creed, color, or national origin. . . .

white boys had been registered and taken to their tents. This seemed to be the established order of procedure at Camp Dix.... This separation of the colored from the whites was completely and rigidly maintained at this camp. . . . Discipline is maintained by imposing extra duty and fines on offenders. The fines are taken only from the $5 a month which the men receive directly.

On the whole, I was gratified rather than disappointed with the CCC. I had expected the worst. Of course it reflects, to some extent, all the practices and prejudices of the U. S. Army. But as a job and an experience, for a man who has no work, I can heartily recommend it.

Poster promoting the U.S. Civilian Conservation Corps

		1950–1965	1965–1975
RELIGION		**1954** Malcolm X Becomes minister of Harlem's Temple 7 **1963** Malcolm X founds the Muslim Mosque	
CULTURE		**1959** Miles Davis records "Kind of Blue" **1960** Louis Armstrong's jazz band tours Africa **1963** James Baldwin publishes *The Fire Next Time* **1965** Alex Haley publishes *The Autobiography of Malcolm X* LeRoi Jones founds the Black Arts Repertory Theater	**1966** San Francisco State University sets up nation's first black studies program **1968** Eldridge Cleaver publishes *Soul on Ice* **1969** Harvard University's African-American Studies program established Robert Chrisman and Nathan Hare start "The Black Scholar" **1970** Imamu Amiri Baraka organizes the Congress of African Peoples **1974** National Council for Black Studies formed
POLITICS & GOVERNMENT		**1954** Brown v.. Board of Education ends "separate but equal" **1955** Brown II decision calls for schools to desegregate with "all deliberate speed" **1957** Federal troops enforce school desegregation in Little Rock, AR **1963** Federal government forces Governor George Wallace to desegregate University of Alabama **1964** Equal Employment Opportunity Commission established	**1965** President Lyndon Johnson first uses the term "affirmative action" Voting Rights Act of 1965 enacted by Congress **1966** Edward Brooke of Massachusetts elected the first black U.S. senator since Reconstruction Black Panther party founded **1967** Thurgood Marshall becomes first black Supreme Court Justice **1968** Kerner Report released
SOCIETY & ECONOMY		**1955** Rosa Parks arrested for refusing to give up her seat on a bus in Montgomery, Ala. **1958** Southern Christian Leadership Conference organized **1960** Black students launch the sit-in movement SNCC founded **1961** Freedom Riders attacked in Alabama **1962** James Meredith admitted to the University of Mississippi **1963** Medgar Evers assassinated Martin Luther King, Jr. delivers "I Have a Dream" speech Baptist church bombed in Birmingham, Ala. **1964** Mississippi Freedom Summer Project Civil rights workers murdered in Mississippi Martin Luther King, Jr. awarded Nobel Peace Prize	**1965** Watts Riot Selma March **1967** Riots in Detroit, Newark, and other cities **1968** Poor People's Campaign Martin Luther King assassinated **1969** Chicago police kill Black Panther leaders Fred Hampton and Mark Clarke **1970** Jackson State killings **1971** Jesse Jackson founds PUSH **1973** National Black Feminist Organization founded

Barbara Jordan

Eldridge Cleaver

Nikki Giovanni

1975–1990	1990–2001	

1978 Lewis Farrakhan becomes leader of the Nation of Islam

1989 Barbara Harris first African-American woman elected bishop of the Episcopal Church

1990 Black Baptists constitute the fourth largest U.S. religious group with 8.7 million members

1991 George A. Stallings consecrated a Roman Catholic bishop

1993 Pope John Paul II aplogizes for the Catholic Church's support of slavery

2000 Vashti M. McKenzie first woman elected bishop of AME church

2001 Bishop Wilton D. Gregory elected President of the United States Conference of Catholic Bishops

1979 Sugar Hill Gang records "Rapper's Delight"

1980 Toni C. Bambara's *Salt Eaters* wins American Book Award

Molete Kete Asante publishes *Afrocentricity*

1982 Alice Walker's *The Color Purple* wins Pulitzer Prize

1984 Prince films "Purple Rain"

1986 "The Oprah Winfrey Show" becomes nationally syndicated

1987 Rita Dove wins Pulitzer Prize for poetry

1988 Temple University becomes first college to offer a Ph.D. in African-American studies

1989 N.W.A. records "Straight Outta Compton"

1990 August Wilson's *The Piano Lesson* wins Pulitzer Prize

1993 Rita Dove becomes Poet Laureate

Toni Morrison becomes the first African American to win Noble Prize for Literature

2007 Forest Whitaker wins the Best Actor Academy Award

1977 Randall Robinson founds TransAfrica

Patricia Harris becomes the first black woman to serve in the Cabinet

1983–1984 Jesse Jackson runs for president

1989 L. Douglas Wilder of Virginia becomes first African-American governor since Reconstruction

1991 Clarence Thomas nominated to the Supreme Court

1996 California approves Proposition 209

2001 Colin Powell becomes first African-American secretary of state

2004 Barack Obama elected to the United States Senate

2005 Condoleezza Rice becomes secretary of state under George W. Bush

1991 Los Angeles Riot after police officers who beat Rodney King are acquitted

1995 Million Man March

1997 Million Woman March

2000 Census records large gains in income and education by African Americans

2005 Hurricane Katrina ravages the city of New Orleans

The Water is Rising Pleas.

21

The Freedom Movement

WHY IS *BROWN V. BOARD OF EDUCATION* (1954)
ONE OF THE MOST IMPORTANT
U.S. SUPREME COURT DECISIONS
OF THE TWENTIETH CENTURY?

HOW DID WHITE SOUTHERNERS' STRATEGY
OF MASSIVE RESISTANCE AFFECT
THE MODERN CIVIL RIGHTS MOVEMENT?

WHAT ROLES DID BLACK WOMEN AND CHILDREN
PLAY IN THE CHALLENGES TO SEGREGATION
AND DISCRIMINATION IN THEIR COMMUNITIES?

WHO WERE THE LEADERS OF
THE MODERN CIVIL RIGHTS MOVEMENT?

HOW DID THE FEDERAL GOVERNMENT SUPPORT,
AND AT TIMES THWART, THE FREEDOM MOVEMENT?

◀ **This black student** at the University of Oklahoma was not allowed to sit in a classroom with white students. It took two Supreme Court decisions to end such segregation at the University of Oklahoma. Corbis-Bettmann

When the history books are written in the future, somebody will have to say, "There lived a race of people, black people, fleecy locks and black complexion, people who had the moral courage to stand up for their rights. And thereby they injected a new meaning into the veins of history and of civilization." And we're gonna do that. God grant that we will do it before it's too late.

—Martin Luther King Jr., December 5, 1955

▼ **Mary McLeod Bethune** pickets outside a drugstore in Washington, D.C.

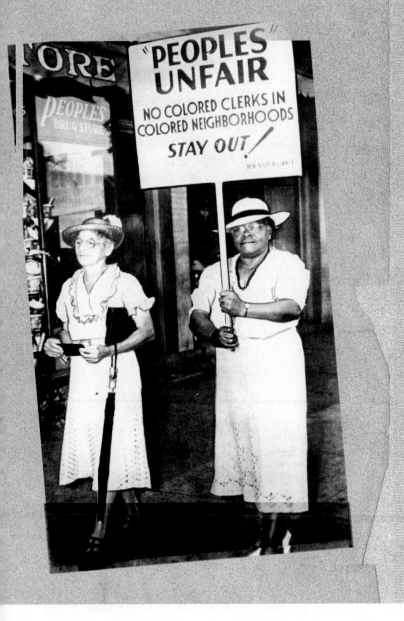

Between 1954 and 1965, the civil rights movement achieved a revolutionary transformation in the legal and social status of African Americans. Bold movements, beginning with the long struggle to overthrow the "separate but equal" doctrine in public schools that triumphed in the *Brown v. Board of Education* decision in 1954, through the Montgomery Bus Boycott of 1955–1956, and culminating in massive protests throughout the South in 1963, 1964, and 1965, changed the face of race relations in the United States. Despite fierce resistance, legally sanctioned segregation, racial discrimination, and disfranchisement fell before a mighty coalition of civil rights groups and their allies. Demonstrations and the pressures of the Cold War compelled high government officials to abandon their early caution. Although racism remained powerful in American life after 1965 and African Americans continued to suffer from economic disadvantages, the significant enlargement of freedom of opportunity and recognition of African-Americans' full citizenship rights transformed America and radiated across the globe.

The heart of the story of the modern civil rights movement is the remarkable courage and tenacity people in their own communities showed in their determination to attack segregation and exclusion from the political process. Behind the charismatic leaders and the powerful spectacles of the NAACP's U.S. Supreme Court victories and the marches and demonstrations captured so dramatically on television were the ordinary citizens who initiated protests, formulated strategies and tactics, and garnered other essential resources that made collective action work. The people's actions were made effective through their families, churches, voluntary associations, political organizations, women's clubs, labor unions, and college organizations and facilities. The sacrifices and experience gained in the previous one hundred years of struggle had, by the mid-1950s, accumulated sufficiently to permit an all-out attack on white supremacy. The civil rights movement would be long and bloody and it would not lead to the Promised Land, but it would profoundly change America.

ACTIVITY
The Civil Rights Movement

The 1950s: Prosperity and Prejudice

For most white Americans, the 1950s ushered in an era of unparalleled prosperity, heightened consumer consumption, and a patriarchal business culture. Affluent white Americans fled to the suburbs, and by 1960 52 percent of Americans owned their own homes. The decade is remembered nostalgically as a time of large stable nuclear families, wives and mothers who stayed at home, and communities untroubled by drugs and juvenile delinquency. It was a time of backyard barbecues and hula hoops, when nightly television shows like *Ozzie and Harriet* and *I Love Lucy* projected a vision of domestic tranquility.

For most black Americans, however, the 1950s were less blissful. American society remained rigidly segregated in housing and in education. Despite the gains African Americans made during the World War II era, Jim Crow still reigned. Although the *Smith v. Allwright* Supreme Court decision in 1944, which declared the "white primary" unconstitutional, helped reenfranchise black voters in Florida, Tennessee, and Texas, Jim Crow restrictions and the ever-present threat of white violence kept millions of African Americans from voting in the deep South. Likewise, although the 1948 *Shelley v. Kramer* U.S. Supreme Court decision, which outlawed the restricted residential covenants that had allowed homeowners to refuse to sell, rent, or lease their property to African Americans, was a significant victory, violence and extralegal practices still made housing integration a distant dream.

More important, most African Americans did not benefit from the economic boom of the 1950s that allowed so many white Americans to purchase homes in the suburbs. Moving into urban centers just as the number of factories and jobs there began to decline, they suffered a higher unemployment rate than any other segment of the population. White workers, fearing for their jobs, felt threatened by competition from unemployed black workers. As urban neighborhoods deteriorated, conditions ripened for a massive explosion.

The Road to *Brown*

In 1954, with the U.S. Supreme Court's decision in *Brown v. Board of Education of Topeka, Kansas,* progress in the desegregation of American society moved from the military into the civilian realm. Ultimately, the *Brown* decision would undermine state-sanctioned segregation in all aspects of American life. The NAACP's legal program of the 1920s and 1930s was largely responsible for this turn of events. In 1940 the NAACP set up the Legal Defense and Educational Fund (NAACP-LDEF) to pursue its assault on the legal foundations of race inequality in American education. Thereafter, the NAACP-LDEF fought segregation and discrimination in education, housing, employment, and politics. In the first years of its existence, attorneys for the fund won stunning victories, including a 1944 U.S. Supreme Court decision, *Smith v. Allwright*, declaring white primaries unconstitutional, and the *Shelley v. Kramer* (1948) decision outlawing restrictive residential covenants. The life and career of one of the NAACP-LDEF lawyers, Constance Baker Motley, symbolizes the struggle that black professionals, both men and women, waged to overcome racial and gender exclusion as well as the coalescence of disparate forces that carried the seeds of the coming revolution. Motley is our guide on the road to *Brown*.

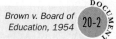
Brown v. Board of Education, 1954   20-2   DOCUMENT

CONSTANCE BAKER MOTLEY AND BLACK LAWYERS IN THE SOUTH

Constance Baker Motley was born in 1921 to immigrant parents, Rachel Huggins and Willoughby Alva Baker, from Nevis, in the British West Indies. She grew up in a tightly knit West Indian community in New Haven, Connecticut. The members of New Haven's black community, including Baker's parents, worked as domestics or in service jobs for Yale University. Baker attended integrated schools and experienced episodic racism, including being refused admission to a local beach and to a roller-skating rink. During her high school years, Baker developed a strong racial consciousness. She recalled, "[M]y interest in civil rights [was] a very early interest which developed when I was in high school. The fact that I was a Black, a woman, and a member of a large, relatively poor family was also the base of this great ambition [to enter the legal profession].

The most important event in her early life was the lecture that George Crawford, a 1903 Yale Law School graduate who worked as an NAACP lawyer in New Haven, gave at the local Dixwell Community Center. The talk concerned the Supreme Court decision in *State of Missouri ex rel. Gaines v. Canada.* Crawford explained that the University of Missouri's law school had denied Gaines admission but had offered to pay his tuition expenses to an out-of-state school. The NAACP Legal Committee under Charles H. Houston's leadership won a victory before the U.S. Supreme Court

Constance Baker Motley endured many hardships and even assaults as she tried school desegregation cases in the South. Here she leaves the federal court in Birmingham after an unsuccessful attempt to force the University of Alabama to accept a black student.

when it ruled that the state had violated the clause in the Fourteenth Amendment mandating that state laws provide equal protection regardless of race. After *Gaines*, states were required to furnish within their borders facilities for legal education for black people equal to those offered for white citizens.

Baker desperately wanted to go to law school, but her family could not even afford to send her to college. For a year and a half after graduation from high school in 1939, Baker earned $50 a month varnishing chairs for a building restoration project under the auspices of the National Youth Administration. In

THE ROAD TO *BROWN*

1938	*Missouri ex rel. Gaines v. Canada*
1948	*Sipuel v. Oklahoma State Board of Regents*
1950	*McLaurin v. Oklahoma*
	Sweatt v. Painter
1954	*Brown v. Board of Education of Topeka*

1938—1954

1940, however, Baker came to the attention of Clarence Blakeslee, a local white businessman and philanthropist who, after hearing her speak at a meeting of black and white community residents, offered to finance her education. She attended Fisk University until 1942 and then transferred to New York University, where she earned a bachelor's degree in economics in 1943. She then became the second black woman ever to attend Columbia University Law School. In 1946, shortly after she finished her legal training, she married former New York University law student Joel Motley and went to work with the NAACP's LDEF.

Constance Baker Motley first met Thurgood Marshall in October 1945 when he hired her as a law clerk during her second year in law school. Marshall assigned her to work on the hundreds of army court-martial cases filed after World War II. Motley recalled, "From the first day I knew that this was where I wanted to be. I never bothered interviewing anywhere else." She added, "But for this fortuitous event, I do not think that I would have gotten very far as a lawyer. Women were simply not hired in those days."

In the late 1940s, the NAACP-LDEF's attack on inequality in graduate education provided the basis for a full-scale assault on segregation. No longer would the organization be satisfied only to push for fulfillment of the promise of "separate but equal" facilities. In 1948 Ada Lois Sipuel was denied admission to the University of Oklahoma Law School because she was black. The U.S. Supreme Court, signaling it was willing to take a more activist stance, quickly heard the case and ordered Oklahoma, in *Sipuel v. Board of Regents of the University of Oklahoma*, to "provide [a legal education] for [Sipuel] in conformity with the equal protection clause of the Fourteenth Amendment and provide it as soon as it does for applicants of any other group." Another case, *Sweatt v. Painter*, which the Supreme Court decided in 1950, began when the University of Texas at Austin attempted to circumvent court orders to admit Heman Sweatt into its law school by creating a separate facility consisting of three basement rooms, a small library, and a few instructors who would lecture to him alone. The court ruled that the University of Texas had deprived Sweatt of intangibles such as "the essential ingredient of a legal education . . . the opportunity for students to discuss the law with their peers and others with whom they would be associated professionally in later life." On the same day the justices ruled in *Sweatt*, they also declared illegal the University of Oklahoma's segregation of George W. McLaurin from white students attending the Graduate School of Education. The University of Oklahoma had admitted McLaurin but made him sit in the hallway at the classroom door, study in a private part of the balcony of the library, and eat in a sequestered part of the lunchroom. When he finally gained a seat in the classroom, it was marked "reserved for colored." In these precedent-setting cases, the U.S. Supreme Court signaled a readiness to reconsider the "separate but equal" doctrine and to redefine the meaning of the "equal protection of the laws" clause. These cases were important stepping-stones on the road to *Brown.*

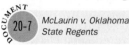

DOCUMENT
20-7 *McLaurin v. Oklahoma State Regents*

A year after the *Sweatt* and *McLaurin* decisions, black parents and their lawyers filed suits in Kansas, South Carolina, Virginia, Delaware, and the District of Columbia asking the courts to apply the qualitative test of the *Sweatt* case to elementary and secondary schools and to declare the "separate but equal" doctrine invalid in public education.

BROWN AND THE COMING REVOLUTION

Black lawyers in the South handling civil rights cases were frequently assaulted. On February 27, 1942, for example, NAACP attorney Leon A. Ransom was attacked by a former deputy sheriff in the hall of the Davidson County Courthouse in Nashville, Tennessee. The *Crisis* reported,

> The attack came when Ransom walked out into the hall from the courtroom where he was sitting with Z. Alexander Looby, local NAACP attorney, on a case involving the exclusion of Negroes from a jury. . . . When the scuffle began, Negroes who would have aided Ransom were held back by a former constable (white) named Hill, who drew his gun and shouted: "We are going to teach these northern Negroes not to come down here raising fancy court questions."

At Ransom's death in 1954, Thurgood Marshall eulogized,

> Negro Americans, whether they know it or not, owe a great debt of gratitude to Andy Ransom and men like him who battled in the courts down a span of years to bring us to the place we now occupy in the enjoyment of our constitutional rights as citizens, in helping to build up the NAACP legal program step by step, in the skill which he gave to individual cases and to the planning of strategy, Dr. Ransom left a legacy to the whole population.

It was no less difficult for a black woman lawyer to venture into the South in search of justice. Black attorney Derrick Bell, who also worked for the LDEF, said of Motley's work,

> Nothing in the Southern lawyers' background could have prepared them for Connie. To them Negro women were either mammies, maids, or mistresses. None of them had ever dealt with a Negro woman on a peer basis, much less on a level of intellectual equality, which in this case quickly became superiority.

Motley was keenly aware of her precarious situation. "Often a southern judge would refer to men attorneys as Mister, but would make a point of calling me 'Connie,' since traditionally Black women in the South were only called by their first name." Housing was another problem. Motley recalled that when in a southern town for a long trial, "I knew that it was going to be impossible to stay in a decent hotel." These lawyers had to depend on the good graces and courage of local people. Motley explained, "Usually in these situations a Black family would agree to put you up. But there was so much publicity involved with civil rights cases that no Black family dared have us—they were too afraid." While in Mississippi arguing a teachers' equalization of salaries case, Motley declared, "A Black doctor invited us to dinner, but that was about it." She privately mused, "I wonder how many lawyers have had the experience of preparing for trial in a flophouse. That was the only room I could get."

In the late 1940s, the black parents of children attending Scott's Branch School in Clarendon County, South Carolina, approached Roderick W. Elliott, the chairman of the school board, with a modest request. There were 6,531 black students and only 2,375 white students enrolled in the county's schools. Although the county had thirty buses to convey the white students to their schools, not one bus was available to black schoolchildren. Some of the black students had to walk eighteen miles round trip each day. Once they arrived they entered buildings heated by wood stoves and lit by kerosene lamps. For a drink of water or to go to the toilet they had to go outdoors.

With the encouragement of AME pastor and schoolteacher Reverend Joseph Armstrong DeLaine, the parents mustered the courage and resolve to petition the school board for buses. Elliott's reply was short: "We ain't got no money to buy a bus for your nigger children." In 1949 DeLaine went to the NAACP officials in Columbia, and Thurgood Marshall was there. On December 20, 1950, Harry Briggs, a navy veteran, and twenty-four other Clarendon County residents

The glaring inequalities between black and white schools underscored the need for social change in American race relations. Black parents and community leaders denounced the broken-down school buildings, outdated secondhand schoolbooks, scarce resources, and inadequate supplies. Public school inequalities mirrored the second-class status of African Americans in American society.

sued the Summerton School District (Clarendon District 22). The case, *Briggs v. Elliott*, was the first legal challenge to elementary school segregation to originate in the South. Meanwhile, however, four other cases in different parts of the country were inexorably advancing through the federal courts. These would be combined into one case that would decide the fate of the *Plessy* doctrine of "separate but equal."

The years of preparation and hardship paid off. Motley worked with a dream team of black lawyers and academics, an inner circle of advisers that included Louis Redding from Wilmington, Delaware; James Nabrit from Washington, D.C.; Robert Ming from Chicago; psychologist Kenneth Clark from New York; and historian John Hope Franklin to prepare the case *Brown v. Board of Education of Topeka* and argue it before the U.S. Supreme Court. Motley, Robert Carter, Jack Greenberg, and Marshall also sought assistance from Spottswood Robinson and Oliver Hill of Richmond, Virginia, and read papers prepared by historians C. Vann Woodward and Alfred Kelly about the original equalitarian intentions of the post–Civil War amendments and other legislation. In his argument, Marshall

appealed to the U.S. Supreme Court to meet the *Plessy* doctrine head on and declare it erroneous.

> It [*Plessy*] stands mirrored today as a legal aberration, the faulty conception of an era dominated by provincialism, by intense emotionalism in race relations . . . and by the preaching of a doctrine of racial superiority that contradicted the basic concept upon which our society was founded. Twentieth century America, fighting racism at home and abroad, has rejected the race views of *Plessy v. Ferguson* because we have come to the realization that such views obviously tend to preserve not the strength but the weakness of our heritage.

By the time Marshall made this argument, black intellectuals, scholars, and activists and their progressive white allies had closed ranks in support of integration. To suggest alternatives as the goal for African Americans was to find oneself swimming against the current.

During late 1953 and early 1954, Chief Justice Earl Warren brought the court in support of Marshall's position. On May 17, 1954, the court ruled unanimously in favor of the NAACP lawyers and their clients that a classification based solely on race violated the Fourteenth Amendment to the U.S. Constitution. In a stirring passage Warren declared,

> We come then to the question presented: Does segregation of children in public schools solely on the basis of race, even though the physical facilities and other 'tangible' factors may be equal, deprive the children of the minority group of equal educational opportunities? We believe that it does. . . . To separate them from others of similar age and qualifications solely because of their race generates a feeling of inferiority as to the status in the community that may affect their hearts and minds in a way unlikely ever to be undone. . . . We conclude that in the field of public education the doctrine of "separate but equal" has no place. Separate educational facilities are inherently unequal.

The *Brown* decision would eventually lead to the dismantling of the entire structure of Jim Crow laws that regulated important aspects of black life in America: movement, work, marriage, education, housing, even death and burial. The *Brown* decision, more than any other case, signaled the emerging primacy of equality as a guide to constitutional decisions. This and subsequent decisions helped advance the rights of other minorities and women. As Motley reflected, "In the *Brown* case and in the decisions that followed, we blazed a trail for others by showing the competence of Black lawyers."

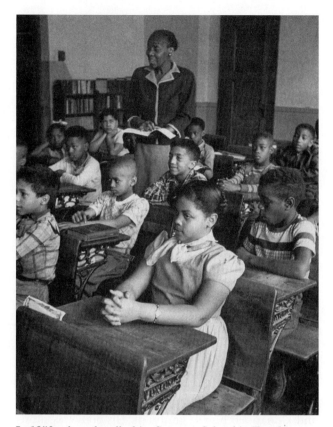

In 1950, when the all-white Summer School in Topeka, Kansas, refused to admit Linda Brown (1943–), her father, Oliver Brown, filed a lawsuit and testified in court that his daughter had to travel an hour and twenty minutes to attend a black school. The Summer School was only seven blocks away but practiced racial exclusion. Linda became the "named plaintiff" in the landmark U.S. Supreme Court case, *Brown v. Board of Education* (1954) that declared unconstitutional laws mandating public school segregation.

Brown II

A year after the 1954 *Brown* decision, in May 1955, the Supreme Court issued a second ruling, commonly known as *Brown II*, which addressed the practical process of desegregation. The Court underscored that the states in the suits should begin prompt compliance with the 1954 ruling, and that this should be done with "all deliberate speed." Many black Americans interpreted this to mean "immediately." White southerners hoped it meant a long time, or never. Ominously, President Eisenhower seemed displeased with the Court's rulings and refused to put the moral authority of his office behind their enforcement.

Nevertheless, in 1955 and early 1956, desegregation proceeded without hindrance in Maryland, Kentucky, Delaware, Oklahoma, and Missouri. Alabama governor Jim Folsom declared that his state would obey the courts and, initially, many other moderate white southern politicians counseled calm and worked to head off a full-scale conflict between their region and the federal government.

MASSIVE WHITE RESISTANCE

White moderates, however, soon found themselves a shrinking minority, as extremists, determined to maintain white supremacy at any cost, prepared for mass resistance to the Court's decisions. The rhetoric of these extremists bordered on hysteria but found a receptive audience among many white people. A young minister from Virginia named Jerry Falwell, for example, explained that black people were the descendants of Noah's son Ham and were destined to be servants because of a curse God had put on him. Falwell also claimed the Supreme Court's decisions were inspired by Moscow. In 1955 leading businessmen, white-collar professionals, and clergy began organizing White Citizens' Councils in virtually every southern city; these were groups dedicated to preserving the southern way of life and the South's "sacred heritage of freedom." The councils used their economic and political power to intimidate black people who challenged segregation. They fired people from their jobs, evicted them from their homes, and refused them credit.

Many white politicians took up the banner of massive resistance. Senator James O. Eastland, from Mississippi, called the *Brown* decision a "monstrous crime." The Virginia legislature closed all public schools in Prince Edward County to thwart integration. Most dramatically, on March 12, 1956, ninety-six southern congressmen led by North Carolina's senator Sam Ervin Jr. and South Carolina's senator Strom Thurmond issued "The Southern Manifesto," vowing to fight to preserve segregation and the southern way of life. The manifesto called the *Brown* decisions an "unwarranted exercise of power by the court, contrary to the Constitution." The only southern senators who refused to sign the "Manifesto" were Albert Gore Sr. of Tennessee and Lyndon B. Johnson of Texas.

The NAACP came under siege after the *Brown* decision as southern states tried to wipe it out of existence. By 1957 nine southern states had filed suit to eradicate the organization. Some states, alleging the NAACP was linked to a worldwide communist conspiracy, made membership illegal. Membership plummeted from

LETTER OF THE MONTGOMERY WOMEN'S POLITICAL COUNCIL TO MAYOR W. A. GAYLE

In this letter threatening a boycott of Montgomery's buses, the Women's Political Council politely asks not for the desegregation of the buses, but only for new regulations that would prevent black riders from being forced to move to accommodate white riders. May 21, 1954

HONORABLE MAYOR W. A. GAYLE
CITY HALL
MONTGOMERY, ALABAMA

Dear Sir:

The Women's Political Council is very grateful to you and the City Commissioners for the hearing you allowed our representative during the month of March, 1954, when the "city-bus-fare-increase case" was being reviewed. There were several things the Council asked for:

1. A city law that would make it possible for Negroes to sit from back toward front, and whites from front toward back until all the seats were taken.

2. That Negroes would not be asked or forced to pay fare at front and go to the rear of the bus to enter.

3. That buses stop at every corner in residential sections occupied by Negroes as they do in communities where whites reside.

We are happy to report that buses have begun stopping at more corners now in some sections where Negroes live than previously. However, the same practices in seating and boarding the bus continue.

Mayor Gayle, three-fourths of the riders of these public conveyances are Negroes. If Negroes did not patronize them, they could not possibly operate.

More and more of our people are already arranging with neighbors and friends to ride to keep from being insulted and humiliated by bus drivers.

There has been talk from twenty-five or more local organizations of planning a city-wide boycott of buses. We, sir, do not feel that forceful measures are necessary in bargaining for a convenience which is right for all bus passengers. We, the Council, believe that when this matter has been put before you and the Commissioners, that agreeable terms can be met in a quiet and in a sensible manner to the satisfaction of all concerned.

128,716 to 79,677, and the association lost 246 branches in the South.

Under these pressures, desegregation ground to a halt. By 1958 thirteen school systems had been desegregated. By 1960, two years later, the total had risen to only seventeen. Massive resistance successfully challenged the possibility of achieving change through court action alone.

THE LYNCHING OF EMMETT TILL

The violent reaction of white southerners to the growing assertiveness of black people found expression in the summer of 1955 in the lynching of fourteen-year-old Emmett Till of Chicago, an event that helped galvanize the emerging civil rights movement. Till was visiting relatives in the small town of Money, Mississippi. On a dare from his friends, he entered Bryant's grocery store, bought candy, and said "Bye, baby" to Carolyn Bryant, the wife of the owner, as he left. Till was unaware how far white people in the town would go to avenge this small breach of white supremacy's racial etiquette. In the middle of the night a few days after the incident, Bryant's husband and brother-in-law arrived at the small home where Till was staying and kidnapped him at gunpoint. His body was subse-

Many of our Southern cities in neighboring states have practiced the policies we seek without incident whatsoever. Atlanta, Macon and Savannah in Georgia have done this for years. Even Mobile, in our own state, does this and all the passengers are satisfied.

Please consider this plea, and if possible, act favorably upon it, for even now plans are being made to ride less, or not at all, on our buses. We do not want this.

Respectfully yours,

The Women's Political Council

Jo Ann Robinson, President

🌿 *What did the Women's Political Council initially hope to accomplish?*

🌿 *What does this letter suggest about the importance of black women's political organizations in the early years of the civil rights movement?*

Source: Stewart Burns, *Daybreak of Freedom: The Montgomery Bus Boycott* (Chapel Hill: University of North Carolina Press, 1997), p. 58.

quently found in the Tallahatchie River tied to a heavy cotton gin fan. Till had a bullet in his head and had been tortured before his murder. Despite overwhelming evidence and the brave testimony of Mose Wright, Till's uncle, and other local black people, an all-white jury acquitted the two men who lynched Till. In early 1956 the murderers sold their confession to *Look* magazine and gloated over their escape from justice. In 2004, new evidence surfaced indicating that ten people may have been involved in the Till lynching.

The Till lynching shaped the consciousness of an entire generation of young African-American activists. Partly this was due to the efforts of Till's mother, Mamie Bradley. Unwilling to let America turn away from this crime, Till's mother had her son's mangled body displayed in an open casket in Chicago. Thousands of mourners paid their respects, and many committed themselves to fighting the system that made this crime possible. Bradley also traveled around the nation speaking to groups on whom her grief had a profound impact. Myrlie Evers, who would later have a role in the movement, remembered how she felt. "I bled for Emmett Till's mother. I know when she came to Mississippi and appeared at the mass meetings how everyone poured out their hearts to her, went into their pockets when people had only two or three pennies, and gave."

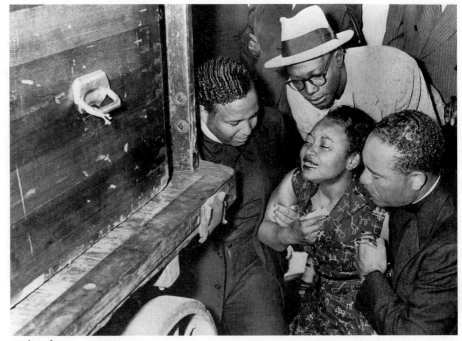

In August 1955, fourteen-year-old Emmet Till was visiting relatives in Money, Mississippi, when he transgressed the line of racial etiquette by speaking to a white woman in a country store. He paid the ultimate price. The lynching of Emmet Till and the subsequent acquittal of his murderers reflected the low regard in which black life was held in the Jim Crow South and the extent to which whites were determined to maintain the racial status quo.

New Forms of Protest: The Montgomery Bus Boycott

Strong local communities formed the core of the civil rights movement, and they were often sparked to action by the deeds of brave and committed individuals. The first and one of the most important expressions of this process occurred in Alabama's small capital city of Montgomery. Blessed with well-organized educational, religious, and other institutions, this city's African-American community of 45,000 was poised to make history.

THE ROOTS OF REVOLUTION

The movement in Montgomery did not emerge out of the blue, although it must have seemed that way to many white residents in the city; it was the result of years of organization and planning by protest groups. In addition to its numerous churches, two black colleges, and other social organizations, the Alabama cap-

ital had a strong core of protest groups. One, the Women's Political Council (WPC), had been founded in 1946 by Mary Frances Fair Burks, chair of Alabama State College English Department, after the all-white League of Women Voters had refused to allow black women to participate in its activities. Although the WPC had only forty members, all middle-class women, its courageous and competent leaders were willing to stand up to powerful white people. The WPC was joined by a chapter of the NAACP led by E. D. Nixon, a Pullman train porter and head of the Alabama chapter of the Brotherhood of Sleeping Car Porters. In 1943 Nixon had founded the Montgomery Voters League, an organization dedicated to helping African Americans navigate Alabama's tortuous voter registration process. In the decade after 1945 these groups searched for a way to mobilize the black community to challenge white power.

The 1954 *Brown* decision seemed to provide a means to destroy segregation and discrimination in the city. Four days after it was announced, Jo Ann Robinson, a professor at Alabama State College, wrote a letter to Montgomery's mayor on behalf of the WPC.

In it she reiterated the complaints of the black community concerning conditions on the city's buses and ended, "Please consider this plea, for even now plans are being made to ride less, or not at all, on our buses." The mayor ignored the warning and the buses remained as segregated as before. All seemed quiet on the surface, but Montgomery's black lawyers and NAACP chapter began laying the groundwork for a test case challenging segregation of the city's bus lines.

On March 2, 1955, a fifteen-year-old girl, Claudette Colvin, was arrested for refusing to give up her seat on a bus to a white person. The WPC was ready to use this incident to initiate the threatened bus boycott, but Nixon dissuaded them. He felt that Colvin, who was unmarried and pregnant, would not be an appropriate symbol around which to organize. He and other activists resolved to wait for another chance.

ROSA PARKS

On Thursday, December 1, 1955, Rosa Parks, a forty-three-year-old department store seamstress and civil rights activist, boarded a city bus and moved to the back where African Americans were required to sit. All seats were taken so she sat in one toward the middle of the bus. When a white man boarded the bus, the driver ordered Parks to vacate her seat for him. There was nothing unusual in this, but on this fateful day, Rosa Parks refused to move. She had not planned to resist on that day, but, as she later said, she had "decided that I would have to know once and for all what rights I had as a human being and a citizen. . . . I was so involved with the attempt to bring about freedom from this kind of thing . . . I felt just resigned to give what I could to protest against the way I was being treated, and felt that all of our meetings, trying to negotiate, bring about petitions before the authorities . . . really hadn't done any good at all." At the time Parks was portrayed as someone who was simply tired, but she had been training for just this kind of challenge for years. When her moment came, she seized it, and with this act of resistance she launched the **Montgomery Bus Boycott** and inspired the modern civil rights struggle for freedom and equality.

The plans of the WPC and NAACP came into play after Parks's arrest for violating Montgomery's transportation laws. She was ordered to appear in court on the following Monday. Meanwhile, E. D. Nixon bailed her out of the city jail and began mobilizing the leadership of the black community behind her. Working in tandem with Nixon, Robinson wrote and circulated a flyer calling for a one-day boycott of the buses followed by a mass meeting of the community to discuss the matter. Robinson took the flyer to the Alabama State College campus, stayed up all night, and, with the help of a colleague, mimeographed thirty thousand copies of it. The WPC had planned distribution routes months earlier, and the next day, Robinson and nearly two hundred volunteers distributed bundles of flyers to beauty parlors and schools, to factories and grocery stores, and to taverns and barbershops throughout the black neighborhoods.

MONTGOMERY IMPROVEMENT ASSOCIATION

On December 5, 1955, the black community did not ride the buses, and the movement had begun. Nixon and other community leaders decided to form a new organization, the Montgomery Improvement Association (MIA), to coordinate the protest; they also selected a twenty-six-year-old minister, Martin Luther King Jr., to act as its president. That evening there was an overflowing mass meeting of the black community at the large Holt Street Baptist Church to decide whether to continue the boycott. King, with barely an hour to prepare, spoke to the crowd and delivered a message that would define the goals of the boycott and the civil rights movement that followed. In his dramatic voice he connected the core values of America and of the Judeo-Christian tradition to the goals of African Americans nationwide as well as in Montgomery.

Mass Meeting Speech **37** *LIVING WORDS*

"We are here this evening," he began,

> for serious business. We are here in a general sense because first and foremost we are American citizens, and we are determined to apply our citizenship to the fullness of its means. . . . You know, my friends, there comes a time when people get tired of being trampled over by the iron feet of oppression. There comes a time, my friends, when people get tired of being flung across the abyss of humiliation, when they experience the bleakness of nagging despair. . . . We are not wrong in what we are doing. If we are wrong, the Supreme Court of this nation is wrong. If we are wrong, the Constitution of the United States is wrong. If we are wrong, God Almighty is wrong. If we are wrong, Jesus of Nazareth was merely a utopian dreamer that never came down to earth. If we are wrong, justice is a lie. Love has no meaning. And we are determined here in Montgomery to work and fight until justice runs down like water, and righteousness like a mighty stream.

MARTIN LUTHER KING JR.

King's speech electrified the meeting, which unanimously decided to stay off the city's buses until the MIA's demands were met. The speech also marked the

PROFILE ❧ ROSA LOUISE MCCAULEY PARKS
(1913–2005)

Rosa McCauley Parks was born on February 4, 1913 to James and Leona (Edwards) McCauley, a carpenter and school teacher, of Tuskegee, Alabama. Her father migrated north when his daughter was two years old. When she was eleven, Rosa attended the Montgomery Industrial School for Girls while living with a widowed aunt. In 1932 Rosa married Raymond Parks, a socially aware young man who worked in the Atlas Barber Shop in Montgomery. They were both active in the efforts to secure the release of the Scottsboro Boys, nine black youths accused of raping two white girls. Rosa Parks enjoyed a full and busy life, working as a self-employed seamstress and serving as the secretary of the Montgomery branch of the NAACP (1943–1956), and as a member of the African Methodist Episcopal Church. In the 1950s she worked as a seamstress at Montgomery Fair, a department store in downtown Montgomery.

On December 1, 1955, Rosa Parks had had enough. When she refused to give up her seat on that fateful day in Montgomery, little could she have anticipated that she would become a living symbol of the African-American quest for freedom, justice, and equality of opportunity. With great dignity and little fanfare, Parks chose to be arrested rather than to comply with the white bus driver's order to move to the back-of-the-bus section reserved for black people. Parks's behavior was thoughtful. Her defiance on this occasion was part of a larger pattern of personal and public resistance. In the 1940s Parks had participated in voter registration campaigns. In 1954, she attended the Highlander Folk School, a training center for social change in Monteagle, Tennessee.

As soon as word of Parks's arrest reverberated through the Montgomery community, JoAnn Robinson and members of the Women's Political Council (WPC) swung into action. On December 2, 1955, Robinson wrote and circulated, with assistance from students and club women, thirty thousand copies of a flyer, declaring that "Another Negro woman has been arrested and thrown in jail because she refused to get up out of her seat on the bus for a white person to sit down. It is the second time since the Claudette Colvin (a pregnant fifteen-year old who had also been arrested for violating the segregation ordinance) case that a Negro woman has been arrested for the same thing. This has to be stopped. Negroes have rights too, for if Negroes did not ride the buses, they could not operate. . . . " Robinson and the WPC asked the community to stay off the buses for a day to show their opposition to bus segregation and their solidarity with Rosa Parks.

The success of the one-day boycott aroused the community and motivated thousands to attend the first mass meeting at the Holt Street Baptist Church and to found, under the leadership of Reverend Martin Luther King Jr., the Montgomery Improvement Association. A year later, December 20, 1956, the U.S. Supreme Court ruled Alabama's state and local segregation laws unconstitutional. In retaliation, the department store fired Parks from her seamstress job. The response was, perhaps, irrelevant.

Parks's resistance ignited the civil rights movement of the 1950s and 1960s. In 1957, Parks, her husband, and her mother moved to Detroit, Michigan, where her brother resided. For a quarter of a century, Rosa Parks worked as a special assistant to Michigan U.S. Congressman John Conyers. In 1979 the NAACP awarded Parks its Spingarn Medal. Detroit has named a street, Rosa Parks Boulevard, in her honor. In keeping with a lifetime commitment to social justice and the pursuit of freedom, at the celebration of her seventy-seventh birthday in 1990 at the Kennedy Center in Washington, D.C., Parks implored the three thousand revelers to "Pray and work for the freedom of Nelson Mandela and all of our sisters and brothers in South Africa."

Until her death on October 24, 2005, at the age of ninety-two, Rosa Parks lived a quiet life in Detroit. Mrs. Parks's casket lay in state in the rotunda of the U.S. Capitol, an honor usually reserved for presidents, for two days as the nation paid its last respects to this extraordinary woman.

Rosa Parks, in this 1999 photograph by Paul Richards, is venerated as ▶ the Mother of the Civil Rights Movement and has remained an important symbol of hope and courage ever since her historic act of resistance on December 1, 1955, in Montgomery, Alabama.

Parks

beginning of King's role as a leader of the civil rights movement. King had been raised in a prominent ministerial family with a long history of standing up for African-American rights. King's grandfather had led a protest to force Atlanta to build its first high school for African Americans. King's father spoke out for African-American rights as pastor of Ebenezer Baptist Church. At age fifteen, King had entered Morehouse College but did not embrace the ministry as his profession until he came under the influence of its president, Dr. Benjamin E. Mays. By age twenty-five, King had been awarded a Ph.D. in theology from Boston University. He moved to Alabama with his wife, Coretta Scott King, to become pastor of Dexter Avenue Baptist Church in Montgomery.

In addition to his verbal artistry, King had the ability to inspire moral courage and to teach people how to maintain themselves under excruciating pressure. King merged Gandhian nonviolence with black Christian faith and church culture to create a unique ideology well suited for the civil rights struggle. King declared that the boycott would continue with or without its leaders because the conflict was not "between the white and the Negro" but "between justice and injustice." He explained to the boycotting community, "If we are arrested every day, if we are exploited every day, if we are trampled over every day, don't ever let anyone pull you so low as to hate them. . . . We must realize so many people are taught to hate us that they are not totally responsible for their hate." King's faith was severely tested. As the boycott proceeded, his home was bombed. Segregationists also bombed Nixon's home and those of two other black clergymen and MIA leaders, Ralph Abernathy and Fred Shuttlesworth, and inflicted violence on many other boycott participants.

WALKING FOR FREEDOM

Although men occupied the top leadership positions in the boycott, women were the key to its effectiveness. The boycott lasted more than a year—381 days—and over its course nearly all the black women previously dependent on the buses to get to work refused to ride them. Some walked twelve miles a day. Others had the support of their white women employers, who provided transportation. And many helped organize an efficient car pool of two hundred vehicles that proved critical to sustaining the boycott. The community at large participated in mass meetings held nightly in local churches. Robinson edited the MIA newsletter. Other women supported the boycott in dozens of ways. Some organized bake sales, and others made door-to-door solicitations to raise the $2,000 per week needed to keep the car pools going.

The boycott took 65 percent of the bus company's business, forcing it to cut schedules, lay off drivers, and raise fares. White merchants also suffered. The bus company, however, could scarcely afford to break the laws of the city that chartered it, and despite the company's losses, the city government refused to capitulate. Officials would not even accede to such a modest demand as a "first come, first served" seating arrangement—like that proposed by the Montgomery Women's Political Council before the boycott began—in which black riders would sit from back to front and white riders from front to back.

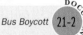
Bus Boycott 21-2 DOCUMENT

Impressive as it was, the boycott by itself could not end segregation on the buses. Black Montgomery needed a two-pronged strategy of mass local pressure and legal recourse through the courts. The legal backing of the federal government was necessary to end Jim Crow. Thus NAACP lawyers and MIA's lawyer Fred Gray filed a suit in the names of Claudette Colvin, Mary Louise Smith, and three other women.

FRIENDS IN THE NORTH

The Montgomery movement was not without allies outside the South. Money poured into the MIA's coffers from concerned Americans. Many northern activists who had long been hoping black southerners would begin just this kind of resistance also swung into action to help. Two people were particularly important at this juncture: Bayard Rustin and liberal Jewish lawyer Stanley Levison. Two and a half months into the boycott, Montgomery officials indicted King and one hundred other leaders on charges of conspiracy to disrupt the bus system. At this time Bayard Rustin arrived in Montgomery and immediately encouraged the leaders to follow Gandhian practice and submit freely to arrest. In a diary entry, Rustin wrote,

> Many of them did not wait for the police to come but walked to the police station and surrendered. Nixon was the first. He walked into the station and said, "You are looking for me? Here I am." This procedure had a startling effect on both the Negro and the white communities. White community leaders, politicians, and police were dumbfounded. Negroes were thrilled to see their leaders surrender without being hunted down. Soon hundreds of Negroes gathered outside the police station and applauded the leaders as they entered, one by one.

Rustin continued working behind the scenes as one of King's most trusted advisers on nonviolent principles and tactics. Stanley Levison and Ella Baker created a group called In Friendship, which raised money for the boycott.

Levison was a wealthy attorney committed to social justice. He had worked with the Communist Party, and Rustin had a long history of association with radical groups. Their influence soon attracted the attention of the Federal Bureau of Investigation, which had long been obsessed with black leaders and organizations. King was not a communist, but FBI director J. Edgar Hoover developed an intense hatred of him and other black leaders. At one point Hoover called King "the most dangerous man in America," and he pressed his subordinates to prove King was a communist and that the civil rights movement was a Moscow-inspired conspiracy. Hoover and his men began tapping King's telephone and hotel rooms and even threatened to expose his extramarital affairs if he did not commit suicide. By the early 1960s, the FBI had stopped warning King when it uncovered threats to his life.

VICTORY

As the bus boycott reached the one-year mark, it was obvious that the all-white city government would not budge, no matter how long the boycott lasted. Any white politician who hoped to remain in office had to defend segregation. King and all the others who suffered through the ordeal grew discouraged and their hopes seemed to fade in November 1956 when it became clear the state courts would soon move to declare the car pools illegal.

Salvation for the movement came from the cases local women and the NAACP had taken to the federal courts. In keeping with the *Brown* precedent, on November 13, 1956, the Supreme Court ordered an end to Montgomery's bus segregation. The *Gayle v. Browder* decision, unlike the *Brown* decision, expressly overturned the 1896 *Plessy v. Ferguson* decision, because like *Plessy* it applied to transportation. Ironically, the ruling was handed down on the same day that the city of Montgomery finally secured a state court injunction to end the MIA car pool. The bus company agreed not only to end segregation but also to hire African-American drivers and to treat all passengers with equal respect.

The city's black community rejoiced. On the morning of December 21, 1956, black citizens of Montgomery boarded the buses and sat wherever they pleased.

No Easy Road to Freedom: 1957–1960

The victory at Montgomery set an example for future protests. It was the result of a highly organized black community led by committed and capable black leaders. These local efforts were bolstered by the advice and involvement of activists outside the South, the attention of a sympathetic national press, and, crucially, intervention from the federal courts. But local victories could only go so far, particularly as white resistance intensified. In the three years following the boycott, black southerners and their allies across the nation prepared for a broader movement. At the same time, federal officials outside the judiciary found they could not ignore the white South's incipient rebellion without grave consequences for the nation and their own power.

MARTIN LUTHER KING AND THE SCLC

By the end of the campaign in Montgomery, Martin Luther King Jr. had emerged as a moral leader of national stature. On the advice of Levison, Rustin, and Ella Baker, he helped create a new organization, the **Southern Christian Leadership Council (SCLC)**, to provide an institutional base for continuing the struggle. The SCLC was a federation of civil rights groups, community organizations, and churches that sought to coordinate all the burgeoning local movements. King assumed leadership of the SCLC, crisscrossing the nation in the ensuing years to build support for the organization and to raise money to fund its activities. Members of the organization also began training black activists, particularly on college campuses, in the tactics of nonviolent protest. Because the ballot was deemed the critical weapon needed to complete school desegregation and secure equal employment opportunity, adequate housing, and equal access to public accommodations, the SCLC focused on securing voting rights for black people. In the three years after the Montgomery bus boycott, the SCLC also aided black communities in applying the lessons of that struggle to challenge bus segregation in Tallahassee (Florida) and Atlanta.

The SCLC shared many of the NAACP's goals, but tensions arose between the two organizations. The NAACP's leadership doubted the effectiveness of the protest tactics favored by the SCLC. They resented having to divert resources away from work on important court cases to defend people arrested in protests and were troubled by the left-wing connections of King's advisers. The fortunes of the NAACP in the South, however, plummeted in the late 1950s as southern states persecuted its members; this left the field to the SCLC. Despite their differences, the SCLC and the NAACP worked together, but the tensions over tactics were never far from the surface.

CIVIL RIGHTS ACT OF 1957

Despite President Eisenhower's tepid response to *Brown*, Congress proved willing to take a modest step toward ending racial discrimination. Buttressing the Supreme Court's desegregation initiatives, it enacted the Civil Rights Act of 1957, the first such legislation since the end of Reconstruction. In a departure from the past, liberals in the Senate were able to end a filibuster by southerners, but the bill they passed was, for all its symbolic import, weak. It created a commission to monitor violations of black civil rights and to propose remedies for infringements on black voting. It upgraded the Civil Rights Section into a division within the Justice Department and gave it the power to initiate civil proceedings against those states and municipalities that discriminated on the basis of race. Although an important step on the long road toward black enfranchisement, this act disappointed black activists because it was not strong enough to counter white reaction and because they felt the Eisenhower administration would not enforce it.

LITTLE ROCK, ARKANSAS

Eisenhower may have had little inclination to support the fight for black rights, but the defiance of Arkansas governor Orville Faubus would soon force him to. At the beginning of the school year in 1957, Faubus posted 270 soldiers from the Arkansas National Guard outside Little Rock Central High School to prevent nine black youths from entering. Faubus was deter-

mined to flout the *Brown* ruling and to maintain school segregation. When a federal district court order forced the governor to allow the children into the school, he simply withdrew the state guard and left the children alone to face a hate-filled mob.

To defend the sovereignty of the federal court and the Constitution, Eisenhower had to act. He sent in 1,100 paratroopers from the 101st Airborne to Little Rock and put the state national guard under federal authority. It was the first time since Reconstruction that troops had been sent to the South to protect the rights of African-American citizens. The troops remained in Little Rock Central High School for the rest of the school year. Governor Faubus closed the Little Rock public schools in 1958–1959. Eight of the nine black students valiantly withstood the abuse, harassment, and curses of segregationists both inside and outside the facility and eventually desegregated the high school. Other young African Americans throughout the South would show similar courage.

Executive Order 10730: Desegregation of Central High School, 1957 **21-4** DOCUMENT

Black Youth Stand Up by Sitting Down

Beginning in 1960, motivated black college students adapted a strategy that CORE had used in the 1940s—the sit-in—and emerged as the dynamic vanguard of the civil rights movement. Their distinctive and independent contributions to the black protest movement accelerated the pace of social change. Before long the movement would inspire an even larger number of northern black and white students.

SIT-INS: GREENSBORO, NASHVILLE, ATLANTA

Early on the morning of February 1, 1960, Ezell Blair Jr., Joseph McNeil, Francis McCain, and David Richmond, all freshmen at North Carolina Agricultural and Technical College (A & T), decided to desegregate local restaurants by sitting at the lunch counter of Greensboro, North Carolina's Woolworth five-and-dime store. Although black people were welcome to spend their money in the store, they were not permitted to dine at the lunch counter, making it a painful symbol of white supremacy. At 4:30 in the afternoon the students sat at the counter. They received no service that day but sat quietly doing their schoolwork until the store closed. The action of these four young men electrified their fellow students, and the next day many others joined them. Soon, black women students from Bennett College and a few white students from

Elizabeth Eckerd, one of nine black students who sought to enroll at Little Rock Central High School in September 1957, endures the taunts of an angry white crowd as she tries to make her way to the school.

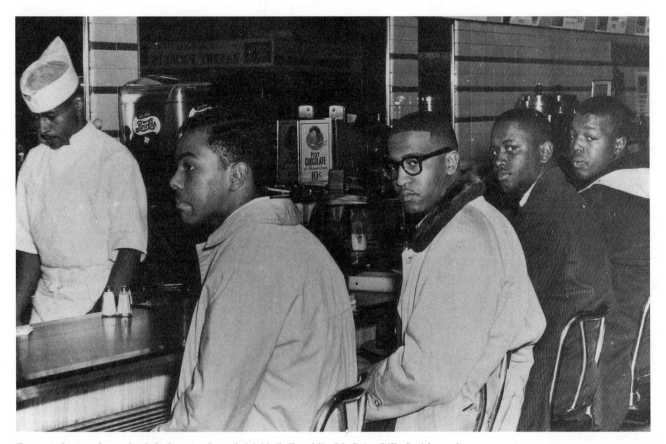

Four students—from the left they are Joseph McNeil, Franklin McCain, Billy Smith, and Clarence Henderson—sit patiently at Woolworth's lunch counter on February 2, 1960, the second day of the sit-in in Greensboro, North Carolina. Although not the first sit-in protest against segregated facilities, the Greensboro action triggered a wave of sit-ins by black high school and college students across the South.

the University of North Carolina Women's College joined the protest, and by the fifth day hundreds of young, studious, neatly dressed African Americans crowded the downtown store demanding their rights.

Like the black people of Montgomery, the students in Greensboro acted with forethought and with the support of their community. They had long debated how they could best participate in the desegregation movement. All four of the black students had been members of NAACP college or youth groups and were aware of the currents of change flowing through the South. Although they began the sit-in on their own, it quickly gained the support of the black community. Many people in the North and West—both black and white—also joined the campaign by picketing local stores of the national chains that approved of segregation in the South. After facing the collective power of the black community and their allies for many months, white businessmen and politicians finally gave in to the black community's demands.

The students at Greensboro were not alone in their desire to strike out at discrimination. Indeed, at Fisk University in Nashville, Tennessee, Diane Nash, John Lewis, Marion Barry, James Bevel, Curtis Murphy, Gloria Johnson, Bernard Lafayette, and Rodney Powell had begun organizing nonviolent workshops before the Greensboro sit-in. Imbued with youthful exuberance and idealism, they determined to follow the Reverend James Lawson's courageous leadership and his teaching on nonviolence and Christian brotherhood. Even better organized than their comrades in North Carolina, they had been undergoing intensive training for a sit-in campaign. Twelve days after the first sit-ins began, the Nashville group swung into action. Hundreds were arrested, and those who sat suffered insults, mob violence, beatings, arrest, and torture while in jail. Nonetheless, they compelled major restaurants to desegregate by May 1960.

Atlanta, Martin Luther King Jr.'s home base and the site of a large African-American community, spawned an even more dramatic movement. It began after Spelman College freshman Ruby Doris Smith persuaded her friends and classmates to launch sit-ins in the city. On March 15, 1960, at Atlanta University, two students, Julian Bond and Lonnie King, executing a carefully orchestrated plan, deployed two hundred sit-in students to ten different eating places. They targeted government-owned property and public places, including bus and train stations and the state capitol, that should have been willing to serve all customers. At the Federal Building, Bond and his classmates attempted to eat in the municipal cafeteria and were arrested. After hours of incarceration they were released. In earlier years, a jail stint had been a mark of shame, but these students returned as heroes to the campus. The Atlanta sit-in students broadened their campaign demands to include desegregation of all public facilities, black voting rights, and equal access to educational and employment opportunities. On September 27, 1961, the Atlanta business and political elite gave in.

Just as in Greensboro, the students in Nashville, Atlanta, and numerous other southern cities won the support of local people who had not been involved in organized resistance before. By April 1960 more than two thousand students from black high schools and colleges had been arrested in seventy-eight southern towns and cities. Local people demonstrated their allegiance to them in numerous ways, but their most effective tactic was the economic boycott. When business began to suffer as a result of the protests, white leaders proved willing to negotiate the racial status quo. By the summer, more than thirty southern cities had set up community organizations to respond to the complaints of local black citizens.

THE STUDENT NONVIOLENT COORDINATING COMMITTEE

Recognizing the significance of the regionwide student action and fearing it would soon melt away, the SCLC's Ella Baker organized a conference for 150 students at her alma mater, Shaw University, in Raleigh, North Carolina. Baker, who managed operations in the SCLC's Atlanta headquarters, chafed under the rigid male leadership of the organization. In contrast, she advocated decentralized leadership and celebrated participatory democracy. Her skepticism about the SCLC struck a chord with the students.

On April 15–17, 1960, delegates representing over fifty colleges and high schools from thirty-seven communities in thirteen states arrived and began discussing how to keep the movement going. Baker

addressed the group in a speech entitled "More Than a Hamburger" and became the midwife of a new organization named the **Student Nonviolent Coordinating Committee (SNCC)**. The newest addition to the roster of civil rights associations adhered to the ideology of nonviolence, but it also acknowledged the possible need for increased militancy and confrontation. More accommodating black leaders, even some of those in the SCLC, objected to the students' use of direct confrontational tactics that disrupted race relations and community peace.

Sit-ins and the Origins of the SNCC, 1960   21-5   DOCUMENT

FREEDOM RIDES

The sit-in movement paved the way for the "**Freedom Rides**" of 1961. CORE's James Farmer and Bayard Rustin resolved it was time for a reprise of their 1947 mission to ride interstate buses and trains in the upper South. That early effort—a planned bus trip from Washington, D.C., to Kentucky—reached only as far as Chapel Hill, North Carolina. There the group of interracial riders met violent resistance, were arrested, and were sentenced to thirty days on a road gang. This new journey tested the Justice Department's willingness to protect the rights of African Americans to use bus terminal facilities on a nonsegregated basis.

The Freedom Rides showed the world how far some white southerners would go to preserve segregation. The first ride ran into trouble on May 4, 1961, when John Lewis, one of the seven black riders, tried to enter the white waiting room of the Greyhound bus terminal in Rock Hill, South Carolina, and was brutally beaten by local white people in full view of the police. The interracial group continued through Alabama toward Jackson, Mississippi, but repeated acts of white violence made escape from Alabama difficult. At Anniston, Alabama, a mob firebombed the bus and beat the escaping riders. A group of local African Americans led by the Reverend Fred Shuttlesworth took many of the shocked and injured riders to Birmingham.

With the police offering no protection, CORE abandoned the Freedom Rides, and all but a few of the original riders left Alabama. But SNCC activists and students in Nashville refused to let the idea die. At least twenty civil rights workers went to Birmingham, where they vowed on May 20 to ride on to Montgomery. John Lewis remained with the group that arrived in Montgomery. Awaiting them was another angry mob of more than a thousand white people, and not a policeman in sight. This time Lewis was knocked unconscious, and all the riders had to be hospitalized. Even a presidential aide assigned to monitor the crisis was injured.

PROFILE ～ ROBERT PARRIS MOSES

Bob Moses, one of the most dedicated and revered young civil rights activists, was a soft-spoken man possessed of a powerful intellect, iron courage, and a rare purity of moral conviction. Born in 1935 in Harlem, Moses was an excellent student. He attended Hamilton College in New York State and from his readings in philosophy there, including works on Buddhism and existentialism, he developed a sophisticated understanding of nonviolent protest, a topic he continued to explore during his graduate studies in philosophy at Harvard University.

When Moses learned of the sit-ins in 1960, he immediately went south to participate. It was a fateful trip during which he met Amzie Moore, one of the World War II veterans who had returned home to make Mississippi safe for democracy. Moore was the vice president of the state conferences of the NAACP branches. The two men developed a deep-seated appreciation for each other's strengths, and Moore soon convinced Moses to center his work in Mississippi. By August 1961 Moses was an SNCC organizer in the small town of McComb, Mississippi. There his group registered black voters. In early 1962 the SNCC activist became the program director of the Council of Federated Organizations (COFO) and remained in the center of the struggle in Mississippi for the next three years.

The violence of white people and the courage of local black people had a profound effect on Moses. In McComb he was arrested, jailed, beaten, and threatened with death. One of the local black people who helped his group was murdered in cold blood by a state senator who was subsequently acquitted of the crime by an all-white jury. Moses respected anyone who had the courage to take a stand after suffering a lifetime of such abuse. He sought to give local people the tools to continue to control their lives long after movement organizers had left.

Although Moses refused to become a formal leader of the SNCC forces in Mississippi, he profoundly affected the movement. The young civil rights worker set an example of nonviolent resistance for other members of SNCC and encouraged the entire organization to avoid developing a hierarchical leadership structure. In late 1963 Moses became the driving force behind the Freedom Summer project and played a central role in persuading SNCC to accept white volunteers from the North. He also stood for principle rather than expediency when he rejected the meager deal offered the Mississippi Freedom Democratic Party (discussed later in the chapter) at the 1964 Democratic Convention. Moses spoke for many young activists when he said in disgust, "You can't trust the political system. I will have nothing to do with the political system any longer."

In 1965 Moses began to drift away from the civil rights movement and toward active opposition to the war in Vietnam. Exhausted from his ordeal in the South and seeking to avoid the draft, he emigrated first to Canada and then to the African nation of Tanzania. Moses returned soon after President Jimmy Carter offered amnesty to draft resisters in 1977 and began teaching math and science to inner-city black children. After receiving a MacArthur Foundation "genius grant," he developed the Algebra Project, which uses many of the empowerment strategies pioneered during the civil rights era to help children and their families gain the education they need in the emerging computer-oriented economy.

Robert "Bob" Moses instructs volunteers for the ▶▶ Freedom Summer campaign of 1964.

Moses

On May 14, in Anniston, Alabama, a white mob firebombed this Freedom Riders' bus and attacked passengers as they escaped the flames.

News services flashed graphic images of the violence around the world, and the federal government resolved to end the bloodletting. Attorney General Robert Kennedy sent four hundred federal marshals to restore law and order. Martin Luther King Jr. and Ralph Abernathy joined the conflict on May 21, as 1,200 men, women, and children met at Abernathy's church. The federal marshals averted further bloodshed by surrounding the building. Only then did Governor John Patterson order the National Guard and state troopers to protect the protesters. When the group arrived in Jackson, Mississippi, white authorities promptly arrested them. By summer's end, more than three hundred Freedom Riders had served time in Mississippi's notorious prisons.

A Sight to Be Seen: The Movement at High Tide

Between 1960 and 1963, the civil rights movement developed the techniques and organization that would finally bring America face to face with the conflict between its democratic ideals and the racism of its politics. Day after day the movement squared off against the die-hard resistance of the white South and created a situation that demanded the president and Congress take action.

THE ELECTION OF 1960

One of the persistent fears of white southerners was that black Americans, if armed with the ballot, would possess the balance of political power. The presidential election of 1960 proved this to be the case. Initially, many African Americans favored the Republican Party's nominee, Richard Nixon, who had advocated strong civil rights legislation. Baseball star Jackie Robinson was a Nixon supporter, as were many other well-known African Americans. It seemed as if the New Deal coalition had weakened and black citizens would reverse their move into the Democratic Party. The Democratic nominee, Massachusetts senator John F. Kennedy, in contrast, had done little to distinguish himself to black Americans in the struggles of the 1950s. As the campaign progressed, however, Kennedy made more sympathetic statements in support of black protests. Meanwhile, Nixon attempted to strengthen his position with white southern voters and remained silent about civil rights issues, even though the Republican Party had a strong pro–civil rights record.

Shortly before the election, Martin Luther King Jr. was sentenced to four months in prison for leading a nonviolent protest march in Atlanta. Kennedy seized the opportunity to telephone King's wife, Coretta Scott King, to offer his support while his brother Robert F. Kennedy used his influence to obtain King's release. These acts impressed African Americans and won their support. African-American voters in key northern cities provided the crucial margin that elected John F. Kennedy. In Illinois, for example, with black voters casting 250,000 ballots for Kennedy, the Democrats carried the state by merely 9,000 votes.

THE KENNEDY ADMINISTRATION AND THE CIVIL RIGHTS MOVEMENT

Early in his administration John F. Kennedy grew concerned about the mounting violence occasioned by the civil rights movement. As the Freedom Rides continued across the deep South, the activists provoked crises and confrontations and forced the federal government to intervene on their behalf. Kennedy's primary interest at this point was to prevent disorder from getting out of hand and to avoid compromising America's position with the developing nations. But Kennedy had little room to maneuver given the continued power of white southerners in his party and in Congress.

Despite these limitations, Kennedy did aid the cause of civil rights. He issued Executive Order 11063, which required government agencies to discontinue discriminatory policies and practices in federally supported housing, and he named Vice President Lyndon B. Johnson to chair the newly established Committee on Equal Employment Opportunity. Kennedy also pleased black Americans when he nominated Thurgood Marshall to the Second Circuit Court of Appeals on September 23, 1961 (although determined opposition in the Senate blocked Marshall's confirmation until September 11, 1963). He named journalist Carl Rowan deputy assistant secretary of state. More than forty African Americans took positions in the new administration, including Robert Weaver, director of the Housing and Home Finance Agency; Mercer Cook, ambassador to Norway; and George L. P. Weaver, assistant secretary of labor. Moreover, Kennedy's brother Robert put muscle into the Civil Rights Division of the Justice Department by hiring an impressive team of lawyers headed by Washington attorney Burke Marshall.

Like Eisenhower, when President Kennedy felt that intractable southern governors were challenging his authority, he acted decisively. On June 25, 1962, one year after James Meredith had filed a complaint of racial discrimination against the University of Mississippi, the U.S. Circuit Court of Appeals for the Fifth Circuit ruled that the university had to admit him. Mississippi governor Ross Barnett vowed to resist the order, but Kennedy sent three hundred federal marshals to uphold it. Thousands of students rioted at the campus; two people died, two hundred were arrested, and nearly half the marshals were injured. Kennedy did not back down. He federalized the Mississippi National Guard to ensure Meredith's admission. Although isolated and harassed throughout his time at Ole Miss, Meredith eventually graduated. Likewise, in June 1963, the Kennedy administration compelled Governor George Wallace of Alabama to allow the desegregation of the University of Alabama.

VOTER REGISTRATION PROJECTS

On June 16, 1961, Robert Kennedy met with student leaders and urged them to redirect their energies to voter registration projects and to lessen their concentration on direct-action activities. He and the Justice Department aides persuaded the students that the free exercise of the ballot would result in profound and significant social change. James Foreman, SNCC's executive director, followed Kennedy's lead. By October 1961 SNCC had joined forces with the NAACP, SCLC, and CORE in the voter education project funded by major philanthropic foundations and administered by the Southern Regional Council. SNCC was responsible for Alabama and Mississippi. Drawing heavily on the expertise of Robert Moses and working closely with a cadre of local leaders like Amzie Moore, head of the NAACP in Mississippi's Cleveland county, and Fannie Lou Hamer of Ruleville, SNCC opened a series of voter registration schools. The "graduates" thereupon attempted to register to vote. These attempts unleashed a wave of white violence and murder across Mississippi.

The Albany Movement

In Albany, Georgia, the burgeoning civil rights movement met sophisticated resistance and experienced its most profound defeat up to that time. The movement in Albany began in the summer of 1961 when SNCC members moved into the city to conduct a voter registration project. Soon representatives of various local groups decided to form a coalition called the Albany Movement and elected osteopath William G. Anderson as its president. The movement's goal quickly expanded from securing the vote to the total desegregation of the town.

In Laurie Pritchett, Albany's police chief, the movement faced an uncommonly sophisticated opponent. Pritchett studied the past tactics of SNCC and King and resolved not to confront the federal government directly and to avoid the kind of violence that brought negative media attention. When students from a black college decided to begin demonstrations by desegregating the bus terminal, Pritchett immediately arrested them after they entered the white waiting room and attempted to eat in the bus terminal dining room. Shrewdly, he charged the students with violating a city ordinance for failing to obey a law enforcement officer. They were not arrested on a federal charge.

The Albany Movement decided to invite King and SCLC to aid them and to overwhelm the police department by filling the jails with protesters. King answered the call. On December 16, 1961, he and more than 250 demonstrators were arrested, joining the 507 people already in jail. The plan was to stay in jail in order to, as Charles Sherrod explained, "break the system down from within. Our ability to suffer was somehow going to overcome their ability to hurt us." King vowed to remain in jail until the city desegregated. Sheriff Pritchett, however, made arrangements to house almost two thousand people in surrounding jail facilities and trained his deputies in the use of nonviolent techniques. Thus Pritchett avoided confrontation, violence, and federal intervention.

BERNICE JOHNSON REAGON ON HOW TO RAISE A FREEDOM SONG

Civil rights activists created a special culture in which black music helped communicate a sense of common purpose, strengthen the resolve to endure hardship and pain, and overcome despair and fear. One of the great singers to emerge out of the Albany Movement was Bernice Johnson Reagon, who today is known internationally as the founder of the a cappella group Sweet Honey in the Rock. During the 1960s she and Cordell Reagon and others formed the SNCC Freedom Singers and traveled the country performing freedom songs. In this statement Reagon describes the significance of song to the civil rights participants.

If you cannot sing a congregational song at full power, you cannot fight in any struggle. . . . It is something you learn.

In congregational singing you don't sing a song—you raise it. By offering the first line, the song leader just offers the possibility, and it is up to you, individually, whether you pick it up or not. . . . It is a big personal risk because you will put everything into the song. It is like stepping off into space. A mini-revolution takes place inside you. Your body gets flushed, you tremble, you're tempted to turn off the circuits. But that's when you have to turn up the burner and commit yourself to follow that song wherever it leads. This transformation in yourself that you create is exactly what happens when you join a movement. You are taking a risk—you are committing yourself and there is no turning back. . . .

Organizing is not gentle. When you organize somebody, you create great anxiety in that person because you are telling them to risk everything. Put yourself in the place of a woman getting by as a hairdresser. You spend your day curling and frying hair, curling and frying. Somebody asks you to put up some civil rights workers in your home. You have to imagine what is going to happen: there may be people shooting up your home; you have to picture the check you get, the car you drive; everything you own, going on the block. You decide to take that risk because this is important enough. . . .

When you get together at a mass meeting you sing the songs which symbolize transformation, which make that revolution of courage inside you. . . . You raise a freedom song.

🌿 *How does Reagon compare singing a freedom song to becoming involved in civil rights protests?*

🌿 *Given the dangers, why did so many ordinary people become involved in the black freedom movement?*

Source: Bernice Johnson Reagon, "We'll Never Turn Back," in *Everybody Says Freedom: A History of the Civil Rights Movement in Songs and Pictures*, edited by Pete Seeger and Bob Reiser (New York: Norton, 1989), p. 82.

On December 18, 1961, two days after King's arrest, the city and the Albany Movement announced a truce. King returned to Atlanta, and the city refused to implement the terms of the agreement. When King and Ralph Abernathy returned to Albany in July 1962 for sentencing on their December arrests, they chose forty-five days in jail rather than admitting guilt by paying a fine. The mass marches resumed, but again Pritchett thwarted King by having him released from jail to avoid negative publicity. The city's attorney then secured a federal injunction to prevent King and the other leaders from demonstrating. Given his dependence on the federal government, King felt he could not violate the injunction and abandoned the protest. For King, the Albany Movement was a failure, his most glaring defeat, and one that called into question the future of the movement.

The Birmingham Confrontation

By early 1963 the movement appeared to be stalled. Black communities in many parts of the South were strong and well organized, but their enormous efforts had achieved only modest changes. It was impossible to overcome the power of southern state and local governments without the intervention of the federal government, but national politicians, including President Kennedy, remained reluctant to act unless faced with open defiance by white people or televised violence against peaceful protesters. King and other black leaders knew that if city governments throughout the South followed the model of Sheriff Pritchett in Albany, the civil rights movement might lose momentum. To rejuvenate the movement, SCLC decided to launch a massive new campaign during 1963, the year of the one hundredth anniversary of the Emancipation Proclamation.

Birmingham, Alabama, a large, tightly segregated industrial city, was chosen as the site for the action. The city was ripe for such a protest, in part because its black community suffered from severe police brutality as well as economic, educational, and social discrimination. The Ku Klux Klan terrorized people with impunity. The black community had, however, developed a strong phalanx of protest organizations called the Alabama Christian Movement for Human Rights (ACMHR) led by the Reverend Fred Shuttlesworth. The ACMHR and SCLC planned a campaign of boycotts, pickets, and demonstrations code-named Project C for Confrontation. Their program would be far more extensive than any before, with demands to integrate public facilities, for guarantees of employment opportunities for black workers in downtown businesses, to desegregate the schools, to improve services in black neighborhoods, and to provide low-income housing. Organizers hoped to provoke the city's public safety commissioner Eugene T. "Bull" Connor, who, unlike Sheriff Pritchett, had a reputation for viciousness. Civil rights leaders believed Connor's conduct would horrify the nation and compel Kennedy to act.

Project C began on the third of April with college students conducting sit-ins. Days later, marches began, and Connor, following the lead of Pritchett, arrested all who participated but avoided overt violence. When the state courts prohibited further protests, King and Abernathy, among others, violated the ruling. They were arrested and jailed on Good Friday, April 12, 1963.

While in jail, King received a letter from eight local Christian and Jewish clergymen who objected to what they considered the "unwise and untimely" protest activities of black citizens. King had smuggled a pen into jail and on scraps of paper, including toilet paper and the margins of the Birmingham *News*, he wrote an eloquent treatise on the use of direct action. His "Letter from Birmingham Jail" was widely published in newspapers and magazines. In it, King dismissed those who called for black people to wait: "I guess it is easy for those who have never felt the stinging darts of segregation to say, 'Wait.' " But, he declared, "freedom is never voluntarily given by the oppressor; it must be demanded by the oppressed." In the letter King also explained, "Nonviolent direct action seeks to create such a crisis and foster such a tension that a community which has constantly refused to negotiate is forced to confront the issue. It seeks so to dramatize the issue that it can no longer be ignored. . . . Any law that degrades human personality is unjust. All segregation statutes are unjust because segregation distorts the soul and damages the personality. It gives the segregator a false sense of superiority and the segregated a false sense of inferiority."

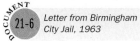

DOCUMENT 21-6 *Letter from Birmingham City Jail, 1963*

King's letter had a powerful national impact, but the Birmingham movement was beginning to lose momentum because many of the protesters were either in jail or could not risk new arrests. At this juncture James Bevel of the SCLC proposed using schoolchildren to continue the protests. Many observers criticized this idea, as did some of those in the movement. But King and other leaders believed it was necessary to risk harm to children in order to ensure their freedom. Thus, on May 2 and 3, 1963, a "children's crusade" involving thousands of youths, some as young as six, marched. This tactic enraged "Bull" Connor and his officers. The police not only arrested the children but flailed away with nightsticks and set vicious dogs on them. On Connor's order, firefighters aimed their powerful hoses at the youngsters, ripping the clothes from backs, cutting flesh, and tumbling children down the street. In the ensuing days many of the children and their parents began to fight back, hurling bottles and rocks at their uniformed tormentors. As the violence escalated, white businessmen became concerned, and the city soon came to the bargaining table.

President Kennedy deployed Assistant Attorney General for Civil Rights Burke Marshall to negotiate a settlement. On May 10, 1963, white businessmen agreed to integrate downtown facilities and to hire black men and women. The following night the KKK bombed the A. G. Gaston Motel, where the SCLC had its headquarters, and the house that belonged to King's brother, the Reverend A. D. King. Black citizens in turn burned cars and buildings and attacked the police. Only intervention by King and other movement leaders prevented a riot. White moderates delivered on the promises and the agreement stuck.

Although the SCLC did not win on every demand, Birmingham was a major triumph and a turning point in the movement. The summer of 1963 saw a massive upsurge in protests across the South, with nearly eight hundred marches, demonstrations, and sit-ins. Ten civil rights protesters were killed and twenty thousand arrested as the white South desperately sought to stem the tide. In one of the most tragic losses for the movement, white extremist Byron de la Beckwith gunned down Medgar Evers in the driveway of his home on June 12, 1963, in Jackson, Mississippi. Evers had been the executive secretary of the NAACP's Mississippi organization and the center of a powerful movement in that city. His cold-blooded murder dramatized the depth of hatred among some white southerners and the lengths to which they would go to prevent change.

A Hard Victory

The sacrifices in Birmingham and the intensification of the movement throughout the South set the stage for Congress to pass legislation for a Second Reconstruction that would at last fulfill the promise of the first.

THE MARCH ON WASHINGTON

The lingering image of Birmingham and the growing number of demonstrations throughout the South compelled action from President Kennedy. On June 11, 1963, he addressed the nation with his strongest statement about civil rights. He declared, "We face . . . a moral crisis as a country and a people. It cannot be

MARCH ON WASHINGTON FOR JOBS AND FREEDOM
AUGUST 28, 1963

LINCOLN MEMORIAL PROGRAM

1. The National Anthem	*Led by* Marian Anderson.
2. Invocation	The Very Rev. Patrick O'Boyle, *Archbishop of Washington.*
3. Opening Remarks	A. Philip Randolph, *Director March on Washington for Jobs and Freedom.*
4. Remarks	Dr. Eugene Carson Blake, *Stated Clerk, United Presbyterian Church of the U.S.A.; Vice Chairman, Commission on Race Relations of the National Council of Churches of Christ in America.*
5. Tribute to Negro Women Fighters for Freedom	Mrs. Medgar Evers
Daisy Bates	
Diane Nash Bevel	
Mrs. Medgar Evers	
Mrs. Herbert Lee	
Rosa Parks	
Gloria Richardson	
6. Remarks	John Lewis, *National Chairman, Student Nonviolent Coordinating Committee.*
7. Remarks	Walter Reuther, *President, United Automobile, Aerospace and Agricultural Implement Wokers of America, AFL-CIO; Chairman, Industrial Union Department, AFL-CIO.*
8. Remarks	James Farmer, *National Director, Congress of Racial Equality.*
9. Selection	Eva Jessye *Choir*
10. Prayer	Rabbi Uri Miller, *President Synagogue Council of America.*
11. Remarks	Whitney M. Young, Jr., *Executive Director, National Urban League.*
12. Remarks	Mathew Ahmann, *Executive Director, National Catholic Conference for Interracial Justice.*
13. Remarks	Roy Wilkins, *Executive Secretary, National Association for the Advancement of Colored People.*
14. Selection	Miss Mahalia Jackson
15. Remarks	Rabbi Joachim Prinz, *President American Jewish Congress.*
16. Remarks	The Rev. Dr. Martin Luther King, Jr., *President, Southern Christian Leadership Conference.*
17. The Pledge	A Philip Randolph
18. Benediction	Dr. Benjamin E. Mays, *President, Morehouse College.*

"WE SHALL OVERCOME"

On August 28, 1963, A. Philip Randolph, John Lewis, James Farmer, Whitney Young, Roy Wilkins, and Martin Luther King Jr., the leaders of the organizations that spearheaded the modern civil rights movement, came together in one of the great mass marches in American history to address issues of jobs and freedom. The program included a tribute to African-American women fighters for freedom and musical performance by great artists such as Marian Anderson, Eva Jessye, and Mahalia Jackson.

met by repressive police action. It cannot be left to increased demonstrations in the streets. It cannot be quieted by token moves or talk. It is a time to act in the Congress, in your state and local legislative body, and above all, in all our daily lives. A great change is at hand, and our task, our obligation, is to make that revolution . . . peaceful and constructive for all." Kennedy subsequently proposed the strongest civil rights bill the country had yet seen, but despite the public's heightened awareness of discrimination, he still could not muster sufficient support in Congress to counter the powerful southern bloc within his own party.

To demonstrate their support for Kennedy's civil rights legislation, a coalition of civil rights organizations—SCLC, NAACP, CORE, SNCC, and the National Urban League—and their leaders resurrected the idea of organizing a march on Washington that A. Philip Ran-

dolph had first proposed in 1941. In 1962 Randolph and Bayard Rustin had proposed a march to protest black unemployment. Their call received a tepid response, but after Birmingham many of the major civil rights organizations reconsidered. Reflecting renewed hope, Randolph christened it a march for "Jobs and Freedom."

In August 1963 nearly 250,000 marchers gathered before the Lincoln Memorial to show their support for the civil rights bill and the movement at large. Throughout the day they sang freedom songs and listened to speeches from civil rights leaders. Finally, late in the afternoon, Martin Luther King Jr. arose, and casting aside his prepared remarks, he delivered an impassioned speech. Most powerfully, King spoke of this vision of the future:

> I say to you today, my friends, that in spite of the difficulties and frustrations of the moment I still have a dream. It is a dream deeply rooted in the American dream. I have a dream that one day this nation will rise up and live out the true meaning of its creed: "We hold these truths to be self-evident; that all men are created equal." I have a dream that one day on the red hills of Georgia the sons of former slaves and the sons of former slave owners will be able to sit down together at the table of brotherhood. I have a dream that one day even the state of Mississippi, a desert state sweltering with the heat of injustice and oppression, will be transformed into an oasis of freedom and justice. I have a dream that my four children will one day live in a nation where they will not be judged by the color of their skin but by the content of their character. I have a dream today. I have a dream that one day the state of Alabama, whose governor's lips are presently dripping with the words of interposition and nullification, will be transformed into a situation where little black boys and black girls will be able to join hands with little white boys and white girls and walk together as sisters and brothers. I have a dream today . . .

King's words did not still the angry opposition of some white southerners. On September 15, 1963, only days after the March on Washington, white racists bombed the 16th St. Baptist Church in Birmingham and killed four little girls attending Sunday school: Addie Mae Collins, Denise McNair, Carole Robertson, and Cynthia Wesley. Chris McNair, the father of the youngest victim, pleaded for calm out of the depth of his own pain: "We must not let this change us into something different than who we are. We must be human." In a similar vein, Martin Luther King Jr. sadly intoned, "The innocent blood of these little girls may well

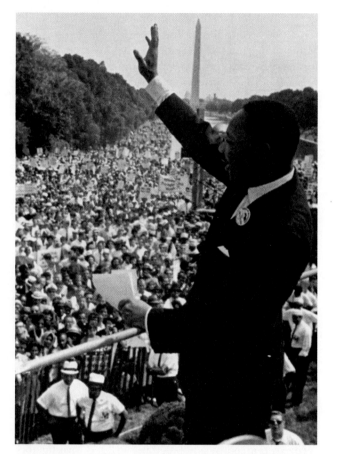

At the height of his moral authority, Martin Luther King Jr. (1929–1968) delivers the memorable "I Have a Dream" speech at the 1963 March on Washington. He conveyed a vision of a future America free of the evil of racism where all God's children would be judged by the content of their character, not the color of their skin. King received the Nobel Peace Prize in 1964, and since 1986 the nation has honored him with a holiday in his name.

serve as the redemptive force that will bring new light to this dark city. . . . Indeed, this tragic event may cause the white South to come to terms with its conscience." The event shook the nation, and combined with the reaction to the assassination of John F. Kennedy in November 1963, set the stage for real change.

THE CIVIL RIGHTS ACT OF 1964

Kennedy's successor Lyndon B. Johnson lobbied hard to secure passage of the landmark Civil Rights Act. Many in the civil rights movement feared that Johnson, a southerner, would back his region's defiance. Nonetheless, only four days after taking the oath of office, Johnson told the nation he planned to support the civil rights bill as a memorial for the slain president. A mas-

ter politician, Johnson pushed the bill through Congress despite a marathon filibuster by its opponents.

The **Civil Rights Act of 1964** was the culmination of the civil rights movement to that time. The act banned discrimination in places of public accommodation, including restaurants, hotels, gas stations, and entertainment facilities, as well as schools, parks, playgrounds, libraries, and swimming pools. The desegregation of public accommodations irrevocably changed the face of American society. The issue of legally mandated racial separation was now settled. The act also banned discrimination by employers and labor unions on the basis of race, color, religion, national origin, and sex in regard to hiring, promoting, dismissing, or making job referrals. The act had strong provisions for enforcement. Most important, it allowed government agencies to withhold federal money from any program permitting or practicing discrimination. This provision had particular import for the desegregation of schools and colleges across the country. The act also gave the U.S. attorney general the power to initiate proceedings against segregated facilities and schools on behalf of people who could not do so on their own. Finally it created the Equal Employment Opportunity Commission to monitor discrimination in employment.

MISSISSIPPI FREEDOM SUMMER

While Congress considered the Civil Rights Act, movement activists renewed their focus on voter registration in the deep South. In the fall of 1963, many CORE and SNCC workers saw segregation crumbling, but they knew that without the ballot, African Americans could never drive racist politicians from office, gain a fair hearing in court, reduce police and mob violence, or get equal services from state and local governments. CORE took responsibility for running registration campaigns in Louisiana, South Carolina, and Florida while the SNCC took on the two most repressive states, Alabama and Mississippi. Mississippi was widely known in the movement as the "toughest nut to crack"—the symbolic center of American racism and white violence. By the summer of 1964, national attention had shifted from Alabama to Mississippi, the site of a massive project known as "Freedom Summer."

The voter registration campaign in Mississippi began in late 1963 when Robert "Bob" Moses mobilized the Council of Federated Organizations (COFO), which had been established in 1961 to aid imprisoned freedom riders. Moses convinced the members of COFO (CORE, SNCC, SCLC, and the NAACP) to sponsor a mock Freedom Election in Mississippi. On Election Day,

VIOLENCE AND THE CIVIL RIGHTS MOVEMENT

MAY 7, 1955	Reverend George Lee killed for leading voter registration drive, Belzoni, Mississippi
AUGUST 13, 1955	Lamar Smith murdered for organizing black voters, Brookhaven, Mississippi
AUGUST 28, 1955	Emmett Louis Till murdered for speaking to white woman, Money, Mississippi
OCTOBER 22, 1955	John Earl Reese slain by night riders opposed to black school improvements, Mayflower, Texas
JANUARY 23, 1957	Willie Edwards Jr. killed by Klan, Montgomery, Alabama
SEPTEMBER 24, 1957	President Eisenhower orders federal troops to enforce school desegregation, Little Rock, Arkansas
APRIL 27, 1959	Mack Charles Parker taken from jail and lynched, Popularville, Mississippi
MAY 14, 1961	Freedom Riders attacked in Alabama while testing compliance with bus desegregation laws
SEPTEMBER 25, 1961	Voter registration worker Herbert Lee killed by a white legislator, Liberty, Mississippi
APRIL 1, 1962	Civil rights groups join forces to launch voter registration drive
APRIL 9, 1962	Roman Ducksworth Jr. taken from bus and killed by police, Taylorsville, Mississippi
SEPTEMBER 30, 1962	Riots erupt when James Meredith, a black student, enrolls at the University of Mississippi; Paul Guihard, European reporter, killed
APRIL 23, 1963	William Lewis Moore slain during one-man march against segregation, Attalla, Alabama
MAY 3, 1963	Birmingham police attack marching children with dogs and fire hoses
JUNE 12, 1963	Medgar Evers, civil rights leader, assassinated, Jackson, Mississippi
SEPTEMBER 15, 1963	Schoolgirls Addie Mae Collins, Denise McNair, Carole Robertson, and Cynthia Wesley die in the bombing of the 16th St. Baptist Church, Birmingham, Alabama
SEPTEMBER 15, 1963	Virgil Lamar Ware killed during racist violence, Birmingham, Alabama
JANUARY 31, 1964	Louis Allen, witness to the murder of a civil rights worker, assassinated, Liberty, Mississippi

1955–1968

eighty thousand disfranchised black people cast ballots for COFO candidates. Impressed with the turnout, Moses and other COFO members believed a massive effort to register voters during the summer of 1964 might break the white monopoly on the ballot box.

After much debate, COFO decided to invite northern white students to participate in the Mississippi project. These students, about one thousand in all, were to be drawn primarily from the nation's most prestigious universities. This move contradicted the movement's emphasis on black empowerment, but COFO leaders calculated that the presence of elite white students in the Magnolia State would attract increased media attention and pressure the federal government to provide protection.

Shortly after the project began, three volunteers, two white New Yorkers—twenty-four-year-old Michael Schwerner and twenty-one-year-old Andrew Goodman—and a black Mississippian, twenty-one-year-old James Chaney, disappeared. Unknown at the time, Cecil Price, deputy sheriff of Philadelphia, Mississippi, had arrested the three on a trumped-up speeding charge. That evening the young men were delivered to a deserted road where three carloads of Klansmen waited. Schwerner and Goodman were shot to death. Chaney was beaten with chains and then shot.

These events were not publicly known until Klan informers, enticed by a $30,000 reward, led investigators to the earthen dam in which Goodman, Schwerner, and Chaney had been buried. The disappearance of the three nonetheless focused national attention on white terrorism. During the summer, approximately thirty homes and thirty-seven churches were bombed, thirty-five civil rights workers were shot at, eighty people were beaten, six were murdered, and more than one thousand were arrested. In the face of this violence, uncertainty, and fear, many SNCC activists rejected Martin Luther King's commitment to nonviolence, the inclusion of white activists in the movement, and the wisdom of integration. Divisions over these issues greatly increased tensions among the groups that made up the movement.

Despite the problems it encountered, the Freedom Summer organized dozens of Freedom Schools and community centers throughout Mississippi. Its efforts mobilized the state's black people to an extent not seen since the first Reconstruction. Many communities began to develop the rudiments of a political movement, one that would grow in coming years.

THE MISSISSIPPI FREEDOM DEMOCRATIC PARTY

Freedom Summer intersected with national politics at the Democratic Party's national convention in August

1964 in Atlantic City, New Jersey. White Mississippians routinely excluded African Americans from the political process, and Robert Moses encouraged COFO to set up the **Mississippi Freedom Democratic Party (MFDP)** to challenge the state's regular Democratic delegation at the convention. Under the leadership of veteran activists Fannie Lou Hamer, Victoria Gray, Annie Divine, and Aaron Henry, the MFDP held its first state convention on August 6. Approximately eighty thousand citizens put their names on the rolls. The convention elected sixty-four delegates who traveled to the national convention to present their credentials.

The MFDP challenge caused considerable difficulty for the Democratic Party. Many liberals wanted to seat the civil rights delegation, but President Lyndon Johnson, who was running for reelection, did not want to alienate white southerners, fearing they would vote for Barry Goldwater, his Republican opponent. Liberal Democratic senator Hubert H. Humphrey, from Minnesota, worked out a compromise calling for Mississippi regulars to be seated if they swore loyalty to the national party and agreed to cast their forty-four votes accordingly. The compromise also provided for the creation of two "at-large" seats to be filled by MFDP members Aaron Henry and Ed King. The rest of the Freedom Democrats could attend the convention as nonvoting guests.

Martin Luther King Jr., Bayard Rustin, and other black leaders counseled acceptance of this compromise. Johnson and the Democrats, they argued, had achieved much of the legislative program favored by the movement, and if the party were returned to power they could do much more. But most of the MFDP delegation, fed up with the violence of Mississippi and unwilling to settle for token representation, rejected the compromise. Many members of the SNCC, bitter and angry, turned their backs on liberalism and cooperation with white people of any political persuasion.

SELMA AND THE VOTING RIGHTS ACT OF 1965

The Civil Rights Act of 1964 contained provisions for helping black voters to register, but white resistance in the deep South had rendered them ineffective. In Alabama, for example, at least 77 percent of black citizens were unable to vote. Their cause was taken up by businesswoman Amelia P. Boynton, owner of an employment and insurance agency in Selma, along with her husband and a high school teacher, the Reverend Frederick Reese, who also led the Dallas County Voters League. These three, with others, fought for black enfranchisement and an end to discriminatory treatment. Their struggle would help pass the Voting Rights Act of 1965, which finally ended the systematic exclusion of African Americans from southern politics.

VIOLENCE AND THE CIVIL RIGHTS MOVEMENT

APRIL 7, 1964	Reverend Bruce Klunder killed protesting construction of segregated school, Cleveland, Ohio
MAY 2, 1964	Henry Hezekiah Dee and Charles Eddie Moore killed by Klan, Meadville, Mississippi
JUNE 21, 1964	Civil rights workers James Chaney, Andrew Goodman, and Michael Schwerner abducted and slain by Klan, Philadelphia, Mississippi
JULY 11, 1964	Lt. Col. Lemuel Penn killed by Klan while driving north, Colbert, Georgia
FEBRUARY 26, 1965	Jimmie Lee Jackson, civil rights marcher, killed by state trooper, Marion, Alabama
MARCH 11, 1965	Selma to Montgomery march volunteer, Reverend James Reeb, beaten to death, Selma, Alabama
MARCH 25, 1965	Viola Gregg Liuzzo killed by Klan while transporting marchers, Selma Highway, Alabama
JUNE 2, 1965	Oneal Moore, black deputy, killed by night riders, Varnado, Louisiana
JULY 18, 1965	Willie Wallace Brewster killed by night riders, Anniston, Alabama
AUGUST 20, 1965	Jonathan Daniels, seminary student, killed by deputy, Hayneville, Alabama
JANUARY 3, 1966	Samuel Younge Jr., student civil rights activist, killed in dispute over whites-only restroom, Tuskegee, Alabama
JANUARY 10, 1966	Vernon Dahmer, black community leader, killed in Klan bombing, Hattiesburg, Mississippi
JUNE 10, 1966	Ben Chester White killed by Klan, Natchez, Mississippi
JULY 30, 1966	Clarence Triggs slain by night riders, Bogalusa, Louisiana
FEBRUARY 2, 1967	Wharlest Jackson, civil rights leader, killed when police fire on protesters, Jackson, Mississippi
FEBRUARY 8, 1968	Students Samuel Hammond Jr., Delano Middleton, and Henry Smith killed when highway patrolmen fire on protesters, Orangeburg, South Carolina
APRIL 4, 1968	Dr. Martin Luther King Jr. assassinated, Memphis, Tennessee

1955–1968

Selma's sheriff James G. Clark worked to block the voter registration activity sponsored by the Boyntons, Reese, and SNCC suffrage workers. By 1964 fewer than 400 of the 15,000 eligible African Americans had registered to vote in Dallas County. President Lyndon Johnson refused requests to deploy federal marshals to the county to protect voter registration workers. Seeking reinforcements, the workers sent a call to Martin Luther King Jr. and the SCLC. King came and was promptly arrested. In mid-February 1965, during a night march in neighboring Perry County, twenty-six-year-old Jimmie Lee Jackson was shot in the stomach as he tried to shield his mother from a beating by a state trooper. His death and the thrashing of several reporters attracted the national media.

PROFILE ∼ FANNIE LOU HAMER (1917–1977)

Fannie Lou Hamer (1917–1977) emerged from the ranks of "local people" in Mississippi to become one of the most powerful leaders and orators of the civil rights movement. Unlike many major leaders, Hamer, the youngest of twenty children, had grown up in extreme poverty and had only a few years of education. She worked and lived as a timekeeper on a plantation in Ruleville, Mississippi. When SNCC workers came to the community for a voting rights campaign, Hamer was one of the first to participate. Despite the great danger of doing so, Hamer supported the civil rights workers because, as she said,

> Nobody ever came out into the country and talked to real farmers and things because this is the next thing this country has done: it divided us into classes, and if you hadn't arrived at a certain level, you wasn't treated no better by blacks than you was by the whites. And it was these kids who broke a lot of that down. They treated us like we were special and we loved 'em. . . . We didn't feel uneasy about our language might not be right or something. We just felt we could talk to 'em. We trusted 'em.

On August 1, 1962, Hamer attempted to register to vote in Indianola, Mississippi. In response, she was fired from her plantation job and evicted from her land. Still, she refused to capitulate and accepted full-time employment as a field secretary for the SNCC, where she worked on the Voter Education Project. This aroused even more police hostility. On June 9, 1963, she and eight other women on their way back from a workshop in South Carolina were arrested by the police in Winona, Mississippi. Hamer was beaten and never fully recovered from the injuries she suffered.

Despite her lack of education, Hamer was a spellbinding orator who had the ability to move not only her friends and neighbors, but the nation as well. Her televised testimony before the 1964 Democratic convention won national support for the MFDP's challenge to the party regulars from Mississippi. The next year Hamer, who had run for the House of Representatives, challenged the seating of the Mississippi congressional delegation. Although unsuccessful, her action helped to reduce tolerance for disfranchisement and paved the way for the Voting Rights Act of 1965.

After 1965, Hamer continued to fight for her people. Although basic civil and voting rights had been won by then, most black people in the Mississippi Delta still lived in deep poverty. In 1968 Hamer sought to address this problem by setting up the nonprofit Freedom Farms Corporation as an agricultural cooperative. With help from northern supporters, the enterprise had some success, but the problems it confronted proved overwhelming. The mixed results of this last campaign, however, cannot diminish the profound changes that Fannie Lou Hamer was so instrumental in bringing about. She died in 1977.

◀ Fannie Lou Hamer, in word and deeds, refused to compromise with racial injustice. This June 1966 photograph by Flip Schule captures Hamer, a tireless organizer, speaking at an evening rally held at Tugaloo College in Mississippi on the last day of the March Against Fear.

Hamer

The SCLC announced plans for a mass march from Selma to Montgomery, the state capital, to begin on Sunday, March 7, 1965. At the forefront of six hundred protesters were King; one of his aides, Hosea Williams; and the chairman of the SNCC, John Lewis. As the marchers approached the Edmund Pettus Bridge, state troopers and Sheriff Clark's county police, in a shocking display of aggression, tear-gassed and beat the retreating marchers while their horses trampled the fallen. Captured in graphic detail by television cameras, this battle became known as "Bloody Sunday." Seizing the moment, King and the activists rescheduled a pilgrimage for March 9. The SCLC leader soon found himself in a dilemma. A federal judge, who was normally supportive of civil rights, had issued an injunction against the march. Moreover, President Johnson and many other key figures in the government urged King not to go through with it. King was reluctant to violate a federal injunction, and he knew he needed Johnson's support to win strong voting rights legislation. But the people of Selma and the hundreds of young SNCC workers would probably march even if King did not.

When the day of the march came, 1,500 protesters marched to the bridge singing "Ain't Gonna Let Nobody Turn Me 'Round" and other freedom songs. To their surprise, King crossed the Pettus Bridge, prayed briefly, and turned around. He had privately made a face-saving compromise with the federal authorities. SNCC workers felt betrayed, and King's leadership suffered. That evening a white Unitarian minister from Boston, James Reeb, was clubbed to death by local white people. His martyrdom created a national outcry and prompted Johnson to act. On March 15 the president, in a televised address to Congress, announced he would submit voter registration legislation. In his address he praised civil rights activists, electrifying them when he invoked the movement's slogan to declare, in his Texas drawl, "We shall overcome."

The protests at Selma and the massive white resistance spurred Congress to pass the **Voting Rights Act of 1965**, which President Johnson signed on August 6. The act outlawed educational requirements for voting in states or counties where less than half the voting age population had been registered on November 1, 1964, or had voted in the 1964 presidential election. It also empowered the attorney general to have the Civil Rights Commission assign federal registrars to enroll voters. The attorney general, Nicholas Katzenbach, immediately deployed federal registrars in nine southern counties. Within months, they had registered approximately 80,000 new voters.

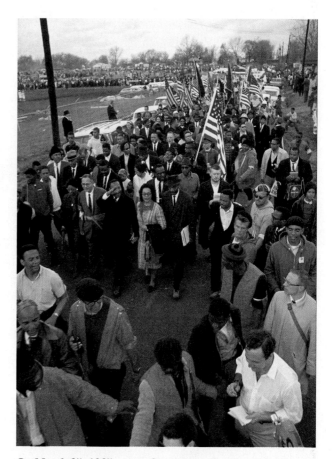

On March 25, 1965, more than two weeks after "Bloody Sunday," when police brutalized civil rights marchers trying to cross Selma's Edmund Pettus Bridge, a second march finally completed the fifty-three-mile trek to Montgomery. Among the leaders are Martin Luther King Jr., Coretta Scott King, Hosea Williams, Bayard Rustin, and Ralph Bunche. The violence preceding this successful march convinced President Johnson, proclaiming "We shall overcome," to submit voting rights legislation to Congress.

In Mississippi, black registrants soared from 28,500 in 1964 to 251,000 in 1968 (see Map 21–1).

Gaining voting rights made a tremendous difference. Before passage of the act, Fannie Lou Hamer had unsuccessfully challenged the seating of the regular Mississippi representatives before the U.S. House of Representatives. In 1968 she was selected as a delegate to the Democratic Party convention. To be sure, southern state legislators resisted the act. They instituted a dazzling array of disfranchisement devices such as gerrymandering, at-large elections, more appointive offices, and higher qualifications for candidates. But the era when white supremacy lay at the core of southern politics was over.

Voting Rights in Mississippi, 1962–1964 21-7 DOCUMENT

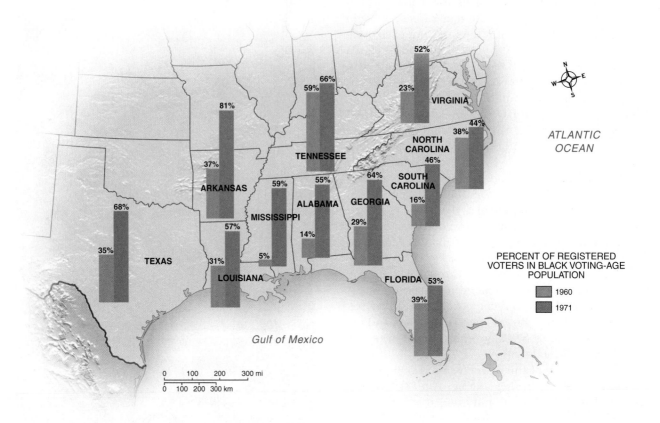

MAP 21–1   THE EFFECT OF THE VOTING RIGHTS ACT OF 1965

The Voting Rights Act enabled millions of previously disfranchised African Americans in the South to vote.

▶▶ *Why was gaining the right to vote so important for southern African Americans?*

CONCLUSION

The two *Brown* decisions ended the legal underpinning of segregation and discrimination and set in motion events that would irrevocably transform the political and social status of African Americans. White southerners resisted the changes unleashed by *Brown*, and as their massive resistance gained momentum, violence against African Americans and their allies exploded. Still, the civil rights movement achieved major successes that depended on many factors. The federal government intervened at crucial moments to enact historic civil rights legislation, issue judgments on behalf of the civil rights protesters, and protect the rule of law with federal marshals and soldiers. Black leaders deliberately pursued strategies to provoke confrontations that would ensure intervention by the federal government and garner widespread media coverage.

For more than a decade, the victorious freedom fighters of the civil rights movement stormed the legal barricades of segregation. The uncompromising struggle of African Americans, their organizations, and their white allies pressured federal officials in the legislative, executive, and judicial branches of government to enact major civil rights legislation, issue executive orders, and deliver judicial decisions that dismantled segregation in the South.

The victories of this era were far reaching, but as they were achieved, new issues arose that would fracture the movement. The civil rights movement had largely been focused on the South. Black northerners already had many of the rights granted by the federal legislation of the era; nonetheless, they still suffered from many forms of discrimination. Addressing their problems required different techniques and new ways of thinking that would emerge over the coming decade.

RECOMMENDED READING

Taylor Branch. *Parting the Waters: America in the King Years, 1954–63.* New York: Simon & Schuster, 1988. Richly researched, lively study that places King at the center of American politics during a critically transformative decade.

Clayborne Carson. *In Struggle: SNCC and the Black Awakening of the 1960s.* Cambridge, MA: Harvard University Press, 1981. One of the best historical studies of the SNCC and the contributions students made to galvanize the civil rights movement.

Vickie Crawford, Jacqueline Rouse, and Barbara Woods, eds. *Women in the Civil Rights Movement: Trailblazers and Torchbearers.* Brooklyn, NY: Carlson Publishing, 1990. An anthology of essays presented at a symposium. The meeting was designed to draw attention to the women whose contributions to the freedom struggle of the 1950s and 1960s are often overlooked or neglected.

Henry Hampton and Steve Fayer, eds. *The Voices of Freedom: An Oral History of the Civil Rights Movement from the 1950s through the 1980s.* New York: Bantam Books, 1990. A remarkable and indispensable oral history of all the participants in the civil rights movement, from the least well known to the internationally celebrated.

Richard Kluger. *Simple Justice: The History of "Brown v. Board of Education" and Black America's Struggle for Equality.* New York: Knopf, 1976; new ed., 2004. An excellent treatment of the historical events leading up to *Brown* and the local individuals whose lives were forever changed because of their resistance to Jim Crow segregation. The new edition includes an illuminating assessment of the fifty years since *Brown*.

Steven F. Lawson. *Running for Freedom: Civil Rights and Black Politics in America since 1941.* Philadelphia: Temple University Press, 1991. A succinct analysis of the politics, legislative measures, and individuals that figured in the successes and failures of the civil rights movement.

Aldon D. Morris. *The Origins of the Modern Civil Rights Movement: Black Communities Organizing for Change.* New York: Free Press, 1984. An important and insightful analysis of the mobilization and organizing strategies pursued by diverse communities for social change that paved the way for the modern civil rights movement.

ADDITIONAL BIBLIOGRAPHY

GENERAL OVERVIEWS OF CIVIL RIGHTS MOVEMENT AND ORGANIZATIONS

Robert Fredrick Burk. *The Eisenhower Administration and Black Civil Rights.* Knoxville: University of Tennessee Press, 1984.

Stewart Burns. *Daybreak of Freedom: The Montgomery Bus Boycott.* Chapel Hill: University of North Carolina Press, 1997.

John Dittmer. *Local People: The Struggle for Civil Rights in Mississippi.* Urbana: University of Illinois Press, 1994.

Adam Fairclough. *To Redeem the Soul of America: The Southern Christian Leadership Conference and Martin Luther King, Jr.* Athens: University of Georgia Press, 1987.

David R. Goldfield. *Black, White and Southern: Race Relations and the Southern Culture, 1940 to the Present.* Baton Rouge: Louisiana State University Press, 1991.

Martin Luther King Jr. *Stride Towards Freedom: The Montgomery Story.* New York: Harper, 1958.

Michael J. Klarman. *From Jim Crow to Civil Rights: The Supreme Court and the Struggle for Racial Equality.* New York: Oxford University Press, 2003.

Steven F. Lawson. *Black Ballots: Voting Rights in the South, 1944–1969.* New York: Columbia University Press, 1976.

Nancy MacLean, *Freedom Is Not Enough: The Opening of the American Workplace.* Cambridge; Harvard University Press, 2006.

Manning Marable. *Race, Reform, and Rebellion: The Second Reconstruction in Black America, 1945–1982.* Jackson: University Press of Mississippi, 1984.

August Meier and Elliot Rudwick. *CORE: A Study of the Civil Rights Movement, 1942–1968.* New York: Oxford University Press, 1973.

Anne Moody. *Coming of Age in Mississippi.* New York: Dial Press, 1968.

Donald G. Nieman. *Promises to Keep: African-Americans and the Constitutional Order, 1776 to the Present.* New York: Oxford University Press, 1991.

Robert J. Norrell. *Reaping the Whirlwind: The Civil Rights Movement in Tuskegee.* New York: Alfred A. Knopf, 1985.

James T. Patterson. *Brown v. Board of Education: A Civil Rights Milestone and Its Troubled Legacy.* New York: Oxford University Press, 2000.

Charles M. Payne. *I've Got the Light of Freedom: The Organizing Tradition and the Mississippi Freedom Struggle.* Berkeley: University of California Press, 1995.

Fred Powledge. *Free at Last? The Civil Rights Movement and the People Who Made It.* Boston: Little, Brown, 1991.

Howell Raines. *My Soul Is Rested: Movement Days in the Deep South Remembered.* New York: Putnam, 1977.

Belinda Robnett. *How Long? How Long? African-American Women in the Struggle for Civil Rights.* New York: Oxford University Press, 1997.

Juan Williams. *Eyes on the Prize: America's Civil Rights Years, 1954–1965.* New York: Viking, 1987.

BLACK POLITICS/WHITE RESISTANCE

Numan V. Bartley. *The Rise of Massive Resistance: Race and Politics in the South during the 1950's.* Baton Rouge: Louisiana State University Press, 1969.

Darlene Clark Hine. *Black Victory: The Rise and Fall of the White Primary in Texas.* Columbia: University of Missouri Press, 2nd ed., 2003.

AFRICAN-AMERICAN EVENTS | NATIONAL EVENTS

• 1954 •

May 17
Supreme Court's *Brown v. Board of Education* decision declares separate but equal education unconstitutional

May 21
Jo Ann Robinson of the Women's Political Council in Montgomery writes to Mayor W. A. Gayle, warning of a possible bus boycott

July 11
First White Citizens Council in Mississippi

• 1955 •

Supreme Court's *Brown II* decision calls for school districts to desegregate immediately or "with all deliberate speed"

The Interstate Commerce Commission outlaws segregated buses and waiting rooms for interstate passengers

August 28
Emmett Till is lynched

December 1
Rosa Parks is arrested for refusing to give up her seat on a Montgomery, Alabama, city bus, beginning Montgomery Bus Boycott

The American Federation of Labor and Congress of Industrial Organizations merge to form the AFL-CIO

• 1956 •

Segregationists in Congress issue the "Southern Manifesto"

November 13
The Supreme Court, in *Gayle v. Browder*, bars segregation in intrastate travel

November
President Dwight D. Eisenhower wins second term as president

• 1957 •

May
Congress passes the Civil Rights Act of 1957, the first in eighty-seven years

September 24
President Eisenhower enforces integration of Little Rock's Central High School with federal troops

Elizabeth Jacoway and David R. Colburn. *Southern Business-men and Desegregation*. Baton Rouge: Louisiana State University Press, 1982.

Doug McAdam. *Freedom Summer*. New York: Oxford University Press, 1988.

Neil R. McMillen. *The Citizen's Council: A History of Organized Resistance to the Second Reconstruction*. Urbana: University of Illinois Press, 1971.

Frank R. Parker. *Black Votes Count: Political Empowerment in Mississippi after 1965*. Chapel Hill: University of North Carolina Press, 1990.

AUTOBIOGRAPHY AND BIOGRAPHY

Daisy Bates. *The Long Shadow of Little Rock: Memoir*. New York: David McKay Co., 1962.

Taylor Branch. *Pillar of Fire: America in the King Years, 1963–65*. New York: Simon & Schuster, 1998.

Eric R. Burner. *And Gently He Shall Lead Them: Robert Parris Moses and Civil Rights in Mississippi*. New York: New York University Press, 1994.

Septima Clark. *Ready from Within: Septima Clark and the Civil Rights Movement*. Navarro, CA: Wild Tree Press, 1986.

Robert S. Dallek. *Flawed Giant: Lyndon Johnson and His Times, 1961–1973*. New York: Oxford University Press, 1998.

Dennis C. Dickerson. *Militant Mediator: Whitney M. Young, Jr., 1921–1971*. Lexington: University Press of Kentucky, 1998.

James Farmer. *Lay Bare the Heart: An Autobiography of the Civil Rights Movement*. New York: Arbor House, 1985.

Cynthia Griggs Fleming. *Soon We Will Not Cry: The Liberation of Ruby Doris Smith Robinson*. Lanham, MD: Rowman & Littlefield, 1998.

David J. Garrow. *Bearing the Cross: Martin Luther King, Jr., and the Southern Christian Leadership Conference*. New York: William Morrow & Company, 1986.

———. *The FBI and Martin Luther King, Jr.* New York: Penguin Books, 1981.

Chana Kai Lee. *For Freedom's Sake: The Life of Fannie Lou Hamer*. Urbana: University of Illinois Press, 1999.

David Levering Lewis. *King: A Critical Biography*. New York: Praeger, 1970.

Genna Rae McNeil. *Groundwork: Charles Hamilton Houston and the Struggle for Civil Rights*. Philadelphia: University of Pennsylvania Press, 1983.

Barbara Ransby. *Ella Baker and the Black Freedom Movement*. Chapel Hill: University of North Carolina Press, 2003.

Jo Ann Gibson Robinson, with David Garrow. *The Montgomery Bus Boycott and the Women Who Started It*. Knoxville: University of Tennessee Press, 1987.

Mark V. Tushnet. *Making Civil Rights Law: Thurgood Marshall and the Supreme Court, 1936–1961*. New York: Oxford University Press, 1994.

Timothy B. Tyson. *Radio Free Dixie: Robert F. Williams and the Roots of Black Power.* Chapel Hill: University of North Carolina Press, 1999.

Juan Williams. *Thurgood Marshall: American Revolutionary.* New York: Times Books, 1998.

REFERENCE WORKS

Charles Eagles, ed. *The Civil Rights Movement in America.* Jackson: University Press of Mississippi, 1986.

Charles S. Lowery and John F. Marszalek, eds. *Encyclopedia of African-American Civil Rights: From Emancipation to the Present.* New York: Greenwood Press, 1992.

TRACING THE ODYSSEY

CIVIL RIGHTS MOVEMENT MUSEUMS

Brown v. Board of Education **National Historic Landmark**, Topeka, Kansas. The Sumner and Monroe Elementary Schools composed the *Brown v. Board of Education* National Historic Landmark. The 1954 *Brown v. Topeka Board of Education* decision written by U.S. Supreme Court Chief Justice Earl Warren removed the legal foundation on which the entire system of racial segregation and discrimination in the South was based and reaffirmed the ideal of the equal protection under the law clause in the Fourteenth Amendment to the U.S. Constitution. The *Brown* decision struck down the 1896 *Plessy v. Ferguson* doctrine of "separate but equal." *Brown* was the culmination of a long struggle waged by the NAACP's team of lawyers headed by Thurgood Marshall and dozens of ordinary citizens in local communities.

Birmingham Civil Rights Institute. Exhibits depict the history of the black freedom struggle. The museum chronicles the dramatic and often violent activities that occurred in Birmingham, Alabama, during the 1960s as black protest confronted massive white resistance.

The Lincoln Memorial, Washington, D.C. The Lincoln Memorial was built to celebrate President Abraham Lincoln and the Civil War (1861–1865) to preserve the Union. It possesses a particular relevance and meaning to African Americans. The Lincoln Memorial was the site of the August 1963 March on Washington during which Martin Luther King delivered his powerful "I Have a Dream" speech.

The Vietnam Veterans Memorial, Washington, D.C. The memorial contains all of the names of Americans who lost their lives in the Vietnam War.

The Martin Luther King Jr. Center for Nonviolent Social Change in Atlanta, Georgia. Founded by Coretta Scott King in 1968 as a living memorial dedicated to the preservation and advancement of the work of her husband, the Martin Luther King Jr. Center for Nonviolent Social Change features exhibits that detail the life and legacy of Martin

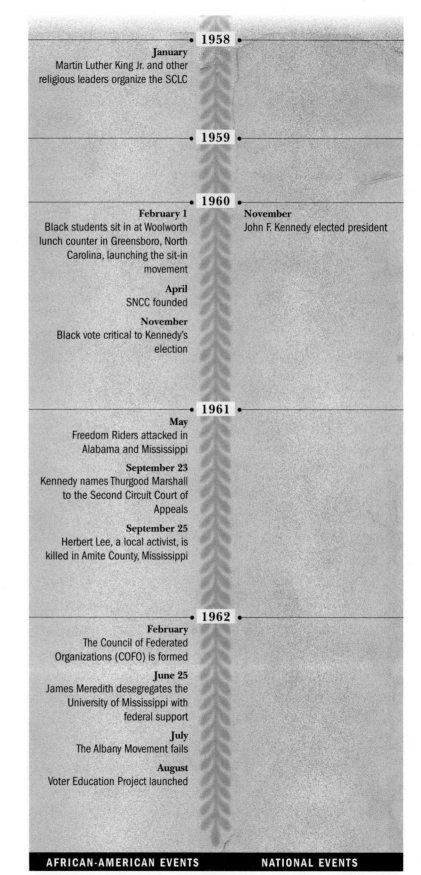

1958

January
Martin Luther King Jr. and other religious leaders organize the SCLC

1959

1960

February 1
Black students sit in at Woolworth lunch counter in Greensboro, North Carolina, launching the sit-in movement

April
SNCC founded

November
Black vote critical to Kennedy's election

November
John F. Kennedy elected president

1961

May
Freedom Riders attacked in Alabama and Mississippi

September 23
Kennedy names Thurgood Marshall to the Second Circuit Court of Appeals

September 25
Herbert Lee, a local activist, is killed in Amite County, Mississippi

1962

February
The Council of Federated Organizations (COFO) is formed

June 25
James Meredith desegregates the University of Mississippi with federal support

July
The Albany Movement fails

August
Voter Education Project launched

AFRICAN-AMERICAN EVENTS   NATIONAL EVENTS

AFRICAN-AMERICAN EVENTS	NATIONAL EVENTS
1963	
April–May Project C highlights racial injustices in Birmingham; King writes his celebrated "Letter from Birmingham Jail"	**November 22** President Kennedy is assassinated Lyndon Johnson succeeds to the presidency
June Federal government compels Alabama governor George C. Wallace to desegregate the University of Alabama	
June 12 Medgar Evers is murdered	
August 17 W. E. B. Du Bois dies in Ghana, Africa, at age ninety-five	
August 28 The March on Washington; Martin Luther King Jr. delivers his "I Have a Dream" speech	
September 15 Ku Klux Klan bombs the 16th Street Baptist Church in Birmingham, Alabama, killing four girls	
December Malcolm X breaks with Elijah Muhammad and the Nation of Islam and founds his own movement, Muslim Mosque	

Luther King Jr. It contains a unique exhibit of his personal memorabilia. The King Library and Archives contains the world's largest existing collection of civil rights materials.

myhistorylab REVIEW, RESEARCH, AND INTERACT

REVIEW QUESTIONS

1. What role did "ordinary" or local people play in the civil rights movement? How did children contribute to the overall struggle for social change?

2. What key issues and events led the federal government to intervene in the civil rights movement? What were the major pieces of legislation enacted, and how did they dismantle legalized segregation?

3. What were the ideologies, objectives, and tactics of the major civil rights organizations and their leaders?

4. What were the human costs of the civil rights movement? Who were some of the people who lost their lives in the struggle?

5. What were the major successes and failures of the freedom movement? What intergenerational tensions plagued the movement? How did the movement transform American politics and society?

Research Navigator.com
RESOURCES FOR COLLEGE RESEARCH ASSIGNMENTS   **www.researchnavigator.com**

Using the tools available in Research Navigator, consider this question:

Compare and contrast nineteenth-century Reconstruction with the "Second Reconstruction" of the mid-twentieth century. Why did the Second Reconstruction have more lasting effects?

INTERACTIVE ACTIVITY

The Civil Rights Movement

A close look at the ideas, events, and people involved in the struggle to end discrimination based on race.

1964

AFRICAN-AMERICAN EVENTS

SNCC launches the Mississippi Freedom Summer Project to promote voter registration

January
Twenty-fourth Amendment to the U.S. Constitution is ratified, outlawing the poll tax

June 21
James E. Chaney, Michael Schwerner, and Andrew Goodman murdered in Mississippi

July 2
Civil Rights Act of 1964 enacted

August
The Mississippi Freedom Democratic Party denied seating at the Democratic National Convention

December
Martin Luther King Jr. wins the Nobel Peace Prize

NATIONAL EVENTS

Equal Employment Opportunity Commission established

1965

March 21
Civil rights marchers walk from Selma to Montgomery after violent confrontation in Selma

August 6
Voting Rights Act of 1965 enacted

Lyndon Johnson outlines the Great Society Program to attack poverty

AFRICAN-AMERICAN EVENTS   **NATIONAL EVENTS**

22

The Struggle Continues, 1965–1980

WHY DID MANY AFRICAN AMERICANS BECOME MORE MILITANT DURING THE 1960s?

WHAT WERE THE CAUSES OF THE URBAN RIOTS OF THE LATE 1960s?

HOW DID THE VIETNAM WAR AFFECT THE GREAT SOCIETY AND AFRICAN AMERICANS?

HOW DID THE BLACK POWER MOVEMENT STIMULATE BLACK CULTURE?

WHAT WERE THE CONTRADICTIONS IN PRESIDENT NIXON'S POLICIES TOWARD AFRICAN AMERICANS AND CIVIL RIGHTS?

WHAT POLITICAL GAINS DID BLACK AMERICANS MAKE DURING THE 1970s?

◄ The raised arm with clinched fist symbolizes both Black solidarity and the major shift from the passive resistance of the Civil Rights Movement to the militant consciousness of the Black Power Movement generation.   Courtesy of the Library of Congress

We must work on two levels. In every city we have a dual society. . . . In every city, we have two economies. In every city, we have two housing markets. In every city, we have two school systems. This duality has brought about a great deal of injustice. . . . Black Power in the positive sense is a psychological call to manhood . . . and a sense of dignity. . . . Black Power is pooling black political resources in order to achieve our legitimate goals. . . . Black Power in its positive sense is a pooling of black economic resources in order to achieve legitimate power. . . . What is necessary now is to see integration in political terms. . . . [T]here are times when we must see segregation as a temporary way-station to the ultimate goal which we seek . . . a truly integrated society where there is shared power.

—Martin Luther King Jr.

Black Power . . . a call for black people in this country to unite, to recognize their heritage, to build a sense of community . . . to define their own goals, to lead their own organizations . . . to reject the racist institutions and values of this society. The concept of Black Power rests on a fundamental premise: *Before a group can enter the open society, it must first close ranks.* [emphasis in the original]

—Stokely Carmichael and Charles V. Hamilton

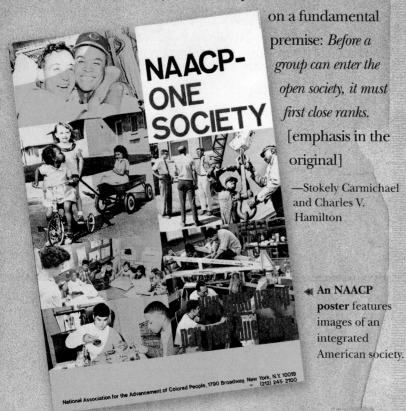

◄ **An NAACP poster** features images of an integrated American society.

When Lyndon Johnson became president in 1963 after John F. Kennedy's assassination, he brought to the office impressive political skills and a determination to reconcile the racial, social, and economic disparities dividing black from white Americans. Johnson's escalation of America's involvement in Vietnam, however, undermined his domestic social policies. Meanwhile, some African Americans lost faith in and patience with American society. In the face of a white backlash against the gains of the civil rights movement, many leaders and scholars—such as Stokely Carmichael and Charles Hamilton—argued for black power and black separatism. Black power, which challenged both the interracialism of the civil rights movement and Johnson's democratic liberalism, became the dominant ideology for many younger activists. King remained ambivalent about black power, preferring to define it as a temporary strategy for black solidarity in the struggle for an integrated society. A. Philip Randolph called black power a "menace to peace and prosperity" and added, "No Negro who is fighting for civil rights can support black power, which is opposed to civil rights and integration." These opposing ideologies represent a generational shift, and the tensions between them frame many of the key events of the post–civil rights movement years.

The Fading Dream of Racial Integration: White Backlash and Black Nationalism

Even though President Johnson easily defeated Republican senator Barry Goldwater, the 1964 election was hardly a mandate for civil rights. In California, for example, voters gave Johnson a decisive victory but also approved an amendment to the state constitution that not only repealed all existing legislation prohibiting discrimination in the sale or rental of housing, but prevented such legislation from ever being enacted in the future. Although the amendment was later struck down by the Supreme Court, its passage suggested that white opposition to racial integration was not confined to the South. When, in 1966, Johnson asked Congress for federal legislation to ban discrimination in housing, a weakened version of his bill died in the Senate. In elections that year, white opposition to civil rights helped elect Republicans, including former movie actor Ronald Reagan as governor of California.

Meanwhile, Alabama governor George Wallace, an outspoken opponent of racial integration and civil rights legislation, was emerging as a national political figure. With limited resources, he had run surprisingly well against Johnson in the 1964 Wisconsin, Indiana, and Maryland Democratic primaries. Heartened by the favorable response he received from northern white voters, Wallace was planning a full-scale presidential race in 1968.

With many white Americans increasingly reluctant to support the goals of the civil rights movement, many black Americans began searching for new approaches to their problems. The reign of terror experienced by COFO (Council of Federated Organizations) workers in Mississippi had undermined the commitment to integration and nonviolence of the civil rights movement and would help radicalize a new, younger generation of activists. Men like Floyd McKissick of the Congress of Racial Equality (CORE) and Stokely Carmichael of the Student Nonviolent Coordinating Committee (SNCC) became disillusioned, rejecting King's moderation, nonviolence, and universalism. The differences between King's SCLC (Southern Christian Leadership Conference) and Carmichael's SNCC grew with each confrontation. Carmichael had argued after the 1964 failure of the Mississippi Freedom Democratic Party that it was time to form an independent black political party. In 1965, after the Selma-to-Montgomery march, he helped found the Lowndes County (Mississippi) Freedom Organization (LCFO). It became the first political organization in the civil rights movement to adopt the symbol of the black panther.

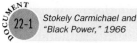

DOCUMENT 22-1 Stokely Carmichael and "Black Power," 1966

Black residents of northern and western cities also lost patience with the slow pace of change. Increasing numbers of young black churchmen castigated mainstream white religious groups for their complicity with racism, demanded reparations, and agitated for substantive power or leadership roles within the governing structures of the National Council of Churches. Out of the interracial conflict and tension emerged a black theology that critiqued racism within white religious groups, and it was followed by a black feminist theology that offered searing critiques of sexism within the black church. Leaders in the development of black theology and the expression of a black nationalist Christianity were theologians James H. Cone, author of *Black Theology and Black Power* (1969), and the Reverend Albert Cleage Jr. of Detroit, who was pastor of the Shrine of the Black Madonna and a passionate advocate of black liberation theology as defined in his books, *Black Christian Nationalism* and *The Black Messiah*. In ways reminiscent of Marcus Garvey, black Christian nationalism argued for black symbols of religious faith. Jesus Christ was, as Reverend Cleage expounded, a black messiah. Black liberation theology asserted the importance of conjoining religious practice and faith with political activism and social change. Growing numbers of young African Americans, along with diverse black religious leaders, dismayed by the great political and economic disparities between themselves and white Americans, became catalysts for an increasingly radical turn in the civil rights movement.

MALCOLM X

After 1965, the year in which he died, no one had more influence on young black activists and the residents of America's ghettoized inner cities than Malcolm X. The son of a Baptist preacher, he was born Malcolm Little in Omaha, Nebraska, and grew up in Lansing, Michigan. His family's home was burned by Klan terrorists, and his father was murdered two years later. His mother was subsequently committed to a mental institution, and welfare agencies separated the children. Malcolm was sent to a juvenile detention home, quit school after the eighth grade, and moved to Boston to live with his sister. There he became involved in the street life of gambling, drugs, and burglary. He was arrested and sentenced to a ten-year prison term in 1946. During the six and a half years he spent in prison, he embraced the teachings of Elijah Muhammad of the Nation of Islam and renounced what he considered his "slave name" to become Malcolm X. In 1954 he became minister of Harlem's Temple Number 7. Articulate, charismatic, and forceful, Malcolm did not believe in nonviolence or advocate integration. His was the voice of the northern urban "second ghettoes." In 1961 he began publishing *Muhammad Speaks*, the official newspaper of the Nation. In *The Autobiography of Malcolm X*, published in 1965 by the writer Alex Haley of *Roots* fame, Malcolm declared,

> Few white people realize that many black people today dislike and avoid spending any more time than they must around white people. This "integration" image, as it is popularly interpreted, has millions of vain, self-exalted white people convinced that black people want to sleep in bed with them—and that's a lie! Oh you can't tell the average white man that the Negro man's prime

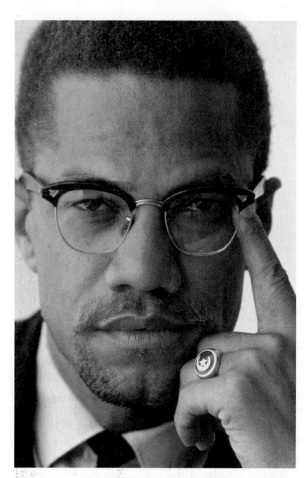

Malcolm X (1925–1965) was eloquent, passionate, and a courageously outspoken champion of black people and a critic of American racism. Today he is an iconic figure memorialized in poems, song, films, books, and operas.

desire isn't to have a white woman—another lie! Like a black brother recently observed to me, "Look, you ever smell one of them wet?"

Malcolm X attracted black people's attention. His dismissal of the goal of racial integration and King's message of redemption through brotherly love resonated with many younger civil rights workers disillusioned by white violence. "The day of nonviolent resistance is over," Malcolm insisted. And in 1964 he declared, "Revolutions are never based upon love-your-enemy, and pray-for-those-who-despitefully-use-you. And revolutions are never waged by singing 'We Shall Overcome.' Revolutions are based on bloodshed."

MALCOLM X'S NEW DEPARTURE

Malcolm X's popularity created tensions between himself and the leadership of the Nation of Islam. He grew disillusioned with Elijah Muhammad's aversion to polit-ical activism, and Elijah Muhammad grew jealous of Malcolm's success. When Malcolm described the Kennedy assassination as a case of "the chickens coming home to roost" (meaning Kennedy was a victim of the same kind of violence that afflicted black people), Elijah Muhammad suspended him. In 1964 Malcolm broke with the Nation of Islam and founded his own organization, the Muslim Mosque, Inc. That same year he went on a pilgrimage to Mecca that profoundly influenced him. He changed his name to El-Hajj Malik El-Shabazz, founded the Organization for Afro-American Unity (after the Organization of African Unity), repudiated the Nation of Islam doctrine that all white people are evil, and began lecturing on the connection between the civil rights struggle in the South and the struggle against colonialism in Africa. On February 14, 1965, assassins associated with the Nation of Islam killed Malcolm X as he addressed an audience in Harlem.

Malcolm's militant advocacy of self-defense, of "overturning systems" that deprive African Americans of basic human rights, helped radicalize other black leaders of the civil rights movement.

STOKELY CARMICHAEL AND BLACK POWER

In 1966 Stokely Carmichael, a native of Trinidad who had been raised in New York City and educated at Howard University, became chairman of the SNCC. By then he had given up on the ideal of interracial collaboration and was determined to move the SNCC toward black nationalism. He dismissed the SNCC's few white staffers, including Bob Zellner, who had been with the organization since its inception.

About this time, James Meredith began a one-man "March Against Fear" from Tennessee to Jackson, Mississippi, to encourage black southerners to register and vote. On this march, he was shot and wounded by white gunmen. In June 1966, after this incident, the SNCC and Carmichael joined with other organizations to complete the march. It was at this time that Carmichael popularized the slogan "Black Power" that was to become SNCC's rallying cry. "The only way we gonna stop them white men from whippin' us," he announced to a cheering crowd, "is to take over. We been saying freedom for six years and we ain't got nothin'. What we gonna start saying is **Black Power**." Carmichael was specific about what black power meant to black southerners:

In Lowndes County [Mississippi], for example, black power will mean that if a Negro is elected sheriff, he can end police brutality. If a black man is elected tax assessor, he can collect and channel funds for the building of better roads and schools serving black people—thus advancing the move from political power into the economic arena. . . . Politically, black power means what it has always meant to SNCC: the coming-together of black people to elect representatives and to force those representatives to speak to their needs. It does not mean merely putting black faces into office.

Critics accused advocates of black power of reverse racism, but Carmichael argued on the contrary that they were promoting positive self-identity, racial pride, and the development of independent political and economic power. There was another more disruptive side of the black freedom movement. All of the organizations suffered internal problems concerning gender roles, relations between white women and black men, and separatism versus integration. As the leaders became more disillusioned about the slow pace of social change, some questioned whether white people belonged in their organizations. In 1968 CORE followed the SNCC's example and ejected its white members, with a resulting loss of financial resources. For various reasons both organizations began to decline, and by the end of the 1960s, SNCC had virtually disappeared.

Martin Luther King had mixed feelings about the ideology of black power. He welcomed its promotion of black political and economic strength, psychological assertiveness, and cultural pride. But when black power degenerated into a mantra of taunts against white people, King denounced it as "a nihilistic philosophy born out of the conviction that the Negro can't win." King also objected to black power's "implicit and often explicit belief in black separatism" and the assertion of its proponents that "there can be a separate Black road to power and fulfillment."

In May 1967 Hubert G. Brown followed Carmichael as head of the SNCC. "H. Rap" Brown, as he became known, raised the militancy of the black power movement's rhetoric to a new level, calling white people "honkies" and the police "pigs." "Violence," he said, was "as American as apple pie." In August 1967 Brown told enthusiastic listeners in the black neighborhood of Cambridge, Maryland, that "black folks built America, and if America don't come around, we're going to burn America down." When a few hours later, a fire erupted in a dilapidated school in the heart of the city's black community, white firemen refused to fight it. Police charged Brown with inciting a riot and committing arson, but he posted bail and fled. Later he was arrested on other charges.

THE NATIONAL COUNCIL OF CHURCHES

Black and white leaders of mainstream religious organizations were transformed by black power. In 1946 the Federal Council of Churches, composed of Protestants, Catholics, and Jews, pledged to work for "a non-

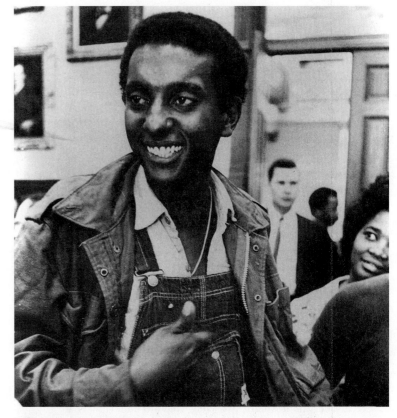

Stokely Carmichael (1941–1998) changed his name to Kwame Turé, a combination of the names of two major African leaders, Kwame Nkrumah and Ahmed Sekou Toure. After he settled in Guinea in 1969, he founded the All-African People's Revolutionary Party.

segregated church and a non-segregated society." Between 1963 and 1965, the National Council of Churches (NCC) contributed financial and moral support to the civil rights movement. In 1963 the NCC founded its Commission on Religion and Race to support the black freedom movement. Although a white-controlled and white-managed operation, three of the eight staff members of the commission were African American: Anna Hedgeman, J. Oscar Lee, and James Breeden. The NCC supported events such as the March on Washington and lobbied for passage of the Civil Rights Act of 1964 and the Voting Rights Act of 1965.

In 1965 the NCC appointed Benjamin Payton as director of the Commission on Religion and Race. Payton, a native of Orangeburg, South Carolina, had been educated at Harvard Divinity School and had earned a Ph.D. at Yale. Payton had taught at Howard University and he was a member of the National Baptist Convention, U.S.A., the largest African-American denomination. Under his stewardship the Commission on Religion and Race was incorporated into the Division of Christian Life and Mission and later became part of

THE BLACK PANTHER PARTY PLATFORM

Huey Newton and Bobby Seale's **Ten-Point Program** *reflects their determination to move from the pursuit of civil rights to a radical restructuring of American society along socialist lines, with work and rewards equally shared.*

October 1966

Black Panther Party, Platform and Program
What We Want, What We Believe

1. We want freedom. We want power to determine the destiny of our Black Community. . .

2. We want full employment for our people. . .

3. We want an end to the robbery of the capitalists of our Black Community. . .

4. We want decent housing fit for shelter of human beings. . .

5. We want education for our people that exposes the true nature of this decadent American society. We want education that teaches us our true history and our role in present-day society. . .

6. We want all Black men to be exempt from military service. . .

7. We want an immediate end to POLICE BRUTALITY and MURDER of Black people. . .

8. We want freedom for all Black men held in federal, state, county and city prisons and jails. . .

9. We want all Black people when brought to trial to be tried in court by a jury of their peer group or people from their Black communities, as defined by the Constitution of the United States. . .

10. We want land, bread, housing, education, clothing, justice, and peace. And as our major political objective, a United Nations supervised plebiscite to be held throughout the Black colony in which only Black colonial subjects will be allowed to participate, for the purpose of determining the will of Black people as to their national destiny.

🌲 *In what ways is the Panthers' Ten-Point Program similar to the Bill of Rights in the U. S. Constitution? How do they differ?*

🌲 *How did the Panthers propose to achieve black liberation? Why did they emphasize studying history? How did the Panthers' program conflict with that of the older civil rights organizations?*

Source: Clayborne Carson et al., eds., *The Eyes on the Prize Civil Rights Reader: Documents, Speeches, and Firsthand Accounts from the Black Freedom Struggle, 1954–1990* (New York: Viking Penguin, 1991), pp. 346–47.

the NCC's Department of Social Justice that included five other special task forces.

Payton had his own views about how organized religion could help address racial problems. He viewed the economic development of black people and their communities as the critical prerequisite to improving national racial relations. In his first address to the National Council, Payton emphasized the need for "a program of economic development to make civil rights real, in housing, employment, education and health care." In July 1966 he convened a small cadre of men that included Gayraud S. Wilmore, who served as the director of the United Presbyterian's Commission on Religion and Race. Out of this gathering emerged the National Commission of Black Churchmen (NCBC), which became a key mainstream ecumenical church group advocating black power concepts and strategies throughout the rest of the 1960s. In May 1967, however, the NCC's Department of Social Justice lost some of its momentum and direction when Payton left to become president of Benedict College, a black Baptist-affiliated college in Columbia, South Carolina.

The black power movement spurred the creation of black caucuses within the predominantly white churches. In February 1968 James Lawson headed the Black Methodists for Church Renewal, a caucus that crystallized within the United Methodist Church. In the same year, the United Presbyterian Church witnessed the formation of the Black Presbyterian United that replaced the Presbyterian Interracial Council. The Episcopal Society for Racial and Cultural Unity, an interracial group, was replaced by an Episcopal Union of Black Clergy and Laity. By the early 1970s, there were nine such caucuses. Within the Roman Catholic Church, black Catholics insisted that the church demonstrate more respect for African-American patterns of worship. All these black religious groups pressed for more black leadership within the denominations. Thus the stage was set for James Forman's **black manifesto**.

In April 1969 James Forman, a former Chicago schoolteacher renowned for his work with the SNCC, addressed the National Black Economic Development Conference in Detroit, sponsored by the Interreligious Foundation for Community Organizations (which was supported by predominantly white churches). Forman demanded that white churches pay $500 million in reparations for their participation in and benefit from American slavery and racial exploitation. His sharply secular critique of American religion precipitated the withdrawal of mainstream white religion groups from active participation in the civil rights movement. These white groups were offended by Forman's black power rhetoric and revolutionary Marxist ideology. Black and other minority groups wanted to share real power within the white-dominated churches. Relations between Blacks and Jews also deteriorated as countercharges circulated of "Jewish racism" and "black anti-Semitism."

The Black Panther Party

The most institutionalized expression of the new black militancy was the Black Panther Party for Self-Defense created by Huey P. Newton and Bobby Seale in Oakland, California, in October 1966. Newton and Seale took the name of the party from the black panther symbol of the Lowndes County Freedom Organization (LCFO). The Black Panthers combined black nationalist ideology with Marxist-Leninist doctrines. Working with white radicals, they hoped to fashion the party into a revolutionary vanguard dedicated to overthrowing capitalist society and ending police brutality. For a few months Stokely Carmichael, who had become estranged from SNCC, aligned himself with the Panthers and was named the party's prime minister. (However, Carmichael soon shifted his interest to Pan-Africanism. He moved to Africa and changed his name to Kwame Turé.) Eldridge Cleaver, the Panthers' minister of education, helped formulate the party's ideology. Cleaver was a convicted rapist who had spent most of his youth in prison, where he became a follower of Malcolm X and began writing the autobiographical essays that would be published as *Soul on Ice* in 1968, the year the party dropped "Self-Defense" from its name. Black people, Cleaver maintained, were victims of col-

onization, not just disfranchised American citizens. Thus integrationism could not meet their needs. They needed, instead, like other colonized peoples, to be liberated. "To achieve these ends," he wrote, "we believe that political and military machinery that does not exist now and has never existed must be created. We need functional machinery that is able to deal with these two interrelated sets of political dynamics which, strictly speaking, make up the total political situation on the North American continent." Cleaver and other top Panther leaders were arrested after a shoot-out with Oakland police in 1968. Cleaver escaped and fled into exile. While abroad, he abandoned his radicalism and became involved with the Republican Party and fundamentalist Christianity after his return to the United States in 1975.

POLICE REPRESSION AND THE FBI'S COINTELPRO

The Panthers, imposing in black leather jackets, berets, and "Afro" haircuts, alarmed white Americans when they took up arms for self-defense and patrolled their neighborhoods to monitor the police. A series of bloody confrontations and shoot-outs in Oakland distracted attention from the Panthers' broader political objectives and community service projects. In Oakland and Chicago, the Panthers arranged free breakfast and health-care programs, worked to instill racial pride, lectured and wrote about black history, and launched some of the earliest drug education programs. These activities were captured in the slogan "Power to the People."

FBI director J. Edgar Hoover was determined to infiltrate, harass, destabilize, and destroy all nationalist groups and their leaders. The FBI cooperated with local law enforcement officials to ridicule and discredit leaders and to undermine and weaken the Black Panther Party. In August 1967 Hoover distributed an explanatory memorandum that detailed the FBI's Counterintelligence Program directed toward black nationalist groups. The purpose, according to the memo, of this new "counterintelligence (**COINTELPRO**) endeavor is to expose, disrupt, misdirect, discredit, or otherwise neutralize the activities of black nationalist, hate-type organizations and groupings, their leadership, spokesmen, membership, and supporters, and to counter their propensity for violence and civil disorder." Undercover agents infiltrated the Panthers and provoked violence and criminal acts. Not that the Panthers were saints. Huey P. Newton, for example, had a long criminal record. He was imprisoned for murder in 1968 but was acquitted and released, only to be charged with murder and assault again in 1974. After fleeing to Cuba to avoid

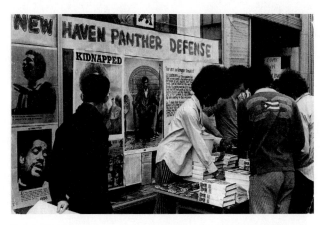

Some members of the Black Panther Party raised funds to pay for the legal fees of those arrested and charged with various offenses, such as Bobby Seale and Ericka Huggins. The Panthers advocated a radical economic, social, and educational agenda that made it the target of a determined campaign of suppression by the police and the FBI.

trial, he returned in 1977 and was again acquitted. He was eventually killed at age forty-two in a drug dispute in Oakland in 1989. Still, the FBI and its counterintelligence agents may have provoked much of the mayhem and violence that became associated with the Black Panther Party. Certainly, COINTELPRO helped shape negative public opinion of black nationalist ideology.

In their effort to destroy the party, law enforcement officials killed an estimated 28 Panthers and imprisoned 750 others. In perhaps the most egregious incident, police in Chicago killed Fred Hampton and Mark Clark in their sleep in a predawn raid on the Illinois Black Panther Headquarters on December 4, 1969. While the police fired hundreds of rounds, only two shots were fired from within the apartment.

PRISONERS' RIGHTS

Despite such repression, black militancy survived in many forms, including the prisoners' rights movement. One of the Black Panthers' social programs had focused on the conditions of black prisoners. By 1970 more than half the inmates in U.S. prisons were African American. In New York State, black Americans were around 70 percent of the prison population. Black activists argued that many African Americans were in jail for political reasons and suffered from unfair sentences and deplorable conditions because of racism and class exploitation.

Angela Davis, an assistant professor of philosophy at the University of California at Los Angeles, became the first black woman to be listed on the FBI's Ten Most Wanted list because of her involvement in prisoners' rights. In 1969 UCLA's board of regents refused to renew her contract, citing her lack of a Ph.D., but in fact they objected to her membership in the Communist Party. During the late 1960s, she had worked on behalf of the Soledad Brothers, three prisoners—George Jackson, John Clutchette, and Fleeta Drumgo—accused of murdering a white guard at Soledad Prison. On August 7, 1970, George Jackson's younger brother, seventeen-year-old Jonathan Jackson, staged a one-man raid on the San Rafael courthouse in Marin County, California, to try to seize hostages to trade for the Soledad Brothers. In the ensuing shootout, Jonathan Jackson, two prisoners, and a judge were killed. Angela Davis, accused of supplying the weapons for the raid, was charged with murder, kidnapping, and conspiracy. She escaped and lived as a fugitive, but she was eventually captured and spent over a year in jail. After a long ordeal and a national "Free Angela" campaign, a jury acquitted Davis. On August 21, 1971, George Jackson was shot and killed at San Quentin

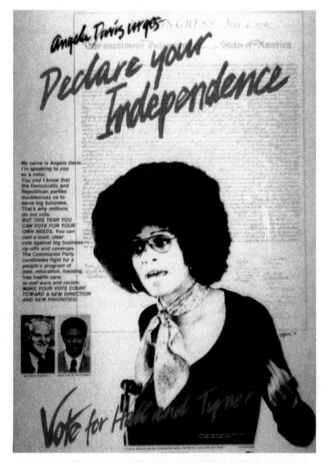

Although the iconic "Afro" is gone, today, Angela Davis continues her forceful advocacy for the rights of prisoners. She serves on the advisory board of the Prison Activist Resource Center and teachers in the History of Consciousness Department at the University of California, Santa Cruz.

Prison by guards who claimed he was trying to escape.

Interview from Prison **40** *LIVING WORDS*

Across the country, prisoners at Attica, a maximum-security prison in northern New York State, began a fast in memory of George Jackson that within days erupted into a full-scale rebellion. On September 9, 1971, 1,200 inmates seized control of half of Attica and took hostages. Four days later, state police and prison guards suppressed the uprising. Tom Wicker, a columnist for the *New York Times*, filed this report:

A task force consisting of 211 state troopers and corrections officers retook Attica using tear gas, rifles, and shotguns. After the shooting was over, ten hostages and twenty-nine inmates lay dead or dying. At least 450 rounds of ammunition had been discharged. Four hostages and eighty-five inmates suffered gunshot wounds that they survived. After initial reports that several hostages had died at the hands of knife-wielding inmates, pathologists' reports revealed that hostages and inmates all died from gunshot wounds. No guns were found in the possession of inmates.

A state commission, assembled in October 1971 to reconstruct the events at Attica, concluded, "With the exception of Indian massacres in the late nineteenth-century, the State Police assault which ended the four-day prison uprising was the bloodiest one-day encounter between Americans since the Civil War."

The Inner-City Rebellions

The militant nationalism of Malcolm X and Stokely Carmichael and the radicalism of the Panthers reflected growing alienation and anger in America's impoverished inner cities. In 1965, 29.1 percent of black households, compared with only 7.8 percent of white households, lived below the poverty line. Almost 50 percent of nonwhite families lived in substandard housing compared with 18 percent of white families. Despite a drop in the number of Americans living in poverty from 38.0 million in 1959 to 32.7 million in 1965, the percentage of poor black people increased from 27.5 percent to 31 percent. In 1965 the black unemployment rate was 8.5 percent, almost twice the white unemployment rate of 4.3. For black teenagers the unemployment rate was 23 percent compared with 10.8 percent for white teenagers. As psychologist Kenneth Clark declared in 1967, "The masses of Negroes are now starkly aware of the fact that recent civil rights victories benefited a very small percentage of middle-class Negroes while their predicament remained the same or worsened."

The passage of civil rights legislation did not resolve these disparities or diminish inner-city alienation. As jobs moved increasingly to suburbs to which inner-city residents could neither travel nor relocate, inner-city neighborhoods sank deeper into poverty. School dropout rates reached epidemic proportions, crime and drug use increased, and fragile family structures weakened. It was these conditions that led militants like the Panthers to liken their neighborhoods to exploited colonies kept in poverty by repressive white political and economic institutions. Few white Americans understood the depths of the black despair that flared into violence each summer between 1965 and 1969, beginning with the Watts rebellion of 1965.

WATTS

In the summer of 1965, a section of Los Angeles called Watts exploded. Watts was 98 percent black. Its residents suffered from overcrowding, unemployment, inaccessible health-care facilities, inadequate public transportation, and increasing crime and drug addiction. Almost 30 percent of the black male population was unemployed. The poverty, combined with anger at the often-brutal behavior of Los Angeles's police force in Watts, proved to be an incendiary combination. On August 11, 1965, a policeman pulled over a young black man to check him for drunk driving. The man was arrested, but not before a crowd gathered. The policeman called for reinforcements, and when they arrived, the crowd pelted them with stones, bottles, and other objects. Within a few hours, Watts was in a total riot.

Governor Pat Brown, a Democrat, sent in the National Guard to restore order, but by the sixth day of the conflagration, Watts had been reduced to rubble and ashes. One reporter commented that Watts looked like Germany at the end of World War II. Thirty-four people had been killed, more than 900 injured, and 4,000 arrested. Total property damage was more than $35 million, equivalent to hundreds of millions of dollars today. The Watts rebellion was the beginning of four summers of uprisings that would engulf cities in the North and Midwest. There were riots in the summer of 1966, but even worse ones erupted in Newark and Detroit in 1967.

The first major urban uprising of the 1960s was in the Watts neighborhood of East Los Angeles in August 1965. It lasted nearly a week and left thirty-four people dead.

NEWARK

Newark, New Jersey, had more than 400,000 inhabitants in 1967. As was true in many other urban areas, white flight to the suburbs in the 1950s and 1960s made Newark a majority black city, but one that operated on an inadequate tax base and under white political control. The city lacked the means to meet its inhabitants' social needs. The school system had deteriorated as unemployment increased. In 1967 Newark had the highest unemployment rate among black men in the entire nation. As tensions flared and police brutality escalated, white officials paid little attention to black people's complaints. On July 12, after a black cab driver in police custody was beaten, protesters gathered at the police station near the Hayes Homes housing project. When a firebomb hit the wall of the station house, the police charged, clubbing the crowd. This triggered one of the most destructive civic rebellions of the period. During four days of rioting, the police and National Guard killed twenty-five black people—most of them innocent bystanders, including two children; a white policeman and fireman were also killed. Widespread looting and arson caused millions of dollars in property damage.

DETROIT

When Detroit erupted a few days after Newark, it caught everyone by surprise except the residents of its inner-city neighborhoods. On the surface Detroit seemed like a model of prosperity and interracial accord. Some of the country's most dynamic popular music flowed from Detroit's Motown recording company. Owned by the astute Berry Gordy, Motown was a classic up-by-the-bootstraps success story. Gordy and his wife Raynoma and their extended family had, by 1967, produced such stars as Diana Ross and Mary Wells. "Before Motown," said Wells, "there were three careers available to a black girl in Detroit—babies, the factories or daywork."

But success like Gordy's was rare among the black migrants and their children, who poured into Detroit during and after World War II. The parents held their disappointment in check, but the children, particularly young men aged between seventeen and thirty-five, sought an outlet for their anger and alienation. Some joined the Nation of Islam; others embraced the Panthers or formed even more radical organizations calling for an all-black nation.

On the night of Saturday, July 23, police raided an after-hours drinking establishment in the center of the black community where more than eighty people were celebrating the return of two veterans from Vietnam. Police efforts to clear the club triggered five days of rioting. Congressman John Conyers, the black U.S. representative for Michigan's First District, knew many of the people in the area and tried to get them to disperse, but they refused. Later, Conyers said, "People were letting feelings out that had never been let out before, that had been bottled up. It really wasn't that they were that mad about an after-hours place being raided and some people being beat up as a result of the closing down of that place. It was the whole desperate situation of being black in Detroit."

Of the fifty-nine urban rebellions that occurred in 1967, Detroit's was the deadliest. Forty-three black people died, most of them shot by members of the National Guard, which had been sent in by Republican governor George Romney. But even the National Guard, combined with two hundred state police and six hundred Detroit police, could not restore order. A reluctant President Johnson had to order 4,700 troops of the elite 82nd and 101st Airborne units to Detroit. Republicans criticized Johnson's move as designed to embarrass Romney, who was a contender for the Republican presidential nomination in 1968. Johnson vehemently denied the charge. Others argued that Johnson's social welfare policies had raised expectations beyond the country's ability or desire to fulfill them and had subsidized the rioters.

THE KERNER COMMISSION

On July 29, 1967, in the wake of the Newark and Detroit riots, Johnson established the National Advisory Commission on Civil Disorders, headed by Illinois governor Otto Kerner. The commission included two black members, Republican senator Edward W. Brooke of Massachusetts (elected in 1966 and the first black senator since Reconstruction) and Roy Wilkins, executive director of the NAACP. In a speech explaining why he had set up the commission, Johnson declared,

> The only genuine, long-range solution for what has happened lies in an attack—mounted at every level—upon the conditions that breed despair and violence. All of us know what those conditions are: ignorance, discrimination, slums, poverty, disease, not enough jobs. We should attack these conditions—not because we are frightened by conflict, but because we are fired by conscience. We should attack them because there is simply no other way to achieve a decent and orderly society in America.

In its final report, released in 1968, the Kerner Commission indicted white racism as the underlying cause of the riots and warned that America was "moving towards two societies, one white, one black—separate and unequal." The commission emphasized that "Negroes firmly believe that police brutality and harassment occur repeatedly in Negro neighborhoods. This belief is unquestionably one of the major reasons for intense Negro resentment against the police." The report added, "Physical abuse is only one source of aggravation in the ghetto. In nearly every city surveyed, the Commission heard complaints of harassment of interracial couples, dispersal of social street gatherings and the stopping of Negroes on foot or in cars without objective basis." The report called for massive government aid to the cities, including funds for public housing, better and more integrated schools, two million new jobs, and funding for a "national system of income supplementation." None of its major proposals was enacted.

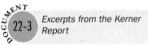
DOCUMENT 22-3 *Excerpts from the Kerner Report*

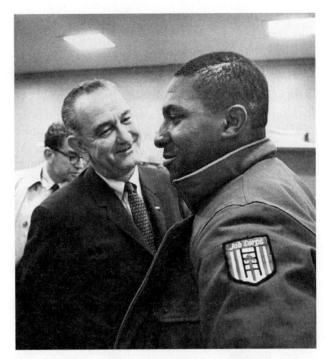

One of the most prominent programs of President Johnson's War on Poverty was the Job Corps, which provided occupational training for poor Americans. In this photo, Johnson speaks with James Truesville at a Job Corps center in Camp Catoctin, Maryland.

Difficulties in Creating the Great Society

The urban riots of the late 1960s undercut support for the broadest attack the federal government had yet waged on the problems of poor Americans, what President Johnson in his election campaign in 1964 had called "the Great Society." Much of the legislation Johnson pushed through Congress in 1964 and 1965—the Medicare program, for example, which provided medical care for the elderly and disabled under the Social Security system or federal aid to education from elementary through graduate schools—remained popular. But the most ambitious Great Society programs—what Johnson called "an unconditional war on poverty"—were controversial and tested the limits of American reform.

Lyndon Johnson was a savvy politician. He had to be to rise from Stonewall, Texas, to the pinnacle of power. But he never lost a deep sympathy for the disadvantaged and the powerless. Entering the House of Representatives in 1937, he had been an enthusiastic New Dealer. Elected to the Senate in 1948, he had refused to sign the Southern Manifesto (see Chapter 21) and, as majority leader, had overcome southern filibusters to win passage of the 1957 and 1960 Civil Rights Acts. As president, he pushed the 1964 Civil Rights Act and the 1965 Voting Rights Act through Congress.

Johnson's concern for the disadvantaged showed itself in the cornerstone of his War on Poverty, the Economic Opportunity Act of 1964. This act created an Office of Economic Opportunity that administered several programs: Head Start to help disadvantaged preschoolers, Upward Bound to prepare impoverished teenagers for college, and Volunteers in Service to America (or VISTA) to serve as a domestic peace corps to help the poor and undereducated across the country. These programs included community-governing boards on which black men and women gained representation, learning such essential political skills as bargaining and organizing.

The War on Poverty was the first government-sponsored effort to involve poor African Americans directly in designing and implementing programs to serve low-income communities. For example, in the New Careers program, residents of poor neighborhoods found jobs as community organizers, day care workers, and teacher aides. The program provided meaningful work, access to education, and critical material resources to poor people, so they would become leaders in their own communities and run for office. The **Community Action Programs (CAPs)** insisted on "maximum feasible participation" by the poor. On another level, the Education Act increased federal funding to colleges and universities and provided low-interest student loans. This initiative increased college enrollments and put higher education within the reach of many more Americans than before.

Johnson faced considerable opposition to CAPs and other Great Society programs. Local politicians, fearing the federal government was subsidizing their opponents and undercutting their power, were especially threatened by programs that empowered the previously disfranchised and dispossessed. Others, reflecting persistent white stereotypes of African Americans, complained that Johnson was rewarding lawlessness and laziness with handouts to the undeserving poor. The black residents of America's inner cities, for their part, had their expectations raised by the promises of the Great Society, only to be frustrated by white backlash and minimal gains. They felt as betrayed by its programs as Johnson's white critics felt robbed by them.

No one will ever know whether Lyndon Johnson could have won his War on Poverty had he been given the resources to do so. As it turned out, the nation's resources were increasingly going into his other war, the war in Vietnam. Statistics tell the story. Government spending, including spending for domestic programs, increased dramatically under Johnson. But most of the money spent on domestic programs during Johnson's presidency, $44.3 billion, went to Social Security benefits, which now included Medicare. Appropriations for the War on Poverty came to only $10 billion. The war in Vietnam, in contrast, consumed $140 billion.

Johnson and the War in Vietnam

Vietnam was a French colony from the 1860s until the Japanese seized it during World War II. After the war the Vietnamese communists, led by Ho Chi Minh, declared independence, but the French, with massive U.S. financial aid, fought to reassert their control from 1945 until they were finally defeated in 1954. In retrospect it is easy to argue that American policy makers should have been more impressed by the failure of the French to defeat the communists in Vietnam. But in 1954, with the French pulling out, the Americans arranged a temporary division of the country into a communist-controlled North Vietnam and a U.S.-supported South Vietnam (which, however, contained many communist guerrillas, called by the Americans "Viet Cong"). The United States ignored the possibility that as guarantor of South Vietnam, it would replace the French as targets for those Vietnamese who were determined to end white colonial domination and unify their country.

For nine years, under Presidents Eisenhower and Kennedy, American aid and advisers propped up the corrupt and incompetent South Vietnamese govern-ment in Saigon. By the time Johnson became president, only the dramatic escalation of American involvement—the bombing of North Vietnam and the introduction of large numbers of American troops into combat in South Vietnam—could keep the South Vietnamese government in power. Johnson himself doubted the advisability of a wholesale American commitment and did not want a foreign war to distract the public's attention or take away resources from the Great Society programs about which he cared so much. "I knew from the start," Johnson claimed later,

that I was bound to be crucified either way I moved. If I left the woman I really loved—the Great Society— in order to get involved with that bitch of a war on the other side of the world, then I would lose everything at home. All my programs. All my hopes to feed the hungry and shelter the homeless. All my dreams to provide education and medical care to the browns and the blacks and the lame and the poor. But if I left that war and let the Communists take over South Vietnam, then I would be seen as a coward and my nation would be seen as an appeaser and we would both find it impossible to accomplish anything for anybody anywhere on the entire globe.

And so, half aware he was entering a quagmire but determined to slug through it, Johnson intervened in Vietnam—gradually, massively, and inexorably.

After an incident involving an alleged North Vietnamese attack on U.S. Navy destroyers in the Gulf of Tonkin in August 1964, Johnson pushed a resolution through Congress that gave him authority to escalate American involvement in Vietnam. In the spring of 1965, he authorized the bombing of selected North Vietnamese targets, but the bombing failed to stop the North Vietnamese from resupplying and reinforcing their forces in the south. The American military presence in South Vietnam then grew rapidly. By the end of 1966, more than 385,000 U.S. troops were stationed there, and by 1968 more than 500,000.

BLACK AMERICANS AND THE VIETNAM WAR

In the mid-1960s, black Americans made up 10 percent of the armed forces. This percentage increased during America's involvement in the Vietnam War. (In the Persian Gulf War in 1991, African Americans were 25 percent of the troops deployed.) Black overrepresentation among the U.S. troops in Vietnam resulted, in large part, from draft deferments for college and graduate students who were predominantly white and middle class (such as Dan Quayle and George W. Bush). Black men and women entered the military for many compelling reasons, in addition to the draft.

One was patriotism. Another was that the military offered educational and vocational opportunities that the children of the working black poor could not otherwise obtain. Still another was Project 100,000.

PROJECT 100,000

In 1966 the U.S. Defense Department launched **Project 100,000** to reduce the high rejection rate of African Americans by the military. The project enabled recruitment officers to accept applicants whom they otherwise would have rejected because of criminal records or lack of skills. The project supplied more than 340,000 new recruits for Vietnam, 136,000 of whom were African Americans. As some have argued, this made the Vietnam War a white man's war but a black man's fight. Although the recruits were promised training and "rehabilitation," they saw more combat duty than regular recruits.

Johnson: Vietnam Destroys the Great Society

By the end of 1967, the nation seemed to be heading toward total racial polarization. In their rage against economic exploitation and police brutality, some inner-city black people had destroyed many of their own neighborhoods. Frightened white people, unable to comprehend black anger, rallied behind those who promised to restore order by any means. The two men who, only a few years before, had seemed the most effective advocates of racial reconciliation—Lyndon Johnson and Martin Luther King Jr.—were both trying to regain the initiative. Each, tragically, ended by alienating himself from the other.

By 1967 Johnson's situation was untenable. He had escalated the war in Vietnam without convincing many Americans it was worth fighting. With misleadingly optimistic claims about the progress of the war, his administration had forfeited public trust and opened what journalists called "the credibility gap." Johnson hoped that, with more bombing and more troops, the Vietnamese communists would give up, but he knew that if Congress had to choose between spending on the war and spending on domestic programs, it would choose the war. After Johnson asked for a tax increase, his Great Society programs met increasing resistance. When, for example, he proposed a special program to exterminate the rats that infested inner-city neighborhoods, congressional opponents turned it into a joke, calling it a "civil rats bill" and proposing to enlist an army of cats.

An even more dramatic example of the ugly mood on Capitol Hill was the House of Representatives expulsion in 1967 of the most prominent African-American

Adam Clayton Powell, Jr. (1908–1972). Beginning in 1954, Powell's Harlem constituency elected him to eleven successive terms in the U.S. House of Representatives. His brilliant leadership of the Education and Labor Committee proved crucial to the successful passage of social reform legislation in the 1960s.

politician in the United States, Adam Clayton Powell Jr. (1908–1972). Pastor of the Abyssinian Baptist Church in Harlem and a longtime civic activist, Powell had first been elected to represent his Harlem district in 1944 and became the foremost champion of civil rights in the House. Because of his seniority he became chairman of the Education and Labor Committee in 1961 and had been instrumental in passing Johnson's education and antipoverty legislation.

Powell gave ammunition to his enemies. He mismanaged the committee's budget, took numerous trips abroad at government expense, and was exiled from his district when threatened with arrest there because of his refusal to pay a slander judgment against him. Yet the sentiment behind his ouster owed much to the dislike he inspired as a champion of minorities and the poor and as a flamboyant black man. The Supreme Court, overruling the House action, upheld his right to his seat, and his Harlem constituents kept him in office until his death.

They Called Each Other "Bloods"

Captain Joseph B. Anderson Jr. of Topeka, Kansas, served as a platoon leader at An Khe, from June 1966 to June 1967, and as company commander in Cambodia, Phouc Vinh, from May 1970 to April 1971, 1st Cavalry Division, U.S. Army. His unit was the subject of The Anderson Platoon, *a 1967 French documentary film.*

Shortly after I got to Vietnam, we got into a real big fight. We were outnumbered at least ten to one. But I didn't know it. I had taken over 1st Platoon of B Company of the 12th Cav. We were up against a Viet Cong battalion. There may have been 300 to 400 of them. And they had just wiped out one of our platoons. At that time in the war, summer of 1966, it was a terrible loss. A bloody massacre.

I was an absolute rarity in Vietnam. A black West Pointer commanding troops. One year after graduation, I was very aggressive about my role and responsibilities as an Army officer serving in Vietnam. I was there to defend the freedom of the South Vietnamese government, stabilize the countryside, and help contain Communism. The Domino Theory was dominant then, predominant as a matter of fact. I was gung ho. And I thought the war would last three years at the most.

There weren't many opportunities for blacks in private industry then. And as a graduate of West Point, I was an officer and a gentleman by act of Congress. Where else could a black go and get that label just like that?

Throughout the Cav, the black representation in the enlisted ranks was heavier than the population as a whole in the United States. One third of my platoon and two of my four squad leaders were black. For many black men, the service, even during a war, was the best of a number of alternatives to staying home and working in the fields or bumming around the streets of Chicago or New York.

There were only a very few incidents of sustained fighting during my tours. Mostly you walked and walked, searched and searched. If you made contact, it would be over in thirty or forty minutes. One burst and then they're gone, because they didn't want to fight or could not stand up against the firepower we could bring with artillery and helicopter gunships.

I had a great deal of respect for the Viet Cong. They were trained and familiar with the jungle. They relied on stealth, on ambush, on their personal skills and wile, as opposed to firepower. They knew it did not pay for them to stand and fight us, so they wouldn't. . . .

What was very clear to me was an awareness among our men that the support for the war was declining in the United States.

Despite opposition in Congress, Johnson did not give up on the Great Society. He knew he could initiate no major programs while the Vietnam War lasted, but he continued to push a variety of measures, including a law to prohibit discrimination in housing. He also named the architect of the NAACP's attack on segregation, Thurgood Marshall, to the Supreme Court in 1967.

Vietnam trapped Johnson. As the hundreds of thousands of people who demonstrated against the war reminded him, Vietnam was incontestably "Lyndon Johnson's war." It was not, he would have replied, the war he had wanted to fight—that was the war against poverty and discrimination—but he was committed to seeing it through. He believed his and the nation's honor were at stake. Even though objective

The gung ho attitude that made our soldiers so effective in 1966, 67, was replaced by the will to survive. They became more security conscious. They would take more defensive measures so they wouldn't get hurt. They were more scared. They wanted to get back home.

Career officers and enlisted men like me did not go back to a hostile environment in America. We went back to bases where we were assimilated and congratulated and decorated for our performance in the conduct of the war.

Personally it was career enhancing. A career Army officer who has not been to war during the war is dead, careerwise. I had done that. I received decorations. Two Silver Stars, five Bronze Stars, eleven Air Medals. . . . But in 1978 I decided I did not want to cool my heels for the next eight to ten years to become a general. . . . I resigned my commission, worked a year as a special assistant to the U.S. Secretary of Commerce, and joined General Motors as a plant manager.

The Anderson Platoon won both an Oscar and an Emmy. As time passes, my memory of Vietnam revolves around the film. I have a print, and I look at it from time to time. And the broadness and scope of my two-year experience narrows down to sixty minutes.

🌲 *How do the experiences of this Vietnam veteran compare with those of black soldiers in World War II?*

🌲 *Why were African-American men attracted to military service? What benefits did they derive from the military, and what does their disproportionate representation in the military suggest about social and economic conditions in black communities?*

Source: "Captain Joseph B. Anderson Jr.," in Wallace Terry, *Bloods: An Oral History of the Vietnam War by Black Veterans* (New York: Ballantine Books, 1984), pp. 219–28.

PROFILE ～ MUHAMMAD ALI

Boxing is a brutal sport. During the 1960s and 1970s, Cassius Clay showed that boxing was also an art, that it could be beautiful, and that the boxer could become a symbol of racial pride, endearing wit, and even love. Born Cassius Marcellus Clay in 1942 in Louisville, Kentucky, Clay went to Rome in 1960, where he won a gold medal as a member of the U.S. Olympic boxing team.

Clay turned the boxing world on its head with audacious declarations of his own greatness as a boxer and beauty as a black man. His defeats of Floyd Patterson and Sonny Liston confirmed the first claim. On February 25, 1964, Clay pounded Liston to become the world heavyweight champion. The next day he announced that he had joined the Nation of Islam and had taken a new name, Muhammad Ali. Explaining his timing of the announcement, he said: "When I joined the Nation in 1961, I figured I'd be pressured if I revealed it, so I kept it quiet for about three years. . . . But after beating Sonny Liston, I was getting more recognition and more power. I revealed it after that fight."

Ali was a master at "playing the dozens," a boasting style that angered his opponents and annoyed white reporters covering his bouts. In 1967, however, it was his refusal to be drafted into the military that brought down on his head the wrath of the boxing establishment and white America. Ali argued that his religion was opposed to military service just as it was against civil rights activism and integration. Muhammad Ali was the new black man who refused to accept the white man's rules about how to behave. He embodied the assertive black consciousness that invaded all forms of social and cultural life in the 1960s and 1970s.

But most black people also adored Ali for other reasons, recalled basketball player Kareem Abdul-Jabbar, who in 1971 discarded the name Lew Alcindor:

When Ali announced his refusal to accept the draft, I thought it was a very brave stand. . . . A meeting to help Ali was called by black athletes back in 1967. We let black people around the country know that we supported Ali. I think by that time Black Americans understood that their presence in Vietnam was highly disproportionate to their percentage of the American population and that the front-line casualties were being absorbed by Black Americans in much greater numbers than they should have.

A federal court found Ali guilty of draft evasion, but he was released on bail pending his appeal. Ali immediately became a popular antiwar speaker. In June 1970 the U. S. Supreme Court overturned his conviction on the grounds that the FBI had placed an illegal wiretap on his telephone.

Actor Harry Belafonte described Ali in admiring terms:

He brought America to its most wonderful and its most naked moment. " I will not play in your game of war. I will not kill in your behalf. What you ask is immoral, unjust, and I stand here to attest to that fact. Now do with me what you will." he said. I mean he was, in many ways, as inspiring as Dr. King, as inspiring as Malcolm. Cassius was a black, young American. Out of the womb of oppression he was our phoenix, he was the spirit of our young. He was our manhood. . . . He was the vitality of what we hoped would emerge. . . . the perfect machine, the wit, the incredible athlete, the facile, articulate, sharp mind on issues, the great sense of humor, which was out of our tradition.

In 1974 Ali fought George Foreman to regain his world heavyweight boxing title. Four years later he lost the title to Leon Spinks. He regained it, retired, then attempted a comeback that ended with his October 2, 1980, loss to Larry Holmes. He was elected to the Boxing Hall of Fame in 1987. In 1996 he lit the Olympic Flame to open the summer games in Atlanta.

Muhammad Ali declared himself "The Greatest," and ▶ for many African Americans he was the epitome of the uncompromised and proud black man.

commentators considered the conflict a stalemate, optimistic reports in 1967, from military commanders and intelligence agents, convinced the president he might yet prevail.

Then, on January 30, 1968, at the start of the Vietnamese new year (called Tet), communist insurgents attacked thirty-six of the forty-four provincial capitals in South Vietnam as well as its national capital, Saigon, where they penetrated the grounds of the American embassy. Although American and South Vietnamese forces quickly recaptured all the territory that was lost and inflicted massive casualties on the enemy, the Tet Offensive was a major psychological blow for the American public, deepening the suspicion that the administration had not been telling the truth about the war. Washington was forced to reconsider its strategy.

On March 31, 1968, President Johnson told the nation he would halt the bombing of North Vietnam to encourage the start of peace negotiations, which began in Paris in May. Then, as if an afterthought, he added that he would not seek renomination as president. Worn out by Vietnam, frustrated in his efforts to achieve the Great Society, the target of bitter criticism, and dispirited by a poor showing in the New Hampshire primary, Lyndon Johnson ended his public career rather than engaging in a potentially bruising renomination battle.

King: Searching for a New Strategy

Like President Johnson, Martin Luther King was attacked on many fronts. Many white people considered him a dangerous radical, whereas black militants considered him an ineffectual moderate. His first response to the urban rebellions in 1965 and 1966 had been to move his campaign to the North to demonstrate the national range of the civil rights movement. In 1966 King and the SCLC set up operations in Chicago at the invitation of the Chicago Freedom Movement. King was confident he would receive the support of the city's white liberals and the entire black community. James Bevel, King's Chicago lieutenant, declared, "We are going to create a new city. . . . Nobody will stop us." His optimism proved unwarranted.

Chicago's powerful, wily mayor Richard Daley viewed King suspiciously from the outset, but he treated him with respect and cautioned the police not to use violence against King's civil rights demonstrators. Because King's movement depended on provoking confrontation, not much happened until King attempted to march into the white ethnic enclave of Marquette Park and the all-white suburb of Cicero.

The ensuing violence attracted the nation's television cameras. Chicago's white liberals joined with King and Daley in negotiating the Summit Agreement on housing, which amounted to a hasty retreat by King in the face of virulent white rage and black militancy. The Chicago strategy was a dismal failure.

But Chicago reinforced two important lessons for King. First, racial discrimination was more than a southern problem: in Chicago he witnessed an intensity of hatred and hostility that surpassed even that of Birmingham. Second, racial discrimination was inextricably intertwined with the country's economic structure. And so he began to think more critically about the need not only to eradicate poverty but to end systemic economic inequality. "What good is it to be allowed to eat in a restaurant," he remarked, "if you can't afford a hamburger?" In the fall of 1967, he announced plans for his most ambitious and militant project, an integrated, nonviolent "Poor People's Campaign" the following spring. According to the plan, tens of thousands of the nation's dispossessed would descend on Washington to focus attention on the disadvantaged members of American society. Among other things, King and his aides wanted a federally guaranteed income policy.

KING ON THE VIETNAM WAR

While planning the **Poor People's Campaign**, King began to attack the war in Vietnam. King rejected what he considered the hypocrisy of the federal government's determination to send black and white men to Vietnam "to slaughter, men, women, and children" while failing to protect black American civil rights protesters in places like Albany, Birmingham, and Selma. His statements that the president was more concerned about winning in Vietnam than winning the "war against poverty" in America turned Johnson against him and further alienated King from many of Johnson's black supporters, including the more traditional civil rights leaders who supported the war in Vietnam. At the same time, the young militants in SNCC, who had already condemned the war, did not rush to embrace him. But King persisted, and by 1968 he had become one of the war's most trenchant critics.

"Conscience and the Vietnam War," 1967 DOCUMENT 22-2

KING'S MURDER

His search for a new strategy led King to a closer involvement with labor issues. In February 1968, attempting to gain union recognition for municipal workers in Memphis, 1,300 members of a virtually all-black sanitation workers local went on strike and together with the local black community boycotted downtown merchants. But Memphis mayor Henry Loeb refused to negotiate. On March 18, 1968, responding to a call from James Lawson, a longtime civil rights activist and the minister of Centenary Methodist Church in Memphis, King went to Memphis to address the striking sanitation workers.

The occasion was marked by violence. Nevertheless, King returned to Memphis on April 3 and delivered his last and perhaps most prophetic speech:

> I would like to live a long life. Longevity has its place. But I'm not concerned about that now. I just want to do God's will. And He's allowed me to go up to the mountaintop, and I've looked over. And I've seen the promised land. I may not get there with you. But I want you to know tonight that we as a people will get to the promised land. So I'm happy tonight. I'm not worried about anything. I'm not fearing any man. "Mine eyes have seen the glory of the coming of the Lord."

The next day King was murdered by James Earl Ray as he stood on the balcony of the Lorraine Motel in Memphis. His assassination unleashed a torrent of civic rage in black communities. More than 125 cities experienced uprisings. By April 11, 46 people were dead, 35,000 were injured, and more than 20,000 had been arrested.

In what seemed to many a belated gesture of racial reconciliation, within days of King's assassination, Congress passed the Civil Rights Act of 1968. Proposed by Johnson two years before, the act outlawed discrimination in the sale and rental of housing and gave the Justice Department authority to bring suits against such discrimination.

King's assassination also boosted support for the SCLC's faltering Poor People's Campaign. The campaign began in May when more than two thousand demonstrators settled into a shantytown they called Resurrection City in Washington, D.C. For more than a month, they marched daily to various federal offices and took part in a mass demonstration on June 19. On June 24, police evicted them, and the campaign ended, leaving an uncertain legacy.

The Black Arts Movement and Black Consciousness

The years between 1967 and 1975 witnessed some of the most intense political and cultural discussions in the history of the black freedom struggle. Black power

stimulated debate about both the future of black politics in the post–civil rights era and the role of black art and artists in the quest for black liberation. Creative people revisited the long-standing issue of whether black art is political or aesthetic. For a decade, discussion about black culture and identity focused on the relationship between art and the artist, and the political movement within the black community. This period became known as the black arts movement. Among the outstanding poets who helped shape the revolutionary movement, introducing new forms of black writing and delivering outspoken attacks on "the white aesthetic" while stressing black beauty and pride, were Sonia Sanchez, Nikki Giovanni, and Don L. Lee (Haki Madhubuti). One of the best examples of Giovanni's militant poems is "The True Import of Present Dialogue, Black vs. Negro," which appeared in her first collection, a self-published volume entitled *Black Feeling, Black Talk* (1967). In a shocking opening line she asked, "nigger/Can you kill/Can you kill/Can a nigger kill/Can a nigger kill a honkie." The poem continues, "Can you kill the nigger/in you/Can you kill your nigger mind/And free your Black hands to/strangle." Sanchez also captured the violence and turbulence of

Imamu Amiri Baraka means "spiritual leader, prince, blessed" in Swahili and is the chosen name of LeRoi Jones. The celebrated "father of the black arts movement" remained prolific, influential, and controversial after five decades of creative engagement in America's "culture war."

the era. In 1970 she published a major collection of poetry entitled, *We a BaddDDD People.* Of equal significance in the development and evolution of this creative flowering was playwright and poet LeRoi Jones.

The formal beginning of the movement was the founding in 1965 of the Black Arts Repertory Theater by LeRoi Jones, who changed his name to Imamu Amiri Baraka in 1967. Jones was the bridge that linked the political and cultural aspects of black power. He had been closely associated with the white avant-garde poets in New York in the 1950s and early 1960s, but he began to change in 1965 from an integrationist to a black cultural nationalist.

The guiding ethos of the black arts movement was the determination of black artists to produce black art for black people and thereby to accomplish black liberation. Baraka declared, "The Black man must seek a Black politics, an ordering of the world that is beneficial to his culture, to his interiorization and judgment of the world. The Black Artist . . . is desperately needed to change the images his people identify with, by asserting Black feeling, Black mind, Black judgment." In 1968 he coedited with Larry Neal the anthology *Black Fire,* which revealed the extent to which black writers and thinkers had rejected the premises of integration in favor of a new black consciousness and nationalist political engagement.

Larry Neal, who was part of the revolutionary action movement, offered a succinct definition of this important dimension of the freedom struggle:

> The Black Arts Movement is radically opposed to any concept of the artist that alienates him from his community. Black Art is the aesthetic and spiritual sister of the Black Power concept. As such, it envisions an art that speaks directly to the needs and aspirations of Black Americans. In order to perform this task, the Black Arts Movement proposes a radical reordering of the western cultural aesthetic. It proposes a separate symbolism, mythology, critique, and iconography. The Black Arts and the Black Power concept both relate broadly to the Afro-American's desire for self-determination and nationhood. Both concepts are nationalistic. One is concerned with the relationship between art and politics; the other with the art of politics.

The black arts movement was criticized because of its celebration of black maleness, its racial exclusivity, and its homophobia. It was never a unified movement in the sense of all black artists speaking in one voice. There was creative dissent and competing visions of freedom. In 1970 Maya Angelou published an autobiographical novel, *I Know Why the Caged Bird Sings,* that unveiled her experience with sexual abuse and the silencing of black women within black communities. Other black women writers would follow suit and in the 1970s create a black women's literary renaissance. Still, prominent integrationist writers agreed with some of the black arts movement's fundamental tenets and were converted to its principles.

The works of Langston Hughes, Lorraine Hansberry, Gwendolyn Brooks, and James Baldwin linked the black cultural renaissances of the 1930s, 1940s, and 1950s to the black arts movement. Brooks, for example, stressed the commitment of artists to community and the importance of the relationship between the artist and her audience. She had consistently supported community-based arts programs, and it seemed natural that she should "convert" to a black nationalist perspective during the 1960s and join forces with younger artists.

But the most popular black writer of the era, especially among white audiences, was James Baldwin. Baldwin was an integrationist. In his work he had resisted the simple inversion of racial hierarchies that characterized some parts of the black power and black arts movements. He wrote, "I think all theories are suspect, that the finest principles may have to be modified, or may even be pulverized by the demands of life, and that one must find therefore, and move through the world hoping that center will guide one aright." Yet in many ways, Baldwin was as alienated and angry as some of the artists identified with black arts.

In *The Fire Next Time* (1963), he concluded with a phrase that echoed through discussions of the rebellions in Watts, Newark, and Detroit. "If we do not now dare everything, the fulfillment of that prophecy, recreated from the bible in song by a slave, is upon us: 'God gave Noah the rainbow sign, No more water, the fire next time!'"

Baldwin was also an unflinching commentator on white racism and had a major impact on public discourse. At one point he told his white readers, "There appears to be a vast amount of confusion on this point, but I do not know many Negroes who are eager to be 'accepted' by white people, still less to be loved by them; they, the blacks, simply don't wish to be beaten over the head by the whites every instant of our brief passage on this planet." And in *No Name in the Street,* Baldwin declared, "I agree with the Black Panther position concerning black prisoners: not one of them has ever had a fair trial, for not one of them has ever been tried by a jury of his peers." He explained: "White middle-class America is always the jury, and they know absolutely nothing about the lives of the people on whom they sit in judgment: and this fact is not altered, on the contrary it is rendered more implacable by the presence of one or two black faces in the jury box."

PROFILE ～ LORRAINE HANSBERRY (1930–1965)

Playwright Lorraine Hansberry was, arguably, the artist/activist who spoke most powerfully to three generations of African Americans. Her play, *A Raisin in the Sun,* has inspired audiences and readers from the 1950s through the civil rights movement to the hip-hop era. Hansberry grew up on the South Side of Chicago and attended the University of Wisconsin, the Art Institute of Chicago, and Roosevelt College (now University) before settling in New York City.

Before achieving national acclaim for *Raisin,* Hansberry worked for Paul Robeson's Harlem newspaper, *Freedom.* In a 1955 essay for the paper, "Life Challenges Negro Youth," she declared, "From the time he is born, the Negro child is surrounded by a society organized to convince him that he belongs to a people whose past is so worthless and shameful that it amounts to no past at all. . . .In a land where the Grace Kelly-Marilyn Monroe monotype 'ideal' is imposed on the national culture, racist logic insists that anything directly opposite—no matter how lovely—is naturally ugly."

In 1953, Hansberry married Robert Nemiroff, but they separated soon after when she told him that she was a lesbian. She and Nemiroff remained close friends and collaborators, however, and the larger world never knew about her sexual identity. Like Bayard Rustin, Hansberry was acutely aware of the homophobia in American society. She disclosed her private life only to a few trusted friends.

In 1965, Hansberry died of pancreatic cancer. Six hundred people attended her funeral, including Malcolm X, James Forman, Nina Simone, Sammy Davis, Jr., Ossie Davis, and Ruby Dee. Martin Luther King Jr. and James Baldwin sent messages. Paul Robeson delivered a eulogy.

A Raisin in the Sun premiered on Broadway in 1959 to rave reviews. Hansberry explained, "I wrote it between my 26th and 27th birthday. One night, after seeing a play I won't mention, I suddenly became disgusted with a whole body of material about Negroes.

Cardboard characters. Cute dialect bits. Or hip-swinging musicals from exotic scores. . . .Even the most sympathetic novel for the Negro. . . happens to have been built around the most offensive character in American literature—who is Uncle Tom." In *Raisin,* Hansberry captured the tribulations of the Younger family's attempt to move from their crowded apartment in Chicago's Bronzeville to a house in the suburbs and what they hope will be a better life. It is a story of upward mobility running up against American racism. Walter Lee Younger wants to use the money from his father's insurance policy to open a liquor store. His mother wants to buy a house for the extended family. His sister wants the money to help pay her tuition to medical school. Their mother prevails and holds the family together even when a friend swindles Walter Lee out of most of the money, and racist neighbors make it clear that the Youngers are not welcome. At the end of the play, the Youngers move into the new home as a united family even though their future there is uncertain.

In 2004, hip-hop impresario Sean (P. Diddy) Combs revived *Raisin* on Broadway and played the role of Walter Lee that Sidney Poitier had played in the original production. Such was the excitement generated by a play still powerfully resonant forty-five years after its premier that the producers recouped their $2.6 million investment within two months. Lorraine Hansberry's writing still inspires individuals to deploy art in the struggle for liberation from the biases and fears that oppress and dehumanize people because of their race, class, gender, and sexual identity.

Hansberry

POETRY AND THEATER

The black arts movement had its greatest and most significant impact in poetry and theater. The movement had three geographical centers: Harlem, Chicago and Detroit, and San Francisco.

The Chicago-based *Negro Digest/Black World*, edited by Hoyt Fuller and published by John Johnson, promoted many of the works of the new generation of creative artists. Fuller, a well-connected intellectual with an exhaustive command of black literature, became editor of the monthly magazine in 1961. In 1970 he changed the name of the magazine to *Black World* to signal the rejection of "Negro" and the adoption of "black" to designate people of African descent. The name change identified African Americans with both the African Diaspora and Africa itself.

In Detroit, Naomi Long Madgett's Lotus Press and Dudley Randall's Broadside Press republished the previous generation of black poets, notably Gwendolyn Brooks, Margaret Walker, and Sterling Brown. In Chicago, poet and literary critic Don L. Lee, who changed his name to Haki Madhabuti, launched Third World Press, which published many of the black arts poets and writers.

LIVING WORDS

41   *Song of the Front Yard*

42   *Liberation/poem*

43   *Woman*

The Chicago-Detroit publishing nexus promoted new poets like Nikki Giovanni, Etheridge Knight, and Sonia Sanchez. These and other poets produced some of the most accomplished and experimental work of the black arts movement. It resonated with the sounds of the African-American vernacular, combining the rhythmic cadences of sermons with popular music and black "street speech" into a spirited new form of poetry that was free, conversational, and militantly cool.

Theater was another prominent genre of the black arts movement. Playwright Ed Bullin edited a special issue of the journal *Drama Review* in the summer of 1968 that featured essays and plays by most of the major activists in black arts, including Sonia Sanchez, Ron Milner, and Woodie King Jr. This volume became the textbook of black arts. In his plays, Bullins, who was greatly influenced by Baraka, portrayed ordinary black life and explored the inner forces that prevented black people from realizing their own liberation and full potential. He showed how racism had deformed the black experience and consciousness. Across the country local black communities formed their own theater groups, including Val Gray Ward's Kuumba Workshop in Chicago and Baraka's Spirit House Theater in New Jersey. These groups reached out to people by hosting seminars, guest appearances, fashion shows, art exhibits, dance recitals, parades, and mass media parties.

On the West Coast, in 1969, Robert Chrisman and Nathan Hare launched *The Black Scholar*, the first serious journal to promote black studies. Chrisman compared the black arts movement with the renaissance in Harlem during the 1920s: "More so than the Harlem Renaissance, in which Black artists were always on the leash of white patrons and publishing houses, the Black Arts movement did it for itself. Black people going out nationally, in mass, saying we are an independent Black people and this is what we produce."

MUSIC

The cultural nationalists in the black arts movement cultivated an appreciation for modern jazz musicians, making them icons of the quest for black freedom. Baraka argued that jazz and other black music was the language that black people developed to give uncensored accounts of their experiences. He and other cultural nationalists believed music could promote black identity and encourage the pride that was vital for political struggle. The music of the jazzmen was often dense and austere, but it could also be powerfully primitive and dazzlingly complex. Above all, the music appeared to challenge Western conceptions of harmony, rhythm, melody, and tone. In jazz you have to improvise, to create your own form of expression by using whatever information inspires you. The emphasis is not on the original, but on individual articulation.

Cultural nationalists perceived jazz to be a self-consciously engaged, economically independent, politically useful art form. Novelist Ralph Ellison put it most succinctly:

> True jazz is an art of individual assertion within and against the group. Each true jazz moment (as distinct from the uninspired commercial performance) springs from a contest in which each artist challenges all the rest; each solo flight, or improvisation, represents (like the successive canvases of a painter) a definition of his identity: as individual, as member of the collectivity and as a link in the chain of tradition.

This outlook explains why Miles Davis's legendary album *Kind of Blue* (1959), one of the most progressive jazz albums ever produced, also became one of the most popular. Davis showed that art could be accessible without sacrificing excellence and rigor. Davis, in the words of one admirer, was able to "dance underwater and not get wet." For black cultural nationalists, Davis projected an image of uncompromising and uncompromised black identity.

Among other intensely celebrated jazz musicians were Charlie Parker, Archie Shepp, Ornette Coleman, Pharoah Sanders, Eric Dophy, Thelonious Monk, and John Coltrane. Playwright Ronald Milner described Coltrane as "a man who through his saxophone before your eyes and ears completely annihilates every single western influence." Coltrane also played the deep, and deeply political, blues of "Alabama" written in response to the Birmingham church bombings.

Jazz, however, tended to appeal to intellectuals. Most black people preferred rhythm and blues, gospel, and soul. During the height of the black consciousness movement, black popular musicians gave performances and concerts to raise funds and to assert racial pride. Aretha Franklin and Ray Charles, for example, allowed SNCC workers to attend their concerts for free. Just as the freedom songs had done, the soul music of the black power era helped unify black people.

No history of the era would be complete without mentioning the performances of the "Godfather of Soul," James Brown, the "Queen of Soul," Aretha Franklin's powerful rendition of the song "R.E.S.P.E.C.T.," and the financial contributions of Berry Gordy of Motown. James Brown's "Say It Loud, I'm Black and I'm Proud" became an anthem for the era. Brown linked sound commercial marketing to social commentary, confronting American racism with racial pride and righteous indignation. He confessed, "I may not do as much as some other individuals who have made it big," but, "you can bet your life that I'm doing the best I can. . . . I owe it to the black community to help provide scholarships, to help children stay in school, to help equip playgrounds and recreation centers, and to keep kids off the streets." Brown was "totally committed to black power, the kind that is achieved not through the muzzle of a rifle but through education and economic leverage."

Berry Gordy contributed to black freedom struggles both artistically and financially. To support King's Chicago movement, Gordy arranged for Stevie Wonder to give a benefit concert at Soldier Field in Chicago. He made cash contributions to black candidates, to the NAACP and its Legal Defense and Educational Fund, and to the Urban League.

With Gordy's encouragement, his performers flirted just enough with black radicalism to gain a patina of militancy. During the late 1960s and early 1970s, the musical and lyrical innovations of the Temptations, Stevie Wonder, and Marvin Gaye reflected Motown's politicization. In an address to one of the sessions launching Jesse Jackson's People United to Save Humanity (PUSH) in 1971, Gordy declared, "I have been fortunate to be able to provide opportunities for young people. . . . Opportunities are supposed to knock once in a lifetime, but too often we have to knock for an opportunity. The first obligation we (as black businessmen) have is to ourselves and our own employees, the second is to create opportunities for others." Musician Curtis Mayfield explained simply, "Our purpose is to educate as well as to entertain. Painless preaching is as good a term as any for what we do."

The Second Phase of the Black Student Movement

The most dramatic expression of militant assertiveness after 1968 occurred among black college students. The black power generation of students was committed to transforming society, although those on predominantly white campuses often, but not always, seemed to be more reformist than revolutionary. Some observers describe the period of activism between 1968 and 1975 as the "second phase" of the black students' movement.

THE ORANGEBURG MASSACRE

The first phase, in this view, was launched by students at southern black colleges in the early 1960s. It began with the sit-ins in Greensboro, North Carolina, and the Freedom Rides, and it culminated in the Mississippi Freedom Summer of 1964. By 1968, however, many of the student organizations that had grown out of the civil rights movement, notably SNCC, were in decline. The massacre of black students at South Carolina State College in Orangeburg on February 8, 1968, marks the end of the first phase and the beginning of the second. Students attending the historically black institution had protested a local bowling alley's whites-only admission policy. When the tension and protests escalated, state officials deployed the highway patrol and National Guard. On the evening of February 8, the students assembled at the front of the campus and taunted the officers; some threw rocks, bricks, and bottles. One officer was hit by a piece of lumber. Later, without warning, nine highway patrolmen opened fire on the students with shotguns. The officers killed three young men and wounded twenty-eight. Most of them were shot in the back. All the officers involved were later acquitted, but a young black activist and SNCC leader, Cleveland Sellers, was convicted of rioting and served nearly a year in prison. He was pardoned in 1993. On February 8, 2001, South Carolina governor James Hodges apologized to a group of survivors who had assembled in Orangeburg.

South Carolina State College Massacre, 1968, Orangeburg, South Carolina. The three young men killed in the Orangeburg Massacre were Henry Smith and Samuel Hammond, both eighteen, and seventeen-year-old high school student, Delano Middleton.

BLACK STUDIES

The second phase owed much of its inspiration to the black power and black arts movements. It began when significant numbers of black students enrolled in predominantly white institutions for the first time. The black students at the white campuses demanded courses in black history, culture, literature, and art as alternatives to the "Eurocentric" bias of the average university curriculum. Many black students also formed all-black organizations, such as the Black Allied Students' Association at New York University and the Black Organization of Students at Rutgers University.

Black students understood that education was essential to empowerment. In 1967 black students accounted for only 2 percent of the total enrollment at predominantly white colleges and universities. This meant that only 95,000 African Americans were among the approximately 5 million full-time undergraduates at these schools. Rutgers University in New Jersey provides a case study. Out of 24,000 baccalaureate degrees it awarded between 1952 and 1967, only about 200 went to African Americans. Federal legislation—especially the Civil Rights Act of 1964 and the Higher Education Act of 1965—outlawed discrimination or segregation in higher education, and by instituting an array of financial aid programs, it spurred colleges and universities to take affirmative action to recruit black students. Where there had been about 100 black undergraduates at Rutgers in 1965, there were more than 400 by 1968, accounting for nearly 3 percent of the undergraduate enrollment.

On the national level, the overall status of black people in education reflected the accomplishments of the classic phase of the civil rights movement, but the black power generation was determined to make its own mark on the struggle. In 1960 only 227,000 black Americans attended the nation's colleges (including those at predominantly black institutions). By the end of the 1960s, enrollments had increased by 100 percent, and in 1977, 1.1 million black students attended America's universities. This was an almost 500 percent increase over 1960. There was wide political diversity among this generation of students, but they shared the sense of being strangers in a white-controlled environment. Many found the campuses hostile, alien places and discovered little there with which they could identify. They resolved to change this situation.

At San Francisco State College, Nathan Hare, formerly a professor at Howard University, and black students demanded not only curriculum changes but the structural transformation of the college. In the 1966–1967 academic year, the Black Student Union (BSU) orchestrated a strike that involved thousands of students of diverse ethnic and racial backgrounds. The students deliberately chose to strike, rather than take over buildings, so they could circulate freely on the campus, increasing their support and maintaining their momentum. Among their demands were the creation of an autonomous degree-granting black studies department and the admission of more black students. The college ultimately did create the first black studies department in 1968, with Hare as its head.

Black students also took over administration buildings at other institutions, demanding not only that the schools offer more black studies courses and programs and hire more black faculty, but often that classrooms and facilities also be made available to local black communities. The upheavals that shut down Columbia University in 1968, for example, began when black student members of the Students Afro-American Society and Students for a Democratic Society demonstrated to block plans to construct a university gymnasium in nearby Morningside Park. The demonstrators argued the gym would impinge on one of the few parks located in Harlem and that it was being built over strenuous objections from the Harlem community.

In 1968, Yale University's Black Student Alliance sponsored a symposium to discuss the need, status, and function of Afro-American studies. Conference organizer Armstead Robinson saw it as the first attempt to create a viable program of Afro-American studies. In December 1968 the faculty voted to make Yale one of the first major universities in the country to institute a degree-granting African-American Studies program. In 1969 Harvard University created an Afro-American Studies Department, and other schools soon followed. In 1969 the Institute of the Black World in Atlanta conducted a project to define the methods and purpose of black studies and then sponsored a black studies directors' seminar. Ron Karenga wrote what remains a major textbook for the new field, *Introduction to Black Studies*. By 1973 some two hundred black studies programs existed in the United States. By the late 1980s, several of the programs, such as those at Cornell, Yale, and UCLA, offered master's degrees in African-American studies. In 1988 Temple University, under the leadership of Molefi Kete Asante, became the first university to offer a Ph.D. in African-American Studies. In 2002, Michigan State University became the sixth to offer the doctorate in the discipline. In 2006 Northwestern University welcomed its first group of five students admitted into the newly created graduate program in African-American Studies.

Still, there is no universally accepted definition of black studies. James E. Turner, founder of Africana Studies at Cornell, viewed it as a collective, interdisciplinary, scholarly approach to the experiences of people of African descent throughout the world. History, in black studies, constituted the foundation for the analysis of common patterns of life that reflected the social conditions of black people. Africana studies or black studies theoreticians have generally agreed on four goals for this new scholarly field: (1) It should develop solutions to the problems facing black people in the African Diaspora; (2) it should provide an analysis of black culture and life that challenges and replaces preexisting Eurocentric models; (3) it should promote social change and educational reform throughout the academy; and (4) it should institutionalize the study of black people as a field with its own theories, methods, ideologies, symbols, language, and culture. In short, the first generation of advocates envisioned black studies as a revolutionary, historically grounded educational reform movement that sought to make the study of African descendants—their culture, problems, worldviews, and spirituality—a serious scholarly endeavor with practical implications for improving black people's lives.

The Election of 1968

In the presidential campaign of 1968, the Democrats provided the excitement but lost the election. In late 1967 Senator Eugene McCarthy of Minnesota entered the race as the antiwar alternative to Lyndon Johnson, but few politicians took him seriously, even though he won several primaries. Robert Kennedy, U.S. senator from New York, was taken seriously, even though by the time he entered the race in mid-March, most of the convention delegates were already pledged to Johnson, and, after Johnson's withdrawal, they quickly transferred their allegiance to Vice President Hubert Humphrey. Whether Kennedy could have gained the nomination will never be known because—in the second traumatic assassination of 1968—he was murdered in June. Grief over his death, bitterness over the war, and personal rivalries spilled over to produce the most tumultuous political convention in modern American history, with Chicago policemen clubbing and gassing antiwar demonstrators.

In November, Republican Richard Nixon narrowly defeated Humphrey 43.1 percent to 42.7 percent in the popular vote and 301 to 191 in the electoral vote. George Wallace, the segregationist ex-governor of Alabama, in his first serious bid for the presidency, won 13.5 percent of the popular vote and forty-six electoral votes. Running as the candidate of the American Independent Party, Wallace denounced civil rights legislation and court-ordered desegregation. He also endorsed the repression of demonstrators and rioters and promised to stamp out communism in Southeast Asia.

The Nixon Presidency

Of all modern presidents, Richard Nixon is probably the hardest to pin down with neat ideological labels. By the standards of the early twenty-first century, much of his record seems progressive. He created the Environmental Protection Agency, endorsed an equal rights amendment to the Constitution that would have prohibited gender discrimination, and signed more regulatory legislation than any other president. His willingness to innovate in policy affecting African Americans can be illustrated by his naming of Daniel Patrick Moynihan, one of Johnson's experts on social policy, to be his domestic policy adviser. But Nixon also pursued a "southern strategy" that realigned the Republican Party with the white southern backlash to civil rights and weakened the New Deal coalition.

THE "MOYNIHAN REPORT" AND FAP

Moynihan first attracted national attention as assistant secretary of labor in the Johnson administration when a confidential memorandum he wrote—loosely organized and full of sweeping generalizations—was leaked to the press. It would later be published as "The Negro Family: The Case for National Action" and is popularly known as the "Moynihan Report." Moynihan's guiding assumption was that civil rights legislation, necessary as it was, would not address the problems of the inner city. There, he argued, the breakdown of the "lower-class" black family had led to the "pathology" of juvenile delinquency, illegitimacy, drug addiction, and poor performance in school. He attributed the vulnerability of the black family to "three centuries of almost unimaginable treatment" by white society: exploitation under slavery, the strain of urbanization, and persistent unemployment.

These forces, he argued, weakened the role of black men and resulted in a disproportionate number of dysfunctional female-headed families. In the most-often repeated passage in the report, Moynihan declared that the black community had been forced into "a matriarchal structure, [which] because it is so out of line with the rest of American society, seriously retards the progress of the group as a whole, and imposes a crushing burden on the Negro male. . . . Obviously, not every instance of social pathology afflicting the Negro community can be traced to the weakness of family structure. . .[but] once or twice removed, it will be found to be the principal source of most of the aberrant, inadequate, or anti-social behavior that did not establish, but now serves to perpetuate the cycle of poverty and deprivation."

Although based on the work of earlier black scholars, such as E. Franklin Frazier, Moynihan's condemnation of "matriarchy" drew fire. Black social scientists, such as Joyce Ladner, Andrew Billingsley, and Carol Stack, countered that the structure of the black family reflected a functional adaptation that black people had made to survive in a hostile and racist American society. Historians Herbert Gutman and John Blassingame argued that Moynihan underestimated the prevalence of two-parent black families in the past. Although many of the criticisms of the report were deserved, they diverted attention from its positive thrust. Moynihan wanted to eliminate poverty and unemployment in the black community, and he recommended vigorous enforcement of the civil rights laws to achieve equality of opportunity. Setting himself apart from other Johnson administration policy makers, Moynihan was one of the first to appreciate how white resentment of the Community Action Program (CAP) and the expansion of the welfare rolls would make both programs politically unfeasible.

Intrigued with Moynihan's independence, Nixon told him to develop a plan to assist poor families. Under the Family Assistance Plan (FAP) that Nixon unveiled in the summer of 1969, each family of four with no wage earner would receive an annual payment of $1,600 plus $800 of food stamps. With its across-the-board guarantee of income, the plan eliminated an oppressive welfare bureaucracy and reduced the invidious comparison between "welfare recipients" and everyone else.

Had it passed, FAP would have preserved and promoted two-parent families by removing the prohibition against assistance to dependent children whose fathers were alive, well, and living at home. It would also have encouraged work by requiring able-bodied recipients to accept jobs or vocational training and by providing benefits to those accepting low-paying jobs. But although the House approved the plan, the Senate, under pressure both from conservatives who objected to any government programs for the poor and from welfare-rights advocates who complained the payments were too low, killed it. Arguably, at least until President Clinton's failed health-care plan in the 1990s, Nixon's FAP was the most significant failed initiative in the history of American social policy.

BUSING

Yet however flexible he might have been on many issues, Nixon was acutely aware that he moved in a changed political environment and particularly in a far more conservative Republican Party than he had when he ran against and lost to John F. Kennedy in 1960. Then, as a presidential candidate, he had had to appease eastern, pro–civil rights liberals led by New York governor Nelson Rockefeller (1908–1979). But in 1968 an influx of southern segregationists whom Barry Goldwater had attracted to the Republican Party in 1964 had to be appeased. Now Nixon chose to court closer relations with South Carolina senator Strom Thurmond, a Republican who had abandoned the Democratic Party in 1964. Thurmond and his allies had demanded that, if elected, Nixon would slow down the process of court-ordered school desegregation in the South. Finally, Nixon could hardly ignore George Wallace, with his racist appeals. In another three-way race in 1972, Wallace might ensure Nixon's defeat.

As a result of these pressures, the Nixon administration perfected its southern strategy and embarked on a collision course with civil rights organizations such as the NAACP, which supported busing to achieve school integration. Thus the major battle over civil rights in the early 1970s was over the federal courts' willingness to implement desegregation goals by busing students across district lines. Nixon used the busing controversy to lure Wallace voters. In 1971 he had advised federal officials to stop pressing to desegregate schools through "forced busing." He argued that such efforts were ultimately "counterproductive, and not in the interest of better race relations."

Educational segregation in the North reflected residential segregation. In Boston, site of some of the most acrimonious busing protests, schools in black neighborhoods received less funding than their white counterparts. Buildings were derelict, seriously overcrowded, and deficient in supplies and equipment, even desks. In 1974 U.S. district judge W. Arthur Garrity ruled in favor of a group of black parents who had filed a class-action suit against the Boston School Committee. The ruling found the school committee guilty of violating the equal protection clause of the Fourteenth Amendment. To achieve racial balance in the Boston schools, the judge ordered the busing of several thousand students between mostly white South Boston, Hyde Park, and Dorchester, and mostly black Roxbury.

White people who opposed busing organized demonstrations and boycotts to prevent their children from being bused into black communities and black children from being bused into white schools. During the first week of busing to achieve desegregation, white students and their mothers clashed with police officers outside South Boston High School. Violence and hostilities continued for weeks despite the arrests of dozens of people and the closing of bars and liquor stores. Sporadic violence persisted for another two years in Boston.

NIXON AND THE WAR

Meanwhile, the war in Vietnam seemed to drag on endlessly, with the peace negotiations that had begun in Paris in May 1968 making no apparent progress. Nixon realized that what most Americans disliked about the war was that it was killing their sons and husbands. So in 1969 he began to phase out direct U.S. involvement in the war. This "Vietnamization," he claimed, was made possible by the growing ability of the South Vietnamese to fight for themselves. What Nixon did not say was that another reason for troop withdrawals was that the morale of American soldiers was plunging rapidly. Drug abuse among troops was widespread, some soldiers had killed their officers, and some of those incidents had racial overtones. Along with his domestic record, Nixon's promise to "wind down the war" was widely popular and assured his reelection. In 1972 he defeated South Dakota senator George McGovern in a landslide.

Few in the Nixon administration, however, took South Vietnamese military capability seriously, and

Nixon, just as much as Johnson, was unwilling to "lose" Vietnam. Between 1969 and 1971, Nixon stepped up the war. Even as American soldiers were being sent home, he escalated the air war dramatically. In the bombing of Cambodia in 1969–1970, for example—which was kept secret from Congress and the public—the United States dropped more bombs than it had on all of Asia in World War II.

But each time Nixon escalated the war—in the spring of 1970 with a joint American-South Vietnamese invasion of Cambodia, in the spring of 1971 with American air support for an invasion of Laos, in the spring of 1972 with the bombing of North Vietnam and the mining of its harbors—opposition to it grew. Antiwar demonstrations kept Nixon off balance and may have deterred him from further escalation.

The most dramatic response to Nixon's escalation in the Vietnam War came after the invasion of Cambodia in April 1970. The invasion triggered antiwar protests on many campuses. In one such protest, on May 4, Ohio National Guardsmen shot and killed four white students at Kent State University. The response of students across the country was electric: the first nationwide student strike in American history. Ten days later in Mississippi, the shooting and killing of two black students at Jackson State University attracted much less attention from either white students or the media. Three years later, at the beginning of 1973, the United States and North Vietnam signed a peace agreement. Congress then prohibited the reintroduction of American troops and the resumption of bombing, and in 1974 began cutting off military aid to the South Vietnamese government. The result of this loss of American support was predictable: in 1975 the communists launched their final offensive, and South Vietnam collapsed.

NIXON'S DOWNFALL

If Nixon assumed the presidency in 1969 with any popular mandate, it was to restore law and order. The disorder that irritated the American public included many things: the inner-city riots, the antiwar demonstrations and campus protests, and the rise in crime. Responding to this mood, Nixon pushed legislation through Congress that gave local law enforcement officials expanded power to use wiretaps and enter premises without advance warning.

But Nixon's personality—a combination of paranoia and ruthlessness—pushed him beyond what the public would tolerate, and even beyond the law itself. He increasingly confused ordinary criminals with principled protesters and his political opponents, and he decided to punish them all. One method was to create an extralegal ring of burglars, operating out of the White House, to gather incriminating information. In June 1972 they were discovered breaking into Democratic National Committee headquarters in the Watergate apartment complex in Washington. Full details emerged in a Senate investigation in 1973–1974, and on August 9, 1974, threatened with impeachment, Nixon resigned. His downfall, however, left no one of his stature or with his flexible attitude toward public policy to resist the takeover of the Republican Party by more ideologically dogmatic conservatives. One early intimation of this was the difficulty Nixon's successor, Gerald Ford, had in securing the 1976 Republican presidential nomination against the right's new hero, former California governor Ronald Reagan.

The Rise of Black Elected Officials

Just as King searched for a new strategy after the victories of the early phase of the civil rights movement, other black leaders mobilized the newly enfranchised black electorate to win political office. After the adoption of the Voting Rights Act of 1965, Vernon Jordan, director of the Voter Education Project, coordinated registration drives and workshops across the South. As he explained, "Too many of these people have been alienated from the political process for too long a time. . .and so we have to . . . teach them what a local government is, how it operates, and try to relate their votes to the things they want."

By 1974 there were 1,593 black elected officials outside the South, and by 1980 the number had risen to 2,455. Although black people in northern cities had been able to vote for a century and had been slowly developing political muscle and winning representation in state legislatures and on municipal councils, they had not been able to command an equal voice in city governance. The rise of black power and the inspiration of the Voting Rights Act, however, signaled a new departure. People now eagerly engaged in the electoral process to achieve a political influence to which their numbers entitled them. In 1967 in Cleveland, where the black population had skyrocketed after World War II, Carl Stokes became the first black mayor of a major American city, winning election with the support of white business leaders and the solid backing of the black community. In the same year prosecutor

Richard G. Hatcher became mayor of Gary, Indiana, where the black population had also increased greatly after the war. Hatcher won by a mere 1,389 votes, garnering 96 percent of the black vote and 14 percent of the white vote.

THE GARY CONVENTION AND THE BLACK POLITICAL AGENDA

These victories made possible one of the most significant events of recent black political history, the Gary convention of 1972. The co-chairs of the convention were Detroit congressman Charles Diggs, Hatcher, and writer and cultural nationalist Amiri Baraka of Newark, New Jersey. Political scientist Ronald Walters, who helped plan the convention, recalled that various ideological factions had to be placated to make the convention work: "The most important thing about 1972 was the fact that it was an election year, so it provided the environment for the politics taking place. So you had two groups of people who saw this as an opportunity to make some very important statements. One of these, of course, was the black nationalist movement led by Amiri Baraka, Maulana Karenga, and others at that time." The nationalists interpreted "black power" to mean that black people should control their own communities and create separate cultural institutions distinct from those of white society. These views clashed with the ideas espoused by the black elected officials represented by Stokes and Hatcher. According to Walters, "It was this body of people who really were contending for the national leadership of the black community in the early seventies. And in the seventies this new group of black elected officials joined the civil rights leaders and became a new leadership class, but there was sort of a conflict in outlook between them and the more indigenous, social, grass roots-oriented nationalist movement."

Hatcher observed that "people had come to Gary from communities all over the United States where they were politically impotent, but . . . they went back home and rolled up their sleeves and dived into the political arena." Approximately eight thousand people gathered to develop an agenda for black empowerment. The discussions about bloc voting, the efficacy of coalitions, and the feasibility of a third party inspired scores of individual African Americans to run for local office. The convention was not homogeneous, however, and no unified black consensus emerged.

Several discussions over strategies to secure common interests revealed deep-seated internal divisions that allowed ancillary issues to provoke even more impassioned disagreement. Coleman Young and other Michigan delegates walked out to protest a proposal calling for African Americans to reject "discriminatory" unions and form their own. Others walked out over a resolution condemning Israel for its "expansionist policy" toward the Palestinians. Others opposed "forced racial integration of schools" through busing, arguing that such practices insulted black students and would cost black teachers their jobs.

The Gary convention was important because it signaled a shift in the political focus of the black community toward electoral politics and away from mass demonstrations and protest measures. Unity continued to elude subsequent conventions, however, and delegates attending the last National Black Convention at Little Rock, Arkansas, in 1974 abandoned the idea of a black political party. Deep ideological differences and institutional cleavages precluded coalitions and cooperation between black nationalists and the rising numbers of black elected officials. These same differences prevented some nationalists and elected officials from taking seriously the 1972 Democratic Party presidential bid of New York congresswoman Shirley Chisholm.

BLACK PEOPLE GAIN LOCAL OFFICES

Despite the demise of the National Black Convention movement, African Americans continued to register impressive gains in electoral politics. A few statistics indicate the success of black politicians. When the leaders first convened the Gary convention, there were thirteen African-American members of Congress; by 1997 there were forty. In 1972 there were 2,427 black elected officials; by 1993 there were 8,106. An amendment to the Voting Rights Act in 1975 enabled minorities to mount court challenges to at-large voting practices that diluted the impact of bloc voting; this helped increase the number of black elected officials. Districts were redrawn with race as the predominant factor in their reconfiguration. On November 5, 1985, state senator L. Douglas Wilder was elected lieutenant governor in Virginia, making him the first African-American lieutenant governor in a southern state since Reconstruction. In 1989 he was elected governor, making him the first black governor of any state since Reconstruction.

Between 1971 and 1975, the number of African-American mayors rose from 8 to 135, leading to the founding of the National Conference of Black Mayors in 1974. In 1973 Coleman Young in Detroit and Thomas Bradley in Los Angeles became the first African-American mayors of cities of more than a million citizens. Bradley won in Los Angeles even though

black people made up only 15 percent of the city's electorate. Ten years later, in 1983, Chicago swore in its first black mayor, Harold Washington. The era of the black elected official had arrived.

Economic Downturn

The 1970s were a decade of recessions and economic instability. Many black people experienced this economic downturn as a depression. During the 1970s, as the gap between the incomes of the upper 20 percent of African Americans and their white counterparts narrowed, the gap between black men and women at the bottom of the economic ladder and their counterparts expanded. Poor black people were losing ground. In 1969 approximately 10 percent of white men and 25 percent of black men earned less than $10,000 (in 1984 constant dollars). In 1984 about 40 percent of black men between age twenty-five and fifty-five earned less than $10,000 compared with 20 percent of comparable white men. Put a different way, between 1970 and 1986, the proportion of black families with incomes of less than $10,000 grew from 26.8 to 30.2 percent. Still, there were some improvements. The black middle class grew. In 1970, 4.7 percent of black families had incomes of more than $50,000; by 1986 the number had almost doubled to 8.8 percent. But in general, the relative economic status of black workers did not improve.

African-American Women in the Workplace 22-5 DOCUMENT

Black Americans and the Carter Presidency

In 1976 the United States celebrated its bicentennial. Flags flew from every flagpole, and fire hydrants were painted red, white, and blue. Tall ships sailed into New York harbor from around the world, and there were more parades than anyone could count. For African Americans, it was an important year, but for another reason. For the first time since 1964, the man most of them voted for was elected president—Jimmy Carter, a former governor of Georgia. Ninety percent of African-American voters favored the soft-spoken, religious Georgia Democrat over incumbent president Gerald Ford. As in 1960 their votes were crucial; without them, Carter could not have even carried his native South.

Presidential Candidate Jimmy Carter on Racial Segregation 22-7 DOCUMENT

The National Black Convention Movement of the Black Power Era

1965	Maulena Karenga founds the US (as opposed to them) Organization in Los Angeles, California; advocates cultural nationalism
1966	Amiri Baraka founds Spirit House Movers and Players in Newark, New Jersey; advocates cultural nationalism
1966	Huey P. Newton and Bobby Seale found the Black Panther Party
1966	Stokely Carmichael embraces and popularizes the term "black power"
1966	Representative Adam Clayton Powell Jr. hosts the first Black Power Conference
1967	Second Black Power Conference, held in Newark, New Jersey, calls for partitioning the United States into separate black and white nations
1968	Third Black Power Conference is held in Philadelphia, Pennsylvania
1969	National Black Economic Development Conference held in Detroit, Michigan
1969	Last Black Power Conference, held in Bermuda, ends in disarray
1970	Congress of Afrikan Peoples, led by Amiri Baraka, is organized in Atlanta, Georgia; adopts the slogan, "It's nation time"
1971	The Reverend Jesse Jackson founds People United to Save Humanity (PUSH) in Chicago, Illinois
1972	National Black Political Convention is held in Gary, Indiana
1973	National Black Feminist Organization is founded by Eleanor Holmes Norton and Margaret Sloan
1974	Last National Black Political Convention is held in Little Rock, Arkansas

1965–1974

BLACK APPOINTEES

Carter acknowledged his debt to the black electorate by appointing African Americans to highly visible posts. He named Patricia Harris secretary of Housing and Urban Development, making her the first black woman to serve in the cabinet. Carter appointed Andrew Young, former congressman from Georgia and a longtime political ally, ambassador to the United Nations. (Young was forced to resign in 1979.) Clifford Alexander Jr. became the secretary of the army.

Eleanor Holmes Norton became the first woman to chair the Equal Employment Opportunity Commission (EEOC). Ernest Green, who had been one of the nine students to desegregate Little Rock's Central High School, was appointed assistant secretary of the Department of Labor. Wade McCree was appointed solicitor general in the Justice Department. Drew Days III became assistant attorney general for civil rights. Historian and former University of Colorado chancellor Mary Frances Berry was appointed assistant secretary for education. Carter also named Louis Martin his special assistant, making him the first African American in a position of influence on the White House staff.

CARTER'S DOMESTIC POLICIES

There are many ways to judge the significance of the Carter presidency to African Americans. Carter's black appointments were practically and symbolically important. Never had so many black men and women occupied positions that had direct and immediate impact on the day-to-day operations of the federal government. Carter also helped cement gains for civil rights. When Congress passed legislation to stop busing for schoolchildren as a means of integrating the schools, Carter vetoed it. He tried to improve fair employment practices by strengthening the enforcement powers of the EEOC. His Justice Department chose cases to prosecute under the Fair Housing Act that involved widespread discrimination, to make the greatest possible impact.

Yet Carter's overall record proved unsatisfactory to most African Americans. Despite a Public Works Employment Act that directed 10 percent of public works funds to minority contractors and helped spur the creation of 585,000 jobs, Carter failed to help Democrats in Congress pass either full-employment or universal health-care bills. He also cut social welfare programs in an attempt to balance the budget, including school lunch programs and financial aid to black students.

Although the sluggish economy undermined Carter's popularity, the event that proved his undoing was the Iran hostage crisis that began in the fall of 1979. For many black people, however, Carter had become a disappointment long before that. They believed he had done little to help them achieve social justice and economic advancement. Still, the nomination of the conservative Ronald Reagan by the Republicans left black voters no alternative to Carter. In the election of 1980, 90 percent of black voters again supported him, but this time they could not prevent his defeat. Carter pulled down scores of Democrats with him, and the Republicans regained the Senate for the first time since 1954.

CONCLUSION

The civil rights movement's victories changed African-American life in particular and American culture in general. The black power and black arts movements continued the struggle for freedom in northern and western urban areas where housing segregation, rising unemployment, and persistent police brutality sparked rebellions that resulted in many deaths and widespread destruction in Watts, Newark, Detroit, and other cities. The black political convention movement did not create a black third party. But one of the most enduring legacies of the era was the rise of black elected officials. Black student militancy persisted despite the destruction of the Black Panther Party. Throughout the late 1960s and 1970s, black students fought to create and institutionalize black studies as a new academic field. The black arts and black consciousness movement opened up new avenues for the expression of black unity and positive black identity. A new generation of black poets, dramatists, and musicians found receptive audiences.

The legislative successes of the early phase of the civil rights movement illuminated how much more needed to be done to achieve a truly egalitarian society. Poor people, black and white, needed jobs, housing, medical care, and education. To varying degrees, Presidents Johnson, Nixon, and Carter attempted to address these needs. Their efforts produced mixed results in the face of a disastrous war in Vietnam and a massive white backlash. In the 1980s Republicans would reap the benefit of the Democratic Party's disarray, and the plight of the poor would deteriorate.

Still, some black intellectuals chose a long view in their assessment of the significance of the post–World War II decades of struggle. Historian and theologian Vincent Harding put it most eloquently:

> It may be that the greatest discovery . . . was the fact that there is no last word in the human struggle for freedom, justice, and democracy. Only the continuing word, lived out by men, women, and children who dance and rest, who wrestle with alligators and stand firm before tanks, and presidents, and drug lords and deep, deep, fears. We learn again that the continuing word remains embedded in those who determined not to be moved, who know, against all odds, that they will overcome, will continue to create a more perfect union, a more compassionate world. The world remains with those who discover, in the midst of unremitting struggle, deep amazing powers within their own lives, power from, power for, the planet.

RECOMMENDED READING

Stokely Carmichael and Charles V. Hamilton. *Black Power: The Politics of Liberation in America.* New York: Vintage Books, 1967. One of the most important books of the era of black power, by Carmichael, who popularized the slogan, and political scientist Hamilton.

Theodore Cross. *The Black Power Imperative: Racial Inequality and the Politics of Nonviolence.* New York: Faulkner Books, 1984. Provides a useful critique of the black power movement and explores the persistence of racial inequality.

Robert Dalleck. *Flawed Giant: Lyndon B. Johnson and His Times 1961–1973.* New York: Oxford University Press, 1998. A definitive biography of President Lyndon Johnson with fresh insights, grounded in exhaustive research.

Henry Hampton and Steve Fayer, eds. *Voices of Freedom: An Oral History of the Civil Rights Movement from the 1950s through the 1980s.* New York: Bantam Books, 1990. Contains the recollections of all the key participants in the critical battles and movements of the three decades that transformed race relations in America.

Michael D. Harris. *Colored Pictures: Race and Visual Representation.* Chapel Hill: University of North Carolina Press, 2003. A splendid study of how race has been represented and visualized, with insightful analyses of arts movements and informative discussions of black painters.

Robert C. Smith. *We Have No Leaders: African Americans in the Post–Civil Rights Era.* New York: State University of New York Press, 1996. A thoughtful critique of the successes and failures of black politics beginning with the National Black Political Convention in Gary, Indiana, in 1972.

Wallace Terry. *Bloods: An Oral History of the Vietnam War by Black Veterans.* New York: Ballantine Books, 1984. One of the best sources for firsthand accounts of the Vietnam War as experienced by black soldiers.

Brian Ward. *Just My Soul Responding: Rhythm and Blues, Black Consciousness, and Race Relations.* Berkeley: University of California Press, 1998. An excellent study of black popular culture during the civil rights and black power movement era.

Craig Hansen Werner. *Playing the Changes: From Afro-Modernism to the Jazz Impulse.* Urbana: University of Illinois Press, 1994. An insightful study of the gospel, blues, and jazz impulse in the writings of key black writers, including James Baldwin and Leon Forrest, during the post–civil rights movement era.

ADDITIONAL BIBLIOGRAPHY

BLACK PANTHERS

Philip S. Foner, ed. *The Black Panther Speaks.* Philadelphia: Lippincott, 1970.

Toni Morrison, ed. *To Die for the People: The Writings of Huey P. Newton.* New York: Writers and Readers Publishing, 1995.

AFRICAN-AMERICAN EVENTS	NATIONAL EVENTS
1965	
1965 Malcolm X assassinated	1965 President Johnson authorizes the bombing of North Vietnam
Watts riot Voting Rights Act of 1965 enacted	1966 National Organization for Women (NOW) is formed
1966 Black Panther Party formed Stokely Carmichael coins the slogan "black power"	
Chicago campaign begins Edward William Brooke of Massachusetts elected the first black U.S. senator since Reconstruction	
Robert C. Weaver becomes first black cabinet officer	
Strike at San Francisco State University results in first black studies program	
1967	
1967 Uprisings in Newark, Detroit, and other cities	1968 North Vietnam launches Tet Offensive
Muhammad Ali refuses to be drafted	U.S. and North Vietnam begin peace talks
Thurgood Marshall confirmed as first black Supreme Court justice	Johnson declines to run for another term
Adam Clayton Powell Jr. denied his seat in Congress	Robert Kennedy assassinated
1968 Kerner Commission Report released	Richard M. Nixon elected president
Poor People's Campaign in Washington, D.C.	Secret bombing of Cambodia
Orangeburg Massacre Martin Luther King Jr. assassinated	
Shirley Chisholm elected to the U.S. House of Representatives	
Carl Stokes elected mayor of Cleveland and Richard Hatcher elected mayor of Gary, Indiana	

Kenneth O'Reilly. *Racial Matters: The FBI's Secret File on Black America, 1960–1972.* New York: Free Press, 1989.

Robert Scheer, ed. *Eldridge Cleaver: Post-Prison Writings and Speeches.* New York: Random House, 1969.

BLACK POWER AND POLITICS

Robert L. Allen. *Black Awakening in Capitalist America.* Trenton, NJ: Africa World Press, 1990.

Elaine Brown. *A Taste of Power: A Black Woman's Story.* New York: Pantheon, 1992.

James H. Cone. *Martin & Malcolm & America: A Dream or a Nightmare.* Maryknoll, NY: Orbis, 1991.

Sidney Fine. *Violence in the Model City: The Cavanagh Administration, Race Relations and the Detroit Riot of 1967.* Ann Arbor: University of Michigan Press, 1989.

James F. Finley Jr. *Church People in the Struggle: The National Council of Churches and the Black Freedom Movement, 1950–1970.* New York: Oxford University Press, 1993.

Frye Gaillard. *The Dream Long Deferred.* Chapel Hill: University of North Carolina Press, 1988.

B. I. Kaufman. *The Presidency of James E. Carter, Jr.* Lawrence: University of Kansas Press, 1993.

Steven Lawson. *In Pursuit of Power: Southern Blacks and Electoral Politics, 1965–1982.* New York: Columbia University Press, 1985.

C. Eric Lincoln. *The Black Muslims in America.* Boston: Beacon Press, 1961.

J. Anthony Lukas. *Common Ground.* New York: Knopf, 1985.

John T. McCartney. *Black Power Ideologies: An Essay in African-American Thought.* Philadelphia: Temple University Press, 1992.

William B. McClain. *Black People in the Methodist Church.* Cambridge, MA: Schenkman, 1984.

Larry G. Murphy. *Down by the Riverside: Readings in African American Religion.* New York: New York University Press, 2000.

William E. Nelson Jr. and Philip J. Meranto. *Electing Black Mayors: Political Action in the Black Community.* Columbus: Ohio State University Press, 1977.

Gary Orfield. *Must We Bus? Segregated Schools and National Policy.* Washington, DC: Brookings Institution, 1978.

Robert A. Pratt. *The Color of Their Skin: Education and Race in Richmond, Virginia, 1954–89.* Charlottesville: University Press of Virginia, 1992.

James R. Ralph Jr. *Northern Protest: Martin Luther King, Jr., Chicago, and the Civil Rights Movement.* Cambridge, MA: Harvard University Press, 1993.

Diane Ravitch. *The Great School Wars.* New York: Basic Books, 1974.

Wilbur C. Rich. *Coleman Young and Detroit Politics.* Detroit, MI: Wayne State University Press, 1989.

Bobby Seale. *Seize the Time.* New York: Random House, 1970.

James Melvin Washington. *Frustrated Fellowship: The Black Baptist Quest for Social Power.* Macon, GA: Mercer University Press, 1986.

Delores S. Williams. *Sisters in the Wilderness: The Challenge of Womanist God-Talk.* Maryknoll, NY: Orbis, 1993.

Gayraud S. Wilmore. *Black Religion and Black Radicalism.* New York: Anchor Press, 1973.

BLACK STUDIES AND BLACK STUDENTS

Talmadge Anderson, ed. *Black Studies: Theory, Method, and Cultural Perspectives.* Pullman: Washington State University Press, 1990.

Jack Bass and Jack Nelson. *The Orangeburg Massacre.* 1970. (1970 new ed. Mason, GA; Mercer Univ. Press, 2003).

William H. Exum. *Paradoxes of Protest: Black Student Activism in a White University.* Philadelphia: Temple University Press, 1985.

Richard P. McCormick. *The Black Student Protest Movement at Rutgers.* New Brunswick, NJ: Rutgers University Press, 1990.

Cleveland Sellers, with Robert Terrell. *The River of No Return: The Autobiography of a Black Militant and the Life and Death of SNCC.* New York: William Morrow, 1987.

CLASS AND RACE

Jack M. Bloom. *Class, Race, and the Civil Rights Movement.* Bloomington: Indiana University Press, 1987.

Martin Gilens. *Why Americans Hate Welfare: Race, Media, and the Politics of Antipoverty Policy.* Chicago: University of Chicago Press, 1999.

Michael Katz. *The Undeserving Poor: From the War on Poverty to the War on Welfare.* New York: Pantheon Books, 1989.

Bart Landry. *The New Black Middle Class.* Berkeley: University of California Press, 1987.

William Julius Wilson. *The Truly Disadvantaged: The Inner City, the Underclass, and Public Policy.* Chicago: University of Chicago Press, 1987.

BLACK ARTS AND BLACK CONSCIOUSNESS MOVEMENTS

William L. Andrews, Frances Smith Foster, and Trudier Harris, eds. *The Oxford Companion to African American Literature.* New York: Oxford University Press, 1997.

James Baldwin. *Notes of a Native Son.* New York: Dial Press, 1955.

———. *Nobody Knows My Name.* New York: Dial Press, 1961.

———. *The Fire Next Time.* New York: Dial Press, 1963.

———. *No Name in the Street.* New York: Dial Press, 1972.

Imamu Amiri Baraka. *Dutchman and the Slave, Two Plays by LeRoi Jones.* New York: William Morrow, 1964.

Samuel A. Hay. *African American Theater: An Historical and Critical Analysis.* Cambridge, MA: Cambridge University Press, 1994.

• 1969 •

AFRICAN-AMERICAN EVENTS

1969
Harvard establishes an Afro-American Studies program

Maulana Karenga publishes *Introduction to Black Studies*

Black Panther leaders Fred Hampton and Mark Clarke killed in Chicago police raid

1970
Jackson State killings

Angela Davis placed on the FBI's Ten Most Wanted list

NATIONAL EVENTS

1970
U.S. incursion into Cambodia

Kent State killings

• 1971 •

1971
Angela Davis arraigned

Jesse Jackson founds People United to Save Humanity (PUSH)

Busing to achieve integration begins

1972
First National Black Political Convention held in Gary, Indiana

Shirley Chisholm makes a bid for the Democratic presidential nomination

Barbara Jordan elected to the House of Representatives

Angela Davis acquitted

1972
Watergate break-in

Nixon reelected president

• 1973 •

1973
Thomas Bradley elected mayor of Los Angeles

Coleman Young elected mayor of Detroit

1974
National Council for Black Studies formed

1974
Watergate hearings

Nixon resigns

• 1975 •

1975
Antibusing protests break out in Boston

1976
Andrew Young named U.S. ambassador to the United Nations

1975
South Vietnam falls

1976
Jimmy Carter elected president

• 1979 •

1979
Andrew Young resigns as U.S. ambassador

1979
Iran hostage crisis begins

1980
Ronald Reagan elected president

AFRICAN-AMERICAN EVENTS   **NATIONAL EVENTS**

LeRoi Jones. *Blues People: Negro Music in White America.* New York: William Morrow, 1963.

LeRoi Jones and Larry Neal, eds. *Black Fire: An Anthology of Afro-American Writing.* New York: William Morrow, 1968.

Frank Kofsky. *Black Nationalism and the Revolution in Music.* New York: Pathfinder Press, 1970.

Larry Neal. *Visions of a Liberated Future: Black Arts Movement Writings.* New York: Thunder's Mouth Press, 1989.

Leslie Catherine Sanders. *The Development of Black Theater in America: From Shadow to Selves.* Baton Rouge: Louisiana State University Press, 1988.

Suzanne E. Smith. *Dancing in the Streets: Motown and the Cultural Politics of Detroit.* Cambridge, MA: Harvard University Press, 2000.

AUTOBIOGRAPHY AND BIOGRAPHY

Imamu Amiri Baraka. *The Autobiography of LeRoi Jones.* New York: Freundlich Books, 1984.

Dennis C. Dickerson. *Militant Mediator: Whitney M. Young, Jr.* Lexington: University Press of Kentucky, 1998.

James Farmer. *Lay Bare the Heart: An Autobiography of the Civil Rights Movement.* New York: Arbor House, 1985.

Jimmie Lewis Franklin. *Back to Birmingham: Richard Arrington, Jr., and His Times.* Tuscaloosa: University of Alabama Press, 1989.

Elliott J. Gorn, ed. *Muhammad Ali: The People's Champ.* Urbana: University of Illinois Press, 1995.

Charles V. Hamilton. *Adam Clayton Powell, Jr.: The Political Biography of an American Dilemma.* New York: Atheneum, 1991.

Hil Haygood. *King of the Cats: The Life and Times of Adam Clayton Powell, Jr.* Boston: Houghton Mifflin, 1993.

David Remnick. *King of the World: Muhammad Ali and the Rise of an American Hero.* New York: Random House, 1998.

Mary Beth Rogers. *Barbara Jordan: American Hero.* New York: Bantam Books, 1998.

Kathleen Rout. *Eldridge Cleaver.* Boston: Twayne Publishers, 1991.

Bobby Seale. *Seize the Time.* New York: Random House, 1970.

Nancy J. Weiss. *Whitney M. Young, Jr., and the Struggle for Civil Rights.* Princeton, NJ: Princeton University Press, 1989.

RETRACING THE ODYSSEY

Motown Museum, Detroit, Michigan. Birthplace of Berry Gordy's Motown Record Corporation, founded in 1957. The "Motown Sound" exemplified the music of such performers as The Jackson Five, Gladys Knight and the Pips, Marvin Gaye, and Stevie Wonder. A sign hangs on the front of the structure, "Hitsville U.S.A.," acknowledging the importance of this state historic site. The museum is composed of two adjoining houses filled with memorabilia

of gold record awards, album covers, costumes, and musical instruments. Visitors are able to view in Studio A the original control booth where hits by the Temptations, Supremes, and other artists were recorded.

DuSable Museum of African-American History, Chicago. In 1961 artist Margaret Goss Burroughs opened, in her home, the Ebony Museum, which moved in 1973 to its present location at Washington Park. It is now one of the nation's major museums of black history, life, and culture. It houses an extensive collection of artifacts, art, books, and civil rights documents and sponsors a diverse array of cultural and educational programs. The DuSable Museum is named in honor of Jean Baptiste Pointe DuSable, a Haitian-born immigrant who arrived in Chicago in 1779 and was the first non-Indian to settle in the area.

Southern Poverty Law Center Civil Rights Memorial, Montgomery, Alabama. The Civil Rights Memorial captures the history of the freedom struggle while ensuring that we do not forget the costs so many paid in the ongoing struggle against racism and social inequality.

The Martin Luther King, Jr. National Historic Site, Atlanta, Georgia. The district is composed of Martin Luther King's birthplace and gravesite. The Ebenezer Baptist Church, where three generations of King men served as pastors, along with an informative National Park Service Visitors Center, provides a detailed overview of King's life. Also in the district is the Martin Luther King, Jr., Center for Non-Violent Social Change, which contains King's personal papers and the records of the Southern Christian Leadership Conference in addition to an oral history collection.

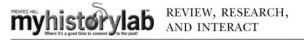

PRENTICE HALL **myhistorylab**   REVIEW, RESEARCH, AND INTERACT

REVIEW QUESTIONS

1. Why did African-American residents of Watts, Newark, and Detroit rebel in 1965–1966? What did these rebellions suggest about the value of the civil rights movement victories?

2. How did the visions and ideals, successes and failures of Martin Luther King Jr. compare with those of Lyndon B. Johnson? Why were these men at odds with each other?

3. What role did African Americans play in the Vietnam War?

4. In what ways can the presidency of Richard Nixon be considered progressive? Which reforms initiated by President Lyndon B. Johnson did Nixon advance once he took office?

5. What were the major ideological concerns of the artists of the black arts movement? To what extent did Baldwin and Amiri Baraka have similar views about art, consciousness, aesthetics, and politics?

6. Why did African Americans not form a third political party? What was the significance of the rise of black elected officials?

7. Why were African Americans disappointed with the presidency of Jimmy Carter?

www.researchnavigator.com

Using the tools available in Research Navigator, consider this question:
What were the key positions of advocates of the black power movement?

PRIMARY SOURCE DOCUMENTS

Black Politics, White Backlash

DID JESSE JACKSON's 1984 AND 1988
PRESIDENTIAL CAMPAIGNS PROVOKE
A WHITE BACKLASH?

WHY DID AFRICAN AMERICANS REMAIN
SO SUPPORTIVE OF BILL CLINTON's PRESIDENCY
AND ATTACHED TO THE DEMOCRATIC PARTY?

HOW DID DEBATES OVER AFFIRMATIVE ACTION,
REPARATIONS, AND WELFARE INFLUENCE
THE POLITICAL REALIGNMENTS OF BLACK
AND WHITE AMERICANS DURING THE REAGAN,
BUSH, AND CLINTON ADMINISTRATIONS?

HOW DID PROMINENT BLACK CONSERVATIVES
ADVANCE THE IDEOLOGICAL, SOCIAL,
AND ECONOMIC AGENDA OF THE REPUBLICAN PARTY?

HOW DID THE EVENTS OF 9/11,
THE WAR IN IRAQ, AND THE IMPACT OF HURRICANE
KATRINA AFFECT BLACK POLITICAL CONSCIOUSNESS?

◀◀ **Many African-American** residents in New Orleans found
themselves stranded literally and figuratively when the levees
broke in the wake of Hurricane Katrina and the federal and
state governments failed to provide prompt and sufficient
relief and rescue efforts.

2006–2008

Many were lost in the struggle for the right to vote: Jimmie Lee Jackson, a young student, gave his life; Viola Liuzzo, a White mother from Detroit, called nigger lover, had her brains blown out at point blank range; [Michael] Schwerner, [Andrew] Goodman and [James] Chaney—two Jews and a Black—found in a common grave, bodies riddled with bullets in Mississippi; the four darling little girls in a church in Birmingham, Alabama. They died that we might have a right to live.

Dr. Martin Luther King Jr. lies only a few miles from us tonight. Tonight he must feel good as he looks down upon us. We sit here together, a rainbow, a coalition—the sons and daughters of slavemasters and the sons and daughters of slaves, sitting together around a common table, to decide the direction of our party and our country. His heart would be full tonight.

We meet tonight at the crossroads, a point of decision. Shall we expand, be inclusive, find unity and power; or suffer division and impotence?

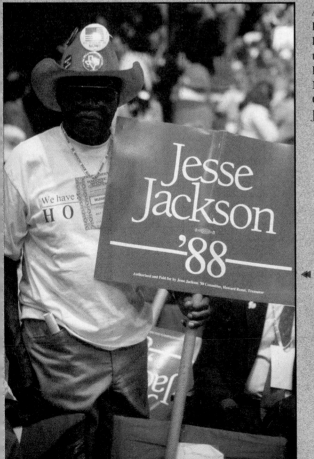

Address by the Reverend Jesse Louis Jackson to the Democratic National Convention, July 19, 1988

◄ A delegate to the 1988 Democratic National Convention holds a sign supporting Jesse Jackson for president.

Jesse Jackson's two bids for the Democratic Party's nomination for president in 1984 and 1988 accomplished many things, but unity was not one of them. In 2007 another African American, U.S. Senator Barack Obama of Illinois, launched his campaign to become the Democratic presidential candidate, challenging Americans to embrace audacity and hope in the face of mounting despair and anguish. The closing decades of the twentieth century were characterized by sharp divisions between white and black Americans and between the Democratic and Republican parties, and by growing economic disparities between working-class and middle-class Americans and the rich. The conservative right used the years of the Carter administration (1977–1981) to create political organizations that supported school prayers, and it attacked women's right to choose and the civil rights claims of gays and lesbians.

Throughout the 1980s white conservatives nurtured and mobilized their base of disillusioned southerners, alienated northerners, and wealthy elites to reverse liberal-progressive policies, such as affirmative action and reforms epitomized by the Voting Rights Act of 1965. Under the leadership of Presidents Ronald Reagan and George H. W. Bush (1981–1993), African America witnessed a consolidation of Republican Party power. As they developed and adhered to a liberal-progressive agenda that emphasized jobs, health care, education, environmental justice, and freedom of opportunity, African Americans chose not to develop a race-conscious third party. Instead, black voters overwhelmingly put their hopes in the Democratic Party.

Thus, not only did the country's party alignment increasingly reflect its racial divisions, but fractures also developed along class lines within the black community. The growing black middle class sought to use electoral politics to share fully in America's educational, social, and political institutions. But not all black Americans benefited equally from the gains of the civil rights movement. The ranks of the black poor swelled as urban areas devastated by the rebellions and riots of the 1960s, job losses, and white flight sank into deep poverty. By 2000, a white conservative backlash combined with inadequate housing, lack of health insurance, resource-starved schools, and reduced funding for welfare and job training programs dampened the expectations and damaged the health and dignity of many poorer black people. Neither Democrats nor Republicans supported a massive urban development and jobs programs for black citizens comparable to the Marshall Plan that had helped rebuild Europe after World War II. In sum, as scholar Nikhil Pal Singh noted, "Despite the growth of a black middle class [during the prosperous 1990s], three decades after the passage of the Civil Rights Act the median net worth of whites—which includes inherited assets as well as income—is a staggering twelve times that of blacks."

Despite the setbacks of the 1980s, African Americans hoped the election in 1992 of William Jefferson (Bill) Clinton to the presidency represented the rise of the rainbow coalition of progressive forces championed in the 1980s by Jesse Jackson. Clinton was undoubtedly a friend to African America, but these hopes were only partly fulfilled. Yet as Donna Brazile, who had worked in Jesse Jackson's campaign and in 2000 would manage Al Gore's doomed race for the White House, wrote, under Clinton the 1990s were a new era of black power. And, despite the conservative triumph in the 2000 elections, the NAACP and other organizations crafted a broad national and international political agenda during the 2004 presidential race, and a generation of new black politicians, such as Barack Obama and Deval Patrick of Massachusetts, addressed the economic, health-care, education, and security concerns of black and white America in a healing new centrist voice.

This chapter explores the complexity, contradictions, ironies, and tensions between race-conscious progressive politics and conservative backlash politics from 1980 to the opening years of the new millennium.

Ronald Reagan and the Conservative Reaction

Beginning in the late 1970s, American politics took a hard turn to the right. This shift profoundly affected African Americans, particularly the poor. With the election of Ronald Reagan (1911–2004) to the presidency in 1980, the executive branch ceased to support expanded civil rights. It also sought to reduce welfare programs, and it staffed key agencies and the federal judiciary with opponents of affirmative action. The now overwhelmingly white Republican Party became increasingly entrenched in the South, ending the Democrats' long dominance in that region. The political landscape of the 1980s and 1990s was thus marked by realignment and a hardening of ideological conflict between liberal and progressive Democrats on one side and conservative Republicans on the other.

Ronald Reagan's defeat of Jimmy Carter in the 1980 presidential election marked the emergence of the New Right as the dominant force in American politics. Reagan possessed charm and the ability to communicate his vision to the American people. His election was the result of more than personal charisma, however. Over the previous decade, many groups unhappy with the changes of the 1960s had developed powerful political organizations that found a home in the Republican Party. These groups included those opposed to equal rights for women, to abortion rights, to the Supreme Court's decisions protecting the rights of the accused and banning compulsory prayer from the public schools, and a range of other issues. White southerners opposed to the changes wrought by the civil rights movement, and white northerners angry at school busing, affirmative action programs, and the tax burden they associated with welfare, were a key part of this coalition.

Richard Viguerie, Why the New Right Is Winning, 1981   23-2   DOCUMENT

DISMANTLING THE GREAT SOCIETY

One of the New Right's goals was to reverse the growth of social welfare programs created during and after the New Deal. To this end, from 1981 to 1992, Reagan and his Republican successor George H. W. Bush cut federal grants to cities in half and terminated programs crucial to the stability of many black families. As the federal government slashed funds earmarked toward redeveloping inner cities and constructing public housing between 1980 and 1992, the percentage of city budgets derived from the federal government declined from 14.3 percent to 5 percent. As a result, inner-city neighborhoods, where 56 percent of poor residents were African American, became more unstable. Reagan advanced a trickle-down theory of economics. He believed that if the financial position of the wealthiest Americans improved, their increased prosperity would percolate through the middle and working classes to the poor. Unemployment statistics soon challenged this theory. By December 1982, the unemployment rate had risen to 10.8, and the rate for African Americans was twice that of white Americans. The real income of the highest-paid 1 percent of the nation, meanwhile, increased from $312,206 to $548,970 during the 1980s.

Growing Inequality

Reagan and Bush often cloaked their intent to undermine rights-oriented policies by appointing black conservatives to key administrative positions. Reagan chose William Bell, for example, to replace the effective Carter appointee Eleanor Holmes Norton as chair of the Equal Employment Opportunity Commission (EEOC). Because Bell had few qualifications for the post, civil rights leaders and organizations immediately protested his appointment. Reagan simply replaced Bell the following year with yet another black conservative, Clarence Thomas, who opposed affirmative action. Thomas reduced the commission's staff and allowed the backlog of affirmative action cases to grow to 46,000 and processing time to increase to ten months.

Reagan similarly tried to change the direction of the U.S. Commission on Civil Rights (CCR), but in this case he met with resistance. Since its creation in 1957, the commission had served as a civil rights watchdog, with no real enforcement powers but with influence on public opinion. Soon after Reagan took office, the CCR began to issue reports critical of his civil rights policies. Reagan responded by trying to load the commission with members sympathetic to his perspective. He replaced the commission's chair, Arthur S. Flemming, who was white, with a black Republican, Clarence Pendleton, former executive director of the San Diego Urban League. The vice chair, however, was Mary Frances Berry, a respected civil rights activist and historian who had been appointed by Carter and who frequently clashed with the new president. In 1984 Reagan tried to remove Berry from the CCR, but she sued in court to retain her position. When she won her case, she became known as "the woman the president could not fire." Nevertheless, the CCR declined to insignificance under Pendleton during the Reagan years.

BLACK CONSERVATIVES

Men like Bell, Thomas, and Pendleton were part of a vocal cadre of black, middle-class, conservative intellectuals, professionals, and politicians who gained prominence during the Reagan years. To augment their influence in the Republican Party, these conservatives cultivated a small, well-educated, articulate group of black men and women intellectuals in addition to black politicians. Prominent black proponents of conservative ideology include Thomas

Sowell, Walter Williams, Shelby Steele, Armstrong Williams, Ward Connerly, and, until he broke with the others in the late 1990s, Glenn Loury. There was a critical difference, however, between elite black Republicans and the black Democratic politicians: black Republicans rarely exercised meaningful power within the party. They were expected to embrace the values and goals set down by the white party leaders. In contrast, elite black Democratic politicians could, and often did, make their influence felt. Moreover, they represented a large and essential constituency within the party.

THE THOMAS–HILL CONTROVERSY

The role of black conservatives was highlighted when, in 1991, President George H. W. Bush nominated Clarence Thomas to the U.S. Supreme Court. Thomas was born in 1948 in rural Georgia. He graduated from Holy Cross College in Massachusetts and Yale Law School. The symbolism of Thomas, who opposed the expansion of civil rights, replacing Thurgood Marshall, the greatest civil rights lawyer of the twentieth century, could not have been more dramatic.

Thomas's nomination precipitated the most public exposure of gender conflict within the black community in history. Marshall had been one of the Court's great liberals and a staunch defender of civil rights. Thomas was a black conservative whose record on civil rights did not endear him either to white liberals or to many within the black community. His credentials for the position were also questionable: he had served only fifteen months as an appellate court judge. However, the black community was loath publicly to contest his nomination or challenge the cynical tokenism of the Bush administration. Still, civil rights organizations expressed grave reservations about the Thomas nomination. The Urban League declared, "We welcome the appointment of an African-American jurist to fill the vacant seat left by Justice [Thurgood] Marshall. Obviously, Judge Thomas is no Justice Marshall. But if he were, this administration would not have appointed him. We are hopeful that Judge Thomas' background of poverty and minority status will lead him to greater identification with those in America who today are victimized by poverty and discrimination. And [we] expect the Senate, in the confirmation hearings, to explore whether he is indeed likely to do so."

The anticipated easy confirmation process derailed when black law professor Anita Hill agreed to appear before the Senate Judiciary Committee, which heard testimony on Thomas's confirmation. Hill accused Thomas of sexually harassing her when she worked for him at the EEOC.

Both Anita Hill and Clarence Thomas were conservative Republicans, and both had earned law degrees at Yale. Hill did not volunteer to testify about Thomas's sexual harassment. She had answered questions put to her in a confidential investigation. When her answers were leaked to the press, she agreed to appear before the committee. Some senators questioned her character and integrity. Thomas charged that he was a victim of a "high-tech lynching" in the media and that Hill's accusations were false. Although many in the black community supported Thomas, progressive feminists, white liberals, and some black people supported Hill. Activist black women were incensed by the treatment that Hill received from the Senate and were determined to voice their opposition to Thomas's political views. Despite the opposition, Thomas won confirmation to the Court by a narrow 52 to 48 majority. On the Court, Thomas has proved to be an archconservative who consistently votes against progressive or liberal causes such as affirmative action.

DEBATING THE "OLD" AND THE "NEW" CIVIL RIGHTS

The Reagan and Bush administrations distinguished between what might be called the "old civil rights law," which they claimed to support, and the "new civil rights law," which they opposed. Developed in the decade between the *Brown* decision and the Voting Rights Act of 1965, the old civil rights law prohibited intentional discrimination, be it legal segregation in the schools, informal discrimination in the workplace, or racially biased restrictions on voting. The new civil rights law is concerned with discriminatory outcomes, as measured by statistical disparities, rather than with discriminatory intent. If, for example, black children overall are disproportionately in all-black schools, or if the workforce in a given firm, compared with the community in which it is located, is disproportionately white (or male), or if elected officials in a multiracial state or municipality are disproportionately white, discrimination is assumed.

The remedies for such historic discrimination, collectively labeled **affirmative action,** tend to be statistical in nature. They include increasing the number of minority pupils, minority employees, or (by redrawing the districts from which they were elected) minority elected officials to correspond to the percentage of the relevant minority population. In employment (and in admissions to colleges and universities), the methods used in reaching these goals became known as affirmative action "guidelines." Sometimes guidelines were imposed by court order; more often they were the result of voluntary efforts by legislatures, government

As a justice on the United States Supreme Court Clarence Thomas has staunchly adhered to conservative values in all of his opinions.

Anita Hill, a law professor at the University of Oklahoma, testified before the U.S. Senate Judiciary Committee Confirmation hearings that Supreme Court nominee Clarence Thomas had sexually harassed her. Thomas was confirmed in spite of these sexual harassment charges.

BLACK WOMEN IN DEFENSE OF THEMSELVES

Within days after Anita Hill appeared before the Senate Judiciary Committee, a group of black women led by Elsa Barkley Brown, Barbara Ransby, and Deborah King raised more than $50,000 to purchase a three-quarter-page ad in the New York Times *to print this statement, "In Defense of Ourselves." Appearing on November 17, 1991, it was signed by 1,603 black women. Five black newspapers— the* San Francisco Sun Reporter, *the* Los Angeles Sentinel, *the* New York City Sun, *the* Atlanta Inquirer, *and the* Chicago Defender—*also published the statement.*

As women of African descent, we are deeply troubled by the recent nomination, confirmation and seating of Clarence Thomas as an Associate Justice of the U.S. Supreme Court. We know that the presence of Clarence Thomas on the Court will be continually used to divert attention away from the historic struggles for social justice through suggestions that the presence of a Black man on the Supreme Court constitutes an assurance that the rights of African Americans will be protected. Clarence Thomas's public record is ample evidence that this will not be true. Further, the consolidation of a conservative majority on the Supreme Court endangers the working class people and the elderly. The seating of Clarence Thomas is an affront not only to African American women and men, but to all people concerned with social justice.

We are particularly outraged by the racist and sexist treatment of Professor Anita Hill, an African American woman who was maligned and castigated for daring to speak publicly of her own experience of sexual abuse. The malicious defamation of Professor Hill insulted all women of African descent and sent a dangerous message to all women who might contemplate a sexual harassment complaint.

We speak here because we recognize that the media are now portraying the Black community as prepared to tolerate the dismantling of affirmative action and the evil of sexual harassment in order to have any Black man on the Supreme Court. We want to make clear that the media have ignored and distorted many African American voices. We will not be silenced.

Many have erroneously portrayed the allegations against Clarence Thomas as an issue of either gender or race. As women of African descent, we understand sexual harassment as both. We further understand that Clarence Thomas outrageously manipulated the legacy of lynching in order to shelter himself from Anita Hill's allegations. To deflect attention away from the reality of sexual abuse in African American women's lives, he trivialized and misrepresented this painful part of African American people's history. This country,

agencies, business firms, and colleges and universities to comply with civil rights laws and court rulings.

AFFIRMATIVE ACTION

Few civil rights policies in the twentieth century have proved more persistently controversial than affirmative action. Many white Americans argue that it runs contrary to the concept of achievement founded on merit and amounts to reverse racial or sexual discrimination. Ironically, because the 1964 Civil Rights Act made gender discrimination in employment illegal, white women have been among the major beneficiaries of affirmative action. But the major advocates of affirmative action have been African Americans, most of whom see it as a

which has a long legacy of racism and sexism, has never taken the sexual abuse of Black women seriously. Throughout U.S. history Black women have been sexually stereotyped as immoral, insatiable, perverse, the initiators in all sexual contacts—abusive or otherwise. The common assumption in legal proceedings as well as in the larger society has been that Black women cannot be raped or otherwise sexually abused. As Anita Hill's experience demonstrates, Black women who speak of these matters are not likely to be believed. In 1991, we cannot tolerate this type of dismissal of any one Black woman's experience or this attack upon our collective character without protest, outrage, and resistance.

As women of African descent, we express our vehement opposition to the policies represented by the placement of Clarence Thomas on the Supreme Court. The Bush administration, having obstructed the passage of civil rights legislation, impeded the extension of unemployment compensation, cut student aid and dismantled social welfare programs, has continually demonstrated that it is not operating in our best interests. Nor is this appointee. We pledge ourselves to continue to speak out in defense of one another, in defense of the African American community and against those who are hostile to social justice no matter what color they are. No one will speak for us but ourselves.

🌿 *Why did the African-American women who signed this letter feel the need to defend themselves?*

🌿 *Why did they oppose the confirmation of Clarence Thomas to the Supreme Court?*

🌿 *Why were they unsympathetic to Thomas's claim that he had been a victim of a "high-tech" lynching?*

Source: *New York Times*, November 17, 1991 p. 53.

remedy for centuries of discrimination. The debate over affirmative action has thus, inevitably, led to racial polarization. It even divided the black community.

President Lyndon Johnson first used the term *affirmative action* in a 1965 executive order that required federal contractors to "take affirmative action" to guarantee that job seekers and employees "are treated without regard to their race, color, religion, sex, or national origin." Much of the credit for compliance with affirmative action belongs to conservative Republican president Richard Nixon. In 1969 Arthur A. Fletcher, a black assistant secretary of labor in the Nixon administration, developed the "Philadelphia Plan," in which firms with federal government contracts in the construction industry would have to set and meet hiring goals for African Americans or be penalized. The plan became a model for subsequent "set-aside" programs that reserved some contracts for minority-owned businesses or that favored the hiring of women and minorities. The process of setting goals and timetables to achieve full compliance with federal civil rights requirements appealed to large corporations and accounted for the early success of affirmative action initiatives.

THE BACKLASH

Although it has produced more litigation, affirmative action in employment has been less controversial than affirmative action in college and university admissions. State higher education institutions have been at the center of the controversy both because they are narrowly bound by the Fourteenth Amendment's prohibitions on racial discrimination and because they, far more than elite private institutions, are the gateways to upward mobility for millions of Americans, white and black. As the 1970s progressed, in the interest both of aiding disadvantaged minorities and of increasing racial and cultural diversity on campus, admissions offices began using different criteria for white and minority admissions. Conservatives called these criteria "racial preferences" and argued that they created new unfairness and white resentment of African Americans.

Negative reaction to affirmative action mushroomed in the late 1970s. The case of *Regents of the University of California v. Bakke* was a key part of this backlash. The medical school at the University of California, as a form of affirmative action, had set aside sixteen of its one hundred places in each entering class for disadvantaged and minority students. They were considered for admission in a separate system. A white student named Alan Bakke sued the university for discrimination after it rejected his application. In 1976 the California Supreme Court ruled he should be admitted to the university, but

SUPREME COURT CASES ON AFFIRMATIVE ACTION IN EMPLOYMENT

1979 *United Steelworkers v. Weber* upholds preferential treatment in hiring and training by private firms

1980 *Fullilove v. Klutznick* upholds government programs that reserve places for minorities

1984 *Memphis Firefighters v. Stotts* rejects a judicial order for retaining less-senior black employees over white employees during layoffs

1986 *Wygant v. Jackson Board of Education* rejects school board's plan for laying off white teachers while retaining less senior black teachers, but it also rejects Reagan administration position that affirmative action be limited to actual victims of discrimination, thus broadly upholding affirmative action

1986 *Local 93 of International Association of Firefighters v. City of Cleveland* upholds promotion of minorities ahead of white applicants with higher test scores and greater seniority

1986 *Local 28 of Sheet Metal Workers v. EEOC* upholds order that union meet minority quota for membership

1987 *U.S. v. Paradise* upholds judicial order imposing racial quotas in hiring and promotions of Alabama state troopers

1987 *Johnson v. Transportation Agency of Santa Clara County* upholds plan that promoted women over men

1987 *American Tobacco Co. v. Patterson* upholds seniority plans in place before 1964 unless discriminatory intent can be shown

1989 *Martin v. Wilks* rules that employees may challenge affirmative action plan after it has gone into effect; this decision is overruled by Congress in the Civil Rights Act of 1991

1989 *Richmond v. J. Croson and Co.* rules that Fourteenth Amendment prohibits set-asides for minority contractors, thus going against spirit of *Weber* and against the letter of *Fullilove v. Klutznick* and implying that all such plans face "strict scrutiny"

1990 *Metro Broadcasting v. FCC* upholds affirmative action plan increasing minority broadcasting owners, returning to *Fullilove*

1995 *Adarand Constructors v. Pena* strikes down a congressional statute requiring 10 percent of federal highway money to go to minority contractors and broadly asserts that any such programs using racial classifications are constitutionally suspect

2003 *Grutter v. Bollinger* upholds the University of Michigan Law School's use of racial preferences in admissions to achieve a more diverse student body

1979–2003

the university appealed to the U.S. Supreme Court, which also ruled in Bakke's favor in 1978. Of the nine justices, five agreed the university violated Bakke's rights. However, other related legal issues were involved, and the court split without a majority on nearly all of them. Only one justice declared that affirmative action cases should be judged on the same strict level of scrutiny applied to "invidious" discrimination. All the other justices stated that race-conscious remedies could be used in some circumstances to correct past discrimination.

California remains the center of the affirmative action storm because of its multiracial population. In 1995 Republican governor Pete Wilson ended affirmative action in state employment. In 1996 California voters approved Proposition 209, the so-called California Civil Rights Initiative, which banned all state agencies from implementing affirmative action programs. The campaign for the proposition was led by Ward Connerly, a conservative black entrepreneur. Born in 1939 in rural Louisiana, he had earned a B.A. from Sacramento State College and had received over $140,000 from state contracts set aside for minority businesses. Nonetheless, Connerly maintained that affirmative action exacerbated the negative stereotyping of African Americans. He and his supporters insisted moreover that affirmative action had failed to address problems of poverty, unemployment, and inadequate education that beset the truly disadvantaged. Instead, it had merely elevated to higher status those least in need of assistance, especially middle-class white women. Finally, Connerly accepted the broader argument that affirmative action assaulted the concept of individual merit and violated core American values of equality and opportunity.

Fifty-four percent of California voters agreed with Connerly, and the U.S. Supreme Court upheld the proposition. Its effect, and that of similar laws or court rulings around the nation, is now known. The number of African Americans and other protected minorities admitted to the University of California system has dropped since the proposition, and the numbers at Berkeley, the University of California's most prestigious campus, fell precipitously. In both California and Texas, which abandoned affirmative action in its university system after a court challenge, administrators have attempted to assure a diverse student body by offering admission to their top schools to all students in the top ranks of their high school class.

On June 23, 2003, the U.S. Supreme Court, in two separate decisions, handed the University of Michigan both a major victory, when it upheld the law school's practice of using race as a criterion in admissions procedures to create a diverse student body, and a defeat,

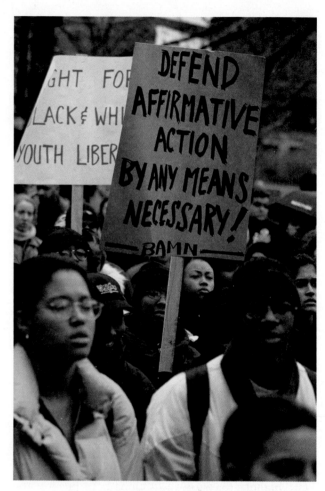

The majority of African Americans defend Affirmative Action as a policy designed to open doors to opportunities in employment and education that had been firmly closed during the long era of Jim Crow segregation and discrimination

when it banned the university from awarding points based on race as a criterion for admitting undergraduates. In the first case, *Grutter v. Bollinge*, a 5–4 decision declared that the University of Michigan Law School could use race to achieve diversity, thus firmly endorsing the long-standing *Bakke* decision written by Justice Powell. Justice Sandra Day O'Connor's majority opinion declared that the equal protection clause of the Fourteenth Amendment to the U.S. Constitution did not prohibit the law school's narrowly tailored use of race in admissions decisions. She was persuaded that the law school acted out of a compelling interest to obtain the educational benefits that accrued from a diverse student population and meaningful integration. However, writing for the majority in the second case, *Gratz v. Bollinger*, Chief Justice Rehnquist appeared to contradict O'Connor's opinion. Rehnquist maintained that in admitting undergraduates the university crossed the line of what was permissable by giving points to black applicants: "The university's policy, which automatically distributed 20 points, or one-fifth of the points needed to guarantee admission, to every single 'underrepresented minority' applicant solely because of race, is not narrowly tailored to achieve the interest in educational diversity that respondents claim justifies their program."

Black Political Activism in the Age of Conservative Reaction

Presidents Reagan and Bush did not completely reverse the advancement of the civil rights agenda. The increased participation of black men and women in the upper echelons of the Democratic Party reflected the extent to which they had overcome political exclusion. In 1964 the nation had only 103 black elected officials; by 1994 there were nearly 8,500. Forty-three African Americans were serving in Congress by 2007. In 1988 Representative William H. Gray of Pennsylvania became the first African American to reach the top ranks of congressional leadership, first as chair of the House Democratic caucus and then in 1989 as majority whip of the House of Representatives. In February 1989 Ronald H. Brown became the first African American to lead a major national political party when he was elected chairman of the Democratic Party. That same year, David Dinkins was elected the first black mayor of New York City. In 1990 Sharon Pratt Dixon (Kelly) was elected mayor of Washington, D.C., becoming the first woman and the first District of Columbia native to serve in that position. By the mid-1990s, black men and women held the mayor's office in four hundred towns and cities. Clearly, the days of black political powerlessness had ended. Or had they?

During the Reagan–Bush era, at least one house of Congress—and often both—was in the hands of the Democrats. Reflecting the importance of African-American voters to the party, Democrats in Congress passed many equal rights laws. Among the most important of these statutes were the Voting Rights Act of 1982, the Civil Rights Restoration Act of 1988, and the Fair Housing Act of 1988. The Civil Rights Restoration Act of 1988 authorized withholding federal funds from an entire institution if any program within it discriminated against women, racial minorities, the aged, or the disabled. The Fair Housing Act of 1988 stipulated that either an individual or the Department of Housing and Urban Development (HUD) could bring a complaint of housing discrimination and authorize administrative judges to investigate housing complaints, issue injunctions and fines, and award punitive damages. These laws and the Civil Rights Act of 1991 were a response to Supreme Court decisions that had narrowed the scope of earlier civil rights legislation.

THE KING HOLIDAY

Many African Americans invested symbolic importance in making Martin Luther King Jr.'s birthday a national holiday, elevating him to the stature of George Washington and Abraham Lincoln, both of whom are honored with a holiday. At first Reagan resisted the idea, but he eventually gave in to pressure from African Americans and their white allies. On January 20, 1985, the United States officially observed Martin Luther King Jr. Day for the first time.

TRANSAFRICA AND THE ANTI-APARTHEID MOVEMENT

Black activism persisted on the international as well as the national front. Much of this effort focused on ending the oppressive conditions of apartheid—the complete social, political, and economic isolation of black people—in South Africa and its glorification of white racial supremacy, an ideology reminiscent of Adolf Hitler's Germany and the American South before the late 1960s.

Randall Robinson, a native of Richmond, Virginia, and a graduate of Harvard Law School who had worked as an assistant for Michigan congressman Charles Diggs, sought to link African-American liberation struggles with those waged by Africans in South Africa and elsewhere. In 1977 he founded TransAfrica to lobby for black political prisoners in South Africa, chief among them Nelson Mandela. In 1984 Robinson was joined by Mary Francis Berry, Eleanor Holmes Norton, and others for a series of sit-ins at the South African Embassy in Washington, D.C., during which hundreds were arrested.

The antiapartheid movement became a major priority for African-American activists. They enlisted the sympathy and help of white Americans on college campuses and pressured many universities into divesting their investments in South Africa. Similar pressures were put on corporations, especially those vulnerable to consumer boycotts. In 1986 the Black Congressional Caucus persuaded its colleagues to enact a U.S. trade embargo against South Africa and sustain it over President Reagan's veto.

In 1990, bowing to international pressure and a souring domestic economy, South African president

Nelson Mandela's release from prison was celebrated around the globe as the event that signaled the final days of South Africa's system of racial apartheid.

F. W. de Klerk removed the ban on the African National Congress, the key opposition party, and a few days afterward ended the twenty-eight-year prison term of its leader, Nelson Mandela. Soon thereafter, South Africa was transformed into a multiracial democracy, and Mandela was elected its president.

Jesse Jackson and the Rainbow Coalition

As Reagan's first term ended, Jesse Jackson announced he would campaign for the presidency of the United States. The first African American to seek the presidential nomination of a major political party was Congresswoman Shirley Chisholm, in 1972. Chisholm had little money and only a small campaign organization, and she was never taken as a serious candidate by her male competitors or the press. Her campaign had nonetheless helped raise the visibility of African-American voters. She captured more than 150 votes on the first ballot at the Democratic National Convention. In the thoroughly male world of presidential politics, however, a black man was a more credible contender.

Jackson's preparation for political battle was not the traditional climb from one elective office to another. Rather, he came up through the ranks of the civil rights movement, working alongside Martin Luther King Jr. in the Southern Christian Leadership Conference (SCLC) and heading Operation Breadbasket, an organization that attempted to mobilize Chicago's black poor. After King's death, Jackson founded People United to Save (later Serve) Humanity (PUSH). This Chicago-based organization induced major corporations with large markets in the black community to adopt affirmative action programs. PUSH-EXCEL, which focused on education, succeeded in raising students' test scores and was given a large grant by the Carter administration.

In 1983, angered by Reagan's social welfare and civil rights rollbacks, Jackson and PUSH began a drive to register black voters. Jackson's charismatic style engendered enthusiasm, especially as the Democratic Party searched for a presidential candidate who could challenge Reagan.

On November 4, 1983, Jackson declared his candidacy for the Democratic nomination and honed an effective style of grassroots mobilization. He began by appealing to what he would call a "rainbow coalition" of people who felt politically marginalized and underrepresented. The **Rainbow Coalition** was composed of diverse groups, including black people, white workers, liberals, Latinos, feminists, students, and environmentalists. Jackson developed a comprehensive economic policy focusing on tax reform, deficit reduction, industrial policy, and employment. The centerpiece of his plan was "Rebuilding America," a program to coordinate government, business, and labor in a national industrial policy. The Jackson platform was well within the tradition of American liberal reform but nonetheless far more progressive than anything his competitors proposed. In January 1984 Jackson gained credentials in international affairs when he traveled to Syria to plead for the release of U.S. Air Force pilot Robert Goodman, who had been held captive there for a year after being shot down in Syrian-controlled airspace. Jackson returned to America in triumph with the freed pilot.

Jackson eventually garnered almost one-fourth of the votes cast in the Democratic primaries and caucuses and one-eighth of the delegates to the convention. His speech to the convention cemented his position as a voice for progressive change and a spiritual heir to both Martin Luther King Jr. and Robert Kennedy. Walter Mondale, Jimmy Carter's vice president, who won the nomination, broke new ground when he made Geraldine Ferraro his running mate and the first woman on a major party's presidential ticket. But many Jackson supporters had hoped Mondale would pick Jackson.

In 1988 the Reverend Jesse Jackson (1941–) addressed the Democratic National Convention. He made two unsuccessful bids for the White House (1984, 1988) but remained a powerful force in the Democratic Party because of his tremendous zeal in registering voters and building coalitions.

In November 1984 black voters overwhelmingly favored the Democratic ticket, but Reagan nonetheless won by a landslide. Mondale carried only his home state of Minnesota and the largely black District of Columbia. Clearly, most white Americans backed Reagan's conservative policies. Undeterred by defeat, Jackson worked to build his Rainbow Coalition, reaching out to a variety of constituencies, including the unemployed, militant trade unionists, small farmers, and gay people. He criticized the Democratic Party's timid opposition to Reagan. Perhaps most important, he also registered enough new voters to help Democrats retain control of the House and regain a majority in the Senate in the 1986 midterm elections.

23-3 Jesse Jackson, Address—Democratic Convention, 1984

By the time Jackson announced he would again run for president in October 1987, he had become a serious contender. He won fifteen presidential primaries and caucuses and garnered seven million votes, one-third of all those cast. His Rainbow Coalition, however, never materialized. His victories in the primaries were based on mobilizing his black supporters; almost all his white support tended to come from college towns and the highly educated. Michael Dukakis, governor of Massachusetts, won the 1988 Democratic nomination.

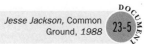

23-5 Jesse Jackson, Common Ground, 1988

Despite Jesse Jackson's voter registration drive and the hopes of the black community, Reagan's vice president, George H. W. Bush, triumphed in the 1988 election. Bush's call for "a kinder, gentler America" was belied by the most memorable feature of his campaign, a polarizing ad that featured Willie Horton, a black convict who had raped a white woman while on furlough from a Massachusetts prison as part of a program approved by Dukakis and his Republican predecessor as governor. Jackson and other black leaders criticized the ad as a blatant appeal to white racism, but Bush would not renounce it.

The general white perception of black men as criminals increased following Bush's election. Even during the Democratic Party's resurgence in the 1990s, the perceptions of black youths as criminals acquired potent political currency, resulting in the mass incarceration of young black men and an increase in police brutality and racial profiling. After the disputed 2000 presidential election, the black community became even more aware of the adverse consequences of mass incarceration because many states deny the right to vote to convicted and incarcerated felons, and 1.8 million of the 4.7 million felons and former felons in the United States are black. Researchers have concluded that "If not for disfranchisement . . . the 2000 presidential election would have been reversed, if former felons in a single state (Florida) had had the right to vote." Moreover, black people, especially black men, are incarcerated in astonishingly high numbers. Not only are African Americans seven times more likely than whites to be in prison, but in 2001, 10 percent of black men in their late twenties were in prison, and more than 30 percent of the young black men who had dropped out of high school had spent time in prison or jail, many for drug-related offenses.

Prison reform activists have sought to draw attention to the brutal conditions that exist within U.S. prisons, especially the violence and high incidence of inmate rape. Yet they have achieved little. In 1994 U.S. Supreme Court justice Clarence Thomas argued, in voting to dismiss claims that prisons failed to protect inmates, that "[p]risons are necessarily dangerous places, they house society's most antisocial and violent people in close proximity with one another. Regrettably, some level of brutality and sexual aggression among [prisoners] is inevitable no matter what the guards do . . . unless all prisoners are locked in their cells twenty-four hours a day and sedated."

Policing the Black Community

In March 1991 Los Angeles police pulled Rodney Glen King from his car after a high-speed chase and beat him with nightsticks. A bystander captured the incident on videotape, which television newscasts broadcast repeatedly, increasing long-simmering anger over police brutality among African Americans in Los Angeles. When a jury of eleven white Americans and one Hispanic American acquitted the four police officers involved in the incident of all but one of the charges brought against them, south-central Los Angeles burst into flames of protest. The verdict highlighted the gulf between the perceptions of white and black Americans about the police and the criminal justice system. Where the mostly white jury had seen the police maintaining law and order, black Americans saw police repression and racism. Fifty-two people were killed in the outbreak that followed the verdict. Arsonists and looters devastated much of the community. Thousands of people were injured, four thousand were arrested, and an estimated half-billion dollars worth of property was damaged or destroyed. The four officers were later retried in federal court on charges of violating King's civil rights. This time juries found two of them guilty and acquitted the other two. Meanwhile, a jury in King's civil suit ordered the city of Los Angeles to pay him $3.8 million in damages.

The Rodney King episode resonated with black men across the country. Earl Ofari Hutchinson suggested why: Black professionals or business owners still tell harrowing tales of being spread-eagle over the hoods of their expensive BMW's or Porsches while the police ran makes on them and tore their cars apart searching for drugs. In polls taken after the Rodney King beating, blacks were virtually unanimous in saying that they believed any black person could have been on the ground that night being pulverized by the police. These were eternal reminders to the "new" black bourgeoisie that they could escape the hood, but many Americans still considered them hoods.

Several such high-profile cases focused public attention on the relation of black communities to white police authorities from the 1980s into the 2000s. Police repression was a long-festering cause of tension and hostility that had been behind many of the riots of the 1960s. On November 16, 1992, two Detroit police officers were formally charged with the murder of Malice Green, a thirty-five-year-old resident of the city. From the late 1990s, the issue exploded into national consciousness with a series of cases. In 1997 a Haitian immigrant, Abner Louima, was beaten and sodomized while in custody at a Brooklyn police station. In 1999 New York police shot Amadou Diallo, a West African immigrant, forty-one times when they mistook his reaching for a wallet for going for a gun. A jury in Albany acquitted the four police officials charged in the Diallo killing. Finally, also in 1999, Patric Dorismond (another Haitian immigrant) was shot and killed after he got into an argument with undercover police officers after he refused to buy drugs from them. In 2006 New York police officers killed unarmed twenty-three-year-old Sean Bell, who was on his way to marry the mother of his two children. Apparently Bell was caught in the middle of an undercover sting operation. Police fired at least fifty bullets into his car. In each instance an enraged black community protested the police profiling as one more instance of bias toward black men and one that targeted other minorities for illegal detention. At a protest rally over Bell's shooting, Rev. Al Sharpton declared, "We cannot allow this to continue to happen. We've got to understand that all of us were in that car."

The videotaped beating of Rodney King by Los Angeles police—shown repeatedly on national television—bolstered charges by African Americans in Los Angeles that they were frequent victims of police brutality. Despite the graphic evidence, the officers were acquitted of using excessive force.

HUMAN RIGHTS IN AMERICA

In October 1998 the human rights group Amnesty International, known for its condemnation of human rights abuse in countries with repressive governments, published a report on police brutality in the United States. The report covered the actions of local and state police, the FBI, the Immigration and Naturalization Service, and the prison system. Its contents came as no surprise to most black Americans or, indeed, to anyone who lived in America's poor urban neighborhoods. The report detailed violations of the UN Code of Conduct for Law Enforcement Officials and the UN Basic Principles on the Use of Force and Firearms. Among the violations reported were:

- the shooting of unarmed suspects fleeing a minor crime scene
- excessive force used on mentally ill or disturbed people
- multiple shootings of a suspect, sometimes after the suspect was apprehended or disabled
- the beating of unresisting suspects
- the misuse of batons, chemical sprays, and electroshock weapons.

These violations all involved the misuse of force during arrests, traffic stops, searches, and so forth. The report also cited sexual abuse of prisoners and the denial of food and water to them. The report noted that while most victims of American law enforcement abuse were members of racial and ethnic minorities, most police officers were white.

It is far too easy to interpret these findings as showing that American police officers, as a group, are racists who use their authority to oppress people they do not like. In fact, the issue of police brutality is not nearly so simple. Police officers are under tremendous pressure and live dangerous lives, in part because of the wide availability of guns in American society. No one can be expected to have perfect judgment about using force, and the cumulative effect of years of dealing with violence can destroy a person's sense of perspective and moral equilibrium.

Neither is the problem of crime by black Americans a simple one. The level of crime in black communities is high. The murder rate, for example, for African Americans in 1997 was seven times that of whites, and black victims accounted for 49 percent of all those murdered, even though African Americans make up only 12 percent of the population. Over 90 percent of those who murder, rape, and assault black people are black themselves. The murder rate for young black men between the ages of fourteen and seventeen tripled between 1976 and 1993. Although this rate, like the rate of violent crime in the country in general, fell in the 1990s, the security of many African Americans remains imperiled.

Crime devastates black neighborhoods. High crime rates raise the costs of business, driving jobs and investment dollars out of those areas most in need of them. Fear of violence leads many in the inner cities to barricade themselves inside their homes. Crime has transformed once vibrant neighborhoods into virtual ghost towns where only the sound of gunfire disturbs the silence of the streets. Filmmaker Spike Lee was shocked when he returned to the Brooklyn neighborhood in which he had grown up to shoot his film *Crooklyn*. He found the streets had become so unsafe that the local children he used as extras had to be taught how to play the games he had played growing up in the 1970s because they had never been allowed to play outside. "Nowadays," Lee reflected after completing the film in 1994, "these kids, they'll shoot you dead in a second and not even think about it. The two big problems are crack and how accessible guns are. And also, you're talking about what Reagan did during his eight years. If I was a parent, I'd be terrified anytime my children left my sight. When I was growing up, I just had to be home by dark." Even Rosa Parks, heroine of the civil rights movement, was not immune to the urban crime wave. In 1994 she was beaten and robbed in her Detroit home by a twenty-eight-year-old unemployed black man. Her assailant recognized Parks but assaulted her anyway.

Being disproportionately the victims of crime, most African Americans have looked to the nation's police departments for aid. Because of their growing political power they have sought, not always successfully, to make the police both responsive to crime and fair in enforcing the laws. One key device for changing the behavior of law enforcement officials has been the appointment of black police chiefs.

The Clinton Presidency

During his first campaign for the presidency, in 1992, black Americans welcomed Arkansas governor Bill Clinton into their churches, schools, and homes. Black citizens and the civil rights leadership warmly embraced Clinton's candidacy against incumbent Republican George H. W. Bush, who had done little to win their loyalty. White Americans, too, were dissatisfied with the Bush presidency. Although he enjoyed high approval ratings in early 1991 following American military success in evicting Iraq from Kuwait in the first Gulf War, by early 1992 his popularity had slumped in the face of an economic downturn. Still, at first, few operatives believed Clinton would unseat Bush.

Shrewdly, however, Clinton positioned himself as a centrist within the mainstream of American politics. This necessitated his at least appearing to place some distance between himself and the liberal-progressive arm of the Democratic Party as represented by Jesse Jackson and the Rainbow Coalition. Undeterred by charges of womanizing, draft evasion, and marijuana smoking, Clinton attacked Bush's record and promised to make government more responsive to the needs of Americans. The strategy catapulted him into the White House. Clinton won in November 1992 with just 43 percent of the popular vote to Bush's 38 percent and third-party candidate H. Ross Perot's 19 percent. However, Clinton garnered 78 percent of the black vote and 39 percent of the white vote in key states including New Jersey, Michigan, New York, Illinois, and California. The election did not present the Democrats with a clear mandate. Although maintaining control of Congress, they gained no seats in the Senate and lost seats in the House. Republicans used the ambiguous outcome to launch a relentless campaign to undermine Clinton's presidency.

Most black people, however, considered Clinton the best president on race issues since Lyndon Johnson. Writer Toni Morrison called Clinton the first black president, and in some circles he was called the first woman president because of his support for equal rights for women, both black and white. Clinton appointed women, including many black women, to 37 percent of the five hundred upper-level positions in the White House and federal bureaucracy. During the campaign, he had visited the riot-torn ruins of south-central Los Angeles, played the saxophone on a black television show, and often worshipped in black churches, where he was warmly received. In Clinton, black Americans had a friend. Indeed, he named his black friends to his transition team: attorney Vernon Jordan as co-chair, Barbara Jordan, William Gray III, and Marian Wright Edelman, founding president of the Children's Defense Fund. Clinton also created a cabinet that mirrored the diversity of the American population—in some cases, such as Hazel O'Leary as secretary of the Department of Energy, Alexis Herman as secretary of labor, and Ron Brown as secretary of commerce, appointing black people to posts that had nothing to do with race. Clinton also gave Washington, D.C., delegate to Congress Eleanor Holmes Norton the prerogative, normally reserved to U.S. senators, of selecting U.S. district court judges, U.S. marshals, and the U.S. attorney for the District of Columbia. Moreover, not only did Clinton appoint many African-American officials and judges, he was the first American president to visit Africa.

"IT'S THE ECONOMY, STUPID!"

In 1996 Clinton became the first Democratic president to win a second term since Franklin Roosevelt. Throughout his two terms in office, Clinton focused attention on the economy, a strategy that won grudging support from moderate Republicans. His objectives were to strengthen the economy and to make more opportunities available for black Americans and other previously excluded groups. Toward these ends, in a significant departure from the policies of his predecessors, he supported a new tax bill that increased the taxes of higher-income Americans. He also advocated expansion of the earned income tax credit to help improve the lives of poor Americans. His college student-aid program increased federal loan benefits. The economy boomed, and when Clinton left office in 2001, the country had the lowest poverty rate in twenty years. The Congressional Black Caucus (CBC) provided critical support for his economic programs. In 1993 CBC chairman Representative Kweisi Mfume of Maryland and the highest-ranking black congressman, Representative John Lewis, delivered the caucus vote that saved Clinton's $500 billion economic budget in both the

HONORING OUR AMERICAN HISTORY

President William Jefferson Clinton is seen here with members of the Little Rock Nine who, as teenagers, defied hostile mobs to desegregate Central High School in Little Rock, Arkansas, in 1957. African Americans claimed Clinton as the first black president, given his comfort around black people and the number of African Americans he considered friends.

House and Senate. In return, black congressmen gained financial support for inner cities, poor families, children, and the elderly. Representative Mfume credited the CBC, for example, for saving the $2.5 billion allocation for food stamps that the Senate sought to eliminate and $3.5 billion for empowerment zones in cities and rural areas.

Unemployment plummeted from 7.2 percent when Clinton took office to 5.5 percent in 1995 and continued to decline in ensuing years. American businesses created ten million new jobs, and many black people who feared they would never gain a foothold in the economy found work, some for the first time. Reduced federal spending and the 1993 tax increase helped cut the annual federal deficit in half. As interest rates fell and the stock market soared, optimistic Americans increased their consumer spending.

CLINTON SIGNS THE WELFARE REFORM ACT

Shortly before his reelection, in August 1996, Clinton signed the Personal Responsibility and Work Opportunity Reconciliation Act, a welfare reform bill. This disappointed many African Americans and political progressives in general. The legislation combined Clinton's own ideas with others espoused in the Republicans' "Contract with America" blueprint for conservative changes. The Republicans had used this platform to win control of both houses of Congress in 1994. The main target of the Personal Responsibility Act was Aid to Families of Dependent Children (AFDC), a program created in 1935 as part of the Social Security Act to prevent children from suffering because of the poverty of their parents. Critics claimed AFDC stipends discouraged poor mothers from finding work, that it was responsible for the breakdown of the family among the nation's poor and did little to reduce poverty. Proponents of the welfare reform bill also insisted the states did not have enough flexibility in administering welfare. The conservative welfare "reform" measure ended guarantees of federal aid to poor children, turning control of such programs over to the states along with allocations of block grants. The act denied benefits to legal immigrants, called for drastic reductions in food stamp appropriations, and limited families to five years of benefits. The law also required most adult welfare recipients to find employment within two years.

There were good reasons to believe the welfare reform bill would not accomplish its sponsors' purposes. Most of the people who would be "encouraged to find work" by having their benefits reduced or cut entirely were among the least employable people in the labor force. A study of people terminated from general assistance in Michigan, for example, revealed that as many as two-thirds remained unemployed. As for the bill's effect on families, it is true that most women on welfare had their first children when they were unmarried teenagers, but little evidence indicates that cutting welfare prevents teenage pregnancies. There is evidence that reforms targeted at improving the collection of child support payments for divorced mothers would reduce welfare costs far more effectively and humanely.

Clinton's support of the welfare act was politically astute and consistent with his centrist ideology. It also immunized him from Republican attacks on the issue and had little impact on his support among African Americans. Clinton endorsed other policies that had negative impact on African Americans but seemed, at least symbolically, to reassure white moderates. He signed a crime bill that allowed local communities to hire more police officers, build more prisons, and implement the three strikes policy of stiffer penalties for those who had at least two prior criminal convictions. He also failed, in the teeth of intense Republican opposition, to enact comprehensive health-care legislation. Yet black support for him remained strong, and Clinton easily defeated his Republican opponent, Senator Robert Dole of Kansas, in 1996.

The preliminary results of the new welfare reform strictures indicated that within a couple of years half of those who had taken jobs had returned to lives of unemployment, poverty, and quiet desperation. As the economy took a downturn in the closing months of Clinton's second term and in the opening years of the new millennium, conditions of poor mothers and children deteriorated steadily. The debate over welfare policy receded to the back burner during the 2000 election campaign and disappeared completely after George W. Bush took office, superseded by the emphasis on tax cuts for the wealthy.

REPUBLICANS CHALLENGE CLINTON

Congressional Republicans and radical conservatives hated Clinton's presidency, and many of them hated Clinton himself. They vowed to take back the White House. Early on, Republicans began raising huge sums of money and energetically organized local constituencies, especially in the South. The Democrats seemed demoralized and did little to mobilize their base, especially in the black community. Their passivity had predictable results. Many African Americans did not vote in the congressional elections in 1994, and the Democrats lost control of Congress. For the first time in forty years, the Republicans could implement

CONDOLEEZZA RICE JUSTIFIES THE IRAQ WAR

Condoleezza Rice was born on November 14, 1954, in Birmingham, Alabama. In 1981 she earned her Ph.D. from the Graduate School of International Studies at the University of Denver. She became a professor of political science at Stanford University in 1981 and later served as provost there for six years. In George H. W. Bush's administration she was an adviser on Soviet and East European affairs in the National Security Council and special assistant to the president for national security affairs. Rice received her most notable appointment when George W. Bush appointed her secretary of state in November 2004.

Instead of a commitment to disarm, Iraq has a high-level political commitment to maintain and conceal its weapons, led by Saddam Hussein and his son Qusay, who controls the Special Security Organization, which runs Iraq's concealment activities. Instead of implementing national initiatives to disarm, Iraq maintains institutions whose sole purpose is to thwart the work of the inspectors. And instead of full cooperation and transparency, Iraq has filed a false declaration to the United Nations that amounts to a 12,200-page lie.

Iraq's declaration even resorted to unabashed plagiarism with lengthy passages of United Nations reports copied word-for-word (or edited to remove any criticism of Iraq) and presented as original text. Far from informing, the declaration is intended to cloud and confuse the true picture of Iraq's arsenal. It is a reflection of the regime's well-earned reputation for dishonesty and constitutes a material breach of United Nations Security Council Resolution 1441, which set up the current inspections programs.

Unlike other nations that have voluntarily disarmed and in defiance of Resolution 1441 Iraq is not allowing inspectors "immediate, unimpeded, unrestricted access" to facilities and people involved in its weapons program. As a recent inspection at the home of an Iraqi nuclear scientist demonstrated, and other sources confirm, material and documents are still being moved around in farcical shell games. The regime has blocked free and unrestricted use of aerial reconnaissance.

Last week's finding by inspectors of 12 chemical warheads not included in Iraq's declaration was particularly troubling. In the past, Iraq has filled this type of warhead with sarin, a deadly nerve agent used by Japanese terrorists in 1995 to kill 12 Tokyo subway passengers and sicken thousands of others.

their conservative agenda, which included rolling back environmental protection policies, reducing taxes for the rich, cutting benefits for the elderly, building a strong military, establishing the primacy of Christianity over other religions, and advancing white supremacy.

Belatedly awake to the peril of black political alienation, some younger Democratic leaders began to fight back. In 1994 Jesse Jackson Jr. won a seat in Congress representing a South Side Chicago district. Jackson outlined a comprehensive social democratic agenda for black America that included full employment, health care, high-quality public education, decent and affordable housing, a safe and sustainable environment, the right to vote, and equality of sexes before the law. Progressive Democrats clearly understood that race was no longer a matter of just black and white people. Many other groups and movements were emerging, including Asian/Pacific Island-Americans, Arab-Americans, and Native Americans. Immigrants groups, especially migrant workers from Mexico, were forming labor organizations to fight for immigrant rights and social justice. But Democrats were now in the congressional minority, and party leaders seemed loathe to knit together these diverse constituencies into viable grassroots organizations and foster solidarity projects and efforts crucial to social change, such as affordable housing, higher-minimum-wage laws, universal health-care coverage, and driver's licenses for immigrants.

Many questions remain about Iraq's nuclear, chemical and biological weapons programs and arsenal and it is Iraq's obligation to provide answers. It is failing in spectacular fashion. By both its actions and its inactions, Iraq is proving not that it is a nation bent on disarmament, but that it is a nation with something to hide. Iraq is still treating inspections as a game. It should know that time is running out.

And a few months later, time did run out and the war with Iraq took over George W. Bush's presidency, much as the first Iraqi war had dominated his father's presidency a decade earlier.

🌲 *Were weapons of mass destruction in Iraq ever found?*

🌲 *In this statement, how is the national security adviser preparing the public for possible conflict with Iraq?*

🌲 *What is the significance of the UN Security Council Resolution 1441?*

Source: Condoleezza Rice, "Why We Know Iraq Is Lying," *New York Times*, January 23, 2003.

While Democrats unraveled, Republicans drew strength from the appointment of Kenneth Starr as an independent counsel to investigate allegations surrounding Bill and Hillary Clinton's investment in an Arkansas land development deal known as Whitewater. Although no proof was found that the Clintons had broken the law, Starr relentlessly pursued every hint or rumor of misdeed. As the investigations escalated, Clinton made the tactical mistake of denying sexual involvement with a White House intern, Monica Lewinsky. The Republicans moved in for the kill. On December 19, 1998, the Republican majority in the House of Representatives narrowly voted to impeach Clinton for perjury and obstruction of justice for tampering with witnesses to conceal his relationship with Lewinsky. But the Senate refused to convict him, and he remained in office. In the midst of the turmoil, Clinton derived solace from the unwavering support of black people, the Congressional Black Caucus, and his friends, including Vernon Jordan and Jesse Jackson.

Black Politics in the New Millennium: The Contested 2000 Presidential Election

The election of 2000 revealed fault lines of culture, geography, race, class, and gender. A gender gap of about 11 percent reflected the fact that men strongly supported Republican candidates and women favored Democratic candidates. The middle of the country and the South voted for Republican Texas governor George W. Bush; Democratic candidate vice president Albert Gore Jr. carried the states of the upper Midwest, the Northeast, and the Pacific Coast. Gays and lesbians voted 70 percent for Gore, whereas those who identified themselves as conservative Christians voted 80 percent for Bush. The campaign focused largely on economic issues—social security, taxes, health care, and education.

Black community leaders and organizations worked hard to register voters and to increase turnout for the 2000 election. The NAACP, for example, spent $9 million on Operation Big Vote. Organizers even registered more than 11,000 inmates in county jails in the South.

GORE V. BUSH

In a hotly contested election, the outcome hung on one state: Florida. In the end, the U.S. Supreme Court, in a 5-to-4 ruling (*Bush v. Gore*, 121 S. Ct. 525 [2000]), decided the issue by halting the recount of ballots in Florida. The Court's majority based its ruling on the Fourteenth Amendment's prohibition of states denying citizens equal protection of the law. The Court insisted the recount had to be stopped because the Florida Supreme Court, which had authorized it, had failed to provide uniform standards for determining the intent of the voters. Bush was declared the winner in Florida by fewer than six hundred votes, which gave him a four-vote majority in the electoral college.

Bill Clinton called *Gore v. Bush* "an appalling decision" and compared its impact on African Americans to the infamous *Dred Scott* and *Plessy v. Ferguson* decisions of the nineteenth century. Indeed, African Americans reported serious discrimination and interference with their voting in Florida. A lawsuit filed in Jacksonville, Florida, claimed that many votes were thrown out as "undervotes" or "overvotes," especially in the four districts with the highest concentration of African Americans in the state. According to the lawsuit, 26,000 ballots were not counted in Duval County, and more than 9,000 of those were cast in largely African-American precincts where Gore had captured more than 90 percent of the vote. Indeed, the U.S. Civil Rights Commission found that tens of thousands of African Americans were disfranchised in Florida. In a draft report, it declared, "African American voting districts were disproportionately hindered by antiquated and error-prone equipment like the punch card ballot system." This meant that more black and low-income voters, who tended to vote Democratic, had their ballots invalidated.

The chair of the commission, Mary Frances Berry, wrote in the *Journal of American History* (Vol. 88, no. 2, September 2001):

> The United States Supreme Court helped undermine the pursuit of equal opportunity by African Americans for most of our history. . . . *Bush v. Gore* was so striking, in part, because the 5–4 majority has been assiduous about deference to state courts and states' rights in general. What the Court has done is to remind us that judges have social and political views that are reflected in their decisions. Each side has used the equal protection clause of the Fourteenth Amendment to convey its policy preferences. But, unlike the majority, in cases involving African American voting and the outcome of the 2000 election, the justices in dissent have remained consistent.

Republican Triumph

In the 2000 elections, Republicans also retained narrow majorities in Congress. *Gore v. Bush* thus not only put George W. Bush in the White House, it also meant that for the first time since 1954, the Republican Party was in control of the presidency and both houses of Congress.

GEORGE W. BUSH'S BLACK CABINET

President Bush was aware that few African Americans had voted for him. But this did not prevent him from appointing well-educated, articulate, and accomplished black men and women to key posts. Such appointments tended to mute black criticism and placate white swing voters who disdained racial exclusion. Bush named General Colin L. Powell to be secretary of state. Powell, the son of Jamaican immigrants, had served as chairman of the Joint Chiefs of Staff (1989–1993), the highest military position in the Department of Defense. During his tenure he oversaw Operation Desert Storm, the victorious 1991 Persian Gulf War. Secretary Powell not only assisted in the formulation of foreign policy, but he also "represented the race." In a speech at Howard University, he expressed pride in his complex role of representing America's universalism on the global stage. "It's just terrific to be able to walk into a room somewhere in Africa, Russia, Asia, and Europe, and you know they're looking at you. You know how they be. They're looking at you and they recognize your position and who you are, and they also recognize that you're black. And it's always a source of inspiration and joy to see people look at me and through me see my country and see what promise my country offers to all people to come to these shores for a better life."

Bush also appointed Condoleezza Rice to be his national security adviser. Rice was the first African American and the first woman to hold this post. During the 2000 election, Rice had formed a strong personal bond with Bush, and this relationship became the foundation of her power in his administration.

An expert on the Soviet Union, Rice had been critical of the Clinton administration's peacekeeping efforts in Bosnia and Haiti. Clinton, she charged, had "assiduously failed" to separate "the important from the trivial . . . we don't need to have the 82nd Airborne escorting kids to kindergarten." But as September 11, 2001, was to show, Rice should have paid closer attention to Samuel Berger, Clinton's national security adviser, when he warned, "America is in a deadly struggle with a new breed of anti-Western jihadist—nothing less than a war . . . as a nation . . . we are engaged in a wholly new battle against an international terrorist network in dozens of countries, which is deeply committed to injuring and destroying the United States and its allies. This is one of the most serious threats the next administration will face."

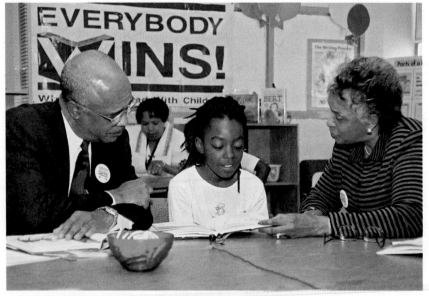

Bush selected Rod Paige to be Secretary of the Department of Education. Paige spearhead a program in which employees of the Department volunteered to mentor students in select schools in the District of Columbia.

EDUCATION REFORM: NO CHILD LEFT BEHIND

During the 2000 campaign, Bush had vowed to reform public education. This was an issue of vital importance to both black and white families. Black parents were especially alarmed over the de facto resegregation of black children in urban schools. Thus many were heartened when Bush selected black Texan Rod Paige as the secretary of education.

Paige introduced the No Child Left Behind Act, an education reform that Bush ardently embraced. This legislation spoke directly to the concerns of white working- and middle-class Americans. It underscored their demand for student and teacher competency testing, that is, the use of testing as an assessment tool to measure performance. The legislation, signed into law in 2002, required all schools to test students at regular intervals in reading, math, and science. States also have to publish the test results and sanction schools whose students fail to do well on the tests. Implicitly the measure rejected integration as a primary social policy objective and retreated from mandatory busing while promoting parents' freedom to enroll their children in the schools of their choice through voucher programs.

Some African Americans, such as Anthony Williams, the mayor of Washington, D.C., supported the school voucher program, arguing that competition with strong schools would force weaker schools to improve their performance. However, Reginald Weaver, the black president of the National Educational Association, argued that the voucher program ignored the needs of most of the students in poor schools. The No Child Left Behind Act, he said, was "a bill that gives $13 million to 2,000 kids who are going to voucher school, and $13 million to 27,000 kids to a charter school, and then $13 million to 167,000 other kids." He concluded, "I think it is political, not educational." No Child Left Behind was soon mired in controversy. Critics, including many conservatives, blasted the measure for setting unrealistic goals and for not including sufficient federal funding to help schools meet the higher standards.

REPARATIONS

While party politics attracted attention, many African Americans shifted their focus to specific issues, including reparations for slavery, and the spread of HIV/AIDS in the United States and in Africa. In 1969 James Foreman, in his "Black Manifesto," called on America's churches and synagogues to collect $500 million as "a beginning of the reparations due us as a people who have been exploited and degraded, brutalized, killed, and persecuted." Although Foreman's call was widely publicized, churches made no serious effort to respond to his demand. Four years later, Boris Bittker, a Yale Law School professor, raised the issue again and argued in *The Case for Black Reparations* that slavery and the persistence of government-sanctioned racial discrimination justified the creation of a program to provide compensation to black Americans. Since 1993 John Conyers, a black Democratic congressman from Detroit, has introduced a bill in every session of Congress—not to pay reparations, but to establish a federal commission to investigate slavery and the legacy of racial discrimination. The bill has never come to the floor of the House of Representatives for a vote.

In 2000 the issue of reparations for slavery was resurrected and finally received widespread attention when Randall Robinson, founder and president of TransAfrica and a graduate of Virginia Union University and the Harvard Law School, published *The Debt: What America Owes to Blacks*. Robinson reasoned that because Jews and Japanese Americans have been compensated for the indignities and horrors they experienced in World War II, African Americans were also due financial indemnification for slavery, for "246 years of an enterprise murderous both of a people and their culture." Robinson maintained that many African Americans still bear the scars of slavery in terms of poor housing, inadequate health care, and insufficient educational opportunities. He insists that reparations would remedy the effect of such inequalities. Temple University professor and Afrocentrist Molefi Asante proposed that instead of "a one-time cash payout" that the American government make long-term commitments for "educational, health care, land or property grants, and a combination of such grants." He elaborated, "What I have argued for is the establishment of some type of organization that would evaluate how reparations would be determined and distributed: the National Commission of African Americans (NCAA) would be the overarching national organization to serve as the clearinghouse for reparations."

Some black writers and journalists adamantly reject arguments that reparations are a realistic resolution of the nation's slave and racist legacy. Two black journalists, William Raspberry and Juan Williams, object to the very idea of reparations. Instead, Raspberry favors a greater investment in education for African Americans, "not because of debts owed to or incurred by our ancestors, but because America needs its citizens to be educated and productive." Williams declared, "The suffering of long-dead ancestors is not a claim check for a bag full of cash. I don't want any money that belongs to any slave. That is obscene. The struggle of African-Americans for civil rights is not about selling out for a check."

In 2004, Ruth Simmons, president of Brown University, the first African American to head an Ivy League university, established a committee to investigate Brown's historic ties to profits from the slave trade and to determine if the university should make reparations. In 2005, Mary Francis Berry published a book, *My Face Is Black Is True*, about Callie House, a former slave, and the Mutual Relief, Bounty, and Pension Association that House and several Baptist ministers organized to fight for compensation for centuries of forced labor. In 1899, House, a washerwoman and mother of six, declared, "If the Government had the right to free us she had a right to make some provision for us and since she did not make it soon after Emancipation she ought to make it, now."

HIV/AIDS IN AMERICA AND AFRICA

As he had done repeatedly with other issues, Jesse Jackson, along with scholars, health-care professionals, social activists, and others, drew attention in the 1980s and 1990s to the HIV/AIDs epidemic and its disastrous impact on black America and in Africa. Jackson believed HIV/AIDs was as much a political issue as it was a matter of health care. His words reflected a mature black internationalism that emphasized the bonds of health and disease across the African Diaspora. He declared,

> As it is in Africa, AIDS is now the leading cause of death for African Americans between twenty-five and forty-four in the United States. Almost two-thirds (63 percent) of all women reported with AIDS are African American; 62 percent of all reported pediatric cases are African-American children; 1 in 50 African-American men and 1 in 160 African-American women are estimated to be HIV infected. Like Africans, many African Americans do not know their HIV status; like Africans, many African Americans cannot access care or afford adequate treatment. Like Africans, many African Americans are in poverty, and many of their communities lack the infrastructure needed to meet the needs of those infected and afflicted by AIDS. Simply speaking, as we begin to understand our commonalities, our differences will no longer be a continent away.

Rodney Hood, former president of the National Medical Association, echoed Jackson's concerns when he wrote, "Racism exists in medicine, especially if you are a person of color. It's very real and it's killing us." Of the fifteen leading causes of death, African Americans have the highest incidence rates in thirteen of the fifteen. Paraphrasing Martin Luther King Jr., Hood concluded, "Of all forms of inequity, injustice in health care is the most shocking and inhumane." (For more on African Americans and health care, see Chapter 24.)

SEPTEMBER 11, 2001

Americans were stunned on September 11, 2001, when terrorists seized four commercial airliners and crashed them into New York's World Trade Center, the Pentagon in Washington, and rural Pennsylvania. Several hundred African Americans perished among the more than three thousand people who died that day.

Leonard Pitts Jr., a black syndicated columnist for the *Miami Herald*, captured the feelings of many Americans when he wrote a rousing defense of the United States and its people against an unknown adversary:

> Did you want to tear us apart? You just brought us together. Let me tell you about my people. We are a vast and quarrelsome family, a family rent by racial, cultural, political and class division, but a family nonetheless. We're frivolous, yes, capable of expending tremendous emotional energy on pop cultural minutiae, a singer's revealing dress, a ball team's misfortune, a cartoon mouse. . . . Some people—you, perhaps—think that any or all of this makes us weak. You're mistaken. We are not weak. Indeed, we are strong in ways that cannot be measured by arsenals.

If the debate over reparations dramatized the separate pasts that black and white Americans have experienced, then September 11, 2001, reminded them of their common future. But the sense of national unity did not last. Less than two years later, as the United States prepared to invade Iraq, activist and scholar Manning Marable wrote of the lessons he had learned from the 9/11 tragedy: "No political ideology, no crusade, no belief in a virtuous cause, can justify the moral bankruptcy of terror. Yet, because of the military actions of our own government, any claims to moral superiority have now disintegrated, in the minds of much of the black and brown world."

WAR

Americans expected President Bush to devise an effective strategy against the Taliban regime in Afghanistan and to destroy Osama bin Laden and the al-Qaeda network, which was responsible for 9/11. The president pledged retribution, and the war in Afghanistan began on October 7, 2001. The Taliban were easily overthrown, but bin Laden and the Taliban leader, Mullah Omar, escaped even though thousands of American troops hunted them in the mountains of Afghanistan.

Still, the Bush administration called its Afghan foray a success even though the Taliban have since launched a new guerrilla war, and much of Afghanistan remains in the control of warlords and insurgents. Critics, such as Richard A. Clarke, the former chief counterterrorism adviser to Presidents Clinton and George W. Bush, argued that the Bush adminstration's real target after 9/11 was not Afghanistan and al-Qaeda but Saddam Hussein's Iraq. Clarke charged that Bush and National Security Adviser Condoleezza Rice had failed to heed the reports of a planned terrorist attack before September 11, 2001.

Al-Qaeda, which claimed responsibility for the bombing of U.S. embassies in Kenya and Tanzania in 1998 and for an attack on the USS *Cole* in Yemen in 2000, should have been the national security priority. Rice denied these charges, but early in 2002 the administration began to shift the nation's attention from Afghanistan to Iraq.

The prospect of war in Iraq aroused mass protests at home and vociferous opposition abroad and at the United Nations, which refused to back the United States despite strenuous lobbying led by Secretary of State Colin Powell. In a speech before the UN Security Council in February 2003, Powell argued, based on what turned out be misleading and possibly distorted intelligence reports, that Saddam not only had weapons of mass destruction, but he also had ties to international terrorist networks, including al-Qaeda. The Security Council was not convinced and voted against the invasion, but the United States invaded Iraq anyway on March 19, 2003. Only Britain gave it significant support.

As in Afghanistan, victory in Iraq appeared to come quickly, and Bush declared the mission there accomplished when Baghdad was occupied after a few weeks of fighting. However, it proved much easier to overthrow Saddam than to pacify Iraq. The country quickly descended into chaos. Insurgents attacked American occupation forces and those Iraqis who cooperated with them. Critics blasted the administration for failing to develop a coherent peace plan. The war, they charged, had actually strengthened terrorism while the failure to secure UN support or to find weapons of mass destruction or establish ties between Saddam and al-Qaeda had damaged America's reputation and credibility and weakened the fabric of international cooperation.

The 2004 Presidential Election

Massachusetts senator John F. Kerry won the Democratic Party's nomination for president in 2004. The war in Iraq dominated other issues, including gay marriage and abortion rights. Kerry selected Senator John Edwards from North Carolina to be his running mate against incumbents George W. Bush and Dick Cheney. While these men campaigned, African Americans registered an important, but subtle, shift in their status within the Democratic Party as it became clear that they would play a key role in determining the outcome of the election.

Condoleeza Rice became the first African American woman in United States history to serve as Secretary of State.

The process of political transformation begun in the 1960s peaked in the 2004 presidential primaries. In these contests African Americans emerged as the most reliable Democratic base and made their views heard and their power acknowledged. They wanted Americans to understand that little divided blacks and whites when it came to regaining the White House. In so doing, African-American leaders skillfully moved away from being considered spokespersons for a small special interest group. In 2004 they demanded acknowledgment of their central role as Democratic standard-bearers. Two of the nine contenders for the Democratic nomination were African Americans: Carol Moseley Braun, former U.S. senator from Illinois, and Rev. Al Sharpton of New York. Braun and Sharpton participated in all of the primary debates before throwing their support to Kerry.

In the spirit of presenting a united front, Braun, Sharpton, and Jesse Jackson addressed the delegates at the Democratic National Convention in Boston. While praising Kerry and attacking Bush, they reiterated their concerns about high black unemployment, the lack of national health-care insurance, and the deteriorating physical conditions of the nation's schools, especially those that served the poor and inner-city residents. And they emphatically attacked the war in Iraq.

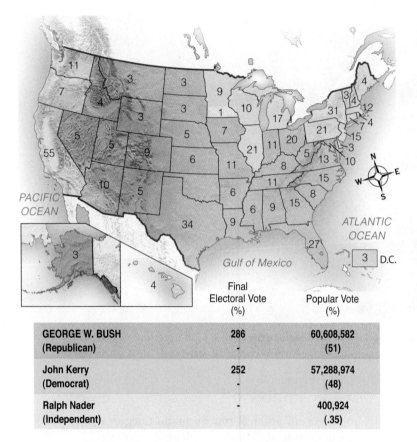

	Final Electoral Vote (%)	Popular Vote (%)
GEORGE W. BUSH (Republican)	286 -	60,608,582 (51)
John Kerry (Democrat)	252 -	57,288,974 (48)
Ralph Nader (Independent)	-	400,924 (.35)

MAP 23–1　The Presidential election results of 2004 revealed that incumbent George W. Bush received over 3 million more votes than did Democratic contender John Kerry. This was a decisive uncontested victory for George W. Bush.

The black star of the convention, however, was the little-known forty-two-year-old state senator from Illinois, Barack Obama, who was running for the U.S. Senate. Obama's keynote speech, claiming that good and efficient government would improve the life chances of all Americans, catapulted him into the limelight.

PRESIDENT BUSH'S SECOND TERM

On November 4, 2004, Americans reelected George W. Bush by a three-million-vote margin (see Map 23–1). After the election Colin Powell resigned. In repayment for her loyalty and experience in international affairs, President Bush appointed Condoleezza Rice to replace Powell as secretary of state. But within months of his victory, Bush's popularity began to plummet. A se-

ries of scandals rocked the administration. But it was Bush's mishandling of the Iraq War and the fumbling and inadequate federal response in 2005 to the devastation wrought by Hurricane Katrina to parts of the Gulf Coast and the city of New Orleans that defined his second term. In the 2006 midterm elections, the Democrats regained control of Congress. Nancy Pelosi became the first woman Speaker of the House, and several African Americans became chairs of House committees. Democrats also captured a majority of the state governorships. One of the new governors, Duval Patrick of Massachusetts, became the second African American to be elected a governor in history.

THE IRAQ WAR

At the outset of his second term, George W. Bush insisted again that America was on the right course in Iraq and that victory would soon be achieved there. Events soon proved him wrong. As the death toll in Iraq mounted—more than 3,500 U.S. troops and tens of thousands of Iraqis had been killed by the summer of 2007 with no end to the casualties in sight—most Americans lost faith in the administration's handling of the conflict, which had become a bloody civil war among Iraq's sectarian and ethnic groups. Civic life in Iraq all but collapsed amid daily suicide bombings, attacks on U.S. troops, kidnappings, murders, and other acts of terrorism. Corruption was rampant. Millions of Iraqis had become refugees. International opinion turned solidly against America.

By 2007, in response to Bush's low poll numbers and the unpopularity of the war, eight Democrats had launched campaigns for their party's presidential nominations. The prospective candidates included a woman, Senator Hillary Rodham Clinton of New York; an African-American, Senator Barack Obama of Illinois; and a Hispanic American, Governor Bill Richardson of New Mexico. This was the most diverse roster of presidential candidates of any party in American history.

HURRICANE KATRINA AND THE DESTRUCTION OF BLACK NEW ORLEANS

Political decisions have consequence. The decision to invade Iraq and the three years of combat there together with questionable appointments to head the agencies charged with providing federal disaster relief left the government unprepared in August 2005 to deal with the catastrophic devastation caused by Hurricane Katrina. Although Katrina also hit the

PROFILE ～ BARACK OBAMA

Barack Obama was born in Honolulu on August 4, 1961. His personal history captures the complexity of identity in contemporary America. Obama's father was an immigrant from Kenya who married a white American from Kansas. When his father abandoned the family to complete his studies at Harvard, two-year-old Barack and his mother moved in with her family. In 1967, Obama and his mother relocated with her second husband to Indonesia, where Obama attended both a Roman Catholic and a Muslim school. Obama and his mother later returned to Hawaii, where he completed high school in 1979.

After high school, Obama entered Occidental College in Los Angeles before graduating from New York's Columbia University in 1983. His father, whom he had seen only once in the interim, died in an automobile accident before his graduation. After a couple of years in the corporate world, Obama moved to Chicago and became a community organizer, working to start a job placement and training center. His experiences as a community organizer taught him "that meaningful change always begins at the grassroots, and that engaged citizens working together can accomplish extraordinary things." He decided to pursue a law degree "to learn power's currency in all its intricacy and detail."

In 1991, Obama graduated from Harvard Law School, where he was the first African-American editor of the *Law Review*. He returned to Chicago and married Michelle Robinson, a native of Chicago's South Side who had also graduated from Harvard Law School. They have two daughters, Malia and Sasha.

In 1996, Obama was elected to the Illinois State Senate, where he voted to ban racial profiling and supported increased funding for child health care. He also helped win passage of a law requiring police to videotape interrogations of suspects in all capital crime cases.

In 2004, as a candidate for the U.S. Senate, Obama electrified the Democratic National Convention with an impassioned keynote speech. He declared, to thunderous applause, "The pundits like to slice-and-dice our country into Red States and Blue States . . . But I've got news for them . . . We worship an awesome God in the Blue States, and we don't like federal agents poking around our libraries in Red States. We coach Little League in the Blue States and have gay friends in the Red States . . . We are one people." A national political star was born.

In the Senate election, Obama coasted to an easy victory over his Republican opponent, black conservative Alan Keyes. His victory made Obama the second African-American man to serve in the U.S. Senate in the twentieth century, and the second black U.S. senator in Illinois history. The freshman senator wasted no time opposing the Iraq War. Indeed, Obama had been a consistent critic of the war since the Bush administration first began to propose it in 2002.

After months of speculation, in February 2007, Obama announced his candidacy to become the presidential nominee of the Democratic Party. He showed himself to be a formidable campaigner, raising enormous amounts of money and attracting enthusiastic support from a wide spectrum of Americans. He addressed many of the key issues—the war in Iraq, health care, public education—that were as important to African Americans as they were to others. Yet some African Americans were ambivalent about his candidacy. When asked to explain this, Obama said, "It's interesting that the people who are most hesitant about this oftentimes are African Americans because they feel protective of me. They're either concerned about the attacks I'd be subjected to or they are skeptical oftentimes that America is prepared to elect a black president."

Obama

CLARENCE PAGE, "WHEN SLUGGISHNESS ISN'T OK"

Columnist Clarence Page wrote about the roles of race, class, and gender in the federal government's incompetent response to the destruction Hurricane Katrina wrought on New Orleans.

It didn't take long for the tragedy of Hurricane Katrina to turn into an eruption about race and class . . .

1. Would the storm victims have been rescued, fed, treated, and evacuated with greater urgency had they been mostly white and middle class instead of black and poor?

2. When state and local authorities made the evacuation of New Orleans a central feature of their response to hurricanes, did they consider that 100,000 to 200,000 people might not have transportation?

3. Did they know that more than 25 percent of the city of 1.5 million lived below the poverty line, as well as the water line?

4. Did they consider that a lot of these folks are sick, or elderly, or badly in need of insulin, or oxygen, or dialysis just to stay alive from day to day?

5. When local authorities put out word that food, fresh water, and other help would be available at the New Orleans Convention Center, did it occur to them that more than 15,000 people would show up, only to discover there was no help at all? Not even a guy with a megaphone or a clipboard?

Hurricane Katrina was the first big test of President Bush's proud invention, the Department of Homeland Security, and it flunked.

🌿 *Given the history of racism and social injustice in the United States, is it legitimate for Page to ask these questions?*

🌿 *Should the federal and state authorities have been better prepared to deal with the consequences of a major flood in New Orleans?*

Source: *Chicago Tribune*, September 4, 2005.

Mississippi and Alabama coasts hard, New Orleans suffered the worst effects. Federal funding for flood control in New Orleans, most of which lies below sea level, had been reduced by 44 percent since 2001 when President Bush took office. State and federal emergency services were so reduced and disorganized that they offered almost no protection in the case of natural disasters. The plan to evacuate New Orleans if a major hurricane threatened the city ignored the fact that most of its poor residents lacked the means to flee. Moreover, one-third (35 percent) of the Louisiana National Guard, who would be needed to furnish aid and keep order in a disaster, was in Iraq.

Obama, The Audacity of Hope 46 LIVING WORDS

What suddenly became apparent to the nation and the world after Katrina struck was that most of the people trapped in New Orleans—abandoned, drowning, rendered homeless, starving, and destitute—were poor and black. New Orleans had been a black-majority city almost since its founding by the French in 1718. Although most black residents of New Orleans had always been poor, the city's black community had produced a rich culture, famous for its food, music, literature, and artistic heritage. In addition to taking more than 1,500 lives in the city, Katrina damaged or destroyed much of that legacy. Historian Mark Naison observed, "Is this what the pioneers of the civil rights movement fought to achieve, a society where many black people are as trapped and isolated by their poverty as they were by segregation laws? . . . If September 11 showed the power of a nation united in response to a devastating attack, Hurricane Katrina reveals the fault lines of a region and a nation, rent by profound social divisions."

William Julius Wilson, The Urban Underclass 23-1 DOCUMENT

Katrina moved ashore on Monday, August 29, 2005, and caused the highest storm surge in U.S. history. It punctured the levees that protected New Orleans in fifty-three places and inundated 80 percent of the city under twenty feet of water. Most of New Orleans's more affluent residents had escaped before the hurricane hit, leaving an estimated 100,000 people, mostly poor and black, to weather the storm. With nowhere else to go and no means with which to get there, thousands of them made their way to the Louisiana Superdome and the Convention Center, where they found wretched conditions—inadequate food, water, electricity, and sanitation. Violence erupted, and chaos loomed. As bad as the hurricane proved to be, the aftermath was worse. As survivors insisted, they may have been poor and black, but they were still American citizens, and not third world refugees as some media figures called them. President Bush cut short his vacation and flew over the wrecked city, but did not visit New Orleans until September 2, when he praised Michael Brown, the director of FEMA (the Federal Emergency Management Agency) for doing "a heck of a job." Since it was already apparent that FEMA's response and Brown's performance were ineffectual, the nation—and black people in particular—was outraged by the president's words. (Brown was forced to resign on September 12 under relentless criticism.) Hip-hop rapper Kanye West departed from the script of a nationally televised program to raise funds for the displaced victims to charge that "George Bush does not care about black people." His comments made Katrina an "Emmett Till" moment for the hip-hop generation.

In the face of government ineptitude, many individuals and groups used their own resources to bring relief to those trapped in New Orleans. Local community organizations mobilized to promote recovery, rebuilding, and renewal. Media stars such as Oprah Winfrey pledged funds to rebuild homes; Jesse Jackson led a caravan to transport hundreds to safety in Chicago. Eleven thousand homeless residents of New Orleans were bused 350 miles away to shelter at the Houston Astrodome. Churches and international relief organizations such as the Red Cross sent supplies, money, and clothes to those who had lost jobs, homes, and loved ones. Universities across the country welcomed students and faculty from historically black institutions such as Dillard University and Xavier University, and professional organizations launched book drives to reconstruct libraries.

Yet this aid could not make up for the failure of the government's response. Today, much of New Orleans remains a disaster area. Whole neighborhoods have disappeared. The city has lost almost half of its pre-Katrina population, and most of the former residents who have not returned are black people. For the first time in centuries, New Orleans may no longer have a black majority. Much of the city still lies in ruins. Crime and poverty are rampant. Some observers wonder if New Orleans will ever recover. As Lawrence Downes wrote in the *New York Times*, May 7, 2007, "New Orleans has been slammed into the 19th century, and it's going to be a long way back." An entire American city along with it a unique and historic black community may have been lost.

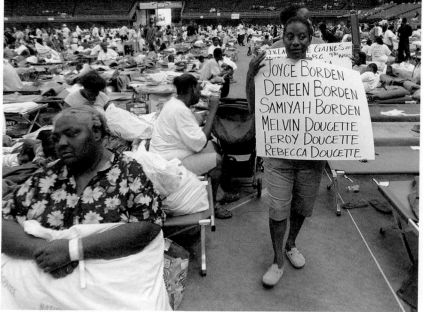

In the aftermath of Hurricane Katrina, New Orleans residents received clothing, food, and shelter in the Houston Astrodome, but many were separated from, or lost contact with, family members. The makeshift signs with names of family, friends, neighbors, and loved ones reflect the desire and urgency to reconnect and rebuild vital relationships and shattered lives.

CONCLUSION

Jesse Jackson, who's Rainbow Coalition reflected a quest for unity amid diversity, asked at the 1988 Democratic convention, "Shall we expand, be inclusive, find unity and power; or suffer division and impotence?" The 2007 Democratic Party primary campaign illustrated the political importance of black Americans and the extent to which the Democratic Party had embraced its diverse constituency. African Americans remained committed to a progressive political agenda that emphasized universal health care, quality education, urban economic development, job training, safe environments, an end to racial profiling and police brutality, and reform of the prison-industrial complex that had disenfranchised so many black Americans and members of other minority groups. At the dawn of the new millennium, black political power had come of age. It marked another stage in the black odyssey toward freedom and the transformation of American society. The Hurricane Katrina disaster, however, reminded the black community exactly how

AFRICAN-AMERICAN EVENTS | NATIONAL EVENTS

1978

1978
U.S. Supreme Court decides
*Regents of the University of
California v. Bakke*

1980

1980
Ronald Reagan is elected president

1981
Recession settles in; Economic
Recovery Tax Act is passed

1982

1984

1984
Jesse Jackson creates Rainbow
Coalition and seeks Democratic
nomination for president

1984
Reagan is reelected

1986

1987
August Wilson wins Pulitzer prize for
his play *Fences*

1988

1988
Jesse Jackson makes second run
for the Democratic nomination for
president

Fair Housing

1988
George H. W. Bush is elected
president of the United States

1989
Ron Brown is elected chairman of
the Democratic Party, the first
African American to lead a major
national political party

1990

1991
Clarence Thomas wins Senate
confirmation to the U.S. Supreme
Court; John Singleton's *Boyz N the
Hood* wins box office success;
Rodney King is beaten by four
white Los Angeles policemen

1991
Operation Desert Storm—against
Iraq—is initiated and ended

1992

1992
Los Angeles riots after King's police
assailants are acquitted; Carol
Mosley-Braun of Illinois is the first
black woman elected to the U.S.
Senate

1992
William Jefferson Clinton is elected
president

1993
Clinton names Ron Brown and
Hazel O'Leary to cabinet

---

precarious life remained for those trapped in poverty and perched at the intersection of race, class, and gender in America.

RECOMMENDED READING

Martha Biondi. "The Rise of the Reparations Movement." *Radical History Review*, 87 (Fall 2003): 5–18. A superb historical overview of the black reparations movement from the Civil War to the present.

Cathy J. Cohen. *The Boundaries of Blackness: AIDS and the Breakdown of Black Politics.* Chicago: University of Chicago Press, 1999. A black political scientist provides a sophisticated and provocative exploration into the social, political, and cultural impact of the AIDS epidemic on the African-American community.

Mary Pattillo, David Weiman, and Bruce Western, eds. *Imprisoning America: The Social Effects of Mass Incarceration.* New York: Russell Sage Foundation, 2004. Important essays that explore the sociological, political, and economic consequences of the mass incarceration of African-American men and other minorities. These studies demonstrate the need for new policies to deal with ex-prisoners, their families, and communities.

Brenda Gayle Plummer, ed. *Window on Freedom: Race, Civil Rights, and Foreign Affairs, 1945–1988.* Chapel Hill: University of North Carolina Press, 2003. An anthology of wide-ranging essays that explore how race and ethnicity complicated U.S. foreign relations during the Cold War.

Deborah Gray White. *Too Heavy a Load: Black Women in Defense of Themselves, 1894–1994.* New York: Norton, 1998. A brilliant study by a black woman historian of black women and the organizations they founded to fight for the ballot, against segregation, and against the sexism and misogyny of contemporary black nationalism.

ADDITIONAL BIBLIOGRAPHY

CULTURE AND RACE STUDIES

Molefi Kete Asante. *Erasing Racism: The Survival of the American Nation.* New York: Prometheus Books, 2003.

Robin D. G. Kelley. *Race Rebels: Culture, Politics, and the Black Working Class.* New York: Free Press, 1994.

Jacob Levenson. *The Secret Epidemic: The Story of AIDS and Black America.* New York: Pantheon, 2004.

Manning Marable. *The Great Wells of Democracy: The Meaning of Race in American Life.* New York: Basic Books, 2002.

Terry McMillan. *Five for Five: The Films of Spike Lee.* New York: Stewart, Tabori & Chang, 1991.

Nikhil Pal Singh. *Black Is a Country: Race and the Unfinished Struggle for Democracy.* Cambridge: Harvard University Press, 2004.

Carol A. Stabile, *White Victims, Black Villains: Gender, Race, and Crime News* in U.S. Culture. New York: Routledge, 2006.

BLACK POLITICS AND ECONOMICS

Mary Frances Berry. *My Face Is Black Is True: Callie House and the Struggle for Ex-Slave Reparations.* New York: Knopf, 2005.

Andrew Billingsley. *Climbing Jacob's Ladder: The Enduring Legacy of African-American Families.* New York: Simon & Schuster, 1993.

Barry Bluestone and Bennett Harrison. *The Deindustrialization of America: Plant Closings, Community Abandonment, and the Dismantling of Basic Industry.* New York: Basic Books, 1982.

Donna Brazile. *Cooking with Grease: Stirring the Pot in American Politics.* New York: Simon & Schuster, 2004.

Michael K. Brown. *Race, Money, and the American Welfare State.* Ithaca, NY: Cornell University Press, 1999.

Robert D. Bullard, Glenn S. Johnson, and Angel O. Torres, eds. *Highway Robbery: Transportation Racism and New Routes to Equity.* Cambridge, MA: South End Press, 2004.

Martin Carnoy. *Faded Dreams: The Politics and Economics of Race in America.* Cambridge, England: Cambridge University Press, 1994.

Dalton Conley. *Being Black, Living in the Red: Race, Wealth, and Social Policy in America.* Berkeley: University of California Press, 1999.

Robert Dallek. *Ronald Reagan: The Politics of Symbolism.* Cambridge, MA: Harvard University Press, 1984.

W. Avon Drake and Robert D. Holsworth. *Affirmative Action and the Stalled Quest for Black Progress.* Urbana: University of Illinois Press, 1996.

Robert Gooding-Williams, ed. *Reading Rodney King: Reading Urban Uprising.* New York: Routledge, 1993.

Lani Guinier. *Tyranny of the Majority: Fundamental Fairness and Representative Democracy.* New York: Free Press, 1995.

Andrew Hacker. *Two Nations: Black and White, Separate, Hostile, Unequal.* New York: Ballantine Books, rev., 1995.

Melissa Victoria Harris-Lacewell. *Barbershops, Bibles, and Bet: Everyday Talk and Black Political Thought.* Princeton: Princeton University Press, 2004.

Charles P. Henry. *Jesse Jackson: The Search for Common Ground.* Oakland, CA: Black Scholar Press, 1991.

Anita Faye Hill and Emma Coleman Jordan, eds. *Race, Gender, and Power in America: The Legacy of the Hill–Thomas Hearings.* New York: Oxford University Press, 1995.

James Jennings. *Welfare Reform and the Revitalization of Inner City Neighborhoods.* East Lansing: Michigan State University Press, 2003.

Peniel E. Joseph. *Waiting 'til the Midnight Hour: A Narrative History of Black Power in America.* New York: Henry Holt and Company, 2006.

Norman Kelley. *The Head Negro in Charge Syndrome: The Dead End of Black Politics.* New York: Nation Books, 2004.

1994

1994
Jesse Jackson Jr. elected to Congress

1994
Midterm elections give Republican Party control of Congress

1996

1996
Clinton is reelected; Clinton signs welfare reform legislation

1998

1998
Clinton is impeached by the House of Representatives

1999
The U.S. Senate acquits Clinton

2000

2000
Donna Brazile manages the presidential campaign of Al Gore

2000
George W. Bush becomes president of the United States

2001
Bush names Condoleezza Rice national security adviser and Colin Powell secretary of state

September 11, 2001
Terrorists demolish the World Trade Center in New York City and attack the Pentagon in Washington

United States invades Afghanistan

No Child Left Behind Act becomes law

2002

2003
Supreme Court upholds use of racial preferences in admission to University of Michigan Law School

2003
United States invades Iraq

2004

2004
Carol Mosely Braun and Al Sharpton run for president

Barack Obama elected to U.S. Senate

Condoleezza Rice appointed secretary of state

2004
George W. Bush reelected president of the United States

2006

2006
James Brown died

2005
Hurricane Katrina devastates New Orleans

2007
Barack Obama runs for president

AFRICAN-AMERICAN EVENTS   **NATIONAL EVENTS**

Douglas S. Massey and Nancy A. Denton. *American Apartheid: Segregation and the Making of the Underclass.* Cambridge, MA: Harvard University Press, 1993.

Adolph Reed Jr. *The Jesse Jackson Phenomenon: The Crisis in Afro-American Politics.* New Haven, CT: Yale University Press, 1986.

Condoleezza Rice. "Why We Know Iraq Is Lying." *New York Times,* January 23, 2003.

Andrea Y. Simpson. *The Tie That Binds: Identity and Political Attitudes in the Post–Civil Rights Generation.* New York: New York University Press, 1998.

Special Issue on Affirmative Action. *The Western Journal of Black Studies,* 27, no. 1 (Spring 2003).

Ronald W. Walters. *Freedom is not Enough: Black Voters, Black Candidates, and American Presidential Politics.* Landam, MD: Rowman & Littlefield Publishers, 2005.

William Julius Wilson. *The Bridge over the Racial Divide: Rising Inequality and Coalition Politics.* Berkeley: University of California Press, 1999.

LIBERATION STUDIES

Derrick Bell. *Faces at the Bottom of the Well: The Permanence of Racism.* New York: Basic Books, 1992.

Michael C. Dawson. *Behind the Mule: Race and Class in African-American Politics.* Princeton, NJ: Princeton University Press, 1994.

W. Marvin Dulaney. *Black Police in America.* Bloomington: Indiana University Press, 1996.

Henry Hampton and Steve Fayer. *Voices of Freedom: An Oral History of the Civil Rights Movement from the 1950s through the 1980s.* New York: Bantam Books, 1990.

Randall Robinson. *The Debt: What America Owes to Blacks.* New York: Plume, 2000.

Cornel West. *Democracy Matters: Wining the Fight against Imperialism.* New York: The Penguin Press, 2004.

BLACK CONSERVATIVES

Thomas Sowell. *Preferential Policies: An International Perspective.* New York: William Morrow, 1990.

Shelby Steele. *A Dream Deferred: The Second Betrayal of Black Freedom in America.* New York: HarperCollins, 1998.

Shelby Steele/CCC. *The Content of Our Character: A New Vision of Race in America.* New York: St. Martin's Press, 1990.

AUTOBIOGRAPHY AND BIOGRAPHY

Marshall Frady. *Jesse: The Life and Pilgrimage of Jesse Jackson.* New York: Random House, 1996.

Barack Obama. *Dreams from My Father: A Story of Race and Inheritance.* New York: Three Rivers Press, 1995, 2004.

Rev. Al Sharpton (with Karen Hunter). *Al on America.* New York: Kensington, 2002.

RETRACING THE ODYSSEY

The *Amistad* Research Center, Tilton Hall, Tulane University, New Orleans. The *Amistad* Center contains manuscripts and art that illuminate the history and culture of diverse ethnic groups and race relations in the United States. Approximately 90 percent of its holdings document the history and records of African Americans' community organizations and struggles. The center also houses records related to religious denominations—Protestant, Catholic, and Jewish. Its art gallery frequently exhibits the work of early black artists, such as Aaron Douglas.

PRENTICE HALL
myhistorylab
Where it's a good time to connect to the past!

REVIEW, RESEARCH, AND INTERACT

REVIEW QUESTIONS

1. To what extent and in what key areas did the Reagan and Bush presidencies nullify or dismantle Great Society legislation? How did African Americans respond to the Republican conservative reaction?

2. What was the significance of Jesse Jackson's campaigns for the Democratic presidential nomination?

3. Compare and contrast the effects on African Americans of the welfare reform legislation passed during Clinton's administration and George W. Bush's No Child Left Behind Act.

4. Why did affirmative action become one of the most contested issues of the 1990s? How did affirmative action in the workplace differ from affirmative action in education?

5. How did the Rodney King case illuminate the different perceptions of black and white Americans of the police and the justice system?

6. To what extent have African Americans become the base of the Democratic Party?

7. How did the Hurricane Katrina disaster expose the fault lines of race, class, and gender in American society?

www.researchnavigator.com

Using the tools available in Research Navigator, consider this question:
What role did racism play in the politics of the 1980s?

PRIMARY SOURCE DOCUMENTS

INTERACTIVE ACTIVITY

Growing Inequality

Over the last twenty-five years, the gap between the rich and poor has substantially widened.

24

African Americans at the Dawn of a New Millennium

WHY ARE SO MANY AFRICAN AMERICANS
LESS WEALTHY AND LESS HEALTHY
THAN WHITE AMERICANS?

WHY HAS RAP MUSIC ACHIEVED
INTERNATIONAL POPULARITY?

WHAT IS AFROCENTRICITY?

WHAT ARE THE STRENGTHS AND TENSIONS
WITHIN THE BLACK CHURCH TODAY?

WHY HAS BLACK IDENTITY BECOME
MORE COMPLICATED AT THE DAWN
OF THE TWENTY-FIRST CENTURY?

◀ **Issues of class,** gender, religion, ethnicity, culture, and
sexuality complicated black racial identity politics at the
dawn of the twenty-first century. The Million Man March and
the Million Woman March reflected the determination to
redefine black identity. Najilah Feanny-Hicks, Corbis/SABA Press Photos, Inc.

What demanding respect for people *as blacks* or *as gays* requires is that there be some scripts that go with being an African-American or having same-sex desires. There will be proper ways of being black and gay: there will be expectations to be met; demands will be made. It is at this point that someone who takes autonomy seriously will want to ask whether we have not replaced one kind of tyranny with another. If I had to choose between Uncle Tom and Black Power, I would, of course, choose the latter. But I would like not to have to choose. I would like other options. The politics of recognition requires that one's skin color, one's sexual body, should be politically acknowledged in ways that make it hard for those who want to treat their skin and their sexual body as personal dimensions of the self. And "personal" does not mean "secret" but "not too tightly scripted," "not too constrained by the demands and expectations of others."

K. Anthonly Appiah ("Racial Identity and Racial Identification," *in* K. Anthony Appiah and Amy Gutmann, *Color Conscious: The Political Morality of Race* [Princeton, NJ: Princeton University Press, 1996])

Identity issues and the struggles of gay and lesbian, black and white Americans for the right to marry occasioned heated debate as the personal became decidely political in the 21st C.

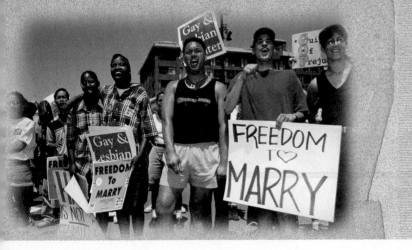

In his 1901 book *The Souls of Black Folk*, W. E. B. Du Bois dreamed of a nation in which black people could be both African and American, embracing their own rich cultural heritage and sharing it with America while becoming full-fledged citizens. This merging of the "two-ness" of the African and American "souls" did not happen in Du Bois's lifetime, but at his death in 1963, the civil rights movement was poised on the edge of its greatest success. Had Du Bois lived to the dawn of the twenty-first century, he would have been both pleased by the progress made toward fulfilling his dream and saddened by the extent to which the ideals of that dream remain unfulfilled.

What Du Bois could not have imagined was the globalization of hip hop, a black youth-generated culture that by the dawn of the twenty-first century had transformed the world into what *National Geographic* has called the "Hip Hop Planet." Hip hop became the latest of a long series of cultural movements improvised by marginalized, impoverished, but creative black young people determined to refashion empowering images of themselves and to critique the impoverished material conditions of their lives in urban America.

In the first decade of the twenty-first century, many African Americans advanced to the top ranks of government, the military, sports, entertainment, business, the professions, and academia. The African "soul" that Du Bois urged black Americans to take pride in moved from the shadowy edges of American culture to its heart, honored for its contributions to the nation's music, language, and fine arts.

As a result of the modern civil rights movement, the nation's legal system prohibits racial segregation, disenfranchisement, and job discrimination. These achievements have enabled millions of black men and women to escape the deep poverty to which nearly all African Americans had been confined when Du Bois wrote his book and in which most of them still remained at his death. Like other Americans, vastly greater numbers of black people now complete high school and college and live healthier and longer lives, although white Americans still, on average, earn more and live longer than their black fellow citizens.

Du Bois would be appalled, however, by the extreme poverty, poor education, addiction, and crime that still afflict much of the black population and by the disassociation of millions of black Americans from the larger opportunities and culture of the nation as a whole. But he might not be surprised by the racism and stereotyping that continue to define the journey of black people in America. African America today is bound together not only in celebration of a common culture and individual achievement, but also by a sense of otherness and threat.

In other words, a two-ness remains a century after Du Bois wrote, but it is complicated both by the successes African Americans have achieved in recent decades and by changes in the nation and in the world. Tensions have always festered between a racially defined identity and the many other ways in which African Americans define themselves. Differences of class, color, belief, and region have divided Americans for centuries. Now, just as Du Bois found two-ness, current observers, such as scholar Anthony Appiah, applaud the possibility of embracing multiple identities linked to sexual preference, religious affiliation, immigration status, and political philosophy. Reconciling all of these self-understandings within a larger racial identity that is complicated by socioeconomic divisions among black people themselves remains the defining struggle of the next phase of the African-American odyssey.

Progress and Poverty: Income, Education, and Health

After the triumphs of the civil rights era, many African Americans made great strides in overcoming the economic and educational disadvantages that had plagued their ancestors. Partly as a result of this progress, they are also living longer, healthier lives. Yet the disparities between the levels of wealth, schooling, and health of African Americans and the white majority, although narrowed, have persisted as a stubborn legacy from centuries of racial oppression. The persistence of black poverty and the social problems that are associated with it erupted into a major controversy among black people in 2004 when Bill Cosby used the fiftieth anniversary of the *Brown* decision to criticize

what he termed "irresponsible black poor parents and their delinquent children." Cosby called for greater "personal responsibility" from middle-class black people who, he argued, should put themselves and their children forward as role models for poor African Americans instead of isolating themselves from the American mainstream and imitating the street culture of the black inner cities. Many black commentators rejected this attack and accused Cosby of "airing the black community's dirty laundry." Black studies scholar Michael Eric Dyson responded to Cosby by emphasizing the complexity of class stratification in black America and its effects on how many black people, especially young black people, behave:

> There are many black middle classes: the one barely a paycheck or two from poverty; the one a notch above, with jobs in the service economy; the one more solidly in the middle, with low-level professional jobs; and one in the upper stratum, with high level professional employment and the esteem such labor yields. Moreover, in strictly literal economic terms; the black definition of class embraces style and behavior as well.

HIGH-ACHIEVING AFRICAN AMERICANS

The years after 1970 witnessed the consolidation of black economic, civic, and political progress. In part, this was exemplified by the prominence of such visible African Americans as entertainer Oprah Winfrey, Bill Clinton's secretary of commerce Ronald Brown, chairman of the Joint Chiefs of Staff and later secretary of state Colin Powell, Powell's successor as secretary of state Condoleezza Rice, professional golfer Tiger Woods, and public intellectual Henry Louis Gates. These people, and many other African Americans, rose to the top of their fields.

As with the American population as a whole, the ultra-rich remained rare in the black community, but their ranks did grow. Oprah Winfrey, Bill Cosby, Michael Jackson, and Michael Jordon acquired immense fortunes as entertainers or athletes. Others in this fortunate few include businessman Robert L. Johnson, founder of Black Entertainment Television (BET), who became the first African American to own a professional basketball team, the Charlotte, North Carolina, Hornets; the late John H. Johnson, publisher of *Ebony* and *Jet* magazines; Berry Gordy, founder of Motown Records; and Russell Simmons, a recording and fashion entrepreneur.

The career of Reginald Lewis illustrates the possibilities open to black people in other industries. Armed

Television mogul Oprah Winfrey is the richest African American woman in the world and she is arguably the most generous. In 2007 she opened a school for girls in Henley-on-Klip, South Africa.

with a degree from Harvard Law School, he first purchased the McCall Pattern Company, and then in 1987 bought Beatrice Foods, an international packaged goods company, for $2.5 billion. At the time it was the largest leveraged buyout in U.S. history, and Lewis became the wealthiest African American. Before his death in 1993, Lewis demonstrated an understanding of the need to give back to his community by donating millions of dollars to Howard University and the NAACP.

AFRICAN AMERICANS' GROWING ECONOMIC SECURITY

The achievements of the most successful African Americans are impressive, but more significant was the increase in job opportunities, income, and wealth for a broad cross section of working African Americans. Before the 1960s nearly all black men worked in the lower rungs of agriculture, construction, transporta-

tion, and manufacturing. Black women were predominantly caged in domestic and food service jobs. Few black men or women had a chance to move to higher-paid and more prestigious skilled or managerial positions, and the wages for all African Americans remained lower than the earnings of white Americans.

Antidiscrimination laws and affirmative action programs allowed millions of black people to climb up the rungs of career ladders. In 1940, for example, only 5.2 percent of black men and 6.4 percent of black women worked in white-collar occupations. By 2000 those figures had risen to 35.3 percent for black men and 62.3 percent for black women. Many black people moved into jobs in government, education, finance, and such professions as the law and medicine, which had largely excluded them.

As a result of these changes, black family income increased dramatically. In 1940 only 1 percent of black families, compared with 12 percent of white families, had incomes at least twice as high as the government's poverty line; by 1998, 50 percent of black families did, compared with 73 percent of white families. The disparity of income between similar families also decreased. In 1960 two-parent black families earned 61 percent as much as two-parent white families, but by 1998 they earned 87 percent as much. This figure is even more impressive when one considers that a larger proportion of black people live in the low-wage South than do white people. On average black women now make 94 percent of what white women earn. The economic boom of the Clinton years from 1993 to 2000 particularly benefited black people. Although the median income of black families remains well below that of white families, it has risen substantially (see Table 24–1).

Although many African-American families made progress in closing the income gap, their average wealth remained far behind that of white families. This was due partly to the centuries-long heritage of poverty during which most black people accumulated little property or other forms of wealth to hand on to their children. It was also closely tied to differences in the proportions of black and white people who owned their own homes, because home ownership is for most American families their primary asset. Only 35 percent of African-American families owned their homes in 1950. This was partly because of low incomes but also due to systematic discrimination. By 2005, thanks to rising incomes, laws that barred discrimination in housing, and government programs, 46.8 percent of African Americans owned their

TABLE 24–1 MEDIAN INCOME OF BLACK AND WHITE HOUSEHOLDS, 1992–2005

	1992	2005	Change	Percentage Increase
White	$39,825	$48,554	$8,729	22
Black	$23,190	$30,858	$7,668	33

Source: U.S. Census Bureau Historical Income Tables—Households.

Growing Inequality

own homes (the figure for white home ownership was 70.7 percent). Still, black households on average held far less in assets than white households.

The Persistence of Black Poverty

Although most African Americans enjoyed greater absolute and relative increases in income, many remained mired in poverty. The poverty rate (in 2007 this meant having an annual income below $20,650 for a family of four) for black people dipped to a low of 22.7 percent during the Clinton boom, but has risen to 23.3 percent during George W. Bush's presidency. Most poor black people are trapped in inner-city neighborhoods plagued by gang warfare, crime, drug and alcohol addiction, and high rates of HIV/AIDS infection.

In the urban impoverished communities where so many of the young live, they are cut off from meaningful participation in the social and economic life of the nation and experience fewer educational and other opportunities that might allow them to escape from poverty. Twenty-three percent of eighteen- and nineteen-year-old African Americans are either not in school or not working, compared with only 10 percent of white people within the same age range. Another large concentration of black poverty is found in depressed rural areas, especially in the South, where mechanization and declining commodity prices for crops have long limited African-American opportunities. Despite cherished myths about rural life, these areas see many of the same social problems as the inner cities. Approximately 40 percent of black rural residents lack high school diplomas as opposed to 20 percent of white rural residents.

The high rate of poverty in the black community disproportionately affects children. In 2000, 53.3 percent of all African Americans under age eighteen lived in families with only one parent, generally with their mother. Partly for this reason, 55.6 percent of black children lived in families at or near the poverty level. Many, if not most, single-parent families headed by females suffer from limited earning capacity, meager public assistance, poor housing, and inferior schools. These conditions often handicap children for the rest of their lives, helping perpetuate poverty from generation to generation. Given their proportion among African-American youth, this is an ominous sign for the future. Marian Wright Edleman, founder of the Children's Defense Fund, captured the plight of the black young when she wrote: "An unlevel playing field from birth contributes to many poor black children getting pulled into a cradle-to-prison-to-death pipeline that we must

dismantle if the clock of racial and social progress is to not turn backwards."

"Talking to Teen Mothers"   **23-6**   DOCUMENT

Poverty persists among urban African Americans in part because of the national economic restructuring that has been under way since the 1960s. **Deindustrialization**, relentless advances in labor-saving technology, and the development of low-wage offshore production have wiped out many jobs that African Americans with limited education and skills once held. The history of Oakland, California, illustrates this process. In the 1940s and 1950s, Oakland attracted a large black population that was employed in everything from canning food to assembling automobiles. Thousands of black laborers unloaded ships at the port or worked in the vast yards and repair facilities of the railroads. By the 1960s, however, manufacturing in Oakland was already in flight to lower-wage areas in the United States or overseas, and the port was mechanized, which sharply reduced both the need for longshoremen and the costs of importing foreign goods. Highways, often built through the heart of black business districts, replaced much of Oakland's rail traffic while displacing residents and undermining neighborhoods.

Conditions Contributing to Poverty   ACTIVITY

By the end of the century, Oakland had become a predominantly residential city through which goods made around the globe would flow but in which relatively little was produced or sold. This shift created wealth for some and provided jobs to many middle-class African Americans, but it left large segments of the once-thriving black districts in the city without legitimate work. This paved the way for the rise of drug-related crime that plagued these parts of the city. The economic boom of the late 1990s did improve the lot of many inner-city residents, with consequent drops in the rate of crime and poverty in Oakland and elsewhere, but the staying power of this renewal remains uncertain.

RACIAL INCARCERATION

The growth in criminal activity in inner-city districts during the 1980s and 1990s and an overwhelming national shift toward aggressive policing and harsher sentencing for those convicted of breaking the law led to a vast increase in the imprisonment rates of African-American men. Incarceration is an increasingly common experience for poor young black men, compounding the barriers to advancement they already face. (For more on black imprisonment, see Chapter 24.) From 1954 to 2005, the black prison population increased by almost 900 percent (see Table 24–2).

TABLE 24–2	RATES OF BLACK INCARCERATION
1954	98,000
1984	288,800
2005	910,000

EDUCATION ONE-HALF CENTURY AFTER *BROWN*

Educational attainment is the key factor that distinguishes the African Americans who achieve economic success from those who do not. Black rates of school completion have advanced tremendously in the past half-century. Many more black youths graduate from high school than ever before. In 1960 only 37.7 percent of African Americans between ages twenty-five and twenty-nine had completed high school, but by 2000, 86.8 percent had, which is close to the 94 percent for white Americans. Black enrollment in college also rose from a mere 136,000 in 1960 to 1,548,000 in 2000. Although still behind white Americans, these rates of achievement place African Americans among the most educated groups of people in the world. African Americans between the ages of twenty-five and thirty-four are now more likely than young adults in Canada, France, Italy, and Britain to have completed high school, and they are more likely than those in Italy, Britain, Germany, and France to have completed college.

Today African-American students pursue education in diverse fields. The Irwin S. Chanin School of Architecture at Cooper Union for the Advancement of Science and Art in New York City offers one path to a brighter future.

Yet despite these encouraging figures, black people who want an education, particularly those in poor inner-city and rural areas, still face severe problems. Schools starved of funds by regressive tax policies and the movement of wealthier people—both black and white—to the suburbs are almost predestined to fail. Affirmative action programs that made a place for African-American students have been cut in California, Texas, and elsewhere, resulting in declining enrollments among black students at the top schools. For impoverished black youth, the combined effect of failing schools and few opportunities results in dropout rates sharply higher than those for more affluent African Americans.

CHALLENGING *BROWN*

For over 50 years, conservative groups have periodically challenged the meaning and intent of the 1954 Supreme Court decision in *Brown v. Board of Education*. In two 2007 decisions, the justices appointed to the Court by both Presidents Bush moved to end the practice of racial classification as a means to achieve racial diversity in public schools. The two cases involved school assignment plans developed by the boards of education in Seattle, Washington and Jefferson County, Kentucky, which includes the city of Louisville. The Seattle school district classified children as white or non-white and used this as the basis for allocating slots to attend the better, or over-subscribed, city high schools. The Jefferson County school district classified children as either black or as "other" and used that to assign students to elementary schools and to inform decisions about transfer requests.

The Court ruled that both plans violated the Fourteenth Amendment to the Constitution, which guarantees equal protection of the laws. Chief Justice John Roberts, writing the majority opinion, declared, "The way to stop discrimination on the basis of race is to stop discriminating on the basis of race." In a separate opinion, Justice Clarence Thomas insisted that, "Racial imbalance is not segregation," adding, "there is no danger of re-segregation."

Joining Roberts and Thomas were Justices Antonin Scalia and Samuel Alito. In his concurring opinion, Justice Anthony Kennedy left open the door for school districts to devise non-racial measures to achieve diversity while limiting the use of racial classification: "Such measures," Kennedy wrote, "may include strategic site selection of new schools; drawing attendance zones with general recognition of neighborhood demographics; allocating resources for special programs; recruiting students and faculty in a targeted fashion; and tracking enrollments, performance, and other statistics by race."

In a spirited dissent, Justice Stephen Breyer called the majority decision a reversal of precedent and a fundamental weakening of *Brown*. Breyer argued that the majority opinion amounted to a retreat from the principle that allowed local school districts to exercise discretion about the best means to end racial segregation, curb re-segregation due to segregated housing patterns, and overcome class division and racial exclusion. (Michigan Congressman John Conyers, Chair of the House Judiciary Committee, echoed Beyer's assessment, called the ruling "shameful" and a "step backward" from *Brown*.)

The Court's decision to outlaw local school and classroom assignment plans designed to achieve diversity based upon racial categorization in Seattle and Louisville could affect hundreds of school districts across the country. School systems will now have to struggle to devise their own strategies to avoid, or reduce racial concentration, to reverse the wide achievement or performance gaps between white and black students on state tests in reading and math, and to resist the re-segregation of schools that has arisen from the growing patterns of housing segregation.

THE HEALTH GAP

As in income and education, African Americans have made significant progress toward living longer, healthier lives, but they still suffer greater incidence of disease and mortality for most major illnesses. In 1970, the first year for which we have statistics, life expectancy was 60 years for black men and 68.3 years for black women. By 2000 it had risen to 68.3 and 75.2 years, respectively. Improvements in the quality of care accessible to black people are partly responsible for these increases, but higher infant mortality rates and greater numbers of deaths from diseases kept them well below the 74.9-year life span for white men and 80.1 years for white women.

Cancer and HIV/AIDS infections are currently among the greatest threats to black health. African-American men are significantly more likely than white men to develop cancer and to die from the disease within five years of diagnosis. Black women have a somewhat lower incidence of cancer than do white women, but those black women who do get the disease die at a higher rate from it than white women do. Cancer is a complicated disease caused by a variety of factors. Some of the higher rate of its incidence among

African Americans is related to risky behaviors common to all impoverished people. These include smoking, heavy drinking, obesity, and a general lack of knowledge about health. A lack of access to health insurance or quality providers compounds the impact of these behaviors. Evidence also indicates that many African Americans mistrust the health-care system and, on the other side, that medical workers tend to treat black cancer patients less aggressively than white patients.

African Americans are more likely to have HIV/AIDS than any other group in the United States. According to *The Covenant with Black America*, a collection of essays by activists and scholars that was published in 2006, "African Americans are 13 percent of the nation's population and account for 56 percent annually of new HIV infections. A quarter of these infections are among people under 25 years of age." Among American women, 63 percent of newly diagnosed HIV/AIDS cases are black. Although HIV/AIDS first spread in the United States primarily among gay men, and unprotected sex between men is still the primary form of transmission, only about one-third of African Americans contract the disease in this manner. Most acquire HIV/AIDS through intravenous drug use and unprotected heterosexual sex.

Although African Americans have had high rates of HIV infection from the beginning of the epidemic, consciousness that this was an important black problem only began to rise in the 1990s. At first the disease was perceived by many black leaders to affect only gay white men and to be relatively less important than the many other crises affecting their community during the 1980s. This began to change when Los Angeles Lakers' star Earvin "Magic" Johnson told the world he had HIV. The deaths of tennis star Arthur Ashe and the young rapper Eric "Eazy-E" Wright also shocked the black community into action.

Identity issues that concerned sexual orientation, feminine and masculine roles, and male/female relationships acquired a new urgency when 2003 reports indicated that African-American women registered more new cases of HIV/AIDS than any other sector of the population. Clearly, heterosexual African-American women sought testing to a greater extent than men. While women received treatment and understanding, their male partners remained in denial and avoided active engagement in programs that could prolong their lives. Eventually questions about the sexual experiences of black men illuminated practices known as the "Down Low." While denying they were gay or bisexual, self-described straight men were having sex with both men and women and spreading the virus that causes HIV/AIDS to their unsuspecting female partners. Several articles in the *New York Times* and in magazines with large black readerships such as *Essence* ignited new conversations about the complex issue of black male sexuality. New books contributed to the long overdue public dialogue. To be sure, writer E. Lynn Harris had done much to expose Down Low behavior in his best-selling novels. In an interview to promote his book, *On the Down Low: A Journey into the Lives of "Straight" Black Men Who Sleep with Men*, HIV activist and educator J. L. King declared,

> Many bisexual men choose not to reveal their sexual orientation because they dread the negative fallout that such a disclosure would likely cause. Homophobia is real. We all witness the harsh words and ridicule to which the gay/lesbian community is subjected. Also, there's tremendous normative pressure to keep closeted about any behavior that exists outside the prevailing social and religious norms. Being judged and ostracized isn't something most folks would sign up for, especially not a DL man whose sense of self is intricately linked to his ability to express masculinity and fulfill the traditional gender expectation assigned to men.

The future of the black community demands open conversation and creative measures to address the HIV/AIDS crisis.

African Americans at the Center of Art and Culture

Cultural triumphs are among the most positive recent developments for black Americans. Beginning in the 1980s, a cultural renaissance emerged in every American community with a substantial African-American presence. Black consciousness institutions proliferated and flourished. They included black history and culture museums, festivals, expositions, publishing houses, bookstores and boutiques, concerts, theaters, and dance troupes. In 1996 *Publishers Weekly* reported that bookstores specializing in African-American books had increased from a dozen a few years earlier to more than two hundred. By 1994 there were African-American publishing companies. In 1998 the National Literary Hall of Fame for Writers of African Descent opened at Chicago State University. Black painters used outdoor murals to celebrate the black experience.

Black playwrights were in the vanguard of this cultural explosion and helped revitalize the American theater. August Wilson had begun writing overtly political work in the 1960s and 1970s but focused on broader themes of race and personality as his work matured. His first great success came in 1984 with the Broadway production of *Ma Rainey's Black Bottom*, which explored the impact of racism in the music industry. He won praise for his powerful use of the rhythmic and symbolic power of black speech. He has since had four other plays on Broadway, two of which won Pulitzer Prizes—*Fences* in 1987 and *The Piano Lesson* in 1990. Charles Fuller has also made race the center of his plays, attacking stereotypes and exploring the complexity of racial identity in modern America. His most well-known play is the 1982 *A Soldier's Tale*, which also won a Pulitzer Prize. It was made into a motion picture titled *A Soldier's Story*, which was nominated for two Academy Awards. George C. Wolfe is a playwright, director, and producer whose achievements helped demolish racial barriers in the theater. His plays, such as *The Colored Museum* and *Jelly's Last Jam*, have won critical acclaim, and he received a Tony Award as best director for *Angels in America* in 1994. His talent and energy were credited with returning the New York Shakespeare Festival to its former glory when he was its director from 1993 to 2004. Anna Deavere Smith has pioneered new forms of theater with her powerful one-woman plays derived from interviews. Her first major success was *Fires in the Mirror*, about tensions between blacks and Jews in Brooklyn's Crown Heights neighborhood. This was followed by *Twilight: Los Angeles 1992*, a powerful portrayal of the Rodney King riots. Smith's achievements in drama and her gifted teaching were rewarded with a MacArthur genius grant in 1996.

The new cultural renaissance differed from the black arts movement of the 1960s and 1970s. The contemporary flowering was more inclusive and more appreciative of women artists. It also included the work of openly gay and lesbian artists, such as documentary filmmaker Marion Riggs, dance choreographer Bill T. Jones, and novelist E. Lynn Harris. Whereas poets and dramatists dominated earlier movements, novelists took center stage in the 1980s. Much of the new work in all fields appeals to white as much as to black audiences, providing new insights into the lives of people of African heritage in a predominantly Eurocentric society.

There were signs of the emergence of a new wave of African-American women novelists as early as 1977 when Toni Morrison's *Song of Solomon* became a Book-of-the-Month-Club selection, the first by a black author since Richard Wright's *Native Son* in 1940. Then Barbara Chase-Riboud made waves with *Sally Hemings* (1979), a fictional treatment of a woman who was both slave to and mistress of President Thomas Jefferson. In 1980 Toni Cade Bambara won the American Book Award for *The Salt Eaters*. At least as significant as these individual books was the founding in 1981 of a new publishing house, Kitchen Table: Women of Color Press. Then, in 1982, Alice Walker won the Pulitzer Prize and the American Book Award for *The Color Purple*, which was later made into a movie by director Steven Spielberg, with Whoopi Goldberg in the starring role. In 1987 poet Rita Dove won the Pulitzer Prize for poetry. In 1993 she became America's poet laureate, and in the same year Toni Morrison became the first African American to win the Nobel Prize for Literature. President Bill Clinton invited Maya Angelou to read one of her poems during his first inauguration.

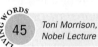

LIVING WORDS
45 *Toni Morrison, Nobel Lecture*

Critics were not the only ones to take an interest in these works. In 1992 novels by three African-American women—Morrison, Walker, and Terry McMillan—made the *New York Times* best-seller list at the same time. In 2001 the works of four African Americans made the *Times* best-seller list and revealed the expanding readership and growing appreciation of black literature across the racial spectrum.

In the first decade of the twenty-first century, African-American performers earned recognition for their work on stage and in film that previous generations would have deemed unthinkable. In 2005, Oprah Winfrey spearheaded a new Broadway production of *The Color Purple*, and more than one million people saw the play in New York before it closed and reopened in Chicago in 2007. Also in 2007, Forrest Whitaker won the Academy Award for best actor for his depiction of Uganda's dictator Idi Amin in *The Last King of Scotland*, and Jennifer Hudson won the academy award for best supporting actress in *Dreamgirls*, which was loosely based on the rise of the Motown singing group the Supremes. Two years earlier Jamie Foxx had won an Oscar for best actor for his role in *Ray*, a film about the singer Ray Charles, and Morgan Freeman won best supporting actor for his role in *Million Dollar Baby*.

THE HIP-HOP NATION

Rap was the most commercially successful genre of black music to emerge in the late twentieth century. It became emblematic of the post–civil rights and black power movement generations of African Americans, known collectively as the hip-hop nation. There are many varieties of rap music. At its least complex, rap is a form of rhythmic speaking in rhyme, hip hop refers

Winner of two Pulitzer Prizes, August Wilson was one of the most successful American playwrights at the end of the twentieth century.

Toni Morrison accepting Nobel Prize. One of the most acclaimed writers in the history of U.S. literature, Toni Morrison's (b. 1931 Lorrain, Ohio, as Chloe Ardelia Woffard) novels are, as a Nobel Prize press release put it, "characterized by visionary force and poetic import, [that] gives life to an essential aspect of American reality." Princeton University literary scholar Valerie Smith described Morrison's work as "always steeped in the realities of the political, social, economic, and historical constraints of African American culture." In 1996 Morrison received the National Book Foundation Medal for Distinguished Contribution to American Letters.

to the backup music for rap that is often composed of excerpts or "samples" from other songs.

ORIGINS OF A NEW MUSIC: A GENERATION DEFINES ITSELF

The rap musical style arose in 1973 in New York City's South Bronx. Its original purpose was to promote musical and dance competitions among the area's inner-city youths who had few outlets for their creative energies. Rap pioneer Kool Herc (aka Clive Campbell) began using simple raps to cover a mix of beats played from two turntables. At the same time, Afrika Bambaataa developed a political version of rap by merging the ideology of the Nation of Islam with the Black Panthers' cultural nationalism. Bambaataa's Zulu Nation promoted competition in break dancing, rapping, and graffiti art and helped spread rap among poor black and Latino neighborhoods.

The first commercial rap hit, "Rapper's Delight" by the Sugar Hill Gang, came out in 1979 and popularized the term **hip-hop**. This was followed by the rise to stardom of Grandmaster Flash and the Furious Five, which grew out of 1970s funk but added rap vocals and the technique of *scratching*—moving a record back and forth under a needle to produce a rhythmic, jarring sound, and manipulating turntable speeds. Much of this music was made primarily for entertainment in the club scene, but some rappers, following the early lead of the spoken-word artists and poets, Amiri Baraka, Gil Scott-Heron, and The Last Poets, offered a political critique of American society wrapped in taunting humor.

LIVING WORDS
44 *Zum Zum (Street and Gangland Rhythms)*

For African-American youths, whom the world had seemingly left behind and ignored, hip-hop became the most important cultural event of their lives. It was a creative medium in which a dispossessed generation could discuss the things that mattered most to them, especially their lives in cities burdened by racial poverty and all which that entailed. In the Reagan years (1981–1989), few middle-class Americans cared to acknowledge the millions left behind in urban decay. Conditions in inner cities worsened during this period, when crack flooded neighborhoods and gang warfare erupted over drug turfs. The "keeping it real" lyrics of hip-hop artists helped forge a sense of community and common destiny among members of a trapped generation. As James McBride wrote in 2007 in *National Geographic*, hip-hop "is a music dipped in the boiling cauldron of race and class."

RAP MUSIC GOES MAINSTREAM

Ironically, white indifference allowed the first hip-hop entrepreneurs to take control of the production, dissemination, and profits connected with this new musical genre. Russell Simmons saw the potential of rap street music in the mid-1970s and recognized that the mainstream entertainment industry was not aware of it. He became a concert promoter, encouraging early rap groups to stay close to the dress styles and language of the inner-city African-American community. In 1984 he and a partner formed Def Jam Records. Their bands, such as RunDMC and Public Enemy, became enormously popular, and many of their albums sold millions of copies. Simmons expanded his business to include marketing hip-hop clothing under the label Phat Pharm and promoting poetry and comedy acts. In 2000 he sold his share of Def Jam for over $100 million. Like Simmons, P. Diddy (aka Sean "Puff Daddy" Combs) found success by working within the mainstream recording industry. Raised in a suburban neighborhood, P. Diddy dropped out of Howard University in 1990 to work for Uptown Records, where his knowledge of the rap scene and instinct for hits fueled a rapid rise to vice president. In 1993 he formed his own company, Bad Boy Records, which was an immediate success.

Commercial success brought new groups to the fore, and the genre changed and grew tremendously during the 1980s and 1990s. Rap bands such as RunDMC, which dominated the charts in the mid-1980s, brought the sound to MTV and to a larger public, which soon came to include white suburban teens. Hip-hop culture quickly spread beyond New York to other African-American urban centers, and each developed a distinctive, and often more graphic, variant of the original. With the music came changes in clothing style, such as baggy, loose-fitting jeans, that trend-hungry fashion designers quickly adopted.

White suburban youths had always been the wealthiest consumers of hip-hop music and its cultural artifacts. By 2000, hip-hop had become a global cultural force and the source of astonishing profits for men such as Russell Simmons and Sean "P. Diddy" Combs—and for white-owned business and music companies. Not surprisingly, the recurrence of the age-old tension between black creativity and white profits fueled new debate. As cultural studies analyst Gregg Tate put it, "Our music, our fashion, our hairstyles, our dances, our anatomical traits, our bodies, our souls continue to be considered ever ripe for the picking and the biting by the same crafty devils who brought you the African slave trade and the Middle Passage."

PROFILE ~ BOB AND ZIGGY MARLEY AND BLACK INTERNATIONALISM

During the 1970s and 1980s, many African Americans relished the music of Bob Marley of Jamaica (1945–1981), embraced his Rastafarian beliefs, and grew dreadlocks like those he wore. Today, Marley enjoys virtually the same heroic stature in the black Diaspora as Martin Luther King Jr. and Nelson Mandela. All three men dedicated their lives to the cause of racial and social justice. King's murder in 1968 occurred when he was most engaged in the struggle to forge workers, the poor, and African Americans into a coalition against racism, poverty, and war. In the decade and a half after King's death, Marley shaped reggae music to liberate the minds of his people from neo-colonial oppression. Across the Atlantic, Nelson Mandela survived twenty-six years in prison before ending racial apartheid in South Africa. Marley and Mandela attracted international audiences and followers at a time when issues affecting black Americans aroused little outside interest. Moreover, Marley's music also deepens our understanding of the birth of hip-hop or rap music that emerged from the inner-city neighborhoods of New York in the 1980s. Hip-hop's subsequent spread around the world signaled the internationalization of African America and helped to unite the black Diaspora.

Marley was a son of the urban ghetto of Trench Town in Kingston, Jamaica's capital city. As a young man he became a Rastafarian, the Jamaican cultural and religious movement that held the black Emperor Haile Selassie of Ethiopia (r. 1930–1974) to be divine and sought to win converts through reason and dialogue. By 1968 Marley was fully engaged in writing and performing music that merged culture, religion, and politics in a way that invited dance but also challenged and excited its listeners' intellect. Especially noteworthy were Marley's three concept albums: *Survival, Uprising,* and *Confrontation,* which brought together the themes that framed his life and work—

celebrating black survival, challenging mental slavery, and constructing new visions for the future through defiance and hope. According to scholar Anthony Bogues, "one not only dances to Marley, but one has to LISTEN to Marley since he is both singing and engaging in social criticism." The lyrics, combined with Marley's conversational style and use of poetry, chants, biblical imagery, and hypnotic offbeat reach across boundaries of class, race, gender, and region.

In "Trench Town" on the *Confrontation* album, Marley sang:

Up a cane river to wash my dread
Upon a rock I rest my head
There I vision through the sea of oppression
Don't make my life a prison
We come from Trench Town...
Can we free our people with music
Lord we free the people with music
We free the people with music, sweet music.

After Marley's untimely death in 1981, his musical mission was taken up to the next step by his son Ziggy. Born in 1968, David Marley, nicknamed "Ziggy" by his father, grew up in Jamaica and the United States. He began playing music at an early age and formed the band Melody Makers with his three siblings shortly after his father's death. Ziggy Marley carried on the reggae tradition but incorporated other sounds from the African Disaspora, including blues rock and hip-hop. In doing so he continues his father's tradition of international engagement and politically informed music.

Source: Anthony Bogues, *Black Heretics, Black Prophets: Radical Political Intellectuals* (New York: Routledge, 2003).

Marley

GANGSTA RAP

The southern California group NWA (Niggas with Attitude) was one of the most successful of the new rap bands coming out in the late 1980s. Their 1988 release of the album *Straight Out of Compton* heralded the rise of **gangsta rap.** Its song "Gansta, Gansta" shocked many observers with its sexist and violent lyrics. Particularly troubling, however, is the persistent objectification of women in hard-core rap music and related films. The widespread use of the terms *bitch* and *ho* by rappers to describe black women reflects broader gender divisions within the black community. Indeed, rap's portrayal of black women as objects and commodities to be used by men—as something less than human—bears an all-too-close resemblance to racist characterizations of black women from the era of slavery.

The emerging voluminous scholarship of hip-hop black studies scholars demonstrates a willingness to tackle the hard questions about gender relations. Many works explore the relationship between hip hop and commercial rap music, suggesting that commercial rap is to hip-hop what orange drink is to orange juice—a watered-down imitation of the real thing. Of particular interest to hip-hop scholars such as T. Denean Sharpley-Whiting and Mark Anthony Neal is the depiction in hip-hop lyrics of black women and of the relationship between men and women and gays and lesbians within the larger society and especially in the hip-hop nation. Sharpley-Whiting asks pointedly,

In 2006, fully clothed Rap artist Lil' Kim performed at the VH1 Hip-Hop Honors in New York City.

"How have hip-hop's lyrics and visual rifts on the acrimonious and sexually charged nature of male-female relationships encouraged the sexual abuse of young black women?" This issue gained national attention in 2007 when white radio talk show host Don Imus referred to the black players on the Rutgers University women's basketball team as a bunch of "nappy-headed hos." His comments inflamed the black community and led Jesse Jackson and Al Sharpton to mobilize a protest that resulted in Imus being fired. Some of his defenders argued that he had merely repeated often heard refrains in rap music. Others insisted that both his derogatory comments and the use of the same words in rap lyrics arose from negative images of black women that were deeply rooted in American culture and needed to be condemned whenever they were used.

It is important to underscore the fact that the rap genre includes many bands that explicitly reject hard-core obscenity and violence. Artists like Queen Latifah, for example, avoid denigrating other African Americans even as they put forward a message of empowerment for black women and men. Other black female hip-hop artists were also in the game. Many, such as Lil' Kim, made sexuality their signature in ways that left little to the imagination.

Even more noteworthy is the extent to which hip-hop has migrated beyond the United States and is now such a global cultural force that commentators talk about a "Hip-Hop Planet." It has influenced music worldwide, particularly across the African Diaspora. France, for example, has a thriving rap music scene. Most of its artists are of Arab, African, or Spanish descent whose music focuses on ethnic and racial discrimination and social criticism. Africa, the Caribbean, and Latin America have also developed rap that builds on indigenous African music. The ability of rap to combine with other musical forms to create compelling hybrids and the global penetration of American popular culture ensures that hip hop will continue to thrive and evolve. In the words of *National Geographic*'s James McBride, "Hip-hop remains . . . a cry of 'I am' from the youth of the world."

AFRICAN-AMERICAN INTELLECTUALS

The struggles of the civil rights and black power movements forced predominantly white academic and cultural institutions to open their doors to African Americans. With a beachhead established, a number of black scholars gained a level of prominence unknown in earlier eras as public intellectuals. These individuals go beyond their roles as academics to participate in public debate on major issues. In the past most public intellectuals were white males. Some African Americans, like the formidable W. E. B. Du Bois and novelists Richard Wright, James Baldwin, and Ralph Ellison, were exceptions, but the voices of most black intellectuals were seldom heard in the mainstream before the 1960s. In the past four decades, however, many of the most prominent public intellectuals to emerge have been African American. Among them are Cornel West, Henry Louis Gates Jr., Molefi Kete Asante, Shelby Steele, William Julius Wilson, Michele Wallace, Ishmael Reed, Stanley Crouch, Charles Johnson, Vonnie McLoyd, John Edgar Wideman, Manning Marable, Adolph Reed, Thomas Sowell, Robin D. G Kelley, Michael Eric Dyson, Nell Irvin Painter, bell hooks, and Anthony Appiah. Their views range across the ideological gamut from Marxist to extreme conservative, but they all strive to define black identity in the United States and to explore the role of race in its social, economic, and political life. Their emergence and the acclaim accorded to them mark the end of America's long refusal to acknowledge the intellectual accomplishments of African Americans.

Many African-American scholars are connected to the black studies programs founded in the late 1960s and early 1970s. Initially marginalized and few in number, these programs now exist in nearly every major university and college. They have become institutionalized—even prized—by institutions that once resisted them. Doctoral degrees are now offered at Northwestern University, Temple University, the University of Massachusetts at Amherst, Harvard, Yale, Michigan State University, and the University of California at Berkeley. Cornell offers a master's degree in the field.

As befits a vibrant intellectual movement, there are several main approaches to understanding the path of African Americans through U.S. history and in contemporary society. Four broad approaches predominate: Afrocentrist, what might be loosely termed "integrationist" or "inclusionist," and, gaining prominence more recently, approaches emphasizing class, gender, and international comparisons and diaspora studies.

AFROCENTRICITY

In the 1980s and 1990s, a philosophy of culture referred to as **Afrocentricity** captured widespread media and academic attention. The philosophy and practice of Afrocentricity had been a prominent feature in the political movement that created black studies, but the

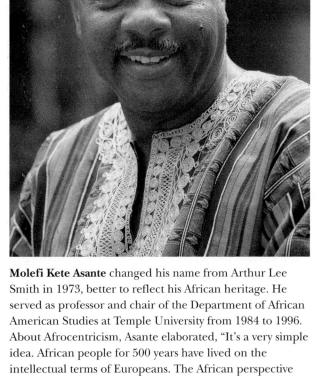

Molefi Kete Asante changed his name from Arthur Lee Smith in 1973, better to reflect his African heritage. He served as professor and chair of the Department of African American Studies at Temple University from 1984 to 1996. About Afrocentricism, Asante elaborated, "It's a very simple idea. African people for 500 years have lived on the intellectual terms of Europeans. The African perspective has finally come to dinner."

emergence of Temple University professor Molefi Kete Asante gave it a presence and a personality. In the 1980s Asante published three books—*Afrocentricity; Kemet: Afrocentricity and Knowledge,* and *The Afrocentric Idea*—in which he argued that an African-centered perspective was needed to reorient African Americans from the Eurocentric periphery to a centered place in their own history. In its most extreme form, Afrocentrists argue that much of European civilization arose out of African origins, particularly the culture of ancient Egypt. They also point to evidence of advanced cultures in other parts of the continent to refute assertions of African cultural inferiority.

Many black educators enthusiastically embraced Afrocentricity as a way to celebrate and reclaim a positive African identity and to unite the peoples of the

African Diaspora. Afrocentrists rejected the idea of America as a melting pot. Assimilation, they argued, meant a rejection of their African cultural heritage. At the heart of this position is an indictment of American ideas and institutions for their complicity in the long oppression of black people.

Afrocentrists have vigorously defended their perspective. Asante explained to his critics, "Afrocentricity is a terribly maligned concept. Afrocentricity is the idea that African people and interests must be viewed as actors and agents in human history, rather than as marginal to the European historical experience—which has been institutionalized as universal." Black historians and social scientists, Afrocentrists argue, have to place Africa and its descendants at the center of their studies to increase appreciation of the contributions of black people in world history.

Many black scholars, however, insist that Afrocentricity is regressive and fosters self-segregation. Writer Earl Ofari Hutchinson, for example, concedes that Asante's ideas merit attention, but he is skeptical about the claims of some Afrocentrist academics. "In their zeal to counter the heavy handed 'Eurocentric imbalance of history,' some have crossed the line between historic fact and fantasy. They've constructed groundless theories in which Europeans are 'Ice People,' 'suffer genetic defects,' or are obsessed with 'color phobias.' They've replaced the shallow European 'great man' theory of history with a feel-good interpretation of history." White and black critics alike caution that the Afrocentrist desire to fabricate "a glorious past" for black people did a disservice to the truth and fostered a narrow notion of race ill suited as a platform for pursuing the study of Africans in America.

AFRICAN-AMERICAN STUDIES MATURES

While the African-American studies department at Temple is the center of the Afrocentric approach and remains one of the largest black studies programs in the nation, many other programs adopt a more ideologically flexible approach. Under the leadership of literary scholar Henry Louis Gates Jr., Harvard University now has the premier program in the integrationist tradition. Gates took charge of the department and the W. E. B. Du Bois Institute in 1991 and has since attracted some of the leading lights of African-American studies from universities around the nation. His goals for the department focus less on recovering a usable past and more on the rigorous multidisciplinary study of the black experience. Gates defines his project in this way: "We're eager to demonstrate that Afro-American studies is an academic department. It is not a place for ethnic cheerleading; it is not a place for a 12-step recovery program to restore your sense of identity. It is a place where one studies an academic discipline in a fashion as rigorous as the study of mathematics or physics, English or history." Apart from intellectual rigor, what binds the department together is a belief that race is a malleable category of identity to be analyzed critically and that effective scholarship in the area is not fundamentally limited by the racial identity of the scholar.

As with American intellectual life as a whole, African-American studies has been influenced by the emergence of scholarship that questions prevailing gender assumptions. Just as the black studies movement challenged racial ideology, women's studies have forced a reconsideration of deeply held gender beliefs and raised historical and social science questions that went unasked in an earlier era. African-American scholars in *womanism* studies, a term popularized by Alice Walker to describe the intellectual projects of women of color, have paid particular attention to the intersections of gender with racial and class hierarchies in shaping the lives of black women. They started journals such as *SAGE* and organizations such as the Association of Black Women Historians, founded by Rosalyn Terborg-Penn and Eleanor Smith. Gradually, their scholarly, literary, historical, and polemical works found readers in the general public and a place in women's studies curricula. As more black women enrolled in college, courses with titles like "Black Women Writers" and "Black Women's History" became part of black studies curricula. The field of black women's history has grown rapidly: scholarly monographs, reference works, anthologies, conferences, and exhibitions have all been devoted to the contribution black women have made to the political struggles and artistic accomplishments of African Americans. Sociologists, literary critics, and historians have explored the role of race, class, and gender in the oppression of marginalized people in American society. In 2007, *The Black Women Family and Gender Journal*, edited by Jennifer Hamer, made its appearance as an official organ of the National Council of Black Studies.

Perhaps most important, scholars have begun to flesh out the larger picture of the black Diaspora. Building on the important work of Philip Curtin, Colin Palmer, Michael Gomez, Thomas C. Holt, and others who have studied the development of the Atlantic slave-labor economy, scholars have begun serious comparisons of the centuries-old African-descended communities throughout the New World and those of more recent African immigrants to Europe. This project is enriching our understanding of African-American history by placing it in the context of a larger global story.

Black Religion at the Dawn of the Millennium

Religion remains at the heart of the African-American experience. Black churches, claiming over 25 million members, remain by far the largest black-controlled institutions in the nation. Houses of worship ranging in size from small storefront operations with a few dozen congregants to massive "mega churches" with many thousands of members are the sinew that binds together nearly every African-American community. The major denominations remain those with ties going back to the nineteenth century. Among the largest are the African American National Baptist Convention of America, Inc., Progressive National Baptist Convention, Inc., African Methodist Episcopal Church, National Missionary Baptist Convention of America, Churches of Christ, and the African Methodist Episcopal Zion Church. Due to immigration from the Caribbean and Africa, African Americans are becoming a larger part of some predominantly white denominations. For example, black worshippers make up more than 9 percent of the American Catholic Church and over 10 percent of the Episcopal Church. Many African-American Catholics and Episcopalians attend predominantly black churches, so there is still truth in Martin Luther King's observation that "11:00 a.m. Sunday morning is the most segregated hour in America," but progress has been made.

African-American men and women have had great success in occupying leadership positions within a variety of predominantly white denominations since the 1960s. Harold R. Perry was consecrated a bishop in the American Roman Catholic Church in 1966, and Bishop Wilton Gregory became the first African American to head the American Catholic bishops in 2002. Recognizing the importance of Africans and African Americans to the future of the church, in 1993 Pope John Paul II apologized for the Catholic Church's support of slavery. African-American John M. Burgess was installed as the first black bishop to head an Episcopal diocese in America in Massachusetts in 1970, followed by John T. Walker in Washington, D.C., in 1977. African Americans made similar gains in other denominations as churches worked to rid themselves of racist practices.

Despite this continuity with the past and the successes of black religious leaders, African-American religious life has changed in the last several decades. Most African Americans remain Protestants, but demographic and social changes within the community have challenged the mainline denominations. One difficulty is the move of middle-class parishioners out of the close-knit urban communities that once supported churches

with people from many different walks of life. Greater levels of education and different life experiences combine with geographical distance to create large suburban mega churches with a distinct character and worship practice. Often Pentecostal, these churches espouse a theology that emphasizes the individual's relationship to God. Their ministers speak to the tensions and anxiety of people with stressful lives and careers or with specific problems such as substance abuse or difficulty with relationships. They also provide community institutions with tremendous services for their parishioners.

Perhaps the best-known minister of this new African-American religious tradition is Bishop T. D. Jakes. Starting in 1980 with a ten-member storefront church in Charleston, West Virginia, he built Potter's House, an enormous ministry with a 28,000-member interracial congregation and 5,000-seat church in Dallas, Texas. In the 1990s Jakes began writing bestselling books such as *Woman, Thou Art Loosed*, which focused on using religion to heal the psychological wounds of modern society. His message is distributed through national seminars, television broadcasts, and the Internet.

BLACK CHRISTIANS ON THE FRONT LINE

Faced with the problems of the black community in the United States and with a changing population, African-American Christians in both traditional and nontraditional religious institutions have developed outreach programs to create supportive communities for the embattled and vulnerable. Some of the new mega churches are located in or near the black inner-city communities and retain a commitment to local action. The Salem Baptist Church in Chicago is a good example. It has over 17,000 members, many of whom are organized to patrol neighborhoods to discourage prostitutes and drug dealers. Reverend James T. Meeks led a political campaign for an antiliquor referendum as a response to the ravages of alcoholism in the community. Similar ministries, often with radio and television broadcasts of services, exist in many other predominantly black communities.

Reverend Eugene Rivers has developed a different approach from that of the mega churches. Along with like-minded former students at Harvard University, he founded the small Azusa Christian Community in a crime-plagued neighborhood in Boston. An evangelical Christian, Rivers believes "the church is the last best hope that black people have," and so he turned a former crack house into a Christian settlement named Ella J. Baker House. Its primary goal, Rivers says, is to keep children from killing one another. He and fellow black clergy formed the 10-Point Coalition and entered into a partnership with the police. The collaboration helped eliminate juvenile murders for two-and-a-half years. Rivers advocates a pragmatic black nationalism aimed at developing a rich, viable black civil society centered on the church.

TENSIONS IN THE BLACK CHURCH

Tensions have arisen within many black churches over their socially conservative message, patriarchal structure, staid ritual, and lack of social engagement. Gender and sexuality are two key areas in which this has been expressed. The black church has long been in accord with other conservative Christian churches in advocating the subordination of women to men. Although most black churchgoers are women, men overwhelmingly dominate visible church leadership. Although a few voices, both male and female, have always challenged patriarchal assumptions in the churches, only in recent decades has the chorus grown too loud to ignore. As theologian, sociologist, and ordained Baptist minister Cheryl Townsend Gilkes puts it, "[t]he cultural maxim 'If it wasn't for the women, you wouldn't have a church,' rises up against male attempts to exclude, ignore, trivialize, or marginalize women in a number of capacities." Some African-American women, particularly of the younger generations, have left the church because of this marginalization. Others, like Gilkes, have stayed to challenge sexism in individual churches and the denominations.

The African Methodist Episcopal (AME) Church has been at the forefront of this movement for reform. Although it has ordained women since 1898, the number of women ministers has only recently grown significant. Now three thousand of its eight thousand ministers are female, and in 2000 it elected Reverend Vashti M. McKenzie bishop of its Southern African district. She took the post after a successful ten-year stint as pastor of Baltimore, Maryland's Payne Memorial Church, whose membership she increased from 300 to 1,700. Upon her election, Bishop McKenzie announced, "The stained glass ceiling has been pierced and broken!" She also connected her achievement to the past efforts of other women. "I stand here tonight, she told the AME convention, "on the shoulders of the unordained, women who serve without affirmation or appointment. I don't stand here alone, but there is a cloud of witnesses who sacrificed, died and gave their best." The achievements of women in the churches have not come without conflict, and this promises to be at the center of black religious life in the twenty-first century.

Black churches also face conflicts over sexuality. Their theology has traditionally limited legitimate sexual activity to monogamous, heterosexual marriages. Baptist minister and University of Pennsylvania professor Michael Eric Dyson lists a number of the challenges for black Christians regarding sexuality: "[t]he guilt and shame that result from unresolved conflicts about the virtues of black sexuality. . . . The role of eroticism in a healthy black Christian sexuality. The revulsion to and exploitation of homosexuals. The rise of AIDS in black communities. The sexual and physical abuse of black women and children by black male church members. The resistance to myths of super black sexuality." Of all of these challenges, those surrounding the HIV/AIDS crisis are most pressing but also the most difficult to address, given the church's traditional refusal to do more than denounce, or remain silent about, nontraditional sexualities.

With the support of the Delta Sigma sorority, family, and the Baltimore, Maryland, church community, Vashti Murphy McKenzie broke through "the stained-glass ceiling" (her words) to become the first woman to be appointed a bishop in the history of the AME Church. She is a graduate of the University of Maryland and earned a master of divinity from Harvard University's Divinity School and a doctorate in ministry at the United Theological Seminary in Dayton, Ohio.

BLACK MUSLIMS

Although still a relatively small phenomenon in African America, Islam has been gaining a significant number of converts. The Nation of Islam is the best known of the many groups comprising African-American Muslims, but in fact its 20,000 to 40,000 members make up only a small percentage of the estimated 1.5 million black American Muslims. After the death of founder Elijah Muhammad in 1975, the Nation of Islam was led by his son Wraith Deen Muhammad, who rejected the racialist aspects of his father's theology for more orthodox, mainstream Sunni Muslim beliefs. He eventually left the organization to found the Muslim American Society, the largest group of African-American Muslims, with perhaps 500,000 members. Many black Muslims have rejected Christianity for what they perceive as its Eurocentric bias and for its former tolerance of slavery, although Islam also had a long history of slave trading in Africa. The clarity and discipline of the Muslim faith and the solidarity they feel with Muslims around the world also attract converts, estimated at about 18,000 per year in the United States.

With growing immigration from Islamic countries, African Americans have become more closely connected to the larger trends of the religion. This is evident in the rise of more orthodox Islam among American blacks. Tensions have arisen between African-American and immigrant Muslims, who make up three-quarters of all American Muslims.

The aftermath of the attacks on the World Trade Center and the Pentagon on September 11, 2001, has left many African-American Muslims conflicted. On the one hand, most deplore the attacks and the ideology that led to them. Imam Abdul Malik Mohammed, for example, declared, "[w]hile the Muslim World has had the Koran and they have recited the Koran and the Koran has dwelled in their hearts . . . I contend that, in view of circumstances that we have witnessed for many years, Mohammed the Prophet is not known to them." He believes that African-American Muslims can lead the way back to a true Islam. On the other hand, many African Americans are troubled by what they perceive to be an indiscriminate anti-Muslim feeling in the United States and are concerned the nation's war on terror might become a holy war against Islam.

Louis Farrakhan and the Nation of Islam

Beginning in the 1980s, the Nation of Islam's minister Louis Farrakhan became a potent source of racial division in the United States. Farrakhan was the younger of

Louis Farrakhan and the Nation of Islam. Always controversial, Farrakhan achieved the greatest feat in the history of black mass mobilization. The actual numbers of black men who heeded his call on October 16, 1995, to attend the Million Man March may forever be in dispute. The figures range from 400,000 to 1.2 million.

two sons of immigrant parents from the West Indies. As a young man, Farrakhan attended a black teachers' college in Winston-Salem, North Carolina, but he dropped out to become a Calypso singer known as the Charmer. In 1955, while performing in Chicago, he heard Elijah Muhammad preach at the Nation of Islam's mosque. This marked a turning point in his life. Farrakhan joined the Nation and quickly ascended within its hierarchy in the wake of Malcolm X's rupture with Elijah Muhammad and subsequent murder in February 1965. Farrakhan became minister of the Harlem Mosque No. 7 and Muhammad's national representative. Farrakhan opposed Wraith Muhammad's move to a more orthodox Islam and was able to take leadership of the Nation of Islam by 1978. In 1982 he purchased a building to publish the Nation of Islam's newspaper, *The Final Call,* and in 1985 he bought and moved into Elijah Muhammad's mansion in Chicago. Under Farrakhan's direction, the Nation developed a number of economic enterprises, including media ventures, restaurants, clothing stores, and companies to provide security for apartment buildings, distribute soap and cosmetics, and manufacture pharmaceuticals. Farrakhan recruited among poor and marginalized urban African Americans and within the black prison population. The national move to the right during the Reagan era complemented the reconstituted Nation's conservative social ideas, which harked back to those advanced by Booker T. Washington at the turn of the century. Like

Elijah Muhammad, Farrakhan downplayed the struggle for political rights. In 1985 he declared:

> God wants us to build a new world order: A new world order based on peace, justice and equality. Where do we start? . . . Physical separation is greatly feared [by whites], and it is not now desired by the masses of black people, but America is not willing to give us eight or ten states, or even one state. Let's be reasonable. . . . If we cannot go back to Africa, and America will not give us a separate territory . . . we should use the blessings that we have received from our sojourn in America to do for ourselves what we have been asking the whites in this nation to do for us.

Until 1984 most white Americans were barely aware of Farrakhan's existence. In that year, however, he broke the Nation of Islam's long-standing tradition of abstaining from politics to support Jesse Jackson's bid for the Democratic presidential nomination and soon ignited a firestorm of controversy. When some Jews took offense at Jackson's off-the-record reference to New York as "Hymietown" during a conversation with two African-American reporters, Farrakhan, whose Fruit of Islam provided security for Jackson's campaign, rose to his defense and made matters worse. On the February 24, 1984, *CBS Evening News*, Farrakhan warned, "I say to the Jewish people, who may not like our brother. It is not Jesse Jackson you are attacking. . . . When you attack him, you are attacking the millions who are lining up with him. You're attacking all of us. . . . Why dislike us? Why attack our champion? Why hurl stones at him? It's our champion. If you harm this brother, what do you think we should do about it?"

In 1984, as in the past, Farrakhan's verbal assaults against Jews, whom he called a principal enemy of African Americans, attracted support from ultra-right-wing anti-Semitic forces and condemnation from Jewish Americans and the Anti-Defamation League. Dredging up anti-Semitic shibboleths reminiscent of Hitler's Germany, Farrakhan blamed Jews for many of the ills plaguing African Americans. Jewish Americans, many of whom had been among the principal allies of African Americans during the civil rights movement, called on African-American organizations and leaders to repudiate Farrakhan and his rhetoric of "Jewish domination and control."

MILLENNIUM MARCHES

In recent years Farrakhan has attempted to move beyond his extremist ideas and reach out to a broader group of African Americans. To this end he called for a Million Man March in Washington, D.C. Farrakhan framed this march as a "Holy Day of Atonement and Reconciliation," meant "to reconcile our spiritual inner beings and to redirect our focus to developing our communities, strengthening our families, working to uphold and protect our civil and human rights, and empowering ourselves through the Spirit of God, more effective use of our dollars, and through the power of the vote."

The estimated 400,000-strong crowd at the October 16, 1995, march made it a symbolic success and generated positive coverage even in the mainstream media. It inspired many black men to become more engaged with their communities and to speak out more forcefully against oppression. On this occasion, the Nation's conservative philosophy of religion, self-respect, family values, community responsibility, and bootstrap capitalism found a responsive audience. Many marchers reported that even though they did not support the Nation of Islam's program, they drew hope from the peaceful solidarity of the gathering.

Yet the goodwill dissipated when, three months after the march, Farrakhan embarked on a World Friendship Tour to Africa and the Middle East. To the consternation of many, he met with the leader of the brutally repressive military regime in Nigeria, General Sani Abacha. At home, Farrakhan's intemperate rhetoric continued to attract attention. In the wake of the Million Man March, however, he failed to forge a coherent strategy to resolve African America's continuing social problems.

Several black intellectuals have expressed their objections to Farrakhan's conservative ideas, none more effectively than political scientist Adolph Reed. According to Reed, Farrakhan "weds a radical oppositional style to a program that proposed private and individual responses to social problems; he endorses moral repressiveness; he asserts racial essentialism; he affirms male authority; and he lauds bootstrap capitalism. . . . His focus on self-help and moral revitalization is profoundly reactionary and meshes perfectly with the victim-blaming orthodoxy of the Reagan/Bush era."

The Million Man March inspired women to organize their own march. Initiated by two Philadelphia women—Phile Chionesu, a small-business owner, and Asia Coney, a public housing activist—on October 25, 1997, an estimated 300,000 black women gathered in Philadelphia to listen to speeches by California congresswoman and president of the Congressional Black Caucus Maxine Waters, rapper Sister Souljah, and South African activist Winnie Mandela. The march was a celebration, a call to unity, and a forum for black women to speak out against domestic violence as well as inadequate access to quality health care and educational opportunities. The march did not garner nearly as much media attention as the Million Man March, perhaps because the organizers were relatively unknown. The March nonetheless symbolized the ongoing struggle of black women to be seen and heard in American society and to counter negative stereotypes and derogatory images of black womanhood. Like the Million Man March, there was little in the way of specific policy demands, but the women marchers did gain a feeling of solidarity. As Detroit real estate agent Gloria Graves put it, "I thought that it was very important that we as black women come together in prayer and unity and the belief that we can bring back the family unit that has been lost. I wanted to meet other strong black women who had the same agenda and be united. It has been just great."

Complicating Black Identity in the Twenty-First Century

The 2000 U.S. census counted 281,421,906 Americans, a 13.2 percent increase from 1990. African-American numbers stood at 34.7 million, or about 12 percent of the total. For the first time in U.S. history, African Americans were no longer the largest minority group: the 35.3 million Americans who identified themselves as Hispanic slightly outnumbered them.

As in the past, most black Americans, 54 percent, live in the South, with about 19 percent in the Midwest, 18 percent in the Northeast, and 10 percent in the West. New York City had the largest black population of any urban area at 2.3 million, followed by Chicago at 1.1 million. Detroit, Philadelphia, and Houston were all in the 500,000 to 1 million range. Looking beyond these raw numbers, however, reveals important information about the evolving nature of African-American identity in an increasingly multiethnic nation.

One of the most important changes in the census was the ability of respondents to choose more than one racial designation for themselves. Since the first census, such classifications have been shaped by the politics of race. Before the Civil War an accurate count of slaves was important because they counted for three-fifths of a person in determining the representation of states. Throughout the nineteenth century, intense fears about miscegenation led census takers to make determinations about the racial character of individuals as black, white, or mixed race. With the rise of segregation in the late nineteenth and early twentieth centuries, the one-drop rule—the belief that any black ancestry, no matter how slight, made a person black—was hard-

ened, and "mulatto" classifications were dropped from the census takers' list of questions. During the early civil rights movement, some groups, such as the ACLU, attempted to remove racial classifications altogether from the census data, reasoning that the only purpose of such distinctions was to disadvantage black people.

The civil rights laws of the 1960s changed the purpose of gathering data by racial classification. It was now necessary to have reliable statistics on racial characteristics of people to combat discrimination. With the rise of affirmative action programs, an individual's identity as an African American could actually be a benefit. The black power movement led many to embrace their identity as African Americans and reject the assimilation implied by abandoning racial categories.

In 1977 the Office of Management and Budget addressed the U.S government's need for standard racial categories with its Statistical Policy Directive 15. This set up the familiar racial classifications: white, black, Asian and Pacific Islander, and Native American. "Hispanic" was chosen to denote an ethnicity and could be selected in addition to one of the four racial categories. Because there is no scientific backing for any biological racial distinctions, these categories are bureaucratic approximations of socially relevant distinctions designed to serve administrative needs. They were not necessarily meant to reflect the complex identities of many individuals included in them. For example, "Asian and Pacific Islander" encompasses individuals from nations with vastly different histories and cultures. The white category includes people descended from Arabs and Turks as well as Europeans. In terms of ethnicity, people now called Hispanic had formerly thought of themselves in terms of national identities, such as Mexican American, Cuban American, and so on, and overlapped with the "black" category for Dominicans and other African-descended people from the former Spanish colonial regions. Over the quarter century after their adoption, these categories became incorporated into identities and social understandings and, in important ways, influenced business and government programs.

Two groups sought to change the categories. The first group saw an end to racial categories as the true legacy of the civil rights movement. These advocates point to the rhetoric of Martin Luther King Jr. and the plain language of the Civil Rights Act of 1964, which forbade any discrimination on the basis of race, as evidence of the need to eliminate racial classifications by the government. Some adherents to this view want to do away with the notion of race altogether. Their goal is a colorblind society that they believe will not be achieved until an individual's race ceases to have a positive or negative impact on access to education, government programs, or employment. Others who advocate this position, however, are ideologically driven conservatives who want to limit the power of the federal government to redress inequality. They have bankrolled state referendums and court cases to end racial classifications and see this as a way to roll back the gains of the civil rights era.

Those who are biracial form a second group opposed to the old classification scheme. Racial mixing is nothing new in America. Under slavery many black women were compelled to bear children to their white masters. There have also been consensual sexual relationships and marriages between African Americans and other ethnic and racial groups. The number of such unions and their social acceptance as legitimate relationships have grown precipitously, however, since the civil rights movement destroyed many of the old racial barriers and the U.S. Supreme Court cast down the last **antimiscegenation** laws in *Loving v. Virginia* in 1967. Although still a small percentage of the total, there are now more than 1.5 million mixed-race marriages in the United States and an increasing number of children growing up in these households. The proportion of mixed-race marriages is much higher among younger generations and seems likely to increase rapidly in the future.

The debate over biracial and multiracial identities rages in the African-American community. One of the most significant concerns is that to make fundamental changes in the classification system will undermine the projects they were designed to advance. As poverty researcher John A. Powell put it, "Without racial statistics, we will not know how distributions of resources affect racial and ethnic groups. Without them, racism, which is still very much a part of our society, will be that much more difficult to eradicate, and that much more likely to remain a societal norm." The programs that use these statistics include the Equal Employment Opportunity Act, the Civil Rights Act of 1964, the Voting Rights Act of 1965, the Public Health Act, the Job Partnership Training Act, the Equal Credit Opportunity Act, the Fair Housing Act, and many others. Some argue that offering mixed-race people the option of not being black might undermine the racial solidarity that has been the basis for black advances. As historian Ibrahim K. Sundiata puts it, "[t]he disaggregation of Blacks would drive a wedge into the community that would only increase the isolation of its most disadvantaged members."

Although only 1.8 million Americans opted for the biracial designation in the 2000 census, its existence does bring into question the nature of racial identity itself. Clearly racism exists, and black Americans experienced centuries of discrimination that distinguishes them from other groups. At the same time, many who would have been considered black under the American system of racial classification no longer think of themselves in the same way and may be increasingly able to assert a multiple identity. The larger pattern of recent immigration that the United States is undergoing undermines what had once been a largely biracial dynamic.

IMMIGRATION AND AFRICAN AMERICANS

Because of immigration restrictions and the general oppression of people of African descent in America, few blacks, either from the Western Hemisphere or Africa, immigrated to the United States before the last few decades. Changes in immigration laws, particularly the landmark 1965 Hart-Cellar Act, which abandoned the racially exclusive restrictions of the past, helped open the door. Military, economic, health, and environmental crises that have roiled Africa and the Caribbean in these years have pushed substantial numbers from these regions through the door. These new African Americans often

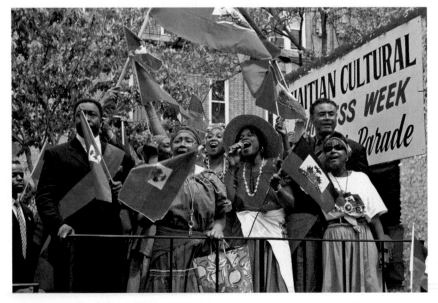

In 2003 the New York Haitian American community celebrated the 200th anniversary of the Haitian Revolution. This Haitian Flag waving group of celebrants congregate on the Eastern Parkway in Brooklyn.

do not fit their identity neatly into the traditional African-American category.

Black people from the West Indies have a long history of immigration to the United States, but their numbers have increased dramatically since the 1960s. During the entire decade of the 1950s, only 123,000 Caribbean people immigrated, but during the 1990s nearly one million did so. The Caribbean islands were one of the main areas of importation for African slaves. The islands' sugar production served as the economic engine of the Spanish, French, Dutch, and British New World empires well into the nineteenth century. These empires all abandoned slavery by the late 1800s, and the retreat of colonialism from the Caribbean in the twentieth century has left a number of micro-nations largely populated by people of African descent whose cultures have remained more influenced by Africa than was true of the United States. Hence African cultural practices were fused with those of the British in Jamaica, the French in Haiti, and the Spanish in Santo Domingo and Cuba. Although a racial hierarchy is not unknown in these societies, racial identity is less important than class and merit-based achievement. Upon immigration, mostly to New York, Florida, and other parts of the East Coast, immigrants from the Caribbean soon learn the importance of race in the United States, but they have also carved out a separate identity from other African Americans. First-generation West Indians tend to have more economic success than native African Americans, in part because employers often favor them. The second generation has often had a more difficult time as the effects of racial discrimination and poor schools take their toll.

Voluntary immigrants from Africa once were few, and before 1980 they were mainly European colonials or from North African nations such as Egypt. In the 1950s only 14,000 Africans came over, but during the 1990s over 350,000 arrived. Most of these new immigrants are men, and they tend to be among the most highly educated of all immigrants. Part of their reason for coming to the United States was the destabilization of many African nations and the persecution of autocratic regimes.

BLACK FEMINISM

The feminist and gay rights movements have challenged traditional ideas of racial identity in recent decades. Both arose as part of the broader "rights revolution" that began with the civil rights movement, but each highlights a different aspect of an individual's identity—gender or sexuality—in addition to race.

A new wave of feminism emerged on the American political landscape in the 1960s and 1970s and transformed gender relations. This movement arose, in part, out of the successes of the African-American civil rights struggle. The 1964 Civil Rights Act outlawed sexual as well as racial discrimination in employment. Although this had not been a goal of the civil rights movement at that time, and its inclusion was meant in part to lessen the law's chance of passage, it helped open discussions of gender oppression that had laid dormant for decades. Many white women activists in the SNCC and other civil rights groups assumed leading roles in the emerging feminist movement, often using the same strategies and tactics that had worked in the fight against racism.

Second-wave feminism achieved many important changes as it gathered adherents in the 1960s and 1970s. The National Organization for Women (NOW), founded in 1966, spearheaded efforts to end job discrimination against women, to expand access to safe and effective birth control, to legalize abortion, and to secure federal and state support for child care. One of the movement's most important early successes was Title IX of the Educational Amendments Act of 1972, which required colleges and universities to ensure equal access for women. Another was the Supreme Court's decision in *Roe v. Wade*, legalizing abortion. Beyond these legislative and judicial victories, the feminist movement has opened up choices for women in nearly every aspect of their lives that traditional gender roles had precluded. It has also engendered a backlash as conservative men and women organized to fight against passage of the Equal Rights Amendment to the Constitution, access to abortion, sex education in schools, and a variety of related issues. This fight has driven much of the political conflict in the United States since the 1970s.

Black women were involved from the start in shaping modern feminism. The core of black feminist thinking is a dual critique of the women's and black liberation movements' core ideology. Black women scholars and writers argued that a critique of patriarchy was incomplete without attention to race and class. Whereas white leaders of the women's movement were silent on race, many male leaders in the African-American freedom movement were all too forthright about their views on gender. As Black Panther leader Elaine Brown put it, "A woman in the Black Power movement was considered at best irrelevant. A woman asserting herself was a pariah." Many believed racial oppression was the primary evil to be fought and that feminism was either a distraction or,

E. LYNN HARRIS

E. Lynn Harris was born in Flint, Michigan, and grew up in Little Rock, Arkansas. He is a best-selling writer whose novels have explored what it is like to be gay and black in America. His first novel, Invisible Life, *was published in 1991. In the following account about his own childhood, Harris is eight years old when he learns a painful lesson about perceptions of sexual difference.*

Easter Sunday, 1964, finally arrived. After my bath, I raced into the tiny room I shared with my two younger sisters and saw the coat laid out on my twin bed. It was red, black, and green plaid with gold buttons. Daddy and I had picked the coat out together at Dundee's Men's Store. I quickly put on my new clothes, and I could see my sisters, Anita and Zettoria, who were five and three, slip on new dresses over their freshly pressed hair. Anita had on a blue taffeta dress, and Shane (our nickname for Zettoria, since her name was so hard to pronounce) had on an identical one in pink. Their dresses were pretty but didn't compare to my coat. After Anita and Shane had accepted their compliments from Daddy, he called me in for inspection. "Where is my little man? Come out here and let Daddy see that new coat," he said. I quickly buttoned up each of the three gold buttons and dashed to the living room for Daddy's endorsement of my outfit. "Look, Daddy. Look at me," I said with excitement as I twirled around like my sisters had a moment before. Suddenly Daddy's bright smile turned into a disgusted frown. What was wrong? Didn't he like my new coat? Had Easter been canceled? "Come here. Stop that damn twirling around," Daddy yelled. I stopped and moved toward Daddy. He was seated on the armless aqua vinyl sofa. Before I reached him, he grabbed me and shouted. "Look at you. You. . . . little sissy with this coat all buttoned up like a little girl. Don't you know better? Men don't button up their coats all the way." Before I could respond or clearly realize what I had done wrong, I saw Daddy's powerful hands moving toward me. His grip was so quick and powerful that I felt the back of my prized coat come apart. A panic filled my tiny body when I saw his hand clutching the fabric. I began to cry as my sisters looked on in horror. I could hear Mama's high heels clicking swiftly as she raced to the living room from the kitchen. "If you don't stop that damn crying, I'm going to make you wear one of your sister's dresses to church." I caught myself and stopped crying. Daddy meant what he said. I would be the laughing stock of the entire neighborhood. . . . I could see all

by encouraging women to be strong and self-reliant, actually undermined the efforts of black men to overcome the emasculating effects of white male power. Black feminists such as Frances Beale countered that racism and sexism had oppressed black women. "It is true," she wrote in 1970, "that our husbands, fathers, brothers and sons have been emasculated, lynched, and brutalized. They have suffered from the cruelest assault on mankind that the world has ever known. However, it is a gross distortion of fact that black women have oppressed black men."

Responding to sexism in the black power movement, many black women writers and activists sought to make the struggle against it as important as that against racism. Between 1973 and 1975, the National Black Feminist Organization (NFBO) articulated many of the concerns specific to black women, from anger with black men for dating and marrying white women; to internal conflict over skin color, hair texture, and facial features; to sexual violence and harassment against black women; to differences in the economic mobility of white and black women. Black feminists also attacked the myth of black matriarchy and stereotypical portrayals of black women in popular culture. Although the organization was short lived, it did break the silence imposed on black women by black liberation movements. Black feminists also helped others talk openly about domestic violence, rape, and sexual harassment in employment. Their political message is best summed up by UCLA law professor Kimberlé Crenshaw: "When feminism does not explicitly oppose racism, and when antiracism does

my friends pointing and laughing at me. I don't remember what I wore that Easter Sunday or many Easters that followed. All I recall is that I wasn't wearing a dress, and I remember what my daddy had said to me. I didn't know what a sissy was and why Daddy despised them so. All I knew was that I was determined never to be one.

🌿 *What does this episode reveal about Harris's father's concept of masculinity and manhood?*

🌿 *Why is this particular Easter Sunday so important to Harris's self-development and sexual identity?*

🌿 *How are Harris's sisters treated differently from him?*

E. Lynn Harris, *What Becomes of the Brokenhearted?* (New York: Doubleday, 2003).

not incorporate opposition to patriarchy, race and gender politics often end up being antagonistic to each other and both interests lose."

GAY AND LESBIAN AFRICAN AMERICANS

The success of the civil rights movement encouraged gays and lesbians to fight openly against the discrimination they had faced for centuries. Their movement was small and quiet until 1969, when gay men at the Stonewall Inn in New York's Greenwich Village violently resisted a police raid. The multiracial crowd's refusal at this bar to go on submitting to the kind of police harassment that homosexuals had long been subjected to in the United States sparked an explosion of activism. By the end of the 1970s, many states and cities had decriminalized homosexual behavior and lifted employment policies that discriminated on the basis of sexuality. Although tensions arose between the lesbian and gay wings of the movement, they worked together to pursue the full range of civil rights enjoyed by heterosexuals despite a persistent and powerful opposition from conservative groups.

Gay, bisexual, lesbian, and transgender African Americans have struggled against their marginality within the larger gay rights movement and homophobia in their own communities. Like the women's movement, the early gay and lesbian rights movement tended to be predominantly white and middle class. Although not explicitly racist, it tended to see racial issues as secondary to or separate from the goal of ending discrimination based on sexual preference.

Despite hostility toward the gay and lesbian rights movement by some African Americans, many black leaders, such as Jesse Jackson, Eleanor Holmes Norton, and John Lewis, and civil rights organizations, such as the NAACP, have embraced its agenda. They do so in part because they accept the analogy between the struggle against repression based on sexual preference and that based on race. The debate between black feminists and gay rights activists, who argue that gender and class identities must be taken into account in political and scholarly analysis, and nationalists, who focus on black identity as primary, continues to rage and will influence our understanding of African-American life in the twenty-first century. As Coretta Scott King put it in a 2002 speech to the National Gay and Lesbian Task Force, "I believe very strongly that all forms of bigotry and discrimination are equally wrong and should be opposed by right-thinking Americans everywhere. Freedom from discrimination based on sexual orientation is surely a fundamental human right in any great

Coretta King at the National Gay/Lesbian Task Force in 2002. Coretta Scott King lived the life of a committed, deeply engaged social reform activist. From 1968 to 1995 she headed the Atlanta-based Martin Luther King Jr. Center for Nonviolent Social Change. She uses her voice to shape opinion and raise awareness about the injustices that black people, women and children, the poor and homeless, and gays and lesbians confront in their daily lives.

democracy, as much as freedom from racial, religious, gender, or ethnic discrimination."

CONCLUSION

The closing of the twentieth century saw remarkable progress for African Americans even as part of the community remained mired in poverty and suffering. African Americans still experience the burden of racism that was so familiar to W. E. B. Du Bois, which prompts collective political action and the maintenance of predominantly black churches, colleges, and social action groups. The black soul that he thought had so much to give America now flows freely through its art, language, and popular culture, especially in hip-hop. At the same time, increasing diversity in the ways that African Americans live their lives has led to differences in how individuals understand their identities. Some, like Anthony Appiah, long for the possibility of asserting those identities in ways not limited by race. The tension between racial, class, gender, sexual, and other identities will shape the African-American odyssey as it moves through the twenty-first century.

AFRICAN-AMERICAN EVENTS	NATIONAL EVENTS
1960	
	1964 Civil Rights Act outlaws sexual discrimination in employment
	1966 National Organization for Women founded
	1969 Stonewall riot in New York
1970	
1973 National Black Feminist Organization founded	
1978 Louis Farrakhan becomes head of Nation of Islam	
1980	
1982 Alice Walker and Charles Fuller win Pulitzer Prizes in fiction and drama	**1980** Ronald Reagan is elected president
1984 Russell Simmons forms Def Jam Records	**1981** Recession settles in; Economic Recovery Tax Act is passed
1987 August Wilson wins Pulitzer Prize for drama	**1984** President Reagan is reelected
1988 "Straight Out of Compton" marks rise of gangsta rap	**1988** George Bush is elected president of the United States

RECOMMENDED READING

Patricia Hill Collins. *Black Feminist Thought: Knowledge, Consciousness, and the Politics of Empowerment.* Boston: Unwin Hyman, 1990. A classic text on black feminist theory and practice by one of black studies' foremost sociologists.

Kent B. Germany. *New Orleans after The Promise: Poverty, Citizenship, and the Search for the Great Society.* Athens: The University of Georgia Press, 2007. A well-researched, thoughtful historical study of the successes and failures of the Great Society programs of the 1960s and 1970s that prefigured the Hurricane Katrina disaster in New Orleans in 2005.

Robin D. G. Kelley. *Yo' Mama Is DysFunkshional!* Boston: Beacon Press, 1998. Insightful essays about America's culture wars and an excellent critique of scholarship about black working-class culture by one of this generation's finest historians.

Ismael Reed. *Airing Dirty Laundry.* Reading, MA: Addison-Wesley, 1993. Provocative, iconoclastic, and entertaining essays by an insightful cultural critic.

Tavis Smiley. *The Covenant with Black America.* Chicago: Third World Press, 2006. An invaluable source on the status of African Americans at the dawn of the twenty-first century and of suggestions for individual and community empowerment programs and strategies.

ADDITIONAL BIBLIOGRAPHY

BLACK CULTURE STUDIES

Anthony Bogues. *Black Heretics, Black Prophets: Radical Political Intellectuals.* New York: Doubleday, 2003.

Brian Cross. *It's Not about a Salary . . . Rap, Race and Resistance in Los Angeles.* London: Verso, 1993.

Michael Eric Dyson. *Between God and Gangsta Rap: Bearing Witness to Black Culture.* New York: Oxford University Press, 1996.

Patricia Liggins Hill, gen. ed. *Call and Response: The Riverside Anthology of the African American Literary Tradition.* New York: Houghton Mifflin, 1969.

Bell Hooks. *Outlaw Culture: Resisting Representations.* New York: Routledge, 1994.

Robin D. G. Kelley. *Race Rebels: Culture, Politics, and the Black Working Class.* New York: Free Press, 1994.

J.L. King. *On the Down Low: A Journey into the Land of "Straight" Black Men Who Sleep with Men.* New York: Broadway Books, 2004.

Terry McMillan. *Five for Five: The Films of Spike Lee.* New York: Stewart, Tabori & Chang, 1991.

Joan Morgan. *When Chickenheads Come Home to Roost: My Life as a Hip-Hop Feminist.* New York: Simon & Schuster, 1999.

Mark Anthony Neal. *New Black Man*. New York: Routledge, 2006.

Kevin Powell. *Who's Gonna Take the Weight? Manhood, Race, and Power in America*. New York: Three Rivers Press, 2003.

Riché Richardson. *From Uncle Tom to Gangsta: Black Masculinity and the U.S. South*. Athens: University of Georgia Press, 2007.

Tricia Rose. *Black Noise: Rap Music and Black Culture in Contemporary America*. Hanover, NH: Wesleyan University Press, 1994.

T. Denean Sharpley-Whiting. *Pimps Up, Ho's Down: Hip Hop's Hold on Young Black Women*. New York: New York University Press, 2007.

Greg Tate. *Flyboy in the Buttermilk*. New York: Fire-Side, 1992.

Deborah Willis. *Reflections in Black: A History of Black Photographers, 1840 to the Present*. New York: Norton, 2000.

IDENTITY STUDIES

K. Anthony Appiah and Amy Guttman. *Color Conscious: The Political Morality of Race*. Princeton: Princeton University Press, 1996.

Molefi Kete Asante. *The Afrocentric Idea*. Philadelphia: Temple University Press, 1987.

Martin Bernal. *Black Athena: The Afroasiatic Roots of Classical Civilization: The Fabrication of Ancient Greece, 1785–1985*. New Brunswick, NJ: Rutgers University Press, 1987.

Jonathan Betsch Cole and Beverly Guy Sheftall. *Gender Talk: The Struggle for Women's Equality in African-American Communities*. New York: Ballantine Books, 2003.

F. James Davis. *Who Is Black? One Nation's Definition*. University Park: Pennsylvania State University Press, 1991.

Charles Harmon, ed. *Double Exposure: Poverty and Race in America*. Armonk, NY: M. E. Sharpe, 1997.

Tsehloane Keto. *Vision, Identity and Time: The Afrocentric Paradigm and the Study of the Past*. Dubuque, IA: Kendall/Hunt, 1995.

Wilson Jeremiah Moses. *Afrotopia: The Roots of African American Popular History*. Cambridge, MA: Cambridge University Press, 1998.

Arthur M. Schlesinger Jr. *The Disuniting of America*. New York: Norton, 1992.

Clarence Walker. *You Can't Go Home Again*. New York: Oxford University Press, 2001.

Cornel West. *Race Matters*. Boston: Beacon Press, 1993.

RACE, GENDER, AND CLASS

Paul M. Barrett. *The Good Black: A True Story of Race in America*. New York: Dutton, 1999.

Lois Benjamin. *The Black Elite: Facing the Color Line in the Twilight of the Twentieth Century*. Chicago: Nelson-Hall, 1991.

1990

AFRICAN-AMERICAN EVENTS

1990
Anna Deveare Smith and August Wilson win Pulitzer Prizes for poetry and drama

1993
Toni Morrison becomes the first black woman to win Nobel Prize for literature

1995
Million Man March

1997
Million Woman March

NATIONAL EVENTS

1990
1.4 million Caribbean and African immigrants move to the United States

1991
Operation Desert Storm against Iraq is initiated and ended

1992
William Jefferson Clinton is elected president of the United States

1994
Midterm elections give Republican Party control of Congress

1996
Clinton is reelected; Clinton signs welfare reform legislation

1998
Clinton is impeached by the House of Representatives

1999
The U.S. Senate acquits Clinton

2000

2000
Vashti M. McKenzie elected first woman AME bishop
African-American college enrollment tops 1.5 million

2001
AIDS becomes a leading cause of death among young African-American men

2002
Wilton Gregory heads U.S. Catholic bishops

2004
Carol Mosely Braun and Al Sharpton run for president
Barack Obama elected to U.S. Senate
Condoleezza Rice appointed secretary of state

2007
Barack Obama runs for president

2000
Hispanics become the largest minority group in the United States

George W. Bush is elected president of United States
Bush names Condoleezza Rice national security advisor and Colin Powell secretary of state

September 11, 2001
Terrorists demolish the World Trade Center and attack the Pentagon

2004
George W. Bush reelected president of the United States

2005
Hurricane Katrina devastates New Orleans

AFRICAN-AMERICAN EVENTS   **NATIONAL EVENTS**

Micheal Eric Dyson. *Has the Black Middle Class Lost Its Mind?* New York: Basic Books, 2005.

Douglas G. Glasgow. *The Black Underclass: Poverty, Unemployment, and Entrapment of Ghetto Youth.* New York: Random House, 1981.

Christopher Jencks. *Rethinking Social Policy: Race, Poverty, and the Underclass.* Cambridge, MA: Harvard University Press, 1992.

Jonathan Kozel. *Savage Inequalities: Children in America's Schools.* New York: Crown, 1991.

Haki R. Madhubuti. *Black Men—Obsolete, Single, Dangerous? Afrikan American Families in Transition: Essays in Discovery, Solution, and Hope.* Chicago: Third World Press, 1990.

Leith Mullings. *On Our Own Terms: Race, Class, and Gender in the Lives of African American Women.* New York: Routledge, 1997.

Steven Shulman, ed. *The Impact of Immigration on African Americans.* New Brunswick, NJ: Transaction Publishers, 2004.

AUTOBIOGRAPHY AND BIOGRAPHY

Amy Alexander, ed. *The Farrakhan Factor: African-American Writers on Leadership, Nationhood and Minister Louis Farrakhan.* New York: Grove Press, 1998.

E. Lynn Harris. *What Becomes of the Broken Hearted?* New York: Doubleday, 2003.

Randall Robinson. *Defending the Spirit: A Black Life in America.* New York: NAL/Dutton, 1998.

Wellington Webb. *The man, the mayor, and the making of modern Denver: An autobiography with Cindy Brovsky.* Golden, Colorado: Fulcrum Publishing, 2007

RETRACING THE ODYSSEY

Harpo Studios, Chicago, Illinois. Harpo Studios is a state-of-the-art film production facility created by Oprah Winfrey. It is also the first multimedia complex owned and operated by an African-American woman.

Rock and Roll Hall of Fame and Museum, Cleveland, Ohio. Among the museum's permanent collection of the five hundred songs that most influenced the development of rock and roll are ones by early blues singers: Otis Redding, Chuck Berry, James Brown, Ray Cook, Ray Charles, Marvin Gaye, and Aretha Franklin.

myhistorylab REVIEW, RESEARCH, AND INTERACT

REVIEW QUESTIONS

1. What social, economic, and material gains did African Americans make after the civil rights era? Why did some black Americans do better than others during this period?

2. Why do white Americans tend to live longer than black Americans? How has the black community dealt with the problems of HIV/AIDS?

3. Who were some of the most important African-American writers, performers, and social critics in the late twentieth century? What is hip-hop, and what is meant by the term the "Hip-Hop Planet"? What is the relationship between rap music and hip-hop?

4. What are the goals of the Afrocentricity movement? Why do many black intellectuals oppose Afrocentricity?

5. Why has the church remained so important to African Americans? How are women's roles changing in the black church? Why has Louis Farrakhan been so controversial?

6. Were the Millenium Marches a success? What did the marches accomplish for those men and women who marched?

7. How has immigration from the Caribbean and Africa affected black America? What factors gave rise to black feminism? What problems do black gays and lesbians face in the black community? How are tensions surrounding class stratification manifested within the black community?

www.researchnavigator.com

Using the tools available in Research Navigator, consider this question:

Who are some of the leading black intellectuals in the American public today?

PRIMARY SOURCE DOCUMENTS

23–6 Elaine Bell Kaplan, "Talking to Teen Mothers"

DATA EXPLORATION

Conditions Contributing to Poverty

The high rate of poverty in the black community disproportionately affects children.

INTERACTIVE ACTIVITY

Growing Inequality

Over the last twenty-five years, the gap between the rich and poor has substantially widened.

SIGNS OF PROTEST IN THE STRUGGLE FOR EQUALITY

The heart of the story of the modern civil rights movement is the remarkable courage and tenacity people in their own communties showed in their determination to attack segregation and exclusion. Ordinary citizens initiated protests, formulated strategies and tactics, and garnered essential resources that made collective action work. The people's actions were made effective through their families, churches, voluntary associations, political organizations, women's clubs, labor unions, and college organizations and facilities. The sacrifices and experience gained in the previous one hundred years of struggle had, by the mid-1950s, accumulated sufficiently to permit an all-out attack on all areas of inequality.

◄ **A. Philip Randolph leads protesters** outside the headquarters of the 1948 Democratic National Convention demanding an end to Jim Crow and desegregation in the U.S. military in Philadelphia, Pennsylvaniz on July 12, 1948.

Demonstrators with the New York Garment Workers Union picket in Times Square with signs demanding a boycott and protesting segregation in the south in April, 1963. ►

Olympic gold and bronze medallists Tommie Smith and John Carlos raise clenched fists while standing on the victory platform in protest for civil rights during the 1968 Olympic Games in Mexico City.

Congress for Racial ► **Equality (CORE)** picketer walks down the main street of Bogalusa, Louisiana, 1965.

The **Silent Parade** of the NAACP protesting the East St. Louis riot and lynching in St. Louis, Missouri, 1917.

Civil rights protesters march in line beside National Guard troops with bayonets in Memphis, Tennessee, 1968.

A young protester marches for jobs near the Lincoln Memorial in Washington, D.C. in August, 1968.

LBJ's GREAT SOCIETY

President Lyndon Johnson launched his Great Society program in 1964 with the intention of raising the standard of living of the lowest portion of American society and at the same time removing the stains of racial bigotry and prejudice that had haunted the nation since before its inception. Modeling his programs after Roosevelt's New Deal, he instituted agencies like Head Start to educate the children of the urban poor and the Job Corps to provide superior training in vocational skills to high school dropouts. The Model Cities program sought to rebuild urban ghettos into livable neighborhoods and viable business districts. The War on Poverty attacked not just the poverty of the ghetto, but rural poverty in the Appalachian Mountains and the backwoods of the South as well.

After almost a hundred years, Congress, under the prodding of Johnson, finally guaranteed the rights of blacks to vote in any state of the Union, but especially in the South where poll taxes, literacy tests, and terror had been used to deny black Americans their constitutional privilege to participate in government as full citizens since Reconstruction.

Examine the mixed record of the Great Society and determine the extent to which it served the aspirations of African American communities. How successful was the Great Society for the political, social, and economic betterment of African Americans?

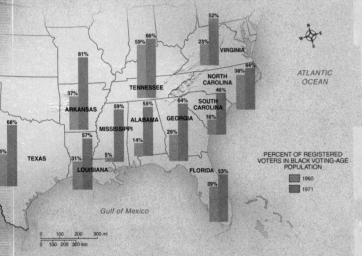

PERCENT OF REGISTERED VOTERS IN BLACK VOTING-AGE POPULATION
- 1960
- 1971

In almost every state of the former Confederacy the participation of blacks in local voting doubled. In the states of the deep South—Louisiana, Mississippi, Alabama, and Georgia—that figure was much larger. By any measure the political side of the Great Society was highly successful.

▶ Voting Rights Act of 1965

AN ACT To enforce the fifteenth amendment to the Constitution of the United States, and for other purposes. Be it enacted by the Senate and House of Representatives of the United States of America in Congress assembled, That this Act shall be known as the "Voting Rights Act of 1965." . . .

SEC. 2. No voting qualification or prerequisite to voting, or standard, practice, or procedure shall be imposed or applied by any State or political subdivision to deny or abridge the right of any citizen of the United States to vote on account of race or color.

▶ Lyndon B. Johnson, Great Society Speech, University of Michigan, Ann Arbor, May 22, 1964

(In). . . your time we have the opportunity to move not only toward the rich society and the powerful society, but upward to the Great Society. The Great Society rests on abundance and liberty for all. It demands an end to poverty and racial injustice, to which we are totally committed in our time. But that is just the beginning. The Great Society is a place where every child can find knowledge to enrich his mind and to enlarge his talents. It is a place where leisure is a welcome chance to build and reflect, not a feared cause of boredom and restlessness. It is a place where the city of man serves not only the needs of the body and the demands of commerce but the desire for beauty and the hunger for community. It is a place where man can renew contact with nature. It is a place which honors creation for its own sake and for what it adds to the understanding of the race. It is a place where men are more concerned with the quality of their goals than the quantity of their goods. But most of all, the Great Society is not a safe harbor, a resting place, a final objective, a finished work. It is a challenge constantly renewed, beckoning us toward a destiny where the meaning of our lives matches the marvelous products of our labor.

▶ Trial of the Chicago Seven, 1969–1970

Transcript of speech by Bobby Seale, Chairman of the Black Panther Party, during the "Days of Rage," Lincoln Park, Chicago, Aug. 27, 1968, introduced in evidence at the Chicago Seven Trial.

So it's very important that we understand the need for organization, cause that's what we deal with. We're not here to be sitting around a jive table vacillating and jiving ourselves. Too many times in the past, the people… get to arguing about whether or not this white racist wall that black people are chained against is real or not…. You're damned right it's real. Because we're chained against this wall.

And we say this here: don't be out there jiving, wondering whether the wall is real or not. . . . Pick up a piece. Pick up a gun. (If). . . you shoot well, all I'm gonna do is pat you on the back and say "Keep shooting."

Now, there are many kinds of guns. Many, many kinds of guns. But the strongest weapon that we have, the strongest weapon that we all each individually have, is all of us. United in opposition. United with revolutionary principles.

So it's very necessary for us to understand the need for functional organization. It's very necessary for us, especially black brothers—listen close—that we have revolutionary principles to guide ourselves by. Because if we just go out in a jive gang, running around in big groups, with rocks and bottles, we're not going to do nothing against 500 pigs with shotguns and .357 Magnums.

What we got to do is functionally put ourselves in organizations. Get every black man in the black community with a shotgun in his home, and a .357 Magnum, and a .45 if he can get it, and an M-1 if he can get it and anything else if he can get it, brothers. Get it and start doing this.

Then, I want to say this here. On the streets, stop running in large groups. That ain't no right tactic. We should run in groups of fours and fives–all around. We cannot continue using these tactics where we lose 3000 arrested or we lose 1 or 200 dead. We gotta stop. So we want to start running in threes, fours, and fives.

Small groups using proper revolutionary tactics. So we can dissemble those pigs who occupy our community, who occupy our community like foreign troops. Black people, we're saying we're lost. We seem to be lost in a world of white racist, decadent America. I'm saying that we have a right to defend ourselves as human beings. And if some pig comes up to us unjustly treating us unjustly, then we have to bring our pieces out and start barbecuing some of that pork.

▶ "Our Nation Is Moving Toward Two Societies, One Black, One White— Separate and Unequal;" Excerpts from the Kerner Report, 1968

Last summer over 150 cities reported disorders in Negro—and in some instances, Puerto Rican— neighborhoods. These ranged from minor disturbances to major outbursts involving sustained and widespread looting and destruction of property. . . .

(In). . . teeming racial ghettos, segregation and poverty have intersected to destroy opportunity and hope and to enforce failure. The ghettos too often mean men and women without jobs, families without men, and schools where children are processed instead of educated, until they return to the street—to crime, to narcotics, to dependency on welfare, and to bitterness and resentment against society in general and white society in particular.

(M)ost whites and many Negroes outside the ghetto have prospered to a degree unparalleled in the history of civilization. Through television—the

LABOR FORCE PARTICIPATION BY RACE AND GENDER, 1960–1975 (PERCENTAGE IN LABOR FORCE)

| Year | African American | | | White | | |
	Total	Male	Female	Total	Male	Female
1960	63.0	80.1	47.2	58.8	82.6	36.0
1965	62.1	77.4	48.1	58.5	80.4	37.7
1970	61.1	74.7	48.9	60.2	79.7	42.0
1975	58.8	70.1	48.7	61.1	78.1	45.4

Source: Bureau of Census, 1977

Statistics include individuals in military service; statistics based on individuals 16 years and older.

universal appliance in the ghetto—and the other media of mass communications, this affluence has been endlessly flaunted before the eyes of the Negro poor and the jobless ghetto youth. . . . Outside the ghetto, many have succeeded in achieving a decent standard of life and in developing the inner resources which give life meaning and direction. Within the ghetto, however, it is rare that either aspiration is achieved.

(Many). . . Negroes have come to believe that they are being exploited politically and economically by the white "power structure." (The). . . result is alienation and hostility toward the institutions of law and government and the white society which controls them. This is reflected in the reach toward racial consciousness and solidarity reflected in the slogan "Black Power.". . . The nation is rapidly moving toward two increasingly separate Americas. Within two decades, this division could be so deep that it would be almost impossible to unite. . . .

Epilogue

A Nation within a Nation

❧

Since the first Africans were brought to these shores in the seventeenth century, black people have been a constant and distinct presence in America. During the prolonged course of the Atlantic slave trade, approximately 600,000 Africans were sold into servitude in what became the United States. By the outbreak of the Civil War in 1861 there were nearly four million African Americans in this country. Today black people number over 30 million and make up slightly over 10 percent of the nation's population.

Initially regarded merely as an enslaved labor force to produce cash crops and not as a people who would or could enjoy an equal role in the political and social affairs of American society, African Americans constituted a separate ethnic, racial, and cultural group. For more than two centuries they remained outcasts.

People of African descent developed decidedly ambivalent relationships with the white majority in America. Never fully accepted and never fully rejected, black people relied on their own resources as they created their own institutions and communities. In 1852 Martin Delany declared, "We are a nation within a nation." A half century later W. E. B. Du Bois observed that the black man wanted to retain his African identity and to be an American as well. "He would not Africanize America, for America has too much to teach the world and Africa. He would not bleach his Negro soul in a flood of white Americanism, for he knows that Negro blood has a message for the world. He simply wishes to make it possible for a man to be both a Negro and an American, without being cursed and spit upon by his fellows, without having the doors of Opportunity closed roughly in his face."

Sometimes in desperation or disgust, some black people have been willing to abandon America or reject assimilation. The slaves who engaged in South Carolina's 1739 Stono rebellion attempted to reach Spanish Florida. As early as 1773, slaves in Massachusetts pledged to go to Africa after emancipation. From the 1790s to the start of the Civil War, visions of nationhood in Africa attracted a minority of African Americans. During the 1920s, Marcus Garvey and the Universal Negro Improvement Association glorified Africa while seeking black autonomy in the United States. By the 1950s, Elijah Muhammad, Malcolm X, and the Nation of Islam attracted black people by emphasizing a separate black destiny.

Yet in spite of the horrors of slavery, the indignity and cruelty of Jim Crow, and the unrelenting violence and discrimination inflicted on people of color, most African Americans have not rejected America but worked and struggled to participate fully in the American way of life. African slaves accepted elements of Christianity, and their descendants found solace in their spiritual beliefs. Black Americans have embraced American principles of brotherhood, justice, fairness, and equality before the law that are embedded in the Declaration of Independence and the Constitution. Again and again, African Americans have insisted that America be America, that the American majority live up to its professed ideals and values.

The nation within a nation has never been homogeneous. There have been persistent class, gender, and color divisions. There have been tensions and ideological conflicts among black leaders and organizations as they sought strategies to overcome racial inequities and white supremacy. Some leaders, such as Booker T. Washington, have emphasized self-reliance and economic advancement, while others, including W. E. B. Du Bois and leaders of the NAACP, have advocated full inclusion in the nation's political, economic, and social fabric.

Furthermore, African Americans have been far more than victims, than an exploited labor force, than the subjects of segregation and stereotypes. They have contributed enormously to the development and character of American society and culture. As slaves, they provided billions of hours of unrequited labor to the American economy. Black people established churches, schools, and colleges that continue to thrive. Black people demonstrated a willingness to fight and die for a country that did not fully accept or appreciate their sacrifices. African Americans have made remarkable and innovative contributions to art, music, folklore, science, politics, and athletics that have shaped and enriched American society.

America is no longer what it was in 1700, 1800, or 1900. Chattel slavery ended in 1865. White supremacy is no longer fashionable or openly acceptable. Legal segregation was prohibited a generation ago. The capacity and willingness of Americans of diverse backgrounds and origins to live together in harmony has vastly improved in recent decades. Although we are now in the twenty-first century, the long odyssey of American people of African descent has not ended, nor will it end in the immediate future. The persistence of urban and rural poverty and the disorganized response of public officials to Hurricane Katrina's destruction of New Orleans remind us of that. Black people continue to help mold and define the United States, but they also continue as "a nation within a nation."

Appendix

THE CONSTITUTION OF THE UNITED STATES OF AMERICA
(with clauses pertaining to the status of African Americans highlighted)

We the people of the United States, in order to form a more perfect union, establish justice, insure domestic tranquility, provide for the common defense, promote the general welfare, and secure the blessings of liberty to ourselves and our posterity, do ordain and establish this Constitution for the United States of America.

ARTICLE I

SECTION 1.   All legislative powers herein granted shall be vested in a Congress of the United States, which shall consist of a Senate and House of Representatives.

SECTION 2.   1. The House of Representatives shall be composed of members chosen every second year by the people of the several States, and the electors in each State shall have the qualifications requisite for electors of the most numerous branch of the State legislature.

2. No person shall be a representative who shall not have attained to the age of twenty-five years, and been seven years a citizen of the United States, and who shall not, when elected, be an inhabitant of that State in which he shall be chosen.

3. Representatives and direct taxes[1] shall be apportioned among the several States which may be included within this Union, according to their respective numbers, which shall be determined by adding to the whole number of free persons, including those bound to service for a term of years, and excluding Indians not taxed, three fifths of all other persons.[2] The actual enumeration shall be made within three years after the first meeting of the Congress of the United States, and within every subsequent term of ten years, in such manner as they shall by law direct. The number of representatives shall not exceed one for every thirty thousand, but each State shall have at least one representative; and until such enumeration shall be made, the State of New Hampshire shall be entitled to choose three, Massachusetts eight, Rhode Island and Providence Plantations one, Connecticut five, New York six, New Jersey four, Pennsylvania eight, Delaware one, Maryland six, Virginia ten, North Carolina five, South Carolina five, and Georgia three.

4. When vacancies happen in the representation from any State, the executive authority thereof shall issue writs of election to fill such vacancies.

5. The House of Representatives shall choose their speaker and other officers; and shall have the sole power of impeachment.

SECTION 3.   1. The Senate of the United States shall be composed of two senators from each State, chosen by the legislature thereof,[3] for six years; and each senator shall have one vote.

2. Immediately after they shall be assembled in consequence of the first election, they shall be divided as equally as may be into three classes. The seats of the senators of the first class shall be vacated at the expiration of the second year, of the second class at the expiration of the fourth year, and of the third class at the expiration of the sixth year, so that one third may be chosen every second year; and if vacancies happen by resignation, or otherwise, during the recess of the legislature of any State, the executive thereof may make temporary appointments until the next meeting of the legislature, which shall then fill such vacancies.[4]

3. No person shall be a senator who shall not have attained to the age of thirty years, and been nine years a citizen of the United States, and who shall not, when elected, be an inhabitant of that State for which he shall be chosen.

4. The Vice President of the United States shall be President of the Senate, but shall have no vote, unless they be equally divided.

5. The Senate shall choose their other officers, and also a president pro tempore, in the absence of the Vice President, or when he shall exercise the office of the President of the United States.

---

[1]See the Sixteenth Amendment.
[2]See the Fourteenth Amendment.

[3]See the Seventeenth Amendment.
[4]See the Seventeenth Amendment.

6. The Senate shall have the sole power to try all impeachments. When sitting for that purpose, they shall be on oath or affirmation. When the president of the United States is tried, the chief justice shall preside: and no person shall be convicted without the concurrence of two thirds of the members present.

7. Judgment in cases of impeachment shall not extend further than to removal from office, and disqualification to hold and enjoy any office of honor, trust or profit under the United States: but the party convicted shall nevertheless be liable and subject to indictment, trial, judgment and punishment, according to law.

SECTION 4. 1. The times, places, and manner of holding elections for senators and representatives, shall be prescribed in each State by the legislature thereof; but the Congress may at any time by law make or alter such regulations, except as to the places of choosing senators.

2. The Congress shall assemble at least once in every year, and such meeting shall be on the first Monday in December, unless they shall by law appoint a different day.

SECTION 5. 1. Each House shall be the judge of the elections, returns and qualifications of its own members, and a majority of each shall constitute a quorum to do business; but a smaller number may adjourn from day to day, and may be authorized to compel the attendance of absent members, in such manner, and under such penalties as each House may provide.

2. Each House may determine the rules of its proceedings, punish its members for disorderly behavior, and, with the concurrence of two thirds, expel a member.

3. Each House shall keep a journal of its proceedings, and from time to time publish the same, excepting such parts as may in their judgment require secrecy; and the yeas and nays of the members of either house on any question shall, at the desire of one fifth of those present, be entered on the journal.

4. Neither House, during the session of Congress, shall, without the consent of the other, adjourn for more than three days, nor to any other place than that in which the two Houses shall be sitting.

SECTION 6. 1. The senators and representatives shall receive a compensation for their services, to be ascertained by law, and paid out of the Treasury of the United States. They shall in all cases, except treason, felony, and breach of the peace, be privileged from arrest during their attendance at the session of their respective Houses, and in going to and returning from the same; and for any speech or debate in either House, they shall not be questioned in any other place.

2. No senator or representative shall, during the time for which he was elected, be appointed to any civil office under the authority of the United States, which shall have been created, or the emoluments whereof shall have been increased, during such time; and no person holding any office under the United States shall be a member of either House during his continuance in office.

SECTION 7. 1. All bills for raising revenue shall originate in the House of Representatives; but the Senate may purpose or concur with amendments as on other bills.

2. Every bill which shall have passed the House of Representatives and the Senate, shall, before it become a law, be presented to the President of the United States; if he approves he shall sign it, but if not he shall return it, with his objections, to that House in which it shall have originated, who shall enter the objections at large on their journal, and proceed to reconsider it. If after such reconsideration two thirds of that House shall agree to pass the bill, it shall be sent, together with the objections, to the other House, by which it shall likewise be reconsidered, and if approved by two thirds of that House, it shall become a law. But in all such cases the votes of both Houses shall be determined by yeas and nays, and the names of the persons voting for and against the bill shall be entered on the journal of each House respectively. If any bill shall not be returned by the President within ten days (Sundays excepted) after it shall have been presented to him, the same shall be a law, in like manner as if he had signed it, unless the Congress by their adjournment prevent its return, in which case it shall not be a law.

3. Every order, resolution, or vote to which the concurrence of the Senate and the House of Representatives may be necessary (except on a question of adjournment) shall be presented to the President of the United States; and before the same shall take effect, shall be approved by him, or being disapproved by him, shall be repassed by two thirds of the Senate and House of Representatives, according to the rules and limitations prescribed in the case of a bill.

SECTION 8. The Congress shall have the power

1. To lay and collect taxes, duties, imposts, and excises, to pay the debts and provide for the common defense and general welfare of the United States; but all duties, imposts, and excises shall be uniform throughout the United States.

2. To borrow money on the credit of the United States;

3. To regulate commerce with foreign nations, and among the several States, and with the Indian tribes;

4. To establish a uniform rule of naturalization, and uniform laws on the subject of bankruptcies throughout the United States;

5. To coin money, regulate the value thereof, and of foreign coin, and fix the standard of weights and measures;

6. To provide for the punishment of counterfeiting the securities and current coin of the United States;

7. To establish post offices and post roads;

8. To promote the progress of science and useful arts, by securing for limited times to authors and inventors the exclusive right to their respective writings and discoveries;

9. To constitute tribunals inferior to the Supreme Court;

10. To define and punish piracies and felonies committed on the high seas, and offenses against the law of nations;

11. To declare war, grant letters of marque and reprisal, and make rules concerning captures on land and water;

12. To raise and support armies, but no appropriation of money to that use shall be for a longer term than two years;

13. To provide and maintain a navy;

14. To make rules for the government and regulation of the land and naval forces;

15. To provide for calling forth the militia to execute the laws of the Union, suppress insurrections and repel invasions;

16. To provide for organizing, arming, and disciplining the militia, and for governing such part of them as may be employed in the service of the United States, reserving to the States respectively, the appointment of the officers, and the authority of training the militia according to the discipline prescribed by Congress;

17. To exercise exclusive legislation in all cases whatsoever, over such district (not exceeding ten miles square) as may, by cession of particular States, and the acceptance of Congress, become the seat of the government of the United States, and to exercise like authority over all places purchased by the consent of the legislature of the State in which the same shall be, for the erection of forts, magazines, arsenals, dockyards, and other needful buildings; and

18. To make all laws which shall be necessary and proper for carrying into execution the foregoing powers, and all other powers vested by this Constitution in the government of the United States, or any department or officer thereof.

SECTION 9.   1. The migration or importation of such persons as any of the States now existing shall think proper to admit, shall not be prohibited by the Congress prior to the year one thousand eight hundred and eight, but a tax or duty may be imposed on such importation, not exceeding ten dollars for each person.

2. The privilege of the writ of habeas corpus shall not be suspended, unless when in cases of rebellion or invasion the public safety may require it.

3. No bill of attainder or ex post facto law shall be passed.

4. No capitation, or other direct, tax shall be laid, unless in proportion to the census or enumeration herein-before directed to be taken.[5]

5. No tax or duty shall be laid on articles exported from any State.

6. No preference shall be given by any regulation of commerce or revenue to the ports of one State over those of another: nor shall vessels bound to, or from, one State be obliged to enter, clear, or pay duties in another.

7. No money shall be drawn from the treasury, but in consequence of appropriations made by law; and a regular statement and account of the receipts and expenditures of all public money shall be published from time to time.

8. No title of nobility shall be granted by the United States: and no person holding any office of profit or trust under them, shall, without the consent of the Congress, accept of any present, emolument, office, or title, of any kind whatever, from any king, prince, or foreign State.

SECTION 10.   1. No State shall enter into any treaty, alliance, or confederation; grant letters of marque and reprisal; coin money; emit bills of credit; make any thing but gold and silver coin a tender in payment of debts; pass any bill of attainder, ex post facto law, or law impairing the obligation of contracts, or grant, any title of nobility.

2. No State shall, without the consent of the Congress, lay any imposts or duties on imports or exports, except what may be absolutely necessary for executing its inspection laws: and the net produce of all duties and imposts laid by any State on imports or exports, shall be for the use of the treasury of the United States; and all such laws shall be subject to the revision and control of the Congress.

3. No State shall, without the consent of the Congress, lay any duty of tonnage, keep troops, or

---

[5]See the Sixteenth Amendment.

ships of war in time of peace, enter into any agreement or compact with another State, or with a foreign power, or engage in war, unless actually invaded, or in such imminent danger as will not admit of delay.

ARTICLE II

SECTION 1.   1. The executive power shall be vested in a President of the United States of America. He shall hold his office during the term of four years, and, together with the Vice President, chosen for the same term, be elected, as follows:

2. Each State shall appoint, in such manner as the legislature thereof may direct, a number of electors, equal to the whole number of senators and representatives to which the State may be entitled in the Congress: but no senator or representative, or person holding any office of trust or profit under the United States, shall be appointed an elector.

The electors shall meet in their respective States, and vote by ballot for two persons, of whom one at least shall not be an inhabitant of the same State with themselves. And they shall make a list of all the persons voted for, and of the number of votes for each; which list they shall sign and certify, and transmit sealed to the seat of the government of the United States, directed to the president of the Senate. The president of the Senate shall, in the presence of the Senate and House of Representatives, open all the certificates, and the votes shall then be counted. The person having the greatest number of votes shall be the President, if such number be a majority of the whole number of electors appointed; and if there be more than one who have such majority, and have an equal number of votes, then the House of Representatives shall immediately choose by ballot one of them for President; and if no person have a majority, then from the five highest on the list the said House shall in like manner choose the President. But in choosing the President, the votes shall be taken by States, the representation from each State having one vote; a quorum for this purpose shall consist of a member or members from two thirds of the States, and a majority of all the States shall be necessary to a choice. In every case after the choice of the President, the person having the greatest number of votes of the electors shall be the Vice President. But if there should remain two or more who have equal votes, the Senate shall choose from them by ballot the Vice President.[6]

3. The Congress may determine the time of choosing the electors, and the day on which they shall give their votes; which day shall be the same throughout the United States.

4. No person except a natural born citizen, or a citizen of the United States, at the time of the adoption of this Constitution, shall be eligible to the office of President; neither shall any person be eligible to the office who shall not have attained to the age of thirty-five years, and been fourteen years a resident within the United States.

5. In case of the removal of the President from office, or of his death, resignation, or inability to discharge the powers and duties of the said office, the same shall devolve on the Vice President, and the Congress may by law provide for the case of removal, death, resignation or inability, both of the President and Vice President, declaring what officer shall then act as President, and such officer shall act accordingly until the disability be removed, or a President shall be elected.

6. The President shall, at stated times, receive for his services a compensation which shall neither be increased nor diminished during the period for which he shall have been elected, and he shall not receive within that period any other emolument from the United States, or any of them.

7. Before he enter on the execution of his office, he shall take the following oath or affirmation:—"I do solemnly swear (or affirm) that I will faithfully execute the office of president of the United States, and will to the best of my ability, preserve, protect and defend the Constitution of the United States."

SECTION 2.   1. The President shall be commander in chief of the army and navy of the United States, and of the militia of the several States, when called into the actual service of the United States; he may require the opinion in writing, of the principal officer in each of the executive departments, upon any subject relating to the duties of their respective offices, and he shall have power to grant reprieves and pardons for offenses against the United States, except in cases of impeachment.

2. He shall have power, by and with the advice and consent of the Senate, to make treaties, provided two thirds of the senators present concur; and he shall nominate, and by and with the advice and consent of the Senate, shall appoint ambassadors, other public ministers and consuls, judges of the Supreme Court, and all other officers of the United States, whose appointments are not herein otherwise provided for, and which shall be established by law; but the Congress may by law vest the appointment of such inferior officers, as they think proper, in the President alone, in the courts of laws, or in the heads of departments.

---

[6]See the Twelfth Amendment.

3. The President shall have power to fill up all vacancies that may happen during the recess of the Senate, by granting commissions which shall expire at the end of their next session.

SECTION 3.   He shall from time to time give to the Congress information of the state of the Union, and recommend to their consideration such measures as he shall judge necessary and expedient; he may, on extraordinary occasions, convene both houses, or either of them, and in case of disagreement between them with respect to the time of adjournment, he may adjourn them to such time as he shall think proper; he shall receive ambassadors and other public ministers; he shall take care that the laws be faithfully executed, and shall commission all the officers of the United States.

SECTION 4.   The President, Vice President, and all civil officers of the United States, shall be removed from office on impeachment for, and conviction of, treason, bribery, or other high crimes and misdemeanors.

ARTICLE III

SECTION 1.   The judicial power of the United States shall be vested in one Supreme Court, and in such inferior courts as the Congress may from time to time ordain and establish. The judges, both of the Supreme and inferior courts, shall hold their offices during good behavior, and shall, at stated times, receive for their services, a compensation, which shall not be diminished during their continuance in office.

SECTION 2.   1. The judicial power shall extend to all cases, in law and equity, arising under this Constitution, the laws of the United States, and treaties made, or which shall be made, under their authority;—to all cases of admiralty and maritime jurisdiction;—to controversies to which the United States shall be a party;[7]— to controversies between two or more States;—between a State and citizens of another State;—between citizens of different States;—between citizens of the same State claiming lands under grants of different States, and between a State, or the citizens thereof, and foreign States, citizens or subjects.

2. In all cases affecting ambassadors, other public ministers and consuls, and those in which a State shall be party, the Supreme Court shall have original jurisdiction. In all the other cases before mentioned, the Supreme Court shall have appellate jurisdiction, both as to law and fact, with such exceptions, and under such regulations as the Congress shall make.

3. The trial of all crimes, except in cases of impeachment, shall be by jury; and such trial shall be held in the State where the said crimes shall have been committed; but when not committed within any State, the trial shall be such place or places as the Congress may by law have directed.

SECTION 3.   1. Treason against the United States shall consist only in levying war against them, or in adhering to their enemies, giving them aid and comfort. No person shall be convicted of treason unless on the testimony of two witnesses to the same overt act, or on confession in open court.

2. The Congress shall have power to declare the punishment of treason, but no attainder of treason shall work corruption of blood, or forfeiture except during the life of the person attained.

ARTICLE IV

SECTION 1.   1. Full faith and credit shall be given in each State to the public acts, records, and judicial proceedings of every other State. And the Congress may by general laws prescribe the manner in which such acts, records and proceedings shall be proved, and the effect thereof.

SECTION 2.   1. The citizens of each State shall be entitled to all privileges and immunities of citizens in the several States.[8]

2. A person charged in any State with treason, felony, or other crime, who shall flee from justice, and be found in another State, shall on demand of the executive authority of the State from which he fled, be delivered up to be removed to the State having jurisdiction of the crime.

3. No person held to service or labor in one State under the laws thereof, escaping into another, shall, in consequence of any law or regulation therein, be discharged from such service or labor, but shall be delivered up on claim of the party to whom such service or labor may be due.[9]

SECTION 3.   1. New States may be admitted by the Congress into this Union; but no new State shall be formed or erected within the jurisdiction of any other State, nor any State be formed by the junction of two or more States, or parts of States, without the consent of the legislatures of the States concerned as well as of the Congress.

2. The Congress shall have power to dispose of and make all needful rules and regulations respecting the territory or other property belonging to the United States; and nothing in this Constitution shall

---

[7]See the Eleventh Amendment.

[8]See the Fourteenth Amendment, Sec. 1.
[9]See the Thirteenth Amendment.

be so construed as to prejudice any claims of the United States, or of any particular State.

SECTION 4.   The United States shall guarantee to every State in this Union a republican form of government, and shall protect each of them against invasion; and on application of the legislature, or of the executive (when the legislature cannot be convened) against domestic violence.

ARTICLE V

The Congress, whenever two thirds of both Houses shall deem it necessary, shall propose amendments to this Constitution, or, on the application of the legislatures of two thirds of the several States, shall call a convention for proposing amendments, which in either case shall be valid to all intents and purposes, as part of this Constitution, when ratified by the legislatures of three fourths of the several States, or by conventions in three fourths thereof, as the one or the other mode of ratification may be proposed by the Congress; Provided that no amendment which may be made prior to the year one thousand eight hundred and eight shall in any manner affect the first and fourth clauses in the ninth section of the first article; and that no State, without its consent, shall be deprived of its equal suffrage in the Senate.

ARTICLE VI

1. All debts contracted and engagements entered into, before the adoption of this Constitution, shall be as valid against the United States under this Constitution, as under the Confederation.[10]

2. This Constitution, and the laws of the United States which shall be made in pursuance thereof; and all treaties made, or which shall be made, under the authority of the United States, shall be the supreme law of the land; and the judges in every State shall be bound thereby, any thing in the Constitution or laws of any State to the contrary notwithstanding.

3. The senators and representatives before mentioned, and the members of the several State legislatures, and all executive and judicial officers, both of the United States and of the several States, shall be bound by oath or affirmation to support this Constitution; but no religious test shall ever be required as a qualification to any office or public trust under the United States.

ARTICLE VII

The ratification of the conventions of nine States shall be sufficient for the establishment of this Constitution between the States so ratifying the same.

[10]See the Fourteenth Amendment, Sec. 4.

Done in Convention by the unanimous consent of the States present the seventeenth day of September in the year of our Lord one thousand seven hundred and eighty-seven, and of the independence of the United States of America the twelfth. In witness whereof we have hereunto subscribed our names.

Articles in addition to, and amendment of, the Constitution of the United States of America, proposed by Congress, and ratified by the legislatures of the several States, pursuant to the fifth article of the original Constitution.

AMENDMENT I [FIRST TEN AMENDMENTS RATIFIED DECEMBER 15, 1791]

Congress shall make no law respecting an establishment of religion, or prohibiting the free exercise thereof; or abridging the freedom of speech, or of the press; or the right of the people peaceably to assemble, and to petition the government for a redress of grievances.

AMENDMENT II

A well regulated militia, being necessary to the security of a free State, the right of the people to keep and bear arms, shall not be infringed.

AMENDMENT III

No soldier shall, in time of peace be quartered in any house, without the consent of the owner, nor in time of war, but in a manner to be prescribed by law.

AMENDMENT IV

The right of the people to be secure in their persons, houses, papers, and effects, against unreasonable searches and seizures, shall not be violated, and no warrants shall issue, but upon probable cause, supported by oath or affirmation, and particularly describing the place to be searched, and the persons or things to be seized.

AMENDMENT V

No person shall be held to answer for a capital or otherwise infamous crime, unless on a presentment or indictment of a grand jury, except in cases arising in the land or naval forces, or in the militia, when in actual service in time of war or public danger; nor shall any person be subject for the same offense to be twice put in jeopardy of life or limb; nor shall be compelled in any criminal case to be a witness against himself, nor be deprived of life, liberty, or property, without due process of law; nor shall private property be taken for public use, without just compensation.

AMENDMENT VI

In all criminal prosecutions, the accused shall enjoy the right to a speedy and public trial, by an impartial jury of the State and district wherein the crime shall have been committed, which district shall have been previously ascertained by law, and to be informed of the nature and cause of the accusation; to be confronted with the witnesses against him; to have compulsory process for obtaining witnesses in his favor, and to have the assistance of counsel for his defense.

AMENDMENT VII

In suits at common law, where the value in controversy shall exceed twenty dollars, the right of trial by jury shall be preserved, and no fact tried by a jury shall be otherwise reexamined in any court of the United States, than according to the rules of the common law.

AMENDMENT VIII

Excessive bail shall not be required, nor excessive fines imposed, nor cruel and unusual punishments inflicted.

AMENDMENT IX

The enumeration in the Constitution of certain rights shall not be construed to deny or disparage others retained by the people.

AMENDMENT X

The powers not delegated to the United States by the Constitution, nor prohibited by it to the States, are reserved to the States respectively, or to the people.

AMENDMENT XI [JANUARY 8, 1798]

The judicial power of the United States shall not be construed to extend to any suit in law or equity, commenced or prosecuted against one of the United States by citizens of another State, or by citizens or subjects of any foreign State.

AMENDMENT XII [SEPTEMBER 25, 1804]

The electors shall meet in their respective States, and vote by ballot for President and Vice President, one of whom, at least, shall not be an inhabitant of the same State with themselves; they shall name in their ballots the person voted for as President, and in distinct ballots, the person voted for as Vice President, and they shall make distinct lists of all persons voted for as President and of all persons voted for as Vice President, and of the number of votes for each, which lists they shall sign and certify, and transmit sealed to the seat of the government of the United States, directed to the President of the Senate;—The President of the Senate shall, in the presence of the Senate and House of Representatives, open all the certificates and the votes shall then be counted;—The person having the greatest number of votes for President, shall be the President, if such number be a majority of the whole number of electors appointed; and if no person have such majority, then from the persons having the highest numbers not exceeding three on the list of those voted for as President, the House of Representatives shall choose immediately, by ballot, the President. But in choosing the President, the votes shall be taken by States, the representation from each State having one vote; a quorum for this purpose shall consist of a member or members from two thirds of the States, and a majority of all the States shall be necessary to a choice. And if the House of Representatives shall not choose a President whenever the right of choice shall devolve upon them, before the fourth day of March next following, then the Vice President shall act as President, as in the case of the death or other constitutional disability of the President. The person having the greatest number of votes as Vice President shall be the Vice President, if such number be a majority of the whole number of electors appointed, and if no person have a majority, then from the two highest numbers on the list, the Senate shall choose the Vice President; a quorum for the purpose shall consist of two thirds of the whole number of Senators, and a majority of the whole number shall be necessary to a choice. But no person constitutionally ineligible to the office of President shall be eligible to that of Vice President of the United States.

AMENDMENT XIII [DECEMBER 18, 1865]

SECTION 1.   Neither slavery nor involuntary servitude, except as punishment for crime whereof the party shall have been duly convicted, shall exist within the United States, or any place subject to their jurisdiction.

SECTION 2.   Congress shall have power to enforce this article by appropriate legislation.

AMENDMENT XIV [JULY 28, 1868]

SECTION 1.   All persons born or naturalized in the United States, and subject to the jurisdiction thereof, are citizens of the United States and of the State wherein they reside. No State shall make or enforce any law which shall abridge the privileges or immunities of citizens of the United States; nor shall any State deprive any person of life, liberty, or property, without due process of law; nor deny to any person within its jurisdiction the equal protection of the laws.

SECTION 2.   Representatives shall be apportioned among the several States according to their respective numbers, counting the whole number of persons in each State, excluding Indians not taxed. But when the right to vote at any election for the choice of electors for President and Vice President of the United States, representatives in Congress, the executive and judicial officers of a State, or the members of the legislature thereof, is denied to any of the male inhabitants of such State, being twenty-one years of age, and citizens of the United States, or in any way abridged, except for participating in rebellion, or other crime, the basis of representation there shall be reduced in the proportion which the number of such male citizens shall bear to the whole number of male citizens twenty-one years of age in such State.

SECTION 3.   No person shall be a senator or representative in Congress, or elector of President and Vice President, or hold any office, civil or military, under the United States, or under any State, who having previously taken an oath, as a member of Congress, or as an officer of the United States, or as a member of any State legislature, or as an executive or judicial officer of any State, to support the Constitution of the United States, shall have engaged in insurrection or rebellion against the same, or given aid or comfort to the enemies thereof. But Congress may by a vote of two thirds of each House, remove such disability.

SECTION 4.   The validity of the public debt of the United States, authorized by law, including debts incurred for payment of pensions and bounties for services in suppressing insurrection or rebellion; shall not be questioned. But neither the United States nor any State shall assume or pay any debt or obligation incurred in aid of insurrection or rebellion against the United States, or any claim for the loss or emancipation of any slave; but all such debts, obligations, and claims shall be held illegal and void.

SECTION 5.   The Congress shall have the power to enforce, by appropriate legislation, the provisions of this article.

AMENDMENT XV [MARCH 30, 1870]

SECTION 1.   The right of citizens of the United States to vote shall not be denied or abridged by the United States or by any State on account of race, color, or previous condition of servitude.

SECTION 2.   The Congress shall have power to enforce this article by appropriate legislation.

AMENDMENT XVI [FEBRUARY 25, 1913]

The Congress shall have power to lay and collect taxes on incomes, from whatever source derived, without apportionment among the several States, and without regard to any census or enumeration.

AMENDMENT XVII [MAY 31, 1913]

The Senate of the United States shall be composed of two senators from each State, elected by the people thereof, for six years; and each senator shall have one vote. The electors in each State shall have the qualifications requisite for electors of the most numerous branch of the State legislature.

When vacancies happen in the representation of any State in the Senate, the executive authority of such State shall issue writs of election to fill such vacancies: Provided, That the legislature of any State may empower the executive thereof to make temporary appointments until the people fill the vacancies by election as the legislature may direct.

This amendment shall not be so construed as to affect the election or term of any senator chosen before it becomes valid as part of the Constitution.

AMENDMENT XVIII[11] [JANUARY 29, 1919]

After one year from the ratification of this article, the manufacture, sale, or transportation of intoxicating liquors within, the importation thereof into, or the exportation thereof from the United States and all territory subject to the jurisdiction thereof for beverage purposes is thereby prohibited.

The Congress and the several States shall have concurrent power to enforce this article by appropriate legislation.

This article shall be inoperative unless it shall have been ratified as an amendment to the Constitution by the legislatures of the several States, as provided in the Constitution, within seven years from the date of the submission hereof to the States by Congress.

AMENDMENT XIX [AUGUST 26, 1920]

The right of citizens of the United States to vote shall not be denied or abridged by the United States or by any State on account of sex.

Congress shall have the power to enforce this article by appropriate legislation.

AMENDMENT XX [JANUARY 23, 1933]

SECTION 1.   The terms of the President and Vice President shall end at noon on the 20th day of January and the terms of Senators and Representatives at noon on the 3d day of January, of the years in which such terms would have ended if this article had not been ratified; and the terms of their successors shall then begin.

SECTION 2.   The Congress shall assemble at least once in every year, and such meeting shall begin at

---

[11]Repealed by the Twenty-first Amendment.

noon on the 3d day of January, unless they shall by law appoint a different day.

SECTION 3.   If, at the time fixed for the beginning of the term of president, the President-elect shall have died, the Vice President-elect shall become President. If a President shall not have been chosen before the time fixed for the beginning of his term, or if the President-elect shall have failed to qualify, then the Vice President-elect shall act as president until a President shall have qualified; and the Congress may by law provide for the case wherein neither a President-elect nor a Vice President-elect shall have qualified, declaring who shall then act as President, or the manner in which one who is to act shall be selected, and such person shall act accordingly until a President or Vice President shall have qualified.

SECTION 4.   The Congress may by law provide for the case of the death of any of the persons from whom, the House of Representatives may choose a President whenever the right of choice shall have devolved upon them, and for the case of the death of any of the persons from whom the Senate may choose a Vice President whenever the right of choice shall have devolved upon them.

SECTION 5.   Sections 1 and 2 shall take effect on the 15th day of October following the ratification of this article.

SECTION 6.   This article shall be inoperative unless it shall have been ratified as an amendment to the Constitution by the legislatures of three-fourths of the several States within seven years from the date of its submission.

AMENDMENT XXI [DECEMBER 5, 1933]

SECTION 1.   The Eighteenth Article of amendment to the Constitution of the United States is hereby repealed.

SECTION 2.   The transportation or importation into any State, Territory, or possession of the United States for delivery or use therein of intoxicating liquors in violation of the laws thereof, is hereby prohibited.

SECTION 3.   This article shall be inoperative unless it shall have been ratified as an amendment to the Constitution by conventions in the several States, as provided in the Consitution, within seven years from the date of the submission thereof to the States by the Congress.

AMENDMENT XXII [MARCH 1, 1951]

No person shall be elected to the office of the President more than twice, and no person who has held the office of President, or acted as President, for more than two years of a term to which some other person was elected President shall be elected to the office of the President more than once.

But this article shall not apply to any person holding the office of President when this article was proposed by the Congress, and shall not prevent any person who may be holding the office of President, or acting as President, during the term within which this article becomes operative from holding the office of President or acting as President during the remainder of such term.

This article shall be inoperative unless it shall have been ratified as an amendment to the Constitution by the legislatures of three-fourths of the several States within seven years from the date of its submission to the States by the Congress.

AMENDMENT XXIII [MARCH 29, 1961]

SECTION 1.   The District constituting the seat of Government of the United States shall appoint in such manner as the Congress may direct.

A number of electors of President and Vice President equal to the whole number of Senators and Representatives in Congress to which the District would be entitled if it were a State, but in no event more than the least populous State; they shall be in addition to those appointed by the States, but they shall be considered, for the purposes of the election of President and Vice President, to be electors appointed by a State; and they shall meet in the District and perform such duties as provided by the twelfth article of amendment.

SECTION 2.   The Congress shall have power to enforce this article by appropriate legislation.

AMENDMENT XXIV [JANUARY 23, 1964]

SECTION 1.   The right of citizens of the United States to vote in any primary or other election for President or Vice President, for electors for President or Vice President, or for Senator or Representative in Congress, shall not be denied or abridged by the United States or any State by reason of failure to pay any poll tax or other tax.

SECTION 2.   The Congress shall have power to enforce this article by appropriate legislation.

AMENDMENT XXV [FEBRUARY 10, 1967]

SECTION 1.   In case of the removal of the President from office or of his death or resignation, the Vice President shall become President.

SECTION 2.   Whenever there is a vacancy in the office of the Vice President, the President shall nominate a Vice President who shall take office upon confirmation by a majority of both Houses of Congress.

SECTION 3.   Whenever the President transmits to the President pro tempore of the Senate and the Speaker of the House of Representatives his written declaration that he is unable to discharge the powers and duties of his office, and until he transmits to them a written declaration to the contrary, such powers and duties shall be discharged by the Vice President as Acting President.

SECTION 4.   Whenever the Vice President and a majority of either the principal officers of the executive departments or of such other body as Congress may by law provide, transmit to the President pro tempore of the Senate and the Speaker of the House of Representatives their written declaration that the President is unable to discharge the powers and duties of his office, the Vice President shall immediately assume the powers and duties of the office as Acting President.

Thereafter, when the President transmits to the President pro tempore of the Senate and the Speaker of the House of Representatives his written declaration that no inability exists, he shall resume the powers and duties of his office unless the Vice President and a majority of either the principal officers of the executive departments or of such other body as Congress may by law provide, transmit within four days to the President pro tempore of the Senate and the Speaker of the House of Representatives their written declaration that the President is unable to discharge the powers and duties of his office. Thereupon Congress shall decide the issue, assembling within

forty-eight hours for that purpose if not in session. If the Congress, within twenty-one days after receipt of the latter written declaration, or, if Congress is not in session, within twenty-one days after Congress is required to assemble, determines by two-thirds vote of both houses that the President is unable to discharge the powers and duties of his office, the Vice President shall continue to discharge the same as Acting President; otherwise, the President shall resume the powers and duties of his office.

AMENDMENT XXVI [JUNE 30, 1971]

SECTION 1.   The right of citizens of the United States who are eighteen years of age or older to vote shall not be denied or abridged by the United States or by any State on account of age.

SECTION 2.   The Congress shall have power to enforce this article by appropriate legislation.

AMENDMENT XXVII[12] [MAY 7, 1992]

No law, varying the compensation for services of the Senators and Representatives, shall take effect until an election of Representatives shall have intervened.

---

[12]James Madison proposed this amendment in 1789 together with the ten amendments that were adopted as the Bill of Rights, but it failed to win ratification at the time. Congress, however, had set no deadline for its ratification, and over the years—particularly in the 1980s and 1990s—many states voted to add it to the Constitution. With the ratification of Michigan in 1992 it passed the threshold of of the states required for adoption, but because the process took more than 200 years, its validity remains in doubt.

Historically Black Four-Year Colleges and Universities

Institution and Location	Year Founded	Land-Grant, Public, or Church-Affiliated Denomination	Institution and Location	Year Founded	Land-Grant, Public, or Church-Affiliated Denomination
Alabama A&M University, Normal, Alabama	1875	Land-grant	Florida A&M University, Tallahassee, Florida	1887	Land-grant
Alabama State University, Montgomery, Alabama	1867	Public	Florida Memorial College, Miami, Florida	1879	Baptist
Albany State University, Albany, Georgia	1903	Public	Fort Valley State College, Fort Valley, Georgia	1895	Land-grant
Alcorn State University, Lorman, Mississippi	1871	Land-grant	Grambling State University, Grambling, Louisiana	1901	Public
Allen University, Columbia, South Carolina	1870	AME	Hampton University, Hampton, Virginia	1868	Private
Arkansas Baptist College, Little Rock, Arkansas	1884	Baptist	Harris-Stowe State College, St. Louis, Missouri	1857	Public
Barber-Scotia College, Concord, North Carolina	1904	Presbyterian	Howard University, Washington, DC	1867	Public
Benedict College, Columbia, South Carolina	1870	Baptist	Huston-Tillotson College, Austin, Texas	1952	United Church of Christ/United Methodist
Bennett College, Greensboro, North Carolina	1873	United Methodist	Jackson State University, Jackson, Mississippi	1877	Public
Bethune-Cookman College, Daytona Beach, Florida	1904	United Methodist	Jarvis Christian College, Hawkins, Texas	1913	Disciple of Christ Christian Church
Bluefield State College, Bluefield, West Virginia	1895	Public	Johnson C. Smith University, Charlotte, North Carolina	1867	Presbyterian
Bowie State University, Bowie, Maryland	1865	Public	Kentucky State University, Frankfort, Kentucky	1886	Land-grant
Central State University, Wilberforce, Ohio	1887	Public	Knoxville College, Knoxville, Tennessee	1875	Presbyterian
Cheyney University, Cheyney, Pennsylvania	1837	Public	Lane College, Jackson, Tennessee	1882	Christian Methodist Episcopal
Claflin College, Orangeburg, South Carolina	1869	United Methodist	Langston University, Langston, Oklahoma	1897	Land-grant
Clark Atlanta University, Atlanta, Georgia	1988	United Methodist	LeMoyne-Owen College, Memphis, Tennessee	1870	United Church of Christ
Concordia College, Selma, Alabama	1922	Lutheran	Lincoln University, Jefferson City, Missouri	1866	Land-grant
Coppin State University, Baltimore, Maryland	1900	Public	Lincoln University, Lincoln, Pennsylvania	1854	Public
Delaware State University, Dover, Delaware	1891	Land-grant	Livingstone College, Salisbury, North Carolina	1879	AME
Dillard University, New Orleans, Louisiana	1930	Congregational/ United Methodist	Miles College, Birmingham, Alabama	1908	Christian Methodist Episcopal
Edward Waters College, Jacksonville, Florida	1866	AME	Mississippi Valley State University, Ita Bena, Mississippi	1946	Public
Elizabeth City State University, Elizabeth City, North Carolina	1891	Public	Morehouse College, Atlanta, Georgia	1867	Baptist
Fayetteville State University, Fayetteville, North Carolina	1867	Public	Morgan State University, Baltimore, Maryland	1867	Public
Fisk University, Nashville, Tennessee	1866	United Church of Christ			

Institution and Location	Year Founded	Land-Grant, Public, or Church-Affiliated Denomination	Institution and Location	Year Founded	Land-Grant, Public, or Church-Affiliated Denomination
Morris Brown College, Atlanta, Georgia	1881	AME	Spelman College, Atlanta, Georgia	1876	Presbyterian
Morris College, Sumter, South Carolina	1908	Baptist	Stillman College, Tuscaloosa, Alabama	1876	Presbyterian
Norfolk State University, Norfolk, Virginia	1935	Public	Talladega College, Talladega, Alabama	1867	United Church of Christ
North Carolina A&T St. U, Greensboro, North Carolina	1892	Land-grant	Tennessee State University, Nashville, Tennessee	1912	Land-grant
North Carolina Central University, Durham, North Carolina	1909	Public	Texas College, Tyler, Texas	1894	Christian Methodist Episcopal
Oakwood College, Huntsville, Alabama	1896	Seventh Day Adventist	Texas Southern University, Houston, Texas	1947	Public
Paine College, Augusta, Georgia	1882	United Methodist	Tougaloo College, Tougaloo, Mississippi	1869	United Church of Christ/United Missionary Society
Paul Quinn College, Dallas, Texas	1872	AME	Tuskegee University, Tuskegee, Alabama	1881	Land-grant
Philander Smith College, Little Rock, Arkansas	1877	United Methodist	University of Arkansas at Pine Bluff, Pine Bluff, Arkansas	1873	Land-grant
Prairie View A&M University, Prairie View, Texas	1878	Land-grant	University of the District of Columbia, Washington, DC	1977	Public
Rust College, Holly Springs, Mississippi	1866	United Methodist	University of Maryland, Eastern Shore, Princess Anne, Maryland	1886	Land-grant
Saint Augustine's College, Raleigh, North Carolina	1867	Episcopal	University of the Virgin Islands, St. Thomas, United States Virgin Islands	1962	Public
Saint Paul's College, Lawrenceville, Virginia	1888	Episcopal	Virginia State University, Petersburg, Virginia	1882	Land-grant
Savannah State College, Savannah, Georgia	1890	Public	Virginia Union University, Richmond, Virginia	1865	Baptist
Selma University, Selma, Alabama	1878	Baptist	Voorhees College, Denmark, South Carolina	1897	Episcopal
Shaw University, Raleigh, North Carolina	1865	Baptist	West Virginia State College, Institute, West Virginia	1891	Public
Sojourner Douglass College, Baltimore, Maryland	1980	Private	Wilberforce University, Wilberforce, Ohio	1856	AME
South Carolina State University, Orangeburg, South Carolina	1896	Land-grant	Wiley College, Marshall, Texas	1873	United Methodist
Southern University and A&M College, Baton Rouge, Louisiana	1880	Land-grant	Winston-Salem State University, Winston-Salem, North Carolina	1892	Public
Southern University at New Orleans, New Orleans, Louisiana	1956	Public	Xavier University of New Orleans, New Orleans, Louisiana	1925	Roman Catholic
Southwestern Christian College, Terrell, Texas	1949	Church of Christ			

PRESIDENTS AND VICE PRESIDENTS OF THE UNITED STATES*

1. George Washington (1789)
   John Adams (1789)

2. John Adams (1797)
   Thomas Jefferson (1797)

3. Thomas Jefferson (1801)
   Aaron Burr (1801)
   George Clinton (1805)

4. James Madison (1809)
   George Clinton (1809)
   Elbridge Gerry (1813)

5. James Monroe (1817)
   Daniel D. Tompkins (1817)

6. John Quincy Adams (1825)
   John C. Calhoun (1825)

7. Andrew Jackson (1829)
   John C. Calhoun (1829)
   Martin Van Buren (1833)

8. Martin Van Buren (1837)
   Richard M. Johnson (1837)

9. William H. Harrison (1841)
   John Tyler (1841)

10. John Tyler (1841)

11. James K. Polk (1845)
    George M. Dallas (1845)

12. Zachary Taylor (1849)
    Millard Fillmore (1849)

13. Millard Fillmore (1850)

14. Franklin Pierce (1853)
    William R. King (1853)

15. James Buchanan (1857)
    John C. Breckinridge (1857)

16. Abraham Lincoln (1861)
    Hannibal Hamlin (1861)
    Andrew Johnson (1865)

17. Andrew Johnson (1865)

18. Ulysses S. Grant (1869)
    Schuyler Colfax (1869)
    Henry Wilson (1873)

19. Rutherford B. Hayes (1877)
    William A. Wheeler (1877)

20. James A. Garfield (1881)
    Chester A. Arthur (1881)

21. Chester A. Arthur (1881)

22. Grover Cleveland (1885)
    T. A. Hendricks (1885)

23. Benjamin Harrison (1889)
    Levi P. Morton (1889)

24. Grover Cleveland (1893)
    Adlai E. Stevenson (1893)

25. William McKinley (1897)
    Garret A. Hobart (1897)
    Theodore Roosevelt (1901)

26. Theodore Roosevelt (1901)
    Charles Fairbanks (1905)

27. William H. Taft (1909)
    James S. Sherman (1909)

28. Woodrow Wilson (1913)
    Thomas R. Marshall (1913)

29. Warren G. Harding (1921)
    Calvin Coolidge (1921)

30. Calvin Coolidge (1923)
    Charles G. Dawes (1925)

31. Herbert C. Hoover (1929)
    Charles Curtis (1929)

32. Franklin D. Roosevelt (1933)
    John Nance Garner (1933)
    Henry A. Wallace (1941)
    Harry S. Truman (1945)

33. Harry S. Truman (1945)
    Alben W. Barkley (1949)

34. Dwight D. Eisenhower (1953)
    Richard M. Nixon (1953)

35. John F. Kennedy (1961)
    Lyndon B. Johnson (1961)

36. Lyndon B. Johnson (1963)
    Hubert H. Humphrey (1965)

37. Richard M. Nixon (1969)
    Spiro T. Agnew (1969)
    Gerald R. Ford (1973)

38. Gerald R. Ford (1974)
    Nelson A. Rockefeller (1974)

39. James E. Carter Jr. (1977)
    Walter F. Mondale (1977)

40. Ronald W. Reagan (1981)
    George H. Bush (1981)

41. George H. Bush (1989)
    James D. Quayle III (1989)

42. William J. Clinton (1993)
    Albert Gore (1993)

43. George W. Bush (2001)
    Richard B. Cheney (2001)

*Year of inauguration.

Glossary of Key Terms and Concepts

54th Massachusetts Regiment: This all-black volunteer infantry regiment was recruited in the Northern states for service with Union military forces in the Civil War. It was made up almost entirely of black men who had been free. It was commanded by white officers.

Abolitionists: Those who sought to end slavery within their colony, state, nation, or religious denomination. By the 1830s the term best applied to those who advocated immediate rather than gradual emancipation.

Acculturation: Change in individuals who are introduced to a new culture.

Affirmative action: Civil rights policy or program that seeks to redress the effects of past discrimination due to race or gender by giving preference to women and minorities in education and employment.

African Methodist Episcopal (AME) Church: Founded in Philadelphia in 1816, it was the first and became the largest independent black church.

Afrocentricists: Scholars who view history from an African perspective.

Afrocentricity: A philosophy of culture that celebrates Africa's role in history and stresses the enduring African roots and identity of black America.

Age of Revolution: A period in Atlantic history that began with the American Revolution in 1776 and ended with the defeat of Napoleonic France in 1815.

Agricultural Adjustment Act (AAA): A federal program that provided subsidies to farmers to grow less to help stabilize prices.

American and Foreign Anti-Slavery Society (AFASS, 1840–1855): An organization of church-oriented abolitionists.

American Anti-Slavery Society (AASS, 1833–1870): The umbrella organization for immediate abolitionists during the 1830s and the main Garrisonian organization after 1840.

American Colonization Society (ACS, 1816–1912): An organization founded in Washington, D.C., by prominent slaveholders. It claimed to encourage the ultimate abolition of slavery by sending free African Americans to its West African colony of Liberia.

American Convention for Promoting the Abolition of Slavery and Improving the Condition of the African Race (1794–1838): A loose coalition of state and local societies, dominated by the Pennsylvania Abolition Society, dedicated to gradual abolition.

American Missionary Association: This religious organization sent teachers and clergymen throughout the South following the Civil War to tend to the spiritual and educational needs of former slaves. It was instrumental in establishing dozens of schools, including Fisk, Hampton, and Avery.

Amistad: A Spanish schooner on which West African Joseph Cinque led a successful slave revolt in 1839.

Animism: The belief that inanimate objects have spiritual attributes.

Asiento: The monopoly over the slave trade from Africa to Spain's American colonies.

Battery Wagner: This defensive fortification guarded Fort Sumter near the entrance to Charleston Harbor in South Carolina. It was the scene in July 1863 of a major Union assault by the 54th Massachusetts Regiment, a black unit. The assault failed, but the bravery and valor of the black troops earned them fame and glory.

Benevolent Empire: A network of church-related voluntary associations designed to fight sin and save souls. It emerged during the 1810s in relationship to the Second Great Awakening.

Berbers: A people native to North Africa and the Sahara Desert.

Black arts movement: Artistic movement that seeks to promote black art by black artists for black people.

Black Cabinet: Informal group of highly placed African-American advisors to President Franklin D. Roosevelt.

Black codes: Laws that were passed in each of the former Confederate states following the Civil War that applied only to black people. While conceding such rights as the right to marry, to contract a debt, or to own property, the codes severely restricted the rights and opportunities of former slaves in terms of labor and mobility.

Black Committee: An organization of prominent black men in the North who assisted in recruiting African Americans to fight for the Union in the Civil War.

Black English (or African-American Vernacular English): A variety of American English that is influenced by West African grammar, vocabulary, and pronunciation.

Black laws: Laws passed in states of the Old Northwest during the early nineteenth century banning or restricting black settlement and limiting the rights of black residents.

Black nationalism: A belief held by some African Americans that they must seek their racial destiny by establishing separate institutions and, perhaps, migrating as a group to a location (often Africa) outside the United States.

Black Panther Party: Black militant organization set up in 1966 by Huey P. Newton and Bobby Seale.

Black studies: Scholarly study of the history and experiences of persons of African descent.

Border ruffians: Pro-slavery advocates and vigilantes from Missouri who crossed the border into Kansas in 1855–1857 to support slavery in Kansas by threatening and attacking antislavery settlers.

Brooks-Sumner Affair: South Carolina congressman Preston Brooks attacked and severely beat Massachusetts Senator Charles Sumner on the floor of the U.S. Senate after

Sumner had denounced the proslavery position of Brooks's uncle, South Carolina Senator Andrew Butler.

Brotherhood of Sleeping Car Porters (BSCP): Black men and women who worked on Pullman passenger coaches on the nation's railroads organized this labor union in 1925 with A. Philip Randolph as its leader. It struggled until the passage in 1935 of the National Labor Relations Act, after which it became one of the powerful unions within the American Federation of Labor (AFL). In 1978 it was absorbed into the Brotherhood of Railway and Airline Clerks.

Brown v. Board of Education of Topeka: Decision by the Supreme Court in 1954 that overturned the "separate but equal" doctrine.

Brownsville Affair: In 1906, a shooting in Brownsville, Texas, was blamed on black soldiers from the 25th Infantry Regiment. President Theodore Roosevelt summarily dismissed 167 black men from the U.S. Army. Later investigations exonerated the men.

Buffalo soldiers: Four regiments of black soldiers that served with the U.S. Army on the western frontier from the 1870s to the 1890s. The Plains Indians called them the buffalo soldiers.

Call-and-response: An African-American singing style rooted in Africa. A solo call tells a story to which a group responds, often with repeated lyrics.

Carpetbagger: The derogatory term used during Reconstruction to describe Northerners who came South following the Civil War to take advantage of political and economic opportunities. They were labeled "carpetbaggers" because they ostensibly carried all of their possessions in a solitary carpetbag.

Cash crop: A crop grown for sale rather than subsistence.

Chattel slavery: A form of slavery in which the enslaved are treated legally as property.

Chicago Renaissance: Flourishing of the arts that made Chicago the center of black culture in the 1940s.

Church of England: A Protestant church established in the sixteenth century as the English national or Anglican church with the English monarch as its head. After the American Revolution, its American branch became the Episcopal Church.

Civil Rights Act, 1866: This act nullified the black codes and made African Americans citizens with the basic rights of life, liberty, and due process. It was passed over President Andrew Johnson's veto. Its main features were subsequently embedded in the Fourteenth Amendment to the Constitution.

Civil Rights Act of 1875: This federal legislation outlawed racial discrimination in public accommodations such as hotels and restaurants, and in transportation, including railroad coaches and steamboats. The Supreme Court invalidated it in 1883.

Civil Rights Act of 1964: Federal law banning discrimination in places of public accommodation.

Civil Rights Act of 1968: Federal law banning discrimination in housing.

Coffle: A file of slaves chained together that was typical of the domestic slave trade.

Colored American (New York, 1837–1842): The leading African-American newspaper of its time.

Colored Farmers' Alliance: A large organization of black southern farmers in the 1880s and 1890s that had as many as one million members who agitated for improved conditions and income for black landowners, renters, and sharecroppers.

Committee for Industrial Organization (CIO): Labor organization that was committed to inter-racial and multiethnic organizing.

Communist Party: Political party formed to promote communism.

Community Action Programs (CAPS): Anti-poverty programs involving "maximum feasible participation" by the poor themselves.

Compromise of 1850: An attempt by the U.S. Congress to settle divisive issues between the North and South, including slavery expansion, apprehension in the North of fugitive slaves, and slavery in the District of Columbia.

Compromise of 1877: This informal arrangement between national Democrats and Republicans settled the disputed presidential election of 1876 by permitting Republican Rutherford B. Hayes to become president while allowing Democrats to complete redemption by taking political control of Louisiana, Florida, and South Carolina.

Congress of Racial Equality: Protest group committed to nonviolent direct action.

Continental Army: The army created by the Continental Congress in June 1775 to fight British troops. George Washington was its commander in chief.

Continental Congress: A representative assembly that first met in October 1775 and served as the de facto central government of the United States during the Revolutionary War.

Contraband: Slaves who escaped to the Union or were captured by Union troops early in the Civil War were considered enemy property or contraband.

Convict lease system: Southern states and communities leased prisoners to privately operated mines, railroads, and timber companies. These businesses forced the prisoners, who were usually black men, to work in brutal, unhealthy, and dangerous conditions. Many convicts died of abuse and disease.

Cotton gin: A simple machine invented by Eli Whitney in 1793 to separate cotton seeds from cotton fiber. It greatly speeded this task and encouraged the westward expansion of cotton-growing in the United States.

Creole: An American brig on which Madison Washington led a successful slave revolt in 1841.

Creoles: Persons of African and/or European descent born in the Americas.

Crop lien: Black and white farmers purchased goods on credit from local merchants. The merchant demanded collateral in the form of a lien on the crop, typically cotton. If the farmer failed to repay the loan, the merchant had the legal right to seize the crop.

Disfranchisement: White southern Democrats devised a variety of techniques in the late nineteenth and early twentieth centuries to prevent black people from voting. Those techniques included literacy tests, poll taxes, and the grandfather clause as well as intimidation and violence.

Divination: A form of magic aimed at telling the future by interpreting a variety of signs.

Domestic slave trade: A trade dating from the first decade of the nineteenth century in American-born slaves purchased primarily in the border South and sent overland or by sea to the cotton-growing regions of the Old Southwest.

Double V campaign: Slogan during World War II that stood for victory over fascism abroad and over racism at home for blacks.

Dred Scott v. Sanford: The 1857 U.S. Supreme Court case that ruled against Missouri slave Dred Scott by declaring that black people were not citizens, that they possessed no constitutional rights, and were considered to be property.

Economic Opportunity Act of 1964: Federal law creating the Office of Economic Opportunity and a number of programs aimed at poor communities.

Emancipation Proclamation: President Abraham Lincoln issued the Preliminary Emancipation Proclamation on September 22, 1862. It declared that slaves in states or portions of states still in rebellion 100 days later would be freed. On January 1, 1863, the Emancipation Proclamation freed slaves in areas of the Confederate states not under Union control.

Enforcement Acts: Also known as the Force Acts, these measures were passed by Congress in the early 1870s to undermine the Ku Klux Klan and other terrorist organizations by authorizing the president to use military force and to suspend the writ of habeas corpus.

Executive Order #8802: Order issued by President Franklin D. Roosevelt in 1941 banning discrimination in employment in defense industries and the federal government.

Executive Order #9346: Order establishing a new Committee on Fair Employment Practices, with greater resources, and direct oversight by the Executive Office of the President.

Executive Order #9981: Order issued by President Harry Truman in 1948 desegregating the armed forces.

Exodusters: Black migrants who left the South during and after Reconstruction and settled in Kansas, often in all-black towns.

Factory: A headquarters for a European company that traded for slaves or engaged in other commercial enterprises on the West African coast.

Fair Employment Practices Committee (FEPC): A committee created by Franklin Roosevelt to investigate complaints of discrimination.

Fair Play Committee: Organization formed to promote black actors in the movie industry and improve the image of blacks in film.

Family Assistance Plan (FAP): Plan giving financial assistance to families with no wage earner.

Federal Arts Project: New Deal agency formed to promote the creation of public art.

Federal Elections bill, 1890: A measure, also known as the Force bill, to protect the voting rights of black men in the South by providing federal supervision of elections. It passed in the House of Representatives but failed in the Senate.

Fetish: A natural object or an artifact believed to have magical power. A charm.

Fifteenth Amendment, 1870: This constitutional amendment stipulated that the right to vote could not be denied on account of race, color, or because a person had been a slave.

First South Carolina Volunteers: This black military unit consisted of former slaves recruited in the South Carolina and Georgia low country in 1862 and 1863 for service with Union military forces in the Civil War.

Fort Pillow: This fort on the east bank of the Mississippi River north of Memphis, Tennessee, was the scene of a massacre of black Union troops as well as some white soldiers and officers by Confederate cavalry in April 1864.

Forty-Niners: The men and women who rushed to California in 1849 after gold had been discovered there.

Fourteenth Amendment, 1868: This amendment ratified during Reconstruction made any person born in the United States a citizen of the United States and of the state in which they lived. It guaranteed citizens the rights of life, liberty, and due process—usually a trial or judicial proceeding—as well as equal protection of the law. It also contained a provision reducing a state's representation in Congress if that state denied the right to vote to any adult males.

Free labor: Mid-nineteenth-century Americans who were free and worked for income or compensation to advance themselves, as opposed to slave labor, which was work done with no financial compensation by people who were not free.

Free papers: Proof of freedom that free black people had to carry at all times in the southern states prior to emancipation. The papers, issued by state governments, identified an individual by name, age, sex, color, height, and so forth.

Free-Soil Party (1848–1853): An almost entirely northern political coalition opposed to the expansion of slavery into western territories. It included former supporters of the Whig, Democratic, and Liberty parties.

Freedmen's Bureau: Congress established the Bureau of Refugees, Freedmen, and Abandoned Lands in February 1865 to assist black and white Southerners left destitute by the Civil War.

Freedmen's Savings Bank: A private financial institution chartered by Congress in 1865. Many black people and organizations deposited funds in the bank, which went bankrupt in 1874.

Freedom Rides: Effort in 1961 to desegregate interstate bus and rail travel.

Freedom suits: Legal cases in which slaves sued their master or master's heirs for freedom.

French and Indian War: A war between Great Britain and its American Indian allies and France and its American Indian allies, fought between 1754 and 1763 for control of the eastern portion of North America.

Fugitive Slave Act of 1793: An act of Congress permitting masters to recapture escaped slaves who had reached the free states and, with the authorization of local courts, return with the slave or slaves to their home state.

Fugitive Slave Law, 1850:   Part of the Compromise of 1850. It required law enforcement officials as well as civilians to assist in capturing runaway slaves.

Gang system: A mode of organizing labor that had West African antecedents. In this system American slaves worked in groups under the direction of a slave driver.

Gansta rap: A genre of rap music characterized by violent and sexist lyrics.

Gary Convention: Meeting of black leaders and organizations in Gary, Indiana to develop an agenda for black empowerment.

Grandfather clause: A method southern states used to disfranchise black men. It stipulated that only men whose grandfathers were eligible to vote were themselves eligible to vote. The U.S. Supreme Court invalidated the grandfather clause in 1915.

Great Dismal Swamp: A heavily forested area on the Virginia–North Carolina border that served as a refuge for fugitive slaves during the eighteenth and nineteenth centuries.

Griot: A West African self-employed poet and oral historian.

Guinea Coast: The southward-facing coast of West Africa, from which many of the people caught up in the Atlantic slave trade departed for the Americas.

Habeas corpus: A court order that a person arrested or detained by law enforcement officers must be brought to court and charged with a crime and not held indefinitely.

Hamburg Massacre: White Democrats attacked black Republicans in July 1876 in the village of Hamburg, South Carolina. Five black men were murdered as the Democrats began a violent effort to redeem the state.

Harlem Renaissance: As New York City became a destination for black migrants before, during, and after World War I, most of them settled in Harlem—a large neighborhood in the northern portion of Manhattan Island—which by the 1920s became a center of African-American cultural activities including literature, art, and music.

Harpers Ferry: *See* John Brown's raid.

Hierarchical: Refers to a social system based on class rank.

Hieroglyphics: A writing system based on pictures or symbols.

Hip-Hop: The back up music for rap. It is also the term for the youth culture that developed with the rise of rap music.

House of Burgesses: A representative body established at Jamestown, Virginia, in 1619.

House Un-American Activities Committee (HUAC):   Congressional committee formed to investigate the activities of communists and "communist sympathizers" in America.

Humanism: The belief that human achievement and interests are more important than theological issues.

Hunting and gathering societies: Small societies dependent on hunting animals and collecting wild plants rather than on agriculture.

Import duties: Taxes on goods brought into a country or colony.

Impressment: During the Civil War, Southern states and the Confederate government required slave owners to provide slaves to work on such public projects as fortifications, roads, and wharves. The owners (not the slaves) were usually compensated for the work.

Incest taboos: Customary rules against sexual relations and marriage within family and kinship groups.

Indigo: A bluish-violet dye produced from the indigo plant.

Industrial Revolution: An economic change that began in England during the early eighteenth century and spread to Continental Europe and the United States. Industry rather than agriculture became the dominant form of enterprise.

Jim Crow: Jump Jim Crow was a nineteenth-century dance ridiculing black people that was transformed by the twentieth century into a term meaning racial discrimination and segregation.

John Brown's raid: Brown's raid on Harpers Ferry, Virginia, in October 1859 failed to lead to a major slave insurrection, but it inflamed the controversy over slavery in the North and South.

Joint-stock companies: Primitive corporations that carried out British and Dutch colonization in the Americas during the seventeenth century.

Kansas-Nebraska Act, 1854:   Legislation introduced by Democratic Senator Stephen Douglas to organize the Kansas and Nebraska territories. It provided for "popular sovereignty," whereby settlers would decide whether slavery would be legal or illegal.

"Know-Nothing Party":   The nickname applied to members of the American Party, which opposed immigration in the 1850s.

Ku Klux Klan: A secret society founded by former Confederates in Pulaski, Tennessee, in 1866. It transformed itself into a terrorist organization during Reconstruction to drive black and white Republicans from political power in southern states. It disappeared by the late nineteenth century but was revived near Atlanta, Georgia, in 1915, as a powerful, white, Anglo-Saxon, Protestant political force in many states outside the South. It was revived again in the 1950s to oppose the civil rights movement.

Liberty Party (1840–1848):   The first antislavery political party. Most of its supporters joined the Free-Soil Party in 1848, although its radical New York wing maintained a Liberty organization into the 1850s.

Lincoln-Douglas debates: Abraham Lincoln and Stephen Douglas debated seven times in the 1858 U.S. Senate race in Illinois. They spent most of their time arguing over slavery, its expansion, the *Dred Scott* decision, and the character of African Americans. Douglas won the election.

Lineage: A type of clan, typical of West Africa, in which members claim descent from a single ancestor.

Lowndes County Freedom Organization (LCFO):   Political organization founded in 1965 by Stokely Carmichael.

Loyalists: Those Americans who, during the Revolutionary War, wished to remain within the British Empire.

Lynching: Killing by a mob without the benefit of a trial or conviction.

Manifest Destiny: A doctrine, prevalent during the nineteenth century, holding that God intended the United

States to expand territorially over all of North America and the Caribbean islands, or over the entire Western Hemisphere.

Manumission: The act of freeing a slave by the slave's master.

March on Washington Movement (MOWM):   Movement created by A. Philip Randolph to pressure the federal government to end discrimination in the defense industry and government.

Market revolution: The process between 1800 and 1860 by which an American economy based on subsistence farming, production by skilled artisans, and local markets changed into an economy marked by commercial farming, factory production, and national markets.

Master class: Slaveholders.

Matrilineal: Descent traced through the female line.

Middle Passage: The voyage of slave ships (slavers) across the Atlantic Ocean from Africa to the Americas.

Mississippi Freedom Democratic Party: Inter-racial group set up to challenge Mississippi's all-white delegation to the Democratic National Convention in 1964.

Missouri Compromise, 1820:   A congressional attempt to settle the issue of slavery expansion in the United States by permitting Missouri to enter the Union as a slave state, admitting Maine as a free state, and banning slavery in the rest of the Louisiana Purchase north of the 36° 30' line of latitude.

Montgomery Bus Boycott: Refusal from 1955 to 1957 of African Americans in Montgomery, Alabama to ride the city's buses until the bus lines were desegregated.

Moral suasion: A tactic endorsed by the American Anti-Slavery Society during the 1830s. It appealed to slaveholders and others to support immediate emancipation on the basis of Christian principles.

Moynihan Report: Report attributing many of the problems of poor black communities to the breakdown of the "lower-class" black family.

Nation of Islam: Religious movement that combines Islam with black nationalism.

National Industrial Recovery Act (NIRA):   Federal law intended to promote the revival of manufacturing by allowing for cooperation among industries.

National Negro Congress (NCC):   Organization founded in 1926 to unite African-American protest groups.

Negro National League: A professional baseball league for black players and teams organized in 1912.

New Deal: Set of policies proposed by the Roosevelt administration in response to the Great Depression.

New York City draft riot: In early July 1863 in opposition to the forthcoming military draft, rioting erupted in New York City. Many of the victims were black men, women, and children.

North Atlantic Treaty Organization: Military alliance formed to counter the threat posed by the Soviet Union and its allies.

North Star: A weekly newspaper published and edited by Frederick Douglass from 1847 to 1851. *Fredrick Douglass's Paper* (1851–1860) succeeded it.

Northwest Ordinance, 1787:   Based on earlier legislation drafted by Thomas Jefferson, it organized the Northwest Territory, providing for orderly land sales, public education, government, the creation of five to seven states out of the territory, and the prohibition of slavery within the territory.

Nuclear family: A family unit consisting solely of one set of parents and their children.

Nullification Crisis (1832–1833):   Arose when the South Carolina legislature declared the United States tariff "null and void" within the state's borders. President Andrew Jackson denounced the action as treasonous and threatened to use military force to uphold national supremacy.

Pan-Africanism: A movement of people of African descent from sub-Saharan Africa in the early twentieth century that emphasized their identity, shared experiences, and the need to liberate Africa from its European colonizers.

Patriarchal: A society ruled by a senior man.

Patrilineal: Descent through the male line.

Patriots: Those Americans who, during the Revolutionary War, favored independence.

Peace Mission Movement: Religious movement led by Father Major Jealous Divine.

Pennsylvania Society for Promoting the Abolition of Slavery (Pennsylvania Abolition Society: 1787–present):   An anti-slavery organization centered in Philadelphia and based on an earlier Quaker society. Exclusively white, it promoted gradual abolition, black self-improvement, freedom suits, and protection of African Americans against kidnapping.

Peonage: The system that forbade southern farmers, usually sharecroppers and renters, who accumulated debts to leave the land until the debt was repaid—often an impossible task. The U.S. Supreme Court outlawed peonage, but many landowners and merchants still forced farmers to remain on the land.

Philadelphia Female Anti-Slavery Society (1833–1870):   A biracial abolitionist organization aligned with the American Anti-Slavery Society. White Quaker women dominated the society, but it included a significant number of black women.

Phonetic script: A writing system based on symbols representing a single sound.

Pidgin: A simplified mixture of two or more languages used to communicate between people who speak different languages.

Plessy v. Ferguson: In 1896 in an 8-to-1 decision, the U.S. Supreme Court ruled that segregation did not violate the equal protection clause of the Fourteenth Amendment. The "separate but equal" doctrine remained the supreme law of the land until the 1954 *Brown vs. Board of Education* decision overturned *Plessy*.

Polygynous family: A family unit consisting of a man, his wives, and their children.

Polytheism: The worship of many gods.

Poor People's Campaign: Project supported by Martin Luther King involving the march of tens of thousands of poor people on Washington.

Popular sovereignty: The residents of a territory (such as Kansas) would vote to legalize or prohibit slavery in that territory.

Populist Party: Also known as the Peoples' Party, the Populists supported inflation, the free and unlimited coinage of silver and gold, government ownership of railroads, telephone, and telegraph companies, and an eight-hour workday. They won state and congressional elections but lost the presidential contests in 1892 and 1896.

Port Royal Experiment: An effort by Northern white missionaries, educators, and businessmen in the Sea Islands near Beaufort, South Carolina, to transform former slaves into educated, reliable, and industrious wage earners. Most of the freedmen did not acquire the land they worked.

Prince Hall Masons: A black Masonic order formed in 1791 in Boston under the leadership of Prince Hall. He became its first grand master and promoted its expansion to other cities.

Project 100,000:   Military project with the goal of reducing the number of African Americans rejected by the military.

Race films: Movies made for African-American audiences in the 1930s and 1940s.

Radical Republicans: Members of the Republican Party during Reconstruction who vigorously supported the rights of African Americans to vote, hold political office, and to have the same legal and economic opportunities as white people.

Rain forest: A dense growth of tall trees characteristic of hot, wet regions.

Rainbow Coalition: Political coalition of African Americans, workers, liberals, feminists, gay people, environmentalists, and others formed by Jesse Jackson in the 1980s.

Reconstruction: The twelve years (1865–1877) following the Civil War, during which the former Confederate states were restored to the Union and former slaves became citizens and gained the right to vote and hold political office. It was also a time of violence and terrorism as many southern white people resisted the change in the status of African Americans.

Reconstruction Acts, 1867:   Led by Radical Republicans, Congress divided the South into five military districts. Each former Confederate state (except Tennessee) was to frame a new state constitution and establish a new state government. The first Reconstruction Act provided for universal manhood suffrage, which granted the right to vote to all adult males, including black men.

Red Scare: The widespread fear among any Americans in the years immediately after World War I from about 1918 to about 1924 that Russia's 1917 Bolshevik Revolution might result in communists attempting to take over the U.S. government.

Redemption: The term used for the process, often violent, by which white conservative Democrats regained political control of a southern state from black and white Republicans during Reconstruction.

Renaissance: A humanist and artistic movement that began in Italy during the late fourteenth century and spread across Europe.

Rochester Convention, 1853:   African-American leaders assembled in Rochester, New York, to discuss slavery, abolition, the recently passed Fugitive Slave Law, and their prospects for life in America.

Savannah: A flat, nearly treeless grassland typical of large portions of West Africa.

Scalawag: The derogatory term used during Reconstruction to identify a native white southerner who supported black and white Republicans. They were considered traitors to their people and the Democratic Party.

Scottsboro Boys: Nine young African-American men unjustly accused of raping two white women in Alabama in 1931. The Supreme Court overturned their convictions in 1937.

Seasoning: The process by which newly arrived Africans were broken in to slavery in the Americas.

Second Great Awakening (1790s–1830s):   A widespread religious revival, centered in the North and upper South, that encouraged reform movements.

Secret societies: Social organizations that have secret ceremonies that only their members know about and can participate in.

Secularism: The belief that the present public welfare should predominate over religion in civil affairs.

Segregation: The separation of people based on their race in the use of such public facilities as hotels, restaurants, restrooms, drinking fountains, parks, and auditoriums. In many instances segregation meant the exclusion of black people.

Semitic: Refers to people who speak languages, such as Arabic and Hebrew, native to southwest Asia.

Sharecropping: The system following the Civil War in which former slaves worked land owned by white people and "paid" for the use of the land and for tools, seeds, fertilizer, and mules by sharing the crop—usually cotton—with the owner.

Shotgun policy: In Mississippi in 1875 white men resorted to violence and intimidation against black and white Republicans to regain political control of the state for conservative Democrats.

Slave power: A term used to indicate the political control exercised by slaveholders over the U.S. government before the Civil War.

Slaver: A ship used to transport slaves from Africa to the Americas.

Sons of Liberty: A secret American organization formed in the Northeast during the summer of 1765 and committed to forcible opposition to the Stamp Act.

Southern Christian Leadership Conference (SCLC):   Organization spearheaded by Martin Luther King, Jr. to provide an institutional base for the Civil Rights Movement.

Southern Homestead Act, 1866:   Congress passed this measure that set aside over 3 million acres of land for former slaves and loyal white Southerners to farm following the Civil War. Most of the land was not fertile or suitable for agriculture, and the act largely failed.

Southern Regional Council (SRC):   Organization that conducted research and focused attention on social, political, and educational inequality in the South.

Spanish Armada: A fleet that unsuccessfully attempted to carry out an invasion of England in 1588.

Special Field Order #15:   General William Tecumseh Sherman issued this military directive in January 1865. It set aside lands along the coast from Charleston, South Carolina, to Jacksonville, Florida, for former slaves. President Andrew Johnson revoked the order six months later.

Spirit possession: A belief rooted in West African religions that spirits may possess human souls.

Student Non-Violent Coordinating Committee (SNCC): Civil rights organization founded by black college students in 1960 at the initiative of Ella Baker.

Syracuse Convention, 1864: A meeting of black leaders in Syracuse, New York, to discuss the future of African Americans following the abolition of slavery. They insisted that black people had earned and deserved the same political and legal rights as white Americans.

Talented Tenth: Term coined by W. E. B. Du Bois for the educated black elite of the late nineteenth and early twentieth centuries. The upper 10 percent was supposed to assume responsibility for the leadership and advancement of the remaining 90 percent of African Americans.

Term slavery: A type of slavery prevalent in the Chesapeake from the late 1700s to the Civil War in which slaves were able to purchase their freedom from their masters by earning money over a number of years.

Terrell law: The Terrell law was a Texas law banning African-American participation in the Democratic primary.

The Great Society: Programs created in response to the problems of poor Americans championed by President Johnson.

Thirteenth Amendment, 1865: This amendment to the U.S. Constitution outlawed slavery and involuntary servitude.

Three-Fifths Clause: A clause in the U.S. Constitution providing that a slave be counted as three-fifths of a free person in determining a state's representation in Congress and the electoral college and three-fifths of a free person in regard to per capita taxes levied by Congress on the states.

Tuskegee Airmen: All-black combat air unit during World War II.

Tuskegee Machine: As the president of Tuskegee Institute, Booker T. Washington developed an extensive network of contacts that gave him extraordinary influence with white political leaders and philanthropists as well as with black businesspeople, journalists, and college presidents.

Tuskegee Study: A medical study by the U.S. Public Health Service of the effects of syphilis on 622 black men. The study ran from 1932 to the 1970s, and the men were given only placebos and no treatment for the disease.

Uncle Tom's Cabin: This antislavery novel by Harriet Beecher Stowe was a best seller in the 1850s and it helped inflame the controversy over slavery.

Underground Railroad: Refers to several loosely organized, semisecret biracial networks that helped slaves escape from the border South to the North and Canada. The earliest networks appeared during the first decade of the nineteenth century; others operated into the Civil War years.

Union League: A social and fraternal organization that stirred political interest and support among black and white Republicans in the South during Reconstruction.

Universal Negro Improvement Association (UNIA): Established in 1914 in Jamaica by Marcus Garvery, it fostered racial pride, African heritage, Christian faith, and economic uplift.

Voting Rights Act of 1965: Federal law banning the methods that had systematically excluded African Americans from registering or voting in southern elections.

Wilmot Proviso: A measure introduced in Congress in 1845 to prohibit slavery in any lands acquired from Mexico. It did not pass.

Biographical Glossary

Ralph David Abernathy (1926–1990)

A civil rights activist, Baptist clergyman, and leader in the modern Civil Rights Movement. Along with Dr. Martin Luther King Jr., Abernathy spearheaded the successful Montgomery Bus Boycott, which brought an end to racial segregation on the city's buses (1956). Was program chief of the Montgomery Improvement Association; was instrumental in the founding of the Southern Christian Leadership Conference (1957); and led numerous marches in Alabama, Georgia, Florida, and North Carolina. His leadership and activism in the Civil Rights Movement contributed to the enactment of the Voting Rights Act of 1964.

Muhammad Ali (1942–)

Born Cassius Marcellus Clay Jr.; was the first heavyweight to regain the title three times. Refused the Selective Service draft and to fight in the Vietnam War and was convicted in federal court, sentenced to five years imprisonment, fined $10,000, and stripped of his boxing title. With the help of NAACP attorneys, Ali's conviction was overturned in the U.S. Supreme Court, and he resumed boxing October 26, 1970. He retired in 1987, and was later inducted into the Boxing Hall of Fame.

King Sunni Ali of Songhai. (r. 1464–1492)

A descendant of a long line of Sunnis, the rulers of the Soninke people. Was instrumental in establishing the largest of the Sudanese empires. Never lost a battle, and under his leadership, the Songhai Empire became larger than Europe and solidly established as a dominant West African power.

Richard Allen (1760–1831)

Enslaved at birth; a noted abolitionist involved in the Underground Railroad Effort. Went on to become a successful businessman, an ordained deacon, and an itinerant preacher for both black and white Methodists. Led the Independent Black Church Movement; founded Philadelphia's Mother Bethel African Church (1794); founded and was the first bishop of the African Methodist Episcopal Church; was responsible for the spread of AME churches across the United States; was a co-founder of the Free African Society (1817); and presided over the first National Negro Convention.

Maya Angelou (1928–)

A poet, writer, and actress; among the most profound African-American writers of the twentieth century. Between 1979 and 1986 had written five autobiographies, each one representing various stages of her life. Also noted for her poems; has published six volumes of poetry since 1971. Wrote a ten-part PBS series, *Black, Blues, Blacks* (1968); a screenplay turned film, *Georgia Georgia* (1971); and *Sister Sister* (1979). Also appeared in Alex Haley's *Roots*. Her national and international fame resulted from her poem "*On the Pulse of Morning*," delivered during President-elect Bill Clinton's 1992 inauguration.

Molefe Asante (1942–)

Born Arthur Lee Smith; developed a reputation as a prolific scholar and co-founder of the concept of afrocentricity. Scholarly works include *Afrocentricity: The Theory of Social Change* (1980); *The Afrocentric Idea* (1987); and *African American Culture* (1998). Has served as editor of the *Journal of Black Studies* and chair of Temple University's African-American Studies department, the first doctorate-granting Black Studies department in the United States.

Crispus Attucks (1723–1770)

A slave who escaped from his owner in 1750. On March 5, 1770, led a multi-racial group of 50–60 working people to march against the British military occupation of Boston and to attack the main guard. Became the first person to die in what is now known as the Boston Massacre.

Ella Baker (1903–1986)

A political activist, organizer, and leading civil rights figure. Held various offices within the national NAACP; was a co-founder of In Friendship (1956), organized to raise funds for the growing civil rights struggle; and belonged to the Southern Christian Leadership Conference (1957) and Mississippi Freedom Democratic Party (1964). Most noted for organizing a conference of black student sit-in leaders at Shaw University (1960), which led to the founding of the Student Non-Violent Coordinating Committee (SNCC).

James Baldwin (1924–1987)

A prolific writer and civil rights activist. Publications include *Go Tell It on the Mountain* (1953), *The Fire Next Time* (1963), and *If Beale Street Could Talk* (1974). Works examined issues of race, class, gender, and sex; he created a literary voice allowing him to emerge as the most popular and most widely read African-American authors of the twentieth century.

Benjamin Banneker (1731–1806)

An inventor, scientist, mathematician, surveyor, author, and abolitionist. In 1761, constructed the first wooden clock that kept accurate time; was also instrumental in surveying the streets of Washington, D.C. Published a series of almanacs from 1791–1802, including *Benjamin Banneker's PA, DE, MD, and VA Almanak* (sic) *and Emphemiris for the Year of Our Lord, 1792.*

Joe Louis Barrow (1914–1981)

The son of Alabama sharecroppers in Lafayette, Alabama; became the world boxing heavyweight champion in 1937, a title he would hold until 1949. Known as "The Brown Bomber," his boxing career spanned more than twenty-five years, winning sixty-eight of seventy-one professional fights with fifty-four knock-outs.

Mary McLeod Bethune (1875–1955)

Born to former slaves; known as an educator, administrator, and noted clubwoman. Established Dayton Normal and Industrial School for Negro Girls (1904) which became Bethune Cookman College (1927). Served as an advisor to five consecutive presidents. Served as director of the New Deal's National Youth Administration's Di-

vision of Negro Affairs (1936–1943); special assistant to the U.S. Secretary of War (1945); president of the National Association of Colored Women from 1924–1928; and founded the National Council of Negro Women in 1935.

Arna Bontemps (1902–1973)

A famous writer, poet, and a prominent figure in the Harlem Renaissance; Bontemps's themes reflected protest, liberation, and race pride. First published works included *Black Thunder* (1936) and *Drums at Dusk* (1939), followed by three other books. Co-authored four books with Jack Conroy and Langston Hughes, and, between 1942 and 1951, a series of original tales for children. Bontemps was the recipient of the *Crisis Magazine* award for *A Black Man Reaping* (1926) and the Alexander Pushkin Award for Poetry (1926 and 1927) for *Golgotha Is a Mountain*; and *The Return*.

Aaron A. Bradley (1815–1881)

Born a slave in South Carolina; insisted that freedmen needed land ownership to ensure their independence. Criticized the Freedmen's Bureau for forcing black people off the land promised by General William T. Sherman's Field Order #15; called for the impeachment of President Andrew Johnson for supporting treasonous Confederate landowners rather than those who had been loyal to the Union.

James Brown (1933–2006)

Once a headliner for Harlem's Apollo Theater; known as "The Godfather of Soul" and "Soul Brother Number One." Recorded more than seventy albums including hit singles *Try Me* (1958), *Cold Sweat* (1967), and *Say It Loud, I'm Black and I'm Proud* (1968), which became the anthem of race pride. Appeared in *The Blues Brothers* and *Rocky IV*, for which he won a Grammy for Best Rhythm and Blues performance for the hit, *Living in America*. Inducted into the Rock 'n' Roll Hall of Fame (1986).

Blanche Kelso Bruce (1841–1898)

Born to a black slave mother and a white plantation owner; in 1864, moved to Hannibal, Missouri, and established Missouri's first school for blacks. While living in Mississippi, held the position of Tallahatchie County registrar of voters and tax assessor; sheriff of Bolivar County; tax collector; supervisor of education; and editor of a local newspaper. Was elected to the Senate in 1874 on the Republican ticket; was appointed in 1881 by President James Garfield to be the register of the Treasury, making him the first African American whose signature was represented on U.S. currency. Later served as the recorder of deeds for Washington, D.C., and again registrar of the Treasury until his death in 1898.

Ralph Bunche (1904–1971)

A federal government official, diplomat, and educator; was the first African American to win the Nobel peace prize. In 1950, received national and international attention for successfully negotiating a cease fire between Egypt and Israel during the Arab-Israeli crisis by crafting the "Four Armistice Agreements." His government service included undersecretary of special political affairs (1957–1967) and undersecretary general, the highest positions ever held by an African American at the United Nations.

Selma Burke (1900–1995)

A nurse, sculptor and educator; noted for sculpturing Franklin Delano Roosevelt's profile on a bronze plaque mounted on the Recorder of Deeds Building in Washington, D.C. (1945) and a bust of Mary McLeod Bethune. Other works include *Grief, Falling Angel, Mother and Child*, and *Torso*, which were made of stone, wood, alabaster and brass, respectively. Established the Selma Burke School of Art in New York (1946).

Anthony Burns (c. 1829–1862)

The subject and center of one of the most notorious cases confronting the Fugitive Slave Law of 1850. A minister who studied Divinity at Oberlin College, Burns immigrated to Canada, where he serviced its fugitive slave community.

Richard Harvey Cain (1825–1887)

Born to free parents; eventually moved to South Carolina, where he was a delegate to the state constitutional convention of 1868 as well as a member of the state senate from 1868 to 1870. Served on the Committee of Agriculture with the Forty-third Congress working for passage of a civil rights bill introduced in 1870. Became a bishop in the A.M.E. Church in 1880 and helped set up Paul Quinn College in Waco, Texas, serving as its president until 1884.

Maude Callen (1898–1990)

A highly competent, dedicated, and well-respected nurse-midwife; delivered babies and provided other forms of medical treatment under the most mundane circumstances to impoverished African Americans in rural Berkeley County, South Carolina. Her work and commitment led to better health among African Americans by providing them access to medical care not otherwise afforded them.

Francis Cardozo (1837–1903)

Born free in Charleston, South Carolina; in 1866, became superintendent of the Avery Normal Institute in Charleston, which was created to train African-American teachers. A political moderate, served as a delegate to the 1868 South Carolina state constitutional convention and later as secretary of state (1868–1872), becoming South Carolina's first African American to hold government office. Was state treasurer for five years until 1887; later appointed to the Treasury Department in Washington, D.C. Worked as the principal of the Colored High School from 1884 to 1896.

Stokely Carmichael (1941–1998)

Known as a civil rights and political activist who rose to prominence during the Civil Rights Movement. Elected SNCC chairman in 1966; coined the phrase "Black Power." Wrote *Stokely Speaks* (1971) and is the co-author of *Black Power* (1967) with Charles V. Hamilton. After leaving SNCC in 1967, became honorary prime minister of the Black Panther Party, quitting in 1969.

William Carney (1840-c. 1901)
Enlisted in the Morgan Guards in 1863, which eventually became part of the 54th Massachusetts regiment, a regiment that saw horrific battle against Fort Wagner; despite being wounded four times, braved enemy bullets to rescue the regiment's flag. Left the service in 1864, moved to New Bedford, Massachusetts, before moving to California. In May 1900, became the first African American to receive the Congressional Medal of Honor.

Eldridge Cleaver (1935–1998)
A writer, radical leader, and a member of the Black Panther Party for Self-Defense. Wrote two significant books, his autobiography and best-seller, *Soul on Ice* (1968), and *Soul on Fire* (1978). While awaiting a return to prison for a parole violation, fled with his wife, also a Black Panther, and their son, to Cuba and later, Algeria, where he founded the international branch of the Black Panther Party.

Daniel Coker (1780–1846)
A prominent abolitionist, black clergyman, and Black Nationalist; wrote an abolitionist pamphlet entitled *A Dialogue Between a Virginian and an African Minister* (1810). In 1816, joined Richard Allen and representatives from five black Methodist societies in Philadelphia to establish the first independent African Methodist Episcopal Church, a meeting that led to the formation of African Bethel Church. Emigrated to Africa in 1820, residing in Liberia and Sierra Leone, working as a missionary, and superintendent of a colony established by the British for recaptured Africans.

Samuel Cornish (1795–1858)
A leading clergyman and founding member of the American Missionary Society; co-founder of the American Anti-Slavery Society (1835); a member of New York City's Vigilance Committee; and wrote *The Colonization Scheme Considered* (1840), opposing the colonization of black people. Established *Freedom's Journal* (1827), the first African-American newspaper in the United States and created the Black Press, which led to the emergence of black newspapers across the country.

Paul Cuffe (1759–1817)
The son of a former slave and Wampanoag Indian; amassed a fortune from whaling, coastal shipping, and trading in the Caribbean and Europe, becoming a wealthy merchant mariner and ship builder. Was a civil rights activist, black nationalist, philanthropist, abolitionist, and successful ship builder. Championed voting rights for blacks and against taxation without representation. Supported the emigration of blacks to Africa, using his own funds to transport 38 people to Sierra Leone, West Africa.

Countee Cullen (1903–1946)
Remembered as one of the finest American poets of the Harlem Renaissance; even before graduating from New York University, his poem *Yet Do I Marvel* was published to critical acclaim. His first collection of poetry, *Color*, was published in 1925 during his senior year. Literary scholars hailed his novel *One Way to Heaven*, published in 1934, as a finely crafted black satire. Cullen spent time as a teacher in the New York City school system before he died.

Angela Davis (1944–)
One of the most celebrated political activists, radicals, controversial figures, and African-American women in U.S. history. In 1970, was listed on the Federal Bureau of Investigation's Ten Most Wanted list for murder, conspiracy, and smuggling guns; her sixteen-month incarceration before her trial led to a nationwide campaign to "Free Angela." Two years later she was acquitted of all charges. Is also the author of several books including *Angela Davis: An Autobiography* (1974) and *Women, Race and Politics* (1989).

Miles Davis (1926–1991)
A jazz trumpeter and composer; was one of the most influential musicians in America during the 1950s and 1960s. Pioneered a style of music called "fusion," a blending of jazz and rock elements; and created the concept of modal jazz, which involves scales instead of chord changes to determine a song's harmony. Popular recordings include *Round about Midnight* (1955); *Milestones* (1958); and *Bitches Brew* (1969).

Martin R. Delaney (1812–1885)
The son of a free black mother and enslaved father; an abolitionist, emigrationist, Civil War veteran, and author. With the passage of the Fugitive Slave Law (1850), advocated black emigration and successfully organized such conferences biennially from 1854–1858 for a proposed settlement in West Africa. Established the *Mystery* (1843–1847), the first African-American newspaper published west of the Allegheny Mountains and was the author of three books and a novel including *The Condition, Elevation, Emigration, and Destiny of the Colored People of the United States, Politically Considered* (1852) and *The Political Destiny of the Colored Race* (1854).

Charles Deslondes (d. 1811)
A native and refugee of St. Domingue, Haiti; organized slaves on surrounding plantations, fugitive slaves, and maroons living in nearby swamps and mountain communities. Led a slave revolt on January 8, 1811, with approximately 180 enslaved men and women, which ended after two days. With twenty other slaves were convicted of insurrection by a tribunal of five plantation owners; were taken to the plantations of their slave owners, where they were shot, beheaded, and their heads placed on poles as a warning to other slaves.

Ayubu Sulieman Diallo of Bondu (c.1701–1773)
Born in Africa where he was enslaved; eventually returned to his family in Africa. Was transported to England in 1733 by James Oglethorpe, director of England's Royal African Company; he returned home only to find a considerable increase in the slave trade, his family suffering, and a gradual invasion of Moroccans. Eventually used his ties to England to assist the Royal African Company in the slave trade, despite his own enslavement.

Father Major J. Divine (1879–1965)
Born George Baker in Savannah, Georgia, to parents who were sharecroppers; founded the Peace Mission Movement in 1930, a non-denominational and interracial organization which attracted people from all walks of life, and established extensions across the United States. Was also a civil rights activist and through his movement challenged racism in America.

Thomas Dorsey (1899–1993)
A gospel music composer and accomplished pianist, called the "Father of Gospel Music;" his notoriety came with composing the song *Take My Hand, Precious Lord* (1932),

one of black gospel music's classics. Established the first publishing house for the exclusive sale of gospel music composed by African Americans in the United States, and was partially responsible for organizing the first National Convention of Gospel Choirs.

Aaron Douglass (1899–1988)
A premier painter and educator; most noted for his painting of murals depicting African-American culture and history at Fisk, Chicago's Sherman Hotel, and Bennett College, Greensboro, North Carolina. Founder of the Carl Van Vechten Art Gallery (1949) at Fisk University. In 1963, was honored by President John F. Kennedy at a reception commemorating the centennial of the Emancipation Proclamation; won the Academy of Arts Outstanding Achievement Award (1972); received a Julius Rosenwald fellowship; and was awarded an honorary degree of Doctor of Fine Arts from Fisk University.

Frederick Douglass (1817–1895)
Born a slave, but went on to become an influential anti-slavery lecturer, author, and journalist. Authored three autobiographies, including the *Narrative of the Life of Frederick Douglass, an American Slave* (1845) and *My Bondage, My Freedom* (1855); founded the *North Star* (1847–1851). Involved in the National Negro Convention Movement and was a supporter of woman's suffrage. Received political appointments during the Reconstruction era including as a U.S. Marshall (1877–1881) and recorder of deeds for the District of Columbia (1881–1886).

W. E. B. Du Bois (1868–1968)
A noted intellectual and great thinker; became the first African American to earn a doctorate from Harvard (1895). An opponent of Booker T. Washington's "accommodation" theory; helped found the Niagara Movement (1905). Noted for his landmark work *The Soul of Black Folk* (1903). In 1909, founded the National Association for the Advancement of Colored People (NAACP) with a group of supporters. In 1961, joined the Communist party, moved to Ghana, and renounced his American citizenship.

Robert Duncanson (c.1821–1872)
The first African-American artist to paint landscapes as an expression of his cultural identity; thirty-five of his fifty-four paintings and portraits were exhibited at the Centennial Exposition sponsored by the Cincinnati Art Museum in 1972. Recognized as the best landscape painter in the West and is most noted for *Land of the Lotus Eaters* (1861).

Katherine Dunham (1909–)
A choreographer and dancer; was the first person to organize a professional black dance troupe of concert caliber (1939). Established three dance schools, the first in Chicago (1931); the Katherine Dunham School for the Arts and Research in New York (1943); and in East St. Louis, the Performing Arts Training Center (1967). Became the first black choreographer for the New York Metropolitan Opera with the Broadway play *Aida* (1963).

Marian Wright Edelman (1939–2006)
A graduate of Yale's Law School; the first African-American woman to pass the Mississippi bar examination. Established the Children's Defense Fund (1973), which focused on the national needs of children including nutrition, child abuse, childcare, and education.

Edward Kennedy "Duke" Ellington (1899–1974)
Considered by many to be the greatest American jazz composer; known as a major force in jazz that continues to this day mainly for his performances at the legendary Cotton Club. His many hits include *Take the A Train* (words and music by Billy Strayhorn), *Satin Doll*, "Rockin' in Rhythm," *Mood Indigo*, *Sophisticated Lady*, and *It Don't Got That Thing if It Ain't Got That Swing*, Awarded the Presidential Medal of Freedom in 1969 and the Legion of Honor by France in 1973, the highest civilian honors of each country.

Robert Brown Elliott (1842–1884)
Born in England; immigrated to the United States, studied law, and opened an office in Columbia, South Carolina. Became a member of the state constitutional convention in 1868 and was later elected to the state house of representatives. Was assistant adjutant general of South Carolina 1869–1871; elected on the Republican ticket to the Forty-second and Forty-third Congresses. Resigned on November 1, 1874, and returned to the South Carolina state house where he served as speaker.

April Ellison (1790–1861)
A mulatto slave who apprenticed to William McCreight, a gin-maker; learned carpentry, blacksmithing, and the maintenance of cotton gins. Established a lucrative gin-making and gin-repair shop in Statesburg, South Carolina which attracted both black and white patrons. One of the South's wealthiest real estate owners who within four years of purchasing his freedom had acquired more success than most white southerners had in a lifetime.

Ralph Ellison (1914–1994)
A writer who gained prominence in 1952, with the publication of *Invisible Man*, considered a "masterwork." Other noted works include a collection of essays and reviews, *Shadow and Act* (1964), *Going to the Territory* (1987), and also a collection of essays which attempted to define the African-American life and culture. Was the recipient of several awards: the National Book Award, the National Newspaper's Publisher's Russwurm Award, and *Chicago Defender* award for *Invisible Man*, all in 1953; and the Medal of Freedom presented by President Lyndon B. Johnson (1969).

Olaudah Equiano (c. 1745–1797)
Born in Nigeria and sold into slavery; purchased his freedom in 1766 from Robert King, a Philadelphia Quaker, becoming an author and working as an abolitionist. He published a narrative about his kidnapping, *The Life of Oladauh Equiano*, a work that enabled readers to understand the horrors of every aspect of slavery and which consisted of eight British editions, one American publication in his lifetime, and ten posthumous editions.

Dr. Matilda A. Evans (1872–1935)
A surgeon; became the first woman licensed to practice medicine in South Carolina. Established Taylor Lane Hospital and Training School in 1901 to provide medical treatment for black families and to train black physicians and nurses. Created the Negro Health Association of South Carolina, a statewide association designed to educate blacks about health-care issues and appropriate treatment. In addition, founded the

Columbia Clinic Association in Columbia, South Carolina, with no charge for patient services.

Medgar Evers   (1925–1963)
Was a symbol of outstanding and dedicated leadership during and after the civil rights era; was Mississippi's first NAACP field director whose responsibility was to investigate the murder of blacks. His fight against Jim Crowism led to the bombing of his home and subsequent assassination, June 12, 1963, which contributed to President John F. Kennedy's request of Congress to enact a comprehensive civil rights law.

James Farmer   (1920–1999) Most noted for his civil rights activities and a leading figure during the 1960s in the Civil Rights Movement; was principal founder and director of the Chicago-based Congress on Racial Equality (CORE) in 1942. Organized the first freedom rides in 1961, designed to desegregate interstate transportation and bus terminals in the South. Worked with the Student Nonviolent Coordinating Committee (SNCC), and was instrumental in planning sit-ins, voter registration drives, and protest marches in the North and South.

James Forten   (1746–1818)
Born free; a businessman, leading abolitionist, and respected leader in Philadelphia's free black community. Abolitionist activities involved petitioning Congress to amend the 1793 Fugitive Slave Law; co-founding the American Anti-Slavery Society (1833); advocating an immediate end to slavery; and using his home as a station on the Underground Railroad. Participated in the first National Negro Convention held in Philadelphia September 1830. In 1832, with other African Americans, petitioned the Pennsylvania State Legislature requesting that it not restrict the immigration of free blacks into the state.

Aretha Franklin   (1942–)
A gospel and rhythm and blues singer; was crowned the "Queen of Soul" in 1968 when her album *Lady Soul* dominated the music charts. Has recorded more than thirty-five albums with seventeen number one hits. Honors include fifteen Grammy Awards; three American Music Awards; the Lifetime Achievement Award from the National Academy of Recording Arts and Sciences (1994); a Grammy Living Legend Award; and the Kennedy Center Honors Award (1994). In 1987, was the first female singer inducted into the Music Hall of Fame.

Elizabeth Freeman   (1744–1811)
Born a slave; was the first slave to file a lawsuit against her slave owner and to be granted her freedom by a state court. The ruling in the lawsuit resulted in the first court decision construing a state constitutional provision as inconsistent with the institution of slavery.

Henry Highland Garnet   (1815–1882)
Born a slave in New Market Maryland but was raised in a free African-American community. A leading abolitionist and religious leader, Garnet used his church—the African Methodist Episcopal Church—as a station on the Underground Railroad. Edited anti-slavery newspapers, the *Clarion* (1842) and *National Watchman* (1847). Was active in the Liberty Party and the Black Convention Movement, and during the 1843 and 1847 conventions, his speech, "Address to the Slaves of the United States of America," urged slaves to strike against their slave owners. Was president of the African Civilization Society (1858) which sought to create a home for "educated and skilled" African Americans in the Niger Valley.

William Lloyd Garrison   (1805–1879)
The son of an itinerant seaman who deserted his family; noted for his staunch abolitionism and reputation as a journalistic crusader. Originally in favor of ridding the United States of free and emancipated African Americans, he later reversed his opinion and founded the New England Anti-Slavery Society in 1832 and co-founded the American Anti-Slavery Society (1833). Was founder and editor of the *Liberator* (1831), an anti-slavery newspaper.

Marcus Garvey   (1887–1940)
Born in Jamaica; started a series of newspapers beginning in 1910. In 1914, founded the Universal Negro Improvement and Conservation Association and African Communities League (UNIA). Most well known for his quest to create a permanent homeland for black people in Africa by seeking to develop Liberia, a plan that never came to fruition due to opposition from European powers with interests in Liberia. In 1929, founded the People's Political Party (PPP), Jamaica's first modern political party to promote workers' rights, education, and aid to the poor.

Henry Louis Gates   (1950–)
African-American literary critic, writer, and scholar; was instrumental in preserving the works of early African-American women in the *Oxford Schomburg Library of Nineteenth-Century Black Women Writers*, a thirty-volume set of books (1988). Has authored, edited, and co-edited a number of important books including the *Norton Anthology of African-American Literature* (1990); *The Encyclopedia of the African and African-American Experience* (1999); and the acclaimed *Signifying Monkey: Towards a Theory of African-American Literary Criticism* (1988). Is director of Harvard University's W. E. B. Du Bois Institute for African and African-American Research.

Jonathan C. Gibbs   (1827–1874)
Born in Philadelphia, Pennsylvania, to well-to-do free parents. After the Civil War, opened a school in North Carolina for freed slaves in North Carolina, before moving to Charleston, South Carolina, where he spent two years campaigning for black rights. In 1867, moved to Florida, taught newly freed slaves, and became the state's highest ranking black official serving as secretary of state (1868), becoming the only African American in the cabinet at that time. Was state superintendent of public instruction in charge of Florida's schools, working to improve the school system.

Mifflin Webster Gibbs   (1823–1915)
Born to well-to-do free parents; worked as an abolitionist and served in the Underground Railroad before becoming a prominent citizen in San Francisco and British Columbia. Edited an abolitionist newspaper and wrote for the leading black newspaper of the day. Was the first African American municipal judge of Little Rock, Arkansas. Served as a delegate to each Republican national convention until 1896, and was appointed United States consul to Madagascar.

Dizzy Gillespie   (1917–1993)
Was one of the greatest jazz trumpeters of the twentieth century and a primary architect of bebop, organizing the first bebop band and establishing the standard for bebop trumpeters. Played with Earl "Fatha" Hines, Billy Eckstein, and Fletcher Hen-

derson. Numerous recordings include classics *Groovin' High* and *A Night in Tunisia*, which he arranged and composed.

Charlotte Forten Grimké   (1837–1914)
Antislavery activist, poet, educator, and abolitionist; noted for the unique journals she kept that chronicled her life as an elite free black woman before the Civil War. Enlisted in the Port Royal Experiment as a teacher in 1862 and taught on Saint Helena Island for two years; an account of her experiences as a teacher on Saint Helena Island was published in the *Atlantic Monthly* in 1864.

Alex Haley   (1921–1992)
A journalist and novelist; best known for his book *Roots: The Saga of an American Family* (1976), which tells the story of his family's beginning in West Africa as enslaved Africans and African Americans, and free people at the Civil War's end. Aired as a television special in 1977, it was considered the single most spectacular educational experience in American race relations. Also noted for writing another bestseller, *The Autobiography of Malcolm X* (1965), which was based on a series of oral interviews with him.

Prince Hall   (1735–1807)
Born to a white English father and a free mother of African and French descent; later became a slave. After becoming free established a business called the "Golden Fleece," which was a leather workshop. Was a businessman, an early abolitionist; activist, civic leader, and masonic organizer. Petitioned the Massachusetts Legislature (1777), to abolish slavery; also established a school for black children. Most noted for founding what became the first African-American Masonic Lodge in America (1787) and the largest and most prestigious fraternal order of African Americans, the Prince Hall Masons.

Fannie Lou Hamer   (1917–1977)
Known as a civil rights activist and grassroots organizer; was a field secretary for SNCC; organized voter registration campaigns; and co-founded the Mississippi Freedom Democratic Party (MFDP) in 1964, which challenged the seating of the all-white Democratic delegation to the 1964 Democratic National Convention, Atlantic City, New Jersey. Also noted for the statement, "I am sick and tired of being sick and tired."

Jupiter Hammon   (1711–c.1806)
An enslaved African; went on to become a Calvinist minister, poet, and writer. On December 25, 1760, became the first published African-American poet in the United States with "An Evening of Thought: Salvation By Christ with Penitential Cries." Other works include: "An Essay on the Ten Virgins" (1779); "A Poem for Children, With Thoughts on Death"; "An Evening's Improvement" with poetical dialogue entitled "The Kind Master and Dutiful Servant," "A Winter Piece," and "An Address to Phillis Wheatley: Ethiopian Poetess in Boston" (1788); and his most recognized work "An Address to the Negroes of the State of New York, Presented to the Free African Society of New York" (1786).

W. C. Handy   (1873–1958)
An African-American blues composer, considered by many as the father of the blues; one of the most influential of American songwriters. Following publication of his autobiography, published a subsequent book on African-American musicians entitled *Unsung Americans Sing*, which was published in 1944. Wrote five books on blues, composers, and Negro spirituals.

Frances Ellen Watkins Harper   (1825–1911)
A pioneering journalist, author of fiction and poetry, professional lecturer, abolitionist, women's rights activist, and noted clubwoman who attained national prominence as a nineteenth-century writer. Primary works include *Poems of Miscellaneous Subjects* (1854); *The Two Offers*, a short story (1859); *Sketches of Southern Life* (1872); and *Iola Leroy or Shadows Uplifted* (1892), a novel. Credited for introducing African-American protest in poetry and noted as the "Empress of Peace and Poet Laureate."

William Hastie   (1904–1976)
A distinguished law professor and civil rights attorney; also served as dean of Howard University Law School. Held a number of high positions in national government, including assistant solicitor of the Department of the Interior; a federal judge of the Danish West Indies (1937); and a civilian aide to the U.S. secretary of war (1941–1943), a post he resigned from on January 5, 1943, in protest of racial discrimination and segregation in the armed forces. Became the first African-American governor of the Virgins Islands (1946) and was appointed a judge on the Third United States Circuit Court of Appeals (1949).

Anita Hill   (1956–)
A law professor, attorney, and government appointee; gained national attention when she accused Clarence Thomas, a nominee to the U.S. Supreme Court, of unwanted explicit sexual remarks and innuendo during a Federal Bureau of Investigation interview. Although Thomas was confirmed on October 15, 1991, Hill's courage shed new light on the issue of sexual harassment in the workplace.

Billie Holiday   (1915–1959)
One of America's most influential jazz singers and greatest musicians; perhaps the greatest jazz singer ever recorded. A soloist, is noted for the hit songs she performed in 1939 *Strange Fruit* and *God Bless the Child*. Also appeared in *Black Singing City Blues* (1935) with Duke Ellington's Symphony. In 1946, performed three songs in the movie *New Orleans* with Louis Armstrong. Her autobiography, *Lady Sings the Blues*, became a full-length film in 1972.

James Mercer Langston Hughes   (1902–1967)
Poet, playwright, and newspaper columnist; also an avid traveler who spent time in Paris, the Soviet Union, and Japan. Is noted for the following works: the poem "The Negro Speaks of Rivers" in the *Crisis*, edited by W. E. B. Du Bois; his first book of poetry, *The Weary Blues* (1926); his first novel, *Not Without Laughter*, (1930); and other novels, short stories, and plays which were influenced by blues and jazz. Hughes's works had a profound influence on the artistic contribution of the Harlem Renaissance of the 1920s. Received a Guggenheim Fellowship in 1935 and was inducted into the National Institute of Arts and Letters in 1961.

Zora Neale Hurston   (1891–1960)
An African-American folklorist and author; studied anthropology at both Barnard College under Franz Boas and Columbia University. In 1931, collaborated with Langston Hughes on the play *Mule Bone*, and published her first novel, *Jonah's Gourd Vine* in 1934. Her best-known work is thought to be *Their Eyes Were Watching God*, her second novel. Hurston's work was out of the mainstream and largely ignored until 1975, when Alice Walker published an article about her in *Ms.* magazine.

Jesse L. Jackson (1941–)

Known for his charisma, great oratory, civil rights activism, and participation in national politics. Founded Operation PUSH (People United to Save Humanity) in Chicago (1971). Established a Rainbow Coalition; ran two U.S. presidential bids in 1984 and 1988, garnering an estimated 3.3 million of 18 million votes and 7 million of 23 million votes, respectively. Noted for the slogans "I Am Somebody" and "Keep Hope Alive," which provided a sense of self and empowerment for many people.

Mahalia Jackson (1912–1972)

A famous gospel singer; won a gold record for the most sales of a gospel record for *Move on Up a Little Higher* and was the official soloist of the National Baptist Convention. Had a weekly radio show on CBS in 1954. Sang at President John F. Kennedy's 1961 inaugural ball; at the 1963 March on Washington, just before Dr. Martin L. King's "I Have a Dream" speech; and at his funeral in 1968, singing Thomas Dorsey's *Take My Hand, Precious Lord.*

James W. Johnson (1871–1938)

Enjoyed an extraordinary life and career serving as U.S. consul in Venezuela and Nicaragua; as secretary of the NAACP; as founder of one newspaper and longtime editor of another; as a lyricist for the Broadway songwriting team of Cole and Johnson Brothers; and as novelist, poet, and anthologist. In 1934, was appointed visiting professor of literature at the New York University School of Education, the first African American to hold a position there.

John Arthur "Jack" Johnson (1878–1946)

Born to former slaves, and better known as Jack Johnson, was the first black heavyweight champion of the World, from 1908 to 1915, and perhaps the best heavyweight of his generation; admitted to the Boxing Hall of Fame in 1954. Flouted conventions regarding the "place" of African Americans in white society. After losing his title in a bout in Cuba in 1920, served a year in prison for allegedly violating the Mann Act because he sent his white girlfriend a railroad ticket to travel from Pennsylvania to Illinois.

Absalom Jones (1746–1818)

Born a slave; was an abolitionist, clergyman, and a leader in Philadelphia's free black community. Became the first African American to petition Congress to abolish slavery and the slave trade in 1797. Other accomplishments include spearheading the Independent Black Church Movement; becoming the first African-American priest ordained by the Protestant Episcopal Church in the United States (1804) and the first minister of St. Thomas African Episcopal Church (1794); co-founding Philadelphia's Free African Society (1787); and founding the Augustine Literary Society (1817).

LeRoi Jones, aka (Imamu Amiri Baraka) (1934–)

A major contributor to the literary field as a poet, author, essayist, playwright, and leader in the Black Arts Movement. Works include *Preface to a Twenty-Volume Suicide Note* (1961); *Home* (1966); *The Dutchman* (1964); and *The Slave* (1965).

Scott Joplin (1867–1917)

A pianist and composer; composed *Maple Leaf Rag*, one of the most popular pieces of "ragtime" music ever recorded. The song boosted Joplin to the top of the list of ragtime performers and moved ragtime into prominence as a musical form. Ragtime music experienced two bursts of popularity, in the early 1950s when it was regarded as nostalgic music from a more innocent time and again in the movie *The Sting.*

Barbara Jordan (1936–1996)

An educator and attorney; most noted for a distinguished political career as a state senator and U.S. congresswoman. In 1966, became the first African American from Texas to be elected to its state senate since 1883; the first African-American senator to chair a major committee (Labor and Management Relations); and the first freshman senator ever named to the Texas Legislative Council. Was unanimously elected pro tempore of the Texas State Legislature in March 1972, and eight months later, elected to the U.S. House of Representatives.

Vernon Jordan (1935–)

A civil rights activist and prominent attorney; noted for helping orchestrate the desegregation of the University of Georgia while serving as field secretary of the Georgia NAACP. Was director of the Southern Regional Council's Education Project (1964–1968); head of the United Negro College Fund; and a delegate to President Lyndon Johnson's White House Conference on Civil Rights. For ten years, was CEO of the National Urban League (1971–1981); his close relationship with Bill Clinton through two presidential terms enabled Jordan to become a power broker in Washington, D.C.

Elizabeth Keckley (c. 1818–1907)

Born a slave who later became a skilled dressmaker; founded The Ladies Contraband Relief Association and enlisted the support of client Mrs. Lincoln to help gather funds and clothing for the poor former slaves. Though sympathetic to the plight of African Americans, felt superior to the people she helped; her memoir, *Behind the Scenes,* published in 1868, reflects her condescending attitude as well as important, firsthand revelations about Mary Lincoln's private life. Died in poverty in 1907 at the Home for Destitute Women and Children in Washington, one of the institutions she had helped to found.

Jamaica Kincaid (1949–)

One of the most important Caribbean writers of her time. Between 1983 and 2005, has published eight fiction books, and eight nonfiction works. They include *At the Bottom of the River* (1983), *Annie John* (1985), and *The Autobiography of My Mother* (1996). Has received numerous awards such as the Morton Dauwen Zabel Award from the American Academy and Institute of Arts and Letters, and Lila Wallace-Reader's Digest Fund writer's award.

Coretta Scott King (1927–2006)

Wife and helpmate of civil rights pioneer, Martin Luther King, Jr. After her husband's assassination, was keynote speaker for the Poor People's Campaign at the Lincoln Memorial (1968); led a march of sanitation workers in Memphis; was successful in her efforts to establish a national holiday in honor of Dr. Martin L. King Jr.; and created the Dr. Martin L. King Jr. Center for Non-Violent Social Change in Atlanta.

Martin Luther King Jr. (1929–1968)

A religious leader, civil rights activist, and author; rose to national prominence for his leadership of the successful Montgomery Bus Boycott, marking the beginning of the Civil Rights Movement. Was co-founder and president of the Southern Christian Leadership Conference; led a series of nonviolent protest marches in the South for black civil rights including Alabama and Georgia; and led the March on Washington, August 28, 1963, to the Lincoln Memorial where he delivered his famous "I Have a Dream" speech. His leadership in the fight for freedom and justice won him the Nobel peace prize (1963) and led to the enactment of the Civil Rights Act of 1964 and Voting Rights Act of 1965. He was assassinated April 4, 1968.

Daisy Lampkin (1884–1965)

Became vice president of *Pittsburgh Courier* in 1929 and was a premiere fundraiser for the NAACP. Active in civic affairs and politics, was affiliated with Pittsburgh's Negro Women's Equal Franchise League; the Republican Party's Women's Division; the National Negro Republican Convention; Pittsburgh's National Association for the Advancement of Colored People. Was active in the Woman Suffrage Movement; was president of Pittsburgh, Pennsylvania's Negro Women's Equal Franchise League; was regional field secretary of the NAACP (1930) and, in 1935, national field secretary.

Lewis Latimer (1848–1928)

Born to fugitive slave parents; became a master draftsmen and inventor. Drafted the patent drawings for Alexander Graham Bell's telephone and earned eight patents during his lifetime for various inventions. In 1918, was a founding member, and the only African-American member, of the Edison Pioneers, a group formed to preserve their memories of those early days working with Thomas Edison.

Spike Lee (1957–)

Most noted as a filmmaker and has produced, directed, written, and acted in all twelve of his films. Films such as *The Jackie Robinson Saga* (1997), *Malcolm X* (1992), *Get On the Bus* (1996), and *Four Little Girls* (1997) are a testament to his extraordinary talent as a filmmaker and desire to bring black history to the big screen. Additionally, has produced more than thirty-five music videos for entertainers such as Anita Baker and rap artists Public Enemy, an estimated twenty-seven commercials, the first with Michael Jordan; and four short films.

Edmonia Lewis (1845–c. 1911)

One of the most prolific American artists of the late nineteenth century and the first African American to gain international fame as a sculptor. Most notable works include a *Bust of Robert Gould Shaw* (1864); *Forever Free* (1867); *Hagar* (1868–1875); and *The Old Arrow-Maker and His Daughter* (1867); and *The Death of Cleopatra* (1876).

John Lewis (1940–)

A prominent civil rights leader; co-founder of the Student Nonviolent Coordinating Committee (SNCC) and its first chairman. Participated in the Southern Christian Leadership Conference's march from Selma to Montgomery; organized Freedom Summer in Mississippi (1964); served on the White House Conference "To Fulfill These Rights" (1966) and on the staff of ACTION to coordinate the volunteer activities of organizations such as VISTA. Was elected to Atlanta's City Council (1981–1986) and in, 1987, to the U.S. House of Representatives representing Georgia's Fifth Congressional District.

Benjamin Lundy (1789–1839)

A white Quaker reformer who devoted his life to ending the institution of slavery. Organized the Union Humane Society (1815); established the *Genius of Universal Emancipation* (1821), an abolitionist journal; and wrote a pamphlet, "*The War in Texas*," an appeal to northerners opposed to political dominance by the South and the expansion of slavery. Worked with John Quincy Adams against the annexation of Texas.

Thurgood Marshall (1908–1993)

Was a judge on the United States Court of Appeals for the Second Circuit in New York (1961); became the first African American appointed solicitor general (1965); and became a U.S. Supreme Court justice (1967). Noted civil rights cases include, but are not limited to, *Smith v. Allwright* (1944), declaring the denial of black voter participation in white primaries to be unconstitutional; *Morgan v. Virginia* (1946), which brought an end to segregation in interstate transportation; *Brown v. Board of Education* (1954), which ended racial segregation in public schools; *Shelly v. Kraemer,* which destroyed restrictive covenants; and *McLaurin v. Missouri,* a successful challenge to the separate-but-equal doctrine. At age 83, retired from the U.S. Supreme Court (1991) after twenty-four years.

King Nzinga Mbemba (Affonso I) of Kongo (r. 1506–1543)

After becoming king, continued relations with the Portuguese which had been started by his father, causing the collapse of his region, Mbanza Kongo; his story is a vivid example of how Europeans came to dominate and colonize African countries. In an effort to control the Portuguese, signed the *Regimento* (1512) which sought to put restrictions on the Portuguese and their actions in the region. By 1568 Mbanza Kongo came under Portuguese rule.

Hattie McDaniel (1898–1952)

A singer, an actress, and vaudeville performer best known for her performance in the classic film *Gone With the Wind* (1939); was the first African American to win an Academy Award. Co-founded the Play Fair Committee to lobby the movie industry. Appeared in approximately 70 films mainly produced by Warner Brothers, United Artists, and 20th Century Fox between 1932–1949, including *Golden West* (1932), her debut film; *Blonde Venus* (1932); *Little Colonel* (1935); and *Showboat* (1936).

Claude McKay (1890–1948)

Born Festus Claudius McKay in Jamaica in 1890; his thoughts and poetic achievements helped set the tone for the Harlem Renaissance. Works include: "If We must Die;" *Spring in New Hampshire* (1920); *Harlem Shadows* (1922); *Home to Harlem* (1928), which quickly became the most popular novel ever written by a black author; short stories "Gingertown" (1932) and "Banana Bottom" (1933); his autobiography *A Long Way from Home* (1937); and the study *Harlem: Negro Metropolis,* (1940).

Terri McMillan (1951–) A writer most noted for her two novels, *Waiting to Exhale* (1995), a best-seller and *How Stella Got Her Groove Back* (1998) which were both turned into films. Other published works include *Mama* (1987) and *Disappearing Acts* (1989).

James Meredith (1933–)

Known for the class action lawsuit against the University of Mississippi in U.S. District Circuit Court of Appeals (1961) which challenged Mississippi's segregation policy with the help of civil rights attorney Constance Baker Motley. The court decided in his favor, and in 1962, Meredith became the first African American to attend the University of Mississippi; his actions led to the desegregation of other southern white colleges and universities.

Oscar Micheaux   (1884–1951)

The son of former slaves; greatest accomplishment was as a producer of all-black films and founder of Oscar Micheaux Corporation, a film company in New York. His films included *The Homesteader* (1919); *Birthright* (1924); *Body and Soul* (1924), featuring Paul Robeson; *The Exile* (1931), which was the first sound motion picture produced by a black film company; and *Veiled Aristocrats* (1932).

Florence Mills   (1895–1927)

Called the "Queen of Happiness"; was one of the most successful entertainers of the 1920s. Was invited to join the Greenwich Village Follies in 1923, making her the first black woman invited to appear in a major white production. Created a major all-black revue, which ran at London's Pavilion Theater and was performed 276 times.

Juanita Jackson Mitchell   (1913–1992)

A prominent attorney; was the first black woman admitted to the Maryland State Bar Association. Successfully litigated several civil rights cases including, in conjunction with the NAACP's Legal Defense Fund, *Robert Mack Bell v. Maryland* in the U.S. Supreme Court ending segregation in the state's restaurants. Was inducted into Maryland's Women's Hall of Fame (1965), and was the recipient of the National Council of Negro Women's Special Distinction in Law award.

Toni Morrison   (1931–2005)

One of the most prolific and influential fiction writers of the twentieth century, and perhaps one of the most important female African-American writers in American history. Most noted published works include *Bluest Eye* (1970), *Song of Solomon* (1977), and *Tar Baby* (1981). Was the recipient of the Pulitzer Prize, the Modern Language Association of American Commonwealth Award in Literature, and Nobel Prize for Literature (making her the first African American to receive this award).

Jelly Roll Morton   (1890–1941)

Born Ferdinand Joseph Lamothe; credited with fusing ragtime and blues and becoming the first jazz composer and theorist to put it on paper. He made his first recordings in 1923 but his career declined over the years due to a variety of reasons. Morton's career received a short reprieve when in 1938 folklorist Alan Lomax recorded Morton in a series of interviews for the Library of Congress, which were later released to the public.

Constance Baker Motley   (1921–2005)

Acquired a national reputation as a prominent civil rights attorney and judge. An attorney for the National Association for the Advancement of Colored People's Legal Defense Education Fund; successfully argued ten civil rights cases in the U.S. Supreme Court, winning nine of them. Was the first black woman elected to the New York State Senate (1964); the first black woman elected Manhattan Borough president (1965); and the first black woman appointed a judge in New York's Federal District Court System (1966).

Elijah Muhammad   (1897–1975)

Born Robert Poole, the son of two former slaves; while in Detroit working for the Chevrolet Corporation joined the Nation of Islam and became a lieutenant of Master Farad Muhammad (Wali Fard). Became leader of the Nation of Islam (Black Muslims) in 1934. Established the Temple of Islam in Chicago; a newspaper, *Muhammad Speaks*, the NOI's official communique; and a private elementary and high school called the University of Islam.

Emperor Mansa Musa   (r. 1312–1337)

The great-nephew of King Sundiata who conquered the Soso people and leveled the former capital of Ghana. Mansa Musa (Emperor Moses) ascended to the throne in 1312, and came to rule the vast empire of Mali; most remembered for his extravagant and historic pilgrimage (*hajj*) to Mecca in 1324 with a vast entourage. Also strengthened Islam, promoted education, trade and commerce in Mali; under his rule, Mali became the largest and richest realm of Africa.

Bob Marley   (1945–1981)

Born in Saint Ann Parish, Jamaica, and a son of the urban ghetto of Trench Town in Kingston, Jamaica's capital city. As a young man he became a Rastafarian, the Jamaican cultural and religious movement. Wrote and performed music that merged culture, religion, and politics in a way that invited dance but also challenged and excited its listeners' intellect. Especially noteworthy concept albums, *Survival, Uprising,* and *Confrontation,* brought together the themes that framed his life and work—celebrating black survival, challenging mental slavery, and constructing new visions for the future through defiance and hope.

Isaac Myers   (1835–1891)

A child of free parents; formed a group of black workers that created a company to buy a shipyard and continue doing business. In 1868, became president of the Colored Caulker's Trades Union Society of Baltimore; was later elected president of the Colored National Labor Union, the first such national organization in American history.

Huey Newton   (1942–1989)

Co-founded the Black Panther Party for Self-Defense, October 15, 1966. Imprisoned for manslaughter after a police officer was killed during an armed confrontation in 1967. As the Black Panther Party's minister of defense, earned a Ph.D. from the University of California, Santa Cruz (1980) writing his dissertation entitled "War Against the Panthers: Study of Repression in America."

Solomon Northup   (c. 1808–1863)

Born free but later enslaved by a slave-trading firm; later reunited with his family in 1853 with the help of a Canadian carpenter, Samuel Bass. The publication of his narrative, *Twelve Years a Slave,* led to the arrest of his kidnappers and speaks to the enormous fear held by northern free blacks about being kidnapped and enslaved.

Jesse Owens   (1913–1980)

A track and field star who during the 1936 Olympics in Berlin, Germany, became the first American in Olympic track and field history to win four gold medals in a single Olympics, destroying German leader Adolf Hitler's notion of Aryan supremacy and proving to the world that African Americans could successfully compete in athletics. In 1976, was awarded the Medal of Freedom by President Gerald Ford, which is the highest honor given a civilian of the United States.

Charlie "Bird" Parker   (1920–1955)

Known as "Yardbird" or "Bird"; became one of the jazz world's greatest legends and one of its most influential improvising jazz soloists. Was the "architect" in the creation and development of "bebop," (1944) also called the "Bebop Movement" or modern jazz, which became the trademark separating African-Amerian musicians from swing bands. Recordings include *Confessin' the Blues* (1941) and *Charlie Bird on the Air* (1944), which sold 81,000 copies.

Rosa Parks   (1918–2005)

Refused to relinquish her seat on a Montgomery bus to a white patron; her subsequent arrest triggered the Montgomery Bus Boycott, December 1, 1955. The boycott that resulted from Parks's action resulted in a U.S. Supreme Court ruling declaring Montgomery's segregated bus system unconstitutional. Known as "The Mother of the Civil Rights Movement."

King Piankhy of Kush   (r. c. 750 B.C.E.)

Was the king of Napata, the capital of Kush; believed to be a direct descendant of the last Egyptian governor of Nubia posted by the pharaohs. Was a great organizer and military commander. Recognized and respected for his military prowess, never lost a battle and was known for fair play. Responsible for founding Egypt's twenty-fifth dynasty.

Pinckney Benton Stewart Pinchback   (1837–1921)

The son of a white planter and his former slave; the first African American to serve as governor of a state (Louisiana). Joined the Republican Party and took an active role in Reconstruction politics; in 1868 voters elected him to the Louisiana state senate. Later became lieutenant governor following the death of Oscar Dunn, the first elected African-American lieutenant governor of a U.S. state.

Colin Powell   (1937–)

Four-Star General; served in both Democratic and Republican administrations under five U.S. presidents—Ronald Reagan, Jimmy Carter, George Bush, Bill Clinton (briefly), and George W. Bush—and was the first African American appointed assistant to the secretary for National Security Affairs (1986); chairman of the Joint Chiefs of Staff (1991), the highest position in the Department of Defense; and U.S. Secretary of State (2001). A highly decorated military veteran, is the recipient of numerous medals including a Purple Heart and the Bronze Star; several civilian awards including the Presidential Medal of Freedom; and several honorary degrees.

Gabriel Prosser   (1775–1800)

Led one of the largest slave revolts in North America, recruiting slaves from funerals and religious meetings with the help of his brother Martin, a minister. An estimated 1,000 people participated in the insurrection, which was foiled by inclement weather and betrayal of two slaves. Was captured in Norfolk, Virginia, tried in court, and convicted of conspiracy and insurrection. Was hanged October 7, 1800, with 26 other insurgents.

Robert Purvis   (1810–1898)

A mulatto who was an abolitionist as a teenager and later, a political activist and co-founder of the American Anti-Slavery Society (1833). Abolitionist activities involved active membership in Philadelphia's Vigilance Committee; financing of the Underground Railroad; hiding fugitive slaves in his home; and using his carriage to transport slaves to the next station. Was a supporter of the Women's Rights Movement and women's suffrage.

Gertrude Pridgett "Ma" Rainey   (1886–1939)

Better known as Ma Rainey and billed as "The Mother of the Blues"; a classic female blues singer and one of the first generation of blues singers to record. Made her first recordings in 1923; signed with Paramount Records, recording some 100 songs between 1923 and 1928, often with top blues artists like Louis Armstrong, Kid Ory, and Fletcher Henderson.

Asa Philip Randolph   (1889–1979)

Known as a tireless champion of equal rights and equal opportunity for more than sixty years. Joined the Socialist party and teamed with Chandler Owen in 1917 to establish *The Messenger,* a radical Harlem magazine. Organized the Brotherhood of Sleeping Car Porters. Was instrumental in President Franklin Delano Roosevelt's signing of Executive Order 8802 (1941), which barred discrimination in defense industries; and President Harry Truman's signing of Executive Order 9981 (1948), which banned segregation in the military. Became vice president when the Congress of Industrial Organizations (CIO) and the AFL merged and became the AFL-CIO in 1955.

James Thomas Rapier   (1837–1883)

Born a free black; in 1866, attended the first Republican convention held in Alabama and was on the committee that framed the platform. Had an unsuccessful bid for secretary of state in 1870 but was appointed assessor of internal revenue in 1871 and state commissioner to the Vienna Exposition by the governor of Alabama in 1873. Was elected to the Forty-third Congress, but lost re-election in 1874 and accepted an appointment as collector of internal revenue for the second district of Alabama, which he served until his death in 1883.

Charlotte Ray   (1850–1911)

Of mixed racial ancestry—including Native American and European—was the first African American woman lawyer in the United States; also the first woman admitted to the bar in the District of Columbia. Taught at both Howard University and in the public school system in Brooklyn, New York.

Hiram Rhodes Revels   (1822–1901)

Born free, the first African American to serve in the United States Senate; completed the unfinished term of Jefferson Davis, the former president of the Confederacy. In the Senate, supported civil rights for blacks. After completing his term in the United States Senate, was named president of Alcorn University.

Condoleezza Rice   (1954–)

The first African-American woman to ever be appointed U.S. Secretary of State, a position she assumed in January 2005. As an educator, is recognized as the first African-American chief academic and budget officer at Stanford University upon being appointed provost, placing her second in command at one of the nation's leading universities. Prominent in national and international politics, she became foreign policy advisor to Republican President George W. Bush.

Paul Robeson   (1898–1976)

Born to a former slave and a mother who came from a distinguished Philadelphia family; athlete, actor, singer, cultural scholar, author, and political activist. Most well known for his acting roles including the lead in Eugene O'Neill's *All God's Chillun Got Wings* (1924) and *The Emperor Jones* (1925). Known for his trademark rendition of *Ol' Man River*. Politically and socially ahead of his time, Robeson believed the famous had a responsibility to fight for justice and peace.

Bill "Bojangles" Robinson (1878–1949)
Born Luther Robinson but called Bojangles because of his ebullience; was a famous tap dancer and stage performer. From 1929 to 1943, worked in ten Hollywood features and some independently produced all-black films. His increasing popularity was the result of four films with (white child actress) Shirley Temple: *The Little Colonel* (1935); *The Littlest Rebel* (1938); *Rebecca of Sunnybrook Farm* (1938); and *Just Around the Corner* (1938). He also performed in *Stormy Weather* with outstanding performer Lena Horne (1943).

Jackie Robinson (1919–1972)
Became the first African American to play major league baseball; on April 4, 1947, broke the color barrier that confined other baseball greats to Negro League baseball teams. During his first season as a first baseman for the Dodgers, was voted National League Rookie of the Year, garnering 124 of 160 votes. In 1949, was voted the National League's most valuable player and also won the batting title. In 1962, was inducted into the Baseball Hall of Fame.

Randall Robinson (1942–)
A political and foreign policy activist; also an author who contributed to the dismantling of apartheid in South Africa. Founder and executive director of Trans-Africa (1977); in 1984, organized daily protests in front of the South African Embassy in Washington, D.C. leading to Congress eventually imposing economic sanctions against the South African government. Also noted for leading the struggle for African-American reparations for slavery and the author of *The Debt: What America Owes to Blacks* (2000).

Frances Rollin (1844–1901)
Raised in the elite antebellum free black community of Charleston; influential in Reconstruction politics. After the war, taught at schools sponsored by the American Missionary Association. Wrote the biography of the black abolitionist leader Martin Delany, the first nonfiction work published in America by a black woman, using the pen name Frank A. Rollin. Later served as a clerk in the General Land Office in Washington, D.C.

Katherine Rollin (1851–1876)
Along with her sister Charlotte, organized a women's right convention in Columbia in 1870 and formed the South Carolina Branch of the American Women's Suffrage Association. One of the five Rollins sisters whose work in the areas of women's rights and women's suffrage in South Carolina broke traditional gender roles.

Bayard Rustin (1910–1987)
An organizer and civil rights activist; most noted for successfully coordinating the 1963 March on Washington where Dr. Martin L. King Jr. delivered his famous "I Have a Dream" speech. Was a field staff member of the Fellowship of Reconciliation (FOR); an officer within the Congress of Racial Equality (CORE); and orchestrated the Journey of Reconciliation (1947).

Peter Salem (1750–1816)
Born a slave; was a veteran of the Revolutionary War, having served gallantly in the Battle of Bunker Hill June 17, 1775. Was the Patriot who fired the shot that killed Major John Pitcairn. Also fought in the battles of Saratoga and Concord, respectively. In his honor, a monument was erected in his memory in Framingham, Massachusetts, and the U. S. Postal Service has issued a Peter Salem stamp in its African-American Heritage series.

Dred Scott (c.1795–1858)
The son of slaves; was the plaintiff in the case of *Scott, a Colored Man v. Emerson 15 MO 57* which was heard in the U.S. Supreme Court and which upheld the lower court's judgment ruling that slaves were not and could never become citizens of the United States. The Dred Scott case created controversy over slavery in the territories, intensified an already growing bitterness between the North and South, and led to increased abolitionist activities.

Bobby Seale (1936–)
A political activist; was one of the most profound black radicals of the 1960s with the formation of the Black Panther Party. Responsible for the organization's growth from a local to a national organization with more than forty chapters and five thousand members in major cities nationwide. With support from the Black Panther Party, unsuccessfully ran for mayor of Oakland in 1973.

William J. Seymour (1870–1922)
Born in Louisiana in 1870; played a key role in church development. Became a proponent of "Pentecostalism," which derives its name from the manifestations of the Holy Spirit found in the Book of Acts; many modern charismatic movements are thought to be outgrowths of Seymour's ministry.

Robert Smalls (1839–1916)
Wheelman of the *Planter*, a dispatch vehicle, which he stole on May 13, 1862, and subsequently delivered to the commanding officer of *Onward*, a Union ship. Entered politics after the Civil War, serving in the state senate from 1868 to 1870. In 1875 voters elected him to the U.S. Congress for the first of five terms; was one of the six black members of the South Carolina constitutional convention of 1895.

Bessie Smith (1894–1937)
Called the "Empress of the Blues; became the most popular singer in the Decade of Jazz, singing in major cities like Atlantic City, Chicago, and Philadelphia. Made almost 200 recordings with her finest recording (and certainly the best known in her day) being *Back Water Blues*, with James P. Johnson.

Charles Spaulding (1874–1952)
One of black America's most successful entrepreneurs; became president of what became North Carolina Mutual Life Insurance Company in 1923. This company became the nation's largest black insurance company under his leadership. Used his wealth and power to salvage black educational institutions such as Shaw University and Virginia Theological Seminary; organizations including the National Negro Business League; and to influence the press, school curriculums, and allocation of public funds.

Mabel K. Staupers (1890–1989) Was a leading nurse and avid civil rights activist; was instrumental in getting black nurses to serve in the U.S. Army and Navy Corps during World War II. In 1908, founded the National Association of Colored Graduate Nurses Association (NACGN); and was responsible for the integration of black women into the American Nurses Association (ANA) in 1948. Was awarded the NAACP's Spingarn Medal in 1951; New York City's Outstanding American Leader and Distinguished Citizen of America Award (1967); and the Howard University Alumni Award (1970).

Maria Miller Stewart (1803–1879)
A native of Hartford, Connecticut; was orphaned at five years old and bound out as a servant in the home of a clergyman where she remained until age fifteen. Wrote and lectured about abolition, morality, and the roles of African-American men and women in American society. Publications and lectures include: *Religion and the Pure Principles of Morality* (1831), *Meditations from the Pen of Mrs. Maria Stewart* (1832), and *An Address Delivered Before the African American Female Intelligence Society of America, A Lecture Delivered at Franklin Hall* (1832). Established a school for black children in Washington, D.C.

Carl Stokes (1927–1996)
A successful politician, broadcast journalist, and attorney; in 1967, became the first African American elected mayor of a major city, Cleveland, Ohio. As mayor, greatest accomplishment was his NOW! program, a multi-million dollar project encouraging citizens to engage various programs to raise funds, establish day care centers, and other endeavors to revive the city. Adopted a fair employment practices act (1969) guaranteeing equal employment opportunities by businesses awarded city contracts; appropriated funds for small and minority-owned businesses; and created the Twenty-first Congressional District Caucus, a vehicle for electing African-American politicians in Cleveland.

Harriet Beecher Stowe (1811–1896)
An educator, abolitionist, and author, who was famous for her controversial anti-slavery novel, *Uncle Tom's Cabin* (1852), which confronted the issues of racism and race theory in the United States. *Uncle Tom's Cabin* was attacked by Southern critics as a grossly false depiction of slavery and their way of life, but became an iconic novel that contributed significantly to the growing opposition of slavery among white northerners.

Sundiata of Mali (c. 1235 CE)
Born physically handicapped at the beginning of the thirteenth century; was the son of Mari Diata, a Mandingo chief of the Keita clan whose family had converted to Islam in the tenth century. Was the legendary leader of the Mandinka people, and upon defeating the Soso people during the Battle of Kirina, created the Empire of Mali. Is credited for consolidating and strengthening the Kingdom of Mali, and in turn, controlling the sources of the gold trade, the foundation of the Mali Empire's prosperity.

Susie King Taylor (1848–1912)
Born a slave; the only black woman to publish her experiences as a black woman who served with the Union's black troops in which she served as a laundress, cook, clerical worker, and nurse. After the war, opened a private school for black children, but the death of her husband and the opening of a public school for black children forced her to seek employment as a domestic servant. Spent much of her later years working in the Woman's Relief Corps, an organization for female Civil War veterans.

Mary Church Terrell (1863–1954)
Born to slaves; helped found the Colored Women's League, addressed delegates at the International Congress of Women in Berlin in German, French, and English, and was an active member of the NAACP. Appointed to the District of Columbia Board of Education in 1895 making her the first female African American to hold such a position. In 1949, became the first black woman admitted to the Washington chapter of the American Association of University Women, thus ending its policy of discrimination.

Clarence Thomas (1948–)
In July 1991, was nominated by President George Bush o the U.S. Supreme Court after the retirement of Chief Justice Thurgood Marshall. Alleged sexual harassment and misconduct toward one of his staff members at the EEOC led to a confirmation hearing on the matter; amidst great controversy, was confirmed a U.S. Supreme Court Justice on October 15, 1991, by a 52-48 vote. Is only the second African American to sit on the U.S. Supreme Court.

Dox Thrash (1892–1965)
A painter and artist; his prints appeared at the New York World's Fair (1939–1940) and the 1940 American Negro Exhibition in Chicago. In 1942 his works were displayed in the Philadelphia Museum of Art and, in 1948, the Smithsonian Institution. Carbographic landscapes include *Deserted Cabin* (1939) and *Boats at Night* (1940); and a graphite drawing of *Man With a Harmonica* (n.d.). Credited for developing a new and more effective lithographic technique called the carborundum print-process, an industrial product made of carbon and silicon crystals.

Jean Toomer (1894–1967)
Born the son of a planter; became a writer and often published in small literary magazines, especially *Dial*. Explored philosophy and meditation; his most important literary contribution was *Cane*, an experimental novel about the black experience, published in 1923.

King Askia Muhammad Toure of Songhai (r. 1492–1528)
The first ruler of the Askia dynasty, succeeding former King Sunni Ali after his death; wielding power for almost thirty-six years, is credited with establishing the Askia dynasty and strengthening the Songhai Empire. King Askia's reign further led to Timbuktu becoming a more prosperous commercial city; its population increasing to more than 100,000 people; and merchants and traders from various parts of Asia and Europe traveling there to exchange their goods for Songhai's gold.

Sojourner Truth (c. 1797–1883)
A former slave, Sojourner Truth was an abolitionist and women's rights activist. Working with leading abolitionists William Lloyd Garrison and Frederick Douglass, she became one of the most popular anti-slavery lecturers during the 1840s and 1850s. Active in the Women's Rights Movement, Truth attended a meeting in Akron, Ohio, where she is noted for stating, "Arn't I a Woman."

Harriet Tubman (1820–1883)

A fugitive slave, abolitionist, nurse, scout, and spy during the Civil War, as well as a social reformer; the most famous conductor on the Underground Railroad. Ignoring the Fugitive Slave Law of 1850 and a $40,000 reward for capture, made an estimated nineteen trips into the South and successfully led 300 slaves to freedom. In her honor, the contributions of private citizens and the African Methodist Episcopal Zion Church led to the construction of the Harriet Tubman Home for Indigent and Aged Negroes (1952). The U.S. Postal Service issued a Harriet Tubman Stamp February 1, 1968, the first in a new Black Heritage USA Series.

Nat Turner (1800–1831)

Born a slave; the son of an African mother and a fugitive slave father. In 1831, led the most significant slave revolt in United States history taking the lives of white men, women, and children. Captured after an initial escape and after a trial, was convicted November 5, 1831, and hanged. His actions created great fear among whites, triggered a series of slave insurrections across the South, led to increased anti-slavery agitation, and the enactment of additional Slave Codes further restricting the mobility and activities of slaves.

Denmark Vesey (c. 1767–1822)

Born a slave; later became an abolitionist who advocated the emancipation of enslaved blacks and racial equality. Led an unsuccessful slave revolt that led to the enactment of several laws in the South Carolina State Legislature restricting the movement of African Americans, including the Negro Seaman Act.

Alice Walker (1944–)

One of America's most profound writers, poets, novelists, and essayists; has won prestigious awards and fellowships such as the Pulitzer Prize for *The Color Purple* (1983); the Lillian Smith Award from the National Endowment for the Arts; the National Institute of Arts and Letters Rosenthal Award; and the Radcliffe Institute and Guggenheim fellowships. Has written five books of poetry, seven novels and short stories, and four collections of prose including *Good Night Willie Lee, I'll See You in the Morning* (1979), *Possessing the Secret of My Joy* (1992), and *In Search of Our Mother's Garden's* (1983).

C. J. Walker (1867–1919)

An African-American businesswoman and philanthropist; perhaps the first female African-American millionaire in the United States. Developed a method for straightening curly hair and hired agents to sell her product door-to-door, calling the company the Madame C.J. Walker Manufacturing Company. Established several Walker Schools of Beauty Culture and insisted on strict health regulations for her staff, long before state cosmetology laws became routine.

David Walker (c. 1796–1830)

The son of a free white mother and enslaved father, Walker was an author, an activist for black civil rights, and an abolitionist. Wrote an *Appeal to Colored Citizens of the World*, also known as *David Walker's Appeal*, which sought to mobilize black organizations and individuals against slavery and racial injustice, to empower black activism, and to encourage slave insurrections against plantation owners. *Appeal* was considered by abolitionists and historians to be "the boldest and most direct appeal on behalf of freedom."

Margaret Walker (1915–1998)

A famous poet, novelist, essayist, and biographer; the author of nine books and recipient of numerous awards. Major works include *For My People* (1937); *Jubilee* (1966); and *A Poetic Equation: Conversations Between Nikki Giovanni and Margaret Walker* (1974) and *Richard Wright: Daemonic Genius* (1988). Founded the Institute for the Study of History, Life, and Culture of Black People at Jackson State University. The recipient of six honorary degrees, several fellowships, the Lifetime Achievement Award for Excellence (1992), and the Living Legacy Award from President Jimmy Carter.

Thomas Wright "Fats" Waller (1904–1943)

The son of a Baptist lay preacher; went on to become an excellent pianist—considered today as one of the very best—as well as a consummate songwriter and entertainer. Before going solo played with many top performers like Bessie Smith and Erskine Tate. Was instrumental in making the film *Stormy Weather* with Lena Horne and Bill Robinson and an all-star band.

Booker T. Washington (1856–1915)

Born into slavery in Virginia in 1856; went on to become one of the most prominent African Americans in the country. Was president of Tuskegee, making it into one of the leading facilities for black education in the United States. Was a proponent of "accommodation," believing that African Americans should accept segregation while learning a trade, a stance that put him in opposition to other African-American leaders of the day, including W. E. B. Du Bois and AME Bishop Henry M. Turner.

Maxine Waters (1938–)

A noted African American and out-spoken politician; was first elected to the California State Assembly in 1976 and re-elected six consecutive terms. She became chairperson of the Democratic Caucus (1984); president of the Congressional Black Caucus; and was appointed the Democratic Party's Chief Deputy Whip.

Ida B. Wells (1862–1931)

Born a slave; was a fearless anti-lynching crusader, suffragist, women's rights advocate, journalist, and speaker. Gained notoriety after pursuing a lawsuit against a railroad company who ejected her after her refusal to give up her seat to a white man. Became an editorial writer and investigative journalist; was a founding member of the NAACP. In 1928, became the first black woman to run for public office in the United States when she threw her name into the Illinois State legislature race.

Cornel West (1953–)

A prolific writer, educator, scholar, and author whose scholarly works have been published in numerous journals including the *Yale Law Journal*, *The Nation*, and *Socialist Review*. Has written at least thirteen books including *Race Matters* (1993), *The Ethical*

Dimensions of Marxist Thought (1991), and *The Future of Race* (1996) with noted scholar Henry Louis Gates Jr. (1996). Currently serves as chair of the African-American Studies Program at Princeton University.

Phillis Wheatley (c. 1753–1784)

Born in Gambia, West Africa and enslaved; became a renowned poet, the first African American and only the second American woman to publish a volume of poetry. In 1773, *Poems on Various Subjects, Religious and Moral* was published in England and brought her international recognition. Other works include her first poem, "*An Elegiac Poem on the Death of the Celebrated Divine . . . George Whitfield*," written in 1770. Of the fifty-five poems she composed, nineteen elegies were about her acquaintances, the Enlightenment, morals, piety, and independence.

William Whipper (1835–1907)

A black attorney from Philadelphia who settled in Beaufort, South Carolina, after the war; one the most controversial figures in Reconstruction era South Carolina. Was a vocal opponent to the disenfranchisement of blacks. Was appointed to circuit court judge, a post the governor refused to endorse despite Whipper's election by the state legislature.

George H. White (1852–1918)

Born a slave; went on to become a prominent attorney in North Carolina and a Post-Reconstruction politician. Elected to the U.S. House of Representatives in 1897 and 1900, the lone African American in Congress and the last ex-slave to hold such an office. Around 1901, established Whitesboro, an all-black New Jersey town and in 1905, moved to Philadelphia and incorporated the People's Savings Bank.

Johnson C. Whittaker (1858–1931)

One of only two black cadets who attended West Point; was at the center of an assault case that led to his discharge from the Armed Forces in which he was accused of lying about the attack. A former slave, Whittaker worked with young people at South Carolina State College and at Douglass High School in Oklahoma City for the rest of his life. In 1995, was posthumously awarded his commission in the United States Army.

August Wilson (1945–2005)

A renowned playwright; of his five most important plays, four were produced on Broadway: *Ma Rainey's Black Bottom* (1983); *Joe Turner's Come and Gone* (1986); *The Piano Lesson* (1987); and *Two Trains Running* (1990). Has won four New York Drama Critics Circle Awards for Best Play; two Pulitzer Prizes; a Tony Award for *Fences* (1985) as best play of the year; and the Drama Desk Best Play Award.

Harriet E. Wilson (1828–1863)

A prolific writer who wrote the first novel published by an African-American woman in the United States: *Our Nig: Or, Sketches from the Life of a Free Black, in a Two Story White House, North* as well as *Showing That Slavery's Shadow's Fall Even There* (1859), which compared and contrasted the lives of northern black domestic workers with southern enslaved blacks. After receiving scant attention for more than 100 years, *Our Nig* was republished in 1983 as an exact reprint of the original 1859 novel.

Oprah Winfrey (1954–)

Recognized as the most successful woman in the history of entertainment; *Forbes* magazine listed her as America's richest entertainer. In 1986, after she boosted *A.M. Chicago*'s ratings, it was renamed *The Oprah Winfrey Show*, which became nationally syndicated under the auspices of King World Productions. In 1989, purchased her own television and movie production studio, HARPO Productions. Also noted for her role as Sophia in *The Color Purple* and the production of two mini-series.

Carter Godwin Woodson (1875–1950)

The son of former slaves; the founder of The Association for the Study of African American Life and History (1915). Published the scholarly book *The Education of the Negro Prior to 1861* (1915), followed by *A Century of Negro Migration* (1918), *The History of the Negro Church* (1927), and *The Negro in Our History*. In January 1916, began the publication of the scholarly *Journal of Negro History* (since 2002, the *Journal of African American History*, now published by Columbia University); other works include *The Mind of the Negro as Reflected in Letters Written During the Crisis, 1800–1860* and *The Mis-Education of the Negro*.

Jonathan J. Wright (1840–1895)

Was the first African American to practice law in Pennsylvania and later in South Carolina. Was elected senator from South Carolina. In 1868, became a member of the South Carolina bar and then an associate justice of the Supreme Court where he served for seven years. Race-inspired criticism for his opinion in *Ex Parte Norris* led to an investigation and his subsequent removal from the Court; after his dismissal, established Claflin College's law department, serving for several years as a college trustee.

Richard Wright (1908–1960)

A major African-American writer; sought to combat racial discrimination in the United States through his essays, lectures, and poetry. Was the author of *Uncle Tom's Children*, *Twelve Million Voices*, and *The Man Who Lived Underground*, but his most popular books were *Black Boy* (1927) and *Native Son* (1940), which was a Book-of-the-Month selection and sold more than one million copies. Founded the South Side Writer's Group in Chicago in 1936 to provide moral support for black writers and criticism of their writings. Was awarded *Story* magazine's prize for *Fire and Cloud* (1938) and the prestigious Spingarn Medal (1941).

Malcolm X (1925–1965)

Born Malcolm Little; joined the Nation of Islam while in prison, going on to become its most renowned and most effective leader. Increased the organization's following from 400 to 10,000 members. Was suspended for remarks about President John F. Kennedy's assassination; made a pilgrimage to Mecca, and upon returning to the states, publicly denounced Elijah Mohammad's teachings and embraced orthodox Islam, which ultimately led to his assassination on February 21, 1965.

Photo and Text Credits

PART TIMELINE I: Images that appear on page xxxii: Tina Chambers © Dorling Kindersley, Courtesy of the National Maritime Museum, London; Courtesy of the Library of Congress; The Library Company of Philadelphia; Library of Congress; The Granger Collection; Library of Congress; The Granger Collection; Abby Aldrich Rockefeller Folk Art Museum, Colonial Williamsburg Foundation, VA; British Museum, London/Bridgeman Art Library, London/SuperStock; Courtesy of the Library of Congress. Images that appear on page 1: Library of Congress; Courtesy of the Massachusetts Historical Society; The Historical Society of Pennsylvania; William Ranney, "The Battle of Cowpens." Oil on canvas. Photo by Sam Holland. Courtesy South Carolina State House.

CHAPTER 1: *Photos:* British Museum, London/Bridgeman Art Library, London/SuperStock, 2; © The British Museum, 4; Dr.Timothy Kendall, 9; Copyright Werner Forman/Art Resource, NY, 10; The Granger Collection, 13; Yoruba Offering Bowl from Ekiti Efon-Alaye, (BON46967) Bonhams, London, UK/Bridgeman Art Library, London/New York, 16; Courtesy of the Library of Congress, 19; Christie's Images Ltd., 2005, 21. *Text:* From Roland Oliver and J.D. Fage, A Short History of Africa, pp. 108–109. Copyright © 1973. Reproduced by permission of Penguin Books Ltd.; Source: Roland Oliver and Caroline Oliver, Africa in the Days of Exploration, 1965, pp. 9–10, 18.

CHAPTER 2: *Photos:* Courtesy of the Library of Congress, 26; Library of Congress, 28; Werner Forman, Art Resource, NY, 30; Culver Pictures, Inc., 35; Courtesy of the Library of Congress, 36, 45; The Granger Collection, 46. *Text:* F 2-1—Estimated Annual Exports of Slaves from Africa, 1500–1700 John Thornton, Africa and Africans in the Making of the Atlantic World, 1400–1680 (New York: Cambridge University Press, 1992), p. 118. Reprinted with the permission of Cambridge University Press, p. 30. T 2-1—Estimated Slave Imports by Destination, 1451–1870; Reprinted Source: From The Slave Trade: The Story of the Atlantic Slave Trade, 1440-1870 by Hugh Thomas, pg. 804, 1997, page 32; Voices—The Journal of a Dutch Slaver, Source: Elizabeth Donnan, ed., Documents Illustrative of the History of the Slave Trade to America, 4 vols. Washington, DC: Carnegie Institute, 1930–35, pp. 1, 141–145, page 40; BRACEY, JOHN H.; SINHA, MANISHA, AFRICAN AMERICAN MOSAIC: A DOCUMENTARY HISTORY FROM THE SLAVE TRADE TO THE TWENTY-FIRST CENTURY, VOLUME ONE: TO 1877, 1st, © 2004. Reproduced by permission of Pearson Education, Inc., Upper Saddle River, New Jersey, page 44.

CHAPTER 3: *Photos:* Courtesy of the Library of Congress, 52; Getty Images Inc.—Hulton Archive Photos, 54; From the collections of the South Carolina Historical Society, 56; Library of Congress, 63; Corbis/Bettmann, 69; Arizona State Library, Archives and Public Records, Archives Division, Phoenix, Neg. # 99-9996, 73; Corbis/Bettmann, 74. *Text:* F 3-1—Africans Brought as Slaves to British North America, 1701–1775; From The American Colonies: From Settlement to Independence, by R.C. Simmons, 1976. New York: David McKay., page 62; F 3-2—Africans as a Percentage of the Total Population of the British American Colonies, 1650–1770, From Time on the Cross: The Economics of Negro Slavery, by Robert W. Fogel and Stanley L. Engerman, 1974., page 71; A Poem by Jupiter Hammon, Source: Dorothy Porten, ed. Early Negro Writing, 1760–1837. 1971 reprint. Baltimore: Black Classic Press, 1995. Reprinted by permission, page 70. Voices—A Description of an Eighteenth-Century Virginia Plantation, Source: From Virginians at Home: Family Life in the Eighteenth Century, by Edmond S. Morgan, pp.53-54, 1952, page 64.

CHAPTER 4: *Photos:* William Ranney, "The Battle of Cowpens." Oil on canvas. Photo by Sam Holland. Courtesy South Carolina State House, 80; Library of Congress, 82; Corbis/Bettmann, 85; Courtesy of the Library of Congress, 87; Library of Congress, 89; The Maryland Historical Society, Baltimore, Maryland, 91; University of Virginia Library, Special Collections Dept., 93; The Granger Collection, 94; Anne S.K. Brown Military Collection, John Hay Library, Brown University, 95; Courtesy, American Antiquarian Society, 98. *Text:* Figure 4-1—The Free Black Population of British North American Colonies in 1750, and of the United States in 1790 and 1800, Source: A Century of Population Growth in the United States. 1790-1900, (1909), p. 80. Data for the 1750 estimated, page 96. Map 4-2—Major Battles of the American War for Independence, Indicating Those in Which Black Troops Participated, Source: Adapted from The Atlas of African-American History and Politics, 1/e by A. Smallwood and J. Elliot, © 1998, page 92. Map 4-3—The Resettlement of Black Loyalists After the American War for Independence, Source: Adapted from The Atlas of African-American History and Politics, 1/e by A. Smallwood and J. Elliot, © 1998, page 97. Voices—Boston's Slaves Link Their Freedom to American Liberty, Source: Gary B. Nash, Race and Revolution. Madison, WI: Madison House, 1990, pp. 173–174. Reprinted by permission, page 89; Voice—Phyllis Wheatley on Liberty and Natural Rights, Source: Roy Finkebine, ed. Sources of the African-American Past: Primary Sources in American History. New York: Addison Wesley Longman, 1997, pp. 22-23, page 90.

CHAPTER 5: *Photos:* Dennis MacDonald, PhotoEdit, Inc., 104; Courtesy of the Library of Congress, 106; Courtesy of the Massachusetts Historical Society, 110; Schomburg Center for Research in Black Culture, The New York Public Library, 117; Delaware Art Museum, 118; The Historical Society of Pennsylvania, 122; Stock Montage, Inc./Historical Pictures Collection, 124; © Curt Teich Postcard Archives, Lake County Discovery Museum, 126. *Text:* T 5-1—Slave Populations in the Mid-Atlantic States, 1790-1860, Source: Philip S. Foner, History of Black Americans, from Africa to the Emergence of the Cotton Kingdom, vol. 1, p. 374. Reproduced with permission of Greenwood Publishing Group, Inc. Westport, CT, page 109. Voices—Absalom Jones Petitions Congress on Behalf of Fugitives Facing Reenslavement, Source: Annals of Congress, 4, Cong., 2 sess. (January 23, 1797), pp. 2015-2018, page 120.

VISUALIZING THE PAST: Images that appear on page 132-133: Hulton Archive, Getty Images; Courtesy of American Antiquarian Society; Courtesy of the Library of Congress; © Dorling Kindersley, Courtesy of the Wilberforce House Museum, Hull; US Dept. of the Interior Museum; Art Resource/Schomburg Center for Research in Black Culture; Wilberforce House © Hull Museums; © Wilberforce House Museum, Hull City Council, UK; Library of Congress

Interpreting the Past: Images that appear on pages 134-135: © 1996 North Wind Pictures; AP Wide World Photos; Library of Congress.

PART TIMELINE II: Images that appear on page 136: Getty Image, Inc.—Liason; Courtesy of the Library of Congress; Corbis/Bettmann; © Wilberforce House Museum, Hull City Council, UK. Uncle Tom and Little Eva, 1853 Robert S. Duncanson. Gift of Mrs. Jefferson Butler and Miss Grace R. Conover. Photograph © 1997 The Detroit Institute of Arts. Images that appear on page 137: Courtesy of the Library of Congress; Frederick Douglass (1817?–95). Oil on canvas, c1844, attr. to E. Hammond. The Granger Collection; Courtesy of the Library of Congress; National Portrait

CHAPTER 6: *Photos:* Library of Congress, 138; Library of Congress, 140; The New York Public Library/Art Resource, N.Y., 141; Chicago Historical Society, 148;; National Archives and Records Administration, 151; South Carolina Department of Parks, Recreation, and Tourism, 152; Courtesy of the Library of Congress, 153; Abby Aldrich Rockefeller Folk Art Museum, Williamsburg, VA, 156. *Text:* Map 6-1—Cotton Production in the South, 1820-1860, Reprinted by permission of Louisiana University Press from Atlas of Antebellum Southern Agriculture by Sam Bowers Hilliard. Copyright © 1984 by Louisiana State Press., page 142. Map 6-2—Slave Population, 1820–1860, Reprinted by permission of Louisiana University Press from Atlas of Antebellum Southern Agriculture by Sam Bowers Hilliard. Copyright © 1984 by Louisiana State Press, page 144 Map 6-4—Population percentages in the Southern states, 1850., Source: Faragher, John Mack; Bihle, Mari Jo; Czitrom, Daniel; Armitage, Susan H., Out of Many: A History of the American People, Combined Volume, 4th edition, © 2003. Reprinted by permission of Pearson Education, Inc. Upper Saddle River, NJ, page 149. T 6-1—United States Slave Population, 1820 and 1860, Copyright © 1974 Slaves Without Masters: The Free Negro in the Antebellum South by Ira Berlin. Reprinted by permission of The New Press. www.thenewpress.com, page 143; Voices—Federick Douglass on the Readiness of Masters to Use the Whip, Source: Roy Finkebine, ed. Sources of the African-American Past: Primary Sources in American History. New York: Addison Wesley Longman, 1997, pp. 43-44, page 150. Voices—A Slaveholder Describes a New Purchase, Source: Tryphena Blanche Holder Fox to Anna Rose Holder, Dec. 27, 1857, Mississippi Department of Archives and History, Jackson, Mississippi, page 154.

CHAPTER 7: *Photos:* Courtesy of the Library of Congress, 164; Manigault Papers, Southern Historical Collection, The Library of the University of North Carolina at Chapel Hill, 166; The Granger Collection, 174; The Granger Collection, New York., 175; Nantucket Historical Association, 177; Photographs and Prints Division. Schomburg Center for Research in Black Culture/Art Resource. The New York Public Library. Astor, Lenox and Tilden Foundations. Photo by H. Rocher, 177; Photographs and Prints Division. Schomburg Center for Research in Black Culture/Art Resource, The New York Public Library. Astor, Lenox and Tilden Foundations, 178; Courtesy of the Library of Congress, 178; Fenimore Art Museum/New York State Historical Association, 180; Courtesy of the Library of Congress, 181; The Maryland Historical Society, Baltimore Maryland, 185; Thomas Waterman Wood, American, 1823–1903, Market Woman, 1858, Oil on canvas, 23-3/8 × 14-1/2 in. Fine Arts Museum of San Francisco, Museum Purchase, Mildred Anna Williams Collection, 1944.8, 187. *Text:* Map 7-1—The Slave , Free, Black and White Population in the United States in 1830, Source: For slave states, Ira Berlin. Slave without Masters: The Free Negro in the Antebellum South (New York: New Press 1971); for free states, Historical Statistics of the United States (Washington GPO, 1960), page 167. T 7-1—Black Population in the States of the Old Northwest, 1800–1840, Table: Black Population in the States of the Old Northwest, 180–1840, p. 104, from In Hope of Liberty: Culture, Community and Protest Among Northern Free Blacks, 1700–1860 by James O. Horton and Lois E. Horton, copyright © 1996 by Oxford University Press, Inc. Used by permission of Oxford University Press, Inc., page 172; T 7-2—Free Black Population of Selected Cities, 1800–1850, Adapted from "The Free Black in Urban America 1800–180: The Shadow of A Dream," by Dr. Leonard P. Curry, p. 250. Copyright © 1981 University of Chicago Press, Chicago, IL. Reprinted by permission of the author, page 173; Voices Maria W. Stewart on the Condition of Black Workers, Source: Maria W. Stewart, "Lecture Delivered at the Franklin Hall, Boston, September 21, 1831," as quoted in Roy Finkenbine, Source of the African American Past: Primary Sources in American History. New York: Addison Wesley Longman, 1997, pp. 30-32, page 176.Voices—The Constitution of the Pittsburgh African Education Society, Source: Dorothy Porten, ed. Early Negro Writing, 1760–1837. 1971 reprint. Baltimore: Black Classic Press, 1995, pp. 120–22. Reprinted by permission, page 182.

CHAPTER 8: *Photos:* The Granger Collection, New York, page 192; © Bettmann/CORBIS, 194; Courtesy of the Library of Congress; Virginia Historical Society, Richmond, Virginia, 200; National Portrait Gallery, Smithsonian Institution, Art Resource, NY, 202; Courtesy of the Library of Congress, 204;Boston Anthenaeum, 205; Stock Montage Inc./Historical Pictures Collection, page 206; Boston Public Library/Rare Books Department, page 207. *Text:* Voices—William Watkins Opposes Colonization,

Source: Herbert Aptheker, ed., A Documentary History of the Negro People in the United States, 1933-1945, 5th ed. New York: Citadel, 1968, pp. 1, 327-328, page 206.

CHAPTER 9: *Photos:* Theo, Kaufmann, "On to Liberty," 1867, Oil on canvas. The Metropolitan Museum of Art. Gift of Erving and Joyce Wolf, 1982 (1982.443.3) Photograph © 1982 The Metropolitan Museum of Art, 212; Corbis/Bettmann, 214; The Granger Collection, 218; Sophia Smith Collection, Smith College, 219; National Portrait Gallery, Smithsonian Institution. Art Resource, N.Y., 220; The Granger Collection, 224; Sophia Smith Collection, Smith College, 227; The Granger Collection,228. *Text:* Voices—Frederick Douglass Describes an Awkward Situation, Source: From The Narrative and Selected Writings (Modern Library College Editions) by Frederick Douglass. Copyright © 1984 Modern Library, page 222.

CHAPTER 10: *Photos:* Courtesy of the Library of Congress, 234; Getty Images Inc.—Hulton Archive Photos, 236; Courtesy of the California History Room, California State Library, Sacramento, California, 238; Courtesy of the Library of Congress, 241, 243; San Francisco Public Library/Gamma Labs, 242; Getty Images, Inc—Liaison, 244; © Ohio Historical Society, 245; Courtesy of the Library of Congress, 246;Corbis/Bettmann, 248; Photographs and Prints Division. Schomburg Center for Research in Black Culture/ Art Resource. The New York Public Library. Astor, Lenox and Tilden Foundations, 251; The Granger Collection, 253. *Text:* Voices—African-Americans Respond to the Fugitive State Law, Source: Vistor Ullman, Martin R. Delaney: The Beginnings of Black Nationaliam. Boston: Beacon Press, 1971, p. 112, page 240.

VISUALIZING THE PAST: Images that appear on page 260: Library of Congress; Courtesy of the Library of Congress; Library of Congress. Images that appear on page 261: Boston Anthenaeum; Library of Congress.

Interpreting the Past: Images that appear on page 262-263: Corbis/Bettmann; Getty Images, Inc.—Hulton Archive Photos.

PART TIMELINE III: Images that appear on page 264: CORBIS-NY; Library of Congress; Corbis/Bettmann; Library of Congress; The Granger Collection, New York; Dave King/Dorling Kindersley © Confederate Memorial Hall, New Orleans. Images that appear on page 265: Moorland-Spingarn Research Center; CORBIS-NY; The Granger Collection; Culver Pictures, Inc.

CHAPTER 11: *Photos:* Courtesy of the Library of Congress, 266; Dave King/Dorling Kindersley © Confederate Memorial Hall, New Orleans, 268; Courtesy of the Library of Congress, 269; Corbis/Bettmann, 272; Courtesy of the Library of Congress, 274; Moorland-Spingarn Research Center, 277; Corbis/Bettmann, 278; Massachusetts Commandery Military Order of the Loyal Legion and The U.S. Army Military History Institute, 280; Courtesy of the Library of Congress, 281; The Granger Collection, 283; Photographs and Prints Division. Schomburg Center for Research in Black Culture. The New York Public Library. Astor, Lenox and Tilden Foundations, 285; Courtesy of the Library of Congress, 286; Culver Pictures, Inc., 287; Harper's Weekly, March 18, 1865. Courtesy of William C. Hine, 290.

CHAPTER 12: *Photos:* Corbis/Bettmann, 296; Courtesy of the Library of Congress, 298, 300, and 301; Courtesy Austin History

Center, 303; The Granger Collection, 305; Courtesy of the Library of Congress, 306; ; Courtesy of Hampton University Archives, 307; The Granger Collection, New York, 313; Courtesy of the Library of Congress, 316; *Text:* Voices—A Freedman's Bureau Commissioner Tells Freed People What Freedom Means, Source: From "The Terrain of Freedom: The Struggle Over the Meaning of Free Labor in the U.S. South," by Ira Berlin et al., History Workshop 22, pp. 108-130, Autumn, 1986, page 302

CHAPTER 13: *Photos:* The Granger Collection, 322; Courtesy of the Library of Congress, 324; The Granger Collection, New York, 325; The Granger Collection, 326; Photographs and Prints Division. Schomburg Center for Research in Black Culture. The New York Public Library. Astor, Lenox and Tilden Foundations, 328; Art Resource/The New York Public Library, Research Libraries, 331; Rutherford B. Hayes Presidential Center, 333; From The Henry Clay Warmoth Papers # 752, Southern Historical Collection, Wilson Library, University of North Carolina at Chapel Hill, 333; Courtesy of the Library of Congress.

VISUALIZING THE PAST Images that appear on page 344: Library of Congress. Images that appear on page 345: Library of Congress.

Intrepeting the Past Images that appear on pages 346-347: Collection of The New-York Historical Society; Courtesy of the Library of Congress; North Wind Picture Archives; Getty Images, Inc.—Hulton Archive Photos.

PART TIMELINE IV Images that appear on page 349: Photographed by Sharon Srchma, courtesy of The American Numismatic Society, New York; Library of Congress; Courtesy of the Library of Congress; Library of Congress; The Granger Collection; Library of Congress. Images that appear on page 349: Courtesy of the Library of Congress; Courtesy of the Hampton University Archives.

CHAPTER 14: *Photos:* Solomon D. Butcher Collection, 350; Library of Congress, 352, 357; Corbis/Bettmann, 359; North Carolina Department of Cultural Resources, 362; Courtesy of the Library of Congress, 364; The Granger Collection, New York, 365: Courtesy of the Library of Congress, 366, 367, 371, and 372; *Text:* The Spread of Disfranchisement, Source: Goldfield, David; Abbott, Carl; Anderson, Virginia DeJohn; Argersinger, Jo Ann E.; Argersinger, Peter H.; Barney, William L.; Weir, Robert M., The American Journey, Combined volume, 3rd Edition, © 2004. Reprinted by permission of Pearson Education, Inc., Upper Saddle River, NJ, page 358; Voices—Cash and Debt for the Black Cotton Farmer, Source: Benjamin Mays, Born to Rebel: An Autobiography. Athens, GA: University of Georgia Press, 1987, pp. 5. *Text:* 6. Reprinted by permission, page 370.

CHAPTER 15: *Photos:* The Erwin E. Smith Collection of the Library of Congress on deposit at the Amon Carter Museum, Fort Worth, Texas, 378; Courtesy of the Library of Congress, 383, 387, and 388; Historical Society, Helena, 391; Museum of the American West Collection, Autry National Center, 393; Courtesy of the Library of Congress, 397; National Park Service, Maggie L. Walker National Historic Site, 389; Courtesy of the Tennessee State Library and Archives, page 401; © 2000 Bettmann/CORBIS, 403; Courtesy of the Library of Congress, 404; *Text:* Voices— Black Men in Battle in Cuba, Source: Willard B. Gatewood, Jr., Smoked Yankees and the Struggle for Empire: Letters from Negro Soldiers, 1898–1902. University of Arkansas Press. Reprinted by permission of the author, page 394. Voices: Thomas E. Miller and the Mission of the Black Land-Grant College, Source: A. Newby, Black Carolinians: A History of Blacks in South Carolina from 1896 to 1968. Columbia, SC: University of South Carolina Press, 1973, p. 263, page 384.

CHAPTER 16: *Photos:* Courtesy of the Library of Congress, 410; Corbis/Bettmann, 412; Brown Brothers, 414; The Granger Collection, New York, 417; Courtesy of the Library of Congress, 420; Special Collections, Cleveland State University Library, 423; James

VanDerZee, "The Wedding Party" Copyright © Donna Mussenden VanDerZee, 424; Schomburg Center for Research in Black Culture/Art Resource, 425; The New York Public Library, Schomburg Center for Research in Black Culture, 427; Surlock Studio Records, Archives Center, National *Text:* Map 16-3—The Expansion of Black Harlem, 1911–1930, from The Harlem Renaissance by Steven Watson, copyright © 1995 by Steven Watson. Used by permission of Pantheon Books, a division of Random House, Inc., page 441.

CHAPTER 17: *Photos:* Courtesy of the Library of Congress, 446 and 448; The Granger Collection, 450; © Carl Van Vechten/Courtesy of the Library of Congress, 453; Gordon Parks, Getty Images Inc.—Hulton Archive Photos, 454; UPI, Corbis/Bettmann, 455; Betsy G. Reyneau. A. Philip Randolph. National Archives, 459; Beinecke Rare Book and Manuscript Library, Yale University, page 463; © Frank Driggs/CORBIS, 449; Frank Driggs Collection, 466; Maryland Historical Society, Baltimore, MD, 467; National Baseball Hall of Fame Library, Cooperstown, N.Y., 468. *Text:* "I, Too, Sing America" (poem by Langston Hughes) from The Collected Poems of Langston Hughes by Langston Hughes, copyright © 1994 by The Estate of Langston Hughes. Used by permission of Alfred A. Knopf, a division of Random House, Inc. Electronic rights by permission of Harold Ober Associates Incorporated, page 448; "Red Silk Stockings" (poem by Langston Hughes), From The Collected Poems of Langston Hughes by Langston Hughes, copyright © 1994 by The Estate of Langston Hughes. Used by permission of Alfred A. Knopf, a division of Random House, Inc. Electronic rights by permission of Harold Ober Associates Incorporated, page 463.

VISUALIZING THE PAST Images that appear on page 472: Corbis/Bettmann; Virginia Historical Society, Richmond, Virginia; The Granger Collection, New York; Courtesy of the Library of Congress. Images that appear on page 473: Alberts, Getty Images Inc.—Hulton Archive Photos; This item is reproduced by permission of The Huntington Library, San Marino, California; Library of Congress.

Interpreting the Past Images that appear on pages 474-475: Corbin/Bettmann; Courtesy of the Library of Congress.

PART TIMELINE V Images that appear on page 476: Library of Congress; Library of Congress; National Archives and Records Administration; NAACP Collection/Library of Congress; Library of Congress. Images that appear on page 477: Library of Congress; Frank Driggs Collection; Courtesy of the Library of Congress.

CHAPTER 18: *Photos:* Margaret Bourke-White/LIFE Magazine © TimePix, 478; Corbis/Bettmann, 480; Doris Ulmann, Schomburg Center for Research in Black Culture/Art Resource, 483; From "A True Likeness: The Black South of Richard Samuel Roberts, 1920–1936 (Bruccoli Clark Layman, 1986), 484; Courtesy of the Library of Congress, 486; Courtesy Mary McLeod Bethune Council House National Historic Site, Washington, DC, 488; Courtesy of the Library of Congress, 493; Scurlock Studios, 491; Getty Images, Inc., 492; © Carl Van Vechten/Courtesy of the Library of Congress, 495; Courtesy of the Library of Congress, 500; National Archives and Records Administration, 503. *Text:* T 18-2—Median Income of Black Families Compared to the Median Income of White Families for Selected Cities, 1935–1936, "Median Income of Black Families . . ." from An American Dilemma: The Negro Problem and Modern Democracy by Gunnar Myrdal. Copyright © 1944, 1962 by Harper & Row Publishers, Inc. Reprinted by permission

HarperCollins Publishers, Inc. page 482; Voices: A Black Sharecropper Details Abuse in the Administration of Agricultural Relief, Table 18-2 "Median Income of Black Families...White Families for Selected Cities, 1935-1936" from AN AMERICAN DILEMMA: THE NEGRO PROBLEM AND MODERN DEMOCRACY by GUNNAR MYRDAL. Copyright © 1944, 1962 by Harper & Row, Publishers, Inc. Reprinted by permission of HarperCollins Publishers, page 494; Voices: Hoboing in Alabama, From Going to the Territory by Ralph Ellison, copyright © 1986 by Ralph Ellison. Used by permission of Random House, Inc., page 502.

CHAPTER 19: *Photos:* © Betmann/Corbis, 508; AP Wide World Photos, 510; Courtesy of the Library of Congress, 511 and 514; © International Negro Press, 1936, 515; Getty Images Inc.—Hulton Archive Photos, 517; Carl Van Vechten/Courtesy of the Library of Congress, 520; © David Lees/CORBIS, 523; Getty Images Inc.—Hulton Archive Photos, 525; Courtesy of the Library of Congress, 526; © CORBIS/Bettmann, 529. *Text:* "The Negro Speaks of Rivers," From The Collected Poems of Langston Hughes by Langston Hughes, copyright © 1994 by The Estate of Langston Hughes. Used by permission of Alfred A. Knopf, a division of Random House, Inc. Electronic rights by permission of Harold Ober Associates Incorporated, page 520; Lyircs from "Strange Fruit", Source: Lyrics by Lewis Allan © 1939 Music Sales Corp (ASCAP). International copyright secured. Reprinted by permission, page 525; Voices— Margaret Walker on Black Culture, Reprinted by permission of Maryemma Graham, page 522.

CHAPTER 20: *Photos:* National Archives and Records Administration, 536; Courtesy of the Library of Congress, 538 and 541; Hon. William H. Hastie, Oil By Sarah Belchet-Swenson, 546; National Archives and Records Administration, 547; National Archives and Records Administration, 549; Courtesy of the Library of Congress, 550; Courtesy of the Moorland-Spingarn Research Center, Howard University, 551; National Archives and Records Administration, 552; © Robert Maass/CORBIS, 555; Michael Barson, 556; Courtesy of the Library of Congress, 559.

VISUALIZING THE PAST Images that appear on page 564: U.S. Air Force; National Archives. Images that appear on pages 564-565: Getty Images Inc.—Hulton Archive Photos. Images that appear on page 543: Getty Images Inc.—Hulton Archive Photos; Courtesy of the Library of Congress; National Archives.

Interpreting the Past: Images that apper on page 566-567: Corbis/Bettmann; Courtesy of the Library of Congress.

PART TIMELINE VI Images that appear on page 568: Andrew Lichtenstein, Aurora & Quanta Productions Inc.; Library of Congress; Stewart Cohen, Index Stock Imagery, Inc.; Corbis/Bettmann; Library of Congress; AP Wide World Photos. Images that appear on page 569: Library of Congress; © Jan Cobb; AP Wide World Photos; Corbis/Bettmann.

CHAPTER 21: *Photos:* UPI, Corbis/Bettmann, 570; Moorland-Spingarn Research Center, 572; UPI, Corbis/Bettmann, 574; © NAACP/Library of Congress, 576; Getty Images, Inc., 577; UPI, Corbis/Bettmann, 579 and 581; AP Wide World Photos, 584; John G. Moebes, News & Record Library, 585;Steve Schapiro, Black Star, 587; UPI Corbis/Bettmann, 588; John F. Kennedy Library, National Archives, document MS 2003-036, 592; AP Wide World Photos, 593; George Ballis, Take Stock-Images of Change, 596; ©1976, Matt Herron/ Take Stock-Images of Change, 597. *Text:* Quote from "I Have A Dream Speech," August 28th, 1963.; Reprinted by arrangement with the Estate of Martin Luther King, Jr., c/o Writers House as agent for the proprietor New York, NY. Copyright 1955 Martin Luther King, Jr., copyright renewed 1991 Coretta Scott King., page 592; Quote from Birmingham Bus Boycott Speech, Dr. Martin Luther King, Jr. December 5, 1955, Reprinted by arrangement with the Estate of Martin Luther King, Jr., c/o Writers House as agent for the proprietor New York, NY. Copyright 1955 Martin Luther King,

Jr., copyright renewed 1991 Coretta Scott King. Page 591; Voices: Bernice Johnson Reagon on How to Raise a Freedom Song, Excerpt from "We'll Never Turn Back" by Bernice Johnson Reagan, edited by Pete Seeger & Bob Reiser, from Everybody Says Freedom: A History of the Civil Rights Movement in Songs and Pictures by Pete Seeger & Bob Reiser. Copyright © 1989 by Pete Seeger and Bob Reiser. Used by permission of W.W. Norton & Company, Inc. page 590; Voices: Letter of the Montgomery Women's Political Council to Mayor W.A. Gayle, Voices—Letter of the Montgomery Women's Political Council to Mayor W.A. Gayle, page 578.

CHAPTER 22: *Photos:* © Betttmann/Corbis All Rights Reserved, 604; Courtesy of the Library of Congress, 606; Getty Images/Time Life Pictures, page 608© Bettmann/Corbis, 609; Leonard Freed, Magnum Photos, Inc., 611; Courtesy of the Library of Congress, 612; AP Wide World Photos, 613; Getty Images Inc.—Hulton Archive Photos, 615; Courtesy of the Library of Congress, 617; Frank Johnston, Black Star, 619; Courtesy of the Library of Congress, 621; © Corbis/Bettmann, 623; AP/Wide World Photos, 626. *Text:* Voices—They Called Each Other Bloods, Source: "Captain Joseph B. Anderson, Jr., in Wallace Terry, Bloods: An Oral History of the Vietnam War by Black Veterans. New York: Ballantine Books, 1984, pp. 219-228, page 618.

CHAPTER 23: *Photos:* Getty Images, 638; S. M. Wakefield, Pearson Education/PH College, 640; Mike Theiler/Reuters, Corbis/Bettmann, 646; AP Wide World Photos, 646; © Neajlah Feanny-Hicks/Corbis All Rights Reserved, 646; © Peter Turnley/Corbis, 648; Paul Conklin, PhotoEdit, 649; Rob Crandall, Stock Boston, 650; Agence France Presse/Getty Images, 652; US Department of Education, 656; © AP/Wide World Photos, 659; © Steve Pope/epa/Corbis All Rights Reserved, 661; Getty Images Inc., 663. *Text:* Voices: Black Women in Defense of Themselves, "Taking Sides Against Ourselves," Rosemary L. Bray, New York Times Magazine, November 17, 1991, p. 53. Reprinted by permission of Elaine Markson Agency, page 644.

CHAPTER 24: *Photos:* Corbis/SABA Press Photos, Inc., 668; Chuck Nacke, Woodfin Camp & Associates, 670; © Kim Ludbrook/ Corbis All Rights Reserved, 672; © Viviane Moos/ Corbis All Rights Reserved, 674; David Burnett, Woodfin Camp & Asscociates, 677; AP Wide World Photos, 677; Getty Images Inc., 680; AP Wide World Photo, 684; David Grossman, The Images Works, 688; National Gay and Lesbian Task Force, 691. *Text:* Profile: Bob and Ziggy Marley and Black Internationalism, Copyright © 2003 from Bibliography: Black Heretics, Black Prophets: Radical Political Intellectuals by Anthony Bogues. Reprinted by permission of Routledge/Taylor & Francis Books, Inc. page 679; Voices: From What Becomes of the Brokenhearted: A Memoir by

E. Lynn Harris, copyright © 2003 by E. Lynn Harris. Used by permission of Doubleday, a division of Random House, Inc., page 690.

VISUALIZING THE PAST Images that appear on page 696: Corbis/Bettmann; Siede Preis, Getty Images, Inc.—Photodisc. Images that appear on page 697: Corbis/Bettmann; Courtesy of the Library of Congress; Getty Images Inc.—Hulton Archive Photos; © Dorling Kindersley.

Interpreting the Past: Images that appear on pages 698-699: Robert Kozloff, AP Wide World Photos; Tom Marotta, UNICEF, Corbis/Bettmann;

Index

SINGLE PC LICENSE AGREEMENT AND LIMITED WARRANTY

READ THIS LICENSE CAREFULLY BEFORE OPENING THIS PACKAGE. BY OPENING THIS PACKAGE, YOU ARE AGREEING TO THE TERMS AND CONDITIONS OF THIS LICENSE. IF YOU DO NOT AGREE, DO NOT OPEN THE PACKAGE. PROMPTLY RETURN THE UNOPENED PACKAGE AND ALL ACCOMPANYING ITEMS TO THE PLACE YOU OBTAINED THEM.

1. GRANT OF LICENSE and OWNERSHIP: The enclosed computer programs <<and data>> ("Software") are licensed, not sold, to you by Pearson Education, Inc. publishing as Pearson Prentice Hall ("We" or the "Company") and in consideration of your purchase or adoption of the accompanying Company textbooks and/or other materials, and your agreement to these terms. We reserve any rights not granted to you. You own only the disk(s) but we and/or our licensors own the Software itself. This license allows you to use and display your copy of the Software on a single computer (i.e., with a single CPU) at a single location for <u>academic</u> use only, so long as you comply with the terms of this Agreement. You may make one copy for back up, or transfer your copy to another CPU, provided that the Software is usable on only one computer.

2. RESTRICTIONS: You may <u>not</u> transfer or distribute the Software or documentation to anyone else. Except for backup, you may <u>not</u> copy the documentation or the Software. You may <u>not</u> network the Software or otherwise use it on more than one computer or computer terminal at the same time. You may <u>not</u> reverse engineer, disassemble, decompile, modify, adapt, translate, or create derivative works based on the Software or the Documentation. You may be held legally responsible for any copying or copyright infringement that is caused by your failure to abide by the terms of these restrictions.

3. TERMINATION: This license is effective until terminated. This license will terminate automatically without notice from the Company if you fail to comply with any provisions or limitations of this license. Upon termination, you shall destroy the Documentation and all copies of the Software. All provisions of this Agreement as to limitation and disclaimer of warranties, limitation of liability, remedies or damages, and our ownership rights shall survive termination.

4. LIMITED WARRANTY AND DISCLAIMER OF WARRANTY: Company warrants that for a period of 60 days from the date you purchase this SOFTWARE (or purchase or adopt the accompanying textbook), the Software, when properly installed and used in accordance with the Documentation, will operate in substantial conformity with the description of the Software set forth in the Documentation, and that for a period of 30 days the disk(s) on which the Software is delivered shall be free from defects in materials and workmanship under normal use. The Company does <u>not</u> warrant that the Software will meet your requirements or that the operation of the Software will be uninterrupted or error-free. Your only remedy and the Company's only obligation under these limited warranties is, at the Company's option, return of the disk for a refund of any amounts paid for it by you or replacement of the disk. THIS LIMITED WARRANTY IS THE ONLY WARRANTY PROVIDED BY THE COMPANY AND ITS LICENSORS, AND THE COMPANY AND ITS LICENSORS DISCLAIM ALL OTHER WARRANTIES, EXPRESS OR IMPLIED, INCLUDING WITHOUT LIMITATION, THE IMPLIED WARRANTIES OF MERCHANTABILITY AND FITNESS FOR A PARTICULAR PURPOSE. THE COMPANY DOES NOT WARRANT, GUARANTEE OR MAKE ANY REPRESENTATION REGARDING THE ACCURACY, RELIABILITY, CURRENTNESS, USE, OR RESULTS OF USE, OF THE SOFTWARE.

5. LIMITATION OF REMEDIES AND DAMAGES: IN NO EVENT, SHALL THE COMPANY OR ITS EMPLOYEES, AGENTS, LICENSORS, OR CONTRACTORS BE LIABLE FOR ANY INCIDENTAL, INDIRECT, SPECIAL, OR CONSEQUENTIAL DAMAGES ARISING OUT OF OR IN CONNECTION WITH THIS LICENSE OR THE SOFTWARE, INCLUDING FOR LOSS OF USE, LOSS OF DATA, LOSS OF INCOME OR PROFIT, OR OTHER LOSSES, SUSTAINED AS A RESULT OF INJURY TO ANY PERSON, OR LOSS OF OR DAMAGE TO PROPERTY, OR CLAIMS OF THIRD PARTIES, EVEN IF THE COMPANY OR AN AUTHORIZED REPRESENTATIVE OF THE COMPANY HAS BEEN ADVISED OF THE POSSIBILITY OF SUCH DAMAGES. IN NO EVENT SHALL THE LIABILITY OF THE COMPANY FOR DAMAGES WITH RESPECT TO THE SOFTWARE EXCEED THE AMOUNTS ACTUALLY PAID BY YOU, IF ANY, FOR THE SOFTWARE OR THE ACCOMPANYING TEXTBOOK. BECAUSE SOME JURISDICTIONS DO NOT ALLOW THE LIMITATION OF LIABILITY IN CERTAIN CIRCUMSTANCES, THE ABOVE LIMITATIONS MAY NOT ALWAYS APPLY TO YOU.

6. GENERAL: THIS AGREEMENT SHALL BE CONSTRUED IN ACCORDANCE WITH THE LAWS OF THE UNITED STATES OF AMERICA AND THE STATE OF NEW YORK, APPLICABLE TO CONTRACTS MADE IN NEW YORK, EXCLUDING THE STATE'S LAWS AND POLICIES ON CONFLICTS OF LAW, AND SHALL BENEFIT THE COMPANY, ITS AFFILIATES AND ASSIGNEES. THIS AGREEMENT IS THE COMPLETE AND EXCLUSIVE STATEMENT OF THE AGREEMENT BETWEEN YOU AND THE COMPANY AND SUPERSEDES ALL PROPOSALS OR PRIOR AGREEMENTS, ORAL, OR WRITTEN, AND ANY OTHER COMMUNICATIONS BETWEEN YOU AND THE COMPANY OR ANY REPRESENTATIVE OF THE COMPANY RELATING TO THE SUBJECT MATTER OF THIS AGREEMENT. If you are a U.S. Government user, this Software is licensed with "restricted rights" as set forth in subparagraphs (a)-(d) of the Commercial Computer-Restricted Rights clause at FAR 52.227-19 or in subparagraphs (c)(1)(ii) of the Rights in Technical Data and Computer Software clause at DFARS 252.227-7013, and similar clauses, as applicable.

Should you have any questions concerning this agreement or if you wish to contact the Company for any reason, please contact in writing: Legal Department, Prentice Hall, 1 Lake Street, Upper Saddle River, NJ 07450 or call Pearson Education Product Support at 1-800-677-6337.